HUMAN RIGHTS ADVOCACY IN THE UNITED STATES

■ ■ ■

by

Martha F. Davis
Professor of Law
Northeastern University School of Law

Johanna Kalb
Associate Professor of Law
Loyola University New Orleans College of Law

Risa E. Kaufman
Executive Director, Human Rights Institute
Lecturer-in-Law
Columbia Law School

AMERICAN CASEBOOK SERIES®

WEST
ACADEMIC
PUBLISHING

Mat #41381199

American Casebook Series is a trademark registered in the U.S. Patent and Trademark Office.

© 2014 LEG, Inc. d/b/a West Academic
    444 Cedar Street, Suite 700
    St. Paul, MN 55101
    1-877-888-1330

West, West Academic Publishing, and West Academic are trademarks of West Publishing Corporation, used under license.

Printed in the United States of America

ISBN: 978-0-314-28656-7

*To Caroline and Mei, for their lessons
in resilience and love*
(MFD)

*To Leo and Thea who inspired
and to Reuben who made it possible*
(JK)

To my parents, with gratitude
(REK)

PREFACE

Why a casebook on human rights advocacy in the United States? And why now?

To our knowledge, this is the first casebook of its kind. From our vantage as human rights scholars and practitioners, the need for such a synthesis has become acute. Knowledge of human rights norms and standards is now required for the responsible practice of law in the U.S., and familiarity with human rights is necessary for lawyers ranging from poverty litigators to corporate legal advisors to judges to legislative counsel. General human rights casebooks are not able to provide a sustained focus on the unique challenges of human rights practice in the U.S. The complications of federalism and constitutionalism, the constraints of legal ethics, the domestic statutory frameworks that incorporate human rights, and the human rights initiatives spearheaded by state and local governments are just a few of the areas that are critical to practitioners in the domestic context. This text fills the void by providing students with the knowledge and tools they need to integrate human rights into their domestic practices.

What's more, having now assembled these materials, we are convinced that this human rights perspective on U.S. law can serve as a platform from which to launch more in-depth study of many areas of domestic law. Human rights law has far greater breadth than traditional first-year offerings, and intersects with constitutional and statutory construction, common law, civil rights law, tribal law, state and local law, corporate law, law firm management, legal ethics and virtually every other aspect of modern law practice in the United States. This is historically rich, compelling material that provides an excellent starting point for further exploration during law school and after.

In developing this casebook, we stand on the shoulders of the many lawyers and other advocates in U.S. history who have viewed human rights as important to the ultimate strength and resilience of our constitutional democracy, and who have used human rights advocacy on behalf of their clients and causes. The list of names stretches back to the beginning of the nation, and includes constitutional framers, abolitionists, feminist lawyers, civil rights activists, labor rights lawyers, and immigration experts. We have tried to weave their stories and give accounts of their advocacy strategies throughout these pages.

As a result of their work, today, it is impossible to avoid the human rights issues being debated across the United States. As we write this, the city of Detroit is threatening to cut off the water supply to needy individuals with unpaid bills, despite statements of concern from U.N. officials; U.S. Representative John Conyers has decried these actions, noting simply that "water is a human right." The United States Interagency Council on Homeless, a federal government body, describes homelessness as a human rights issue. And litigants before both federal and state courts are increasingly presenting human rights arguments, pressing issues ranging from affirmative action to marriage equality.

The chapters in this textbook are divided into three general categories. First, Chapters I through IV set out an overarching framework for U.S. human rights advocacy. Second, Chapters V through VII build on that introduction to examine in greater depth the ways in which human rights norms and standards are used in domestic advocacy given the constraints of federalism and the constitutional emphasis on negative rights. Third, Chapters VIII through XI address specific advocacy strategies and techniques, along with special ethics challenges faced by human rights lawyers.

Each chapter includes notes and questions that both expand upon and probe the material excerpted in the text. We have also included extensive case studies that provide concrete examples of the challenges and opportunities of using human rights in domestic advocacy. In the initial chapter, "A Framework for U.S. Human Rights Advocacy," we develop a case study on the human rights challenges to sentences of juvenile life without parole. Chapter III, entitled "The United States and U.N. Human Rights Treaties," includes a case study of litigation challenging the detention of Haitian refugees. Case studies in subsequent chapters address issues including the human right to housing; the human right to health and the Affordable Care Act; advocacy in the Inter-American system addressing violence against women; state level immigration laws; human rights challenges to U.S. counterterrorism practices; the Native American tribes' use of human rights mechanisms; and human rights challenges after Hurricanes Katrina and Rita.

In addition to these case studies, many of the readings are drawn from examples of actual U.S. human rights advocacy. We believe that students will gain a great deal from exposure to primary materials such as briefs, comments, local resolutions, complaints and compliance reports, in addition to secondary analyses that frame and synthesize the material. To further develop lawyering and advocacy skills, we include a number of Skills Exercises that draw on these materials to engage students in the actual work of domestic human rights advocacy, from devising a strategic human rights advocacy campaign to advising a corporation under the Guiding Principles on Business and Human Rights. With these components, the book easily lends itself to a variety of settings, including traditional seminars, clinics, and other experiential courses

As human rights lawyers ourselves, developing the material for this textbook has been a labor of love. Our fondest hope is that this textbook will help equip law students and lawyers to carry on the domestic development of human rights norms that have been a hallmark of U.S. advocacy for centuries. But we also know that this book is a first step along that road, and we welcome comments and critiques as we refine the material for future editions. Please feel free to contact any of us with your suggestions, criticism and yes, even praise. Like those who came before us, we are committed to this project for the long haul.

Martha F. Davis,
Northeastern University School of Law,
m.davis@neu.edu

Johanna Kalb,
Loyola University New Orleans College of Law,
jkalb@loyno.edu

Risa E. Kaufman,
Columbia Law School,
risa.kaufman@law.columbia.edu

July 2014

ACKNOWLEDGMENTS

The authors are grateful to the many individuals who provided feedback, research and other critical support for this book. In particular, we are thankful to the following colleagues, collaborators, and friends who provided valuable comments on drafts of the manuscript and otherwise helped to shape its content: Cathy Albisa, Daniel Belasco, Caroline Bettinger-López, Sarah Cleveland, Harlan Cohen, Kaitlin Cordes, Jamil Dakwar, Davida Finger, Julie Goldscheid, Alice Henkin, Deena Hurwitz, Tarek Ismael, Sarah Knuckey, Deb LaBelle, Connie de la Vega, Hope Metcalf, Sarah Paoletti, John Pollock, Deborah Popowski, Bill Quigley, Judith Resnik, JJ Rosenbaum, Peter Rosenblum, Jeffrey Selbin, Cindy Soohoo, Erin Foley Smith, Eric Tars, Jonathan Todres, JoAnn Kamuf Ward, and Deborah Weissman. We are grateful, too, to Columbia Law School and Dean David Schizer, to Loyola University New Orleans College of Law, Dean Maria Pabón López, and Associate Dean John Lovett, and to Northeastern University School of Law, Dean Jeremy Paul, and Dean Emily Spieler, for supporting this effort. Stephen Caruso, Rick Doyon and Greta Moseson provided indispensable administrative assistance. Jootaek "Juice" Lee provided skilled reference assistance.

The following individuals provided excellent research assistance, without which this project would not have been possible: Amy Elmgren, Katherine Carey, Hannah Adams, Patrick Reagin, Kaki Johnson, Greg Dorchak, Ruth Harper, Laurel Goldstein, Ariel Woodard-Stephens, Scheagbe Grigsby, Atenas Madico, Van Huynh, Lizzy Foydel and Ariana Sarfarazi.

Additionally, we are deeply thankful for our families, who have supported and encouraged our work on this project.

Finally, we would like to acknowledge our gratitude to the following authors and publishers who kindly granted us permission to reprint copyrighted material:

Alabama Law Review and Penny Venetis, for excerpts from Penny M. Venetis, *Making Human Rights Treaty Law Actionable in the United States: The Case for Universal Implementing Legislation*, 63 Ala. L. Rev. 97 (2011), © 2011, reprinted with permission of the Alabama Law Review and Penny Venetis.

Alabama Media Group, for excerpts from Joey Kennedy, *Editorial: Bear Witness to a Wrong, Then Tell All*, Birm. News, Dec, 18, 2001, © 2001, reprinted with permission of the Alabama Media Group.

Alice Henkin, for excerpts from Louis Henkin, *International Law as Law in the United States*, 82 Mich. L. Rev. 1555 (1984), ©1984, reprinted with permission of Alice Henkin.

The American Bar Association, for excerpts from American Bar Association Report Accompanying ABA Resolution Endorsing the UN Guiding Principles on Business and Human Rights (2012); and for excerpts from ABA Model Rules of Professional Conduct (2013), © 2013 by the American Bar Association, reprinted with the permission of the ABA. Copies of ABA Model Rules of Professional Conduct, 2008 Edition are available from Service Center, American Bar Association, 321 North Clark Street, Chicago, IL 60654, 1-800-285-2221. This information or any or portion thereof may not be copied or disseminated in any form or by any means or stored in an electronic database or retrieval system without the express written consent of the American Bar Association.

American Civil Liberties Union, for excerpts from American Civil Liberties Union, *United States Compliance with the International Covenant on Civil and Political Rights: Shadow Report to the Fourth Periodic Report by the United States* (Sept. 13, 2013), © 2013, reprinted with permission of the American Civil Liberties Union; and American Civil Liberties Union and Columbia Law School Human Rights Institute, *The United States' Compliance with the International Covenant on Civil and Political Rights: Suggested List of Issues to Country Report Task Force on the United States* (Dec. 28, 2012), © 2012, reprinted with permission of the American Civil Liberties Union and the Columbia Law School Human Rights Institute.

Amnesty International, for Amnesty International, *"Will I Be Next?"*: *U.S. Drone Strikes in Pakistan* (Oct. 22, 2013), © 2013 by Amnesty International, 1 Easton Street, London WC1X 0DW, United Kingdom, http://www.amnesty.org, reprinted with permission of Amnesty International.

The American Law Institute, for excerpts from Restatement (3d) of Foreign Relations Law of the United States, © 1987, reprinted with permission of the American Law Institute. All rights reserved.

The American Prospect, for excerpts from Cass Sunstein, *Economic Security: A Human Right*, Am. Prospect, Sept. 20, 2004, © 2004, reprinted with permission of The American Prospect.

American Society of International Law, for excerpts from Roger P. Alford, *Misusing International Sources to Interpret the Constitution*, 98 Am. J. Int'l L. 57 (2004), © 2004, reprinted with permission of American Journal of International Law, conveyed through Copyright Clearance Center, Inc., and Roger P. Alford; for excerpts from Curtis A. Bradley, *Intent, Presumptions, and Non-Self-Executing Treaties*, 102 Am. J. Int'l L. 540 (2008), © 2008, reprinted with permission of American Journal of

International Law, conveyed through Copyright Clearance Center, Inc., and Curtis A. Bradley; for excerpts from Hilary Charlesworth, Christine Chinkin, & Shelley Wright, *Feminist Approaches to International Law*, 85 Am. J. Int'l L. 613 (1991), © 1991, reprinted with permission of American Journal of International Law, conveyed through Copyright Clearance Center, Inc.; for excerpts from Louis Henkin, *U.S. Ratification of Human Rights Conventions: The Ghost of Senator Bricker,* 89 Am. J. Int'l L. 341 (1995), © 1995, reprinted with permission of American Journal of International Law, conveyed through Copyright Clearance Center, Inc.; for excerpts from Oscar Schachter, *Human Dignity as a Normative Concept*, 77 Am. J. Int'l L. 848 (1983), © 1983, reprinted with permission of American Journal of International Law, conveyed through Copyright Clearance Center, Inc.; and for excerpts from Carlos Manuel Vázquez, *Less Than Zero?*, 102 Am. J. Int'l L. 563 (2008), © 2008, reprinted with permission of American Journal of International Law, conveyed through Copyright Clearance Center, Inc., and Carlos Manuel Vázquez.

Curtis A. Bradley, for excerpts from *The Treaty Power and American Federalism*, 97 Mich. L. Rev. 390 (1998), © 1998, reprinted with permission of Curtis A. Bradley.

The Brookings Institute, for excerpts from Ted Piccone, *Catalysts for Rights: The Unique Contribution of the UN's Independent Experts on Human Rights* (2010), © 2010 The Brookings Institute, reprinted with permission of The Brookings Institute.

Cambridge University Press, for excerpts from Davida Finger and Rachel E. Luft, *No Shelter: Disaster Politics in Louisiana and the Struggle for Human Rights*, *in* Human Rights in the United States: Beyond Exceptionalism, (Shareen Hertel & Kathryn Libal eds. 2011), © 2011, reprinted with permission of Cambridge University Press, Davida Finger, and Rachel E. Luft; and for excerpts from Cathy Albisa, *Drawing Lines in the Sand: Building Economic and Social Rights Norms in the United States*, *in* Human Rights in the United States: Beyond Exceptionalism, (Shareen Hertel & Kathryn Libal eds. 2011), © 2011, reprinted with permission of Cambridge University Press.

Vincent Carroll, for excerpts from Editorial, *On Point: Usurping Justice*, Rocky Mtn. News, Mar. 2, 2007, and Editorial, *A Phony Human Rights Case*, Rocky Mtn. News, Oct. 14, 2007, reprinted with the permission of Vincent Carroll.

The Center for Economic and Social Rights, for excerpts from *Brief for the Center for Economic and Social Rights et al. as Amici Curiae Supporting Petitioner*, Sojourner v. New Jersey Social Services, 803 A.2d 1165 (N.J. 2003) (No. 52981), reprinted with permission of the Center for Economic and Social Rights.

Clearinghouse Review: Journal of Poverty Law and Policy, for excerpts from Martha F. Davis, *Human Rights in the Trenches: Using International Human Rights Law in Everyday Legal Aid Cases*, 41 Clearinghouse Rev. 414 (2007); first published in 41 Clearinghouse Review: Journal of Poverty Law and Policy 414 (Nov.—Dec. 2007), © 2007 Sargent Shriver National Center on Poverty Law, reprinted with permission of Martha F. Davis and Sargent Shriver National Center on Poverty Law; for excerpts from Eric Tars, *Who Knows What Lurks in the Hearts of Human Rights Violators? The Shadow (Reporter) Knows— Human Rights Shadow Reporting: A Strategic Tool for Domestic Justice*, 42 Clearinghouse Rev. 475 (2009), first published in 42 Clearinghouse Review: Journal of Poverty Law and Policy 475 (Jan.—Feb. 2009), © 2009 Sargent Shriver National Center on Poverty Law, reprinted with permission of Eric Tars and Sargent Shriver National Center on Poverty Law; for excerpts from Caroline Bettinger-López, *The Inter-American Human Rights System, A Primer*, 42 Clearinghouse Rev. 581 (2009); first published in 42 Clearinghouse Review: Journal of Poverty Law and Policy 581 (Jan.—Feb. 2009), © 2009 Sargent Shriver National Center on Poverty Law, reprinted with permission of Caroline Bettinger-López and Sargent Shriver National Center on Poverty Law; and for excerpts from J. Peter Sabonis, *Using a Human Rights Framework at the Maryland Legal Aid Bureau*, 44 Clearinghouse Rev. 450 (2011), © 2011 Sargent Shriver National Center on Poverty Law, reprinted with permission of J. Peter Sabonis and Sargent Shriver National Center on Poverty Law.

Clinical Law Review and Dina F. Haynes, for excerpts from Dina F. Haynes, *Client-Centered Human Rights Advocacy*, 13 Clinical L. Rev. 379 (2006), © 2006, reprinted with permission of Clinical Law Review and Dina F. Haynes.

Columbia Human Rights Law Review, for excerpts from Deborah Weissman, The Human Rights Dilemma, 35 Colum. Hum. Rts. L. Rev. 259 (2004), © 2004, first published in Columbia Human Rights Law Review, reprinted with permission of Columbia Human Rights Law Review and Deborah Weissman; and for excerpts from Martha F. Davis, *Human Rights and the Model Rules of Professional Conduct: Intersection and Integration*, 42 Colum. Hum. Rts. L. Rev. 157 (2010), © 2010, reprinted with permission of Columbia Human Rights Law Review and Martha F. Davis.

Columbia Law Review, for excerpts from Louis Henkin, *Rights: American and Human*, 79 Colum. L. Rev. 405 (1979), © 1979, reprinted with permission of Columbia Law Review and Alice Henkin.

Columbia Law School Human Rights Institute, for excerpts from Columbia Law School Human Rights Institute, *Stakeholder Report on U.S. Human Rights Treaty Ratification, Joint Submission to the United*

Nations Universal Periodic Review, Ninth Session of the Working Group on the Universal Periodic Review, Human Rights Council (2010), © 2010, reprinted with permission of the Columbia Law School Human Rights Institute.

Columbia University Press, for excerpts from Louis Henkin, The Age of Rights (1990), © 1990, reprinted with permission of Columbia University Press and Alice Henkin.

The Constitutional Court of South Africa, for excerpts from State v. T. Makwanyane and Another, 1995 (3) SALR 391 (CC) (S. Afr.)), reprinted with permission of the Constitutional Court of South Africa.

Cornell Law Review, for excerpts from Oona A. Hathaway, Spencer Amdur, Celia Choy, Samir Deger-Sen, John Paredes, Sally Pei & Haley Nix Proctor, *The Treaty Power: Its History, Scope, and Limits*, 98 Cornell L. Rev. 239, 325 (2013), © 2013, reprinted with permission of Cornell Law Review and authors.

Council on Foreign Relations, for excerpts from *Public Opinion on Global Issues, Chapter 16: U.S. Opinion on Human Rights* (Dec. 6, 2011). Produced by CFR's International Institutions and Global Governance program. © 2011, reprinted with permission of the Council on Foreign Relations.

Scott Cummings, for excerpts from *The Internationalization of Public Interest Law*, 57 Duke L. J. 891 (2008), © 2008, reprinted with permission of Scott Cummings.

Martha F. Davis and The Leadership Conference on Civil and Human Rights, for excerpts from *Brief of Amici Curiae The Leadership Conference on Civil and Human Rights et al. in Support of Respondents Regarding Medicaid Expansion*, State of Florida v. United States Dep't of Health and Hum,. Serv. (No. 11–400), 567 U.S. ___ (2012), reprinted with permission of Martha F. Davis and The Leadership Conference on Civil and Human Rights.

Fernando Garcia, for excerpts from *Human Rights and Immigration in the U.S.: An Experience of Border Immigrant Communities*, 22 Georgetown Imm. L. J. 405 (2008), © 2008, reprinted with permission of Fernando Garcia.

Fordham Law Review, for excerpts from Alan Jenkins & Kevin Hsu, *American Ideals and Human Rights: Findings from New Public Opinion Research by the Opportunity Agenda*, 77 Fordham L. Rev. 439 (2008), © 2008, reprinted with permission of Fordham Law Review and Alan Jenkins.

The Green Bag, for excerpts from Jack Landman Goldsmith, *International Human Rights Law and the United States*, 1 Green Bag 2d 165 (1998), © 1998, reprinted with permission of The Green Bag.

Steven Groves, for excerpts from Steven Groves, *The Inequities of the U.N. Committee on the Elimination of Racial Discrimination*, Heritage Foundation Backgrounder (Aug. 7, 2008); Steven Groves, *Ratification of the Disabilities Convention Would Erode American Sovereignty*, Heritage Foundation Backgrounder (Apr. 26, 2010); and *Women's Rights are Human Rights: U.S. Ratification of the Convention on the Elimination of All Forms of Discrimination Against Women: Hearing before the U.S. Sen. Comm. on Hum. Rts and the Law*, 111th Cong. (2010) (statement of Steven Groves), reprinted with permission of Steven Groves.

Harvard Human Rights Journal, for excerpts from David Kennedy, *The International Human Rights Movement; Part of the Problem?*, 15 Harv. Hum. Rts. J. 101 (2002), © 2002, reprinted with permission of Harvard Human Rights Journal and David Kennedy, permission conveyed through Copyright Clearance Center, Inc.; and excerpts from Diane F. Orentichler, *Bearing Witness: The Art and Science of Human Rights Factfinding*, 3 Harv. Hum. Rts. J. 83 (1990), © 1990, reprinted with permission of Harvard Human Rights Journal, conveyed through Copyright Clearance Center, Inc., and Diane F. Orentichler.

Harvard International Law Journal, for excerpts from Curtis A. Bradley, *Unratified Treaties, Domestic Politics, and the U.S. Constitution*, 48 Harv. Int'l L. J. 309 (2007), © 2007, reprinted with permission of Harvard International Law Journal, conveyed through Copyright Clearance Center, Inc., and Curtis A. Bradley; and for excerpts from Makua wa Mutua, *Savages, Victims, and Saviors: The Metaphor of Human Rights*, 42 Harv. Int'l L. J. 201 (2001), © 2001, reprinted with permission of Harvard International Law Journal, conveyed through Copyright Clearance Center, Inc., and Makua wa Mutua.

Harvard Journal of Gender and Law, formerly the Harvard Women's Law Journal and Tracy E. Higgins, for excerpts from Tracy E. Higgins, *Anti-Essentialism, Relativism and Human Rights*, 19 Harv. Women's L. J. 89 (1996), © 1996, reprinted with permission of Harvard Journal of Gender and Law, conveyed through Copyright Clearance Center. Inc., and Tracy E. Higgins.

Harvard Law Review for excerpts from Curtis A. Bradley and Jack L. Goldsmith, *Customary International Law as Federal Common Law: A Critique of the Modern Position*, 110 Harv. L. Rev. 815 (1997), © 1997, reprinted with permission of Harvard Law Review, conveyed through Copyright Clearance Center, Inc.; excerpts from Harold Hongju Koh, *Is International Law Really State Law?*, 111 Harv. L. Rev. 1824 (1998), © 1998,. reprinted with permission of Harvard Law Review and Harold

Hongju Koh, conveyed through Copyright Clearance Center, Inc.; excerpts from Vicki C. Jackson, *Constitutional Comparisons: Convergence, Resistance, Engagement*, 119 Harv. L. Rev. 109 (2005), © 2005, reprinted with permission of Harvard Law Review, conveyed through Copyright Clearance Center, Inc.; excerpts from Carlos Manuel Vazquez, *Treaties as Law of the Land: The Supremacy Clause and the Judicial Enforcement of Treaties*, 122 Harv. L. Rev. 599 (2008), © 2008, reprinted with permission of Harvard Law Review, conveyed through Copyright Clearance Center, Inc., and Carlos Manuel Vazquez.

Human Rights Advocates, for excerpts from, *Brief for Human Rights Advocates et al. as Amici Curiae in Support of Respondents*, Fisher v. University of Texas at Austin, 133 S.Ct. 2411 (2013) (No. 11–345) (Constance de la Vega and Neil Popović, Counsel), reprinted with permission of Human Rights Advocates, Constance de la Vega, and Neil Popović.

Human Rights Brief, for excerpts from Aryeh Neier, *Social and Economic Rights; A Critique*, 13 No. 2 Hum. Rts. Brief 1 (2006), © 2006, reprinted with permission of Human Rights Brief and Aryeh Neier.

Human Rights Watch, *No Way to Live: Alabama's Immigrant Law* (2011), © 2011 Human Rights Watch. All rights reserved. Reprinted with permission of Human Rights Watch.

Indiana Law Journal, for excerpts from Martha F. Davis and Johanna Kalb, *Oklahoma and Beyond: Understanding The Wave of State Anti-Transnational Law Initiatives*, 87 Ind. L. J. Supp. 1 (2011), © 2011, reprinted with permission of Indiana Law Journal, Martha F. Davis, and Johanna Kalb.

The International Bar Association, for excerpts from *Guidelines for International Human Rights Fact-Finding Visits and Reports (The Lund-London Guidelines)* (2009), © 2009 International Bar Association, London, UK and Raoul Wallenberg Institute of Human Rights and Humanitarian Law, Lund, Sweden, reprinted with the permission of the International Bar Association and the Raoul Wallenberg Institute of Human Rights and Humanitarian Law; and for excerpts from the *International Principles on Conduct for the Legal Profession* (2011), © 2011 International Bar Association, London, UK, reprinted by permission of the International Bar Association.

International Journal of Civil Society Law, for excerpts from Kerstin Martins, *NGOS in the UN System: Examining Formal and Informal Mechanisms of Interaction*, 2 Int'l J. Civ. Soc. L. 10 (2004), © 2004, reprinted with the permission of Kerstin Martins and the International Journal of Civil Society Law.

The Japan Federation of Bar Associations, for excerpts from *Basic Regulations for Attorneys' Duties* (Bengoshi shokumu kihon kitei) (Nov. 10, 2004), reprinted with permission of JFBA.

Johns Hopkins University Press, for excerpts from Kenneth Roth, *Defending Economic, Social and Cultural Rights: Practical Issues Faced by an International Human Rights Organization*, 26 Hum. Rts. Q. 63 (2004), © 2004 Johns Hopkins University Press, reprinted with permission of Johns Hopkins University Press and Kenneth Roth; and excerpts of Leonard S. Rubenstein, *How International Human Rights Organizations Can Advance Economic, Social and Cultural Rights: A Response to Kenneth Roth*, 26 Hum. Rts. Q. 845 (2004), © 2004 Johns Hopkins University Press, reprinted with permission of Johns Hopkins University Press.

JurisNet LLC, for excerpts from Hilary Charlesworth & Christine Chinkin, The Boundaries of International Law: A Feminist Analysis (2000), © 2000, reprinted with permission of JurisNet LLC.

Journal of Human Rights Practice, for excerpts from A.C. Finnegan et al., *Negotiating Politics and Culture: The Utility of Human Rights For Activists Organizing in the United States*, 2 J. of Hum. Rts. Practice 307 (2010), © 2010, reprinted with permission of Journal of Human Rights Practice, conveyed through Copyright Clearance Center, and authors.

Risa E. Kaufman, for excerpts from *By Some Other Means: Considering the Executive's Role in Fostering Subnational Human Rights Compliance*, 33 Cardozo L. Rev. 1971 (2012), © 2012, reprinted by permission of Risa E. Kaufman.

Law & Society Review, for excerpts from Sally Engle Merry et al., *Law From Below: Women's Human Rights and Social Movements in New York City*, 44 Law & Soc'y Rev. 101 (2010), © 2010, reprinted with permission of the Law & Society Review, conveyed through Copyright Clearance Center.

The Law Society Gazette (England and Wales), for excerpts from Jonathan Goldsmith, *When Human Rights and Clients' Rights Conflict*, 24 Sept. 2012, © 2012, reprinted with permission of the Law Society Gazette (England and Wales).

Jessica Lenahan, for excerpts from *Guest Commentary, Failing Victims of Violence*, Denver Post, Aug. 28, 2011, © 2011, reprinted with permission of Jessica Lenahan.

Michael W. Lewis, for excerpts from *The Misleading Human Rights Watch and Amnesty International Reports on Drones*, Opinio Juris (Nov. 8, 2013, 12:28 PM), http://opiniojuris.org, reprinted with permission of Michael W. Lewis.

Gillian MacNaughton, for excerpts from *Untangling Equality and Non-discrimination to Promote the Right to Health Care for All*, 11 Health & Hum. Rts.: An Int'l J. 47 (2009), © 2009, reprinted with permission of Gillian MacNaughton. This article was first published in Health and Human Rights: An International Journal.

Maryland Legal Aid Bureau, Inc., for excerpts from *Complaint to the U.N. Special Rapporteur on Extreme Poverty and Human Rights regarding the U.S. failure to protect legal service providers' access to migrant farmworkers* (Dec. 13, 2012), reprinted with permission of Maryland Legal Aid Bureau, Inc.

Mariah McGill, for excerpts from *Human Rights from the Grassroots Up: Vermont's Campaign for Universal Health Care,* 14 Health & Hum. Rts.: An Int'l J. 106 (2012), © 2012, reprinted with permission of Mariah McGill. This article was first published in Health and Human Rights: An International Journal.

The Hon. Margaret H. Marshall, for excerpts from *"Wise Parents Do Not Hesitate To Learn From Their Children": Interpreting State Constitutions in an Age of Global Jurisprudence*, 79 N.Y.U. L. Rev. 1633 (2004), © 2004, reprinted with permission of Hon. Margaret H. Marshall.

Missouri Law Review, for excerpts from Margaret E. McGuinness, *Foreward*, 46 Mo. L. Rev. 921 (2008), © 2008, reprinted with permission of Margaret McGuinness and Missouri Law Review.

National Law Center on Homelessness & Poverty, for excerpts from National Law Center on Homelessness & Poverty, "Simply Unacceptable": Homelessness and the Human Rights to Housing in the United States 2011 (June 2011), © 2011, reprinted with permission of National Law Center on Homelessness & Poverty.

New Orleans Workers' Center for Racial Justice, for excerpts from STAND with Dignity, *Through My Eyes: Louisiana's First Independent Evacuation Monitoring Report* (Aug. 2009), reprinted with permission of the NOWCRJ.

New York City Bar Association, for excerpts from *Brief of New York City Bar Association, et al. as Amici Curiae in support of Plaintiffs,* Valdez et al. v. City of New York, 960 N.E.2d 356 (N.Y. 2011), reprinted with permission of the New York City Bar Association.

The New York University Journal of Law & Social Change, for excerpts from *The Spirit of Our Times: State Constitutions and International Human Rights*, 30 N.Y.U. Rev. L. & Soc. Change 359 (2006), © 2006, reprinted with permission of the New York University Journal of Law & Social Change and Martha F. Davis.

North Carolina Law Review, for excerpts from Julian G. Ku, *The State of New York Does Not Exist: How the States Control Compliance with International Law*, 82 N.C.L. Rev. 457 (2004), © 2004, reprinted with permission of North Carolina Law Review and Julian G. Ku.

Northeastern University Law Journal, for excerpts from Risa E. Kaufman, *Framing Economic, Social and Cultural Rights at the U.N.*, 4 Northeastern U.L.J. 407 (2012), © 2012, reprinted with permission of Northeastern University Law Journal and Risa E. Kaufman; and for excerpts from Katharine G. Young, *Redemptive and Rejectionist Frames: Framing Economic, Social and Cultural Rights for Advocacy and Mobilization in the United States*, 4 Northeastern U.L.J. 323 (2013), © 2013, reprinted with permission of Northeastern University Law Journal and Katharine G. Young.

Notre Dame Law Review, for excerpts from Ingrid Wuerth, *The Alien Tort Statute and Federal Common Law: A New Approach*, 85 Notre Dame L. Rev. 1931 (2010). This article first appeared in Vol. 86 Notre Dame Law Review, Pages 1938–39 (2010), © 2010 Notre Dame Law Review, reprinted with permission of Notre Dame Law Review, University of Notre Dame. The publisher bears responsibility for any errors which have occurred in reprinting or editing.

Ohio Northern University Law Review, for excerpts from William Quigley, *Reflections of Community Organizers: Lawyering for Empowerment of Community Organizations*, 21 Ohio N. Univ. L. Rev. 455 (1995), © 1995, reprinted with permission of William Quigley and Ohio Northern University Law Review.

The Opportunity Agenda, for excerpts from *Talking Human Rights in the United States: A Communications Toolkit from the Opportunity Agenda* (2009), © 2009, reprinted with permission of The Opportunity Agenda; and from excerpts of *How to Discuss Specific Social Justice Issues Within a Human Rights Framework: Public Opinion Research Findings* (2009), © 2009, reprinted with permission of The Opportunity Agenda.

Oxford University Press, for excerpts from Norman Dorsen, *The Relevance of Foreign Legal Materials in U.S. Constitutional Cases: A Conversation between Justice Antonin Scalia and Justice Stephen Breyer*, 3 Int'l J. Con. L. 519 (2005), © 2005, reprinted with the permission of the International Journal of Constitutional Law and Norman Dorsen.

Penn State Law Review, for excerpts from Johanna Kalb, *Human Rights Treaties in State Courts: The International Prospects of State Constitutionalism After Medellin*, 115 Penn. St. L. Rev. 1051 (2011), © 2011, reprinted with permission of Penn State Law Review and Johanna Kalb.

Princeton University Press, for excerpts from Michael Ignatieff, *Introduction: American Exceptionalism and Human Rights*, *in* Exceptionalism and Human Rights (Michael Ignatieff, ed. 2005), © 2005, reprinted with permission of Princeton University Press.

Regents of the University of California, for excerpts from Joan Fitzpatrick, *The International Dimension of U.S. Refugee Law*, 15 Berkeley J. Int'l L. 1 (1997), © 1997 by the Regents of the University of California, reprinted from the Berkeley Journal of International Law by permission of the Regents of the University of California.

Risa E. Kaufman, for excerpts from *By Some Other Means: Considering the Executive's Role in Fostering Subnational Human Rights Compliance*, 33 Cardozo L. Rev. 1971 (2012), © 2012, reprinted by permission from Risa E. Kaufman.

Cynthia Soohoo, Catherine Albisa and Martha F. Davis, for excerpts from Paul Gordon Lauren, *A Human Rights Lens on U.S. History: Human Rights at Home and Human Rights Abroad*, in Bringing Human Rights Home, Vol. 1 (Soohoo et al. eds. 2008); for excerpts from Elizabeth Borgwardt, *FDR's Four Freedoms and Wartime Transformations in America's Discourse of Rights* in Bringing Human Rights Home, Vol. 1 (Soohoo et al. eds. 2008); for excerpts from Carol Anderson, *A "Hollow Mockery": African Americans, White Supremacy, and the Development of Human Rights in the United States* in Bringing Human Rights Home, Vol. 1 (Soohoo et al. eds. 2008); for excerpts from Cynthia Soohoo, *Human Rights and the Transformation of the "Civil Rights" and "Civil Liberties" Lawyer* in Bringing Human Rights Home, Vol. 2 (Soohoo et al. eds. 2008); for excerpts from Margaret Huang, *"Going Global": Appeals to International and Regional Human Rights Bodies* in Bringing Human Rights Home, Vol. 2 (Soohoo et al. eds. 2008); for excerpts from Martha F. Davis, *Thinking Globally, Acting Locally: States, Municipalities, and International Human Rights* in Bringing Human Rights Home, Vol. 2 (Soohoo et al. eds. 2008); and for excerpts from Greg Asbed, *Coalition of Immokalee Workers: "Golpear a Uno Es Golpear a Todos!" To Beat One of Us is to Beat Us All!* in Bringing Human Rights Home, Vol. 3 (Soohoo et al. eds. 2008); © 2008, Praeger Publishers, reprinted with permission of Cynthia Soohoo, Catherine Albisa, Martha F. Davis and Praeger Publishers.

Southern Center for International Studies, for excerpts from *Remarks by Sandra Day O'Connor, Associate Justice, United States Supreme Court* (Oct. 28, 2003), reprinted with permission of the Southern Center for International Studies, http://www.southerncenter.org/.

Stanford Law Review, for excerpts from Helen Hershkoff, *"Just Words": Common Law and the Enforcement of State Constitutional Social and Economic Rights*, 62 Stanford L. Rev. 1521 (2009), © 2009, reprinted with permission of Stanford Law Review, conveyed through Copyright Clearance Center, Inc.; excerpts from Harold Hongju Koh, *On American Exceptionalism*, 55 Stanford L. Rev. 1479 (2003), © 2003, reprinted with permission of Stanford Law Review, conveyed through Copyright Clearance Center, Inc.; and excerpts from Judith Resnik & Julie Suk, *Adding Insult to Injury: Questioning the Role of Dignity in Conceptions of Sovereignty*, 55 Stanford L. Rev. 1921 (2003), © 2003, reprinted with permission of Stanford Law Review, conveyed through Copyright Clearance Center, Inc.

SUR International Journal on Human Rights, for excerpts from Barbora Bukovska, *Perpetrating Good: Unintended Consequences of International Human Rights Advocacy*, 9 SUR Int'l J. on Hum. Rts. 7 (2008), © 2008, reprinted with permission of SUR International Journal on Human Rights and Barbora Bukovska.

The United Nations, for the text of the Universal Declaration of Human Rights (10 Dec. 1948), U.N.G.A. Res. 217 A (III) (1948); the International Covenant on Civil and Political Rights (New York, 16 Dec. 1966) 999 U.N.T.S. 171 and 1057 U.N.T.S. 407, *entered into force* 23 Mar. 1976 [the provisions of article 41 (Human Rights Committee) entered into force 28 Mar. 1979]; the International Covenant on Economic, Social and Cultural Rights (New York, 16 Dec. 1966) 993 U.N.T.S. 3, *entered into force* 3 Jan. 1976; the Convention on the Rights of Persons with Disabilities (New York, 13 Dec. 2006) 2515 U.N.T.S. 3, *entered into force* 3 May 2008; the International Convention on the Elimination of All Forms of Racial Discrimination (New York, 7 Mar. 1966) 660 U.N.T.S. 195, 5 I.L.M. 352 (1966), *entered into force* 4 Jan. 1969; the Convention on the Elimination of All Forms of Discrimination Against Women (Dec. 18, 1979), 1249 U.N.T.S. 13, *entered into force* 3 Sept. 1982; the Convention against Torture and Other Cruel, Inhuman or Degrading Treatment or Punishment (New York, 10 Dec. 1984) 1465 U.N.T.S. 85, 23 I.L M. 1027 (1984), *as modified by* 24 I.L.M. 535 (1985), *entered into force* 26 June 1987; the Convention on the Rights of the Child (New York, 20 Nov. 1989) 1577 U.N.T.S. 3, 28 I.L.M. 1448 (1989), *entered into force* 2 Sept. 1990; the Optional Protocol to the Convention on the Rights of the Child on the involvement of children in armed conflict (New York, 25 May 2000) UN Doc.A/54/RES/263, *entered into force* 12 Feb. 2002; and the Optional Protocol to the Convention on the Rights of the Child on the sale of children, child prostitution and child pornography (New York, 25 May 2000) UN Doc. A/54/RES/263, *entered into force* 18 Jan. 2002; the United Nations Declaration on the Rights of Indigenous Peoples (13 Sept. 2007), U.N.G.A. Res. 61/295 (2007), © United Nations, reprinted with permission of the United Nations.

The United Nations, for excerpts from the Charter of the United Nations (San Francisco, 26 June 1945), 3 Bevans 1153, 59 Stat. 1031, T.S.

No. 993, *entered into force* 24 Oct. 1945; the Convention on the Recognition and Enforcement of Foreign Arbitral Awards (New York, 10 June 1958) 330 U.N.T.S. 3; 21 U.S.T. 2517; T.I.A.S. No. 6997, *entered into force* 7 June 1959; for excerpts from the Vienna Convention on the Law of Treaties (Vienna, 23 May 1969) 1155 U.N.T.S. 331, *entered into force* 27, Jan. 1980; for excerpts from the Basic Principles on the Role of Lawyers, Eighth United Nations Congress on the Prevention of Crime and the Treatment of Offenders, Havana, 27 August to 7 September 1990, U.N. Doc. A/CONF.144/28/Rev.1 at 118 (1990); for excerpts from the Professional Training Series No. 7: Training Manual on Human Rights Monitoring (U.N. Office of the High Commissioner for Human Rights, 2001); for excerpts from the Bangalore Principles of Judicial Conduct, United Nations Centre for International Crime Prevention (2002); for excerpts from the Report of the UN Special Rapporteur on violence against women, its causes and consequences, 59th sess. CHR, U.N. Doc. E/CN.4/2003/75/Add.2 (Jan. 14, 2003) (by Radhika Coomaraswamy); for excerpts from the Human Rights Committee, General Comment 32, Art. 14: Right to equality before courts and tribunals and to a fair trial (ninetieth session, 2007), U.N. Doc. CCPR/C/GC/32 (2007); for excerpts from the Concluding Observations of the Committee on the Elimination of Racial Discrimination: United States of America. 8/05/2008. A/56/18, CERD/C/USA/CO/6; for excerpts from the Report of the UN Special Rapporteur on racism, xenophobia and related forms of intolerance, 11th sess. HRC, U.N. Doc. A/HRC/11/36/Add.3 (April 28, 2009) (by Doudou Diene); for excerpts from the Report of the Working Group on the Universal Periodic Review, United States of America, UN Human Rights Council (4 Jan. 2011); the Special Representative of the Secretary-General on the issue of human rights and transnational corporations and other business enterprises, 17th sess. HRC, U.N. Doc. A/HRC/17/31 (Mar. 21, 2011) (by John Ruggie); for excerpts from the Report of the UN Special Rapporteur on the human right to safe drinking water and sanitation, 18th sess. HRC, U.N. Doc. A/HRC/18/33/Add.4 (August 2, 2011) (by Catarina de Albuquerque); for excerpts from the Report of the UN Special Rapporteur of the Human Rights Council on torture and other cruel, inhuman or degrading treatment or punishment, 66th sess. GA, U.N. Doc. A/66/268 (August 5, 2011) (by Juan E. Méndez); for excerpts from the Letter from Catarina de Albuquerque, U.N. Special Rapporteur on the human right to safe drinking water and sanitation, to Mayor Kevin Johnson, City of Sacramento, 2012; for excerpts from the Report of the UN Special Rapporteur on Extreme Poverty and Human Rights, 67th sess. GA, U.N. Doc. A/67/278 (August 9, 2012) (by Magdalena Sepúlveda Carmona); for excerpts from the Report of the UN Special Rapporteur on adequate housing as a component of the right to an adequate standard of living, 22nd sess. HRC, U.N. Doc. A/HRC/22/46 (Dec. 24, 2012) (by Raquel Rolnik); for excerpts from the Report of the UN

Special Rapporteur on the Independence of Judges and Lawyers, 23rd sess. HRC, U.N. Doc. A/HRC/23/43 (Mar. 15, 2013) (by Gabriela Knaul); for excerpts from the UN Human Rights Committee, List of Issues in Relation to the Fourth Periodic Report of the United States of America (CCPR/C/USA/4 and Corr. 1 (April 29, 2013); and for excerpts from UN Human Rights Committee, List of Issues in Relation to the Fourth Periodic Report of the United States of America, Addendum: Replies of the United States of America to the List of Issues, U.N. Doc. CCPR/C/USA/4 and Corr.1 (July 5, 2013), © United Nations, reprinted with permission of the United Nations.

U.S. Human Rights Network, for excerpts from U.S. Human Rights Network, *A Summary of U.S. NGO Responses to the U.S. 2007 Combined Periodic Reports to the International Committee on the Elimination of All Forms of Racial Discrimination* (Feb. 2008), © 2008, reprinted with permission of the U.S. Human Rights Network, and for excerpts from U.S. Human Rights Network, *Summary Submission to the U.N. Universal Periodic Review* (2010), © 2010, reprinted with permission of the U.S. Human Rights Network.

University of California Irvine Law Review, for excerpts from Christopher A. Whytock, Donald Earl Childress III, & Michael D. Ramsey, *After Kiobel: International Human Rights Litigation in State Courts and Under State Law*, 3 U.C. Irvine L. Rev. 1 (2013), © 2013, reprinted with permission of U.C. Irvine Law Review and authors. This article was first published in the U.C. Irvine Law Review.

University of Pennsylvania Press, for excerpts from Philip Alston, *Putting Economic, Social and Cultural Rights Back on the Agenda of the United States*, *in* The Future of Human Rights (William Schultz ed. 2008), © 2008, reprinted with permission of University of Pennsylvania Press and Philip Alston.

Utah Law Review, for excerpts from Harold Hongju Koh, *Refugees, the Courts, and the New World Order*, 1994 Utah. L. Rev. 999 (1994), © 1994, reprinted with permission of Utah Law Review.

Villanova Law Review, for excerpts from Sarah H. Cleveland, *Crosby and the "One Voice" Myth in U.S. Foreign Relations*, 46 Vill. L. Rev. 975 (2001), © 2001, reprinted with permission of Villanova Law Review and Sarah H. Cleveland.

Yale Journal of International Law, for excerpts from David Sloss, *The Domestication Of International Human Rights: Non-Self Executing Declarations and Human Rights Treaties*, 24 Yale J. Int'l L. 129 (1999), © 1999, reprinted with permission of Yale Journal of International Law; and for excerpts from Rebecca Ingber, *Interpretation Catalysts and Executive Branch Legal Decisionmaking*, 38 Yale J. Int'l L. 359 (2013),

© 2013, reprinted with permission of Yale Journal of International Law and Rebecca Ingber.

Yale Law Journal and Judith Resnik, for excerpts from Judith Resnik, *Law's Migration: American Exceptionalism, Silent Dialogues, and Federalism's Multiple Ports of Entry*, 115 Yale L.J. 1564 (2006), © 2006, reprinted with permission of Yale Law Journal, conveyed through Copyright Clearance Center, Inc., and Judith Resnik.

A Note on Editing

No case is reprinted unedited. Omissions are identified with ellipses or brackets, but there is no identification where only case citations or other authorities are deleted. Case citations do not include subsequent history denying review. Where a holding other than the one for which the case is cited has been overruled or limited by statute or a later case, that is not shown. Internal quotes are sometimes omitted from quotations within cases for ease of reading.

SUMMARY OF CONTENTS

TABLE OF CONTENTS

TABLE OF CASES

The principal cases are in bold type.

HUMAN RIGHTS ADVOCACY IN THE UNITED STATES

CHAPTER I

A FRAMEWORK FOR U.S. HUMAN RIGHTS ADVOCACY

∎ ∎ ∎

I. INTRODUCTION

For lawyers working to advance human rights in the United States, human rights norms and strategies are mutually dependent and reinforcing, creating an integrated framework for advocacy. Human rights lawyers in the United States draw upon the standards embodied in international human rights law, including human rights treaties and customary international law, as a basis for assessing governments' (and, in some cases, private actors') obligations to protect, respect, and fulfill basic rights. Further, they engage a set of human rights tools, including human rights documentation and the mechanisms of the United Nations and Inter-American human rights system, to create pressure on the relevant actors to close the gap between universal human rights standards and domestic practice. Effective human rights lawyering requires deep understanding of the possibilities and limitations of both.

In this introductory chapter, we first explore the norms, standards, and textual sources that underlie the practice of domestic human rights law in the 21st Century, along with some critiques that reveal the challenges and limitations of the human rights framework. We then turn to an overview of the human rights strategies that lawyers and other advocates use to advance human rights protections in the United States. Through a case study of advocacy efforts to challenge the sentencing of juveniles to life in prison without the possibility of parole (JLWOP), we explore how lawyers in the United States are drawing on human rights norms to assess the legitimacy of the practice under international law and using cross-cutting human rights strategies to leverage international, national and local pressure to end it.

By exploring the doctrinal and normative bases for domestic human rights advocacy alongside an example of human rights strategies at work in the U.S., this chapter introduces the relationship between doctrine and practice to develop a foundation for your study of human rights work in the United States.

II. DEFINING HUMAN RIGHTS NORMS
FOR U.S. ADVOCACY

The concept of human rights is neither new nor novel. Human rights have long animated legal institutions and social movements, including both the American and French Revolutions. While cross-cultural comparisons are always treacherous, general concepts of human rights are found in most, if not all, major religions—for example, the Hindu Vedas, the Babylonian Code of Hammurabi, the Bible, the Quran (Koran), and the Analects of Confucius all address questions of people's duties, rights, and responsibilities from a perspective of shared humanity.

There are multiple accounts of the origins of human rights as a political force and as a social movement.[1] Former slave, orator, statesman, and activist Frederick Douglass is among those credited with the early articulation of "human rights" as a legal concept, supporting individual claims against the government or private actors. In particular, Douglass began in the 1850s to mount the argument that since blacks were humans, they were entitled to the rights that natural law mandated and that the United States recognized in its Declaration of Independence and Constitution. Douglass recognized the universality of the human rights concept, and extended it to women's rights as well, writing that in denying women's right to vote "not merely the degradation of woman and the perpetuation of a great injustice happens, but the maiming and repudiation of one-half of the moral and intellectual power of the government of the world."[2] Further, Douglass's arguments went beyond civic participation and examined access to economic, social, and cultural rights. As Douglass wrote in the December 1, 1866 issue of the Atlantic Magazine, "No republic is safe that tolerates a privileged class, or denies to any of its citizens equal rights and equal means to maintain them."[3]

At the same time that Douglass recognized and honed nascent legal claims based on human rights concepts, he was also well aware of the power of human rights to contribute to organizing, and of the importance of political organizing to successful social change. As Douglass famously observed, "If there is no struggle, there is no progress. Those who profess to favor freedom, and deprecate agitation, are men who want crops without plowing up the ground, they want rain without thunder and

---

[1] *See, e.g.*, Human Rights in the Twentieth Century (Stefan-Ludwig Hoffman, ed., 2010); Lynn Hunt, Inventing Human Rights (2007); Micheline R. Ishay, The History of Human Rights: From Ancient Times to the Globalization Era (2004); Hans Joas, The Sacredness of the Person: A New Genealogy of Human Rights (2013); Samuel Moyn, The Last Utopia (2012); and Aryeh Neier, The International Human Rights Movement: A History (2012).

[2] Frederick Douglass, Life and Times of Frederick Douglass 575 (Park Publishing 1882).

[3] Frederick Douglass, *Reconstruction*, The Atlantic (Dec. 1, 1866) *available at* http://www.theatlantic.com/magazine/archive/1866/12/reconstruction/304561/.

lightning."[4] Douglass lived to see the impact of his activism in the adoption of the 13th, 14th, and 15th amendments to the U.S. Constitution, and in the initial strides made in the Reconstruction era following the Civil War. However, Douglass died decades before the seeds that he planted bore fruit in post-World War II efforts to enshrine human rights into both international and domestic law.

In the ashes of World War II, many of the world's nations came together to articulate firmer guidelines and boundaries for government activity. Formal adoption of human rights concepts into law required a level of definition and precision beyond the human rights rhetoric of earlier times. In this section, we will explore what, precisely, is meant by human rights in the contemporary era, and the general sources of human rights law. We will also examine some critiques of human rights, which help illuminate both the promise and the limits of this approach for domestic advocacy.

A. HUMAN RIGHTS IN THE MODERN ERA

The first attempt at drafting an international instrument defining and protecting human rights in the wake of World War II was undertaken by the nations of the Americas.[5]

In April 1948, the Ninth International Conference of American States approved the American Declaration of the Rights and Duties of Man. Human rights declarations, such as the American Declaration and the Universal Declaration of Human Rights, consist of a set of guiding but non-binding basic human rights principles adopted by parties in order to develop consensus and articulate norms that may later ripen into legally binding treaties.

The American Declaration's preamble provides that:

> All men are born free and equal, in dignity and in rights, and, being endowed by nature with reason and conscience, they should conduct themselves as brothers one to another.

> The fulfillment of duty by each individual is a prerequisite to the rights of all. Rights and duties are interrelated in every social and political activity of man. While rights exalt individual liberty, duties express the dignity of that liberty.

---

[4] Frederick Douglass, West India Emancipation Speech (Aug. 3, 1857). For more background on the role of human rights in the abolition movement, see Jenny Martinez, The Slave Trade and the Origins of International Human Rights Law (2012).

[5] The earlier League of Nations (1919–1946) also reflected the influence of human rights concepts. The drafting history of the League indicates that a range of human rights issues were considered for inclusion in the League's charter, though only protections for labor and women, particularly trafficking, were ultimately articulated in its founding documents. See Pamela Bromley, *Human Rights and the League of Nations: How Ideas About Human Rights Came to Be Included in the Charter and Work of the League of Nations* (Mar. 20, 2008) (paper prepared for the annual meeting of the Western Political Science Association, San Diego, CA), *available at* http://www.allacademic.com/meta/p237945_index.html.

Duties of a juridical nature presuppose others of a moral nature which support them in principle and constitute their basis.

Inasmuch as spiritual development is the supreme end of human existence and the highest expression thereof, it is the duty of man to serve that end with all his strength and resources.

Since culture is the highest social and historical expression of that spiritual development, it is the duty of man to preserve, practice and foster culture by every means within his power.

And, since moral conduct constitutes the noblest flowering of culture, it is the duty of every man always to hold it in high respect.

American Declaration of the Rights and Duties of Man, preamble, O.A.S. Res. XXX, adopted by the Ninth International Conference of American States (April 1948), *reprinted* in Basic Documents Pertaining to Human Rights in the Inter-American System, OEA/Ser.L.V./II.82 doc.6 rev. 1 at 17 (1992).

Finalized just a few months after the American Declaration, the Universal Declaration of Human Rights, the product of a post-World War II effort to create a lasting peace, defines human rights as follows:

Article I: All human beings are born free and equal in dignity and rights. They are endowed with reason and conscience and should act towards one another in a spirit of brotherhood.

Universal Declaration of Human Rights, G.A. Res. 217 (III) A, U.N. Doc. A/RES/217(III) (Dec. 10, 1948).

In the following passage, the late Professor Louis Henkin offers a more comprehensive distillation of the contemporary understanding of human rights. As you read this passage, consider the implications that flow from Professor Henkin's explication of human rights.

LOUIS HENKIN, THE AGE OF RIGHTS
1–5 (1990).

Individual rights as a political idea draws on natural law and its offspring, natural rights. In its modern manifestation that idea is traced to John Locke, to famous articulations in the American Declaration of Independence and in the French Declaration of the Rights of Man and of the Citizen, and to realizations of the idea in the United States Constitution and its Bill of Rights and in the constitutions and laws of modern states.

The idea of human rights that has received currency and universal (if nominal) acceptance in our day owes much to these antecedents but it is discrete and different from them. The contemporary version does not ground or justify itself in natural law, in social contract, or in any other political theory. In international instruments representatives of states declare and recognize human rights, define their content, and ordain their consequences within political societies and in the system of nation-states. The justification of human rights is rhetorical, not philosophical. Human rights are self-evident, implied in other ideas that are commonly intuited and accepted. Human rights are derived from accepted principles, or are required by accepted ends-societal ends such as peace and justice; individual ends such as human dignity, happiness, fulfillment.

What the pattern of declared norms amounts to, the idea it reflects, is nowhere articulated. I attempt to do so here, not as a philosophical construct, but as a distillation of what underlies national and international instruments.

Human rights are rights of individuals in society. Every human being has, or is entitled to have, "rights"-legitimate, valid, justified claims-upon his or her society; claims to various "goods" and benefits. Human rights are not some abstract, inchoate "good"; they are defined, particular claims listed in international instruments such as the Universal Declaration of Human Rights and the major covenants and conventions. They are those benefits deemed essential for individual well-being, dignity, and fulfillment, and that reflect a common sense of justice, fairness, and decency. In the constitutional jurisprudence of the United States, as we shall see, individual rights have long been thought of as consisting only of "immunities," as limitations on what government might do to the individual. Human rights, on the other hand, include not only these negative "immunity claims" but also positive "resource claims," claims to what society is deemed required to do for the individual. They include liberties-freedom from (for example, detention, torture), and freedom to (speak, assemble); they include also the right to food, housing, and other basic human needs.

Human rights are universal: they belong to every human being in every human society. They do not differ with geography or history, culture or ideology, political or economic system, or stage of societal development. To call them "human" implies that all human beings have them, equally and in equal measure, by virtue of their humanity—regardless of sex, race, age; regardless of high or low "birth," social class, national origin, ethnic or tribal affiliation; regardless of wealth or poverty, occupation, talent, merit, religion, ideology, or other commitment. Implied in one's humanity, human rights are inalienable and imprescriptible: they cannot be transferred, forfeited, or waived; they cannot be lost by having been usurped, or by one's failure to exercise or assert them.

Human rights are rights; they are not merely aspirations, or assertions of the good. To call them rights is not to assert, merely, that the benefits indicated are desirable or necessary; or, merely, that it is "right" that the individual shall enjoy these goods; or even, merely, that it is the duty of society to respect the immunity or provide the benefits. To call them "rights" implies that they are claims "as of right," not by appeal to grace, or charity, or brotherhood, or love; they need not be earned or deserved. The idea of rights implies entitlement on the part of the holder in some order under some applicable norm; the idea of human rights implies entitlement in a moral order under a moral law, to be translated into and confirmed as legal entitlement in the legal order of a political society. When a society recognizes that a person has a right, it affirms, legitimates, and justifies that entitlement, and incorporates and establishes it in the society's system of values, giving it important weight in competition with other societal values.

Human rights imply the obligation of society to satisfy those claims. The state must develop institutions and procedures, must plan, must mobilize resources as necessary to meet those claims. Political and civil rights require laws, institutions, procedures, and other safeguards against tyranny, against corrupt, immoral, and inefficient agencies or officials. Economic and social rights in modern society require taxation and spending and a network of agencies for social welfare. The idea of human rights implies also that society must provide some system of remedies to which individuals may resort to obtain the benefits to which they are entitled or be compensated for their loss. Together, the affirmation of entitlement, the recognition by society of an obligation to mobilize itself to discharge it, and the implication of remedy, all enhance the likelihood that the right will be realized, that individuals will actually enjoy the benefits to which they are entitled.

Human rights are claims upon society. These claims may derive from moral principles governing relations between persons, but it is society that bears the obligation to satisfy the claims. Of course, the official representatives of society must themselves respect individual freedoms and immunities; political society must also act to protect the individual's rights against private invasion. As regards claims to economic and social benefits, society must act as insurer to provide them if individuals cannot provide them for themselves. Thus, government must protect me from assault by my neighbor, or from wolves, and must ensure that I have bread or hospitalization; in human rights terms my rights are against the state, not against the neighbor or the wolves, the baker, or the hospital. The state may arrange to satisfy my claims by maintaining domestic laws and institutions that give me, say, rights and remedies in tort against my neighbor, or administrative remedies against a corrupt, misguided, or inefficient bureaucrat, or access to public schools or health services. Those legal rights and remedies against individuals or agencies within society give effect to my human rights claims upon society.

The idea of human rights has implications for the relation of the individual's rights to other public goods. It is commonly said that human rights are "fundamental." That means that they are important, that life, dignity, and other important human values depend on them; it does not mean that they are "absolute," that they may never be abridged for any purpose in any circumstances. Human rights enjoy a prima facie, presumptive inviolability, and will often "trump" other public goods. Government may not do some things, and must do others, even though the authorities are persuaded that it is in the society's interest (and perhaps even in the individual's own interest) to do otherwise; individual human rights cannot be lightly sacrificed even for the good of the greatest number, even for the general good of all. But if human rights do not bow lightly to public concerns, they may be sacrificed if countervailing societal interests are important enough, in particular circumstances, for limited times and purposes, to the extent strictly necessary. The Universal Declaration recognizes that rights are subject to limitations determined by law "for the purpose of securing due recognition and respect for the rights and freedoms of others and of meeting the just requirements of morality, public order, and the general welfare in a democratic society" (Art. 29[2]).

The idea of rights accepts that some limitations on rights are permissible but the limitations are themselves strictly limited. Public emergency, national security, public order are weighty terms, bespeaking important societal interests, but they are not to be lightly or loosely invoked, and the conception of national security or public order cannot be so large as to swallow the right. Derogations are permitted only in time of a public emergency that threatens the life of the nation, not as a response to fears (warranted or paranoid) for other values, or for the security of a particular regime. Even in an authentic emergency, a society may derogate from rights only to the extent strictly required by the exigencies of the situation, and even such necessary derogations must not involve invidious inequalities, and may not derogate from basic rights: they must not invade the right to life, or involve torture or cruel, inhuman punishment, slavery or servitude, conviction of crime under ex post facto laws, denial of rights as a person before the law, or violate freedom of thought, conscience, or religion. Moreover, considerations of public emergency permitting derogations, or of national security or public order permitting limitations on certain rights, refer to a universal standard, monitored by external scrutiny and judgment.

In sum, the idea of human rights is that the individual counts—independent of and in addition to his or her part in the common good. Autonomy and liberty must be respected, and the individual's basic economic-social needs realized, as a matter of entitlement, not of grace or discretion (even by wise and benevolent authority, or even by "the people"). The individual has obligations to others and to the community, and society may ask all individuals to give up some of their rights for the rights of others and for the common good, but there is a core of individuality that cannot be invaded or sacrificed. And all individuals count equally. An individual's right can be sacrificed to another's right only when choice is inevitable, and only according to some principle of choice reflecting the comparative value of each right. No particular individual can be singled out for particular sacrifice, except at random or by some other "neutral principle," consistent with the spirit of equal protection of the laws.

I have referred to rights as claims upon society, not against society. In the ideology of rights, human rights are not "against society," against the interest of society; on the contrary, the good society is one in which individual rights flourish, and the promotion and protection of every individual's rights are a public good. There is an aura of conflict between individual and society only in that individual rights are asserted against government, against those who represent society officially, and because the human rights idea often requires that an individual's right be preferred to some other public good. But this apparent conflict between individual and society is specious; in the longer, deeper view, the society is better if the individual's rights are respected.

. . .

NOTES & QUESTIONS

1.   Professor Louis Henkin, widely credited with founding the field of human rights law, was also insistent in training the lens of human rights on the United States' own practices. He noted, in 1979, that, in the cathedral of human rights, "the United States has not been a pillar . . . only a 'flying buttress'—supporting them from the outside." Louis Henkin, *Rights: American and Human*, 79 Colum. L. Rev. 405, 421 (1979). A prolific author of many influential books, Professor Henkin served as the chief reporter for the Third Restatement of the Foreign Relations Law of the United States (1987) which, by 2007, had been cited in eighteen U.S. Supreme Court decisions and over 250 decisions by the courts of appeals. *See* Ruth Bader Ginsburg, *Letters Honoring Louis Henkin*, 38 Colum. L. Rev. 467 (2007). For an oral history of Professor Henkin, see Catherine Powell, *Louis Henkin and Human Rights: A New Deal at Home and Abroad*, *in* 1 Bringing Human Rights Home: A History of Human Rights in the United States 57 (Soohoo et al. eds., 2008).

2.   Henkin describes a set of characteristics of human rights, for example, that they are "universal" and "do not differ with geography or history, culture or ideology, political or economic system, or stage of societal development." Louis Henkin, The Age of Rights 2 (1990). What types of rights can you envision meeting his criteria? Are there any potential problems or pitfalls with defining human rights in this way?

3. How does Henkin conceive of the role of the state in ensuring human rights? Does his view of the state require a particular model of governance?

4. Why does Henkin emphasize that these guarantees are not amorphous principles but rather clearly articulated legal rights?

As the Henkin excerpt indicates, a central concept embedded in human rights is the understanding of the dignity of all people. In the following excerpt, Professor Oscar Schachter opines on the meaning of "dignity" and its relevance to the concept of human rights. How does the concept of "dignity" as articulated by Schachter inform the content of human rights as described by Henkin?

OSCAR SCHACHTER, "HUMAN DIGNITY AS A NORMATIVE CONCEPT"
77 Am. J. of Int'l L.848, 849–52 (1983).

We do not find an explicit definition of the expression "dignity of the human person" in international instruments or (as far as I know) in national law. Its intrinsic meaning has been left to intuitive understanding, conditioned in large measure by cultural factors. When it has been invoked in concrete situations, it has been generally assumed that a violation of human dignity can be recognized even if the abstract term cannot be defined. "I know it when I see it even if I cannot tell you what it is."

In some situations an abstract definition is not needed; but it is not entirely satisfying to accept the idea that human dignity cannot be defined or analyzed in general terms. Without a reasonably clear general idea of its meaning, we cannot easily reject a specious use of the concept, nor can we without understanding its meaning draw specific implications for relevant conduct.

An analysis of dignity may begin with its etymological root, the Latin "dignitas" translated as worth (in French, "valeur"). One lexical meaning of dignity is "intrinsic worth." Thus, when the UN Charter refers to the "dignity and worth" of the human person, it uses two synonyms for the same concept. The other instruments speak of "inherent dignity," an expression that is close to "intrinsic worth."

What is meant by "respect" for "intrinsic worth" or "inherent dignity" of a person? "Respect" has several nuanced meanings: "esteem," "deference," "a proper regard for," "recognition of." These terms have both a subjective aspect (how one feels or thinks about another) and an objective aspect (how one treats another). Both are relevant to our question, but it seems more useful to focus on the latter aspect for purposes of practical measures.

One general answer to our question is suggested by the Kantian injunction to treat every human being as an end, not as a means. Respect for the intrinsic worth of every person should mean that individuals are not to be perceived or treated merely as instruments or objects of the will of others. This proposition will probably be generally acceptable as an ideal. There may be more questions about its implications. I shall suggest such implications as corollaries of the general proposition.

The first is that a high priority should be accorded in political, social and legal arrangements to individual choices in such matters as beliefs, way of life, attitudes and the conduct of public affairs. Note that this is stated as a "high priority," not an absolute rule. We may give it more specific content by applying it to political and psychological situations. In the political context, respect for the dignity and worth of all persons, and for their individual choices, leads, broadly speaking, to a strong emphasis on the will and consent of the governed. It means that the coercive rule of one or the few over the many is incompatible with a due respect for the dignity of the person. It also means that governments are not to use coercion to impose beliefs and attitudes on those subject to their rule or to extend their authority into areas of human life that are essentially personal and familial. The question of the proper boundaries between the public and the private, and between the sphere governed by the "general will" and that left to the individual remains to be answered in particular cases. But the idea that such boundaries need to be drawn and that an appropriate priority should be accorded to individual choices is not without significance. It clearly runs counter to many existing political ideologies and practices.

The conception of respect for dignity suggested above can also be given more specific meaning by applying it to actions of psychological significance. Indeed, nothing is so clearly violative of the dignity of persons as treatment that demeans or humiliates them. This includes not only attacks on personal beliefs and ways of life but also attacks on the groups and communities with which individuals are affiliated. Official statements that vilify groups or hold them up to ridicule and contempt are an especially dangerous form of psychological aggression resulting in a lack of respect by others for such groups and, perhaps even more insidious, destroying or reducing the sense of self-respect that is so important to the integrity of every human. We can also point to the widespread practice of using psychogenic drugs or other forms of psychological coercion to impose conformity and ideological obedience. These should clearly be seen as violations of the inherent dignity of the person. Put in positive terms, respect for the intrinsic worth of a person requires a recognition that the person is entitled to have his or her beliefs, attitudes, ideas and feelings. The use of coercion, physical or psychological, to change personal beliefs is as striking an affront to the dignity of the person as physical abuse or mental torture.

Our emphasis on respect for individuals and their choices also implies proper regard for the responsibility of individuals. The idea that people are generally responsible for their conduct is a recognition of their distinct identity and their capacity to make choices. Exceptions may have to be made for those incapable of such choices . . . or in some cases for those under severe necessity. But the general recognition of individual responsibility, whether expressed in matters of criminal justice or civic duties, is an aspect of the respect that each person merits as a person. It is also worth noting as a counterpart that restraint is called for in imputing responsibility to individuals for acts of others such as groups of which they are members. In general, collective responsibility is a denigration of the dignity of the individual, a denial of a person's capacity to choose and act on his or her responsibility.

We do not by this last comment mean to separate individuals sharply from the collectivities of which they are a part. Indeed, we believe that the idea of human dignity involves a complex notion of the individual. It includes recognition of a distinct personal identity, reflecting individual autonomy and responsibility. It also embraces a recognition that the individual self is a part of larger collectivities and that they, too, must be considered in the meaning of the inherent dignity of the person. We can readily see the practical import of this conception of personality by considering political orders that, on the one hand, arbitrarily override individual choice and, on the other, seek to dissolve group ties. There is also a "procedural" implication in that it indicates that every individual and each significant group should be recognized as having the capacity to assert claims to protect their essential dignity.

We are led more deeply into the analysis of human dignity when we consider its relation to the material needs of human beings and to the ideal of distributive justice. Few will dispute that a person in abject condition, deprived of adequate means of subsistence, or denied the opportunity to work, suffers a profound affront to his sense of dignity and intrinsic worth. Economic and social arrangements cannot therefore be excluded from a consideration of the demands of dignity. At the least, it requires recognition of a minimal concept of distributive justice that would require satisfaction of the essential needs of everyone.

Some would probably go beyond this and contend that substantial equality is a necessary condition of respect for the intrinsic worth of the human person. "Each person is as good as every other" may be inferred as a plausible maxim. In particular, relations of dominance and subordination would be viewed as antithetical to the basic ideal. If this is so, great discrepancies in wealth and power need to be eliminated to avoid such relations. However, the counterargument can be made that such egalitarian objectives cannot be realized without excessive curtailment of individual liberty and the use of coercion. This familiar confrontation of conflicting political philosophies need not be pursued here, but it is worth noting that demands for the respect of human dignity will almost surely lead into the continuing debate between advocates of equality and advocates of freedom.

These observations on the meaning of respect for the inherent dignity of the human being suggest the far-reaching implications of an ideal that has not yet been given substantial specific content. At the same time, our analysis indicates that a determinate core of meaning may be elucidated that is in keeping with widely accepted (though not universally accepted) values. This core of meaning has not been formulated as an explicit definition. To do so would result in another highly abstract formula. What is important is the extent to which the analysis leads to more concrete acceptable norms of conduct.

. . .

NOTES & QUESTIONS

1.   What is the relationship between the concept of dignity and the protection of human rights? Can we rely on the notion of dignity to help define what "counts" as a human right? Or is dignity itself too amorphous a concept?

2.   Although the concept of dignity was not included in the U.S. Constitution as a supplement or complement to the fundamental rights of equality and liberty, the U.S. Supreme Court has repeatedly drawn on the concept of dignity in its jurisprudence. Professors Judith Resnik and Julie Suk note that, "[d]uring the eighteenth and nineteenth centuries, the Supreme Court mentioned the word 'dignity' only in terms of entities such as sovereigns and courts. Moving forward to the twentieth century . . . the word becomes linked to persons. It was not until the 1940s—the decade of World War II and the Universal Declaration of Human Rights—that the Court embraced dignity as something possessed by individuals." Judith Resnik & Julie Chi-hye Suk, *Adding Insult to Injury: Questioning the Role of Dignity in Conceptions of Sovereignty*, 55 Stan. L. Rev. 1921, 1934 (2003). For example, Justice Frank Murphy, dissenting in the World War II era case of *Korematsu v. United States*, stated that the policy of Japanese exclusion and internment would "adopt one of the cruelest of the rationales used by our enemies to destroy the dignity of the individual and to encourage and open the door to discriminatory actions against other minority groups in the passions of tomorrow." 323 U.S. 219, 240 (1944). *See* Maxine D. Goodman, *Human Dignity in Supreme Court Jurisprudence*, 84 Neb. L. Rev. 749, 754–55 (2006). The U.S. Supreme Court has since drawn upon or referenced the concept of dignity in cases addressing 8th Amendment protections against cruel and unusual treatment; 4th amendment protections against unreasonable searches and seizures; and the equality and due process guarantees of the

5th and 14th amendments. For example, in *Planned Parenthood v. Casey*, 505 U.S. 833 (1992), *Lawrence v. Texas*, 539, U.S. 558 (2003), and *United States v. Windsor*, 133 S. Ct. 2675 (2013), the majority opinions of Justice Kennedy identified human dignity as a touchstone when addressing rights of procreation, abortion, sexual relations, privacy and marriage. *See* Judith Resnik & Julie Chi-hye Suk, *Adding Insult to Injury: Questioning the Role of Dignity in Conceptions of Sovereignty* 55 Stan. L. Rev. 1921, 1935 (2003). *See also* The Constitution of Rights: Human Dignity and American Values (Michael J. Meyer & William A. Parent eds., 1992); Libby Adler, *The Dignity of Sex,* 17 U.C.L.A. Women's L.J. 1 (2008); Christopher A. Bracey, *Dignity in Race Jurisprudence,* 7 U. Pa. J. Const. L. 669 (2005); Erin Daly, *Human Dignity in the Roberts Court: A Story of Inchoate Institutions, Autonomous Individuals, and the Reluctant Recognition of a Right*, 37 Ohio N.U. L. Rev. 381 (2011); Leslie Meltzer Henry, *The Jurisprudence of Dignity*, 160 U. Pa. L. Rev. 169 (2011); Johanna Kalb, *Litigating Dignity: A Human Rights Framework*, 74 Alb. L. Rev. 1725 (2011); Judith Resnik, *Law's Migration: American Exceptionalism, Silent Dialogues, and Federalism's Multiple Ports of Entry*, 115 Yale L.J. 1564, 1594–97 (2006); Reva B. Siegel, *Dignity and the Politics of Protection: Abortion Rights under Casey/Carhart*, 117 Yale L.J. 1694 (2008); and Stephen J. Wermiel, *Law and Human Dignity: The Judicial Soul of Justice Brennan*, 7 Wm. & Mary Bill Rts. J. 223 (1998).

   3.   While the term "human rights" is found in neither the U.S. nor state constitutions, the term "dignity" is found in several state constitutions. The right to dignity is included in the constitutions of Montana, Louisiana, Illinois, and the Commonwealth of Puerto Rico. For example, Article 2, Section 4 of the Montana State Constitution provides:

> Individual dignity: The dignity of the human being is inviolable. No person shall be denied the equal protection of the laws. Neither the state nor any person, firm, corporation, or institution shall discriminate against any person in the exercise of his civil or political rights on the basis of race, color, sex, culture, social origin or condition, or political or religious ideas.

See also Ill. Const. art. 1, § 20; La. Const. art. 1, § 3; P.R. Const. art. 2, § 1. Professor Vicki Jackson has detailed the international influences behind the right to individual dignity clauses in the Puerto Rico and Montana Constitutions and courts' interpretation of the clauses. *See* Vicki C. Jackson, *Constitutional Dialogue and Human Dignity: States and Transnational Constitutional Discourse*, 65 Mont. L. Rev. 15 (2004). *See also* Matthew O. Clifford & Thomas P. Huff, *Some Thoughts on the Meaning and Scope of the Montana Constitution's "Dignity" Clause with Possible Applications*, 61 Mont. L. Rev. 301 (2000); Heinz Klug, *The Dignity Clause of the Montana Constitution: May Foreign Jurisprudence Lead the Way to an Expanded Interpretation?*, 64 Mont. L. Rev. 133 (2003). Is international law an appropriate source for state courts to consider in interpreting state constitutional dignity clauses? If so, how might advocates urge U.S. state court judges to draw on international human rights law in interpreting the dignity clauses in their state constitutions? We will revisit these questions in more detail in **Chapter VI**.

B. FORMALIZING HUMAN RIGHTS

In the aftermath of the atrocities of World War II, national governments seeking to crystalize and protect human rights organized new international and regional legal systems by forming the United Nations, the Organization of American States, and the Council of Europe, each of which included as its purpose the protection and promotion of human rights. Each of these systems likewise created human rights instruments setting forth a comprehensive set of rights and establishing mechanisms for their protection and promotion.[6]

The United Nations has played a particularly important role in the development of modern human rights law. The organization has its origins in the Atlantic Charter, an agreement between the United States and Great Britain envisioning a post-World War II world and setting out common principles for international collaboration to establish a lasting peace. Echoing themes from Roosevelt's January 1941 Four Freedoms speech to Congress, which will be discussed in **Chapter II**, the Atlantic Charter articulated the "desire to bring about the fullest collaboration between all nations in the economic field with the object of securing, for all, improved labor standards, economic advancement and social security," and "to see established a peace which will afford to all nations the means of dwelling in safety within their own boundaries, and which will afford assurance that all the men in all the lands may live out their lives in freedom from fear and want."[7] President Franklin Delano Roosevelt and Prime Minister Winston Churchill signed the Atlantic Charter on August 14, 1941, onboard a ship off the coast of Newfoundland, prior to the United States' entry into the war in December 1941. Six months later, twenty-six allied countries signed the Declaration by United Nations, pledging support for the Charter, followed in 1943 by the Moscow Declaration, which recognized the need for the creation of an international organization to maintain peace and security.[8]

The structure and scope of the United Nations was developed over the course of the Dumbarton Oaks Conference in Washington D.C., from August through October 1944. At the conference, the United States, Great Britain, Soviet Union, and China reached consensus on a preliminary blueprint, later supplemented by the Yalta Conference, for what would

---

[6]   The African human rights system, created under the African Union, is a more recent regional human rights system. It is composed of the African Commission on Human and Peoples' Rights and the African Court on Human and Peoples' Rights.

[7]   Atlantic Charter, U.S.-U.K., Aug. 14, 1941.

[8]   For a more detailed accounting of the history leading to the U.N. Charter, and the U.S. role in the creation of the United Nations, see Ruth B. Russell, A History of the United Nations Charter: The Role of the United States, 1940-1945 (1958).

become the United Nations. The next year, in April 1945, representatives from fifty nations met in San Francisco, resulting in the Charter of the United Nations, the treaty establishing the United Nations and setting forth its underlying purposes and principles.

Article 1 of the U.N. Charter states as a purpose of the U.N. "[t]o achieve international co-operation in solving international problems of an economic, social, cultural, or humanitarian character, and in promoting and encouraging respect for human rights and for fundamental freedoms for all without distinction as to race, sex, language, or religion."[9] Article 55 pledges the U.N. to promote "universal respect for, and observance of, human rights and fundamental freedoms for all without distinction as to race, sex, language, or religion."[10]

While the U.N. Charter contains several explicit references to international human rights, the Charter itself did not include a bill of international human rights. Instead, it established the Social and Economic Council, authorized to "make recommendations for the purpose of promoting respect for, and observance of, human rights and fundamental freedoms for all,"[11] and tasked with establishing a commission to promote human rights.[12] The Council created the Commission on Human Rights, which was responsible for drafting what would become the Universal Declaration of Human Rights.

The Universal Declaration of Human Rights (UDHR), adopted by the U.N. General Assembly on December 10, 1948, set forth norms recognizing and promoting dignity, fairness, and opportunity for all people to meet their basic needs. The principles articulated in the Universal Declaration and approved by forty-eight countries, with eight abstentions, became the basis for the universal human rights treaties. Though not legally binding, the UDHR is considered to be the most widely accepted international human rights instrument.

THE UNIVERSAL DECLARATION OF HUMAN RIGHTS
G.A. res. 217 (III) A, U.N. Doc. A/RES/217(III) (Dec. 10, 1948).

Article 1.

All human beings are born free and equal in dignity and rights. They are endowed with reason and conscience and should act towards one another in a spirit of brotherhood.

---

[9] U.N. Charter art. 1, para. 3.

[10] *Id.* at art. 55.

[11] *Id.* at art. 62, para. 2.

[12] *Id.* at art. 68.

Article 2.

Everyone is entitled to all the rights and freedoms set forth in this Declaration, without distinction of any kind, such as race, colour, sex, language, religion, political or other opinion, national or social origin, property, birth or other status.

Furthermore, no distinction shall be made on the basis of the political, jurisdictional or international status of the country or territory to which a person belongs, whether it be independent, trust, non-self-governing or under any other limitation of sovereignty.

Article 3.

Everyone has the right to life, liberty and security of person.

Article 4.

No one shall be held in slavery or servitude; slavery and the slave trade shall be prohibited in all their forms.

Article 5.

No one shall be subjected to torture or to cruel, inhuman or degrading treatment or punishment.

Article 6.

Everyone has the right to recognition everywhere as a person before the law.

Article 7.

All are equal before the law and are entitled without any discrimination to equal protection of the law. All are entitled to equal protection against any discrimination in violation of this Declaration and against any incitement to such discrimination.

Article 8.

Everyone has the right to an effective remedy by the competent national tribunals for acts violating the fundamental rights granted him by the constitution or by law.

Article 9.

No one shall be subjected to arbitrary arrest, detention or exile.

Article 10.

Everyone is entitled in full equality to a fair and public hearing by an independent and impartial tribunal, in the determination of his rights and obligations and of any criminal charge against him.

Article 11.

Everyone charged with a penal offence has the right to be presumed innocent until proved guilty according to law in a public trial at which he has had all the guarantees necessary for his defence.

No one shall be held guilty of any penal offence on account of any act or omission which did not constitute a penal offence, under national or international law, at the time when it was committed. Nor shall a heavier penalty be imposed than the one that was applicable at the time the penal offence was committed.

Article 12.

No one shall be subjected to arbitrary interference with his privacy, family, home or correspondence, nor to attacks upon his honour and reputation. Everyone has the right to the protection of the law against such interference or attacks.

Article 13.

Everyone has the right to freedom of movement and residence within the borders of each State.

Everyone has the right to leave any country, including his own, and to return to his country.

Article 14.

Everyone has the right to seek and to enjoy in other countries asylum from persecution.

This right may not be invoked in the case of prosecutions genuinely arising from nonpolitical crimes or from acts contrary to the purposes and principles of the United Nations.

Article 15.

Everyone has the right to a nationality.

No one shall be arbitrarily deprived of his nationality nor denied the right to change his nationality.

Article 16.

Men and women of full age, without any limitation due to race, nationality or religion, have the right to marry and to found a family. They are entitled to equal rights as to marriage, during marriage and at its dissolution.

Marriage shall be entered into only with the free and full consent of the intending spouses.

The family is the natural and fundamental group unit of society and is entitled to protection by society and the State.

Article 17.

Everyone has the right to own property alone as well as in association with others.

No one shall be arbitrarily deprived of his property.

Article 18.

Everyone has the right to freedom of thought, conscience and religion; this right includes freedom to change his religion or belief, and freedom, either alone or in community with others and in public or private, to manifest his religion or belief in teaching, practice, worship and observance.

Article 19.

Everyone has the right to freedom of opinion and expression; this right includes freedom to hold opinions without interference and to seek, receive and impart information and ideas through any media and regardless of frontiers.

Article 20.

Everyone has the right to freedom of peaceful assembly and association.

No one may be compelled to belong to an association.

Article 21.

Everyone has the right to take part in the government of his country, directly or through freely chosen representatives.

Everyone has the right to equal access to public service in his country.

The will of the people shall be the basis of the authority of government; this will shall be expressed in periodic and genuine elections which shall be by universal and equal suffrage and shall be held by secret vote or by equivalent free voting procedures.

Article 22.

Everyone, as a member of society, has the right to social security and is entitled to realization, through national effort and international co-operation and in accordance with the organization and resources of each State, of the economic, social and cultural rights indispensable for his dignity and the free development of his personality.

Article 23.

Everyone has the right to work, to free choice of employment, to just and favourable conditions of work and to protection against unemployment.

Everyone, without any discrimination, has the right to equal pay for equal work.

Everyone who works has the right to just and favourable remuneration ensuring for himself and his family an existence worthy of human dignity, and supplemented, if necessary, by other means of social protection.

Everyone has the right to form and to join trade unions for the protection of his interests.

Article 24.

Everyone has the right to rest and leisure, including reasonable limitation of working hours and periodic holidays with pay.

Article 25.

Everyone has the right to a standard of living adequate for the health and well-being of himself and of his family, including food, clothing, housing and medical care and necessary social services, and the right to security in the event of unemployment, sickness, disability, widowhood, old age or other lack of livelihood in circumstances beyond his control.

Motherhood and childhood are entitled to special care and assistance. All children, whether born in or out of wedlock, shall enjoy the same social protection.

Article 26.

Everyone has the right to education. Education shall be free, at least in the elementary and fundamental stages. Elementary education shall be compulsory. Technical and professional education shall be made generally available and higher education shall be equally accessible to all on the basis of merit.

Education shall be directed to the full development of the human personality and to the strengthening of respect for human rights and fundamental freedoms. It shall promote understanding, tolerance and friendship among all nations, racial or religious groups, and shall further the activities of the United Nations for the maintenance of peace.

Parents have a prior right to choose the kind of education that shall be given to their children.

Article 27.

Everyone has the right freely to participate in the cultural life of the community, to enjoy the arts and to share in scientific advancement and its benefits.

Everyone has the right to the protection of the moral and material interests resulting from any scientific, literary or artistic production of which he is the author.

Article 28.

Everyone is entitled to a social and international order in which the rights and freedoms set forth in this Declaration can be fully realized.

Article 29.

Everyone has duties to the community in which alone the free and full development of his personality is possible.

In the exercise of his rights and freedoms, everyone shall be subject only to such limitations as are determined by law solely for the purpose of securing due recognition and respect for the rights and freedoms of others and of meeting the just requirements of morality, public order and the general welfare in a democratic society.

These rights and freedoms may in no case be exercised contrary to the purposes and principles of the United Nations.

Article 30.

Nothing in this Declaration may be interpreted as implying for any State, group or person any right to engage in any activity or to perform any act aimed at the destruction of any of the rights and freedoms set forth herein.

NOTES & QUESTIONS

1.   Is the UDHR sufficiently clear about the content and scope of the human rights protections it covers? What do the discussions of dignity and human rights offered by Professors Henkin and Schachter add? What else would you want to know about the nature of the rights protected?

2.   In what ways do the provisions of the UDHR differ from the U.S. Constitution, and in particular from the Constitution's Bill of Rights?

3.   As suggested above, the United States played a fundamental role in the development of the United Nations and the UDHR. President Roosevelt's 1941 State of the Union address, articulating the "four essential freedoms," was memorialized in the Universal Declaration's Preamble, which states that, "the freedom of speech and belief and freedom from fear and want have been proclaimed as the highest aspiration of the common people." Universal Declaration of Human Rights preamble, G.A. Res. 217 (III) A, U.N. Doc. A/RES/217(III) (Dec. 10, 1948). From January 1947 until the UDHR's adoption in December 1948, Eleanor Roosevelt chaired the Commission on Human Rights and played a key role in the Declaration's drafting process. For more detailed histories of the UDHR and the United States' role in developing and drafting the declaration, see Mary Ann Glendon, A World Made New: Eleanor Roosevelt and the Universal Declaration of Human Rights (2001); Johannes Morsink, The Universal Declaration of Human Rights: Origins, Drafting and Intent (1999).

4. In 1993, the member states of the United Nations adopted the Vienna Declaration and Programme of Action at the World Conference on Human Rights in Vienna, reasserting their commitment to human rights contained in the U.N. Charter and the Universal Declaration of Human Rights. The declaration reaffirms that "all human rights derive from the dignity and worth inherent in the human person," and that "[a]ll human rights are universal, indivisible and interdependent and interrelated." World Conference on Human Rights, June 14–25, 1993, *Vienna Declaration and Programme of Action*, U.N. Doc. A/Conf.157/23 (July 12, 1993). What does it mean for human rights to be universal, interdependent, interrelated, and indivisible? What practical impact might these concepts have in advocacy around human rights concerns in the United States?

5. Historian Samuel Moyn argues that, contrary to common understanding of the importance of the UDHR in ushering in the era of human rights, until the mid-1970s, the term "human rights" was merely rhetorical. It wasn't until the 1970s, he argues, that a genuine social movement emerged around human rights. He states that this emergence was due to the "collapse of other, prior utopias . . . that promised a free way of life, but led into bloody morass, or offered emancipation from empire and capital, but suddenly came to seem like dark tragedies rather than bright hopes." Samuel Moyn, The Last Utopia: Human Rights in History 8 (2010). In this context, he argues, human rights "surged" because it provided "a pure alternative in an age of ideological betrayal and political collapse." *Id.* What are the implications of this argument? Note that Moyn's argument has sparked some critique. *See, e.g.*, Philip Alston, *Does the Past Matter? On the Origins of Human Rights*, 126 Harv. L. Rev. 2043 (2013) (reviewing Jenny Martinez, The Slave Trade and the Origins of International Human Rights Law (2012)) (characterizing Moyn as arguing that human rights "emerged in the 1970s seemingly from nowhere"); Jenny Martinez, *Response: Human Rights and History*, 126 Harv. L. Rev. F. 221 (May 20, 2013), http://harvardlawreview.org/2013/05/human-rights-and-history/ (characterizing Moyn's work as a sort of "Big Bang" theory of human rights).

Although the UDHR sets forth guiding principles addressing the full panoply of rights, for political and historical reasons explored later in this chapter and in **Chapter II**, economic, social, and cultural rights and civil and political rights were grouped into separate core treaties.[13] Thus, along with the UDHR, two key treaties form the International Bill of Rights: the International Covenant on Civil and Political Rights (ICCPR)[14] and the International Covenant on Economic, Social and

---

[13] *See* Carol Anderson, Eyes off the Prize: The United Nations and the African American Struggle for Human Rights, 1944–1955 (2003); Hope Lewis, *"New" Human Rights: U.S. Ambivalence Towards the International Economic and Social Rights Framework, in* 1 Bringing Human Rights Home 103 (Cynthia Soohoo et al. eds., 2008).

[14] International Covenant on Civil and Political Rights, Dec. 16, 1966, 999 U.N.T.S. 171 [hereinafter ICCPR].

Cultural Rights (ICESCR).[15] In total, nine core U.N. treaties are currently in force to protect and promote human rights, alongside other international and regional treaties and other documents that protect human rights (see chart below). We will explore many of these, along with the process for and impact of ratifying treaties in the United States, in **Chapter III**. The text of many of these treaties is set forth in the Appendix section.

Core U.N. Human Rights Treaties

Treaty	Description	Signed by the U.S.	Ratified by the U.S.
International Covenant on Economic, Social, and Cultural Rights (ICESCR)	The ICESCR is the principal human rights treaty regarding economic, social and cultural rights. It protects the rights to housing, work, social security, the highest attainable standard of health, and the continuous improvement of living conditions. It also prohibits all forms of discrimination in the enjoyment of these rights.	Yes	No
International Covenant on Civil and Political Rights (ICCPR)	The ICCPR protects a broad range of civil and political rights, including the right to life, freedom of association, the right to be free from torture and slavery, non-discrimination, and certain fair trial rights.	Yes	Yes

---

[15] International Covenant on Economic, Social and Cultural Rights, Dec. 16, 1966, 099 U.N.T.S. 3 [hereinafter ICESCR].

Treaty	Description	Signed by the U.S.	Ratified by the U.S.
International Convention on the Elimination of All Forms of Racial Discrimination (ICERD or CERD)	The ICERD, or CERD, is the principal human rights treaty on racial discrimination. The treaty specifically prohibits discrimination in the areas of voting, education, health, housing, property, social security and employment, among others.	Yes	Yes
Convention on the Elimination of All Forms of Discrimination Against Women (CEDAW)	The CEDAW is the principal human rights treaty on sex discrimination, which provides for women's equal access to—and equal opportunities in—private, political and public life.	Yes	No
Convention on the Rights of the Child (CRC)	The CRC is the principal human rights treaty on the rights of children. Though the U.S. has not ratified the Convention, it is the most widely ratified treaty in the international human rights system.	Yes	The United States has not ratified the CRC, but it has ratified two optional protocols (OPs) to the CRC, including OP on Sale of Children and OP on Children in Armed Conflict

Treaty	Description	Signed by the U.S.	Ratified by the U.S.
Convention Against Torture and other Cruel, Inhuman or Degrading Treatment or Punishment (CAT)	The CAT requires states to take effective measures to prevent and punish torture under any circumstances (even wartime) and also forbids states from sending individuals to other countries if there is reason to believe they will be tortured.	Yes	Yes
Convention on the Rights of Persons with Disabilities (CRPD)	The CRPD promotes disabled persons' rights to equal protection, equal participation, and accessibility, and provides special protection for women and children with disabilities.	Yes	No
International Convention on the Protection of the Rights of All Migrant Workers and Members of their Families (ICMW)	The ICMW protects the fundamental rights of both documented and undocumented migrants.	No	No
International Convention for the Protection of All Persons from Enforced Disappearances	The most recent U.N. human rights treaty, the ICPPED protects against forced disappearance.	No	No

NOTES & QUESTIONS

1.   The core universal human rights treaties clarify and expand upon the human rights principles set out in the UDHR. There are other sources which delineate human rights obligations, as well. The Convention on the Prevention and Punishment of the Crime of Genocide ("The Genocide Convention"), adopted by the U.N. General Assembly in 1948, entered into force in 1951, and ratified by the United States in 1988, defines and establishes genocide as an international crime. The Geneva Conventions regulate the conduct of armed conflict to protect human rights. Many of the conventions of the International Labour Organization (the ILO), including the fourteen that are ratified by the United States, include human rights provisions addressing issues such as forced labor, the right to organize, and the right to collective bargaining. The Universal Declaration of the Rights of Indigenous Peoples, which the U.N. General Assembly adopted in 2007 and the United States endorsed in 2010, is a non-binding international instrument which sets forth important understandings about the rights of indigenous peoples, including rights of equality, self-determination, property and cultural integrity. The human rights instruments of the regional Inter-American human rights system, discussed in **Chapter VIII**, are likewise relevant to the United States. These include the American Declaration, the American Convention on the Rights and Duties of Man, the Additional Protocol to the American Convention in the Area of Economic, Social and Cultural Rights (Protocol of San Salvador), and the Inter-American Convention on the Prevention, Punishment and Eradication of Violence Against Women (Convention of Belem do Para). Other regional human rights documents can be instructive in determining the content of human rights norms, including the European Convention for the Protection of Human Rights and Fundamental Freedoms and the African Charter on Human and Peoples' Rights. Customary international law, discussed in depth in **Chapter IV**, is also an important source of human rights law. Judicial decisions by international and domestic courts, and statements, reports, and analysis by international human rights experts, scholars, and others are sources of human rights law, as well.

2.   As noted above, although the UDHR addresses the full panoply of rights (civil, political, economic, social, and cultural), rights are grouped into two separate core treaties: the ICCPR (focusing on civil and political rights) and the ICESCR (focusing on economic, social, and cultural rights). While the international community has repeatedly reaffirmed the notion that all human rights must be accorded equal respect,[16] some tension exists with respect to the priority of civil and political versus economic, social, and

---

[16] For example, the 1993 World Conference on Human Rights in the Vienna Declaration and Programme of Action stated that "The international community must treat human rights globally in a fair and equal manner, on the same footing, and with the same emphasis." World Conference on Human Rights, June 14–25, 1993, *Vienna Declaration and Programme of Action*, ¶ 5, U.N. Doc. A/Conf.157/23 (July 12, 1993).

cultural rights. As Professors Hilary Charlesworth and Christine Chinkin describe:

> The development of human rights law through the UN is often, if controversially, described in terms of "generations". The first generation of rights consists of civil and political rights. First generation rights are typically characterised as rights that can be claimed by individuals against governments. Such rights protect against arbitrary interference by the state. Civil and political rights may be described as "negative" in that they require abstention by the state from particular acts, such as torture, arbitrary deprivation of life, liberty and security. . . . The core of first generation rights is the preservation of the autonomy of the individual. The major general document of the first generation of rights is the ICCPR.

> The second generation of rights comprises economic, social and cultural rights. These are rights, such as those to health, housing and education, that require positive activity by the state to ensure their protection. They assume an active, interventionist role for governments and can be claimed by individuals and groups to secure their subsistence, with dignity, as human beings. The most detailed definition of second generation rights is in the ICESCR. The comparative justiciability of the first and second generation rights is often raised in debates about the implementation of human rights. Can governments be held accountable for violations of economic, social and cultural rights in the same way as they can for violations of civil and political rights? How can causal links be established between alleged violations of economic and social rights and state actions, or inaction? What standard of compliance is required—is it a general standard, or does it depend on the level of economic development of the state concerned?

> The third generation of rights encompasses peoples', or collective, rights, such as the rights to self-determination, development and peace, that can only be claimed by groups, rather than by individuals. Claims of peoples' rights can be made against the international community, as well as particular nation states. The guarantee of collective rights assumes both that the benefits will flow to individuals within the group and that the interests of all members of the group will coincide. Many of the third generation rights are contained in "soft" law instruments, such as UN General Assembly declarations and resolutions.

. . .

> The generational metaphor in human rights law is controversial. First, very few rights fall neatly into a single category. For example, the right to freedom of thought, conscience and religion appears to be a quintessential individual civil right.

However, people form their thoughts and beliefs through shared ideas drawn from within their culture and express them, even internally, through their shared language. Culture and language are at the heart of peoples' rights, and peoples can only be sustained through adequate standards of living, education and health—economic and social rights. Second, the metaphor implies a hierarchy in the development of human rights within the international community. It is largely the product of cold war politics and decolonisation. Northern states have typically regarded civil and political rights as the most crucial for international protection and many commentators from the North still regard them as the paradigm against which all newer claims of rights must be measured. Indeed, some assert that civil and political rights are the only possible form of international human rights. Civil and political rights fit easily into liberal accounts of rights because they attach to the individual and provide a buffer against governmental action. Nations of the South have usually given the strongest statements of support for economic, social and cultural rights and group or peoples' rights, particularly the right to development. The argument is sometimes made that economic under-development makes concern with civil and political rights irrelevant or, indeed, destructive in the context of fragile states. In turn, the status of third generation rights has been regularly challenged in the North. The apparent end of the cold war allowed the Vienna Conference to attempt to resolve this debate by the very general prescription that "all human rights are universal, indivisible and interdependent and interrelated" and that they must accordingly be treated "in a fair and equal manner, on the same footing, and with the same emphasis".

Hilary Charlesworth and Christine Chinkin, The Boundaries of International Law: A Feminist Analysis 203–07 (2000).

What do you think accounts for the generational approach to human rights internationally? Do you think this prioritization persists? Do you see evidence of it within the United States? In **Chapter VII**, we will discuss the implications of, and challenges posed by, the approach within the United States with respect to economic, social and cultural rights, including the United States' failure to ratify the core treaty on ESC rights.

C. CRITIQUING HUMAN RIGHTS

While the U.N. instruments refer to human rights as a universal and unified whole, for many observers, human rights is a contested field with internal contradictions raising numerous political and ideological dilemmas. Critiques of human rights come from activists, academics, and other human rights professionals who argue that inconsistency and oversimplification of the human rights discourse has profound implications for advocacy goals and political realities.

This section introduces some of the core critiques regarding how human rights are defined and operationalized.

i.   Feminist Critiques

A strong critique of the traditional human rights paradigm comes from feminist scholars, who assert that the traditional definitions and frameworks for approaching human rights fail to account for women's experiences and perspectives and inadequately address the systemic nature of women's subordination. As you read the following, consider whether you agree with the concerns raised by the authors, whether there are specific issues or areas where these concerns are particularly evident, and whether there are ways in which the critiques might inform lawyers' and other advocates' engagement with "human rights."

HILARY CHARLESWORTH, CHRISTINE CHINKIN, AND SHELLY WRIGHT, "FEMINIST APPROACHES TO INTERNATIONAL LAW"
85 Am. J. of Int'l L. 613, 625–34 (1991).

The normative structure of international law has allowed issues of particular concern to women to be either ignored or undermined. For example, modern international law rests on and reproduces various dichotomies between the public and private spheres, and the "public" sphere is regarded as the province of international law. One such distinction is between public international law, the law governing the relations between nation-states, and private international law, the rules about conflicts between national legal systems. Another is the distinction between matters of international "public" concern and matters "private" to states that are considered within their domestic jurisdiction, in which the international community has no recognized legal interest. Yet another is the line drawn between law and other forms of "private" knowledge such as morality.

At a deeper level one finds a public/private dichotomy based on gender. One explanation feminist scholars offer for the dominance of men and the male voice in all areas of power and authority in the western liberal tradition is that a dichotomy is drawn between the public sphere and the private or domestic one. The public realm of the work place, the law, economics, politics and intellectual and cultural life, where power and authority are exercised, is regarded as the natural province of men; while the private world of the home, the hearth and children is seen as the appropriate domain of women. The public/private distinction has a normative, as well as a descriptive, dimension. Traditionally, the two spheres are accorded asymmetrical value: greater significance is attached to the public, male world than to the private, female one. The distinction drawn between the public and the private thus vindicates and makes natural the division of labor and allocation of rewards between the sexes. Its reproduction and acceptance in all areas of knowledge have conferred primacy on the male world and supported the dominance of men.

. . .

What force does the feminist critique of the public/private dichotomy in the foundation of domestic legal systems have for the international legal order? Traditionally, of course, international law was regarded as operating only in the most public of public spheres: the relations between nation-states. We argue, however, that the definition of certain principles of international law rests on and reproduces the public/private distinction. It thus privileges the male world view and supports male dominance in the international legal order.

The grip that the public/private distinction has on international law, and the consequent banishment of women's voices and concerns from the discipline, can be seen in the international prohibition on torture. The right to freedom from torture and other forms of cruel, inhuman or degrading treatment is generally accepted as a paradigmatic civil and political right. It is included in all international catalogs of civil and political rights and is the focus of specialized United Nations and regional treaties. The right to be free from torture is also regarded as a norm of customary international law-indeed, like the prohibition on slavery, as a norm of *jus cogens*.

The basis for the right is traced to "the inherent dignity of the human person." Behavior constituting torture is defined in the Convention against Torture as

> any act by which severe pain or suffering, whether physical or mental, is intentionally inflicted on a person for such purposes as obtaining from him or a third person information or a confession, punishing him for an act he or a third person has committed or is suspected of having committed, or intimidating or coercing him or a third person, or for any reason based on discrimination of any kind, when such pain or suffering is inflicted by or at the instigation of or with the consent or acquiescence of a public official or other person acting in an official capacity.

This definition has been considered broad because it covers mental suffering and behavior "at the instigation of" a public official. However, despite the use of the term "human person" in the Preamble, the use of the masculine pronoun alone in the definition of the proscribed behavior immediately gives the definition a male, rather than a truly human, context. More importantly, the description of the prohibited conduct relies on a distinction between public and private actions that obscures injuries to their dignity typically sustained by women. The traditional canon of human rights law does not deal in categories that fit the experiences of women. It is cast in terms of discrete violations of rights and offers little redress in cases where there is a pervasive, structural denial of rights.

The international definition of torture requires not only the intention to inflict suffering, but also the secondary intention that the infliction of suffering will fulfill a purpose. Recent evidence suggests that women and children, in particular, are victims of widespread and apparently random terror campaigns by both governmental and guerrilla groups in times of civil unrest or armed conflict. Such suffering is not clearly included in the international definition of torture.

A crucial aspect of torture and cruel, inhuman or degrading conduct, as defined, is that they take place in the public realm: a public official or a person acting officially must be implicated in the pain and suffering. The rationale for this limitation is that "private acts (of brutality) would usually be ordinary criminal offenses which national law enforcement is expected to repress. International concern with torture arises only when the State itself abandons its function of protecting its citizenry by sanctioning criminal action by law enforcement personnel." Many women suffer from torture in this limited sense. The international jurisprudence on the notion of torture arguably extends to sexual violence and psychological coercion if the perpetrator has official standing. However, severe pain and suffering that is inflicted outside the most public context of the state-for example, within the home or by private persons, which is the most pervasive and significant violence sustained by women-does not qualify as torture despite its impact on the inherent dignity of the human person. Indeed, some forms of violence are attributed to cultural tradition. The message of violence against women, argues Charlotte Bunch, is domination:

> [S]tay in your place or be afraid. Contrary to the argument that such violence is only personal or cultural, it is profoundly political. It results from the structural relationships of power, domination, and privilege between men and women in society. Violence against women is central to maintaining those political relations at home, at work, and in all public spheres.

States are held responsible for torture only when their designated agents have direct responsibility for such acts and that responsibility is imputed to the state. States are not considered responsible if they have maintained a legal and social system in which violations of physical and mental integrity are endemic. In its draft articles on state responsibility, the International Law Commission did not widen the concept of imputability to incorporate such acts. A feminist perspective on human rights would require a rethinking of the notions of imputability and state responsibility and in this sense would challenge the most basic assumptions of international law. If violence against women were considered by the international legal system to be as shocking as violence against people for their political ideas, women would have considerable support in their struggle.

. . .

Some branches of international law have recognized and addressed issues relating to women. Various International Labour Organisation Conventions focus on women. A growing literature on these conventions examines the assumptions they make about the role of women, the topics they cover, and their approach to the position of women.

The Women's Convention is the most prominent international normative instrument recognizing the special concerns of women. But the terms of the Convention and the way it has been accepted by states prompt us to ask whether it offers a real or chimerical possibility of change.

The Women's Convention has been ratified or acceded to by almost two-thirds of the members of the United Nations. Article 1 defines "discrimination against women" as

> any distinction, exclusion or restriction made on the basis of sex which has the effect or purpose of impairing or nullifying the recognition, enjoyment or exercise by women, irrespective of their marital status, on a basis of equality of men and women, of human rights and fundamental freedoms in the political, economic, social, cultural, civil or any other field.

Although the Convention goes further than simply requiring equality of opportunity and covers the more contentious concept of equality of result, which justifies affirmative action programs and protection against indirect discrimination, the underlying assumption of its definition of discrimination is that women and men are the same. Most international commentators treat this model of equality as uncontroversial. But the notions of both equality of opportunity and equality of result accept the general applicability of a male standard (except in special circumstances such as pregnancy) and promise a very limited form of equality: equality is defined as being like a man. "Man," writes Catharine MacKinnon, "has become the measure of all things." In this analysis, equality can be achieved in a relatively straightforward way by legally requiring the removal of identifiable barriers to the rise of women to the same status as men: equality is achievable within the social and legal structures as they are now. This assumption ignores the many real differences and inequities between the sexes and the significant barriers to their removal.

. . .

Certainly, the separate focus on women in the Women's Convention is beneficial in some respects. Attention is drawn to issues of distinct concern to women (for example, trafficking in women and prostitution) and to the fact that not all women have the same problems (for example, rural women have special needs). The reporting provisions require that state parties focus on the steps they have taken to implement the goals of the Convention so that discrimination against women does not become submerged in general human rights issues. The Convention also provides an important mix of civil, political, economic and social rights.

The Women's Convention, however, establishes much weaker implementation procedures than those of other human rights instruments of apparently universal applicability such as the International Convention on the Elimination of All Forms of Racial Discrimination and the Covenant on Civil and Political Rights. More generally, the specialized nature of the Women's Convention has been used by "mainstream" human rights bodies to justify ignoring or minimizing women's perspectives. They can assure themselves that, since these problems are scrutinized elsewhere, their organizations are relieved from the task. Yet the impact on women and men of many provisions of, for example, the Covenant on Civil and Political Rights may not be the same.

States have made a significant number of reservations and declarations of understanding when becoming parties to the Women's Convention. Article 28(1) permits ratification subject to reservations, provided the reservations are not "incompatible with the object and purpose of the present Convention" (Article 28(2)). No criteria are given for the determination of incompatibility. Over 40 of the 105 parties to the Convention have made a total of almost a hundred reservations to its terms. Many of these reservations were motivated by the conflict between some interpretations of Islam and the notion of sexual equality. They take the form of limiting the reserving state's obligations under the Convention to the taking of steps compatible with Islamic law and customs. Both general reservations and reservations to specific provisions have been made that are regarded by other state parties as incompatible with the overall object and purpose of the Convention. Other reservations concern national religious or customary laws that restrict women's inheritance and property rights; nationality laws that do not accord women the same rights as men to acquire, change or retain their nationality upon marriage; and laws limiting women's economic opportunities, freedom of movement and choice of residence.

The pattern of reservations to the Women's Convention underlines the inadequacy of the present normative structure of international law. The international community is prepared to formally acknowledge the considerable problems of inequality faced by women, but only, it seems, if individual states are not required as a result to alter patriarchal practices that subordinate women. Members of the CEDAW Committee, which monitors the implementation of the Convention but does not have jurisdiction to determine the compatibility of reservations with it, have questioned representatives of state parties about their reservations. The biennial meetings of the state parties, however, have not taken action to obtain an authoritative determination on the compatibility of the reservations with the object and purpose of the Convention. The numerous reservations made to the Women's Convention stand in stark contrast to the four substantive reservations made to the Convention on the Elimination of All Forms of Racial Discrimination and suggest that discrimination against women is somehow regarded as more "natural" and acceptable than racial discrimination.

. . .

TRACY E. HIGGINS, "ANTI-ESSENTIALISM, RELATIVISM, AND HUMAN RIGHTS"
19 Harv. Women's L. J. 89, 93–97, 101–105 (1996).

Despite the general consensus reflected in the Declaration, differences have persisted over the scope and priorities of the international human rights agenda, differences that are translated with surprising frequency into the rhetoric of universality versus cultural relativism, imperialism versus self-determination. Notwithstanding the language of universality, the question remains: To what extent may a state depart from international norms in the name of culture? Both the Covenant on Economic, Social and Cultural Rights and the Covenant on Civil and Political Rights contribute to this tension in their recognition of the importance of the collective right to self-determination. These documents do not clearly resolve the degree to which citizens, exercising their right of self-determination, may subordinate other protected rights in the interest of security, development, or culture.

Apart from any ambiguities in human rights instruments themselves, non-Western states have argued that the very hierarchy of human rights established in those instruments privileges civil and political rights over economic, social and cultural rights in a way that is biased toward both Western political traditions and the wealth of Western states relative to the rest of the world. Strategic enforcement of existing standards, coupled with the persistence of discrimination and economic inequality in Western nations, have further called into question the adequacy of Western concepts of civil and political rights to ensure human well-being. Finally, postmodernism and identity politics within the academy have contributed to the critique of universalism by questioning its very philosophical foundations.

. . .

Opposing the various theories offered as justifications for the existence of universal human rights, cultural relativism reflects skepticism about the availability of universal norms. Like universalism, cultural relativism takes a number of different forms. Generally speaking, however, cultural relativists are committed to one or both of the following premises: that knowledge and truth are culturally contingent, creating a barrier to cross-cultural understanding; and that all cultures are equally valid. Combined with the empirical observation of cultural diversity worldwide, these two premises lead to the conclusion that human rights norms do not transcend cultural location and cannot be readily translated across cultures. The two premises of cultural relativism deprive human rights advocates of both a transcendent justification for human rights standards (i.e., notwithstanding disagreement, human rights exist as a product of the human condition) and a hope for consensus (by bridging the barriers of cultural difference). Cultural relativism raises the possibility that the category "human" is no longer sufficient to enable cross-cultural assessment of human practices or the actions of states.

. . .

The influence of the universalist/relativist divide on the politics of human rights is perhaps nowhere more evident than in debates over women's rights as human rights. Cultural relativists have targeted feminism itself as a product of Western ideology and global feminism as a form of Western imperialism. Ironically, cultural relativists have accused feminist human rights activists of imposing Western standards on non-Western cultures in much the same way that feminists have criticized states for imposing male-defined norms on women. The complexity of this debate has sown confusion among feminist human rights activists, undermining the effectiveness of the global feminist movement.

. . .

Although feminists have criticized the adequacy of traditional human rights, they have less frequently attacked the universality of those rights. Rather, recognizing the threat that cultural defenses pose to women's rights, as defined from a Western feminist perspective, feminists have most often argued for an expansion of both the scope and the applicability of human rights standards. Indeed, feminist efforts to expand the scope of human rights violations to include harms women suffer as a result of cultural norms or religious practices pose an even greater threat to cultural integrity than do traditional human rights standards. This increased scrutiny of the culture and its most central institutions, the church and the family, have made advocates of a global feminism a target of cultural relativists.

In addition to criticism from cultural relativists, this cross-cultural approach to women's oppression has not been immune from criticism within the feminist community. Such cross-cultural analysis depends upon very broad assumptions about women's lives and experiences and therefore raises important empirical questions regarding the extent to which women's oppression is similarly constituted across cultures. It also raises issues about the formulation of those empirical questions themselves. An essentialist approach generally begins with the experiences of white, middle-class, educated, heterosexual women. Such an approach tends to attribute commonly shared forms of oppression to gender and specific forms of oppression to other sources such as race, class, or sexual orientation. Consequently, an essentialist approach risks becoming a least common denominator approach, allowing relatively privileged women's experiences to define the feminist agenda. This tendency, in turn, creates division among women. In short, when feminists aspire to account for women's oppression through claims of cross-cultural commonality, they construct the feminist subject through exclusions, narrowing her down to her essence. And, as Judith Butler has observed, "those excluded domains return to haunt the 'integrity' and 'unity' of the feminist 'we'."

Responding to this division, anti-essentialist feminists have attempted to rethink both the various descriptions of gender oppression that have been offered and the assumption that gender oppression can be described meaningfully along a single axis. Instead, they have focused on local, contextualized problems of gender oppression. In this sense, anti-essentialism's criticism of general accounts of women's oppression parallels cultural relativism's critique of universal theories of human rights. Like cultural relativism, feminist anti-essentialism seems to lead to the conclusion that gender inequality cannot be explained cross-culturally.

Thus, despite the general inclination of feminist human rights activists to side with universalists, feminist theory, specifically anti-essentialism, does resonate with relativists' concern over cultural imperialism. Indeed, global feminists' tendency to take for granted the adequacy of their own standards—reflected in their simultaneous insistence on both the inadequacy of traditional human rights norms and the universal application of amended, feminist standards—is precisely the tendency that generated the anti-essentialist critique within feminism itself.

Notwithstanding this resonance, some feminists have cautioned that radical anti-essentialism, like cultural relativism, threatens to undermine the central goal of feminist human rights advocacy: to identify and criticize systems of inequality and injustice that transcend cultural, political, and geographic boundaries. The assumption that gender is culturally contingent not only calls into question universalist notions of gender justice but also renders problematic a feminist critique of legal institutions and legal reform outside of narrow, localized experience. To the extent that feminist anti-essentialism questions the use of cross-cultural categories, it threatens to undermine the identification of broad structures of inequality premised on gender.

It is perhaps this concern that has left feminist advocates on the international level much more reluctant than feminists within the United States to accept the implications of anti-essentialism. At least within a single state, cultural commonalities and legal institutions provide a common framework within which difference can be contained. On the international level, the parameters of such a framework are much more difficult to identify. Moreover, adherence to a universalist approach has been relatively successful for feminist human rights advocates. Although the effort to develop Western notions of justice has proceeded largely without women's participation—and indeed at times with the assumption that they are incapable of reason—women have made identifiable legal gains on the international level by resorting to claims of justice and equality. Feminists therefore fear that without an objectively defensible basis for evaluating the status of women, women will be left with power alone to dictate the outcome of competing claims of truth. That prospect most frightens those who are most oppressed.

A feminist approach to international human rights therefore leads in two apparently conflicting directions at once: (1) increased awareness universally of the importance of cultural and economic rights for women, including such issues as the structure of the family; and (2) increased respect for cultural difference based on an awareness of the partiality of perspective, a skepticism of universal claims of authenticity. Is the tension irreconcilable? Does a feminist commitment to resist imperialism, a commitment born of women's own experience of powerlessness under patriarchy, leave us without a standard by which to condemn abuses of women throughout the world?

Increasingly aware of the diversity of women's experience, sympathizing with the claim that universalism may be barely disguised ethnocentrism, and embracing in large part a position of epistemological skepticism, feminists are faced with a dilemma. Should they move to expand human rights to encompass women's experience as though it were monolithic or, recognizing women's differences, reject the universality of human rights divorced from cultural context? The latter conclusion risks undermining feminist critiques of cultural practices that are deeply harmful to women. Women are economically disempowered in the name of culture. They are denied the right to be educated, to travel, to seek paid employment, to divorce. They are denied legal protection against domestic violence, including spousal murder. They are subject to painful, often dangerous surgery to ensure female chastity. Together these practices and countless others create and sustain cultures of male privilege across the globe. Feminists must therefore respond to relativist or anti-essentialist arguments and take seriously issues of cultural difference without surrendering a critical stance toward the many forms of women's oppression.

. . .

NOTES & QUESTIONS

1.   A major early feminist critique of human rights, as articulated by Charlesworth, Chinkin, and Wright, questioned its focus on state responsibility and the dichotomy between the public and private, and consequent failure to address issues related to violence against women in the hand of non-state actors. The issue of violence against women has subsequently been addressed by both international and regional human rights systems. In 1993, the U.N. General Assembly adopted the Declaration on the Elimination of Violence Against Women. The Beijing Declaration and Platform for Action, adopted at the 1995 Women's Conference in Beijing, articulates violence against women as a human rights issue and focuses on the role that states play in creating and sustaining the conditions that lead to and allow for such violence. *See* Fourth World Conference on Women, *Beijing Declaration and Platform for Action*, Sept. 4–15, 1995, Annex I, ch IV, 125–30, U.N. Doc. A/CONF.177/20 and A/CONF.177/20/Add.1 (Sept. 15, 1995); Declaration on the Elimination of Violence Against Women, G.A. Res. 48/104, U.N. Doc. A/RES/48/104 (Dec. 20, 1993). Subsequent human rights bodies and experts have articulated the link between discrimination, violence, and due diligence, holding states responsible for failing to protect women from domestic violence acts perpetrated by non-state actors. *See* Special Rapporteur on Violence Against Women, its Causes and Consequences, *State Responsibility for Eliminating Violence Against Women*, Human Rights Comm'n, U.N. Doc. A/HRC/23/49 (May 14, 2013) (by Rashida Manjoo). *See also Jessica Gonzales v. United States*, Case 12.626, Inter-Am. Comm'n H.R., Report No. 52/07, OEA/Ser.L/V/II.128, doc. 19 (2007). Can you think of other rights that may be neglected in the absence of a specific focus on issues that impact women's lives? What are the advantages and disadvantages of generating human rights standards that focus on the lives of women? Consider for example, the critiques of the CEDAW set out in the excerpts above.

2.   At a later point in her article, Professor Higgins states that, "[f]or feminists, the challenge is simultaneously to reject universalist human rights

claims that fail to account for difference and to embrace a normative conception of gender justice that is critical of patriarchy across cultures." 19 Harv. Women's L.J. at 105. Can these two seemingly contradictory concerns be reconciled? Consider the practice referred to in the global North as "female genital mutilation." Is this a gender-based human rights violation? How should these kinds of determinations be made, and by whom? *See* Hope Lewis, *Between Irua and "Female Genital Mutilation": Feminist Human Rights Discourse and the Cultural Divide*, 8 Harv. H. Rts. J. 1 (1995).

3.   For other feminist perspectives on international human rights law, see Catherine A. MacKinnon, Are Women Human?: And Other International Dialogues (2006); Charlotte Bunch, *Women's Rights as Human Rights: Toward a Re-Vision of Human Rights*, 12 Human Rts. Q. 486 (1990); Rebecca Cook, *Women's International Human Rights Law: The Way Forward*, 15 Hum. Rts. Q. 230 (1993).

ii.   Cultural Relativism and Essentialism

The excerpt by Professor Tracy Higgins refers to legal theorists who offer a critique of human rights that challenges the notion of their universality. These critical legal theorists assert that the human rights movement and framework are inherently Eurocentric and thus impose cultural norms and contribute to cultural essentialism. In the following article, Professor Makau wa Mutua offers a critique of the human rights movement as constructing a narrative "that depicts an epochal contest pitting savages . . . against victims and saviors;" in other words pitting good against evil in a way that evokes and reifies stereotypes. What are the implications of this savage-victim-savior (SVS) narrative? What might an alternative narrative look like, and how it might be constructed?

MAKAU WA MUTUA, "SAVAGES, VICTIMS, AND SAVIORS: THE METAPHOR OF HUMAN RIGHTS"
42 Harv. Int'l L. J. 201, 202–09 (2001).

The first dimension of the prism depicts a savage and evokes images of barbarism. The abominations of the savage are presented as so cruel and unimaginable as to represent their state as a negation of humanity. The human rights story presents the state as the classic savage, an ogre forever bent on the consumption of humans. Although savagery in human rights discourse connotes much more than the state, the state is depicted as the operational instrument of savagery. States become savage when they choke off and oust civil society. The "good" state controls its demonic proclivities by cleansing itself with, and internalizing, human rights. The "evil" state, on the other hand, expresses itself through an illiberal, anti-democratic, or other authoritarian culture. The redemption or salvation of the state is solely dependent on its submission to human rights norms.

The state is the guarantor of human rights; it is also the target and *raison d'etre* of human rights law.

But the reality is far more complex. While the metaphor may suggest otherwise, it is not the state per se that is barbaric but the cultural foundation of the state. The state only becomes a vampire when "bad" culture overcomes or disallows the development of "good" culture. The real savage, though, is not the state but a cultural deviation from human rights. That savagery inheres in the theory and practice of the one-party state, military junta, controlled or closed state, theocracy, or even cultural practices such as the one popularly known in the West as female genital mutilation (FGM), not in the state per se. The state itself is a neutral, passive instrumentality—a receptacle or an empty vessel—that conveys savagery by implementing the project of the savage culture.

The second dimension of the prism depicts the face and the fact of a victim as well as the essence and the idea of victimhood. A human being whose "dignity and worth" have been violated by the savage is the victim. The victim figure is a powerless, helpless innocent whose naturalist attributes have been negated by the primitive and offensive actions of the state or the cultural foundation of the state. The entire human rights structure is both anticatastrophic and reconstructive. It is anticatastrophic because it is designed to prevent more calamities through the creation of more victims. It is reconstructive because it seeks to re-engineer the state and the society to reduce the number of victims, as it defines them, and prevent conditions that give rise to victims. . . .

The third dimension of the prism is the savior or the redeemer, the good angel who protects, vindicates, civilizes, restrains, and safeguards. The savior is the victim's bulwark against tyranny. The simple, yet complex promise of the savior is freedom: freedom from the tyrannies of the state, tradition, and culture. But it is also the freedom to create a better society based on particular values. In the human rights story, the savior is the human rights corpus itself, with the United Nations, Western governments, INGOs, and Western charities as the actual rescuers, redeemers of a benighted world. In reality, however, these institutions are merely fronts. The savior is ultimately a set of culturally based norms and practices that inhere in liberal thought and philosophy.

The human rights corpus, though well-meaning, is fundamentally Eurocentric, and suffers from several basic and interdependent flaws captured in the SVS [savage-victim-savior] metaphor. First, the corpus falls within the historical continuum of the Eurocentric colonial project, in which actors are cast into superior and subordinate positions. Precisely because of this cultural and historical context, the human rights movement's basic claim of universality is undermined. Instead, a historical understanding of the struggle for human dignity should locate the impetus of a universal conception of human rights in those societies *subjected* to European tyranny and imperialism. Unfortunately, this is not part of the official human rights narrative. Some of the most important events preceding the post-1945, United Nations-led human rights movement include the anti-slavery campaigns in both Africa and the United States, the anti-colonial struggles in Africa, Asia, and Latin America, and the struggles for women's suffrage and equal rights throughout the world. But the pioneering work of many non-Western activists and other human rights heroes are not acknowledged by the contemporary human rights movement. These historically important struggles, together with the norms anchored in non-Western cultures and societies, have either been overlooked or rejected in the construction of the current understanding of human rights.

Second, the SVS metaphor and narrative rejects the cross-contamination of cultures and instead promotes a Eurocentric ideal. The metaphor is premised on the transformation by Western cultures of non-Western cultures into a Eurocentric prototype and not the fashioning of a multicultural mosaic. The SVS metaphor results in an "othering" process that imagines the creation of inferior clones, in effect dumb copies of the original. For example, Western political democracy is in effect an organic element of human rights. "Savage" cultures and peoples are seen as lying outside the human rights orbit, and by implication, outside the regime of political democracy. It is this distance from human rights that allows certain cultures to create victims. Political democracy is then viewed as a panacea. Other textual examples anchored in the treatment of cultural phenomena, such as "traditional" practices that appear to negate the equal protection for women, also illustrate the gulf between human rights and non-liberal, non-European cultures.

Third, the language and rhetoric of the human rights corpus present significant theoretical problems. The arrogant and biased rhetoric of the human rights movement prevents the movement from gaining cross-cultural legitimacy. This curse of the SVS rhetoric has no bearing on the substance of the normative judgment being rendered. A particular leader, for example, could be labeled a war criminal, but such a label may carry no validity locally because of the curse of the SVS rhetoric. In other words, the SVS rhetoric may undermine the universalist warrant that it claims and thus engender resistance to the apprehension and punishment of real violators.

The subtext of human rights is a grand narrative hidden in the seemingly neutral and universal language of the corpus. For example, the U.N. Charter describes its mandate to "reaffirm faith in fundamental human rights, in the dignity and worth of the human person, in the equal rights of men and women and of nations large and small." This is certainly a noble ideal. But what exactly does that terminology mean here? This phraseology conceals more than it reveals. What, for example, are fundamental human rights, and how are they determined? Do such rights have cultural, religious, ethical, moral, political, or other biases? What exactly is meant by the "dignity and worth" of the human person? Is there an essentialized human being that the corpus imagines? Is the individual found in the streets of Nairobi, the slums of Boston, the deserts of Iraq, or the rainforests of Brazil? In addition to the Herculean task of defining the prototypical human being, the U.N. Charter puts forward another pretense-that all nations "large and small" enjoy some equality. Even as it ratified power imbalances between the Third World and the dominant American and European powers, the United Nations gave the latter the primary power to define and determine "world peace" and "stability." These fictions of neutrality and universality, like so much else in a lopsided world, undergird the human rights corpus and belie its true identity and purposes. This international rhetoric of goodwill reveals, just beneath the surface, intentions and reality that stand in great tension and contradiction with it.

. . .

Fourth, the issue of power is largely ignored in the human rights corpus. There is an urgent need for a human rights movement that is multicultural, inclusive, and deeply political. Thus, while it is essential that a new human rights movement overcome Eurocentrism, it is equally important that it also address deeply lopsided power relations among and within cultures, national economies, states, genders, religions, races and ethnic groups, and other societal cleavages. Such a movement cannot treat Eurocentrism as the starting point and other cultures as peripheral. The point of departure for the movement must be a basic assumption about the moral equivalency of all cultures. . . .

The fifth flaw concerns the role of race in the development of the human rights narrative. The SVS metaphor of human rights carries racial connotations in which the international hierarchy of race and color is reintrenched and revitalized. The metaphor is in fact necessary for the continuation of the global racial hierarchy. In the human rights narrative, savages and victims are generally non-white and non-Western, while the saviors are white. This old truism has found new life in the metaphor of human rights. But there is also a sense in which human rights can be seen as a project for the redemption of the redeemers, in which whites who are privileged globally as a people—who have historically visited untold suffering and savage atrocities against non-whites-redeem themselves by "defending" and "civilizing" "lower," "unfortunate," and "inferior" peoples. The metaphor is thus laced with the pathology of self-redemption.

As currently constituted and deployed, the human rights movement will ultimately fail because it is perceived as an alien ideology in non-Western societies. The movement does not deeply resonate in the cultural fabrics of non-Western states, except among hypocritical elites steeped in Western ideas. In order ultimately to prevail, the human rights movement must be moored in the cultures of all peoples.

The project of reconsidering rights, with claims to their supremacy, is not new. The culture of rights in the present milieu stretches back at least to the rise of the modern state in Europe. It is that state's monopoly of violence and the instruments of coercion that gave rise to the culture of rights to counterbalance the abusive state. . . . The critique of human rights should be based not just on American or European legal traditions but also on other cultural milieus. The indigenous, non-European traditions of Asia, Africa, the Pacific, and the Americas must be central to this critique. The idea of human rights—the quest to craft a universal bundle of attributes with which all societies must endow all human beings—is a noble one. The problem with the current bundle of attributes lies in their inadequacy, incompleteness, and wrong-headedness. There is little doubt that there is much to celebrate in the present human rights corpus just as there is much to quarrel with. In this exercise, a sober evaluation of the current human rights corpus and its language is not an option—it is required.

. . .

Professor David Kennedy has catalogued prevailing critiques of the human rights movement as a way to encourage what he calls a "more pragmatic attitude" towards human rights. In the following excerpt, he focuses in particular on the critique that, despite its claims of universality, human rights is born of a particular context and ideology. What are the implications of this critique on the validity and strength of the human rights framework?

DAVID KENNEDY, "THE INTERNATIONAL HUMAN RIGHTS MOVEMENT: PART OF THE PROBLEM?"
15 Harv. Hum. Rts. J. 101, 111–16 (2002).

Human Rights Expresses the Ideology, Ethics, Aesthetic Sensibility and Political Practice of a Particular Western Eighteenth-through Twentieth-Century Liberalism

Tainted origins. Although there are lots of interesting analogies to human rights ideas in various cultural traditions, the particular form these ideas are given in the human rights movement is the product of a particular moment and place. Post-enlightenment, rationalist, secular,

Western, modern, capitalist. From a pragmatist point of view, of course, tainted origins are irrelevant. That human rights *claims* to be universal but *is really* the product of a specific cultural and historical origin says nothing—unless that specificity exacts costs or renders human rights less useful than something else. The human rights tradition might itself be undermined by its origin—be treated less well by some people, be less effective in some places—just as its origin might, for other audiences, accredit projects undertaken in its name. This is the sort of thing we might strategize about—perhaps we should downplay the universal claims, or look for parallel developments in other cultural traditions, etc.

The movement's Western liberal origins become part of the problem (rather than a limit on the solution) when particular difficulties general to the liberal tradition are carried over to the human rights movement. When, for example, the global expression of emancipatory objectives in human rights terms narrows humanity's appreciation of these objectives to the forms they have taken in the nineteenth- and twentieth-century Western political tradition. One cost would be the loss of more diverse and local experiences and conceptions of emancipation. Even within the liberal West, other useful emancipatory vocabularies (including the solidarities of socialism, Christianity, the labor movement, and so forth) are diminished by the consolidation of human rights as the international expression of *the* Western liberal tradition. Other costs would be incurred to the extent the human rights tradition could be seen to carry with it particular down sides of the liberal West.

Down sides of the West. That the emancipations of the modern West have come with costs has long been a theme in critical writing— alienation, loss of faith, environmental degradation, immorality, etc. Seeing human rights as part of the Western liberal package is a way of asserting that at least some of these costs should be attributed to the human rights tradition. This might be asserted in a variety of ways. If you thought secularism was part of what is bad about the modern West, you might assert that human rights shares the secular spirit, that as a sentimental vocabulary of devotion it actively displaces religion, offering itself as a poor substitute. You might claim that the enforcement of human rights, including religious rights, downgrades religion to a matter of private and individual commitment, or otherwise advances the secular project. To the extent human rights can be implicated in the secular project, we might conclude that it leaves the world spiritually less well off. Other criticisms of the modern liberal West have been extended to human rights in a parallel fashion.

In particular, critics have linked the human rights project to liberal Western ideas about the relationships among law, policies, and economics. Western enlightenment ideas that make the human rights movement part of the problem rather than the solution include the following: the economy *pre-exists* politics, politics *pre-exists* law, the private *pre-exists* the public, just as the animal pre-exists the human, faith pre-exists reason, or the feudal preexists the modern. In each case, the second term is fragile, artificial, a human creation and achievement, and a domain of choice, while the first term identifies a sturdy and natural base, a domain outside human control.

Human rights encourages people to seek emancipation in the vocabularies of reason rather than faith, in public rather than private life, in law rather than policies, in politics rather than economics. In each case, the human rights vocabulary overemphasizes the difference between what it takes as the (natural) base and as the (artificial) domain of emancipation, and underestimates the plasticity of what it treats as the base. Moreover, human rights is too quick to conclude that emancipation *means* progress forward from the natural passions of politics into the civilized reason of law. The urgent need to develop a more vigorous human politics is sidelined by the effort to throw thin but plausible nets of legal articulation across the globe. Work to develop law comes to be seen as an emancipatory end in itself, leaving the human rights movement too ready to articulate problems in political terms and solutions in legal terms. Precisely the reverse would be more useful. The posture of human rights as an emancipatory political project that extends and operates within a domain above or outside policies—a political project repackaged as a form of knowledge-delegitimates other political voices and makes less visible the local, cultural, and political dimensions of the human rights movement itself.

As liberal Western intellectuals, we think of the move to rights as an escape from the unfreedom of social conditions into the freedom of citizenship, but we repeatedly forget that there is also a loss. A loss of the experience of belonging, of the habit of willing in conditions of indeterminacy, innovating collectively in the absence of knowledge, unchanneled by an available list of rights. This may represent a loss of either the presence of experience itself, experience not yet channeled and returned to the individual as the universal experience of a right holder, or of the capacity to deploy other vocabularies that are more imaginative, open, and oriented to future possibility.

The West and the rest. The Western/liberal character of human rights exacts particular costs when it intersects with the highly structured and unequal relations between the modern West and everyone else. Whatever the limits of modernization in the West, the form of modernization promoted by the human rights movement in third world societies is too often based only on a fantasy about the modern/liberal/capitalist west. The insistence on more formal and absolute conceptions of property rights in transitional societies than are known in the developed West is a classic example of this problem—using the authority of the human rights movement to narrow the range of socio-economic choices available in developing societies in the name of "rights" that do not exist in this unregulated or compromised form in any developed western democracy.

At the same time, the human rights movement contributes to the framing of political choices in the third world as oppositions between "local/traditional" and "international/modern" forms of government and modes of life. This effect is strengthened by the presentation of human rights as part of belonging to the modern world, but coming from some place outside political choice, from the universal, the rational, the civilized. By strengthening the articulation of third world politics as a choice between tradition and modernity, the human rights movement impoverishes local political discourse, often strengthening the hand of self-styled "traditionalists" who are offered a common-sense and powerful alternative to modernisation for whatever politics they may espouse.

. . .

NOTES & QUESTIONS

1.   Do you agree with the critiques articulated by Mutua and/or Kennedy? Are they relevant in the context of "home-grown" advocacy to address human rights concerns within the United States? What are the implications of these critiques for the validity of human rights as a frame for addressing rights violations in the United States?

2.   A related critique of human rights lawyering is the propensity of the attorney-client relationship to perpetuate inequalities and hierarchies and contribute to "victim essentialization." For a discussion of how human rights clinicians might engage this critique by examining structural and historical sources of human rights crises and bridge international human rights lawyering with domestic poverty and community lawyering, see Caroline Bettinger-López et al., *Redefining Human Rights Lawyering Through the Lens of Critical Theory: Lessons for Pedagogy and Practice*, 18 Geo. J. on Poverty L. and Pol'y 337 (2011). What is the relevance of this critique for human rights lawyers working domestically?

3.   For additional perspectives on cultural relativism and human rights, see Josiah A.M. Cobbah, *African Values and the Human Rights Debate: An African Perspective*, 9 Hum. Rts. Q. 309 (1987); Ratna Kapur, *Human Rights in the 21st Century: Take a Walk on the Dark Side*, 28 Sydney L. Rev. 665 (2006); Bilahari Kausikan, *Asia's Different Standard*, 92 Foreign Pol'y 24 (1983); Raimundo Panikkar, *Is the Notion of Human Rights a Western Concept*, 120 Diogenes 75 (1982); Gayatri C. Spivak, *Righting Wrongs*, 103 S. Atlantic Q. 523 (2004).

III.   USING HUMAN RIGHTS STRATEGIES TO ADVANCE U.S. ADVOCACY

As we explored in the previous sections, the human rights framework offers lawyers in the United States an important set of internationally accepted norms and standards to draw upon in challenging domestic laws, practices and policies. These sources are at the core of the human rights framework. But they are only part of the human rights approach to advocacy. Just as central is the set of tools that human rights offers lawyers in the U.S. working to advance domestically-focused advocacy on a wide range of issues.

Many of these strategies are cross-cutting and independent of specific mechanisms or tools. For example, advocates in the United States have found that human rights concepts and framing are effective for organizing, mobilizing, and supporting social movements to address and respond to the needs of impacted communities. We examine this approach in **Chapter X**.

Other strategies involve domestic mechanisms, such as U.S. courts. For example, lawyers can draw on international law in litigation in U.S. courts by citing to human rights treaties as persuasive authority urging a particular interpretation of a federal or state constitutional provision. We will explore this strategy in depth in **Chapters V** and **VI**. Advocates can also urge state and local officials to implement human rights treaties more directly by conducting human rights audits and impact assessments. We discuss this and other strategies aimed at state and local actors in **Chapter VI**. And advocates can engage in human rights fact-finding and documentation, shining the light on abuses and violations through human rights reporting. **Chapter IX** examines this strategy.

Lawyers working to advance human rights in the United States also engage a set of tools and strategies offered by the international and regional human rights systems. The international human rights system is grounded in the mechanisms of the United Nations. The United States has ratified three of the core U.N. human rights conventions: the International Covenant on Civil and Political Rights (ICCPR), the Convention Against Torture and other Cruel, Inhuman or Degrading Treatment (CAT), and the Convention on the Elimination of All Forms of Racial Discrimination (CERD). It has also ratified two of the optional protocols to the Convention on the Rights of the Child (CRC), including the optional protocols on the sale of children and on children in armed conflict. One of the obligations that the United States accepts when it ratifies a human rights treaty is periodic reporting to a U.N. committee comprised of human rights experts, known as a "treaty body." Advocates in the United States can use these treaty reviews as an opportunity to raise human rights concerns with both the U.S. government and the experts comprising the treaty bodies and urge specific reforms based on commitments the U.S. made in ratifying the human rights treaties. Although the findings and recommendations of the treaty bodies generally are not binding, advocates can incorporate them back into their domestic advocacy efforts, for example by offering them as persuasive authority in litigation before U.S. courts or lobbying the government to implement policy changes.

Other U.N. mechanisms, including U.N. Special Procedures and the Universal Periodic Review (UPR), offer opportunities for U.S. advocates to raise human rights concerns on the international stage and leverage international attention into domestic advocacy efforts, independent of U.S. ratification of particular human rights treaties. Special Procedures are human rights experts charged with evaluating and addressing human rights concerns in specific countries or pertaining to particular thematic issues. The UPR, established by the United Nations' Human Rights Council in 2006, requires that each country belonging to the U.N. undergo a "peer review" of its human rights record by the other member states once every four years.

The following essay provides a brief introduction to the U.N. human rights system, as well as the regional Inter-American human rights system. We explore U.S. advocacy strategies for engaging these systems in greater depth in **Chapter VIII**.

MARGARET HUANG, " 'GOING GLOBAL': APPEALS TO INTERNATIONAL AND REGIONAL HUMAN RIGHTS BODIES"
2 Bringing Human Rights Home 105, 106–13 (Cynthia Soohoo et al. eds., 2008).

The international human rights system is a complex arena, including actors at the regional and international level. There are essentially three categories of international human rights institutions accessible to U.S. advocates: those created by the United Nations Charter and/or subsequent resolutions adopted by the U.N. member states (also known as the Charter-based bodies); those established through the adoption and ratification of international human rights treaties (also known as the treaty-based bodies); and those established by regional institutions, such as the Organization of the American States (known as the Inter-American human rights system). . . .

United Nations Charter-based Institutions

The United Nations was established with the adoption of its Charter at the San Francisco Conference in June 1945. In early proposals for the international organization, the United States and the other leading Allies of World War II sought to limit references to individual rights, hoping to preserve national sovereignty and limit interventions into domestic affairs. But a concerted response led by governments from smaller, often former colonial countries and non-governmental organizations won the day. Citing the failure of the Treaty of Versailles signed after World War I to prevent further bloodshed, and motivated by the horrors and devastation wrought by World War II, human rights advocates succeeded in their demands that the U.N. Charter emphasize the protection and promotion of human rights. As Paul Gordon Lauren has noted, "The U.N. Charter explicitly drew a connection between human well-being and international peace, reiterated support for the principle of equal rights and self-determination, and committed the organization to promote universal respect for, and observance of, human rights and fundamental freedoms without discrimination—'for all'."

. . .

U.S. domestic advocates [were] active participants in the [UN Commission for Human Rights] for many years, particularly since the late 1990s. For instance, in 1999, the National Coalition to Abolish the Death Penalty took its campaign to the Commission, calling for international pressure to end the practice of executions in the United States. During that same session, advocates from Louisiana made the first formal intervention on environmental racism as a human rights violation before the Commission, highlighting the failure of the U.S. government to protect its citizens from grave human rights violations of the right to health and other abuses. In 2000, advocates fighting racism in the criminal justice system, including the National Association of Criminal Defense Lawyers and the NAACP Legal Defense and Education Fund, participated in a delegation to the Commission. Since that time, many other U.S. organizations have asked the Commission to examine issues including poverty in the U.S., violence against women, the right to housing, and discrimination against migrant workers.

In 2005, U.N. Secretary-General Kofi Annan laid out a vision of reform for the U.N.'s human rights system. Because of political disputes and the actions of some member states seeking to prevent the Commission from addressing critical human rights violations, Annan proposed to replace the [U.N. Commission on Human Rights] with a new body, the Human Rights Council (HR Council), which would serve as a subsidiary body to the General Assembly. (In U.N. terms, the Council is considered more important than the Commission because it reports to a higher department—the General Assembly. . . .) After several months of negotiation, and despite U.S. government objections, the General Assembly approved the creation of the HR Council in April 2006.

. . .

Many of the rest of the U.N.'s Charter-based institutions fall under the purview of the Office of the High Commissioner for Human Rights (or OHCHR). . . . The mandate of the High Commissioner is to serve as the U.N. official with principal responsibility for United Nations human rights activities, including providing advisory services and technical assistance to U.N. member states; engaging in a dialogue with governments to secure respect for all human rights; and coordinating all human rights activities within the U.N. system. The High Commissioner oversees a staff of more than five hundred in offices around the world, with the great majority working at the headquarters for the U.N.'s human rights system in Geneva, Switzerland.

[T]he OHCHR provides support to several Special Procedures, or human rights experts, which are currently divided into two categories: one group of experts holds thematic mandates, such as the use of torture or violence against women, while the second group is tasked with monitoring the human rights situation in a particular country or territory. Special Procedures can have different designations, including "Special Rapporteur," "Independent Expert," or in some cases a "Working Group" which usually has five members representing the five regions recognized by the U.N. (Asia, Africa, Latin America, Eastern Europe, and "Western Europe & Others"—where the U.S. is represented). Each of the Special Procedures submits an annual report to the United Nations, documenting violations covered by her or his mandate and making recommendations to Member States and U.N. officials on how to stop or remedy the violations.

. . .

United Nations Treaty-based Institutions

During the last sixty years, U.N. Member States have negotiated and adopted . . . core human rights treaties to protect and promote human rights around the world.

. . .

Once a country has ratified a treaty, the government is required to submit periodic reports on its compliance with the treaty's obligations to the treaty monitoring body—a committee of independent human rights experts. For U.S. activists, the reporting process offers an important opportunity to highlight the human rights situation in the country and to demand policy and legal reforms that would bring the U.S. government into compliance with its international legal obligations . . . . As part of the official reviews of each of these reports, civil society groups have collaborated to submit "shadow reports" to the U.N. Committees. Shadow reports are information, analysis, and recommendations provided by non-governmental organizations about specific human rights abuses in the country being reviewed.

. . .

The Inter-American Human Rights System

Founded in 1948, the Organization of American States (OAS) is a regional forum to facilitate multilateral cooperation and discussion among the countries of the Western Hemisphere. With thirty-five member states (though Cuba has actually been suspended from participation since 1962), the OAS works to promote democracy, protect human rights, and confront problems such as terrorism, poverty, corruption, and the illegal trade in drugs. The OAS has two primary mechanisms for protecting human rights: the Inter-American Commission on Human Rights (the Inter-American Commission) and the Inter-American Court of Human Rights (Inter-American Court). The Inter-American Commission is based in Washington, DC, and the Inter-American Court is housed in San Jose, Costa Rica. Under the OAS Charter, all member countries are bound by the provisions of the *American Declaration of the Rights and Duties of Man*, placing them under the jurisdiction of the Inter-American Commission. Because the U.S. government has not ratified the *American Convention on Human Rights* and has therefore not accepted the jurisdiction of the Inter-American Court, U.S. advocates have primarily focused their advocacy efforts at the Inter-American Commission.

The Inter-American Commission is composed of seven independent human rights experts, elected to serve by the General Assembly of the OAS. Commission members carry out fact-finding missions to OAS member states, investigate individual complaints of human rights violations, and monitor the general human rights situation in the countries of the Americas. Similar to the U.N. system, the Inter-American Commission has the authority to appoint Special Procedures, each with a mandate to examine a particular human rights problem such as the Special Rapporteurship on the Rights of Persons Deprived of their Liberty and the Special Rapporteurship on the Rights of Afro-Descendants. Civil society advocates from across the region, including the United States, work with the special procedures to bring attention to rights violations in their country and to pressure governments to take action.

Over the last several decades, U.S. activists have brought a number of petitions to the Inter-American Commission, many of them focused on death penalty sentences. But since the 1990s, cases have been reviewed on a much wider range of issues, including the indefinite detention of Cubans sent to the U.S. in the Mariel boatlift of 1980; the interdiction of Haitians seeking asylum in the U.S.; the U.S. military invasions of Grenada and Panama; the rights of indigenous peoples to their tribal lands; the voting rights of the residents of the District of Columbia; violations of the rights of the poor through welfare reform initiatives; the rights of undocumented migrant workers; and the practice of sentencing juveniles to life-without-parole.

Additionally, the Inter-American Commission has adopted a new procedure of holding "thematic hearings," not to be used for individual cases but rather to educate the Commission Members about a pattern or increasing trend in human rights violations. U.S. activists have used this procedure to request a number of hearings on issues specific to the U.S., including racial disparities caused by mandatory minimum sentencing practices; the failure of the government to protect victims of Hurricanes Katrina and Rita, and the gross exploitation of migrant workers in the reconstruction efforts after the hurricanes in the Gulf region; and increasing racial segregation in the public education system.

. . .

In the following passage, we explore these and other possible human rights strategies through the example of advocacy efforts in the United States to end the practice of sentencing juveniles to life in prison without the possibility of parole. As you read the following case study, notice how the different strategies overlap and how they draw and depend upon the human rights norms and texts discussed in the previous section. Reflect, too, on the critiques of human rights, and whether the example explored here reinforces, challenges, or responds to those critiques. Ask yourself whether all of the strategies discussed in this section are unique to human rights advocacy, or whether at least some are more generally applicable to traditional domestic public interest lawyering. What makes these "human rights" strategies?

IV. CASE STUDY: CHALLENGING JUVENILE LIFE WITHOUT PAROLE: HOW HAS HUMAN RIGHTS MADE A DIFFERENCE?[17]

Introduction

Human rights standards and strategies play an important role in social justice legal advocacy in the United States. Human rights help frame new arguments, offer new venues for challenging existing policies and practices, provide opportunities for coalition-building, and afford new means to bring attention to rights violations. One example of human

---

[17] This case study is adapted from Columbia Law School Human Rights Institute, Challenging Juvenile Life Without Parole: How Has Human Rights Made a Difference? (2014), available at the Columbia Law School Human Rights Institute's website, http://web.law. columbia.edu/human-rights-institute. Erin Foley Smith, project attorney with the Human Rights Institute, researched the case study and is the primary author. The study is based upon research and interviews with a number of human rights advocates. Complete citations and acknowledgements are included in the online version of the report.

rights strategies at work in the U.S. is found in advocates' efforts to end a practice unique to the United States: sentencing juveniles to life in prison without the possibility of parole.

In 42 states in the United States, a child who commits a crime can be sentenced to life in prison without the possibility of parole. There are currently approximately 2,500 individuals serving life sentences for crimes they committed when they were below eighteen years of age. For years, advocates have been working to end this practice, which is typically called juvenile life without parole, or "JLWOP."

In the past ten years, human rights strategies have played an important role in challenging states' use of the sentence. Human rights have contributed to increased media attention on the issue, two U.S. Supreme Court decisions limiting the practice, and legislative changes at the state level. This case study, based on interviews with a number of advocates working to end the practice, explores how human rights standards and strategies have helped to advance advocacy strategies to end JLWOP.

Status of JLWOP Under U.S., Foreign, and International Law

In the United States, two recent U.S. Supreme Court decisions have limited the practice of JLWOP. In 2010, in *Graham v. Florida*,[18] the Court struck down a state law that allowed juveniles convicted of a non-homicide offense to be sentenced to life imprisonment without the possibility of parole, finding that such laws violate the Eighth Amendment's prohibition on cruel and unusual punishment. In 2012, in *Miller v. Alabama*,[19] the Court further held that the Eighth Amendment forbids a sentencing scheme that mandates life imprisonment without the possibility of parole for juveniles convicted of homicide-related crimes. Following the *Miller* and *Graham* decisions, a juvenile convicted of a homicide offense may be sentenced to life without parole if the sentencing scheme follows certain processes, including considering the youth and individual characteristics of the offender.

The United States is currently the only country in the world that sentences juveniles to life without the possibility of parole. A 2012 study identified nine countries, including the United States, whose laws could potentially allow for a JLWOP sentence. However, there are no known cases of the sentence being imposed outside the U.S.

The practice of sentencing juvenile offenders to life without parole is widely condemned under international law. International human rights experts have found that such sentences violate the three core human rights treaties ratified by the U.S.—the International Covenant on Civil

---

[18]   560 U.S. 48 (2010).
[19]   132 S. Ct. 2455 (2012)

and Political Rights (the "ICCPR"), the Convention Against Torture (the "CAT"), and the Convention on the Elimination of All Forms of Racial Discrimination (the "CERD"). The Convention on the Rights of the Child (the "CRC")—ratified by every country in the world, other than South Sudan, Somalia, and the United States—expressly prohibits JLWOP. Demonstrating international opposition to JLWOP, the United Nations General Assembly has called for immediate abrogation of JLWOP sentences every year since 2006. JLWOP sentences have also been rejected by regional human rights bodies, which monitor human rights compliance in the Americas.

Human Rights Strategies Used in JLWOP Advocacy

Advocates in the United States have used a wide variety of human rights strategies to end juvenile life without parole sentences, ranging from explicit references to international human rights treaties in litigation in U.S. courts to reshaping the language people use to discuss crimes committed by juveniles. As the examples below demonstrate, advocates have engaged human rights frameworks to advance and supplement a variety of traditional advocacy strategies, including litigation, media campaigns, and legislative advocacy, particularly with state and local officials. They have also taken the cause to the international community and documented the scope of JLWOP and its impact on individuals, families, and communities. Not all of these strategies cite to human rights law—or, indeed, even include the term "human rights"—but they are grounded in fundamental human rights principles, including fairness, equality, and human dignity, which are laid out in the Universal Declaration of Human Rights and numerous human rights treaties. As a general matter, leveraging human rights strategies requires assessing the audience and determining the most effective strategies and language. This is particularly the case in the context of the United States, where courts, policy makers, and the public may not be familiar with the international framework and how it applies to U.S. practice.

Citing to Foreign and International Practice

As noted above, juvenile life without parole sentences are widely condemned in both foreign and international law. Advocates have found that educating U.S. judges and policymakers about international law and the fact that the U.S. stands alone in imposing these sentences can help encourage the elimination of JLWOP here.

In Courts

Citing to international and foreign law in briefs to U.S. federal and state courts informs U.S. judges about the way in which the U.S. is an outlier with regards to the practice and demonstrates alternative approaches that have been used elsewhere.

Lawyers and advocates have invoked foreign practice and international law in briefs to the U.S. Supreme Court, as well as in state courts and lower federal courts. A group of human rights organizations and bar associations, including Amnesty International, Human Rights Watch, Human Rights Advocates, the Center for Constitutional Rights, and Columbia Law School's Human Rights Institute, filed *amicus* briefs in both *Graham v. Florida*, and *Miller v. Alabama*, urging the U.S. Supreme Court to consider international and foreign law and practice in its interpretation of the Eighth Amendment's clause prohibiting cruel and unusual punishment. Advocates have submitted appellate briefs and *amicus* briefs citing foreign and international law and practice in a number of state court cases challenging JLWOP, including in California, Massachusetts, and Pennsylvania.

At the federal level, references to foreign and international law have historically been most effective in cases dealing with the Eighth Amendment's prohibition on cruel and unusual punishment. In *Graham v. Florida*, this approach yielded some success, as Justice Kennedy's majority opinion acknowledged the fact that JLWOP sentences have been "rejected the world over."[20] The Court continued its "longstanding practice" of looking "beyond our Nation's borders for support for its independent conclusion that a particular punishment is cruel and unusual."[21] The Court explained the role of foreign and international law in its decision as follows:

> The question before us is not whether international law prohibits the United States from imposing the sentence at issue in this case. The question is whether that punishment is cruel and unusual. In that inquiry, the overwhelming weight of international opinion against life without parole for nonhomicide offenses committed by juveniles provides respected and significant confirmation for our own conclusions.[22]

State courts have been a site for successful advocacy based on international and comparative law and practice, as well. A 2014 report co-authored by The Opportunity Agenda and Northeastern University School of Law's Program on Human Rights and the Global Economy details how state courts consider and apply international human rights law. The report finds that "some state courts have considered and affirmatively used international law as persuasive authority for the interpretation of state constitutions, statutes, and common law. Further,

---

[20] 560 U.S. at 80.

[21] *Id.*

[22] *Id.* at 81,

individual judges regularly draw on human rights norms in concurring or dissenting opinions."[23]

For example, in *Diatchenko v. District Attorney for Suffolk District*,[24] Massachusetts' highest court referenced international and foreign law in the context of a decision involving JLWOP. In *Diatchenko*, the court found that *Miller v. Alabama*'s prohibition on mandatory JLWOP sentences applies retroactively and held that discretionary imposition of a JLWOP sentence violates the Massachusetts state constitutional prohibition against cruel and unusual punishment. In its decision, the court stated, "In concluding that the imposition of a sentence of life in prison without the possibility of parole on juveniles under the age of eighteen violates the constitutional prohibition against 'cruel or unusual punishment[ ]' in art. 26, we join a world community that has broadly condemned such punishment for juveniles."[25] The court went on to say, "As John Adams recognized over 215 years ago, we belong to an international community that tinkers toward a more perfect government by learning from the successes and failures of our own structures and those of other nations."[26]

Understanding that some state courts may be wary of citing to foreign and international law, advocates engaging this strategy are careful to research courts' precedents, including individual judges' opinions—especially at the appellate level—to determine whether a particular court is likely to be receptive to arguments based on foreign and international law. Where a court has been receptive in the past, advocates cite those cases to encourage the court to consider foreign and international law again in their case.

For example, Naoka Carey, Executive Director of Citizens for Juvenile Justice, which works to improve the juvenile justice system in Massachusetts, states:

> The Massachusetts judiciary tends to be open to hearing international arguments. In some states this would backfire, but we don't have that issue here. Our judiciary tends to be much more open to international law arguments than our state legislature because judges are more familiar with international law and have a framework for understanding how it is relevant in our cases.

---

[23] The Opportunity Agenda & Northeastern University School of Law's Program on Human Rights and the Global Economy, "Human Rights in State Courts 2014," 4 http://opportunity agenda.org/files/field_file/2014.2.06.HumanRightsinStateCourts.pdf.

[24] 466 Mass. 655 (Mass. 2013).

[25] *Id.* at 671 n.16.

[26] *Id.* (citing J. Adams, Preface, A Defence of the Constitutions of Government of the United States of America (1797)). John Adams was the principal author of the Massachusetts Constitution, the oldest functioning written constitution in the world.

Some advocates note that elected state court judges may be less receptive to foreign and international law arguments than appointed judges, because they fear that reliance on such sources could be used against them in a future election. Furthermore, some appellate judges are known to be hostile to foreign and international law arguments, and advocates report avoiding such arguments before those judges for at least two reasons: first, they want to make those arguments that will be most effective for their case and therefore avoid arguments they know will be rejected or will raise unnecessary controversy, and second, they want to avoid the risk of an opinion that sets a negative precedent.

This reflects the reality that there is some resistance within the U.S. to comparing U.S. practice to other countries, with making international agreements binding on the U.S., and with submitting U.S. practice to scrutiny by international bodies, such as the United Nations. Therefore, arguments based on international and foreign law are not always persuasive. For example, Justice Scalia has rejected citations to foreign law. In his dissent in *Lawrence v. Texas*, a case challenging Texas' "Homosexual Conduct" law, Justice Scalia disapproved of Justice Kennedy's citation to foreign law in the majority opinion.[27] In *Miller v. Alabama*, nineteen U.S. states and the territory of Guam filed an *amicus* brief urging the Supreme Court to, among other things, refrain from considering foreign law in deciding the case. In *Graham v. Florida*, sixteen members of the U.S. House of Representatives filed an *amicus* brief arguing that the CRC is not binding on the United States, and that the U.S. does not violate any other treaty obligations by sentencing juveniles to life without parole.

Furthermore, some states have gone so far as to pass legislation barring state courts from considering international, foreign, and, in some cases, Sharia law. Such an amendment to the Oklahoma Constitution was struck down as violating the U.S. constitution. Nevertheless, at least sixteen states introduced similar bills in 2013.

Advocates are thus strategic in how they incorporate international and foreign law in U.S. litigation. As Alicia D'Addario of Equal Justice Initiative notes:

> We look closely at how and whether human rights influences the judiciary, and we tailor our arguments based on our audience. Because we represent individual children in challenging sentences that condemn them to die in prison, it is very important that we make the arguments that will be most effective for our client in a particular case.

---

[27]   539 U.S. 558, 598 (2003) (Scalia, J., dissenting).

With Policymakers and Media

Legislators may also be receptive to arguments based on comparative foreign and international law. Deb LaBelle, a Michigan attorney working to end the imposition of JLWOP, notes:

> U.S. citizens and lawmakers often want to believe that the U.S. is a leader in human rights, and it can be powerful for them to discover instances where we lag far behind. When we presented the statistics, Michigan lawmakers were shocked to discover that the U.S. is such an outlier on the issue of juvenile life without parole.

For this same reason, comparative law arguments can also be effective with the media. Advocates note that the media tend not to be interested in specific language from human rights treaties, but that they are interested in hearing how the U.S. compares to other countries.

Challenging JLWOP in Regional and International Forums

Human rights open new venues for challenging unfair treatment that may nevertheless be consistent with U.S. law. Seizing this opportunity, advocates have used regional and international forums to challenge JLWOP sentences in the United States, specifically the Inter-American Commission on Human Rights and the U.N. human rights treaty bodies. The findings and recommendations of these bodies can be used in U.S. courts and in meeting with federal, state, and local policymakers, as noted above.

Inter-American Commission on Human Rights

At the regional level, the U.S. is a member of the Organization of American States (OAS) and has human rights obligations emanating from the American Declaration on the Rights and Duties of Man (the "American Declaration") and the OAS Charter. Compliance with these obligations is monitored by the Inter-American Commission on Human Rights. The Commission hears cases, holds thematic and country specific-hearings upon request, and issues reports on human rights issues.

The Commission has rejected JLWOP sentences as a violation of human rights norms. In a 2011 report from the Commission's Rapporteurship on the Rights of the Child, the rapporteur found that "a sentence of life imprisonment for children under the age of 18 makes it impossible to achieve the purposes that punishment under the juvenile justice system is intended to serve, such as the child's rehabilitation and his or her reintegration into society." He called on countries to "eliminate all forms of life imprisonment in the case of offenders under the age of 18." More recently, the Inter-American Court of Human Rights decided a case, *Mendoza et al. v. Argentina*, involving Argentina's use of *sentencias perpetuas*—sentences under which juveniles serve at least 20 years in prison before they are eligible for parole.[28] The Inter-American Court found that these sentences were a violation of human rights.

Currently pending before the Inter-American Commission on Human Rights is a case challenging JLWOP in the state of Michigan. *Hill v. United States*,[29] which has been brought by the American Civil Liberties Union, the American Civil Liberties Union of Michigan, and Columbia Law School's Human Rights Clinic, alleges that the laws and practices of the state of Michigan, by which thirty-two petitioners were charged and tried, and the imposition of their life without parole sentences violate provisions of the American Declaration, including their rights to special protection; to be free from cruel, infamous, or unusual punishment and to humane treatment; as well as their guarantees to due process and equality under the law. The case also alleges that the petitioners' rights to education and their implicit rights to rehabilitation have been violated. The initial petition in the case was filed in 2006, and the Commission held a hearing on the merits of the case in March 2014. The case itself has offered opportunities to raise public awareness and has provided the petitioners a platform to vindicate their human rights.

Although the findings of the U.N. treaty bodies and of the Inter-American Commission on Human Rights are not directly enforceable in U.S. courts, advocates can use these recommendations as a tool to push for change in the United States. Strong language from these bodies can be helpful with the media in demonstrating to the public where the U.S. stands in comparison to the rest of the world, and it can also be useful in litigation before state and federal courts. JoAnn Kamuf Ward, of Columbia Law School's Human Rights Institute, explains:

> International and regional mechanisms, including the Inter-American Commission, offer a venue for U.S. advocates to establish human rights norms that we can use in domestic advocacy. Through this feedback loop, we bring our human rights issues to regional and international bodies, for recognition that certain policies or practices do not comport with human rights. The findings and recommendations of human rights experts can then bolster advocacy efforts here at home.

The *Mendoza* case at the Inter-American Court, discussed above, is one example of this "feedback loop." In September 2012, the Human Rights Clinic at Columbia Law School submitted an *amicus* brief to the Inter-American Court calling for the elimination of all forms of juvenile life sentences based on the American Declaration, the American Convention, and international and comparative human rights standards.

---

[28] Mendoza et al. v. Argentina, Preliminary Objections, Merits, and Reparations, Judgment, Inter-Am. Ct. H.R. (ser. C) No. 260, ¶ 154 (May 14, 2013).

[29] Case 12.866, Inter-Am. Comm'n H.R.

The brief provided relevant rules and guidelines from the international and European legal systems and urged the Court to develop clear standards providing that all juvenile sentences must include regular and realistic opportunities for review and release. The Inter-American Court's findings—that juvenile sentences must be "as short as possible," of determinate length, and subject to periodic review, and that children must be released once their imprisonment is no longer required—can now be used in the U.S. case before the Inter-American Commission and in U.S. advocacy efforts.

The Inter-American Commission case has also presented avenues for coalition-building and grassroots mobilization. In preparation for the public hearing on the *Hill* case before the Commission in March 2014, advocacy organizations and academic institutions, including the University of San Francisco School of Law, NAACP Legal Defense and Educational Fund, Human Rights Watch, Amnesty International, and Georgetown Law's Human Rights Institute, in partnership with several law firms, prepared *amicus* briefs for the Commission's consideration on a range of topics relating to JLWOP, including its disparate impact, international standards prohibiting JLWOP, and the relationship between JLWOP and the trend of moving juveniles into the adult criminal justice system.[30] Furthermore, because Commission hearings offer an opportunity for live testimony, a number of advocates and officials offered their testimony, including Congressman John Conyers and retired Michigan judge Fred Mester, in addition to some of the petitioners themselves, via video testimony. The Campaign for the Fair Sentencing of Youth also submitted written testimony for the hearing, offering a state-by-state breakdown of individuals serving JLWOP. The media coverage of the hearing provided further opportunities for education and advocacy.

U.N. Treaty Bodies

At the international level, countries are required to periodically report to the U.N. treaty bodies responsible for overseeing the implementation of the human rights treaties they have ratified. As noted above, for the United States, this includes the ICCPR, the CAT, and the CERD. JLWOP sentences have been found to violate all three of these treaties.

In 2014, the U.N. Human Rights Committee, which monitors countries' implementation of the ICCPR, stated that sentencing children to life without parole does not comply with article 24 (1) of the Covenant, which guarantees rights for children, and recommended that the United

---

[30] The *amicus* briefs are available through the Columbia Law School Human Rights Institute website at http://web.law.columbia.edu/human-rights-institute/inter-american-human-rights-system/jlwop.

States "prohibit and abolish all juvenile life without parole sentences irrespective of the crime committed."

The U.N. Committee Against Torture, which monitors implementation of the CAT, recommended in the course of its 2006 review of the United States that the U.S. "address the question of sentences of life imprisonment of children, as these could constitute cruel, inhuman or degrading treatment or punishment" in violation of Article 16 of the CAT.

Finally, in its 2008 review of the United States, the U.N. Committee on the Elimination of Racial Discrimination, which monitors the implementation of the CERD, noted the racially discriminatory effect of JLWOP sentencing in the U.S., indicating that the practice is incompatible with Article 5 of the treaty, guaranteeing the right to equality before the law.

Through the shadow reporting process, advocacy organizations and coalitions, including the U.S. Human Rights Network and Human Rights Watch, have used recent U.S. reports to these treaty bodies to raise concerns at the international level about JLWOP, and the treaty bodies have responded with strong language condemning the practice, as quoted above, and calling for the U.S. to take action to eliminate the practice.

In addition to the "feedback loop" described above, treaty body reviews provide an additional benefit, as described by Connie de la Vega of University of San Francisco School of Law:

> When these international bodies review our country, U.S. officials are forced to stand up and answer for JLWOP, and it forces them to acknowledge how far out of sync we are with the international community. This realization alone can be valuable because these officials may otherwise have no occasion to discover just how universally this practice has been condemned. This realization may ultimately inspire officials to make a change.

Documentation

A core human rights approach is to document abuses, including through reliable statistics as well as personal narratives, in order to build a record that shows how policies perpetuate injustice. Advocates working to end JLWOP sentencing are using this strategy. Prior to recent documentation efforts, comprehensive statistics on JLWOP were unavailable. In the past several years, advocates have documented state and national trends in juvenile life without parole sentencing, including analyses of the race, personal histories, and crimes of offenders in several reports.

The results of these documentation efforts have been powerful. For example, Human Rights Watch has issued multiple reports on JLWOP, collecting data on individuals serving life without parole sentences for crimes they committed before they turned 18. The data demonstrate that approximately 2,500 individuals are currently serving such sentences. Human Rights Watch's data also revealed serious racial disparities in the imposition of JLWOP: the organization found that in California, an African-American youth arrested for murder is over five times more likely to receive a sentence of life without parole than a white youth arrested for murder. Human Rights Watch used this data to demonstrate the racially disparate impact of JLWOP to the Committee on the Elimination of Racial Discrimination, and the Committee took note of this disparity in its 2008 review of the United States' compliance with the CERD. The U.N. thus offered an international platform to echo the findings of U.S. advocates, and the U.N. statements have since been used in *amicus* briefs and policy advocacy.

As part of their documentation efforts, advocates have interviewed those serving JLWOP sentences to give a more complete picture of their personal histories, the crimes they were convicted of (and their roles), and their experiences in prison. While the U.S. has consistently claimed before international human rights bodies that it imposes JLWOP sentences only in exceptional circumstances, the data and stories collected by advocates paint a different picture, showing a greater magnitude of sentencing. Stories of offenders' experiences in prison also highlight offenders' capacity for rehabilitation and support claims that they should be eligible to have their sentences reviewed. Narratives about the underlying crimes also demonstrate that sentences are meted out in a way that does not necessarily reflect culpability, demonstrating that sentencing is influenced by myriad factors, including the defense lawyer, the prosecutor, whether other perpetrators entered pleas, as well as race and gender.

Courts have been receptive to the statistics and personal narratives made available through these documentation efforts. Justice Kennedy's majority opinion in *Graham v. Florida* cited human rights-based reports in support of the Court's decision to end JLWOP for non-homicide offenses.

And personal narratives from offenders serving JLWOP sentences have been used to demonstrate their humanity and to show that JLWOP sentences have not been reserved for the "worst of the worst." For example, in working to change California law regarding JLWOP, advocates used Sara Kruzan's story extensively in media and legislative advocacy. Kruzan, who was sixteen years old when she killed the man who had raped her when she was twelve and had later lured her into prostitution, was tried as an adult and sentenced to life in prison without the possibility of parole. Kruzan expressed remorse for her crime and spoke of her commitment to educate herself and to play a positive role in society.

The documentation strategy for JLWOP brings into relief both a strength and a challenge of the human rights framework: the universality of human rights prohibits the sentencing of any person under age 18 to life without the possibility of parole, regardless of the nature of the underlying offense. It may be most compelling to describe the most sympathetic stories in order to persuade people that JLWOP should be eliminated. For example, the story of a thirteen year-old first-time offender serving JLWOP because he or she participated in a crime in which an adult co-defendant killed a rival gang member may elicit more sympathy than the story of a seventeen year-old with a long criminal history who murdered a mother and her children. But the prohibition on JLWOP applies equally to both offenders. Alison Parker of Human Rights Watch acknowledges this challenge:

> The reality is that children can and do commit very serious crimes. We don't attempt to gloss over that in our reports, and in fact it was important to us to acknowledge this fact. As a human rights organization, we believe strongly that there must be accountability for these kinds of crimes. But accountability for crimes committed by children does not in any way require sentencing them to life without the possibility of parole.

Reframing the Issue

Focusing the human rights lens on the practice of JLWOP enables a new vocabulary for discussing the issue. People under the age of 18 are considered children under international law, and referring to them as children as opposed to "juveniles" or even "teen killers," as some refer to them, can re-orient how people conceive of those sentenced to JLWOP. Framing JLWOP as an issue of children's rights can humanize and "un-demonize" them. Reminding people that they are children can also help open the door to other core human rights concepts, such as dignity and redemption. In a 2013 op-ed in the Washington Post, Jody Kent Lavy, director and national coordinator of the Campaign for the Fair Sentencing of Youth, employed this human rights language, referring throughout to children, second chances, dignity, and American values.

Talking about redemption and the rights of children to second chances has proven powerful with conservative and faith-based communities, opening the door to new avenues of collaboration and the ability to form unique coalitions. Jody Kent Lavy says, "Our organization's Statement of Principles refers to youth, fairness, rehabilitation, and redemption. Referring to human rights and also to our Statement of Principles has been effective in engaging new communities, including faith communities, the American Correctional Association, the national PTA, and more." In fact, a group of 25 religious organizations and individuals submitted an *amicus* brief in *Graham v. Florida*, urging the Court to find JLWOP sentences unconstitutional. The brief discusses redemption, rehabilitation, and forgiveness, and it cites the CRC, U.N. resolutions condemning JLWOP, and the general international consensus against JLWOP in favor of its position.

Finally, framing concerns about JLWOP in terms of equality and fairness has also been effective, particularly when reinforced through the documentation efforts demonstrating racial disparities in the imposition of JLWOP sentences. Nicole Porter, Director of Advocacy for The Sentencing Project, observes:

> The Sentencing Project refers to both 'fairness' and 'human rights' in advocating for fair and effective sentencing practices. However, we have found that the narrative and language of fairness really resonate with people across demographics in the United States, whereas explicitly referring to 'human rights' or international treaty standards is not as effective with certain audiences.

Working with those Most Impacted

Traditional human rights work is grounded in the experiences of those directly affected by government policies that violate human rights. In the case of JLWOP, human rights advocates work directly with individuals serving JLWOP sentences and also with the victims of their crimes, or their families. Much of the pushback against eliminating JLWOP sentences, or against making the Supreme Court decisions curtailing them retroactive in effect, comes from those concerned about the rights of crime victims and their families. But human rights advocates have found that many victims' families are also against JLWOP. Although these families have been affected by serious crimes, they support the idea that children may warrant special treatment in the criminal justice system and should have the opportunity for rehabilitation. These families have proven to be powerful voices before courts, legislators, and the media. Groups of victims' families came together to submit *amicus* briefs in both *Graham v. Florida* and *Miller v. Alabama*, urging the Court to find JLWOP sentences unconstitutional. An organization representing victims' families also submitted briefs in both cases urging the opposite result.

In efforts to reform California state law regarding JLWOP, advocates established a working group drawing from a broad range of actors, including family members of victims and family members of individuals serving JLWOP sentences, as well as human rights advocates, people of faith, law professors, and former prosecutors. In 2010, the working group established a sub-group called the Victims' Perspective Committee, which was tasked with ensuring that the group was incorporating victims' needs and perspectives as advocacy efforts moved forward. The working group also created a healing dialogue and action group, which held several meetings with family members of both victims and offenders, in which participants were guided in compassionate listening and then divided into small groups to share their stories. These groups not only created an opportunity for healing and understanding, but also assisted in developing strong advocates. Elizabeth Calvin of Human Rights Watch explains:

> Following the dialogue sessions, we asked those who were interested to join us in Sacramento to help with our legislative efforts to end the use of life without parole sentences for youth. We set up small groups—each of which included a family member of a victim, a family member of an offender, and an advocate—to meet with legislators. It meant that policymakers sat down to meet with the mother of someone who had been murdered there with the mother of someone convicted of murder. At the time, the voice of victims in Sacramento was largely constrained to a narrow perspective, one focused on retribution, so to have a surviving family member there asking for sentences that reflect mercy and restraint was new in and of itself. But to have that person sitting next to, and in relationship with the mother of someone convicted of murder blew away traditional concepts of "us" and "them." It was very powerful. There was another benefit, though, which was equally important in my opinion. Through the Healing Dialogue and Action process we create opportunities for healing but also build leadership among those who have been most impacted by violence and a broken criminal justice system. Advocacy for change must be grounded in and guided by the people most affected by the problems. I'm excited that after passage of these bills, the Healing Dialogue and Action group is moving forward with more dialogues and opportunities for action.

The efforts in California have resulted in two recent legislative changes. Senate Bill 9 allows those who were under the age of 18 at the time of their crime and who were sentenced to life without parole to request a new sentencing hearing. It was passed in 2012 and became California law in January 2013. Senate Bill 260 is considerably broader and requires a parole board to review the cases of people who were under the age of 18 at the time their crime was committed and who were tried as an adult and sentenced to an adult prison sentence. It was passed in 2013 and became California law in January 2011.

Beyond Advocacy—Talking with Incarcerated Individuals

Finally, invoking human rights law, language, strategies, and forums has also been helpful in working with individuals serving JLWOP sentences. Offenders gain hope and dignity from learning that their sentences have been so widely condemned outside the United States, from discovering more information about others serving the same sentence, and from hearing their cases discussed in terms of children's rights and capacity for redemption. Advocates report that offenders feel validation from these sources, even where there is no hope that their own sentence will be reviewed, partly because they hope that other children will be spared their fate. Deb LaBelle explains:

> It's been very powerful in talking to youth serving life without parole to explain that [their] sentences constitute a human rights violation, to tell them that they are right to feel that this is wrong, that no other country sentences youth to these kinds of sentences. They really embrace the human rights language and care about the fact that children in other countries are not subject to these sentences.

Human rights mechanisms can also give a voice to individuals serving JLWOP sentences. For example, as noted above, some petitioners in the case before the Inter-American Commission had the opportunity to testify before the Commission via video. Participating in the case and telling their stories provided these individuals with a sense of empowerment.

Conclusion

Advocates have leveraged a broad range of human rights strategies in working to end juvenile life without parole sentences. While these sentences are still permissible in certain instances in the U.S. today, their use has been limited by recent Supreme Court decisions, and advocacy for legislative changes remains underway. As the examples cited in this case study demonstrate, using human rights standards and strategies in JLWOP advocacy has had the additional benefit of helping advocates to identify new partners and to build new coalitions and alliances, including with faith-based groups and victims' groups. Human rights strategies and frameworks will continue to play a role as advocates advance their work on this issue, through educating decision makers about foreign and international practice, documenting and sharing statistics and stories of those affected, representing the perspectives of victims and their families, advocating before regional and international forums, and changing the language used to describe juvenile life without parole and those affected by it.

NOTES & QUESTIONS

1. What is the "value added" of human rights in efforts to challenge the practice of sentencing juveniles to life in prison without the possibility of parole? Does this case study persuade you that human rights played a role in the litigation and policy successes described at the beginning of the case study? What, if anything, about the strategies described is unique to a human rights approach?

2. Is there anything particular about the practice of JLWOP that lends itself to a human rights approach? Are there other issues that you think might be particularly ripe for or aided by a human rights approach?

3. Recall Henkin's discussion of "human rights," and Schachter's discussion of "dignity." Do the advocacy strategies described in the JLWOP case study reflect the concepts and normative concerns that those passages discuss? In what ways? Are there particular human rights principles that animate these strategies?

4. Recall the feminist critiques and concerns about cultural relativism and essentialism discussed in the previous section. Do any of the strategies described in this case study raise concerns similar to those articulated in the critiques? Do any of the strategies appear to be informed by the critiques, or perhaps answer some of the concerns that they raise? Are there ways in which the advocacy strategies might better account for the concerns raised in those critiques? Do these strategies raise any other concerns for you?

CHAPTER II

THE PLACE OF "HUMAN RIGHTS" IN THE UNITED STATES

■ ■ ■

The United States has played a key role in the development of modern human rights law. Further, since the nation's inception, United States' society and culture have been profoundly influenced by concepts of human rights. At the same time, United States policy has often reflected deep ambivalence toward international human rights norms, especially as applied to the United States itself. This chapter examines these paradoxes and tensions in greater depth, as a precursor to a more nuanced understanding of contemporary human rights practice in the United States. Section I addresses the role of human rights in the nation's founding, in the guises of both constitutional law and customary international law. Section II looks to the turn toward, and then away from explicit human rights norms in the 20th century, beginning with President Franklin Roosevelt's famous "Four Freedoms" speech embracing human rights to the Cold War era. This section also examines the impact of these developments on the practice of public interest law. Finally, Section III sets out more contemporary debates concerning American exceptionalism and the U.S. role in the global community.

I. HUMAN RIGHTS IN THE FOUNDATIONAL ERA

A. FOUNDING PHILOSOPHIES

In the United States, the role of human rights norms in defining individuals' relationship to the state is contested. Illustrative of those tensions, human rights in the U.S. is susceptible to at least two competing narratives. On the one hand, a concept of human rights is at the very core of the American experiment. It was a quest for human rights that spurred the Pilgrims, the Huguenots, the Quakers and others seeking religious freedom to turn to the American colonies as a place of refuge. A concern for individual rights also triggered the American Revolution, as American patriots decried government oppression and lack of access to democratic participation.

At the same time, the contradictions in American human rights implementation and practice—tantamount to complete transgression of such rights—have also been apparent from the very beginnings of this nation. With few exceptions, European immigrants' treatment of America's native peoples violated concepts of human rights on a grand scale—with significant political, economic, social and cultural impacts that continue today.[1] Further, even those Europeans who sought religious freedom in the emerging nation were often persecuted and unable to fully participate in community governance.[2] African slavery, a part of the American experience from the early days, posed a clear human rights travesty, yet compromises in the drafting of the U.S. Constitution perpetuated slavery as a legal practice for nearly a century after the nation's founding.[3]

Importantly, despite deep American ambivalence and conflicting practices concerning human rights over the centuries, the Declaration of Independence plainly recognizes the important role of international law in confirming the legitimacy of the United States as a new nation. The Declaration's familiar opening stanza states:

> When in the Course of human events, it becomes necessary for one people to dissolve the political bands which have connected them with another, and to assume among the powers of the earth, the separate and equal station to which the Laws of Nature and of Nature's God entitle them, *a decent respect to the opinions of mankind* requires that they should declare the causes which impel them to the separation (emphasis added).

Human rights historian Professor Paul Gordon Lauren traces the wide-ranging intellectual origins of the American concept of human rights while also capturing its contradictions in the excerpt below. Immediately following, Professor Louis Henkin trains a narrower, and perhaps more cynical, legal scholar's eye on the nation's founding documents and their incorporation of human rights norms. As you read these selections, consider whether Professors Lauren and Henkin generally agree or disagree about the important role of human rights in the foundational era.

---

[1] Barbara Gurr, *We are a People in the World: Native Americans and Human Rights*, in Human Rights in Our Own Backyard: Injustice and Resistance in the United States 105 (William T. Amaline, et al., eds., 2011).

[2] *See* The First Prejudice: Religious Tolerance and Intolerance in Early America (Chris Beneke & Christopher S. Grenda, eds., 2010).

[3] *See, e.g.*, George Anastaplo, *Slavery and the Constitution: Explorations,* 20 Tex. Tech L. Rev. 677 (1989); David Waldstreicher, *The Mansfieldian Moment: Slavery, The Constitution, and American Political Traditions,* 43 Rutgers L.J. 471 (2013).

PAUL GORDON LAUREN, "A HUMAN RIGHTS LENS ON
U.S. HISTORY: HUMAN RIGHTS AT HOME AND
HUMAN RIGHTS ABROAD"

1 Bringing Human Rights Home 1, 3–5, (Cynthia Soohoo, et al., eds., 2008).

Early American colonists did not find it at all strange to borrow ideas and practices from England and from the broader European intellectual movement known as the Enlightenment. They argued that they were the inheritors and beneficiaries of the rights that had evolved through the Magna Carta of 1215 on the limitations upon royal government and legal protections for certain individual liberties, the Habeas Corpus Act of 1679 establishing the right to be protected against arbitrary detention, and the landmark English Bill of Rights of 1689 with its specific provisions of civil and political rights such as free elections, freedom of speech, religious toleration, trial by jury, and prohibitions against cruel and unusual punishment. These rights, among others, they had read in the seminal *Second Treatise of Government* written by philosopher John Locke, were "natural rights" derived from "natural law." As such, they should apply not just to the continent of Europe, but to "common humanity" and "governments throughout the world." All people are born, Locke declared,

> with a title to perfect freedom and uncontrolled enjoyment of all the rights and privileges of the law of nature equally with any other man or number of men in the world and have by nature a power not only to preserve his property—that is his life, liberty, and estate—against the injuries and attempts of other men, but to judge and punish the breaches of that law in others.

From this premise it followed that people formed governments to preserve these rights, not to surrender them. As a consequence, governments received their powers from the governed with whom they signed a contract. Any government that acted in such a way as to violate these natural rights, wrote Locke in passages widely quoted with approval among colonists in North America chafing under English rule, therefore dissolved the contract and gave people a right to resist.

The ideas about natural law and natural rights articulated by Locke and by other philosophers and writers such as Jean-Jacques Rousseau, Baron de Montesquieu, Marquis de Condorcet, Voltaire, and Denis Diderot from France, David Hume from England, Francis Hutcheson from Scotland, Immanuel Kant from Prussia, and Cesare Beccaria from Milan, among others, heavily influenced the thinking of many of the founders of the early American republic. They drew not only upon the general ideas, but sometimes even the specific language from the other side of the Atlantic. Delegates to the First Continental Congress of 1774, for example, borrowed the words of the *philosophes* of the Enlightenment about "the immutable laws of nature" and "the principles of the English constitution" to assert that the inhabitants of the colonies were "entitled to life, liberty, and property." George Mason did the same in composing the celebrated Virginia Declaration of Rights, forcefully arguing that "all men are by nature equally free and independent, and have certain inherent rights." Thomas Jefferson knew and utilized the same sources, especially when writing the memorable words of the Declaration of Independence of July 4, 1776:

> We hold these truths to be self-evident, that all men are created equal, that they are endowed by their Creator with certain unalienable rights, that among these are life, liberty, and the pursuit of happiness. That to secure these rights, governments are instituted among men, deriving their just powers from the consent of the governed. That whenever any form of government becomes destructive of those ends, it is the right of the people to alter or to abolish it, and to institute a new government.

These words helped to launch the American Revolutionary War. When that long and painful war finally ended, the task at hand was not to fight and destroy but rather to debate and create. More specifically, the critical undertaking was to institute a new government by consent and to provide for the protection of what were perceived to be the unalienable or natural rights of its citizens, although there was no precise agreement upon exactly what these might entail. The definition of "human rights" would be one that evolved through time and circumstance. The Constitution of 1787 began this process by establishing a federal government with a separation of powers and checks and balances and by enshrining the political rights of voting and of holding office. Many citizens throughout the new republic, however, believed that the Constitution, as it then stood, said far too little about protecting individual rights. They worried not only about threats and abuses that might originate from the government, but also—and very significantly— from a tyranny of the majority. As one of the central founders James Madison expressed it: "In republican government the majority, however composed, ultimately give the law. Whenever therefore an apparent interest or common passion unites a majority, what is to restrain them from unjust violations of the rights and interests of the minority, or of individuals?" Such questions, and the fears and concerns they expressed, as well as the Declaration of the Rights of Man and Citizen that appeared with the outbreak of the French Revolution in 1789, energized rights advocates to mobilize a vigorous, contentious, and lengthy campaign throughout the new country for the purpose of adding amendments to the Constitution that specifically addressed and enumerated critical civil rights.

As a result of their efforts, the first ten amendments, collectively known as the Bill of Rights, were added to the Constitution in 1791. They established the legal foundation for the protection of human rights in the United States. Unlike earlier declarations of rights that used words like "ought" and "should," the amendments employed the word "shall" as a command. Thus, the powerful First Amendment enumerated the freedom of conscience and expression by explicitly stating: "Congress shall make no law respecting an establishment of religion, or prohibiting the free exercise thereof; or abridging the freedom of speech, or of the press; or the right of the people peacefully to assemble; and to petition the Government for a redress of grievances." Other amendments established that people shall be secure in their persons and possessions against unreasonable searches and seizures; shall enjoy the right to a speedy and public trial, a trial by jury, and legal counsel; shall not be compelled to provide witness against themselves; shall not be deprived of life, liberty, or property without due process of law; and shall be protected against excessive fines or cruel and unusual punishment.

Those advocates who had actively campaigned on behalf of rights and supported the inclusion of the Bill of Rights into the Constitution could take justifiable pride in the fact that these protections now became an integral part of the law of the land. They could hardly know, of course, just how important or what kinds of controversies they would generate through time, especially when its provisions were invoked as a rallying cry by those who fell outside its protection and during periods of crisis, national emergency, or war. Some Americans of the early republic even hoped that the provisions they had created would make a significant contribution to human rights by setting an example and inspiring others throughout the world to do the same. As Jefferson himself noted earlier, "a bill of rights is what the people are entitled to against every government on earth."

At times, they did inspire. The early American articulation of human rights certainly went on to influence scores of Europeans of contemporary and subsequent generations, many Asians and Africans in the process of decolonization during the twentieth century, and a number of significant and more recent international efforts. At other times, however, they provided little inspiration for emulation at all, especially when it was clear that they were not fully applied in practice at home. Activists and observers at home and from abroad were quick to point out that the human rights provisions in the much-heralded Constitution and Bill of Rights, for example, did not apply to everyone. Among the many not protected were women, the unpropertied, slaves, indigenous peoples, and children. This fact, they noted, demonstrated a glaring gap between early American vision and American reality.

. . .

LOUIS HENKIN, "RIGHTS: AMERICAN AND HUMAN"
79 Colum. L. Rev. 405, 405–07 (1979).

In speaking of American rights, I shall refer to American constitutional rights, and American constitutionalism. You will notice, however, that I shall quote not from the Constitution but from the Declaration of Independence, a document now reserved for ceremonial occasions; I shall draw on early *state* constitutions—those of Virginia and Massachusetts—now known only to students of history. In fact, those of you who have looked into the American Constitution recently may not recall much evidence for what I say. In particular, the concept of rights is barely hinted at in the Constitution—only in one phrase in the preamble, and in another in one of the early amendments. This, I suggest, is because, at its conception and at birth, the United States Constitution was not an authentic, full-blown, expression of American constitutionalism.

Let me explain this heresy. It contributes to understanding our Constitution to keep in mind its genealogy. In 1776, with independence, the thirteen colonies became thirteen states, each with a state constitution and a state government. These constitutions and governments were the direct descendants of the Declaration of Independence, realizing its political theory, carrying out its political promises.

The U.S. Constitution came thirteen years later. It was not only "come-lately," but was at best only a collateral heir of the Declaration of Independence, deriving not from it, but from a concurrent and parallel development. At the time that the colonies were moving to independence and to self-government, they also moved to union: on the same day in June 1776 that a committee was appointed to draft a declaration of independence, another committee was appointed to draft articles of union. The Articles of Confederation were also conceived in 1776, although they did not come into effect until a few years later. In 1787 those wise men we now call the Constitutional Fathers came to Philadelphia under instructions to improve the Articles of Confederation. But they went beyond their instructions, abandoned the Articles, and produced in its stead the United States Constitution.

It is not only historically, but spiritually, and conceptually, too, that the United States Constitution descended not from the Declaration, but from the Articles. At the Constitutional Convention, the focus was not on principles of government, and the relation of individual to society—to which the Declaration had spoken—but on the needs and uses of union, which the Articles had addressed. The new Constitution did not replace, subsume, or modify the state constitutions and the state governments; only the *links between* states were transformed, into a small superstructure of government over, and above, the state governments, to form a "more perfect Union."

And so, one may say, while the state constitutions descended from the Declaration and its principles of self-government, the U.S. Constitution descended from the Articles and its concerns with union. American principles of government and American constitutionalism were alive and well-formed before confederation and they remained largely unaffected by it. In principle, and perhaps in fact, constitutional government would have remained alive and well, had the new-born States abandoned the effort to confederate and gone thirteen separate ways; had they become two or three confederacies instead of one; or had confederation survived and succeeded under the Articles, and the Constitution had never been born.

This brief genealogical excursion will explain why, unlike the Declaration and the state constitutions, the U.S. Constitution articulates no political theory and contains little political rhetoric. All the political theory in the Constitution is that implied in the fact of a written constitution, and in the words "We the People . . . ordain and establish this Constitution. . . ." All the rhetoric is in a few borrowed, undefined, references to "Justice" and the "Blessings of Liberty." There was no bill of rights—of course: individual rights were not implicated in the issues of union that were the concern of the new superstructure of government. Powers were allocated to different, more-or-less separate, branches of the new government, but there is no articulation and justification of the philosophy of separation-of-powers, as there is in the early Virginia and Massachusetts constitutions. Even federalism, which was, of course, original, is not articulated or justified in principle, and owed less to Locke and Montesquieu than to the brief experience of our ancestors with confederation, to their fears and needs, and to their political compromises, emerging—in Charles and Mary Beard's phrase—as "the mosaic of their second choices."

As the price of ratification, we know, opponents exacted the promise of a bill of rights, and one was added shortly after the new government was formed. Even with the Bill of Rights, however, the United States Constitution lacked much of what we identify with American constitutionalism. It took nationalizing influences in American life, legitimized by nationalistic interpretations of the Constitution; it took the Civil War, and the constitutional amendments that constituted the peace treaty ending it; it took another American contribution—the Supreme Court—to establish the United States government, the United States Constitution, and especially American constitutional rights, as we know them today. Perhaps it took even the genetic defects of our Constitution, including a less-than-clear theory of government and of rights, to give us greater room for growth and development under that same, hardly amended Constitution.

. . .

NOTES & QUESTIONS

1.   Professor Lauren, a historian, articulates a more expansive view of human rights' role in America's founding than does Professor Henkin, a lawyer and legal scholar. For example, Professor Lauren looks at influences from far beyond the nation's own borders. Does that expansive view, supported by historical documentation if not constitutional text, provide a justification for contemporary legal theories that would incorporate human rights norms into domestic federal law—for example, claims that the federal constitution should protect a right to education? How should a lawyer treat this broad historic context if it is not reflected in constitutional text itself?

2.   Professor Henkin also argues for an expansive interpretation of the Constitution, concluding that later developments such as the Civil War and Reconstruction are an appropriate frame for viewing the constitutional text. But why don't the narrow origins of the Constitution, as Professor Henkin describes them, suggest that the Constitution should continue to be viewed as a document with an inherently narrow purpose, even as the text is amended in modest ways over time? Is Professor Henkin too dismissive of his own historical account of the Constitution as a limitation on government, including the Supreme Court?

3.   Professor Henkin notes that the original state constitutions, which preceded the federal constitution, were more in the tradition of the Declaration of Independence in recognizing individual human rights. Among other things, still today, the Massachusetts Constitution articulates a right to education, Massachusetts Constitution of 1780, Ch. 5, Sec. 2, and the Virginia Constitution explicitly recognizes unenumerated "inherent rights" which cannot be stripped away by government. Va. Const. 1776, Art. 1. Is the dichotomy between state and federal constitutions suggested by these textual distinctions sensible? Are states better situated than the federal government to be responsive to their population's concerns and to recognize and protect individual rights?

B. THE JUDICIAL BRANCH AND HUMAN RIGHTS: *THE PAQUETE HABANA*

As both Professors Lauren and Henkin note, the original U.S. Constitution was primarily concerned with the institutional structures necessary to establish a working government. While early amendments to the Constitution added provisions addressing individual rights through the Bill of Rights, the more evocative rhetoric of the Declaration of Independence was never replicated in the Constitutional text. However, the Constitution does include the Supremacy Clause in Article VI, Clause 2. The Clause provides:

> This Constitution, and the Laws of the United States which shall be made in pursuance thereof; *and all treaties made, or which shall be made, under the authority of the United States, shall be the supreme law of the land*; and the judges in every state shall be bound thereby, anything in the constitution or laws of any state to the contrary notwithstanding (emphasis added).

This statement seems to clearly establish treaties—including human rights treaties—as the supreme law of the land, though as discussed in **Chapter III**, it is not quite as clear as all that. At least, though, there is a constitutional text to point to when the status and implementation of treaties are at issue in U.S. courts. But what about customary international law that is not incorporated into a treaty? As we will discuss in further detail in **Chapter IV**, under the international law regime, well-established practices of nations can become binding on nations through their wide international acceptance and consistent conforming practice. Contemporary examples of customary international law norms include the prohibitions on genocide, slavery and torture. The domestic status of customary international law is a strong indication of a nation's acceptance of human rights norms and its recognition of the legitimacy of international law outside of the more contract-based treaty system. Yet the Supremacy Clause does not explicitly address the status of customary international law within the U.S. legal structure.

The U.S. Supreme Court turned to this issue in 1900, building on the sentiments underlying the Declaration of Independence as well as the Constitution's Supremacy Clause. In *The Paquete Habana*, the Court held that customary international law—in this case, the prize law, which governs the treatment of items such as ships captured during war—was the relevant law of decision when fishing vessels sailing under a Spanish flag were captured by U.S. ships off the coast of Florida, then sold at auction. The court began its opinion with a lengthy discussion of the jurisdiction of U.S. courts. Having concluded that the federal Judiciary Acts extend Supreme Court appellate jurisdiction to such disputes, the Court turned to a discussion of the law of decision, finding that international law—and particularly, customary international law established by the law of nations—governed this dispute in the domestic courts.

THE PAQUETE HABANA

Supreme Court of the United States, 1900.
175 U.S. 677.

By an ancient usage among civilized nations, beginning centuries ago, and gradually ripening into a rule of international law, coast fishing vessels, pursuing their vocation of catching and bringing in fresh fish, have been recognized as exempt, with their cargoes and crews, from capture as prize of war.

International law is part of our law, and must be ascertained and administered by the courts of justice of appropriate jurisdiction as often as questions of right depending upon it are duly presented for their determination. For this purpose, where there is no treaty and no controlling executive or legislative act or judicial decision, resort must be had to the customs and usages of civilized nations, and, as evidence of these, to the works of jurists and commentators who by years of labor, research, and experience have made themselves peculiarly well acquainted with the subjects of which they treat. Such works are resorted to by judicial tribunals, not for the speculations of their authors concerning what the law ought to be, but for trustworthy evidence of what the law really is.

. . .

This review of the precedents and authorities on the subject appears to us abundantly to demonstrate that at the present day, by the general consent of the civilized nations of the world, and independently of any express treaty or other public act, it is an established rule of international law, founded on considerations of humanity to a poor and industrious order of men, and of the mutual convenience of belligerent states, that coast fishing vessels, with their implements and supplies, cargoes and crews, unarmed and honestly pursuing their peaceful calling of catching and bringing in fresh fish, are exempt from capture as prize of war.

. . .

This rule of international law is one which prize courts administering the law of nations are bound to take judicial notice of, and to give effect to, in the absence of any treaty or other public act of their own government in relation to the matter.

. . .

MR. JUSTICE FULLER, with MR. JUSTICE HARLAN and MR. JUSTICE McKENNA, dissenting:

The district court held these vessels and their cargoes liable because it was not "satisfied that as a matter of law, without any ordinance, treaty, or proclamation, fishing vessels of this class are exempt from seizure."

This court holds otherwise, not because such exemption is to be found in any treaty, legislation, proclamation, or instruction granting it, but on the ground that the vessels were exempt by reason of an established rule of international law applicable to them, which it is the duty of the court to enforce.

I am unable to conclude that there is any such established international rule, or that this court can properly revise action which must be treated as having been taken in the ordinary exercise of discretion in the conduct of war.

In cannot be maintained "that modern usage constitutes a rule which acts directly upon the thing itself by its own force, and not through the sovereign power."

. . .

It is needless to review the speculations and repetitions of the writers on international law. Ortolan, De Boeck, and others admit that the custom relied on as consecrating the immunity is not so general as to create an absolute international rule; Heffter, Calvo, and others are to the contrary. Their lucubrations may be persuasive, but not authoritative.

In my judgment, the rule is that exemption from the rigors of war is in the control of the Executive. He is bound by no immutable rule on the subject. It is for him to apply, or to modify, or to deny altogether such immunity as may have been usually extended.

Exemptions may be designated in advance, or granted according to circumstances, but carrying on war involves the infliction of the hardships of war, at least to the extent that the seizure or destruction of enemy's property on sea need not be specifically authorized in order to be accomplished.

Being of opinion that these vessels were not exempt as matter of law, I am constrained to dissent from the opinion and judgment of the court; and my brothers Harlan and McKenna concur in this dissent.

NOTES & QUESTIONS

1. What is the actual disagreement between the majority and dissenting justices in the *Paquete Habana*? Do the justices disagree over a substantive point of international customary law, or over the question of whether U.S. law incorporates established customary international law, or over the circumstances of the seizure itself? For the historical context of *The Paquete Habana*, see William S. Dodge, *The Paquete Habana: Customary International Law as Part of Our Law*, *in* International Law Stories 175

(John E. Noyes, et al. eds., 2007). *See also* Jordan J. Paust, *Paquete and the President: Rediscovering the Brief for the United States*, 34 Va. J. Int'l L. 981 (1994). For an overview of "prize law," see 11 J.H.W. Verzijl *et al.*, International Law in Historical Perspective: The Law of Maritime Prize v–vi (1992).

2.   The majority concludes that U.S. law does recognize customary international law and that customary international law is controlling, at least in the absence of overriding domestic law. What authority might the majority cite to support the conclusion that "international law is part of our law"? Since the subject matter of the *Paquete Habana* does not itself involve human rights but the prize law, should the Court's general conclusion really be understood to encompass human rights norms? Keep in mind that the contemporary human rights documents that we look to today for guidance as to the content of human rights norms, such as the UDHR, did not exist when the *Paquete Habana* was decided in 1900.

3.   Is the U.S. Supreme Court competent to determine what international practices constitute customary international law? What should the members of the Court be guided by, first, in assessing their own competence and second, in ascertaining the content of customary international law? Is the Court's task in this regard any more difficult (or legally questionable) when the question is whether human rights norms constitute customary international law than, for example, whether the law of the sea constitutes customary international law? **Chapter IV** discusses the contemporary status of customary international law, including the complicating factor of the U.S. federal system, in greater depth.

II.   AMERICAN RIGHTS AND HUMAN RIGHTS IN THE 20TH CENTURY

The past century has seen a tremendous growth in the definition, codification and institutionalization of international human rights law. The following section examines the ways in which these developments both challenge and build on domestic U.S. law.

A.   HUMAN RIGHTS AND CONSTITUTIONAL INTERPRETATION

The American justice system faced new complications in the 20th century. The challenges of the Reconstruction Era had already resulted in expanded powers for the federal government through the 13th, 14th, and 15th Amendments to the United States Constitution. But the American tradition, still reflected in the core provisions of the Constitution, was one of limited government, more focused on policing the boundaries of separation of powers and federalism than expanding individual rights.

A more affirmative vision of government, however, was apparent in the growing international human rights regime that took hold during and immediately after World War II. Louis Henkin squarely identified the conceptual and political challenges this created for the United States, writing:

> American constitutional rights were born in the eighteenth century out of European ideas and antecedents. International human rights, born during the Second World War from revulsion at the horrors of Hitler, drew heavily on American constitutionalism (and on related constitutional developments in Europe and Latin America), but took also from a different ideology, *i.e.*, from socialism and other commitments to the welfare state. American constitutionalism developed in its own national climate, and was nurtured and maintained by home-grown institutions. International human rights were developed by representatives of different nations, in a complex, unorganized political process; they are designed for diverse national societies, maintained by diverse national institutions, and monitored in uncertain, small ways by primitive international procedures, in a loose international political system.

> . . .

> [In the U.S.,] [g]overnment was to be a watchman, a policeman. That would leave the individual free to pursue his happiness. While the Constitution was ordained, as the preamble tells us, to "establish Justice" and to "promote the general Welfare," those phrases should not be read with twentieth-century preconceptions nurtured in a "welfare state." For the Framers, justice and the general welfare would be the result of the kind of government to be established, a government committed to the accepted, limited purposes. It was not the business of government to provide the people with the "welfare-state" kind of welfare; instead, government was to leave the individual free to pursue such welfare himself.

> . . .

> Like American rights, international human rights also, inevitably, implicate the purposes for which governments are created; but—unlike American rights originally—international rights surely do *not* reflect a commitment to government for limited purposes only. On the contrary, born after various socialisms were established and spreading, and after commitment to welfare economics and the welfare state was

nearly universal, international human rights imply a conception of government as designed for many purposes and seasons. The rights deemed to be fundamental include not only freedoms which government must not invade, but also rights to what is essential for human well-being, which government must actively provide or promote. They imply a government that is activist, intervening, and committed to economic-social planning for the society, so as to satisfy economic-social rights of the individual.

Louis Henkin, *Rights: American and Human*, 79 Colum. L.Rev. 405, 407–11 (1979).

B. HUMAN RIGHTS AND GOVERNMENT OBLIGATIONS

Professor Henkin differentiates between American rights as originally conceived (narrow and reactive) and international rights (broad and affirmative). But as Professor Henkin recognizes at a later point in the article, there is powerful evidence that the idea of affirmative government obligations to ensure individual rights is home-grown as well (though not constitutionally protected). In particular, the challenges of the Great Depression helped reshaped the American public's expectations of government toward a more affirmative stance. In the face of this national economic crisis, the federal government's role grew beyond defending the nation's borders to include—through the Social Security Act of 1935, the National Labor Relations Act of 1935, and the Fair Labor Standards Act of 1938—protecting individual rights to work, welfare, and sustenance. Reflecting these changes, President Franklin D. Roosevelt's 1944 State of the Union Address articulated the "Freedom from Want" as one of the basic freedoms essential to the preservation of the union, along with a robust defense and respect for civil liberties. As set out in the excerpt below, his address, one of the most famous speeches of the 20th century, makes clear the domestic grounding for the social and economic rights that are generally associated with international human rights norms. As you read it, note how President Roosevelt interweaves national security issues, a traditional federal government role that was much on Americans' minds in 1944, and social and economic rights.

FRANKLIN DELANO ROOSEVELT, ADDRESS TO CONGRESS
("THE FOUR FREEDOMS SPEECH")

January 6, 1941.

Mr. President, Mr. Speaker, Members of the Seventy-seventh Congress:

... Every realist knows that the democratic way of life is at this moment being directly assailed in every part of the world—assailed either by arms, or by secret spreading of poisonous propaganda by those who seek to destroy unity and promote discord in nations that are still at peace.

During sixteen long months this assault has blotted out the whole pattern of democratic life in an appalling number of independent nations, great and small. The assailants are still on the march, threatening other nations, great and small.

Therefore, as your President, performing my constitutional duty to "give to the Congress information of the state of the Union," I find it, unhappily, necessary to report that the future and the safety of our country and of our democracy are overwhelmingly involved in events far beyond our borders.

. . .

The need of the moment is that our actions and our policy should be devoted primarily—almost exclusively—to meeting this foreign peril. For all our domestic problems are now a part of the great emergency.

. . .

The Nation takes great satisfaction and much strength from the things which have been done to make its people conscious of their individual stake in the preservation of democratic life in America. Those things have toughened the fibre of our people, have renewed their faith and strengthened their devotion to the institutions we make ready to protect.

Certainly this is no time for any of us to stop thinking about the social and economic problems which are the root cause of the social revolution which is today a supreme factor in the world.

For there is nothing mysterious about the foundations of a healthy and strong democracy. The basic things expected by our people of their political and economic systems are simple. They are:

Equality of opportunity for youth and for others.

Jobs for those who can work.

Security for those who need it.

The ending of special privilege for the few.

The preservation of civil liberties for all.

The enjoyment . . . of the fruits of scientific progress in a wider and constantly rising standard of living.

These are the simple, basic things that must never be lost sight of in the turmoil and unbelievable complexity of our modern world. The inner and abiding strength of our economic and political systems is dependent upon the degree to which they fulfill these expectations.

. . .

In the future days, which we seek to make secure, we look forward to a world founded upon four essential human freedoms.

The first is freedom of speech and expression—everywhere in the world.

The second is freedom of every person to worship God in his own way—everywhere in the world.

The third is freedom from want—which, translated into world terms, means economic understandings which will secure to every nation a healthy peacetime life for its inhabitants-everywhere in the world.

The fourth is freedom from fear—which, translated into world terms, means a world-wide reduction of armaments to such a point and in such a thorough fashion that no nation will be in a position to commit an act of physical aggression against any neighbor—anywhere in the world.

That is no vision of a distant millennium. It is a definite basis for a kind of world attainable in our own time and generation. That kind of world is the very antithesis of the so-called new order of tyranny which the dictators seek to create with the crash of a bomb.

. . .

This nation has placed its destiny in the hands and heads and hearts of its millions of free men and women; and its faith in freedom under the guidance of God. Freedom means the supremacy of human rights everywhere. Our support goes to those who struggle to gain those rights or keep them. Our strength is our unity of purpose. To that high concept there can be no end save victory.

———————

Roosevelt's "Four Freedoms" speech uses the phrase "human rights" only once—"Freedom means the supremacy of human rights everywhere"—yet the speech has been cited frequently and authoritatively as a source for understanding the status and scope of human rights in the U.S., particularly economic and social rights.[4] Roosevelt himself expanded on the Four Freedoms in subsequent public statements and, with the help of artist Norman Rockwell, posters depicting the Four Freedoms became iconic American images, with

———————

[4] *See* Cass Sunstein, The Second Bill of Rights: FDR's Unfinished Revolution (2004); Elizabeth Borgwardt, *"When You State a Moral Principle, You Are Stuck With It": The 1941 Atlantic Charter as a Human Rights Instrument*, 46 Va. J. Int'l L. 501, 506 (2006).

Freedom from Want shown as a family sharing an enormous roast turkey around a holiday dining table. In the excerpt below, historian Elizabeth Borgwardt situates Roosevelt's Four Freedoms speech in its larger post-war and global political context, examining the way in which the speech stimulated dialogue and positioned the U.S. role in human rights implementation both domestically and internationally. As you read this excerpt, consider the ways in which this political context contributed to the emerging meaning of "human rights" on the world stage.

ELIZABETH BORGWARDT, "FDR'S FOUR FREEDOMS AND WARTIME TRANSFORMATIONS"

1 Bringing Human Rights Home 31, 40–44 (Cynthia Soohoo, et al., eds. 2008).

[A]s a figure of speech, "human rights" entered the lexicon of educated readers and influential commentators as a readily understood shorthand in the World War II era, both in the United States and internationally. More importantly, the term's meaning shifted as it entered general use.

Before the war, the phrase occasionally appeared as a somewhat disfavored variation of the much older locution, "rights of man." In arguing that the basic conception of the rights of man first crystallized in the French revolutionary era, historian Lynn Hunt explains that such rights "require three interlocking qualities: rights must be natural (inherent in human beings); equal (the same for everyone); and universal (the same everywhere)." Even given this essential conceptual framework, however, up through the interwar era, the term "human rights" was seldom used in the United States. It appears occasionally as a synonym for what was then the narrower legal term "civil rights"—which in the interwar era in the United States usually meant controversies relating to the Bill of Rights or specialized fields such as labor rights. By the end of World War II, however, the term "human rights" was serving as a caption for the so-called fundamental freedoms meant to differentiate the Allies from their totalitarian rivals.

Traditional civil rights such as freedom of speech and religion were a lesser, included subset of these fundamental freedoms, which drew on natural law concepts to paint a vision of what scholar of ethics and public affairs Paul Lauren calls "certain basic and inherent rights" to which all individuals were entitled "simply by virtue of being human." For example, for the political theorist Hannah Arendt, the wartime encounter with totalitarianism "demonstrated that human dignity needs a new guarantee which can be found only in a new political principle, in a new law on earth, whose validity this time must comprehend the whole of humanity." Legal scholar Richard Primus explains that what he calls a "resurgence of normative foundationalism" soon resulted in "a new vocabulary of 'human rights' " which linked wartime political commitments with "a broader idea rarely seen in the generation before the war but ascendant thereafter: that certain rights exist and must be respected regardless of the positive law." Lynn Hunt agrees that "human rights only become meaningful when they gain political content," and wartime America supplied the concrete political experiences to transform these much older ideas.

While the precise measurement of such a sea-change is necessarily inexact, one way of highlighting this shift in American political thought would be to examine the *New York Times Index* for the years 1936 to 1956. In 1936, there is no "human rights" heading at all. In 1937, the term makes a tentative appearance with two articles, one on property rights and one on labor rights. By 1946, the term is listed as a separate heading, referring the reader to "civil rights," where there are approximately 150 articles we would recognize as addressing human rights-related topics. In 1956, the human rights heading is no longer cross-referenced to civil rights, but rather to a whole new conceptual universe, "freedom and human rights," under which heading there are over 600 articles.

There is arguably something of a time lag for such an amorphous shift to be reflected in the index of a general-interest newspaper. Indeed, if there were a "moment" when the term acquired its modern meaning, a strong candidate would be the signing of the initial "Declaration by United Nations" on January 1, 1942. This document explicitly "multilateralized" the war aims of the August 1941 Atlantic Charter, and was a product of the second major Churchill-Roosevelt summit, code-named Arcadia, held in mid-December 1941 to early January 1942. . . .

In this January 1942 Declaration by United Nations, the twenty-six Allies began by affirming the "common program of purposes and principles . . . known as the Atlantic Charter." The United Nations coalition went on to assert that they were fighting to secure "decent life, liberty, independence, and religious freedom" as against the "savage and brutal forces seeking to subjugate the world." These nations pledged to cooperate in order "to preserve human rights and justice in their own lands as well as in other lands."

The term "human rights" had been absent from the December 25 draft of the Declaration by United Nations. It was likely added in response to a memo from Harry Hopkins, who wrote that: "another sentence should be added including a restatement of our aims for human freedom, justice, security, not only for the people in our own lands but for all the people of the world." He continued, "I think a good deal of care should be given to the exact words of this and I do not think the reference to the Atlantic Charter is adequate."

Incorporating the Atlantic Charter by explicit reference, the final version of the Declaration by United Nations is the first multilateral statement of the four key elements of a new, anti-Axis reading of the term "human rights." These four elements included (1) highlighting traditional political rights as core values; (2) incorporating a broader vision of so-called Four Freedoms rights, which included references to economic justice; (3) suggesting that the subjects of this vision included individuals as well as the more traditional unit of sovereign nation-states (by means of the Atlantic Charter phrase referencing "all the men in all the lands"); and finally, (4) emphasizing that these principles applied domestically as well as internationally. This was a fresh formulation of a much older term, and all four of these elements continue to inform our modern conception of the term "human rights" today.

There is, of course, a heartbreaking irony in the timing of the United Nations' ringing phrases, which were circulated worldwide during the same month in 1942 as the infamous Wannsee Conference was held among Nazi Germany's wartime leaders. Again with bitter irony, January 1942 is also the very same month that federal officials decided forcibly to "relocate"—under what were effectively POW conditions—some 127,000 persons of Japanese ancestry in the continental United States, roughly two-thirds of whom were American citizens. Such horrifying contrasts only emphasize why it is important continually to juxtapose discussions of words with an examination of lived realities. Reacting to the Declaration of the United Nations, Mohandas Gandhi wrote to Roosevelt in July 1942: "I venture to think that the Allied Declaration that the Allies are fighting to make the world safe for freedom of the individual and for democracy sounds hollow, so long as India, and for that matter, Africa are exploited by Great Britain, and America has the Negro problem in her own home." . . . Gandhi's letter underscores how aware historical actors themselves often were of these yawning gaps between rhetoric and reality. . . .

This transformation of human rights as a label—from narrow and domestic ideas about civil rights to a broader and internationalized vision of fundamental freedoms—is an unusually clear example of how a conceptual change may be reflected in a rhetorical shift. In short, human rights as a locution achieved what might be called a kind of "cultural traction" in the United States during this era—a congruence with the newly reshaped worldview not only of elite opinion makers, but also of what was then a fairly recently identified demographic growing up between elite and mass opinion, a widening group of citizens known at the time as "the attentive public."

. . .

The infusion of these human rights ideas into traditional American conceptions of the national interest resulted in something new under the sun in mid-1940s America. The human rights ideas embedded in the Four Freedoms and the Atlantic Charter—as well as in the 1942 Declaration of the United Nations, the document which further internationalized the Charter—had reshaped the concept of the national interest by injecting an explicitly moral calculus. While international initiatives infused with moralistic ideas were hardly a new development, now mobilized and mainstream constituencies were arguably paying attention and reacting in a way they had not before. These vocal constituencies were quick to shout about the betrayal of the "principles of the Atlantic Charter" when confronted with the cold realities of U.S. policies that ignored British colonialism, strengthened *status quo* ideologies such as national sovereignty, or facilitated racial segregation and repression.

New Zealand Prime Minister Peter Fraser echoed many of America's allies when he repeatedly invoked "the principles of the Atlantic Charter" which "must be honoured because thousands have died for them." As he elaborated in a 1944 speech to the Canadian parliament linking the Atlantic Charter and the Four Freedoms: "Your boys, boys of New Zealand, South Africa, India, the United States and all the united nations have given their lives that the four freedoms—freedom of speech, freedom of religion, freedom from fear and freedom from want—may be established and the masses of the people given greater opportunities than ever before." He then warned, "Unless we strive to carry out those principles we shall be undoing in peace what has been won on the battlefield."

Similarly, after an early four-power draft of the United Nations Charter was circulated in October 1944, one of the main objections by "smaller" countries not invited to these negotiations was the absence of an explicit discussion of a role for human rights, especially economic and social rights. Representatives of Australia and New Zealand met in Wellington in November 1944 and developed a joint proposal calling for a greater role for expanded provisions on economic and social rights; Poland and Denmark offered proposals to append the 1941 Atlantic Charter to the draft of the United Nations Charter; Norway wanted to append the 1942 "Declaration by United Nations," multilateralizing the Atlantic Charter and explicitly referencing human rights.

Probably the most trenchant human rights-related critique of the draft world charter came from an assembly of nineteen Latin American nations convened at Chapultepec castle near Mexico City in February–March 1945, when Bolivia, Cuba, and Mexico sought to annex an international bill of rights to the UN's proposed "constitution." The delegation from Nicaragua admonished that "the peace and security of the world" now depended on "all nations, large and small, now adopting in their international relations . . . solid principles of equality and justice, of liberty and law," while the delegation from Cuba submitted an extensive "Declaration of the International Rights and Duties of the Individual" which the conference voted to append to the other suggestions to be forwarded to the inaugural San Francisco UN conference. Conference president Ezequiel Padilla, who had formerly served as Mexico's attorney general and as a revolutionary leader under Pancho Villa, explained that wartime solidarity needed to be converted "into a solidarity of peace; a solidarity that considers the poverty of the people, its social instability, its malnutrition."

By the end of the war, the iconic status of the Four Freedoms and the Atlantic Charter had itself become a sort of "entangling alliance" in its own right, in the evocative image of historian Lloyd Gardner. Especially in the realm of social and economic rights, images of "war aims" and "what we are fighting for" contributed to both creating and raising expectations about the justice and legitimacy of any proposed postwar order, much to the inconvenience—and occasional annoyance—of the Allied officials charged with planning for a postwar world.

. . .

NOTES & QUESTIONS

1.   Professor Borgwardt, a historian, asserts that the U.S. turn toward human rights in the 1940s resulted in "something new under the sun"—a national interest shaped by moral imperatives. But however strong this narrative, can historical developments or State of the Union speeches legitimately reshape the individual claims on the government that undergird the text of our United States Constitution? Is something more required to effect sweeping changes?

2.   FDR's Four Freedoms speech was made at a time when the world was watching, and the speech took account of the international context of the historic moment facing the United States. Professor Borgwardt notes similar human rights sentiments articulated at the time in Latin American nations, in New Zealand, and in international fora. Does the *Paquete Habana* help explain how these developments might ripen into U.S. law?

3.   Historian Samuel Moyn has challenged Professor Borgwardt's account of the rise of human rights. As we saw in **Chapter I**, he argues that contemporary human rights concepts are of much more recent origin, traceable to the 1970s, and that the use of the phrase "human rights" in the 1940s was incidental and particular to post-war political concerns. *See* Samuel Moyn, *Human Rights in History*, The Nation (Aug. 30/Sept. 6, 2010). Moyn states that "The Universal Declaration was less the annunciation of a new age than a funeral wreath laid on the grave of wartime hopes." *Id.* Moyn traces the origins of human rights to the 1970s in part because of the surge of activism led by non-governmental organizations (NGOs) around human rights issues at that time, as well as the high level of national discourse on the issue, led by President Jimmy Carter. While the more commonly accepted

narrative of human rights emerging from the post-Holocaust ashes is powerful, Moyn rejects it as a "myth," arguing that "the true history of human rights matters most of all so that we can confront their prospects today and in the future." *Id.* What is lost and what is gained by adopting Moyn's version of history? In citing the 1970s activities of NGOs as indicative of human rights' "arrival" in the 1970s, does Moyn give too little weight to the earlier human rights activism of the NAACP and the National Women's Party, described below?

C. HUMAN RIGHTS AND DOMESTIC ADVOCACY

i.   American Exceptionalism and Advocacy for Racial Justice

As the phrase "human rights" gained meaning in legal and political spheres through the 1940s, advocates working on behalf of various constituencies took note and incorporated these new developments into their work. International human rights advocacy by domestic groups was not new. Alice Paul and the National Women's Party mounted significant international efforts before and after the ratification of the 19th amendment in 1921 to pressure the U.S. to expand women's rights domestically.[5] Similarly, the Universal Negro Improvement Association led by Marcus Garvey petitioned the League of Nations in 1922 to bring international attention to the plight of African Americans in the U.S. and to step up domestic pressure for change.[6] In 1923, Deskaheh, a Cayuga leader, orchestrated the submission to the League of a petition concerning the status and treatment of the Iroquois by the Canadian government.[7] But in the 1940s, the strengthening of the international human rights regime, the U.S.'s prominent role in creating and upholding it, and the post-War political exigencies that led to these developments, created new openings for advocates to enlist human rights norms in their work. In the excerpt below, historian Carol Anderson discusses the ways in which, during this period, racial justice advocates from the NAACP incorporated human rights norms and mechanisms into their strategic initiatives to achieve domestic equality for African Americans. Yet as Professor Anderson concludes, this period was short-lived. The story continues with the excerpt authored by Professor Cynthia Soohoo, who describes the

---

[5]   See Martha F. Davis, *Not So Foreign After All: Alice Paul and International Women's Rights*, 16 New Eng. Int'l L.J. 1 (2010).

[6]   Marcus Garvey, *Enclosure: Petition of the Universal Negro Improvement Association and African Communities League to The League of Nations*, The Hague (July 20, 1922), reprinted in The Marcus Garvey and Universal Negro Improvement Association Papers: Africa for the Africans—June 1921—December 1922–Volume IX, 535 (Robert A. Hill, ed., 1995).

[7]   Deskaheh remained in Geneva for over a year, but the League refused to consider the petition. Though the specific dispute raised by the petition was with the Canadian government, it had significant implications for the United States as traditional home of many members of the Iroquois nation. *See* Laurie Meijer Drees, *Nationalism, the League of Nations, and the Six Nations of Grand River*, 10 Native Studies Rev. 75 (1995).

backlash embodied in the U.S. Senate's Bricker Amendment and the politics surrounding its consideration.

As you read these selections, consider why the resistance to human rights has been so strong in the U.S., the source of the resistance, and whether different advocacy strategies might have been more successful in diffusing that resistance.

CAROL ANDERSON, "A 'HOLLOW MOCKERY': AFRICAN AMERICANS, WHITE SUPREMACY, AND THE DEVELOPMENT OF HUMAN RIGHTS IN THE UNITED STATES"

1 Bringing Human Rights Home 75, 80–93 (Cynthia Soohoo, et al., eds., 2008).

The war and the language of war proved an important vehicle in the [NAACP's] fight to make human rights a viable force in the United States. . . . The Atlantic Charter's language was specific enough, eloquent enough, and vague enough to envelope a range of interpretations. African Americans clearly saw it as a way out of no way. The second and third points of the Atlantic Charter, for example, spoke of self-determination, that all people had the right to choose their own government. . . .

The Atlantic Charter offered more than mere self-determination, however. The fifth point in that historic document truly seemed to be the dawn of a new world order. The United States and Britain pledged "to bring about the fullest collaboration between all nations in the economic field with the object of securing, *for all,* improved labor standards, economic advancement and social security." The phrase "for all" was unintentionally but decidedly revolutionary. The leaders seemed to promise that the world's citizens would finally have human rights—better working conditions, better and increasing pay, and a safety net of economic security. The British and American leadership had grasped that it was the destabilization in the world markets, which had then avalanched into the Great Depression, that had made Hitler so appealing to the Germans. Roosevelt and Churchill were determined that never again would a nation's economy be so ravaged that the only way out of darkness was through a raving demagogue like Adolf Hitler. Although this may have been the intention of the president and prime minister, African Americans, whose living conditions were simply appalling, interpreted this as a pledge by the federal government to remove the barriers that had systematically prevented them from reaping the benefits from centuries of the unpaid and barely paid hard labor, which had built the wealthiest nation on earth.

. . .

It is within this framework of the Four Freedoms and human rights that the African American leadership soon began "formulating a program of post war needs for the American Negro." At the top of that list was "first-class citizenship" as defined by "basic civil rights" such as "the right to vote in all parts of the country." There was also a recurring emphasis on "essential economic rights" such as the "right to compete in fields of employment on equal levels," "the right to work," "the right to remuneration for work on the basis of merit and performance," and "the right to advance in rank and salary in terms of ability and productive contribution." In addition, African Americans sought the right to "unsegregated and unrestricted housing" and the "right to live without the burdens and embarrassments that are provoked by the unwarranted segregation" in education, health care, and in public accommodations. . . .

[In 1947, the NAACP] . . . petitioned the UN Commission on Human Rights to investigate the conditions under which African Americans lived and died in the United States. In doing so the NAACP made the disastrous error of overestimating its allies and underestimating its opposition. The petition, however, was first-rate. *An Appeal to the World,* written under Du Bois's leadership, stated that although "there is general agreement that the 'fundamental human rights' which" members of the "United Nations are pledged to promote . . . 'without distinction as to race,' include Education, Employment, Housing and Health" it is clear that "the Negro in the United States is the victim of wide deprivation of each of these rights." In his chapter of the petition, Washington Bureau chief and trained sociologist, Leslie S. Perry, began first and foremost with the right to education because, he noted, "those who would continue to exploit the Negro, politically and economically have first tried to keep his mind in shackles."

The petition had, therefore, carefully documented the gross disparities in educational attainment, opportunity, quality, and funding. It had noted that in school districts where African Americans comprised over 75 percent of the school-age population, only $2.12 per capita was spent on them as opposed to $28.50 per white student. The Association had further documented that in 1943–1944, while the United States was at war with the Nazis, Southern states spent 111 percent more on white students than black. Mississippi led the way, of course, with a staggering 499 percent difference between its funding of black and white schools. Moreover, because of the South's insistence on paying black teachers significantly less than white ones, African Americans lost $25 million per year in wages, which in 2005, would equal nearly $1.6 billion annually. As statistic after statistic rolled through the pages of the NAACP's petition to the United Nations about state-sponsored racial inequality—in education, in employment, in housing, in health care—one U.S. diplomat at the United Nations insisted that the Jim Crow Leader of the Free World could not afford to be exposed as a "nation of hypocrites" and he used his influence to bury the petition deep within the UN bureaucracy.

Additional opposition came from "friend of the Negro," NAACP board member, and chair of the UN Commission on Human Rights Eleanor Roosevelt. In an article and a series of letters . . . she emphasized that the NAACP had made a big mistake in going to the UN to air African Americans' grievances because the petition played into the Soviets' hands, and, she intimated, the only petitions the USSR ever supported were those authored by known communist-dominated groups. . . . She firmly believed that the "colored people in the United States . . . would be better served in the long run if the NAACP Appeal were not placed on the Agenda." Then, in the ultimate lesson, Roosevelt submitted her resignation from the NAACP board of directors. Although she did not mention the petition that she had helped squash, the timing of her resignation seemed to carry with it a very distinct, ominous message. White, of course, pleaded with her to reconsider. The Association "would suffer irreparable loss if you were to resign." She held firm. He begged her again. "[U]nder no circumstances would we want you to resign from the Board. Your name means a great deal to us." His pleas, astutely, never mentioned the UN but only how much needed to be done domestically and how only she had the clout to make that happen. Roosevelt eventually agreed to stay. And White began to seriously rethink the NAACP's investment in the struggle for human rights. Indeed, the following year, as part of the growing fissure between Du Bois and him, which was then buttressed by the hard, cold reality of Roosevelt's displeasure with *An Appeal to the World,* White announced to a State Department official that the NAACP "had no intention" of pressing its case ever again before the United Nations.

. . .

In many ways, that retreat from human rights, particularly as the civil rights movement erupted in Alabama [ ] in 1955, bequeathed an agenda for equality that was too restricted to even ask the right question, much less provide the answer, about the root cause of systemic and perpetual inequality.

. . .

CYNTHIA SOOHOO, "HUMAN RIGHTS AND THE
TRANSFORMATION OF THE 'CIVIL RIGHTS' AND
'CIVIL LIBERTIES' LAWYER"
2 Bringing Human Rights Home 71, 74–77 (Cynthia Soohoo, et al., eds., 2008).

By the 1950s, NAACP leadership had essentially given up on international human rights advocacy, focusing instead on domestic civil and political rights claims. Any demands for economic and social rights were left to the black left. When the Civil Rights Congress (CRC) filed a petition with the UN in 1951 based on many of the same underlying facts as the NAACP petition, it failed to gain the support of the black community, and many prominent African Americans, including NAACP leadership denounced it.

. . .

During the same period, U.S. lawyers also tried to incorporate international human rights law into legal arguments in U.S. courts. In a review of Supreme Court civil rights cases from 1946–1955, legal scholar Bert Lockwood found that lawyers frequently raised the U.S.'s human rights and antidiscrimination obligation under the UN Charter. Briefs submitted by progressive legal organizations such as the ACLU, the U.S. government, and occasionally by the parties themselves, argued that the UN Charter evidenced the high principles to which the United States had subscribed including public policy against discrimination. . . . The U.S. government briefs opposing segregation also frequently emphasized the negative impact that segregation had on world opinion. For example, in a case challenging segregated dining cars on railroads, the United States argued that "in our foreign relations, racial discrimination, as exemplified by segregation, has been a source of serious embarrassment . . . Our position and standing before the critical bar of world opinion are weakened if segregation not only is practiced in this country but also is condoned by federal law."

The high-water mark for judicial recognition of UN Charter obligations came in the 1948 Supreme Court case *Oyama v. California,* in which the Supreme Court considered a challenge to California's Alien Land Law. The law prohibited aliens ineligible for citizenship from owning agricultural land, and, at the time, Japanese citizens were ineligible for naturalization. Four Supreme Court justices (one less than a majority), in two separate concurring opinions, indicated that the law was unconstitutional and inconsistent with the human rights obligations the United States undertook when it ratified the UN Charter.

However, in 1950, a California appellate court went too far. In *Sei Fujii v. State,* the court issued a decision overturning the Land Law based on the UN Charter's human rights and nondiscrimination provisions, stating that the treaty invalidated conflicting state laws. By suggesting that the UN Charter imposed enforceable legal obligations superseding inconsistent state law, the *Sei Fujii* decision played right into the hands of opponents of the UN such as Frank Holman, a former president of the American Bar Association, and Senator John W. Bricker of Ohio. Holman portrayed the UN and human rights treaties as threats to U.S. sovereignty and tools to erode states' rights. He argued that human rights treaties were a plot to promote communism and impose socialism on the U.S. *Sei Fujii* provoked an outpouring a criticism. Lockwood describes it as "the legal shot heard around the nation. Perhaps no other decision of a state appellate court received as much attention in the legal periodicals." In 1952, the California Supreme Court responded by repudiating the appellate court's reasoning, stating that the charter "represents a moral commitment of foremost importance" but the human rights and nondiscrimination provisions relied on by the plaintiff "were not intended to supersede existing domestic legislation, and we cannot hold that they operate to invalidate the alien land law."

. . .

The *Sei Fujii* case, the UN petitions, and opposition to U.S. ratification of the Convention on the Prevention and Punishment of the Crime of Genocide (Genocide Convention) fueled domestic backlash against the UN and human rights treaties in the 1950s led by Senator Bricker and Frank Holman. Concerned about the potential of the UN Charter and future human rights treaties to impact domestic law, Bricker attempted to amend the Constitution to limit the president's power to ratify treaties. Although the amendments proposed by Bricker concerned the division of power between the President and Congress and the state and federal government, as illustrated by contemporaneous debate, support for the amendment was fueled by concern that human rights treaties would be used to dismantle segregation, which was being defended as state prerogative.

The battle over U.S ratification of the Genocide Convention in the 1950s was a focal point for this struggle. In the aftermath of the Holocaust, one of the first items on the international agenda was the drafting of the Genocide Convention. Despite a context in which a convention denouncing genocide would appear a reasonable undertaking by the international community, Southern senators adamantly opposed U.S. ratification, because they feared it was a "back-door method of enacting federal anti-lynching legislation." Holman belittled the Genocide Convention arguing that accidentally running over a "Negro child" could be grounds for an overseas trial for genocide and argued that the treaties could lead to the "nullifying of statutes against mixed marriages."

The Bricker amendment was narrowly defeated in the Senate. In order to head off further criticism of and attacks on the president's foreign relations power, the Eisenhower administration agreed that it would not seek ratification of the Genocide Convention or any other human rights treaty. The U.S. Senate did not take up ratification of human rights treaties until the waning days of the Cold War.

. . .

After World War II, the international community concluded that an international commitment to protect human rights was necessary to sustain peace and ensure fundamental rights. Progressive lawyers in the United States recognized the potential that the twin tools of universally recognized human rights standards and international pressure could have on social justice work in the United States, particularly on the issues of racial discrimination and segregation. In response to this threat to their interests, U.S. isolationists and defenders of a segregated South formed an effective alliance. In the context of the Cold War, they were able to both narrow the rights claims domestic activists could make and the venues in which they made them. As legal historian Mary Dudziak writes:

> The primacy of anticommunism in postwar American politics and culture left a very narrow space for criticism of the status quo. By silencing certain voices and by promoting a particular vision of racial justice, the Cold War led to a narrowing of acceptable civil rights discourse. The narrow boundaries of Cold War—era civil rights politics kept discussions of broad-based social change, or a linking of race and class, off the agenda.

. . .

While the confluence of domestic civil rights struggles and the Cold War in the 1940s and 1950s was a unique time in U.S. history, the period captures a continuing tension with the use of international human rights law in the United States. The UN Charter (and later the human rights treaties that would finally be ratified by the United States in the 1990s) created a legal and moral imperative for the United States to alter its conduct. In the 1940s and 1950s, this imperative was intensified as the world watched to see how the United States would respond as segregation was challenged by the civil rights movement. At the same time, anti-internationalist sentiment and fear of the erosion of domestic sovereignty made it difficult for courts and the public to accept claims that the United States was legally bound to domestically enforce human rights treaties. As a result, any influence on Supreme Court decisions was indirect. As Lockwood states, "Courts, disposed to move in the direction of correcting the American dilemma, were on firmer ground to buttress the change with a domestic constitutional cloak of legitimacy than to rely on such a radical notion as international human rights law."

. . .

NOTES & QUESTIONS

1.   These contributions by Professors Anderson and Soohoo begin to raise questions about the role of law in domestic human rights advocacy efforts. How does the use of the human rights legal norms differ from the use of human rights rhetoric by advocates? In the examples above, which

approach—rhetorical or legal—was more effective in achieving advocates' goals?

2.   Do you see a recurring dynamic in these advocacy stories—progress toward human rights goals, followed by a backlash? What triggers this response? For more examples, see Gerald N. Rosenberg, The Hollow Hope: Can Courts Bring About Social Change? (1991); Michael J. Klarman, From Jim Crow to Civil Rights: The Supreme Court and the Struggle for Racial Equality 196–225 (2004); and Carlos A. Ball, *The Backlash Thesis and Same-Sex Marriage: Learning From Brown v. Board of Education and its Aftermath*, 14 Wm. & Mary Bill Rts. J. 1493 (2006). Is there a way for advocates to avoid this dynamic? Or maybe they should not avoid it—does this back and forth have positive implications for organizing and advocacy?

3.   What is the legacy of the early history of human rights in terms of advocacy opportunities and strategies available to U.S. advocates? How might the history recounted in Anderson's and Soohoo's essays inform future strategies, including campaigns for human rights treaty ratification, implementation and enforcement? To be more concrete, what might advocates for U.S. ratification of the U.N. Convention on the Rights of Persons with Disabilities learn from this history? For general background on the politics surrounding the Disabilities Convention in the U.S., see Tracy R. Justesen & Troy R. Justesen, *An Analysis of the Development and Adoption of the United Nations Convention Recognizing the Rights of Individuals with Disabilities: Why The United States Refuses to Sign this UN Convention*, 14 Hum. Rts. Brief 36 (2006) and Tara J. Melish, *The UN Disability Convention: Historic Process, Strong Prospects, and Why the U.S. Should Ratify*, 14 Hum. Rts. Brief 37 (2006).

---

ii. Public Interest Advocacy

The NAACP's civil rights litigation victories captured the attention of a broad range of public interest advocates, who throughout the 1960s and '70s sought to use domestic impact litigation to similar effect addressing women's rights, poverty rights, the rights of Mexican Americans and Asian Americans, and the rights of other ethnic minorities. These lawyers were, like the NAACP Legal Defense and Educational Fund, Inc. (LDF) advocates, profoundly affected by the shadow that Cold War politics cast on human rights arguments. Yet it is clear today—and it is indeed the basis for this book—that things are changing, and that domestic lawyers are increasingly using international law and human rights mechanisms in their advocacy. Professor Scott Cummings surveys a wide range of public interest lawyers—including immigrants' rights, women's rights and environmental rights lawyers—to analyze the reasons for the gradual internationalization of public interest law through the late 20th and early 21st centuries. Growing interest in human rights approaches is only one factor in this internalization, since the matters handled by public interest lawyers are also heavily influenced by increased international communication, travel and trade; for example, North American Free Trade Agreement (NAFTA), which creates a free trade zone between the United States, Canada and Mexico, is an external development that has pushed labor lawyers to look to international standards.[8] However, Professor Cummings posits that perceived limits of domestic law and absence of federal government support for more progressive domestic policies have also contributed to increased attention to human rights approaches. As you read Cummings' work, think about whether you agree with his assertion that human rights advocacy is a figurative last stop on the line of public interest advocacy that began with *Brown v. Board of Education.*

SCOTT CUMMINGS, "THE INTERNATIONALIZATION OF PUBLIC INTEREST LAW"
57 Duke L. J. 891, 900–1005 (2008).

The pivotal moment for the law reform movement came in *Brown v. Board of Education*, which validated the test-case strategy of the NAACP Legal Defense and Educational Fund (NAACP LDF) with the Supreme Court's sweeping repudiation of school segregation. The LDF model of law reform defined the second phase of legal activism, which lasted through the 1970s and—because of its association with efforts to promote the interests of politically vulnerable social groups—came to be identified with the concept of "public interest law." The success of liberal lawyers in using the courts as a fulcrum to leverage political change brought resources and status to a new sector of legal organizations promising to use federal court litigation to promote progressive reform. Yet, while the public interest law movement developed as a distinctively American project, its evolution was framed by the emergence of a human rights system outside U.S. borders and the changing stream of immigrants within. The United States was a primary architect of human rights in the postwar era, contributing to the formation of the United Nations (UN), whose Charter proclaimed "respect for human rights," and helping to draft the Universal Declaration of Human Rights. While the United States sought to use human rights to cultivate anticommunist allies abroad, the creation of the human rights system emboldened activist groups at home, who saw it as a way to force the U.S. government to put

---

[8]   North American Free Trade Agreement Implementation Act, Pub. L. No. 103–182 (1993). For discussion on the impact of NAFTA, see Tamara Kay, NAFTA and the Politics of Labor Transnationalism (2011). Also, the University of Miami's Inter-American Law Review devoted a journal issue to the impact of regional trade agreements on human rights and the rule of law, including coverage of NAFTA. See the introduction to the symposium, describing the various contributions to the volume, Robert Shawn Hogue, *Introduction*, 42 Miami Inter-Am L. Rev. ix (2011).

its principles into practice. The NAACP, sensitive to the dynamics of Cold War politics, brought its civil rights agenda to the UN in the late 1940s and early 1950s in an effort to internationalize the civil rights struggle, submitting a petition to the newly formed UN Commission on Human Rights challenging the "barbaric" practice of U.S. discrimination against blacks. Additional human rights efforts ensued, as lawyers from the NAACP LDF, the ACLU, and other groups attempted to draw international attention to racial discrimination through the inclusion of human rights claims in civil rights cases during the 1940s and 1950s. But this human rights approach was de-emphasized in the 1950s in part to avoid the red-baiting that destroyed other civil rights groups, but also because of the building momentum for domestic legalism, dramatized by *Brown*, and cultivated by U.S. policymakers eager to avoid international embarrassment. Successive legal victories and the passage of the civil rights laws bolstered the domestic trend, which—though never exclusive—became the defining mode of legal engagement during the public interest period.

. . .

As the rule-of-law movement abroad underscores, the public interest impulse outside U.S. borders is articulated in the language of human rights, which proponents seek to embed in embryonic legal systems to counter the deregulatory thrust of market integration and to assert in international political institutions (like the UN) as a bulwark against the power of international financial institutions (like the WTO). Human rights is thus viewed as a way to infill the multiple fissures in global governance with laws of uniform consistency—to globalize a set of universal political norms to act as a countervailing force against economic globalization. For U.S. public interest lawyers, the interest in "bringing human rights home," represents the optimism of this international human rights movement, but also a pragmatic acknowledgment of the limits of domestic law to produce political change at home. The picture of American public interest lawyers—who a generation ago championed the transformation of domestic law for progressive ends—now turning to human rights as a master frame for social change highlights the contrasting fortunes of public interest law at home and its human rights counterpart abroad. It also suggests the strong influence of changing U.S. policy on the circuitous path of human rights domestication. Whereas the international human rights system promoted in the Cold War era was, in part, a way to *export* American-style public interest law to activists in foreign countries resisting authoritarian regimes, the current U.S. human rights movement represents an effort by public interest lawyers to *import* the very norms and methods built through international struggle to contest what they view as the erosion of domestic legal standards resulting from new American policy imperatives: market integration, conservatism, and the War on Terror.

. . .

As these campaigns reach for international authority to achieve domestic results, they highlight the gap that separates the contemporary domestic human rights movement from public interest law in its initial phase. Whereas early public interest law sought to enlist the federal government as a liberal ally in combating discriminatory state practice and regulating private business, domestic human rights has emerged as a vehicle for contesting the now conservative centers of federal power by turning to human rights institutions as a potentially progressive alternative. In this sense, the field of domestic human rights is an expression of public interest law's resilience—a reinterpretation of goals and strategies in the face of political realignment. But by the same token, it is also a reflection of the relative weakness of public interest law, unable to fully achieve its aims through the domestic channels that it pioneered four decades ago.

. . .

NOTES & QUESTIONS

1.   Professor Cummings draws a contrast between the *Brown*-era lawyers who tried to work *with* the federal government to enforce civil rights at the state level and contemporary public interest lawyers *challenging* the federal government in international forums. How do federalism issues complicate this description? What posture do public interest lawyers operating in the international sphere maintain vis-à-vis *state* and *local* governments? We return to this question in **Chapter VI**.

2.   Does advocacy in the international law setting, *i.e.*, through the U.N. treaty monitoring bodies, and special procedures, inevitably mean adopting an adversarial posture towards the U.S. government? Might public interest lawyers use international fora strategically to strengthen and support existing factions within the federal government, rather than always critiquing federal policy? We will explore these questions in greater depth in **Chapter VIII**.

III. CONTEMPORARY RELATIONSHIP TO HUMAN RIGHTS—U.S. EXCEPTIONALISM

As domestic public interest lawyers shape their advocacy work to protect individual rights, larger U.S. international policy positions may have a profound effect on the extent to which they can effectively utilize international human rights law and norms in their day to day advocacy. American exceptionalism has been observed and defined by many scholars and commentators, and one particular challenge for domestic advocates is the perceived double-standard that the United States has adopted with respect to the implementation of human rights abroad and at home. As Michael Ignatieff observes,

> [s]ince 1945 America has displayed exceptional leadership in promoting international human rights. At the same time, however, it has also resisted complying with human rights standards at home or aligning its foreign policy *with* these standards abroad. Under some administrations, it has promoted human rights as if they were synonymous with American values, while under others, it has emphasized the superiority of American values over international standards. This combination of leadership and resistance is what defines American human rights behavior as exceptional.

Michael Ignatieff, Exceptionalism and Human Rights 113 (2005).

United States' policies of human rights exceptionalism may seem far away from domestic civil rights, environmental and immigration advocacy, but the connection between foreign policy and domestic human rights is closer than it may first appear; the issues come together around the question of government accountability for human rights violations and abuses, and also affect the ability of domestic advocates to bring international mechanisms to bear on more local human rights concerns.

In the excerpt below, Harold Koh, a professor of law as well as a former federal government official, argues that American exceptionalism has many facets, not all of which are negative. The Statement on Human Rights Day which follows, issued by President-elect Obama in 2008, seems to align with the ideals that Koh articulates, emphasizing the positive possibilities of exceptionalism. As you read these selections, think about how the various forms of American exceptionalism in the international arena may help or hinder domestic advocates.

HAROLD HONGJU KOH, "ON AMERICAN EXCEPTIONALISM"
55 Stan. L. Rev. 1479, 1483–88 (2003).

I prefer to distinguish among four somewhat different faces of American exceptionalism, which I call, in order of ascending opprobrium: distinctive rights, different labels, the "flying buttress" mentality, and double standards. In my view, the fourth face—double standards— presents the most dangerous and destructive form of American exceptionalism.

By distinctiveness, I mean that America has a *distinctive rights culture,* growing out of its peculiar social, political, and economic history. Because of that history, some human rights, such as the norm of nondiscrimination based on race or First Amendment protections for speech and religion, have received far greater emphasis and judicial protection in America than in Europe or Asia. So, for example, the U.S. First Amendment is far more protective than other countries' laws of hate speech, libel, commercial speech, and publication of national security information. But is this distinctive rights culture, rooted in our American tradition, fundamentally inconsistent with universal human rights values? On examination, I do not find this distinctiveness too deeply unsettling to world order. The judicial doctrine of "margin of appreciation," familiar in European Union law, permits sufficient national variance as to promote tolerance of some measure of this kind of rights distinctiveness.

Similarly, America's tendency to use *different labels* to describe synonymous concepts turns out to be more of an annoyance than a philosophical attack on the rest of the world. When I appeared before the Committee Against Torture in Geneva to defend the first United States report on U.S. compliance with the Torture Convention, I was asked the reasonable question why the United States does not "maintain a single, comprehensive collation of statistics regarding incidents of torture and cruel, inhuman or degrading treatment or punishment," a universally understood concept. My answer, in effect, was that the myriad bureaucracies of the federal government, the fifty states, and the territories *did* gather statistics regarding torture and cruel, inhuman, or degrading treatment, but we called that practice by different labels, including "cruel and unusual punishment," "police brutality," "section 1983 actions," applications of the exclusionary rule, violations of civil rights under color of state law, and the like. Refusing to accept the internationally accepted human rights standard as the American legal term thus reflects a quirky, nonintegrationist feature of our cultural distinctiveness (akin to our continuing use of feet and inches, rather than the metric system). But different labels don't necessarily mean different rules. Except for some troubling post-September 11 backsliding, the United States generally accepts the prohibition against torture, even if it calls that prohibition by a different name.

Third, I believe that lumping all of America's exclusionary treaty practices—e.g., nonratification, ratification with reservations, and the non-self-executing treaty doctrine—under the general heading of "American exemptionalism" misses an important point: that not all the ways in which the United States exempts itself from global treaty obligations are equally problematic. For example, although the United States has a notoriously embarrassing record for the late ratification, nonratification, or "Swiss cheese ratification" of various human rights treaties, as my colleague Oona Hathaway has empirically demonstrated, the relevant question is not nonratification but *noncompliance* with the underlying norms, a problem from which the rest of the world tends to suffer more than the United States. Many countries adopt a strategy of ratification without compliance; in contrast, the United States has adopted the perverse practice of human rights *compliance without ratification*. So, for example, during the thirty-seven years after the United States signed, but before it was ratified, the Genocide Convention, no one plausibly claimed that U.S. officials were committing genocide. This was simply another glaring example of American compliance without ratification.

This third face of American exceptionalism Louis Henkin long ago dubbed "America's *flying buttress* mentality." Why is it, he asked, that in the cathedral of international human rights, the United States is so often seen as a flying buttress, rather than a pillar, willing to stand outside the structure supporting it, but unwilling to subject itself to the critical examination and rules of that structure? The short answer is that compliance without ratification gives a false sense of freedom. By supporting and following the rules of the international realm most of the time, but always out of a sense of political prudence rather than legal obligation, the United States tries to have it both ways. On the one hand, it enjoys the appearance of compliance. On the other, it maintains the illusion of unfettered sovereignty. It is a bit like the driver who regularly breaks the speed limit but rarely gets a ticket, because he uses radar detectors, cruise control, ham radios, and similar tricks to stay just this side of the law. He complies, but does not obey, because to obey visibly would mean surrendering his freedom and admitting to constraints, while appearing "free" better serves his self-image than the more sedate label of being law-abiding.

Like "distinctive rights" and "different labels," the flying buttress mentality is ultimately more America's problem than the world's. For example, it is a huge embarrassment that only two nations in the world-the United States and Somalia, which until recently did not have an organized government-have not ratified the Convention on the Rights of the Child. Nevertheless, this ultimately is more America's loss than that of the world. Why? Because the United States rarely gets enough credit for the large-scale moral and financial support that it actually gives to children's rights around the world, in no small part because of its promiscuous failure to ratify a convention with which it actually complies in most respects. But once one weighs in the unfavorable alignment of proratification votes in the Republican-controlled Senate, and considers the amount of political capital that U.S. activists would require to obtain the sixty-seven votes needed for ratification any time soon, one soon concludes that children's rights advocates are probably better off directing their limited energies not toward ratification, but rather, toward real strategies to reduce the exploitation of child labor or to expand the prohibitions in the child-soldiers protocol. This brings me to the fourth and most problematic face of American exceptionalism: when the United States actually uses its exceptional power and wealth to promote a *double standard*. The most problematic case is not distinctive American rights culture, a taste for different labels, or a flying buttress mentality, but rather, when the United States proposes that a different rule should apply to itself than applies to the rest of the world. Recent well-known examples include such diverse issues as the International Criminal Court, the Kyoto Protocol on Climate Change, executing juvenile offenders or persons with mental disabilities, declining to implement orders of the International Court of Justice with regard to the death penalty, or claiming a Second Amendment exclusion from a proposed global ban on the illicit transfer of small arms and light weapons. In the post-9/11 environment, further examples have proliferated: America's attitudes toward the global justice system, holding Taliban detainees on Guantanamo without Geneva Convention hearings, and asserting a right to use force in preemptive self-defense, about all of which I will say more shortly.

For now, we should recognize at least four problems with double standards. The first is that, when the United States promotes double standards, it invariably ends up not on the higher rung, but on the lower rung with horrid bedfellows—for example, with such countries as Iran, Nigeria, and Saudi Arabia, the only other countries that have not in practice either abolished or declared a moratorium upon the imposition of the death penalty on juvenile offenders. This appearance of hypocrisy undercuts America's ability to pursue an affirmative human rights agenda. Worse yet, by espousing the double standard, the United States often finds itself co-opted into either condoning or defending other countries' human rights abuses, even when it previously criticized them (as has happened, for example, with the United States critique of military tribunals in Peru, Russia's war on Chechen "terrorists," or China's crackdown on Uighur Muslims). Third, the perception that the United States applies one standard to the world and another to itself sharply weakens America's claim to lead globally through moral authority. This diminishes U.S. power to persuade through principle, a critical element of American "soft power." Fourth, and perhaps most important, by opposing the global rules, the United States can end up undermining the legitimacy of the rules themselves, not just modifying them to suit America's purposes. The irony, of course, is that, by doing so, the United States disempowers itself from invoking those rules, at precisely the moment when it needs those rules to serve its own national purposes.

Having focused until now on the negative faces of American exceptionalism, I must address a fifth, much-overlooked dimension in which the United States is genuinely exceptional in international affairs.

Looking only at the half-empty part of the glass, I would argue, obscures the most important respect in which the United States has been genuinely exceptional, with regard to international affairs, international law, and promotion of human rights: namely, in its *exceptional global leadership* and activism. To this day, the United States remains the only superpower capable, and at times willing, to commit real resources and make real sacrifices to build, sustain, and drive an international system committed to international law, democracy, and the promotion of human rights. Experience teaches that when the United States leads on human rights, from Nuremberg to Kosovo, other countries follow. When the United States does not lead, often nothing happens, or worse yet, as in Rwanda and Bosnia, disasters occur because the United States does not get involved.

. . .

STATEMENT OF PRESIDENT-ELECT OBAMA ON HUMAN RIGHTS DAY 2008

The United States was founded on the idea that all people are endowed with inalienable rights, and that principle has allowed us to work to perfect our union at home while standing as a beacon of hope to the world. Today, that principle is embodied in agreements Americans helped forge—the Universal Declaration of Human Rights, the Geneva Conventions, and treaties against torture and genocide—and it unites us with people from every country and culture.

When the United States stands up for human rights, by example at home and by effort abroad, we align ourselves with men and women around the world who struggle for the right to speak their minds, to choose their leaders, and to be treated with dignity and respect. We also strengthen our security and wellbeing, because the abuse of human rights can feed many of the global dangers that we confront—from armed conflict and humanitarian crises, to corruption and the spread of ideologies that promote hatred and violence.

So on this Human Rights Day, let us rededicate ourselves to the advancement of human rights and freedoms for all, and pledge always to live by the ideals we promote to the world.

———

Professor Koh critiques the policy of American exceptionalism from the left and urges greater coherence and adherence to human rights principles. Do you agree with his critique? What about his characterization of the positive aspects of exceptionalism?

Some scholars defend American exceptionalism as a rational approach to foreign policy that ultimately has little impact on human rights internationally, and no impact on domestic human rights protections. Professor Goldsmith, whose work is excerpted below, has been a leading proponent of this view.

JACK LANDMAN GOLDSMITH, "INTERNATIONAL HUMAN RIGHTS LAW AND THE UNITED STATES DOUBLE STANDARD"
1 Green Bag 2d 365, 369–73 (1998).

. . . [T]he U.S. government uses the international human rights system to measure the legitimacy of foreign governmental acts, but it systematically declines to hold domestic acts to the same legal scrutiny.

To understand the significance of the double standard, it is first necessary to understand the special enforcement logic and poor enforcement record of international human rights law.

Much of international law is largely self-enforcing because nations receive mutually beneficial gains from compliance. A good example is the law of diplomatic immunity. Whether by treaty or customary law, the immunity of ambassadors has been viewed as a necessary prerequisite to successful diplomatic intercourse since at least the beginning of the nation-state. This law persists because of the mutual advantage it brings. Nations forgo the relatively small benefit of enforcing local laws against foreign diplomats in order to realize the broader benefits that accrue from relations with foreign nations. But unless both nations provide immunity, neither will do so and both will be worse off. The model here is the iterated prisoners' dilemma. Nations involved in indefinite relationships will forgo private, short-term advantage to achieve superior long-term benefits that can only be gained by mutual cooperation.

International human rights law is not self-enforcing in this way. If two nations are not inclined for purely domestic reasons to provide a certain level of individual rights protection to their citizens, they gain nothing from a mutual promise to provide greater protection to their citizens. Assuming for the moment an absence of independent international incentives (such as forgone economic aid, threat of military intervention, or diplomatic ostracization), a nation that violates its citizens' human rights will have no incentive to comply with more restrictive international human rights norms.

For this reason, the efficacy of international human rights law in a nation not otherwise inclined to obey this law depends on the willingness of other nations to sanction non compliance. The problem is that nations rarely expend the military or economic resources needed to alter the way another nation treats its citizens. Severe public sanctions for violations of human rights are usually limited to two situations in which nations have special enforcement incentives. The first occurs when one nation's human rights violations threaten significant adverse consequences for another nation. This explains the United States' intervention in the former Yugoslavia and Haiti.

A second context for likely human rights enforcement is when a government receives domestic political benefits from unilateral enforcement, and the costs of such enforcement—in economic or military terms—are low. Examples of this phenomenon are U.S. economic sanctions against weak and unpopular countries like Cuba and Myanmar. In general, nations will not enforce international human rights law if enforcement is costly and the strategic benefits of enforcement are low or uncertain. This explains the paucity of human rights law enforcement against China and Saudi Arabia.

There are of course more subtle sanctioning methods. Although nations regularly fail to comply with international human rights law, no nation publicly declares a prerogative to commit human rights abuses against its citizens, and every nation takes steps to avoid exposure of, or at least to justify, such abuse. This phenomenon reflects the human rights community's success in making human rights a matter of international concern, as well as more effective communication tools for exposing human rights abuses. Today exposure of a nation's human rights abuses can result in a variety of low-level sanctions. It can, for example, lead to ostracization of elites along the many points of diplomatic and economic interaction. Or it can cause an increase in pressure for broader sanctions by interested groups in other countries. For example, Christian groups are putting enormous pressure on Congress to sanction governments that commit acts of religious persecution, and non-governmental organizations often pressure corporations to alter business practices in countries that abuse human rights. These relatively low-level responses to human rights abuses have varying effects on the behavior of nations that violate human rights. At the margin they must have some effect, for some nations otherwise inclined to violate international standards do take steps to avoid exposure of illegal acts, and often engage in sporadic and nominal acts of compliance (such as releasing a dissident prisoner or announcing new human rights aspirations). But this effect is often indiscernible, and confirms international human rights law's generally poor enforcement record.

Underenforcement of international human rights law feeds noncompliance with that law. The content of human rights treaties is significantly influenced by human rights activists within governments and progressive organizations such as the United Nations General Assembly, Human Rights Watch, and Amnesty International. For this reason among others, the human rights treaties presented for national ratification are invariably more protective of human rights than domestic legal systems. Weak and sporadic enforcement means that a nation can through ratification minimize the stigma of non-ratification at little if any cost to its domestic political arrangement.

There is even less reason for a nation not to ratify an aspirational human rights treaty if, as many academic commentators believe, customary international law independently imposes on the nation certain human rights obligations regardless of whether it has ratified a treaty in which the obligation might also be found. These factors help explain why the Civil and Political Rights Covenant has been ratified by such human rights champions as Afghanistan, Algeria, Columbia, Croatia, Guatemala, Iraq, North Korea, Libya, Serbia, and Sudan. China, too, recently announced that it would ratify the Covenant.

We can now better understand how and why the United States perpetuates the double standard. The explanation is not subtle. The United States declines to embrace international human rights law because it can. Like other nations, the United States wants the benefits from an international human rights regime with as little disruption as possible to its domestic political order. Unlike most other nations, the United States' paramount economic and military power, combined with its dominance of international institutions, means that it is largely immune from both formal international sanctions and the variety of less formal, lower-level sanctions. General satisfaction with domestic human rights protections, combined with a suspicion of international processes, mean that NGO and foreign government attempts to stigmatize the United States for noncompliance with human rights law fall flat.

This explanation for the double standard does not, of course, speak to its normative attractiveness. Many criticize the standard as hypocritical. This charge, however, is too casually made. Hypocrisy is the act of professing virtues that one does not hold. The United States does not typically urge substantive standards on other countries that it does not itself abide by. It does not, for example, claim that other countries violate human rights law when they execute minors for capital crimes. The United States tends only to press those human rights norms abroad that its domestic law protects at home.

Moreover, despite its unwillingness to enforce international human rights law against U.S. officials, the United States remains one of the greatest protectors of individual rights in the world by virtue of its domestic constitutional and democratic processes. Many human rights activists contend that the United States nonetheless violates international human rights law with respect to immigration practices, police abuse, custodial treatment and conditions, the death penalty, and discrimination. There is always room for the United States to improve on these and other human rights fronts. But the charge that the United States violates *international law* in these respects is almost always an exaggeration. This charge is usually based on a non-rigorous understanding of international law that eschews its fundamental grounding in state consent. The many reservations, understandings, and declarations to human rights treaties that these activists complain about are designed to ensure that the United States does not consent to international obligations that it cannot abide by domestically. It is precisely to avoid hypocrisy that the United States resists certain international human rights obligations. The notion that the United States is nonetheless bound by a customary international law of human rights because of an international consensus to which it does not adhere represents a radical and thus far unaccepted conception of international law.

If the United States' double standard evinces hypocrisy, it is because the United States urges other nations to embrace international human rights treaties that the United States itself either does not ratify or does not enforce domestically. Even here the double standard is not necessarily hypocritical. International law's treatment of nations as equals is a fiction. There is much less moral and political justification for imposing human rights obligations on the United States than there is for imposing these obligations on Myanmar or China or Rwanda. International human rights law is primarily designed for nations with domestic institutions that do not hold the promise for generating adequate human rights protections.

But perhaps there is a connection between the United States' failure to embrace international human rights law and the poor compliance records of nations that abuse human rights. Perhaps the United States' failure to subject itself to these international processes undermines its moral authority to enforce human rights. It is not at all clear, however, that the efficacy of international human rights law depends on moral authority in this way. Compliance with human rights law depends on the costs of non-compliance. Effective coercive measures are usually carried out by or with the support of the United States, usually after a careful calculation that the benefits to the United States' strategic position outweigh the costs of enforcement. The efficacy of these measures is not likely to be affected by the extent to which the United States itself engages the international human rights law process. The success of U.S. sanctions in Bosnia, or the United States' ability to bestow (or withhold) status in international organizations, is unaffected by the United States practice of executing juvenile murderers or its failure to ratify the Rights of the Child Convention.[9]

[9 Editors' Note: The U.S. practice regarding execution of juveniles has changed since this article was published *See, e.g.*, Roper v. Simmons, 543 U.S. 551 (2005).].

The United States double standard might undermine the effectiveness of international human rights law in a different way. The international human rights movement presents its aspirational moral and political goals as a form of law. The purposeful space between law and compliance is then used as a basis for pressuring governments (through the various methods discussed above) into ratcheting up their human rights protections. The effectiveness of this pressure might depend on the perceived legitimacy of human rights law. And the U.S. double standard might undermine this legitimacy by revealing the legal system itself to be little more than an exercise in international politics. On this view, the U.S. double standard reduces the gravitational moral pull of human rights law.

There is little evidence that compliance with human rights law depends on the perceived legitimacy of the international legal system, as opposed to the legitimacy of particular moral norms—such as a prohibition on torture—that might or might not be instantiated in an international law binding on a particular nation. China has not yet signed the Civil and Political Rights Convention, and cannot reasonably be viewed as having embraced an international custom of protecting civil and political rights.

But it is nonetheless a frequent focus of criticism for violating the civil rights of its citizens, because these acts are viewed as morally wrong independent of their illegality. It is true, of course, that criticism of a country's human rights record is often dressed up in the language of illegality. But this rhetoric rarely depends on careful arguments about legality, and both the content and sources of international human rights law are much too diffuse for illegality to be the criterion of opprobrium it is in domestic legal systems. It is the moral quality of the acts in question, not their illegality that actually triggers the international community's opprobrium. The successful characterization of an act as "illegal" can of course change perceptions about the moral worth of the act, but it is moral worth, and not legality, that counts.

Finally, even if the United States double standard does affect the legitimacy of the international human rights law system, it does not follow that, as many believe, the United States should incorporate international human rights law into its domestic system. This demand is unrealistic because of the widespread domestic opposition to international human rights law. It also ignores two other possible responses that are both more realistic and more sensitive to the relative costs of particular institutional arrangements.

One possible response is that international human rights law is too ambitious. This law could, and perhaps should, narrow its legitimacy gap by modifying its universalistic pretensions and lowering its aspirations.

Many of the reasons for United States resistance to international human rights law—distrust of international institutions, desire to maintain local cultural and political difference, satisfaction with domestic political systems, preservation of sovereignty and the related benefits of self-government—explain other countries' resistance to this law. It is unclear which regime leads to more effective respect for human rights: One that is extremely ambitious, but suffers a legitimacy deficit because of the inevitable gap between aspiration and compliance; or one that is less ambitious but suffers less of a legitimacy gap. Criticisms of the United States double standard rarely consider the latter option, but if legitimacy is the goal, modesty might be the most effective option. The point here is something that critics of the double standard tend to ignore: international human rights law inevitably involves a trade-off between ambition and legitimacy.

A second possible response is that the United States should stop enforcing human rights norms against other countries. Such a course would alleviate any hypocrisy that inheres in the double standard. But it would harm the promotion of international human rights. A United States double standard is in this sense preferable to no enforcement at all. This shows that the pertinent question to ask about the double standard is not whether it is good or bad. The pertinent question is whether it is better or worse than the feasible alternatives. Without United States enforcement pressure, international human rights law would be even less efficacious than it already is. And there would be no United States enforcement if the United States were itself subject to the same potential sanctions it imposes on others. The United States double standard is one price the international community pays for the important benefit of United States enforcement. Fortunately, the United States does not need external legal processes or the threat of external sanctions in order to provide its citizens and residents with prodigious human rights protections.

NOTES & QUESTIONS

1.   These excerpts from Professors Koh and Goldsmith make clear how complicated the notion of American exceptionalism is, and how directly it is tied to American foreign policy interests. Given that, are domestic advocates going far beyond their expertise and into dangerous waters when they press the U.S. to more fully incorporate human rights norms into U.S. law and to honor such commitments on the international stage was well? Should domestic groups defer to the government's foreign policy expertise, much as the Supreme Court does? And should that area of deference—i.e., foreign policy—be drawn broadly? For more background on foreign affairs deference in the judicial context, see Jonathan I. Charney, *Judicial Deference in Foreign Relations*, 83 Am. J. Int'l L. 805 (1989). *See also* Michael P. Fix & Kirk A. Randazzo, *Judicial Deference and National Security: Applications of*

the Political Question and Act of State Doctrines, 6 Democracy and Security 1 (2010).

2.   Professor Koh argues that we should not forget the positive aspects of exceptionalism, and the leadership that the U.S. often takes on human rights issues internationally. Do the positive aspects of American exceptionalism and America's international "leadership" on human rights answer the concerns of human rights advocates? Assuming that the U.S. will continue to take leadership on human rights issues when it is politically advantageous, what is the role of advocates in securing U.S. commitments to human rights both domestically and abroad when the political benefits are not clear, and where the U.S. might not take action in the absence of external pressures?

3.   Decrying perceived U.S. human rights violations after September 11, 2011—such as targeted drone strikes—former President Jimmy Carter asserted that "[t]he United States is abandoning its role as a global champion of human rights." Jimmy Carter, *Op-Ed: A Cruel and Unusual Record*, New York Times, June 24, 2012. President Carter invoked the UDHR, pointing out that the U.S. played a leading role in its creation and citing it as a benchmark from which the U.S. should not derogate. Why might the former President want to ground his charges against current U.S. policies in the provisions of the UDHR? How does his assertion draw on the positive aspects of American exceptionalism, as articulated by Professor Koh? Do you think this is an effective critique?

———————

In 2006, the U.N. General Assembly led an effort to restructure some of the U.N.'s human rights monitoring and compliance apparatus. Among these, the longstanding Human Rights Commission was replaced by a new Human Rights Council. In 2009, the U.S. ran for a seat on the new Council. As part of its candidacy, the U.S. made an explicit set of commitments to the international community, listed below. As you will see, most of these commitments are external to the U.S., yet some focus on goals for domestic policy.

Also in 2006, the U.N. adopted a new method of monitoring nations' human rights compliance: the Universal Periodic Review (UPR). The UPR process is a full review of the human rights record of all countries that are members of the United Nations, in which all member countries participate. Forty-eight member states are reviewed each year by the other U.N. member states. The stated goal of the UPR is to advance human rights; address human rights violations; encourage countries to fulfill their treaty obligations; ensure that recommendations by treaty bodies are implemented; provide technical assistance to countries implementing recommendations; and to share best practices for advancing human rights. We explore the UPR in greater depth in **Chapter VIII**.

The U.S.'s first UPR took place in 2010. As part of this process, members of U.S. civil society had an opportunity to comment on the U.S.'s adherence to human rights. An excerpt from the civil society UPR report to the U.N. Human Rights Council is included below. As you read the commitments made by the U.S. in 2009, juxtaposed with the inputs from U.S. civil society at the time of the U.S.'s first periodic review in 2010, consider the impacts of American exceptionalism on domestic constituencies.

Following these U.N.-related documents is a report from the Opportunity Agenda summarizing Americans' understanding of and familiarity with human rights concepts. In 2008, the Opportunity Agenda undertook an empirical study of this question through polling data. As you read the findings from the Opportunity Agenda's study, consider whether the polling data indicates strong support for human rights at home, at least at the conceptual level, and whether it might be read to indicate that at least the aspect of exceptionalism that completely exempts U.S. domestic policy from human rights scrutiny is on the wane.

U.S. HUMAN RIGHTS COMMITMENTS AND PLEDGES ON JOINING THE U.N. HUMAN RIGHTS COUNCIL
(2009).

The deep commitment of the United States to championing the human rights enshrined in the Universal Declaration of Human Rights is driven by the founding values of our nation and the conviction that international peace, security and prosperity are strengthened when human rights and fundamental freedoms are respected and protected. As the United States seeks to advance human rights and fundamental freedoms around the world, we do so cognizant of our own commitment to live up to our ideals at home and to meet our international human rights obligations. We therefore make the following pledges:

Commitment to advancing human rights in the United Nations system

1. The United States commits to continuing its efforts in the United Nations system to be a strong advocate for all people around the world who suffer from abuse and oppression, and to be a stalwart defender of courageous individuals across the globe who work, often at great personal risk, on behalf of the rights of others.

2. The United States commits to working with principled determination for a balanced, credible and effective United Nations Human Rights Council to advance the purpose of the Universal Declaration of Human Rights. To that same end, in partnership with the

international community, we fully intend to promote universality, transparency and objectivity in all of the Council's endeavours. The United States commits to participating fully in the universal periodic review process and looks forward to the review in 2010 of its own record in promoting and protecting human rights and fundamental freedoms in the United States.

3.   The United States is committed to advancing the promotion and protection of human rights and fundamental freedoms in the General Assembly and the Third Committee, and in this vein intends to actively participate in the 2011 review by the General Assembly of the work of the Human Rights Council.

4.   The United States is also committed to the promotion and protection of human rights through regional organizations. Through our membership in the Organization for Security and Cooperation in Europe and the Organization of American States, the United States commits to continuing efforts to uphold human rights and fundamental freedoms, and to strengthening and developing institutions and mechanisms for their protection. In particular recognition of its human rights commitments within the Inter-American system, the United States strongly supports the work of the Inter-American Commission on Human Rights.

5.   The United States recognizes and upholds the vital role of civil society and human rights defenders in the promotion and protection of human rights and commits to promoting the effective involvement of non-governmental organizations in the work of the United Nations, including the Human Rights Council, and other international organizations

6.   As part of our commitment to the principle of universality of human rights, the United States commits to working with our international partners in the spirit of openness, consultation and respect and reaffirms that expressions of concern about the human rights situation in any country, our own included, are appropriate matters for international discussion.

. . .

Commitment to advancing human rights, fundamental freedoms, and human dignity and prosperity internationally

1.   The United States commits to continuing to support States in their implementation of human rights obligations, as appropriate, through human rights dialogue, exchange of experts, technical and interregional cooperation, and programmatic support of the work of non-governmental organizations.

2.   The United States commits to continuing its efforts to strengthen mechanisms in the international system established to

advance the rights, protection and empowerment of women through, for example, supporting the full implementation of Security Council resolutions 1325 (2000) and 1820 (2008), on women, peace and security, and all relevant General Assembly resolutions, particularly 61/143 and 63/155, on the intensification of efforts to eliminate all forms of violence against women; supporting the work of the Commission on the Status of Women; and supporting the work of the Inter-American Commission on Women.

3. The United States commits to continuing to promote respect for workers' rights worldwide, including by working with other Governments and the International Labour Organization (ILO) to adopt and enforce regulations and laws that promote respect for internationally recognized worker rights and by providing funding for technical assistance projects designed to build the capacity of worker organizations, employers and Governments to address labour issues, including forced labour and the worst forms of child labour, such as child soldiering, workplace discrimination, and sweatshop and exploitative working conditions.

4. The United States commits to continuing to advocate a victim-centered and multidisciplinary approach to combating all forms of trafficking in persons and to restoring the dignity, human rights and fundamental freedoms of human trafficking victims.

5. The United States commits to continuing to promote freedom of religion for individuals of all beliefs, particularly members of minority and vulnerable religious groups, through dedicated outreach, advocacy, training and programmatic efforts.

6. The United States is committed to continuing to promote human rights in the fight against HIV/AIDS in a variety of ways, including through promoting the rights of people living with HIV/AIDS, fighting against stigma and discrimination, and supporting women's rights. The United States is committed to preventing suffering and saving lives by confronting global health challenges through improving the quality, availability and use of essential health services.

7. The United States is committed to continuing its leadership role in promoting voluntary corporate social responsibility and business and human rights initiatives globally. The United States intends to convene Government, civil society and business stakeholders for the purpose of seeking joint solutions in respect of business and human rights, and to serve as an active participant in key multi-stakeholder initiatives such as the Voluntary Principles on Security and Human Rights.

8. Recognizing the essential contributions of independent media in promoting the fundamental freedom of expression, exposing human rights abuses and promoting accountability and transparency in governance, the United States commits to continuing to champion freedom of expression

and to promote media freedom and the protection of journalists worldwide.

9.   We are dedicated to combating both overt and subtle forms of racism and discrimination internationally. The United States is party to the International Convention on the Elimination of All Forms of Racial Discrimination, and is committed to seeing the goals of this covenant fully realized. Particular emphasis should be placed not only on eliminating any remaining legal barriers to equality, but also on confronting the reality of continuing discrimination and inequality within institutions and societies.

Commitment to advancing human rights and fundamental freedoms in the United States

1.   The United States executive branch is committed to working with its legislative branch to consider the possible ratification of human rights treaties, including but not limited to the Convention on the Elimination of All Forms of Discrimination against Women and ILO Convention No. 111 concerning Discrimination in Respect of Employment and Occupation.

2.   The United States is committed to meeting its United Nations treaty obligations and participating in a meaningful dialogue with treaty body members.

3.   The United States is committed to cooperating with the human rights mechanisms of the United Nations, as well as the Inter-American Commission on Human Rights and other regional human rights bodies, by responding to inquiries, engaging in dialogues and hosting visits.

4.   The United States is also strongly committed to fighting racism and discrimination, and acts of violence committed because of racial or ethnic hatred. Despite the achievements of the civil rights movement and many years of striving to achieve equal rights for all, racism still exists in our country and we continue to fight it.

5.   The United States is committed to continuing to promote human prosperity and human rights and fundamental freedoms of all persons within the United States, including through enforcement of the Americans with Disabilities Act and its amendments, engaging religious and community leaders in upholding religious freedom and pluralism, and encouraging the members of the private sector to serve as good corporate citizens both in the United States and overseas.

––––––––––––––

During the U.S.'s UPR review in 2010, many domestic advocacy organizations prepared reports on a wide range of human rights concerns within the United States. These reports were summarized for submission to the U.N. Human Rights Council by the U.S. Human Rights Network, a non-governmental coordinating group for domestic human rights organizations. The following excerpt highlights the issues of administration of justice and the right to work, among the many issues raised by U.S. advocates.

SUMMARY SUBMISSION TO THE U.N. UNIVERSAL PERIODIC REVIEW, THE U.S. HUMAN RIGHTS NETWORK
(2010).

Administration of justice, including impunity and the rule of law

12. The U.S. continues to fall short of its human rights obligations in the administration of justice, particularly in relation to: racially disparate sentencing, sentencing of juveniles to life without parole, and collateral consequences of felony convictions; conditions of confinement that violate an incarcerated women's reproductive rights, and rights of prisoners with psychosocial disabilities; treatment of individuals in supermax facilities; and, treatment of political prisoners. Furthermore, the Prison Litigation Reform Act presents significant barriers to prison oversight.

13. Racial profiling persists in the U.S. where policies and programs that allow for, or incentivize the use of racial profiling in criminal, immigration, and national security law enforcement proliferate, despite U.S. obligations under the ICERD, the ICCPR, and the UDHR to ensure the non-derogable right of all people under its jurisdiction to be free from discrimination.

14. Dozens of political prisoners who were victimized by the U.S. government's political repression against African-Americans, Puerto Ricans, and Native American communities continue to languish in prison and endure solitary confinement, poor medical health care, various other forms of abuse, and perfunctory parole hearings resulting in routine denial of release. These violations have repeated themselves in the post-9/11 era under the guise of national security.

. . .

Right to work and to just and favourable conditions of work

18. While the U.S. has recently undertaken renewed efforts to secure workplace rights and reduce unemployment at the aggregate level, the prevalence of exploitative, subsistence-only jobs combined with persistent unemployment rates [persists].

19. Employment promotion measures have not yielded a sufficient number of jobs for jobseekers: Recently, the American Recovery and Reinvestment Act (ARRA) has created and saved jobs, and extended

benefits to vulnerable populations, but did not employ direct employment programs to create new jobs.

20. Anti-discrimination laws do not fully comply with ICERD: The U.S. has a number of laws that protect against discrimination in employment, however, the definition of discrimination in current law does not meet the standard in Article 1 (1) of ICERD, and is inadequate in addressing policies and practices that appear neutral but put people of particular racial, ethnic or national origin at a disadvantage compared with other persons in the enjoyment of the right to work. For example, most state laws allow employers to refuse to hire people with a criminal record including people who were arrested but never convicted. Given the persistent practice of racial profiling, and disproportionate arrest based on race, this practice has a disproportionate negative effect on African Americans. In application, Title VII of the Civil Rights Law of 1964, which prohibits employment discrimination, does not apply to employers with less than 15 employees, and thus sectors that tend to have fewer employees are *de facto* excluded.

21. Insufficient workplace accommodation for pregnancy and parenting: The Pregnancy Discrimination Act offers incomplete protection for pregnant women in the workplace, because federal courts have interpreted the Act narrowly, leaving many allowable grounds to fire a pregnant worker. Furthermore, the U.S. is the only industrialized country with no mandated maternity leave policy. The Family and Medical Leave Act guarantees up to 12 weeks unpaid leave for some workers, but because it is unpaid, many workers cannot afford to take advantage of it.

22. Federal labor laws exclude many low-wage workers: Domestic workers, agricultural workers, and independent contractors—workers who are often low-wage, and predominantly women and racial/ethnic minorities in the case of domestic workers—are exempt from the full protection of labor laws creating uneven standards across labor sectors. The Fair Labor Standards Act (FLSA), which establishes minimum wage and overtime pay guidelines, excludes live-in domestic workers. As a matter of policy, the Occupational Safety and Health Act (OSHA) excludes domestic workers, depriving them of the right to a safe and healthy work environment, among other rights. Furthermore, because labor laws assign rights to "employees"—a status narrowly defined— employers often misclassify employees as independent contractors or subcontractors denying them workplace protections.

23. Inadequate protection of the of basic workplace rights: The absence of public oversight in high-violation industries has precipitated the lowering of standards in the labor market as a whole. The few existing legal protections against workplace violations are not adequately enforced.

. . .

———————

The UPR process demonstrates that advocates have much to say about the U.S.'s failure to comply with human rights norms. The advocates cited here represent many important domestic constituencies. But how widespread is popular engagement with these issues, and what do Americans as a whole really think about human rights? The Opportunity Agenda set out to answer these questions using social science methodologies. As you read this excerpt, consider whether you would characterize these results as positive or negative for advocates working in this arena.

ALAN JENKINS AND KEVIN HSU, "AMERICAN IDEALS AND HUMAN RIGHTS: FINDINGS FROM NEW PUBLIC OPINION RESEARCH FROM THE OPPORTUNITY AGENDA"
77 Fordham L. Rev. 439, 445–49 (2008).

Analysis of the research resulted in four main findings: (1) the concept of human rights is clear and positive for Americans; (2) the public places many social justice issues in a human rights framework; (3) perceptions of the role of government complicate support for human rights; and (4) communicating about international treaties is a long-term challenge.

A. *The Concept of Human Rights Is Clear and Positive for Americans*

Perhaps the most striking research finding is that a large majority of Americans strongly believe in human rights, specifically in the notion that "every person has basic rights regardless of whether their government recognizes those rights or not," with 80% of those surveyed agreeing with that statement, and 62% agreeing strongly. Similarly, very few respondents believed that rights stem solely from the government deciding to afford them to an individual; only 19% agreed that "rights are given to an individual by his or her government." These findings are consistent with a survey conducted ten years earlier in which 76% of respondents agreed that "every person has basic rights common to all human beings" and only 17% "believed rights are given by government." Nor do Americans see human rights as inherently international or foreign; 81% agree that "we should strive to uphold human rights in the U.S. because there are people being denied . . . human rights in our country." This finding, that the American public is "very comfortable with the term human rights," was also reflected in the focus groups, confirming that, while the issue of human rights is an infrequent topic of discussion for most Americans, it is one that they are fully comfortable having.

Americans not only believe in human rights as a concept, they also believe that the United States should be working to improve human rights at home, with 77% strongly agreeing that government should "protect" human rights for everyone, and 69% strongly agreeing that government should "provide" human rights. Addressing human rights problems aggressively is not a top priority for most Americans, however. Only 27% believe that, compared to other challenges facing the country, human rights should be put "near the top of the list," and half of respondents believe instead that we should "[m]ove cautiously, trying to make regular progress on human rights problems."

B.   *Americans Place Many Social Justice Issues in a Human Rights Framework*

Just as the public shows broad support for the general concept of human rights, Americans are also open to viewing specific social justice issues through a human rights lens and consider many substantive freedoms and guarantees to be human rights. The national survey asked respondents whether each of fifteen social justice principles and issue areas "should be considered a human right." That inquiry found three tiers of support, which we discuss below.

1.   Social Justice Issues as Human Rights

There is broad and emphatic public recognition of social justice guarantees related to equal opportunity, nondiscrimination, and freedom from abuse by law enforcement as human rights. Nearly all Americans found the following protections to be human rights, with over eight in ten "strongly agree[ing]" that they are human rights: equal opportunity regardless of gender (86%), equal opportunity regardless of race (85%), fair treatment in the criminal justice system for the accused (83%), freedom from discrimination (83%), freedom from torture or abuse by law enforcement (83%), and equal access to quality public education (82%). Focus group findings suggest that these protections are particularly closely aligned with the values of dignity, fairness, and opportunity that Americans identify with the notion of human rights. Each right, moreover, has roots in the U.S. Constitution, and Americans see the protection of these rights as building upon human rights guarantees.

In the "second tier," only slightly smaller majorities of the public also recognized the following four guarantees to be human rights, with over six in ten "strongly agree[ing]" that they are human rights: access to health care (72%), living in a clean environment (68%), fair pay for workers to meet their basic needs for food and housing (68%), and keeping personal behavior and choices private (60%). Most of these guarantees relate to the opportunity for people to meet their basic human needs, indicating public support for positive rights alongside negative prohibitions against discrimination. Support for protection of privacy in personal behavior may have served as a proxy for such issues as contraception and same-sex intimacy.

The "third tier" represents guarantees which were recognized by a majority of respondents, but for which only approximately half of respondents "strongly agree" that they are human rights: equal opportunities regardless of whether you are gay or lesbian (79% total agree; 57% "strongly"), freedom from extreme poverty (78%; 52% "strongly"), adequate housing (77%; 51% "strongly"), ensuring economic opportunity (77%; 47% "strongly"), and the right to an abortion (64%; 40% "strongly").

Within this tier, the issue of abortion as a human right produced the most evenly split result, with 40% strongly supporting a human right to abortion, 24% only somewhat supporting the notion that abortion is a human right, and 35% believing that abortion should not be a human right. Majorities of liberals (58%), Democrats (53%), and residents of the Northeast (50%) strongly recognized a human right to abortion, whereas majorities of Republicans (52%) and conservatives (51%), and a plurality of residents of the South (44%) believe that abortion should not be considered a human right. Though this final tier of issues received less "strong" support than the other ten issues, there is still significant support for approaching these issues from a human rights framework.

2.   Specific Contemporary U.S. Problems as Human Rights Violations

In addition to inquiring whether Americans view social justice issues as human rights, the research also examined whether Americans consider six specific, ongoing situations in the United States to be human rights violations. Respondents were asked to state whether they strongly agreed, somewhat agreed, somewhat disagreed, or strongly disagreed that each of the following was a human rights violation-with the percentages for total "agree" and "strongly agree" listed, respectively, in parentheses: police stop and search based solely on race or ethnicity (84%; 70%), lack of quality education for children in poor communities (81%; 62%), torturing prisoners suspected of terrorism (67%; 43%), treatment of New Orleans residents after Hurricane Katrina (60%; 41%), and denying "illegal immigrants" access to medical care (49%; 24%). These results indicate that Americans are amenable to a human rights framework not only for broad values or high-level thinking about social justice, but also as applied to specific, real-life problems.

A particular pair of survey results bears further discussion. While 72% of Americans strongly agree that access to health care is a human right, the public is split regarding the proposition that denial of access to medical care for undocumented immigrants is a human rights violation, with 49% of Americans saying that it is. More of the public strongly disagrees with the latter proposition (32%) than strongly agrees (24%). This reflects the sharp division in the United States around the issue of immigration.

These results no doubt reflect the current divisive debate about immigration reform and the future of undocumented immigrants. For example, there are deep demographic and ideological distinctions in how different groups responded to the question of immigrants and medical care. Yet, the disconnect in overall responses to the two survey items does raise questions about the extent to which audiences view all human rights as inalienable and universal.

Overall, however, this research demonstrates that Americans are open to thinking about domestic social justice issues in a human rights framework. Some areas of social justice work gain stronger support for consideration through a human rights lens than others, but each of the fifteen issues tested garnered at least a plurality of strong support. Majorities of Americans also viewed a variety of contemporary social problems as human rights violations, with the exception of denial of access to medical care for undocumented immigrants, which provided a divided response.

C.   *Americans Have Mixed Beliefs About the Role of Government*

Given Americans' acceptance of human rights as a concept and as a set of substantive protections, it is not surprising that the public also believes that government should play a role in upholding those human rights. Large majorities of the public "strongly agree" that the government should be both a "protector" (77%) and "provider" (69%) of human rights, and 67% "strongly" or "somewhat" agree that such protection and provision of rights may require expansion of government assistance programs in areas such as housing, food, health care, and jobs.

This belief in the need for government action, however, is tempered by Americans' belief in the role of "personal responsibility." For example, Americans are evenly split in assigning responsibility for poverty, with 47% believing that poverty results from personal lack of effort, while 48% believe that it results from circumstances beyond the control of those who are impoverished. While a majority agrees that the expansion of government assistance for jobs is required to protect and provide human rights, nearly two-thirds (64%) disagree that it is the government's responsibility to "provide a job to everyone who wants one."

Significantly, despite recognizing a need to expand government assistance programs, nearly three-quarters (71%) of the public believes that poor people have become too dependent on government programs. These mixed views-a strong belief in a role for government in upholding human rights and a strong concern that the poor are insufficiently self-reliant-suggest that communications that begin with the values and goals of human rights protection, then move to the specific governmental action needed, will garner greater public support than those that begin with government programs and mechanisms. Similarly, the research shows that framing government as "protector" rather than "provider" of rights increases support for enforcement, irrespective of the right in question. This is not to say that advocates and others concerned with human rights in the United States should not speak in specifics, but rather that in *starting* conversations and framing the issues at stake, the values and goals inherent in human rights such as dignity and fairness will be more effective in engaging audiences than immediately delving into the details or mechanisms of government action that is required.

. . .

NOTES & QUESTIONS

1. The Opportunity Agenda's work on Americans' understanding and acceptance of human rights raises many questions. For example, the survey data indicates that most Americans believe that the government does not have a responsibility to provide work to those who seek jobs. Does this confirm the idea that there is no democratic authority for government to implement such a program? Further, even in those instances where a majority believes that government has greater responsibilities—such as health care—isn't a constitutional amendment required to create an *obligation* on the part of the government?

2. In recent years, U.S. advocates have actively critiqued the U.S. before international bodies, as the submission to the U.N. UPR process demonstrates. Should domestic advocates be concerned about undermining U.S. foreign policy interests when they critique the U.S. in such international forums? Or should they adopt the same aggressive posture that is typical in domestic advocacy? For another perspective on NGO advocacy in the UPR process, see Lawrence Moss, *Opportunities for Nongovernmental Organization Advocacy in the Universal Periodic Review Process at the UN Human Rights Council*, 2 Hum. Rts. Practice 122 (2010). Moss views the UPR as an exceptional opportunity to increase the on-the-ground effectiveness of advocates, and suggests that "NGOs can engage in a continuous cycle of advocacy built around UPR."

3. Who is the audience for the advocates' UPR submission to the U.N.? Are there multiple audiences? What strategic purpose does the advocacy report serve? Is there a possibility that it could be counterproductive to advocates' ultimate goals? Importantly, the UPR process is one that is being used to review every member of the U.N. There may be important lessons to be learned from the experiences of other nations and other advocates as the UPR process continues to develop. Some possible resources include Elaine Dewhurst and Noelle Higgins, *Ireland and the Universal Periodic Review: A Two-Way Process*, 1 Socio-Legal Studies Rev. 140 (2010), and Elaine Harrington, *Canada, the United Nations Human Rights Council, and Universal Periodic Review*, 18 Const. Forum 79 (2009). We will return to the discussion of the UPR in **Chapter VIII**.

CHAPTER III

THE UNITED STATES AND THE U.N. HUMAN RIGHTS TREATIES

∎ ∎ ∎

I.   THE STATUS OF HUMAN RIGHTS TREATIES IN DOMESTIC LAW

Much of modern human rights law is codified in treaties. The United States' relationship with these instruments has always been deeply contradictory. As discussed in **Chapter II**, the United States played an instrumental role in developing the core human rights instruments in the years following World War II. Nonetheless, it refused to ratify any of them for decades and still lags behind most Western democracies in its willingness to accept international human rights obligations.

This ambivalent relationship has posed a challenge for domestic human rights advocacy. As we saw in the previous chapter, while the U.S. government regularly raises human rights concerns in its foreign policy, it has been less willing to acknowledge the relevance of these principles domestically. Still, as illustrated in many examples throughout this book, over the last several decades, a growing movement of activists has pushed for greater U.S. engagement with the major international treaty instruments and has pursued strategies for enforcing their guarantees.

The materials in this chapter examine the ongoing doctrinal debates surrounding the implementation and enforcement of human rights treaty law in the United States. Part I begins by exploring the debates around U.S. participation in the U.N. treaty regimes, focusing particularly on the multi-decade efforts to ratify the Convention on the Elimination of All Forms of Discrimination Against Women (CEDAW) and the newer movement to ratify the Convention on the Rights of Persons with Disabilities (CRPD). This Part then reviews the ways in which the Senate has limited the nation's commitments to the treaties that it has ratified through the use of reservations, understandings, and declarations. Building on this discussion, Part II examines the challenges advocates face when attempting to enforce treaty rights in U.S. courts. Finally, Part III examines the ongoing debate over the scope of the treaty power and evaluates how successful Congress has been in its efforts to implement the United States' international human rights commitments.

A. THE RATIFICATION DEBATES: CEDAW AND CRPD

The United States has signed seven of the core U.N. human rights treaties, but has only ratified three of them: the International Covenant on Civil and Political Rights (ICCPR); the Convention on the Elimination of All Forms of Racial Discrimination (CERD); and the Convention Against Torture and other Cruel, Inhuman or Degrading Treatment or Punishment (CAT). The U.S. has signed, but not ratified the CEDAW, the CRPD, the International Covenant on Economic, Social and Cultural Rights, and the Convention on the Rights of the Child (CRC), although it has ratified two of the optional protocols to the CRC. The chart set out in **Chapter I** shows the status of each of these instruments in international and U.S. national law.

In addition to these core U.N. human rights treaties, there are a number of other international instruments that help to shape the United States' human rights obligations. These include the Genocide Convention, which defines and establishes genocide as an international crime, the Geneva Conventions, which regulate the conduct of armed conflict to protect human rights, and the conventions of the International Labour Organization (the ILO), which include provisions on issues such as forced labor, the right to organize and the right to collective bargaining. The human rights instruments of the regional Inter-American human rights system, which will be discussed in **Chapter VIII**, are likewise relevant to understanding the United States' human rights commitments. These include the American Declaration, the American Convention on the Rights and Duties of Man, the Additional Protocol to the American Convention in the Area of Economic, Social and Cultural Rights (Protocol of San Salvador) and the Inter-American Convention on the Prevention, Punishment and Eradication of Violence Against Women (Convention of Belem do Para).

Once a treaty is ratified, Article VI, Clause 2 of the Constitution provides that it is the "supreme Law of the Land," which gives it status equivalent to a federal statute. The path to ratification is, however, challenging because it requires both the president's signature and a vote of approval by two-thirds of the U.S. Senate.[1] This supermajority requirement acts as a significant check on presidential power and ensures that the interests of the states are well-represented in treaty-making process. Moreover, as a practical matter, it means that successful treaties must usually have significant bipartisan support.

The Convention on the Elimination of All Forms of Discrimination Against Women is one of the treaties that the United State has *not*

---

[1] The Constitution provides that the president "shall have Power, by and with the Advice and Consent of the Senate, to make Treaties, provided two-thirds of the Senators present concur." *See* Const. Art. II, § 2.

ratified. The United States' complicated history with the U.N. human rights treaties is exemplified by its relationship with CEDAW. The U.S. was very involved with the drafting of CEDAW, and the treaty was signed by President Jimmy Carter in 1980 shortly after it was opened for signature.

Today, the United States is one of only a small handful of countries that has failed to fully accept CEDAW. The Senate Foreign Relations Committee held hearings on CEDAW on several occasions between 1988 and 2002, but the Convention was never considered by the full Senate. In 2010, the Senate Judiciary Subcommittee on Human Rights held hearings on the ratification of CEDAW, but failed to take further action. The following are statements and testimony presented during this hearing. As you review these materials, and the text of CEDAW included in the Appendix, consider the reasons offered by the witnesses for and against ratification of the treaty. How do they characterize the impact of ratification on the United States?

STATEMENT OF SENATOR RICHARD DURBIN, "WOMEN'S RIGHTS ARE HUMAN RIGHTS: U.S. RATIFICATION OF THE CONVENTION ON THE ELIMINATION OF ALL FORMS OF DISCRIMINATION AGAINST WOMEN (CEDAW)"

Hearing of the Human Rights and Law Subcommittee (Nov. 18, 2010).

Last December, this Subcommittee held the first-ever Congressional hearing on U.S. compliance with our human rights treaty obligations. Today, we focus on a treaty that the United States has not yet ratified: the Convention on the Elimination of All Forms of Discrimination Against Women (CEDAW).

This is the first Senate hearing on CEDAW since 2002. And this is the first time the Judiciary Committee has ever held a hearing on whether to ratify a human rights treaty. CEDAW is the only treaty to focus on the human rights of women. It addresses issues like violence against women, sex trafficking, the right to vote, and access to education.

Why is CEDAW needed? Because the human rights of women and girls are violated at an alarming rate all over the world. To take just one example, violence against women is at epidemic levels. In South Asia, countless women and girls have been burned with acid, including Afghan girls attacked by the Taliban for the simple act of attending elementary school. And literally hundreds of thousands of women have been raped in the Democratic Republic of Congo and other conflict situations. This Subcommittee explored this horrible phenomenon in a 2008 hearing on rape as a weapon of war.

CEDAW is not a cure-all for these atrocities, but it has had a real impact in improving the lives of women and girls around the world. For example:

CEDAW has led to the passage of laws prohibiting violence against women in countries like Afghanistan, Ghana, Mexico, and Sierra Leone.

It led to women being granted the right to vote in Kuwait.

It helped give women the right to inherit property in Kenya, Kyrgyzstan, and Tajikistan.

CEDAW has been ratified by 186 of 193 countries. Sadly, the United States is one of only seven countries in the world that has failed to ratify CEDAW, along with Iran, Somalia, and Sudan. CEDAW was transmitted to the Senate 30 years ago. Twice, in 1994 and 2002, a bipartisan majority in the Senate Foreign Relations Committee reported the treaty to the Senate floor, but the Senate has never voted on CEDAW.

Under Presidents Reagan, George H.W. Bush, and Clinton, the United States ratified similar agreements on genocide, torture, and race. It is time to renew this proud bipartisan tradition and join the rest of the world in demonstrating our commitment to women's rights.

Let's be clear. The United States does not need to ratify CEDAW to protect the rights of American women and girls. Women have fought a long and difficult struggle for equal rights in the United States, with many victories along the way. To name just a few:

- The 19th Amendment, giving women the right to vote, in 1920.
- Title IX, prohibiting discrimination in education, in 1972.
- The Pregnancy Discrimination Act, in 1978.
- The Violence Against Women Act, in 1994.
- The election of the first woman Speaker of the U.S. House of Representatives in 2007.
- Passage of the Lilly Ledbetter Fair Pay Act just last year.

Of course, the struggle for women's rights continues. Every year, millions of American women and girls are subjected to domestic violence, rape, and human trafficking. And women who work full-time still earn only 77 cents for every dollar that a man makes. That is why it is so unfortunate that the Paycheck Fairness Act failed to pass yesterday.

However, the robust women's rights protections in U.S. law in many ways exceed the requirements of CEDAW. Even opponents of CEDAW acknowledge that ratifying CEDAW wouldn't change U.S. law in any way.

So why should the United States ratify CEDAW? Because CEDAW will enhance our ability to advocate for women and girls around the world. Throughout our history, the United States has done more to advance human rights than any other country in the world. But now some are questioning our commitment to women's rights because we have failed to ratify CEDAW.

Yesterday I received a letter from retired Justice Sandra Day O'Connor, the first woman ever to serve on the Supreme Court. Justice O'Connor supports ratifying CEDAW and here is what she says:

"The Senate's failure to ratify CEDAW gives other countries a retort when U.S. officials raise issues about the treatment of women, and thus our non-ratification may hamper the effectiveness of the United States in achieving increased protection for women worldwide."

Justice O'Connor is right. We need to ratify CEDAW so that we can more effectively lead the fight for women's rights in corners of the globe where women and girls are subjected to the most extreme forms of violence and degradation simply for exercising their fundamental human rights.

CEDAW is about giving women all over the world the chance to enjoy the same freedoms and opportunities that American women have struggled long and hard to achieve. Women have been waiting for 30 years. The United States Senate should ratify this treaty without further delay.

STATEMENT OF STEVEN GROVES, THE HERITAGE FOUNDATION, "WOMEN'S RIGHTS ARE HUMAN RIGHTS: US RATIFICATION OF THE CONVENTION ON THE ELIMINATION OF ALL FORMS OF DISCRIMINATION AGAINST WOMEN (CEDAW)"

Hearing of the Human Rights and Law Subcommittee (Nov. 18, 2010).

Mr. Chairman and members of the Committee:

Thank you for inviting me to testify before you today regarding the Convention on the Elimination of All Forms of Discrimination against Women (CEDAW).

Ratification of CEDAW would neither advance U.S. national interests within the international community nor enhance the rights of women in the United States. Domestically, CEDAW membership would not improve our existing comprehensive statutory framework or strengthen our enforcement system for the protection of women's rights.

Within the international sphere, the United States need not become party to the Convention to demonstrate to the rest of the world its commitment to women's rights at home or abroad. Becoming a member of CEDAW would produce, at best, an intangible and dubious public diplomacy benefit.

Moreover, it does not serve the interests of the United States to periodically submit its record on women's rights to scrutiny by a committee of gender experts that has established a record of promoting policies that do not comport with existing American norms and that encourages national governments to engage in social engineering on a massive scale. The United States should become party to a treaty only if membership would advance U.S. national interests. For a human rights treaty such as CEDAW, national interests may be characterized in both domestic and international terms. Only if U.S. membership in CEDAW would advance the cause of women's rights domestically and further U.S. national interests in the world should the United States consider ratification of the treaty.

Domestically, ratification of CEDAW is not needed to end gender discrimination nor advance women's rights. The United States already has effective avenues of enforcement in place to effectively combat discrimination based on sex.

. . .

––––––––––––

Despite its poor record of ratification, the United States has continued to sign most of the major human rights treaties. Most recently, in 2009, President Barack Obama signed the Convention on the Rights of Persons with Disabilities. On May 17, 2012, the CRPD was referred to the Senate Committee on Foreign Relations. The full text of the CRPD is included in the Appendix. As you read the letter of transmittal sent from the White House to the Senate, consider the arguments that President Obama raises in favor of ratification and compare those to the statements made in the CEDAW hearings.

PRESIDENT BARACK OBAMA, LETTER OF TRANSMITTAL TO THE SENATE OF THE UNITED STATES
May 17, 2012.

To the Senate of the United States:

I transmit herewith, for advice and consent of the Senate to its ratification, the Convention on the Rights of Persons with Disabilities, adopted by the United Nations General Assembly on December 13, 2006, and signed by the United States of America on June 30, 2009 (the "Convention"). . . .

Anchored in the principles of equality of opportunity, nondiscrimination, respect for dignity and individual autonomy, and inclusion of persons with disabilities, the Convention seeks to promote, protect, and ensure the full and equal enjoyment of all human rights by persons with disabilities. While Americans with disabilities already enjoy these rights at home, U.S. citizens and other individuals with disabilities frequently face barriers when they travel, work, serve, study, and reside in other countries. The rights of Americans with disabilities should not end at our Nation's shores. Ratification of the Disabilities Convention by the United States would position the United States to occupy the global leadership role to which our domestic record already attests. We would thus seek to use the Convention as a tool through which to enhance the rights of Americans with disabilities, including our veterans. Becoming a State Party to the Convention and mobilizing greater international compliance could also level the playing field for American businesses, who already must comply with U.S. disability laws, as well as those whose products and services might find new markets in countries whose disability standards move closer to those of the United States.

Protection of the rights of persons with disabilities has historically been grounded in bipartisan support in the United States, and the principles anchoring the Convention find clear expression in our own domestic law. As described more fully in the accompanying report, the strong guarantees of nondiscrimination and equality of access and opportunity for persons with disabilities in existing U.S. law are consistent with and sufficient to implement the requirements of the Convention as it would be ratified by the United States.

I recommend that the Senate give prompt and favorable consideration to this Convention and give its advice and consent to its ratification, subject to the reservations, understandings, and declaration set forth in the accompanying report.

BARACK OBAMA.

———————

The full Senate voted on ratification of the CRPD on December 4, 2012. Sixty-one senators voted in favor of ratification, but the measure failed since it required approval by a two-thirds majority.

NOTES & QUESTIONS

1.   Consider the readings in this section. What do they tell you about what motivates the United States' participation in human rights treaty regimes? What kinds of arguments do treaty proponents make in order to promote ratification? Can you think of other arguments in favor of ratification that are not reflected in the CEDAW and CRPD debates? Why might they not appear in the testimony?

2.   Why do you think Senator Durbin is so forceful in his statement that ratification of CEDAW won't change U.S. law? What concerns might other advocates for treaty ratification have about that message?

3.   Debates over the ratification of human rights treaties often draw on the language of American exceptionalism. As Professor Deborah Weissman has observed in the context of CEDAW:

> [B]oth proponents and detractors of the treaty have invoked the concept of American exceptionalism to advance their positions. Opponents of CEDAW have generally argued that the treaty threatens to affect women's interests adversely. . . . But perhaps more telling is the fact that treaty proponents have also expressed their position in terms that may be said to conflict with human rights values. Supporters of ratification have framed their arguments in terms that denigrated other cultures and geopolitical regions, while exempting the United States from the problems that women suffer worldwide. . . . These arguments have been consistent throughout the debates—ratification of CEDAW is required to alleviate suffering almost everywhere in the world except the United States.

Deborah Weissman, *The Human Rights Dilemma*, 35 Colum. Hum. Rts. L. Rev. 259, 326 (2004). Review the statements in support of the ratification of CEDAW and CRPD. Can you identify any examples of the phenomenon that Professor Weissman is describing in the excerpts above? Why might human rights proponents use this language?

4.   The recent debates over the ratification of CEDAW and CPRD have generally split along party lines, with Democrats in support and Republicans opposed. Why do you think that this is the case? How do the debates over the ratification of these treaties intersect with the domestic political dialogue? See, for example, the arguments made by former Senator and Republican presidential candidate Rick Santorum, a prominent opponent of the treaty. Rick Santorum; *U.N. Disabilities Treaty Would've Had Bureaucrats Unseat Parents*, The Daily Beast (Dec. 5, 2012).

5.   How has ratification and implementation of human rights treaties impacted conditions in other nations? The International Center for Research on Women has documented the ways in which CEDAW has been used to end violence and trafficking in women and girls; improve conditions for women's economic opportunity; increase women's political participation; and promote women's equality. *See* ICRW, *Recognizing Rights, Promoting Progress: The Global Impact of the Convention of the Elimination of All Forms of Discrimination Against Women* (2010). In Bangladesh and India, courts cited CEDAW in opinions concluding that women have the right to be free of sexual harassment in the workplace. In Kenya, Tanzania, and Uganda, courts have invoked CEDAW to defeat the application of discriminatory customary or common law norms. In Mexico and Saudi Arabia, CEDAW has been used as the basis for drafting new laws that eliminate institutionalized sex discrimination and end violence against women. In many countries, the ratification of CEDAW and the treaty reporting processes have provided a forum for advocacy and organization on behalf of women. Would ratification

have a similar effect on law and policy in the United States? What laws and policies can you think of that might be subject to challenge if CEDAW were ratified?

6.   Progressive groups and individuals in the U.S. have expressed differing views on what the domestic impact of CEDAW ratification might be, primarily due to the package of reservations, understandings, and declarations that the Senate includes to limit the nation's international commitments when ratifying treaties. We will study these in greater depth in the next section. Many groups, like the YWCA and the Leadership Conference on Civil and Human Rights, stress that ratifying CEDAW would not require changes to U.S. law, but primarily would have the effect of reinforcing U.S. international leadership on women's issues and create the opportunity for periodic reporting on U.S. efforts to achieve women's equality within the United States. Others, such as Janet Benshoof, the founder of the Center for Reproductive Rights, argue that CEDAW ratification should include a commitment to make the legal and policy changes necessary to ensure domestic equality. *See, e.g.*, Janet Benshoof, *U.S. Ratification of CEDAW: An Opportunity to Radically Reframe the Right to Equality Accorded Women Under the U.S. Constitution*, 35 N.Y.U. Rev. L. & Soc. Change 103, 121–124 (2011); *see also* Lisa A. Crooms, *Families, Fatherlessness, and Women's Humans Rights: An Analysis of the Clinton Administration's Public Housing Policy as a Violation of the Convention on the Elimination of All Forms of Discrimination Against Women*, 36 Brandeis J. Fam. L. 1, 5 (1997/98). Are these differences simply matters of strategy or do these groups have different conceptions of the domestic role of international law?

SKILLS EXERCISE

You work for an advocacy organization that has the mission of advancing the civil rights of persons with disabilities. The organization is developing a campaign to support a renewed effort to ratify the CRPD. Draft a short memorandum outlining what you see as the best strategy for framing the benefits of ratifying the treaty. Consider which potential benefits you would want to publicize as part of the ratification campaign and to which audiences. Are there advantages to ratification that you would not want to include as part of your public campaign? Why? Refer to the Appendix for the full text of the CRPD.

B. LIMITING THE IMPACT OF RATIFICATION— RESERVATIONS, UNDERSTANDINGS, AND DECLARATIONS

As discussed in the previous section, the United States has only ratified four of the major human rights treaties. Yet even when the Senate has accepted these instruments, it has still found ways to limit their domestic effect. Each time the Senate has adopted a human rights treaty, it has attached a package of reservations, understandings, and declarations, or "RUDs." These RUDs purport to cabin the United States' commitment to these treaties in various ways, although their legality has been questioned in the academic literature.[2] Reservations are specific stipulations that limit the United States' agreement to be bound to the obligations imposed by the treaty. For example, as you will see in the readings that follow, the United States took a reservation with respect to the provision of the International Covenant on Civil and Political Rights that banned the execution of juveniles under the age of eighteen. That ratification reservation expressed the United States' decision not to comply with that particular provision of the treaty. Understandings are interpretive statements that clarify the United States' view of the meaning of the treaty, and declarations are statements of policy or purpose related to issues raised by the treaty. By contrast to reservations, understandings and declarations do not alter the legal commitments created by ratification.

RUDs are not unique to the United States and other nations also take RUDs when ratifying treaties. Yet the United States is notable for the breadth of its RUDs. As you read through the following section, consider what concerns and values are expressed by the RUDs and what motivates their inclusion.

In 1992, the United States ratified the ICCPR. Prior to the Senate vote on the treaty, the Committee on Foreign Relations prepared and submitted the following report on its proposed RUDs to guide the senators' deliberations on ratification.

U.S. SENATE EXECUTIVE REPORT 102–23
102d Cong., 2d Sess. (Mar. 24, 1992).

MARCH 24, 1992. . . .

Mr. PELL, from the Committee on Foreign Relations, submitted the following

REPORT

The Committee on Foreign Relations to which was referred the International Covenant on Civil and Political Rights, adopted unanimously by the United Nations General Assembly on December 16, 1966, and signed on behalf of the United States on October 5, 1977, having considered the same, reports favorably thereon with 5 reservations, 5 understandings, 4 declarations, and 1 proviso, and

---

[2] *See* M. Cherif Bassiouni, *Reflections on the Ratification of the International Covenant on Civil and Political Rights by the United States Senate*, 42 DePaul L. Rev. 1169 (1993).

recommends that the Senate give its advice and consent to ratification thereof.

I. PURPOSE

The Covenant guarantees a broad spectrum of civil and political rights, rooted in basic democratic values and freedoms, to all individuals within the territory or under the jurisdiction of the States Party without distinction of any kind, such as race, gender, ethnicity, et cetera. The Covenant obligates each State Party to respect and ensure these rights, to adopt legislative or other necessary measures to give effect to these rights, and to provide an effective remedy to those whose rights are violated. The Covenant also establishes a Human Rights Committee to oversee compliance and investigate reports of noncompliance made by one Party against another.

. . .

III. COMMITTEE COMMENTS

The International Covenant on Civil and Political Rights is one of the fundamental instruments created by the international community for the global promotion and protection of human rights. Over 100 States, including the member states of the European Community, Canada, and other traditional U.S. allies, have ratified the Covenant. In view of the leading role that the United States plays in the international struggle for human rights, the absence of U.S. ratification of the Covenant is conspicuous and, in the view of many, hypocritical. The Committee believes that ratification will remove doubts about the seriousness of the U.S. commitment to human rights and strengthen the impact of U.S. efforts in the human rights field. The rights enumerated in the Covenant, such as freedom of thought, conscience, religion, and expression, the right to vote, and the right to a fair trial, are the cornerstones of a democratic society. The historical changes in the Soviet Union and Eastern Europe have created an opportunity for democracy to grow and take hold. By ratifying the Covenant at this time, the United States can enhance its ability to promote democratic values and the rule of law, not only in Eastern Europe and the successor states of the Soviet Union but also in those countries in Africa and Asia which are beginning to move toward democratization.

. . .

VII. EXPLANATION OF BUSH ADMINISTRATION CONDITIONS

The Bush Administration submitted its proposed reservations, understandings and declarations to the Committee on November 21, 1991. At the same time, the Administration submitted the following explanation of its proposals.

INTERNATIONAL COVENANT ON CIVIL AND POLITICAL RIGHTS

Explanation of Proposed Reservations, Understandings and Declarations

GENERAL COMMENTS

In general, the substantive provisions of the Covenant are consistent with the letter and spirit of the United States Constitution and laws, both state and federal. Consequently, the United States can accept the majority of the Covenant's obligations and undertakings without qualification.

In a few instances, however, it is necessary to subject U.S. ratification to reservations, understandings or declarations in order to ensure that the United States can fulfill its obligations under the Covenant in a manner consistent with the United States Constitution, including instances where the Constitution affords greater rights and liberties to individuals than does the Covenant. Additionally, a few provisions of the Covenant articulate legal rules which differ from U.S. law and which, upon careful consideration, the Administration declines to accept in preference to existing law. Specific proposals dealing with both situations are included below.

. . .

FORMAL RESERVATIONS

1.   Free speech (article 20)

Although Article 19 of the Covenant specifically protects freedom of expression and opinion, Article 20 directly conflicts with the First Amendment by requiring the prohibition of certain forms of speech and expression which are protected under the First Amendment to the U.S. Constitution (i.e., propaganda for war and advocacy of national, racial or religious hatred that constitutes incitement to discrimination, religious hatred that constitutes incitement to discrimination, hostility or violence). The United States cannot accept such an obligation.

Accordingly, the following reservation is recommended:

Article 20 does not authorize or require legislation or other action by the United States that would restrict the right of free speech and association protected by the Constitution and laws of the United States.

. . .

2.   Article 6 (capital punishment)

Article 6, paragraph 5 of the Covenant prohibits imposition of the death sentence for crimes committed by persons below 18 years of age and on pregnant women. In 1978, a broad reservation to this article was proposed in order to retain the right to impose capital punishment on any person duly convicted under existing or future laws permitting the imposition of capital punishment. The Administration is now prepared to accept the prohibition against execution of pregnant women. However, in light of the recent reaffirmation of U.S. policy towards capital punishment generally, and in particular the Supreme Court's decisions upholding state laws permitting the death penalty for crimes committed by juveniles aged 16 and 17, the prohibition against imposition of capital punishment for crimes committed by minors is not acceptable. Given the sharply differing view taken by many of our future treaty partners on the issue of the death penalty (including what constitutes "serious crimes" under Article 6(2)), it is advisable to state our position clearly.

Accordingly, we recommend the following reservation to Article 6:

The United States reserves the right, subject to its Constitutional constraints, to impose capital punishment on any person (other than a pregnant woman) duly convicted under existing or future laws permitting the imposition of capital punishment, including such punishment for crimes committed by persons below eighteen years of age.

. . .

3.   Article 7 (torture/punishment)

Article 7 provides that no one shall be subjected to torture or to cruel, inhuman or degrading treatment or punishment or be subjected without his free consent to medical or scientific experimentation. Since the United States is already proceeding toward ratification of the more detailed Convention Against Torture and Other Cruel, Inhuman or Degrading Treatment or Punishment on the basis of several carefully crafted reservations, declarations and understandings, it will be made clear in the record that we interpret our obligations under Article 7 of the Covenant consistently with those we have undertaken in the Torture Convention.

We believe it is advisable to take, with respect to the Covenant, an identical reservation with regard to the meaning of "cruel, inhuman and degrading treatment or punishment." Because the Bill of Rights already contains substantively equivalent protections, and because the Human Rights Committee (like the European Court of Human Rights) has adopted the view that prolonged judicial proceedings in cases involving capital punishment could in certain circumstances constitute such treatment, U.S. ratification of the Covenant should be conditioned upon a reservation limiting our undertakings in this respect to the prohibitions of the Fifth, Eighth and/or Fourteenth Amendments. This would also have the effect of excluding such other practices as corporal punishment and solitary confinement, both of which the Committee has indicated might, depending on the circumstances, be considered contrary to Article 7. (Most of the Committee's interpretive statements under Article 7 have focused on such practices as torture, disappearances, extrajudicial killings and incommunicado detention.)

To ensure uniformity of interpretation between the Covenant and the Torture Convention on this point, we recommend the following reservation:

The United States considers itself bound by Article 7 to the extent that "cruel, inhuman or degrading treatment or punishment" means the cruel and unusual treatment or punishment prohibited by the Fifth, Eighth and/or Fourteenth Amendments to the Constitution of the United States.

. . .

UNDERSTANDINGS

1.   Article 2(1), 4(1) and 26 (non-discrimination)

The very broad anti-discrimination provisions contained in the above articles do not precisely comport with long-standing Supreme Court doctrine in the equal protection field. In particular, Articles 2(1) and 26 prohibit discrimination not only on the basis of "race, colour, sex, language, religion, political or other opinion, national or social origin, property, birth" but also on any "other status." Current U.S. civil rights law is not so open-ended; discrimination is only prohibited for specific statuses, and there are exceptions which allow for discrimination. For example, under the Age Discrimination Act of 1975, age may be taken into account in certain circumstances. In addition, U.S. laws permit additional distinctions, for example between citizens and non-citizens and between different categories of non-citizens, especially in the context of the immigration laws.

In interpreting the relevant Covenant provisions, the Human Rights Committee has observed that not all differentiation of treatment constitutes discrimination, if the criteria for such differentiation are reasonable and objective and if the aim is to achieve a purpose which is legitimate under the Covenant. In its General Comment on non-discrimination, for example, the Committee noted that the enjoyment of rights and freedoms on an equal footing does not mean identical treatment in every instance.

Notwithstanding the very extensive protections already provided under U.S. law and the Committee's interpretive approach to the issue, we recommend the following understanding:

The Constitution and laws of the United States guarantee all persons equal protection of the law and provide extensive protections against discrimination. The United States understands distinctions based upon race, colour, sex, language, religion, political or other opinion, national or social origin, property, birth or any other status—as those terms are used in Article 2, paragraph 1 and Article 26—to be permitted which such distinctions are, at minimum, rationally related to a legitimate governmental objective. The United States further understands the prohibition in paragraph 1 of Article 4 upon discrimination, in time of public emergency, based "solely" on the status of race, colour, sex, language, religion or social origin not to bar distinctions that may have a disproportionate effect upon persons of a particular status.

. . .

5.   Article 50 (federalism)

In light of Article 50 ("The provisions of the present Covenant shall extend to all parts of federal States without any limitations or exceptions"), it is appropriate to clarify that, even though the Covenant will apply to state and local authorities, it will be implemented consistent with U.S. concepts of federalism.

The following recommended understanding is a modification of the understanding adopted on the same point in connection with the Torture Convention:

The United States understands that this Convention shall be implemented by the Federal Government to the extent that it exercises legislative and judicial jurisdiction over the matters covered therein, and otherwise by the State and local governments; to the extent that State and local governments exercise jurisdiction over such matters, the Federal Government shall take measures appropriate to the Federal system to the end that the competent authorities of the State or local governments may take appropriate measures for the fulfillment of the Convention.

The proposed understanding serves to emphasize domestically that there is no intent to alter the constitutional balance of authority between the State and Federal governments or to use the provisions of the Covenant to "federalize" matters now within the competence of the States. (During the negotiation of the Covenant, the "federal-state" issue assumed some importance because there were legally justified practices, at the State and local level, which were both manifestly inconsistent with the Covenant and beyond the reach of Federal authority under the law in force at that time; that is no longer the case.)

A reservation is not necessary with respect to Article 50 since the intent is not to modify or limit U.S. undertakings under the Covenant but rather to put our future treaty partners on notice with regard to the implications of our federal system concerning implementation. Moreover, an attempt to reserve to this article would likely prove contentious. For example, in the face of objections from other States Parties, Australia recently withdrew its initial reservation to Article 50 (to the effect that implementation of the Covenant would be a matter for the authorities of its constituent States where the subject-matter was within the States' legislative, executive and judicial jurisdiction), replacing it with a declaration that, since it has a federal system, the Covenant will be implemented by Commonwealth, State and Territorial authorities having regard to their respective constitutional powers and arrangements concerning their exercise. The proposed understanding is similarly intended to signal to our treaty partners that the U.S. will implement its obligations under the Covenant by appropriate legislative, executive and judicial means, federal or state as appropriate, and that the Federal Government will remove any federal inhibition to the States' abilities to meet their obligations.

DECLARATIONS

1.   Non-self-executing treaty

For reasons of prudence, we recommend including a declaration that the substantive provisions of the Covenant are not self-executing. The intent is to clarify that the Covenant will not create a private cause of action in U.S. courts. As was the case with the Torture Convention, existing U.S. law generally complies with the Covenant; hence, implementing legislation is not contemplated.

We recommend the following declaration, virtually identical to the one proposed in 1978 as well as the one adopted by the Senate with respect to the Torture Convention:

The United States declares that the provisions of Articles 1 through 27 of the Covenant are not self-executing.

. . .

The Senate adopted the ICCPR in 1992 with the RUDs proposed by the Foreign Relations Committee and has included similar RUDs when ratifying each of the human rights treaties. In the following excerpt, Professor Henkin offers his interpretation of what motivates these limitations on the nation's human rights commitments.

LOUIS HENKIN, "U.S. RATIFICATION OF HUMAN RIGHTS
CONVENTIONS: THE GHOST OF SENATOR BRICKER"

89 Am. J. Int'l L. 341, 341–58 (1995).

U.S. Policy on Human Rights Conventions

The package of reservations, understandings and declarations the
United States has been attaching to its ratifications of human rights
conventions appears to be guided by several "principles":

1.   The United States will not undertake any treaty obligation that
it will not be able to carry out because it is inconsistent with the United
States Constitution.

2.   United States adherence to an international human rights treaty
should not effect—or promise—change in existing U.S. law or practice.

3.   The United States will not submit to the jurisdiction of the
International Court of Justice to decide disputes as to the interpretation
or application of human rights conventions.

4.   Every human rights treaty to which the United States adheres
should be subject to a "federalism clause" so that the United States could
leave implementation of the convention largely to the states.

5.   Every international human rights agreement should be "non-
self-executing."

I address each of these "principles" in turn.

Constitutional Limitations on Treaties

Under accepted United States constitutional jurisprudence, treaties
are subject to constitutional limitations: none of the three branches—the
Executive, the Congress, or the courts—can give effect to a treaty
provision that is inconsistent with the Constitution. Therefore, a
reservation to avoid an obligation that the United States could not carry
out because of constitutional limitations is appropriate, indeed necessary.

Such a reservation may have been required when the United States
ratified the International Covenant on Civil and Political Rights, in
respect of the obligation in Article 20 to prohibit war propaganda and
"racial hate speech." In that case, however, had the executive branch been
disposed to avoid entering a reservation, it might have contented itself
with an "understanding" that would construe Article 20 as requiring only
that a state party prohibit speech that incites to unlawful action. That,
indeed, is the plausible interpretation of Article 20(2), and as so
understood could be implemented by the United States under the
Constitution.

Again, in respect of the Race Convention, the United States by
reservation refused any international obligation to ensure against private

discrimination on account of race "except as mandated by the Constitution and laws of the United States." If behind that reservation were the fear that the Convention might be construed to forbid discrimination by individuals that falls within their zone of "privacy" (autonomy) protected by the Constitution, a narrow reservation (or understanding) to that effect would have been appropriate. Instead, the United States entered a reservation that seems designed not to avoid constitutional difficulties but to resist change in United States law.

Rejecting Higher International Standards

By its reservations, the United States apparently seeks to assure that its adherence to a convention will not change, or require change, in U.S. laws, policies or practices, even where they fall below international standards. For example, in ratifying the International Covenant on Civil and Political Rights, the United States refused to accept a provision prohibiting capital punishment for crimes committed by persons under eighteen years of age. In ratifying the Torture Convention, the United States, in effect, reserved the right to inflict inhuman or degrading treatment (when it is not punishment for crime), and criminal punishment when it is inhuman and degrading (but not "cruel and unusual").

Reservations designed to reject any obligation to rise above existing law and practice are of dubious propriety: if states generally entered such reservations, the convention would be futile. The object and purpose of the human rights conventions, it would seem, are to promote respect for human rights by having countries—mutually—assume legal obligations to respect and ensure recognized rights in accordance with international standards. Even friends of the United States have objected that its reservations are incompatible with that object and purpose and are therefore invalid.

By adhering to human rights conventions subject to these reservations, the United States, it is charged, is pretending to assume international obligations but in fact is undertaking nothing. It is seen as seeking the benefits of participation in the convention (e.g., having a U.S. national sit on the Human Rights Committee established pursuant to the Covenant) without assuming any obligations or burdens. The United States, it is said, seeks to sit in judgment on others but will not submit its human rights behavior to international judgment. To many, the attitude reflected in such reservations is offensive: the conventions are only for other states, not for the United States.

As in the case of "constitutional" reservations, moreover, U.S. reservations designed to refuse higher international standards are more extravagant than called for by their purpose. For example, in ratifying the Covenant, the United States did not reserve only the right to execute a person who committed a capital crime at age seventeen; by the terms used, the United States reserved the right to execute any child, of any age. In ratifying the Race Convention, the United States reserved not only an individual's right to discriminate on matters within his/her constitutional zone of privacy; what was reserved would seem to allow the United States to permit, even to require, private racial discrimination and de facto segregation in any circumstances.

The ICJ Reservation

The United States has proposed a reservation to the clause, included in several conventions, pursuant to which a state party may bring a dispute as to the interpretation or application of the convention to the International Court of Justice. The Clinton administration reserved on the "ICJ clause" in ratifying the Race Convention, as President Bush did for the Torture Convention, as President Reagan did in ratifying the Genocide Convention.

. . .

Administration testimony before the Senate Foreign Relations Committee on the Race Convention justified such a reservation as "prudent," presumably to avoid frivolous or *mala fide* charges against the United States. Critics will construe such "prudence" as meaning that the United States recognizes that it may not be in compliance with the provisions of those conventions, even with whatever obligations might be left for the United States after its reservations.

The "Federalism" Clause

The "federalism" clause attached to U.S. ratifications of human rights conventions has been denominated an "understanding," a designation ordinarily used for an interpretation or clarification of a possibly ambiguous provision in the treaty. The federalism clause in the instruments of ratification of the human rights conventions is not an understanding in that sense, but may be intended to alert other parties to United States intent in the matter of implementation.

In several instances after the Second World War, some "federal states" proposed the addition to particular conventions of special clauses qualifying their obligation; such a clause found its way into the Refugee Convention. But in general the majority of states refused to agree to special treatment for federal states, and some conventions expressly rejected "limitations or exceptions" for federal states.

The United States has proposed "federalism" clauses in the past, presumably to assuage "states' rights" sensibilities. At one time, the United States sought to limit its obligations under particular treaties to those matters that were "within the jurisdiction" of the federal Government, and to exclude any international obligation as to matters subject to the jurisdiction of the states. Some early versions of the federal-state clause reflected a misapprehension about "the jurisdiction" of the federal Government, as regards the reach of both its treaty power and congressional legislative power. There are no significant "states' rights" limitations on the treaty power. There is little that is not "within the jurisdiction of the United States," i.e., within the treaty power, or within the legislative power of Congress under the Commerce Power, under its authority to implement the Fourteenth Amendment, or under its power to do what is necessary and proper to carry out its treaty obligations. In time, recognizing that virtually any matter governed by treaty was "within the jurisdiction" of the United States, the executive branch took to declaring that the convention shall be implemented by the federal Government to the extent that it "exercises jurisdiction" over matters covered by the treaty, leaving to the states implementation of matters over which the states exercise jurisdiction.

Such a statement is deeply ambiguous. The federal Government exercises jurisdiction over all matters covered in a human rights convention, if only by making the treaty. It exercises jurisdiction over such matters because Congress has the power to legislate, and has legislated, in respect of them. In any event, as a matter of international treaty law, such a statement is not an "understanding" or a reservation, and raises no international difficulties. International law requires the United States to carry out its treaty obligations but, in the absence of special provision, does not prescribe how, or through which agencies, they shall be carried out. As a matter of international law, then, the United States could leave the implementation of any treaty provision to the states. Of course, the United States remains internationally responsible for any failure of implementation.

The "federalism" declarations that have been attached to human rights conventions thus serve no legal purpose. But some see such declarations as another sign that the United States is resistant to international human rights agreements, setting up obstacles to their implementation and refusing to treat human rights conventions as treaties dealing with a subject of national interest and international concern.

The Non-Self-Executing Declaration

The United States has been declaring the human rights agreements it has ratified to be non-self-executing. The U.S. practice of declaring human rights conventions non-self-executing is commonly seen as of a piece with the other RUDs. As the reservations designed to deny international obligations serve to immunize the United States from external judgment, the declaration that a convention shall be non-self-executing is designed to keep its own judges from judging the human rights conditions in the United States by international standards. To critics, keeping a convention from having any effect as United States law confirms that United States adherence remains essentially empty.

The non-self-executing declaration has been explained—and justified—as designed to assure that changes in U.S. law will be effected only by "democratic processes"—therefore, by legislation, not by treaty. That argument, of course, impugns the democratic character of every treaty made or that will be made by the President with the consent of the Senate.

Whatever may be appropriate in a special case, as a general practice such a declaration is against the spirit of the Constitution; it may be unconstitutional. Article VI of the Constitution provides expressly for lawmaking by treaty: treaties are declared to be the supreme law of the land. The Framers intended that a treaty should become law *ipso facto,* when the treaty is made; it should not require legislative implementation to convert it into United States law. In effect, lawmaking by treaty was to be an alternative to legislation by Congress.

Nothing in the Constitution or in the history of its adoption suggests that the Framers contemplated that some treaties might not be law of the land. That was a later suggestion by John Marshall, because he found that some promises *by their character* could not be "self-executing": when the United States undertook to do something in the future that could be done only by legislative or other political act, the treaty did not—could not—carry out the undertaking. Marshall did not contemplate that treaty undertakings that could be given effect as law by the Executive and the courts, or by the states, should not be carried out by them, but might be converted into promises that Congress would legislate. Surely, there is no evidence of any intent, by the Framers (or by John Marshall), to allow the President or the Senate, by their *ipse dixit,* to prevent a treaty that by its character *could* be law of the land from becoming law of the land.

. . .

In any event, declaring a treaty—here a human rights convention—non-self-executing achieves the worst of both systems. A human rights convention, like other treaties, goes to the Senate for its consent, where— "undemocratically"—a third of the members (plus one) can reject the convention. But unlike treaties generally, human rights conventions would later, after Senate consent and U.S. ratification, require going to the Senate again, as well as to the House, for implementing legislation, involving additional, often extended delays and obstacles to carrying out United States international obligations.

Consider the record to date. President Truman signed the Genocide Convention and transmitted it to the Senate in 1949. Thirty-five years later, President Reagan asked the Senate to consent to the Convention with reservations. Congress finally enacted implementing legislation in 1988 and the Convention came into force for the United States in 1989.

In 1988 President Reagan sought Senate consent to United States ratification of the Convention against Torture with reservations, and with a declaration that it shall not be self-executing. The executive branch apparently decided that the Convention should not be ratified until Congress enacted implementing criminal legislation required by the Convention. Congress finally enacted such legislation in April 1994 and the United States ratified the Torture Convention in October 1994.

In 1992 the United States adhered to the International Covenant on Civil and Political Rights with reservations, and with a declaration that it shall not be self-executing. The Bush administration made no move to seek implementing legislation; its spokesman suggested that legislation would not be sought, and that none was necessary, because, as a result of the substantive reservations, United States adherence would require no change in United States law. The Clinton administration has not sought legislation to implement the Covenant and none seems to be in prospect. Apparently, the Covenant will continue to have less than full legal effect as the law of the land for courts in the United States.

Similarly, the United States has declared the Race Convention non-self-executing and the Clinton administration has indicated it will not seek implementing legislation.

The pattern of non-self-executing declarations threatens to subvert the constitutional treaty system. That, for the present at least, the non-self-executing declaration is almost exclusively a concomitant of U.S. adherence to human rights conventions will appear to critics as an additional indication that the United States does not take such conventions seriously as international obligations.

. . .

NOTES & QUESTIONS

1.   Professor Henkin suggests that RUDs adopted for the purpose of ensuring that the United States does not have to improve its domestic law to meet international standards are of "dubious propriety." The Human Rights Committee, which monitors implementation of the ICCPR, has gone further, stating that this type of reservation may be invalid under the Vienna Convention on the Law of Treaties. Article 19(3) of that Convention provides that States may not make reservations that are incompatible with the object and purpose of the treaty. *See* United Nations, *Vienna Convention on the Law of Treaties*, May 23, 1969, 1155 U.N.T.S. 331. The Committee explains:

> The intention of the Covenant is that the rights contained therein should be ensured to all those under a State's party's

jurisdiction. . . . Domestic laws may need to be altered properly to reflect the requirements of the Covenant; . . . . Reservations often reveal a tendency of States not to want to change a particular law. And sometimes that tendency is elevated to a general policy. Of particular concern are widely formulated reservations which essentially render ineffective all Covenant rights which would require any change in national law to ensure compliance with Covenant obligations. No real international rights or obligations have thus been accepted. . . .

See Human Rights Committee, Issues Relating to Reservations Made Upon Ratification or Accession to the Covenant or the Optional Protocols thereto, or in relation to declarations under Article 41 of the Covenant, General Comment No. 24(52), para. 12, U.N. Doc. CCPR/C/21/Rev.1/Add.6 (Nov. 2, 1994).

2.   As you have learned, the United States has never ratified a human rights treaty without extensive RUDs. What are the domestic concerns that inspired the inclusion of the RUDs? Do you agree with Professor Henkin's characterization of them? Do any of the RUDs seem more or less justifiable or problematic?

3.   Each time CEDAW has been considered for ratification, the Senate Foreign Relations Committee and the Administration in power have proposed that it be adopted with RUDs. In addition to the now standard ratification limitations described in the excerpt above by Professor Henkin, the following RUDs have been proposed for CEDAW:

(1) The Constitution and laws of the United States establish extensive protections against discrimination, reaching all forms of governmental activity as well as significant areas of non-governmental activity. However, individual privacy and freedom from governmental interference in private conduct are also recognized as among the fundamental values of our free and democratic society. The United States understands that by its terms the Convention requires broad regulation of private conduct, in particular under Articles 2, 3, and 5. The United States does not accept any obligation under the Convention to enact legislation or take any other action with respect to private conduct except as mandated by the Constitution or laws of the United States.

(2) Current U.S. law contains substantial provisions for maternity leave in many employment situations but does not require paid maternity leave. Therefore, the United States does not accept an obligation under Article 11(2)(b) to introduce maternity leave with pay or with comparable social benefits without loss of former employment, seniority or social allowances.

(3) The United States understand that Article 12 permits States Parties to determine which healthcare services are appropriate in

connection with family planning, pregnancy, confinement, and the post-natal period, as well as when the provision of free services is necessary, and does not mandate the provision of particular services on a cost-free basis.

(4) Nothing in this Convention shall be construed to reflect or create any right to abortion and in no case should abortion be promoted as a method of family planning.

What do you think motivates the inclusion of these particular RUDs? Review the text of CEDAW and consider whether they are necessary to achieve the goals of their proponents. Janet Benshoof, an international human rights lawyer, has argued that ratification of CEDAW with these RUDs would be damaging, both domestically and internationally. *See* Janet Benshoof, *Twisted Treaty Shafts U.S. Women*, On the Issues (Winter 2009). *See also* Ann M. Piccard, *U.S. Ratification of CEDAW: From Bad to Worse?* 28 Law & Ineq. 119 (2010). Why might that be the case? Do you think ratification of CEDAW with these RUDs is a goal worth pursuing? Countries are able to eliminate or alter RUDs once they have ratified a treaty. For example, Australia eliminated one of the RUDs that it had initially taken with respect to CEDAW after the nation adopted a policy of equality for women in Australia's military. The United States has not removed RUDs that it has previously attached to human rights treaties, including RUDs that have been rendered moot by subsequent U.S. Supreme Court jurisprudence.

4.   The CRPD was also brought to the full Senate for consideration with a package of RUDs, one of which was a federalism reservation. The reservation provides: "To the extent that state and local governments exercise jurisdiction over issues covered by the convention, U.S. obligations under the convention are limited to the U.S. government taking measures appropriate to the federal system, such as enforcement under the ADA, with the ultimate objective of full implementation of the convention." How does this provision differ from the federalism understanding included with the ICCPR? What is the impact of adopting a federalism "reservation" rather than a federalism "understanding"?

5.   The CRPD RUDs also include the following unique understandings:

(1) Economic, Social, and Cultural Rights. The United States understands the convention prevents discrimination on the basis of disability with respect to economic, social, and cultural (ESC) rights, insofar as such rights are recognized and implemented under U.S. federal law.

(2) Equal Employment Opportunity. U.S. law protects persons with disabilities against unequal pay, including the right to equal pay for equal work. The United States understands that the convention does not require adoption of a comparable framework for persons with disabilities.

What do you think motivates the ESC rights understanding? What impact do you think it would have, if CRPD was eventually ratified? Compare the CEDAW and CRPD RUDs with those attached to the ICCPR. Why do you think these treaties inspired RUDs that focus on particular substantive protections?

6. Given that the U.S. has never ratified a human rights treaty without RUDs, should advocates of the CRPD and CEDAW who nevertheless oppose the RUDs set forth above continue to focus on ratification as a goal? Why or why not?

7. How does the use of broad RUDs impact the United States' credibility on the international stage? In an earlier passage of the excerpted article, Professor Henkin observed that the United States' use of RUDs has "evoked criticism abroad and dismayed supporters of ratification in the United States." Louis Henkin, *U.S. Ratification of Human Rights Conventions: The Ghost of Senator Bricker*, 89 Am. J. Int'l L. 341, 341 (1995). Professor Cherif Bassiouni has argued that the "Senate's practice of de facto rewriting treaties, through reservations, declarations, understandings, and provisos, leaves the international credibility of the United States shaken and its reliability as a treaty-negotiating partner with foreign countries in doubt." M. Cherif Bassiouni, *Reflections on the Ratification of the International Covenant on Civil and Political Rights by the United States Senate*, 42 DePaul L. Rev. 1169, 1173 (1993). By contrast, Professor Jack Goldsmith has observed that the U.S. behavior is not unique, and that in fact, other liberal democracies "take reservations to important human rights treaties, decline to make these treaties domestically enforceable, and generally show a preference for local and regional human rights norms and institutions over international ones." Jack Goldsmith, *The Unexceptional U.S. Human Rights RUDs*, 3 U. St. Thomas L.J. 311, 312 (2005). Assuming Professor Goldsmith is correct, does that justify the United States' continued use of RUDs?

C. WHAT EFFECT? THE PROBLEM OF UNRATIFIED TREATIES

As described above, the United States has signed but not ratified a number of human rights treaties, including CEDAW, CRC, ICESCR, and CRPD. In some cases, a treaty may remain in this state of legal limbo for decades. In the first excerpt below, Professor Bradley explains how this phenomenon occurs and describes the domestic effect of these instruments during the period after signing but before ratification. The following passage, excerpted from an *amicus* brief to the Supreme Court in *Roper v. Simmons*,[3] illustrates the nature of the U.S.'s international obligations under signed, but unratified treaties.

---

[3]   543 U.S. 551 (2005).

CURTIS A. BRADLEY, "UNRATIFIED TREATIES, DOMESTIC
POLITICS, AND THE U.S. CONSTITUTION"

48 Harv. Int'l L.J. 307, 309–14 (2007).

I.   The Phenomenon of Signed but Unratified Treaties

Throughout its history, the United States has signed numerous treaties that it has not subsequently ratified. This phenomenon has been especially evident in the last several decades, during which time the United States has signed, but has not yet ratified, a variety of important multilateral treaties. These treaties include significant human rights agreements such as the International Covenant on Economic, Social, and Cultural Rights (signed in 1977); the American Convention on Human Rights (signed in 1977); the Convention on the Elimination of All Forms of Discrimination Against Women (signed in 1980); and the Convention on the Rights of the Child (signed in 1995). They also include important environmental treaties such as the Kyoto Protocol to the United Nations Framework Convention on Climate Change (signed in 1998); the Rio Convention on Biological Diversity (signed in 1993); and an agreement revising the seabed mining provisions of the Law of the Sea Convention (signed in 1994). Another set of treaties that have been signed but not ratified, much discussed in connection with the post-September 11 war on terrorism, are the First and Second Additional Protocols to the Geneva Conventions (signed in 1977). Finally, the United States has signed but not ratified a number of private international law treaties.

. . .

There are a number of reasons why the United States may sign but not ratify a treaty. The president might submit a treaty to the Senate and have it defeated there, although this happens only rarely. . . . More likely, a president might withhold submission of the treaty to the Senate because of perceived opposition in that body, perhaps with the hope that the Senate's position—and perhaps its composition—would change. This appears to have been the case, for example, with the Convention on the Rights of the Child, which the Clinton Administration signed in 1995 but did not submit to the Senate. In addition, a president may submit a treaty to the Senate and have it languish there, once its supporters in the Senate realize that they do not have sufficient votes for advice and consent. . . . A president might also sign a treaty without being committed to ratification, perhaps in an effort to stay involved in subsequent negotiations related to the treaty or in the institutions established by the treaty, or for symbolic political benefits.

Yet another reason why a treaty might be signed by the United States but remain unratified is a change in policy that occurs as a result of a new presidential administration. Such a change of policy has occurred on a number of occasions. For example, President Carter signed the SALT II nuclear reduction treaty in 1979, but the Reagan Administration announced in 1982 that the United States had no intention of ratifying that treaty. Secretary of State Alexander Haig explained to the Senate Foreign Relations Committee that "[t]his proposal has been abandoned by this administration," and that "we consider SALT II dead and have so informed the Soviets."

. . .

II. Legal Effect of Signing a Treaty

Under international law, a nation does not become a party to a treaty until it expresses its "consent to be bound." Traditionally, this consent could be expressed in a variety of ways, including through a nation's signature of the treaty.

. . .

Today, although signing is not typically viewed as a manifestation of consent to be bound to a treaty, many international law academics and lawyers contend that signing does impose certain obligations on the signatory country. This contention is based on a provision in the Vienna Convention, a treaty that regulates the formation, interpretation, and termination of treaties. Article 18 of the Vienna Convention states that a nation that signs a treaty is "obliged to refrain from acts which would defeat the object and purpose" of the treaty "until it shall have made its intention clear not to become a party to the treaty." Although the United States has not ratified the Vienna Convention, executive branch officials have stated on a number of occasions that they view much of the Convention as reflecting binding customary international law. Moreover, when the executive branch initially sought Senate ratification of the Vienna Convention, State Department officials specifically described the Article 18 object and purpose obligation as a codification of customary international law, and State Department officials have since repeated this description.

. . .

_____

BRIEF OF THE EUROPEAN UNION AND MEMBERS OF THE INTERNATIONAL COMMUNITY AS AMICI CURIAE IN SUPPORT OF RESPONDENT ROPER V. SIMMONS

Supreme Court of the United States, 2004.
2004 WL 1619203 at *13–17.

In the view of the [European Union], a significant number of treaties, including a number ratified or signed by the United States, prohibit the execution of persons under the age of 18 at the time of their offenses. The bodies charged with interpretation of those treaties also support this view.

The United Nations Convention on the Rights of the Child ("CRC") is the most widely ratified human rights treaty in the world. All Member States of the United Nations barring two, some 192 nations, have ratified the CRC. No other human rights instrument has achieved this level of global recognition. The U.S. and Somalia are the only two nations that have not ratified the CRC. The U.S. signed the CRC in February of 1995, and Somalia signed the CRC in May of 2002, indicating its intent to ratify. As stated in Article 18 of the Vienna Convention on the Law of Treaties . . . a nation is obliged to "refrain from acts which would defeat the object and purpose of the treaty after signature and prior to ratification." Although the United States is not a party to the Vienna Convention, the U.S. Department of State has recognised it as the authoritative guide to current treaty law and procedure. This provision would therefore be taken into account when examining whether the actions of a State, which had signed but not ratified the CRC, were contrary to the object and purpose of the Treaty.

Article 37(a) of the CRC prohibits the execution of juvenile offenders. It provides that "[n]either capital punishment nor life imprisonment without possibility of release shall be imposed for offences committed by persons below eighteen years of age. . . ." A Report of the Secretary General, U.N. ESCOR, Economic and Social Council, Subst. Sess., U.N. Doc. E/2000/3 at 21 ¶ 90 (2000), notes that in all but 14 States parties to the CRC, national laws prohibit the imposition of the death penalty on persons who committed the offense when under 18 years of age.

In May of 2002, the United Nations General Assembly unanimously adopted an extensive resolution, "A World Fit For Children", in which the body declared that "we acknowledge that the Convention on the Rights of the Child, the most universally embraced human rights treaty in history . . . contain[s] a comprehensive set of international legal standards for the protection and well-being of children." The document further calls upon the Governments of all States, "in particular States in which the death penalty had not been abolished, to comply with the obligations they have assumed under relevant provisions of international human rights instruments, including in particular Articles 37 and 40 of the Convention on the Rights of the Child and Articles 6 and 14 of the International Covenant on Civil and Political Rights".

Some 152 nations have ratified the International Covenant on Civil and Political Rights ("ICCPR"). Article 6(5) of the ICCPR specifically forbids the use of the death penalty against those under 18 at the time of the crime: "Sentence of death shall not be imposed for crimes committed by persons below eighteen years of age . . . ." The United States signed the

ICCPR in 1979 and ratified it in 1992 with a reservation to Article 6(5), stating that "the United States reserves the right, subject to its Constitutional constraints, to impose capital punishment on any person (other than a pregnant woman) duly convicted under existing or future laws permitting the imposition of capital punishment, including such punishment for crimes committed by persons below eighteen years of age," and a more general declaration that the provisions of Articles 1 through 27 of the Covenant were not self-executing. As articulated in Article 19 of the Vienna Convention, a State may, when ratifying a treaty, formulate a reservation, but the reservation must not be "incompatible with the object and purpose of the treaty."

Article 4(2) of the ICCPR states that no derogation can be made from Article 6 even in times of public emergency, thus indicating that Article 6 is seen to be inherent to the object and purpose of the ICCPR. The EU notes that the United States has made no reservation to Article 4(2).

The Human Rights Committee ("HRC") is the treaty body that monitors and reports on matters relating to the ICCPR. By ratifying the ICCPR, the United States has expressly recognized the authority of the HRC. A number of federal courts also have explicitly recognized the HRC's authority in matters of the ICCPR's interpretation. . . .

In General Comment No. 24 (52), U.N. Doc. CCPR/C/21/Rev.1/Add.6 (1994), the HRC states, in relevant part:

> 6.   . . . [W]here a reservation is not prohibited by the treaty or falls within the specified permitted categories, a State may make a reservation provided it is not incompatible with the object and purpose of the treaty.
>
> . . .
>
> 8.   Reservations that offend peremptory norms would not be compatible with the object and purpose of the Covenant. Although treaties that are mere exchanges of obligations between States allow them to reserve *inter se* application of rules of general international law, it is otherwise in human rights treaties, which are for the benefit of persons within their jurisdiction. Accordingly, provisions in the Covenant that represent customary international law (and *a fortiori* when they have the character of peremptory norms) may not be the subject of reservations. Accordingly, a State may not reserve the right (. . .) to execute children (. . .).
>
> . . .
>
> 10. . . . While there is no automatic correlation between reservations to non-derogable provisions, and reservations which

offend against the object and purpose of the Covenant, a State has a heavy onus to justify such a reservation.

. . .

18. . . . The normal consequence of an unacceptable reservation is not that the Covenant will not be in effect at all for a reserving party. Rather, such a reservation will generally be severable, in the sense that the Covenant will be operative for the reserving party without benefit of the reservation.

In 1995, the HRC applied General Comment No. 24 to the first U.S. report on domestic compliance with the ICCPR and found that the U.S. reservation to Article 6(5) was incompatible with the object and purpose of the treaty. It recommended that the U.S. withdraw the reservation.

. . .

NOTES & QUESTIONS

1.   Article 18 of the Vienna Convention on the Law of Treaties provides:

A State is obliged to refrain from acts which would defeat the object and purpose of a treaty when:

(a) it has signed the treaty or has exchanged instruments constituting the treaty subject to ratification, acceptance or approval, until it shall have made its intention clear not to become a party to the treaty; or

(b) it has expressed its consent to be bound by the treaty, pending the entry into force of the treaty and provided that such entry into force is not unduly delayed.

United Nations, *Vienna Convention on the Law of Treaties*, art. 18, May 23, 1969, 1155 U.N.T.S. 331.

As Professor Bradley explains, advocates have relied on Article 18 in a wide range of cases to argue that domestic law violates the United States' obligations based on unsigned treaties. *See, e.g., The European Community, et al., v. RJR Nabisco, et al.*, No. 03–1427, Supplemental Brief for Petitioners (arguing that the court had a duty not to violate the object and purpose of the unsigned Framework Convention on Tobacco Control); *Ehrlich v. Am. Airlines, Inc.*, 360 F.3d 366, 373 n. 7 (2d Cir. 2004) (arguing an object and purpose claim based on the Convention for the Unification of Certain Rules for International Carriage by Air, S. Treaty Doc. No. 106–45, May 28, 1999); *United States v. Royal Caribbean Cruises*, 11 F. Supp.2d 1358, 1369 (S.D. Fla. 1998) (involving a claim under the unratified United Nations Convention on the Law of the Sea).

How does the *amicus* brief of the international community rely on Article 18 to argue that the United States' policy of executing persons under eighteen years old violated its international obligations? Review the material on RUDs *supra*. How does this brief argue that the United States' reservation to the ICCPR on the juvenile death penalty is invalid?

2.   While the Executive's constitutional authority to sign international agreements has generally been unquestioned, Professor David Moore has recently argued that the President's unilateral assumption of international obligations in the interim period before completing the constitutional process for adopting a new treaty is unconstitutional. *See* David H. Moore, *The President's Unconstitutional Treatymaking*, 59 UCLA L. Rev. 598 (2012). Why might this be the case?

3.   Given the impact that signed, but unratified treaties have on domestic law under Article 18 of the Vienna Convention on the Law of Treaties, is there a strategic benefit for advocates to continue to push the executive branch to sign new instruments that have little chance of being ratified? Are there any risks to this strategy?

II.   ENFORCING TREATY RIGHTS IN UNITED STATES COURTS

The ratification of a treaty creates international obligations for the United States. With respect to the human rights treaties, ratification indicates to the other state parties to the treaty that the United States government has committed to protecting certain rights at home. Each of the ratified human rights treaties requires the United States to undergo a regular review before the treaty body responsible for monitoring each state party's compliance with its treaty commitments. **Chapter VIII** sets out how this review process works.

In addition to the international obligations they create, ratified treaties are the "supreme law of the land,"[4] with a status equivalent to federal law. Nonetheless, enforcing human rights treaties in domestic courts is challenging. The United States has ratified each human rights treaty with the understanding that these instruments are "non-self-executing." Whether a treaty is self-executing or non-self-executing determines what effect the treaty has on domestic law upon ratification, but the exact scope of this effect has been a subject of longstanding (and confusing) academic debate. Nonetheless, as early as 1829, the Supreme Court in *Foster v. Neilson*,[5] introduced the idea that some types of treaties might not be enforceable by domestic courts without some action by Congress. It therefore distinguished between a treaty "that operates of itself without the aid of any legislative provision" and one that would

---

[4]   Const. Art. VI, cl. 2.

[5]   27 U.S. 253 (1829).

require execution by the Legislature before it can become a rule for the Court.[6]

Since *Foster*, both courts and commentators have assumed that treaties can be either "self-executing" or "non-self-executing," but there has been substantial uncertainty both about how a court should decide whether a particular instrument is non-self-executing, and what effect that decision has on the treaty's status in domestic law. The materials in this section explore the contours of both of these debates.

A. DEFINING NON-SELF-EXECUTION

What does it mean for a treaty to be non-self-executing? This excerpt from Professor Sloss describes different possible understandings of the impact of the non-self-execution determination on a court's ability to enforce the treaty in a pending case.

DAVID SLOSS, "THE DOMESTICATION OF INTERNATIONAL HUMAN RIGHTS: NON-SELF EXECUTING DECLARATIONS AND HUMAN RIGHTS TREATIES"
24 Yale J. Int'l L. 129, 130–52 (1999).

III. The Meaning of the Term "Not Self-Executing"

When courts hold that a particular treaty provision is "not self-executing," they generally refuse to apply the treaty provision in the manner that the litigant invoking the provision wishes it to apply. However, this consistent refusal masks an underlying conceptual confusion about the meaning of the term. A 1948 memorandum prepared for the Department of State Legal Adviser stated that, "An examination of adjudicated cases and of some treatises and of some of the law reviews has failed to disclose a clear definition of the term 'Self-Executing Treaty.'" Three years later, Professor Myres McDougal stated that, "this word 'self-executing' is essentially meaningless, and . . . the quicker we drop it from our vocabulary the better for clarity and understanding." Nevertheless, despite repeated exhortations by scholars to either clarify or dispense with the concept of self-execution, courts continue to employ the term, and the ambiguity surrounding its usage has only increased with the passage of time.

. . .

The various non-self-execution concepts are divided into two groups: (1) those concepts that preclude altogether the direct judicial application of non-self-executing treaty provisions; and (2) those concepts that limit the direct judicial application of non-self-executing treaty provisions to certain types of claims and/or certain types of litigants.

---

[6] *Id.* at 314.

. . .

A. Concepts That Preclude Direct Judicial Application

[C]ertain concepts of non-self-execution would preclude altogether the direct judicial application of non-self-executing treaty provisions. This Section briefly describes two such concepts.

1. Automatic Incorporation

When courts say that a particular treaty provision is self-executing, they sometimes mean that it is automatically incorporated into domestic law upon ratification of the treaty. Under this interpretation, the statement that a treaty provision is not self-executing means that it has no status as domestic law in the absence of implementing legislation.

The earliest use of the term "self-executing" in this sense appears to have been in *Whitney v. Robertson*. There, the Supreme Court stated that:

> When the [treaty] stipulations are not self-executing they can only be enforced pursuant to legislation to carry them into effect. . . . If the treaty contains stipulations which are self-executing, that is, require no legislation to make them operative, to that extent they have the force and effect of a legislative enactment. . . .

Under this concept of self-execution, self-executing treaty provisions are automatically incorporated into domestic law upon treaty ratification; non-self-executing provisions have no domestic legal status in the absence of implementing legislation, even if they are obligatory as a matter of international law.

. . .

2. The Foster Concept of Non-Self-Execution

Although *Foster v. Neilson* does not use the term "self-executing," the case is widely regarded as the source of the distinction in United States law between self-executing and non-self-executing treaties. In *Foster*, Chief Justice John Marshall stated that some treaties are addressed "to the political, not the judicial department; and the legislature must execute the contract [i.e., the treaty] before it can become a rule for the Court." Thus, Marshall distinguished between: (1) treaties that address themselves to the judicial department, which can be applied directly by the courts (self-executing); and (2) treaties that address themselves to the political branches, which require legislative implementation before they can provide a rule of decision for the judiciary (non-self-executing).

. . .

No treaty provision can be directly applicable unless it is also automatically incorporated—that is, judges cannot rely on a provision as a rule of decision if it has no status as domestic law. However, the fact that a treaty provision is automatically incorporated into domestic law does not necessarily mean that judges can rely on it to provide a rule of decision in a case. For example, an arms control treaty provision that obligates the United States to destroy certain missiles is not directly applicable by the judiciary, because it manifestly "addresses itself to the political, not the judicial department." The fact that the provision is not directly applicable by the judiciary, however, does not mean that it is without domestic legal force. It is analogous to a statute that authorizes funds for missile production—such a statute has domestic legal force, but it does not provide a rule of decision for the courts.

Thus, under the *Foster* concept of self-execution, a non-self-executing treaty has domestic legal force, but it cannot be applied directly by the judiciary.

. . .

B. Concepts That Permit Direct Judicial Application in Some Cases

The preceding Section described concepts of non-self-execution that share one common feature: courts are precluded from applying non-self-executing treaty provisions directly as a rule of decision. In contrast, this Section describes two concepts of non-self-execution that would permit direct judicial application of non-self-executing treaty provisions in some cases, depending on the nature of the claim and/or the identities of the litigants. It is important to emphasize that, to the best of the author's knowledge, no U.S. court has ever held a treaty provision to be non-self-executing and then applied it directly to decide a case. However, courts often apply treaty provisions directly to cases before them without considering whether the treaty provision is self-executing. Moreover, courts frequently discuss the concept of non-self-execution in terms that imply the possibility of direct judicial application in some cases.

. . .

2. The "Private Cause of Action" Concept of Non-Self-Execution

In analyzing the domestic legal effect of treaties, courts have frequently linked the concept of self-execution with the concept of a private right of action, or a private cause of action. Similarly, state court decisions analyzing whether state constitutional provisions are "self-executing" have also linked the concept of self-execution to the concept of a private cause of action.

The statement that a treaty is not self-executing, in the sense that it does not create a private cause of action, does not mean that the treaty cannot be applied directly by the courts. As Professor Vázquez has stated:

[A] treaty that does not itself confer a right of action . . . is not for that reason unenforceable in the courts. A right of action is not necessary if the treaty is being invoked as a defense. Moreover, treaties have long been enforced pursuant to common law forms of action. Furthermore, there are a number of possible federal statutory bases for rights of action to enforce treaties, the most important being section 1983 and the APA. Only if there is no other basis for the right of action should it be necessary to locate a right of action in the treaty itself.

Thus, under the "private cause of action" concept, like the standing concept, the self-execution inquiry turns on whether a particular litigant may invoke a treaty provision in a particular case. However, the fact that a treaty provision is not self-executing, in the sense that it does not create a private cause of action, does not preclude direct judicial application of the provision in all cases.

From a policy standpoint, the "private cause of action" concept makes sense in cases where the treaty makers wish to prevent the treaty from being utilized to create new avenues of litigation, while still permitting judicial enforcement of the treaty in other contexts to help ensure compliance with treaty obligations.

. . .

The Supreme Court's most recent discussion of the complicated problem of non-self-execution came in *Medellín v. Texas*.[7] Jose Ernesto Medellín, an 18-year old citizen of Mexico, participated in the gang rape and murder of two girls in Houston, Texas. He was arrested five days later and signed a confession after receiving the *Miranda* warning. Under the Vienna Convention on Consular Relations, a treaty that the United States has signed and ratified, Medellín was also entitled to have the Mexican consulate notified of his arrest. Texas officials did not advise him of that right.

Medellín was convicted and sentenced to death in 1997. He appealed, and raised the violation of his Vienna Convention rights as part of his appeal, but the conviction was upheld by the state trial court and by the Texas Court of Criminal Appeals. In 2003, Medellín filed a petition for writ of habeas corpus in the federal district court, which was denied on the ground that his Vienna Convention claim had not been raised during trial and was thus procedurally defaulted.

Also in 2003, Mexico brought a suit against the United States in the International Court of Justice, arguing that the United States had

---

[7]   552 U.S. 491 (2008).

violated its duties under the Vienna Convention by failing to notify 51 Mexican citizens of their consular notification rights. Under the terms of the Optional Protocol to the Vienna Convention on Consular Relations Concerning the Compulsory Settlement of Disputes, which the United States had also signed and ratified, the ICJ had jurisdiction to resolve disputes over compliance with the convention. Medellín was one of the 51 nationals named in the suit. In 2004, the ICJ held in *Case Concerning Avena and Other Mexican Nationals*,[8] that the named Mexican citizens were entitled to review and reconsideration of their convictions and sentences. Following the judgment, the United States withdrew from the Optional Protocol.

On appeal to the U.S. Court of Appeals for the Fifth Circuit, Medellín raised the ICJ's *Avena* ruling, but was denied relief. He then petitioned the U.S. Supreme Court, which granted *certiorari*. Before the Court could hear the case, however, President George W. Bush issued a Memorandum for the Attorney General ordering the state courts to review the convictions and sentences of the Mexican nationals named in the *Avena* judgment.

Following the issuance of the Memorandum, the U.S. Supreme Court dismissed the writ of *certiorari* as improvidently granted. Medellín returned to the Texas Court of Criminal Appeals to enforce the President's memorandum, but was denied relief. He then petitioned for *certiorari* and the Court again granted the writ to consider both (1) whether the President had the authority to order state courts to comply with *Avena*, and (2) whether state courts were required under the Constitution to give effect to the *Avena* judgment. In reaching a decision on the second question, the Court was required to consider whether judgments of the ICJ are self-executing. Ultimately, it determined that they are not. But in the course of reaching this conclusion, the Court made several statements that seemed to indicate that a non-self-executing treaty has no domestic legal effect at all. Sections of the *Medellín* decision are excerpted later in this chapter. In the article excerpt below, Professor Vázquez explains the constitutional problems with this understanding of the Court's opinion.

CARLOS MANUEL VÁZQUEZ, "TREATIES AS LAW OF THE LAND: THE SUPREMACY CLAUSE AND THE JUDICIAL ENFORCEMENT OF TREATIES"

122 Harv. L. Rev. 599, 648–51 (2008).

The Court in *Medellín* noted that "the label 'self-executing' has on occasion been used to convey different meanings," but it made clear that "[w]hat we mean by 'self-executing' is that the treaty has automatic

---

8   2004 I.C.J. 12 (Judgment of March 31).

domestic effect as federal law upon ratification." "Conversely, a 'non-self-executing' treaty does not by itself give rise to domestically enforceable federal law." This and many similar statements in the opinion suggest that the majority understood that the effect of a determination that a treaty is non-self-executing is that the obligations imposed by the treaty as a matter of international law lack the force of domestic law. If so, the Court was endorsing a view that had been repeated by many lower courts and commentators but had never before been endorsed by the Court itself. It is a claim that has not received the scrutiny deserved by a statement so directly at odds with the constitutional text.

The Supremacy Clause declares that "all" treaties are the "supreme Law of the Land." This provision thus takes the international obligations imposed on the United States by its treaties and gives them the force of domestic law. Exceptions can legitimately be interpolated for treaties that are invalid or have been superseded by subsequent statutes. For example, a treaty that purports to accomplish what is beyond the treaty power lacks the force of domestic law because, to that extent, it is invalid. Similarly, though a treaty superseded by a statute continues to bind the United States internationally, it is considered repealed as a matter of domestic law. There is no basis, however, for denying the force of domestic law to a treaty that imposes an obligation on the United States that is not beyond the treaty power or otherwise invalid and has not been superseded by a statute.

The *Medellín* majority did not attempt to square the view that non-self-executing treaties lack the force of domestic law with the text of the Supremacy Clause. As support for this characterization, it merely cited *Foster*'s statement that, if a treaty is self-executing, it must be regarded in the courts as the equivalent of an act of the legislature. But *Foster* never said that non-self-executing treaties lack the force of domestic law. Rather, it characterized such treaties as laws "addresse[d] to" the political branches rather than the courts. When a treaty is addressed to the legislature, as the Court concluded in *Foster*, then it is clearly not the equivalent of an act of the legislature, as legislatures do not typically pass laws obligating themselves to pass specified other laws in the future. Moreover, such a treaty is not to be "regarded in [the] courts" at all, because courts in our constitutional system lack the power to require the legislature to legislate. Such a treaty is thus not judicially enforceable because of the particular nature of the obligation it imposes, not because it lacks the force of domestic law.

To be sure, a treaty addressed to the legislature lacks virtually all of the attributes that we usually associate with a "law." For example, it is not enforceable in courts, and can be violated by the norm-subject with impunity. I share the majority's skepticism about the legal status of such a norm. But the difficulty of understanding how a non-self-executing treaty can be said to be a "law" in any recognizable sense should have led the Court to question the concept of non-self-execution, not to ignore the constitutional text. Non-self-execution, after all, originated as an alternative holding in a subsequently overruled decision and was never again the clear basis for denial of relief by the Supreme Court. The *Medellín* majority instead appeared to treat *Foster's* alternative holding as sacrosanct and barely took notice of the constitutional text.

Notwithstanding the suggestions throughout the opinion that non-self-executing treaties lack the force of domestic law, *Medellín* is susceptible to a narrower interpretation. At several points, the Court said that non-self-executing treaties were not "enforceable" domestic law. Only this narrower understanding of *Medellín* avoids a direct conflict with the constitutional text. For this reason, even the Solicitor General of Texas, who argued the case on behalf of the State, disavows the broader interpretation.

Indeed, the *Medellín* majority itself implicitly recognized that Article 94 of the U.N. Charter had some effect as domestic law. In deciding that the President lacked the power to order the state of Texas to comply with the ICJ's judgment in *Avena*, the majority applied Justice Jackson's familiar tripartite test from *Youngstown Sheet & Tube Co. v. Sawyer*. The majority concluded that the President's power was at its lowest ebb because he was acting in the face of a non-self-executing treaty, which, in its view, reflected a decision by the treatymakers that enforcement of the treaty would require an act of legislation. Thus, as applied by the majority, Article 94 had the domestic legal effect of reducing the President's power to act unilaterally. In this part of its opinion, the majority seems to reach the same conclusion regarding Article 94 of the U.N. Charter that the Court in *Foster* reached with respect to Article 8 of the Adams-Onís Treaty: in both cases, the treaty had domestic legal force but was "addressed to" the legislature and hence required legislative implementation before it could be enforced in the courts. As discussed above, this understanding reconciles *Foster*-type non-self-execution (albeit uneasily) with the constitutional text.

One scholar who has embraced a narrow interpretation of *Medellín* on this point has suggested that the Court should be understood to have held that a non-self-executing treaty is not judicially enforceable domestic law. This gets it almost right. If non-self-executing treaties are "laws" addressed to the political branches, then they are not judicially enforceable. But a more precise definition is required. Some treaties are not judicially enforceable because the obligation they impose is not one for the courts at all. But there was little doubt in either *Foster* or *Medellín* that compliance with the relevant obligations would require the involvement of courts at some point. The question was whether judicial enforcement had to be preceded by action from the political branches. In the words of *Medellín*, a self-executing treaty is one that is "immediate[ly]" or "direct[ly]" or "automatic[ally]" enforceable in the courts. When we say that a treaty is non-self-executing in the Foster sense, therefore, what we mean is that such a treaty is enforceable in the courts only indirectly—that is, pursuant to implementing legislation or other appropriate action by the political branches. The treaty is the supreme law of the land, but it is "addressed to" the political branches rather than the courts.

. . .

NOTES & QUESTIONS

1.   Is the distinction that Professor Vázquez identifies important? As a practical matter, what is the difference between determining that a treaty has no domestic effect and a holding that the treaty is the supreme law of the land, but is addressed to the political branches? As a human rights advocate, why might this matter to you, given that all of the major instruments have been designated as non-self-executing?

2.   In attaching the non-self-executing RUD when ratifying the ICCPR, the Senate averred that "the intent is to clarify that the Covenant will not create a private cause of action in U.S. courts." Is there are way to reconcile this characterization, endorsed by the Senate, with the *Medellín* court's conclusions? Why didn't the Court give greater deference to the political branches in determining the meaning of "non-self-execution"?

3.   In addition to ratifying the major human rights treaties with a non-self-execution provision, the United States has never ratified a treaty in a way that would allow persons within its jurisdiction to bring allegations of human rights violations directly to the treaty body for adjudication. Seven of the human rights treaty bodies, including three for treaties the United States has ratified (ICCPR, CERD, and CAT), have individual complaint mechanisms; however, the U.S. has not acceded to them. The general purpose of these procedures is to allow an individual or a group to complain to the treaty committee about a state's violation of its treaty obligations. While the enforcement power of these committees is limited, they may validate the allegation that a human rights violation has occurred. In limited circumstances, they may recommend financial compensation for the complainants, even though these findings are not enforceable in national or international courts. For more information regarding individual complaint mechanisms, *see* Alexandra R. Harrington, *Don't Mind the Gap: The Rise of Individual Complaint Mechanisms Within International Human Rights Treaties*, 22 Duke J. Comp. & Int'l L. 153 (2012). What is the impact of the United States' inclusion of the non-self-execution provision and its failure to consent to be subject to the individual complaint mechanisms?

B. DETERMINING WHETHER A TREATY
IS NON-SELF-EXECUTING

As the previous section indicates, a court's determination that a treaty is non-self-executing significantly limits its domestic effect. At a minimum, it means that courts cannot directly enforce the rights the instrument protects. Thus a very important question in treaty analysis is how a court should decide whether a treaty is non-self-executing. Is the inclusion of a ratification declaration that a treaty is non-self-executing conclusive in this analysis? To understand how courts have approached this question, compare the decision of the District Court for the Eastern District of Washington in *White v. Paulsen* with the Supreme Court's decision a decade later in *Medellín v. Texas*.

WHITE V. PAULSEN

United States District Court, Eastern District of Washington, 1998.
997 F. Supp. 1380.

WHALEY, DISTRICT JUDGE.

Before the Court is Defendant C. Alvin Paulsen's Motion to Dismiss which has been joined by Defendants General Electric Company, Battelle Memorial Institute, Rhay, and Conte. Defendants' motion seeks dismissal of the White and McClellan Plaintiffs' "crimes against humanity" cause of action, which pertains to radiation experiments that Plaintiffs allege were conducted on them without their informed consent while they were prisoners in the custody of the State of Washington. As is discussed more fully below, Defendants' motion is granted, and this cause of action is dismissed, because Plaintiffs' allegations do not correspond to a federal private right of action for violations of international law's prohibition of "crimes against humanity."

Discussion

. . .

In the context of this motion, the central issue is whether Plaintiffs' cause of action "arises under" any of the sources of federal law identified in § 1331. Put slightly differently, because § 1331 is a pure jurisdictional statute that does not, on its own, create a private right of action for all violations of federal law, the critical question is whether a right of action is created by some other source of federal law. Thus, for jurisdiction to exist under § 1331 over Plaintiffs' "crimes against humanity" cause of action, a source of federal law other than § 1331 must give rise to a private right of action for the violations of international law they allege.

Plaintiffs contend there are two such sources: the law of nations, as it is incorporated into the laws of the United States, and treaties to which the United States is a party. These arguments are addressed separately.

. . .

Where Congress has not enacted authorizing legislation, a treaty gives rise to a private right of action only if it is "self-executing"; i.e., if it either expressly or impliedly creates a private right of action to enforce rights described in the treaty.

There is no set test for determining whether a treaty is self-executing; different courts have come up with various descriptions of factors relevant to this inquiry. The Ninth Circuit has expressly stated that its subordinate courts must look to relevant "contextual factors," including:

> the purposes of the treaty and the objectives of its creators, the existence of domestic procedures and institutions appropriate for direct implementation, the availability and feasibility of alternative enforcement methods, and the immediate and long-range social consequences of self—or non-self-execution.

Of these four non-exclusive factors, "it is the first factor that is critical to determine whether an executive agreement is self-executing, while the other factors are most relevant to determine the extent to which the agreement is self-executing."

Plaintiffs contend two treaties to which the United States is a party contain self-executing prohibitions on torture that incorporate non-consensual medical experimentation: the . . . International Covenant on Civil and Political Rights ("ICCPR"), and the Convention Against Torture and Other Cruel, Inhuman or Degrading Treatment or Punishment. To date, however, no court that has considered either of these treaties has found them to be self-executing. Moreover, both of these treaties expressly require that party-states take steps under their municipal laws to enforce the rights described in those treaties, suggesting strongly that parties to these agreements did not intend for them to be self-executing. *See Foster v. Neilson,* 27 U.S. (2 Pet.) 253, 314, 7 L.Ed. 415 (1829) ("[W]hen the terms of [a treaty] import a contract, when either of the parties engages to perform a particular act, the treaty addresses itself to the political, not the judicial department; and the legislature must execute the contract before it can become a rule for the Court."), *overruled on other grounds, United States v. Percheman,* 32 U.S. (7 Pet.) 51, 8 L.Ed. 604 (1833).

For example, although Article 2 of the ICCPR expressly addresses the duty of party-states to enforce the rights described in the ICCPR, it does not purport to expressly or implicitly create a private right of action for violations of those rights. On its face, Article 2 creates no express right, discussing only what the party-states have agreed to do to give effect to the rights discussed in the ICCPR. Moreover, the language is couched in terms of further actions that States agree to undertake, thereby suggesting that the agreement is subject to further domestic action rather than self-executing. Additionally, Article 2 expressly recognizes that the treaty imposes no obligation to take further action if effective remedies exist, non-judicial or otherwise, and also provides that the remedy need not be judicial in nature. Indeed, to the extent that Article 2 addresses itself to a requirement for a judicial remedy, it states only that its parties must "develop the possibilities of a judicial remedy." From this language, it is apparent that the parties to the ICCPR did not intend for its provisions to be self-executing in the sense of automatically creating a private right of action cognizable by citizens of a State.

Supporting this conclusion is the fact that the United States Senate expressly declared that the relevant provisions of the ICCPR were not self-executing when it addressed this issue in providing advice and consent to the ratification of the ICCPR. While this declaration may not carry controlling weight on this issue, the view of the Senate is entitled to substantial deference given the role the United States Constitution confides in the Senate with regard to the process of making treaties the law of the United States. Additionally, with respect to the Torture Convention, it is relevant that Congress has created a private right of action for torture, an action that would be unnecessary if these treaties were self-executing.

Finally, the existence of the various domestic law remedies discussed above counsels against reading into these treaties an intent to create a domestic private right of action.

Given these considerations, the Court concludes that neither of these treaties is a self-executing treaty that gives rise to a private right applicable to the allegations at issue in this case.

. . .

Now compare the court's reasoning in *White v. Paulsen* with the following excerpt from the *Medellín* decision, in which the Court determined that decisions of the ICJ in *Avena* are non-self-executing.

MEDELLÍN V. TEXAS

Supreme Court of the United States, 2008.
552 U.S. 491.

Medellín first contends that the ICJ's judgment in *Avena* constitutes a "binding" obligation on the state and federal courts of the United States. He argues that "by virtue of the Supremacy Clause, the treaties requiring compliance with the *Avena* judgment are *already* the 'Law of the Land' by which all state and federal courts in this country are 'bound.' Accordingly, Medellín argues, *Avena* is a binding federal rule of decision that pre-empts contrary state limitations on successive habeas petitions.

No one disputes that the *Avena* decision—a decision that flows from the treaties through which the United States submitted to ICJ jurisdiction with respect to Vienna Convention disputes—constitutes an *international* law obligation on the part of the United States. But not all international law obligations automatically constitute binding federal law enforceable in United States courts. The question we confront here is whether the *Avena* judgment has automatic *domestic* legal effect such that the judgment of its own force applies in state and federal courts.

This Court has long recognized the distinction between treaties that automatically have effect as domestic law, and those that—while they constitute international law commitments—do not by themselves function as binding federal law. The distinction was well explained by Chief Justice Marshall's opinion in *Foster v. Neilson,* which held that a treaty is "equivalent to an act of the legislature," and hence self-executing, when it "operates of itself without the aid of any legislative provision." When, in contrast, "[treaty] stipulations are not self-executing they can only be enforced pursuant to legislation to carry them into effect." In sum, while treaties "may comprise international commitments . . . they are not domestic law unless Congress has either enacted implementing statutes or the treaty itself conveys an intention that it be 'self-executing' and is ratified on these terms."

A treaty is, of course, "primarily a compact between independent nations." It ordinarily "depends for the enforcement of its provisions on the interest and the honor of the governments which are parties to it." "If these [interests] fail, its infraction becomes the subject of international negotiations and reclamations. . . . It is obvious that with all this the judicial courts have nothing to do and can give no redress." Only "[i]f the treaty contains stipulations which are self-executing, that is, require no legislation to make them operative, [will] they have the force and effect of a legislative enactment."

Medellín and his *amici* nonetheless contend that the Optional Protocol, United Nations Charter, and ICJ Statute supply the "relevant obligation" to give the *Avena* judgment binding effect in the domestic courts of the United States. Because none of these treaty sources creates binding federal law in the absence of implementing legislation, and because it is uncontested that no such legislation exists, we conclude that the *Avena* judgment is not automatically binding domestic law.

A

The interpretation of a treaty, like the interpretation of a statute, begins with its text. Because a treaty ratified by the United States is "an agreement among sovereign powers," we have also considered as "aids to its interpretation" the negotiation and drafting history of the treaty as well as "the postratification understanding" of signatory nations. As a signatory to the Optional Protocol, the United States agreed to submit disputes arising out of the Vienna Convention to the ICJ. The Protocol provides: "Disputes arising out of the interpretation or application of the [Vienna] Convention shall lie within the compulsory jurisdiction of the International Court of Justice." Of course, submitting to jurisdiction and agreeing to be bound are two different things. A party could, for example, agree to compulsory nonbinding arbitration. Such an agreement would require the party to appear before the arbitral tribunal without obligating the party to treat the tribunal's decision as binding.

The most natural reading of the Optional Protocol is as a bare grant of jurisdiction. It provides only that "[d]isputes arising out of the interpretation or application of the [Vienna] Convention shall lie within the compulsory jurisdiction of the International Court of Justice" and "may accordingly be brought before the [ICJ] . . . by any party to the dispute being a Party to the present Protocol." The Protocol says nothing about the effect of an ICJ decision and does not itself commit signatories to comply with an ICJ judgment. The Protocol is similarly silent as to any enforcement mechanism.

The obligation on the part of signatory nations to comply with ICJ judgments derives not from the Optional Protocol, but rather from Article 94 of the United Nations Charter—the provision that specifically addresses the effect of ICJ decisions. Article 94(1) provides that "[e]ach Member of the United Nations *undertakes to comply* with the decision of the [ICJ] in any case to which it is a party." 59 Stat. 1051 (emphasis added). The Executive Branch contends that the phrase "undertakes to comply" is not "an acknowledgement that an ICJ decision will have immediate legal effect in the courts of U.N. members," but rather "a *commitment* on the part of U.N. Members to take *future* action through their political branches to comply with an ICJ decision."

We agree with this construction of Article 94. The Article is not a directive to domestic courts. It does not provide that the United States "shall" or "must" comply with an ICJ decision, nor indicate that the Senate that ratified the U.N. Charter intended to vest ICJ decisions with immediate legal effect in domestic courts. Instead, "[t]he words of Article 94 . . . call upon governments to take certain action." In other words, the U.N. Charter reads like "a compact between independent nations" that "depends for the enforcement of its provisions on the interest and the honor of the governments which are parties to it."

The remainder of Article 94 confirms that the U.N. Charter does not contemplate the automatic enforceability of ICJ decisions in domestic courts. Article 94(2)—the enforcement provision—provides the sole remedy for noncompliance: referral to the United Nations Security Council by an aggrieved state.

The U.N. Charter's provision of an express diplomatic—that is, nonjudicial—remedy is itself evidence that ICJ judgments were not meant to be enforceable in domestic courts. And even this "quintessentially *international* remed[y]," is not absolute. First, the Security Council must "dee[m] necessary" the issuance of a recommendation or measure to effectuate the judgment. Second, as the President and Senate were undoubtedly aware in subscribing to the U.N. Charter and Optional Protocol, the United States retained the unqualified right to exercise its veto of any Security Council resolution.

This was the understanding of the Executive Branch when the President agreed to the U.N. Charter and the declaration accepting general compulsory ICJ jurisdiction.

If ICJ judgments were instead regarded as automatically enforceable domestic law, they would be immediately and directly binding on state and federal courts pursuant to the Supremacy Clause. Mexico or the ICJ would have no need to proceed to the Security Council to enforce the judgment in this case. Noncompliance with an ICJ judgment through exercise of the Security Council veto—always regarded as an option by the Executive and ratifying Senate during and after consideration of the U.N. Charter, Optional Protocol, and ICJ Statute—would no longer be a viable alternative. There would be nothing to veto. In light of the U.N. Charter's remedial scheme, there is no reason to believe that the President and Senate signed up for such a result.

In sum, Medellín's view that ICJ decisions are automatically enforceable as domestic law is fatally undermined by the enforcement structure established by Article 94. His construction would eliminate the option of noncompliance contemplated by Article 94(2), undermining the ability of the political branches to determine whether and how to comply with an ICJ judgment. Those sensitive foreign policy decisions would instead be transferred to state and federal courts charged with applying an ICJ judgment directly as domestic law. And those courts would not be empowered to decide whether to comply with the judgment—again, always regarded as an option by the political branches—any more than courts may consider whether to comply with any other species of domestic law. This result would be particularly anomalous in light of the principle that "[t]he conduct of the foreign relations of our Government is committed by the Constitution to the Executive and Legislative—'the political'—Departments."

. . .

JUSTICE BREYER, with whom JUSTICE SOUTER and JUSTICE GINSBURG join, dissenting.

The Constitution's Supremacy Clause provides that "all Treaties . . . which shall be made . . . under the Authority of the United States, shall be the supreme Law of the Land; and the Judges in every State shall be bound thereby." The Clause means that the "courts" must regard "a treaty . . . as equivalent to an act of the legislature, whenever it operates of itself without the aid of any legislative provision."

In the *Avena* case the International Court of Justice (ICJ) (interpreting and applying the Vienna Convention on Consular Relations) issued a judgment that requires the United States to reexamine certain criminal proceedings in the cases of 51 Mexican nationals. The question here is whether the ICJ's *Avena* judgment is enforceable now as a matter of domestic law, *i.e.,* whether it "operates of itself without the aid" of any further legislation.

The United States has signed and ratified a series of treaties obliging it to comply with ICJ judgments in cases in which it has given its consent to the exercise of the ICJ's adjudicatory authority. Specifically, the United States has agreed to submit, in this kind of case, to the ICJ's "compulsory jurisdiction" for purposes of "compulsory settlement." And it agreed that the ICJ's judgments would have "binding force . . . between the parties and in respect of [a] particular case." President Bush has determined that domestic courts should enforce this particular ICJ judgment. And Congress has done nothing to suggest the contrary. Under these circumstances, I believe the treaty obligations, and hence the judgment, resting as it does upon the consent of the United States to the ICJ's jurisdiction, bind the courts no less than would "an act of the [federal] legislature."

I

. . .

The critical question here is whether the Supremacy Clause requires Texas to follow, *i.e.,* to enforce, this ICJ judgment. The Court says "no." And it reaches its negative answer by interpreting the labyrinth of treaty provisions as creating a legal obligation that binds the United States internationally, but which, for Supremacy Clause purposes, is not automatically enforceable as domestic law.

. . .

The majority places too much weight upon treaty language that says little about the matter. The words "undertak[e] to comply," for example, do not tell us whether an ICJ judgment rendered pursuant to the parties' consent to compulsory ICJ jurisdiction does, or does not, automatically become part of our domestic law. To answer that question we must look instead to our own domestic law, in particular, to the many treaty-related cases interpreting the Supremacy Clause.

. . .

B

1

The case law provides no simple magic answer to the question whether a particular treaty provision is self-executing. But the case law does make clear that, insofar as today's majority looks for language about "self-execution" in the treaty itself and insofar as it erects "clear statement" presumptions designed to help find an answer, it is misguided.

The many treaty provisions that this Court has found self-executing contain no textual language on the point. Few, if any, of these provisions are clear. Those that displace state law in respect to such quintessential state matters as, say, property, inheritance, or debt repayment, lack the "clea[r] state[ment]" that the Court today apparently requires. This is also true of those cases that deal with state rules roughly comparable to the sort that the majority suggests require special accommodation. These many Supreme Court cases finding treaty provisions to be self-executing cannot be reconciled with the majority's demand for textual clarity.

Indeed, the majority does not point to a single ratified United States treaty that contains the kind of "clea[r]" or "plai[n]" textual indication for which the majority searches. . . . And that is not because the United States never, or hardly ever, has entered into a treaty with self-executing provisions. The case law belies any such conclusion. Rather, it is because the issue whether further legislative action is required before a treaty provision takes domestic effect in a signatory nation is often a matter of how that Nation's domestic law regards the provision's legal status. And that domestic status-determining law differs markedly from one nation to another. As Justice Iredell pointed out 200 years ago, Britain, for example, taking the view that the British Crown makes treaties but Parliament makes domestic law, virtually always requires parliamentary legislation. On the other hand, the United States, with its Supremacy Clause, does not take Britain's view. And the law of other nations, the

Netherlands for example, directly incorporates many treaties concluded by the executive into its domestic law even without explicit parliamentary approval of the treaty.

The majority correctly notes that the treaties do not explicitly state that the relevant obligations are self-executing. But given the differences among nations, why would drafters write treaty language stating that a provision about, say, alien property inheritance, is self-executing? How could those drafters achieve agreement when one signatory nation follows one tradition and a second follows another? Why would such a difference matter sufficiently for drafters to try to secure language that would prevent, for example, Britain's following treaty ratification with a further law while (perhaps unnecessarily) insisting that the United States apply a treaty provision without further domestic legislation? Above all, what does the absence of specific language about "self-execution" prove? It may reflect the drafters' awareness of national differences. It may reflect the practical fact that drafters, favoring speedy, effective implementation, conclude they should best leave national legal practices alone. It may reflect the fact that achieving international agreement on *this* point is simply a game not worth the candle.

In a word, for present purposes, the absence or presence of language in a treaty about a provision's self-execution proves nothing at all. At best the Court is hunting the snark. At worst it erects legalistic hurdles that can threaten the application of provisions in many existing commercial and other treaties and make it more difficult to negotiate new ones.

2

The case law also suggests practical, context-specific criteria that this Court has previously used to help determine whether, for Supremacy Clause purposes, a treaty provision is self-executing. The provision's text matters very much. But that is not because it contains language that explicitly refers to self-execution. . . . Drafting history is also relevant. But, again, that is not because it will explicitly address the relevant question. Instead text and history, along with subject matter and related characteristics will help our courts determine whether, as Chief Justice Marshall put it, the treaty provision "addresses itself to the political . . . department[s]" for further action or to "the judicial department" for direct enforcement.

In making this determination, this Court has found the provision's subject matter of particular importance. Does the treaty provision declare peace? Does it promise not to engage in hostilities? If so, it addresses itself to the political branches. Alternatively, does it concern the adjudication of traditional private legal rights such as rights to own property, to conduct a business, or to obtain civil tort recovery? If so, it may well address itself to the Judiciary. Enforcing such rights and setting their boundaries is the bread-and-butter work of the courts.

One might also ask whether the treaty provision confers specific, detailed individual legal rights. Does it set forth definite standards that judges can readily enforce? Other things being equal, where rights are specific and readily enforceable, the treaty provision more likely "addresses" the judiciary.

Alternatively, would direct enforcement require the courts to create a new cause of action? Would such enforcement engender constitutional controversy? Would it create constitutionally undesirable conflict with the other branches? In such circumstances, it is not likely that the provision contemplates direct judicial enforcement.

Such questions, drawn from case law stretching back 200 years, do not create a simple test, let alone a magic formula. But they do help to constitute a practical, context-specific judicial approach, seeking to separate run-of-the-mill judicial matters from other matters, sometimes more politically charged, sometimes more clearly the responsibility of other branches, sometimes lacking those attributes that would permit courts to act on their own without more ado. And such an approach is all that we need to find an answer to the legal question now before us.

C

Applying the approach just described, I would find the relevant treaty provisions self-executing as applied to the ICJ judgment before us.

. . .

NOTES & QUESTIONS

1. Scholars have offered different views on whether *Medellín* constitutes a radical departure from the Court's earlier case law on determining self-execution. Professor Carlos Vázquez has argued that:

> There is substantial ground for rejecting a reading of *Medellín* as requiring evidence that the treaty was intended to have the force of domestic law. If such evidence were required, few, if any, treaties— and no multilateral treaties—would be self-executing. States rarely, if ever, address a treaty's status as domestic law in the treaty itself. Such a test would accordingly conflict with many, many Supreme Court decisions, stretching back to the 1790s, that have applied unexecuted treaties, including decisions the majority in *Medellín* purported not to disturb. The portions of the majority opinion purporting to require affirmative evidence of an intent to give the treaty domestic legal force are thus in conflict with the portions of the same opinion recognizing that "some international agreements are self-executing" and purporting not to disturb decisions enforcing

treaties that lack "provisions clearly according [them] domestic effect."

Carlos Manuel Vázquez, *Less Than Zero?*, 102 Am. J. Int'l L. 563, 570–71 (2008). In contrast, Curtis Bradley has suggested that:

> When a treaty provision expressly provides for legislative implementation or addresses a matter within the exclusive regulatory prerogatives of Congress (such as the appropriation of money), there is little dispute that it is non-self-executing. In other cases, the determination of whether a treaty provision is self-executing can depend on the phrasing and context of the provision.

In *Foster*, the Court concluded that a provision in a treaty between the United States and Spain stipulating that land grants made by Spain before the treaty "shall be ratified and confirmed" was non-self-executing because it was phrased in "the language of contract." The Court explained that "when the terms of the stipulation import a contract, when either of the parties engages to perform a particular act, the treaty addresses itself to the political, not the judicial department; and the legislature must execute the contract before it can become a rule for the Court." The Court later changed its mind about the effect of this treaty provision after examining the Spanish version, the English translation of which stated in relevant part that the prior land grants "shall remain ratified and confirmed." The Court nevertheless employed a text-centered approach in both instances.

As in *Foster*, the Court in *Medellín* focused heavily on the text of the relevant treaties in considering whether they were self-executing. In particular, the Court construed the phrase "undertakes to comply" in Article 94(1) of the United Nations Charter, a phrase that is addressed to potential ICJ judgments that may or may not be rendered with respect to a particular state, as not being "a directive to domestic courts." As the Court noted, Article 94(1) "does not provide that the United States 'shall' or 'must' comply with an ICJ decision, nor indicate that the Senate that ratified the U.N. Charter intended to vest ICJ decisions with immediate legal effect in domestic courts." The Court also observed that the remainder of Article 94, which provides for potential enforcement of ICJ decisions through the UN Security Council, "does not contemplate the automatic enforceability of ICJ decisions in domestic courts."

There is nothing new about treating future-oriented treaty language that is directed generically at the states parties rather than at their courts as suggestive of non-self-execution. The Supreme Court did precisely that in *Foster*, and lower courts have also pointed to future-oriented language as evidence of non-self-execution.

. . .

Although not a departure from Supreme Court precedent, the Court's approach to self-execution in *Medellín* is a departure to some extent from the approach that had been adopted by several lower courts starting in the 1970s. These courts had applied multifactored tests to evaluate whether a treaty or treaty provision was self-executing. . . . The dissenters in *Medellín* advocated something like this approach, pursuant to which courts would rely on "practical, context-specific criteria" in determining whether a treaty provision was self-executing. The Court rejected this multifactored inquiry on the grounds that it would be too indeterminate and would improperly "assign to the courts—not the political branches—the primary role in deciding when and how international agreements will be enforced."

At the same time, the difference between the multifactored approach and the majority's approach in *Medellín* should not be overstated. Many of the factors that the dissent in *Medellín* proposed for consideration, such as the subject matter of the treaty, the level of specificity of the treaty provision, and the views of the political branches, are likely to be relevant even under the majority's approach, which . . . looks to whether the president and the Senate intended the treaty to be self-executing. What the majority appears to have been objecting to was not these factors per se, but rather their application in a way that would render a treaty provision self-executing in some cases but not self-executing in others. The Court notes, for example, that "[i]t is hard to believe that the United States would enter into treaties that are sometimes enforceable [in U.S. courts] and sometimes not." A multifactored approach, however, could be applied more categorically, so that a treaty provision would be either self-executing or not in all cases, avoiding this concern.

Curtis A. Bradley, *Intent, Presumptions, and Non-Self-Executing Treaties*, 102 Am. J. Int'l L. 540, 541–43 (2008).

Which reading do you think more accurately captures the majority opinion in *Medellín*? How would you articulate the test for self-execution after this case? Both authors appear to resist the idea that *Medellín* requires textual evidence for self-execution within the treaty itself. Why do you think that is the case?

SKILLS EXERCISE

The United States is party to the United Nations Conference of International Commercial Arbitration Convention on the Recognition and Enforcement of Foreign Arbitral Awards. Review the following excerpt from the Convention. After *Medellín*, how would you determine whether this

Convention is self-executing? Is there other information you would need to consider beyond the text of the instrument?

Article I

1. This Convention shall apply to the recognition and enforcement of arbitral awards made in the territory of a State other than the State where the recognition and enforcement of such awards are sought, and arising out of differences between persons, whether physical or legal. It shall also apply to arbitral awards not considered as domestic awards in the State where their recognition and enforcement are sought.

2. The term "arbitral awards" shall include not only awards made by arbitrators appointed for each case but also those made by permanent arbitral bodies to which the parties have submitted.

3. When signing, ratifying or acceding to this Convention, or notifying extension under article X hereof, any State may on the basis of reciprocity declare that it will apply the Convention to the recognition and enforcement of awards made only in the territory of another Contracting State. It may also declare that it will apply the Convention only to differences arising out of legal relationships, whether contractual or not, which are considered as commercial under the national law of the State making such declaration.

Article II

1. Each Contracting State shall recognize an agreement in writing under which the parties undertake to submit to arbitration all or any differences which have arisen or which may arise between them in respect of a defined legal relationship, whether contractual or not, concerning a subject matter capable of settlement by arbitration.

2. The term "agreement in writing" shall include an arbitral clause in a contract or an arbitration agreement, signed by the parties or contained in an exchange of letters or telegrams.

3. The court of a Contracting State, when seized of an action in a matter in respect of which the parties have made an agreement within the meaning of this article, shall, at the request of one of the parties, refer the parties to arbitration, unless it finds that the said agreement is null and void, inoperative or incapable of being performed.

Article III

Each Contracting State shall recognize arbitral awards as binding and enforce them in accordance with the rules of procedure of the territory where the award is relied upon, under the conditions laid down in the following articles. There shall not be imposed substantially more onerous conditions or higher fees or charges on the recognition or enforcement of arbitral awards to which this Convention applies than are imposed on the recognition or enforcement of domestic arbitral awards.

Article IV

1.   To obtain the recognition and enforcement mentioned in the preceding article, the party applying for recognition and enforcement shall, at the time of the application, supply:

(a) The duly authenticated original award or a duly certified copy thereof;

(b) The original agreement referred to in article II or a duly certified copy thereof.

2.   If the said award or agreement is not made in an official language of the country in which the award is relied upon, the party applying for recognition and enforcement of the award shall produce a translation of these documents into such language. The translation shall be certified by an official or sworn translator or by a diplomatic or consular agent.

Article V

1.   Recognition and enforcement of the award may be refused, at the request of the party against whom it is invoked, only if that party furnishes to the competent authority where the recognition and enforcement is sought, proof that:

(a) The parties to the agreement referred to in article II were, under the law applicable to them, under some incapacity, or the said agreement is not valid under the law to which the parties have subjected it or, failing any indication thereon, under the law of the country where the award was made; or

(b) The party against whom the award is invoked was not given proper notice of the appointment of the arbitrator or of the arbitration proceedings or was otherwise unable to present his case; or

(c) The award deals with a difference not contemplated by or not falling within the terms of the submission to arbitration, or it contains decisions on matters beyond the scope of the submission to arbitration, provided that, if the decisions on matters submitted to arbitration can be separated from those not so submitted, that part of the award which contains decisions on matters submitted to arbitration may be recognized and enforced; or

(d) The composition of the arbitral authority or the arbitral procedure was not in accordance with the agreement of the parties, or, failing such agreement, was not in accordance with the law of the country where the arbitration took place; or

(e) The award has not yet become binding on the parties, or has been set aside or suspended by a competent authority of the country in which, or under the law of which, that award was made.

2.   Recognition and enforcement of an arbitral award may also be refused if the competent authority in the country where recognition and enforcement is sought finds that:

(a) The subject matter of the difference is not capable of settlement by arbitration under the law of that country; or

(b) The recognition or enforcement of the award would be contrary to the public policy of that country.

III.   IMPLEMENTING LEGISLATION

Even prior to *Medellín*, federal and state courts generally refused to enforce non-self-executing human rights treaties whether raised directly by plaintiffs in civil cases or defensively in criminal cases. Given that the United States has made an international commitment to these treaties, how can the federal government ensure that the rights that they protect are honored domestically? In *Medellín*, Chief Justice Roberts noted that Congress is capable of passing implementing legislation to give non-self-executing treaties domestic effect.[9] The question for this section is whether the Chief Justice is correct in this assertion. Are there any limitations on Congressional authority to pass legislation implementing a human rights treaty? And has Congress passed legislation that has been effective in domesticating the nation's human rights commitments?

A.   THE POWER TO IMPLEMENT

The scope of Congress's power to implement treaties was determined almost a century ago in *Missouri v. Holland*, which examined the constitutionality of a statute passed to ensure compliance with a treaty regulating the treatment of migratory birds. In the following excerpt, Professor McGuinness sets out the historical backdrop to this important decision. An excerpt from the *Missouri v. Holland* opinion follows.

MARGARET E. MCGUINNESS, "FOREWORD"
73 Mo. L. Rev. 921, 922–24 (2008).

The story behind the case [of *Missouri v. Holland*] begins with a classic collective action problem: regulating the hunting of migratory birds. When European settlers arrived on this continent hundreds of species of migratory birds dominated the North American skies. By the late 19th Century, the unregulated hunting of migratory birds for their meat and plumage (satisfying the then-high demand for feathers for

---

[9]   552 U.S. 491, 521–522 (2008).

women's millinery) had reduced populations of many species to desperately low levels. Migratory birds were especially vulnerable due to their habit of nesting in great numbers, making them an easy target for market hunters looking to take the highest quantity in the most efficient manner possible. The plight of the now-extinct Ectopistes migratorius, or passenger pigeon, is illustrative. They were once the most populous species of bird in North America; naturalists estimate that there were as many as five billion passenger pigeons in North America at the time of the arrival of the Europeans. They were so numerous that flocks of the migrating birds could stretch up to a mile wide and over 300 miles long, and were so densely clustered that they were reported to blot out the sun for hours or even days at a time. Yet, by the end of the 19th Century, passenger pigeons had been hunted to the brink of extinction.

Prior to 1900, no federal law regulated the capture of migratory birds. Instead, a patchwork of state and territorial laws regulated bird hunting and resale. The states and territories faced a classic tragedy of the commons. Bird hunting filled a commercial need, which incentivized states to permit capture and incentivized hunters to violate or evade the hunting rules in other states. Absent coordination of hunting rules among the states and territories, overhunting was leading to near-extinction of some bird populations, including insectivorous species essential to agriculture. The movement for national regulation started from the ground up, with state game officials finding common cause with state and national conservation organizations and sportsmen's organizations (forefathers of the modern environmental NGOs). They were joined by the Department of Agriculture, which was increasingly focused on the devastating effect of the depletion of insectivorous birds on crop yields.

The result of this alignment of interests was the Lacey Act of 1900, which made it illegal to engage in interstate transport of birds or wildlife taken in violation of state or territorial law. The weak enforcement provisions of the Lacey Act, however, proved inadequate to the task. Congress got tougher with the passage of the Weeks-McLean law of 1913, which deemed all migratory game and insectivorous birds that passed through the borders of any state or territory to be within the custody of the U.S. Government, and prohibited the destruction or taking of those migratory species. As many of its proponents feared would happen, two federal courts declared the Weeks-McLean statute unconstitutional as outside Congress' enumerated powers, and rejected, in accordance with Court precedent at the time, the argument that regulation of game found within the borders of a State could be accomplished through the Commerce Clause. By that time, Senator Elihu Root—who just a few years earlier had founded the American Society of International Law— had suggested the use of a treaty as a solution to any constitutional infirmities. In reaction to these court decisions, the United States negotiated and the Senate approved the Migratory Bird Treaty with Great Britain, acting on behalf of Canada, in 1916. Congress passed the implementing statute—the Migratory Bird Treaty Act—in 1918, and President Woodrow Wilson signed the Act in July of that year. The Act prohibited the hunting, killing, or subsequent sale or shipment of the birds protected by the Migratory Bird Treaty.

Later that year President Wilson set sail for the Paris Peace conference with a new adviser in tow, a young native Missourian and law professor from the University of Missouri named Manley O. Hudson. Hudson would go on to teach at Harvard, replace former Secretary of State Frank Billings Kellogg as justice on the League of Nation's Permanent Court of International Justice, and advise the drafters of the UN Charter and the Statute of the International Court of Justice. As the peace negotiations opened in Paris (promising, not for the last time, a new world order under international law) opponents of the new Weeks-McLean law, which included commercial hunters and some avid recreational hunters concerned about federal oversight of their sport, looked for a challenge. They found it when the federal game warden, Ray Holland, arrested and indicted some Missourians caught with ducks hunted out of season for violating the new statute.

The State of Missouri sought to enjoin further action by Holland. The federal district court of the Western District of Missouri dismissed Missouri's application for an injunction, and in so doing remarked that, without the treaty, the Act would have been unconstitutional. It is from this opinion that the State of Missouri appealed to the Supreme Court. The Court upheld the treaty and the implementing statute by a vote of 7–2.

. . .

STATE OF MISSOURI V. HOLLAND

Supreme Court of the United States, 1920.
252 U.S. 416.

MR. JUSTICE HOLMES delivered the opinion of the Court.

This is a bill in equity brought by the State of Missouri to prevent a game warden of the United States from attempting to enforce the Migratory Bird Treaty Act of July 3, 1918, . . . and the regulations made by the Secretary of Agriculture in pursuance of the same. The ground of the bill is that the statute is an unconstitutional interference with the rights reserved to the States by the Tenth Amendment, and that the acts of the defendant done and threatened under that authority invade the sovereign right of the State and contravene its will manifested in statutes. The State also alleges a pecuniary interest, as owner of the wild birds within its borders and otherwise, admitted by the Government to be sufficient, but it is enough that the bill is a reasonable and proper means to assert the alleged quasi sovereign rights of a State. A motion to dismiss was sustained by the District Court on the ground that the Act of Congress is constitutional. The State appeals.

On December 8, 1916, a treaty between the United States and Great Britain was proclaimed by the President. It recited that many species of birds in their annual migrations traversed many parts of the United States and of Canada, that they were of great value as a source of food and in destroying insects injurious to vegetation, but were in danger of extermination through lack of adequate protection. It therefore provided for specified closed seasons and protection in other forms, and agreed that the two powers would take or propose to their lawmaking bodies the necessary measures for carrying the treaty out. The above mentioned act of July 3, 1918, entitled an act to give effect to the convention, prohibited the killing, capturing or selling any of the migratory birds included in the terms of the treaty except as permitted by regulations compatible with those terms, to be made by the Secretary of Agriculture. Regulations were proclaimed on July 31, and October 25, 1918. It is unnecessary to go into any details, because, as we have said, the question raised is the general one whether the treaty and statute are void as an interference with the rights reserved to the States.

To answer this question it is not enough to refer to the Tenth Amendment, reserving the powers not delegated to the United States, because by Article 2, Section 2, the power to make treaties is delegated expressly, and by Article 6 treaties made under the authority of the United States, along with the Constitution and laws of the United States made in pursuance thereof, are declared the supreme law of the land. If the treaty is valid there can be no dispute about the validity of the statute under Article 1, Section 8, as a necessary and proper means to execute the powers of the Government. The language of the Constitution as to the supremacy of treaties being general, the question before us is narrowed to an inquiry into the ground upon which the present supposed exception is placed.

It is said that a treaty cannot be valid if it infringes the Constitution, that there are limits, therefore, to the treaty-making power, and that one such limit is that what an act of Congress could not do unaided, in derogation of the powers reserved to the States, a treaty cannot do. An earlier act of Congress that attempted by itself and not in pursuance of a treaty to regulate the killing of migratory birds within the States had been held bad in the District Court. Those decisions were supported by arguments that migratory birds were owned by the States in their sovereign capacity for the benefit of their people, and that under cases like *Geer v. Connecticut*, . . . this control was one that Congress had no power to displace. The same argument is supposed to apply now with equal force.

Whether the two cases cited were decided rightly or not they cannot be accepted as a test of the treaty power. Acts of Congress are the supreme law of the land only when made in pursuance of the Constitution, while treaties are declared to be so when made under the authority of the United States. It is open to question whether the authority of the United States means more than the formal acts prescribed to make the convention. We do not mean to imply that there are no qualifications to the treaty-making power; but they must be ascertained in a different way. It is obvious that there may be matters of the sharpest exigency for the national well being that an act of Congress could not deal with but that a treaty followed by such an act could, and it is not lightly to be assumed that, in matters requiring national action, 'a power which must belong to and somewhere reside in every civilized government' is not to be found. What was said in that case with regard to the powers of the States applies with equal force to the powers of the nation in cases where the States individually are incompetent to act. We are not yet discussing the particular case before us but only are considering the validity of the test proposed. With regard to that we may add that when we are dealing with words that also are a constituent act, like the Constitution of the United States, we must realize that they have called into life a being the development of which could not have been foreseen completely by the most gifted of its begetters. It was enough for them to realize or to hope that they had created an organism; it has taken a century and has cost their successors much sweat and blood to prove that they created a nation. The case before us must be considered in the light of our whole experience and not merely in that of what was said a hundred years ago. The treaty in question does not contravene any prohibitory words to be found in the Constitution. The only question is whether it is forbidden by some invisible radiation from the general terms of the Tenth Amendment. We must consider what this country has become in deciding what that amendment has reserved.

The State as we have intimated founds its claim of exclusive authority upon an assertion of title to migratory birds, an assertion that is embodied in statute. No doubt it is true that as between a State and its inhabitants the State may regulate the killing and sale of such birds, but it does not follow that its authority is exclusive of paramount powers. To put the claim of the State upon title is to lean upon a slender reed. Wild birds are not in the possession of anyone; and possession is the beginning of ownership. The whole foundation of the State's rights is the presence within their jurisdiction of birds that yesterday had not arrived, tomorrow may be in another State and in a week a thousand miles away. If we are to be accurate we cannot put the case of the State upon higher ground than that the treaty deals with creatures that for the moment are within the state borders, that it must be carried out by officers of the

United States within the same territory, and that but for the treaty the State would be free to regulate this subject itself.

As most of the laws of the United States are carried out within the States and as many of them deal with matters which in the silence of such laws the State might regulate, such general grounds are not enough to support Missouri's claim. Valid treaties of course 'are as binding within the territorial limits of the States as they are elsewhere throughout the dominion of the United States.' No doubt the great body of private relations usually fall within the control of the State, but a treaty may override its power.

. . .

Here a national interest of very nearly the first magnitude is involved. It can be protected only by national action in concert with that of another power. The subject matter is only transitorily within the State and has no permanent habitat therein. But for the treaty and the statute there soon might be no birds for any powers to deal with. We see nothing in the Constitution that compels the Government to sit by while a food supply is cut off and the protectors of our forests and our crops are destroyed. It is not sufficient to rely upon the States. The reliance is vain, and were it otherwise, the question is whether the United States is forbidden to act. We are of opinion that the treaty and statute must be upheld.

Decree affirmed.

———

The *Holland* decision prompted a domestic backlash. Critics of the decision were concerned that its expansive interpretation of the treaty power posed a threat to American federalism. *Holland* appeared to give the federal government the ability to evade any limits placed on its domestic powers by linking its legislation to an international treaty. These concerns were heightened when a state court in California invalidated California's Alien Land Law, which prohibited aliens ineligible for citizenship from owning agricultural land, as inconsistent with the U.N. Charter's human rights and non-discrimination provisions. In *Sei Fujii*, the state court reasoned that "[t]he position of this country in the family of nations . . . demands that every State in the Union accept and act upon the [U.N.] Charter according to its plain language and its unmistakable purpose and intent," and thus concluded that the treaty invalidated the conflicting state law.[10]

Although *Sei Fujii* was eventually overturned, the decision added to the fears that the treaty power would be used to threaten the rights of

---

[10] Sei Fujii v. State, 217 P.2d 481 (Cal. Dist. Ct. App. 1950).

states. As we saw in **Chapter II** and earlier in this chapter, in the 1950s, a series of proposals were introduced that would have amended the Constitution to limit the treaty powers. Collectively, the proposals were referred to as the "Bricker Amendment" after Senator John W. Bricker in 1951, who along with leaders of the American Bar Association, was a key proponent of the measure. During the first hearings on the amendment, Senator Bricker explained that "[t]he primary purpose of [the Amendment] is to prohibit the use of the treaty as an instrument of domestic legislation for surrendering national sovereignty."[11] As discussed in **Chapter II**, some commentators have suggested, however, that the Amendment supporters were primarily concerned about the impact that adoption of the U.N. human rights conventions could have on the practices of racial segregation in the Southern States.

The proposed constitutional amendments failed, although one version came within a single vote of Senate approval. In order to ensure that the measure was defeated, the Eisenhower Administration agreed not move forward with ratification of any of the human rights instruments. Concern about the scope of the treaty power also faded when, during in the New Deal era, the Supreme Court adopted an expansive reading of Congress's commerce and other powers. Because the federal government's domestic lawmaking powers were so broad, defining and limiting the scope of the treaty power became less important.

In the last two decades, however, the Supreme Court has demonstrated a renewed willingness to enforce limitations on Congress's domestic powers, particularly with respect to regulation of the states. In *United States v. Lopez*,[12] the Court for the first time in decades invalidated a federal statute on the grounds that it exceeded Congressional authority under the Commerce Clause. Two years later, the Court found that the Religious Freedom Restoration Act exceeded Congress's remedial powers under the Fourteenth Amendment.[13] Following these and the subsequent "New Federalism" cases, a number of prominent scholars have argued that Congress's implementing powers under the treaty power should be subject to these same limitations. The excerpt from Professor Bradley below makes this argument.

---

[11] Treaties and Executive Agreements: Hearing on S.J. Res. 130 Before a Subcomm. of the Senate Comm. on the Judiciary, 82d Cong. 1 (1952) (statement of Sen. John Bricker).

[12] 514 U.S. 549 (1995).

[13] *See* City of Boerne v. Flores, 521 U.S. 507 (1997).

CURTIS A. BRADLEY, "THE TREATY POWER AND AMERICAN FEDERALISM"

97 Mich. L. Rev. 390, 450–61 (1998).

Historically, it often was assumed that the treaty power was appropriate only for certain externally oriented subjects. As the distinction between foreign and domestic affairs wanes, however, it becomes increasingly difficult to maintain any meaningful subject matter limitation. As a result, I argue that it makes more sense today to focus on structural federalism limitations on the treaty power, and, for a variety of reasons, I argue that the treaty power should be subject to the same federalism limitations that apply to Congress's legislative powers. In other words, my argument is that the federal government should not be able to use the treaty power (or executive agreement power) to create domestic law that could not be created by Congress.

. . .

A. Reviving a Subject Matter Limitation

One option for protecting federalism in this context would be to revive a subject matter limitation on the treaty power.

. . .

There are two possibilities here. The first would be to limit the treaty power to matters usually the subject of treaties at the time the Constitution was adopted. This was one of the limitations suggested by Jefferson. This suggested limitation has never received much acceptance, however. Moreover, as a policy matter, this limitation would seem to be highly undesirable. Not only would it exclude U.S. participation in human rights treaties, it also would presumably exclude U.S. participation in treaties relating to the environment, terrorism, and private international law, to name a few subjects. Moreover, it is doubtful that this limitation could be justified even under a strict originalist interpretation of the Constitution. There is no evidence that the Founders intended the treaty power to be frozen to 1780s issues, and the inflexibility such a limitation would impose on the national government makes it highly unlikely that the Founders would have had such an intent. And, of course, other constitutional powers—such as the commerce power—have not been limited in this fashion.

The other possibility would be to limit the treaty power to matters that are truly "international" in nature. . . . Although this approach may deserve further exploration, it suffers from a substantial problem: Today, almost any issue can plausibly be labeled "international." Given the globalization of trade, technology, and travel, among other things, nations are indisputably connected to each other in a variety of ways. As a result, "domestic" actions by nations are often matters of concern to the international community. As Professor Tribe has observed, "[w]ith global interdependence reaching across an ever broadening spectrum of issues," any requirement that the treaty power be restricted to matters of international concern "seems unlikely to prove a serious limitation."

This may be true even in the area of human rights. Human rights is, of course, a matter today of international negotiation and agreement. Unlike some proponents of the nationalist view, I do not find that fact alone dispositive of the question whether this subject falls within the scope of the federal government's treaty power. If it were dispositive, it would mean that the federal government's power in this regard would be determined entirely by the international community rather than by domestic-law standards, something at odds with this country's "dualist" approach to international law. Nevertheless, it is difficult to dispute that, in this day and age, how one nation treats its citizens has international effects. These effects may be direct and physical—for example, an influx of refugees, or instability in the region. Or they may be more abstract and emotional—for example, a sense of moral outrage, or an empathetic loss. Anyone who has observed recent events in Tiananmen Square, Somalia, or Rwanda will find it difficult to deny the existence of such effects.

But perhaps a focus on effects is not the right test. Another test would be a focus on need. The question here might be whether the issue requires international cooperation in order to be addressed. This is, after all, how the Court described the migratory bird treaty at issue in *Holland*. Under this test, human rights treaties might be suspect, since their implementation involves action by individual governments within their territories rather than cooperative action. But this line is fuzzy at best. It is arguable that there is in fact a demonstrable need for cooperative international action to address even "domestic" issues such as human rights. Without reciprocal agreements, along with international monitoring and other enforcement mechanisms, many nations might well continue to engage in human rights abuses. Perhaps treaties are required to obtain results even here. To be sure, the proliferation of human rights treaties has not eliminated human rights abuses in the countries that have ratified them, but it is certainly possible that it has helped improve conditions.

In any event, even if there were a workable distinction in theory between international and domestic matters, it seems unlikely that U.S. courts would feel competent to contradict the political branches on this issue. It is far from clear, for example, what standard the courts could use to draw such a line.

. . .

[T]he line between what is domestic and what is international is difficult to define, the scope of what can plausibly be labeled international has grown substantially in recent years, and courts as a result are unlikely to restrict the treaty power much, if at all, based on this distinction. If federalism is to be protected in the treaty context, another approach must be found.

B. Parity with Federal Legislation

Another option for protecting federalism, and the option I favor, would be to subject the treaty power to the same federalism restrictions that apply to Congress's legislative powers. Under this approach, the treaty power would not confer any additional regulatory powers on the federal government, just the power to bind the United States on the international plane. Thus, for example, it could not be used to resurrect legislation determined by the Supreme Court to be beyond Congress's legislative powers.

. . .

[T]here are several conceptual and doctrinal reasons why it may make sense today to subject treaties to the same federalism limitations as federal statutes. First, unlike traditional treaties that were generally bilateral and addressed the relations between nations, both the form and substance of modern treaty law resembles domestic legislation. As discussed above, treaty law today regulates the relations between nations and their citizens, it covers many of the same subjects as domestic law, and it is even made in a kind of legislative way, through mechanisms such as multilateral drafting conferences.

Second, as the Restatement (Second) of Foreign Relations Law recognized, the immunity of the treaty power from states'-rights limitations is premised on the existence of a meaningful distinction between the foreign and the domestic. Yet proponents of the nationalist view themselves, probably correctly, deny that we can continue to make this distinction. Once that is denied, however, there is a much stronger case, based upon the limited and enumerated powers doctrine, for subjecting the treaty power to the same limitations that apply to other federal law.

Third, there is strong doctrinal support for the equal treatment of federal statutes and treaties. Since at least the late 1800s, the Supreme Court has consistently held that treaties and federal statutes have an equal status in the U.S. system, such that, in the case of a conflict, the last in time is the controlling domestic law. This well-settled equality of treaties and federal statutes supports treating them as equal as well for federalism purposes. As the Supreme Court has observed, its decisions "generally have regarded treaties as on much the same plane as acts of Congress, and as usually subject to the general limitations in the Constitution." Indeed, not treating them the same with respect to federalism limitations presents a doctrinal puzzle: If treaties can be made that go beyond what Congress could do pursuant to its legislative powers, then what happens to Congress's ability to supersede the treaty with subsequent legislation? As William Mikell explained many years ago:

> If, however, a treaty were made which affected the reserved rights of the states, it is, to say the least, doubtful if such a treaty could be abrogated at all without the consent of the President, for Congress having no power to pass a law, affecting the reserved rights of the states, could enact no law either in affirmance or derogation of the treaty.

. . .

In sum, there is a strong case—based on history, doctrine, and policy—for subjecting the treaty power to the same federalism limitations that apply to Congress's legislative powers. This approach would involve overruling some of the reasoning in *Holland*, but that reasoning has become questionable in light of changes in both the nature of treaty-making and the scope of federal legislative power . . . Importantly, this proposal would not interfere substantially with the treaty power. It might preclude some of the broadest intrusions on state power, . . . , but it would leave the political branches with substantial flexibility to conclude and implement international agreements in the national interest.

. . .

NOTES & QUESTIONS

1.   Are you persuaded by Professor Bradley's argument that it is important to impose federalism limitations on the treaty power? Does history suggest that it is necessary? In a recent article, Professor Oona A. Hathaway and her co-authors argued that these legal limits are unnecessary because there are already mechanisms in place that prevent federal abuse of the treaty power. They explain:

> The Treaty Clause has served its purpose—perhaps too well. It has prevented the passage of all but a handful of Article II treaties each year since the Founding. The political, structural, and diplomatic checks that the Framers put in place have served to create a system of federal accommodation that does not require intervention by the courts. Top-down federalism accommodates federalism concerns through self-restraint by the federal government institutions. The President and the Senate actively work to accommodate federalism concerns by rejecting treaties that would impinge on state prerogatives, modifying treaties to address federalism concerns, providing for state implementation of treaties, and by declining to compel state agencies to carry out treaty obligations. This operates alongside bottom-up federalism—accommodation of federalism

concerns by states that play a direct and active role in shaping the international lawmaking process. In a variety of areas, states have been on the front lines of implementing treaties and thus played an active role in their interpretation and in determining when and how the treaty will affect the states.

Oona A. Hathaway, Spencer Amdur, Celia Choy, Samir Deger-Sen, John Paredes, Sally Pei & Haley Nix Proctor, *The Treaty Power: Its History, Scope, and Limits*, 98 Cornell L. Rev. 239, 325 (2013).

2.   The scope of both the Treaty Power and Congress's authority under the Necessary and Proper Clause came before the Supreme Court again in the 2013–2014 term in *Bond v. United States*, 134 S. Ct. 2077 (2014). After learning that her best friend was pregnant and that her own husband of fourteen years was the father, Carol Ann Bond sought revenge. A trained microbiologist, Bond spread mixtures of toxic chemicals on her former friend's mail, mailbox, car door, and other surfaces. Eventually caught in the act by postal inspectors' surveillance cameras, Bond was charged with two counts of possessing and using a chemical weapon in violation of 18 U.S.C. § 229(a)(1), the federal criminal statute enacted to implement the United States' treaty obligations under the 1993 Chemical Weapons Convention. Bond responded to the charges in part by arguing that the treaty could not constitutionally give the federal government the power to criminalize purely domestic or "local" acts. Citing *Missouri v. Holland*, a unanimous panel on the Third Circuit Court of Appeals rejected Bond's claim.

Bond petitioned for *certiorari*, arguing *inter alia* that treaty implementing legislation "is subject to the same basic constraints and rules of construction as other federal legislation" and inviting the Court to overrule *Holland*. Brief for Petitioner, *Bond v. United States*, 2013 WL 1963862 *38 (2013). A group of former State Department Legal Advisers filed an *amicus* brief, arguing that adopting Bond's view of the Treaty power would undermine the United States' foreign policy.

The national government is responsible for the United States' compliance with all treaties. The Framers of the Constitution provided a centralized treaty power specifically to ensure that the United States would be capable of implementing and complying with its international obligations. . . .

Petitioner's brief ignores the important role of treaty compliance in the President's management of foreign affairs. Unless the federal government has ample authority to ensure compliance with treaties, the President cannot effectively conduct foreign policy and present the United States as "one nation . . . in respect to other nations."

In order to fulfill its international obligations, the federal government must have the ability to implement treaties. Many treaties are not self-executing. States may fail to pass or enforce necessary legislation, and the federal government cannot require states to do so. As a result, the interest of full compliance sometimes compels the United States to implement a treaty through federal measures.

Nowhere is the importance of federal legislation more evident than in U.S. efforts to combat the international drug trade. Stopping the sale of illicit narcotics has been among the United States' most important foreign relations priorities for decades. In a concerted effort to limit the international production and supply of certain dangerous drugs, the United States joined the 1961 Single Convention on Narcotic Drugs, . . . ; the 1971 Convention on Psychotropic Substances, Feb. 21, 1971, . . . ; and the 1988 Convention Against Illicit Traffic in Narcotic Drugs and Psychotropic Substances, . . . Congress enacted the Controlled Substances Act, in large part to implement U.S. obligations under the 1961 Convention . . . Since then, Congress periodically has enacted new legislation to implement other obligations under subsequent conventions related to narcotics. The United States relies on these federal statutes to remain in compliance with international agreements.

Federal implementing legislation is particularly important in light of recent state referenda decriminalizing marijuana, a drug that is outlawed by international conventions. Thus, federal implementing legislation serves as an essential backstop that saves the United States from non-compliance with its treaty obligations. Were the United States to fail to comply with the international narcotics conventions that it has long championed, the United States would have little basis to complain if other countries failed to satisfy their own obligations.

. . .

Many U.S. treaty obligations require not only federal implementing legislation but also federal enforcement. The Convention on the Prohibition of the Development, Production, Stockpiling and Use of Chemical Weapons and on their Destruction is one such example. Where states decline to prosecute the use of chemical weapons, the federal government may need to enforce the Chemical Weapons Convention Implementation Act, in order to protect national interests. Just as drug sales may pose national or international concerns, so may the use of chemical weapons. And the greater the opportunity for individuals to use chemical weapons with impunity, the greater the opportunity for terrorists to learn about and use chemical weapons themselves.

Moreover, treaty compliance is a two-way street. If the use of chemical weapons goes unenforced here in the U.S., then the nation loses critical leverage should Pakistan, for example, decline to fulfill its obligations under the Chemical Weapons Convention to investigate and prosecute arguably "local" conduct in its autonomous tribal regions. The same is true for numerous other important national security treaty implementing regimes.

Conduct that may appear to be purely "local" when viewed in isolation can actually have a much broader impact. The federal government is better positioned than the states to appreciate the national and international consequences of certain law enforcement actions. And it is the political branches—not the courts—that have the competence to set national and foreign policy.

Brief of Former State Dep't Legal Advisers as Amici Curiae in Support of Respondents at *5–9, *Bond v. United States*, 134 S.Ct. 373 (2013) (No. 12–158), 2013 WL 4518602.

The *Bond* Court ultimately declined to reach the constitutional question regarding the scope of the Treaty Power and Congress' authority under the Necessary and Proper Clause to enact implementing legislation touching on issues traditionally within the jurisdiction of state and local government. Writing for the Court, Chief Justice Roberts noted an ambiguity in the scope of the Chemical Convention Implementation Act and turned to what he characterized as the "well-established" principle that courts must find that Congress intended to override the traditional state/federal balance before construing an otherwise ambiguous statute to do so. Concluding that there was no "clear indication" that Congress intended the Act to cover Bond's "purely local" crime, the Court held that the Act did not cover Ms. Bond's conduct. Justices Alito, Scalia, and Thomas concurred only in the Court's judgment. Each wrote separately to argue for narrower limits on the scope of the Treaty Power and Congress' authority under the Necessary and Proper Clause.

B. DESIGNING IMPLEMENTING LEGISLATION

Despite the broad grant of legislative authority authorized by *Missouri v. Holland*, Congress has only passed implementing legislation for two of the major human rights treaties, the Genocide Convention and the Convention Against Torture. However, even these statutes have been criticized for their failure to fully realize the commitments the United States made when ratifying these instruments. In the excerpt below, Professor Venetis highlights the challenges posed by human rights implementation legislation through an examination of the Convention Against Torture.

PENNY M. VENETIS, "MAKING HUMAN RIGHTS TREATY LAW
ACTIONABLE IN THE UNITED STATES: THE CASE FOR
UNIVERSAL IMPLEMENTING LEGISLATION"
63 Ala. L. Rev. 97, 119–30 (2011).

The United States ... enacted implementing legislation for the Convention Against Torture (CAT), but in a piecemeal package that has watered down the treaty. Like other human rights treaties ratified by the United States, the CAT was ratified in 1994 with multiple RUDs, including a non-self-executing reservation covering Articles 1–16. Those RUDs nullify the treaty's obligations and language.

Despite the CAT's comprehensive nature and unequivocal message that torture violates fundamental human rights, the CAT's implementing legislation is so weak that over a decade after it was ratified by the United States, our government was engaged in a serious debate over whether U.S. operatives could torture while engaged in the "War on Terror."

. . .

The greater majority of the CAT is dedicated to fleshing out the obligations of state parties. The treaty's provisions ... place strong burdens on the treaty's parties to eradicate torture [requiring state parties to take effective action to prevent acts of torture, to criminalize acts of torture within its legal system, to fully investigate allegations of torture, and to offer victims of torture fair compensation].

. . .

Unlike other international agreements or public declarations prohibiting torture, Article 1 of CAT actually provides a general definition of torture:

> [A]ny act by which severe pain or suffering, whether physical or mental, is intentionally inflicted on a person for such purposes as obtaining from him or a third person information or a confession, punishing him for an act he or a third person has committed or is suspected of having committed, or intimidating or coercing him or a third person, or for any reason based on discrimination of any kind, when such pain or suffering is inflicted by or at the instigation of or with the consent or acquiescence of a public official or other person acting in an official capacity. It does not include pain or suffering arising only from, inherent in or incidental to lawful sanctions.

Actions falling short of this definition may constitute cruel, inhumane, or degrading treatment outlined in Article 16 of the treaty. Under Articles 1 and 4 of the CAT, the definition of torture, as the working definition of the treaty, must be written into the criminal codes of State parties.

Articles 4 and 5 respectively require State parties to "ensure that all acts of torture are offences under its criminal law" and "take such measures as may be necessary to establish its jurisdiction over [these] offences."

Thus, as a state party, the United States must "ensure that all acts of torture are offences under its criminal law," as required by Article 4 in these following jurisdictions specified by Article 5:

(a) When the offences are committed in any territory under its jurisdiction or on board a ship or aircraft registered in that State;

(b) When the alleged offender is a national of that State;

(c) When the victim is a national of that State if that State considers it appropriate.

Yet, Congress ignored these directives and did not enact legislation criminalizing torture in the United States. Instead, Congress presumed that acts that would violate CAT would already "be covered by existing applicable federal and state statutes." For example, statutes criminalizing assault, manslaughter, and murder were thought to put the United States in compliance, at least nominally.

But these domestic criminal provisions, while punishing specific crimes that a torturer might commit while torturing, do not explicitly punish torture. This is significant. By failing to implement all provisions of the CAT domestically, Congress left open the question of whether torture itself was illegal. Congress never explicitly outlawed torture as a crime inside the United States, even though the treaty requires state parties to "ensure that all acts of torture are offences under its criminal law."

. . .

[This gap between CAT and its implementing legislation was exposed during the War on Terror.] The infamous, top-secret "Torture Memos" drafted by John Yoo and signed by Jay Bybee during 2002–2005 are now public knowledge. The memos, which served the basis for a professional misconduct probe of their drafters by Attorney General Eric Holder, Jr. five years later, depict an administration worried about breaking the law.

Specifically, the memos sought to answer whether "certain [enhanced] interrogation methods," namely waterboarding, violated the Federal Torture Statute, 18 U.S.C. §§ 2340–2340B. Unfortunately, the Federal Torture Statute does not implement, verbatim, the CAT's definition of torture. CAT's strong language broadly condemns intentionally inflicted "severe pain or suffering, whether physical or mental" for purposes of obtaining information or a confession. The Federal Torture Statute does not adopt this definition, but rather, itemizes the definition of "severe mental pain or suffering." As clarified by the fourth Torture Memo (a letter from John Yoo to then-Attorney General Alberto Gonzalez), the definition of torture in CAT need not apply, because a U.S. reservation to CAT adopts the language of the Federal Torture Statute.

More important, however, is how the Torture Memos relied on a U.S. reservation to CAT regarding the requisite mens rea. Similar to the Genocide Convention, CAT requires the torturer to have "general intent," whereas the U.S. reservation requires "specific intent." Because of the heightened mens rea requirement, a Memo concludes that "even if the defendant knows that severe pain will result from his actions, if causing such harm is not his objective, he lacks the requisite specific intent." Thus, according to the Torture Memos, a suspect can be waterboarded 183 times in one month (nearly six times a day), if causing harm is "not [the] objective." In fact, one of the Memos "discuss[ed] the potential [for] the President to approve the maiming, drugging or applying 'scalding water, corrosive acid or caustic substance' on detainees."

After declassification and public release of the Torture Memos, Congress sought to formulate specific detainee interrogation practices and debated whether to make torture illegal. Even the outspoken torture critic, Senator John McCain, who was tortured at the "Hanoi Hilton" during the Vietnam War, sided with the Bush administration and voted not to restrict CIA interrogation methods that, under any honest interpretation, constitute torture. Other congressional representatives publicly condemned the use of torture generally, but backed CIA interrogation methods, like waterboarding, with full knowledge that the United States prosecuted Japanese soldiers for torture in World War II for similar acts.

. . .

This embarrassing and shameful national debate about whether torture is or should be illegal could not take place if the CAT had been ratified and fully implemented into the legal infrastructure of the United States. The world had already defined torture in the CAT. The United States' non-self-executing RUD allowed Congress to redefine it, and water it down to such a level that permitted the Abu Ghraib and other similar atrocities to take place without significant legal repercussions.

For these reasons alone it is necessary to enact comprehensive, universal legislation to implement U.S. treaty obligations. That legislation must fully incorporate human rights treaties (as they were negotiated and worded with other nations) into the U.S. legal infrastructure. As shown by the haphazard implementation of the . . . Convention Against Torture, leaving it to Congress to enact implementing legislation for each treaty allows Congress to alter each treaty significantly, and to handpick only portions of the already-negotiated treaties for implementation.

. . .

NOTES & QUESTIONS

1.   Why do you think that the Genocide Convention and the CAT are the only U.N. human rights treaties to have been domestically enforced through implementing legislation? What accounts for the divergence between the treaty instruments and the implementing legislation that Congress passed to enforce the Genocide Convention and the CAT?

2.   How would you design implementing legislation for the ICCPR and CERD, given the problems that Professor Venetis describes with the CAT implementing legislation? What challenges would you face in translating these instruments into domestic law?

C. CASE STUDY: THE HAITIAN REFUGEE LITIGATION

The law of asylum is one of the most international areas of U.S. national law, with significant human rights implications. The major international treaty governing the treatment of refugees is the 1951 United Nations Convention Relating to the Status of Refugees. The Convention defines a "refugee" as a person who "owing to a well-founded fear of being persecuted for reasons of race, religion, nationality, membership of a particular social group or political opinion" is unable or unwilling to return to the country of his or her nationality. Convention Relating to the Status of Refugees, July 28, 1951, art. 1(A)(2), 19 U.S.T. 6259, 6261 (entered into force Apr. 22, 1954) The Convention was adopted in response to the horrors of World War II and restricted the definition of "refugee" to those who became refugees prior to January 1, 1951. In 1967, a new Protocol Relating to the Status of Refugees (Protocol) came into force, which obligated states to apply the substantive protections of the Convention to refugees without geographical or temporal limitation. *See* Protocol Relating to the Status of Refugees, Jan. 31, 1967, 19 U.S.T. 6223 (entered into force Oct. 4, 1967). Although the United States has never ratified the Convention, its ratification of the Protocol means that the nation is required to comply with the substantive provisions of the Convention. The cornerstone of the Convention is Article 33, which prohibits "refoulement"—the return of a person to a place where s/he faces persecution. The protection against refoulement applies except when the person poses a threat to national security or the safety of the community.

In 1980, Congress passed the Refugee Act to implement the United States' obligations under the Convention. The legislative history of the Refugee Act explicitly acknowledges the Congress' intent to bring national law into conformity with international law, specifically with respect to Article 1 (refugee status) and Article 33 of the Convention. The House Judiciary Committee described the amendments as necessary to ensure "that U.S. statutory law clearly reflects our legal obligations under international agreements."[14]

Despite its international underpinnings, American refugee law does not always conform to the treaty regime. As noted by Professor Joan Fitzpatrick, "[a]djudicators adhere to no consistent methodology to conform domestic and international law, and they sometimes display appalling disregard for the fundamental premises of refugee protection. The gap between available domestic protection and the imperatives of international obligation results in a serious denial of justice to many asylum-seekers."[15]

Why has this gap developed between the protections offered by the domestic and international legal regimes? In *Sale v. Haitian Centers Council*,[16] the United States Supreme Court was asked to determine whether an Executive Order authorizing the Coast Guard to repatriate all fleeing Haitians detained on the high seas violated either domestic or international law. The *Sale* case has a lengthy and interesting history. On September 30, 1991, Jean Bertrand Aristide, the first democratically elected president in Haitian history, was deposed in a military coup. Following the coup, hundreds of Haitians were subject to persecution because of their political beliefs and thousands were forced in hiding. In subsequent months, the United States Coast Guard interdicted over 34,000 Haitians attempting to flee the country. The Department of Defense created temporary facilities at the United States Naval Base in Guantánamo, Cuba, to accommodate the detained Haitians while they were screened for full eligibility for refugee status. The facilities were limited, however, and soon overwhelmed. On May 22, 1992, the United States Navy determined that no additional migrants could safely be accommodated at Guantánamo.

With the number of detained Haitians increasing and the facilities at Guantánamo filled to capacity, President George H.W. Bush issued an Executive Order stating that the U.S. government would no longer conduct even a limited screening process to determine whether the detained Haitians were eligible for refugee status. The *Sale* litigation challenged the legality of that decision under the Refugee Act and the Protocol. It was litigated by Professor Harold Hongju Koh and the students of the Allard K. Lowenstein International Human Rights Clinic

---

[14] H.R. Rep. No. 96–608, at 18 (1979).

[15] Joan Fitzpatrick, *The International Dimension of U.S. Refugee Law*, 15 Berkeley J. Int'l Law 1, 3 (1997).

[16] 509 U.S. 155 (1993).

at Yale Law School, in partnership with attorneys from both private law firms and national civil rights organizations.[17]

As you read the opinion below, consider how the Court weighs and weights the different sources of authority when interpreting the Immigration and Nationality Act and the Convention.

SALE V. HAITIAN CENTERS COUNCIL, INC.
Supreme Court of the United States, 1993.
509 U.S. 155.

JUSTICE STEVENS delivered the opinion of the Court.

The President has directed the Coast Guard to intercept vessels illegally transporting passengers from Haiti to the United States and to return those passengers to Haiti without first determining whether they may qualify as refugees. The question presented in this case is whether such forced repatriation, "authorized to be undertaken only beyond the territorial sea of the United States," violates § 243(h)(1) of the Immigration and Nationality Act of 1952 (INA or Act). We hold that neither § 243(h) nor Article 33 of the United Nations Protocol Relating to the Status of Refugees applies to action taken by the Coast Guard on the high seas.

. . .

III

Both parties argue that the plain language of § 243(h)(1) is dispositive. It reads as follows:

> "The Attorney General shall not deport or return any alien (other than an alien described in section 1251(a)(4)(D) of this title) to a country if the Attorney General determines that such alien's life or freedom would be threatened in such country on account of race, religion, nationality, membership in a particular social group, or political opinion."

Respondents emphasize the words "any alien" and "return"; neither term is limited to aliens within the United States. Respondents also contend that the 1980 amendment deleting the words "within the United States" from the prior text of § 243(h), obviously gave the statute an extraterritorial effect. This change, they further argue, was required in order to conform the statute to the text of Article 33.1 of the Convention, which they find as unambiguous as the present statutory text.

---

[17] For two first-hand accounts of this litigation, *see* Harold Hongju Koh, *Refugees, the Courts, and the New World Order*, 1994 Utah L. Rev. 999 (1994) and Victoria Clawson *et al*, *Litigating as Law Students: An Inside Look at Haitian Centers Council*, 103 Yale L.J. 2337 (1994). *See also* Brandt Goldstein, Storming the Court (2005).

Petitioners' response is that a fair reading of the INA as a whole demonstrates that § 243(h) does not apply to actions taken by the President or Coast Guard outside the United States; that the legislative history of the 1980 amendment supports their reading; and that both the text and the negotiating history of Article 33 of the Convention indicate that it was not intended to have any extraterritorial effect.

We shall first review the text and structure of the statute and its 1980 amendment, and then consider the text and negotiating history of the Convention.

A. The Text and Structure of the INA

Although § 243(h)(1) refers only to the Attorney General, the Court of Appeals found it "difficult to believe that the proscription of § 243(h)(1)—returning an alien to his persecutors—was forbidden if done by the attorney general but permitted if done by some other arm of the executive branch." Congress "understood" that the Attorney General is the "President's agent for dealing with immigration matters," and would intend any reference to her to restrict similar actions of any Government official. As evidence of this understanding, the court cited 8 U.S.C. § 1103(a). That section, however, conveys to us a different message. It provides, in part:

> "The Attorney General shall be charged with the administration and enforcement of this chapter and all other laws relating to the immigration and naturalization of aliens, *except insofar as this chapter or such laws relate to the powers, functions, and duties conferred upon the President, the Secretary of State, the officers of the Department of State, or diplomatic or consular officers. . . .*" (Emphasis added.)

Other provisions of the Act expressly confer certain responsibilities on the Secretary of State, the President, and, indeed, on certain other officers as well. The 1981 and 1992 Executive Orders expressly relied on statutory provisions that confer authority on the President to suspend the entry of "any class of aliens" or to "impose on the entry of aliens any restrictions he may deem to be appropriate." We cannot say that the interdiction program created by the President, which the Coast Guard was ordered to enforce, usurped authority that Congress had delegated to, or implicated responsibilities that it had imposed on, the Attorney General alone.

The reference to the Attorney General in the statutory text is significant not only because that term cannot reasonably be construed to describe either the President or the Coast Guard, but also because it suggests that it applies only to the Attorney General's normal responsibilities under the INA. The most relevant of those responsibilities for our purposes is her conduct of the deportation and exclusion hearings in which requests for asylum or for withholding of deportation under § 243(h) are ordinarily advanced. Since there is no provision in the statute for the conduct of such proceedings outside the United States, and since Part V and other provisions of the INA obviously contemplate that such proceedings would be held in the country, we cannot reasonably construe § 243(h) to limit the Attorney General's actions in geographic areas where she has not been authorized to conduct such proceedings. Part V of the INA contains no reference to a possible extraterritorial application.

Even if Part V of the Act were not limited to strictly domestic procedures, the presumption that Acts of Congress do not ordinarily apply outside our borders would support an interpretation of § 243(h) as applying only within United States territory. The Court of Appeals held that the presumption against extraterritoriality had "no relevance in the present context" because there was no risk that § 243(h), which can be enforced only in United States courts against the United States Attorney General, would conflict with the laws of other nations. We have recently held, however, that the presumption has a foundation broader than the desire to avoid conflict with the laws of other nations.

Respondents' expansive interpretation of the word "return" raises another problem: It would make the word "deport" redundant. If "return" referred solely to the destination to which the alien is to be removed, it alone would have been sufficient to encompass aliens involved in both deportation and exclusion proceedings. And if Congress had meant to refer to all aliens who might be sent back to potential oppressors, regardless of their location, the word "deport" would have been unnecessary. By using both words, the statute implies an exclusively territorial application, in the context of both kinds of domestic immigration proceedings. The use of both words reflects the traditional division between the two kinds of aliens and the two kinds of hearings. We can reasonably conclude that Congress used the two words "deport" and "return" only to make § 243(h)'s protection available in both deportation and exclusion proceedings. Indeed, the history of the 1980 amendment confirms that conclusion.

. . .

IV

. . .

When the United States acceded to the Protocol in 1968 . . . the INA already offered *some* protection to both classes of refugees. It offered *no* such protection to any alien who was beyond the territorial waters of the United States, though, and we would not expect the Government to assume a burden as to those aliens without some acknowledgment of its dramatically broadened scope. Both Congress and the Executive Branch gave extensive consideration to the Protocol before ratifying it in 1968; in all of their published consideration of it there appears no mention of the possibility that the United States was assuming any extraterritorial obligations. Nevertheless, because the history of the 1980 Act does disclose a general intent to conform our law to Article 33 of the Convention, it might be argued that the extraterritorial obligations imposed by Article 33 were so clear that Congress, in acceding to the Protocol, and then in amending the statute to harmonize the two, meant to give the latter a correspondingly extraterritorial effect. Or, just as the statute might have imposed an extraterritorial obligation that the Convention does not (the argument we have just rejected), the Convention might have established an extraterritorial obligation which the statute does not; under the Supremacy Clause, that broader treaty obligation might then provide the controlling rule of law. With those possibilities in mind we shall consider both the text and negotiating history of the Convention itself.

Like the text and the history of § 243(h), the text and negotiating history of Article 33 of the United Nations Convention are both completely silent with respect to the Article's possible application to actions taken by a country outside its own borders. Respondents argue that the Protocol's broad remedial goals require that a nation be prevented from repatriating refugees to their potential oppressors whether or not the refugees are within that nation's borders. In spite of the moral weight of that argument, both the text and negotiating history of Article 33 affirmatively indicate that it was not intended to have extraterritorial effect.

A.   The Text of the Convention

Two aspects of Article 33's text are persuasive. The first is the explicit reference in Article 33.2 to the country in which the alien is located; the second is the parallel use of the terms "expel or return," the latter term explained by the French word "refouler."

The full text of Article 33 reads as follows:

"Article 33.—Prohibition of Expulsion or Return ('refoulement')

"1.   No Contracting State shall expel or return ('refouler') a refugee in any manner whatsoever to the frontiers of territories where his life or freedom would be threatened on account of his race, religion, nationality, membership of a particular social group or political opinion.

"2.   The benefit of the present provision may not, however, be claimed by a refugee whom there are reasonable grounds for regarding as a danger to the security of the country in which he is, or who, having been convicted by a final judgment of a particularly serious crime, constitutes a danger to the community of that country." Convention Relating to the Status of Refugees.

Under the second paragraph of Article 33 an alien may not claim the benefit of the first paragraph if he poses a danger to the country in which he is located. If the first paragraph did apply on the high seas, no nation could invoke the second paragraph's exception with respect to an alien there: An alien intercepted on the high seas is in no country at all. If Article 33.1 applied extraterritorially, therefore, Article 33.2 would create an absurd anomaly: Dangerous aliens on the high seas would be entitled to the benefits of 33.1 while those residing in the country that sought to expel them would not. It is more reasonable to assume that the coverage of 33.2 was limited to those already in the country because it was understood that 33.1 obligated the signatory state only with respect to aliens within its territory.

Article 33.1 uses the words "expel or return ('refouler')" as an obvious parallel to the words "deport or return" in § 243(h)(1). There is no dispute that "expel" has the same meaning as "deport"; it refers to the deportation or expulsion of an alien who is already present in the host country. The dual reference identified and explained in our opinion in *Leng May Ma v. Barber* suggests that the term "return ('refouler')" refers to the exclusion of aliens who are merely " 'on the threshold of initial entry.' "

This suggestion—that "return" has a legal meaning narrower than its common meaning—is reinforced by the parenthetical reference to *"refouler,"* a French word that is *not* an exact synonym for the English word "return." Indeed, neither of two respected English-French dictionaries mentions *"refouler"* as one of many possible French translations of "return." Conversely, the English translations of *"refouler"* do not include the word "return." They do, however, include words like "repulse," "repel," "drive back," and even "expel." To the extent that they are relevant, these translations imply that "return" means a defensive act of resistance or exclusion at a border rather than an act of transporting someone to a particular destination. In the context of the Convention, to "return" means to "repulse" rather than to "reinstate."

The text of Article 33 thus fits with [the] understanding that " 'expulsion' would refer to a 'refugee already admitted into a country' and that 'return' would refer to a 'refugee already within the territory but not yet resident there.' Thus, the Protocol was not intended to govern parties' conduct outside of their national borders." From the time of the Convention, commentators have consistently agreed with this view.

The drafters of the Convention and the parties to the Protocol—like the drafters of § 243(h)—may not have contemplated that any nation would gather fleeing refugees and return them to the one country they had desperately sought to escape; such actions may even violate the spirit of Article 33; but a treaty cannot impose uncontemplated extraterritorial obligations on those who ratify it through no more than its general humanitarian intent. Because the text of Article 33 cannot reasonably be read to say anything at all about a nation's actions toward aliens outside its own territory, it does not prohibit such actions.

. . .

V

Respondents contend that the dangers faced by Haitians who are unwillingly repatriated demonstrate that the judgment of the Court of Appeals fulfilled the central purpose of the Convention and the Refugee Act of 1980. While we must, of course, be guided by the high purpose of both the treaty and the statute, we are not persuaded that either one places any limit on the President's authority to repatriate aliens interdicted beyond the territorial seas of the United States.

It is perfectly clear that 8 U.S.C. § 1182(f), grants the President ample power to establish a naval blockade that would simply deny illegal Haitian migrants the ability to disembark on our shores. Whether the President's chosen method of preventing the "attempted mass migration" of thousands of Haitians—to use the Dutch delegate's phrase—poses a greater risk of harm to Haitians who might otherwise face a long and dangerous return voyage is irrelevant to the scope of his authority to take action that neither the Convention nor the statute clearly prohibits. As we have already noted, Acts of Congress normally do not have extraterritorial application unless such an intent is clearly manifested. That presumption has special force when we are construing treaty and statutory provisions that may involve foreign and military affairs for which the President has unique responsibility.

. . .

The judgment of the Court of Appeals is reversed.

It is so ordered.

JUSTICE BLACKMUN, dissenting.

When, in 1968, the United States acceded to the United Nations Protocol Relating to the Status of Refugees, it pledged not to "return (*'refouler'*) a refugee in any manner whatsoever" to a place where he would face political persecution. In 1980, Congress amended our immigration law to reflect the Protocol's directives. Today's majority nevertheless decides that the forced repatriation of the Haitian refugees is perfectly legal, because the word "return" does not mean return, because the opposite of "within the United States" is not outside the

United States, and because the official charged with controlling immigration has no role in enforcing an order to control immigration.

I believe that the duty of nonreturn expressed in both the Protocol and the statute is clear. The majority finds it "extraordinary," that Congress would have intended the ban on returning "any alien" to apply to aliens at sea. That Congress would have meant what it said is not remarkable. What is extraordinary in this case is that the Executive, in disregard of the law, would take to the seas to intercept fleeing refugees and force them back to their persecutors—and that the Court would strain to sanction that conduct.

I

I begin with the Convention, for it is undisputed that the Refugee Act of 1980 was passed to conform our law to Article 33, and that "the nondiscretionary duty imposed by § 243(h) parallels the United States' mandatory *non-refoulement* obligations under Article 33.1. . . ." The Convention thus constitutes the backdrop against which the statute must be understood.

A

Article 33.1 of the Convention states categorically and without geographical limitation:

> "No Contracting State shall expel or return ('*refouler*') a refugee in any manner whatsoever to the frontiers of territories where his life or freedom would be threatened on account of his race, religion, nationality, membership of a particular social group or political opinion."

The terms are unambiguous. Vulnerable refugees shall not be returned. The language is clear, and the command is straightforward; that should be the end of the inquiry. Indeed, until litigation ensued, the Government consistently acknowledged that the Convention applied on the high seas.

The majority, however, has difficulty with the treaty's use of the term "return ('*refouler*')." "Return," it claims, does not mean return, but instead has a distinctive legal meaning. For this proposition the Court relies almost entirely on the fact that *American* law makes a general distinction between *deportation* and *exclusion*. Without explanation, the majority asserts that in light of this distinction the word "return" as used in the treaty somehow must refer only to "the exclusion of aliens who are . . . 'on the threshold of initial entry.'"

. . .

I find this tortured reading unsupported and unnecessary. The text of the Convention does not ban the "exclusion" of aliens who have reached some indeterminate "threshold"; it bans their "return." It is well settled that a treaty must first be construed according to its "ordinary meaning." The ordinary meaning of "return" is "to bring, send, or put (a person or thing) back to or in a former position." Webster's Third New International Dictionary 1941 (1986). That describes precisely what petitioners are doing to the Haitians. By dispensing with ordinary meaning at the outset, and by taking instead as its starting point the assumption that "return," as used in the treaty, "has a legal meaning narrower than its common meaning," the majority leads itself astray

. . .

Article 33.1 is clear not only in what it says, but also in what it does not say: It does not include any geographical limitation. It limits only where a refugee may be sent "to," not where he may be sent from. This is not surprising, given that the aim of the provision is to protect refugees against persecution.

Article 33.2, by contrast, *does* contain a geographical reference, and the majority seizes upon this as evidence that the section as a whole applies only within a signatory's borders. That inference is flawed. Article 33.2 states that the benefit of Article 33.1

> "may not . . . be claimed by a refugee whom there are reasonable grounds for regarding as a danger to the security of the country in which he is, or who, having been convicted by a final judgment of a particularly serious crime, constitutes a danger to the community of that country."

The signatories' understandable decision to allow nations to deport criminal aliens who have entered their territory hardly suggests an intent to permit the apprehension and return of noncriminal aliens who have not entered their territory, and who may have no desire ever to enter it. One wonders what the majority would make of an exception that removed from the Article's protection all refugees who "constitute a danger to their families." By the majority's logic, the inclusion of such an exception presumably would render Article 33.1 applicable only to refugees with families.

Far from constituting "an absurd anomaly," the fact that a state is permitted to "expel or return" a small class of refugees found within its territory but may not seize and return refugees who remain outside its frontiers expresses precisely the objectives and concerns of the Convention. Nonreturn is the rule; the sole exception (neither applicable nor invoked here) is that a nation endangered by a refugee's very presence may "expel or return" him to an unsafe country if it chooses. The tautological observation that only a refugee already in a country can pose a danger to the country "in which he is" proves nothing.

. . .

II

A

Like the treaty whose dictates it embodies, § 243(h) of the Immigration and Nationality Act of 1952 (INA) is unambiguous. It reads:

> "The Attorney General shall not deport or return any alien . . . to a country if the Attorney General determines that such alien's life or freedom would be threatened in such country on account of race, religion, nationality, membership in a particular social group, or political opinion."

"With regard to this very statutory scheme, we have considered ourselves bound to assume that the legislative purpose is expressed by the ordinary meaning of the words used." Ordinary, but not literal. The statement that "the Attorney General shall not deport or return any alien" obviously does not mean simply that the person who is the Attorney General at the moment is forbidden personally to deport or return any alien, but rather that her agents may not do so. In the present case the Coast Guard without question is acting as the agent of the Attorney General. "The officers of the Coast Guard insofar as they are engaged . . . in enforcing any law of the United States shall . . . be deemed to be acting as agents of the particular executive department . . . charged with the administration of the particular law . . . and . . . be subject to all the rules and regulations promulgated by such department . . . with respect to the enforcement of that law." The Coast Guard is engaged in enforcing the immigration laws. The sole identified purpose of Executive Order No. 12807 is to address the "serious problem of persons attempting to come to the United States by sea without necessary documentation and otherwise illegally." The Coast Guard's task under the order is "to enforce the suspension of the entry of undocumented aliens by sea and the interdiction of any defined vessel carrying such aliens." The Coast Guard is authorized to return a vessel and its passengers *only* "when there is reason to believe that an offense is being committed against the United States immigration laws, or appropriate laws of a foreign country with which we have an arrangement to assist."

The majority suggests indirectly that the law which the Coast Guard enforces when it carries out the order to return a vessel reasonably believed to be violating the immigration laws is somehow not a law that the Attorney General is charged with administering. That suggestion is baseless. Under 8 U.S.C. § 1103(a), the Attorney General, with some exceptions, "shall be charged with the administration and enforcement of this chapter and all other laws relating to the immigration and naturalization of aliens. . . ." The majority acknowledges this designation, but speculates that the particular enforcement of immigration laws here may be covered by the exception for laws relating to "'the powers, functions, and duties conferred upon the President, the Secretary of State, the officers of the Department of State, or diplomatic or consular officers. . . .'" The majority fails to point out the proviso that directly follows the exception: "*Provided, however,* That . . . the Attorney General . . . shall have the power and duty to control and guard the boundaries and borders of the United States against the illegal entry of aliens. . . ." There can be no doubt that the Coast Guard is acting as the Attorney General's agent when it seizes and returns undocumented aliens.

. . .

The laws that the Coast Guard is engaged in enforcing when it takes to the seas under orders to prevent aliens from illegally crossing our borders are laws whose administration has been assigned to the Attorney General by Congress, which has plenary power over immigration matters. Accordingly, there is no merit to the argument that the concomitant legal restrictions placed on the Attorney General by Congress do not apply with full force in this case.

. . .

C

That the clarity of the text and the implausibility of its theories do not give the majority more pause is due, I think, to the majority's heavy reliance on the presumption against extraterritoriality. The presumption runs throughout the majority's opinion, and it stacks the deck by requiring the Haitians to produce "affirmative evidence" that when Congress prohibited the return of "any" alien, it indeed meant to prohibit the interception and return of aliens at sea.

The judicially created canon of statutory construction against extraterritorial application of United States law has no role here, however. It applies only where congressional intent is "unexpressed." Here there is no room for doubt: A territorial restriction has been deliberately deleted from the statute.

Even where congressional intent is unexpressed, however, a statute must be assessed according to its intended scope. The primary basis for the application of the presumption (besides the desire—not relevant here—to avoid conflict with the laws of other nations) is "the commonsense notion that Congress generally legislates with domestic concerns in mind." Where that notion seems unjustified or unenlightening, however, generally worded laws covering varying subject matters are routinely applied extraterritorially.

In this case we deal with a statute that regulates a distinctively international subject matter: immigration, nationalities, and refugees. Whatever force the presumption may have with regard to a primarily domestic statute evaporates in this context. There is no danger that the Congress that enacted the Refugee Act was blind to the fact that the laws it was crafting had implications beyond this Nation's borders. The "commonsense notion" that Congress was looking inwards—perfectly valid in a case involving the Federal Tort Claims Act, such as *Smith,—* cannot be reasonably applied to the Refugee Act of 1980.

In this regard, the majority's dictum that the presumption has "special force" when we construe "statutory provisions that may involve foreign and military affairs for which the President has unique responsibility," is completely wrong. The presumption that Congress did not intend to legislate extraterritorially has *less* force—perhaps, indeed, no force at all—when a statute on its face relates to foreign affairs. What the majority appears to be getting at, as its citation to *United States v. Curtiss-Wright Export Corp.,* 299 U.S. 304, 57 S.Ct. 216, 81 L.Ed. 255 (1936) is that in some areas, the President, and not Congress, has sole constitutional authority. Immigration is decidedly not one of those areas. " '[O]ver no conceivable subject is the legislative power of Congress more complete. . . .' " And the suggestion that the President somehow is acting in his capacity as Commander in Chief is thwarted by the fact that nowhere among Executive Order No. 12807's numerous references to the immigration laws is that authority even once invoked.

If any canon of construction should be applied in this case, it is the well-settled rule that "an act of congress ought never to be construed to violate the law of nations if any other possible construction remains." *Murray v. Schooner Charming Betsy,* (1804). The majority's improbable construction of § 243(h), which flies in the face of the international obligations imposed by Article 33 of the Convention, violates that established principle.

III

The Convention that the Refugee Act embodies was enacted largely in response to the experience of Jewish refugees in Europe during the period of World War II. The tragic consequences of the world's indifference at that time are well known. The resulting ban on *refoulement,* as broad as the humanitarian purpose that inspired it, is easily applicable here, the Court's protestations of impotence and regret notwithstanding.

The refugees attempting to escape from Haiti do not claim a right of admission to this country. They do not even argue that the Government has no right to intercept their boats. They demand only that the United States, land of refugees and guardian of freedom, cease forcibly driving them back to detention, abuse, and death. That is a modest plea, vindicated by the treaty and the statute. We should not close our ears to it.

I dissent.

NOTES & QUESTIONS

1.   The United Nations High Commissioner for Refugees submitted an *amicus* brief in *Sale* in support of the respondents, but the Court rejected its interpretation of the Refugee Convention. Professor Fitzpatrick suggests that American judges are typically unfamiliar with and resistant to implementing international standards, even when the directive to do so is clear. *See* Joan Fitzpatrick, *The International Dimension of U.S. Refugee Law*, 15 Berkeley J. Int'l L. 1, 24–25 (1997). Why might that be the case? If Professor Fitzpatrick is correct, what are the implications for the nation's participation in international legal regimes? What can human rights advocates do to address these systemic barriers?

2.   The Refugee Act is one of a small number of statutes that directly incorporates international treaty language into U.S. domestic law. *See* John F. Coyle, *Incorporative Statutes and the Borrowed Treaty Rule*, 50 Va. J. Int'l L. 655, 659 (2010). Does that impact the way the Court interprets the statute? Do the majority and the dissenting judges in *Sale* differ in the way they view the relationship between the international convention and the national implementing legislation? Review this chapter's discussion of implementing legislation in Section III.B. Does this case study on the Refugee Convention offer any lessons of statutory design for implementing the U.N. human rights treaties?

3.   The year after the *Sale* decision, the Clinton Administration helped to broker an accord between the coup leaders and President Aristide, which provided that Aristide would return to Haiti by October 30, 1993; however, as the deadline approached it became clear that the coup leaders would not honor the agreement. Violence and human rights violations surged. The Clinton Administration began enforcing a blockade off the coast of Haiti, while the Coast Guard continued to intercept and return fleeing boat people.

Meanwhile, the Clinton administration was facing increasing criticism, both domestically and internationally, for its handling of Haiti. As a candidate, Bill Clinton had criticized the Bush Administration's interdiction policy. Once in office, however, he continued to defend it before the Supreme Court, undermining his Administration's public commitments to promoting human rights. In March 1994, the Congressional Black Caucus, important allies of the Administration on other policy matters, sent the president a letter demanding that he revise the nation's policy on Haiti. Human rights groups brought a challenge before the Inter-American Commission on Human Rights claiming that the U.S. policy was in violation of the American Declaration of the Rights and Duties of Man and the American Convention on Human Rights. The United Nations High Commissioner for Refugees, an important U.S. ally in resolving refugee crises around the globe, continued to criticize American policy, calling the *Sale* decision "a setback to modern international refugee law." UN High Commissioner for Refugees Responds to U.S. Supreme Court Decision in Sale v. Haitian Centers Council, 32 I.L.M. 1215, 1215 (1993). In May 1994, "fac[ing] the unappetizing prospect of rallying regional and global support for coercive isolation of the Haitian regime, while simultaneously pursuing a refugee policy that many of those allies viewed as repugnant," Harold Hongju Koh, *Refugees, the Courts, and the New World Order*, 1994 Utah L. Rev. 999, 1018 (1994), the Clinton Administration abandoned the repatriation policy that the Supreme Court had upheld only a year earlier and adopted one more consistent with international law.

4.   The question of extraterritorial application of human rights protections is a recurring theme. We next encounter the issue in **Chapter IV**, regarding the federal Alien Tort Statute.

CHAPTER IV

CUSTOMARY INTERNATIONAL LAW IN U.S. COURTS

■ ■ ■

I. INTRODUCTION

In addition to treaties, custom is an important source of human rights law. Customary international law (CIL) is defined in the Restatement (Third) of the Foreign Relations Law of the United States as international law that "results from a general and consistent practice of states followed by them from a sense of legal obligation."[1] While this definition is well-established, it poses a number of challenges for advocates attempting to make arguments based on CIL norms in U.S. courts. How many nations must accept or engage in a practice (and for how long) for it to be continuous and systematic? How does an advocate prove that state behavior is motivated by a "sense of legal obligation"? And, assuming that such an international rule exists, how does it interact with contradictory state or federal law?

This chapter examines the role of customary international law in domestic human rights advocacy. Part II begins with the question of how U.S. courts identify and define customary international law norms. These materials further describe the ongoing debate over the status of customary international law within the U.S. legal system. Part III then examines the primary ways in which advocates have attempted to enforce CIL in U.S. courts, through the *Charming Betsy* canon of statutory construction and the Alien Tort Statute.

As you review the materials in this chapter, consider how customary international law intersects with the U.N. human rights treaties you have already studied. Has the codification of some human rights law made CIL more or less relevant for advocates? How should U.S. courts consider claims based on norms that are not yet the subject of treaties—or that are included in treaties that the United States has not yet ratified? As an advocate, when and how would you choose to raise a customary international law claim?

---

[1] Restatement (Third), § 102(2) (1987).

II. DEFINING CUSTOMARY INTERNATIONAL LAW

A. THE RESTATEMENT (THIRD)

The first challenge in applying customary international law is determining its existence. The following two sections from the Restatement (Third) of Foreign Relations Law explain how a rule or principle becomes customary international law and detail the evidence that a litigant must present to a court to make the case that this legalization process has occurred.

RESTATEMENT (THIRD) OF FOREIGN RELATIONS LAW, § 102

Restatement of the Law—The Foreign Relations Law of the
United States American Law Institute (1987).

§ 102 Sources of International Law

(1) A rule of international law is one that has been accepted as such by the international community of states;

(a) in the form of customary law;

(b) by international agreement; or

(c) by derivation from general principles common to the major legal systems of the world.

(2) Customary international law results from a general and consistent practice of states followed by them from a sense of legal obligation.

(3) International agreements create law for the states parties thereto and may lead to the creation of customary international law when such agreements are intended for adherence by states generally and are in fact widely accepted.

(4) General principles common to the major legal systems, even if not incorporated or reflected in customary law or international agreement, may be invoked as supplementary rules of international law where appropriate.

Comment:

. . .

b. *Practice as customary law.* "Practice of states," . . . includes diplomatic acts and instructions as well as public measures and other governmental acts and official statements of policy, whether they are unilateral or undertaken in cooperation with other states. . . . Inaction may constitute state practice, as when a state acquiesces in acts of another state that affect its legal rights. The practice necessary to create customary law may be of comparatively short duration, but . . . it must be "general and consistent." A practice can be general even if it is not universally followed; there is no precise formula to indicate how widespread a practice must be, but it should reflect wide acceptance among the states particularly involved in the relevant activity. Failure of a significant number of important states to adopt a practice can prevent a principle from becoming general customary law. . . . A principle of customary law is not binding on a state that declares its dissent from the principle during its development.

c.   Opinio juris. For a practice of states to become a rule of customary international law it must appear that the states follow the practice from a sense of legal obligation . . . ; a practice that is generally followed but which states feel legally free to disregard does not contribute to customary law. A practice initially followed by states as a matter of courtesy or habit may become law when states generally come to believe that they are under a legal obligation to comply with it. It is often difficult to determine when that transformation into law has taken place. . . .

d.   Dissenting views and new states. Although customary law may be built by the acquiescence as well as by the actions of states and become generally binding on all states, in principle a state that indicates its dissent from a practice while the law is still in the process of development is not bound by that rule even after it matures. Historically, such dissent and consequent exemption from a principle that became general customary law has been rare. A state that enters the international system after a practice has ripened into a rule of international law is bound by that rule.

. . .

i.   International agreements codifying or contributing to customary law. . . . Some multilateral agreements may come to be law for non-parties that do not actively dissent. That may be the effect where a multilateral agreement is designed for adherence by states generally, is widely accepted, and is not rejected by a significant number of important states. A wide network of similar bilateral arrangements on a subject may constitute practice and also result in customary law. If an international agreement is declaratory of, or contributes to, customary law, its termination by the parties does not of itself affect the continuing force of those rules as international law. However, the widespread repudiation of the obligations of an international agreement may be seen as state practice adverse to the continuing force of the obligations.

. . .

k.   Peremptory norms of international law (jus cogens). Some rules of international law are recognized by the international community of states as peremptory, permitting no derogation. These rules prevail over and invalidate international agreements and other rules of international law in conflict with them. Such a peremptory norm is subject to modification only by a subsequent norm of international law having the same character.

. . .

Restatement (Third) Foreign Relations Law, § 103

Restatement of the Law—The Foreign Relations Law of the
United States American Law Institute (1987).

§ 103   Evidence of International Law

(1) Whether a rule has become international law is determined by evidence appropriate to the particular source from which that rule is alleged to derive (§ 102).

(2) In determining whether a rule has become international law, substantial weight is accorded to

(a) judgments and opinions of international judicial and arbitral tribunals;

(b) judgments and opinions of national judicial tribunals;

(c) the writings of scholars;

(d) pronouncements by states that undertake to state a rule of international law, when such pronouncements are not seriously challenged by other states.

. . .

Comment:

a. Primary and secondary evidence of international law. Section 102 sets forth the "sources" of international law, *i.e.*, the ways in which a rule or principle becomes international law. This section indicates the means of proving, for example, in a court or other tribunal, that a rule has become international law by way of one or more of the sources indicated in § 102.

. . .

b. Judicial and arbitral decisions. . . . [T]o the extent that decisions of international tribunals adjudicate questions of international law, they are persuasive evidence of what the law is. The judgments and opinions of the International Court of Justice are accorded great weight. Judgments and opinions of international tribunals generally are accorded more weight than those of domestic courts, since the former are less likely to reflect a particular national interest or bias, but the views of national courts, too, generally have the weight due to bodies of presumed independence, competence, impartiality, and authority.

. . .

c.   *Declaratory resolutions of international organizations.* States often pronounce their views on points of international law, sometimes jointly through resolutions of international organizations that undertake to declare what the law is on a particular question, usually as a matter of general customary law. International organizations generally have no authority to make law, and their determinations of law ordinarily have no special weight, but their declaratory pronouncements provide some evidence of what the states voting for it regard the law to be. The evidentiary value of such resolutions is variable. Resolutions of universal international organizations, if not controversial and if adopted by consensus or virtual unanimity, are given substantial weight.

. . .

B. CUSTOMARY INTERNATIONAL LAW NORMS AND JURISPRUDENCE

The determination of whether a CIL rule exists often falls to the courts when litigants raise claims or defenses based on these principles in domestic suits. In *Filartiga v. Pena-Irala*, the Second Circuit Court of Appeals was asked to consider whether the prohibition on torture violates customary international law. The case was brought under a provision of the Judiciary Act of 1789, codified at 28 U.S.C. § 1350, known as the Alien Tort Statute ("ATS"). Under that provision, enacted by the First Congress, district courts have original jurisdiction over "all causes where an alien sues for a tort only (committed) in violation of the law of nations." As you read the *Filartiga* decision, consider whether and how its analysis and the evidence it considers conform to the standard set out in the Restatement. Note that *Filartiga* was decided before the Convention Against Torture came into force.

FILARTIGA V. PENA-IRALA
United States Court of Appeals for the Second Circuit, 1980.
630 F.2d 876.

The appellants, plaintiffs below, are citizens of the Republic of Paraguay. Dr. Joel Filartiga, a physician, describes himself as a longstanding opponent of the government of President Alfredo Stroessner, which has held power in Paraguay since 1954. His daughter, Dolly Filartiga, arrived in the United States in 1978 under a visitor's visa, and has since applied for permanent political asylum. The Filartigas brought this action in the Eastern District of New York against Americo Norberto

Pena-Irala (Pena), also a citizen of Paraguay, for wrongfully causing the death of Dr. Filartiga's seventeen-year old son, Joelito.

. . .

The appellants contend that on March 29, 1976, Joelito Filartiga was kidnapped and tortured to death by Pena, who was then Inspector General of Police in Asuncion, Paraguay. Later that day, the police brought Dolly Filartiga to Pena's home where she was confronted with the body of her brother, which evidenced marks of severe torture. As she fled, horrified, from the house, Pena followed after her shouting, "Here you have what you have been looking for for so long and what you deserve. Now shut up." The Filartigas claim that Joelito was tortured and killed in retaliation for his father's political activities and beliefs.

. . .

In July of 1978, Pena sold his house in Paraguay and entered the United States under a visitor's visa. . . . [He was] living in Brooklyn, New York, when Dolly Filartiga, who was then living in Washington, D. C., learned of [his] presence. Acting on information provided by Dolly, the Immigration and Naturalization Service arrested Pena and his companion, both of whom were subsequently ordered deported on April 5, 1979 following a hearing. They had then resided in the United States for more than nine months.

Almost immediately, Dolly caused Pena to be served with a summons and civil complaint at the Brooklyn Navy Yard, where he was being held pending deportation. The complaint alleged that Pena had wrongfully caused Joelito's death by torture and sought compensatory and punitive damages of $10,000,000. The Filartigas also sought to enjoin Pena's deportation to ensure his availability for testimony at trial. The cause of action is stated as arising under "wrongful death statutes; the U.N. Charter; the Universal Declaration on Human Rights; the U.N. Declaration Against Torture; the American Declaration of the Rights and Duties of Man; and other pertinent declarations, documents and practices constituting the customary international law of human rights and the law of nations," as well as 28 U.S.C. s 1350, Article II, sec. 2 and the Supremacy Clause of the U. S. Constitution.

. . .

II

Appellants rest their principal argument in support of federal jurisdiction upon the Alien Tort Statute, 28 U.S.C. s 1350, which provides: "The district courts shall have original jurisdiction of any civil action by an alien for a tort only, committed in violation of the law of nations or a treaty of the United States." Since appellants do not contend that their action arises directly under a treaty of the United States, a threshold question on the jurisdictional issue is whether the conduct alleged violates the law of nations. In light of the universal condemnation of torture in numerous international agreements, and the renunciation of torture as an instrument of official policy by virtually all of the nations of the world (in principle if not in practice), we find that an act of torture committed by a state official against one held in detention violates established norms of the international law of human rights, and hence the law of nations.

. . .

The *Paquete Habana*, 175 U.S. 677, 20 S.Ct. 290, 44 L.Ed. 320 (1900), reaffirmed that

> where there is no treaty, and no controlling executive or legislative act or judicial decision, resort must be had to the customs and usages of civilized nations; and, as evidence of these, to the works of jurists and commentators, who by years of labor, research and experience, have made themselves peculiarly well acquainted with the subjects of which they treat. Such works are resorted to by judicial tribunals, not for the speculations of their authors concerning what the law ought to be, but for trustworthy evidence of what the law really is.

Modern international sources confirm the propriety of this approach.

Habana is particularly instructive for present purposes, for it held that the traditional prohibition against seizure of an enemy's coastal fishing vessels during wartime, a standard that began as one of comity only, had ripened over the preceding century into "a settled rule of international law" by "the general assent of civilized nations." Thus it is clear that courts must interpret international law not as it was in 1789, but as it has evolved and exists among the nations of the world today.

The requirement that a rule command the "general assent of civilized nations" to become binding upon them all is a stringent one. Were this not so, the courts of one nation might feel free to impose idiosyncratic legal rules upon others, in the name of applying international law. Thus, in *Banco Nacional de Cuba v. Sabbatino*, 376 U.S. 398 (1964), the Court declined to pass on the validity of the Cuban government's expropriation of a foreign-owned corporation's assets, noting the sharply conflicting views on the issue propounded by the capital-exporting, capital-importing, socialist and capitalist nations.

The case at bar presents us with a situation diametrically opposed to the conflicted state of law that confronted the *Sabbatino* Court. Indeed, to paraphrase that Court's statement, there are few, if any, issues in international law today on which opinion seems to be so united as the limitations on a state's power to torture persons held in its custody.

The United Nations Charter (a treaty of the United States) makes it clear that in this modern age a state's treatment of its own citizens is a matter of international concern. It provides [in Article 55]:

> With a view to the creation of conditions of stability and well-being which are necessary for peaceful and friendly relations among nations ... the United Nations shall promote ... universal respect for, and observance of, human rights and fundamental freedoms for all without distinctions as to race, sex, language or religion.

And further:

> All members pledge themselves to take joint and separate action in cooperation with the Organization for the achievement of the purposes set forth in Article 55.

While this broad mandate has been held not to be wholly self-executing, this observation alone does not end our inquiry. For although there is no universal agreement as to the precise extent of the "human rights and fundamental freedoms" guaranteed to all by the Charter, there is at present no dissent from the view that the guaranties include, at a bare minimum, the right to be free from torture. This prohibition has become part of customary international law, as evidenced and defined by the Universal Declaration of Human Rights, General Assembly Resolution 217 (III)(A) (Dec. 10, 1948) which states, in the plainest of terms, "no one shall be subjected to torture." The General Assembly has declared that the Charter precepts embodied in this Universal Declaration "constitute basic principles of international law."

Particularly relevant is the Declaration on the Protection of All Persons from Being Subjected to Torture. ... The Declaration expressly prohibits any state from permitting the dastardly and totally inhuman act of torture. Torture, in turn, is defined as "any act by which severe pain and suffering, whether physical or mental, is intentionally inflicted by or at the instigation of a public official on a person for such purposes as ... intimidating him or other persons." The Declaration goes on to provide that "(w)here it is proved that an act of torture or other cruel, inhuman or degrading treatment or punishment has been committed by or at the instigation of a public official, the victim shall be afforded redress and compensation, in accordance with national law." This Declaration, like the Declaration of Human Rights before it, was adopted without dissent by the General Assembly.

These U.N. declarations are significant because they specify with great precision the obligations of member nations under the Charter.

Since their adoption, "(m)embers can no longer contend that they do not know what human rights they promised in the Charter to promote." Moreover, a U.N. Declaration is, according to one authoritative definition, "a formal and solemn instrument, suitable for rare occasions when principles of great and lasting importance are being enunciated." Accordingly, it has been observed that the Universal Declaration of Human Rights "no longer fits into the dichotomy of 'binding treaty' against 'non-binding pronouncement,' but is rather an authoritative statement of the international community." Thus, a Declaration creates an expectation of adherence, and "insofar as the expectation is gradually justified by State practice, a declaration may by custom become recognized as laying down rules binding upon the States." Indeed, several commentators have concluded that the Universal Declaration has become, in toto, a part of binding, customary international law.

Turning to the act of torture, we have little difficulty discerning its universal renunciation in the modern usage and practice of nations. The international consensus surrounding torture has found expression in numerous international treaties and accords. . . . The substance of these international agreements is reflected in modern municipal *i.e.* national law as well. Although torture was once a routine concomitant of criminal interrogations in many nations, during the modern and hopefully more enlightened era it has been universally renounced. According to one survey, torture is prohibited, expressly or implicitly, by the constitutions of over fifty-five nations, including both the United States and Paraguay. Our State Department reports a general recognition of this principle:

> There now exists an international consensus that recognizes basic human rights and obligations owed by all governments to their citizens. . . . There is no doubt that these rights are often violated; but virtually all governments acknowledge their validity.

We have been directed to no assertion by any contemporary state of a right to torture its own or another nation's citizens. Indeed, United States diplomatic contacts confirm the universal abhorrence with which torture is viewed:

> In exchanges between United States embassies and all foreign states with which the United States maintains relations, it has been the Department of State's general experience that no government has asserted a right to torture its own nationals. Where reports of torture elicit some credence, a state usually responds by denial or, less frequently, by asserting that the conduct was unauthorized or constituted rough treatment short of torture.

. . .

Having examined the sources from which customary international law is derived the usage of nations, judicial opinions and the works of jurists we conclude that official torture is now prohibited by the law of nations. The prohibition is clear and unambiguous, and admits of no distinction between treatment of aliens and citizens. . . . The treaties and accords cited above, as well as the express foreign policy of our own government, all make it clear that international law confers fundamental rights upon all people vis-à-vis their own governments. While the ultimate scope of those rights will be a subject for continuing refinement and elaboration, we hold that the right to be free from torture is now among them.

. . .

NOTES & QUESTIONS

1.   Note that *Filartiga* was decided prior to the publication of the Third Restatement. Does the *Filartiga* opinion nevertheless apply the standards set out in the Restatement for evaluating plaintiff's claim that torture violates the law of nations? Do you agree with the court's conclusion? Does the Restatement provide a clear and workable test for identifying CIL norms?

2.   Once a CIL norm is established, it binds all States. There is an exception, however, for States that clearly and persistently objected to the standard or practice prior to the point at which it "hardened" into CIL. *See* Ted Stein, *The Approach of the Different Drummer: The Principle of the Persistent Objector in International Law*, 26 Harv. Int'l L.J. 457, 457 (1985). To claim persistent objector status, a State must affirmatively communicate its opposition to the norm to the international community; maintaining silence or adopting or adhering to a contrary practice is insufficient. *See* Lynn Loschin, *The Persistent Objector and Customary Human Rights Law: A Proposed Analytical Framework*, 2 U.C. Davis J. Int'l L. & Pol'y 147, 150–51 (1996). A CIL norm may be overridden by treaty with respect to the signatory nations. *See* Int'l L. Comm'n, [195], 2 Y.B. Int'l L. Comm'n 154–55, U.N. Doc. A/CN.4/63/1953. A small set of international norms, referred to as "peremptory" or "*jus cogens*" norms are said to arise from nearly universal practice and to permit no exception—even for persistent objectors—and they may not be overridden by treaty. Commonly cited examples of *jus cogens* norms include genocide, slavery, and torture.

Prior to the Supreme Court's decision in *Roper v. Simmons*, 543 U.S. 551 (1995), which held the juvenile death penalty unconstitutional, numerous commentators had argued that the practice violated CIL. By the time of the *Roper* decision, the United States was the only country in the world that permitted the execution of juveniles. Only the United States and Somalia had refused to ratify the Convention on the Rights of the Child, which prohibited the use of capital punishment on persons who committed crimes prior to the age of 18. Despite this evidence of state practice, no U.S. federal or state court accepted a defendant's argument that the execution of a juvenile violated CIL.

In *Servin v. Nevada*, the Supreme Court of Nevada considered and rejected the defendant's argument that his execution would violate international law because the United States had ratified the ICCPR with a reservation claiming the continued ability to impose the death penalty on juvenile offenders. The Court nonetheless found the imposition of the death penalty excessive in this case. Concurring in the judgment, Justice Rose wrote:

> I concur with the majority's conclusion that the death penalty was excessive when applied to Servin, but I believe that an additional ground for ruling out the death penalty for this minor is that customary international law precludes the most extreme penalty for juvenile offenders.
>
> At first blush, the U.S. Senate's reservation to the International Covenant on Civil and Political Rights (ICCPR) seems completely incompatible with the object and purpose of the treaty. However, three factors convince me that the Senate's reservation has continued viability. First, the ICCPR does not expressly prohibit reservations or make reference to the object-and-purpose test. Second, it is reported that there is a "widespread state practice in support of reservations to human rights treaties" and that "approximately one-third of the parties to the ICCPR made reservations to over a dozen substantive provisions." Third, while 11 of the 146 nations objected to the Senate's reservation because it violated the basic purpose of the treaty, none of the objections were raised within the twelve months after the communication of the United States' reservation, and therefore, the reservation is deemed accepted under the Vienna Convention. . . .
>
> This is not the end of the hunt in the international law arena, however, because Servin also argues that assessing the death penalty upon juveniles violates an international customary law norm. His argument is that a proposition becomes so accepted among a great many nations that it becomes an international law norm, and therefore, should be recognized as customary international law and bind all nations. Two of the legal authorities who argue such a position are Professor Harold Koh and Professor Louis Henkin.
>
> Professors Koh and Henkin contend that customary international law is federal law and supercedes state law that is inconsistent. "Once customary norms have sufficiently crystallized, courts should presumptively incorporate them into federal common law, unless" federal directives specifically oust the norm. Without contrary federal directives, bona fide rules of customary international law

become federal law unless the United States affirmatively protested the norm before the norm matured.

Several commentators make persuasive arguments that it is customary international law that juveniles should not be executed. "[T]here is an emerging customary international law under which capital punishment of juveniles is prohibited." Indeed, there appears to be overwhelming support among the majority of nations to ban the imposition of the death penalty for juvenile offenders. Notably, this support appears to be influencing several states within the United States to also ban the death penalty for juveniles.

While there are other respected legal authorities that reach the contrary conclusion, I am persuaded that banning the execution of juveniles is a customary international norm and this ban should be recognized as binding on the United States. In my view, this is an additional reason to reduce Servin's penalty to life imprisonment without the possibility of parole.

Servin v. State, 117 Nev. 775, 794–96, 32 P.3d 1277, 1290–92 (2001) (Rose, J., concurring).

3.   As Justice Rose's opinion indicates, the United States could be bound by a CIL norm that it had explicitly rejected in the context of ratifying a treaty. Is that problematic? Could the United States have been exempt from that CIL rule as a "persistent objector"? What other information would you want to know to answer that question? Could the prohibition on the execution of juveniles be a *jus cogens* rule? Why or why not?

4.   The American Law Institute is now in the process of developing the Restatement Fourth of Foreign Relations Law. As you read the remaining materials in this Chapter, consider whether and how the standards for identifying and proving a customary international law norm have changed since 1987. Which elements of the Restatement Third might have to be revisited?

SKILLS EXERCISE

Is there a customary international law norm against child labor? Draft a short strategy memorandum outlining the evidence that you would consider and the sources you would consult in order to determine whether such a norm exists in international law.

III.   CUSTOMARY INTERNATIONAL LAW IN THE U.S. LEGAL SYSTEM

Assuming that a customary international law norm exists, what effect does it have on domestic law in the United States? As Justice Rose explains in *Servin*, the academic debate centers on whether CIL is a form of federal law that can preempt state law (or even contrary federal law).

As you read the excerpts below, consider the implications of this debate on inter-branch relationships in the federal government, on federalism, and on the nation's participation in the international legal system.

LOUIS HENKIN, "INTERNATIONAL LAW AS LAW IN THE UNITED STATES"

82 Mich. L. Rev. 1555, 1556–69 (1984).

[How does international law fit into the hierarchy of United States law?] Since it is law not enacted by Congress, and the principles of that law are determined by judges for application in cases before them, customary international law has often been characterized as 'federal common law' and has been lumped with authentic federal common law— the law made by federal judges under their constitutional power or under authority delegated by Congress.

In fact, however, to call international law federal common law is misleading. It is *like* federal common law in that both have the status of federal law for purposes of supremacy to state law. And it is *like* federal common law in that determinations of customary international law by the Supreme Court are law in the United States and binding on the states. But it is not federal common law in other significant respects. Unlike federal common law, customary international law is not made and developed by the federal courts independently and in the exercise of their own law-making judgment. In a real sense federal courts *find* international law rather than make it, as was not true when courts were applying the 'common law,' and as is clearly not the case when federal judges make federal common law pursuant to constitutional or legislative delegation. The courts determine international law for their purposes, but the determinants are not their own judgments or the precedents of U.S. courts. In principle, the courts interpret law that exists independently of them, law that is 'legislated' through the political actions of the governments of the world's States. It is determined primarily and more authoritatively by international courts and with equal authority by domestic courts of other countries. And it is the executive branch, far more than the courts, that acts for the United States to help legislate customary international law.

In general, it may not be important whether international law when applied by the courts is properly characterized as 'common law' or merely described as 'like common law in important respects.' But the loose characterization of the law of nations as common law has led—I think—to jurisprudential conclusions that are unwarranted. For a while, we have seen, referring to our customary international law as common law misled judges in diversity cases, causing them to treat international law as state rather than federal law. Recently, because they assumed that international law is, or is like, judge-made common law, a few lawyers have tended to relegate it to the subordinate status that federal common law has in the hierarchy of federal law—lower than that of treaties or statutes of the United States. In particular, they have argued that even if the United States has fully participated in and has supported the creation of a rule of customary law, such law is not self-executing, is not domestic law in the United States, and the courts should not give it effect in the face of an earlier treaty or statute of the United States. Presumably, this view would also hold that the President cannot give effect to customary law in the face of an earlier treaty or act of Congress, although he is free to make and must give domestic effect to a treaty in the face of an earlier act of Congress.

To understand that view, and why I have doubts about it, one must recall the accepted jurisprudence as it relates to the categories of federal law. The Constitution, we know, is supreme law. Acts of Congress and treaties of the United States are 'inferior' to the Constitution. A statute inconsistent with the Constitution is invalid; a treaty inconsistent with the Constitution may be binding internationally but will not be enforced as law in the United States. The language of the Supremacy Clause of the Constitution has been read to imply that laws and treaties of the United States are not only supreme over state law, but are equal in status and authority to each other. It is not unconstitutional for Congress to enact law inconsistent with a treaty of the United States; it is not unconstitutional for the President, with the consent of the Senate, to make a treaty inconsistent with an earlier act of Congress. And in the case of inconsistency between a statute and a treaty, the later one will be given effect by the courts and by the executive.

The place of federal common law, of federal law made by judges pursuant to their inherent constitutional authority or to authority delegated them by Congress, has not been conclusively determined. In principle, any authority exercised by the courts under their own constitutional authority ought to be equal to the authority of Congress or of the treaty-makers, and their 'enactments' entitled to equal weight; here too the later-in-time might prevail in case of conflict. But the common law tradition that judges are bound by acts of the legislature, whether earlier or later, has discouraged the view that law made by judges pursuant to their own constitutional authority is equal in status to legislation, and that federal courts can make federal law inconsistent with an earlier act of Congress. Ironically, law made by courts not on their own constitutional authority but pursuant to authorization by Congress would presumably draw on congressional authority and like a later act of Congress could supersede earlier legislation.

Assuming that authentic federal common law cannot be made and given effect in the face of an earlier inconsistent treaty or act of Congress, some have suggested that the same is true also of customary international law. There is no authority for that view. The status of customary international law in the law of the United States in relation to treaties or acts of Congress has not been authoritatively determined. And, in principle, the argument for according customary law equal authority, and for applying the later-in-time rule to it as well, is not unpersuasive. In international law, customary law and treaties are of equal authority and the later in time will prevail in case of inconsistency, when the parties so intend. The obligations of the United States under customary law are of the same status as its treaty obligations; for the United States in its relations with other nations a later principle of customary law would supersede a treaty obligation if so intended. In U.S. law, both treaties and customary law are law of the United States just as statutes are; like statutes, both are superior to state law. Treaties, it is established, are equal in status to statutes, and subject to the later-in-time principle; why should customary international law be of lower status?

. . .

The process by which customary law is created is hardly certain and remains somewhat mysterious. Courts are often reluctant to conclude that a principle has become customary law, and they may be even more reluctant to do so when the principle would be contrary to earlier congressional legislation. But where the existence of the principle is clear, and the world, including the United States, is living by it, there seems to be no compelling reason to require courts to treat it as lesser law and to refuse to give it effect until Congress repeals the earlier statutory provision.

It is not that international law is superior to an act of Congress; in U.S. law, this is not true. But customary law is 'self-executing,' and like a self-executing treaty it is equal in authority to an act of Congress for domestic purposes. An old act of Congress need not stand in the way of U.S. participation in the development of customary law and courts need not wait to give effect to that development until Congress repeals the older statute. As with respect to a treaty, Congress can at any time legislate to supersede the development for purposes of domestic law.

. . .

That international law is part of the law of the United States is asserted and accepted today as it was at our national beginnings. But nations, and the law of nations, and the United States and its place among nations, are different today; the nominal continuity in our jurisprudence masks radical development, much of it in our time. It is right that the law of nations, which is the responsibility of the U.S.

nation, should be seen as incorporated in our national jurisprudence as national (federal) law. It seems right that courts of the United States should not assert a final say as to how the nation shall behave in respect of its obligations to other nations, and should not command Congress or the President to comply with international norms. For me, it seems right too that the courts should continue to give effect to developments in international law to which the United States is party, unless Congress is moved to reject them as domestic law in the United States.

. . .

The view of customary international law outlined by Professor Henkin was well-accepted until the late 1990s, when Professors Bradley and Goldsmith set out a vigorous challenge in the Harvard Law Review. As you review the excerpt below, consider what concerns about international law motivate these authors' critique, and how their concept of the judicial role in international law enforcement differs from that expressed by Professor Henkin.

CURTIS A. BRADLEY & JACK L. GOLDSMITH, "CUSTOMARY INTERNATIONAL LAW AS FEDERAL COMMON LAW: A CRITIQUE OF THE MODERN POSITION"
110 Harv. L. Rev. 815, 816–76 (1997).

The traditional conception of CIL was that it resulted from "a general and consistent practice of states followed by them from a sense of legal obligation." Both the "state practice" and "sense of legal obligation" requirements reflected the notion that international law was grounded in state consent. To ensure that states had consented to a CIL rule, the passage of a substantial period of time was generally required before a practice could become legally binding. Furthermore, CIL, like international law generally, primarily governed relations among nations, not the relations between a nation and its citizens.

The post-World War II era has witnessed a dramatic transformation in the nature of CIL lawmaking. Conceptually, one of the results of the Nuremberg trials was that the individual, and not just the state, came to be viewed as a significant subject of international law. Structurally, the establishment of the United Nations and other international organizations made it easier for nations to meet and express their views about the content of international law. These organizations also facilitated the proliferation of multilateral treaties on a wide range of subjects, including human rights. Such changes, not surprisingly, have influenced the nature of CIL.

Perhaps the most significant change in the nature of CIL is that it is less tied to state practice. International and U.S. courts now rely on General Assembly resolutions, multilateral treaties, and other international pronouncements as evidence of CIL without rigorous examination of whether these pronouncements reflect the actual practice of states. [I]n *Filartiga*, the Second Circuit relied extensively on declarations and treaties as evidence of a CIL rule against torture, although it recognized that such a rule did not necessarily comport with state practice.

· · ·

Another difference between the traditional and the new CIL is that the latter can develop very rapidly. The International Court of Justice has stated that "the passage of only a short period of time is not necessarily, or of itself, a bar to the formation of a new rule of customary international law." The accelerated process of CIL lawmaking is due in part to improvements in communication, which have "made the practice of states widely and quickly known." It is also due to the fact that discrete events such as pronouncements of international organizations and the promulgation of multilateral treaties are treated as evidence of CIL.

· · ·

Finally, the content of CIL has changed. In particular, CIL is now viewed as regulating many matters that were traditionally regulated by domestic law alone. By far the largest such body of new CIL concerns human rights. There is widespread agreement that CIL now protects the rights to be free from genocide, slavery, summary execution or murder, "disappearance," "cruel, inhuman, or degrading treatment," "prolonged arbitrary detention," and "systematic racial discrimination." An intergovernmental human rights committee recently asserted that CIL also protects "freedom of thought, conscience and religion," a presumption of innocence, a right of pregnant women and children not to be executed, and a right to be free from expressions of "national, racial, or religious hatred." A prominent human rights organization's list of "potential candidates for rights recognized under customary international law" includes "the right to free choice of employment; the right to form and join trade unions; and the right to free primary education, subject to a state's available resources." The list continues to grow. As a leading authority on international human rights has observed, "[g]iven the rapid continued development of international human rights, the list as now constituted should be regarded as essentially open-ended. . . . Many other rights will be added in the course of time."

In sum, the new CIL differs from traditional CIL in several fundamental ways. It is less tied to state practice, it can develop rapidly, and it increasingly purports to regulate a state's treatment of its own citizens. With these points in mind, we now consider some of the implications of the claim that CIL is federal common law.

. . .

Prior to *Erie*, federal courts applied a common law (which included CIL) that did not emanate from a particular sovereign authority, and they determined the content of this common law independently of state courts. The Court in *Erie* effectively "overruled [this] particular way of looking at law" and replaced it with another. *Erie*'s new conception of law, and of the constitutional role of the federal courts in applying law, bears upon the claims of the modern position in several ways.

The first way in which *Erie* is relevant to the modern position is in its embrace of legal positivism. In rejecting the notion of a general common law in the federal courts, the Court explained that "law in the sense in which courts speak of it today does not exist without some definite authority behind it." This strand of *Erie* requires federal courts to identify the sovereign source for every rule of decision. Because the appropriate "sovereigns" under the U.S. Constitution are the federal government and the states, all law applied by federal courts must be either federal law or state law. After *Erie*, then, a federal court can no longer apply CIL in the absence of some domestic authorization to do so, as it could under the regime of general common law.

. . .

The second way in which *Erie* pertains to the modern position concerns its embrace of a legal realist view of judicial decisionmaking. . . . The recognition that courts "make" law when they engage in common law decisionmaking . . . formed a basis for the Court's conclusion that the development of an independent general common law by federal courts was "an unconstitutional assumption of powers."

. . .

The final way in which *Erie* is relevant to the modern position concerns the "new" federal common law to which the decision gave rise. *Erie* did not eliminate the lawmaking powers of federal courts—it changed them. Federal court development of general common law was illegitimate not because it was a form of lawmaking, but rather because it was unauthorized lawmaking. Thus, federal judicial lawmaking is consistent with *Erie* if it is legitimately authorized. Since *Erie*, federal courts have determined that such authorization exists in a variety of circumstances. Is it within the federal judiciary's authority, after Erie, to apply CIL as federal common law? We now turn to this question.

. . .

There is "considerable uncertainty" concerning the proper scope of the post-Erie federal common law. The Supreme Court's federal common law decisions do not lend themselves to ready synthesis. As a result, both the Court and commentators sometimes "explain" federal common law by simply listing categories, or "enclaves," of federal common law decisions.

The uncertainty regarding the proper scope of federal common law is grounded more in the application of first principles than in the principles themselves. Courts and scholars generally agree that federal common law must be authorized in some fashion by the Constitution or a federal statute. This principle flows from Erie's requirement that all law applied by federal courts must derive from a domestic sovereign source. It is precisely the grounding of federal common lawmaking in a federal sovereign source that makes the new federal common law, unlike the pre-Erie general common law, binding on the states.

Is there domestic federal authorization for federal courts to interpret and apply CIL as federal law in the wholesale fashion contemplated by the modern position? Nothing on the face of the Constitution or any federal statute authorizes such a practice. Article III of the Constitution does not even list CIL as a basis for the exercise of federal judicial power, much less authorize federal courts to incorporate CIL wholesale into federal law. Nor does Article VI list CIL as a source of supreme federal law. Article I does authorize Congress to define and punish offenses against the law of nations, and Congress has exercised this and related powers to incorporate select CIL principles into federal statutes. But Congress has never purported to incorporate all of CIL into federal law. And Congress's selective incorporation would be largely superfluous if CIL were already incorporated wholesale into federal common law, as advocates of the modern position suggest.

CIL's alleged federal law status also departs dramatically from generally accepted limitations on federal common law. The modern position claims that the common law powers of federal courts provide the federal authority for transforming CIL into domestic federal law. But the modern position also claims that CIL applies wholesale as federal common law and that federal courts must apply whatever CIL requires. The problem with this latter claim . . . is that, under the modern position, the federal law status of CIL simply cannot be based upon the common law powers of federal courts. If, according to the modern position, federal courts must apply whatever CIL requires, then it is illogical also to assert that they exercise the political or legal authority that transforms CIL into federal law. In other words, the modern position at bottom assumes that U.S. courts apply CIL in the absence of any domestic authorization. Viewed in this way, the modern position has the structure of pre-*Erie* general common law, with the important difference that the CIL that applies in the absence of a domestic authorization has the status and collateral consequences of federal law. As explained above, however, the notion that federal courts may apply any law, including CIL, without domestic authorization cannot survive *Erie*.

In addition, the modern position that CIL is federal common law is in tension with basic notions of American representative democracy. When a federal court applies CIL as federal common law, it is not applying law generated by U.S. lawmaking processes. Rather, it is applying law derived from the views and practices of the international community. The foreign governments and other non-U.S. participants in this process "are neither representative of the American political community nor responsive to it." Indeed, under modern conceptions of CIL, CIL rules may be created and bind the United States without any express support for the rules from the U.S. political branches. Nonetheless, as federal law, such CIL would preempt state law and, under certain formulations of the modern position, might bind the President and supersede prior inconsistent federal legislation.

. . .

NOTES & QUESTIONS

1.   Bradley and Goldsmith begin their article by noting how CIL has changed in the post-World War II era. Why do you think that this expansion of CIL prompted a reconsideration of the role of CIL in U.S. law? What structural and political concerns might motivate this critique?

2.   Bradley and Goldsmith's article launched a vigorous debate in the academy. The following year, Professor Harold Koh published a response in the Harvard Law Review in which he took on their concern that "unelected federal judges apply customary international law made by the world community at the expense of state prerogatives. In this context, of course, the interests of the states are neither formally nor effectively represented in the lawmaking process." Koh writes:

> "So what else is new?" As Professor Neuman has noted, because federal courts have applied customary international law since the beginning of the Republic, "one might think it was rather late to claim that judicial application of customary international law was in principle inconsistent with the American understanding of democracy." Moreover, there is absolutely nothing new about unelected judges applying law that was made elsewhere . . . Every court in the United States—including the state courts that Bradley and Goldsmith champion—applies law that was not made by its own polity whenever the court's own choice-of-law principles so direct. Nor is there anything inherently undemocratic about judges applying norms of customary law that were made outside the United States. This, too, is something that American judges have done since the beginning of the Republic, whenever they declared

rules of customary international law to be part of "general common law."

. . .

When construing customary international law, federal courts arguably exercise less judicial discretion than when making other kinds of federal common law, as their task is not to create rules willy-nilly, but rather to discern rules of decision from an existing corpus of customary international law rules. Here, Bradley and Goldsmith charge that state interests are not formally or effectively represented in the customary international lawmaking process. But insofar as customary international law rules arise from traditional State practice, the United States has been, for most of this century, the world's primary maker of and participant in this practice. Increasingly, multilateral treaty drafting processes and fora such as the United Nations, regional fora, standing and ad hoc intergovernmental organizations, and diplomatic conferences have become the driving forces in the creation and shaping of contemporary international law. In nearly all of these organizations and fora, the United States ranks among the leading participants.

Notwithstanding the executive branch domination of foreign affairs, in every foreign policy decisionmaking process, one can find multiple channels for congressional participation and state representation. These include, but are not limited to, such oversight and input mechanisms as hearings, markups, congressional consultations, committee approval devices, and the like. When customary international law rules arise from a treatymaking process, or from a treaty regime, congressional interests are often directly represented at the negotiating table. Even when Members of Congress are not allowed to participate directly in such treaty negotiations, the knowledge that any negotiated agreement must return to Congress for ratification necessarily pervades the executive branch's negotiating position.

Bradley and Goldsmith nowhere explain why explicit federal legislation—a process notoriously dominated by committees, strong-willed individuals, collective action problems, and private rent-seeking—is invariably more democratic than the judge-driven process they criticize. Nor do they explain why state courts would act more democratically than federal courts in deciding customary international law cases. The Founders recognized that "democratic" values are poorly served by permitting the courts of one state of the Union to issue rulings that could potentially embroil the entire nation in international controversies. If, for example, a Massachusetts judge issued a ruling on head-of-state immunity that triggered an international dispute between the U.S. and the United Kingdom, the citizens of every other state would potentially suffer from the unelected state judge's actions. Even under Bradley and Goldsmith's standards, it is hard to imagine a more undemocratic result.

Under the traditional view, federal common law rules of customary international law are perennially subject to a democratic check: supervision, revision, and endorsement by the federal political branches.

Harold Hongju Koh, *Is International Law Really State Law?*, 111 Harv. L. Rev. 1824, 1851–55 (1998).

How do you respond to Bradley and Goldsmith's argument that viewing CIL as federal common law is anti-democratic? Do you find Koh's pragmatic response persuasive?

3.   Professor Koh also points to a practical problem with rejecting the position that CIL is federal law:

Bradley and Goldsmith mount virtually no arguments explaining why fifty state courts and legislatures should be free to reject, modify, reinterpret, selectively incorporate, or completely oust customary international law rules from domestic law. Under Bradley and Goldsmith's view, absent an explicit and unambiguous directive from a federal statute or treaty, state courts or legislatures could simply refuse to incorporate into state law customary international rules regarding the non-execution of pregnant women or the immunity of visiting heads of state. Alternatively, each state could adopt its own parochial answer to each of these questions. Thus, for example, the Bradley and Goldsmith theory would allow Massachusetts to deny the customary international law protection of head-of-state immunity to Queen Elizabeth on tort claims arising out of events in Northern Ireland, whereas the forty-nine other states could choose instead to grant the Queen every conceivable variant of full or partial immunity. Yet surely, such issues raise precisely the kind of "basic choice regarding the competence and function of the Judiciary and the National Executive in ordering our relationships with other members of the international community" that the Supreme Court held "must be treated exclusively as an aspect of federal law."

Harold Hongju Koh, *Is International Law Really State Law?*, 111 Harv. L. Rev. 1824, 1828–29 (1998).

How do you think Bradley and Goldsmith would respond to this critique? Do you think that this is a real problem? Are there other ways to ensure that CIL is uniformly enforced throughout the United States?

4.   Professor Julian Ku has argued that states actually do exercise substantial control over the nation's compliance with its international law obligations. He explains:

States control the implementation of international obligations in several different ways. First, state courts have always exercised substantial control over the interpretation of international law largely free from federal supervision. For instance, state courts applying the doctrine that "the law of nations is part of the common law" have incorporated customary international law through their independent common lawmaking powers. State courts have actually played a crucial role in the initiation as well as development of certain doctrines of customary international law without any supervision or intervention from the federal courts.

Second, state legislatures may enact legislation intended to comply with international obligations stemming from either customary international law or treaties. In some cases, state legislatures have passed such measures at the urging of the federal government and, in other cases, they have acted at the urging of foreign governments themselves. State implementation of treaties is often crucial from a functional perspective, if the treaty is either non-self-executing or involves areas of law, such as probate law, for which federal institutions are poorly equipped to regulate. Additionally, state legislatures may adopt "model codes" or "uniform laws" promulgated at either the national or international level that are intended to create a uniform system of laws across national borders. Although this last mechanism does not technically involve the "incorporation of" international law, it is one example of how states are participating in an international effort—independent of the federal government—to unify certain areas of the law.

Third, state governors exercise their powers to enforce or comply with international obligations, both customary and treaty-based. In some cases, governors act to enforce customary international law obligations while in other cases, governors have acted to enforce treaty obligations. Sometimes the governors have acted at the request of the federal government while at other times, the governors appear to be exercising their own independent judgment on whether and how to comply with international law obligations.

Julian G. Ku, *The State of New York Does Exist: How the States Control Compliance with International Law*, 82 N.C. L. Rev. 457, 476–78 (2004).

Ku offers three areas in which states have traditionally controlled compliance with the nation's international law obligations: enforcing consular rights in estate proceedings; regulating the taxation of foreign state property; and protecting the CIL and treaty rights of aliens within their jurisdiction. Does Ku's evidence weaken Koh's argument regarding the importance of treating CIL as federal common law? If not, why not?

IV. ENFORCING CUSTOMARY INTERNATIONAL LAW

Despite the academic interest in CIL, it appears only rarely in domestic litigation. Under longstanding Supreme Court precedent, customary international law applies only "where there is no treaty, and no controlling executive or legislative act or judicial decision. . . ."[2] As a result, CIL rarely is invoked to provide the binding rule of decision in modern disputes. Nonetheless, it is still an important tool of human rights litigation. This section examines two significant ways in which human rights advocates have attempted to raise and enforce customary international law norms in U.S. courts—through the *Charming Betsy* canon and through the Alien Tort Statute.

A. CHARMING BETSY

In an 1804 decision, *Murray v. The Schooner Charming Betsy*, the Supreme Court explained that "an act of Congress ought never to be construed to violate the law of nations if any other possible construction remains." Since then, the *Charming Betsy* canon of statutory construction has been applied regularly by the Supreme Court and by lower federal courts and codified in the Restatement (Third) of Foreign Relations. Human rights advocates have relied on the *Charming Betsy* canon to argue that federal laws should be interpreted in ways that are consistent with customary international law norms.

The excerpt below from the federal district court's opinion in *Beharry v. Reno* demonstrates how a court can apply the *Charming Betsy* canon in interpreting a statute. Don Beharry entered the United States in 1982 when he was seven years old as a lawful permanent resident. Following a criminal conviction for robbery in 1996, the Immigration and Naturalization Service commenced deportation proceedings. Because of the robbery, the immigration courts found that Beharry was not eligible for discretionary relief from deportation. He then filed a writ of *habeas corpus* challenging his deportation as inconsistent with international law.

---

[2] The Paquete Habana, 175 U.S. 677, 700 (1900). *See also* Garcia-Mir v. Meese, 788 F.2d 1446, 1453 (11th Cir. 1986) ("public international law is controlling only" in the absence of controlling positive law or judicial precedent).

BEHARRY V. RENO

United States District Court, Eastern District of New York, 2002.
183 F.Supp.2d 584.

D. Customary International Law

. . .

2. Authority of Customary International Law

United States courts may not ignore the precepts of customary international law. This concept has been most clearly embodied in admiralty cases, where domestic law may directly clash with customary international law. The Supreme Court has long recognized the principle that in admiralty United States courts are "bound by the law of nations, which is part of the law of the land."

Like admiralty, immigration law is founded on international law. The Supreme Court has repeated that the basis for Congress's extremely broad power over aliens comes not from the Constitution itself, but from international law. "*It is an accepted maxim of international law* that every sovereign nation has the power, as inherent in sovereignty, and essential to self-preservation, to forbid the entrance of foreigners within its dominions." It is because of international norms that Congress has such broad authority.

. . .

Since Congress's power over aliens rests at least in part on international law, it should come as no shock that it may be limited by changing international law norms.

. . .

United States courts should interpret legislation in harmony with international law and norms wherever possible. "An act of Congress ought never to be construed to violate the law of nations if any other possible construction remains." *Charming Betsy,* 6 U.S. at 118, 2 Cranch 64. This opinion was authored by Chief Justice John Marshall. Marshall and other members of that court were of the generation that had written the Constitution.

. . .

Congress may override provisions of customary international law. This rule interacts with the "Charming Betsy" principle to create a principle of clear statement: since Congress may overrule customary international law (*Paquete Habana*), but laws are to be read in conformity with international law where possible (*Charming Betsy*), it follows that in order to overrule customary international law, Congress must enact domestic legislation which both postdates the development of a customary international law norm, and which clearly has the intent of repealing that norm.

The need to harmonize domestic and international law is well recognized.

. . .

Where a statute appears to contradict international law, an appropriate remedy is to construe the statute so as to resolve the contradiction. Customary international law is legally enforceable unless superceded by a clear statement from Congress. Such a statement must be unequivocal. Mere silence is insufficient to meet this standard.

3. Provisions of the Convention on the Rights of the Child as Customary International Law

The CRC has been adopted by every organized government in the world except the United States. This overwhelming acceptance is strong reason to hold that some CRC provisions have attained the status of customary international law. As at least one court of appeals had explicitly stated, "international human rights instruments . . . are evidence of customary international law."

While the CRC is relatively new, it contains many provisions codifying longstanding legal norms. It states that "the family . . . should be afforded the necessary protection and assistance" and that "in all actions concerning children . . . the best interests of the child shall be a primary consideration." CRC, Preamble and Art. 3. These provisions of the CRC are not so novel as to be considered outside the bounds of what is customary. Similar doctrines have long been a part of our law. . . . They are also applied by other nations. For example, there is an extensive jurisprudence in Europe supporting judicial enforcement of the right to family integrity. Given its widespread acceptance, to the extent that it acts to codify longstanding, widely-accepted principles of law, the CRC should be read as customary international law. "The rights to be free from arbitrary interference with family life and arbitrary expulsion are part of customary international law."

Congress's failure to ratify the CRC is not a sufficiently clear statement to constitute repudiation of the customary international law principles contained in and underlying this treaty. This ruling of law does not mean that other, more novel sections of the CRC must be adopted as customary international law. This is especially true for some novel sections of the CRC which Congress has specifically sought to repudiate, such as provisions intended to regulate the application of the death penalty.

. . .

IV. Application of Law to Facts

A. *Relief Under the Immigration and Naturalization Act*

Petitioner is ineligible for relief under a narrow and wooden construction of the INA.

. . .

C. *Relief Under Customary International Law*

As noted above, the CRC, because of its broad acceptance, collects and articulates customary international law. It is a codification of now longstanding, uniformly-accepted legal principles. If read as the government suggests, the INA would violate the principles of customary international law that the best interests of the child must be considered where possible. Categoric denial of a hearing and thus of any consideration of the child's interests in all cases of theft where the sentence exceeds a year is not in compliance with that international mandate.

It is not disputed that Congress could override this norm of customary international law if it chose to do so. It has not expressed a clear intent to overrule this principle of customary international law which is otherwise binding upon United States courts. "The statutes under which Mr. Beharry is being deported [do] not explicitly authorize the separation of an alien from immediate family members." The court construes the statute in conformity with international law, as mandated by the *Charming Betsy* doctrine.

D. *Appropriate Remedy*

As now interpreted and implemented against this petitioner, the statute would violate treaty obligations and customary international law. It is appropriate to interpret the statute in a way which does not violate international law. Since both statutes and international law are enforceable under the Constitution's Supremacy Clause, the statute should be construed in conformity with international law to avoid a constitutional issue if "fairly possible." In this task the court should make the minimal changes necessary to bring the statute into compliance.

Section 212(h) of the Immigration and Naturalization Act allows discretionary relief from deportation for aliens who have established seven years of residence in the United States, and who have family members in the United States who would suffer "extreme hardship" if the alien is removed.

The most narrowly targeted way to bring the INA into compliance with international law requirements is to read into section 212(h) a requirement of compliance with international law. Those aliens eligible for section 212(h)—those who have seven years or more of residence, and whose removal would cause an "extreme hardship" to legally present family members—are already a carefully selected group with close ties to this country. It would be a violation of international law to categorically deny to all members of this group who have been denominated after their crime was committed as "aggravated felons," relief under the provision. The statutory provision "No waiver shall be provided . . . if . . . the alien has been convicted of an aggravated felony" should be narrowly construed so as to accord with international law. That can be done by ruling that section 212(h) waivers are available for aliens, including petitioner, who meet its stringent requirements of seven years residence and "extreme hardship" to family—if these aliens have been convicted of an "aggravated felony" as defined after they committed their crime, but which was not so categorized when they committed the crime.

It should be emphasized that such an interpretation does not constitute a ruling that petitioner cannot be deported. He is only entitled to a hearing at which a broad discretion to exclude may be exercised by the INS.

. . .

V. Conclusion

The writ is granted. The I.N.S. is ordered to conduct a hearing under section 212(h) to determine whether petitioner may remain in the United States. The judgment is stayed pending completion of appellate proceedings if any.

———————

The district court's decision was reversed by the U.S. Court of Appeals for the Second Circuit on other grounds, as that court determined that Beharry had failed to exhaust his administrative remedies.[3]

NOTES & QUESTIONS

1.   How did customary international law influence the court's decision in *Beharry*? Do you agree with the court's methodology and the outcome of the case? Note that the court relied heavily on the CRC, a treaty that the United States has not ratified. Is that appropriate under the principles of the Vienna Convention on the Law of Treaties (see **Chapter III**), or is it an example of federal judges ignoring a directive from the political branches in order to make new law?

2.   The *Beharry* court was receptive to the *Charming Betsy* argument raised by petitioner. In *Serra v. Lappin*, a panel of the Ninth Circuit offered a much more cabined view of the appropriate use of the doctrine. In *Serra*, a group of current and former federal prisoners argued that their low pay

———————

[3]   *See* Beharry v. Ashcroft, 329 F.3d 51 (2d Cir. 2003).

violated the Fifth Amendment and various sources of international law, including customary international law. The Court responded:

> Plaintiffs assert that "the customs and usages" of the nations of the world, as revealed in these and other sources, form customary international law entitling them to higher wages. This claim fails because customary international law is not a source of judicially enforceable private rights in the absence of a statute conferring jurisdiction over such claims. Plaintiffs can point to no statute that brings their claim within our purview.

> . . .

> We have allowed ourselves a few sidelong glances at the law of nations . . . by applying the canon of statutory construction that "[w]here fairly possible, a United States statute is to be construed as not to conflict with international law or with an international agreement with the U.S." The canon is derived from Chief Justice Marshall's statement that

>> an act of Congress ought never to be construed to violate the law of nations if any other possible construction remains, and consequently can never be construed to violate neutral rights, or to affect neutral commerce, further than is warranted by the law of nations as understood in this country.

Murray v. The Schooner Charming Betsy, 6 U.S. (2 Cranch) 64 (1804). The *Charming Betsy* canon is not an inviolable rule of general application, but a principle of interpretation that bears on a limited range of cases. Mindful that "Congress has the power to legislate beyond the limits posed by international law," we do not review federal law for adherence to the law of nations with the same rigor that we apply when we must review statutes for adherence to the Constitution. We invoke the *Charming Betsy* canon only where conformity with the law of nations is relevant to considerations of international comity. We decline to determine whether Plaintiffs' rates of pay were in violation of the law of nations because this case meets neither condition for applying the canon.

First, the purpose of the *Charming Betsy* canon is to avoid the negative "foreign policy implications" of violating the law of nations, and Plaintiffs have offered no reason to believe that their low wages are likely to "embroil[ ] the nation in a foreign policy dispute." That the courts should ever invoke the *Charming Betsy* canon in favor of United States citizens is doubtful, because a violation of the law of nations as against a United States citizen is unlikely to bring about the international discord that the canon guards against. In *The Charming Betsy,* the status of the ship's owner as a Danish subject, and thus a neutral in the conflict between the United States and France, was critical to the Court's conclusion that the Non-

Intercourse Act of 1800 should not be interpreted to permit the seizure and sale of his ship. We have never employed the *Charming Betsy* canon in a case involving exclusively domestic parties and domestic acts, nor has the Supreme Court. As a general rule, domestic parties must rely on domestic law when they sue each other over domestic injuries in federal court. We need not consider whether the statutory and regulatory regime of federal inmate compensation conflicts with the law of nations because Plaintiffs, as United States citizens and residents, have not demonstrated that their low wages have any possible ramifications for this country's foreign affairs.

Second, "[t]he *Charming Betsy* canon comes into play only where Congress's intent is ambiguous," and there is nothing ambiguous about the complete discretion that Congress vested in the Attorney General with regard to inmate pay. Congress is not constrained by international law as it is by the Constitution. As a result, "we are bound by a properly enacted statute, provided it be constitutional, even if that statute violates international law." Because the statutes giving the Attorney General discretion over prisoner pay grades are unambiguous, there is no reason for this court to decide whether they accord with the law of nations. Thus, the district court did not err in dismissing Plaintiffs' complaint.

Serra v. Lappin, 600 F.3d 1191, 1198–200 (9th Cir. 2010).

The Ninth Circuit has significantly limited the use of the *Charming Betsy* canon. Given what you have learned about its origin and purpose, are these limitations appropriate?

3.   The debate over the legal status of customary international law has led some judges to conclude that the *Charming Betsy* canon is obsolete. *See Al-Bihani v. Obama*, 619 F.3d 1 (D.C. Cir. 2010) (Kavanaugh, J. concurring in denial of rehearing *en banc*):

[T]he problems with applying *Charming Betsy* are equally substantial. There was a good argument for interpreting statutes in light of customary international law in the days before *Erie*, when customary-international-law principles were considered part of the general common law that all federal courts could enforce. *See, e.g.*, John F. Manning, *Deriving Rules of Statutory Interpretation from the Constitution*, 101 Colum. L. Rev. 1648, 1680 n. 146 (2001) ("To the extent that courts applying the law of nations believed that they were implementing a preexisting body of customary law, they may have felt somewhat greater freedom to exercise such independent common law powers in relation to statutes."). After *Erie* and particularly after *Sosa*, however, it is clear that customary-international-law norms, like non-self-executing treaties, are not part of domestic U.S. law. Congress has incorporated customary international law into domestic U.S. law on numerous occasions, including in statutes related to war. Thus, when Congress does not act to incorporate those norms into domestic U.S. law, such non-incorporation presumably reflects a deliberate congressional choice. And it likewise makes sense to conclude that Congress would not want courts to smuggle those norms into domestic U.S. law through the back door by using them to resolve questions of American law. As the Seventh Circuit has stated, use of the *Charming Betsy* canon "so as to effectively incorporate customary international law into federal statutes when the political branches of our government may have rejected the international law at issue seems dubious at best." *Sampson v. Federal Republic of Germany,* 250 F.3d 1145, 1153 (7th Cir. 2001); *see also* Curtis A. Bradley & Jack L. Goldsmith, *Customary International Law as Federal Common Law: A Critique of the Modern Position,* 110 Harv. L. Rev. 815, 871–72 (1997) (affording customary international law its proper status is arguably inconsistent with the *Charming Betsy* canon); Curtis A. Bradley, *The* Charming Betsy *Canon and Separation of Powers: Rethinking the Interpretive Role of International Law,* 86 Geo. L.J. 479, 536 (1997) ("the redefinition of federal court power after *Erie*" "compel[s] reexamination of" the *Charming Betsy* canon); Note, *The* Charming Betsy *Canon, Separation of Powers, and Customary International Law,* 121 Harv. L. Rev. 1215, 1221–22 (2008) ("courts arguably violate the separation of powers when they cabin congressional lawmaking power with a canon that draws force from a body of law that has no constitutional origin and does not promote any competing constitutional value").

After *Erie,* and particularly after *Sosa* and *Medellín,* courts should not invoke the *Charming Betsy* canon to conform federal statutes to non-self-executing treaties and customary international law. Invocation of the *Charming Betsy* canon in such circumstances constitutes an "indirect, 'phantom' use of international law" that can "have the same effect as direct incorporation of international law." Bradley, *The* Charming Betsy *Canon,* 86 Geo. L.J. at 483. Applying *Charming Betsy* to customary international law and non-self-executing treaties would create an "international law-based, quasi-constitutional 'penumbra' that crowds out and inhibits congressional lawmaking." Note, *The* Charming Betsy *Canon,* 121 Harv. L.Rev. at 1222.

Judge Kavanaugh assumes that Congressional inaction should be interpreted as a rejection of the customary international law rule. Is this a defensible presumption? What would be the implications of this rule for U.S. compliance in the international law legal system?

B. THE ALIEN TORT STATUTE

As the *Filartiga* case set out above demonstrates, customary international law is regularly raised in modern human rights cases brought pursuant to the Alien Tort Statute (ATS). Until the last few decades, this provision was rarely invoked as a basis for federal jurisdiction. Its significance as a tool for redressing human rights violations only became apparent with the Second Circuit's 1980 decision in *Filartiga v. Pena-Irala, see* Section II(B) *supra.*

Following *Filartiga,* several circuits applied its holding to award damages for human rights violations that occurred abroad. These decisions recognized a core set of customary international human rights norms that could be redressed under the ATS as "violation[s] of the law of nations," including summary execution, disappearance, war crimes, crimes against humanity, slavery, and arbitrary detention. Initially, these cases received minimal attention because most of the defendants were foreign nationals and most cases resulted in default judgments that could not be enforced. Then, in the late 1990s, advocates began to bring suits against multinational corporations alleging that they had committed human rights abuses or were complicit in human rights violations of state actors. For example, in *Doe v. Unocal,*[4] Burmese plaintiffs alleged that the defendant oil corporation had colluded in the commission of human rights violations by the Burmese military in order to further an oil pipeline project.

Not surprisingly, the proliferation of these cases against multinational corporations generated a reaction from the American business community, which began to actively oppose the use of the ATS as a tool of corporate accountability. The growing controversy also helped to prompt a shift in the views of the executive branch. While the Carter Administration had filed a brief in *Filartiga* supporting the use of the ATS to redress violations of customary international human rights law, when the U.S. Supreme Court ultimately took up the issue in *Sosa v. Alvarez-Machain,* the George W. Bush Administration filed a brief opposing jurisdiction.

The *Sosa* case came to the Court with a long and complicated history. In 1985, Enrique Camarena-Salazar, an agent of the U.S. Drug Enforcement Agency, was tortured and murdered by drug traffickers in Mexico. Alvarez, a doctor, was indicted in the United States. He was accused of participating in the crime by helping to keep Camarena-Salazar alive during the torture. Unable to extradite Alvarez to stand trial, the DEA hired a group of Mexican nationals to kidnap him and bring him across the border into Texas. The lower courts dismissed the criminal indictment against Alvarez, holding that the illegal kidnapping constituted "outrageous governmental conduct," but the Supreme Court reversed, holding that the manner of his seizure did not impact the

---

[4]   395 F.3d 932 (9th Cir. 2002), *opinion vacated and reh'g en banc granted,* 395 F.3d 978 (9th Cir. 2003).

federal courts' jurisdiction. The case was remanded for a trial, which ultimately ended with a judgment of acquittal in 1992.

Alvarez then filed a civil suit for damages against Jose Francisco Sosa, one of the Mexican nationals responsible for his arrest and detention, as well as against several DEA agents and the U.S. government. Most of the claims and defendants were dismissed, leaving only Sosa and the U.S. government. The district court ultimately dismissed the claim against the federal government, but entered a $25,000 judgment against Sosa for arbitrary arrest and detention. A three-judge panel of the Ninth Circuit affirmed the ATS judgment, but reinstated the claim against the United States. The Ninth Circuit then agreed to hear the case *en banc* and in a divided decision, affirmed the panel. The Supreme Court granted *certiorari* and rendered a judgment on the merits. The excerpt that follows sets out the Court's reasoning on the purpose and use of the ATS.

SOSA V. ALVAREZ-MACHAIN
Supreme Court of the United States, 2004.
542 U.S. 692.

JUSTICE SOUTER delivered the opinion of the Court.

. . .

Alvarez has also brought an action under the ATS against petitioner Sosa, who argues (as does the United States supporting him) that there is no relief under the ATS because the statute does no more than vest federal courts with jurisdiction, neither creating nor authorizing the courts to recognize any particular right of action without further congressional action. Although we agree the statute is in terms only jurisdictional, we think that at the time of enactment the jurisdiction enabled federal courts to hear claims in a very limited category defined by the law of nations and recognized at common law. We do not believe, however, that the limited, implicit sanction to entertain the handful of international law *cum* common law claims understood in 1789 should be taken as authority to recognize the right of action asserted by Alvarez here.

A

. . .

The parties and *amici* here advance radically different historical interpretations of this terse provision. Alvarez says that the ATS was intended not simply as a jurisdictional grant, but as authority for the creation of a new cause of action for torts in violation of international law. We think that reading is implausible. As enacted in 1789, the ATS gave the district courts "cognizance" of certain causes of action, and the term bespoke a grant of jurisdiction, not power to mold substantive law. The fact that the ATS was placed in § 9 of the Judiciary Act, a statute otherwise exclusively concerned with federal-court jurisdiction, is itself support for its strictly jurisdictional nature.

. . .

But holding the ATS jurisdictional raises a new question, this one about the interaction between the ATS at the time of its enactment and the ambient law of the era. Sosa would have it that the ATS was stillborn because there could be no claim for relief without a further statute expressly authorizing adoption of causes of action. *Amici* professors of federal jurisdiction and legal history take a different tack, that federal courts could entertain claims once the jurisdictional grant was on the books, because torts in violation of the law of nations would have been recognized within the common law of the time. We think history and practice give the edge to this latter position.

1

"When the United States declared their independence, they were bound to receive the law of nations, in its modern state of purity and refinement." In the years of the early Republic, this law of nations comprised two principal elements, the first covering the general norms governing the behavior of national states with each other: "the science which teaches the rights subsisting between nations or states, and the obligations correspondent to those rights," or "that code of public instruction which defines the rights and prescribes the duties of nations, in their intercourse with each other." This aspect of the law of nations thus occupied the executive and legislative domains, not the judicial.

The law of nations included a second, more pedestrian element, however, that did fall within the judicial sphere, as a body of judge-made law regulating the conduct of individuals situated outside domestic boundaries and consequently carrying an international savor. To Blackstone, the law of nations in this sense was implicated "in mercantile questions, such as bills of exchange and the like; in all marine causes, relating to freight, average, demurrage, insurances, bottomry . . . ; [and] in all disputes relating to prizes, to shipwrecks, to hostages, and ransom bills.". . . And it was the law of nations in this sense that our precursors spoke about when the Court explained the status of coast fishing vessels in wartime grew from "ancient usage among civilized nations, beginning centuries ago, and gradually ripening into a rule of international law. . . ." *The Paquete Habana.*

There was, finally, a sphere in which these rules binding individuals for the benefit of other individuals overlapped with the norms of state relationships. Blackstone referred to it when he mentioned three specific offenses against the law of nations addressed by the criminal law of England: violation of safe conducts, infringement of the rights of ambassadors, and piracy. An assault against an ambassador, for example, impinged upon the sovereignty of the foreign nation and if not adequately redressed could rise to an issue of war. It was this narrow set of violations of the law of nations, admitting of a judicial remedy and at the same time threatening serious consequences in international affairs, that was probably on minds of the men who drafted the ATS with its reference to tort.

2

Before there was any ATS, a distinctly American preoccupation with these hybrid international norms had taken shape owing to the distribution of political power from independence through the period of confederation. The Continental Congress was hamstrung by its inability to "cause infractions of treaties, or of the law of nations to be punished," and in 1781 the Congress implored the States to vindicate rights under the law of nations. In words that echo Blackstone, the congressional resolution called upon state legislatures to "provide expeditious, exemplary and adequate punishment" for "the violation of safe conducts or passports, . . . of hostility against such as are in amity . . . with the United States, . . . infractions of the immunities of ambassadors and other public ministers . . . [and] infractions of treaties and conventions to which the United States are a party." The resolution recommended that the States "authorise suits . . . for damages by the party injured, and for compensation to the United States for damage sustained by them from an injury done to a foreign power by a citizen." Apparently only one State acted upon the recommendation, but Congress had done what it could to signal a commitment to enforce the law of nations.

. . .

The Framers responded by vesting the Supreme Court with original jurisdiction over "all Cases affecting Ambassadors, other public ministers and Consuls." U.S. Const., Art. III, § 2, and the First Congress followed through. The Judiciary Act reinforced this Court's original jurisdiction over suits brought by diplomats, created alienage jurisdiction, and, of course, included the ATS, § 9.

. . .

There is no record of congressional discussion about private actions that might be subject to the jurisdictional provision, or about any need for further legislation to create private remedies; there is no record even of debate on the section. Given the poverty of drafting history, modern commentators have necessarily concentrated on the text, remarking on the innovative use of the word "tort." . . . But despite considerable scholarly attention, it is fair to say that a consensus understanding of what Congress intended has proven elusive.

Still, the history does tend to support two propositions. First, there is every reason to suppose that the First Congress did not pass the ATS as a jurisdictional convenience to be placed on the shelf for use by a future Congress or state legislature that might, someday, authorize the creation of causes of action or itself decide to make some element of the law of nations actionable for the benefit of foreigners. The anxieties of the preconstitutional period cannot be ignored easily enough to think that the statute was not meant to have a practical effect.

. . .

The second inference to be drawn from the history is that Congress intended the ATS to furnish jurisdiction for a relatively modest set of actions alleging violations of the law of nations. Uppermost in the legislative mind appears to have been offenses against ambassadors, violations of safe conduct were probably understood to be actionable, and individual actions arising out of prize captures and piracy may well have also been contemplated. But the common law appears to have understood only those three of the hybrid variety as definite and actionable, or at any rate, to have assumed only a very limited set of claims. As Blackstone had put it, "offences against this law [of nations] are principally incident to whole states or nations," and not individuals seeking relief in court.

. . .

In sum, although the ATS is a jurisdictional statute creating no new causes of action, the reasonable inference from the historical materials is that the statute was intended to have practical effect the moment it became law. The jurisdictional grant is best read as having been enacted on the understanding that the common law would provide a cause of action for the modest number of international law violations with a potential for personal liability at the time.

IV.

We think it is correct, then, to assume that the First Congress understood that the district courts would recognize private causes of action for certain torts in violation of the law of nations, though we have found no basis to suspect Congress had any examples in mind beyond those torts corresponding to Blackstone's three primary offenses: violation of safe conducts, infringement of the rights of ambassadors, and piracy. We assume, too, that no development in the two centuries from the enactment of § 1350 to the birth of the modern line of cases beginning with *Filartiga v. Pena-Irala,* has categorically precluded federal courts from recognizing a claim under the law of nations as an element of common law; Congress has not in any relevant way amended § 1350 or limited civil common law power by another statute. Still, there are good reasons for a restrained conception of the discretion a federal court should exercise in considering a new cause of action of this kind. Accordingly, we think courts should require any claim based on the present-day law of nations to rest on a norm of international character accepted by the civilized world and defined with a specificity comparable to the features of the 18th-century paradigms we have recognized. This requirement is fatal to Alvarez's claim.

. . .

Alvarez's detention claim must be gauged against the current state of international law, looking to those sources we have long, albeit cautiously, recognized.

> "[W]here there is no treaty, and no controlling executive or legislative act or judicial decision, resort must be had to the customs and usages of civilized nations; and, as evidence of these, to the works of jurists and commentators, who by years of labor, research and experience, have made themselves peculiarly well acquainted with the subjects of which they treat. Such works are resorted to by judicial tribunals, not for the speculations of their authors concerning what the law ought to be, but for trustworthy evidence of what the law really is." *The Paquete Habana.*

To begin with, Alvarez cites two well-known international agreements that, despite their moral authority, have little utility under the standard set out in this opinion. He says that his abduction by Sosa was an "arbitrary arrest" within the meaning of the Universal Declaration of Human Rights. And he traces the rule against arbitrary arrest not only to the Declaration, but also to article nine of the International Covenant on Civil and Political Rights to which the United States is a party, and to various other conventions to which it is not. But the Declaration does not of its own force impose obligations as a matter of international law. And, although the Covenant does bind the United States as a matter of international law, the United States ratified the Covenant on the express understanding that it was not self-executing and so did not itself create obligations enforceable in the federal courts. Accordingly, Alvarez cannot say that the Declaration and Covenant themselves establish the relevant and applicable rule of international law. He instead attempts to show that prohibition of arbitrary arrest has attained the status of binding customary international law.

Here, it is useful to examine Alvarez's complaint in greater detail. As he presently argues it, the claim does not rest on the cross-border feature of his abduction. Although the District Court granted relief in part on finding a violation of international law in taking Alvarez across the border from Mexico to the United States, the Court of Appeals rejected that ground of liability for failure to identify a norm of requisite force prohibiting a forcible abduction across a border. Instead, it relied on the conclusion that the law of the United States did not authorize Alvarez's arrest, because the DEA lacked extraterritorial authority under 21 U.S.C. § 878, and because Federal Rule of Criminal Procedure 4(d)(2) limited the warrant for Alvarez's arrest to "the jurisdiction of the United States." It is this position that Alvarez takes now: that his arrest was arbitrary and as such forbidden by international law not because it infringed the prerogatives of Mexico, but because no applicable law authorized it.

Alvarez thus invokes a general prohibition of "arbitrary" detention defined as officially sanctioned action exceeding positive authorization to detain under the domestic law of some government, regardless of the circumstances. Whether or not this is an accurate reading of the Covenant, Alvarez cites little authority that a rule so broad has the status of a binding customary norm today. He certainly cites nothing to justify the federal courts in taking his broad rule as the predicate for a federal lawsuit, for its implications would be breathtaking. His rule would support a cause of action in federal court for any arrest, anywhere in the world, unauthorized by the law of the jurisdiction in which it took place, and would create a cause of action for any seizure of an alien in violation of the Fourth Amendment, supplanting the actions under 42 U.S.C. § 1983, and *Bivens v. Six Unknown Fed. Narcotics Agents,* 403 U.S. 388 (1971), that now provide damages remedies for such violations. It would create an action in federal court for arrests by state officers who simply exceed their authority; and for the violation of any limit that the law of any country might place on the authority of its own officers to arrest. And all of this assumes that Alvarez could establish that Sosa was acting on behalf of a government when he made the arrest, for otherwise he would need a rule broader still.

Alvarez's failure to marshal support for his proposed rule is underscored by the Restatement (Third) of Foreign Relations Law of the United States (1986), which says in its discussion of customary international human rights law that a "state violates international law if, as a matter of state policy, it practices, encourages, or condones . . . prolonged arbitrary detention." Although the Restatement does not explain its requirements of a "state policy" and of "prolonged" detention, the implication is clear. Any credible invocation of a principle against arbitrary detention that the civilized world accepts as binding customary international law requires a factual basis beyond relatively brief detention in excess of positive authority. Even the Restatement's limits are only the beginning of the enquiry, because although it is easy to say that some policies of prolonged arbitrary detentions are so bad that those who enforce them become enemies of the human race, it may be harder to say which policies cross that line with the certainty afforded by Blackstone's three common law offenses. In any event, the label would never fit the reckless policeman who botches his warrant, even though that same officer might pay damages under municipal law.

Whatever may be said for the broad principle Alvarez advances, in the present, imperfect world, it expresses an aspiration that exceeds any binding customary rule having the specificity we require. Creating a private cause of action to further that aspiration would go beyond any residual common law discretion we think it appropriate to exercise. It is enough to hold that a single illegal detention of less than a day, followed by the transfer of custody to lawful authorities and a prompt arraignment, violates no norm of customary international law so well defined as to support the creation of a federal remedy.

. . .

The judgment of the Court of Appeals is *Reversed*.

NOTES & QUESTIONS

1.   Review the Henkin-Bradley/Goldsmith-Koh exchange above. Which position does the *Sosa* Court adopt with respect to the status of customary international law? Many commentators argued that the decision confirmed that customary international is federal common law. One ATS expert, Professor Ralph Steinhardt, stated that CIL "was and [after *Sosa*] remains an area in which no affirmative legislative act is required to 'authorize' its application in U.S. courts." Ralph G. Steinhardt, *Laying One Bankrupt Critique to Rest: Sosa v. Alvarez-Machain and the Future of International Human Rights Litigation in U.S. Courts*, 97 Vand. L. Rev. 2241, 2259 (2004). Perhaps not surprisingly, Professors Bradley and Goldsmith have disagreed, arguing that *Sosa* stands for the proposition that "CIL is incorporated into federal law . . . only when its incorporation has been authorized either by the structure of the Constitution or by the political branches, and it is to be applied interstitially in a manner consistent with the relevant policies of the political branches." Curtis A. Bradley, Jack L. Goldsmith & David H. Moore, *Sosa, Customary International Law and the Continuing Relevance of Erie*, 120 Harv. L. Rev. 869, 935–36 (2007). Which argument do you think finds more support in the text of the decision?

2.   The *Sosa* Court affirmed that "federal courts should not recognize private claims under federal common law for violations of any international law norm with less definite content and acceptance among civilized nations than the historical paradigms familiar when [the ATS] was enacted," namely "violation of safe conducts, infringement of the rights of ambassadors, and piracy." *See* Sosa, 542 U.S. at 724. Compare this standard with the standard for determining rules of CIL provided in the Restatement (Third). Does this decision limit the set of CIL claims that are available through the ATS?

After *Sosa*, the pace of ATS litigation picked up considerably, particularly against corporate defendants. By 2011, plaintiffs had filed over 150 cases against corporate defendants and were beginning to experience some victories. In 2005, the parties in the *Unocal* case settled and issued the following statement:

> The parties to several lawsuits related to Unocal's energy investment in the Yadana gas pipeline project in Myanmar/Burma announced today that they have settled their suits. Although the terms are confidential, the settlement will compensate plaintiffs and provide funds enabling plaintiffs and their representatives to develop programs to improve living conditions, health care and education and protect the rights of people from the pipeline region. These initiatives will provide substantial assistance to people who may have suffered hardships in the region. Unocal reaffirms its principle that the company respects human rights in all of its activities and commits to enhance its educational programs to further this principle. Plaintiffs and their representatives reaffirm their commitment to protecting human rights.

One report suggested that the Unocal settlement was for $30 million.[5] In 2008, two courts entered judgments for plaintiffs in their cases against corporate defendants.[6] Then, in 2009, days before the start of trial, Royal Dutch Shell agreed to a $15.5 million settlement in a suit alleging that the company had taken part in human rights abuses in the oil rich region of the Niger Delta.[7] While many ATS cases were dismissed, the statute appeared to be an increasingly powerful tool for ensuring international corporate accountability. And even when plaintiffs lost in court, the cases helped to support broader transnational advocacy campaigns. As the plaintiffs' lawyers in the cases against Coca Cola explained:

> [Litigation] . . . served to focus a broader campaign seeking to persuade [Coca-Cola] to accept responsibility for violence in its bottling plants, wholly apart from any potential legal liability . . . The campaign is using factual information developed from the investigations connected to the litigation, as well as traditional

---

[5]   *See* A Milestone for Human Rights, Bus. Wk., Jan. 24, 2005.

[6]   *See* Aguilar v. Imperial Nurseries, 2008 WL 2572250 (D. Conn. 2008) (settlement for $7.7 million); Licea v. Curacao Drydock Co., Inc., 584 F.Supp. 2d 1355 (S.D. Fla. 2008) (settlement for $80 million).

[7]   *See* Jad Mouawad, Shell to Pay $15.5 Million to Settle Nigerian Case, N.Y. Times, June 9, 2009.

human rights reports, to support specific demands that Coca-Cola respond to the violence.[8]

Then in 2010, the Second Circuit decided another case brought by Nigerian nationals against Royal Dutch Petroleum and Shell Transport and Trading alleging human rights violations in Nigeria. A divided panel in *Kiobel v. Royal Dutch Petroleum*, held that corporations cannot be held liable for violations of CIL. As you read the excerpts from the court's opinion, consider whether and how the Second Circuit's approach to identifying CIL norms changed since *Filartiga*.

KIOBEL V. ROYAL DUTCH PETROLEUM CO.
United States Court of Appeals for the Second Circuit, 2010.
621 F.3d 111.

JOSE A. CABRANES, CIRCUIT JUDGE:

. . .

[T]his appeal presents a question that has been lurking for some time in our ATS jurisprudence. Since our first case upholding claims brought under the ATS in 1980, *see Filartiga v. Pena-Irala,* 630 F.2d 876 (2d Cir.1980), our Court has never directly addressed whether our jurisdiction under the ATS extends to civil actions against corporations.

. . .

II. Corporate Liability Is Not a Norm of Customary International Law

To attain the status of a rule of customary international law, a norm must be "specific, universal, and obligatory." Defining such norms "is no simple task," as "[c]ustomary international law is discerned from myriad decisions made in numerous and varied international and domestic arenas." The sources consulted are therefore of the utmost importance. As the Supreme Court re-emphasized in *Sosa,* we look to "those sources we have long, albeit cautiously, recognized":

> '[W]here there is no treaty, and no controlling executive or legislative act or judicial decision, resort must be had to the *customs and usages of civilized nations;* and, as evidence of these, to the works of jurists and commentators, who by years of labor, research and experience, have made themselves peculiarly well acquainted with the subjects of which they treat. Such works are resorted to by judicial tribunals, not for the

---

[8] Jonathan C. Drimmer & Sarah R. Lamoree, *Think Globally, Sue Locally: Trends and Out-of-Court Tactics in Transnational Tort Actions,* 29 Berkeley J. Int'l L. 456, 514–15 (2011) (quoting Cheryl Holzmeyer, *Human Rights in an Era of Neoliberal Globalization: The Alien Tort Claims Act and Grassroots Mobilization in Doe v. Unocal,* 43 Law & Soc'y Rev. 271, 291 (2009)).

speculations of their authors concerning what the law ought to be, but for trustworthy evidence of what the law really is.'

Agreements or declarations that are merely aspirational, and that "do[ ] not of [their] own force impose obligations as a matter of international law," are of "little utility" in discerning norms of customary international law.

. . .

With those principles in mind, we consider whether the sources of international law reveal that corporate liability has attained universal acceptance as a rule of customary international law.

A. International Tribunals

Insofar as international tribunals are established for the specific purpose of imposing liability on those who violate the law of nations, the history and conduct of those tribunals is instructive. We find it particularly significant, therefore, that no international tribunal of which we are aware has *ever* held a corporation liable for a violation of the law of nations.

1. The Nuremberg Tribunals

The Charter of the International Military Tribunal, commonly known as the "London Charter," authorized the punishment of the major war criminals of the European Axis following the Second World War. The London Charter and the trials at Nuremberg that followed are collectively the single most important source of modern customary international law concerning liability for violations of fundamental human rights. . . .

It is notable, then, that the London Charter, which established the International Military Tribunal at Nuremberg, granted the Tribunal jurisdiction over *natural persons only.*

. . .

[T]he subsequent United States Military Tribunals, established under Control Council Law No. 10, prosecuted *corporate executives* for their role in violating customary international law during the Second World War, but not the corporate entities themselves. This approach to liability can be seen most clearly in the tribunal's treatment of the notorious I.G. Farben chemical company ("I.G. Farben").

The refusal of the military tribunal at Nuremberg to impose liability on I.G. Farben is not a matter of happenstance or oversight. This corporation's production of, among other things, oil, rubber, nitrates, and fibers was harnessed to the purposes of the Nazi state, and it is no exaggeration to assert that the corporation made possible the war crimes and crimes against humanity perpetrated by Nazi Germany, including its infamous programs of looting properties of defeated nations, slave labor, and genocide:

> The depth of the partnership [between the Nazi state and I.G. Farben] was reached at Auschwitz, the extermination center [in Poland], where four million human beings were destroyed in accordance with the "Final Solution of the Jewish Question," Hitler's plan to destroy an entire people. Drawn by the almost limitless reservoir of death camp labor, I.G. [Farben] chose to build a great industrial complex at Auschwitz for the production of synthetic rubber and oil.

. . .

Twenty-four executives of Farben were charged, *inter alia,* with "Planning, Preparation, Initiation, and Waging of Wars of Aggression and Invasions of Other Countries"; "Plunder and Spoliation"; and "Slavery and Mass Murder." But the I.G. Farben corporate entity was not charged, nor was it named in the indictment as a criminal organization. In issuing its judgment, the tribunal pointedly observed that "the corporate defendant, Farben, is not before the bar of this Tribunal and cannot be subjected to criminal penalties in these proceedings."

. . .

In declining to impose corporate liability under international law in the case of the most nefarious corporate enterprise known to the civilized world, while prosecuting the men who led I.G. Farben, the military tribunals established under Control Council Law No. 10 expressly defined liability under the law of nations as liability that could not be divorced from *individual* moral responsibility. It is thus clear that, at the time of the Nuremberg trials, corporate liability was not recognized as a "specific, universal, and obligatory" norm of customary international law.

We turn now to international tribunals convened since Nuremberg to determine whether there is any evidence that the concept of corporate liability has coalesced into a "specific, universal, and obligatory" norm.

2.   International Tribunals Since Nuremberg

Since Nuremberg, international tribunals have continually declined to hold corporations liable for violations of customary international law. For example, the charters establishing both the International Criminal Tribunal for the former Yugoslavia ("ICTY") and the International Criminal Tribunal for Rwanda, or ("ICTR") expressly confined the tribunals' jurisdiction to "natural persons."

. . .

More recently, the Rome Statute of the ICC also limits that tribunal's jurisdiction to "natural persons." Significantly, a proposal to grant the ICC jurisdiction over corporations and other "juridical" persons was advanced by the French delegation, but the proposal was rejected. As commentators have explained, the French proposal was rejected in part because "criminal liability of corporations is still rejected in many national legal orders" and thus would pose challenges for the ICC's principle of "complementarity." The history of the Rome Statute therefore confirms the absence of any generally recognized principle or consensus among States concerning corporate liability for violations of customary international law.

In sum, modern international tribunals make it abundantly clear that, since Nuremberg, the concept of corporate liability for violations of customary international law has not even begun to "ripen[ ]" into a universally accepted norm of international law.

B. International Treaties

Treaties "are proper evidence of customary international law because, and insofar as, they create *legal obligations* akin to contractual obligations on the States parties to them." Although all treaties ratified by more than one State provide *some* evidence of the custom and practice of nations, "a treaty will only constitute *sufficient proof* of a norm of *customary international law* if an overwhelming majority of States have ratified the treaty, *and* those States uniformly and consistently act in accordance with its principles."

. . .

That a provision appears in one treaty (or more), therefore, is not proof of a well-established norm of *customary* international law.

One district court in our Circuit erroneously overvalued the importance of a number of international treaties in finding that corporate liability has attained the status of customary international law. None of the treaties relied upon in the district court's 2003 *Presbyterian Church* opinion have been ratified by the United States, and most of them have not been ratified by other States whose interests would be most profoundly affected by the treaties' terms. Those treaties are therefore insufficient—considered either individually or collectively—to demonstrate that corporate liability is universally recognized as a norm of customary international law.

Even if those specialized treaties had been ratified by an "overwhelming majority" of states—as some recent treaties providing for corporate liability have been—the fact that those treaties impose obligations on corporations in the context of the treaties' particular subject matter tells us nothing about whether corporate liability for, say, violations of *human rights,* which are not a subject of those treaties, is universally recognized as a norm of *customary international law.* Significantly, to find that a treaty embodies or creates a rule of customary international law would mean that the rule applies beyond the limited subject matter of the treaty and *to nations that have not ratified it.* To construe those treaties as so-called "law-making" treaties—that is, treaties that codify existing norms of customary international law or crystallize an emerging rule of customary international law—would be wholly inappropriate and without precedent.

As noted above, there is no historical evidence of an existing or even nascent norm of customary international law imposing liability on corporations for violations of human rights. It cannot be said, therefore, that those treaties on specialized questions codify an existing, general rule of customary international law.

. . .

It bears underscoring that the purpose of the ATS was not to encourage United States courts to create new norms of customary international law unilaterally. Instead, the statute was rooted in the ancient concept of comity among nations and was intended to provide a remedy for violations of customary international law that "threaten[ ] serious consequences in international affairs." Unilaterally recognizing new norms of customary international law—that is, norms that have not been universally accepted by the rest of the civilized world—would potentially create friction in our relations with foreign nations and, therefore, would contravene the international comity the statute was enacted to promote.

We conclude, therefore, that the relatively few international treaties that impose particular obligations on corporations do not establish corporate liability as a "specific, universal, and obligatory" norm of customary international law

. . .

C. Works of Publicists

Although the works of publicists (*i.e.,* scholars or "jurists") can be a relevant source of customary international law, "[s]uch works are resorted to by judicial tribunals, not for the speculations of their authors concerning what the law ought to be, but for trustworthy evidence of what the law really is."

In light of the evidence discussed above, it is not surprising that two renowned professors of international law, Professor James Crawford and Professor (now Judge) Christopher Greenwood, forcefully declared in litigation argued before this panel on the same day as this case that customary international law does not recognize liability for corporations that violate its norms. According to Professor Crawford, "no national court [outside of the United States] and no international judicial tribunal has so far recognized corporate liability, as opposed to individual liability, *in a civil or criminal context* on the basis of a violation of the law of nations or customary international law." Even those who favor using the ATS as a means of holding corporations accountable for human rights violations reluctantly acknowledge that "the universe of international criminal law does not reveal any prosecutions of corporations per se."

Together, those authorities demonstrate that imposing liability on corporations for violations of customary international law has not attained a discernible, much less universal, acceptance among nations of the world in their relations *inter se*. Because corporate liability is not recognized as a "specific, universal, and obligatory" norm, it is not a rule of customary international law that we may apply under the ATS. Accordingly, insofar as plaintiffs in this action seek to hold only corporations liable for their conduct in Nigeria (as opposed to individuals within those corporations), and only under the ATS, their claims must be dismissed for lack of subject matter jurisdiction.

. . .

LEVAL, CIRCUIT JUDGE (concurring only in the judgment):

The majority opinion deals a substantial blow to international law and its undertaking to protect fundamental human rights. According to the rule my colleagues have created, one who earns profits by commercial exploitation of abuse of fundamental human rights can successfully shield those profits from victims' claims for compensation simply by taking the precaution of conducting the heinous operation in the corporate form. Without any support in either the precedents or the scholarship of international law, the majority take the position that corporations, and other juridical entities, are not subject to international law, and for that reason such violators of fundamental human rights are free to retain any profits so earned without liability to their victims.

Adoption of the corporate form has always offered important benefits and protections to business—foremost among them the limitation of liability to the assets of the business, without recourse to the assets of its shareholders. The new rule offers to unscrupulous businesses advantages of incorporation never before dreamed of. So long as they incorporate (or act in the form of a trust), businesses will now be free to trade in or exploit slaves, employ mercenary armies to do dirty work for despots, perform genocides or operate torture prisons for a despot's political opponents, or engage in piracy—all without civil liability to victims. By adopting the corporate form, such an enterprise could have hired itself out to operate Nazi extermination camps or the torture chambers of

Argentina's dirty war, immune from civil liability to its victims. By protecting profits earned through abuse of fundamental human rights protected by international law, the rule my colleagues have created operates in opposition to the objective of international law to protect those rights.

. . .

According to the majority, in cases where the norms of the law of nations were violated by a corporation (or other juridical entity), compensatory damages *may be awarded under the ATS against the corporation's employees,* natural persons who acted in the corporation's behalf, *but not against the corporation* that commanded the atrocities and earned profits by committing them. The corporation, according to my colleagues, has not violated international law, and is indeed incapable of doing so because international law does not apply to the conduct of corporations.

. . .

The majority contend . . . that unambiguous jurisprudence "lead[s] inescapably" to their conclusion. . . . The argument depends on its observation that international *criminal* tribunals have been established without jurisdiction to impose *criminal punishments* on corporations for their violations of international law. From this fact the majority contend an inescapable inference arises that international law does not govern corporations, which are therefore free to engage in conduct prohibited by the rules of international law with impunity.

There is no logic to the argument. The reasons why international tribunals have been established without jurisdiction to impose *criminal* liability on corporations have to do solely with the theory and the objectives of *criminal punishment,* and have no bearing on civil compensatory liability. The view is widely held among the nations of the world that criminal punishments (under domestic law, as well as international law) are inappropriate for corporations. This view derives from two perceptions: First, that criminal punishment can be theoretically justified only where the defendant has acted with criminal intent—a condition that cannot exist when the defendant is a juridical construct which is incapable of having an intent; and second, that criminal punishments are pointless and counterproductive when imposed on a fictitious juridical entity because they fail to achieve the punitive objectives of criminal punishment. For these reasons many nations in their domestic laws impose criminal punishments only on natural persons, and not on juridical ones. In contrast, the imposition of civil liability on corporations serves perfectly the objective of civil liability to compensate victims for the wrongs inflicted on them and is practiced everywhere in the world. The fact that international tribunals do not impose *criminal punishment* on corporations in no way supports the inference that corporations are outside the scope of international law and therefore can incur no *civil compensatory liability* to victims when they engage in conduct prohibited by the norms of international law.

. . .

The majority then argue that the absence of a universal practice among nations of imposing civil damages on corporations for violations of international law means that under international law corporations are not liable for violations of the law of nations. This argument is as illogical as the first and is based on a misunderstanding of the structure of international law. The position of international law on whether civil liability should be imposed for violations of its norms is that international law takes no position and leaves that question to each nation to resolve. International law, at least as it pertains to human rights, consists primarily of a sparse body of norms, adopting widely agreed principles prohibiting conduct universally agreed to be heinous and inhumane. Having established these norms of prohibited conduct, international law says little or nothing about how those norms should be enforced. It leaves the manner of enforcement, including the question of whether there should be private civil remedies for violations of international law, almost entirely to individual nations. While most nations have not recognized tort liability for violations of international law, the United States, through the ATS, has opted to impose civil compensatory liability on violators and draws no distinction in its laws between violators who are natural persons and corporations. The majority's argument that national courts are at liberty to award civil damages for violations of international law solely against natural persons and not against corporations has no basis in international law and, furthermore, nullifies the intention of international law to leave the question of civil liability to be decided separately by each nation.

The majority's asserted rule is, furthermore, at once internally inconsistent and incompatible with Supreme Court authority and with our prior cases that awarded damages for violations of international law. The absence of a universally accepted rule of international law on tort damages is true as to defendants who are natural persons, as well as to corporations. . . . If the absence of a universally accepted rule for the award of civil damages against corporations means that U.S. courts may not award damages against a corporation, then the same absence of a universally accepted rule for the award of civil damages against natural persons must mean that U.S. courts may not award damages against a natural person. But the majority opinion concedes (as it must) that U.S. courts may award damages against the corporation's employees when a corporation violates the rule of nations. Furthermore, our circuit and others have for decades awarded damages, and the Supreme Court in

Sosa made clear that a damage remedy does lie under the ATS. The majority opinion is thus internally inconsistent and is logically incompatible with both Second Circuit and Supreme Court authority.

. . .

The rule in cases under the ATS is quite simple. The law of nations sets worldwide norms of conduct, prohibiting certain universally condemned heinous acts. That body of law, however, takes no position on whether its norms may be enforced by civil actions for compensatory damages. It leaves that decision to be separately decided by each nation. The ATS confers on the U.S. courts jurisdiction to entertain civil suits for violations of the law of nations. In the United States, if a plaintiff in a suit under the ATS shows that she is the victim of a tort committed in violation of the norms of the law of nations, the court has jurisdiction to hear the case and to award compensatory damages against the tortfeasor. That is what the Supreme Court explained in *Sosa*. No principle of domestic or international law supports the majority's conclusion that the norms enforceable through the ATS—such as the prohibition by international law of genocide, slavery, war crimes, piracy, etc.—apply only to natural persons and not to corporations, leaving corporations immune from suit and free to retain profits earned through such acts.

I am in full agreement that *this* Complaint must be dismissed. It fails to state a proper legal claim of entitlement to relief. . . . I therefore agree with the majority that the claims against the Appellants must be dismissed, but not on the basis of the supposed rule of international law the majority have fashioned.

NOTES & QUESTIONS

1.   Does the majority opinion apply the standards for defining and proving a CIL norm that are set out in the Restatement (Third)? If not, how would you describe the differences in its approach? What kind of evidence does the Second Circuit consider persuasive?

2.   The majority and the dissent in *Kiobel* disagree over whether international or domestic law applies to the question of corporate liability in ATS cases. This dispute sheds some light on why the modernist-revisionist debate about the status of CIL is of continued significance in ATS cases. As Professor Ingrid Wuerth explains,

> [ATS] cases call upon domestic courts to translate international norms into domestic civil litigation, which often means applying norms developed in international criminal law to domestic civil law and wrestling with questions of individual, corporate, and secondary liability that are in some state of evolution and flux in customary international law. . . . Doctrinally, courts and commentators have struggled to determine whether international law or domestic

federal common law governs [these questions]. . . . In fact, neither alternative is fully convincing. These questions are critical to the scope of ATS, because they help define the kind of injury that is actionable. The statute is designed to redress violations of international law, and it would thus be odd to conclude that these issues should be resolved without reference to international law. On the other hand, international law is still developing in these areas, to some extent because international law relies itself on domestic law and international tribunals to help develop these doctrines through enforcement. It would thus be odd to conclude that they must be resolved in *toto* with no relationship to domestic law.

Ingrid Wuerth, *The Alien Tort Statute and Federal Common Law: A New Approach*, 85 Notre Dame L. Rev. 1931, 1938–39 (2010).

Wuerth advocates for a third way that adopts neither the modernist or revisionist approaches. She says that "[t]reading these as questions of federal common law that are developed with reference to international law is a better approach in ATS cases. It is also doctrinally superior because it avoids the threshold question of which kind of law to apply and allows courts to focus on the more significant questions: the content of domestic and international law, and the intentions of Congress and the executive branch." *Id.* at 1939. Do you find Wuerth's approach compelling? How do you think the other authors you have read would respond?

Kiobel petitioned for *certiorari*, which was granted by the Supreme Court. The case was argued in the 2011 term on the issue of corporate liability under the ATS.

Approximately a week after oral argument, the Supreme Court issued an order setting the case for reargument and ordering supplemental briefing on the question of "whether and under what circumstances the Alien Tort Statute, 28 U.S.C. § 1350, allows courts to recognize a cause of action for violations of the law of nations occurring within the territory of a sovereign other than the United States." The case was reheard during the 2012 term, and in April 2013, the Court issued a unanimous, but splintered decision affirming the Second Circuit's dismissal of the case, but never addressing the question of corporate liability.

KIOBEL V. ROYAL DUTCH PETROLEUM CO.

Supreme Court of the United States, 2013.
133 S.Ct. 1659.

CHIEF JUSTICE ROBERTS delivered the opinion of the Court.

Petitioners, a group of Nigerian nationals residing in the United States, filed suit in federal court against certain Dutch, British, and Nigerian corporations. Petitioners sued under the Alien Tort Statute, 28 U.S.C. § 1350, alleging that the corporations aided and abetted the Nigerian Government in committing violations of the law of nations in Nigeria. The question presented is whether and under what circumstances courts may recognize a cause of action under the Alien Tort Statute, for violations of the law of nations occurring within the territory of a sovereign other than the United States.

. . .

II

Passed as part of the Judiciary Act of 1789, the ATS was invoked twice in the late 18th century, but then only once more over the next 167 years. The statute provides district courts with jurisdiction to hear certain claims, but does not expressly provide any causes of action. We held in *Sosa v. Alvarez-Machain,* however, that the First Congress did not intend the provision to be "stillborn." The grant of jurisdiction is instead "best read as having been enacted on the understanding that the common law would provide a cause of action for [a] modest number of international law violations." We thus held that federal courts may "recognize private claims [for such violations] under federal common law." The Court in *Sosa* rejected the plaintiff's claim in that case for "arbitrary arrest and detention," on the ground that it failed to state a violation of the law of nations with the requisite "definite content and acceptance among civilized nations."

The question here is not whether petitioners have stated a proper claim under the ATS, but whether a claim may reach conduct occurring in the territory of a foreign sovereign. Respondents contend that claims under the ATS do not, relying primarily on a canon of statutory interpretation known as the presumption against extraterritorial application. That canon provides that "[w]hen a statute gives no clear indication of an extraterritorial application, it has none," and reflects the "presumption that United States law governs domestically but does not rule the world."

This presumption "serves to protect against unintended clashes between our laws and those of other nations which could result in international discord." As this Court has explained:

For us to run interference in . . . a delicate field of international relations there must be present the affirmative intention of the Congress clearly expressed. It alone has the facilities necessary to make fairly such an important policy decision where the possibilities of international discord are so evident and retaliative action so certain." The presumption against extraterritorial application helps ensure that the Judiciary does not erroneously adopt an interpretation of U.S. law that carries foreign policy consequences not clearly intended by the political branches.

We typically apply the presumption to discern whether an Act of Congress regulating conduct applies abroad. The ATS, on the other hand, is "strictly jurisdictional." It does not directly regulate conduct or afford relief. It instead allows federal courts to recognize certain causes of action based on sufficiently definite norms of international law. But we think the principles underlying the canon of interpretation similarly constrain courts considering causes of action that may be brought under the ATS.

Indeed, the danger of unwarranted judicial interference in the conduct of foreign policy is magnified in the context of the ATS, because the question is not what Congress has done but instead what courts may do. This Court in *Sosa* repeatedly stressed the need for judicial caution in considering which claims could be brought under the ATS, in light of foreign policy concerns. As the Court explained, "the potential [foreign policy] implications . . . of recognizing. . . . causes [under the ATS] should make courts particularly wary of impinging on the discretion of the Legislative and Executive Branches in managing foreign affairs." These concerns, which are implicated in any case arising under the ATS, are all the more pressing when the question is whether a cause of action under the ATS reaches conduct within the territory of another sovereign.

These concerns are not diminished by the fact that *Sosa* limited federal courts to recognizing causes of action only for alleged violations of international law norms that are " 'specific, universal, and obligatory.' " As demonstrated by Congress's enactment of the Torture Victim Protection Act of 1991, identifying such a norm is only the beginning of defining a cause of action. See *id.,* § 3 (providing detailed definitions for extrajudicial killing and torture); *id.,* § 2 (specifying who may be liable, creating a rule of exhaustion, and establishing a statute of limitations). Each of these decisions carries with it significant foreign policy implications.

The principles underlying the presumption against extraterritoriality thus constrain courts exercising their power under the ATS.

III

Petitioners contend that even if the presumption applies, the text, history, and purposes of the ATS rebut it for causes of action brought under that statute. It is true that Congress, even in a jurisdictional provision, can indicate that it intends federal law to apply to conduct occurring abroad. But to rebut the presumption, the ATS would need to evince a "clear indication of extraterritoriality." It does not.

To begin, nothing in the text of the statute suggests that Congress intended causes of action recognized under it to have extraterritorial reach. The ATS covers actions by aliens for violations of the law of nations, but that does not imply extraterritorial reach—such violations affecting aliens can occur either within or outside the United States. Nor does the fact that the text reaches "*any* civil action" suggest application to torts committed abroad; it is well established that generic terms like "any" or "every" do not rebut the presumption against extraterritoriality.

. . .

Nor does the historical background against which the ATS was enacted overcome the presumption against application to conduct in the territory of another sovereign. We explained in *Sosa* that when Congress passed the ATS, "three principal offenses against the law of nations" had been identified by Blackstone: violation of safe conducts, infringement of the rights of ambassadors, and piracy. The first two offenses have no necessary extraterritorial application. Indeed, Blackstone—in describing them—did so in terms of conduct occurring within the forum nation. . . .

. . .

The third example of a violation of the law of nations familiar to the Congress that enacted the ATS was piracy. Piracy typically occurs on the high seas, beyond the territorial jurisdiction of the United States or any other country. Petitioners contend that because Congress surely intended the ATS to provide jurisdiction for actions against pirates, it necessarily anticipated the statute would apply to conduct occurring abroad.

Applying U.S. law to pirates, however, does not typically impose the sovereign will of the United States onto conduct occurring within the territorial jurisdiction of another sovereign, and therefore carries less direct foreign policy consequences. Pirates were fair game wherever found, by any nation, because they generally did not operate within any jurisdiction. We do not think that the existence of a cause of action against them is a sufficient basis for concluding that other causes of action under the ATS reach conduct that does occur within the territory of another sovereign; pirates may well be a category unto themselves.

. . .

Finally, there is no indication that the ATS was passed to make the United States a uniquely hospitable forum for the enforcement of international norms. As Justice Story put it, "No nation has ever yet pretended to be the custos morum of the whole world. . . ." It is implausible to suppose that the First Congress wanted their fledgling Republic—struggling to receive international recognition—to be the first. Indeed, the parties offer no evidence that any nation, meek or mighty, presumed to do such a thing.

The United States was, however, embarrassed by its potential inability to provide judicial relief to foreign officials injured in the United States. Such offenses against ambassadors violated the law of nations, "and if not adequately redressed could rise to an issue of war." The ATS ensured that the United States could provide a forum for adjudicating such incidents. Nothing about this historical context suggests that Congress also intended federal common law under the ATS to provide a cause of action for conduct occurring in the territory of another sovereign.

Indeed, far from avoiding diplomatic strife, providing such a cause of action could have generated it. Recent experience bears this out. Moreover, accepting petitioners' view would imply that other nations, also applying the law of nations, could hale our citizens into their courts for alleged violations of the law of nations occurring in the United States, or anywhere else in the world. The presumption against extraterritoriality guards against our courts triggering such serious foreign policy consequences, and instead defers such decisions, quite appropriately, to the political branches.

We therefore conclude that the presumption against extraterritoriality applies to claims under the ATS, and that nothing in the statute rebuts that presumption. "[T]here is no clear indication of extraterritoriality here," and petitioners' case seeking relief for violations of the law of nations occurring outside the United States is barred.

IV

On these facts, all the relevant conduct took place outside the United States. And even where the claims touch and concern the territory of the United States, they must do so with sufficient force to displace the presumption against extraterritorial application. Corporations are often present in many countries, and it would reach too far to say that mere corporate presence suffices. If Congress were to determine otherwise, a statute more specific than the ATS would be required.

The judgment of the Court of Appeals is affirmed.

It is so ordered.

JUSTICE KENNEDY, concurring.

The opinion for the Court is careful to leave open a number of significant questions regarding the reach and interpretation of the Alien Tort Statute. In my view that is a proper disposition. Many serious concerns with respect to human rights abuses committed abroad have been addressed by Congress in statutes such as the Torture Victim Protection Act of 1991 (TVPA), and that class of cases will be determined in the future according to the detailed statutory scheme Congress has enacted. Other cases may arise with allegations of serious violations of international law principles protecting persons, cases covered neither by the TVPA nor by the reasoning and holding of today's case; and in those disputes the proper implementation of the presumption against extraterritorial application may require some further elaboration and explanation.

. . .

JUSTICE BREYER, with whom JUSTICE GINSBURG, JUSTICE SOTOMAYOR and JUSTICE KAGAN join, concurring in the judgment.

I agree with the Court's conclusion but not with its reasoning. The Court sets forth four key propositions of law: First, the "presumption against extraterritoriality applies to claims under" the Alien Tort Statute. Second, "nothing in the statute rebuts that presumption." Third, there "is no clear indication of extraterritoria[l application] here," where "all the relevant conduct took place outside the United States" and "where the claims" do not "touch and concern the territory of the United States . . . with sufficient force to displace the presumption." Fourth, that is in part because "[c]orporations are often present in many countries, and it would reach too far to say that mere corporate presence suffices."

Unlike the Court, I would not invoke the presumption against extraterritoriality. Rather, guided in part by principles and practices of foreign relations law, I would find jurisdiction under this statute where (1) the alleged tort occurs on American soil, (2) the defendant is an American national, or (3) the defendant's conduct substantially and adversely affects an important American national interest, and that includes a distinct interest in preventing the United States from becoming a safe harbor (free of civil as well as criminal liability) for a torturer or other common enemy of mankind. In this case, however, the parties and relevant conduct lack sufficient ties to the United States for the ATS to provide jurisdiction.

. . .

Application of the statute in the way I have suggested is consistent with international law and foreign practice. Nations have long been obliged not to provide safe harbors for their own nationals who commit such serious crimes abroad.

Many countries permit foreign plaintiffs to bring suits against their own nationals based on unlawful conduct that took place abroad.

Other countries permit some form of lawsuit brought by a foreign national against a foreign national, based upon conduct taking place abroad and seeking damages. Certain countries, which find "universal" criminal "jurisdiction" to try perpetrators of particularly heinous crimes such as piracy and genocide, also permit private persons injured by that conduct to pursue *"actions civiles,"* seeking civil damages in the criminal proceeding. Moreover, the United Kingdom and the Netherlands, while not authorizing such damages actions themselves, tell us that they would have no objection to the exercise of American jurisdiction in cases such as *Filartiga* and *Marcos.*

. . .

III

Applying these jurisdictional principles to this case, however, I agree with the Court that jurisdiction does not lie. The defendants are two foreign corporations. Their shares, like those of many foreign corporations, are traded on the New York Stock Exchange. Their only presence in the United States consists of an office in New York City (actually owned by a separate but affiliated company) that helps to explain their business to potential investors. The plaintiffs are not United States nationals but nationals of other nations. The conduct at issue took place abroad. And the plaintiffs allege, not that the defendants directly engaged in acts of torture, genocide, or the equivalent, but that they helped others (who are not American nationals) to do so.

Under these circumstances, even if the New York office were a sufficient basis for asserting general jurisdiction, it would be farfetched to believe, based solely upon the defendants' minimal and indirect American presence, that this legal action helps to vindicate a distinct American interest, such as in not providing a safe harbor for an "enemy of all mankind." Thus I agree with the Court that here it would "reach too far to say" that such "mere corporate presence suffices."

I consequently join the Court's judgment but not its opinion.

NOTES & QUESTIONS

1. Justice Kennedy provided the fifth vote for applying the presumption against extraterritoriality to the ATS. In his short concurrence, he suggested that other human rights cases would arise in the future that could properly be brought under the ATS. What do you think he meant by this statement? Can you envision human rights cases that would survive

Kiobel? See Ingrid B. Wuerth, *The Supreme Court and the Alien Tort Statute: Kiobel v. Royal Dutch Petroleum Co.*, 107 AM. J. INT'L L. (2013). The Court did not address the Second Circuit's holding on corporate liability. Can you envision a case against a corporation that would still be actionable?

    2.   In 2012, the Center for Constitutional Rights filed an ATS lawsuit on behalf of Sexual Minorities Uganda against the President of Abiding Truth Ministries, Scott Lively. The suit alleges that Lively's involvement in anti-gay efforts in that country violates the CIL rule against persecution, i.e., the "international and severe deprivation of fundamental rights contrary to international law by reason of the identity of the group or collectivity." While a motion to dismiss was pending, the Supreme Court decided *Kiobel*. Following the decision, Lively filed a notice of supplemental authority arguing that the case should be dismissed because the ATS does not apply to conduct that occurred entirely outside the United States. On August 14, 2013, the district court denied Lively's motion to dismiss. With respect to Lively's *Kiobel* argument, the Court explained:

> Two facts alleged in this case distinguish it from *Kiobel*. First, unlike the British and Dutch corporations, Defendant is an American citizen residing within the venue of this court in Springfield, Massachusetts. Second, read fairly, the Amended Complaint alleges that the tortious acts committed by Defendant took place to a substantial degree within the United States, over many years, with only infrequent actual visits to Uganda. The fact that the impact of Defendant's conduct was felt in Uganda cannot deprive Plaintiff of a claim. Defendant's alleged actions in planning and managing a campaign of repression in Uganda from the United States are analogous to a terrorist designing and manufacturing a bomb in this country, which he then mails to Uganda with the intent that it explode there. The Supreme Court has made clear that the presumption against the extraterritorial application of a statute comes into play only where a defendant's conduct lacks sufficient connection to the United States. *Kiobel* elaborated on this theme. As Chief Justice Roberts stated in his opinion, the issue in that case was "whether a claim may reach conduct occurring in the territory of a foreign sovereign." In the final paragraph of his decision, he emphasized that the Court's holding applied to a factual scenario where "all the relevant conduct took place outside the United States." Where conduct occurred solely abroad, "mere corporate presence," he concluded, did not touch and concern the United States "with sufficient force to displace the presumption against extraterritorial application."

>   . . .

> This is not a case where a foreign national is being hailed into an unfamiliar court to defend himself. Defendant is an American citizen located in the same city as this court. The presumption

against extraterritoriality is based, in large part, on foreign policy concerns that tend to arise when domestic statutes are applied to foreign nationals engaging in conduct in foreign countries. An exercise of jurisdiction under the ATS over claims against an American citizen who has allegedly violated the law of nations in large part through actions committed within this country fits comfortably within the limits described in *Kiobel*. Indeed, the failure of the United States to make its courts available for claims against its citizens for actions taken within this country that injure persons abroad would itself create the potential for just the sort of foreign policy complications that the limitations on federal common law claims recognized under the ATS are aimed at avoiding. Under the law of nations, states are obliged to make civil courts of justice accessible for claims of foreign subjects against individuals within the state's territory. . . .

Sexual Minorities Uganda v. Lively, No. 12–cv–30051–MAP, 2013 WL 4130756 at *13–14 (D. Mass. Aug. 14, 2013). What does the *Sexual Minorities Uganda* case suggest about the future of ATS litigation?

3.   All nine justices in *Kiobel* appeared to reject the idea that U.S. courts should provide a venue for the redress of injuries that lack a connection to this country. Do you agree with this position? Why or why not? If the defendant is found to have violated the law of nations, should connection to a particular national jurisdiction matter? *See* Jordan J. Paust, *Kiobel, Corporate Liability, and the Extraterritorial Reach of the ATS*, 53 Va. J. Int'l L. Dig. 18 (2012).

4.   With growing substantive and procedural barriers to litigating in federal courts, attention has increasingly focused on the possibilities of pursuing human rights claims in state courts and using state law. As Professors Whytock, Childress, and Ramsey have explained:

> Among the potential attractions of state courts and state law, human rights claimants might be able to avoid application of the federal *forum non conveniens* doctrine and strict federal pleading standards, and in some cases they may find a more sympathetic judge or jury. Since "[t]he same conduct that constitutes a violation of international human rights norms usually also violates the law of the place where it occurred and the law of the forum state," plaintiffs might be able to avoid Sosa's limitations on the types of international law violations over which the ATS provides jurisdiction by pleading their claims under state or foreign law. Moreover, by pleading human rights claims as domestic tort claims rather than violations of international law—for example, assault and battery or intentional infliction of emotional harm rather than torture, or wrongful death instead of extrajudicial execution— plaintiffs might be able to avoid limits on corporate liability of international law violations. . . .

Christopher A. Whytock, Donald Earl Childress III, & Michael D. Ramsey, *After Kiobel: International Human Rights Litigation in State Courts and Under State Law*, 3 U.C. Irvine L. Rev. 1, 5–6 (2013) (quoting Beth Stephens et al. International Human Rights Litigation in U.S. Courts 120 (2d ed. 2008)). What other advantages and disadvantages do you see to pursuing these types of human rights claims in state courts?

CHAPTER V

USING FOREIGN AND INTERNATIONAL LAW AS PERSUASIVE AUTHORITY

■ ■ ■

I. INTRODUCTION

Ratified treaties and customary international law provide human rights standards that bind the United States. Nonetheless, as the preceding chapters have illustrated, enforcing these sources of international human rights law in domestic courts is challenging. In light of this, advocates have sometimes found it more effective to raise foreign and international law as educational, persuasive or informational in adjudication, rather than offering it as a binding rule of decision for the court.

Some courts, at both the state and federal levels, have been receptive to these arguments. This chapter focuses on the practice in federal courts; the use of foreign and international law in state courts will be discussed in **Chapter VI**. In recent years, the United States Supreme Court has cited foreign and international law in a handful of controversial decisions related to the death penalty, gay rights, and federalism. This development has prompted a heated debate among policymakers and academics about the wisdom and propriety of considering non-U.S. law in constitutional adjudication. Members of both the Senate and the House have responded by introducing legislation to ban the use of foreign authority, and recent Supreme Court nominees have been closely questioned about their positions on the citation of foreign authority. Given the political sensitivities of raising arguments based on foreign and international law, even as persuasive authority, human rights advocates have to be strategic about when and how to invoke these sources.

This Chapter introduces the uniquely American debate over the practice of looking abroad for inspiration and ideas. Part II begins with excerpts of two of the Supreme Court decisions that launched the recent controversy, *Roper v. Simmons* and *Graham v. Florida*. The readings in Part III then offer a variety of perspectives on the debate, between the justices themselves and among academics. The materials offer different explanations of the reasons for citing foreign and international law and different assessments of its impact. Finally, Part III examines how advocates draw upon these materials in domestic human rights litigation.

II. THE SUPREME COURT'S CITATION OF FOREIGN AND INTERNATIONAL LAW

Before considering the debate over the citation of foreign and international law, it is important to have a sense of how the Court engages in the practice. As you review two of the Court's most well-known and controversial cases in this regard, *Roper v. Simmons* and *Graham v. Florida*, consider what work the references to international law and foreign practice are doing in these decisions. How significant are these citations to the outcomes of the cases? Do you believe that they are dispositive? Why does the Court believe that international standards and comparative practices are relevant to these cases? Can you imagine the same logic applying to other parts of the Constitution, or are these decisions in some way unique?

ROPER V. SIMMONS
Supreme Court of the United States, 2005.
543 U.S. 551.

JUSTICE KENNEDY delivered the opinion of the Court.

This case requires us to address, for the second time in a decade and a half, whether it is permissible under the Eighth and Fourteenth Amendments to the Constitution of the United States to execute a juvenile offender who was older than 15 but younger than 18 when he committed a capital crime. In *Stanford v. Kentucky,* 492 U.S. 361, 109 S.Ct. 2969, 106 L.Ed.2d 306 (1989), a divided Court rejected the proposition that the Constitution bars capital punishment for juvenile offenders in this age group. We reconsider the question.

. . .

II

The Eighth Amendment provides: "Excessive bail shall not be required, nor excessive fines imposed, nor cruel and unusual punishments inflicted." The provision is applicable to the States through the Fourteenth Amendment. As the Court explained in *Atkins,* the Eighth Amendment guarantees individuals the right not to be subjected to excessive sanctions. The right flows from the basic " 'precept of justice that punishment for crime should be graduated and proportioned to [the] offense.' " By protecting even those convicted of heinous crimes, the Eighth Amendment reaffirms the duty of the government to respect the dignity of all persons.

The prohibition against "cruel and unusual punishments," like other expansive language in the Constitution, must be interpreted according to its text, by considering history, tradition, and precedent, and with due regard for its purpose and function in the constitutional design. To implement this framework we have established the propriety and affirmed the necessity of referring to "the evolving standards of decency that mark the progress of a maturing society" to determine which punishments are so disproportionate as to be cruel and unusual.

. . .

III

A

The evidence of national consensus against the death penalty for juveniles is similar, and in some respects parallel, to the evidence *Atkins* [*v. Virginia*] held sufficient to demonstrate a national consensus against the death penalty for the mentally retarded. When *Atkins* was decided, 30 States prohibited the death penalty for the mentally retarded. This number comprised 12 that had abandoned the death penalty altogether, and 18 that maintained it but excluded the mentally retarded from its reach. By a similar calculation in this case, 30 States prohibit the juvenile death penalty, comprising 12 that have rejected the death penalty altogether and 18 that maintain it but, by express provision or judicial interpretation, exclude juveniles from its reach. *Atkins* emphasized that even in the 20 States without formal prohibition, the practice of executing the mentally retarded was infrequent. Since *Penry,* only five States had executed offenders known to have an IQ under 70. In the present case, too, even in the 20 States without a formal prohibition on executing juveniles, the practice is infrequent. Since *Stanford,* six States have executed prisoners for crimes committed as juveniles. In the past 10 years, only three have done so: Oklahoma, Texas, and Virginia. In December 2003 the Governor of Kentucky decided to spare the life of Kevin Stanford, and commuted his sentence to one of life imprisonment without parole, with the declaration that " '[w]e ought not be executing people who, legally, were children.' " By this act the Governor ensured Kentucky would not add itself to the list of States that have executed juveniles within the last 10 years even by the execution of the very defendant whose death sentence the Court had upheld in *Stanford v. Kentucky.*

There is, to be sure, at least one difference between the evidence of consensus in *Atkins* and in this case. Impressive in *Atkins* was the rate of abolition of the death penalty for the mentally retarded. Sixteen States that permitted the execution of the mentally retarded at the time of *Penry* had prohibited the practice by the time we heard *Atkins*. By contrast, the rate of change in reducing the incidence of the juvenile death penalty, or in taking specific steps to abolish it, has been slower. Five States that allowed the juvenile death penalty at the time of *Stanford* have abandoned it in the intervening 15 years—four through legislative enactments and one through judicial decision.

Though less dramatic than the change from *Penry* to *Atkins* ("telling," to borrow the word *Atkins* used to describe this difference), we still consider the change from *Stanford* to this case to be significant. As noted in *Atkins,* with respect to the States that had abandoned the death penalty for the mentally retarded since *Penry,* "[i]t is not so much the number of these States that is significant, but the consistency of the direction of change." The number of States that have abandoned capital punishment for juvenile offenders since *Stanford* is smaller than the number of States that abandoned capital punishment for the mentally retarded after *Penry;* yet we think the same consistency of direction of change has been demonstrated. Since *Stanford,* no State that previously prohibited capital punishment for juveniles has reinstated it.

. . .

As in *Atkins,* the objective indicia of consensus in this case—the rejection of the juvenile death penalty in the majority of States; the infrequency of its use even where it remains on the books; and the consistency in the trend toward abolition of the practice—provide sufficient evidence that today our society views juveniles, in the words *Atkins* used respecting the mentally retarded, as "categorically less culpable than the average criminal."

B

A majority of States have rejected the imposition of the death penalty on juvenile offenders under 18, and we now hold this is required by the Eighth Amendment.

Because the death penalty is the most severe punishment, the Eighth Amendment applies to it with special force. Capital punishment must be limited to those offenders who commit "a narrow category of the most serious crimes" and whose extreme culpability makes them "the most deserving of execution."

. . .

Three general differences between juveniles under 18 and adults demonstrate that juvenile offenders cannot with reliability be classified among the worst offenders. First, as any parent knows and as the scientific and sociological studies respondent and his *amici* cite tend to confirm "[a] lack of maturity and an underdeveloped sense of responsibility are found in youth more often than in adults and are more understandable among the young. These qualities often result in impetuous and ill-considered actions and decisions." It has been noted that "adolescents are overrepresented statistically in virtually every category of reckless behavior." In recognition of the comparative immaturity and irresponsibility of juveniles, almost every State prohibits those under 18 years of age from voting, serving on juries, or marrying without parental consent.

The second area of difference is that juveniles are more vulnerable or susceptible to negative influences and outside pressures, including peer pressure. This is explained in part by the prevailing circumstance that juveniles have less control, or less experience with control, over their own environment.

The third broad difference is that the character of a juvenile is not as well formed as that of an adult. The personality traits of juveniles are more transitory, less fixed.

These differences render suspect any conclusion that a juvenile falls among the worst offenders. The susceptibility of juveniles to immature and irresponsible behavior means "their irresponsible conduct is not as morally reprehensible as that of an adult." Their own vulnerability and comparative lack of control over their immediate surroundings mean juveniles have a greater claim than adults to be forgiven for failing to escape negative influences in their whole environment.

. . .

IV

Our determination that the death penalty is disproportionate punishment for offenders under 18 finds confirmation in the stark reality that the United States is the only country in the world that continues to give official sanction to the juvenile death penalty. This reality does not become controlling, for the task of interpreting the Eighth Amendment remains our responsibility. Yet at least from the time of the Court's decision in *Trop,* the Court has referred to the laws of other countries and to international authorities as instructive for its interpretation of the Eighth Amendment's prohibition of "cruel and unusual punishments."

As respondent and a number of *amici* emphasize, Article 37 of the United Nations Convention on the Rights of the Child, which every country in the world has ratified save for the United States and Somalia, contains an express prohibition on capital punishment for crimes committed by juveniles under 18. No ratifying country has entered a reservation to the provision prohibiting the execution of juvenile offenders. Parallel prohibitions are contained in other significant international covenants.

Respondent and his *amici* have submitted, and petitioner does not contest, that only seven countries other than the United States have executed juvenile offenders since 1990: Iran, Pakistan, Saudi Arabia, Yemen, Nigeria, the Democratic Republic of Congo, and China. Since then each of these countries has either abolished capital punishment for juveniles or made public disavowal of the practice. In sum, it is fair to say that the United States now stands alone in a world that has turned its face against the juvenile death penalty.

Though the international covenants prohibiting the juvenile death penalty are of more recent date, it is instructive to note that the United Kingdom abolished the juvenile death penalty before these covenants came into being. The United Kingdom's experience bears particular relevance here in light of the historic ties between our countries and in light of the Eighth Amendment's own origins. The Amendment was modeled on a parallel provision in the English Declaration of Rights of 1689, which provided: "[E]xcessive Bail ought not to be required nor excessive Fines imposed; nor cruel and unusual Punishments inflicted." As of now, the United Kingdom has abolished the death penalty in its entirety; but, decades before it took this step, it recognized the disproportionate nature of the juvenile death penalty; and it abolished that penalty as a separate matter. In 1930 an official committee recommended that the minimum age for execution be raised to 21. Parliament then enacted the Children and Young Person's Act of 1933, which prevented execution of those aged 18 at the date of the sentence. And in 1948, Parliament enacted the Criminal Justice Act, prohibiting the execution of any person under 18 at the time of the offense. In the 56 years that have passed since the United Kingdom abolished the juvenile death penalty, the weight of authority against it there, and in the international community, has become well established.

It is proper that we acknowledge the overwhelming weight of international opinion against the juvenile death penalty, resting in large part on the understanding that the instability and emotional imbalance of young people may often be a factor in the crime. The opinion of the world community, while not controlling our outcome, does provide respected and significant confirmation for our own conclusions.

Over time, from one generation to the next, the Constitution has come to earn the high respect and even, as Madison dared to hope, the veneration of the American people. The document sets forth, and rests upon, innovative principles original to the American experience, such as federalism; a proven balance in political mechanisms through separation of powers; specific guarantees for the accused in criminal cases; and broad provisions to secure individual freedom and preserve human dignity. These doctrines and guarantees are central to the American experience and remain essential to our present-day self-definition and national identity. Not the least of the reasons we honor the Constitution, then, is because we know it to be our own. It does not lessen our fidelity to the Constitution or our pride in its origins to acknowledge that the express affirmation of certain fundamental rights by other nations and peoples simply underscores the centrality of those same rights within our own heritage of freedom.

. . .

The Eighth and Fourteenth Amendments forbid imposition of the death penalty on offenders who were under the age of 18 when their crimes were committed. The judgment of the Missouri Supreme Court setting aside the sentence of death imposed upon Christopher Simmons is affirmed.

It is so ordered.

. . .

JUSTICE SCALIA with whom THE CHIEF JUSTICE and JUSTICE THOMAS join, dissenting.

In urging approval of a constitution that gave life-tenured judges the power to nullify laws enacted by the people's representatives, Alexander Hamilton assured the citizens of New York that there was little risk in this, since "[t]he judiciary . . . ha[s] neither FORCE nor WILL but merely judgment." But Hamilton had in mind a traditional judiciary, "bound down by strict rules and precedents which serve to define and point out their duty in every particular case that comes before them." Bound down, indeed. What a mockery today's opinion makes of Hamilton's expectation, announcing the Court's conclusion that the meaning of our Constitution has changed over the past 15 years—not, mind you, that this Court's decision 15 years ago was *wrong,* but that the Constitution *has changed.* The Court reaches this implausible result by purporting to advert, not to the original meaning of the Eighth Amendment, but to "the evolving standards of decency," of our national society. It then finds, on the flimsiest of grounds, that a national consensus which could not be perceived in our people's laws barely 15 years ago now solidly exists. Worse still, the Court says in so many words that what our people's laws say about the issue does not, in the last analysis, matter: "[I]n the end our own judgment will be brought to bear on the question of the acceptability of the death penalty under the Eighth Amendment." The Court thus proclaims itself sole arbiter of our Nation's moral standards—and in the course of discharging that awesome responsibility purports to take guidance from the views of foreign courts and legislatures. Because I do not believe that the meaning of our Eighth Amendment, any more than the meaning of other provisions of our Constitution, should be determined by the subjective views of five Members of this Court and like-minded foreigners, I dissent.

I

In determining that capital punishment of offenders who committed murder before age 18 is "cruel and unusual" under the Eighth Amendment, the Court first considers, in accordance with our modern (though in my view mistaken) jurisprudence, whether there is a "national consensus," that laws allowing such executions contravene our modern "standards of decency." We have held that this determination should be based on "objective indicia that reflect the public attitude toward a given sanction"—namely, "statutes passed by society's elected representatives."

. . .

[T]he Court dutifully recites this test and claims halfheartedly that a national consensus has emerged since our decision in *Stanford*, because 18 States—or 47% of States that permit capital punishment—now have legislation prohibiting the execution of offenders under 18, and because all of 4 States have adopted such legislation since *Stanford*.

Words have no meaning if the views of less than 50% of death penalty States can constitute a national consensus. Our previous cases have required overwhelming opposition to a challenged practice, generally over a long period of time.

. . .

Relying on such narrow margins is especially inappropriate in light of the fact that a number of legislatures and voters have expressly affirmed their support for capital punishment of 16- and 17-year-old offenders since *Stanford*. Though the Court is correct that no State has lowered its death penalty age, both the Missouri and Virginia Legislatures—which, at the time of *Stanford,* had no minimum age requirement—expressly established 16 as the minimum. The people of Arizona and Florida have done the same by ballot initiative. Thus, even States that have not executed an under-18 offender in recent years unquestionably favor the possibility of capital punishment in some circumstances.

. . .

III

Though the views of our own citizens are essentially irrelevant to the Court's decision today, the views of other countries and the so-called international community take center stage.

The Court begins by noting that "Article 37 of the United Nations Convention on the Rights of the Child, which every country in the world has ratified *save for the United States* and Somalia, contains an express prohibition on capital punishment for crimes committed by juveniles under 18." The Court also discusses the International Covenant on Civil and Political Rights (ICCPR), which the Senate ratified only subject to a reservation that reads:

"The United States reserves the right, subject to its Constitutional constraints, to impose capital punishment on any person (other than a pregnant woman) duly convicted under existing or future laws permitting the imposition of capital punishment, including such punishment for crimes committed by persons below eighteen years of age."

Unless the Court has added to its arsenal the power to join and ratify treaties on behalf of the United States, I cannot see how this evidence favors, rather than refutes, its position. That the Senate and the President—those actors our Constitution empowers to enter into treaties, see Art. II, § 2—have declined to join and ratify treaties prohibiting execution of under—18 offenders can only suggest that *our country* has either not reached a national consensus on the question, or has reached a consensus contrary to what the Court announces. That the reservation to the ICCPR was made in 1992 does not suggest otherwise, since the reservation still remains in place today. It is also worth noting that, in addition to barring the execution of under—18 offenders, the United Nations Convention on the Rights of the Child prohibits punishing them with life in prison without the possibility of release. If we are truly going to get in line with the international community, then the Court's reassurance that the death penalty is really not needed, since "the punishment of life imprisonment without the possibility of parole is itself a severe sanction," gives little comfort.

It is interesting that whereas the Court is not content to accept what the States of our Federal Union *say,* but insists on inquiring into what they *do* (specifically, whether they in fact *apply* the juvenile death penalty that their laws allow), the Court is quite willing to believe that every foreign nation—of whatever tyrannical political makeup and with however subservient or incompetent a court system—in fact *adheres* to a rule of no death penalty for offenders under 18. Nor does the Court inquire into how many of the countries that have the death penalty, but have forsworn (on paper at least) imposing that penalty on offenders under 18, have what no State of this country can constitutionally have: a *mandatory* death penalty for certain crimes, with no possibility of mitigation by the sentencing authority, for youth or any other reason. I suspect it is most of them. To forbid the death penalty for juveniles under such a system may be a good idea, but it says nothing about our system, in which the sentencing authority, typically a jury, always can, and almost always does, withhold the death penalty from an under—18 offender except, after considering all the circumstances, in the rare cases where it is warranted. The foreign authorities, in other words, do not even speak to the issue before us here.

More fundamentally, however, the basic premise of the Court's argument—that American law should conform to the laws of the rest of the world—ought to be rejected out of hand. In fact the Court itself does not believe it. In many significant respects the laws of most other countries differ from our law—including not only such explicit provisions of our Constitution as the right to jury trial and grand jury indictment, but even many interpretations of the Constitution prescribed by this Court itself. The Court-pronounced exclusionary rule, for example, is distinctively American. When we adopted that rule in *Mapp v. Ohio,* (1961), it was "unique to American jurisprudence." *Bivens v. Six Unknown Fed. Narcotics Agents* (1971) (Burger, C. J., dissenting). Since then a categorical exclusionary rule has been "universally rejected" by other countries, including those with rules prohibiting illegal searches and police misconduct, despite the fact that none of these countries "appears to have any alternative form of discipline for police that is effective in preventing search violations." England, for example, rarely excludes evidence found during an illegal search or seizure and has only recently begun excluding evidence from illegally obtained confessions. Canada rarely excludes evidence and will only do so if admission will "bring the administration of justice into disrepute." The European Court of Human Rights has held that introduction of illegally seized evidence does not violate the "fair trial" requirement in Article 6, § 1, of the European Convention on Human Rights.

The Court has been oblivious to the views of other countries when deciding how to interpret our Constitution's requirement that "Congress shall make no law respecting an establishment of religion. . . ." Amdt. 1. Most other countries—including those committed to religious neutrality—do not insist on the degree of separation between church and state that this Court requires. For example, whereas "we have recognized special Establishment Clause dangers where the government makes direct money payments to sectarian institutions," countries such as the Netherlands, Germany, and Australia allow direct government funding of religious schools on the ground that "the state can only be truly neutral between secular and religious perspectives if it does not dominate the provision of so key a service as education, and makes it possible for people to exercise their right of religious expression within the context of public funding." England permits the teaching of religion in state schools. Even in France, which is considered "America's only rival in strictness of church-state separation," "[t]he practice of contracting for educational services provided by Catholic schools is very widespread."

And let us not forget the Court's abortion jurisprudence, which makes us one of only six countries that allow abortion on demand until the point of viability. Though the Government and *amici* in cases following *Roe v. Wade,* (1973), urged the Court to follow the international community's lead, these arguments fell on deaf ears.

The Court's special reliance on the laws of the United Kingdom is perhaps the most indefensible part of its opinion. It is of course true that we share a common history with the United Kingdom, and that we often consult English sources when asked to discern the meaning of a constitutional text written against the backdrop of 18th-century English law and legal thought. If we applied that approach today, our task would be an easy one. As we explained in *Harmelin v. Michigan* (1991), the "Cruell and Unusuall Punishments" provision of the English Declaration of Rights was originally meant to describe those punishments "'out of [the Judges'] Power'"—that is, those punishments that were not authorized by common law or statute, but that were nonetheless administered by the Crown or the Crown's judges. Under that reasoning, the death penalty for under—18 offenders would easily survive this challenge. The Court has, however—I think wrongly—long rejected a purely originalist approach to our Eighth Amendment, and that is certainly not the approach the Court takes today. Instead, the Court undertakes the majestic task of determining (and thereby prescribing) *our* Nation's *current* standards of decency. It is beyond comprehension why we should look, for that purpose, to a country that has developed, in the centuries since the Revolutionary War—and with increasing speed since the United Kingdom's recent submission to the jurisprudence of European courts dominated by continental jurists—a legal, political, and social culture quite different from our own. If we took the Court's directive seriously, we would also consider relaxing our double jeopardy prohibition, since the British Law Commission recently published a report that would significantly extend the rights of the prosecution to appeal cases where an acquittal was the result of a judge's ruling that was legally incorrect. We would also curtail our right to jury trial in criminal cases since, despite the jury system's deep roots in our shared common law, England now permits all but the most serious offenders to be tried by magistrates without a jury.

The Court should either profess its willingness to reconsider all these matters in light of the views of foreigners, or else it should cease putting forth foreigners' views as part of the *reasoned basis* of its decisions. To invoke alien law when it agrees with one's own thinking, and ignore it otherwise, is not reasoned decisionmaking, but sophistry.

The Court responds that "[i]t does not lessen our fidelity to the Constitution or our pride in its origins to acknowledge that the express affirmation of certain fundamental rights by other nations and peoples simply underscores the centrality of those same rights within our own heritage of freedom." To begin with, I do not believe that approval by "other nations and peoples" should buttress our commitment to American principles any more than (what should logically follow) disapproval by "other nations and peoples" should weaken that commitment. More importantly, however, the Court's statement flatly misdescribes what is going on here. Foreign sources are cited today, *not* to underscore our "fidelity" to the Constitution, our "pride in its origins," and "our own [American] heritage." To the contrary, they are cited *to set aside* the centuries-old American practice—a practice still engaged in by a large majority of the relevant States—of letting a jury of 12 citizens decide whether, in the particular case, youth should be the basis for withholding the death penalty. What these foreign sources "affirm," rather than repudiate, is the Justices' own notion of how the world ought to be, and their diktat that it shall be so henceforth in America. The Court's parting attempt to downplay the significance of its extensive discussion of foreign law is unconvincing. "Acknowledgment" of foreign approval has no place in the legal opinion of this Court *unless it is part of the basis for the Court's judgment*—which is surely what it parades as today.

. . .

Five years after *Roper*, the Court was asked to consider the constitutionality of imposing sentences of life in prison without the possibility of parole on juveniles who had committed crimes other than homicide. As you read the following excerpt, consider whether and how the Court's method of invoking international norms and foreign practice changed between these cases.

GRAHAM V. FLORIDA
Supreme Court of the United States, 2010.
560 U.S. 48.

JUSTICE KENNEDY delivered the opinion of the Court.

There is support for our conclusion in the fact that, in continuing to impose life without parole sentences on juveniles who did not commit homicide, the United States adheres to a sentencing practice rejected the world over. This observation does not control our decision. The judgments of other nations and the international community are not dispositive as to the meaning of the Eighth Amendment. But " '[t]he climate of international opinion concerning the acceptability of a particular punishment' " is also " 'not irrelevant.' " The Court has looked beyond our Nation's borders for support for its independent conclusion that a particular punishment is cruel and unusual. *See, e.g., Roper*, 543 U.S., at 575–578, 125 S.Ct. 1183.

. . .

Today we continue that longstanding practice in noting the global consensus against the sentencing practice in question. A recent study concluded that only 11 nations authorize life without parole for juvenile offenders under any circumstances; and only 2 of them, the United States and Israel, ever impose the punishment in practice. An updated version of the study concluded that Israel's "laws allow for parole review of juvenile offenders serving life terms," but expressed reservations about how that parole review is implemented. But even if Israel is counted as allowing life without parole for juvenile offenders, that nation does not appear to impose that sentence for nonhomicide crimes; all of the seven Israeli prisoners whom commentators have identified as serving life sentences for juvenile crimes were convicted of homicide or attempted homicide.

Thus, as petitioner contends and respondent does not contest, the United States is the only Nation that imposes life without parole sentences on juvenile nonhomicide offenders. We also note, as petitioner and his *amici* emphasize, that Article 37(a) of the United Nations Convention on the Rights of the Child, Nov. 20, 1989, 1577 U.N.T.S. 3 (entered into force Sept. 2, 1990), ratified by every nation except the United States and Somalia, prohibits the imposition of "life imprisonment without possibility of release . . . for offences committed by persons below eighteen years of age." As we concluded in *Roper* with respect to the juvenile death penalty, "the United States now stands alone in a world that has turned its face against" life without parole for juvenile nonhomicide offenders.

The State's *amici* stress that no international legal agreement that is binding on the United States prohibits life without parole for juvenile offenders and thus urge us to ignore the international consensus. These arguments miss the mark. The question before us is not whether international law prohibits the United States from imposing the sentence at issue in this case. The question is whether that punishment is cruel and unusual. In that inquiry, "the overwhelming weight of international opinion against" life without parole for nonhomicide offenses committed by juveniles "provide[s] respected and significant confirmation for our own conclusions."

The debate between petitioner's and respondent's *amici* over whether there is a binding *jus cogens* norm against this sentencing practice is likewise of no import. The Court has treated the laws and practices of other nations and international agreements as relevant to the Eighth Amendment not because those norms are binding or controlling but because the judgment of the world's nations that a particular sentencing practice is inconsistent with basic principles of decency demonstrates that the Court's rationale has respected reasoning to support it.

. . .

NOTES & QUESTIONS

1.   The Court uses international law sources, including treaties and comparative law sources, such as the decisions of other nations' courts, in its analysis *Roper* and *Graham*. Does the Court seem to place more value on international legal standards or on the practices of other nations? Do you find one to be more persuasive then the other? Based on what you learned about the United States' treaty commitments in **Chapter III**, should the Court give more weight to treaties? Professor Karen Knop has argued that many national courts are "blurring . . . international and comparative law . . . and looking at all international law through lens of comparative law." Karen Knop, *Here and There: International Law in Domestic Courts*, 32 N.Y.U. J. Int'l L. & Pol. 501, 525 (2005). Does this accurately characterize the United States Supreme Court's practice? If so, why do you think this might be occurring?

2.   Is the citation of international and foreign law sources dispositive in the *Roper* and *Graham* decisions? How important are the references to the Court's reasoning? If you conclude that they are not essential to the outcome of the case, why does the Court include them? To what audiences do you think they are directed?

3.   Justice Scalia strongly criticizes the majority's references to foreign and international law in *Roper*. What purposes does he believe they serve in the Court's opinions? What is the nature of his objection to their use? Is his position persuasive? Do you think that the Court's *Graham* opinion addresses the concerns raised in Justice Scalia's *Roper* dissent?

4.   In both *Roper* and *Graham*, *amicus* briefs were filed describing the relevant international law instruments and the practice of the international community. Do you think these kinds of arguments are more strategically made in an *amicus* brief? Why or why not?

5.   In 2012, the Court revisited the question left open in *Graham*, namely, whether the Eighth Amendment prohibits mandatory imposition of life in prison without the possibility of parole sentences for juveniles convicted of homicide-related offenses. Again, a number of human rights advocates filed *amicus* briefs in the case urging the U.S. Supreme Court to consider international and foreign law and practice in its interpretation of the Eighth Amendment's clause prohibiting cruel and unusual punishment. In addition, nineteen U.S. states and the territory of Guam filed an *amicus* brief urging the Supreme Court to, among other things, refrain from considering foreign law in deciding the case. (It should be noted that in *Graham*, sixteen members of the U.S. House of Representatives filed an amicus brief arguing that the CRC is not binding on the United States, and that the U.S. does not violate any other treaty obligations by sentencing juveniles to life without parole.) In its decision, *Miller v. Alabama*, 132 S. Ct 2455 (2012), the Court held that the 8th Amendment does, indeed, prohibit mandatory JLWOP sentences in homicide cases. Yet, in contrast to *Graham*, the Court did not cite to international or foreign law in its decision. Why do

you think the Court declined to reference international and foreign law in its consideration of the case?

6.   The Supreme Court has not reserved its use of foreign and international to its Eighth Amendment jurisprudence. For example, in *Lawrence v. Texas*, 539 U.S. 558 (2003), the United States Supreme Court cited the case law of the European Court of Human Rights and the statutory law of Britain in finding that criminal punishment of consensual sodomy violates the liberty interests protected under the Due Process Clause of the Fourteenth Amendment. *Id.* at 572–73.

7.   While the citation of foreign and international law has recently become controversial, its use stretches back to the nation's earliest days. Foreign law was cited in some of the Supreme Court's most significant decisions, including the concurring and dissenting opinions in *Dred Scott v. Sandford*, as well as in the Court's opinions in the anti-polygamy case, *Reynolds v. United States*, the Legal Tender Cases, and the Selective Draft Cases. *See* Steven G. Calabresi & Stephanie Dotson Zimdahl, *The Supreme Court and Foreign Sources of Law: Two Hundred Years of Practice and the Juvenile Death Penalty Decision*, 47 Wm. & Mary L. Rev. 743, 754 (2005). One empirical account of the Supreme Court's decisions suggests that while the practice dates back to the founding, it has been steadily increasing in recent years. *See id. C.f.* Sarah H. Cleveland, *Our International Constitution*, 31 Yale J. Int'l L. 1, 11–88 (2006) (cataloging the numerous and significant ways in which the Court has drawn on foreign and international law in cases throughout its history). Another empirical account, which expands the scope of study to all federal court decisions, concludes that the practice is venerable but that the incidence of foreign citation has not increased. *See generally* David T. Zaring, *The Use of Foreign Decisions by Federal Courts: An Empirical Analysis*, 3 J. Emp. Leg. Stud. 297 (2006). Assuming that these authors are correct that this practice is not new, should that allay any of the concerns raised by Justice Scalia?

III.   THE FOREIGN CITATION DEBATE

The debate between the Justices over the use of foreign and international law has continued outside of the courtroom. In the excerpts below, three current and former Supreme Court Justices discuss their views on the consideration of foreign and international law. As you review these materials, consider whether the Justices' explanations for their use of, or opposition to, the citation of foreign and international law is reflected in the opinions in *Roper* and *Graham* (bearing in mind that both of those majority opinions in these cases were authored by Justice Kennedy).

REMARKS BY SANDRA DAY O'CONNOR ASSOCIATE JUSTICE, UNITED STATES SUPREME COURT

Southern Center for International Studies.
(Oct. 28, 2003).

The impressions we create in this world are important and can leave their mark. A friend of mine tells the story of a bus driver who was becoming angry but still kept his composure when a woman passenger made many complaints during the trip. She was rude and made the trip very unpleasant for those around her. It wasn't until the driver opened the door at her stop to let her off the bus that the driver said, "Lady, you left something behind." She turned and snarled, "And what was it I left behind?" The driver smiled and said softly, "A bad impression."

On the whole, the United States judicial system leaves a favorable impression around the world. But when it comes to the impression created by the treatment of foreign and international law in United States courts, the jury is still out. A skeptic of the relevance of non-U.S. law to the United States legal system would begin by asking why judges and lawyers should divert their attention from the intricacies of the Employee Retirement Income Security Act, or the Americans with Disabilities Act, or the Bankruptcy Code, to the principles and decisions of foreign and international law. The reason, of course, is globalization. No institution of government can afford any longer to ignore the rest of the world. One-third of our gross domestic product is internationally derived. We operate today under a large array of international agreements and organizations directly impacting judicial decisionmaking, including the U.N. Convention on Contracts for the International Sale of Goods, NAFTA, the World Trade Organization, the Hague Conventions on Collection of Evidence Abroad and on Service of Process, and the New York Convention on Enforcement of Arbitral Awards. But globalization is much more than simply these agreements and organizations. Globalization also represents a greater awareness of, and access to, peoples and places far different from our own. The fates of nations are more closely intertwined than ever before, and we are more acutely aware of the connections.

The word "globalization" has many connotations, some positive and some negative. These varying views are reflective of both the potential of globalization to increase world harmony, and the risk that globalization will suppress desirable differences and become no more than a tool for imposing the preferences of powerful nations like our own upon the rest of the world. Harnessing the good that can come from our increasingly global world while avoiding these pitfalls requires those with power and influence in our country to develop a greater knowledge and understanding of what is happening outside our nation's borders.

This is true of courts as much as it is of any other governmental body. There is talk today about the "internationalization of legal relations." We are already seeing this in American courts, and should see it increasingly in the future. This does not mean, of course, that our courts can or should abandon their character as domestic institutions. But conclusions reached by other countries and by the international community, although not formally binding upon our decisions, should at times constitute persuasive authority in American courts—what is sometimes called "transjudicialism".

American courts have not, however, developed as robust a transnational jurisprudence as they might. Many scholars have documented how the decisions of the Court on which I sit have had an influence on the opinions of foreign tribunals. One scholar has even remarked that:

> When life or liberty is at stake, the landmark judgments of the Supreme Court of the United States, giving fresh meaning to the principles of the Bill of Rights, are studied with as much attention in New Delhi or Strasbourg as they are in Washington, D. C., or the State of Washington, or Springfield, Illinois.

This reliance, however, has not been reciprocal. There has been a reluctance on our current Supreme Court to look to international or foreign law in interpreting our own Constitution and related statutes. While ultimately we must bear responsibility for interpreting our own laws, there is much to be learned from other distinguished jurists who have given thought to the difficult issues we face here.

For instance, the Court on which I sit has held for more than 200 years that Acts of Congress should be construed to be consistent with international law absent clear expression to the contrary. Somewhat surprisingly, however, this doctrine is rarely invoked in the Court's decisionmaking. I can think of only two cases during my now more than 20 years on the Court that have relied upon this interpretive principle.

We have also, historically, declined to consider international law and the law of other nations when interpreting our own constitution. We are sometimes asked to do so, particularly when dealing with Eighth Amendment challenges to the death penalty. Litigants claiming that the execution of those who were juveniles at the time they committed the crime violates the International Covenant on Civil and Political Rights as well as general international norms are sometimes before us.

But the first indicia of change have appeared. Two terms ago, in *Atkins v. Virginia*, we considered the constitutionality of executing individuals who are mentally retarded. Several of the briefs submitted to the Supreme Court focused on the practice in other nations, and one "friend of the court" brief from a group of American diplomats discussed the difficulties posed for their missions by American death penalty practice. The Court's opinion in *Atkins* made note of the fact that "within the world community, the imposition of the death penalty for crimes committed by mentally retarded offenders is overwhelmingly disapproved."

Solicitude for the views of foreign and international courts also appeared in last term's decision in *Lawrence v. Texas*. In ruling that consensual homosexual activity in one's home is constitutionally protected, the Supreme Court relied in part on a series of decisions from the European Court of Human Rights. I suspect that with time, we will rely increasingly on international and foreign law in resolving what now appear to be domestic issues, as we both appreciate more fully the ways in which domestic issues have international dimension, and recognize the rich resources available to us in the decisions of foreign courts.

Doing so may not only enrich our own country's decisions; it will create that all important good impression. When U. S. courts are seen to be cognizant of other judicial systems, our ability to act as a rule-of-law model for other nations will be enhanced.

. . .

Because of the scope of the problems we face, understanding international law is no longer just a legal specialty; it is becoming a duty.

. . .

THE RELEVANCE OF FOREIGN LEGAL MATERIALS IN U.S. CONSTITUTIONAL CASES: A CONVERSATION BETWEEN JUSTICE ANTONIN SCALIA AND JUSTICE STEPHEN BREYER

3 Int'l J. Con. L. 519, 520–541 (2005).

[Professor Norman] Dorsen:

. . .

When we talk about the use of foreign court decisions in U.S. constitutional cases, what body of foreign law are we talking about? Are we limiting this to foreign constitutional law? . . . . What about cases involving international law, such as the interpretation of treaties, including treaties to which the U.S. is a party?

When we talk about the use of foreign court decisions in U.S. law, do we mean them to be authority or persuasive, or merely rhetorical? If, for example, foreign court decisions are not understood to be precedent in U.S. constitutional cases, they nevertheless strengthen the sense that U.S. assures a common moral and legal framework with the rest of the world? If this is so, is that in order to strengthen the legitimacy of a decision within the U.S., or to strengthen a decision's legitimacy in the rest of the world?

. . .

So, I invite our distinguished guests to respond to any or none of those points, and to make whatever comments they wish in conversation.

[Justice] Scalia: Well, most of those questions should be addressed to Justice Breyer because I do not use foreign law in the interpretation of the United States Constitution. [Laughter.] Now, I will use it in the interpretation of a treaty. In fact, in a recent case I dissented from the Court, including most of my brethren who like to use foreign law, because this treaty had been interpreted a certain way by several foreign courts of countries that were signatories, and that way was reasonable—although not necessarily the interpretation I would have taken as an original matter. But I thought that the object of a treaty being to come up with a text that is the same for all the countries, we should defer to the views of other signatories, much as we defer to the views of agencies—that is to say defer if it's within ball park, if it's a reasonable interpretation, though not necessarily the very best.

But you are talking about using foreign law to determine the content of American constitutional law—to be sure we're on the right track, that we have the same moral and legal framework as the rest of the world. But we *don't* have the same moral and legal framework as the rest of the world, and never have. If you told the framers of the Constitution that we're to be just like Europe, they would have been appalled. And if you read the Federalist Papers, they are full of statements that make very clear the framers didn't have a whole lot of respect for many of the rules in European countries.

. . .

[T]ake our abortion jurisprudence: we are one of only six countries in the world that allows abortion on demand at any time prior to viability. Should we change that because other countries feel differently? Or, maybe a more pertinent question: Why *haven't* we changed that, if indeed the Court thinks we should be persuaded by foreign law? Or do we just use foreign law selectively? When it agrees with what the justices would like the case to say, we use the foreign law, and when it doesn't agree we don't use it.

. . .

What's going on here? Do you want it to be authoritative? I doubt whether anybody would say, "Yes, we want to be governed by the views of foreigners." Well if you don't want it to be authoritative, then what is the criterion for citing it? That it agrees with you? I don't know any other criterion to bring forward.

So, that may answer none of your questions, but that's what I wanted to say. [Laughter.]

. . .

[Justice] Breyer:

. . .

I believe, and I suspect Justice Scalia also believes, that the United States differs from some other nations in that law here is not handed down from on high, not even from the Supreme Court. Rather, law emerges from a complex interactive democratic process. We justices play a limited role in that process. But we are part of it. So are lawyers, law professors, students and ordinary citizens. The process amounts to a kind of conversation. . . . Law emerges from that messy but necessary conversational process. We judges participate in that conversation, when we decide cases and we can do so, too, when we speak more generally about the law and about the decision-making process itself.

. . .

The best example arose at a seminar where several professors, a member of Congress, a senator, and another judge and I were discussing relationships among the branches of government. The congressman began to criticize the Supreme Court's use of foreign law in its decisions. At first, I was uncertain what he had in mind. After a time I understood that he was discussing the issue that Justice Scalia and I disagree about. I said, "Well, your criticism seems aimed at me." I added that, when I refer to foreign law in cases involving a constitutional issue, I realize full well that the decisions of foreign courts do not bind American courts. Of course they do not. But those cases sometimes involve a human being working as a judge concerned with a legal problem, often similar to problems that arise here, which problem involves the application of a legal text, often similar to the text of our own Constitution, seeking to protect certain basic human rights, often similar to the rights that our own Constitution seeks to protect.

. . .

I said to the congressman, "If I have a difficult case and a human being called a judge, though of a different country, has had to consider a similar problem, why should I not read what that judge has said? It will not bind me, but I may learn something." The congressman replied, "Fine. You are right. Read it. Just don't cite it in your opinion." [Laughter.]

. . .

I added, "Let me be a little bit more frank. In some foreign countries, people are struggling to establish institutions that will help them protect democracy and human rights despite earlier undemocratic or oppressive governmental traditions. . . . The United States has prestige in this area. Foreign courts refer to our decisions. And if we sometimes refer to their decisions, the references may help these struggling institutions. The references show that we read, and are interested in, their reactions to similar legal problems.

. . .

The congressman's point—and he had a point—is similar to the point that Justice Scalia makes. Once we start to refer to foreign opinions, how do we know we can keep matters under control? How do we know we have referred to opinions on both sides of the issue? How do we know we have found all that might be relevant? The answers to these questions lie in the nature of the judicial process. . . . We must rely upon judicial integrity to assure a fair and comprehensive reading of any relevant foreign materials. . . . Of course, I hope that I, or any other judge, would refer to materials that support positions that the judge disfavors as well as those he favors.

. . .

Scalia: I don't know what it means to express confidence that judges will do what they ought to do, after having read the foreign law. My problem is I don't know what they ought to do. What is it that they ought to do? Why is it that foreign law would be relevant to what an American judge does when he interprets—interprets, not writes—the Constitution?

Now, my theory of what to do when interpreting the American Constitution is to try to understand what it meant, what it was understood by the society to mean when it was adopted. And I don't think it has changed since then.

. . .

If you have that philosophy, obviously foreign law is irrelevant with one exception: old English law—because phrases like "due process" and the "right of confrontation" were taken from English law, and were understood to mean what they meant there. So the reality is I use foreign law more than anybody on the Court. But it's all old English law.

. . .

That's my approach to interpreting the Constitution. Justice Breyer doesn't have my approach. He applies . . . the notion that the Constitution is not static. It doesn't mean what the people voted for when it was ratified. Rather, it changes from era to era to comport with—and this is a quote from our cases, "the evolving standards of decency that mark the progress of a maturing society." I detest that phrase . . . because I'm afraid that societies don't always mature. Sometimes they rot. What makes you think that, you know, human progress is one upwardly inclined plane; every day, in every way, we get better and better? It seems to me that the purpose of the Bill of Rights was to prevent change, not to encourage it and have it written into a Constitution.

Anyway, let's assume you buy into the evolving Constitution. Still and all, what you're looking for as a judge . . . using that theory is what? The standards of decency of American society—not the standards of decency of the world, not the standards of decency of other countries that don't have our background, that don't have our culture, that don't have our moral views. Of what conceivable value as indicative of *American* standards of decency would foreign law be?

. . .

The only way in which it makes sense to use foreign law is if you have a third approach to the interpretation of the Constitution, to wit: "I as a judge am not looking for the original meaning of the Constitution, nor for the current standards of decency of American society; I'm looking for what is the best answer to this social question in my judgment as an intelligent person. And for that purpose I take into account the views of other judges, throughout the world."

Let me ask the law students here: Do you think you're representative of American society? Do you not realize you are a small layer of cream at the top of the educational system, and that your views on innumerable things are not the views of America at large? And doesn't it seem somewhat arrogant for you to say, when you later become judges, I can make up what the moral values of America should be on all sorts of issues, such as penology, the death penalty, abortion, whatever? . . . . I frankly don't want to undertake that responsibility. I don't want to do it with foreign law, and I don't want to do it without foreign law. I sleep very well at night, because I read old English cases. [Laughter.] And there's my answer.

Breyer: That's a good answer. Indeed, I think you have identified something that understandably worries many people.

. . .

Scalia: One of the difficulties of using foreign law is that you don't understand what the surrounding jurisprudence is. So that you can say, for example, "Russia follows *Miranda*," but you don't know that Russia doesn't have an exclusionary rule.

And you say every other country of the world thinks that holding somebody for twelve years under sentence of death is cruel and unusual punishment, but you don't know that these other countries don't have habeas corpus systems which allow repeated applications to state and federal court, so that the reason it takes twelve years here is because the convicted murderer himself continues to file appeals that are continuously rejected.

In England, before they abolished the death penalty. . . . that sentence would be carried out within two weeks. So I mean that's the reason twelve years seems extraordinary to them. It's extraordinary because we've been so sensitive to the problem of an erroneous execution that we allow repeated habeas corpus applications. I just don't think it's comparable. It's just not fair to compare the two.

But most of all, what does the opinion of a wise Zimbabwe judge or a wise member of the House of Lords law committee—what does that have to do with what Americans believe? It's irrelevant unless you really think it's been given to *you* to make this moral judgment, a very difficult moral judgment? And so in making it for yourself and for the whole country, you consult whatever authorities you want. Unless you have that philosophy, I don't see how it's relevant at all.

Breyer: Well, it's relevant in the sense I described. A similar kind of person, a judge, with similar training, tries to apply a similar document with similar language . . . in a society that is somewhat similarly democratic and protective of basic human rights. England is not the moon, nor is India.

. . .

Dorsen: . . . .

The question to Justice Breyer is a variant of something that Justice Scalia said in his opening comments. Is it fair to criticize you and other members of the court who do refer to foreign sources, even though they do not consider them binding, that they refer in general to cases that support the positions they are taking? For example, in cases of the death penalty, in cases of abortion, in cases of other controversial issues, I'm not sure I see as many citations to East Asian courts, to South American courts, to Islamic courts. And is it a fair criticism that there's a certain selectivity that is result-oriented in the way foreign references are considered by you and those who agree with you?

Breyer: Yes, it's a fair criticism. We have referred to opinions of India's Supreme Court. But I confess that fewer opinions from other Asian nations come to our attention, because we're not going to refer to as many Asian courts at the moment, though we refer to India as an Asian court, because fewer come to our attention.

. . .

The criticism can be encapsulated in Judge Harold Leventhal's remark: Using legislative history is like looking at a cocktail party to try to identify your friends. [Laughter.] But if a judge does, in fact, use legislative history or foreign material in that way, the judge is not doing his or her job. . . . And if a judge is not conscientious, he will have many opportunities for distortion. But if you are not conscientious, why become a judge? What would be the pleasure or reward in entering a profession that prizes integrity, honesty, doing the job properly? The pleasure certainly does not lie in the pay [Laughter.]

. . .

Scalia: That can't be the only explanation for not using other foreign sources—that we don't know what the other countries say. In my dissent in *Lawrence*, the homosexual sodomy case, I observed that the court cited only European law; it pointed out that every European country has said you cannot prohibit homosexual sodomy.

Of course, they said it not as a consequence of some democratic ballot but by decree of the European Court of Human Rights. . . . It had not been done democratically. Nonetheless, it was true that throughout all of Europe, it was unlawful to prohibit homosexual sodomy. The court did not cite the rest of the world. It was easy to find out what the rest of the world thought about it. I cited it in my dissent. The rest of the world was equally divided.

. . .

I mean, it lends itself to manipulation. It invites manipulation. You know, I want to do this thing; I have to think of some reason for it. . . . I have to cite *something*. [Laughter.] I can't cite a prior American opinion because I'm overruling two centuries of practice. I can't cite the laws of the American people because, in fact, only eighteen of the thirty-eight states that have capital punishment say that you cannot leave it to the jury whether the person is mentally deficient and whether that should count. So my goodness, what am I going to use?

. . .

I have a decision by an intelligent man in Zimbabwe or anywhere else and you put it in there and you give the citation. By God, it looks lawyerly! [Laughter.] And it lends itself to manipulation. It just does.

. . .

Question: I'm a little embarrassed because my comments really are not in the form of a question because I think that the heart of the issue is really the function of the judge. Justice Scalia has said this many times.

The question is, what is the role of the judge? And there is a very sharp disagreement here.

. . .

Breyer:

. . .

Our disagreement often concerns, not the role of the judge, which is, of course, to apply the law, but about the importance of explicit rules. Some believe that too few rules and too few clear approaches may mean judges with too much power, more power than an unelected judge should possess in a democracy. If a legal rule, or a decision-making practice, is too open-ended, it may permit judges to substitute their own subjective views for the views of the legislature. And that substitution runs counter to the principle of democracy. I recognize the problem.

Nonetheless, a legal rule, or a decision-making practice, that is not at all open-ended can produce a cure that is worse than the disease. Legal rules that are inflexible, that do not adjust adequately to changing circumstances, produce law that is divorced from life.

No one wants to divorce the law from life, and nobody wants unelected judges who routinely substitute their subjective views for those of elected officials. Some believe the former is the greater danger; some believe the latter is of the greater danger. There is no magic solution to the problem.

. . .

Question: To you first, Justice Breyer. Justice Scalia responded to a question by saying, go ahead, read all these things as much as you want, but why do you have to put them in your opinions. I'd be interested to hear a response to that, because I think all of your arguments are very strong in terms of the usefulness of reading this material, but they don't necessarily translate to the opinions.

. . .

Breyer: I do not often put references to foreign materials in my opinions. I do so occasionally when I believe that a reference will help lawyers, specialists, or the public at large better understand the issues or the views expressed in my opinions. If the foreign materials had a significant impact on my thinking, they may belong in the opinion because an opinion should be transparent. It should reflect my actual thinking.

Question: Justice Scalia has raised the concern, and has really put centrally, the concern that citing foreign law is an invitation to judicial elites to impose their own moral and social views. And yet neither Justice Scalia nor Justice Breyer has directly addressed a deeper concern about these materials; namely, that it's not about elite imposition as such, but instead that these legal materials have no democratic provenance, they have no democratic connection to this legal system, to this constitutional system, and thus lack democratic accountability as legal materials.

. . .

Scalia: They're your materials; you defend them. [Laughter.]

Breyer: The point is interesting. It is common for an opinion to refer to material that, as you describe it, has no "democratic provenance." Blackstone has no democratic provenance. Law professors have no democratic provenance. Yet I read and refer to treatises and I read and refer to law review articles. My opinion is meant to reflect my actual method of reaching a legal conclusion; and references to those legal materials that had significance and will help the reader understand.

. . .

NOTES & QUESTIONS

1.   What reasons are offered by Justice Breyer and Justice O'Connor for considering foreign and international law in their decisionmaking? Are they the same?

2.   To what extent does the debate over foreign and international law sources relate to different conceptions of the role of a judge? Do Justices Scalia, Breyer, and O'Connor differ in their ideas about the sources of judicial authority and areas of judicial competence? How are these idea reflected in the debate over "looking abroad"?

3.   During the debate, it is suggested to Justice Breyer that he should read foreign sources, but not reference them. Justice Scalia agrees with this "solution" in a part of the discussion not included in the excerpt. Would reading without citing foreign materials alleviate Justice Scalia's stated concerns about the practice? Justice Breyer responds that he thinks that it is important for judges to be transparent. Do you agree?

4.   Justice O'Connor suggests that the Supreme Court's failure to acknowledge relevant international law creates a bad impression on the global stage. For an example of this phenomenon, *see* Claire L'Heureux-Dube, *The Importance of Dialogue: Globalization and the International Impact of the Rehnquist Court*, 34 Tulsa L.J. 15 (1998), in which this former Canadian Supreme Court Justice criticizes the U.S. Supreme Court's insularity and failure to acknowledge relevant Canadian jurisprudence. In some ways, this rationale for citing international precedent sounds more like judicial participation in foreign relations than law. Interestingly, the Justice Department has cited foreign relations and international opinion as a

relevant consideration for the Supreme Court, most notably in its *amicus* brief in *Brown v. Board of Education*. *See* Mary Dudziak, Cold War Civil Rights: Race and the Image of American Democracy (2d ed. 2011). In that brief, the DOJ noted the way in which American apartheid was being used against the U.S. in Cold War propaganda, and then urged the Supreme Court to mandate racial equality in public education. This would certainly be a valid concern for the Congress or the President, but is such foreign opinion a relevant consideration when the Court considers a domestic issue?

———————

References to foreign and international law have also prompted a heated scholarly debate. As you read the excerpts from Professors Jackson and Alford below, consider how these accounts differ or build upon the positions of the justices.

VICKI C. JACKSON, "CONSTITUTIONAL COMPARISONS: CONVERGENCE, RESISTANCE, ENGAGEMENT"
119 Harv. L. Rev. 109, 111–18 (2005).

I.   Constitutions and the Transnational: Three Models

Although references to foreign law go way back in U.S. constitutional history, there is considerably more to refer to now. Before World War II, other countries offered experience in governance, but much less in the way of justiciable constitutional law. An era of human rights-based constitutionalism was born in the global constitutional moment that followed the defeat of Nazism, producing international human rights law and more tribunals issuing reasoned constitutional decisions. Sources of law from beyond U.S. boundaries continue to grow. While some are binding (such as ratified treaties), others are plainly not, including the domestic constitutional law of foreign countries, which nonetheless some national courts find relevant as "persuasive" or "relational" authority. The U.S. Supreme Court has gone from being one of the only to one of many constitutional courts in the world, a change producing both opportunities for common learning and occasions for anxiety. As Chief Justice Rehnquist extrajudicially commented, "now that constitutional law is solidly grounded in so many countries . . . it's time the U.S. courts began looking to the decisions of other constitutional courts to aid in their own deliberative process." The question is not whether but how constitutional adjudication responds to this growing corpus.

A.   The Models

At least three models might broadly describe the relationships between domestic constitutions and law from transnational sources. Justice Scalia accused the Court in *Roper* of assuming the desirability of convergence with other nations' laws—the Convergence Model. He proposed instead an approach that relishes resistance by national constitutions to outside influence—the Resistance Model. Neither of these models, standing alone, is a good fit with our constitutional practices. Rather, the Constitution can best be viewed as a site of engagement with the transnational, informed but not controlled by consideration of other nations' legal norms and the questions they put to interpreters of our specifically national constitution—the Engagement Model.

The Convergence Model sees national constitutions as sites for implementation of international law or for development of transnational norms. . . . The South African Constitution explicitly requires that international law be taken into account when interpreting constitutional rights and specifically authorizes its courts to consider foreign law, manifesting a vision of the constitution as a site for possible convergence with transnational constitutional, or international, norms. Even without so explicit a mandate, courts in a number of other countries look to foreign or international law for guidance in resolving domestic constitutional questions.

Constitutions can also provide a basis for resistance to, or differentiation from, foreign law or practice. Outside the United States, domestic constitutions' provisions for national ownership or control of resources have functioned as a basis for resisting globalization's economic pressures. Within this country, federalism has been advanced as an affirmative reason to resist constitutionalizing human rights norms derived from transnational sources. Justice Scalia's position is more aggressive, sometimes evincing a kind of willful indifference to foreign law in constitutional interpretation and insisting that "comparative analysis [is] inappropriate to the task of interpreting a constitution."

Third, constitutional law can be understood as a site of engagement between domestic law and international or foreign legal sources and practices. On this view, the constitution's interpreters do not treat foreign or international material as binding, or as presumptively to be followed. But neither do they put on blinders that exclude foreign legal sources and experience. Transnational sources are seen as interlocutors, offering a way of testing understanding of one's own traditions and possibilities by examining them in the reflection of others'. The foundational case on judicial review is illustrative: In *Marbury v. Madison*, the written character of the Constitution was used to differentiate the U.S. government from Britain's and justify the legitimacy of judicial review, while the Court also drew affirmatively on British traditions of suing the King to define the "essence of civil liberty."

. . .

It is this third model of comparison as engagement or interlocution that *Roper* [*v. Simmons*] illustrates. Both the majority and Justice

O'Connor were willing to look to outside law and practice to interrogate their judgment of whether the punishment is constitutionally disproportionate in the United States, but only after considering more important factors, including state law and practice. For Justice Kennedy, foreign law, practice, and reasoning—though not "controlling"—helped to confirm the Court's judgment based on the weight of state practices and its view of the moral capacities of adolescents. . . . Each of these Justices preserved an Eighth Amendment methodology in which the law and practices of the states held first place in the analysis—not a stance conducive to a commitment to converge with international or transnational norms.

B.   In Praise of Engagement

. . .

Engagement with transnational legal sources may helpfully interrogate understanding of our own Constitution in several ways, three of which I discuss here.

First, to the extent constitutional systems perform similar functions, similar concerns may arise about the consequences of interpretive choices. If more than one interpretation of the Constitution is plausible from domestic legal sources, approaches taken in other countries may provide helpful empirical information in deciding what interpretation will work best here.

. . .

Second, comparisons can shed light on the distinctive functioning of one's own system. Foreign constitutional courts sometimes consider U.S. case law but decline to follow it, demonstrating that engagement with foreign law need not lead to its adoption. Our Court, no less than others, can draw such distinctions. Considering the questions other systems pose may sharpen understandings of how we are different.

. . .

Third, foreign or international legal sources may illuminate "suprapositive" dimensions of constitutional rights, as when constitutional text or doctrine requires contemporary judgments about a quality of action or freedom—the "reasonableness" of a search, the "cruelty" of a punishment. Many modern constitutions include individual rights that protect similar values at an abstract level, often inspired by human rights texts. Such rights, although embedded in particular national constitutions, have "universal" aspects, reflecting "the inescapable ubiquity of human beings as a central concern" for any legal system and widespread (though not universal) aspirations for law to constrain government treatment of individuals.

. . .

ROGER P. ALFORD, "MISUSING INTERNATIONAL SOURCES TO INTERPRET THE CONSTITUTION"

98 Am. J. of Int'l L. 57, 58–59, 61, 64, 67–69 (2004).

The first misuse of international sources . . . occurs when the "global opinions of humankind" are ascribed constitutional value to thwart the domestic opinions of Americans. To the extent that value judgments are a source of constitutional understandings of community standards, in the hierarchical ranking of relative values domestic majoritarian judgments should hold sway over international majoritarian values. Using global opinions as a means of constitutional interpretation dramatically undermines sovereignty by utilizing the one vehicle—constitutional supremacy—that can trump the democratic will reflected in state and federal legislative and executive pronouncements.

Treaty norms embodied in canonical human rights instruments are a reflection of an international majoritarian perspective on what is required of a good and just society. Internalization of these norms through treaty adherence and legislative enactments furthers that majoritarian objective, and it does so consistently with domestic sovereignty concerns. But occasionally, as with capital punishment, the international majoritarian impulse is not consistent with the domestic majoritarian impulse. The values inherent in national sovereignty and the objectives reflected in international and foreign sources clash. If international majoritarian values cannot find expression through the political branches, advocates resort to the courts. But in the courts, overcoming sovereign values reflected in legislative enactments can be achieved only through constitutional supremacy. Hence the strategy to utilize international law to interpret the Constitution. If what is good and just cannot be achieved by democratic governance, then it shall be foisted upon the governed through constitutional interpretation.

. . .

The second misuse of international sources occurs when treaties are elevated to a status they do not enjoy under our federal system. The entire edifice of constitutional law rests on the foundation that the acts of the political branches are subject to and limited by the Constitution. Proposing that international law be part of the canon of constitutional material improperly empowers the political branches to create source materials—treaties and executive agreements—that serve as interpretive inputs to the process of constitutional decision making.

. . .

The third misuse of international sources occurs when the Court references them haphazardly, relying on only those materials that are readily at its fingertips. In the international legal arena, where the Court has little or no expertise, the Court is unduly susceptible to selective and incomplete presentations of the true state of international and foreign affairs. If the suggestion is that international sources may "cast an empirical light on the consequences of different solutions to a common legal problem," it is incumbent upon the Court to engage in empirical rather than haphazard comparativism. It is far from evident that this is what the Court is doing.

. . .

A final misuse occurs when international and foreign materials are used selectively. In a country that "considers itself the world's foremost protector of civil liberties," what is perhaps most surprising about the enthusiasm for comparativism is the assumption that it will enhance rather than diminish basic human rights in this country. This assumption is either blind to our visionary leadership, deaf to the discord in the international instruments, or selectively mute in giving voice to only certain topics for comparison.

A variety of constitutional liberties are ripe for comparison—property rights, establishment of religion, abortion, procedural due process, free speech—but query whether these subjects are on the agenda for comparative analysis. One may surmise that they are not, and the reason may well be that selective comparativism promotes the goal, to quote Justice Oliver Wendell Holmes, of having the Constitution become "the partisan of a particular set of ethical . . . opinions, which by no means are held *semper ubique et ab omnibus*." Put simply, international sources are proposed for comparison only if they are viewed as rights enhancing. To the extent that a comparative analysis supports government interests in lessening civil liberties—or at least certain civil liberties—international sources will likely be ignored.

. . .

Selective utilization of international sources is perhaps expected of advocates. But if the Supreme Court takes liberties with the comparative material in order to promote only certain liberties, few will find its approach persuasive. If international and foreign sources are arrows in the quiver of constitutional interpretation, those arrows should pierce our constitutional jurisprudence to produce results that we celebrate and that we abhor. Put simply, if we are all comparativists now, the results will by no means herald a capacious enhancement of civil liberties in this country.

. . .

As Justice O'Connor indicates, consideration of foreign and international law is not an uncommon practice among global constitutional courts. The South African Constitutional Court is among the leaders in drawing on comparative jurisprudence in its constitutional decisionmaking, in part because of a constitutional mandate which requires the Court to consider international law and permits it to consider foreign law. Below is an excerpt from that Court's extensive discussion of foreign and international law in *State v. Makwanyane and Another*, a constitutional challenge to the application of the death penalty. In the full opinion, the Court cites extensively from multiple international instruments and from a number of foreign courts. In this selection, the Court explains its approach to examining foreign and international law, and applies this view to the American example.

As you read, consider whether and how the use of foreign and international law by the South African Constitutional Court (SACC) differs from the United States Supreme Court's practice. Would adopting the techniques used by the SACC help to allay some of the domestic critics' concerns? Why or why not?

STATE V. T. MAKWANYANE AND ANOTHER

Constitutional Court of Republic of South Africa, 1995.
Case No. CCT/3/94.

International and Foreign Comparative Law

The death sentence is a form of punishment which has been used throughout history by different societies. . . . The movement away from the death penalty gained momentum during the second half of the present century with the growth of the abolitionist movement. In some countries it is now prohibited in all circumstances, in some it is prohibited save in times of war, and in most countries that have retained it as a penalty for crime, its use has been restricted to extreme cases. . . . Today, capital punishment has been abolished as a penalty for murder either specifically or in practice by almost half the countries of the world including the democracies of Europe and our neighbouring countries, Namibia, Mozambique and Angola. In most of those countries where it is retained, as the Amnesty International statistics show, it is seldom used.

In the course of the arguments addressed to us, we were referred to books and articles on the death sentence, and to judgments dealing with challenges made to capital punishment in the courts of other countries and in international tribunals. The international and foreign authorities are of value because they analyse arguments for and against the death sentence and show how courts of other jurisdictions have dealt with this vexed issue. For that reason alone they require our attention. They may also have to be considered because of their relevance to *section* 35(1) of the Constitution, which states:

> In interpreting the provisions of this Chapter a court of law shall promote the values which underlie an open and democratic society based on freedom and equality and shall, where applicable, have regard to public international law applicable to the protection of the rights entrenched in this Chapter, and may have regard to comparable foreign case law.

. . .

In dealing with comparative law, we must bear in mind that we are required to construe the South African Constitution, and not an international instrument or the constitution of some foreign country, and that this has to be done with due regard to our legal system, our history and circumstances, and the structure and language of our own Constitution. We can derive assistance from public international law and foreign case law, but we are in no way bound to follow it.

Capital Punishment in the United States of America

. . .

Although challenges under state constitutions to the validity of the death sentence have been successful, the federal constitutionality of the death sentence as a legitimate form of punishment for murder was affirmed by the United States Supreme Court in *Gregg v. Georgia*. Both before and after *Gregg*'s case, decisions upholding and rejecting challenges to death penalty statutes have divided the Supreme Court, and have led at times to sharply-worded judgments. The decisions ultimately turned on the votes of those judges who considered the nature of the discretion given to the sentencing authority to be the crucial factor.

Statutes providing for mandatory death sentences, or too little discretion in sentencing, have been rejected by the Supreme Court because they do not allow for consideration of factors peculiar to the convicted person facing sentence, which may distinguish his or her case from other cases. For the same reason, statutes which allow too wide a discretion to judges or juries have also been struck down on the grounds that the exercise of such discretion leads to arbitrary results. In sum, therefore, if there is no discretion, too little discretion, or an unbounded discretion, the provision authorising the death sentence has been struck down as being contrary to the Eighth Amendment; where the discretion has been "suitably directed and limited so as to minimise the risk of wholly arbitrary and capricious action," the challenge to the statute has failed.

Arbitrariness and Inequality

Basing his argument on the reasons which found favour with the majority of the United States Supreme Court in *Furman v. Georgia*, Mr Trengove contended on behalf of the accused [in this case, that] the unbounded discretion [to impose the death penalty] vested . . . in the Courts, makes [this section of the Criminal Procedure Act] unconstitutional.

. . .

Under our court system questions of guilt and innocence, and the proper sentence to be imposed on those found guilty of crimes, are not decided by juries. In capital cases, where it is likely that the death sentence may be imposed, judges sit with two assessors who have an equal vote with the judge on the issue of guilt and on any mitigating or aggravating factors relevant to sentence; but sentencing is the prerogative of the judge alone. The Criminal Procedure Act allows a full right of appeal to persons sentenced to death, including a right to dispute the sentence without having to establish an irregularity or misdirection on the part of the trial judge. The Appellate Division is empowered to set the sentence aside if it would not have imposed such sentence itself, and it has laid down criteria for the exercise of this power by itself and other courts.

. . .

Mitigating and aggravating factors must be identified by the Court, . . . Due regard must be paid to the personal circumstances and subjective factors which might have influenced the accused person's conduct, and these factors must then be weighed up with the main objects of punishment, which have been held to be: deterrence, prevention, reformation, and retribution. In this process "[e]very relevant consideration should receive the most scrupulous care and reasoned attention", and the death sentence should only be imposed in the most exceptional cases, where there is no reasonable prospect of reformation and the objects of punishment would not be properly achieved by any other sentence.

There seems to me to be little difference between the guided discretion required for the death sentence in the United States, and the criteria laid down by the Appellate Division for the imposition of the death sentence

. . .

The argument that the imposition of the death sentence under [the Act] is arbitrary and capricious does not, however, end there. It also focuses on what is alleged to be the arbitrariness inherent in the application of [the Act] in practice. Of the thousands of persons put on trial for murder, only a very small percentage are sentenced to death by a trial court, and of those, a large number escape the ultimate penalty on appeal. At every stage of the process there is an element of chance. The outcome may be dependent upon factors such as the way the case is investigated by the police, the way the case is presented by the prosecutor, how effectively the accused is defended, the personality and particular attitude to capital punishment of the trial judge and, if the matter goes on appeal, the particular judges who are selected to hear the case. Race and poverty are also alleged to be factors.

Most accused facing a possible death sentence are unable to afford legal assistance, and are defended under the *pro deo* system. The defending counsel is more often than not young and inexperienced, frequently of a different race to his or her client, and if this is the case, usually has to consult through an interpreter. *Pro deo* counsel are paid only a nominal fee for the defence, and generally lack the financial resources and the infrastructural support to undertake the necessary investigations and research, to employ expert witnesses to give advice, including advice on matters relevant to sentence, to assemble witnesses, to bargain with the prosecution, and generally to conduct an effective defence. Accused persons who have the money to do so, are able to retain experienced attorneys and counsel, who are paid to undertake the necessary investigations and research, and as a result they are less likely to be sentenced to death than persons similarly placed who are unable to pay for such services.

. . .

The differences that exist between rich and poor, between good and bad prosecutions, between good and bad defence, between severe and lenient judges, between judges who favour capital punishment and those who do not, and the subjective attitudes that might be brought into play by factors such as race and class, may in similar ways affect any case that comes before the courts, and is almost certainly present to some degree in all court systems. Such factors can be mitigated, but not totally avoided, by allowing convicted persons to appeal to a higher court. . . . What also needs to be acknowledged is that the possibility of error will be present in any system of justice and that there cannot be perfect equality as between accused persons in the conduct and outcome of criminal trials. We have to accept these differences in the ordinary criminal cases that come before the courts, even to the extent that some may go to gaol when others similarly placed may be acquitted or receive non-custodial sentences. But death is different, and the question is, whether this is acceptable when the difference is between life and death.

· · ·

In the United States, the Supreme Court has addressed itself primarily to the requirement of due process. Statutes have to be clear and discretion curtailed without ignoring the peculiar circumstances of each accused person. Verdicts are set aside if the defence has not been adequate, and persons sentenced to death are allowed wide rights of appeal and review. This attempt to ensure the utmost procedural fairness has itself led to problems. The most notorious is the "death row phenomenon" in which prisoners cling to life, exhausting every possible avenue of redress, and using every device to put off the date of execution, in the natural and understandable hope that there will be a reprieve from the Courts or the executive. It is common for prisoners in the United States to remain on death row for many years, and this dragging out of the process has been characterised as being cruel and degrading. The difficulty of implementing a system of capital punishment which on the one hand avoids arbitrariness by insisting on a high standard of procedural fairness, and on the other hand avoids delays that in themselves are the cause of impermissible cruelty and inhumanity, is apparent. Justice Blackmun, who sided with the majority in *Gregg*'s case, ultimately came to the conclusion that it is not possible to design a system that avoids arbitrariness. To design a system that avoids arbitrariness and delays in carrying out the sentence is even more difficult.

The United States jurisprudence has not resolved the dilemma arising from the fact that the Constitution prohibits cruel and unusual punishments, but also permits, and contemplates that there will be capital punishment. The acceptance by a majority of the United States Supreme Court of the proposition that capital punishment is not per se unconstitutional, but that in certain circumstances it may be arbitrary, and thus unconstitutional, has led to endless litigation. Considerable expense and interminable delays result from the exceptionally-high standard of procedural fairness set by the United States courts in attempting to avoid arbitrary decisions. The difficulties that have been experienced in following this path, to which Justice Blackmun and Justice Scalia have both referred, but from which they have drawn different conclusions, persuade me that we should not follow this route.

· · ·

NOTES & QUESTIONS

1.   How do Professors Jackson and Alford differ in their assessment of the practice of "looking abroad?" Do the critiques they offer distinguish between using international and foreign law, or do they conflate these sources? Are their critiques more valid with respect to one set of sources over another? Which account do you find more persuasive?

2.   Do the scholarly accounts of the purpose of foreign references align with those offered by the Justices themselves? What might account for any differences?

3.   How would you describe the differences between the way the U.S. Supreme Court and the South African Constitutional Court rely on foreign and international law in their decision-making?

4.   One reason that the South African Constitutional Court may be so adept in its comparative law analysis is that its justices "have the benefit of up to five clerks selected from applicants around the world" in addition to their South African clerks. Ursula Bentele, *Mining for Gold: The Constitutional Court of South Africa's Experience with Comparative Constitutional Law*, 37 Ga. J. Int'l Comp. L. 219, 244 (2009). The Supreme Court of Israel also has a practice of hiring foreign law clerks. *See, e.g.,* Foreign Clerks with the Supreme Court of Israel, http://elyon1.court.gov.il/eng/Clerking_opportunities/main.html. Would this approach make sense for the United States Supreme Court?

IV.   USING FOREIGN AND INTERNATIONAL LAW IN HUMAN RIGHTS ADVOCACY

Given the controversy surrounding the citation of foreign and international law, advocates must be strategic about when and how to invoke these standards in domestic litigation. Below is an excerpt from an *amicus* brief filed in *Fisher v. Texas*, a recent Supreme Court case considering the constitutionality of affirmative action in higher education. The brief raises international and foreign law for the Court's consideration.

In 2008, Abigail Fisher, a Caucasian high school senior, was denied admission to the University of Texas at Austin (UT Austin). Fisher did not qualify for admission under the University's Top Ten Percent (TTP) plan, which provides for automatic admission for any state resident who graduates in the top ten percent of his or her high school class. In the year Fisher applied, students admitted under the TTP filled over eighty percent of the seats in the first year class.

The remaining spots were filled based on consideration of the applicants' scores on an academic index and a personal achievement index. Race was included as one component of the student's personal achievement index, which also included factors such as the applicant's extracurricular activities, work experience, community service, and the socio-economic status of her family. Fisher was denied admission and filed a lawsuit arguing that the University's admissions policy violated the Equal Protection Clause of the Fourteenth Amendment.

The suit was filed only five years after the Supreme Court, by a narrow 5–4 vote, upheld the affirmative action policy of the University of

Michigan Law School in *Grutter v. Bollinger*.[1] The Court held that the law school could consider race as one factor in its admissions process as part of its efforts to create a diverse class. Fisher argued that UT Austin's admissions policy went further than *Grutter* allows because the TTP program created sufficient diversity in the student body without any consideration of race. UT Austin argued that its admissions policy was very similar to the one endorsed by the *Grutter* Court, and that its limited use of race was necessary to ensure that the class included a "critical mass" of minority students in its student body.

By the time this case reached the Supreme Court, Justice O'Connor, who authored the majority opinion in *Grutter*, had been replaced by the more conservative Justice Samuel Alito. Many observers were concerned that the Court's decision to grant *certiorari* in *Fisher* would mean the end of affirmative action in higher education. Approximately 90 briefs, representing a broad range of interests, were filed with the Court. The brief excerpted below was filed on behalf of several human rights advocacy organizations.

As you read this material, consider why the advocates may have chosen to raise foreign and international law and practice in this case. What are the potential benefits and risks of this strategy?

BRIEF OF *AMICI CURIAE* HUMAN RIGHTS ADVOCATES ET AL. IN SUPPORT OF RESPONDENTS FISHER V. UNIVERSITY OF TEXAS AT AUSTIN

Supreme Court of the United States, 2013.
133 S. Ct. 2411.

ARGUMENT

I. INTERNATIONAL AND COMPARATIVE FOREIGN LAW ARE RELEVANT TO THE SUPREME COURT'S CONSIDERATION OF THE CONSTITUTIONALITY OF THE UNIVERSITY OF TEXAS' ADMISSIONS PROGRAM

While the constitutionality of the University of Texas's undergraduate admissions program is largely bound up in domestic law and Fourteenth Amendment jurisprudence, examining the permissibility of holistic considerations of race in admissions decisions in the international context would continue the Court's "longstanding practice" of looking at international and foreign law to affirm and inform constitutional interpretation. *Graham v. Florida*, 130 S. Ct. 2011, 2033 (2010).

---

[1]   539 U.S. 306 (2003).

The Declaration of Independence itself speaks to the significance of other nations:

> When, in the course of human events, it becomes necessary for one people to dissolve the political bands which have connected them with another, and to assume among the powers of the earth, the separate and equal station to which the laws of nature and of nature's God entitle them, a *decent respect to the opinions of mankind* requires that they should declare the causes which impel them to the separation.

The Declaration of Independence para. 1 (U.S. 1776) (emphasis added).

Thomas Jefferson, drafter of the Declaration of Independence, had a keen appreciation for international opinion and law. He had a broad understanding of eighteenth century political thought, and was greatly influenced by European Enlightenment philosophers and their understanding of ancient Greek democracy and the Roman Republic. John Adams, too, understood the need to select the best the world had to offer in order to create a better government, and he believed that international opinion should inform the new nation's laws and institutions.

In urging courts to afford the requisite "decent respect to the opinions of mankind" Justice Blackmun explained that:

> [T]he early architects of our Nation understood that the customs of nations—the global opinions of mankind-would be binding upon the newly forged union. John Jay, the first Chief Justice of the United States, observed . . . that the United States "had, by taking a place among the nations of the earth, become amenable to the laws of nations."

Harry A. Blackmun, *The Supreme Court and the Law of Nations,* 104 Yale L.J. 39, 39 (1994) (footnotes omitted). This Court has recognized that history and noted that:

> For two centuries we have affirmed that the domestic law of the United States recognizes the law of nations. It would take some explaining to say now that federal courts must avert their gaze entirely from any international norm intended to protect individuals.

Sosa v. Alvarez-Machain, 542 U.S. 692, 729–30 (2004) (citations omitted).

In recent decisions, the Court has referred to international standards and has invoked U.S. treaty obligations, particularly when human rights issues arise. *Roper v. Simmons,* 543 U.S. 551, 576–77 (2005) (citing the United Nations Convention on the Rights of the Child as well as other nations' practices in abolishing juvenile death penalty); *see also Lawrence v. Texas,* 539 U.S. 558, 572–73, 578–79 (2003) (referencing a decision from the European Court of Human Rights in finding Texas's sodomy law unconstitutional); . . . . Thus, the Court recognizes the relevance of international law even when it is not directly binding. The relevance is even stronger in situations where the United States is party to a treaty.

Members of the Court have invoked international legal obligations in discussions of race conscious policies in higher education, in particular. In *Grutter,* the concurrence explained that the Court's decision to uphold the University of Michigan Law School's race-conscious admissions program comported with the United States' obligations under The Convention on the Elimination of All Forms of Racial Discrimination (CERD) to enact " 'special and concrete measures' " to guarantee equal protection and enjoyment of human rights for all races. . . . Particularly with respect to the CERD and the International Covenant on Civil and Political Rights (ICCPR), treaties which the United States has ratified, the United States has assumed international legal obligations that should inform the Court's analysis here.

II. CONSIDERATIONS OF RACE IN ADMISSIONS DECISIONS ARE CONSISTENT WITH THE UNITED STATES' INTERNATIONAL HUMAN RIGHTS COMMITMENTS

A. Human Rights Treaties Ratified by the United States Require the Adoption of Race-Conscious Measures

The United States has ratified two international human rights treaties that support, and indeed require, the race-conscious measures that are at issue in this case: the CERD and the ICCPR. Under the Supremacy Clause of the Constitution, these treaties are the supreme law of the land, U.S. Const., art. VI, cl. 2, and state and local government share responsibility with the federal government for upholding the United States' human rights treaty commitments. The ratification of these treaties creates binding international legal obligations for the United States to uphold and implement the principles of the CERD and the ICCPR.

1. *Considerations of Race Are Consistent with the CERD*

CERD was ratified by the U.S. in 1994, and obligates parties to the treaty "to adopt all necessary measures for speedily eliminating racial discrimination in all its forms and manifestations" and to "undertake to prevent, prohibit and eradicate all [racially discriminatory] practices."

CERD requires state parties to take affirmative steps to accomplish these goals. Article 1(4) states that:

> Special measures taken for the sole purpose of securing adequate advancement of certain racial or ethnic groups or individuals requiring such protection as may be necessary in order to ensure

such groups or individuals equal enjoyment or exercise of human rights and fundamental freedoms shall not be deemed racial discrimination.

Article 2(2) reiterates this requirement, providing that States shall take "special and concrete measures" to help guarantee full freedom and protection under the law for groups and individuals of all races. These special measures are limited in that they cannot lead to "unequal or separate rights for different racial groups," and are to end after the intended objectives have been achieved.

The CERD treaty body, the CERD Committee, has explained that special measures should include laws, policies, or practices that can affect areas such as housing, education, employment, and general participation in public life. UN Comm. on the Elimination of Racial Discrimination (CERD), *General Recommendation No. 32, The meaning and scope of special measures in the International Convention on the Elimination of All Forms [of] Racial Discrimination (Gen. Recommendation No. 32)*, U.N. Doc. No. CERD/C/GC/32 24 (Sept. 24, 2009), *available at* http://www.unhcr.org/refworld/docid/4adc30382.html. These laws or policies should be implemented by parties to address the situation of disfavored groups, and should work towards both *de jure* and *de facto* equality for all races. The obligation for parties to "secure human rights and fundamental freedoms on a nondiscriminatory basis" requires that parties address not just intentional discrimination, but also discriminatory effects. Such affirmative or positive actions should be "appropriate to the situation to be remedied, be legitimate, necessary in a democratic society, respect the principles of fairness and proportionality, and be temporary." The emphasis of the programs adopted as special measures should be to "correct [ ] present disparities and . . . prevent[ ] further imbalances from arising."

When reviewing countries' compliance with the convention, the CERD Committee has often raised the importance of special measures, particularly in the field of education. Requests for states to initiate or enhance special measures to promote greater equality in education are common in the CERD Committee's annual reports.

Importantly, the Committee has also made numerous references to concerns about access to higher education in particular, underscoring the recognition that inequalities at the university level are within the purview of the treaty, and that addressing those inequalities is part of the parties' legal obligations.

The United States' policies on education have been the subject of concern for the CERD Committee, as well. In its report to the Committee in 2007, the U.S. cited "race-conscious educational admission policies and scholarships" as evidence of the country's *compliance* with article 2(2) and specifically mentioned the *Grutter* decision as an example of that compliance. CERD, *Reports submitted by States parties under article 9 of the Convention: International Convention on the Elimination of all Forms of Racial Discrimination: 6th periodic reports of States parties due in 2005: add.: United States of America* ¶¶ 128, 131, U.N. Doc. CERD/C/USA/6 (Oct. 24, 2007), *available at* http://www.unhcr.org/ref world/docid/4785e8be2.html. Nevertheless, in the Concluding Observations commenting on its review of the United States' report, the Committee responded that the United States had not done enough to enact special measures to eradicate *de facto* discrimination in schools, recommending that the United States:

> undertake further studies to identify the underlying causes of de facto segregation and racial inequalities in education, with a view to elaborating effective strategies aimed at promoting school desegregation and providing equal educational opportunity in integrated settings for all students. In this regard, the Committee recommends that the State party take all appropriate measures [to allow] school districts to voluntarily promote school integration through the use of carefully tailored special measures adopted in accordance to article 2, paragraph 2, of the Convention.

Although the Concluding Observations referred specifically to Supreme Court decisions that limit the consideration of individual students' race in K-12 school assignment, it is clear that the CERD Committee is cognizant and concerned about racial equality in American schools generally. Compounded with the numerous recommendations for special measures in higher education throughout CERD's evaluations of other nations, it is clear that parties to CERD, including the United States, are obligated under the treaty to take all necessary measures, including positive action, to end *de facto* segregation—and thus to promote equal opportunity—in all levels of education, as part of the parties' legal obligations. Thus holistic considerations of race in higher education admissions decisions are consistent with the United States' international legal obligations under CERD, and indeed can be defended on the grounds that they implement the United States' treaty obligations.

2. Considerations of Race Are Permissible and Encouraged under The International Covenant on Civil and Political Rights

The United States ratified the ICCPR in 1992. The treaty obligates member states to protect the human dignity of individuals by upholding "equal and inalienable rights" within their territories. The Covenant requires states parties to protect individual rights "without distinction of any kind, such as race, colour, sex, language, religion," and provides that "the law shall prohibit any discrimination and guarantee to all persons equal and effective protection against discrimination on any ground."

In its 2006 review of U.S. compliance with the ICCPR, the Human Rights Committee (HRC) expressed concern over "de facto racial segregation in public schools," and reminded the U.S. of its obligations under articles 2 and 26 to guarantee effective protection against practices with discriminatory *effects*. The Committee recommended that the U.S. conduct investigation into racial segregation in schools and "take remedial steps." . . . In the United States' report to the Human Rights Committee in 2011 regarding its compliance with its commitments under the ICCPR, the U.S. State Department highlights the Court's consideration of education-specific affirmative action plans and guidance issued by the Departments of Education and Justice to assist educational institutions in pursuing policies to achieve diversity and avoid racial isolation, as evidence of the United States' compliance under ICCPR article 2. In doing so, the government acknowledges that special measures in higher education serve to uphold the "equal and inalienable rights" championed in the ICCPR and further the U.S.'s compliance with its international obligations under that treaty.

B.   Other Independent Human Rights Experts Have Recommended Considerations of Race in Higher Education to Address Inequality

The United Nations Working Group of Experts on People of African Descent has also raised concerns about minority access to higher education in the United States. In a report to the U.N. Human Rights Council concerning its visit to the United States in January 2010, the Working Group found that "the challenges faced by people of African descent in this country related mainly to disproportionately high levels of unemployment, generally lower income levels than the rest of the population, access to education (especially to higher levels of education) and quality of education." The Working Group suggested that the United States continue the initiatives already in place to remedy inequality in the education system, and also create "positive action policies to achieve parity of educational conditions among students of African descent and those of the majority population."

C.   The University Of Texas' Holistic Race Conscious Approach To Admissions Is Consistent With International Treaty Obligations And Recommendations

As explained in *Fisher,* the University of Texas seeks to admit a "critical mass" of minority students to its undergraduate programs through a holistic, individualized admissions process. The University contends that its program, which looks at a combination of factors concerning each applicant, including race, comports with the Supreme Court's decision in *Grutter,* which allows programs that involve a "narrowly tailored use of race in admissions decisions to further a compelling interest in obtaining the educational benefits that flow from a diverse student body."

Along with adhering to constitutional requirements under the Equal Protection Clause, the University of Texas' admissions program is also permissible according to international treaty obligations, including those of CERD articles 1(4) and 2(2) concerning special measures to eliminate racial discrimination. As explained above, under CERD, special measures must be "goal-directed programmes which have the objective of alleviating and remedying the disparities in the enjoyment of human rights and fundamental freedoms affecting particular groups and individuals, protecting them from discrimination." *Gen. Recommendation No. 32*, ¶ 22. The University of Texas's program seeks to promote equal opportunity in higher education for students of all races by ensuring a critical mass of under-represented minorities who otherwise would be less likely to be admitted due to the entrenched (and documented) discrimination against minorities in the United States' educational system.

Moreover, CERD requires that states implement special and concrete measures, "when the circumstances so warrant," in order to ensure that all racial groups are granted full and equal human rights. Thus, CERD does not require a finding of purposeful discrimination, only discriminatory effects. As the Fifth Circuit explained, the admissions program is warranted in light of a low number of minority students attending the University. After conducting studies to assess whether the university was fully obtaining the educational benefits of diversity that result from a critical mass of underrepresented minority students, the University implemented a program that would consider race as one of many factors in deciding which applicants to admit. The policy has led to "noticeable results,", and thus complies with CERD's requirements that special measures be "appropriate to the situation to be remedied, legitimate . . . [and] respect the principles of fairness and proportionality."

Moreover, the University has shown that these special measures are necessary in a democratic society, as achieving a critical mass of racial minorities in higher education will help to "'promote "cross-racial understanding," "break down racial stereotypes," enable students to better understand persons of other races, better prepare students to function in a multi-cultural workforce, [and] cultivate the next set of national leaders'" These measures are not discriminatory: the CERD Committee has explained that measures that take into account individuals who are in disadvantaged situations, like the measures at issue here, are "not an exception to the principle of non-discrimination but are integral to its meaning and essential to the [CERD] project of eliminating racial discrimination and advancing human dignity and effective equality." The University of Texas's admissions program is a necessary component of instituting nondiscrimination in the United States, as required by the CERD.

Finally, although there is no established end date to the University's program, both informal and formal review processes ensure that the policy adheres to CERD's mandate that special measures be temporary.

III. OTHER JURISDICTIONS AFFIRM THE USE OF RACE-CONSCIOUS APPROACHES TO PROMOTE EQUALITY AND NON-DISCRIMINATION

In addition to furthering the United States' compliance with its international legal obligations, the University of Texas' race-conscious admissions program comports with affirmative action measures permitted in, and endorsed by, other jurisdictions.

The European Court of Justice, for instance, has endorsed "positive action" programs to promote equality between men and women. In two cases, the European Court has upheld German initiatives that give priority to women in promotion decisions in positions where women were underrepresented. The programs under review in [these cases] were intended to counteract unequal opportunities for a disadvantaged group, regardless of the presence of intentional discrimination. The European Court found that the German policies lawfully pursued this legitimate social objective and utilized means that were proportionate in relation to the real needs of the disadvantaged group.

Along with the European Court of Justice, national courts in other jurisdictions have upheld affirmative action measures, specifically in relation to racial disparities in higher education. Most recently, the Federal Supreme Court of Brazil, that nation's highest court of appeals on constitutional matters, declared a race-conscious policy in student admissions at the University of Brasilia (UNB) to be constitutional. Just as the University of Texas program aims to promote diversity in the university setting, the Brazilian court found that UNB's affirmative action program was necessary to "set a plural and diversified academic environment."

Courts in South Africa have also upheld race-conscious measures in higher education. In one case, an Indian woman who was denied admission to a medical school challenged the school's affirmative action program that was aimed at benefiting historically-disadvantaged African students. The court rejected the claim, stating that the experience of African students in the country required specific compensation and thus the program was not discriminatory under the South African constitution.

Other countries permit affirmative action programs as a matter of law. For instance, India's national constitution was amended in 2005 to affirm that the nation would allow affirmative action in higher education: "Nothing in [the constitution's anti-discrimination provisions] shall prevent the State from making any special provision, by law, for the advancement of any socially and educationally backward classes of citizens or for [disadvantaged castes and tribes]." India Const, art. 15, cl. 5. Similarly, the Canadian constitution guarantees equal protection under the law, and explains that this guarantee "does not preclude any law, program or activity that has as its object the amelioration of conditions of disadvantaged individuals or groups including those that are disadvantaged because of race, national or ethnic origin, colour, religion, sex, age or mental or physical disability." Canadian Charter of Rights and Freedoms, Part I of the Constitution Act, 1982 § 15(2), being Schedule B to the Canada Act, 1982, c.11 (U.K.). In addition, statutes in New Zealand and Australia permit affirmative action measures in those countries. These examples evidence the willingness by other countries that are also parties to the CERD and the ICCPR to endorse race-conscious programs. They should inform the Court's consideration here.

. . .

In June 2013, nearly nine months after oral argument, the Court issued its decision in *Fisher*. In a 7–1 opinion (Justice Kagan was recused), the Court reiterated that a university's use of affirmative action in its admissions must meet the stringent "strict scrutiny" standard—and thus, that courts reviewing these programs must confirm that the university's use of race is necessary to create a diverse student body.[2] The case was remanded to the lower court to determine whether UT Austin could make this showing. On remand, the Fifth Circuit Court of Appeals, applying strict scrutiny, upheld the constitutionality of UT Austin's admissions plan.[3]

NOTES & QUESTIONS

1.   What are the ways in which this brief tries to convince the Court that foreign and comparative sources of authority are relevant and valid? How, if at all, do these reasons track to those offered by Justices Breyer and O'Connor in their defense of the practice?

2.   What level of authority is assigned to the foreign and international legal sources in this brief? Do the authors clearly distinguish between those standards that bind the United States and those that do not?

3.   Neither international nor foreign law were cited in the Supreme Court's opinion in *Fisher,* nor mentioned at oral argument. Does that mean

---

[2]   Fisher v. University of Texas at Austin, 133 S. Ct. 2411 (2013).
[3]   Fisher v. University of Texas at Austin, 2014 WL 3442449 (5th Cir. Jul. 15, 2014).

that this advocacy was not successful? Why might it make sense to file this type of brief, even if the impact on the court is difficult to measure? What audiences other than the Court are advocates trying to reach?

4. Why do you think these advocates chose to raise foreign and international law arguments in *Fisher*? Notably, similar *amicus* briefs were filed in several other affirmative action cases before the Supreme Court, and Justice Ginsburg cited international law sources in her concurrence in *Grutter v. Bollinger*. Are there particular cases in which these kinds of briefs may be more relevant? As an advocate, what qualities in a case would make you more likely to decide to file a comparative or international law brief?

SKILLS EXERCISE

A federal class action lawsuit has been filed against the state of California challenging the prolonged use of solitary confinement in its prisons as violating the Eighth and Fourteenth Amendment.

You work for a national human rights organization. The plaintiffs' attorneys in the California case have approached the leadership of your organization to ask if they intend to file an *amicus* brief before the district court in the case. *In addition to the materials in this chapter*, your supervisor has given you the research file below and asked you for a memorandum that addresses the following questions:

Whether this is an appropriate case for an international and comparative human rights brief? Is so, what are the strongest arguments? What are the potential downsides? And, what additional research would you want to conduct as you make your evaluation?

Research Materials

International Covenant on Civil and Political Rights

G.A. res. 2200A (XXI), 21 U.N. GAOR Supp. (No. 16) at 52, U.N. Doc A/6316, 999. U.N.T.S. 171, *entered into force* Mar. 23, 1976.

Preamble

The States Parties to the present Covenant,

Considering that, in accordance with the principles proclaimed in the Charter of the United Nations, recognition of the inherent dignity and of the equal and inalienable rights of all members of the human family is the foundation of freedom, justice and peace in the world,

Recognizing that these rights derive from the inherent dignity of the human person,

Recognizing that, in accordance with the Universal Declaration of Human Rights, the ideal of free human beings enjoying civil and political freedom and freedom from fear and want can only be achieved if conditions are created whereby everyone may enjoy his civil and political rights, as well as his economic, social and cultural rights,

Considering the obligation of States under the Charter of the United Nations to promote universal respect for, and observance of, human rights and freedoms,

Realizing that the individual, having duties to other individuals and to the community to which he belongs, is under a responsibility to strive for the promotion and observance of the rights recognized in the present Covenant,

Agree upon the following articles:

. . .

Article 7

No one shall be subjected to torture or to cruel, inhuman or degrading treatment or punishment.

. . .

Article 10

1. All persons deprived of their liberty shall be treated with humanity and with respect for the inherent dignity of the human person.

. . .

CONVENTION AGAINST TORTURE AND OTHER CRUEL, INHUMAN OR DEGRADING TREATMENT OR PUNISHMENT
10 December 1984, U.N.T.S. 1465.

The States Parties to this Convention,

Considering that, in accordance with the principles proclaimed in the Charter of the United Nations, recognition of the equal and inalienable rights of all members of the human family is the foundation of freedom, justice and peace in the world,

Recognizing that those rights derive from the inherent dignity of the human person,

Considering the obligation of States under the Charter, in particular Article 55, to promote universal respect for, and observance of, human rights and fundamental freedoms,

Having regard to article 5 of the Universal Declaration of Human Rights and article 7 of the International Covenant on Civil and Political Rights, both of which provide that no one shall be subjected to torture or to cruel, inhuman or degrading treatment or punishment,

Having regard also to the Declaration on the Protection of All Persons from Being Subjected to Torture and Other Cruel, Inhuman or Degrading Treatment or Punishment, adopted by the General Assembly on 9 December 1975,

Desiring to make more effective the struggle against torture and other cruel, inhuman or degrading treatment or punishment throughout the world,

Have agreed as follows:

. . .

Article 1

1. For the purposes of this Convention, the term "torture" means any act by which severe pain or suffering, whether physical or mental, is intentionally inflicted on a person for such purposes as obtaining from him or a third person information or a confession, punishing him for an act he or a third person has committed or is suspected of having committed, or intimidating or coercing him or a third person, or for any reason based on discrimination of any kind, when such pain or suffering is inflicted by or at the instigation of or with the consent or acquiescence of a public official or other person acting in an official capacity. It does not include pain or suffering arising only from, inherent in or incidental to lawful sanctions.

2. This article is without prejudice to any international instrument or national legislation which does or may contain provisions of wider application.

INTERIM REPORT OF THE SPECIAL RAPPORTEUR OF THE HUMAN
RIGHTS COUNCIL ON TORTURE AND OTHER CRUEL, INHUMAN
OR DEGRADING TREATMENT OR PUNISHMENT

5 August 2011, U.N. Doc. A/66/268.

. . .

C. *Definition*

25. There is no universally agreed upon definition of solitary confinement. The Istanbul Statement on the Use and Effects of Solitary Confinement defines solitary confinement as the physical isolation of individuals who are confined to their cells for 22 to 24 hours a day. In many jurisdictions, prisoners held in solitary confinement are allowed out of their cells for one hour of solitary exercise a day. Meaningful contact with other people is typically reduced to a minimum. The reduction in stimuli is not only quantitative but also qualitative. The available stimuli

and the occasional social contacts are seldom freely chosen, generally monotonous, and often not empathetic.

26. Solitary confinement is also known as "segregation", "isolation", "separation", "cellular", "lockdown", "Supermax", "the hole" or "Secure Housing Unit (SHU)", but all these terms can involve different factors. For the purposes of this report, the Special Rapporteur defines solitary confinement as the physical and social isolation of individuals who are confined to their cells for 22 to 24 hours a day. Of particular concern to the Special Rapporteur is prolonged solitary confinement, which he defines as any period of solitary confinement in excess of 15 days. He is aware of the arbitrary nature of the effort to establish a moment in time which an already harmful regime becomes prolonged and therefore unacceptably painful. He concludes that 15 days is the limit between "solitary confinement" and "prolonged solitary confinement" because at that point, according to the literature surveyed, some of the harmful psychological effects of isolation can become irreversible.

D. *Legal framework*

27. International and regional human rights bodies have taken different approaches to address the underlying conditions of social and physical isolation of detainees, and whether such practices constitute torture or cruel, inhuman or degrading treatment or punishment. For example, while the European Court of Human Rights has confronted solitary confinement regimes with regularity, the United Nations Human Rights Committee and the Inter-American Court of Human Rights have most extensively addressed the related phenomenon of incommunicado detention. For the purposes of this report, the Special Rapporteur will highlight the work of universal and regional human rights bodies on solitary confinement only.

1.   International level

General Assembly

28. In 1990, the General Assembly adopted resolution 45/111, the Basic Principles for the Treatment of Prisoners. Principle 7 states that efforts to abolish solitary confinement as a punishment, or to restrict its use, should be undertaken and encouraged.

29. In the same year, the General Assembly adopted resolution 45/113, the United Nations Rules for the Protection of Juveniles Deprived of their Liberty. In paragraph 67 the Assembly asserted that "All disciplinary measures constituting cruel, inhuman or degrading treatment shall be strictly prohibited, including . . . solitary confinement or any other punishment that may compromise the physical or mental health of the juvenile concerned".

United Nations treaty bodies

30. The Human Rights Committee, in paragraph 6 of its General Comment No. 20, noted that prolonged solitary confinement of the detained or imprisoned person might amount to acts prohibited by article 7 of the International Covenant on Civil and Political Rights. In its concluding observations on Rwanda, the Human Rights Committee recommended that "The State party should put an end to the sentence of solitary confinement. . . ."

31. The Committee against Torture has recognized the harmful physical and mental effects of prolonged solitary confinement and has expressed concern about its use, including as a preventive measure during pretrial detention, as well as a disciplinary measure. The Committee has recommended that the use of solitary confinement be abolished, particularly during pretrial detention, or at least that it should be strictly and specifically regulated by law (maximum duration, etc.) and exercised under judicial supervision, and used only in exceptional circumstances, such as when the safety of persons or property is involved. The Committee has recommended that persons under the age of 18 should not be subjected to solitary confinement.

32. The Subcommittee on Prevention of Torture and Other Cruel, Inhuman or Degrading Treatment or Punishment has pointed out that prolonged solitary confinement may amount to an act of torture and other cruel, inhuman or degrading treatment or punishment and recommended that solitary confinement should not be used in the case of minors or the mentally disabled. The Subcommittee has also recommended that a medical officer should visit prisoners held in solitary confinement every day, on the understanding that such visits should be in the interests of the prisoners' health. Furthermore, prisoners held in solitary confinement for more than 12 hours should have access to fresh air for at least one hour each day. In view of the condition of solitary confinement, the Subcommittee has pointed out that beds and proper mattresses should be made available to all inmates, including prisoners held in solitary confinement.

33. The Committee on the Rights of the Child, in its General Comment No. 10 (2007), emphasized that "disciplinary measures in violation of article 37 [of the Convention on the Rights of the Child] must be strictly forbidden, including . . . closed or solitary confinement, or any other punishment that may compromise the physical or mental health or well-being of the child concerned." Moreover, the Committee has urged States parties to prohibit and abolish the use of solitary confinement against children.

2.   Regional level

European Court of Human Rights

34. In its evaluation of cases of solitary confinement, the European Court of Human Rights considers the rationale given by the State for the imposition of social and physical isolation. The Court has found violations of article 3 of the European Convention on Human Rights where States do not provide a security-based justification for the use of solitary confinement. In circumstances of prolonged solitary confinement, the Court has held that the justification for solitary confinement must be explained to the individual and the justification must be "increasingly detailed and compelling" as time goes on.

35. Through its jurisprudence, the European Court of Human Rights emphasizes that certain procedural safeguards must be in place during the imposition of solitary confinement, for example, monitoring a prisoner's physical well-being, particularly where the individual is not in good health and having access to judicial review.

36. The level of isolation imposed on an individual is essential to the European Court of Human Rights' assessment of whether instances of physical and mental isolation constitute torture or cruel, inhuman or degrading treatment or punishment. A prolonged absolute prohibition of visits from individuals from outside the prison causes suffering "clearly exceeding the unavoidable level inherent in detention." However, where the individual can receive visitors and write letters, have access to television, books and newspapers and regular contact with prison staff or visit with clergy or lawyers on a regular basis, isolation is "partial", and the minimum threshold of severity—which the European Court of Human Rights considers necessary to find a violation of article 3 of the European Convention on Human Rights—is not met. Nevertheless, the Court has emphasized that solitary confinement, even where the isolation is only partial, cannot be imposed on a prisoner indefinitely.

Inter-American System on Human Rights

37. The jurisprudence on solitary confinement within the Inter-American System on Human Rights is more conclusive than within the bodies discussed above. Since its earliest judgments, the Inter-American Court of Human Rights has found that certain elements of a prison regime and certain physical prison conditions in themselves constitute cruel and inhuman treatment, and therefore violate article 5 of the American Convention on Human Rights, which recognizes the right to the integrity of the person. For example, the Court held that "prolonged isolation and deprivation of communication are in themselves cruel and inhuman treatment, harmful to the psychological and moral integrity of the person and a violation of the right of any detainee to respect for his inherent dignity as a human being". The Court has additionally

addressed physical conditions of detention, asserting that "isolation in a small cell, without ventilation or natural light, . . . [and] restriction of visiting rights . . . , constitute forms of cruel, inhuman and degrading treatment".

38. The Court has additionally recognized that solitary confinement results in psychological and physical suffering that may contribute to treatment that constitutes torture. In at least one case, the Court has identified the physical conditions of solitary confinement, including "a small cell with no ventilation or natural light", and a prison regime where a detained individual "is held for 23 and a half hours a day . . . , [and] permitted to see his relatives only once a month, but could have no physical contact with them", when coupled with other forms of physical and psychological aggression, in sum may constitute physical and psychological torture.

39. In its analysis of solitary confinement, the Court has noted that even when used in exceptional circumstances, procedural safeguards must be in place. For example, "the State is obliged to ensure that the detainee enjoys the minimum and non-derogable guarantees established in the [American] Convention and, specifically, the right to question the lawfulness of the detention and the guarantee of access to effective defense during his incarceration". Similarly, the Inter-American Commission on Human Rights has consistently held that all forms of disciplinary action taken against detained persons must comport with the norms of due process and provide opportunity for judicial review.

. . .

G.   *Prolonged or indefinite solitary confinement*

57. The use of prolonged or indefinite solitary confinement has increased in various jurisdictions, especially in the context of the "war on terror" and "a threat to national security". Individuals subjected to either of these practices are in a sense in a prison within a prison and thus suffer an extreme form of anxiety and exclusion, which clearly supersede normal imprisonment. Owing to their isolation, prisoners held in prolonged or indefinite solitary confinement can easily slip out of sight of justice, and safeguarding their rights is therefore often difficult, even in States where there is a strong adherence to rule of law.

58. When a State fails to uphold the Standard Minimum Rules for the Treatment of Prisoners during a short period of time of solitary confinement, there may be some debate on whether the adverse effects amount to cruel, inhuman or degrading treatment or punishment or torture. However, the longer the duration of solitary confinement or the greater the uncertainty regarding the length of time, the greater the risk

of serious and irreparable harm to the inmate that may constitute cruel, inhuman or degrading treatment or punishment or even torture.

59. The feeling of uncertainty when not informed of the length of solitary confinement exacerbates the pain and suffering of the individuals who are subjected to it. In some instances, individuals may be held indefinitely during pretrial detention, increasing the risk of other forms of cruel, inhuman or degrading treatment or punishment or torture.

60. Most studies fail to specify the length of time after which solitary confinement becomes prolonged. While the term may be undefined, detainees can be held in solitary confinement from a few weeks to many years. For example, in Kazakhstan, individuals can be held in solitary confinement for more than two months. Some detainees have been held in solitary confinement facilities for years, without any charge and without trial, and in secret detention centres where isolation is used as an integral part of interrogation practices. In a joint report on the situation of detainees at Guantánamo Bay, experts found that although 30 days of isolation was the maximum period permissible, some detainees were returned to isolation after very short breaks over a period of up to 18 months.

61. There is no international standard for the permitted maximum overall duration of solitary confinement. In A.B. v. Russia, the European Court of Human Rights held that detaining an individual in solitary confinement for three years constituted a violation of article 3 of the European Convention on Human Rights. By contrast, in the United States of America, it is reported that two prisoners have been held in solitary confinement in a Louisiana prison for 40 years after failed attempts at judicial appeal of the conditions of their confinement. As explained in paragraph 26 above, the Special Rapporteur finds that solitary confinement exceeding 15 days is prolonged.

. . .

K.   *When solitary confinement amounts to torture and other cruel, inhuman or degrading treatment or punishment*

70. Because of the absence of witnesses, solitary confinement increases the risk of acts of torture and other cruel, inhuman or degrading treatment or punishment. Given its severe adverse health effects, the use of solitary confinement itself can amount to acts prohibited by article 7 of the International Covenant on Civil and Political Rights

. . .

82. The Special Rapporteur calls upon States to respect and protect the rights of persons deprived of liberty while maintaining security and

order in places of detention. He recommends that States conduct regular reviews of the system of solitary confinement. In this context, the Special Rapporteur reiterates that States should refer to the Istanbul Statement on the Use and Effects of Solitary Confinement as a useful tool in efforts to promote the respect and protection of the rights of detainees.

83. The Special Rapporteur calls upon States to ensure that all persons deprived of their liberty are treated with humanity and respect for the inherent dignity of the human person as protected by article 10, paragraph 1, of the International Covenant on Civil and Political Rights. The Special Rapporteur refers to the Standard Minimum Rules for the Treatment of Prisoners and recommends that States increase the level of psychological, meaningful social contact for detainees while in solitary confinement.

84. The Special Rapporteur urges States to prohibit the imposition of solitary confinement as punishment—either as a part of a judicially imposed sentence or a disciplinary measure. He recommends that States develop and implement alternative disciplinary sanctions to avoid the use of solitary confinement.

85. States should take necessary steps to put an end to the practice of solitary confinement in pretrial detention. The use of solitary confinement as an extortion technique during pretrial detention should be abolished. States should adopt effective measures at the pretrial stage to improve the efficiency of investigation and introduce alternative control measures in order to segregate individuals, protect ongoing investigations, and avoid detainee collusion. States should abolish the use of solitary confinement for juveniles and persons with mental disabilities. Regarding disciplinary measures for juveniles, the Special Rapporteur recommends that States should take other measures that do not involve the use of solitary confinement. In regard to the use of solitary confinement for persons with mental disabilities, the Special Rapporteur emphasizes that physical segregation of such persons may be necessary in some cases for their own safety, but solitary confinement should be strictly prohibited.

. . .

87. Indefinite solitary confinement should be abolished.

88. It is clear that short-term solitary confinement can amount to torture or cruel, inhuman or degrading treatment or punishment; it can, however, be a legitimate device in other circumstances, provided that adequate safeguards are in place. In the opinion of the Special Rapporteur, prolonged solitary confinement, in excess of 15 days, should be subject to an absolute prohibition.

89. The Special Rapporteur reiterates that solitary confinement should be used only in very exceptional circumstances, as a last resort, for as short a time as possible. He emphasizes that when solitary confinement is used in exceptional circumstances, minimum procedural safeguards must be followed. These safeguards reduce the chances that the use of solitary confinement will be arbitrary or excessive, as in the case of prolonged or indefinite confinement. They are all the more important in circumstances of detention where due process protections are often limited, as in administrative immigration detention. Minimum procedural safeguards should be interpreted in a manner that provides the greatest possible protection of the rights of detained individuals.

. . .

CHAPTER VI

STATE AND LOCAL IMPLEMENTATION

■ ■ ■

I. INTRODUCTION

States and local governments play a significant role in ensuring the United States meets its international human rights treaty commitments. Although the Constitution gives the federal government the exclusive authority to enter into treaties with foreign powers, the United States regularly ratifies human rights treaties with the understanding that states and localities are responsible for implementation in areas traditionally under their jurisdiction, such as criminal justice, housing, and education.

Each time the Senate has given its advice and consent to ratify a major human rights treaty, it has done so with the understanding that:

> [T]his Covenant shall be implemented by the Federal Government to the extent that it exercises legislative and judicial jurisdiction over the matters covered therein, and otherwise by the state and local governments; to the extent that state and local governments exercise jurisdiction over such matters, the Federal Government shall take measures appropriate to the Federal system to the end that the competent authorities of the state or local governments may take appropriate measures for the fulfillment of the Covenant.[1]

Similarly, when the United States issued its first report to the United Nations Human Rights Committee regarding its compliance with the ICCPR, the federal government reiterated that it is:

> A government of limited authority and responsibility. . . . [and that] state and local governments exercise significant responsibilities in many areas, including matters such as education, public health, business organization, work conditions, marriage and divorce, the care of children and exercise of the ordinary police power . . . Some areas covered by the Covenant fall into this category.

---

[1] 140 Cong. Rec. 14326 (1994) (recognizing that state and local governments shall implement obligations under the CERD in areas within their jurisdiction). *See also* 138 Cong. Rec. 8071 (1992) (similar understanding for the ICCPR); 136 Cong. Rec. S17,486 (daily ed. Oct. 27, 1990) (similar understanding for the CAT).

U.S. Department of State, *Initial Report of the United States of America to the U.N. Committee on Human Rights Concerning the International Covenant on Civil and Political Rights* (Aug. 24, 1994).

The report then explained that the United States had, through its ratification process, put other governments worldwide on notice that the "United States will implement its obligations under the Covenant by appropriate legislative, executive and judicial means, federal or state, and that the federal government will remove any federal inhibition to the abilities of the constituent states to meet their obligations in this regard."[2]

Under international law, this kind of delegation is permissible, and indeed anticipated. Still, under international law, the national government retains responsibility for ensuring compliance with international obligations. For example, Article 50 of the ICCPR states that "[t]he provisions of the present Covenant shall extend to all parts of federal States without any limitations or exceptions." And Article 2 of the CERD states that "[e]ach State party undertakes to engage in no act or practice of racial discrimination against persons, groups of persons or institutions and to ensure that all public authorities and public institutions, national and local, shall act in conformity with this obligation."

To date, however, the United States federal government's attempts to require state and local actors to engage with, and implement, these treaty instruments have been limited. As noted in **Chapter III**, the United States ratifies most human rights treaties with a declaration that the treaty is non-self-executing. The United States has enacted federal legislation implementing the Convention Against Torture and the Genocide Convention, but not the other core human rights treaties that it has ratified. Thus, most treaty commitments are not directly enforceable in federal and state courts. And Supreme Court jurisprudence makes clear that without federal legislation, the President has limited authority to require states to comply with human rights treaty obligations. In particular, in *Medellín v. Texas*,[3] discussed in greater detail in **Chapter III** and below, the Court held that the executive branch is unable to compel states to comply with non-self-executing treaties absent implementing legislation.

Notwithstanding the lack of federal direction and coordination, states and cities are increasingly active participants in advancing human rights, both domestically and abroad. States and cities have a long history of engaging in efforts to influence human rights in foreign countries,

---

[2]   U.S. Department of State, *Initial Report of the United States of America to the U.N. Committee on Human Rights Concerning the International Covenant on Civil and Political Rights* (Aug. 24, 1994).

[3]   552 U.S. 491 (2008).

including through state legislation mandating divestment in rights-abusing countries and regimes. States and localities are embracing, and in some cases integrating, more internally focused human rights activities to influence *domestic* policy and practice, as well. This chapter explores both the successes and challenges of these domestically focused efforts.

Following this Introduction, Part II of this chapter reviews the ways in which advocates are using international human rights law and comparative foreign law to support litigation strategies in state courts and examines judicial responses to these efforts. As might be expected, state courts often follow the federal Supreme Court in considering comparative and international sources—for example, when reviewing challenges to the constitutionality of punishment practices that are also governed by the federal Eighth Amendment. And because state constitutions often include different and more expansive rights guarantees than the federal constitution, many more of the most innovative uses of comparative and international human rights law are occurring at the state level, as state jurists interpret their own constitutional documents independent of federal constraints.

Part III moves beyond the courts to examine the ways in which state and local legislators and are engaging with human rights norms and instruments to impact domestic policy and practice. Through legislative and policy initiatives, states and cities are pressuring the federal government to expand and deepen its human rights agenda, while also offering concrete examples of how broad human rights principles can be realized as a matter of local policy.

Throughout, this chapter examines the political and doctrinal challenges to these types of efforts. Minimal federal coordination of human rights treaty implementation at the state and local level has resulted in somewhat *ad hoc* subnational engagement. Moreover, doctrinal uncertainty about federal pre-emption and the extent to which states and cities may constitutionally participate in questions of foreign affairs lurk in the background of some of these local initiatives. Finally, concerns about protecting American sovereignty and values have, in some quarters, led to grassroots political opposition to the United States' participation in international human rights treaty regimes and state court judges' consideration of international and foreign law.

This chapter illustrates the complexities of realizing the nation's human rights commitments within our federalist system. As you read, consider both the advantages and disadvantages of this decentralized approach.

II. FOREIGN AND INTERNATIONAL LAW IN STATE COURTS

State courts have a significant role to play in implementing the nation's international human rights obligations. Under the Supremacy Clause, treaties are the "Supreme Law of the Land," binding on the "Judges in every State."[4] This gives ratified treaties "a legal status equivalent to enacted federal statutes. As such, they prevail over previously enacted federal law (to the extent of any conflict) and over any inconsistent state or federal law."[5] The Supremacy Clause may also require states to implement customary international law, particularly in areas of law traditionally within their jurisdiction. Professor Julian Ku has demonstrated that in fact state courts have been engaged in such activities for decades in the areas of trusts and estates and family law.[6]

Even absent a formal mandate, state courts may consider international and foreign sources when interpreting their own constitutions, particularly those provisions that have parallels in international treaty instruments and modern constitutions from around the world. State courts may also consider transnational sources in interpreting state statutes and in developing state common law. In these instances, where federal law gives little or no direction to state courts, transnational law may be an important source of guidance. This section examines the ways in which state courts are engaging with—both adopting and at times rejecting—international human rights claims and arguments.

A. INTERNATIONAL LAW AS DIRECT AUTHORITY

i. Raising Treaty Obligations in State Courts: *Commonwealth v. Gautreaux*

In 2011, the Massachusetts Supreme Judicial Court was asked to order a new trial for a citizen of the Dominican Republic on the grounds that he had not been informed of his right under a U.S.-ratified international treaty, the Vienna Convention on Consular Relations (VCCR), to have his consulate notified at the time of his arrest in the United States.

At the time this case came before the Massachusetts Supreme Judicial Court, the domestic law regarding the enforcement of the VCCR was in something of a muddle. The International Court of Justice had

---

[4]   U.S. Const. art. VI, cl. 2.

[5]   U.S. Department of State, *Initial Report to the Committee on the Elimination of Racial Discrimination* (Oct. 10, 2000).

[6]   *See generally* Julian Ku, *Customary International Law in State Courts*, 42 Va. J. Int'l L. 265 (2001).

recently held in *Case concerning Avena and Other Mexican Nationals (Mex. v. U.S.)*,[7] that the United States had violated its obligations under the VCCR by failing to ensure the right of consular notification to a class of Mexican nationals facing criminal proceedings in the United States. It had ordered the United States to provide "review and reconsideration" of their sentences. Nonetheless, when José Medellín, a Mexican national on death row in Texas, tried to rely on the ICJ judgment to obtain review of his conviction and death sentence through a habeas petition, the United States Supreme Court, in *Medellín v. Texas*, concluded that while the ICJ judgment "creates an international law obligation on the part of the United States, it does not of its own force constitute binding federal law that preempts state restrictions"—in this case, the Texas procedural law barring Mr. Medellín's effort to raise the consular notification issue in a post-conviction habeas petition.[8]

Concurring with the majority in the *Medellín* case, Justice Stevens went on to discuss the practical meaning of the international law obligation recognized by the majority. Justice Stevens noted that the Court's decision did not absolve the United States or the State of Texas of the need to meet their international obligations. He explained:

> Even though the ICJ's judgment in *Avena* is not "the supreme Law of the Land," no one disputes that it constitutes an international law obligation on the part of the United States. . . . Under the express terms of the Supremacy Clause, the United States' obligation to "undertak[e] to comply" with the ICJ's decision falls on each of the States as well as the Federal Government. One consequence of our form of government is that sometimes States must shoulder the primary responsibility for protecting the honor and integrity of the Nation. Texas' duty in this respect is all the greater since it was Texas that—by failing to provide consular notice in accordance with the Vienna Convention—ensnared the United States in the current controversy. Having already put the Nation in breach of one treaty, it is now up to Texas to prevent the breach of another.

Medellín v. Texas, 552 U.S. 491, 536 (2008) (Stevens, J., concurring).

Texas did not take up Justice Stevens' plea to protect the nation's international integrity. Instead, José Medellín was executed on August 5, 2008, without judicial examination of the impact that denial of his consular rights had on his initial trial and conviction.

When the same issue arose in Massachusetts, the state's Supreme Judicial Court took a different tack. As you read Justice Cordy's opinion in *Commonwealth v. Gautreaux*, consider how the Massachusetts court

---

[7] 2004 I.C.J. 12 (Mar. 31).

[8] 552 U.S. 491, 522–23 (2008).

views its role in ensuring that the United States meets its international treaty obligations under the VCCR.

COMMONWEALTH V. GAUTREAUX

Supreme Judicial Court of Massachusetts, 2011.
941 N.E.2d 616.

CORDY, J.:

The defendant, Amaury Gautreaux, was born in the Dominican Republic in 1980 and moved to the United States when he was fourteen years of age. His primary language is Spanish and he has never become fluent in English. He is not a United States citizen. On August 27, 2003, he pleaded guilty in the Lawrence District Court to criminal charges arising out of three arrests. Pursuant to a plea bargain struck with the Commonwealth, the defendant received an eleven-month sentence to a house of correction suspended for eighteen months, during which period he was placed on probation. Approximately five years later, on May 26, 2008, the defendant was once again arrested, and on July 8, 2008, he received an order of deportation from the United States Department of Homeland Security. In February, 2009, he moved . . . to vacate his guilty plea and for a new trial.

In his motion, the defendant claimed that he was never notified of his right as a foreign national to have his consulate informed of his arrests in violation of art. 36 of the Vienna Convention on Consular Relations, April 24, 1963, 21 U.S.T. 77, T.I.A.S. No. 6820 (art. 36 or Vienna Convention).

. . .

1.   *Article 36 of the Vienna Convention on Consular Relations.*

The Vienna Convention, negotiated in 1963, governs the establishment of consular relations between nation States (States) and defines the functions of a consulate. The Vienna Convention was ratified by the United States in 1969. Once ratified, the Vienna Convention became the "supreme Law of the Land" and binding on the States of the United States. The United States also signed the Optional Protocol to the Vienna Convention Concerning the Compulsory Settlement of Disputes, April 24, 1963, 21 U.S.T. 325, 596 U.N.T.S. 487 (Optional Protocol), which established that the International Court of Justice (ICJ) would have jurisdiction over disputes regarding compliance by the signatory States with the provisions of the Vienna Convention, and made its decisions binding on the parties before it.

Article 36 sets out the procedure to be followed when a foreign national is arrested or detained. It provides in pertinent part that a foreign national shall be notified "without delay" of "his rights," including his right to have authorities of the detaining State notify his consulate of his detention. Once requested to do so, such authorities shall inform the detainee's consulate of his detention "without delay." Thereafter, consular officers shall be free to communicate with and have access to the detainee and to arrange for his legal representation. The Vienna Convention further provides that the rights and obligations it contains "shall be exercised in conformity with the laws and regulations of the receiving State," and that these laws and regulations must "enable full effect" to be given to the intended purposes of art. 36. In order to enable the full effect to be given to art. 36, we conclude that the notifications it requires must be incorporated into the protocols of the State and local law enforcement agencies of Massachusetts.

The Vienna Convention is silent as to remedy for the failure in individual cases to adhere to the provisions of art. 36, where the detainee is subsequently convicted of a crime. We have never determined whether the consular notification requirement of the Vienna Convention confers individual rights on foreign nationals that are judicially enforceable. . . . In *Breard v. Greene*, the United States Supreme Court stated that the Vienna Convention "arguably confers on an individual the right to consular assistance following arrest," but has since avoided the question. Circuit Courts of the United States Appeals that have decided the question have answered inconsistently. Other Federal District and State courts have weighed in, also with varied results.

Consequently, while it remains far from clear whether art. 36 confers rights on individuals judicially enforceable by them under American law, it is unquestioned that an enforceable right exists for signatory States. The International Court of Justice (ICJ) has heard three cases where signatory States have challenged the application (or lack of application) by the United States of art. 36. The ICJ issued decisions in both *LaGrand* and *Avena,* binding on the United States.

In *LaGrand,* the ICJ concluded that art. 36 of the Vienna Convention not only confers rights on signatory States, but also grants "individual rights" to the States' nationals that "may be invoked in this Court by the national State of the detained person."

. . .

Subsequently, in the *Avena* case, the ICJ found that the United States had violated its obligations under art. 36 with regard to a large number of Mexican nationals arrested and subsequently convicted of crimes in Texas. As reparation, the United States was required to provide, "by means of its own choosing, review and reconsideration of the convictions and sentences of the [foreign] nationals" that takes into account the violation of rights set forth in art. 36. The ICJ did not limit its holding to the case at hand; indeed, it took care to "re-emphasize a point of importance" that "the fact that in this case the Court's ruling has concerned only Mexican nationals cannot be taken to imply that the conclusions reached by it in the present Judgment do not apply to other foreign nationals finding themselves in similar situations in the United States."

Although a decision of the ICJ is not binding on this court, it is entitled to respectful consideration. The ICJ is the judicial organ designated to resolve disputes regarding implementation of the Vienna Convention, and as signatory to the Optional Protocol, the United States agreed to be bound by its decisions. We acknowledge and accept the conclusion of the ICJ regarding the obligation that art. 36 creates when clear violations of its notice protocols have been established, that is, to provide some process by which the soundness of a subsequent conviction can be reviewed in light of the violation.

Under our procedural rules, a postconviction review may be obtained at any time by filing a motion for a new trial pursuant to rule 30(b). That was the manner in which relief was sought in this case. In such a post trial proceeding, it is incumbent on the foreign national to demonstrate that the failure to comply with art. 36 of the Vienna Convention gave rise to a substantial risk of a miscarriage of justice. "A substantial risk of a miscarriage of justice exists when we 'have a serious doubt whether the result of the [proceeding] might have been different had the error not been made.' "

To demonstrate a substantial risk of a miscarriage of justice in this context, a defendant must show that it is likely that if he had been notified of the rights provided in Article 36 of the Vienna Convention, the result of the criminal proceeding would have been different. At a minimum, this means that the defendant must establish that his consulate would have assisted him in a way that likely would have favorably affected the outcome of his case.

In support of his claim, the defendant asserts that had he "known of his right to consular notification and assistance he would have sought that assistance and presumably, at least, have been advised of the necessity of taking great care in seeking to understand his attorney, the proceedings against him and ways in which he might accomplish this (i.e. his right to an interpreter, etc.)." He has, however, produced no evidence of the practices and protocols of the Dominican Republic Consulate (consulate), or of the advice and assistance it would have provided on notification of the detention of one of its citizens. An assumption with respect to such matters is not evidence, and is woefully insufficient to demonstrate that the outcome of the defendant's case—his pleading guilty to a significantly reduced set of charges with no sentence of incarceration—likely would have been different, had he been informed of his right to have his consulate so notified.

. . .

NOTES & QUESTIONS

1.   In *Medellín*, the United States Supreme Court held that the ICJ judgment requiring "review and reconsideration" did not create a federal legal obligation that state courts were bound to apply. Nonetheless, as Justice Stevens indicated, nothing in the Court's decision prevents states from honoring the ICJ's judgment and curing the international legal violations they caused. Does the decision in *Gautreaux* do as Justice Stevens urges? Was the Massachusetts Supreme Judicial Court the appropriate state actor to remedy the Vienna Convention violation? Other state actors are available. For example, in *Torres v. Mullin*, an Oklahoma case arising under the Vienna Convention, the sentence of one defendant of Mexican nationality was repeatedly upheld by the state courts but was ultimately commuted by the Oklahoma Governor. The Governor noted that the ICJ's ruling in *Avena* and international attention to the case played a role in his decision. *See Mexican on Okla. Death Row Gets Clemency*, NBC News (May 13, 2004, 7:45 PM),   http://www.nbcnews.com/id/4972850/ns/us_news-crime_and_courts/t/ mexican-okla-death-row-gets-clemency/#.UoA9v41qrR0.   *See also* Sandra Babcock, *The Limitations of International Law: Efforts to Enforce Rulings of the International Court of Justice in U.S. Death Penalty Cases*, 62 Syracuse L. Rev. 183, 189–92 (2012). In some states, legislators have acted. For example, California has adopted its own state-level consular notification law that brings its practices into compliance with the Vienna Convention. Cal. Penal Code § 834c (West 2014).

2.   For additional state court decisions considering alleged violations of the Vienna Convention on Consular Relations post-*Medellín*, see *Alberran v. State*, 96 So.3d 131 (Ala. Crim. App. 2011) (denying defendant's request to suppress evidence of police statement when police had failed to notify him of his right to consular notification on grounds that VCCR violations do not create a judicially enforceable right); *State v. Ramos,* 297 P.3d 2151 (Okla. Crim. App. 2013) (holding that suppression of evidence is not a proper remedy for VCCR Article 36 violations, in part because *Miranda* rights confer "the same or similar protections"); *Contreras v. State*, 324 S.W.3d 789 (Tex. App. 2010) (holding that the VCCR does not create a procedural due process right "requiring police to inform a foreign national of the right to contact his consulate before beginning a custodial interrogation" and that "suppression of statements was not a remedy for any violation of the Vienna Convention"). *See also Virgin Islands v. Milosavljevic*, Crim. No. ST–09–CR–582, 2010 WL 3746176 (V.I. Super. Ct. Sept. 16, 2010) (holding that VCCR vested defendant with "individually enforceable rights" but denying defendant's motion to dismiss for violation of the VCCR because he failed to show that his case had been prejudiced as a result of this violation).

3.   In *Gautreaux*, the Massachusetts court, giving "respectful consideration" to the ICJ judgment in *Avena*, noted that the remedy for a

violation of the VCCR was a post-conviction review in which the defendant must show that the failure to comply with Article 36 "gave rise to a substantial risk of a miscarriage of justice." The Court ultimately held that the defendant failed to demonstrate that the outcome of his case likely would have been different had he been informed of his right to notify his consulate. Other countries have held that the suppression of evidence is the appropriate remedy for a violation of the VCCR, and have employed a similar standard requiring a showing that the violation resulted in prejudice. *See* Brief for Petitioner Mario A. Bustillo at 32–33, *Sanchez-Llamas v. Oregon*, 548 U.S. 331 (2006) (No.05–51) (citing courts in Canada, Australia, Germany and the United Kingdom).

ii. Raising Customary International Law in State Courts

Federal courts have historically been viewed as friendlier fora than state courts for civil rights claims. In recent years, the diversity of state courts and the opportunities created by the presence of constitutional provisions guaranteeing economic and social rights have resulted in an increased focus by advocates on state courts as sites for protecting and promoting rights. One strategy involves raising human rights through claims under customary international law. As discussed in **Chapter IV**, customary international law is defined as a general practice accepted as law. In order for a norm to become customary international law, countries must follow it out of a sense of legal obligation, not as a matter of policy. Though the United States has not ratified the core human rights treaties protecting economic, social and cultural rights, such as the International Covenant on Economic, Social and Cultural Rights and the Convention on the Rights of the Child, these treaties are widely ratified around the world. Indeed, the United States is one of only three countries that have not ratified the Convention of the Rights of the Child (the other two being South Sudan and Somalia, with Somalia indicating its intention to ratify). Advocates have raised the norms contained in these treaties in state courts by asserting that they amount to customary international law. Consider the example of *Sojourner v. New Jersey Social Services.*

In 2003, advocates filed a state court challenge to New Jersey's "family cap," a policy denying additional welfare benefits to children born while their mothers were receiving welfare. Under most circumstances, state welfare programs provide families with cash assistance grants that vary in amount according to family size. Now found in over twenty states, New Jersey was the first to amend its state welfare program to deny an incremental increase in benefits to children born into families already receiving public assistance benefits. In introducing the measure to the New Jersey legislature in 1992, the measure's sponsor declared that the law was "intended to discourage [welfare] recipients from having additional children during the period of their welfare dependence."[9]

Also known as the Child Exclusion, the controversial policy was earlier upheld by the federal Third Circuit Court of Appeals. In *C.K. v. Shalala*, the plaintiffs challenged the policy on grounds that it violated the federal Administrative Procedure Act and equal protection and privacy rights under the federal Constitution. The federal district court hearing the case rejected the federal constitutional claims on grounds that the provision met the "rational basis" test required of social welfare legislation.[10] Advocates then sought to challenge the provision in state court, invoking the New Jersey State Constitution's privacy and equal protection provisions. When the case reached the New Jersey Supreme Court, advocates filed an *amicus* brief arguing that the policy violated both customary international law and established treaty obligations to which states were required to conform. In particular, *amici* argued that the Child Exclusion violated customary international law as embodied in the Convention on the Rights of the Child (CRC). The United States has not ratified the CRC, but would nevertheless be bound by the provisions of the treaty if they constitute customary international law. This argument is set out below:

AMICI CURIAE BRIEF FOR THE CENTER FOR ECONOMIC AND SOCIAL RIGHTS ET AL., SOJOURNER V. NEW JERSEY SOCIAL SERVICES
Supreme Court of New Jersey, 2002.
803 A.2d 1165.

Due to the nature of our federal system, the reach of international human rights standards must extend beyond the federal judiciary and become part of state jurisprudence as well. First, . . . state, not national, governments primarily regulate the economic and social fields. Second, the federal government—through the treaty ratification process and other representations on the international stage—has committed the individual States to meeting US human rights obligations.

. . .

[Third], human rights treaties specifically require the availability of judicial remedies for violations. Therefore, unless there is State court participation in the implementation of human rights standards, the US

---

[9]   *See* Risa E. Kaufman, *State ERAs in the New Era: Securing Poor Women's Equality by Eliminating Reproductive Based Discrimination*, 24 Harv. Women's L. J. 191, 205–07 (2001) (citing Statement of Assemblyman Bryant).

[10]   C.K. v. Shalala, 883 F.Supp. 991 (D.N.J. 1995), *aff'd sub nom.*, C.K. v. New Jersey Department of Health and Human Services, 92 F.3d 171 (3d Cir. 1996).

will fall short of meeting its human rights obligations and maintaining credibility on the international stage.

These considerations also apply with regards to international customary human rights law. US courts have recognized that certain human rights norms have attained the status of customary law, in particular the norms contained in the Convention on the Rights of the Child. . . . As in the case of treaties, many of these customary law norms apply to the economic and social fields primarily regulated by the States. Without State implementation, the US would also fall short of meeting this set of obligations.

Moreover, State courts are no strangers to the use of customary human rights law. There are numerous examples of State court decisions that have relied upon or cited these standards to interpret domestic law.

. . .

The Child Exclusion was enacted with the intention of dissuading poor women from having additional children. It was intended as an incentive for women on welfare to be "responsible" and not have additional children, and as a penalty on those who gave birth nonetheless. The CRC prohibits enacting legislation for this purpose under two different articles. Article 2 states that:

> State Parties shall take all appropriate measures to ensure that the child is protected against all forms of discrimination or punishment on the basis of the status, activities, expressed opinions or beliefs of the child's parents, legal guardians, or family members.

The Child Exclusion constitutes a discrimination and penalty based on the activities of the child's parents, i.e. having children while on welfare, and on the status of the child's parents, i.e. welfare recipients. Moreover, in cases where a parent has religious beliefs that prevent her from controlling the timing of her children's birth, the Child Exclusion also constitutes a discrimination and penalty against a child for his or her parent's beliefs.

Article 3 of the CRC also requires that "the best interest of the child shall be a primary consideration" in any action "undertaken by . . . legislative bodies. . . ." The legislative history of the Child Exclusion reflects a chilling dearth of concern for the children born into those families receiving welfare. Indeed, there appears to be no indication that the interest of the affected children was considered at all. Moreover, by its very nature a legislative act that excludes poor children from receiving necessary assistance cannot be considered in the best interest of those children.

. . .

NOTES & QUESTIONS

1. The New Jersey Supreme Court considering the *Sojourner* case acknowledged the international law argument in a footnote in its opinion rejecting the challenge to the Child Exclusion. The Court asserted that it need not address the argument because it was not raised below, and that in any event, the Child Exclusion policy did not violate any obligations of the state under international human rights law. The Court proceeded to uphold the Child Exclusion policy under the New Jersey State Constitution. Is the Court correct that the argument was waived because it was not presented to the lower court? What reasons might advocates have for presenting human rights arguments to a court, even if it is unlikely that the court will view them favorably? Why do you think the CIL argument in *Sojourner* was presented in an *amicus* brief rather than in the parties' main brief?

2. Customary international law arguments are difficult to make because of the inherent uncertainty surrounding the scope and content of customary international law. Consider the materials we studied in **Chapter IV**. Even if the Convention on the Rights of the Child does embody customary international law, can that law be binding on nations absent some affirmative act on the State's part to incorporate such law? Can it be binding on States that persistently object to ratifying the treaty?

3. Was it necessary for the *Sojourner amici* to assert customary international law in order to urge the Court to consider the human rights norms contained in the CRC when weighing the constitutionality of the Child Exclusion? How else might advocates have brought these norms before the Court?

4. In 2014, the United Kingdom Court of Appeals considered a similar case, *SG and Others v. Secretary of State for Work and Pensions*, [2014] EWCA Civ 156. At issue in the case was a general cap on housing benefits, which the U.K. litigants challenged on grounds that the cap particularly discriminated against women, with special burdens on single mothers facing domestic violence. As in *Sojourner*, the plaintiffs raised human rights concerns under the Convention on the Rights of the Child. The Court held, however, that the government's actions were rational, and that human rights law did not create any affirmative right to housing. Does the Court's holding indicate anything about the merits of the *Sojourner amici*'s customary international law argument? Is it relevant that, as a policy matter, other countries may be reducing their social welfare supports at the same time that individual states in the U.S. are implementing measures like the Child Exclusion?

5. The plaintiff in this case, Sojourner, was a pseudonym for a representative of a group of low-income women affected by the Child Exclusion. Her real identity was kept under seal by the court because she was concerned about facing hostility should her name become known. The Child Exclusion policy still stands in New Jersey as well as more than twenty other states and has now affected thousands of parents and children in the

state and nationwide. Aside from litigation, how might the human rights claims articulated in the *amicus* brief aid those impacted by the policy in organizing and advocating for themselves? In what other fora might they pursue human rights claims against the state of New Jersey?

B. USING INTERNATIONAL AND FOREIGN LAW AS PERSUASIVE AUTHORITY IN STATE COURTS

Perhaps because of the complexities of bringing claims based on treaty and customary international law, advocates more frequently raise international human rights norms indirectly, as a source of persuasive authority for state courts to consider in their decision-making. This section reviews the different ways in which these sources are invoked and examines the normative debate surrounding their use in state court decision-making.

i. Justifications for Raising International and Foreign Law in State Courts

In 1977, U.S. Supreme Court Justice William Brennan sparked a rethinking of state court adjudication when he argued in the Harvard Law Review that state constitutions should be construed independently of the federal constitution, to provide greater protection for individual rights.[11] In recent decades, judges, academics, and advocates have suggested that international human rights law might offer a rich source for this kind of constitutional interpretation, particularly for protections that have international, but no federal analogues—for example those related to social and economic rights, such as education and housing. As you review the following passages from Professor Martha Davis and former Chief Justice Margaret Marshall of the Massachusetts Supreme Judicial Court, evaluate their arguments for using international law and the decisions of foreign courts in state constitutional interpretation.

MARTHA DAVIS, "THE SPIRIT OF OUR TIMES: STATE
CONSTITUTIONS AND INTERNATIONAL HUMAN RIGHTS"
30 N.Y.U. Rev. L. & Soc. Change 359, 371–74 (2006).

Even where no binding transnational law is at issue, state courts can appropriately reference transnational law. For example, some state laws have been crafted in the shadow of, and were thus influenced by, international agreements such as the Universal Declaration of Human Rights. As a result, many state constitutions reject federal constitutional constructions in favor of transnational formulations of rights. In some

---

[11] William J. Brennan, Jr., *State Constitutions and the Protection of Individual Rights*, 90 Harv. L. Rev. 489 (1977). *See also* Burt Neuborne, *Foreword: State Constitutions and the Evolution of Positive Rights*, 20 Rutgers L.J. 881 (1988).

instances, the origins of the language and the genesis of concerns expressed are the same. But even when such direct connections are not apparent, the similarities between international law provisions and state constitutional provisions granting affirmative rights support using transnational human rights norms to interpret state law.

Many state constitutions articulate rights that are not mentioned in the federal constitution, such as positive rights to welfare, health, education, and the right to work. Positive rights to welfare—wholly lacking at the federal level—are "among the most common positive rights in state constitutions." One of the most specific of these provisions, article XVII of the New York State Constitution, states that "the aid, care and support of the needy are public concerns and shall be provided by the state . . . in such manner and by such means" as the legislature shall determine. Explicit rights to education, also absent from the federal constitution, are also found in many state constitutions. For example, the Constitution of North Dakota states that "the legislative assembly shall provide for a uniform system of free public schools throughout the state." Though health is less often directly addressed in discrete provisions of state constitutions, there are a number of pertinent state constitutional sections. For example, Alaska's constitution, adopted at the time of statehood in 1959, provides for the public health of state inhabitants. Hawaii's constitution also states that "the State shall provide for the protection and promotion of the public health." Finally, many state constitutions also address the affirmative right to work and the right to organize as members of trade unions. For example, the New York State Constitution states "employees shall have the right to organize and to bargain collectively through representatives of their own choosing." Several state constitutions also specifically address working hours and working conditions.

These state constitutional provisions and the laws that implement them are direct analogues to international law approaches that encourage or mandate affirmative attention to areas of economic and social well-being. Like the state constitutional provisions set out above, the International Covenant on Economic, Social and Cultural Rights (ICESCR) addresses education, stating that "[t]he States Parties to the present Covenant recognize the right of everyone to education." The ICESCR also specifies the requisite steps for ensuring the public health, including reduction of infant mortality, improvement of industrial hygiene, prevention of disease, and provision of medical services. Labor rights are directly addressed in article 22 of the ICCPR, which states "[e]veryone shall have the right to freedom of association with others, including the right to form and join trade unions for the protection of his interests." The ICESCR addresses work conditions in greater detail than the ICCPR, mandating that States Parties provide "[f]air wages," "[a] decent living," "[s]afe and healthy working conditions," "[e]qual opportunities for everyone to be promoted," and "[r]est, leisure and reasonable limitation of working hours."

There are often dramatic similarities between the language and content of state constitutions and international human rights instruments. For example, in the area of welfare, the ICESCR provides that States Parties "recognize the right of everyone to social security, including social insurance," and "the right of everyone to an adequate standard of living for himself and his family, including adequate food, clothing and housing, and to the continuous improvement of living conditions." Hawaii's constitution tracks these sentiments, providing for financial assistance, medical assistance, and social services for persons in need, as well as economic security for the elderly. It also grants the state power to provide housing, slum clearance, and development and rehabilitation of substandard areas. Kentucky's constitution, amended in 1985, also specifically addresses social insurance, directing the general assembly to "prescribe such laws as may be necessary for the granting and paying of old persons an annuity or pension." . . . . These provisions' meanings on the international stage cannot easily be differentiated from the meaning of similar provisions in state constitutions. It is therefore appropriate for state courts to look to transnational law for guidance when construing state constitutions.

. . .

THE HON. MARGARET H. MARSHALL, " 'WISE PARENTS DO NOT HESITATE TO LEARN FROM THEIR CHILDREN': INTERPRETING STATE CONSTITUTIONS IN AN AGE OF GLOBAL JURISPRUDENCE"

79 N.Y.U. L. Rev. 1633, 1636, 1639–43 (2004).

Dialogue among the world's constitutional jurists is now commonplace.

. . .

Why all this global cross-pollination concerning individual rights, and why now? Advances in information technology of course play a part. The decisions of constitutional courts worldwide are only a mouse click away. But in my view, the key factor giving rise to global interest in individual rights is the growing recognition that every person—every person—is endowed with fundamental rights that no government can extinguish. Coupled with this understanding is a development I consider to be one of the most striking and profound in world politics over the last several decades: the emerging consensus in the world's democracies that a written charter of rights, enforced by an independent judiciary, is central to the protection of personal liberty.

. . .

For nearly two hundred years, the United States stood, constitutionally speaking, in splendid isolation. Yes, we shared a common language of the common law with other English-speaking nations. Yes, our legislative law-making branch mirrored, for example, the United Kingdom's bicameral House of Lords and House of Commons. But our tripartite system of government was unique, and so, in consequence, was our constitutional jurisprudence. On momentous questions concerning the fundamental rights guaranteed by our state and federal constitutions, we had little to learn from courts like Britain's, in which the word of Parliament was supreme.

. . .

But over the past two decades, our isolation has given way. Now every newly independent, and many older, democracies around the world have adopted the idea of a written charter of rights enforced by independent judges. Even Britain, that great bastion of parliamentary sovereignty, undertook in 2000 to give the provisions of the European Convention on Human Rights the full force of law in domestic courts.

. . .

As state court judges, we know that we owe our allegiance to both the state and the federal constitutions. We are less accustomed to seeing ourselves as part of the wider world. It is unfair, I think, to ascribe our reluctance to look at foreign constitutional law to provincialism or lack of respect. A state constitution is the product of the democratic aspirations of people united by a highly localized culture and history. Fiscal concerns and the press of dealing with ninety-five percent of our nation's litigation may restrict a state court judge's time and resources. Yet in many ways, state judges are uniquely positioned to take advantage of the significant potential of comparative constitutional law. First, our federal system has, in Chief Justice Shirley Abrahamson's words, "made seasoned comparatists of all of us." As a state court judge, I have frequent occasion to look to the constitutional law of fifty other American jurisdictions, even though other states' interpretations of their constitutions have no precedential weight for Massachusetts. They do, however, provide guidance, perspective, inspiration, reassurance, or cautionary tales. How odd, then, when one stops to think of it: A novel issue of constitutional law will send us, our clerks, and counsel to the library to uncover any possible United States source of authority—including the note of a second-year law student. But in our search for a useful legal framework, we ignore the opinion of a prominent constitutional jurist abroad that may be directly on point.

Second, state court judges work actively in the open tradition of the common law. *Erie Railroad Co. v. Tompkins* removed much of the traditional common-law role from the federal courts, but what Holmes described as expounding from experience is the quintessential role of a state court judge. Third, in contrast to our federal Constitution, many state constitutions contain "positive liberty" clauses. Like the federal Constitution, state constitutions, of course, protect individuals from unlawful government action. But they also have provisions concerning a particular benefit. For example, in Massachusetts, New Hampshire, and New York, state constitutional provisions concerning access to public education have resulted in complex litigation that implicates a host of issues—constitutional, statutory, and common law.

As charters of "positive liberty," some state constitutions may bear close affinity to the new constitutions of other democracies. Here is one example among many: Article 23 of the Canadian Charter of Rights and Freedoms contains guarantees not only concerning access to primary and secondary education, but also the right to receive that education in either English or French. In interpreting constitutional claims concerning bilingual education here, we may have much to learn from looking beyond our national borders to a country where such jurisprudence already is being developed.

No doubt there are many areas of American state constitutional law that are so robust and well developed, so self-contained, that in most cases they are unlikely to benefit from consideration of foreign sources. For example, Massachusetts constitutional law in the areas of search and seizure, separation of powers, takings, and jury instructions is as extensive and well wrought as any. But other emerging issues seem to call for the broadest comparative analysis. In those circumstances, there is much room for fruitful transnational inquiry.

. . .

The United States Supreme Court has been strongly criticized for relying on international and comparative law in some of its recent constitutional cases. Congressional committees have held several hearings on this practice, and both Houses of Congress have considered (and ultimately rejected) legislative proposals to limit federal judicial consideration of foreign or international sources.

In **Chapter V**, we encountered Professor Roger Alford's article discussing the potential misuse of international and foreign law in U.S. constitutional interpretation. Alford's critique is levied primarily at the use, or misuse, of international and foreign law by federal court judges in their interpretation of the U.S. Constitution. State judges are, however, differently situated than federal court judges. In the excerpt below, Professor Davis addresses the major critiques of comparative citation and suggests why they are less relevant to state court judging. As you read, consider whether Alford's critique is relevant to state courts' consideration of international and foreign law.

MARTHA DAVIS, "THE SPIRIT OF OUR TIMES: STATE CONSTITUTIONS AND INTERNATIONAL HUMAN RIGHTS"
30 N.Y.U. Rev. L. & Soc. Change 359, 376–84 (2006).

Opponents of international citation have articulated four rationales for limiting judicial reliance on transnational law:

• Reliance on international and comparative law impinges on the executive's foreign relations and foreign policy role;

• Citation to international and comparative law violates rules of constitutional construction that limit the sources on which judges can rely to domestic sources contemporary to the Constitution's framing;

• Reliance on transnational law undermines democratic participation by giving undue authority over American law to foreign courts; and

• Given the differences in legal systems and cultures, United States judges may not be competent to properly interpret and construe international authority, with the result that judges will "cherry-pick" transnational citations that support their own views, giving those decisions distorted significance.

Whatever persuasive value these points might have on the federal level, they fail to take into account the differences between the federal and state constitutional contexts.

a. Impinging on the Executive's Role

The federal constitution grants the executive branch authority over foreign relations. This delegation of authority ensures that the United States speaks with one voice when addressing foreign policy issues. Given the fact that the American system includes three coordinate branches of government, granting Congress or the Supreme Court the power to independently develop foreign relations principles, to negotiate treaties, or to participate in international fora alongside the executive could have a disastrous impact on foreign relations.

[A]ny concerns that may be raised by federal court citation of transnational authority are diminished on the state level since the possibility that a single state court's pronouncement would be mistaken for national policy is remote. In addition, any concern that a state court's citation of transnational law would impinge on the state's own executive branch of government is mitigated by several factors. First, certainly no branch of state government has principal constitutional or institutional responsibility for foreign relations. Second, because most state constitutions do not draw strict lines between state governmental branches, a state court citing transnational law does not impinge on the core responsibilities of the other branches. Finally, the ease with which state constitutions may be revised, and the role of popular participation in their amendment, enables the political process to limit any perceived misuse of judicial power.

State constitutions are amended frequently and often with popular participation. For example, the Iowa Constitution has been amended an average of once every three years since its adoption. Alabama's constitution has been amended at least 618 times since 1819, and California's has been amended at least 493 times. By 1995, the nation had seen 230 state constitutional conventions, in which 146 constitutions and some 6000 amendments were adopted. Even when they are generated by the legislature or a constitutional convention, state constitutions and constitutional amendments are often ultimately passed by popular referendum.

. . .

Where state constitutions are easily revised, and where the revision process encourages popular participation, give-and-take among the branches and with the electorate is a real possibility. Thus, while federal courts might arguably be required to tread lightly in areas that are reserved to the executive branch, such as foreign relations, state courts have more flexibility because the state's executive branch, its legislature, and the state's citizens are in a position to respond relatively rapidly to any court decisions they think are misguided.

b.   Improper Sources

Opponents of the use of international law in federal adjudication have also asserted that such sources are simply improper, as they undermine the determinative role that the domestic sources relied upon by the Constitution's "framers" should play in constitutional interpretation. . . . [A] heated debate has taken place primarily on the federal level. This is because, again, state constitutions differ from their federal counterpart in both history and text. A state constitution that is adopted by popular referendum does not have "framers" in the same sense as does the federal constitution. While relying on the framers in the federal context limits the relevant sources a court may examine when interpreting the federal constitution, the analogous approach in the state context has the potential to widen the inquiry to any factor that might have influenced the electorate to approve the constitution and to open the process to a wide range of interpretive approaches. The significant role of a state's citizens in its constitution's framing means that constitutional history cannot be strictly limited to statements of amendment sponsors or other official actors. Rather, relevant interpretive material may be wide-ranging, reflecting social trends, economic concerns, and other factors that motivate individual members of the electorate.

Further, many states have amended their constitutions and adopted state constitutional provisions relatively recently, at a time when state legislators certainly knew of the international precedents and trends that inform contemporary lawmaking. As a result, the transnational sources relevant to state constitutional construction may be quite contemporary. For example, Iowa and Florida added prohibitions of sex discrimination to their state constitutions in 1998, eighteen years after the United States signed the Convention on the Elimination of All Forms of Discrimination Against Women (CEDAW), and three years after the Beijing Conference at which then-First Lady Hillary Clinton spoke about the importance of global women's rights. Hawaii's state constitutional provision extending financial assistance and medical and social services to persons in need was added in 1978, the year after President Carter signed the ICESCR. Even those state constitutional provisions adopted decades earlier may reflect not only a reaction against the passivity of the United States Constitution in the face of persistent poverty, racism, or sexism, but an appreciation of the international and transnational alternatives to the status quo.

Importantly, the framers of the federal constitution and those responsible for drafting state constitutions possessed a similar interest in transnational law. There is ample evidence that both sets of drafters surveyed other constitutional approaches and made choices based on information about their success or failure, taking national or state values into account.

. . .

c.   Lack of Democratic Participation

Those opposed to domestic citation of transnational precedent also argue that reliance on foreign law undermines the democratic will by extending undue authority over domestic law to foreign courts. There are at least two counterarguments to this assertion. First, the relative populism of state constitutions weakens accusations of countermajoritarianism in the state context. At that level, the degree of interplay between voters, legislative drafters, and judges renders the likelihood of any foreign court "capturing" the state legal structure extremely remote. Second, the countermajoritarian objection misunderstands the potential role of transnational law. Such law is only binding when the United States affirmatively acknowledges its force by ratifying a treaty or enacting a statute, or in the case of customary international law where the principle is so overwhelmingly accepted and respected that it rises to the level of binding law. Otherwise, judges may look to transnational law for guidance, but they are not bound by it, and a judge might as easily reject a foreign court's approach as accept it.

. . .

d. Lack of Competence

Finally, opponents of the role of transnational law question judges' competence to interpret transnational law sources. Specifically, they suggest that judges may erroneously give such sources undue weight, unreasonably preferring them to domestic interpretive sources. The answer to such a challenge is not to place some relevant sources of ideas and interpretation "out of bounds," but to provide sufficient judicial education so that judges can properly evaluate the full range of sources relevant to their interpretive task.

By suggesting that judges are not competent to evaluate and apply transnational law to domestic cases, some critics distinguish legislative drafters or framers from courts. They maintain that international law may properly be consulted in the course of drafting legislation, but not while interpreting the law. This argument, however, mistakes the task in which the court is engaged when it relies on transnational law to aid its interpretation of constitutional provisions. Certainly, courts do not approach fact-gathering in the same way as legislatures. When resolving a case or controversy, a court is focused on elucidating the facts particular to the parties before it, while a legislature is looking to uncover facts that will contribute to broader policy development.

But legislatures and courts also use law differently. Legislatures or constitutional framers may gather information about international and comparative law much the same way that they compile statistics or individual testimony—as an aid to development of broad-based policy. In contrast, courts survey transnational laws as an aid to legal interpretation and proper resolution of a particular case. Further, the ways in which federal or state courts might use transnational law when adjudicating a particular case—to shed empirical "light" on how a common standard might be applied, to construe a "parallel rule," and to explicate a "community standard"—are consistent with traditional methods of constitutional analysis and interpretation.

While these uses of transnational law are traditional and widely accepted, it may be the case that some judges avoid using transnational law because they are not sufficiently familiar with its sources—a problem that is already being remedied through judicial education. Indeed, the question of judicial competence in the transnational law arena is increasingly a relic of an earlier time. In law schools today, international law, including human rights law, is one of the fastest growing areas of the curriculum.

. . .

For those judges educated before the "globalization" of law school, or those whose law school education did not provide a solid grounding in transnational law, continuing judicial education courses on these topics are also becoming far more common. Such education can contextualize transnational law for judges, and provides a forum where they may discuss different approaches with others who are engaged in similar endeavors.

This is not to say that judges will never go astray in resolving legal issues, whether they are looking to transnational law or limiting their inquiry to domestic sources. But in the event that high court judges make an irreversible interpretive mistake and give undue weight or distorted meaning to transnational law, state constitutions can be amended to remedy the mistake with relative ease. As discussed above, state constitutions are not beyond the reach of voters to the degree that the United States Constitution is, and citizens operating at the state level have a meaningful opportunity to debate and amend their governing documents to reflect their evolving intentions.

. . .

NOTES & QUESTIONS

1.   Professor Davis argues for consideration of international treaty law in state constitutional interpretation. Chief Justice Marshall's article is directed at uses of foreign and comparative law in adjudication. Is there a bright line between these two categories? What distinguishes them? Does the distinction matter when courts are considering these sources? For example, is there greater concern about inappropriate state and local involvement in foreign affairs when state courts consider international law than when they invoke comparative examples? For other articles authored by state court jurists on the relevance of international and comparative law to their work, see Shirley S. Abrahamson & Michael J. Fischer, *All the World's a Courtroom: Judging in the New Millennium*, 26 Hofstra L. Rev. 273 (1997); Cathy Hollenberg Serrette, *Invoking International Human Rights Law in Litigation: A Maryland Judge's Perspective*, 45 Clearinghouse Rev. 238 (2011); Penny J. White, *Legal, Political, and Ethical Hurdles to Applying*

International Human Rights Law in the State Courts of the United States (and Arguments for Scaling Them), 71 U. Cin. L. Rev. 937 (2003). *See also* Florence Roisman, *Using International and Foreign Human Rights Law in Public Interest Advocacy*, 18 Ind. Int'l & Comp. L. Rev. 1 (2008).

2. When examining comparative material, which foreign decisions should be given the most persuasive value by state court judges? Chief Justice Marshall sat on the Massachusetts Supreme Judicial Court. Should she give more weight to decisions from England and Canada, countries which share legal history and geography, respectively, with Massachusetts, than she gives to decisions of France or Japan? What approach should a justice of the California Supreme Court take, given the state's shared border with Mexico and strong ties to Pacific Rim nations? *See Roper v. Simmons*, 543 U.S. 551, 607–30 (2005) (Scalia, J. dissenting); Rex D. Glensy, *Which Countries Count: Lawrence v. Texas and the Selection of Foreign Persuasive Authority*, 45 Va. J. Int'l L. 357 (2005).

3. If a state court judge considers an international or foreign law source in reaching a conclusion concerning state law, should the judge be obliged to cite that source even if there is ample support for the judge's conclusion without the citation? Is transparency important? What is to be gained by including such citations in an opinion? What are the risks? Are the risks different when the court is considering international human rights law versus foreign law? Are there other factors that might affect whether and when a judge should take international and foreign law into consideration? Keep in mind that some states have enacted statutes barring state court judges from considering foreign or international law. *See* Martha F. Davis and Johanna Kalb, *Oklahoma and Beyond: Understanding the Wave of State Anti-Transnational Law Initiatives*, 87 Ind. L.J. Supp. 1 (2011). We discuss these provisions in greater detail later in this chapter. Also pertinent to this calculus is the fact that many state court judges are elected and may be concerned about the impact of a controversial citation on their retention. *See, e.g.,* Chris Bonneau, The Federalist Soc'y, A Survey of Empirical Evidence Concerning Judicial Elections 7–8 (Mar. 14, 2012), *available at* http://www.fed-soc.org/publications/detail/a-survey-of-empirical-evidence-concerning-judicial-elections (noting persuasive evidence that judges consider the likelihood of reelection when making judicial decisions, yet questioning whether this is problematic).

4. In her *Wise Parents* article, Chief Justice Marshall concludes that "[p]articipating in the global conversation about human liberty will keep our courts a vital part of the local community we serve and of the world community into which we and our constituents are now so tightly woven." Others have also written about the phenomenon of global judicial dialogue. *See* Sarah K. Harding, *Comparative Reasoning and Judicial Review*, 28 Yale J. Int'l L. 409 (2003); Claire L'Heureux-Dube, *The Importance of Dialogue: Globalization and the International Impact of the Rehnquist Court*, 34 Tulsa L.J. 15 (1998–1999); Anne-Marie Slaughter, *A Typology of Transjudicial Communication*, 29 U. Rich. L. Rev. 99 (1994–1995). Assuming that Chief

Justice Marshall's conclusion is true, and that global dialogue between judges is important, is it a sufficient reason for state courts to look beyond domestic law to international and foreign law for guidance and ideas? Why should state court judges be participating in that international dialogue?

5.   Professor Davis argues that the critiques of comparative citation leveled at federal judges are less applicable to state judges and justices. Does Professor Davis address Professor Alford's concern that judges use international and foreign law selectively, only proposing comparisons that are "rights enhancing," and ignoring comparative analysis that would result in the lessening of human rights? Is this a matter of judicial competence and training, or rather a hazard of the comparative approach more generally?

ii. International and Foreign Law as Persuasive Authority in State Constitutional Interpretation

Although relatively few in number, some state courts have used foreign and international law as persuasive authority in significant constitutional cases. In this section, we review several such instances.

In the following case, the Oregon Supreme Court was asked to consider whether requiring prisoners to undergo a "pat-down" by guards of the opposite sex violated Article 1, Section 13 of the Oregon Constitution, which states: "No person arrested, or confined in jail, shall be treated with unnecessary rigor." The Court concluded that except in exceptional circumstances, cross-gender touching of a prisoner's intimate areas did violate this provision of the state constitution. Justice Linde's discussion of international law as support for his conclusion is excerpted below. As you read this and the excerpts that follow, ask yourself what work is being done by these references to foreign and international law in each of the opinions.

STERLING V. CUPP
Supreme Court of Oregon, 1981.
625 P.2d 123.

LINDE, J.:

It is widely recognized, first, that even convicted prisoners retain claims to personal dignity, and also that under the conditions of arrest and imprisonment the relation between the sexes poses particularly sensitive issues. These assumptions underlie most contemporary statements of the relevant standards for penal institutions. Thus the Federal Standards for Corrections published by the Department of Justice postulate that "(e)ach facility develops and implements policies and procedures governing searches and seizures to ensure that undue and unnecessary force, embarrassment or indignity to the individual is avoided." Specifically, when body searches are required, "staff personnel avoid unnecessary force and strive to preserve the dignity and integrity of the inmate." Issues of dignity or embarrassment and indignity arising from sexual differences traditionally have been stated with a view of the rights of female prisoners. Standards for jails published by the Department's Bureau of Prisons stress, in connection with searches of newly admitted prisoners, that "(n)aturally, admission for women should be completely separate from that for men and should be conducted by female staff members." They continue with the advice that "(t)he following conditions must be met if difficulties are to be avoided in jails housing both male and female prisoners:

"1. Women prisoners must be completely separated from male prisoners, with no possibility of communication by sight or sound.

"2. All supervision of female prisoners must be by female employees. In the larger jail a full-time matron should provide constant supervision. Smaller jails may have a part-time matron who retains the key to the women's section and is on call as needed.

"3. Male employees must be forbidden to enter the women's section unless they are accompanied by the matron."

These federal standards reflect principles also found in nonofficial sources, such as the American Bar Association's Standards of Criminal Justice and the American Correctional Association's Manual of Correctional Standards. Indeed, the same principles have been a worldwide concern recognized by the United Nations and other multinational bodies. [FN 21][12]

> [FN 21: Universal Declaration of Human Rights, proclaimed "as a common standard of achievement" under the directive to "promote . . . universal respect for, and observance of, human rights" in Article 55 of the United Nations Charter, states in Article 5: "No one shall be subjected to torture or to cruel, inhuman or degrading treatment or punishment." In the later International Covenant of Civil and Political Rights, this principle is repeated in Part III, Article 7 and further spelled out and expanded in Part III, Article 10:
>
> "1. All persons deprived of their liberty shall be treated with humanity and with respect for the inherent dignity of the human person.
>
> "2. (a) Accused persons shall, save in exceptional circumstances, be segregated from convicted persons, and shall be subject to separate treatment appropriate to their status as unconvicted persons;

---

[12] The opinion's lengthy Footnote 21 is included in brackets in the text here for ease of reference.

"(b) Accused juvenile persons shall be separated from adults and brought as speedily as possible for adjudication.

"3. The penitentiary system shall comprise treatment of prisoners the essential aim of which shall be their reformation and social rehabilitation. Juvenile offenders shall be segregated from adults and be accorded treatment appropriate to their age and legal status."

The formulation of the Universal Declaration is used in Article 3 of the European Convention for the Protection of Human Rights and Fundamental Freedoms. It was applied by the European Court of Human Rights in Ireland v. United Kingdom, judgment of Jan. 18, 1978 Series A no. 25 reprinted in 17 Int'l Legal Materials 680 (1978) (detention and interrogation practices held violative of art. 3). In the American Convention on Human Rights the same formulation is followed by the sentence "All persons deprived of their liberty shall be treated with respect for the inherent dignity of the human person." American Convention on Human Rights, art. 5, s 2. The Standard Minimum Rules for the Treatment of Prisoners adopted by the First United Nations Congress on the Prevention of Crime and the Treatment of Offenders in 1955 and approved by the Economic and Social Council in 1957 (Resolution 663C (XXIV)) provide for the separation of male and female prisoners (Rule 8(a)) and for minimizing conditions "which tend to lessen the responsibility of the prisoners or the respect due to their dignity as human beings." (Rule 60(1).) Contained in the Report of the First United Nations Congress on the Prevention of Crime and the Treatment of Offenders (U.N.Pub., No.: 1956. IV. 4), reproduced in Compendium of Model Correctional Legislation and Standards at Compendium IV–10, IV–13 (American Bar Association and Council of State Governments, 1972). This expression of the United Nations in turn had antecedents in the League of Nations. *See* S. Rubin, The Law of Criminal Correction 286 n. 7 (1963). The history of these standards and their application is reviewed in Skoler, World Implementation of the United Nations Standard Minimum Rules for Treatment of Prisoners, 10 Jnl. Int.L. & Econ. 453 (1975).]

The various formulations in these different sources in themselves are not constitutional law. We cite them here as contemporary expressions of the same concern with minimizing needlessly harsh, degrading, or dehumanizing treatment of prisoners that is expressed in article I, section 13. Thus the questions to be considered are whether a practice of body searches including sexually intimate areas by officers of the opposite sex, even though the prisoner remains clothed, constitutes a cognizable indignity and if so, whether it is justified by necessity.

. . .

In *Moore v. Ganim*, the Connecticut Supreme Court considered whether the Connecticut State Constitution imposed an affirmative obligation on the state to provide basic subsistence benefits to indigent residents. The plaintiffs had been denied basic benefits—termed General Relief—as part of a statewide curtailing of such support. The majority of the Court denied the plaintiffs' claim, ruling that there was no affirmative obligation to provide support under the Connecticut Constitution. In a concurrence, excerpted below, the Court's Chief Justice Ellen Peters opined that the history and practice of the state, along with contemporary international norms, did support such an affirmative obligation. Compare her discussion of international law to Justice Linde's discussion in *Sterling*.

MOORE V. GANIM
Supreme Court of Connecticut, 1995.
660 A.2d 742.

PETERS, C.J., concurring.

I disagree with the majority that recognition of the constitutional right asserted here will fetter legislative attempts to establish reasonable eligibility requirements. Moreover, in my view, our duty to construe the state constitution requires us to undertake [a] plenary analysis . . . which includes consideration of issues of morality, policy and value.

Contemporary economic, sociological, legal and moral considerations overwhelmingly support the recognition of a qualified right to some limited form of governmental assistance to assure minimal support for our poor citizens. A right to governmental support is even more important today than it was 350 years ago, when our forebears recognized the right. In their largely agricultural society, with a vast, unsettled western frontier, paid work presumably was available to everyone who wanted it. In today's postindustrial society, on the other hand, almost all jobs that pay a living wage require skills or educations that many poor people neither possess nor have the economic resources to acquire. There also is no longer any opportunity to "go west," homestead new land, and grow the food necessary for survival.

Finding a governmental obligation of minimal subsistence in the constitution also is justified by our contemporary notions about democracy and universal suffrage. Although the constitution of 1818 did not so provide, our state constitution now extends the suffrage to all adults, regardless of race, gender, or economic circumstances. Individuals who have no food, clothing, shelter or medical care will, in all likelihood, be severely hampered in their ability to vote or otherwise to participate in the political process. The right to minimal subsistence can therefore be justified as necessary to ensure that the unsheltered poor-a truly discrete and insular minority group-have access to the political process.

These contemporary economic circumstances and contemporary conceptions of democracy already have led the international community to incorporate a right to subsistence into the international law of human rights. For example, article 25(1) of the Universal Declaration of Human Rights declares that "[e]veryone has the right to a standard of living adequate for the health and well-being of himself and of his family, including food, clothing, housing and medical care and necessary social services, and the right to security in the event of unemployment, sickness, disability, widowhood, old age or other lack of livelihood in circumstances beyond his control."

Article 11(1) of the International Covenant on Economic, Social and Cultural Rights (International Covenant), which supersedes the Universal Declaration of Human Rights for the 104 states that are parties to it, similarly provides that "[t]he States Parties to the present Covenant recognize the right of everyone to an adequate standard of living for himself and his family, including adequate food, clothing and housing, and to the continuous improvement of living conditions. The States Parties will take appropriate steps to ensure the realization of this right. . . ."

Although the United States is not a party to the International Covenant, and although no right to subsistence may yet apply to this country as part of customary international law, the wide international agreement on at least the hortatory goals identified in the human rights documents strongly supports the plaintiffs' claim.

. . .

In sum, our constitutional framers, the contemporary academy, and the international community all support the conclusion that the government may not stand idle while its poorest residents die in the streets because of lack of food, shelter, clothing or medical care. The government has wide discretion in implementing its constitutional obligation and in imposing reasonable conditions on the provision of minimal support. The government, nonetheless, has a constitutional obligation to provide minimal subsistence.

In *In re Mark C.H.*, a New York County surrogate's court considered the applicability of international law in deciding whether constitutional due process requires that the guardianship appointment for a severely disabled and autistic person be subject to a requirement of periodic reporting and review.

IN RE MARK C.H.

New York County Surrogate's Court, 2010.
906 N.Y.S.2d 419.

GLEN, J.:

In addition to the more familiar liberty and property rights protection offered by the Fourteenth Amendment, international human rights norms derived from treaties signed and ratified by the United States have relevance to the instant case and, more broadly, the situation of persons with intellectual disabilities, by virtue of the Supremacy Clause.

In 2006 the United Nations General Assembly adopted the Convention and Optional Protocol on the Rights of Persons with Disabilities. According to a handbook for parliamentarians drafted by the Office of the United Nations High Commissioner for Human Rights, the purpose of the Disability Convention is to "reaffirm the dignity and worth of every person with a disability, and to provide States with an effective legal tool to end the injustice, discrimination, and violation of rights that confront most persons with disabilities." The United States became a signatory on July 24, 2009.

Article 12 of the Disability Convention protects a disabled person's rights to "equal recognition before the law," with the goal of affirming that persons with disabilities have the right to recognition everywhere as persons before the law, and that they enjoy legal capacity on an equal basis with others in all aspects of life. States may act in order to support disabled individuals who are exercising their legal capacities; other Articles provide a plethora of rights of persons with disabilities that implicate 17-A guardianships.

To the extent that Article 12 recognizes the state's "power to act to support disabled individuals," it requires that signatories:

> shall ensure that all measures that relate to the exercise of legal capacity provide for appropriate and effective safeguards to prevent abuse. . . . Such safeguards shall ensure that measures relating to the exercise of legal capacity respect the rights, will and preferences of the person, are free of conflict of interest and undue influence, are proportional and tailored to the person's circumstances, apply for the shortest time possible and are

subject to regular review by a competent, independent and impartial authority or judicial body.

Thus, as a matter of international human rights law, state interventions, like guardianships, pursuant to parens patriae power, must be subject to periodic review to prevent the abuses which may otherwise flow from the state's grant of power over a person with disabilities such as those covered by SCPA Article 17-A. Because the Disability Convention has not yet been ratified by the Senate, a state's obligations under it are controlled by the Vienna Convention on the Law of Treaties, which requires signatories "to refrain from acts which would defeat [the Disability Convention's] object and purpose." Arguably, granting guardianships (especially plenary guardianships) over persons with mental retardation and developmental disability with absolutely no review provisions defeats the "object[s] and purpose" of a Convention intended to "protect against the injustice . . . and violation of rights" confronting persons with intellectual disabilities. In any case, courts and the Legislature should be aware that, if and when the Disability Convention is ratified, the state's obligations with regard to the various rights guaranteed by the Convention will be affirmative ("A party may not invoke the provisions of its internal law as justification for its failure to perform a treaty" [Art. 27 of the Vienna Convention, 8 ILM at 690]), and current Article 17-A will be problematic at best.

It should also be noted that the United States has long since ratified the International Covenant on Civil and Political Rights (ICCPR). While the ICCPR nowhere deals explicitly with persons with intellectual disabilities, it provides for "the right of self determination," (Art. 1); "liberty of movement," including "the right to choose one's own residence," (Art. 12); freedom from "arbitrary or unlawful interference with . . . privacy" (Art. 17); and "freedom of association with others" (id.). Similarly, although there is no specific requirement of periodic review when the state exercises its parens patriae power, the ICCPR require signatories "to take the necessary steps . . . to adopt . . . measures as may be necessary to give effect to the rights recognized" by the ICCPR (Art. 2, para. 2). It is difficult to see how the state can meet that obligation in the case of Art. 17-A guardianships without some provision for monitoring the guardians appointed by the state, and the wards it has undertaken to protect.

Finally, whatever the treaty obligations already assumed, or likely to be assumed if and when the Disability Convention is ratified, international adoption of protection of the rights of persons with intellectual and other disabilities, including the right to periodic review of burdens on individual liberty, is entitled to "persuasive weight" in interpreting our own laws and constitutional protections[,] it further supports the conclusion that any guardianship statutes, including 17-A, must contain provisions for periodic review or be found constitutionally wanting.

. . .

NOTES & QUESTIONS

1.   What impact do the foreign and international citations have in these decisions? Were any of them necessary to the court's holding or the individual justice's opinion? If not, why did the court or individual justice include them? Which of the decisions above articulates the strongest, most persuasive argument based on international or foreign law? Are some sources that the courts reference more persuasive than others?

2.   Despite the increasing interest among scholars and advocates in state court consideration of international and transnational law, its incidence is still relatively unusual. Professor Johanna Kalb has observed that there is some uncertainty among state jurists about what level of authority human rights treaties should be given in their decision-making. She explains:

> Some state courts view the treaty law as binding, but consistent with federal and state constitutional law such that any action lawful under domestic law is automatically consistent with international law. Others simply reject entirely the notion that treaty-based claims can be raised by private parties. The complexities go beyond the self-execution debate, however, as state courts attempt to understand their own particular relationship with these treaties. Justice Houston drew attention to this problem in a concurring opinion in *Ex parte Pressley*, a case in which the court was asked to invalidate the death sentence of a juvenile offender based on the ICCPR. The majority relied upon a ratification reservation which reserved for "[t]he United States" the ability to impose capital punishment on any person other than a pregnant woman "subject to its constitutional constraints." Justice Houston, in concurrence, noted that "the United States" was referred to as single entity and he thus expressed his concern that the reservation was applicable only to the federal government. Nonetheless, he reluctantly joined the majority's conclusion, noting that the U.S. Supreme Court had denied a petition for *certiorari* in a similar case from the Nevada Supreme Court, which split 3–2 in rejecting the juvenile defendant's claim that his execution violated the ICCPR.

> Uncertainty with how international human rights law claims should be treated in state courts may partially explain the somewhat odd pattern in which they appear. Although one might expect citations to ratified treaties (as the law of the land) to be far more frequent than the unratified treaties, the pattern is actually more complex. The ratified treaties are cited more often than the unratified treaties; however, the Universal Declaration on Human Rights, which is a non-binding aspirational statement of shared

principles, is cited both more frequently than any of the ratified treaties with the exception of the ICCPR and more often than any of the signed but as yet unratified treaties. . . .

Some of the cases suggest actual confusion among jurists (or perhaps among the parties appearing before them) about the status of these instruments in domestic law. In *In re Julie Anne*, an Ohio court held that parents were restrained from smoking in front of minor child. The court noted that under the United Nations Convention on the Rights of the Child (CRC), courts of law, state legislatures, and administrative agencies have a duty as a matter of human rights law to reduce children's compelled exposure to tobacco smoke. But the court mistakenly suggested that the CRC had been ratified by the U.S. In other instances, state courts' ambiguity about the treaty's status may be purposeful. In a 2007 case by the Supreme Court of Hawai'i, the court relied on the Convention on the Elimination of All Forms of Discrimination against Women (CEDAW) to reach its holding that the state constitutional right to privacy does not prevent the criminalization of prostitution. The court noted that the consensus in the international community is that prostitution has negative consequences, and that the U.S. has agreed to "take all appropriate measures, including legislation, to suppress all forms of traffic in women and exploitation of prostitution of women." The court did not explain, however, that the U.S. has failed to ratify CEDAW, despite noting that several other countries have ratified it and referencing a link to the UN Division on the Advancement of Women that explains the status of the treaty in each state. Thus, it seems plausible that the court wished to downplay the treaty's formal status.

To the extent that the human rights treaties do appear in state court jurisprudence, they are only rarely used as scholars have suggested as a source for non-binding but persuasive authority in state constitutional or statutory interpretation. The frequency with which these treaties are cited appears to have increased over the years, but the change has predominately resulted from an increase in the parties' reliance on these instruments as binding authority that prohibits the imposition of a particular type of criminal sanction. Although the parties have often been quite creative in their framing of these arguments, courts around the country have generally been dismissive of the claim that they are bound by even the ratified instruments, although the reasons for their rejection of these sources have varied.

Johanna Kalb, *Human Rights Treaties in State Courts: The International Prospects of State Constitutionalism After Medellín*, 115 Penn St. L. Rev. 1051, 1056–59 (2011).

Assuming Professor Kalb's assessment is correct, what could advocates do to assist state courts in their consideration of international and comparative human rights law?

3.   In 2008, the California Supreme Court held that a ban on same-sex marriage violated the state constitution. The Court observed that:

> It is noteworthy that the California and federal Constitutions are not alone in recognizing that the right to marry is not properly viewed as simply a benefit or privilege that a government may establish or abolish as it sees fit, but rather that the right constitutes *a basic civil or human right of all people*. Article 16 of the Universal Declaration of Human Rights, adopted by the United Nations General Assembly in 1948, provides: "Men and women of full age, without any limitation due to race, nationality, or religion, have the right to marry and to found a family. . . . [¶] . . . [¶] The family is the natural and fundamental unit of society and is entitled to protection by society and the State." Numerous other international human rights treaties similarly recognize the right "to marry and to found a family" as a basic human right (Internat. Covenant on Civil and Political Rights, art. 23; see European Convention for the Protection of Human Rights and Fundamental Freedoms, art. 12; Amer. Convention on Human Rights, art. 17), and the constitutions of many nations throughout the world explicitly link marriage and family and provide special protections to these institutions. (*See* Wardle, *Federal Constitutional Protection for Marriage: Why and How* (2006) 20 BYU J. Pub. L. 439, 453–461 [describing constitutional provisions of other nations].)

In re Marriage Cases, 183 P.3d 384, 426 n.41 (Cal. 2008).[13]

The California Supreme Court also cited opinions of Canada and South Africa as illustrative of the give-and-take between judicial and legislative branches in the area of marriage rights. Do these references increase the persuasiveness of the Court's decision? Is there something special or different—or universal—about the right to marriage that makes international law particularly pertinent?

4.   Consider again the customary international law argument raised by *amici* in *Sojourner v. New Jersey Social Services*, discussed earlier in this chapter. Was it necessary for the *amici* to assert customary international law

---

[13] Following the California Supreme Court's decision, in November 2008, California voters approved Proposition 8, amending the California Constitution to limit marriage to opposite-sex couples. A decision by the U.S. District Court for the Northern District of California found that the provision was unconstitutional under the U.S. Constitution's Due Process and Equal Protection Clauses and permanently enjoined California officials from enforcing the law. Perry v. Schwarzenegger, 704 F. Supp. 2d 921 (N.D. Cal. 2010). California officials decided not to appeal the ruling, but proponents of Proposition 8 did. The U.S. Supreme Court eventually dismissed an appeal of the lower court's ruling on grounds that the proponents of the provision lacked standing to appeal, leaving the district court's decision intact without addressing the merits of the case. Hollingsworth v. Perry, 133 S.Ct. 2652 (2013).

in order to make their argument that the New Jersey Child Exclusion is counter to the human rights norms set forth in the Convention on the Rights of the Child? Do you think the New Jersey Supreme Court would have found their brief more persuasive if they had instead urged the Court to take the CRC into account as persuasive authority in interpreting the New Jersey Constitution's equal protection clause?

5. Should there be any limits on a court's consideration of international and foreign law in state constitutional interpretation? For example, is it more appropriate for courts to derive general principles from international human rights law in interpreting a constitutional provision than adopt a human rights treaty body's application of international human rights law in a particular context, particularly with respect to treaties that the United States has not ratified?

iii. International and Foreign Law as Persuasive Authority in State Statutory and Common Law Interpretation

Thus far, we have examined the utility of international and foreign law in state constitutional interpretation. State courts are also called upon to interpret statutory protections and obligations and to develop the common law, a task that rests on the assumption that judges will draw from a range of relevant sources to craft an approach appropriate to the particular jurisdiction. Do the arguments for and against considering foreign and international law have more or less weight in the statutory and common law contexts? In this section, consider whether there is a normative or persuasive difference in using such sources for statutory and common law interpretation versus constitutional interpretation.

First, in *Boehm v. Superior Court*, the California Court of Appeals was asked to consider whether the Merced County government's reduction of welfare assistance benefits violated the state's welfare statute (General Assistance, or "GA" program), which mandates the provision of subsistence benefits. In reading the following excerpt, consider the persuasive effect of the Court's discussion of the Universal Declaration of Human Rights in interpreting the statutory requirement that the county provide for minimum subsistence.

BOEHM V. SUPERIOR COURT

California Court of Appeals, 1986.
178 Cal.App.3d 494.

HAMLIN, J.:

GA is a program of last resort for indigent and disabled persons unable to qualify for other kinds of public benefits. GA is often the only means by which they can obtain the basic necessities. The program is unique because the responsibility for funding and administering it rests entirely upon individual county governments.

Section 17000 provides that "Every county ... *shall relieve and support all* incompetent, poor, indigent persons, and those incapacitated by age, disease, or accident, lawfully resident therein, when such persons are not supported and relieved by their relatives or friends, by their own means, or by state hospitals or other state or private institutions." Section 17001 imposes a mandatory duty on each county to adopt standards of aid and care for the indigent and dependent poor. Counties do, however, have discretion to determine eligibility for, the type and amount of, and conditions to be attached to, indigent relief. The courts have no authority to interfere ". . . in the absence of a clear showing of fraud or arbitrary or capricious conduct. . . ."

Nonetheless, a county's discretion can be exercised only within fixed boundaries and consistent with the underlying purpose of the statutes which impose the duty. Section 10000 outlines the statutory purpose and legislative intent of division 9 (§§ 10000–18971), which contains the provisions governing GA (§§ 17000–17410).

"The purpose of this division is to provide for protection, care, and assistance to the people of the state in need thereof, and to promote the welfare and happiness of all of the people of the state by providing appropriate aid and services to all of its needy and distressed. It is the legislative intent that aid shall be administered and services provided promptly and humanely, with due regard for the preservation of family life, and without discrimination on account of race, national origin or ancestry, religion, sex, marital status, or political affiliation; and that aid shall be so administered and services so provided, to the extent not in conflict with federal law, as to encourage self-respect, self-reliance, and the desire to be a good citizen useful to society." (§ 10000.) Sections 10000, 17000, and 17001 are to be interpreted along with section 11000, which states, "The provisions of law relating to a public assistance program shall be fairly and equitably construed to effect the stated objects and purposes of the program."

. . .

The County *must* set GA standards of aid and care that provide benefits necessary for basic survival.

. . .

Minimum subsistence, at the very least, must include allocations for housing, food, utilities, clothing, transportation and medical care. The State of California includes these items among the necessities for a low income family on which it bases changes in the cost of living.

. . .

The Universal Declaration of Human Rights provides: "Everyone has the right to a standard of living adequate for the health and well being of himself and of his family, including food, clothing, housing and medical care and necessary social services, and the right to security in the event of unemployment, sickness, disability, widowhood, old age or other lack of livelihood in circumstances beyond his control." Universal Declaration of Human Rights, art. 25(1).

Indeed, it defies common sense and all notions of human dignity to exclude from minimum subsistence allowances for clothing, transportation and medical care. Such allowances are essential and necessary to " 'encourage [self-respect and] self-reliance' . . . in a 'humane' manner consistent with modern standards." Without a clothing allowance, recipients must wear tattered clothing and worn out shoes. The lack of adequate and decent clothing and essential transportation is damaging both to recipients' self-respect and their ability to obtain employment. Finally, to leave recipients without minimum medical assistance is inhumane and shocking to the conscience.

We conclude that the GA grant fixed by the County must include an appropriate allowance for each of the basic necessities of life: food, clothing, housing (including utilities), transportation and medical care. If the GA grant fails to provide for any of those needs, the omission must be based on a study that demonstrates the need omitted will be satisfied by some other program available to the GA recipients. Nothing less will satisfy the requirements of sections 10000, 17000 and 17001 when fairly and equitably construed as required by section 11000.

. . .

NOTES & QUESTIONS

1. How does the Court's discussion of the Universal Declaration of Human Rights in *Boehm* aid in its interpretation of the state's welfare statute? Does the Court's reference to "human dignity" and the UDHR aid in understanding the plain meaning of the statute, or help to interpret the legislative intent of the statute? Compare the California Court of Appeal's use of international human rights law in *Boehm* to Chief Justice Peters' exploration of human rights law in her concurrence in the state constitutional case of *Moore v. Ganim*. Does one have a more persuasive impact than the other? If so, what accounts for the difference? Is there something particularly relevant or useful about international and foreign law in the interpretation of constitutional and statutory rights pertaining to economic and social rights? *See King v. State*, 818 N.W.2d 1, 60–62 (Iowa 2012) (Appel, J., dissenting) (citing the UDHR in stating that "education is essential to the development of

an autonomous individual that is the essence of human dignity" and should be deemed protected under the Iowa constitution).

2.   In *Grimes v. Kennedy Kreiger Institute*, 782 A.2d 807 (Md. 2001), the Court of Appeals of Maryland considered negligence actions brought against a research institute by children who allegedly developed lead poisoning while participating in a research study run by the institute. Relying extensively on the Nuremberg Code, the Court held that, in certain circumstances, informed consent can create a special relationship giving rise to greater duties, the breach of which can support a judicial cause of action. The Court noted that the Nuremberg Code, which evolved in the aftermath of "the atrocities performed in the name of science during the Holocaust, and other happenings in the World War II era," was, "at least in significant part . . . the result of legal thought and legal principles, as opposed to medical or scientific principles, and thus should be the preferred standard for assessing the legality of scientific research on human subjects. Under it, duties to research subjects arise." 782 A.2d at 835. Rejecting the defendants' claims that parental consent was sufficient in this case, the Court stated that the "Nuremberg Code specifically requires researchers to make known to human subjects of research 'all the inconveniences and hazards reasonably to be expected; and the effects upon his health or person which may possibly come from his participation in the experiment.' " *Id*. at 849.

Why might the Court have turned to the Nuremberg Code in considering the appropriate standards in this negligence case? Is the Court's reliance on international materials in this context any more or less persuasive than the examples, above, of courts' consideration of international law and foreign law in state constitutional interpretation? Do you think that the Court's reliance on this international standard is appropriate? What else might you want to know about the case and/or the relevant precedent in evaluating the Court's reliance on the Nuremberg Code?

3.   In addition to raising international and comparative law in cases involving interpretation of state constitutional provisions and in cases involving statutory and common law interpretation, advocates have also sought to engage an international human rights frame to inform judicial rule making. One example is in advocacy surrounding the right to counsel in civil cases. In many states, state supreme courts issue binding rules that lay out the requirements that state courts must follow in appointing counsel. As with state or municipal legislation, these rules may be guided by human rights norms. In 2012, when the Wisconsin Supreme Court considered expanding civil counsel as part of its rulemaking process, the Court heard testimony on both international and foreign law in this area. In the end, the Wisconsin court did not alter its rules, but the hearing did provide a forum for considerable judicial education on this issue, and the court endorsed a pilot project to test the appointment of civil counsel in certain cases involving significant human needs, such as sustenance, safety, shelter, health, and child custody. *See* Wisconsin Supreme Court Order No. 10–08, 2012 WI 14 (Feb. 24, 2012) *available at* http://www.wicourts.gov/sc/rulhear/Display

Document.html?content=html&seqNo=7859. Would state courts' reliance on international law in their rulemaking role raise the same concerns that have been leveled against citations in judicial opinions? Are there strategic reasons that advocates for a right to civil counsel might choose to pursue an administrative rule change rather than litigation seeking a reinterpretation of the state constitution? In which forum would human rights arguments be more effective?

———————

Reliance on international and human rights law might also be useful for state court judges engaged in common law decision making in areas where there is no explicit state action. In the following excerpt, Professor Helen Hershkoff argues that state constitutional social and economic rights can and should exert influence on a state's common law decision making. As you read, consider whether her arguments in favor of state courts engaging constitutional economic and social rights protections when determining questions of common law where there is no state action applies equally to state court consideration of international and foreign law in common law decision making.

Helen Hershkoff, " 'Just Words': Common Law and the Enforcement of State Constitutional Social and Economic Rights"
62 Stan. L. Rev. 1521, 1528–30, 1547–55 (2009).

State common law has long served as a modality for the enforcement of public norms: whether through the public law tort or the doctrine of reasonableness, state courts traditionally import constitutional values into areas of private life that are considered to be immune from constitutional regulation under the federal state action doctrine. This form of common law constitutionalism—not to be conflated with the federal practice of a similar name—works through private law pathways to interpret and extend public norms to private activity. Whether a similar practice exists of state courts' indirectly enforcing social and economic rights through common law portals raises a significant but unanswered question.

. . .

[U]nderstanding the pathways through which state constitutional positive norms may influence common law doctrine offers new insight into the relation between law and social change, an area that has generated significant disagreement. Law skeptics often disparage constitutional litigation as a weak mechanism for progressive change. For those interested in using law to improve conditions for the poor and marginalized, the general conclusions are grim: constitutional rights do little to encourage distributive justice or to uproot entrenched poverty, and the common law is seen as likewise ineffective. This Article questions such pessimism. Law does not exclusively determine the shape of private relationships, but neither is it irrelevant. Economic and social relations are created and sustained by common law rules, and common law courts remain open to revise those rules. I argue that state constitutional socio-economic provisions offer a source of interpretive material from which state judges may reconsider and reform existing doctrine on a case-by-case basis.

[A] better appreciation of the interpretive effects of state constitutional social and economic rights may hold prescriptive possibility as a way to reorient federal constitutional doctrine toward concerns of material well being. It is widely recognized that the Federal Constitution, conceived as a "charter of negative rather than positive liberties," takes as its starting point common law entitlements which it protects against state action. A common law baseline informs federal constitutional doctrine, determining such issues as whether something is property for due process protection, whether a medical decision falls within the protected zone of autonomy, or whether intimate activity deserves protection as expression or on the basis of privacy. However, common law rules can evolve and change, and as they do, they potentially may reshape federal constitutional doctrine. A prime example is the common law's treatment of common callings and the contribution of that approach to federal anti-discrimination doctrine. Over time, the indirect effect of social and economic rights on common law development may create new understandings that "presage" federal constitutional rights.

. . .

[In the following section, Professor Hershkoff draws on foreign judicial practice, principles of federalism, and an expressive theory of law to support the practice of state courts according indirect effect to state constitutional positive rights in common law decision making.]

Commentators typically assume that American constitutionalism does not incorporate the practice of indirect constitutional effect. . . . The absence of horizontal effect from American constitutionalism often is explained by the federal state action doctrine and the Court's view that federal constitutional rights bind only government actors. However, the fact that a law lacks direct coercive effect does not foreclose it from having influence in other dimensions.

. . .

In addition, the federal system's adherence to the state action doctrine does not bind the states in their state law decision making;

indeed, federalism and the distinct institutional position of the states tilt in favor of a different interpretive approach.

. . .

A.   Indirect Constitutional Effect and Interpretive Practice Abroad

Discussions about the horizontal effect of constitutional rights typically turn to foreign courts for illustration. Even in countries where private relations are immune from constitutional oversight, some national courts nevertheless recognize the indirect effect of constitutional norms on the interpretation and application of private law duties and relations. This form of indirect effect is not limited to conventional civil liberties—so-called negative rights—but also extends to positive and third-generation social and economic rights.

Examples from abroad usually draw from Germany, where the principle of Drittwirkung has been applied to accord the Basic Law— which, among other rights, protects as "inviolable" the "dignity of man"— an "impact on third parties" in a court's interpretation of private law doctrine. The adjective "radiating" often is used to describe the interpretive effect of the Basic Law, which is said to provide "a yardstick for measuring and assessing all actions in the areas of legislation, public administration, and adjudication," such that "[e]very provision of private law must be compatible with the system of values, and every such provision must be interpreted in this spirit."

. . .

The judicial practice of according indirect effect to public norms is present even in some countries that have adopted an explicit doctrine of "non-application" that formally insulates private law from the direct application of constitutional doctrine. In Canada, for example, the Charter of Rights and Freedoms, adopted in 1982, together with the Canada Constitution, serves as "supreme law," so that "any law that is inconsistent" with either document is "of no effect." The Supreme Court of Canada has made it clear, however, that the Charter applies to common law decision making only where state action is present, and that "the order of a court" is not "governmental action" for these purposes. Nevertheless, even in a private law matter, a judge deciding a case is "bound by the Charter" so that "the Charter is far from irrelevant to private litigants whose disputes fall to be decided at common law."

. . .

In both Germany and Canada, public norms thus influence the direction of private law decision making, and courts are obliged to take these norms into account even where state action is absent.

. . .

B.   Indirect Constitutional Effect and Federalism

The fact that the Article III system has not embraced the theory of indirect constitutional effect does not foreclose state judicial systems from adopting a different interpretive approach. Indeed, some commentators see it as an interpretive "failure" for state judiciaries to proceed in lockstep with the federal. State courts are not required to conform to Article III judicial practice, and the institutional context of their decision making differs significantly from that of the U.S. Supreme Court in overseeing state court judgments. Unlike the Article III courts, which lack general authority to develop common law applicable in the states, state courts have plenary authority to do so, and they explicitly engage in a form of interest balancing that sits comfortably with European-style proportionality analysis. Moreover, concerns of federalism which constrain decision making by unelected federal judges, lack applicability at the state level, where many judges are elected or appointed for fixed terms, and their decisions are localized, conditional, and not burdened by the presumptive finality accorded to Supreme Court decisions relative to the political branches.

The presence of explicit socio-economic rights in a state constitution further differentiates the context of state judicial decisions from their federal counterparts. Although the history and motivation of state constitutional reform differs from state to state, in significant instances reformers amended their state documents in order to regulate private interests that appeared to be impeding or obstructing liberty and well being. Similar concerns lay behind the post-World War II inclusion of socio-economic rights in national constitutions, and it is in these nations that commentators have found a relaxed state action requirement to be more prevalent. Moreover, to the extent that Article III courts hesitate to enforce social and economic rights because of institutional concerns related to unelected judges' mandating their policy views for all times and for all states, this problem is avoided by the minimalist approach of the common law, which favors—to borrow from Cass R. Sunstein—"a long series of case-by-case judgments, highly sensitive to particulars."

C.   Indirect Constitutional Effect and Expressivism

Finally, a state court's engagement with the indirect effect of constitutional positive rights is consistent with the structural nature of social and economic norms understood through an expressive theory of law. The expressivist approach, as leading exponents put it, focuses on ensuring that government actors take account of "particular goals or purposes as reasons for particular actions." The expressive theory builds on a large interdisciplinary literature about norms that helps to explain the important, noncoercive function of law in creating incentives, influencing attitudes, shaping relations, and conveying the importance of particular values over others despite the absence of a direct method of enforcement. Although "norm" lacks a consistent definition, overall it loosely signifies an appreciation for law as "a guide to conduct that somehow, in some way, transcends the purely optional." Constitutional socio-economic provisions encompass this norm-like status, in the sense of articulating "a desired set of social outcomes."

. . .

State constitutional socio-economic rights fit comfortably within [the] conception of rights as constitutive of a shared polity. They aim not only to secure the material improvement of a single claimant, but also to protect a particular kind of political culture that values a shared interest in specified public goods such as free public schooling or safe workplaces. Discussions of positive rights often overlook their structural significance and instead focus solely on the material benefit that such rights confer upon an individual claimant. . . .

Expressivism reframes social and economic rights in ways that illuminate their structural significance to the collective polity. Consider, for example, a state constitutional right to work. A right of this sort can take a number of forms: a right to job security, to join a union, to decide not to join a union, to enjoy workplace safety, or to be guaranteed a fair minimum wage. Certainly the right sustains an individual's well being, and supports the claimant's efforts to secure a good life. But the right to work—and the security of knowing that one cannot be fired for "speaking out"—also sustains a collective interest in a political culture that encourages a plurality of public views and respects the dignity of all members of the polity.

The emphasis on the expressive nature of socio-economic rights, and thus their structural importance, should not obscure the individual interests that are at stake whenever such a right is invoked. Admittedly, the structural aspect of a right may run counter to the individual's interest, just as an individual may press an interest that runs counter to that of another individual. The principle of indirect effect attempts to mediate this conflict, first, by according legal weight to the claimant's demand, rather than treating it only as a need or a desire, and then by balancing the dueling interests using the traditional balancing test that is indigenous to common law reasoning.

. . .

NOTES & QUESTIONS

1. Do you think that the same arguments Professor Hershkoff makes in favor of state courts drawing on positive state constitutional rights in

common law decision making are relevant to the question of whether state courts should draw on international and foreign law in common law decision making? Are there particular instances when this might be appropriate, for example in the realm of economic and social rights?

2.   For further discussion of this approach, see Martha F. Davis, *Public Rights, Global Perspectives and Common Law*, 36 Ford. Urb. L.J. 653 (2009). For a specific application of this common law approach, see Florence Roisman, *The Right to Remain: Common Law Protections for Security of Tenure*, 86 N.C.L. Rev. 817 (2009).

iv. State and Local Resistance to International & Foreign Law

Perhaps reflecting the increasing interest by lawyers and judges in considering international and foreign law in state court proceedings, in recent years, legislators in a number of states have proposed laws which seek to prohibit state courts from considering international, foreign and, in some cases, Sharia law. A successful example emerged in 2010, when Oklahoma voters approved State Question 755, amending Oklahoma's constitution to prohibit state court judges from "considering or using" foreign, international, and Sharia law in making judicial determinations.[14] The amendment was enjoined from going into effect, on grounds that it violated the First Amendment.[15] Despite the Tenth Circuit's finding that the provision was unconstitutional, similar amendments and legislation have been proposed in over twenty other states. Many of these state initiatives track the Constitution Restoration Act of 2004,[16] a proposed federal bill that would have prohibited federal courts from relying upon, *inter alia*, foreign or international law in interpreting and applying the U.S. Constitution.

As you read the following passage, consider what is motivating this backlash against the use of international and foreign law in state courts, what impact these initiatives might have, and what strategies advocates might consider to minimize their impact.

MARTHA F. DAVIS AND JOHANNA KALB, "OKLAHOMA AND BEYOND: UNDERSTANDING THE WAVE OF STATE ANTI-TRANSNATIONAL LAW INITIATIVES"
87 Ind. L. J. Supp. 1, 9–15 (2011).

[After suggesting that Oklahoma's Save Our State Amendment and others like it are motivated by (1) anti-Islamic sentiment and a perceived need to defend Christian values; (2) concern over state and foreign

---

[14] Save Our State Amendment, H.R.J. Res. 1056, 52d Leg., Reg. Sess. (Okla. 2010) (amending article 7, section 1 of the Oklahoma state constitution).

[15] Awad v. Ziriax, 670 F.3d 1111 (10th Cir. 2012).

[16] S. 2082, 108th Cong. § 201 (2004).

sovereignty; (3) fear of judicial activism; and (4) a belief in American exceptionalism, the authors turn to the legal and policy implications of these anti-transnational initiatives.]

The impact of the proposed anti-transnational initiatives, should they be widely enacted, would be dramatic and devastating to our legal system. The proposals undermine principles of federalism, since our constitutional structure requires that state courts, in some instances, consider and apply both international and foreign law. The federal government has been careful to preserve that sphere of state authority. Further, as described below, the practical impact of these measures will likely be negative for state and local governments, businesses, and individuals operating in today's global economy. While the legal consequences vary with the exact language of the proposal, the following discussion highlights the common challenges they present.

A.   Anti-Transnational Law Initiatives Undermine Our Federalism

Treaties

The U.S. Constitution provides that "all Treaties . . . shall be the supreme Law of the Land." Thus, a treaty that has been signed by the President and approved by a two-thirds majority of the Senate has the status of federal law. Moreover, state constitutions "almost always explicitly or implicitly acknowledge the binding nature of ratified treaties." The prominence accorded to treaties in both the federal and state constitutions reflects the understanding that "if the United States [is] to bargain effectively, the national government must not only have the power to conclude treaties but [also] to compel states to observe them."

Some of the treaties that the United States has signed regulate the behavior of national governments, such as those in the area of arms control and trade relations. Increasingly, however, as the world becomes more integrated through globalization, international treaty law has developed to protect the rights of individuals at home and when traveling and working abroad, as well as to facilitate business transactions occurring across national borders. For example, the United States is party to the Vienna Convention on Consular Relations, which guarantees Americans detained while traveling abroad in signatory countries the right to notify the consulate. The United States has also signed numerous investment treaties that protect the property of U.S. corporations located in other countries and guarantee these companies equal access to those countries' courts in the event of disputes. These kinds of international instruments often overlap with areas of state regulation and control.

Mindful that joining these international regimes may inhibit state prerogatives, the U.S. government has been selective about the treaties it adopts and thoughtful in its approach to implementation of those treaties.

In some cases, this approach has meant ratifying a treaty with specific provisions preserving states' authority to control compliance with the instrument's obligations. For example, in adopting the Convention on the Elimination of All Forms of Racial Discrimination and the International Covenant on Civil and Political Rights, the Senate included a federalism understanding which reserves the power to implement these treaties to the states to the extent that they touch on historic areas of state control. In other instances, the federal government has worked collaboratively with the states to implement its international obligations through state law. For example, rather than passing federal legislation to implement the Convention Providing a Uniform Law on the Form of the International Will, the State Department has worked to amend the Uniform Probate Code to bring it into compliance with the Convention, and has encouraged states to adopt the amendments. The federal government is sensitive to the impact of these international instruments on state law and engages with the states in their implementation in order to limit encroachment on their authority. Anti-transnational initiatives interfere with the nuanced and dynamic relationship that the federal government and states have built, and continue to build, on these issues.

Customary International Law

In addition to treaties, some customary international law norms are binding in the United States as federal common law. Customary international law is made up of legal rules developed out of the shared practice of a majority of nations acting out of a sense of legal obligations. Historically, states have played a significant independent role in incorporating customary international law into their own common law in order, for example, to properly distribute the property of deceased foreign nationals or to resolve tax claims related to the property of foreign sovereigns. Because state courts have been willing and able to resolve these questions of customary international law, the federal government has often deferred to their authority to do so rather than setting a binding federal standard and requiring the states to comply. Anti-international initiatives threaten this flexibility. Their passage would force the federal government to adopt legislation to ensure enforcement of customary international law in the states, which would limit state court creativity and autonomy.

Comity

In addition to preventing state courts from considering transnational law, many of the proposed bills would prevent judges from considering foreign law, including the judgments of the courts of other nations. This would put an end to a common practice in state courts that dates back to this country's founding. Under the doctrine of comity, state courts have often voluntarily deferred to the judgments of foreign courts unless doing so would contradict the state's public policy. The U.S. Supreme Court has described the practice as neither a matter of absolute obligation, on the one hand, nor of mere courtesy or good will upon the other. But it is the recognition which one nation allows within its territory to the legislative, executive or judicial acts of another nation, having due regard both to international duty and convenience, and to the rights of its own citizens or of other persons who are under the protection of its laws.

Based on the principle of comity, state courts regularly consider the decisions of foreign courts when resolving family law, estate, or contract disputes involving the activities of Americans while abroad or of foreign nationals living in the United States. For example, courts have chosen to honor or enforce the custodial and financial decisions made by a foreign court when entering a divorce decree after one or both of the parties move to the United States. The states' ability to consider and defer to these foreign judgments prevents unnecessary tensions in the nation's foreign relations and prevents state courts from being used unfairly by parties who have received an adverse determination elsewhere.

Thus, the states have always had a significant role to play in mediating the relationship between international, foreign, and domestic law, both independently in the exercise of their own sovereignty and as required by federal law. The federal government has acknowledged the states' role in fulfilling the United States' legal commitments and has often deferred to state autonomy in this area. Preventing the judiciary from considering international law claims disrupts this cooperative relationship between the states and the federal government. If implemented, these measures would prevent states from fulfilling their obligations under the U.S. Constitution and would create tensions in the United States' relations with other nations.

B.   Policy Implications for American Citizens and Businesses

Undermining International Reciprocity and Domestic Predictability

The decision to forbid state jurists from considering international law also has serious consequences both for that state's residents and businesses, and for the United States as a whole. A single state's refusal to permit its courts to enforce the United States' international obligations puts the entire nation's credibility at risk, with potentially devastating results for the country's ability to protect its citizens and businesses. On a wide range of matters, including the detection and prevention of terrorism, the regulation of trade and monetary policy, and the protection of the environment, the success of the United States' efforts depends upon its ability to follow through on its international commitments.

Furthermore, sending the message that the United States will not observe its international obligations may prevent U.S. citizens and businesses from receiving those protections when working or traveling internationally or transnationally. For example, if they are arrested while traveling abroad, U.S. citizens may no longer be assured of their right to notify the consulate, if state courts are unwilling to provide a remedy when state law enforcement officers fail to grant this right reciprocally to foreign nationals.

Businesses may also find it more difficult to enter into international transactions if the courts of their state are unwilling to uphold their obligation to apply international law. According to Professor Peter Krug of the University of Oklahoma, "successful international business transactions require, and benefit from, a firmly-established legal infrastructure that provides adequate comfort—legal certainty—for those who wish to participate in the global marketplace." After the Oklahoma amendment, for example, foreign businesses may decline to enter into contracts with Oklahoma companies if state courts refuse to apply the United Nations Convention on Contracts for the International Sale of Goods (CISG) instead of the Uniform Commercial Code (UCC) when considering a contract dispute arising between an Oklahoman and a foreign business. Similarly, foreign companies may be concerned about ending up in litigation in state courts if that means that they are denied the protection of the treaties on judicial assistance to which the United States is a party, like the Hague Convention on the Taking of Evidence Abroad in Civil or Commercial Matters. The resulting uncertainty in the business environment will discourage international relationships with state businesses, which is likely to have an economic cost to the state and to the nation. Finally, even in states which have yet to enact these anti-transnational law provisions, the proposals themselves may create sufficient uncertainty to encourage companies to site their transactions elsewhere.

Limiting Contractual Freedom of Business and Individuals

Beyond the issues of reciprocity in foreign courts and stability at home, these initiatives interfere with the ability of businesses and individuals to designate the law—foreign or domestic—that will be applied to enforce or interpret their agreements. Perhaps corporate parties are involved in a series of transactions, some of which are governed by foreign law, and the parties want the contracts to be construed and enforced consistently. Or perhaps individual parties have concurred on a contractual arbitration clause designating law outside of the United States as the applicable decisional law in a will or prenuptial agreement for reasons of religion or because of family considerations. In either case, an Oklahoma-type provision would undermine the parties' ability to seek enforcement of these consensual contractual arrangements in a state's courts, since the courts would be precluded from considering foreign law even when the parties agreed on its application.

For businesses dealing with global transactions and incorporating foreign legal regimes, the inability to rely on domestic courts for enforcement is a very serious impediment. It is no wonder, then, that some of the more recent state legislative proposals include exemptions for businesses. While perhaps assuaging the concerns of the business community, these proposals would create a disturbing two-tiered system wherein individuals effectively have less contractual freedom than corporate interests. A corporation could look to the state courts to enforce a contract incorporating French law, while an individual could not.

In sum, much of the international law to which the United States is committed exists to protect American citizens and companies in their international and transnational interactions, and to preserve their freedom of contract in an increasingly diverse and globalized world. Even a single state's decision to forbid its jurists from doing their part in meeting the United States' international obligations will place these protections at risk for all Americans.

Judicial Independence

In addition to the threat that the anti-transnational law proposals pose to the state and the nation's participation in the international legal framework, they also have immediate consequences for the independence and autonomy of state judiciaries. The consideration and adoption of these initiatives, even in their mildest forms, will likely have a chilling effect on judicial deliberation. In an age when state judges are increasingly the subjects of targeted electoral campaigns based on their judicial opinions, these initiatives send the messages to judges that they will be punished for their consideration of international or foreign law.

Judicial independence is a constitutive principle of the United States government. As Justice Sandra Day O'Connor has explained:

> [t]he Founders of our Nation, having narrowly escaped the grasp of a tyrannical government, saw fit to render federal judges independent of the political departments with respect to their tenure and salary as a way of ensuring that they would not be beholden to the political branches in their interpretation of laws and constitutional rights.

At the state level, judges are selected by a variety of different mechanisms, including, as is the case in Oklahoma, by election. Despite the variation, there is some consistency; in each of the fifty states, judges are elevated to, and removed from, the bench according to established and transparent rules. A jurist selected for the bench decides the cases that arise according to the law of the state and the nation without interference in the decision-making process. The independence of U.S. judges is admired internationally and has been replicated in new democracies around the world.

The anti-transnational law initiatives threaten the independence of state judges by instructing them that certain law is beyond the scope not just of their enforcement powers, but beyond their ability to consider in their deliberations. By directing judges how to decide the cases before them, these proposals purport to constrain judges in their decision making in a way that is historically unprecedented in this country and threatens the core values animating our judicial system. Moreover, these proposals handicap state judges and justices from considering potentially informative sources in order to reach the best outcomes in the cases before them. Jurists in every state draw regularly on the comparative experience of other states and of the federal government in their decision making. In some circumstances, however, the relevant parallel experience may come from beyond national boundaries, or the state standard to be interpreted may require an examination of the national or international consensus. For example, California statutes provide that a person exporting electronic waste to foreign countries must do so "in accordance with applicable United States or applicable international law." Similarly, Alaska law prohibits commercial fishing of halibut in a manner inconsistent with the regulations of the International Pacific Halibut Commission, a public international organization established by a convention between Canada and the United States. The amendment cuts Oklahoma's jurists off from the world of comparative experience, impoverishes the development of the state's statutory law, and undermines its constitutional and common law jurisprudence.

. . .

NOTES & QUESTIONS

1. For detailed status reports on proposed state law provisions banning state courts from considering international, foreign and/or Sharia law, see Bill Raftery, *Jurisdiction Archive*, Gavel to Gavel, http://gavel togavel.us/category/jurisdiction/.

2. What consideration should lawyers give to the potential for political backlash when weighing whether to bring arguments based on international or foreign law in state courts? How should judges weigh the possibility as they consider how to write their opinions? What impact might the possibility of such backlash have on the way a judge decides a case or authors an opinion? Consider that forty states use general elections either to select appellate court judges for each term or to determine whether to retain a judge who has finished a fixed term. *See* American Judicare Society, *Methods of Judicial Selection*, http://www.judicialselection.us/judicial_selection/ methods/selection_of_judges.cfm?state. The practice of judicial elections has been criticized as compromising judicial independence and impartiality. *See* Kenneth J. Aulet, *It's Not Who Hires You But Who Can Fire You: The Case Against Retention Elections*, 44 Colum. J. L. & Soc. Probs. 589 (2011);

Lawrence Baumm, *Judicial Elections and Judicial Independence: The Voters' Perspective*, 64 Ohio State L.J. 13, 16–17 (2003); Bronson D. Bills, *A Penny for the Courts' Thoughts? The High Price of Judicial Elections*, 3 NW J. L. & Soc. Pol'y 29 (2008).

3.   For additional commentary on the constitutionality of state law provisions that bar consideration of foreign and international law by state court judges, see John T. Parry, *Oklahoma's Save Our State Amendment and the Conflict of Laws*, 65 Okla. L. Rev. 1 (2012), and Penny M. Venetis, *The Unconstitutionality of Oklahoma's SQ 755 and Other Provisions Like It That Bar State Courts from Considering International Law*, 59 Clev. St. L. Rev. 189 (2011).

SKILLS EXERCISE

You work for a human rights organization that seeks to support litigation challenging a 2008 Louisiana parish ordinance prohibiting homeowners from renting a property to anyone other than a blood relative. The parish, which has a predominantly white population, abuts a predominantly African-American parish. The residents of the neighboring parish were overwhelmingly displaced following Hurricanes Katrina and Rita.

The parish council's stated purpose in enacting the blood-relative ordinance was to re-establish "pre-existing neighborhoods," and to maintain "integrity," "quality of life," "family atmosphere" and "quiet enjoyment" of "long established neighborhoods."

Yet, the parish's blood-relative requirement had a disproportionate impact on the ability of African-Americans to find rental housing in the parish. African-Americans owned only 4% of owner-occupied housing in the parish. By contrast, whites owned approximately 93% of all owner-occupied single-family housing in the parish. Moreover, African-American households in the parish are twice as likely as white households to seek rental housing.

The Fair Housing Alliance (FHA), a local non-government organization, brought a lawsuit in Louisiana state court challenging the ordinance on behalf of a group of rental property owners. The United States Supreme Court has held that in order to prevail on an Equal Protection claim under the Federal Constitution, the plaintiff must prove that a public policy was adopted with the specific intent to discriminate based on race.[17] Lacking this kind of evidence, FHA brought the suit under Article I, Section 3 of the Louisiana Constitution of 1974 which provides the following:

Right to Individual Dignity:

No person shall be denied the equal protection of the laws. No law shall discriminate against a person because of race or religious ideas, beliefs or affiliations. No law shall arbitrarily, capriciously, or

---

[17] *See, e.g.*, Washington v. Davis, 426 U.S. 229 (1976).

unreasonably discriminate against a person because of birth, age, sex, culture, physical condition or political ideas or affiliations. Slavery and involuntary servitude are prohibited except in the latter case as punishment for crime.

FHA argued that the provision should be read more expansively than the federal Constitution to invalidate this policy that disproportionately affects African-Americans from finding housing in the community.

The organization that you work for plans to submit an *amicus* brief arguing that the Louisiana courts should consider the United States' obligations under international law in interpreting the Individual Dignity clause in this case. Your supervisor has given you the research materials below and asked you to draft a short memorandum setting out the arguments that should be included in the brief.

As you familiarize yourself with these materials consider the following questions:

(1) How will you argue that the Louisiana state court should consider the United States' international obligations in interpreting the state constitution?

(2) What status do these different materials have in domestic law? What level of consideration should they be given by Louisiana state courts? Consider whether and how you would distinguish between the research sources.

(3) The Louisiana state constitutional provision is titled the "Right to Individual Dignity." Dignity is a very important concept in international human rights law. How can you use the reference to dignity in the Louisiana Constitution to argue for a broader reading of its equal protection provision?

(4) This case was initiated in the aftermath of Hurricane Katrina, which displaced tens of thousands of Gulf Coast residents. The right to housing is well-recognized under international human rights law. How should this context impact the Louisiana courts' consideration of the Individual Dignity clause in this case?

Research Materials

UNIVERSAL DECLARATION OF HUMAN RIGHTS (DECLARATION)

G.A. Res. 217 (III) A, U.N. Doc. A/810 (Dec. 10, 1948).

Preamble

Whereas recognition of the inherent dignity and of the equal and inalienable rights of all members of the human family is the foundation of freedom, justice and peace in the world,

. . .

The General Assembly proclaims THIS UNIVERSAL DECLARATION OF HUMAN RIGHTS as a common standard of achievement for all peoples and all nations, to the end that every individual and every organ of society, keeping this Declaration constantly in mind, shall strive by teaching and education to promote respect for these rights and freedoms and by progressive measures, national and international, to secure their universal and effective recognition and observance, both among the peoples of Member States themselves and among the peoples of territories under their jurisdiction.

Article 1.

All human beings are born free and equal in dignity and rights. They are endowed with reason and conscience and should act towards one another in a spirit of brotherhood.

Article 2.

Everyone is entitled to all the rights and freedoms set forth in this Declaration, without distinction of any kind, such as race, colour, sex, language, religion, political or other opinion, national or social origin, property, birth or other status.

. . .

Article 7.

All are equal before the law and are entitled without any discrimination to equal protection of the law. All are entitled to equal protection against any discrimination in violation of this Declaration and against any incitement to such discrimination.

. . .

Article 25.

(1) Everyone has the right to a standard of living adequate for the health and well-being of himself and of his family, including food, clothing, housing and medical care and necessary social services, and the right to security in the event of unemployment, sickness, disability, widowhood, old age or other lack of livelihood in circumstances beyond his control.

. . .

INTERNATIONAL CONVENTION ON THE ELIMINATION
OF ALL FORMS OF RACIAL DISCRIMINATION

Dec. 21, 1965, 660 U.N.T.S. 195. [CERD].

The States Parties to this Convention,

. . .

Considering that the Universal Declaration of Human Rights proclaims that all human beings are born free and equal in dignity and rights and that everyone is entitled to all the rights and freedoms set out therein, without distinction of any kind, in particular as to race, colour or national origin,

Considering that all human beings are equal before the law and are entitled to equal protection of the law against any discrimination and against any incitement to discrimination,

. . .

Have agreed as follows:

Article 1

1.   In this Convention, the term "racial discrimination" shall mean any distinction, exclusion, restriction or preference based on race, colour, descent, or national or ethnic origin which has the purpose or effect of nullifying or impairing the recognition, enjoyment or exercise, on an equal footing, of human rights and fundamental freedoms in the political, economic, social, cultural or any other field of public life.

. . .

Article 2

1.   States Parties condemn racial discrimination and undertake to pursue by all appropriate means and without delay a policy of eliminating racial discrimination in all its forms and promoting understanding among all races, and, to this end:

(a) Each State Party undertakes to engage in no act or practice of racial discrimination against persons, groups of persons or institutions and to ensure that all public authorities and public institutions, national and local, shall act in conformity with this obligation;

. . .

(c) Each State Party shall take effective measures to review governmental, national and local policies, and to amend, rescind or nullify any laws and regulations which have the effect of creating or perpetuating racial discrimination wherever it exists;

(d) Each State Party shall prohibit and bring to an end, by all appropriate means, including legislation as required by circumstances, racial discrimination by any persons, group or organization;

. . .

Article 5

In compliance with the fundamental obligations laid down in article 2 of this Convention, States Parties undertake to prohibit and to eliminate racial discrimination in all its forms and to guarantee the right of everyone, without distinction as to race, colour, or national or ethnic origin, to equality before the law, notably in the enjoyment of the following rights:

. . .

(i) The right to freedom of movement and residence within the border of the State;

. . .

(iii) The right to housing;

. . .

————————

The U.S. ratified the CERD with a "federalism understanding" which provides:

> That the United States understands that this Convention shall be implemented by the Federal Government to the extent that it exercises jurisdiction over the matters covered therein, and otherwise by the state and local governments. To the extent that state and local governments exercise jurisdiction over such matters, the Federal Government shall, as necessary, take appropriate measures to ensure the fulfillment of the Convention.

140 Cong. Rec. S7634–02 (daily ed. June 24, 1994).

————————

The CERD requires each state party to submit regular reports to the United Nations Committee on the Elimination of Racial Discrimination regarding its compliance. The Committee then issues observations based on these reports. In 2008, the Committee offered the following observation regarding the United States' obligation to consider the disparate impact of its federal, state, and local policies on different racial, ethnic, or national groups:

COMMITTEE ON THE ELIMINATION OF RACIAL DISCRIMINATION,
CONSIDERATION OF REPORTS SUBMITTED BY STATES PARTIES
UNDER ARTICLE 9 OF THE CONVENTION, CONCLUDING
OBSERVATIONS OF THE COMMITTEE ON THE REPORT OF THE
UNITED STATES OF AMERICA, U.N. DOC. CERD/C/USA/CO/6

(May 8, 2008). para 10.

The Committee reiterates the concern expressed in . . . its previous concluding observations of 2001 that the definition of racial discrimination used in the federal and state legislation and in court practice is not always in line with that contained in article 1, paragraph 1, of the Convention, which requires States parties to prohibit and eliminate racial discrimination in all its forms, including practices and legislation that may not be discriminatory in purpose, but in effect. In this regard, the Committee notes that indirect, or de facto—discrimination occurs where an apparently neutral provision, criterion or practice would put persons of a particular racial, ethnic or national origin at a disadvantage compared with other persons, unless that provision, criterion or practice is objectively justified by a legitimate aim and the means of achieving that aim are appropriate and necessary (art.1 (1)).

The Committee recommends that the State party review the definition of racial discrimination used in the federal and state legislation and in court practice, so as to ensure, in light of the definition of racial discrimination provided for in article 1, paragraph 1, of the Convention— that it prohibits racial discrimination in all its forms, including practices and legislation that may not be discriminatory in purpose, but in effect.

. . .

NOTES & QUESTIONS

1.   This skills exercise is based on a real case, *Greater New Orleans Fair Housing Action Center v. St. Bernard Parish*, which was filed in U.S. District Court for the Eastern District of Louisiana in 2006. For a history of the resulting litigation, *see* Greater New Orleans Fair Housing Action Center, www.gnofairhousing.org/.

The complaint alleged that St. Bernard Parish violated the federal Fair Housing Act, the federal Civil Rights Acts of 1866 and 1871, and the Equal Protection Clause of the Fourteenth Amendment. Why do you think that the plaintiff chose to file in federal court rather than state court and to limit its claims to those based in federal statutory and constitutional law? What questions must advocates consider when deciding which forum is most appropriate for international human rights-based arguments?

2.   Recall from the discussion in **Chapter I** that the constitutions of Montana and Puerto Rico also include protections for human dignity. These references have origins in the international human rights movement. Puerto

Rico's constitution was adopted shortly after World War II, "at a time when the international community was converging on the centrality of human dignity as a fundamental value." Vicki C. Jackson, *Constitutional Dialogue and Human Dignity: States and Transnational Constitutional Discourse*, 65 Mont. L. Rev. 15, 26 (2004). Its provision was modeled on the Universal Declaration of Human Rights and other transnational documents. *See id.* at 23–26.

Twenty years later, Puerto Rico's dignity provision served as inspiration for delegates to the Montana Constitutional Constitution who sought to strengthen state constitutional protections against discrimination. *Id.* at 21–22. Judges in Montana and Puerto Rico have relied upon this legislative history in interpreting their constitutions to provide protections beyond those guaranteed in the federal constitution. *Id.* at 27–39.

Louisiana's inclusion of an individual dignity clause was inspired in part by Montana's constitutional text. *See* Mary Anne Wolf, *Louisiana's Equal Protection Guarantee: Questions about the Supreme Court Decision Prohibiting Affirmative Action*, 58 La. L. Rev. 1209, 1223 (1998). Given this shared history, how could you use comparative information from other U.S. states to argue for an expansive reading of the Louisiana constitution? *See* Johanna Kalb, *Litigating Dignity: A Human Rights Framework*, 74 Alb. L. Rev. 1725 (2011).

III. HUMAN RIGHTS IMPLEMENTATION BY STATE AND LOCAL GOVERNMENTS

In addition to state court judges, other state and local officials, including legislators, law enforcement, administrators, and human rights commissions, can play a role in implementing human rights locally. Indeed, elected and appointed officials at the state, city, county and municipal levels are developing tools and techniques to address local problems, influence local, state and national policy, and generally promote and protect human rights within local communities. This section explores the appropriateness and utility of these inwardly-focused endeavors, as well as strategies that state and local officials are using to "bring human rights home." In the subsequent section, we explore doctrinal concerns with state and local initiatives that are more "outwardly" focused, explicitly seeking to influence the policies and practices of other countries. Query, however, whether it is possible to draw a clear line between outwardly and inwardly focused state and local human rights activities.

A. THE CASE FOR LOCAL IMPLEMENTATION

Before turning to the ways in which state and local officials are engaging with international human rights law, we need to ask whether states and cities *should* have a role in the local implementation of human rights. A traditional model of U.S. federalism places this responsibility solely within the jurisdiction of the federal government. As Professor Martha Davis notes:

> Mayors, governors, city councils, and state legislatures are not usually associated with foreign affairs. The United States Constitution states that the federal government has the power to make treaties, and it has been widely accepted that this authority encompasses a more general "foreign affairs power." A large share of that power rests with the executive branch. While the Constitution also reserves some residual powers to be exercised by the states or "the people," the argument that the nation must speak with one voice on issues of international concern has reinforced the idea that there is little role for the divergent perspectives of individual states and cities in the world of international relations.

Martha F. Davis, *Thinking Globally, Acting Locally: States, Municipalities, and International Human Rights, in* 2 Bringing Human Rights Home 127, 127–28 (Cynthia Soohoo et al. eds., 2008).

Nonetheless, as state and local governments have become increasingly engaged in human rights activities, this traditional division of labor has been challenged in both scholarship and practice. This section explores the potential benefits of viewing international human rights as crossing the boundaries of federal, state and local jurisdiction.

As you review the following passage by Professor Judith Resnik, assess her arguments for local involvement in human rights treaty implementation. How does she envision state and municipal participation? Which actors are involved and what kinds of initiatives have they adopted?

JUDITH RESNIK, "LAW'S MIGRATION: AMERICAN EXCEPTIONALISM, SILENT DIALOGUES, AND FEDERALISM'S MULTIPLE PORTS OF ENTRY"
115 Yale L.J. 1564, 1576, 1580, 1636–42, 1655–56, 1667–70 (2006).

States and localities—through city councils, state legislatures, national organizations of local officials, and courts—serve as both importers and exporters of law. The conceit that United States law is basically bounded is inaccurate. Rather, laws (like people) migrate, and seepage is everywhere. The courts are only one stop along the way.

. . .

With such permeability, the origins of rules blur. While certain legal precepts are foundational to the United States, one should label them "made in the USA" knowing that—like other "American" products—their parts and designs are also produced abroad. The questions are not if or whether non-United States law will have an effect but rather (1) how, when, and through which actors lessons from abroad will be brought home; and (2) how, when, and through which actors the United States will attempt to affect the law and practices of nations and of international organizations.

. . .

State courts and city councils, as well as administrators and other executive branch officials, are important participants in the process of absorption. Although the United States has yet to ratify CEDAW, a few cities have adopted aspects of it as local law. San Francisco has, for example, called for a review of laws to identify systematic and structural discrimination against women and girls.

. . .

As these many actors, at national and local levels, in and outside formal legal structures, embrace propositions like racial and gender equality, new understandings become entrenched, even if what obligations flow from commitments to equality remain contested. When successfully incorporated at these various levels, Americans come to think of these precepts as internal to the American project.

. . .

The prospect of the United States ratifying CEDAW has sparked considerable anxiety in some quarters. . . . Consistent with the historical practice of asserting "domestic" authority as a barrier to transnational lawmaking, these concerns are sometimes couched in the language of jurisdiction—that CEDAW is particularly pernicious because it undermines the rightful place of state governance of personal status relationships. As one opponent put it, joining would entail "surrendering American domestic matters to the norm setting of the international community."

. . .

States' rights are one set of prerogatives delineated by opponents of CEDAW; adherence to gender roles (also a battle about boundaries) is another. Opposition to CEDAW is predicated on both kinds of border claims, as is exemplified by testimony given in 2002 at Senate subcommittee hearings on CEDAW. A speaker testifying on behalf of the Heritage Foundation accused the United Nations of being part of a "campaign to undermine the foundations of society—the two-parent married family, the religions that espouse the primary importance of marriage and traditional sexual morality, and the legal and social structures that protect these institutions."

Those charges are predicated on disagreement with CEDAW's call for both women and men to take responsibility for the "upbringing and development of their children." CEDAW does expect state parties to enable women to have access to a host of activities beyond family life. Moreover, because CEDAW defines discrimination to include any "distinction, exclusion, or restriction made on the basis of sex" that works an inequality in any field ("political, economic, social, cultural, [or] civil") its inquiries are far-reaching, seeking accounts of how gender affects safety, education, health, employment, recreation and sports, government benefits, and political power. From this perspective, the Heritage Foundation and other critics have correctly identified (if hyperbolically attacked) CEDAW's challenge to a conception of women as obliged first and foremost to their households and to a conception of the United States as not required to account to other organizations or nations. If having to respond to questions is an affront to a nation's sovereignty, critics' concerns have a basis for their argument. Were the United States to ratify it, this country—like nations around the world—would be required to send its representatives to reply to questions by the twenty-three members of the CEDAW Committee about compliance with treaty provisions.

Further, opponents have understood that CEDAW's aspirations surpass the current requirements of federal constitutional law on gender equality. Not only is affirmative action appropriate under CEDAW, but the definition of what constitutes inequality differs from current American constitutional law. CEDAW focuses on the purpose and effect on women of laws or actions rather than on the intent of a particular legal rule. In addition, CEDAW applies to private as well as public actors, as CEDAW aspires to reach all aspects of one's life, from households to labor markets to governments, from early education to old age. Similarly, although the United States Supreme Court narrowly rejected an effort by Congress to give women victims of violence access to redress in federal courts, resolutions of the United Nations frame violence as a "manifestation of historically unequal power relations between men and women, which have led to domination over and discrimination against women by men and to the prevention of the full advancement of women" and as a "crucial social mechanism[ ] by which women are forced into a subordinate position compared with men."

b.   National Action Gaining Support for CEDAW at the Local Level

Concerned about the United States's reluctance to embrace CEDAW, the General Federation of Women's Clubs, the Women's Institute for Leadership Development for Human Rights (WILD), along with Amnesty

International, many church groups, and other NGOs, initiated a drive to have states and localities enact resolutions calling for the United States to ratify CEDAW. Some one hundred and ninety civic, religious, educational, environmental, and legal organizations have built a coalition that provides model resolutions for localities to "recognize" equal rights, to "eschew all forms of discrimination on the basis of sex," and to endorse efforts to obtain U.S. ratification. As of 2004, forty-four cities, eighteen counties, and sixteen states have passed or considered legislation relating to CEDAW, with yet others contemplating action.

Most of those provisions are expressive or hortatory, calling for the United States to ratify CEDAW. Some local adaptations have varied the text of the model resolution to insist on either the propriety of local action or (echoing a theme of exceptionalism) the special role of America as a human rights leader. For example, noting it was "the home of the Liberty Bell and Independence Hall," the City of Philadelphia asserted the "appropriate and legitimate role" that localities have in "affirming the importance of international law in our own communities as a universal norm and to serve as guides for public policy." Burlington, Vermont went further, addressing "the greatly increased interdependence of the people of the world" and its understanding that "we are citizens of the world with responsibilities extending beyond the boundaries of our city, state, and nation, as demonstrated through [the] Sister Cities Program."

Such "ratification" resolutions are the most common form of local engagement with CEDAW, but a few jurisdictions have done more, directly implementing some of CEDAW's precepts. San Francisco is the most prominent, making aspects of CEDAW its own domestic law.

. . .

[T]he discussion now focused on the legitimacy of judicial importation should take into account how "foreign" precepts make their way into American law through ports of entry other than courts. The legal literature needs to address the incorporation or absorption of transnational or non-American law through regulation, administrative action, and legislation shaped by government actors nationally, locally, and inter-regionally. In doing that analytic work, appreciation of United States federalism should animate presumptions of concurrency of state and federal action, rather than exclusivity of national authority.

. . .

Because the contemporary debate has posited the international comparative exercise as a source of liberalism that welcomes judicial elaboration and enforcement of rights, I have focused on the expansion of rights through various transnational efforts, such as CEDAW . . . , that are innovative when compared to facets of American law. Yet, under the domestic regimes of many nations, women and the environment have sometimes made more progress. As Justice Scalia cautioned in *Roper*, foreign innovations are not intrinsically rights-expanding.

Moreover, many commentators criticize international bodies and domestic governments for their failures in responding to acute problems, such as the pandemics of AIDS and of hunger, as well as to the sadly ordinary violence, poverty, and illiteracy that lace women's lives around the world. Indeed, several of the countries that have ratified CEDAW are identified with consistently oppressive conditions for women. Further, international institutions and law have only begun to think about the intersecting forms of discrimination and, according to many commentators, continue to marginalize programs focused on women.

Similarly, while I have mapped the local initiatives attempting to bring transnational insights home, activism at that level does not inevitably fall on the "progressive" side of a ledger. CEDAW proponents in the 1990s have gone to local legislatures, but so did Bricker activists in the 1950s. They succeeded in 1954 in the Texas State Senate, which passed a resolution petitioning Congress to submit the Bricker amendment to the states for ratification. Since the 1960s, mobilization by conservative groups has wrought an impressive transformation now well chartered by social scientists. As Lisa McGirr has detailed, the "men and women who rejected the liberal vision and instead championed individual economic freedom and a staunch social conservativism" have had a significant impact, with recent examples including bans on gay marriages and legislation to limit access to abortions.

. . .

In short, institutional voices in a host of jurisdictions, public and private, can and do shift their tones. The [American Bar Association] was once run by sovereigntists who dominated the Bricker amendment hearings. Today, the ABA plays a leadership role in promoting transnational efforts to enhance human rights, including urging ratification by the United States of CEDAW. The [National League of Cities], now generating women's global leadership networks, was also the organization that campaigned against federal regulation of workers' benefits and minimum wages. Moreover as the National Association of Attorneys General took stances supportive of regulation, a subgroup, a Republican National Association of Attorneys General, has spun off. Political scientists discussing the idea of "capture" have dozens of case studies to cite, as all genres of jurisdiction offer opportunities for those with the wherewithal and insight to use them.

Thus, neither the kind of jurisdiction nor the territorial space occupied by a polity produces rights of a particular kind. Renouncing a claim of a "jurisdictional imperative," I am likely to disappoint nationalists and federalists, sovereigntists and internationalists alike. Jurisdictions do not make rights, but people do—through collective action and repeated iterations, some democratic and some not. Further, that work proceeds without the capacity to be self-contained. Promoters of nation-states have relied on the conceit of boundaries as they forged governments during a period of world history in which that level of governance seemed able to offer a set of services and protections for those within its borders. The impulse to assert a robust persona for the nation-state and bright lines of jurisdictional competencies stems from a fear, fairly grounded, that with border blurring comes a loss of identity. But if America ever had a period that could be called its heyday (pick any one), it was always permeated by ideas and peoples from abroad. Just as individuals constantly defy the immigration laws to enter the United States illegally, so law seeps in—acknowledged or not.

Once norm entrepreneurs let go of an assumption that any one level of power—the international, the transnational, the national, or the local—can be an ongoing source of any particular political stance, they have to understand the necessity to work at multiple sites. That is costly and time-consuming, even as it may be generative of democratic practices and enable shifting understandings as communities compare their own judgments with those of others. Such multiplicity is a source of opportunity, as gaps in governance and alternative governments are spaces in which all power-seekers, be they entrenched or newly fabricated, try to gain toe-holds. Jurisdiction, from this perspective, functions as a form of oppression, as an obstacle to reform, and as a source of opportunity for those seeking to redefine rights that will require dislodging long-entrenched definitions of the bounded roles assigned to women, men, and governments.

· · ·

NOTES & QUESTIONS

1.   Professor Catherine Powell, too, has written on the importance of state and local efforts to implement human rights treaties. Catherine Powell, *Dialogic Federalism: Constitutional Possibilities for Incorporation of Human Rights Law in the United States*, 150 U. Pa. L. Rev. 245 (2001). Stating that local implementation of human rights can help to overcome the "democratic deficit" inherent in international law, Powell urges greater partnership between federal and local governments, with the federal government playing a strong coordinating function. This, she notes, "may convert weakly-legitimated norms developed at the international level into norms that are more strongly legitimated at a local level." *Id*. at 265. Professor Powell also argues that direct incorporation of human rights at the local level can help to address concerns about the federal government acting in areas traditionally within state and local control.

2.   Do   you   agree   with   Professors   Powell   and   Resnik   that implementation and internalization of human rights at the state and local level is beneficial? If so, is it useful only because national implementation efforts are stalled, or would there be a value in subnational participation even if the federal government was more fully engaged?

3.   Resnik focuses on the dual-pronged value of state and local efforts to implement human rights: bolstering the legitimacy of human rights norms and facilitating their internalization. Do you think that the CEDAW activity she describes at the state and local level has the potential to counter federal apathy and antipathy towards ratification of the Convention? In what ways?

4.   What are the implications of Professor Resnik's observation that local activism is not always "progressive" and more rights protective? What are the advocacy implications of her assertion that "[j]urisdiction . . . functions as a form of oppression, as an obstacle to reform, and as a source of opportunity for those seeking to redefine rights?" 115 Yale L.J. at 1670.

5.   Do you think that local implementation of human rights treaties might provide an effective counter to the argument that human rights treaties undermine U.S. sovereignty and federalism interests more generally? Consider this excerpt from an organization opposing U.S. ratification of the Convention on the Rights of Persons with Disabilities:

> Ceding Authority to an International Committee: To monitor implementation, human rights treaties usually establish a "committee of experts" to review reports from states parties on their compliance. The "experts" on such committees are not elected democratically; rather, each is appointed by a state party, regardless of that state's human rights record. States parties are required to submit periodic reports (usually every four years) to the committee detailing their compliance with the particular treaty. For example, the Human Rights Committee oversees state compliance with the provisions of the International Covenant on Civil and Political Rights, and the Committee on the Rights of the Child monitors compliance with the Convention on the Rights of the Child. The Disabilities Convention established the Committee on the Rights of Persons with Disabilities (CRPD Committee), which is charged with reviewing periodic reports and making "such suggestions and general recommendations on the report as it may consider appropriate."

. . .

> In general, UN human rights treaty committees have frequently made demands of states parties that fall well outside of the legal, social, economic, and cultural traditions and norms of those states parties. This has especially been the case with the United States. For instance, in February 2008, the Committee on the Elimination of Racial discrimination reviewed the U.S. record

on racial discrimination and issued a report directing the United States to change its policies on a series of political causes completely divorced from the issues of race and racial discrimination. Specifically, the committee urged the United States to guarantee effective judicial review to the foreign unlawful enemy combatants held at the Guantánamo Bay detention facility, prevent U.S. corporations from abusing the rights of indigenous populations in other countries, place a moratorium on the death penalty, restore voting rights to convicted felons, and take action on other matters completely unrelated or only tangentially related to racial discrimination.

The committees overseeing the enforcement of other human rights treaties to which the United States is not a party often recommend changes in policies that are outside of traditional American norms. For example, the committee that oversees the Convention on the Elimination of All Forms of Discrimination Against Women (CEDAW) regularly advocates that states decriminalize prostitution, radically expand access to abortion, devalue the role of women as mothers, reduce parental authority, and implement strict numerical gender quotas in the government and private sectors.

The U.S. has ample reason to expect that the experts on the CRPD Committee will disregard U.S. sovereignty and embark on similar forays in pursuit of a broader agenda of social and cultural engineering unrelated to disabilities.

Steven Groves, *Ratification of the Disabilities Convention Would Erode American Sovereignty*, Heritage Foundation Backgrounder, No. 2406, April 26, 2010, at 5–6, *available at* http://s3.amazonaws.com/thf_media/2010/pdf/bg_2406.pdf (footnotes omitted).

6. Professor Tara Melish notes that state and local implementation is consistent with the principle of subsidiarity. Tara J. Melish, *From Paradox to Subsidiarity: The United States and Human Rights Treaty Bodies*, 34 Yale J. Int'l L. 389, 428 (2009). This principle, central to the human rights framework, embraces the importance of local decision-making and implementation. As Melish notes, the principle of subsidiarity is foundational to international law, and articulates the shared responsibility and relationship between international, national and subnational entities for the "shared project of ensuring human rights protection for all individuals." *Id.* at 438 (citing Paola G. Carozza, *Subsidiarity as a Structural Principle of International Human Rights Law*, 97 Am. J. Int'l L. 38, 38 n.1 (2003)). The human rights system is designed to monitor human rights conditions and interfere only when domestic or local institutions are unable or ineffective to address human rights concerns. *Id.* at 452. By respecting and enabling the primacy of local institutions, the human rights system ensures that human rights values and approaches reflect the concerns and needs of local

communities, allowing for a more "authentic," effective, and relevant approach to rights protection. *Id.* at 453. How might Professor Melish's articulation of shared federal/state/local responsibility ease concerns that human rights treaties erode federalism and sovereignty?

7. Does state and local implementation erode the universality of human rights? As Professor Louis Henkin noted, human rights are intended to be universal, "belonging to every human being in every society," regardless of "geography or history, culture or ideology, political or economic system, or stage of societal development." Louis Henkin, The Age of Rights 2–3, 16–17 (2d ed. 1996). If human rights are meant to encourage adherence to a set of universally accepted norms such as dignity, justice, equality and fairness, is there a danger in disrupting this universality though diverse state and local approaches at implementation?

In answering this question, would it change your view to know that human rights treaty law allows for and anticipates some amount of variation in treaty interpretation and application? For example, countries typically ratify treaties with significant reservations, understandings, and declarations limiting or modifying their effect, although there are limits to the extent to which countries can dilute the content and scope of human rights treaties through this process. In addition, particularly with respect to the economic and social rights treaties, signatories anticipate that countries will realize rights "progressively," rather than all at once and immediately. The European Court of Human Rights has recognized the inevitability of variation in interpretation of and compliance with human rights treaties, in particular the European Convention on Human Rights, by adopting the doctrine of "margin of appreciation" to grant deference to member-states' formulation of human rights obligations. *See* Judith Resnik, *Comparative (In)Equalities: CEDAW, the Jurisdiction of Gender, and the Heterogeneity of Transnational Law Production*, 10 Int'l J. Con. L. 531, 547 (2012) (citing the example of *Handyside v. United Kingdom*, 24 Eur. Ct. H.R. (ser. A) at 47, 49 (1976)). How do these structural mechanisms for allowing diversity in implementation square with the goal of universality? Might they promote wider acceptance and adherence to human rights?

B. STRATEGIES FOR IMPLEMENTING HUMAN RIGHTS AT THE LOCAL LEVEL

As suggested by the above section, states and localities are increasingly embracing a range of human rights activities to influence domestic policy and practice. Some draw upon the Universal Declaration of Human Rights, generally, as a set of guiding principles for rights protection. Others adopt resolutions urging or endorsing human rights treaties that the United States has yet to ratify. Still others fashion more wholesale approaches to incorporating human rights principles into local government functions. This section explores some of these strategies to influence human rights policy and practice. What is the potential effectiveness and impact of each of the strategies discussed? How can advocates ensure that the measures discussed here are implemented in a meaningful way?

i. Aspirational Commitments to Human Rights

A number of states and localities have adopted resolutions affirming the importance of human rights and their allegiance to human rights principles and expressing support for specific international conventions.

Consider two approaches:

CARRBORO, NORTH CAROLINA BOARD OF ALDERMAN, A RESOLUTION ADOPTING THE UNIVERSAL DECLARATION OF HUMAN RIGHTS AS GUIDING PRINCIPLES

Resolution No. 89/2008–2009 (April 21, 2009).

WHEREAS, Carrboro is a leader among American cities in advancing human rights and human dignity; and

WHEREAS, Carrboro promotes an engaged citizenry that cares for the human rights and dignity of others; and

WHEREAS, the Human Rights Center of Chapel Hill and Carrboro have petitioned the Board of Aldermen to adopt the Universal Declaration of Human Rights, promulgated by the United Nations General Assembly on December 10, 1948 and signed and agreed to by all countries, including the United States; and

WHEREAS, having been promulgated in 1948, Carrboro acknowledges that certain principles set forth in the Universal Declaration of Human Rights should be updated as follows:

a. The preamble, in paragraph two, should make reference to "humankind" rather than "mankind";

b. Article 2 should also contain the statuses of ethnicity, sexual orientation and gender identity or gender expression;

c. Article 10 should acknowledge the rights of all persons to enter into civil marriage with their partner of choice, regardless of gender;

d. Article 16(1) should make reference to "people" rather than "men and women." It should add "ethnicity" to the limitation clause.

e. Article 16(3) makes reference to "family." It should be noted that the definition of "family" has evolved greatly since 1948. Historically it was known as "the basic unit in society traditionally consisting of two parents rearing their children," while today it further includes "any of various social units differing from but regarded as equivalent to the traditional family."

f.   Article 25(2) should be revised to include "fatherhood" and should delete the reference to "born in or out of wedlock."

g.   Throughout the document, any reference to "his," "him" or "himself" should be stated "them" or "themselves" in order to be gender inclusive.

WHEREAS, the principles set forth in the Universal Declaration of Human Rights (*with clarification above*) will guide the spirit of the laws, practices, and policies carried out with and on behalf of the residents of Carrboro; and

WHEREAS, the Human Rights Center has asked that the Board appoint an advisory committee to report to the Board on a semi-annual basis about the condition of human rights.

NOW, THEREFORE, BE IT RESOLVED:

Section 1. The Board hereby adopts the Universal Declaration of Human Rights as guiding principles.

Section 2. This resolution shall become effective upon adoption.

CITY COUNCIL OF CHICAGO, EXPRESSION OF SUPPORT FOR CONVENTION ON THE RIGHTS OF THE CHILD
Res. No. R2009–143 (Feb. 11, 2009).

WHEREAS, the City of Chicago has demonstrated a sustained commitment toward ensuring the realization of human rights for all, including rights for women, laborers, and the homeless; and

WHEREAS, the City of Chicago has high aspirations and standards for its children and families and is constantly seeking ways to improve their lives and ensure an environment that protects children's health; and

WHEREAS, the City of Chicago is one of only two U.S. cities distinguished as a UNICEF Child Friendly City; and

WHEREAS, The Convention on the Rights of the Child was adopted by the United Nations General Assembly on November 20, 1989 and became effective as an international treaty on September 2, 1990; and

WHEREAS, The Convention on the Rights of the Child is the only international human rights treaty to recognize the vital role of the family and the parent child relationship; and

WHEREAS, the United States and Somalia are the only two countries that have not ratified the Convention on the Rights of the Child; and

WHEREAS, the adoption of the Convention on the Rights of the Child enhances Chicago's stature as a municipal leader in promoting the care and well-being of children; and

WHEREAS, the adoption of the Convention on the Rights of the Child by the City Council is consistent with Chicago's past support of securing fundamental rights for the most vulnerable; and

WHEREAS, the adoption of the Convention on the Rights of the Child affirms Chicago's commitment to protect children and promote their rights; and

WHEREAS, the Convention would provide a single, comprehensive framework within which the diverse arms of the Chicago city government can assess and address, in a consistent manner, the rights and protections of our children; now, therefore

IT IS RESOLVED, that the Mayor and members of the City Council of Chicago, gathered here on the 11th day of February, 2009 A.D., do hereby affirm their support of the Convention on the Rights of the Child; and,

IT IS FURTHER RESOLVED, that the Mayor and members of the City Council of Chicago will advance policies and practices that are in harmony with the principles of the Convention on the Rights of the Child in all city agencies and organizations that address issues directly affecting the City's children.

NOTES & QUESTIONS

1.   The Carrboro resolution is unique in that it seeks to bring the language contained in the 1948 UDHR up to date, for example making it gender inclusive and sensitive to a range of family structures. Does the need to update the UDHR suggest something about its continued relevance? Does its adaptability to local norms strengthen or weaken its relevance as a universal document?

2.   What does it mean for a city to adopt the UDHR as a set of guiding principles? How might advocates use the language in the resolution to urge a particular policy or practice? For example, how might advocates seeking to challenge a city's practice of criminalizing homelessness engage the language of a local UDHR resolution?

3.   Carrboro's resolution does not create legal obligations for the town, but it does include a potential implementation mechanism. Reflecting input from local advocates, namely the Human Rights Center of Carrboro and Chapel Hill, the resolution calls for an advisory body to monitor and report to

the Board on human rights conditions in the town. If established in the future, the advisory body could encourage the town to use the resolution proactively, and identify areas where local policies comply with the principles of the UDHR and where more work is needed.

Even without the advisory board in place, the Carrboro resolution has been invoked by members of the community as a basis for voicing their concerns to the Board, such as attempts to close a community center that served the town's immigrant population. It has also been cited as support for local resolutions encouraging fair trade. *See* Columbia Law School Human Rights Institute, *Bringing Human Rights Home: How State and Local Governments Can Use Human Rights to Advance Local Policy* (Dec. 2012), *available at* http://web.law.columbia.edu/sites/default/files/microsites/human-rights-institute/files/Bringing%20Human%20Rights%20Home.pdf.   How might the resolution have been drafted to provide more "teeth" for enforcement? Why do you think the resolution was drafted in the way that it was?

4.   Is the Chicago resolution more enforceable than the Carrboro resolution? How might children's rights advocates in Chicago invoke the language of the CRC resolution in support of their policy efforts and individual clients?

5.   Aspirational resolutions often result from sustained and grassroots advocacy from affected communities and dedicated human rights advocates. As its text reveals, the Carrboro resolution was the result of efforts by a local advocacy group, the Human Rights Center of Carrboro and Chapel Hill. The Chicago resolution was similarly the result of collaboration among local advocates. A broad coalition of organizations participated and helped fashion the resolution as a tool to help address a range of issues, from dignity in schools and youth homelessness to police mistreatment of youth and gang violence. With support from the Commissioner of the Department of Family and Support Services, the Mayor of Chicago introduced the resolution, and it was adopted by the City Council in 2009. How might such local community involvement aid in implementation of the resolutions? Does community involvement help build legitimacy for such measures, bolstering Professor Powell's and Resnik's suggestion that local implementation of human rights helps to overcome the democratic deficit of human rights law?

6.   Short of pledging to draw upon human rights treaties as guiding principles, several states and localities have adopted resolutions supporting U.S. ratification of specific treaties. *See, e.g.,* City Council of Philadelphia, Resolution Supporting U.S. Ratification of CEDAW, Phil. Pa. Res. 980148 (Mar. 12, 1998); Joint Resolution, JRS 33, 1997–98 Legislature (Vt. 1997) (urging the U.S. ratification of the CRC). How might advocates draw upon such resolutions in state and local advocacy around issues pertaining to the rights contained in these treaties? What impact might these resolutions have on national efforts to ratify human rights treaties? Do they, and resolutions such as the Chicago resolution discussed above, create the potential for

political backlash? Note that there is a growing trend of state legislatures approving resolutions opposing U.S. ratification of the Convention on the Rights of the Child, discussed *infra* **Part D**.

———————

Complementing and recognizing the growing number of resolutions and other actions affirming local governments' commitment to human rights, in June 2013, the U.S. Conference of Mayors, which is comprised of the mayors of over 1300 cities in the United States, adopted a resolution committing its members to uphold and promote international human rights locally.

UNITED STATES CONFERENCE OF MAYORS, RESOLUTION, PROMOTING AND ENCOURAGING INTERNATIONAL HUMAN RIGHTS

Adopted Resolutions, 81st Annual Meeting (June 2013).

WHEREAS, the United States has played a prominent role in promoting international human rights since the founding of the United Nations in 1945; and

WHEREAS, international human rights are articulated in the Universal Declaration of Human Rights and a broad range of laws, norms and values that recognize and promote the fundamental humanity and dignity of every person, as well as the necessity of fairness and opportunity for all people, and that enable people to meet their basic needs and to enjoy basic civil, political, social, economic and cultural rights; and

WHEREAS, there is an international human rights system, of which the United States is a part, which includes a framework of charters, treaties, court cases and laws, and international monitoring bodies, all of which are recognized and accepted by the vast majority of the global community of nations and individuals; and

. . .

WHEREAS, the United States has emphasized its commitment to human rights at home and abroad, which requires it to assess domestic conditions in light of universally accepted standards, take steps to promote and protect the full range of human rights, and engage constructively with international human rights institutions; and

WHEREAS, a basic tenet of the human rights framework is that human rights must start at home, and must involve and reflect the needs and expertise of local communities, and that governments have an affirmative obligation to respect, protect and fulfill these rights; and

WHEREAS, mayors are on the front lines of ensuring equality, combating discrimination and enabling access to affordable housing, healthcare and education, among other human rights issues; and

WHEREAS, The United States Conference of Mayors has endorsed international agreements, including the Vienna Declaration in Support of Cost Effective and Evidence-Based Drug Policy and supported United Nations Conferences, such as Rio +20; and led cities in a global effort to comply with the Kyoto Protocol through its Climate Protection Agreement; and

WHEREAS, The United States Conference of Mayors is committed to ensuring that cities around the world initiate and share innovative ideas and programs; and has encouraged international exchanges; and

. . .

WHEREAS, a majority of people in the United States believe that human rights include equal opportunities regardless of gender and race, being treated fairly in the criminal justice system, freedom from discrimination, freedom from torture or abuse by law enforcement, equal access to quality public education, access to health care, living in a clean environment; fair pay for workers to meet the basic needs for food and housing; and keeping personal behavior and choices private; and

WHEREAS, The United States Conference of Mayors has promoted policies to address fundamental human rights and needs, including health, poverty reduction, homelessness, equality for LGBT persons, non-citizens and disparities in incarceration rates; and

WHEREAS, as has been demonstrated in numerous cities, including Seattle, Washington, Salt Lake City, Utah, Los Angeles, California, Eugene, Oregon and El Paso, Texas, international human rights can provide a powerful framework for, and play an instrumental role in, efforts by cities to ensure opportunity and equality for their communities,

NOW, THEREFORE, BE IT RESOLVED, The United States Conference of Mayors recognizes and affirms the importance of the international human rights principles of dignity, equality and opportunity; and

BE IT FURTHER RESOLVED members of The United States Conference of Mayors commit to uphold and promote international human rights, in collaboration with state and local government agencies and officials, as well as local communities; and

BE IT FURTHER RESOLVED members of the United States Conference of Mayors commit to explore opportunities to incorporate international human rights into local policy and practice, and to support broader efforts to advance human rights principles locally.

NOTES & QUESTIONS

1.   Compare the USCM resolution to the Carrboro, North Carolina and Chicago, Illinois resolutions. Does the USCM resolution commit its members to uphold or consider any specific human rights treaties or take any particular action? What considerations do you think went into drafting the resolution?

2.   What is the potential impact or utility of the USCM's resolution? How might advocates draw on the resolution in advocating with local officials around human rights concerns?

ii.   Reframing Local Concerns as Human Rights Issues

Going a step beyond aspirational statements, some states and localities are framing specific local concerns as human rights issues and invoking human rights law in crafting solutions for particular local problems. In November 2011, the City Council of Madison, Wisconsin passed a resolution declaring that housing is a human right. The resolution cites statistics concerning the prevalence of homelessness in Madison, recognizes that homelessness and poverty are systemic and interrelated problems, particularly for people of color, those in the LGBTQ community, the elderly, and immigrants, and notes the links between employment, mental health, and housing. The resolution further acknowledges that because the U.S. has ratified the ICCPR and the CERD, these treaties have the force of law and require government action.

COMMON COUNCIL OF CITY OF MADISON, THAT HOUSING BE
RECOGNIZED AS A HUMAN RIGHT, AND THAT THE CITY OF
MADISON WILL WORK WITH DANE COUNTY, SURROUNDING
MUNICIPALITIES, AND COMMUNITY PARTNERS TO DEVELOP A
HOUSING PLAN AND ADDRESS HOUSING ISSUES
IN THE REGION

Res. 11–00984 (Nov. 29, 2011).

WHEREAS, in 2009 in Dane County, 2,413 individuals in families were turned away from shelter, 92% of those were individuals with families, and 94% of turned-away families were rejected due to lack of shelter space or lack of funds to pay for motel vouchers; and

. . .

WHEREAS, in 2008, 776 children attending schools in Madison were homeless; and

WHEREAS, homelessness impacts a disproportionate number of people of color in Dane County, with 71% in shelter identifying as non-white, 83% of families, 64% of single women, 54% of single men and 48%

of unaccompanied youth identified as non-white, and African Americans make up the largest minority group; and

WHEREAS, in the U.S., 20%–40% of homeless youth identify as lesbian, gay, bi-sexual, transgender and/or queer (LGBTQ), while only 3%–5% of the overall youth population identifies as LGBTQ; 44% of gay homeless youth are African-American and 26% of gay homeless youth identify as Latino; 62% of transgender homeless youth are African-American and 20% of transgender homeless youth are Latino; and LGBTQ youth are twice as likely to be the victims of sexual crimes while homeless; and

WHEREAS, immigrants are more likely to face barriers to enforcing their housing rights including language barriers, cultural mistrust, fear of government agencies, fear of retaliation, lack of familiarity with applicable laws, and lack of familiarity with judicial and administrative procedures for enforcing their rights; and

WHEREAS, in 2009, 69 persons in the Dane County shelter system were 62 years and older and AARP reports that in the U.S. in 2001, 18% of homeowners and 38% of renters over the age of 65 spent more than one half of their monthly income on housing; and

. . .

WHEREAS, unstable housing causes children to suffer from slowed development, emotional problems, and underachievement in education; and

. . .

WHEREAS, the U.S. has ratified the International Covenant on Civil and Political Rights (ICCPR), giving it the force of law, which protects individuals from discrimination based on property and economic status; and

WHEREAS, the UN Human Rights Committee has asked our government to take "adequate and adequately implemented" measures to remedy the human rights abuse of having a 12% African-American population but having African-Americans making up 50% of all homeless in the U.S.; and

WHEREAS, the U.S. has ratified the Convention on the Elimination of All Forms of Racial Discrimination (CERD), which requires the government to eliminate all racially discriminatory effects of government laws and rules; and

WHEREAS, the City of Madison, as a recipient of federal funds for housing and development, has an obligation to affirmatively further fair housing; and

WHEREAS, the United States has signed onto the Universal Declaration of Human Rights, which provides that "Everyone has the right to a standard of living adequate for the health and well-being of himself and of his family, including . . . housing . . ."; and

WHEREAS, the human right to housing includes legal security of tenure, availability of services and infrastructure, affordability, habitability, accessibility, location, and cultural adequacy; and

WHEREAS, we join the efforts of Washington D.C., Cook County, Illinois, Minneapolis, New York City and Los Angeles to recognize and progressively realize the human right to housing at the local level;

NOW, THEREFORE, BE IT RESOLVED that housing be recognized as a human right and that all people who desire a place of shelter and stable long-term housing be prioritized to have this basic need met both temporarily and permanently. In doing so, the City of Madison recommits to the goals in its Comprehensive Plan that call for the availability of safe, decent and sanitary and distinctive housing for all residents as well as the objectives and policies that accompany that goal. The City of Madison also recommits to the goals and objectives in the Community Plan to Prevent and End Homelessness in Dane County.

BE IT FURTHER RESOLVED that the City of Madison will initiate the process of developing a Housing Plan and consider creating a staff position that will be responsible for housing policy.

NOTES & QUESTIONS

1.   The Madison resolution is part of a larger effort to establish a human right to housing in the United States. Advocates are working to establish a strong record documenting housing rights violations under international law, including through visits of U.N. experts, treaty reporting, and the Universal Periodic Review. *See* Eric S. Tars & Déodonné Bhattarai, *Opening the Door to Housing*, 45 Clearinghouse Rev. 197 (2011). Do you think the Madison resolution is effective in re-framing the "local" problem of homelessness as an international human rights concern? Given the limited protections for economic and social rights under the U.S. Constitution, what is the added value of framing homelessness as a human rights concern?

2.   What does it mean for Madison to "progressively realize" the human right to housing? Local groups that supported the Madison resolution wanted to ensure that it would lead to concrete action and worked with city council members to include mechanisms for implementation. This includes calling on the City to create a new staff position to oversee a needs assessment and responsive housing strategy, and to strive to use public funds to increase affordable, available housing to address the local concerns about housing and homelessness. How effective do you think these mechanisms will be in

implementing the promise of the right to housing in Madison? Are there other provisions that would have given the measure more teeth?

3.   For an analysis of the impact of the Madison Right to Housing resolution upon the two-year anniversary of its passage, *see* Staff Editorial, *Madison Marks Two Years Since Passing Housing Rights Resolution*, The Madison Times, Nov. 26, 2013, http://legacy.themadisontimes.com/news_details.php?news_id=3341.

4.   Several cities, including Cincinnati, Ohio, Baltimore, Maryland, and Miami, Florida, have adopted resolutions declaring that freedom from domestic violence is a human right, grounded in international instruments, including the UDHR, and declaring that state and local governments bear responsibility for securing that right. *See, e.g.,* Cincinnati City Council, Res. 47–2011 (Oct. 5, 2011). These resolutions' articulation of domestic violence as a human rights concern is a departure from its more traditional framing under domestic law as a crime, a tort, a due process and equal protection violation, and as a civil rights concern. What is the added value of framing domestic violence as a human rights concern? Is there something unique about the role of state and local officials in protecting against domestic violence? We revisit these resolutions in **Chapter VIII**.

iii. Conducting Human Rights Based Audits and Impact Assessments

A number of governments are using human rights standards as benchmarks to understand the potential impact of their policies and decisions, to measure program effectiveness, and to identify barriers to reaching intended beneficiaries. These assessments encourage state and local authorities to weigh human rights concerns when formulating and executing policies.

San Francisco provided an early example of such local implementation of human rights principles. In 1998, San Francisco adopted a local ordinance implementing the human rights norms and principles of the Convention on the Elimination of All Forms of Discrimination Against Women (CEDAW), requiring that government agencies and departments in San Francisco implement the standards of the CEDAW and "integrate gender equity and human rights principles into all of its operations."[18] Under the ordinance, the city must eradicate all policies that discriminate, including those that have a discriminatory impact, and proactively identify barriers to the exercise of human rights. The ordinance also calls for human rights education for city departments and employees. The Commission on the Status of Women is designated as the implementing agency and is required to conduct gender analyses of

---

[18] S.F., Cal., Admin. Code ch. 12K.4(a) (2011) (Local Implementation of the United Nations Convention on the Elimination of All Forms of Discrimination Against Women (CEDAW), Ordinance No. 128–98 (Apr. 13 1998)).

the budget, services and employment practices of selected city departments to identify barriers and discrimination against women. That ordinance has been amended to include reference to the CERD and the need to recognize intersections of race and gender discrimination.[19]

As a result of the gender analyses, the Commission identified myriad discriminatory practices, raising awareness around the need for policy changes to benefit both women and men. Consider the following excerpt from a report by the San Francisco Department on the Status of Women analyzing the impact of the CEDAW ordinance ten years after its enactment.

SAN FRANCISCO DEPARTMENT ON THE STATUS OF WOMEN, CEDAW IN ACTION: LOCAL IMPLEMENTATION IN THE CITY AND COUNTY OF SAN FRANCISCO

5, 7–8, 11 (2010).

In 1999, the CEDAW Task Force selected 2 departments to undergo the first gender analyses:

- The Department of Public Works was selected for its large size, non-traditional employment opportunities for women, and provision of public infrastructure services such as street construction and building design.

- The Juvenile Probation Department, which serves youth in the criminal justice system and operates Juvenile Hall, provided an opportunity to examine service provision to an increasing population of young women involved in the criminal justice system.

First and foremost, the very process of conducting a CEDAW gender analysis created a new awareness of gender-related issues at both departments. Most departmental personnel were not only receptive to the analysis as a proactive approach to eliminating discrimination, but some staff members, on their own initiative, began to change the way they evaluated their policies and programs to serve all persons more effectively.

Top management at the Juvenile Probation Department stated that the gender analysis had a decisive impact on agency operations by helping promote gender specific services for girls at Juvenile Hall. A

---

[19] S.F., Cal., Admin. Code ch. 12K.3 (2011) (stating that, "[i]n implementing CEDAW, the City recognizes the connection between racial discrimination, as articulated in the International Convention on the Elimination of All Forms of Racial Discrimination [CERD], and discrimination against women"); *id.* at ch. 12K.1(e) (recognizing that discrimination based on gender is "interconnected and often overlaps with discrimination based on race and other criteria"); *id.* at ch. 12K.1(f)(3) (stating the "the need to consider the intersection of gender and race in particular recognizing the unique experiences of women of color").

specific "Girls Unit" was later created in Juvenile Hall to provide gender specific, trauma-focused services for girls whose needs, it was found, were not being addressed by programming that was originally created for boys.

Through the gender analysis, staff at the Department of Public Works acknowledged that service delivery impacts women and men differently. For example, women's safety at night depended on such factors as the number and the placement of streetlights in the City. It was pointed out that a lack of curb cuts on sidewalk corners impacted women disproportionately. Curb cuts facilitate the work of caregivers to the very young in strollers as well as to the elderly or disabled who are wheelchair bound. These caregivers are commonly women. Staff also recognized the need to make specific efforts to recruit women into non-traditional employment positions.

After completing these 2 gender analyses, the CEDAW Task Force reviewed carefully which 5 new departments would follow best on the work of the previous 2 departments.

Adult Probation Department: This department provides services for and monitors individuals on probation. Workplace flexibility issues came to the forefront of the analysis.

The department found that after a new telecommuting policy was instituted to the 18-member investigations unit, it became one of the most productive units. It was clear that telecommuting, or the ability to have flexibility in work location, helped retain and recruit staff because it made it easier for those with caretaking responsibilities to manage their work and family lives. This program thus helped both the employees and the department create an efficient and productive work environment. This information led the department to expand the telecommuting and flexible work policies option for its employees.

. . .

Case Study: The Department of the Environment

. . .

The following are some of the highlights from the original gender analysis and the 2009 update the Department of the Environment presented to the Commission on the Status of Women:

Recruitment and Retention of Diverse Employees

• The Department surveyed all employees in order to get feedback about issues of concern. This process revealed that many employees wanted the opportunity to provide direct feedback about all aspects of Departmental functions. Now the Departmental leadership conducts annual staff surveys and responds directly to comments made during their annual staff retreat.

• Many Department positions are non-traditional jobs for women and minorities. When the original gender analysis was conducted, women held 33% of professional positions, while the labor pool data showed that the available labor pool of women professionals in these relevant areas was 48%. The Department also only had one person of color in a professional level position. In February 2009, the Department reported significant increases in the number of women and minority employees. Out of 68 employees, 69% are currently women and 39% are minorities. These numbers reflect expanded recruitment efforts to ensure that women and minorities are part of the applicant pool.

Grants: The CEDAW gender analysis led the Department to start analyzing grants in a more holistic way. In addition to examining whether a grant achieves the agency's environmental goals, staff also now looks at which communities and individuals receive grant monies dispersed by the Department in order to ensure equitable distribution of public monies across diverse communities. The Department reviews who holds leadership positions at grantee organizations and who is hired with monies granted by the Department. The Department is also, for the first time, working with the City's Economic and Workforce Development agency to place low income individuals in training positions for non-traditional jobs.

Flexible Work Policies:

• When the Department began its CEDAW review, senior managers were also considering whether to adopt an "Emergency Ride Home" program to encourage use of alternative transportation in the City. This program provides a free or low-cost ride home in cases of emergency for any employee working in San Francisco who used an alternative form of transportation to get to work that day (e.g., carpooling, public transit, bicycling, and walking). The gender analysis findings helped provide the justification and impetus for the program by noting that it would greatly benefit those with caregiving responsibilities (predominantly women). As of 2009, the Department's program has expanded significantly, and the agency now assists private sector companies throughout San Francisco in creating similar programs.

• The Department also offers 2 popular flex-time programs. The 9/80 program allows employees to choose to work eight 9-hour days and one 8-hour day in a 2 week period so that they can have the tenth day off. The Department's flex-time program allows employees to begin their work days any time between 6:30 and 9:30 a.m. As of February 2009, 51 of the 68 employees use the 9/80 program and 42 employees use the flex-time program. The Department has found that these various scheduling options have increased employee productivity.

- The Department of the Environment used the gender analysis tool and its findings to not only create individual programs and policies to improve the lives of employees and constituents, but also to create a culture of gender equality and freedom from discriminatory practices that has continued to expand as the Department grows.

. . .

The San Francisco Gender Equality Principles Initiative

San Francisco's CEDAW Ordinance states that "there is a need to work toward implementing the principles of CEDAW in the private sector." It also calls for gender analysis of private entities to the extent permitted by the law. The first 10 years of CEDAW implementation in San Francisco focused on assessing and improving gender equality within government entities. As the City approached the 10th anniversary of the CEDAW Ordinance, the Department on the Status of Women decided to focus its efforts on promoting CEDAW principles in the private sector through the San Francisco Gender Equality Principles Initiative (GEP Initiative). The GEP Initiative is a partnership between the Department on the Status of Women, Calvert Group, Ltd., one of the largest families of socially responsible mutual funds in the United States, and Verité, an international labor and human rights monitoring organization.

The GEP Initiative is a groundbreaking program that helps companies around the world achieve greater gender equality and build more productive workplaces through practical implementation of the Gender Equality Principles (GEP). The GEP are a set of aspirational principles focusing on 7 fundamental gender equality issue areas:

- Employment and Compensation
- Work-Life Balance and Career Development
- Health, Safety and Freedom from Violence
- Management and Governance
- Business, Supply Chain, and Marketing Practices
- Civic and Community Engagement
- Transparency and Accountability

The GEP Initiative provides companies with practical standards, tools, and resources that can be used to improve gender equality from the factory floor to the boardroom.

In 2008–2009, the initial year of the project, 18 of the San Francisco Bay Area's largest companies and nonprofits joined the GEP Initiative, including Deloitte, IBM, McKesson, The San Francisco Foundation, Charles Schwab, and Symantec.

Between 2008–2010 the GEP Initiative has been hosting quarterly roundtables, each one focused on 1 of the 7 principles, to foster peer-to-peer discussion between companies on best practices and challenges related to promoting gender equality. The companies work with the GEP Initiative partners to create self-assessment tools and compile resources to help private sector companies implement innovative policies and practices related to gender equality.

The GEP is based on the Calvert Women's Principles. These 2 documents form the basis of the Women's Empowerment Principles, a set of global women's principles that are being developed by the United Nations Global Compact. They have also shaped the Gender in Sustainability Reporting Guide of the International Finance Corporation (IFC), a member of the World Bank Group, and the Global Reporting Initiative (GRI).

. . .

NOTES & QUESTIONS

1. A primary goal of the San Francisco ordinance is to promote government accountability for gender equality. *See* San Francisco Department on the Status of Women, CEDAW in Action: Local Implementation in the City and County of San Francisco 12 (2010). Does the above report suggest that the measure achieves that objective? In what ways? Is the San Francisco CEDAW ordinance a local human rights implementation success story?

2. As the report reflects, the San Francisco Department on the Status of Women is using its CEDAW authority to develop and promote human rights standards for both the public and the private sector. What is the potential impact of this approach on the private sector? Do you think this is an appropriate vehicle for encouraging human rights compliance by businesses? What might be some of the challenges of implementation?

3. Other localities have considered and adopted similar approaches. Drawing from the UDHR, the government of Eugene, Oregon has developed a tool, called the "triple bottom line framework," which encourages city decision makers to take into account the environmental, equity and economic impacts and benefits of policy proposals, budget choices, and other city projects and initiatives. This assessment tool prioritizes the protection and fulfillment of the full panoply of rights in the UDHR. *See* City of Eugene, Triple Bottom Line Framework, *available at* https://www.eugene-or.gov/index.aspx?NID= 512. The tool has informed policy decisions related to the assessment of brownfield sites and transportation investments. *See* City of Eugene Sustainability Commission, Meeting Agenda (Mar. 20, 2013), http://www.eugene-or.gov/ArchiveCenter/ViewFile/Item/2277. It has also influenced programming and budget allocations within the city's recreation department. *See* City of Eugene Library, Recreation and Cultural Services, 2010 Annual

Report, *available at* http://issuu.com/cityofeugenerecreation/docs/eugenelrcs annualreport2010web.

4.   In New York City, the proposed New York City Human Rights in Government Operations Audit Law (Human Rights GOAL) seeks to integrate human rights principles of dignity and equality (based on the CERD and the CEDAW) into local policy and practice by requiring that the city train its personnel in human rights, undertake a human rights analysis of the operations of each city department, program and entity, and create action plans for how the city will integrate human rights principles. *See* N.Y., N.Y., File No. Int. 0731–2008 (as introduced by New York City Council Members Mar. 12, 2008). The bill would create a taskforce comprised of community and government representatives to oversee its implementation and would provide avenues for community participation in the development of the human rights analysis and action plan. Despite significant support from grassroots and national advocacy groups, and a strong contingent of city council co-sponsors, the measure was stalled for years during former Mayor Bloomberg's tenure. What might account for political opposition to the measure? What strategies might its supporters use to overcome the opposition? We return to these questions in **Chapter X**.

5.   A number of cities, in the United States and internationally, are self-proclaimed "human rights cities." Human rights cities explicitly commit themselves to using human rights norms and strategies to improve local governance, for example by informing city policies or specific initiatives. *See* Stephen P. Marks *et al.*, Human Rights Cities: Civic Engagement for Societal Development (2008), *available at* http://www.pdhre.org/Human_Rights_ Cities_Book.pdf. In the United States, Pittsburgh, Washington D.C., Eugene, and Boston are all examples of cities which have designated themselves as human rights cities. International associations also promote the creation of human rights cities around the world. United Cities and Local Governments (UCLG) actively promotes human rights at the local level and fosters the creation of human rights cities. *See Adoption in Florence of the Global Charter-Agenda for Human Rights in the City*, *News*, United Cities and Local Governments (Dec. 16, 2011, 7:35 PM), http://www.uclg.org/en/media/news/ adoption-florence-global-charter-agenda-human-rights-city.   The   World Human Rights Cities Forum gathers representatives, including U.N. experts, academics, and representatives from human rights cities around the world to discuss strategies and "good practices" for implementing human rights at the local level. International examples of human rights cities include Graz, Australia, Edmonton, Canada, and Rosario, Argentina.

iv.   Reporting on Local Compliance with Human Rights Treaties

State and local officials have also begun to engage in human rights treaty reporting, using periodic reporting to the U.N. human rights treaty bodies as an opportunity to assess their own compliance with human rights principles. Berkeley, California was the first U.S. city to file periodic reports on its fulfillment of obligations under treaties the United States has ratified. It has used reporting to highlight the City's efforts to address homelessness, as well as to note achievement gaps in education and LGBT concerns, among others. The California State Assembly recently followed suit, passing legislation that calls on the state Attorney General to "publicize the text" of the ICCPR, the ICERD and the ICAT, and requests that state and local officials prepare the required periodic reports for the U.N. Committees overseeing implementation of these treaties.[20]

NOTES & QUESTIONS

1.   What is the value of treaty reporting in promoting state and local government accountability for human rights? What is the potential impact of state and local officials contributing data and information to official U.S. reports to the United Nations? Should state and local officials report directly to the U.N. bodies, rather than contribute to the U.S. State Department's reports? Why or why not? We will return to these questions in **Chapter VIII**.

2.   Professor David Kaye suggests that states can play an even greater role in implementation of U.S. human rights treaty obligations through direct incorporation of the ratified treaties into state law, allowing individuals to bring actions in state court for state violation of the treaties' substantive provisions. *See* David Kaye, *State Execution of the International Covenant on Civil and Political Rights*, 3 U.C. Irvine L. Rev. 95 (2013). What are some of the potential benefits and challenges of this approach?

C. THE ROLE OF STATE, LOCAL AND TRIBAL HUMAN RIGHTS COMMISSIONS

There are over 150 state and local commissions or agencies mandated by state, county or city governments to enforce human and civil rights, and/or to conduct research, training, and public education and issue policy recommendations on human intergroup relations and civil and human rights. Many state and local commissions date back to the 1940s and 1950s, when human rights and race relations commissions were established to address racial tension and violence that was erupting around the country. Others were formed later, in the 1960s and 1970s, in reaction to the civil rights movement and in response to calls to eradicate racial discrimination. In addition to state and local commissions, the Navajo Nation recently established a human rights commission to protect and promote the human rights of Navajo Nation citizens. Although these commissions go by different names and have varying missions, they all generally operate to prevent and eliminate discrimination through a

---

[20] Assemb. Con. Res. No. 129, Leg., 2009–10 Reg. Sess. (Cal. 2010) (Relative to International Treaties).

variety of means, including enforcing anti-discrimination laws and engaging in community education and training in an effort to prevent discrimination from occurring.

State, local, and tribal human rights and human relations commissions are increasingly interested in undertaking human rights activity, as well. For example, the City of Portland, Oregon's Human Rights Commission has incorporated the Universal Declaration of Human Rights into its bylaws. The Eugene, Oregon City Council voted to broaden its Human Rights Commission's mandate to explicitly support and promote the full range of human rights within the Universal Declaration of Human Rights. Even prior to this official change in mandate, the Commission engaged in community education and outreach efforts, as well as conducted trainings for city advisory boards, commissions, staff, and managers, raising awareness about the potential for an international human rights framework to advance the equality and dignity of local residents. In 2014, the Tennessee Human Rights Commission held a series of state-wide hearings on the status of human rights in the state. The umbrella organization of state and local human rights and human relations agencies, the International Association of Official Human Rights Agencies (IAOHRA), has adopted resolutions proclaiming support for domestic incorporation of human rights treaties, with its membership pledging to undertake actions to integrate human rights standards and strategies into their daily functioning.

NOTES & QUESTIONS

1. Why might state, local, and tribal human rights commissions offer particularly promising opportunities for local implementation of human rights? Is there something particular to their relationship with other government agencies and their non-elected status that might help or hinder their efforts in this regard?

2. How else might state, local, and tribal human rights and human relations commissions work to implement human rights? Risa Kaufman has suggested that these bodies could: (1) monitor and document human rights issues; (2) assess local policy and practice in light of international standards; (3) engage in human rights education; (4) incorporate human rights principles into advocacy efforts; (5) investigate human rights complaints; and (6) coordinate and implement local policy to integrate human rights principles. *See* Risa E. Kaufman, *State and Local Commissions as Sites for Domestic Human Rights Implementation, in* Human Rights in the United States 89 (Shareen Hertel & Kathryn Libal eds., 2010). What impact would adopting these strategies have on the role and mission of these bodies within their own communities?

D. CHALLENGES TO HUMAN RIGHTS IMPLEMENTATION BY STATE AND LOCAL GOVERNMENTS

Their potential notwithstanding, state and local governments face some limitations in their ability to engage in human rights activity and implement human rights norms and commitments at the local level. These challenges include doctrinal, political, and pragmatic concerns. As you read the following material, consider whether the value of the human rights approaches and activities discussed above is diminished or curtailed by these limitations, and what arguments exist for strengthening the possibilities of local human rights implementation.

i. Pre-emption

One potential concern with the state and local initiatives discussed in this section is that they interfere with, and thus are preempted by, the federal government's plenary foreign affairs powers. Indeed, the U.S. Supreme Court has invalidated state efforts to promote other countries' human rights compliance, holding that such activities infringe on the foreign-relations powers of the federal government. In *Crosby v. National Foreign Trade Council*, the Court held that state efforts to ban state procurement as a means of protesting foreign violations of human rights was preempted by a federal law similarly imposing sanctions, thus infringing on the federal prerogative to "speak with one voice" on foreign relations. Relatedly, the Court held in *American Insurance Association v. Garamendi*, that an Executive branch agreement with foreign countries preempted a state law forcing disclosure of insurance companies operating during World War II. As you read the following excerpts from these two cases, consider what state interests were being advanced by the state laws at issue. Consider too, the nature of the conflict that the Court found in each case, and whether similar conflicts might arise or exist with respect to the more "inwardly" focused state and local activities discussed previously in this chapter.

CROSBY V. NATIONAL FOREIGN TRADE COUNCIL

Supreme Court of the United States, 2000.
530 U.S. 363.

JUSTICE SOUTER delivered the opinion of the Court.

The issue is whether the Burma law of the Commonwealth of Massachusetts, restricting the authority of its agencies to purchase goods or services from companies doing business with Burma, is invalid under the Supremacy Clause of the National Constitution owing to its threat of frustrating federal statutory objectives. We hold that it is.

I

In June 1996, Massachusetts adopted "An Act Regulating State Contracts with Companies Doing Business with or in Burma (Myanmar)," 1996 Mass. Acts 239, ch. 130. The statute generally bars state entities from buying goods or services from any person (defined to include a business organization) identified on a "restricted purchase list" of those doing business with Burma.

. . .

In September 1996, three months after the Massachusetts law was enacted, Congress passed a statute imposing a set of mandatory and conditional sanctions on Burma. See Foreign Operations, Export Financing, and Related Programs Appropriations Act, 1997, § 570, 110 Stat. 3009–166 to 3009–167. . . .

First, it imposes three sanctions directly on Burma. It bans all aid to the Burmese Government except for humanitarian assistance, counternarcotics efforts, and promotion of human rights and democracy. The statute instructs United States representatives to international financial institutions to vote against loans or other assistance to or for Burma, and it provides that no entry visa shall be issued to any Burmese Government official unless required by treaty or to staff the Burmese mission to the United Nations. These restrictions are to remain in effect "[u]ntil such time as the President determines and certifies to Congress that Burma has made measurable and substantial progress in improving human rights practices and implementing democratic government."

Second, the federal Act authorizes the President to impose further sanctions subject to certain conditions. He may prohibit "United States persons" from "new investment" in Burma, and shall do so if he determines and certifies to Congress that the Burmese Government has physically harmed, rearrested, or exiled Daw Aung San Suu Kyi (the opposition leader selected to receive the Nobel Peace Prize), or has committed "large-scale repression of or violence against the Democratic opposition."

. . .

Third, the statute directs the President to work to develop "a comprehensive, multilateral strategy to bring democracy to and improve human rights practices and the quality of life in Burma." He is instructed to cooperate with members of the Association of Southeast Asian Nations (ASEAN) and with other countries having major trade and investment interests in Burma to devise such an approach, and to pursue the additional objective of fostering dialogue between the ruling State Law and Order Restoration Council (SLORC) and democratic opposition groups.

As for the procedural provisions of the federal statute, the fourth section requires the President to report periodically to certain congressional committee chairmen on the progress toward democratization and better living conditions in Burma as well as on the development of the required strategy. And the fifth part of the federal Act authorizes the President "to waive, temporarily or permanently, any sanction [under the federal Act] . . . if he determines and certifies to Congress that the application of such sanction would be contrary to the national security interests of the United States."

On May 20, 1997, the President issued the Burma Executive Order, Exec. Order No. 13047, 3 CFR 202 (1997 Comp.). He certified for purposes of § 570(b) that the Government of Burma had "committed large-scale repression of the democratic opposition in Burma" and found that the Burmese Government's actions and policies constituted "an unusual and extraordinary threat to the national security and foreign policy of the United States," a threat characterized as a national emergency. The President then prohibited new investment in Burma "by United States persons," any approval or facilitation by a United States person of such new investment by foreign persons, and any transaction meant to evade or avoid the ban.

. . .

III

A fundamental principle of the Constitution is that Congress has the power to preempt state law. Even without an express provision for preemption, we have found that state law must yield to a congressional Act in at least two circumstances. When Congress intends federal law to "occupy the field," state law in that area is preempted. And even if Congress has not occupied the field, state law is naturally preempted to the extent of any conflict with a federal statute. We will find preemption where it is impossible for a private party to comply with both state and federal law, and where "under the circumstances of [a] particular case, [the challenged state law] stands as an obstacle to the accomplishment and execution of the full purposes and objectives of Congress." What is a sufficient obstacle is a matter of judgment, to be informed by examining the federal statute as a whole and identifying its purpose and intended effects[.]. . . .

Applying this standard, we see the state Burma law as an obstacle to the accomplishment of Congress's full objectives under the federal Act. We find that the state law undermines the intended purpose and "natural effect" of at least three provisions of the federal Act, that is, its delegation of effective discretion to the President to control economic sanctions against Burma, its limitation of sanctions solely to United States persons and new investment, and its directive to the President to proceed diplomatically in developing a comprehensive, multilateral strategy toward Burma.

A

First, Congress clearly intended the federal Act to provide the President with flexible and effective authority over economic sanctions against Burma. Although Congress immediately put in place a set of initial sanctions (prohibiting bilateral aid, support for international financial assistance, and entry by Burmese officials into the United States), it authorized the President to terminate any and all of those measures upon determining and certifying that there had been progress in human rights and democracy in Burma. It invested the President with the further power to ban new investment by United States persons, dependent only on specific Presidential findings of repression in Burma. And, most significantly, Congress empowered the President "to waive, temporarily or permanently, any sanction [under the federal Act] . . . if he determines and certifies to Congress that the application of such sanction would be contrary to the national security interests of the United States."

This express investiture of the President with statutory authority to act for the United States in imposing sanctions with respect to the Government of Burma, augmented by the flexibility to respond to change by suspending sanctions in the interest of national security, recalls Justice Jackson's observation in *Youngstown Sheet & Tube Co. v. Sawyer,* 343 U.S. 579, 635 (1952): "When the President acts pursuant to an express or implied authorization of Congress, his authority is at its maximum, for it includes all that he possesses in his own right plus all that Congress can delegate." Within the sphere defined by Congress, then, the statute has placed the President in a position with as much discretion to exercise economic leverage against Burma, with an eye toward national security, as our law will admit. And it is just this plenitude of Executive authority that we think controls the issue of preemption here. The President has been given this authority not merely to make a political statement but to achieve a political result, and the fullness of his authority shows the importance in the congressional mind of reaching that result. It is simply implausible that Congress would have gone to such lengths to empower the President if it had been willing to compromise his effectiveness by deference to every provision of state statute or local ordinance that might, if enforced, blunt the consequences of discretionary Presidential action.

And that is just what the Massachusetts Burma law would do in imposing a different, state system of economic pressure against the Burmese political regime. . . . [T]he state statute penalizes some private action that the federal Act (as administered by the President) may allow, and pulls levers of influence that the federal Act does not reach. But the point here is that the state sanctions are immediate. This unyielding application undermines the President's intended statutory authority by making it impossible for him to restrain fully the coercive power of the national economy when he may choose to take the discretionary action open to him, whether he believes that the national interest requires sanctions to be lifted, or believes that the promise of lifting sanctions would move the Burmese regime in the democratic direction. Quite simply, if the Massachusetts law is enforceable the President has less to offer and less economic and diplomatic leverage as a consequence.

. . .

B

Congress manifestly intended to limit economic pressure against the Burmese Government to a specific range. The federal Act confines its reach to United States persons, imposes limited immediate sanctions, places only a conditional ban on a carefully defined area of "new investment," and pointedly exempts contracts to sell or purchase goods, services, or technology. These detailed provisions show that Congress's calibrated Burma policy is a deliberate effort "to steer a middle path."

The State has set a different course, and its statute conflicts with federal law at a number of points by penalizing individuals and conduct that Congress has explicitly exempted or excluded from sanctions.

. . .

The conflicts are not rendered irrelevant by the State's argument that there is no real conflict between the statutes because they share the same goals and because some companies may comply with both sets of restrictions. The fact of a common end hardly neutralizes conflicting means, and the fact that some companies may be able to comply with both sets of sanctions does not mean that the state Act is not at odds with achievement of the federal decision about the right degree of pressure to employ. Sanctions are drawn not only to bar what they prohibit but to allow what they permit, and the inconsistency of sanctions here undermines the congressional calibration of force.

C

Finally, the state Act is at odds with the President's intended authority to speak for the United States among the world's nations in developing a "comprehensive, multilateral strategy to bring democracy to and improve human rights practices and the quality of life in Burma." Congress called for Presidential cooperation with members of ASEAN and other countries in developing such a strategy, directed the President to encourage a dialogue between the Government of Burma and the democratic opposition, and required him to report to the Congress on the progress of his diplomatic efforts. As with Congress's explicit delegation to the President of power over economic sanctions, Congress's express command to the President to take the initiative for the United States among the international community invested him with the maximum authority of the National Government, in harmony with the President's own constitutional powers. This clear mandate and invocation of exclusively national power belies any suggestion that Congress intended the President's effective voice to be obscured by state or local action.

Again, the state Act undermines the President's capacity, in this instance for effective diplomacy. It is not merely that the differences between the state and federal Acts in scope and type of sanctions threaten to complicate discussions; they compromise the very capacity of the President to speak for the Nation with one voice in dealing with other governments. We need not get into any general consideration of limits of state action affecting foreign affairs to realize that the President's maximum power to persuade rests on his capacity to bargain for the benefits of access to the entire national economy without exception for enclaves fenced off willy-nilly by inconsistent political tactics. When such exceptions do qualify his capacity to present a coherent position on behalf of the national economy, he is weakened, of course, not only in dealing with the Burmese regime, but in working together with other nations in hopes of reaching common policy and "comprehensive" strategy.

. . .

IV

The State's remaining argument is unavailing. It contends that the failure of Congress to preempt the state Act demonstrates implicit permission. The State points out that Congress has repeatedly declined to enact express preemption provisions aimed at state and local sanctions, and it calls our attention to the large number of such measures passed against South Africa in the 1980's, which various authorities cited have thought were not preempted. The State stresses that Congress was aware of the state Act in 1996, but did not preempt it explicitly when it adopted its own Burma statute. The State would have us conclude that Congress's continuing failure to enact express preemption implies approval, particularly in light of occasional instances of express preemption of state sanctions in the past.

The argument is unconvincing on more than one level. A failure to provide for preemption expressly may reflect nothing more than the settled character of implied preemption doctrine that courts will dependably apply, and in any event, the existence of conflict cognizable under the Supremacy Clause does not depend on express congressional recognition that federal and state law may conflict. The State's inference of congressional intent is unwarranted here, therefore, simply because the silence of Congress is ambiguous. Since we never ruled on whether state and local sanctions against South Africa in the 1980's were preempted or otherwise invalid, arguable parallels between the two sets of federal and state Acts do not tell us much about the validity of the latter.

V

Because the state Act's provisions conflict with Congress's specific delegation to the President of flexible discretion, with limitation of sanctions to a limited scope of actions and actors, and with direction to develop a comprehensive, multilateral strategy under the federal Act, it is preempted, and its application is unconstitutional, under the Supremacy Clause.

The judgment of the Court of Appeals for the First Circuit is affirmed.

———————

Three years after striking the Massachusetts Burma law, the Supreme Court addressed the constitutionality of a California law requiring that any insurer doing business in the state must disclose information about insurance policies sold in Europe during and around the time of World War II. The law was aimed at identifying misappropriated Holocaust-era assets. The Court considered the California statute in light of the federal government's foreign affairs powers, particularly in relation to federal executive agreements pertaining to European insurers. As you read the decision, consider the Court's application of *Crosby* to this set of facts.

AMERICAN INSURANCE ASSOCIATION V. GARAMENDI

Supreme Court of the United States, 2003.
539 U.S. 396.

JUSTICE SOUTER delivered the opinion of the Court.

California's Holocaust Victim Insurance Relief Act of 1999 (HVIRA or Act) requires any insurer doing business in that State to disclose information about all policies sold in Europe between 1920 and 1945 by the company itself or any one "related" to it. The issue here is whether HVIRA interferes with the National Government's conduct of foreign relations. We hold that it does, with the consequence that the state statute is preempted.

A

The Nazi Government of Germany engaged not only in genocide and enslavement but theft of Jewish assets, including the value of insurance policies, and in particular policies of life insurance, a form of savings held by many Jews in Europe before the Second World War. Early on in the Nazi era, loss of livelihood forced Jews to cash in life insurance policies prematurely, only to have the government seize the proceeds of the repurchase, and many who tried to emigrate from Germany were forced to liquidate insurance policies to pay the steep "flight taxes" and other levies imposed by the Third Reich to keep Jewish assets from leaving the country. Before long, the Reich began simply seizing the remaining policies outright. . . . After the war, even a policy that had escaped confiscation was likely to be dishonored, whether because insurers denied its existence or claimed it had lapsed from unpaid premiums during the persecution, or because the government would not provide heirs with documentation of the policyholder's death.

. . .

These confiscations and frustrations of claims fell within the subject of reparations, which became a principal object of Allied diplomacy soon after the war. . . . [T]he United States was among the parties to an agreement [the Paris Agreement] to share seized assets with other western allies as settlement, as to each signatory nation, of "all its claims and those of its nationals against the former German Government and its Agencies, of a governmental or private nature, arising out of the war."

The effect of the Paris Agreement was curtailed, however, and attention to reparations intentionally deferred, when the western Allies moved to end their occupation and reestablish a sovereign Germany as a buffer against Soviet expansion.

. . .

In the meantime, the western Allies placed the obligation to provide restitution to victims of Nazi persecution on the new West German Government. . . . Despite a payout of more than 100 billion deutsch marks as of 2000, these measures left out many claimants and certain types of claims, and [after reunification of East and West Germany] . . . class-action lawsuits for restitution poured into United States courts against companies doing business in Germany during the Nazi era.

These suits generated much protest by the defendant companies and their governments, to the point that the Government of the United States took action to try to resolve "the last great compensation related negotiation arising out of World War II." From the beginning, the Government's position . . . stressed mediated settlement "as an alternative to endless litigation" promising little relief to aging Holocaust survivors. Ensuing negotiations at the national level produced the German Foundation Agreement . . . in which Germany agreed to enact legislation establishing a foundation funded with 10 billion deutsch marks contributed equally by the German Government and German companies, to be used to compensate all those "who suffered at the hands of German companies during the National Socialist era."

The willingness of the Germans to create a voluntary compensation fund was conditioned on some expectation of security from lawsuits in United States courts, and after extended dickering President Clinton put his weight behind two specific measures toward that end. First, the Government agreed that whenever a German company was sued on a Holocaust-era claim in an American court, the Government of the United States would submit a statement that "it would be in the foreign policy interests of the United States for the Foundation to be the exclusive forum and remedy for the resolution of all asserted claims against German companies arising from their involvement in the National Socialist era and World War II." Though unwilling to guarantee that its foreign policy interests would "in themselves provide an independent legal basis for dismissal," that being an issue for the courts, the Government agreed to tell courts "that U.S. policy interests favor dismissal on any valid legal ground." On top of that undertaking, the Government promised to use its "best efforts, in a manner it considers appropriate," to get state and local governments to respect the foundation as the exclusive mechanism.

As for insurance claims specifically, both countries agreed that the German Foundation would work with the International Commission on Holocaust Era Insurance Claims (ICHEIC) [which would] . . . negotiate with European insurers to provide information about unpaid insurance policies issued to Holocaust victims and settlement of claims brought under them. It has thus set up procedures for handling demands against participating insurers.

. . .

B

While these international efforts were underway, California's Department of Insurance began its own enquiry into the issue of unpaid claims under Nazi-era insurance policies, prompting state legislation designed to force payment by defaulting insurers.

. . .

State legislative efforts culminated the next year with passage of Assembly Bill No. 600, the first section of which amended the State's Code of Civil Procedure to allow state residents to sue in state court on insurance claims based on acts perpetrated in the Holocaust and extended the governing statute of limitations to December 31, 2010. The section of the bill codified as HVIRA, at issue here, requires "[a]ny insurer currently doing business in the state" to disclose the details of "life, property, liability, health, annuities, dowry, educational, or casualty insurance policies" issued "to persons in Europe, which were in effect between 1920 and 1945." The duty is to make disclosure not only about policies the particular insurer sold, but also about those sold by any "related company," including "any parent, subsidiary, reinsurer, successor in interest, managing general agent, or affiliate company of the insurer," whether or not the companies were related during the time when the policies subject to disclosure were sold. Nor is the obligation restricted to policies sold to "Holocaust victims" as defined in the Act, § 13802(a); it covers policies sold to anyone during that time. The insurer must report the current status of each policy, the city of origin, domicile, or address of each policyholder, and the names of the beneficiaries, all of which is to be put in a central registry open to the public. The mandatory penalty for default is suspension of the company's license to do business in the State, and there are misdemeanor criminal sanctions for falsehood in certain required representations about whether and to whom the proceeds of each policy have been distributed.

. . .

[I]n November 1999, Deputy Secretary [of Treasury] Eizenstat wrote to the insurance commissioner of California that although HVIRA "reflects a genuine commitment to justice for Holocaust victims and their families, it has the unfortunate effect of damaging the one effective means now at hand to process quickly and completely unpaid insurance claims from the Holocaust period, the [ICHEIC]."

. . .

III

The principal argument for preemption made by petitioners and the United States as *amicus curiae* is that HVIRA interferes with foreign policy of the Executive Branch, as expressed principally in the executive agreements with Germany, Austria, and France. The major premises of the argument, at least, are beyond dispute. There is, of course, no question that at some point an exercise of state power that touches on foreign relations must yield to the National Government's policy, given the "concern for uniformity in this country's dealings with foreign nations" that animated the Constitution's allocation of the foreign relations power to the National Government in the first place.

Nor is there any question generally that there is executive authority to decide what that policy should be. Although the source of the President's power to act in foreign affairs does not enjoy any textual detail, the historical gloss on the "executive Power" vested in Article II of the Constitution has recognized the President's "vast share of responsibility for the conduct of our foreign relations." While Congress holds express authority to regulate public and private dealings with other nations in its war and foreign commerce powers, in foreign affairs the President has a degree of independent authority to act.

At a more specific level, our cases have recognized that the President has authority to make "executive agreements" with other countries, requiring no ratification by the Senate or approval by Congress, this power having been exercised since the early years of the Republic. Making executive agreements to settle claims of American nationals against foreign governments is a particularly longstanding practice. . . . and has received congressional acquiescence throughout its history, [thus] the conclusion "[t]hat the President's control of foreign relations includes the settlement of claims is indisputable."

· · ·

Generally, then, valid executive agreements are fit to preempt state law, just as treaties are, and if the agreements here had expressly preempted laws like HVIRA, the issue would be straightforward. But petitioners and the United States as *amicus curiae* both have to acknowledge that the agreements include no preemption clause, and so leave their claim of preemption to rest on asserted interference with the foreign policy those agreements embody. Reliance is placed on our decision in *Zschernig v. Miller,* 389 U.S. 429 (1968).

· · ·

It is a fair question whether respect for the executive foreign relations power requires a categorical choice between the contrasting theories of field and conflict preemption . . . but the question requires no answer here. . . . [T]he likelihood that state legislation will produce something more than incidental effect in conflict with express foreign policy of the National Government would require preemption of the state law. And since on this view it is legislation within "areas of . . . traditional competence" that gives a State any claim to prevail, it would be reasonable to consider the strength of the state interest, judged by standards of traditional practice, when deciding how serious a conflict must be shown before declaring the state law preempted. Judged by these standards, we think petitioners and the Government have demonstrated a sufficiently clear conflict to require finding preemption here.

IV

A

· · ·

The situation created by the California legislation calls to mind the impact of the Massachusetts Burma law on the effective exercise of the President's power, as recounted in the statutory preemption case, *Crosby v. National Foreign Trade Council,* 530 U.S. 363 (2000). HVIRA's economic compulsion to make public disclosure, of far more information about far more policies than ICHEIC rules require, employs "a different, state system of economic pressure," and in doing so undercuts the President's diplomatic discretion and the choice he has made exercising it. Whereas the President's authority to provide for settling claims in winding up international hostilities requires flexibility in wielding "the coercive power of the national economy" as a tool of diplomacy, HVIRA denies this, by making exclusion from a large sector of the American insurance market the automatic sanction for noncompliance with the State's own policies on disclosure. . . . The law thus "compromise[s] the very capacity of the President to speak for the Nation with one voice in dealing with other governments" to resolve claims against European companies arising out of World War II.[14]

Crosby's facts are replicated again in the way HVIRA threatens to frustrate the operation of the particular mechanism the President has chosen. The letters from Deputy Secretary Eizenstat to California officials show well enough how the portent of further litigation and sanctions has in fact placed the Government at a disadvantage in obtaining practical results from persuading "foreign governments and foreign companies to participate voluntarily in organizations such as ICHEIC." In addition to thwarting the Government's policy of repose for companies that pay through the ICHEIC, California's indiscriminate disclosure provisions place a handicap on the ICHEIC's effectiveness (and raise a further irritant to the European allies) by undercutting European privacy protections. It is true, of course, as it is probably true of all elements of HVIRA, that the disclosure requirement's object of obtaining compensation for Holocaust victims is a goal espoused by the National Government as well. But "[t]he fact of a common end hardly neutralizes conflicting means," and here HVIRA is an obstacle to the success of the National Government's chosen "calibration of force" in dealing with the Europeans using a voluntary approach.

B

The express federal policy and the clear conflict raised by the state statute are alone enough to require state law to yield. If any doubt about the clarity of the conflict remained, however, it would have to be resolved in the National Government's favor, given the weakness of the State's interest, against the backdrop of traditional state legislative subject

---

[14] It is true that the President in this case is acting without express congressional authority. . . . But in *Crosby* we were careful to note that the President possesses considerable independent constitutional authority to act on behalf of the United States on international issues, and conflict with the exercise of that authority is a comparably good reason to find preemption of state law.

matter, in regulating disclosure of European Holocaust-era insurance policies in the manner of HVIRA.

. . .

[T]here is no serious doubt that the state interest actually underlying HVIRA is concern for the several thousand Holocaust survivors said to be living in the State. But this fact does not displace general standards for evaluating a State's claim to apply its forum law to a particular controversy or transaction, under which the State's claim is not a strong one.

. . .

But should the general standard not be displaced, and the State's interest recognized as a powerful one, by virtue of the fact that California seeks to vindicate the claims of Holocaust survivors? The answer lies in recalling that the very same objective dignifies the interest of the National Government in devising its chosen mechanism for voluntary settlements, there being about 100,000 survivors in the country, only a small fraction of them in California. As against the responsibility of the United States of America, the humanity underlying the state statute could not give the State the benefit of any doubt in resolving the conflict with national policy.

C

The basic fact is that California seeks to use an iron fist where the President has consistently chosen kid gloves. We have heard powerful arguments that the iron fist would work better, and it may be that if the matter of compensation were considered in isolation from all other issues involving the European Allies, the iron fist would be the preferable policy. But our thoughts on the efficacy of the one approach versus the other are beside the point, since our business is not to judge the wisdom of the National Government's policy; dissatisfaction should be addressed to the President or, perhaps, Congress. The question relevant to preemption in this case is conflict, and the evidence here is "more than sufficient to demonstrate that the state Act stands in the way of [the President's] diplomatic objectives."

. . .

The judgment of the Court of Appeals for the Ninth Circuit is reversed.

NOTES & QUESTIONS

1. What conflicts between state and federal law did the Court identify in *Crosby* and *Garamendi*? Do you agree with the Court's analysis in *Crosby* that the Massachusetts Burma law compromised the executive's ability to

speak with "one voice" regarding the country's foreign relations? Professor Sarah Cleveland levels the following critique of the Court's decision:

> The 'one-voice' doctrine is a myth. It finds little support in the constitutional framework, which divides the foreign relations powers among the three federal branches, and even less in the actual practice of the government. Congress and the President have full power to expressly preempt state and local interference with foreign affairs, and they have exercised that power on occasion. But even more often they have tolerated, deferred to or even encouraged state and local measures impacting on foreign affairs. Neither Congress nor the President had expressly preempted the Massachusetts law at issue in *Crosby*, despite ample opportunity to do so. Quite to the contrary, repeated actions by both branches suggested an intent to tolerate the Massachusetts law. In the face of our constitutional history and this substantial evidence of federal practice, it was improper for the Court to preempt the statute on its own.

Sarah H. Cleveland, Crosby *and the "One Voice" Myth in U.S. Foreign Relations*, 46 Vill. L. Rev. 975, 975 (2001).

2.   Prior to *Crosby*, during the South African apartheid era, numerous states, cities, and counties in the United States enacted laws requiring divestment in or limiting procurement from companies doing business with South Africa's apartheid regime. Only one legal challenge was considered, pertaining to Baltimore City ordinances requiring that city pension funds divest their holdings in companies doing business with South Africa. The Maryland Court of Appeals (the state's highest court) upheld the ordinances, holding, *inter alia,* that they were not preempted by the federal Comprehensive Anti-Apartheid Act, did not intrude on the federal government's exclusive power to conduct foreign policy, and did not violate the Commerce Clause. *Board of Trustees v. City of Baltimore*, 562 A.2d 720 (Md. 1989). In its decision, the Court noted that "the Ordinances embody the City's moral condemnation of racial discrimination. The use of pension funds arguably to support racial discrimination in South Africa is an issue of deep concern, not only to the pension systems' members and beneficiaries but also to all citizens of Baltimore who are sensitive to slavery's persistent legacy." *Id*. at 755. The Court characterized these as "unique and profound local concerns." *Id*. The U.S. Supreme Court denied *certiorari* in the case. Previously, U.S. Attorney General Ed Meese had issued an Attorney General opinion concluding that state and local South African laws were a constitutional exercise of states' rights to spend and invest their own funds. Constitutionality of South African Divestment Statutes Enacted by State and Local Governments, 10 Op. O.L.C. 49, 54–55 (Apr. 9, 1986). *See* Martha F. Davis, *Thinking Globally, Acting Locally: States, Municipalities, and International Human Rights, in* 2 Bringing Human Rights Home 127, 130–31 (Cynthia Soohoo et al. eds., 2008).

The Massachusetts Burma Law and similar state and local Burma laws, as well as the state and local South African divestment measures, were followed by federal measures addressing similar concerns. What does this suggest about the value and role of state and local efforts to promote human rights in other countries, and the impact of state and local efforts on federal law and policy?

3. Interestingly, Congress authorized state and local divestment measures in enacting the Sudan Accountability and Divestment Act of 2007, Pub. L. No. 110–174, 121 Stat. 2516, thereby explicitly allowing precisely the type of state and local action that was challenged in *Crosby* and *Garamendi* and held to be within the exclusive orbit of the federal government under its foreign affairs powers. *See* Robert B. Ahdieh, *Foreign Affairs, International Law and the New Federalism: Lessons From Coordination*, 73 Mo. L. Rev. 1185, 1193–94 (2008). Does this undermine or support the Court's reasoning in *Crosby* and *Garamendi*?

4. A number of commentators have suggested that the facts and the Court's analysis in *Crosby* and *Garamendi* suggest that the Court's preemption doctrine in this area is limited to the context of state and local activities intended to influence the actions of other nations. *See* Gaylynn Burroughs, *More Than an Incidental Effect on Foreign Affairs: Implementation of Human Rights by State and Local Governments*, 30 N.Y.U. Rev. L. & Soc. Change 411, 436–39 (2006); Martha F. Davis, *Upstairs, Downstairs: Subnational Incorporation of International Human Rights Law at the End of an Era*, 77 Fordham L. Rev. 411, 435–38 (2008); Judith Resnik, *The Internationalism of American Federalism: Missouri and Holland*, 73 Mo. L. Rev. 1105, 1142–43 (2008); Judith Resnik, *Law's Migration: American Exceptionalism, Silent Dialogues, and Federalism's Multiple Ports of Entry*, 115 YALE L. J. 1564, 1654–55 (2006); Lesley Wexler, *Take the Long Way Home: Sub-Federal Integration of Unratified and Non-Self-Executing Treaty Law*, 28 Mich. J. Int'l L. 1, 44–46 (2006). Are the state and local examples examined earlier in this chapter sufficiently different from those at issue in *Crosby* and *Garamendi*? What distinguishes them from those that were invalidated by the Court?

5. Do some of the state and local examples discussed in this chapter potentially tread more closely on the federal government's foreign affairs powers or jeopardize its ability to "speak in one voice" on foreign affairs than others? For example, do resolutions and laws seeking to implement unratified treaties at the local level contradict U.S. policy to *not* ratify a particular treaty? What about with respect to ratified treaties, where Congress has failed to enact legislation implementing the treaty?

6. The question of state and local authority to implement human rights overlaps with the federal government's authority to enact implementing legislation for ratified treaties touching on areas traditionally within the jurisdiction of state and local government. As we discussed in **Chapter III**, in *Missouri v. Holland*, 252 U.S. 416 (1920), the Supreme Court

affirmed that the Treaty Power authorizes the federal government to ratify treaties covering a large swath of activities, even those touching on traditional state functions. A corollary of the holding is that if a treaty is ratified pursuant to a valid exercise of the Treaty Power, resulting national legislation implementing the treaty is valid, as well. As discussed in **Chapter III**, the petitioner in *Bond v. United States*, 134 S.Ct. 2077 (2014), challenged this central aspect of *Missouri v. Holland*. Yet the Court in *Bond* declined to address the constitutional issue of Congress's authority to enact implementing legislation reaching traditional state functions, and instead decided the case by construing the statute at issue narrowly, so as not to interfere with traditionally local concerns. 134 S. Ct. at 2082.

ii. Coordination and Capacity

Although many state and local governments are eager to, or at least interested in, implementing human rights norms and principles at the local level, they face many practical constraints on their ability to do so, including resource limitations, lack of education and training on human rights, and lack of coordination and information sharing among sister jurisdictions. What strategies might state and local governments employ to overcome these limitations, and what role should the federal government play in encouraging and supporting state and local human rights efforts?

RISA E. KAUFMAN, "BY SOME OTHER MEANS: CONSIDERING THE EXECUTIVE'S ROLE IN FOSTERING SUBNATIONAL HUMAN RIGHTS COMPLIANCE"

33 Cardozo L. Rev. 1971, 1980–85, 2003–06 (2012).

The United States is increasingly engaging with the international human rights system and embracing the domestic incorporation of human rights obligations. It reports more regularly to human rights treaty bodies, extends invitations to U.N. experts to visit the United States on fact-finding missions, engages in briefing and arguments at the Inter-American Human Rights Commission, and, most recently, showcases its robust engagement with the UPR as a model for other countries.

However, this federal engagement at the international level is not coupled with parallel engagement at the state and local level. The United States currently lacks a national human rights institution to regularly monitor human rights conditions at the subnational level, and it lacks a coordinated approach to ensure that human rights commitments are transmitted to, or implemented by, subnational government officials. This gap in monitoring, implementation and coordination potentially leaves state and local officials unaware of and compromised in their ability to adhere to human rights commitments made by the U.S., a deficiency recognized both nationally and internationally.

. . .

[In addition to lacking a national human rights monitoring body] [t]he United States . . . has no focal point charged with coordinating state and local governments' implementation of human rights treaties. In 1998, former President Clinton signed Executive Order 13107, creating the Interagency Working Group on the Implementation of Human Rights Treaties to undertake a range of functions to oversee domestic implementation of the various U.N. treaties ratified by the United States. The Bush administration abandoned the working group and replaced it with a Policy Coordinating Committee, which, by most accounts, was never fully operationalized. The Obama administration has convened a . . . policy-coordinating committee to engage in treaty reporting and the UPR. However, the working group has no explicit mandate to coordinate and engage with state and local officials. Similarly, the State Department office that was created to liaise with state and local officials on foreign policy issues is not mandated to engage on issues related to domestic implementation of human rights.

Nevertheless, the Obama administration has made some strides towards greater engagement with state and local officials regarding human rights implementation. [The] legal adviser to the State Department has sent official communications to state governors, attorneys general and state and local human rights and human relations commissioners, apprising them of the human rights treaties that the United States has ratified and seeking their input on U.S. reports to U.N. treaty monitoring bodies. Administration officials have spoken about international human rights obligations at gatherings of state and local human rights and human relations commission staff. In its most recent report to the U.N. Human Rights Committee, the expert committee that monitors countries' compliance with the International Covenant on Civil and Political Rights (ICCPR), the administration recognized the importance of state and local officials in meeting the United States' obligations under the treaty by appending a catalogue of state, local, and tribal human rights agencies and programs that "play a critical role in U.S. implementation of the human rights treaties to which the United States is a party[.]"

However, these efforts and acknowledgments have not been coupled with robust monitoring, coordinated and affirmative outreach efforts, or incentives. Many state and local officials thus lack the necessary information . . . to implement [their] human rights obligations.

. . .

Their potential notwithstanding, there are limitations to state and local governments' ability to bring the United States into compliance with its treaty obligations. To be sure, there are challenges posed by political resistance. . . . At a more basic and pragmatic level, state and local officials have limited information about human rights standards, obligations and best practices, as well as limited resources to conduct human rights monitoring and to engage in implementation.

. . .

[S]tate and local officials, including commissions, have articulated significant barriers to engaging in [human rights-related activity]. Most of these human rights activities occur on an *ad hoc* basis; there is no centralized clearinghouse of information regarding good or effective practices, or mechanisms to coordinate commissions in their efforts to report human rights concerns and to address their impact. Resources for commissions come from governmental as well as private sources, yet are often scarce, with budgets being cut in ways that compromise the commissions' ability to monitor and enforce even domestic laws. Indeed, although commission staff express an interest in deepening their involvement with and use of international human rights, they note that financial and other resource limitations constrain their ability to do so. . . . There is a need . . . for wider collection and dissemination of information regarding effective state and local initiatives that seek to address human rights concerns and implement human rights obligations. Moreover, funding is necessary to support such initiatives.

. . .

NOTES & QUESTIONS

1.   Given that Congress has failed to enact implementing legislation for the human rights treaties ratified by the United States, and given the Court's holding in *Medellín* that, in the absence of implementing legislation, the President cannot compel states to comply with treaties, what should the federal government's role be in ensuring that state and local governments comply with the United States' human rights treaty commitments? Is the federal government powerless to act? And does the federal government have a role to play in encouraging state and local implementation of human rights with respect to treaties that the United States has signed but not yet ratified? For recommendations on how the federal government might support and coordinate state and local human rights compliance, see Robert B. Ahdieh, *Foreign Affairs, International Law, and the New Federalism: Lessons From Coordination*, 73 Mo. L. Rev. 1185, 1229 (2008); Martha F. Davis, *The Spirit of Our Times: State Constitutions and International Human Rights*, 30 N.Y.U. Rev. L. & Soc. Change 359, 389 (2006); Johanna Kalb, *Dynamic Federalism in Human Rights Treaty Implementation*, 84 Tul. L. Rev. 1025, 1055, 1064 (2010); Risa E. Kaufman, *"By Some Other Means": Considering the Executive's Role in Fostering Subnational Human Rights Compliance*, 33 Cardozo L. Rev. 1971 (2012); Tara J. Melish, *From Paradox to Subsidiarity:*

The United States and Human Rights Treaty Bodies, 34 Yale J. Int'l L. 389, 456–61 (2009); Catherine Powell, *Dialogic Federalism: Constitutional Possibilities for Incorporation of Human Rights Law in the United States*, 150 U. Pa. L. Rev. 245 (2001).

2. How might lawyers and other advocates encourage the federal government to take a more active and supportive role in state and local human rights implementation?

In 2010, then State Department Legal Adviser Harold Hongju Koh sent letters to the state governors, attorney generals, and state and local human rights commissions informing them of treaties that the United States has ratified, and their obligations under the treaties. As you read the following letter to state governors, consider how state and local officials might respond upon receiving such a letter, and what additional information or resources they might require in order to uphold the United States' treaty obligations.

MEMORANDUM FROM HAROLD HONGJU KOH, LEGAL ADVISER, TO STATE GOVERNORS, U.S. HUMAN RIGHTS TREATY REPORTS

January 20, 2010.

This electronic communication contains information on several human rights treaties to which the United States is party, and which are implemented through existing laws at all levels of government (federal, state, insular and local). To promote knowledge of these treaties in the United States, we would appreciate your forwarding this communication to your Attorney General's office, and to the departments and offices that deal with human rights, civil rights, housing, employment and related issues in your administration.

Specifically, this memorandum provides background information on five human rights treaties to which the United States is a party and on which the United States has filed reports with the United Nations from 2005–2008: the Convention Against Torture and other Cruel, Inhuman or Degrading Treatment or Punishment (CAT); the International Covenant on Civil and Political Rights (ICCPR); the International Convention on the Elimination of All Forms of Racial Discrimination (CERD); and two optional protocols to the Convention on the Rights of the Child—the Optional Protocol on the Involvement of Children in Armed Conflict and the Optional Protocol on the Sale of Children, Child Prostitution, and Child Pornography (CRC Optional Protocols). The United States is party to each of these treaties and, pursuant to obligations under each of these treaties, is obliged to submit reports to treaty monitoring bodies on the implementation of U.S. obligations thereunder. Because U.S. treaty obligations may apply to all levels of government throughout the territory of the United States and because of the important issues of U.S. law and practice addressed in our reports, we wish to make you and the appropriate members of your staff aware of these reports.

United States obligations under the ICCPR, CERD, and the CRC Optional Protocols are implemented under existing law; in other words, prior to becoming a party to each of these treaties, the U.S. State Department, coordinating with other relevant agencies, reviewed the treaties and relevant provisions of U.S. law and determined that existing laws in the United States were sufficient to implement the treaty obligations, as understood or modified by reservations, understandings, or declarations made by the United States at the time of ratification in order to ensure congruence between treaty obligations and existing U.S. laws. With regard to the CAT, Congress passed specific implementing legislation. Although these treaties do not give rise directly to individually enforceable rights in U.S. courts, the United States is bound under international law to implement all of its obligations under these treaties and takes these obligations very seriously.

As noted above, among these obligations are requirements to submit to the United Nations periodic reports of the actions the United States has taken in implementation of these treaties. Subsequent to submission of the reports, representatives of the United States (and in some cases representatives of the states) met with the relevant United Nations committees involved to present these reports, answer questions, and provide further information. In the context of these reports and meetings, the United Nations committees have expressed interest in confirming that the existence and substance of these treaties is made known throughout the territory of the United States. For example, one of these committees expressly urged the United States to "make government officials, the judiciary, federal and state law enforcement officials, teachers, social workers and the public in general aware about the responsibilities of the State party under the Convention." Because implementation of these treaties may be carried out by officials at all levels of government (federal, state, insular, and local) under existing laws applicable in their jurisdictions, we want to make sure that the substance of these treaties and their relevance to the United States is known to appropriate governmental officials and to members of the public.

I have attached to this memorandum links to the State Department and other websites containing the relevant treaties, the reports submitted by the United States, committee responses ("Concluding Observations"), and other relevant documents. We ask that you transmit these links to the appropriate offices in your organization or department.

NOTES & QUESTIONS

1.   What might be the Legal Adviser's goal in transmitting this letter to state governors? Is it sufficiently detailed to achieve its goal? What other information might be useful? How might state governors respond upon receiving the letter?

2.   The Legal Adviser sent a similar letter to the members of the International Association of Official Human Rights Agencies (IAOHRA). How might advocates leverage these letters in their advocacy with state and local officials around human rights concerns?

3.   More recently, in February 2014, Principal Deputy Legal Adviser Mary McLeod sent a letter to the Governors outlining the upcoming treaty review processes. According to McLeod, U.S. human rights obligations "are implemented not only by the federal government, but also through the dedicated efforts of state, local, insular, and tribal governments throughout our country, in areas such as protecting the civil and political rights of our citizens, combating racial discrimination, and protecting children from harms such as pornography and prostitution." In addition to sharing information about the treaties, she encouraged further give-and-take, adding that "[t]he federal government will continue to need your help in the future in implementing our human rights obligations, consulting with the public about these issues, and identifying areas for improvement." The letter was copied to the National Governors Association, the National Conference of Mayors, the National Association of Counties, the National Association of Attorneys General, and the IAOHRA. Having sent this letter, what sort of follow-up from the federal government would be appropriate and effective?

iii. Backlash: State and Local Opposition to Ratification

Earlier in this chapter, we discussed the political backlash against state court consideration of international human rights and the law of foreign courts. State and local efforts to engage in human rights activities have led to similar political forms of backlash. For example, despite, or perhaps in reaction to, state and local resolutions urging the United States to ratify human rights treaties, several state legislatures have approved resolutions opposing U.S. ratification of human rights treaties.

Consider this Resolution, approved by the Alabama Legislature in 2011:

URGING THE MEMBERS OF THE UNITED STATES SENATE TO
OPPOSE RATIFICATION OF THE UNITED NATIONS
CONVENTION ON THE RIGHTS OF THE CHILD

SJR 65, Reg. Sess. 2011 (Ala. 2011).

WHEREAS, the right of the parents to direct the upbringing and education of their children is a fundamental right protected by the Constitution of the United States and the State of Alabama; and

WHEREAS, our nation has long pursued the path of relying first and foremost on parents to meet the real and necessary needs of children; and

WHEREAS, the United States Supreme Court in Wisconsin v. Yoder, 406 U.S. 205 (1972), has held that "This primary role of the parents in the upbringing of their children is now established beyond debate as an enduring American tradition"; and

WHEREAS, children are best served by the continued practice of requiring proper proof of harm before the government intervenes in the family to override parental decisions in any sphere of the child's upbringing; and

WHEREAS, certain members of the United States Senate have called upon the Secretary of State and the President to forward to them the United Nations Convention on the Rights of the Child for ratification; and

WHEREAS, Article VI of the Constitution of the United States provides that treaties that are ratified by the United States Senate become a part of the "supreme law of the land" and that state laws and constitutions are subservient to the treaties; and

WHEREAS, virtually all law that applies to children and families in Alabama is state law; and

WHEREAS, by virtue of the federal Supremacy Clause all Alabama laws regarding children would be overridden if there is a conflict with this treaty if ratified; and

WHEREAS, the Congress of the United States would acquire primary jurisdiction to legislate to meet our nation's legal obligation to comply with the treaty if ratified, thereby shifting from Alabama and her sister states to the Congress of the United States powers not formerly delegated which are currently reserved to the states under the Tenth Amendment to the United States Constitution; and

WHEREAS, the treaty is subject to the general rule of international law that "custom" is binding law in many circumstances, rendering the text of a treaty as an unreliable guide to its future meaning; and

WHEREAS, the United Nations Committee on the Rights of the Child at periodic intervals publishes "General Comments" which are substantive additions to the obligations of state parties already under the Convention; and

WHEREAS, the United Nations Committee on the Rights of the Child makes regular determinations of the meaning and the application of the treaty, and it would hold these interpretations to be binding on the Congress of the United States and the courts of the United States when interpreting and enforcing the treaty; and

WHEREAS, this represents a wholesale abandonment of the ultimate sovereignty of the United States on matters within the scope of the treaty; and

WHEREAS, this abandonment violates the core principle of our self-government: To-wit, only American Legislatures and the people themselves have the moral authority to make law for America; and

WHEREAS, the substance of the treaty as interpreted and applied by this official United Nations tribunal:

1. Bans all corporal punishment, including reasonable spanking by parents.

2. Gives the government review authority of a broad scope of parental decisions without the necessity of proving that the parents are unfit or have harmed the child.

3. Allows children and government to override reasonable and ordinary decisions concerning the religious upbringing of the child.

4. Allows the government the ability to review any parental decision concerning the education of their child, even if that decision fully complies with the law of Alabama.

5. Requires a level of socialized spending programs for the supposed needs of children, which in too many cases simply employ more government workers, that would bankrupt any American state.

6. Grants to children a legally enforceable right to leisure and many other particular "rights" that are contrary to American traditions and common sense;

Now therefore, BE IT RESOLVED BY THE LEGISLATURE OF ALABAMA, BOTH HOUSES THEREOF CONCURRING, That the State of Alabama hereby condemns the United Nations Convention on the Rights of the Child.

BE IT FURTHER RESOLVED, that the State of Alabama urges the United States Senate to reject its ratification.

NOTES & QUESTIONS

1.   What weight should the U.S. Senate give to the Alabama resolution in considering whether to give its advice and consent to ratify the CRC?

2.   How might advocates urging U.S. ratification of the CRC respond to the Alabama resolution and similar measures?

3.   Does the potential that similar resolutions might be adopted in other states counsel against advocacy efforts to organize local support for U.S. ratification of human rights treaties?

SKILLS EXERCISES

1.   Refer to the Skills Exercise at the end of Section II. You are a housing advocate at FHA. You have determined that the Louisiana courts are unlikely to be receptive to your arguments for a broad reading of the Louisiana State Constitution's Individual Dignity clause. Drawing on the same source materials, as well as the examples provided above, outline a plan for a human rights advocacy campaign to promote more equitable access to housing at the local level. Consider which state or local institutions might be most receptive and why. Consider, too, which modes of advocacy and state and local implementation mechanisms discussed in this chapter might make progress towards addressing FHA's concerns.

2.   You work for the mayor of your home town. The mayor has asked you to draft a resolution on a local human rights concern impacting the town. It is her hope that this resolution will appeal to a broad array of constituents and also make a positive impact on local policy. Further, the mayor is a member of the U.S. Conference of Mayors and is interested in implementing the 2013 USCM resolution, and thus has asked that you explicitly include human rights principles.

Given your deep human rights expertise, the mayor has asked you to determine which sources of human rights to include and the human rights standards and language that will be most compelling to local stakeholders. The mayor has also asked you to include mechanisms for local implementation.

Draft a 2–3 page local resolution on a human rights issue of your choice. As you draft the resolution, think through the following questions: How can you effectively develop the connection between the local context and international human rights?; How can you effectively articulate the issue as a human rights concern?; What human rights sources will be most compelling?; How can the resolution ensure or at least encourage implementation and local change to advance human rights?; How can the resolution minimize the potential for backlash?

CHAPTER VII

THE INTERDEPENDENCE OF RIGHTS: ADVANCING ECONOMIC, SOCIAL AND CULTURAL RIGHTS ALONGSIDE CIVIL AND POLITICAL RIGHTS IN THE U.S.

■ ■ ■

I. INTRODUCTION

A. ECONOMIC, SOCIAL AND CULTURAL RIGHTS IN THE U.S. LEGAL SYSTEM

A strength of the human rights framework is its recognition of the interdependence of rights and the opportunities it offers U.S. advocates to promote economic, social, and cultural rights on equal footing with civil and political rights within the United States.

The United States has a strong tradition of protecting civil and political rights. The Bill of Rights to the Constitution protects virtually the same set of rights contained in the ICCPR, with a few exceptions. And the anti-discrimination protections of the CERD are similar to, though broader than, the protections included in the U.S. Constitution's equal protection clause. Missing from the U.S. Constitution, however, is strong protection for economic, social and cultural (ESC) rights. Indeed, the U.S. Supreme Court has declined to find a fundamental right to subsistence benefits under the U.S. Constitution. And the Court consistently analyzes federal constitutional challenges to social and economic welfare legislation using a lenient, rational basis approach, thereby granting great deference to legislatures in this realm,[1] although, as discussed *infra*, many state constitutions contain more substantive economic and social rights protections.[2]

---

[1] *See, e.g.*, Dandridge v. Williams, 397 U.S. 471 (1970).

[2] A good illustration of this dichotomy is the litigation challenging public education financing in Texas. In federal court, applying the U.S. Constitution, the disparities in educational offerings based on wealth were upheld as rational, in part because there was no federal constitutional right to education. San Antonio v. Rodriguez, 411 U.S. 1 (1973). In contrast, the state Supreme Court, applying the state constitutional provision guaranteeing public education to the same facts, applied a higher standard of review and ordered changes to the public education financing scheme. Edgewood Independent School District v. Kirby, 777 S.W.2d 391 (1989).

In contrast, international human rights documents, including the UDHR, call for the protection of the full panoply of rights. The core human rights treaty addressing ESC rights, the International Covenant on Economic, Social and Cultural Rights (ICESCR), protects the enjoyment of all economic, social and cultural rights, including the right to work, the right to just and favorable conditions of work, the right to form and join trade unions, the right to social security and social insurance, the right to an adequate standard of living including adequate food, clothing, and housing, the right to the highest attainable standard of health, and the right to an education. Article 2(1) of the Covenant states that:

> Each State party to the present Covenant undertakes to take steps . . . to the maximum of its available resources, with a view to achieving progressively the full realization of the rights recognized in the present Covenant by all appropriate means, including particularly the adoption of legislative measures.

Though the United States is credited with helping to ensure that ESC rights were included in the UDHR, the United States has signed but not yet ratified the ICESCR. It has likewise signed but not yet ratified most of the other core human rights treaties containing explicit protections for ESC rights, including the Convention on the Elimination of All Forms of Discrimination Against Women (CEDAW), the Convention on the Rights of the Child (CRC), and Convention on the Rights of Persons with Disabilities (CRPD). Despite the United States' failure to ratify these treaties, advocates have developed creative strategies to frame and promote ESC rights within the United States to address issues including housing, healthcare, education, food and clean water.

B. THE CONTENT OF ECONOMIC, SOCIAL, AND CULTURAL RIGHTS

Though the human rights framework protects ESC rights on equal footing with civil and political rights, the treaties and treaty bodies articulate the nature of ESC rights somewhat differently than civil and political rights. Unlike the ICCPR and the CERD, the ICESCR requires that states "take steps" to the maximum of their available resources in order to achieve "progressively" the full realization of the rights contained in the treaty. The ICESCR contains a non-discrimination provision, as well, obligating states to guarantee the enjoyment of ESC rights without discrimination and to ensure the equal rights of men and women to the enjoyment of these rights.[3] While governments may realize ESC rights progressively, the Committee on Economic, Social and Cultural Rights, the treaty body with oversight of the ICESCR, has interpreted the

---

[3] ICESCR, art. 2(2).

Covenant to impose an immediate obligation on states in several respects, including: the immediate obligation of non-discrimination; to "take steps" immediately to ensure that people's enjoyment of economic and social rights improves over time; and to satisfy certain minimum core obligations, including access to employment, minimum essential food, basic shelter housing and sanitation, and adequate supply of safe drinking water.[4] Governments also have an immediate obligation of non-retrogression, which requires that once a particular level of enjoyment of rights has been realized, it must be maintained.

In addition, governments have a responsibility to respect, protect and fulfill economic, social and cultural rights.[5] The obligation to respect means that a state may not interfere directly or indirectly with the enjoyment of ESC rights. The obligation to protect means that a state must prevent violations of rights by third parties. And the obligation to fulfill requires that states take the appropriate legislative, administrative, budgetary, judicial and other measures to ensure the enjoyment of ESC rights.

The Committee has also issued a series of general comments and findings that further explicate the content of economic, social and cultural rights. For example, the Committee has stated that the right to health, guaranteed in Article 12 of the ICESCR and in other international documents, ensures the right to the highest attainable standard of physical and mental health; it does not guarantee the right to be healthy, but rather the right to enjoy facilities, goods, services and conditions necessary for the realization of health. It affords special protections for maternal, child and reproductive health, disabled persons, ethnic minorities, indigenous populations, the elderly, and persons with HIV/AIDS. Components of the right to health include availability, accessibility, acceptability, appropriateness and quality.[6]

The civil and political rights treaties ratified by the United States contain important economic, social and cultural rights protections, as well. For example, the CERD specifically prohibits discrimination with respect to the enjoyment of economic, social, and cultural rights. In particular, Article 5 of the CERD protects against discrimination in the enjoyment of, *inter alia*, the right to work, the right to form and join trade unions, the right to housing, the right to public health, medical care, social security, and social services, the right to education and training, and the right to equal participation in cultural activities.

---

[4]   U.N. Comm. on Econ., Soc. & Cultural Rights [hereinafter, CESCR], General Comment No. 3: The Nature of States Parties' Obligations.

[5]   *See, e.g.*, The Maastricht Guidelines on Violations of Economic, Social and Cultural Rights, II (6).

[6]   CESCR, General Comment 14: The Right to the Highest Attainable Standard of Health.

The ICCPR, too, contains protections ensuring equality and non-discrimination. Like the CERD, Article 26 of the ICCPR protects against instances of disparate impact discrimination, and thus extends its protections to many groups that may be disproportionately represented among the poor, including minorities, women, and people with disabilities.

In this chapter, we explore the opportunities for, and challenges of, using a human rights framework to advocate for economic, social and cultural rights in the United States. Professor Tara Melish has argued that "[t]here are ... virtually no substantive issues arising under the CEDAW, CRC, and ICESCR that cannot in some way be addressed under the ICCPR, CERD, and CAT supervisory procedures."[7] Do you agree? If so, then why have advocates not made more progress on these issues? What might they do differently or in addition? Following this Introduction, Part II provides a brief history of the United States' stance on ESC rights. Part III discusses some of the common critiques of ESC rights advocacy. Parts IV and V look at strategies that U.S. advocates are embracing in order to promote and protect ESC rights within the United States. Part V features a case study and skills exercise drawn from this material.

II.   THE UNITED STATES' STANCE ON ECONOMIC, SOCIAL AND CULTURAL RIGHTS

The United States has a history of ambivalence concerning ESC rights. Though instrumental in ensuring their inclusion in the UDHR, the U.S. has not broadly embraced ESC rights domestically. In the materials that follow, consider the history of ESC rights in the United States. What accounts for the United States' reluctance to embrace ESC rights fully? What is the legacy of this history?

President Roosevelt is widely credited with articulating the interrelated nature of human rights and setting forth a blueprint for the rights later contained in the Universal Declaration of Human Rights. We read Roosevelt's highly influential 1941 "Four Freedoms" speech in **Chapter II**. Regarding his 1944 State of the Union speech excerpted below, Cass Sunstein has stated:

> Roosevelt's speech has had a large international influence; the Second Bill of Rights should be seen as a leading American export. The Universal Declaration of Human Rights, written in the shadow of FDR and accepted by the UN General Assembly in 1948, explicitly includes social and economic guarantees. The United States enthusiastically supported the declaration (but

---

[7]   Tara Melish, *From Paradox to Subsidiarity: The United States and Human Rights Treaty Bodies*, 34 Yale J. Int'l L. 389, 430 (2009).

has been exceptionally unusual in refusing to ratify the International Covenant on Economic, Social, and Cultural Rights, which would help to enforce social and economic guarantees). Many constitutions include social and economic guarantees in a way that can be traced directly to Roosevelt's speech.

Cass Sunstein, *Economic Security: A Human Right*, The American Prospect, Sept 20, 2004.

As you read this excerpt, consider why Roosevelt's sentiments may have been more influential abroad than at home.

PRESIDENT FRANKLIN D. ROOSEVELT, STATE OF THE UNION ADDRESS
January 1944.

This Nation in the past two years has become an active partner in the world's greatest war against human slavery.

We have joined with like-minded people in order to defend ourselves in a world that has been gravely threatened with gangster rule.

But I do not think that any of us Americans can be content with mere survival. Sacrifices that we and our allies are making impose upon us all a sacred obligation to see to it that out of this war we and our children will gain something better than mere survival.

We are united in determination that this war shall not be followed by another interim which leads to new disaster—that we shall not repeat the tragic errors of ostrich isolationism—that we shall not repeat the excesses of the wild twenties when this Nation went for a joy ride on a roller coaster which ended in a tragic crash.

. . .

The one supreme objective for the future, which we discussed for each Nation individually, and for all the United Nations, can be summed up in one word: Security.

And that means not only physical security which provides safety from attacks by aggressors. It means also economic security, social security, moral security—in a family of Nations.

. . .

In this war, we have been compelled to learn how interdependent upon each other are all groups and sections of the population of America.

Increased food costs, for example, will bring new demands for wage increases from all war workers, which will in turn raise all prices of all things including those things which the farmers themselves have to buy. Increased wages or prices will each in turn produce the same results. They all have a particularly disastrous result on all fixed income groups. . . .

It is our duty now to begin to lay the plans and determine the strategy for the winning of a lasting peace and the establishment of an American standard of living higher than ever before known. We cannot be content, no matter how high that general standard of living may be, if some fraction of our people—whether it be one-third or one-fifth or one-tenth—is ill-fed, ill-clothed, ill housed, and insecure.

This Republic had its beginning, and grew to its present strength, under the protection of certain inalienable political rights—among them the right of free speech, free press, free worship, trial by jury, freedom from unreasonable searches and seizures. They were our rights to life and liberty.

As our Nation has grown in size and stature, however—as our industrial economy expanded—these political rights proved inadequate to assure us equality in the pursuit of happiness.

We have come to a clear realization of the fact that true individual freedom cannot exist without economic security and independence. "Necessitous men are not free men." People who are hungry and out of a job are the stuff of which dictatorships are made.

In our day these economic truths have become accepted as self-evident. We have accepted, so to speak, a second Bill of Rights under which a new basis of security and prosperity can be established for all regardless of station, race, or creed.

Among these are:

The right to a useful and remunerative job in the industries or shops or farms or mines of the Nation;

The right to earn enough to provide adequate food and clothing and recreation;

The right of every farmer to raise and sell his products at a return which will give him and his family a decent living;

The right of every businessman, large and small, to trade in an atmosphere of freedom from unfair competition and domination by monopolies at home or abroad;

The right of every family to a decent home;

The right to adequate medical care and the opportunity to achieve and enjoy good health;

The right to adequate protection from the economic fears of old age, sickness, accident, and unemployment;

The right to a good education.

All of these rights spell security. And after this war is won we must be prepared to move forward, in the implementation of these rights, to new goals of human happiness and well-being.

America's own rightful place in the world depends in large part upon how fully these and similar rights have been carried into practice for our citizens. For unless there is security here at home there cannot be lasting peace in the world.

. . .

I ask the Congress to explore the means for implementing this economic bill of rights—for it is definitely the responsibility of the Congress so to do.

. . .

Our fighting men abroad—and their families at home—expect such a program and have the right to insist upon it. It is to their demands that this Government should pay heed rather than to the whining demands of selfish pressure groups who seek to feather their nests while young Americans are dying.

The foreign policy that we have been following—the policy that guided us at Moscow, Cairo, and Teheran—is based on the common sense principle which was best expressed by Benjamin Franklin on July 4, 1776: "We must all hang together, or assuredly we shall all hang separately."

. . .

NOTES & QUESTIONS

1.   The 2nd Bill of Rights that Roosevelt called for was never enacted. It should be noted that in invoking a 2nd Bill of Rights, Roosevelt did not propose a constitutional amendment incorporating these rights. Rather, he intended that Congress implement the bill of rights by statute. What is the practical difference between enshrining these rights in the constitution and protecting them statutorily? Why do you think Roosevelt sought the latter and not the former?

2.   In **Chapter II**, we read Historian Carol Anderson's account of how, in the Cold War era after the drafting of the UDHR, the United States distanced itself from human rights, and in particular economic and social rights. She attributes this to the United States' desire to shield the South's Jim Crow policies from international scrutiny and criticism. She recounts

how African American leaders nevertheless took seriously Roosevelt's articulation of the Four Freedoms, including the recognition and promise of social and economic rights, and framed their own battle against poverty and economic inequality within the United States in terms of a human rights vision for a "new world order" denouncing all oppression, particularly inequities in health care, education, housing and employment. Carol Anderson, *A Hollow Mockery*, *in* 1 Bringing Human Rights Home, 76–83 (Cynthia Soohoo, *et al.*, eds., 2008). In 1947, the NAACP prepared a petition to the U.N. Commission on Human Rights challenging racial inequities, including educational inequities, in the United States. The leadership of the NAACP sought Eleanor Roosevelt's assistance in introducing this petition, in her capacity as both the chair of the U.N. Human Rights Commission and an NAACP board member, but she refused. *Id.* at 90. *See also* Carol Anderson, Eyes Off the Prize: The United Nations and the African American Struggle for Human Rights, 1944–1955 (2003) (detailing history of African American leadership's efforts to challenge racial segregation and inequality through human rights frame). Further, according to Anderson, white Southern politicians, threatened by the impact that recognition of ESC rights would have on Jim Crow and its progeny, lobbied hard to restrict the U.N. Charter's limitations on government sovereignty, resulting in the State Department's agreement to separate the political and civil rights contained in proposed U.N. treaties from economic and social rights. The result is the twin human rights treaties—the ICCPR and the ICESCR, and the U.S.'s eventual, though still ambivalent, embrace of the rights contained in one but not the other. What is the impact of this history on contemporary efforts to advocate for economic, social and cultural rights in the United States? Do you think that the rights contained in the ICESCR are still controversial within the United States? If so, why?

In the following essay, Professor Philip Alston, a former expert member of the U.N. Committee on Economic, Social and Cultural Rights, and, at the time of this writing, the U.N. Special Rapporteur on extreme poverty and human rights, describes the United States' stance on ESC rights through the end of the administration of President George W. Bush. As you read, consider whether the U.S.'s position has changed in the intervening years.

PHILIP ALSTON, "PUTTING ECONOMIC, SOCIAL AND CULTURAL RIGHTS BACK ON THE AGENDA OF THE UNITED STATES"
The Future of Human Rights 120, 120–27 (William Schultz, ed., 2008).

Despite the UN's insistence that all human rights are "indivisible and interdependent and interrelated," the reality is that civil and political rights (CPR) have dominated the international agenda while economic, social, and cultural rights (ESCR) have been accorded second-class status.

This is not to say that ESCR have not been the subjects of long and noisy rhetorical campaigns championed in particular by developing countries, or that the UN and other actors have not mounted a significant number of initiatives designed to promote and enhance the status of these rights. The bottom line remains, however, that ESCR continue to enjoy an inferior status and that endeavors to enhance that status have often been blocked.

. . .

Economic, Social, and Cultural Rights Before Bush

President Franklin Delano Roosevelt is often credited with having first launched the specific proposals that led to the inclusion of ESCR in the Universal Declaration of Human Rights. In developing the notion of freedom from want into a proposed "second Bill of Rights" for the United States, Roosevelt urged the recognition of "the right of every family to a decent home; the right to adequate medical care and the opportunity to achieve and enjoy good health; the right to adequate protection from the economic fears of old age, sickness, accident, and unemployment; [and] the right to a good education."

President Harry Truman supported including ESCR in the Universal Declaration and it was under his auspices that Eleanor Roosevelt participated in the early and crucial phases of the drafting of the International Covenant on Economic, Social and Cultural Rights (ICESCR). President Dwight Eisenhower, under the impetus of the debates surrounding the Bricker amendment, repudiated both that draft covenant and the draft of the International Covenant on Civil and Political Rights (ICCPR) but neither he nor other opponents of the UN's human rights aspirations expressed special animus toward the covenant that dealt with ESCR.

The administration of President Lyndon Johnson not only participated in the resumed drafting of the ICESCR but also voted in favor of its adoption in 1966 by the UN General Assembly. And the same administration supported the inclusion of economic and social rights provisions in the International Convention on the Elimination of All Forms of Racial Discrimination.

In 1975, President Gerald Ford signed the Helsinki Accords, which proclaimed that the participating states would "promote and encourage the effective exercise of civil, political, economic, social, cultural and other rights and freedoms all of which derive from the inherent dignity of the human person and are essential for his free and full development.'" By agreeing to a follow-up declaration, adopted in Vienna in January 1989 by the Conference on Security and Cooperation in Europe, the United States joined other countries in recognizing that the promotion of ESCR "is of paramount importance for human dignity and for the attainment of the legitimate aspirations of every individual." Accordingly the United States said it would guarantee the "effective exercise" of economic, social, and cultural rights and consider acceding to the ICESCR.

The administration of President Jimmy Carter embraced ESCR as a central part of its human rights policy; Carter signed the ICESCR in 1978 and transmitted it to the Senate for its advice and consent. Although hearings were held which included coverage of the ICESCR, the Senate took no action in relation to it.

One of the first acts of President Ronald Reagan's administration in the human rights field was to signal a clear and straightforward policy of opposition to economic and social rights. The earliest and best known statement of policy was included in the introduction written in 1982 by the new assistant secretary of state for human rights and humanitarian affairs, Elliott Abrams, and published in the State Department's annual review of human rights practices around the world. This report explicitly removed the treatment of economic and social rights, which had previously been included in the reports. Abrams subsequently offered several justifications for the policy change. The most significant was that the inclusion of these rights blurred "the vital core of human rights." The distinction he drew was between economic and social rights, which he portrayed as "goods [which] the government ought to encourage over the long term," and civil and political rights, which are "rights" [that] the government has an absolute duty to respect at any time. The second reason given was that economic and social rights are easily exploited for propaganda purposes by unscrupulous governments whose real aim is to avoid respect for civil and political rights. Because such abuses have occurred, the more prudent path was seen to be to deny the very existence of economic and social rights.

The administration of George H. W. Bush was considerably less ideologically engaged, at least overtly, in its opposition to these rights but, when it advanced (and achieved) the ratification of the Covenant on Civil and Political Rights in 1992, no thought was given to advocating concurrent action on the "other" covenant.

The administration of President Bill Clinton initially proclaimed an inclusive approach that included a commitment to support ESCR in international fora and to promote U.S. ratification of the covenant. As a result, one of its first major international acts was to participate in the consensus emerging from the 1993 Vienna World Conference on Human Rights, which proclaimed that "all human rights are universal, indivisible and interdependent and interrelated. The international community must treat human rights globally in a fair and equal manner, on the same footing, and with the same emphasis." Fairly soon thereafter, however, the Clinton administration began to distance itself from its original embrace of ESCR and adopted a number of policies effectively designed to marginalize them.

It reluctantly signed on to the Convention on the Rights of the Child (CRC) but the fact that this treaty contained a number of provisions giving effect to ESCR was often cited as a reason for not proceeding with ratification. This was rather ironic since most of the relevant formulations had in fact been significantly watered down at the insistence of the Reagan administration during the process of drafting the CRC in the 1980s. At the end of the day, the Clinton policy was an uneasy combination of affirming its general support, at least in principle, for ESCR while creating considerable difficulties in relation to most efforts undertaken in UN forums to make progress in relation to specific rights. It also made no attempt to promote ratification of the ICESCR, insisting only that its priority was to achieve ratification of the Convention on the Elimination of All Forms of Discrimination against Women.

The Bush Administration and Economic and Social Rights

The administration of President George W. Bush has not diverged fundamentally from the policies towards ESCR that its predecessors had developed since 1982. "Goods" such as food, housing, education, and water are acknowledged to be desirable components of an adequate standard of living but they do not constitute "human rights" in the full sense of the term. Thus there can be no claim to their realization as a matter of right on the part of those who are being denied those "goods" even if the denial threatens the individuals' survival. Despite this, the United States regularly invokes the Universal Declaration (with its clear recognition of ESCR) in relation to other states.

Because the administration has not adopted any comprehensive policy statements relating to economic and social rights, its views must be discerned from the various speeches and interventions made by U.S. officials in the context of debates and votes within the relevant international forums. The most important of these has been the UN Commission on Human Rights up until 2006, and subsequently the Human Rights Council. Close inspection reveals that the Bush administration has varied its attitude toward economic and social rights significantly in the course of its first seven years.

At least four separate concerns relating to economic, social, and cultural rights motivate the United States position, although they are usually expressed together as though they were part of a seamless whole. They are 1) a belief in the chronological priority of civil and political rights; 2) an objection to the terminological equivalence of the different sets of rights; 3) a concern over what might be termed the "internationalization of responsibility" for failures to meet economic and social rights; and 4) a concern about the justiciability of economic and social rights.

. . .

One of the most important elements in the United States position is that, while the United Nations refers to all rights as human rights and does not contest abstract assertions of their indivisibility, the United States insists that the two sets of rights are fundamentally different from one another. Thus, for example, in a statement on the right to food, the United States emphasized that it must be seen as "a goal or aspiration to be realized progressively" and that it translates into "the opportunity to secure food; it is not a guaranteed entitlement." Or as the U.S. representative to the 2003 meeting of the UN Commission on Human Rights expressed the difference, economic and social rights "are aspirational; [civil and political rights] inalienable and immediately enforceable."

. . .

It seems that the U.S. position of insisting that economic and social rights are merely "aspirational" is to be taken literally. These rights are not to be considered rights in any moral, legal, or administrative sense since they do not give rise to any specific obligations in those spheres. Rather, they are matters to which individuals might aspire, if they so wish. And the role of a government is to ensure that no one stands in the way—in the sense of positively obstructing—the opportunity to seek those rights.

. . .

———————

In March 2011, the administration of President Barak Obama made a major policy statement on economic, social and cultural rights in the speech by a State Department official, set out below. In this passage, consider the difference between the Obama Administration's articulation of its commitment to economic, cultural and social rights and the views of the previous administration, as described by Professor Alston.

MICHAEL H. POSNER, ASSIST. SEC., BUREAU OF DEMOCRACY,
HUMAN RIGHTS AND LABOR, ADDRESS TO THE AMERICAN
SOCIETY OF INTERNATIONAL LAW, "THE FOUR
FREEDOMS TURN 70"

March 24, 2011.

Although the freedom from want is not explicitly contained in the U.S. Constitution, concern about the economic wellbeing of the American populace is deeply embedded in our nation's history and culture.

After all, in the Preamble to the Constitution, the Framers aimed to "promote the general welfare." From our earliest days, state laws and constitutions sought to promote our people's economic security. And the American Dream is predicated on the belief that allowing individuals to flourish is the best way for our nation to flourish.

Nevertheless, the United States has had reservations about the international debate on economic, social and cultural rights

. . .

The United States has taken steps to provide for economic, social and cultural rights but we understand them in our own way and, at any given time, we meet them according to our domestic laws—laws that emerge from a political system based on representative democracy, free speech and free assembly.

But since the founding of the U.N., some Americans have worried that the international movement to recognize economic, social and cultural rights would obligate us to provide foreign assistance commitments that went beyond what was decided by the U.S. This has never been true. Human rights law doesn't create an obligation to any particular level of foreign assistance.

The U.S. is a leading contributor to global efforts to alleviate poverty and promote development—not because we have an obligation to but because it is in our interest. We do this through our bilateral aid programs, through our multilateral contributions, and through the American people—who annually contribute financially and through voluntary service to development and humanitarian activities around the world.

. . .

Some have also been concerned that using the language of human rights could create new domestic legal obligations that would be enforceable though the courts and tie the hands of Congress and the states. But we have been careful to ensure that any international agreements we endorse protect the prerogatives of the federal government, as well as those of our states and localities.

Under the U.S. federal system, states take the lead on many economic, social and cultural policies. For example, all 50 states are committed through their constitutions to providing education for all children. But our federal Constitution makes no mention of rights to education, health care, or social security.

Nevertheless, as my late friend and mentor Professor Louis Henkin wrote, once economic and social rights are granted by law, they cannot be taken away without due process. And these rights also fall under the general requirement that government act rationally and afford equal protection under the law.

Our government's commitment to provide for the basic social and economic needs of our people is clear, and it reflects the will of the American people.

The people ask us to care for the sick . . . and we do. In 2009, our nation spent nearly $900 billion on Medicare and Medicaid. And as you know, last year the administration passed and signed the Affordable Care Act to expand access to health care in America.

They ask us to provide shelter for the destitute . . . and we do. In the wake of the housing crisis, last year the federal government committed almost $4 billion to target homelessness.

They ask us to educate every child, including those with physical and learning disabilities . . . and we do. This year alone, federal, state and local governments will spend close to $600 billion on education.

Some of our suspicion of the international focus on economic, social and cultural rights springs from the misuse of these demands in earlier times. For decades, the Soviet states and the Non-Aligned Movement critiqued the United States for a perceived failure to embrace economic and social rights. They used the rhetoric of economic, social and cultural rights to distract from their human rights abuses. They claimed economic rights trumped political rights, while in fact failing to provide either. We have prioritized political and civil rights because governments that are transparent and respect free speech are stable, secure and sustainable— and do the most for their people.

It is time to move forward. The Obama administration takes a holistic approach to human rights, democracy and development. Human rights do not begin after breakfast. But without breakfast, few people have the energy to make full use of their rights. As Martin Luther King once noted, an integrated lunch counter doesn't help the person who can't afford to eat there.

Therefore, we will work constructively with like minded delegations to adopt fair and well-reasoned resolutions at the UN that speak to the issues of economic, social and cultural rights and are consistent with our own laws and policies.

We will do this understanding that these goals must be achieved progressively, given the resources available to each government. But we will also stress that nothing justifies a government's indifference to its own people. And nothing justifies human oppression—not even spectacular economic growth.

When negotiating language on these resolutions and in our explanations of position, we will be guided by the following five considerations:

- First, economic, social and cultural rights addressed in U.N. resolutions should be expressly set forth, or reasonably derived from, the Universal Declaration and the International Covenant on Economic, Social and Cultural Rights. While the United States is not a party to the Covenant, as a signatory, we are committed to not defeating the object and purpose of the treaty.

- Second, we will only endorse language that reaffirms the "progressive realization" of these rights and prohibits discrimination.

- Third, language about enforcement must be compatible with our domestic and constitutional framework.

- Fourth, we will highlight the U.S. policy of providing food, housing, medicine and other basic requirements to people in need.

- And fifth, we will emphasize the interdependence of all rights and recognize the need for accountability and transparency in their implementation, through the democratic participation of the people.

At the same time, the U.S. will not hesitate to reject resolutions that are disingenuous, at odds with our laws, or contravene our policy interests. Just because a resolution is titled "a right to food" doesn't mean it is really about the right to food. Resolutions are not labeling exercises. Rather, they are about substance.

Finally, we will push back against the fallacy that countries may substitute human rights they like for human rights they dislike, by granting either economic or political rights. To assert that a population is not "ready" for universal human rights is to misunderstand the inherent nature of these rights and the basic obligations of governments.

All Four Freedoms are key to the Obama administration approach to human rights, national security and sustainable global prosperity. . . .

Freedom from want in foreign policy today means a U.S. leadership role in a global food security initiative that aims to help subsistence farmers expand their production and developing countries to develop their markets. It also means being the world's leader in global health—providing treatment for those infected by HIV, and strengthening health systems in developing countries. It also includes our recent pledge of $150 million in economic aid and democracy assistance to Egypt to help during this time of transition.

For our domestic policy today, freedom from want means this Administration will keep fighting to bring health care to more Americans, improve education to make our country more competitive, and continue to provide unemployment benefits for those who need them. Despite our budget constraints, we will continue to invest in the future of the American people.

We will also continue to urge other countries to invest in a better future for their citizens. And we stand willing to assist by pursuing an approach to development that respects human rights, involves local stakeholders, promotes transparency and accountability, and builds the institutions that underpin sustainable democracy.

This is in our moral interest, our political interest and our strategic interest. President Obama, in his National Security Strategy, put it in terms Franklin Roosevelt would have approved:

> "Democracy does not merely represent our better angels," the President said, "It stands in opposition to aggression and injustice, and our support for universal rights is both fundamental to American leadership and a source of strength in the world."

NOTES & QUESTIONS

1.   As Secretary Posner notes, although the United States has not yet ratified core ESC rights treaties, as a signatory it nevertheless has international obligations with respect to each. Specifically, a country that has signed a treaty has an obligation "to refrain from acts which would defeat the object and purpose of a treaty" until it expresses its intention not to become a party. Vienna Convention on the Law of Treaties art. 18, Jan. 27, 1980, 1155 U.N.T.S. 331. While the United States is not a party to the Vienna Convention, it recognizes that many of the Convention's provisions have become customary international law and has signaled its intention to abide by the principles contained in treaties it has signed. *See* Vienna Convention on the Law of Treaties, U.S. Dep't of State, http://www.state.gov/s/l/treaty/faqs/70139.htm (last visited August 20, 2014). How might this fact be useful to advocates engaged in ESC rights advocacy in the United States?

2.   Does Secretary Posner's speech represent a "success" for U.S. advocates who had been urging the United States to take a stronger and more positive stance on ESC rights? Is it a forceful articulation of economic, social and cultural rights in the United States? How is it qualified? How is it different from the stance taken under the previous administration, as described by Philip Alston? How might advocates draw upon Secretary Posner's speech in policy advocacy with the federal government? How might they critique it?

III.   THE CHALLENGES OF ENGAGING IN ECONOMIC, SOCIAL AND CULTURAL RIGHTS ADVOCACY

A common criticism of ESC rights is that the standards contained in the ICESCR are vague, and that the rights themselves are non-justiciable and thus incapable of being enforced. These concerns, alongside the U.S.'s failure to ratify the core ESC rights treaties, pose particular challenges for U.S. advocates seeking to engage in ESC rights advocacy. The following excerpts explore these critiques and suggest some responses.

ARYEH NEIER, "SOCIAL AND ECONOMIC RIGHTS: A CRITIQUE"
13 Hum. Rts. Brief 1, 1–3 (2006).

By way of introduction, let me first make clear that I favor a fairer distribution of the world's resources; however, I believe that the effort to achieve fairer distribution has to take place through the political process. For the most part, although there may be some small exceptions, it cannot take place through the assertion of rights. I do not think that rights are an abstract concept. I think they are a contract between a citizen and a state, or a citizen and her community, and that a citizen has to be able to enforce her side of that contract.

. . .

The concern I have with economic and social rights is when there are broad assertions of the sort that appear in the Universal Declaration of Human Rights or that appear in the South African Constitution, which speak broadly of a right to shelter or housing, a right to education, a right to social security, a right to a job, and a right to health care. There, I think, we get into territory that is unmanageable through the judicial process and that intrudes fundamentally into an area where the democratic process ought to prevail.

These issues ought to be debated by everyone in the democratic process, with the legislature representing the public and with the public influencing the legislature in turn. To suggest otherwise undermines the very concept of democracy by stripping from it an essential part of its role.

Indeed, whenever you get to these broad assertions of shelter or housing or other economic resources, the question becomes: What shelter, employment, security, or level of education and health care is the person entitled to? It is only possible to deal with this question through the process of negotiation and compromise. Not everybody can have everything. There have to be certain decisions and choices that are made when one comes to the question of benefits, and a court is not the place where it is possible to engage in that sort of negotiation and compromise. It is not the place where different individuals come forward and declare their interests and what they are willing to sacrifice for those interests. That is the heart of the political process; only the political process can handle those questions.

Consider the question of health care. One person needs a kidney transplant to save her life, another needs a heart-bypass operation, and still another needs life-long anti-retroviral therapy. All of these are life-saving measures, but they are expensive. Then there is the concern about primary health care for everyone. If you are allocating the resources of a society, how do you deal with the person who says they need that kidney transplant or that bypass or those anti-retroviral drugs to save their life when the cost of these procedures may be equivalent to providing primary health care for a thousand children? Do you say the greater good for the greater number, a utilitarian principle, and exclude the person whose life is at stake if they do not get the health care that they require? I do not believe that is the kind of thing a court should do. Rather, I think that many different considerations need to be taken into account, and that only through a process of negotiation can an outcome be reached that, although it might not satisfy everybody, allows society to grapple with questions that affect a whole community of people.

. . .

Part of my concern with this question of so-called economic and social rights is that I am a believer in very strong civil and political rights: the right to free speech, the right to assemble, the right not to be tortured, etc. Those rights have to mean exactly the same thing every place in the world. With social and economic "rights," however, it is inevitable that they are going to be applied differently in different places. That is, if you are talking about one country with extensive resources and one that is very poor, there is not going to be the same right to shelter or to health care. Resource allocation has to come into play in determining what is going to be provided, and it is appropriate that countries should deal with these matters in different ways depending upon their resources.

But suppose that one takes that same idea—that different stages of development mean different things for each country—and applies it to the concept of civil and political rights. . . . Therefore, I think it is dangerous to allow this idea of social and economic rights to flourish, particularly because there will always be different stages of development and different resources to consider in determining benefits.

Another way in which the idea of social and economic rights is dangerous is that you can only address economic and social distribution through compromise, but compromise should not enter into the adjudication of civil and political rights. I do not want a society to say that it cannot afford to give individuals the right to speak or publish freely, or the right not to be tortured. Instead, I want to be able to argue as strenuously as possible for these rights and say it does not matter what your other concerns are. Everybody is entitled to speak. No one may be tortured, no matter the situation. We know that there are many people who argue that there are considerations that ought to allow governments to torture somebody because of "exigent circumstances." But I do not want to legitimize compromises as far as civil and political rights are concerned. Putting economic and social rights on the same plane as civil and political rights implicitly takes an area where compromise is essential and brings that into the process of rights adjudication.

. . .

Finally, I would say that it is important to recognize how significant civil and political rights are in dealing with economic and social inequities. . . . Civil and political rights can be tremendously significant . . . and often are crucial when dealing with economic and social inequities. Accordingly, I believe it is important to ensure that civil and political rights are as strong as possible. This is not only because of their intrinsic significance, and not only because of their essential role in making the democratic process possible, but because civil and political rights, although not an ultimate solution to the unfair distribution of resources, are among the most effective ways to address social and economic injustice.

NOTES & QUESTIONS

1.   In his essay, Aryeh Neier, the former president of the Open Society Institute and a former executive director of both Human Rights Watch and the American Civil Liberties Union, expresses a high degree of skepticism about the utility and validity of ESC rights. What is the basis of these concerns? To what extent do you agree with these critiques?

2.   One of Neier's concerns with ESC rights is that they are context-specific. He asks, essentially: "What does it mean for a country to take steps to realize ESC rights to 'the maximum of available resources?' What does 'progressive realization' mean in the context of the United States? What is a 'minimum core?'" How might the context-specific nature of ESC rights pose a challenge for U.S. advocates?

3.   Neier is particularly concerned with the enforceability of ESC rights. In general, questions regarding domestic judicial enforcement of ESC rights take two forms: (1) concerns based on democratic legitimacy (i.e., are antimajoritarian courts overstepping their proper limits when they enforce ESC rights?); and (2) concerns based on judicial competencies (i.e., do domestic adjudicators have a sufficient understanding of ESC rights to render competent decisions?). Professor Helen Hershkoff has argued forcefully that the democratic objection weakens considerably when state courts are enforcing democratically-adopted state constitutional provisions addressing ESC rights. Helen Hershkoff, *Positive Rights and State Constitutions: The Limits of Federal Rationality*, 112 Harv. L. Rev. 1131 (1999). As to competence, national systems elsewhere are proving that they can enforce these rights, with standards for monitoring and enforcing ESC rights emerging from national courts including the South African Constitutional Court and the Canadian Court, and regional institutions such as the Inter-American Commission and Court. Do these developments answer Neier's concern?

4.   Post-reconciliation, South Africa adopted a constitution which includes explicit protections for social and economic rights and requires courts to consider international law in interpreting the constitution. Thus, the South African Constitutional Court is at the forefront of developing a jurisprudence on the justiciability of ESC rights. One way in which the South African Constitutional Court differs from the U.N. Committee on Economic, Social and Cultural Rights, however, is in the Court's seeming rejection of the minimum core obligation in favor of a "reasonableness review" for evaluating claims. Specifically, the Court asks whether the means that the government has chosen are reasonably capable of facilitating the realization of the rights in question. For example, in *Republic of South Africa & Others v. Grootboom*, the South African Constitutional Court evaluated a government housing program in light of the constitutional right of everyone to have access to adequate housing, concluding that a government program that failed to account for the needs of society's worst off was unreasonable. *Republic of S. Africa & Others v. Grootboom* 2001 (46) SA 1 (CC) (S. Afr.) http://www.saflii. org/za/cases/ZACC/2000/19.pdf. *See also Minister for Health v. Treatment Action Campaign* 2002 (5) SA 721 (CC) (S. Afr.), available at http://www. saflii.org/za/cases/ZACC/2002/15.html (holding that Government is required "to devise and implement . . . a comprehensive and coordinated programme to realize progressively the rights of pregnant women and their newborn children to have access to health services to combat mother-to-child transmission of HIV"); Eric C. Christiansen, *Adjudicating Non-Justiciable Rights: Socio-Economic Rights and the South African Constitutional Court*, 38 Colum. Hum. Rts. L. Rev. 321 (2007); Marius Pieterse, *Possibilities and Pitfalls in the Domestic Enforcement of Social Rights: Contemplating the South African Experience*, 26 Hum. Rts. Q. 882 (2004); Lucy A. Williams, *The Right to Housing in South Africa: An Evolving Jurisprudence*, 45 Colum. H.Rts. L. Rev. 816 (2014). What might be the practical effect of this difference

in interpretation? What is the relevance of South Africa's jurisprudence to U.S. advocates engaged in work to promote economic and social rights?

5. Although the U.S. Constitution does not contain explicit and substantive protections for economic, social and cultural rights, many U.S. state constitutions do, and state courts are often called upon to adjudicate them. For example, the New York Court of Appeals, which is New York's highest court, has on many occasions been asked to interpret New York Constitution's Article 17, which requires the state to provide for the "aid, care and support of the needy," and the state constitution's Education Article, which provides for what the Court has interpreted as the right to a "sound basic education." *Bd. of Ed. Levittown Free Union Sch. Dist. v. Nyquist*, 453 N.Y.S.2d 643, 653 (1982). In *Jiggetts v. Grinker*, 554 N.Y.S.2d 92 (1990), the Court was presented with the question of whether the state commissioner of social services has a duty to establish adequate shelter allowances for poor people in the state. The Court first addressed the question of whether the issue was justiciable, and found that it was, because the state social services law mandates that the executive establish adequate grants. The Court went on to hold that public assistance shelter allowances for families with minor children in New York City must bear a reasonable relation to the actual cost of housing, remanding the question of what is reasonable and adequate to the trial court (and resulting in years of subsequent litigation on the question). In *Campaign for Fiscal Equity v. New York*, 769 N.Y.S.2d 106 (2003), the Court of Appeals addressed the question of whether the state system for funding schools in New York City violates state constitutional guarantees for education. In holding that the state must ascertain the actual cost of providing a sound basic education in New York City and reform the system to ensure that every school in the city has the resources necessary for providing the opportunity, the Court stated: "We have neither the authority, nor the ability, nor the will, to micromanage education financing. By the same token . . . it is the province of the Judicial branch to define, and safeguard, rights provided by the New York State Constitution, and order redress for violation of them." *Id.* at 125. Professor Cass Sunstein suggests that the Court of Appeal's adjudication of these cases suggests that "a degree of judicial enforcement of [Roosevelt's second bill of rights] is indeed possible—that courts can take some steps toward protecting reasonable judgments by the legislature." Cass Sunstein, The Second Bill of Rights, FDR's Unfinished Revolution and Why We Need it More Than Ever (2004). What relevance might the jurisprudence from South Africa, Canada, and other national courts, as well as general comments from the U.N. Committee on Economic, Social and Cultural Rights have in litigation and other advocacy efforts to promote the rights to education and housing in New York?

6. For more discussion and critique regarding the issue of how national courts and regional institutions approach the question of justiciability of ESC rights, see Laurence Burgorgue-Larsen, *Economic and Social Rights*, *in* The Inter-American Court of Human Rights 612 (Laurence Burgorgue-Larsen & Amaya Ubeda de Torres eds., Rosalind Greenstein

trans., 2011); Courting Social Justice: Judicial Enforcement of Social and Economic Rights in the Developing World (Daniel M. Brinks & Varun Gauri eds., 2008); Justiciability of Economic and Social Rights: Experiences from Domestic Systems (Fons Coomans ed., 2006); Ida Koch, Human Rights as Indivisible Rights: The Protection of Socio-Economic Demands Under the European Convention on Human Rights (2009); Aoife Nolan, Bruce Porter, & Malcolm Langford, The Justiciability of Social and Economic Rights: An Updated Appraisal (Ctr. Hum. Rts. & Global Just, Working Paper No. 15, 2007); Social Rights Jurisprudence: Emerging Trends in International and Comparative Law (Malcolm Langford ed., 2008); Diane A. Desierto, *Justiciability of Socio-Economic Rights: Comparative Powers, Roles, and Practice in the Philippines and South Africa*, 11 Asian-Pac. L. & Pol'y J. 114 (2010).

In the following excerpt, Kenneth Roth, the executive director of Human Rights Watch, discusses the challenges of ESC related advocacy mounted by a human rights organization which engages primarily in documentation, analysis and exposure ("naming and shaming"). As you read this passage, consider whether you agree that effective advocacy through naming and shaming on ESC-related issues requires clarity of the three elements he identifies.

KENNETH ROTH, "DEFENDING ECONOMIC, SOCIAL AND CULTURAL RIGHTS: PRACTICAL ISSUES FACED BY AN INTERNATIONAL HUMAN RIGHTS ORGANIZATION"
26 Hum. Rts. Q. 63, 63–72 (2004).

Over the last decade, many have urged international human rights organizations to pay more attention to economic, social and cultural (ESC) rights. I agree with this prescription, and for several years Human Rights Watch has been doing significant work in this realm. However, many who urge international groups to take on ESC rights have a fairly simplistic sense of how this is done. Human Rights Watch's experience has led me to believe that there are certain types of ESC issues for which our methodology works well and others for which it does not. In my view, understanding this distinction is key for an international human rights organization such as Human Rights Watch to address ESC rights effectively. Other approaches may work for other types of human rights groups, but organizations such as Human Rights Watch that rely foremost on shaming and the generation of public pressure to defend rights should remain attentive to this distinction.

. . .

In my view, the most productive way for international human rights organizations, like Human Rights Watch, to address ESC rights is by building on the power of our methodology. The essence of that methodology, as I have suggested, is not the ability to mobilize people in the streets, to engage in litigation, to press for broad national plans, or to provide technical assistance. Rather, the core of our methodology is our ability to investigate, expose, and shame. We are at our most effective when we can hold governmental (or, in some cases, nongovernmental) conduct up to a disapproving public. Of course, we do not have to wait passively for public morality to coalesce on a particular issue; we can do much to shape public views by exposing sympathetic cases of injustice and suggesting a moral analysis for understanding them. In the end, the principal power of groups like Human Rights Watch is our ability to hold official conduct up to scrutiny and to generate public outrage. The relevant public is best when it is a local one—that is, the public of the country in question. Surrogate publics can also be used if they have the power to shape the policies of a government or institution with influence over the officials in question, such as by conditioning international assistance or trade benefits, imposing sanctions, or pursuing prosecution.

. . .

In my view, to shame a government effectively—to maximize the power of international human rights organizations like Human Rights Watch—clarity is needed around three issues: violation, violator, and remedy. We must be able to show persuasively that a particular state of affairs amounts to a violation of human rights standards, that a particular violator is principally or significantly responsible, and that a widely accepted remedy for the violation exists. If any of these three elements is missing, our capacity to shame is greatly diminished. We tend to take these conditions for granted in the realm of civil and political rights because they usually coincide.

. . .

In the realm of ESC rights, the three preconditions for effective shaming operate much more independently. (For these purposes, I exclude the right to form labor unions and bargain collectively since while codified in the International Covenant on Economic, Social and Cultural Rights (ICESCR), this right functions more as a subset of the civil and political right to freedom of association.) I accept, for the sake of this argument, that indicia have been developed for subsistence levels of food, housing, medical care, education, etc. When steady progress is not being made toward realizing these subsistence levels, one can presumptively say that a "violation" has occurred.

But who is responsible for the violation, and what is the remedy? These answers flow much less directly from the mere documentation of an ESC rights violation than they do in the civil and political rights realm. . . .

Similar confusion surrounds discussions of appropriate remedies. Vigorously contested views about "structural adjustment" are illustrative. Is structural adjustment the cause of poverty, through its forced slashing of public investment in basic needs, or is it the solution by laying the groundwork for economic development? Supporting evidence can be found on both sides of this debate. When the target of a shaming effort can marshal respectable arguments in its defense, shaming usually fails.

The lesson I draw from these observations is that when international human rights organizations such as Human Rights Watch take on ESC rights, we should look for situations in which there is relative clarity about violation, violator, and remedy.

Broadly speaking, I would suggest that the nature of the violation, violator, and remedy is clearest when it is possible to identify arbitrary or discriminatory governmental conduct that causes or substantially contributes to an ESC rights violation.

. . .

If one accepts that international human rights organizations like Human Rights Watch are at our most powerful in the realm of ESC rights when we focus on discriminatory or arbitrary conduct rather than matters of pure distributive justice, guidance for our ESC work is provided. An important part of our work should be to shape public opinion gradually so that it tends to see ESC issues not only in terms of distributive justice but also in terms of discriminatory or arbitrary conduct.

. . .

It has been clear for many years that the movement would like to do more in the ESC realm. Yet despite repeated professions of interest, its work in this area remains limited. Part of the reason, of course, is expertise; the movement must staff itself somewhat differently to document shortfalls in such matters as health or housing than to record instances of torture or political imprisonment. But much of the reason, I suspect, is a sense of futility. International human rights activists see how little impact they have in taking on matters of pure distributive justice so they have a hard time justifying devoting scarce institutional resources for such limited ends. However, if we focus our attention on ESC policy that can fairly be characterized as arbitrary or discriminatory, I believe our impact will be substantially larger. And there is nothing like success to breed emulation.

Thus, when outsiders ask international human rights organizations such as Human Rights Watch to expand our work on ESC rights, we should insist on a more sophisticated and realistic conversation than has been typical so far. It is not enough, we should point out, to document ESC shortcomings and to declare a rights violation. Rather, we should ask our interlocutors to help us identify ESC shortcomings in which there is relative clarity about the nature of the violation, violator, and remedy, so that our shaming methodology will be most effective. As we succeed in broadening the number of governmental actions that can be seen in this way, we will go a long way toward enhancing the ESC work of the international human rights movement-work that, we all realize, is essential to our credibility.

. . .

NOTES & QUESTIONS

1.   What is the basis of Roth's concern about Human Rights Watch's engagement in advocacy around economic, social and cultural rights? Do you agree that the victim-violator-remedy framework is required for effective advocacy through naming and shaming on ESC related issues? Are there alternative approaches, both to naming and shaming on ESC related issues, and to advocacy approaches on ESC rights more generally? How are Roth's concerns relevant to U.S. NGOs, or to some subset of U.S. NGOs?

2.   Consider the response to Kenneth Roth written by Leonard Rubenstein, the executive director of Physicians for Human Rights:

At a minimum, international human rights organizations, especially those based in the United States, should promote the centrality of economic, social, and cultural rights in creating a just society at home. They should use the credibility and influence they have developed and find creative ways to confront resistance to the acceptance of housing, health care, and economic security as matters of right.

. . .

I agree that naming and shaming can be adapted to certain violations of economic, social, and cultural rights, both at the national and international levels. Most obviously, documentation and exposure of discrimination against women and racial, religious, and ethnic groups in education, health, and economic life is an essential strategy for forcing action by states to eliminate it. Documentation, analysis, and exposure are also desperately needed to show how certain economic and trade policies of wealthy countries and international financial institutions violate the requirements of the Covenant on Economic, Social, and Cultural Rights and bring devastating harms to people in poor countries.

Naming and shaming as a strategy and method can be enormously powerful in this realm.

. . .

Ken Roth, however, not only argues for the utility of naming and shaming as a productive strategy to further economic, social, and cultural rights; he appears to say that, given their skills and track record, it is the only appropriate method for international human rights organizations to use. Moreover, he contends that in the area of economic, social, and cultural rights, naming and shaming can only be successful if applied narrowly, to practices that can be fairly characterized as arbitrary or discriminatory. Otherwise, he says, it will be difficult to identify the violation, violator, and remedy that are essential to an effective naming and shaming strategy.

He is certainly correct that international human rights organizations must be rigorous and unsentimental in applying their resources and skills to advancing economic, social, and cultural rights. I believe, however, that a full account of both the nature of economic, social, and cultural rights and the actions needed to realize them suggest roles beyond naming and shaming, both for domestic and international human rights organizations.

. . .

First, in collaboration with organizations in developing countries, they should engage in analysis and lobbying to influence the design of systems of services so they fulfill the rights at stake. Second, they should advocate for the resources essential to fulfill economic, social, and cultural rights. Third, their monitoring activities—the naming and shaming—should be premised on specific obligations states have, rather than being restricted to conduct that is arbitrary or discriminatory, to assure attention to some of the most serious, chronic violations of economic, social, and cultural rights. This is not, of course, an exclusive list of potential areas of engagement.

Leonard S. Rubenstein, *How International Human Rights Organizations Can Advance Economic, Social and Cultural Rights: A Response to Kenneth Roth*, 26 Hum. Rts. Q. 845, 845–49 (2004).

Do you agree with this critique? Are there additional advocacy strategies that U.S. and international NGOs can engage in order to promote ESC rights within the United States?

IV. THEORETICAL APPROACHES TO ADVANCING THE FULL SPECTRUM OF RIGHTS IN THE U.S.

The debates outlined above notwithstanding, there are pockets of movement and some models of advocacy utilizing human rights frameworks to further ESC rights in the United States. The excerpts below address the theoretical challenges identified by advocates involved in this work. Practical challenges and models are addressed in Section V.

The theoretical challenges to ESC rights advocacy in the U.S. are significant. First, there is tremendous cultural resistance to the essential idea that governments are under an affirmative obligation to ensure economic, social and cultural rights. Second, beyond the cultural resistance, there is the difficulty of reconciling human rights approaches with the longstanding domestic law that privileges civil and political rights and limits government to negative obligations.

The first selection below, by Cathy Albisa, focuses on the cultural challenges. In particular, she examines the ways in which "constitutive commitments" emerge socially and culturally before they are ultimately reflected in law. Among other things, she draws comparisons between the development of U.S. anti-discrimination laws and government commitments involving ESC rights. While she remains essentially optimistic, Albisa's "long" view of the ESC rights movement in the U.S. measures the movement's progress in reshaping culture over decades, lifespans and even centuries rather than single campaigns.

As you read Albisa's selection, ask yourself whether cultural norms are able to change more quickly than she posits? The rapidly increasing acceptance of same-sex marriage offers an example. Significant legal changes in marriage equality have come about in less than a decade.[8] Haven't those legislative reforms and court decisions rested on equally rapid cultural changes? How might Albisa distinguish this example and explain why ESC rights are on such a relatively slow track?

---

[8] *See, e.g.*, William Eskridge, *Backlash Politics: How Constitutional Litigation has Advanced Marriage Equality in the United States*, 93 B.U. L. Rev. 275 (2013); Mary Ziegler, *The Terms of the Debate: Litigation, Argumentative Strategies and Coalitions in the Same-Sex Marriage Struggle*, 39 Fla. St. U. L. Rev. 467 (2012).

CATHY ALBISA, "DRAWING LINES IN THE SAND: BUILDING
ECONOMIC AND SOCIAL RIGHTS NORMS
IN THE UNITED STATES"

Human Rights in the United States: Beyond Exceptionalism,
68, 75–86 (Shareen Hertel & Kathryn Libal eds., 2011).

Prior to the welfare reform efforts of the mid-1990s, [Louis] Henkin observed that our "welfare system and other rights granted by legislation are so deeply embedded as to have near constitutional sturdiness." Has this assertion really withstood the test of time? Have we established a right to public assistance, or to education, or to be free of racial discrimination in employment or public accommodations, or to be protected when joining a labor union, or to Social Security?

That any child in the United States has a formal right to education is probably the most indisputable of the previous claims. . . . The notion of education as a constitutive commitment can be attributed in large part to the common schools movement of the early part of the twentieth century. Every state constitution includes a right to education of some sort, and even the Supreme Court has found support for the right to education in instances of discrimination and absolute exclusion. Although the right to education in our domestic law is not as robust as that found in the international domain and has significant limitations, it is true that no class of children can be excluded formally from any state school system (although informally children are often pushed out through abusive suspension and expulsion policies). On the contrary, children are—for the most part—legally required to attend school.

Almost equally indisputable are the rights protected in the Civil Rights Act of 1964. These include the right to be free from discrimination based on race or sex in employment and public accommodations. Racial discrimination in general has become a thoroughly discredited social approach. Although we accept disparate impacts in many areas of life, it is no longer politically acceptable to formally treat similarly situated people differently. Thus, de jure discrimination has gone the way of flogging for minor offenses—a historical horror we are happy to leave behind. . . . There is a social consensus on the validity of nondiscrimination norms—a consensus that applies even to elected politicians.

Is the right to join a labor union also a constitutive commitment? The right to join a union is indeed constitutionally protected as part of the First Amendment. But in contemporary practice, this protection does not mean that the right to unionize obligates the government to protect individuals against retaliation for joining a union. First, the right is not universal. Farm workers and domestic workers are explicitly excluded from national laws that protect against retaliation for joining a union.

Second, there are still many public officials who are explicitly anti-union. It is publicly acceptable to take the position that unions are bad for the economy and for the nation as a whole.

Although there are some constraints on what public officials can promote regarding anti-unionization, these are not parallel to the absolute lines drawn around racial discrimination in the public sphere. Not surprisingly, the labor movement has suffered major setbacks and defeats since the 1980s, with rates of unionization plummeting.

Finally, has Social Security for the elderly become a constitutive commitment? There are high levels of popular support for Social Security through government-managed retirement programs, and there was considerable outcry when President George W. Bush proposed to privatize it. Yet I am still skeptical that access to Social Security has achieved the status of an enduring right in the United States. Social Security pensions are not universal. Unless you pay into the system, you are not entitled to any support. Current reversals in the fortunes of the stock market make government-run pension programs seem the wiser choice for stability and peace in old age—but this is a practical argument, not a moral imperative. Rights are the things we protect despite arguments about practicality. If the elderly had a right to Social Security, then it would not matter if they were undocumented or had simply recently arrived in the United States as refugees or legal immigrants. Indeed, it would not matter whether they had paid into the system for any reason. It would simply be their right to enjoy basic economic security in old age. I suspect that Social Security is perceived more as a contractual obligation than as a basic human right. Public officials who openly seek to privatize it are not demonized as morally repugnant. Although people might be outraged at the threat of privatization, officials who promote it are not deemed outrageous (as racists are) but rather simply wrong.

The remaining parts of our social safety net are on far more fragile ground than Social Security. . . . [T]he entitlement to welfare was dismantled amid the reforms of 1996. Other aspects of the safety net are also attacked fairly regularly, including health coverage for the poor (Medicaid). But none of this should be terribly surprising, given that there has never been a social consensus that these programs confer or protect any sort of fundamental rights.

Unlike the Civil Rights Act, the legislative history of welfare is marked by phrases like "family assistance," "temporary assistance," "support," and later "personal responsibility," "transition," and "work." Although in substance welfare differs little from a right depending on the scope of the entitlement, it is radically distinct in terms of social perceptions. From its inception, welfare has been associated far more with charity than rights. Additionally, welfare programs have not been universal. A person could be extremely poor and still not be eligible for cash assistance if she or he did not have children. Such benefits are not attached to the individual but rather to the family. If basic economic security were thought of as a right, it would make no sense to exclude any category of people.

After the reforms of 1996, it became impossible to argue that welfare was any sort of right. There was no guarantee of receiving welfare if the state ran out of funds. Moreover, recipients became ineligible for welfare after a certain number of months—even if the need remained severe. In many states, additional children did not receive assistance if they were born into a family that already received welfare support. . . . The stated purpose of the 1996 reforms was to push people off the rolls. By this measure, the law was stunningly successful.

In sum, I believe we have achieved some constitutive commitments—specifically, education and the right to be free from de jure discrimination in private employment, housing, and public accommodations. I would include in the latter category sex discrimination. (Although I have not touched on it in this chapter, discrimination against the disabled is moving in the direction of a constitutive commitment.) I also believe that there are rights—such as joining a union and economic security in old age—where we have laid part of the foundation. These are considered significant human interests and have far more defenders than detractors. But there are also rights that remain disparaged—access to welfare and other social safety net programs—that matter most to the most vulnerable and excluded in our society.

. . .

We have much further to go before the full range of economic and social rights become constitutive commitments in the United States. Constitutive commitments can be divided into three categories: those that are explicitly recognized in the Constitution, those that have been interpreted as part of the Constitution through case law, and those that have been adopted through legislation and deep social consensus. Because the current Supreme Court is unlikely to render judgments grounded in human rights, and because constitutional change is daunting even under more favorable circumstances, the idea of forging a strategy to create constitutive commitments that fall outside the constitutional sphere is particularly appealing.

Doing so would require articulating the minimum elements of a constitutive commitment and then intentionally building layers of social consensus around and investment in such commitments. Important questions to ask include:

- Is it universal (or at least universal for some stage of life, such as for children or the elderly)?

- Is it equitable and equal, meaning does each person receive the same level of guarantee for the right—including those with particular needs? (A contrary example would be different tiers of health insurance for different people.)

- Is the language associated with it inclusive of the concept of rights and does it imply permanence?

- Is it socially unacceptable to deny its legitimacy as a right?

- Is it enforceable?

- Was it adopted after significant social changes and/or social movements?

Universality is key because it defines the basic essence of a human right. Moreover, it is what distinguishes a right from an interest—or in the even more pejorative term often used in the United States, a special interest. A right is held by everyone, regardless of his or her particular interest in it. Equity and equality on the one hand, and universality on the other, represent two sides of the same coin. Equity, in particular, raises the bar to the point where not only should each person be able to realize all their rights, but resources should be used in a way that prioritizes what each person or group needs to do so. Additionally, the language of rights, if it reflects a social consensus, increases the likelihood that it would be socially unacceptable for a public figure to argue against the right at stake, which makes the right practically immune from attack.

A constitutive commitment must also be reflected in some vehicle for enforcement against violations. Just because it may be socially unacceptable to attack a right in principle does not mean that it will not be consistently violated in practice. If a right is unenforceable, it loses credibility, and there is far less reason for anyone to be invested in protecting it. Thus, a genuine commitment must include an enforcement strategy.

Finally, "rights are born of wrongs," and here is where social movements play a critical role in transforming economic and social rights into constitutive commitments in the United States. Unless recognition of a right is the result of a sustained social movement activism, its foundation is far too unsteady.

. . .

So how do we create the language, legitimacy, and social buy-in necessary to create constitutive commitments for economic and social rights? At a minimum, advocacy and organizing strategies must break the isolation of the poor by creating platforms for leadership and the kind of storytelling that reclaims a person's dignity. This requires furiously rejecting the "victim advocacy model"—where an advocacy group "shows" a victim's side of the story, and then the "victim" falls silent while their representatives speak about solutions. Part of the story must include poor people themselves creating and conveying an image of the solution. Poor people must also become both the harbingers of the future definition of rights and stakeholders who engage in the conversation over how those ideals should be represented in the legal system.

This strategy for building constitutive commitments is grounded in the relationship and interactions between culture, law, and social movements. It requires working at multiple levels, lest short-term gains be swept away in the blink of an election cycle. In the daily work of activists, it means finding ways to scale the walls that exist between the poorest communities and the sites where decisions are made. Walls turned on their sides, after all, are bridges. Once we build and cross them, the conversation can never be the same again.

Creating alliances across social sectors and communities combined with consensus on what we want to achieve will dramatically increase the likelihood that constitutive commitments on economic and social rights take hold in the United States. The conceptual framework of human rights is essential to building that consensus: universality, interdependence of rights, public accountability, equity, equality, and participation. We can build those alliances by being willing to let the poor lead themselves and by committing to provide all the tools necessary for them to succeed. Constitutive commitments are not built in one or two election cycles. This is decades-long work. Perhaps the most important ingredient is sustained commitment to the vision and the approach. Changing a law might easily be characterized as an advocacy project. Changing a culture, however, must be a life's work.

NOTES & QUESTIONS

1.   The civil rights movement of the 1960s mentioned by Albisa is well known, but there was also a welfare rights movement during the same era. The National Welfare Rights Organization spearheaded advocacy efforts, led by low income mothers on welfare as well as organizers, lawyers and other supporters. Though the movement had some successes, it was short-lived and virtually all its successes have been undermined by subsequent welfare cuts and restrictions. Stigma, lack of funding, and the difficulty of sustaining poor people's activism in the face of daily challenges all contributed to the short-lived nature of the organized campaign. *See generally* Martha F. Davis, Brutal Need: Lawyers and the Welfare Rights Movement (1996); Felicia Kornbluh, The Battle for Welfare Rights (2007). Albisa calls for a new movement led by low income people, but how does she propose to overcome

these same hurdles in the 21st century? Would an explicitly human rights framework for organizing and mobilization help this effort, or simply marginalize poor people further and cut off their alliances with other domestic movements that are not human rights-based?

2.   Albisa's idea that cultural change occurs over life-spans also suggests that new generations must build on the work of prior generations to incorporate ESC rights into public consciousness and acceptance. Is that a realistic goal? What steps would you suggest to ensure that sort of "baton passing" across generations of activists working for ESC rights?

———————

Beyond the cultural hurdles facing ESC rights advocates are the legal hurdles that lawyers and clients must confront. There is difficulty in translation: human rights law often utilizes language and concepts that are unfamiliar in the domestic context. And there is difficulty in implementation: domestic law provides little protection for ESC rights, and is resistant to interpretations that would incorporate ESC rights.

One approach to this challenge is to try to reconcile international and domestic legal concepts. In the excerpt that follows, Professor Gillian McNaughton takes on this task in the area of health care and equality. First, she carefully parses international and domestic legal sources to ascertain the possible meanings of equality in the health care context, identifying both bloc inequality and individual one-to-one equality as possible approaches. Finding that both of these approaches to equality may include a substantive component, she then brings this new understanding to bear on the status of the right to health in the United States. Noting that domestic law typically does not recognize poverty as a valid "bloc" for measuring inequality, she suggests that the concept of individual one-to-one equality may support positive government obligations and domestic extension of health care rights.

Though both Cathy Albisa and Gillian MacNaughton are lawyers, in many ways, MacNaughton's careful legal analysis is 180 degrees away from Albisa's call for organizing and cultural change. As you read this excerpt, consider whether you share MacNaughton's faith in the power of law. Consider, too, whether there is a way to embrace both approaches simultaneously.

GILLIAN MACNAUGHTON, "UNTANGLING EQUALITY AND NON-DISCRIMINATION TO PROMOTE THE RIGHT TO HEALTH CARE FOR ALL"

11 Health and Human Rights: An Int'l J. 47, 52–56 (2009).

Inequalities in health care systems implicate the right to health, which is enshrined in the majority of national constitutions, the

Constitution of the World Health Organization, and many international human rights treaties. The Universal Declaration of Human Rights includes the right to health as a component of the right to an adequate standard of living. The ICESCR also contains the right to health and requires the countries that are parties to the Covenant to "recognize the right of everyone to the enjoyment of the highest attainable standard of physical and mental health." Additionally, the Covenant calls for countries to take steps, for example, to reduce infant mortality, to improve environmental conditions, to ensure workplace safety, to prevent and treat epidemics, and to secure health care services for all.

. . .

Importantly, parties to the Covenant must ensure equal access for all to health care and the underlying determinants of health. Accordingly, payment for health care services must be based on the principle of equity, meaning that "poorer households should not be disproportionately burdened with health expenses as compared to richer households." Additionally, health resource allocations should not favor expensive curative health care, often accessible to only a privileged few, at the expense of primary and preventative health care, benefiting the larger population.

The Covenant acknowledges that governments have constraints due to limited resources and thus allows for progressive realization of the right to health; however, it imposes an immediate obligation upon governments to guarantee the exercise of the right to health without discrimination of any kind. Further, governments have the immediate obligation "to ensure equitable distribution of all health facilities, goods and services."

Like the Human Rights Committee, the Committee on Economic, Social and Cultural Rights is troubled by bloc inequalities, and it is particularly disturbed by inequalities that adversely impact poor people.

. . .

In General Comment No. 20 on non-discrimination, the Committee highlights several areas of concern with health care systems. For example, the Committee states, "In relation to young persons, unequal access by adolescents to sexual and reproductive health information and services amounts to discrimination." Denial of access to health insurance on the basis of health status may also amount to discrimination.

Further, the exercise of rights should not be qualified by a person's place of residence. Thus, governments must ensure "even distribution in the availability and quality of primary, secondary and palliative health care facilities" in all localities and regions, including urban and rural areas. Overall, the Committee's approach to non-discrimination and equality seeks to eliminate bloc inequalities, both formal and substantive. It understands "other status" to be flexible and commonly recognizes new blocs for social groups that are vulnerable and suffer marginalization.

Beyond the Committee's work, Paul Hunt, UN Special Rapporteur on the right to health from 2002 to 2008, also elaborated on the content of the right to health and, in particular, on a right-to-health approach to health systems. In his 2008 Annual Report to the Human Rights Council, he stated:

> At the heart of the right to the highest attainable standard of health lies an effective and integrated health system encompassing health care and the underlying determinants of health, which is responsive to national and local priorities, and accessible to all. Without such a health system, the right to the highest attainable standard of health can never be realized.

Hunt also expressed his views on equality and non-discrimination as core features of a health system. In the same report, he stated that governments have "a legal obligation to ensure that a health system is accessible to all without discrimination," and "that disadvantaged individuals and communities enjoy, in practice, the same access as those who are more advantaged." Accordingly, both the Committee on Economic, Social and Cultural Rights and the Special Rapporteur on the right to health consider equality and non-discrimination to be important features of a human rights-respecting health system. Additionally, they are both acutely concerned with ensuring that adequate resources are allocated to health systems so that poor people have access to equal health facilities, goods, and services. These concerns might be addressed by promoting the ideas that economic status is a prohibited ground of discrimination and that positive equality requires health systems to offer the same health facilities, goods, and services to all. Both ideas may help to equalize health care systems.

. . .

Bloc Equality

The idea of bloc equality is well illustrated in the 1954 case, Brown v. Board of Education, in which the US Supreme Court held that a state law segregating children in the public schools on the basis of race, even if the physical facilities and other tangible factors were equal, deprives minority children of equal education opportunities in violation of the Equal Protection Clause of the US Constitution. Today, such a two-tiered system of schools that discriminates on the basis of race also would . . . violate the non-discrimination provisions in the ICESCR and the ICCPR, which came into effect in 1976.

Tiered health care systems also exist in many countries. In apartheid South Africa, for example, the two-tiered health care system was race-based in a similar fashion to the two-tiered school system in the US case. Health care systems are, however, more often tiered on the basis of economic status. Indeed, the World Bank has supported "segmenting out" middle-and high-income groups into private health insurance schemes, leaving the public sector health services to focus on poor people. Such a segmented health care system results in separate health care systems for rich and poor people. Not surprisingly, segmentation is likely to result in unequal health services, reflecting and reinforcing socioeconomic inequalities.

Individual one-to-one equality

There is no single case that exemplifies the right to one-to-one equality in the way that Brown v. Board of Education exemplifies the right to bloc equality.

Several less well-known cases brought under state constitutions in the US, however, have required one-to-one equality in school financing. In *Brigham v. State of Vermont*, for example, the Vermont Supreme Court ruled that the state system for funding public education, which was largely based on local property taxes and resulted in wide disparities in funding per pupil across school districts, violated the Common Benefits Clause of the Vermont Constitution. In that case, the 1995 per-pupil spending varied from US$2,979 to US$7,726, depending on the school district. Further, the richer school districts taxed themselves at a lower rate than the poorer districts and still achieved revenues allowing more than twice the funding per student. This school financing system failed to protect individual one-to-one equality of the students in violation of the right to equality under the Vermont Constitution. Several state supreme courts in the US have reached similar conclusions.

The Constitutional Court of South Africa, in *Mashavha v. President of the Republic of South Africa*, reached a similar conclusion concerning unequal disbursement of disability benefits across the provinces. In that case, the Court held invalid a presidential proclamation made under the Interim Constitution that assigned administration of social services to provincial governments. The Court recognized that, historically, gross inequalities had been legally imposed on the basis of race and also on the basis of geographical area, and that therefore, "the need for equality could not be ignored" in interpreting the Interim Constitution. Accordingly, the Court stated that it would offend human dignity and the fundamental right of equality to allow higher old age pensions or child benefits in one province than was allowed in another. Such a system would "create different classes of citizenship and divide South Africa into favoured and disfavoured areas." In so doing, the Court recognized a right to individual one-to-one equality with respect to social benefits.

The Human Rights Committee and the Committee on Economic, Social and Cultural Rights both view such sharp disparities in spending on health care or education across geographic locations as discrimination. Yet, neither committee has explicitly called for one-to-one equality in spending. In general, the notion of such individual one-to-one equality is rarely recognized outside the US. At the federal level in the US, where social rights are generally not recognized, one-to-one equality is primarily applicable to civil and political rights, like the right to vote.

There has been some success, as demonstrated by the school funding cases, under state constitutions, all of which recognize at least some social rights. Although several state constitutions contain some form of a right to health, they have received little interpretation by the courts. The best possibilities for developing a positive right to equality in health care may be under these state constitutions or others that include welfare provisions. Even where there is no substantive provision on health or welfare, however, the positive right to equality is still applicable in any area in which the government regulates.

. . .

Similarly, many individual claims for publicly funded health benefits implicate the positive right to equality, when a decision results in the claimant receiving a benefit that others do not receive. Such violations of one-to-one equality may also amount to violations of bloc equality when such individual claims are widespread. In Brazil, for example, poorer individuals may not have equal access to the medicines that wealthier individuals obtain from the public health care system, given that the latter have better access to courts and are able to bring right-to-health claims, which are routinely granted. As Siri Gloppen notes, individual claims for the right to health may skew health spending in favor of more privileged sectors of society, reducing the overall equity of the system.

Courts should balance this collective right to equality in health care against individual claims for health benefits. The positive right to one-to-one equality provides this balance by requiring that benefits available to one be available to all. Accordingly, both equality rights and social rights, particularly for poorer people, could be advanced at the international level by the human rights treaty bodies, as well as at the national level by courts, adopting the notion of one-to-one equality, especially in the vast majority of countries that recognize social rights.

. . .

NOTES & QUESTIONS

1.   What value-added does the international human rights perspective bring to Professor McNaughton's analysis? Why look to international human rights norms when U.S. cases like *Brown v. Board* and *Brigham v. State of Vermont* provide domestic support for differing approaches to equality?

2.   Professor McNaughton mentions in passing that "although several state constitutions contain some form of a right to health, they have received little interpretation by the courts." In contrast to these health clauses, every state constitution has an equality provision and all have been interpreted by the courts in a wide range of contexts. Might McNaughton's analysis linking equality with health care access pave the way for more judicial consideration of health care rights? Would it be equally relevant in states that do not have health provisions in their constitutions?

3.   General Comment No. 14 of the Committee on Economic, Social and Cultural Rights states that "the right to health must be understood as a right to the enjoyment of a variety of facilities, goods, services and conditions necessary for the realization of the highest attainable standard of health." Further, it clarifies that the right to health includes both timely and appropriate health care and the underlying determinants of health, such as potable water, adequate sanitation, nutritious food, secure housing, healthy working and environmental conditions, and access to health-related education and information. Are all of these determinants of health susceptible to an equality analysis? While the meaning of "potable" may be clear and ascertainable, what about the terms "healthy," or "nutritious," or "adequate"? For example, can a government or a court realistically use an equality standard to determine if there is access to nutritious food? For more discussion of this issue, see Angela Duger, et al., *A Human Rights-Based Approach to Food Security*, 46 Clearinghouse Rev. 202 (2012).

4.   In *Drawing Lines*, Cathy Albisa argues that the movement toward acceptance of ESC rights should be led by those most affected. Would grassroots activists or other representatives of the constituent groups that Albisa identifies find Professor McNaughton's analysis useful in their organizing on these issues? Or are the ideas about different concepts of equality too subtle to support organizing? If so, what productive use can movement lawyers make of McNaughton's analysis?

V.   PRACTICE-ORIENTED APPROACHES TO INTEGRATING A HUMAN RIGHTS FRAME INTO ESC RIGHTS ADVOCACY

Advocates working to advance ESC rights in the United States must eventually move beyond theory to implementation. Many of advocates' practical approaches to ESC rights implementation are discussed in other chapters. They include: systematic integration of human rights norms into state court litigation concerning ESC rights such as education, health and housing; engagement of U.N. mechanisms to raise ESC rights issues in conjunction with federal government treaty reporting; and enactment of local and state resolutions and ordinances incorporating human rights norms and standards.

Yet moving from theory to practice is not always easy. For example, even when human rights law could enhance and support domestic arguments, advocates acting in a representational capacity must make strategic decisions based on their client's interests. When a judge is hostile to international human rights law, ethical considerations may dictate that an advocate hold back.

The step before that strategic decision is, however, determining whether human rights law is relevant at all. In the excerpt below, Professor Davis analyzes a poverty law case and examines the ways in which an international human rights perspective might have enhanced the domestic arguments made by the legal aid lawyers handling the case. As she acknowledges, whether or not to use these materials is a strategic decision that will depend on the venue, the judge, and the client's interests. However, she tries to make a case that international human rights law has something to contribute to local legal aid and legal services advocacy. As you read this excerpt, consider whether her argument is successful, or whether this exercise simply drives home Cathy Albisa's point that cultural change must come before more legalistic efforts?

MARTHA F. DAVIS, "HUMAN RIGHTS IN THE TRENCHES: USING INTERNATIONAL HUMAN RIGHTS LAW IN EVERYDAY LEGAL AID CASES"

41 Clearinghouse Rev. 414, 414–20 (2007).

[W]hile lofty international human rights principles and ringing phrases such as "human dignity" may seem appropriate references in appellate cases challenging serious and systemic wrongs, they can seem tone-deaf—and perhaps even counter-productive—in the halls of housing court or in a fair hearing. When domestic public interest lawyers participate in trainings on using international human rights as an advocacy tool, this question almost always comes up: Can advocacy of international human rights principles really play a useful role in run-of-the-mill legal aid cases? It would be nice to respond with a simple, resounding "yes." But the question deserves a more nuanced answer. Certainly, from a "big picture" view of legal work on behalf of low-income clients, international human rights are relevant to even the most mundane and local case. When lawyers take on individual benefit cases, for example, they contribute to a larger effort to protect the economic and social rights of individuals—rights seldom recognized under U.S. law but central to international human rights law.

. . .

So what are the right occasions? How can you use human rights in day-to-day practice? While no legal aid case is "generic," I describe a few representative cases below. [Editors' Note: Only one is excerpted here.]

. . .

Government Benefits: Work, Education, and Training

Case Example: Ms. P, a 24-year-old single mother of two, approached a legal aid office for help. A survivor of domestic violence, she had escaped a life-threatening situation only to be faced with hunger and homelessness after her public assistance application was denied. She needed to obtain the benefits to which she was entitled and, because she lacked skills, to participate in an education and training program in place of a work assignment.

Analysis: Given the benefits law relating to education and training, access to such programs may be severely restricted. Ms. P's ability to continue receiving benefits while participating in such programs will likely turn on an administrator's discretion or, if the matter is appealed, on a judge's interpretation of state law. However, relevant international human rights standards could (1) frame the issues sympathetically, (2) encourage a judge or administrator to exercise discretion favorably and, or instead, to interpret the relevant statute generously, and (3) lay the groundwork for systemic change in policies that limit access to education and training.

First, as a domestic violence survivor, Ms. P has particular international law claims that enhance her arguments for access to education and training. Over the last twenty-five years, the United Nations has ratified at least one international human rights treaty—the International Covenant on Civil and Political Rights—that recognizes the right to government protection from and remedies for domestic violence perpetrated by private actors.

Two even more widely accepted treaties—signed but not ratified by the United States—similarly protect women and children: the Convention on the Elimination of All Forms of Discrimination Against Women and the Convention on the Rights of the Child. Through its ratification of the Charter of the Organization of American States, the United States is held to the standards of the American Declaration of the Rights and Duties of Man as well as the charter. The Inter-American Convention on the Prevention, Punishment, and Eradication of Violence Against Women, a regional treaty implementing the Declaration which the United States has yet to ratify, also recognizes women's right to be free from domestic violence and requires governments to take measures to prevent, investigate, and punish such acts.

While these treaties hold national governments directly accountable for dealing with domestic violence, states and localities also have obligations under international law. As an initial matter, under international human rights law each national government subject to a treaty must ensure that treaty principles are implemented throughout its political subdivisions. In the United States the principal mechanism for ensuring compliance with ratified treaties is the Supremacy Clause. Many state constitutions explicitly acknowledge the supremacy of ratified treaties and impose an independent obligation on state governments to implement a treaty's provisions once the national government takes action to adopt it.

The International Covenant on Civil and Political Rights, the Convention on Elimination of All Forms of Discrimination Against Women, the Convention on the Rights of the Child, and the Inter-American treaty, which establish nations' obligation to adopt affirmative measures to combat and remedy domestic violence, offer considerable support for adequate welfare benefits and for education and training programs to ensure that women have the economic means to end violent relationships and to protect their children from the dire impact of violence. In Ms. P's case, however, the government apparently did little or nothing to prevent the violence in the first place and is now compounding its initial failure by making it difficult for Ms. P to achieve the economic independence that she needs to support her family without further reliance on the batterer.

At the very least, this inaction violates the government's obligation to bring its system into compliance with the International Covenant on Civil and Political Rights, which the United States has ratified, and the Convention on the Rights of the Child, many provisions of which U.S. courts have recognized as customary international law. For example, the International Covenant on Civil and Political Rights recognizes domestic violence as a form of sex discrimination and accordingly requires that governments take affirmative steps to curtail it in order to achieve greater social equality.

Similarly, Article 26 of the Convention on the Rights of the Child specifically deals with a child's right to benefit from social security, "taking into account the resources and the circumstances of the child," including the potential for domestic violence in the home. A lawyer representing Ms. P might want to use these international human rights principles as a way to frame the issues, particularly to underscore the government's role in perpetuating the impact of the violence and aggravating Ms. P's current problems.

Second, even aside from her experiences of domestic violence, Ms. P can cite international law to support her argument for access to adequate education and training. While the United States has ratified none of the relevant treaties, and therefore is not legally bound by them, the treaties nevertheless contribute to the weight that should be given to Ms. P's claims.

International human rights law deals extensively with vocational education and training as a component of both the right to work and the right to a basic education. As early as 1946, the Universal Declaration of Human Rights provided that "[t]echnical and professional education shall be made generally available." The International Covenant on Economic, Social and Cultural Rights, completed in 1966, expanding on the Universal Declaration's earlier formulation and addressing the right to work, provides that "the full realization of this right shall include technical and vocational guidance and training programmes, policies and techniques to achieve steady economic, social and cultural development and full and productive employment under conditions safeguarding fundamental political and economic freedoms to the individual."

Article 13 of this covenant, dealing with the right to education, also refers to vocational training programs. Further, under the general comment issued by the Committee on Economic, Social, and Cultural Rights in 1999 to elucidate the meaning of these provisions, "[t]echnical and vocational education (TVE) forms part of both the right to education and the right to work (art. 6 (2)). . . . [T]he Committee takes the view that [technical and vocational education] forms an integral element of all levels of education."

The committee stated that vocational and professional training programs "should be understood as a component of general education" and that such training is needed because, among other reasons, "[i]t enables students to acquire knowledge and skills which contribute to their personal development, self-reliance and employability and enhances the productivity of their families and communities, including the State party's economic and social development." The committee particularly noted the relationship between vocational training and the anti-discrimination provisions found elsewhere in the International Covenant on Economic, Social, and Cultural Rights, supporting "programmes which promote the [technical and vocational education] of women, girls, out-of-school youth, unemployed youth, the children of migrant workers, refugees, persons with disabilities and other disadvantaged groups."

In Ms. P's case, a legal aid advocate might seek exercise of discretion under state law to permit Ms. P to pursue education and training. Combined with a range of equitable arguments to pursue education and possible domestic legal authority—such as a state constitutional provision on education, state antidiscrimination laws that extend to victims of domestic violence, and policy pronouncements favoring workforce development made by the state legislature and state program administrators—international human rights law's strong statements about the fundamental nature of training and education may help Ms. P individually and may lay the groundwork for more general advocacy.

The posture of Ms. P's case presents an opportunity to raise international human rights principles affirmatively. In an initial submission appealing to her caseworker's discretion or in a petition seeking a review of denial of access to education and training, an advocate might cite the international law making government accountable for failing to eliminate the violence confronting Ms. P and then use that framework to strengthen her claim for services in the wake of the domestic violence. Reference to the human rights status of education and training may also highlight the significance of this issue and show that Ms. P's claims are entirely consistent with needs that are recognized globally, particularly for families disrupted by violence.

The human rights law relating to education and training may also support more generalized advocacy on the issue. Several grassroots groups around the nation have focused their efforts on expanding welfare recipients' access to education and training, particularly postsecondary education. International human rights principles offer the groups an additional tool as they seek policy changes that would expand access to these programs. For example, proponents of educational options for benefit recipients might appeal to international bodies such as the Human Rights Committee (perhaps through the shadow reporting process), the U.N. Special Rapporteur on the Right to Education, the U.N. Special Rapporteur on Violence Against Women, or the Inter-American Commission Rapporteur on the Rights of Women, as a way to put additional pressure on states and the federal government to expand access to education and training. Advocates could also seek a general hearing on the issue before the Inter-American Commission on Human Rights.

Merely focusing on Ms. P's individual circumstances, without appeal to broader international human rights principles, will have little impact on the many clients who share her concerns. Enlisting international human rights law in support of Ms. P's case may also contribute to broader efforts on behalf of legal aid clients who need access to education and training programs in order to leave poverty permanently.

. . .

While Professor Davis speculates on how human rights materials might be used by legal aid lawyers, the Maryland Legal Aid Bureau (MLAB), a state wide organization providing free civil legal services for low-income people throughout Maryland, has moved from theoretical implementation to actual implementation: it adopted a human rights framework in its mission statement and has taken steps to integrate human rights into its daily practices. Leading up to this shift, MLAB conducted focus groups and surveys of its clients, concluding that the human rights framework was ultimately more responsive to the clients' needs and interests than other possibilities grounded in domestic law. Having taken this step, MLAB is now working out the particulars. Among the questions being asked are, how should this mission be implemented, given MLAB's scarce resources as an NGO serving the poor? For example, must human rights law play a role in every case? And what role should MLAB play in the international arena, holding the U.S. accountable for respecting their clients' human rights? What steps should MLAB take to be a human rights employer—perhaps applying the Guiding Principles on Business and Human Rights, discussed in **Chapter XI**, to their staffing policies? On a positive and perhaps unexpected note, MLAB staffers report that the human rights framework has facilitated conversations and collaboration across units so that, for example, housing attorneys and government benefit attorneys can connect their work through use of a human rights lens. The following excerpt written by MLAB's former assistant director of advocacy, Peter Sabonis, puts their work in a human rights context. As you read this, consider the drawbacks and benefits of this reframing from the perspectives of MLAB and MLAB's clients.

J. PETER SABONIS, USING A HUMAN RIGHTS FRAMEWORK AT THE MARYLAND LEGAL AID BUREAU

44 Clearinghouse Rev. 450, 451–58 (2011).

To us, international human rights treaties were not tickets to more client-friendly United Nations and regional forums, although those forums could be utilized where necessary or appropriate. They also were not supremacy clause trump cards to be played in court when our own statutes failed to provide remedies, although again this was an option.

We saw incorporating human rights treaties into our work first as a mind-set that revived the best of our legal services roots. Most of our current attorneys were not alive when the federal Legal Services Program was created to be a tool in a national antipoverty initiative that emphasized maximum feasible participation by the relevant communities. Our advocates are more familiar with the federal restrictions on systemic advocacy and the idea that we exist primarily to give resource-strapped clients simple access to justice in courts or administrative forums. The community immersion and law reform that dominated the early history of the legal services movement now seem reserved for a small group of heroic lawyers or programs.

Beginning with the premise that clients, because of their own humanity, are entitled to civil and economic rights, we hoped to trigger both systemic and individual advocacy that was characteristic of our early history: aggressive, creative, client-centered, and movement-oriented.

Building a Human Rights Framework for Systemic Work

Catherine Albisa, executive director of the National Economic and Social Rights Initiative, spoke at a programwide kickoff event in October 2009 and assisted us in constructing our human rights framework. Albisa acknowledged that our effort was akin to "building an airplane while you fly it," but she gave us some principles that have been helpful in guiding our thinking in both systemic and individual advocacy to date:

- *What is the value added in raising a human rights argument? Does it make my claim stronger? And if it does not, does it present an opportunity to use this legal and policy tool without compromising my case or project?* If the answer to the last two of these questions is "no," then the human rights framework is used only as an analytical starting point.

- *Just say it—to judges, legislators, clients, advocates, and one another.* As Albisa said to us, "if we who believe in these rights are not willing to say whenever and wherever we can that these are fundamental human rights and that the government has a sacred responsibility to protect them, then we aren't likely to make much progress."

- *Work in a multifaceted way, with a movement focus.* In Albisa's words: "It is not just a court strategy, or a press strategy, or an organizing strategy. It has to happen on all fronts simultaneously so that we can create social assumptions about what people have a right to expect and what government has an obligation to do." Albisa adds: "The activists aren't just all working in their own silos; they are coordinating to create social movement in multiple sectors at once."

Thoughtful critics of human rights have historically expressed concern that rights-based strategies emphasize litigation and lobbying at the expense of more democratic and radical grassroots activism. Similarly these critics are concerned that advocates like us do not understand the politics-and-economics interplay that actually determines rights, and, even if any human "economic" rights are secured in court or legislatures, this interplay will lead to an inevitable "implementation gap" between right and reality.

These concerns are legitimate, and we at the Maryland Legal Aid Bureau are trying to formulate our own approaches by recognizing these pitfalls and dynamics. We hope to be savvy and engage in a praxis of action and reflection informed by a structural analysis of socioeconomic forces. We also hope to glean lessons from those who have previously battled (with or without success) to realize civil or economic rights.

While every era presents its own opportunities and political dynamics, most successful campaigns to realize previously unrecognized rights have involved organization. Organized people are often the only weapon that can defeat the organized resources that often oppose social change. Legal services to low-income persons can actively facilitate this organization or passively undermine it.

Thus our first priority involved educating our legal advocates about how organization and mobilization help in achieving significant social change. On a more concrete level, we prioritized the representation of client-based groups who were pursuing goals compatible with our own. We also challenged our advocates, particularly those in communities without active organizing, to be creative in using legal education, outreach, and assistance to bring clients with common interests into contact with one another and with concerned activists. In short, we started to use the human rights bridge to link lawyers and organizers.

Surprisingly our attempts to encourage organization raised more apprehension than adopting the human rights advocacy goals themselves. Many advocates and at least one major funder, accustomed to the proverbial tension between systemic and individual casework in legal services, expressed concern that we had sharply tipped the balance between the two to the systemic side at the cost of ignoring individual client needs.

We have assuaged them, however, with our belief that our framework will eventually transform this traditional systemic-individual dichotomy. While group representation and organizing may divert time from direct representation, these activities can facilitate organization and advocacy that might not directly involve the Maryland Legal Aid Bureau but may result in significant systemic change. Representing or educating individual clients, and linking them with other individuals with similar issues and interests (through methods consistent with our ethical responsibilities), maximizes the opportunity for organization to develop. For better or for worse, we have a commodity—legal services and knowledge—that is valuable and needed by the communities we serve. The way we deliver this commodity can either facilitate community organization or ignore it.

· · ·

The Maryland Legal Aid Bureau is an ideal candidate for reporting human rights violations across the state. To date, we have not characterized the presenting problems of our clients as human rights violations, but this is changing. The stories we hear daily about the denial or termination of housing, health care, and food and income assistance, or about the denials of employment and living wages, will be gathered, we hope, into annual reports to be submitted as part of the Universal Periodic Review. In short, our database of 45,000 annual intakes is an ideal source for monitoring state compliance with human rights obligations. We hope that, to maximize statewide impact, this can be coordinated with other Maryland organizations and advocacy campaigns.

We are also confident that our advocates and their communities will continue to find creative ways to use the human rights framework. Framing client stories and community challenges with a human rights perspective certainly holds great promise in giving policy advocacy positions moral weight; it also has a track history of sparking the kind of client involvement necessary to achieve systemic change.

Of course, accomplishing this in a state-wide, LSC-funded program that is more geared toward triaging requests for legal services is ongoing. New attorneys are introduced to our human rights framework during interviews with our executive leadership, and all new staff members receive instruction during our daylong program orientation. Program task forces organized by subject matter (i.e., housing, public benefits, employment, family, and consumer law) or by client population (elders, children, limited-English proficiency) discuss human rights principles germane to their advocacy efforts. Our website has a repository of human rights materials, with a particular focus on the body of scholarship supporting the applicability of economic human rights in the United States. We give new clients a brochure explaining the human rights framework. While much remains to be done to incorporate the framework fully into our service delivery structure and outreach strategies, we have a unit devoted to statewide advocacy and support that will ensure that human rights goals guide our systemic advocacy in the interim.

. . .

For some, a human rights framework for legal services advocacy is perhaps too visionary, but its honesty and focus assist our analysis and work. While the stories of our clients differ, the common theme is the unjust distribution of community, state, and national resources. Advocacy for economic human rights puts these resource issues squarely on the public policy table and guides states in making more equitable distributions. Clever and creative legal and policy arguments alone will not change the fact that resource distribution decisions are controlled by those with political and economic power. But the organization and mobilization of our clients and allies to counter this power is happening in a number of communities. This movement is using human rights to transform clients, communities, and public policy. We would do well to follow their lead and craft our advocacy strategies accordingly.

NOTES & QUESTIONS

1.   As yet, few legal aid or legal services offices have followed MLAB's lead in adopting a human rights mission. Does it matter what framework or mission these offices adopt so long as they are doing the same work, providing representation to poor people facing legal issues? Should a legal aid office only adopt a human rights mission if the office's clients frame their needs in that way?

2.   Despite the mantra of the indivisibility of rights, civil rights frameworks for activism and action are often seen as competing with human rights frameworks. For example, a number of legal services offices have explicitly adopted a civil rights—not human rights—framework for their work. *See, e.g.*, Bill Kennedy, *et al.*, *Framing in Race-Conscious, Antipoverty Advocacy: A Science-Based Guide to Delivering Your Most Persuasive Message*, 43 Clearinghouse Rev. 408 (2010). Similarly, long-time civil rights lawyers may be wary of framing their work in human rights terms, fearing that they will lose purchase in domestic venues that are more familiar with civil rights frameworks. Is there a way to avoid this sense of competition and to reconcile these approaches?

3.   Professor Davis urges domestic lawyers to be creative in integrating international human rights arguments into even the most local of cases. Her assertions have a "make the road by walking" quality, suggesting that human rights materials offered in cases today can help educate judges for future cases. But can lawyers legitimately and ethically take these future cases into account when they are representing a client in the present, who may not benefit from reference to human rights and whose interests may not include the hoped-for long-term results?

———————

Domestic ESC rights advocates also regularly use international mechanisms to expand attention to ESC rights at home. While the United States has not ratified the principal treaty addressing ESC rights (the ICESCR), U.S.-ratified treaties such as CERD and the ICCPR encompass some ESC rights. Further, the Universal Periodic Review process and the reports of U.N. Special Procedures may be more wide-ranging in their commentary on U.S. human rights compliance; because they are not limited to U.S. treaty obligations, UPR reviews and Special Procedures' reports may highlight issues relating to U.S. implementation of ESC rights. Advocates have used all of these mechanisms—treaty monitoring, the UPR review, and Special Procedures' visits and reports to focus attention on ESC rights in the U.S.

In the following excerpt, previewing strategies we will explore in greater detail in **Chapter VIII**, Risa Kaufman describes several recent U.N. treaty monitoring reviews of the United States, their results and the domestic uses made of the treaty bodies' work.

RISA E. KAUFMAN, "FRAMING ECONOMIC, SOCIAL, AND CULTURAL RIGHTS AT THE U.N."
4 Northeastern U.L.J. 407, 413–23 (2012).

Unable to directly enforce human rights treaties in U.S. courts, human rights advocates nevertheless leverage ICCPR and CERD's broad approach to equality and non-discrimination to highlight the interrelated and interdependent nature of rights. These advocates draw international, national, and local attention to core ESC concerns. Specifically, by engaging in U.N.-based advocacy through the treaty reporting process, ESC rights advocates take advantage of unique opportunities to engage with international mechanisms and government officials, and push for concrete recommendations around ESC concerns, which can be incorporated into domestic advocacy efforts.

An important obligation that the United States accepts when it ratifies a human rights treaty is periodic reporting to a committee of independent experts. This treaty review process provides civil society actors with an opportunity to document human rights concerns through "shadow reports," which are submitted to treaty monitoring bodies to supplement the government's official report and place public pressure on the government to comply with its treaty commitments. In addition, treaty reviews offer advocates opportunities to engage with government officials, particularly through civil society consultations. Advocates can draw upon the concluding observations ultimately issued by the treaty monitoring bodies by submitting observations as persuasive support in administrative and litigation advocacy efforts and by raising general public awareness concerning ESC issues addressed during the course of the review.

Recent examples illustrate this approach. During the 2008 review of the United States for its compliance with the CERD, advocates used the occasion to bring the issue of access to healthcare and racial discrimination to the attention of the CERD Committee. A shadow report filed by a coalition of organizations documented the extent of racial and ethnic health disparities in the United States and the key structural forces underlying the disparities, including residential segregation, access to health insurance and quality care, and the health effects of race-based discrimination. In its Concluding Observations, the CERD Committee noted its concern that a "large number of persons belonging to racial, ethnic and national minorities still remain without health insurance and face numerous obstacles to access to adequate health care and services." The Committee recommended that the United States:

> [A]ddress the persistent health disparities affecting persons belonging to racial, ethnic and national minorities, in particular by eliminating the obstacles that currently prevent or limit their access to adequate health care, such as lack of health insurance, unequal distribution of health care resources, persistent racial discrimination in the provision of health care and poor quality of public health care services.

Similarly, housing advocates submitted a shadow report to the CERD Committee highlighting the epidemic of homelessness and substandard housing in the United States, noting the disproportionate number of African Americans who are homeless and the fact that racial minorities constitute a disproportionate percentage of people living in substandard housing and suffering severe rent burdens. The CERD Committee urged the United States to address these concerns by reducing residential segregation based on race, ethnicity, and national origin. Similarly, noting that a disproportionate number of homeless people in the United States are African American, the Human Rights Committee recommended that the United States bring an end to de facto and "historically generated" racial discrimination.

In the shadow reporting effort surrounding the United States' 2006 review under the ICCPR, gender advocates raised issues of pay inequity, lack of family support policies, and employment discrimination as a means of highlighting women's poverty. The Human Rights Committee's recommendations for the United States included a recommendation that the government provide equality and equal protection for women, particularly in the area of employment.

Advocates have incorporated these observations and recommendations in subsequent advocacy efforts to add authority to their claims. In the litigation context, U.S. advocates recently cited the CERD Committee's concerns related to disparities in access to healthcare in briefs to the U.S. Supreme Court, supporting federal legislation to reform the U.S. health care system. Two *amicus* briefs filed by civil and human rights advocates in the Supreme Court litigation concerning the constitutionality of the Patient Protection and Affordable Care Act cited to the CERD Committee's Concluding Observations to bolster their assertions that the Act is necessary to promote equal opportunity in the United States and represents an important effort by the United States to abide by its human rights commitments.

In the non-litigation context, the National Law Center on Homelessness and Poverty submitted a letter in early 2008 to the New Orleans Housing and Human Needs Committee addressing a proposed anti-camping ordinance that would disproportionately affect the homeless. NLCHP drew on the recommendations made by the CERD Committee to lend weight to its argument that the ordinance would have an unfair and disparate impact on displaced African Americans.

As these examples reflect, through the equality and non-discrimination provisions of core civil and political rights treaties ratified by the United States, advocates are able to raise the profile of ESC concerns and focus international attention on these issues. Moreover, framing ESC issues through the non-discrimination and equality lens has the benefit of showcasing the interrelated and interdependent nature of economic, social, cultural, and political rights, underscoring that, in order to achieve dignity, equality, and freedom, every person must be able to meet his or her basic needs.

. . .

Advocates have been particularly successful using U.N.-based advocacy to mobilize grassroots and civil society more generally around ESC rights issues. For example, in the lead up to the United States' review by the U.N. Committee on Racial Discrimination, the U.S. Human Rights Network, an alliance of social justice organizations, coordinated a coalition of 400 grassroots and national social justice organizations to draft and submit a 600-page shadow report with chapters addressing ESC concerns, including homelessness, health, education, social security, labor and employment, and the government's response to Hurricane Katrina. In addition, the Network organized a delegation of 125 activists to travel to Geneva, Switzerland to observe the U.S. review and lobby the CERD Committee members on their concerns. Similar civil society mobilization and coordination occurred in the lead up to the United States UPR [Universal Periodic Review]. Advocacy communities hosted and participated directly in conversations with federal government officials through on-site consultations held in nine cities around the country. At the New York City consultation, for example, advocates discussed issues related to housing, employment and labor, education, and health.

. . .

U.N.-based ESC rights advocacy has also been successful in broadening the conversation around ESC rights within the United States, particularly with federal government officials. Housing rights advocates credit their deep involvement with the UPR with "opening the door to discussion [with federal housing officials] about housing as a human right in the United States." Recently, advocates have been invited to participate in a roundtable discussion with the State Department about actions it can take on ESC issues at the U.N. Human Rights Council.

Indeed, recent reports and statements by the U.S. government indicate a shift towards openness and acceptance, though limited, of ESC rights in the United States.

. . .

NOTES & QUESTIONS

1.   United States advocates seeking to raise ESC-related issues before human rights treaty monitoring bodies must do so primarily through the treaties' equality and non-discrimination provisions. What are the limitations of an advocacy strategy that frames core ESC concerns in this way? For example, does such framing allow advocates to draw on the specific standards and obligations for ESC rights included in the core ESC treaties and those developing in international jurisprudence? How might advocates compensate for this potential limitation?

2.   In addition to the treaty bodies and the UPR process, advocates are also engaging the U.N. Special Procedures mechanism to advance ESC-related advocacy in the United States. We explore this strategy in **Chapter VIII**.

3.   As part of their human rights strategy on these issues, domestic ESC advocates engage directly with federal policymakers. Unlike most developed nations, the United States does not have a national human rights institution that might take leadership in responding to and implementing the recommendations of the international human rights bodies. However, in 2006, the U.S. Senate established a new Subcommittee on Human Rights and the Law under the Senate Judiciary Committee. The subcommittee's jurisdiction encompasses: (1) Human rights law and policies; (2) Enforcement and implementation of human rights laws; (3) Judicial proceedings regarding human rights laws; and (4) Judicial and executive branch interpretations of human rights laws. The subcommittee has held a number of hearings on issues including business and human rights, and human trafficking. On December 16, 2009, the subcommittee held a landmark hearing on "The Law of the Land: U.S. Implementation of Human Rights Treaties." Dozens of domestic NGOs submitted written testimony to the subcommittee, many of them highlighting ESC rights issues such as housing and education and making ample use of the Concluding Observations directed to the U.S. during the CERD and ICCPR reviews. Advocates are engaging directly with federal agency officials around ESC rights, as well. For example, advocates from the National Law Center on Homelessness and Poverty have incorporated treaty body recommendations into their policy advocacy with officials at the U.S. Interagency Council on Homelessness. As a result, agency officials have embraced a human rights framework to address and prevent homelessness. *See* Liz Osborn, *3 Reasons to Address Homelessness as a Human Rights Issue*, USICH Blog (Apr. 14, 2014), *available at* http://usich.gov/blog/3-reasons-to-address-homelessness-as-a-human-rights-issue.

VI. CASE STUDY AND SKILLS EXERCISE: RIGHT TO HOUSING

One of the substantive areas receiving sustained attention from ESC rights advocates in the United States is housing. The following case study illustrates the multiple ways that advocates are using human rights norms in their domestic work. Part A provides background on the international law establishing the right, the domestic work being done to bring that right home, and the comparative examples supporting the right. Then building on this real-life background, Part B poses a hypothetical advocacy challenge.

A. CASE STUDY: THE HUMAN RIGHT TO HOUSING[9]

i. International Law

A human right to housing has been frequently recognized in international documents and has also been acknowledged by the United States on the international stage. In particular, the Universal Declaration of Human Rights, which the United States signed in 1948, provides that the "right to a standard of living adequate for the health and well-being of himself and his family," includes a right to housing.[10] This provision echoes President Roosevelt's inclusion of housing as an important element of his "Second Bill of Rights," set out in the 1944 State of the Union address.

As a matter of international law, the right to housing was first codified in the International Covenant on Economic, Social and Cultural Rights (ICESCR) in 1966. Article 11 of the ICESCR provides that "[t]he States Parties to the present Covenant recognize the right of everyone to an adequate standard of living for himself and his family, including adequate food, clothing and housing and to the continuous improvement of living conditions. The States Parties will take appropriate steps to ensure the realization of this right, recognizing to this effect the essential importance of international cooperation based on free consent." In 1991, the Committee on Economic, Social, and Cultural Rights, which oversees the implementation of the ICESCR, issued its General Comment 4 on the right to adequate housing, defining and elaborating on the right to adequate housing. In General Comment 4, the Committee specified that the right consists of seven elements: (1) legal security of tenure, (2) availability of services, materials, facilities, and infrastructure, (3) affordability, (4) habitability, (5) accessibility, (6) a location in a place

---

[9] Sections A(i) and (ii) have been adapted from National Law Center on Homeless and Poverty, "Simply Unacceptable": Homelessness and the Human Right to Housing in the United States (2011).

[10] Universal Declaration of Human Rights, G.A. Res. 217, U.N. GAOR, 3d Sess., pt. 1, art. 25(1), U.N. Doc. A/810 (1948).

with access to employment options, healthcare facilities, schools, child care centers, and other social facilities, and (7) with a housing design that is culturally adequate.

The United States signed the ICESCR in 1977, but the Senate has never ratified it. Other treaties the U.S. has signed, but not ratified, also recognize aspects of the right to adequate housing either explicitly or through support for the right to an adequate standard of living. These include the Convention on the Elimination of All Forms of Discrimination Against Women,[11] the Convention on the Rights of the Child,[12] and the Convention Relating to the Status of Refugees.[13] The International Convention on the Protection of the Rights of All Migrant Workers and Members of their Families,[14] and the International Labour Organization Convention No. 117 concerning Social Policy,[15] which the U.S. has not signed, also recognize aspects of the right to housing.

The United States has, however, ratified the International Covenant on Civil and Political Rights (ICCPR) and the International Convention on the Elimination of All Forms of Racial Discrimination (ICERD). These

---

[11] International Convention on the Elimination of All Forms of Discrimination Against Women, art. 14(2)(h), opened for signature Dec. 18, 1979 (Article 14(2)): "States Parties shall take all appropriate measures to eliminate discrimination against women in rural areas in order to ensure, on a basis of equality of men and women, that they participate in and benefit from rural development and, in particular, shall ensure to such women the right . . . (h) to enjoy adequate living conditions, particularly in relation to housing, sanitation, electricity and water supply, transport and communications."

[12] Convention on the Rights of the Child, arts. 16(1) and 27(3), opened for signature Nov. 20, 1989 (Article 16(1): "No child shall be subject to arbitrary or unlawful interference with his or her privacy, family, home or correspondence, nor to unlawful attacks on his or her honour and reputation"; and Article 27(3): "States Parties in accordance with national conditions and within their means shall take appropriate measures to assist parents and others responsible for the child to implement this right and shall in case of need provide material assistance and support programmes, particularly with regard to nutrition, clothing and housing").

[13] Convention relating to the Status of Refugees, art. 21, opened for signature July 28, 1951 (Article 21: "As regards housing, the Contracting States, in so far as the matter is regulated by laws or regulations or is subject to the control of public authorities, shall accord refugees lawfully staying in their territory treatment as favourable as possible and, in any event, not less favourable than that accorded to aliens generally in the same circumstances").

[14] International Convention on the Protection of the Rights of All Migrant Workers and Members of Their Families, art. 43(1)(d), opened for signature Dec. 18, 1990 (Article 43(1): "Migrant workers shall enjoy equality of treatment with nationals of the State of employment in relation to . . . (d) Access to housing, including social housing schemes, and protection against exploitation in respect of rents").

[15] International Labour Organization Convention No. 117 concerning Social Policy, arts. 2, 4(d) and 5(2) (Article 2: "The improvement of standards of living shall be regarded as the principal objective in the planning of economic development"; Article 4: "The measures to be considered by the competent authorities for the promotion of productive capacity and the improvement of standards of living of agricultural producers shall include . . . (d) the supervision of tenancy arrangements and of working conditions with a view to securing for tenants and labourers the highest practicable standards of living and an equitable share in any advantages which may result from improvements in productivity or in price levels"; Article 5(2): "In ascertaining the minimum standards of living, account shall be taken of such essential family needs of the workers as food and its nutritive value, housing, clothing, medical care and education").

treaties obligate the United States to ensure freedom from discrimination in housing on the basis of race, gender, disability, and other statuses.

Significantly, the right to housing does not create a positive duty to provide a home to every individual free of charge. Further, the right does not require states to immediately fulfill the right; rather, they are charged with "progressive realization" of the right. Under the ICESCR, States Parties are bound to "take steps" to the "maximum of [their] available resources" to "progressively" but "fully" realize the right to adequate housing "by all appropriate means, including the adoption of legislative measures." "Maximum of available resources" has been defined as requiring that States show that "every effort has been made to use all resources that are at its disposal in an effort to satisfy, as a matter of priority," its obligations. However, each right contains a "core minimum content" and immediately enforceable aspects, such as the prohibition on discrimination, the provision of shelter for homeless people and protection against forced eviction.

ii. International Human Rights and U.S. Housing Law and Practice

The United Nations has monitored the United States' record on housing and homelessness for many years. In 2006, the U.N. Human Rights Committee reviewed the U.S. government for compliance with the ICCPR, including aspects of the treaty relevant to housing. The Committee's Concluding Observations took particular note of racial disparities in housing, expressing concern "that some 50% of homeless people are African American although they constitute only 12% of the U.S. population." The Committee recommended that the government "take measures, including adequate and adequately implemented policies, to bring an end to such de facto and historically generated racial discrimination." It further noted that, "[i]n the aftermath of Hurricane Katrina, [the U.S.] should increase its efforts to ensure that the rights of poor people and in particular African-Americans, are fully taken into consideration in the reconstruction plans with regard to access to housing."

In 2008, the U.N. Committee on the Elimination of Racial Discrimination (CERD) reviewed the United States for compliance with the International Convention on the Elimination of All Forms of Racial Discrimination (ICERD). Domestic organizations again submitted multiple reports on housing discrimination, prompting the CERD members to compare segregated housing conditions in the U.S. to apartheid South Africa. The CERD recommended the U.S. government: (i) support the development of public housing complexes outside poor, racially segregated areas; (ii) eliminate the obstacles that limit affordable housing choice and mobility for beneficiaries of Section 8 Housing Choice

Voucher Program; and (iii) ensure the effective implementation of legislation adopted at the federal and state levels to combat discrimination in housing, including the phenomenon of "steering" and other discriminatory practices carried out by private actors, as well as "increase its efforts in order to facilitate the return of persons displaced by Hurricane Katrina to their homes, if feasible, or to guarantee access to adequate and affordable housing, where possible in their place of habitual residence."

Also in 2008, the U.N.'s Special Rapporteur on Racism visited eight cities across the United States on his first official mission to the country. Housing advocates organized site visits, and the Rapporteur's resulting report raised concerns about housing segregation and the racially disparate impact of policing patterns on homeless communities of color. Other U.N. Special Rapporteurs have been similarly active in the United States. In 2009, the U.N. Special Rapporteur on the right to adequate housing conducted an official visit to the United States. And in 2012, following her own visit to the U.S., the U.N. Rapporteur on the Human Right to Safe Drinking Water and Sanitation issued a letter to the Mayor of Sacramento expressing concern regarding the city's failure to adequately address sanitation needs of a local homeless community.[16]

During 2010, the United States government underwent its first-ever comprehensive human rights review under the U.N.'s Universal Periodic Review mechanism. Leading up to the U.N. review, hundreds of advocates testified before representatives from the U.S. Department of Housing and Urban Development and other government agencies during a consultation process initiated by the U.S. government. At the U.N. review in November 2010, U.N. member states made dozens of specific housing, homelessness, and poverty-related recommendations.

When the U.N. Human Rights Committee again reviewed the United States for its ICCPR compliance in 2014, the Committee identified specific concerns about criminalization of homelessness. The Committee urged the United States to "engage with state and local authorities to . . . [a]bolish the laws and policies criminalizing homelessness at state and local levels," and to "intensify efforts to find solutions for the homeless, in accordance with human rights standards."

iii. Comparative Precedents

While U.S. courts have been reluctant to find housing rights in either state or federal constitutions, the South African judiciary has taken a different approach. In 2001, the South African Constitutional Court's

---

[16] This advocacy initiative is discussed further in **Chapter XIII**. For more background, see Mona Towatao & Colin Bailey, *Toward a Human Rights Framework in Homelessness Advocacy: Bringing Clients Face to Face with the United Nations*, 45 Clearinghouse Rev. 169 (2011).

decision in *South Africa v. Grootbroom*[17] departed from earlier South African precedent and held the national government to its international obligations to provide adequate housing. *Grootbroom* is perhaps the most cited economic and social rights case in the world, paving the way for subsequent successful rights claims in South Africa and elsewhere. The Constitutional Court laid the foundation for the justiciability of the obligation to progressively realize economic and social rights. It further indicated that it would review implementation of these rights on the basis of the "reasonableness" test, exercising deference to the implementing government, where appropriate, at the stage of remedy. The ruling placed the adjudication of economic and social rights within a framework familiar to courts in all common law jurisdictions while elevating the lower rationality review standard previously adopted in South African cases.

The case arose when a community of squatters, evicted from an informal settlement outside of Capetown, set up rudimentary shelters of plastic and other materials at a sports center near a local community center. They lacked basic sanitation or electricity. The group brought an action under sections 26 (the right of access to adequate housing) and 28 (children's right to basic shelter) of the South African Constitution seeking action by various levels of government. The High Court, relying on the principles of judicial deference established in earlier cases found that the government respondents had taken "reasonable measures within available resources to achieve the progressive realisation of the right to have access to adequate housing"—as required by s. 26(2) of the Constitution. However, because the right of children to shelter in article 28 was not subject to the condition of available resources, the High Court held that the applicants were entitled to be provided with basic shelter. On appeal, the Constitutional Court found no violation of s. 28 but found instead a violation of the right to adequate housing in s. 26. The Court held that section 26 obliges the state to devise and implement a coherent, co-ordinated housing programme and that in failing to provide for those in greatest need the government had failed to take reasonable measures to progressively realize the right to housing. The Court ordered that the local and national governments "devise, fund, implement and supervise measures to provide relief to those in desperate need." The South African Human Rights Commission agreed to monitor the governments' implementation of this order.

The decision had a major impact on housing policy in South Africa. Most municipalities added a "*Grootboom* allocation" to their budgets to address the needs of those in desperate need. The applicants were provided with basic amenities as a result of a settlement reached prior to the hearing of the case by the Constitutional Court. Yet the results of the

---

[17] 2001 (1) SA 46 (CC).

decision for the particular community that initiated the lawsuit were disappointing, as further legal action was required to enforce the remedy against the local government.

In some other jurisdictions, legislative approaches to housing rights, rather than litigation, have borne fruit. For example, both Scotland and France have adopted the right to housing through legislative initiatives. Scotland's comprehensive housing plan defines the "homeless" as not only those without a home, but more broadly as those who live in housing that is dangerous, overcrowded, temporary, or unsuitable for long-term residence. It also covers individuals who are at risk of domestic violence, do not have access to accommodation, and even "people who live in a boat or motor home and have no place to park."[18] Eligibility for assistance is determined by whether the household became homeless intentionally, and whether they are connected to the locality from which they are requesting help. Individuals and families who meet these requirements can petition a local authority to provide assistance. Additional components of the law include protections from eviction and foreclosure, and a "mortgage to rent" scheme, in which a registered "social landlord" purchases a house being foreclosed upon, and agrees to rent it back to the family residing in it.

In France, the *droit au logement opposable* ("inalienable right to housing that a court cannot deny"), commonly known as DALO, was passed in 2007.[19] The law was modeled on the Scottish legislation in that it applies to a broad range of people with housing issues, and compels the government to provide housing through local authorities.[20] An individual entitled to housing under DALO can file suit against the government for a failure to fulfill its obligations and petition for redress, as the law gives courts the authority to uphold this right. Nevertheless, this ambitious legislation has a number of shortcomings. For example, an estimated 600,000 families are eligible for "priority" consideration under DALO, yet funding for the law is insufficient to meet this need, and the supply of housing is inadequate. Additionally, the process for exercising their rights is unclear to many homeless families. Finally, eviction protections are not consistently enforced. Still, the French legislation provides an affirmative, and potentially enforceable, framework for a national right to housing.

---

[18]   Eric S. Tars & Caitlin Egleson, *Great Scot!: The Scottish Plan to End Homelessness and Lessons for the Housing Rights Movement in the United States*, 16 Geo. J. on Poverty L. & Pol'y 187 (2009).

[19]   Thomas Byrne & Dennis P. Culhane, *The Right to Housing: An Effective Means for Addressing Homelessness?*, 14 U. Pa. J. L. & Soc. Change 379 (2011).

[20]   Kyra Olds, *The Role of Courts in Making the Right to Housing a Reality Throughout Europe: Lessons from France and the Netherlands*, 28 Wis. Int'l L.J. 170 (2010).

iv. Local Resolutions in the U.S.

In the United States, state and local governments are joining the effort to advance housing rights. For example, in September 2011, Madison, Wisconsin joined several other U.S. subnational governments, including Cook County, Illinois, Minneapolis, Minnesota, and Washington, D.C., in adopting a local human rights resolution. The prefatory sections of the Madison resolution set out devastating statistics concerning the impact of housing inadequacy in Madison, and cite the rights and obligations in the ICCPR, the ICERD and the UDHR. Madison's Resolution then recognizes housing as a human right and commits the city to a process for addressing housing needs. The Madison Resolution is excerpted in **Chapter VI**. Citing the Madison Resolution, the American Bar Association's House of Delegates adopted a resolution in August 2013 drawing on international human rights norms and urging "governments to promote the human right to adequate housing for all."[21]

B. SKILLS EXERCISE: HUMAN RIGHT TO HOUSING

i.   The Facts and the Challenge

The End Homelessness Law Center (EHLC), a nonprofit law firm with a national focus is located in Columbia, the capital city of the fictional 51st state of Lincoln. EHLC has long advocated for recognition of a human right to housing in the United States. However, courts have held that neither the federal constitution nor the Lincoln state constitution recognizes a right to affordable and adequate housing. Similarly, the Columbia City Charter is silent on any local government obligation to ensure access to adequate housing. You are a new staff attorney at EHLC, and it is your job to take this campaign to the next level. After reviewing the preceding materials and those below, develop the next stage of a plan to use international human rights law to support the EHLC's campaign for recognition and implementation of a human right to housing on the local, state, and/or national levels. You can focus efforts on litigation, legislative advocacy, organizing, media work or any other combination of advocacy tools.

ii.   The Law: Selected Domestic Constitutional and Charter Provisions

There are no housing rights explicitly recognized in the federal or state constitutions, or in the Columbia City Charter, but the provisions set out below might be relevant to such rights.

---

[21] *See* ABA Res. 117 (2013), *available at* http://www.americanbar.org/content/dam/aba/administrative/homelessness_poverty/resolution117.authcheckdam.pdf.

U.S. Constitution:

> Preamble: We the People of the United States, in Order to form a more perfect Union, establish Justice, insure domestic Tranquility, provide for the common defence, promote the general Welfare, and secure the Blessings of Liberty to ourselves and our Posterity, do ordain and establish this Constitution for the United States of America

> . . .

> Amendment X: The powers not delegated to the United States by the Constitution, nor prohibited by it to the states, are reserved to the states respectively, or to the people.

> . . .

> Amendment XIV, Section 1: All persons born or naturalized in the United States, and subject to the jurisdiction thereof, are citizens of the United States and of the state wherein they reside. No state shall make or enforce any law which shall abridge the privileges or immunities of citizens of the United States; nor shall any state deprive any person of life, liberty, or property, without due process of law; nor deny to any person within its jurisdiction the equal protection of the laws.

Lincoln State Constitution:

> Art. 2, s. 1: All persons are born equally free, and have certain natural, inherent and inalienable rights, among which are the rights of enjoying and defending life and liberty, of acquiring, possessing and protecting property, and of seeking and obtaining safety and happiness.

> s. 2: No person shall be deprived of life, liberty or property without due process of law; nor shall any person be denied equal protection of the laws. Equality of rights under law shall not be denied on account of the sex of any person.

> s. 3: The enumeration in this constitution of certain rights shall not be construed to deny, impair or disparage others retained by the people.

Columbia City Charter:

> Preamble: We, the People of Columbia, establish this Charter to secure the benefits of local governance and to provide for the general health, safety and welfare of our community. In so doing, we build a government that meets the needs of the people it serves and whose character it reflects. Our government shall further cooperation, encourage leadership, solicit our input and

support the active participation of our residents in their governance. Our government shall be effective and accountable and shall promote equal rights and representative democracy. Our government shall provide public education that enables all residents to acquire the knowledge and skills necessary to participate fully in Columbia's civic, intellectual, cultural and economic life, in order to enrich and strengthen our community and our common future.

Art. 1, Grant of Powers to the City:

Sec. 1: The inhabitants of the City of Columbia shall continue to be a body politic and corporate by the name of the City of Columbia, and shall have, exercise, and enjoy all the rights, immunities, powers, privileges, and franchises and shall be subject to all the duties, liabilities and obligations provided for herein, or otherwise, pertaining to or incumbent upon such city as a municipal corporation or to the inhabitants or municipal authorities thereof; and may enact reasonable by-laws, regulations, and ordinances for municipal purposes, not inconsistent with the Constitution and laws of the State of Lincoln.

Sec. 2: The administration of all the fiscal, prudential, and municipal affairs of the City of Columbia shall be vested in the Columbia City Council, except the general management, care, conduct, and control of the schools of such city which shall be vested in a board of public education.

NOTES & QUESTIONS

1. In crafting the next stage of ELHC's campaign for a domestic human right to housing, how will you define a "right to housing"? What alternative definitions might you reject and why? Are the federal and state constitutional provisions helpful in defining this right, or are they largely irrelevant? Does the Columbia City Charter provide any toehold for claiming a right to housing? If so, can that right be expanded beyond Columbia?

2. In crafting your plan, how will you balance immediate successes and results with long-term strategies for change? Do you feel that you are acting on behalf of a client or client group, or are you unconstrained by client obligations?

3. How, if at all, will you engage the private sector in achieving adequate housing and eradicating homelessness? Is international law useful in defining the private sector role and encouraging private sector work in this area?

4. Assuming that your campaign achieves some success and a human right to housing is recognized, how will you ensure that the new housing rights for individuals living in Columbia, Lincoln or the United States are implemented and enforced?

CHAPTER VIII

ENGAGING INTERNATIONAL AND REGIONAL MECHANISMS FOR DOMESTIC ADVOCACY

∎ ∎ ∎

I. INTRODUCTION

The United Nations and the regional Inter-American human rights systems have emerged as important avenues of advocacy for social justice lawyers in the United States. Mechanisms offered by these systems provide not only alternative fora, but also unique opportunities for collaboration among U.S. civil society groups and engagement with the international community and domestic policy makers. International and regional mechanisms offer platforms for advocates to raise human rights concerns on the national and international stage and leverage international attention to advance advocacy back home. Taken together, U.N. and regional human rights mechanisms offer a range of opportunities for advocates to elevate the profile of issues within communities, with government officials and in the international arena.

The following materials explore the challenges of, and opportunities offered by, these systems. Each section provides a detailed picture of U.S. advocates engaging with international and regional human rights mechanisms. Part II begins with an exploration of the United Nations human rights system. The section first discusses the human rights treaty monitoring bodies and then moves into an exploration of the U.N. Charter-based mechanisms, including the Universal Periodic Review and the U.N. Special Procedures. It examines, too, the appropriate role of civil society, including academic institutions, community groups, and non-governmental organizations (NGOs), in the U.N. system. Part III of this chapter turns to the Inter-American human rights system, with a particular focus on the Inter-American Commission on Human Rights, the primary regional human rights body in which the United States participates. It concludes with two case studies: one focused on advocacy in the Inter-American system concerning violence against women, and another exploring the Western Shoshone People's use of regional and international human rights mechanisms to protect their ancestral lands.

As you read this chapter, reconsider whether and how the United States' failure to ratify core human rights treaties impacts the utility of engaging with international and regional mechanisms, and what strategies lawyers have devised to compensate. What are the comparative advantages and disadvantages of engaging with the different mechanisms? How can advocates leverage gains made in one forum into efforts in another? And, how can lawyers leverage and translate "success" in international and regional fora back home in the United States?

II. U.N. MECHANISMS

A. U.N. HUMAN RIGHTS TREATY MONITORING BODIES

The United States has ratified three of the core international human rights treaties: the International Covenant on Civil and Political Rights (ICCPR), the International Convention on the Elimination of All Forms of Racial Discrimination (CERD); and the Convention Against Torture and Other Cruel, Inhuman or Degrading Treatment of Punishment (CAT). It has also ratified two of the optional protocols to the Convention on the Rights of the Child (CRC), those dealing with the sale of children as well as children in armed conflict. These treaties, covering a wide range of human rights concerns, establish mechanisms enabling advocates to engage with international human rights experts and their own government officials.

Each U.N. human rights treaty establishes a committee of experts to oversee member countries' implementation of their treaty obligations. These committees (also known as treaty bodies) monitor countries' treaty compliance through a periodic review process, issue general comments interpreting the meaning and scope of the treaty provisions, and, in the case of several of the treaty bodies, evaluate individual complaints where a member country has accepted the complaint mechanism or ratified the relevant optional protocol to the treaty.

Although the United States has not accepted the individual complaints function of any of the core treaties that it has ratified, the United States is nevertheless obligated to engage in periodic reporting to each treaty body with jurisdiction over a treaty it has ratified. Thus, the United States periodically reports to the U.N. Human Rights Committee (which reviews compliance with the ICCPR), the Committee on the Elimination of Racial Discrimination (which monitors implementation of the CERD), the Committee Against Torture (which oversees implementation of the CAT), and the Committee on the Rights of the Child (which monitors compliance with the CRC and its three optional protocols). The review process offer an occasion for advocates to engage with their own government and with the U.N. system on issues of domestic import.

The treaty review process begins when the country subject to review submits its official report on compliance to the treaty monitoring body. Although each committee has its own procedures, in the course of its examination of the official country report and preparation for the review, the treaty body will often prepare a list of issues (or themes) and questions to guide the review. (Countries accepting the Optional Reporting Procedures of the Committee Against Torture and the Human Rights Committee receive this list prior to submitting their country reports. The United States has recently accepted both of these new procedures.) With respect to at least a few of the treaty bodies, advocates have the opportunity to suggest issues or themes and influence the questions put before the country undergoing review. In some cases, the country under review submits a written response to the list of issues or themes prior to the in-person review session.

The review itself is a public session, intended to serve as an in-person dialogue between treaty experts and the government to identify human rights concerns and potential solutions. At the end of a review, the treaty body issues concluding observations highlighting specific areas of concern and setting forth recommendations for the reporting country.[1]

The treaty review process offers multiple opportunities for advocates in the United States to engage with the treaty bodies in an effort to influence their concluding observations and recommendations. For example, advocates can submit issue papers and lobby members of a treaty body to influence the issues, themes, and questions the committee poses to the United States prior to the in-person review. In advance of the review, advocates can also document domestic human rights concerns by submitting more in-depth "shadow reports" as a means of supplementing or clarifying information provided by the government in its official report. Furthermore, advocates who are able to travel to the review (usually held in Geneva, Switzerland) can observe the in-person session, hold "side events," and otherwise lobby the committee members in order to focus attention during the review on issues of particular concern to civil society.

In addition, treaty reviews offer openings for advocates to engage directly with government officials. For instance, the Obama administration adopted the practice of holding consultation meetings with civil society prior to drafting its official report for review by a treaty body and at other points in the review process. At these consultations and in follow-up communications, advocates can draw attention to and urge government action on specific issues.

---

[1] For more background information on this process, see Michael O'Flaherty, *The Concluding Observations of United Nations Human Rights Treaty Bodies*, 6 Hum. Rts. L. Rev. 27 (2006).

Advocates can be creative in working to implement the concluding observations and recommendations resulting from the treaty review, as well. For example, advocates can request that local officials hold public hearings to consider the concluding observations in light of local policy and practice, offer treaty bodies' observations as support for domestic administrative and litigation advocacy efforts, and, through media and other outreach, raise general public awareness on issues addressed during the course of the review.

We begin this section by examining materials related to the United States' compliance with the CERD. The United States ratified the CERD in 1994, but did not submit its initial report to the Committee that monitors compliance with the treaty until 2000. The United States submitted its first follow-up report in 2007. In the lead up to that review, which took place in Geneva in 2008, 128 advocacy organizations worked collectively to create twenty-six working groups and produce a 600 page shadow report to the CERD Committee. In 2008, the CERD Committee issued a set of forty-six concluding observations, noting concern and offering recommendations on issues including racial segregation in housing, disparities in access to health care and in the criminal justice system, the death penalty, and the treatment of foreign detainees held as "enemy combatants." As you read the following excerpts from the government's report to the CERD Committee, the civil society shadow report, and the resulting concluding observations, reflect on what role U.S. advocates played in shaping the review and the resulting recommendations, and how advocates might be able to parlay the treaty body's findings back into domestic advocacy around issues of discrimination, including disparities in housing and health. As you read the excerpt from the U.S. report to the CERD Committee in 2013, addressing similar issues in relation to the more recent U.S. CERD review, think about what might account for the differences in the U.S. government's approach to the issues between the 2007 and 2013 reviews.

U.S. DEPARTMENT OF STATE, "PERIODIC REPORT OF THE UNITED STATES OF AMERICA TO THE U.N. COMMITTEE ON THE ELIMINATION OF RACIAL DISCRIMINATION CONCERNING THE INTERNATIONAL CONVENTION ON THE ELIMINATION OF ALL FORMS OF RACIAL DISCRIMINATION"

(April 2007).

Factors Affecting Implementation

52. As noted in the Initial U.S. Report, the United States has made significant progress in the improvement of race relations over the past half-century. Due in part to the extensive constitutional and legislative framework that provides for effective civil rights protections, overt

discrimination is far less pervasive than it was in the early years of the second half of the Twentieth Century. As the United States continues to become an increasingly multi-ethnic, multi-racial, and multi-cultural society, many racial and ethnic minorities have made strides in civic participation, employment, education, and other areas.

53. Nonetheless, significant challenges still exist. Subtle, and in some cases overt, forms of discrimination against minority individuals and groups continue to plague American society, reflecting attitudes that persist from a legacy of segregation, ignorant stereotyping, and disparities in opportunity and achievement. Such problems are compounded by factors such as inadequate understanding by the public of the problem of racial discrimination, lack of awareness of the government-funded programs and activities designed to address it, lack of resources for enforcement, and other factors.

. . .

Measures taken to review governmental, national and local policies and to amend, rescind or nullify any laws and regulations that have the effect of creating or perpetuating racial discrimination wherever it exists

81. Article 2 (1) (c) requires States parties to "take effective measures to review governmental, national and local policies . . . which have the effect of creating or perpetuating racial discrimination" and to "amend, rescind or nullify any laws and regulations" that have such effects.

82. The United States continues to satisfy these obligations through its ongoing legislative and administrative processes at all levels of government, as well as through court challenges brought by governmental and private litigants. Laws and regulations in the United States are under continuous legislative and administrative revision and judicial review.

. . .

Measures taken to give effect to the undertaking to prohibit and bring to an end, by all appropriate means, including legislation as required by the circumstances, racial discrimination by any persons, group or organization

. . .

106. *Health.* The Minority Health and Health Disparities Research and Education Act was enacted in November of 2000 to address the fact that, despite progress in overall health in the nation, continuing disparities exist in the burden of illness and death experienced by some minority groups, compared to the U.S. population as a whole. Although a

higher number of non-Hispanic White residents fall in the medically
underserved category, higher proportions of racial and ethnic minorities
are represented among that group. The law establishes a National Center
on Minority Health and Health Disparities in the National Institutes of
Health (NIH) within the U.S. Department of Health and Human Services
(HHS). The Center is to oversee basic and applied research on health
disparities, and to provide grants to Centers of Excellence for Research,
Education, and Training to train members of minority health-disparity
populations as professionals in biomedical and/or behavior research. The
act also requires the Agency for Healthcare Research and Quality
(AHRQ) in HHS to conduct research to: (1) identify populations for which
there are significant disparities in quality, outcomes, cost, or use of
healthcare services; (2) identify causes of and barriers to reducing
healthcare disparities, by taking into account such factors as
socioeconomic status, attitudes toward health, language spoken, extent of
education, area and community of residence, and other factors; and (3)
conduct research and run demonstration projects to identify, test, and
evaluate strategies for reducing or eliminating health disparities. Finally,
the act calls for a national campaign to inform the public and health-care
professionals about health disparities, with specific focus on minority and
underserved communities.

107.   In response to Congressional mandate, HHS/AHRQ published
two annual reports. . . . Together, [these reports] assess the quality of,
and existing disparities in, care provided to the American people. The
reports have led to on-line state forums, where states can identify the
strengths and weaknesses of their health systems over time, and compare
their performance on selected measures with other states, regionally, and
nationally. [The reports] track performance on a number of measures and
operate as tools to improve the quality of future health care. Providing a
benchmark of health-care performance helps policy makers at all levels
target their resources to improve the status of health care, and to
diminish disparities of care in minority and vulnerable populations.

108.   The HHS Health Resources and Services Administration's
Health Center Program, which has been a major component of its healthcare safety net for U.S. indigent populations for more than 40 years, is
leading initiatives to increase health-care access in the most needy
communities. The underserved health center patients include migrant
and seasonal farm workers; homeless individuals; people living in rural
areas; large numbers of unemployed persons; and substance abusers,
among others. Approximately two-thirds of the patients are minorities.

109.   Maternal and Child Health Block Grants deliver health care to
pregnant women and to children, including children with special healthcare needs. The funds support vital immunizations and newborn
screening services, and also pay for transportation and case management

to help families access care. These legislated responsibilities are consistent with the current emphasis of HHS on reducing racial differences, building capacity and infrastructure for child health, and ensuring quality care.

. . .

The right to public health, medical care, social security and social services

. . .

258. *Health care.* Notwithstanding the strong overall care provided by the U.S. health-care system, the Initial U.S. Report described a number of disparities in the prevalence of certain diseases and conditions among racial and ethnic groups, many of which continue to exist since 2000. For example, for American Indians and Alaska Natives, the prevalence of diabetes is more than twice that for all adults in the United States, and for African Americans, the age-adjusted death rate for cancer was approximately 25 percent higher than for White Americans in 2001. Disparities are also seen in women's health issues, such as infant mortality and low birth weight. Although infant mortality decreased among all races during the 1980–2000 time period, the Black-White gap in infant mortality widened. During the same period, however, the Black-White gap with regard to low birth weight infants decreased.

259. To understand such disparities better, in 1999 Congress requested the Institute of Medicine (IOM) of the National Academy of Sciences to: (1) assess the extent of racial and ethnic disparities in health-care, assuming that access-related factors, such as insurance status and the ability to pay for care, are the same; (2) identify potential sources of these disparities, including the possibility that overt or subtle biases or prejudice on the part of health-care providers might affect the quality of care for minorities; and (3) suggest intervention strategies. The IOM issued its report in March of 2002. According to the report, the vast majority of studies indicated that minorities are less likely than Whites to receive needed care, including clinically necessary procedures, in certain types of treatment areas. Disparities were found in treatment for cancer, cardiovascular disease, HIV/AIDS, diabetes, and mental illness, and were also seen across a range of procedures, including routine treatments for common health problems.

260. The study looked at possible explanations for such disparities, including subtle differences in the way members of different racial and ethnic groups respond to treatment, variations in help-seeking behavior, racial differences in preferences for treatment, cultural or linguistic barriers, the fragmentation of health-care systems, and possible unintentional bias on the part of well-intentioned health-care workers.

Based on the findings, the IOM recommended a comprehensive, multi-level strategy to eliminate disparities. This would include cross-cultural education and training; policy and regulatory changes to address fragmentation of health plans along socioeconomic lines; health-system interventions to promote the use of clinical-practice guidelines; language and cultural interpretation where needed; and the collection of further data to refine the understanding of the problem.

261. HHS Secretary Michael O. Leavitt has reaffirmed his Department's commitment to eliminating racial and ethnic disparities in health care, and the Department has moved forward on a number of IOM's recommendations, including initiatives to:

- Develop a communication strategy aimed at raising awareness of racial and ethnic disparities among consumers, providers, state and local governments, and community-based and other organizations;

- Promote the collection of health data and the strengthening of data infrastructure to enable the identification and monitoring of health status among U.S. racial and ethnic minorities;

- Emphasize the centrality of patient/provider communications;

- Strengthen U.S. capacity to prepare health professionals to serve minority populations and to increase the diversity of the health-related workforce; and

- Integrate cross-cultural education into the training of all current and future health professions.

262. HHS has also made elimination of health disparities affecting racial and ethnic minority populations, including women's health issues, a critical goal of Healthy People 2010, the nation's public-health agenda for the current decade. As part of this effort, in 2001, HHS and the ABC Radio Networks launched an initiative denominated "Closing the Health Gap." This educational campaign is designed to make health an important issue among racial and ethnic minority populations. Originally launched in African American communities, the campaign was expanded in 2003 to include Hispanic Americans, American Indians and Alaska Natives, Asian Americans, and Native Hawaiians and Pacific Islanders.

. . .

263. In January 2006, HHS hosted the second National Leadership Summit for Eliminating Racial and Ethnic Disparities in Health. The conference included over 2,000 participants and featured more than 96 workshops and special institutes on current and emerging health issues

in the areas of: health-care access, utilization, and quality; health care and the public workforce; research, data, and evaluation; health information technology; health disparities across the lifespan; and culture, language, and health literacy. The Summit served as a vehicle for highlighting, promoting, and applying the knowledge experience and expertise of community-based organizations and other partners across the nation toward more strategic and effective actions. The Summit also served as a launching point for the creation of a national action agenda to eliminate racial and ethnic disparities in health.

. . .

Submissions by human rights advocacy organizations to the CERD Committee paint a different picture of U.S. compliance with its human rights treaty obligations. The following excerpt is from the NGO summary document submitted by the U.S. Human Rights Network, a national coalition of organizations engaged in domestic human rights advocacy. As you read, compare its characterization of health disparities in the United States and the U.S. government's efforts to address them, with the U.S. government's report. And reflect on the approach adopted by the CERD Committee in the Concluding Observations following the NGO report.

U.S. HUMAN RIGHTS NETWORK, A SUMMARY OF U.S. NGO RESPONSES TO THE U.S. 2007 COMBINED PERIODIC REPORTS TO THE INTERNATIONAL COMMITTEE ON THE ELIMINATION OF ALL FORMS OF RACIAL DISCRIMINATION
(Feb. 2008).

Art. 5(e)(iv) Right to public health, medical care, social security and social services

118. The "persistent disparities" in health that were noted by the Committee in its 2001 Concluding Observations have not significantly abated. Of particular concern are widening disparities in infant mortality between black and white populations, and continuing disparities in cancer mortality, diabetes, heart disease and overall life expectancy. The U.S. government has also failed to collect data on racial disparities in health care as required by the Convention or to provide adequate resources to federal agencies charged with monitoring compliance.

119. Racial and ethnic disparities in health outcomes in the U.S. are caused not only by structural inequities in our health care systems, but also by a wide range of social and environmental determinants of health. The Convention recognizes and encompasses this dual analysis in the area of public health. As used in article 5, "public health" includes not

only health care systems but also the underlying social and environmental factors affecting health.

120. The U.S. government's claim that "[s]ubstantial progress has been made in addressing disparities in . . . access to health care . . . over the years" is belied by persistent and dramatic racial disparities in infant and maternal mortality rates, life expectancy, and prevalence and survival rates of cancer, HIV-AIDS, and heart disease shocking in a country of the United States' wealth and resources. For instance, the U.S. boasts one of the highest maternal mortality rates in the Western world, with African American women nearly 4 times more likely to die in childbirth than white women; the infant mortality rate among Native Americans in the U.S. is 150% greater than the white population; and African Americans and Native Americans' life expectancy is a full 6 years less than that of the overall population.

121. The efforts cited by the U.S. government as evidence of its compliance with its obligations under the Convention in the arena of health care are grossly under resourced, and [focus] almost exclusively on individual behaviors while failing to address systemic factors driving health disparities, including obstacles to access to health care such as lack of health insurance, unequal distribution of health care resources, and poor quality public health care.

122. Persistent effects of historical de jure segregation in health care facilities, ongoing racial discrimination in the provision of health care, and the effects of racial segregation in housing and persistent racial disparities in the placement and remediation of hazardous and toxic industries and facilities are also factors that contribute to racialized health disparities. Laws such as the 1946 Hill-Burton legislation, which provided federal funding for construction of racially exclusionary hospitals, produced grossly unequal services subsidized with tax dollars, leaving a legacy of segregated health care. Moreover, since its initial report to the Committee, the U.S. Government has adopted legislation further limiting access to quality health care for low income people of color, in violation of its obligations under the Convention.

123. The disproportionate lack of health insurance among minority families and children is a critical element contributing to these disparities; moreover, a substantial body of evidence demonstrates that racial and ethnic minorities receive a lower quality and intensity of health care than white patients, even when they are insured at the same levels and present with the same types of health problems. There is also increasing evidence that race-based discrimination itself is not only emotionally hurtful but also physiologically damaging to minority Americans hereby leading to unique adverse health impacts.

124. A particularly egregious example of this type of rights violation is experienced by Native people. They are subject to disproportionate impacts of toxic industries, including gold and uranium mines, sited near or on reservation lands. They are also affected by significant under resourcing of federally funded Indian Health Services both on reservations and in urban centers.

125. Another example is found in the state of health rights in those Gulf Coast communities devastated by Hurricanes Katrina and Rita. The U.S. Department of Health and Human Services and other governmental authorities have failed to re-open public health care facilities, and have contributed to an increase in the number of deaths due to the lack of medical services. Hurricane-related environmental impacts, such as arsenic contamination of sediment and debris disposal, have been a burden on communities of color who have been denied public health protection by the U.S. Environmental Protection Agency.

126. Contrary to the Committee's General Recommendation No. XXV, the Periodic Report largely fails to address the intersection between racial and gender discrimination. . . . For example, women of color in the United States fare significantly worse than white women in every aspect of reproductive health. African American women are nearly four times more likely to die in childbirth than white women and 24 times more likely to be infected with HIV/AIDS. These disparities result from a range of government actions and inactions, from the failure to address high rates of uninsured women of color to restrictions on public funding for sexual and reproductive health services. Women of color, who are more economically disadvantaged than white women and more likely to rely on government funded health insurance, are disproportionately impacted by federal and state policies that restrict access to and public funding for sexual and reproductive health care. . . .

127. U.S. environmental policies have also failed to address racial disparities in health. The key federal civil rights law addressed to "unintentional" racial disparities in government programs (Title VI of the Civil Rights Act of 1964) was recently rendered unenforceable by the U.S. Supreme Court in a 2001 decision, and Congress has not yet responded to repair the law. In addition, the federal Environmental Protection Agency has failed to implement the 1994 Executive Order on Environmental Justice, and its own internal complaint system for adjudicating race-based complaints is ineffective.

128. Recent government policies have further perpetuated disparities in health care access for many racial and ethnic minorities. Although the government funds Medicaid and other health insurance safety net programs, recent federal laws such as the Personal Responsibility and Work Opportunity Reconciliation Act of 1996

(PRWORA), i.e. welfare reform, and the Deficit Reduction Act of 2005 (DRA) have negatively affected the health insurance status of low-income people of color. Rather than increasing access to health care for racial minorities, these policies have restricted access and are exacerbating racial disparities in health care, particularly for women and children.

. . .

COMMITTEE ON THE ELIMINATION OF RACIAL
DISCRIMINATION, CONSIDERATION OF REPORTS SUBMITTED BY
STATES PARTIES UNDER ARTICLE 9 OF THE CONVENTION,
CONCLUDING OBSERVATIONS: UNITED STATES OF AMERICA

U.N. Doc. CERD/C/USA/CO/6 (May 8, 2008).

A. *Introduction*

2. The Committee welcomes the reports, and the opportunity to continue an open and constructive dialogue with the State party. The Committee also expresses appreciation for the detailed responses provided to the list of issues, as well as for the efforts made by the high-level delegation to answer the wide range of questions raised during the dialogue.

B. *Positive aspects*

3. The Committee welcomes the acknowledgement of the multi-racial, multi-ethnic, and multi-cultural nature of the State party.

4. The Committee notes with satisfaction the work carried out by the various executive departments and agencies of the State party which have responsibilities in the field of the elimination of racial discrimination, including the Civil Rights Division of the U.S. Department of Justice, the Equal Employment Opportunity Commission (EEOC) and the Department of Housing and Urban Development (HUD).

. . .

8. The Committee notes with satisfaction the *National Partnership for Action to End Health Disparities for Ethnic and Racial Minority Populations*, created in 2007, as well as the various programmes adopted by the U.S. Department of Health and Human Services (HHS) to address the persistent health disparities affecting low-income persons belonging to racial, ethnic and national minorities.

. . .

C. *Concerns and recommendations*

10. The Committee reiterates the concern expressed in paragraph 393 of its previous concluding observations of 2001 (A/56/18, paras. 380–407) that the definition of racial discrimination used in the federal and

state legislation and in court practice is not always in line with that contained in article 1, paragraph 1, of the Convention, which requires States parties to prohibit and eliminate racial discrimination in all its forms, including practices and legislation that may not be discriminatory in purpose, but in effect. In this regard, the Committee notes that indirect—or *de facto*—discrimination occurs where an apparently neutral provision, criterion or practice would put persons of a particular racial, ethnic or national origin at a disadvantage compared with other persons, unless that provision, criterion or practice is objectively justified by a legitimate aim and the means of achieving that aim are appropriate and necessary. (Article 1 (1))

The Committee recommends the State party to review the definition of racial discrimination used in the federal and state legislation and in court practice, so as to ensure—in light of the definition of racial discrimination provided for in article 1, paragraph 1, of the Convention—that it prohibits racial discrimination in all its forms, including practices and legislation that may not be discriminatory in purpose, but in effect.

. . .

32. While noting the wide range of measures and policies adopted by the State party to improve access to health insurance and adequate health care and services, the Committee is concerned that a large number of persons belonging to racial, ethnic and national minorities still remain without health insurance and face numerous obstacles to access to adequate health care and services. (Article 5 (e) (iv))

The Committee recommends that the State party continue its efforts to address the persistent health disparities affecting persons belonging to racial, ethnic and national minorities, in particular by eliminating the obstacles that currently prevent or limit their access to adequate health care, such as lack of health insurance, unequal distribution of health care resources, persistent racial discrimination in the provision of health care and poor quality of public health care services. The Committee requests the State party to collect statistical data on health disparities affecting persons belonging to racial, ethnic and national minorities, disaggregated by age, gender, race, ethnic or national origin, and to include it in its next periodic report.

33. The Committee regrets that despite the efforts of the State party, wide racial disparities continue to exist in the field of sexual and reproductive health, particularly with regard to the high maternal and infant mortality rates among women and children belonging to racial, ethnic and national minorities, especially African Americans, the high incidence of unintended pregnancies and greater abortion rates affecting

African American women, and the growing disparities in HIV infection rates for minority women. (Article 5 (e) (iv))

The Committee recommends that the State party continue its efforts to address persistent racial disparities in sexual and reproductive health, in particular by:

(i) improving access to maternal health care, family planning, pre- and post-natal care and emergency obstetric services, *inter alia* through the reduction of eligibility barriers for Medicaid coverage;

(ii) facilitating access to adequate contraceptive and family planning methods; and

(iii) providing adequate sexual education aimed at the prevention of unintended pregnancies and sexually-transmitted infections.

. . .

The next time the United States submitted a periodic report to the U.N. CERD Committee was in June 2013, under a new presidential administration. Below is an excerpt from the report addressing disparities in access to health care and treatment. How does it compare to the United States' previous submission and the CERD Committee's recommendations?

U.S. DEPARTMENT OF STATE, "PERIODIC REPORT OF THE UNITED STATES OF AMERICA, TO THE UNITED NATIONS COMMITTEE ON THE ELIMINATION OF RACIAL DISCRIMINATION, CONCERNING THE INTERNATIONAL CONVENTION ON THE ELIMINATION OF ALL FORMS OF RACIAL DISCRIMINATION"

(June 2013).

133. *Non-discrimination regarding public health, medical care, social security and social services. Disparities in access and treatment.* With regard to Article 5 and paragraph 32 of the Committee's Concluding Observations, under Title VI of the Civil Rights Act of 1964, discrimination on the basis of race, color or national origin, including action that has a disparate impact on members of minorities, has long been prohibited in all federally funded hospitals and health care facilities. HHS and DOJ vigorously enforce these laws, and HHS collects and analyzes statistics on health care disparities. Every year since 2003, HHS has produced the National Healthcare Quality Report (NHQR) and the National Healthcare Disparities Report (NHDR), which track the level of

health care quality, access, and disparities for the nation. Data are based on more than 200 health care measures categorized in areas such as access to care, efficiency of care, effectiveness of care, and health system infrastructure for racial and ethnic minority and low income groups and other priority populations, such as residents of rural areas and persons with disabilities. These analyses indicate that, in many cases, health care quality in America could be improved. The gap between best possible care and that which is routinely delivered remains substantial. The analyses also indicate that, despite substantial efforts to improve health care for all, disparities based on race and ethnicity, socioeconomic status and other factors persist at unacceptably high levels.

134. According to the 2011 reports, improvements in health care quality continue to progress at a slow rate—about 2.5% a year. Few disparities in quality of care are narrowing, and almost no disparities in access to care are getting smaller. Overall, Blacks/African Americans and Hispanics/Latinos received worse care than Whites for about 40% of measures, and Asian Americans and American Indians and Alaska Natives received worse care than Whites for about 30% of measures. Poor people received worse care than high-income people for about 50% of measures.

135. Some minor improvements in health disparities have occurred. For example, since 1990, the gap in life expectancy between White males and Black/African American males narrowed from eight years to five years, and the gap in life expectancy between White females and Black/African American females decreased from six years to four years.

136. In 2011, HHS also released the HHS CDC Health Disparities and Inequalities Report—United States, 2011—the first in a series of periodic assessments that highlight health disparities by various characteristics, including race and ethnicity. This report, which represents a milestone in CDC's history of work to eliminate disparities, addresses disparities in health care access, exposure to environmental hazards, mortality, morbidity, behavioral risk factors, disability status, and social determinants of health. It finds that in recent decades the nation has made substantial progress in improving U.S. residents' health and reducing health disparities. Yet health disparities by race and ethnicity, along with other social characteristics, still persist. For example, persons who live and work in low socioeconomic circumstances are at increased risk for premature mortality, morbidity, unhealthy behaviors, reduced access to healthcare, and inadequate quality of care. Environmental hazards, such as inadequate and unhealthy housing and unhealthy air quality, likewise affect health outcomes. The study found that the highest infant mortality was for non-Hispanic Black/African American women, with a rate 2.4 times that for non-Hispanic White women. With regard to coronary heart disease, Black/African American

women and men had much higher coronary heart disease rates in the 45–74 age group than women and men of the three other races. Likewise, obesity rates were lower for Whites than for Blacks/African Americans and Hispanic/Latino Americans.

137.   The report recommends that health disparities be addressed with dual intervention strategies related to health and social programs and, more broadly, access to economic, educational, employment, and housing opportunities. The dual strategy includes making national and locally determined interventions universally available as well as making targeted interventions available to populations with specific needs. To address health disparities and inequalities at the national, state, tribal, and local levels, the CDC is leading an effort to compile and publish evidence-based and promising practices and strategies used by CDC-funded programs to address some of the persistent health disparities and inequalities highlighted in the HHS CDC Health Disparities and Inequalities Report. These practices and strategies will serve as a resource for practitioners at all levels in their efforts to address health disparities and inequalities.

. . .

138.   The United States is committed to improving access to quality health care for all, and to reducing and eventually eliminating these disparities. For many years the United States has provided government benefits programs to address health care, such as Medicare and Medicaid. Hundreds of hospitals that are federally funded under the Hill-Burton Act are obligated to provide free or reduced-cost health care, regardless of an individual's ability to pay. In addition, the Emergency Medical Treatment and Labor Act requires Medicare-participating hospitals to provide, regardless of ability to pay, a medical screening examination when a request is made for emergency treatment, and also to provide the individual stabilizing treatment or an appropriate transfer if the hospital is unable to stabilize the individual within its capacity.

139.   The [Patient Protection and Affordable Care Act], which was upheld by the U.S. Supreme Court, *National Federation of Independent Business et al. v. Sebelius*, 132 S. Ct. 2566 (2012), is intended to help reduce health care disparities, inter alia, by: (1) expanding insurance coverage; (2) promoting preventive and wellness services; (3) improving chronic disease management; (4) increasing access to Community Health Centers, which provide comprehensive primary health care to patients regardless of ability to pay; (5) strengthening the cultural competency skills of health care professionals; (6) promoting implementation of HHS's April 2011 Action Plan to Reduce Racial and Ethnic Health Disparities and; (7) increasing the diversity of the health care workforce. Under the ACA, it is estimated that as many as 5.4 million Hispanics/Latinos, 3.8

million Blacks/African Americans, and 2 million Asian Americans who would otherwise be uninsured will gain coverage by 2016 through the expansion of Medicaid eligibility and creation of Affordable Insurance Exchanges; that 1.3 million young adult members of minority groups . . . have gained coverage because they are now able to stay on their parents' insurance through age 26; and that 45.1 million women can receive recommended preventive services without having to pay a co-pay or deductible. Under the ACA's expansion of the Community Health Centers program, more than 8,500 service delivery sites provide health care to more than 20 million patients throughout the United States and its territories—approximately 35% of patients served are Hispanic/Latino and 25% are Black/African American. In May 2012 HHS announced awards of $728 million to build, expand and improve community health centers nationwide—part of a $9.5 billion five-year expansion plan under the ACA. The ACA has also helped nearly to triple the number of clinicians in the National Health Service Corps, a network of primary care providers who receive scholarships and loan repayment in exchange for working in underserved communities. Black/African American physicians make up about 17.8% of the Corps, a percentage that greatly exceeds their 6.3% share of the national physician workforce.

140. In 2011, HHS released its Action Plan to Reduce Racial and Ethnic Health Disparities, outlining the goals and actions it will take to reduce racial and ethnic health disparities, building on the ACA. At the same time, the National Partnership for Action to End Health Disparities (NPA) released its National Stakeholder Strategy for Achieving Health Equity, which complements the Action Plan by providing a roadmap for public and private sector initiatives and partnerships to address disparities. The NPA is intended to mobilize a comprehensive, community-driven, and sustained approach to combating health disparities and to move the nation toward achieving health equity, http://minorityhealth.hhs.gov/npa/. In February 2013, under the leadership of HHS/OCR, HHS released its 2013 Language Access Plan, ensuring that LEP individuals have meaningful access to HHS programs, including Medicare and those established under Title I of the ACA.

141. Healthy People 2020 is an ambitious, yet achievable, disease prevention/health promotion agenda to improve the health of all Americans throughout the decade ending in 2020 and to achieve health equity, eliminate disparities, and improve the health of the Nation during that period. HHS grants more than $14.2 million to universities and medical schools to study and implement more effective health strategies among racial and ethnic minority populations. It also has programs to improve the cultural and linguistic competency of health care providers, such as the HHS/OCR Medical Schools National Initiative, which has worked with 18 medical schools to develop the flagship course, "Stopping

Discrimination Before It Starts: The Impact of Civil Rights Laws on Healthcare Disparities—A Medical School Curriculum."

142.   With regard to Native American health disparities, the Obama Administration understands and seeks to support the priority tribal leaders place on improving the delivery of health care services in their communities. The Indian Health Service (IHS) has engaged for many years with federally recognized tribes. The Obama Administration achieved a 29% increase in funding for the IHS during the last 4 years, in addition to $500 million provided to the IHS under the Recovery Act. Under the Indian Health Care Improvement Act, which was made permanent by the ACA, IHS is addressing priorities identified by tribes, including long-term care, behavioral health, diabetes/dialysis, and improving the collaboration and coordination of services for veterans eligible for services of both the Department of Veterans Affairs (VA) and IHS. In consultation with tribal leaders, HHS and DOI are also working together to combat a full range of social issues affecting health in Indian Country.

. . .

NOTES & QUESTIONS

1.   The United States' official reports for the CERD Committee both recognize racial disparities in health within the United States and provide details concerning the government's attempts to document these disparities and address them. Who is the audience for the U.S. government's official reports? Is there more than one intended audience? What might the United States be trying to achieve through its detailed recitation of initiatives addressing disparities in health? Does the United States' recitation of initiatives demonstrate fulfillment of its treaty obligations? What other information would be useful in assessing compliance?

2.   How does the NGO shadow report's framing and articulation of disparities in health and access to health care in the United States differ from the official U.S. account in 2007? Do you think the NGO submission is effective in how it frames the issue and critiques the U.S. response to health disparities? In what ways could it be made more effective?

3.   What evidence does the NGO submission offer to back up its assertions? What should the standard of proof be for such submissions?

4.   How would you characterize the Committee's recommendations in 2008? Are they sufficiently directive and specific to address the concerns raised in the NGO submissions and acknowledged by the Committee? Do they take account of the United States' political system of separation of powers, its federalist structure, and sovereignty interests? What weight does the CERD Committee appear to give to the NGO submission on disparities in health?

5. How does the 2013 U.S. report to the CERD Committee compare with the previous administration's submission in 2007? What might account for the differences? How does the report respond to the CERD Committee's previous recommendations? How might U.S. advocates respond to the government's 2013 report?

6. The equality and non-discrimination provisions contained in the civil and political rights provisions of treaties ratified by the United States are broader than the U.S. Constitution's Equal Protection guarantees. The CERD addresses discrimination by protecting against distinctions and exclusions that have the *purpose or effect* of impairing the enjoyment of human rights or fundamental freedoms. *See* CERD, art. 1, para. 1. Article 5 of the CERD obligates State parties "to prohibit and to eliminate racial discrimination in all its forms and to guarantee the right of everyone, without distinction as to race, colour, or national or ethnic origin, to equality before the law." The CERD Committee has interpreted these non-discrimination provisions broadly, recognizing that policies that have a disparate impact, but not necessarily discriminatory intent, may violate norms of non-discrimination. *See* Committee on the Elimination of All Forms of Racial Discrimination, General Recommendation 14, U.N. Doc. A/48/18 at 114 (1994). In interpreting the equality and non-discrimination provisions of Article 26 of the ICCPR, the Human Rights Committee draws on definitions in the CERD and the Convention on the Elimination of All Forms of Discrimination Against Women (CEDAW), and, thus, the ICCPR's equality and non-discrimination provision, too, covers instances of disparate impact discrimination.

This broad understanding of discrimination stands in contrast to the U.S. Supreme Court's interpretation of the Fifth and Fourteenth Amendments' Equal Protection Clauses, which the Court has read as a narrow protection against intentional discrimination. *Washington v. Davis*, 426 U.S. 229, 240 (1979) (holding that "the invidious quality of a law claimed to be racially discriminatory must ultimately be traced to a racially discriminatory purpose"); *Personnel Administrator of Massachusetts v. Feeney*, 442 U.S. 256, 258 (1979) (holding that a plaintiff alleging discrimination in violation of the Equal Protection Clause must prove that the action was "at least in part 'because of,' not merely 'in spite of,' its adverse effects upon an identifiable group"). While many U.S. laws and regulations appear on their face to offer protection from actions that have discriminatory impact, U.S. Supreme Court jurisprudence has eroded the ability of individuals to enforce these protections. *See, e.g., Alexander v. Sandoval*, 532 U.S. 275, 293 (2001) (holding that there is no private right of action for individuals to enforce Title VI of the Civil Rights Act's disparate impact regulations; rather, only intentional acts of discrimination can be the basis of a private law suit). Enforcement of these provisions thus often rests with the U.S. Department of Justice and the civil rights offices of other federal agencies. What advocacy opportunities might the CERD's recognition of disparate impact claims offer to U.S. lawyers seeking to challenge racial disparities? How might U.S. lawyers draw on the CERD in advocacy with government officials? In its Concluding Observations regarding the U.S. review, the CERD Committee noted concern over the Supreme Court's intent requirement. How might this concern be addressed by the federal executive branch? By Congress? What weight should the U.S. Supreme Court give to the CERD Committee's recommendations as the Court is called upon to construe U.S. anti-discrimination laws?

7.   As mentioned, in addition to conducting periodic reviews, many of the U.N. treaty bodies also have authority to receive individual complaints regarding human rights concerns. However, because the United States has not recognized or authorized the individual complaints function of any of the treaties it has ratified, the treaty bodies do not have authority to consider individual complaints lodged against the United States. The exception is the CERD Committee's relatively recent mechanism, the Early Warning and Urgent Action Procedures, whereby the CERD Committee can investigate situations requiring immediate attention to prevent or limit the scale or number of serious violations of the Convention. This mechanism has been invoked by indigenous communities to protect the traditional land of the Western Shoshone people and to challenge the security wall built by the U.S. along the U.S.-Mexico border. *See, e.g.,* Western Shoshone People of the Timbisha Shoshone Tribe, Winnemucca Indian Colony and Yomba Shoshone Tribe, Second Request of Urgent Action under Early Warning Procedure to the Committee on the Elimination of Racial Discrimination of the United Nations, In Relation to the United States of America (July 29, 2005); Committee for the Elimination of Racial Discrimination, Early Warning and Urgent Action Procedure, Decision 1 (68), United States of America (March 2006). We explore this advocacy effort in greater detail at the end of the chapter.

8.   For a general overview of the treaty monitoring bodies and opportunities for engagement, see International Service for Human Rights, *Simple Guide to the U.N. Treaty Bodies* (2009); Office of the High Commissioner for Human Rights & The United Nations Non-Governmental Liaison Services, *The United Nations Human Rights System: How to Make it Work For You*, UNCTAD/NGLS/2008/2 (2008).

———————

The human rights treaty review process can be an opportunity for civil society to seek clarification or definitive statements from the U.S. government on questions of policy or practice. The following excerpts from the fourth periodic review of the United States by the U.N. Human Rights Committee for its compliance with the ICCPR illustrates the dialogue that can occur between civil society, the treaty monitoring body, and the government.

What follows is an NGO submission to the U.N. Human Rights Committee seeking to influence its "List of Issues" to the U.S.

Government by urging the Committee to include questions regarding specific U.S. counterterrorism practices. As you read the excerpt and the materials that follow, consider what is gained from the back and forth between the Committee, the government, and civil society prior to the in-person review.

Columbia Law School Human Rights Institute and American Civil Liberties Union, United States' Compliance with the International Covenant on Civil and Political Rights, Suggested List of Issues to Country Report Task Force on the United States

(Dec. 28, 2012).

Targeted Killings Through Drone Strikes in Pakistan, Yemen and Somalia (Article 6 (arbitrary deprivation of right to life); Article 4 (non-derogation from, *inter alia*, Article 6); Article 2(3) (right to effective remedy))

I.   Issue Summary

The U.S. government is engaged in targeted killings through drone strikes (and other aircraft) in Pakistan, Yemen, Somalia and elsewhere, which have resulted in the deaths of thousands of people. U.S. practice is characterized by secrecy and an unwillingness even to engage directly with concerns about civilian harm, let alone to provide accountability for civilian deaths and injury. Despite calls for disclosure from U.N. experts and non-governmental organizations, the U.S. government uses vague and shifting legal standards, and fails to disclose the basis for strikes or the steps it takes to minimize harm to civilians and investigate reported violations of international humanitarian law and human rights law.

The government carries out targeted killings outside of recognized armed conflict largely through the Central Intelligence Agency (CIA) and the military's Joint Special Operations Command (JSOC), two highly secretive organizations that often evade public scrutiny. On the one hand, the government stalls transparency and accountability by claiming in litigation that the CIA's involvement in the drone program is a state secret and that disclosure would cause grave harm to national security. On the other hand, government officials tout the effectiveness of the program in anonymous leaks to the press—a forum in which claims of lawfulness and low civilian casualties cannot be tested meaningfully.

U.S. disclosure about measures to protect civilians and ensure legal compliance is especially crucial in light of troubling reports about civilian casualties from strikes in Pakistan and Yemen. Although there has not been a large-scale study based on ground reporting, several organizations have credibly made civilian casualty estimates that are significantly higher than those the U.S. government has suggested in anonymous leaks.

In some areas, the U.S. government reportedly "counts all military-age males in a strike zone as combatants" who may be targeted—a standard reported by the New York Times in May 2012 and which the U.S. government has never disputed. This standard would lead the government to systematically undercount potential civilian casualties and would violate international law.

Moreover, there are numerous reports of U.S. "double-tap" strikes—those occurring after the initial strike to ensure that all individuals present in a "kill box," or designated area, are killed. The practice has reportedly resulted in the deaths of rescuers; in the context of armed conflict, deliberate targeting of rescuers would be a war crime, as U.N. expert Christof Heyns stated in June 2012. Both in and outside of armed conflict, killing of rescuers violates human rights law.

Despite calls by U.N. experts we describe below, the U.S. government does not disclose whether it conducts effective investigations after strikes to determine the identity of individuals killed, nor does it disclose the results of any such investigations. Moreover, we know of no U.S.-sponsored system of amends, reparation or compensation for strike victims or their families in Pakistan, Yemen or Somalia.

Top U.S. officials invoke both the doctrine of self-defense and international humanitarian law as legal justification for the targeted killing program. But the U.S. legal framework is ambiguous and appears to conflate self-defense principles related to the permissibility of using force (*jus ad bellum*) with humanitarian law principles regarding how force should be exercised in the targeting of particular individuals (*jus in bello*). It also applies international humanitarian law's more permissive regime for the use of lethal force in situations where there is no recognized armed conflict, while refusing to recognize the international human rights standards that properly apply.

What one official has termed a "flexible understanding of imminence" appears to have replaced the strict limitations on the use of lethal force under both international human rights and humanitarian law (assuming humanitarian law were properly to apply). This interpretation appears to have enlarged the scope of who the U.S. views as lawfully subject to direct attack, with officials variously saying that they target individuals who pose a "significant threat" or "an actual ongoing threat," and incorporate in imminence "the relevant window of opportunity to act." Thus, even if imminence were the relevant standard, these malleable and shifting partial definitions are so broad as to rob the term of meaning.

II. Concluding Observations by the Human Rights Committee

The Human Rights Committee has not previously addressed U.S. targeted killings through drone strikes (or other aircraft). U.S. drone strikes in Pakistan began in 2004 and in Yemen the first reported strike was in 2002, but the government accelerated these strikes dramatically starting in 2008. In its first review of Yemen since then, in March 2012, the Human Rights Committee addressed questions to Yemen about targeted killings through drone strikes conducted by the U.S. on its territory. One Committee member asked "how the Government was engaging in that matter, which was clearly a violation of the right to life." Yemen's Minister of Human Rights responded, describing the "lack of transparency" and "the current situation, whereby civilians had been killed by unmanned vehicles."

In 2006, the Committee recommended the United States acknowledge the applicability of the Covenant to actions taken with respect to individuals under its jurisdiction but outside U.S. territory, as well as its applicability in times of war.

III. U.S. Government Report

The Human Rights Committee has not previously asked the government to address U.S. targeted killings through drone strikes (or other aircraft).

Regarding extraterritorial application of the ICCPR, the government's position is that article 2(1) of the Covenant only applies to individuals both within the territory and jurisdiction of the State Party. The U.S. does not take the position that the Convention is suspended in times of war.

IV. Other U.N. Body Recommendations

In March 2012, U.N. Special Rapporteur on extrajudicial, summary or arbitrary executions Christof Heyns called on the United States to "clarify the rules that it considers to cover targeted killings"; the "procedural safeguards in place to ensure in advance that targeted killings comply with international law"; and "the measures taken after such killing to ensure that its legal and factual analysis is correct." Heyns emphasized: "Disclosure of these killings is critical to ensure accountability, justice and reparation for victims or their families." He called on the U.S. to disclose data on civilian casualties from drone strikes; "the measures or strategies applied to prevent casualties"; "the measures in place to provide prompt, thorough, effective and independent public investigation of alleged violations" of international humanitarian law and human rights.

These comments echoed recommendations made by Heyns' predecessor Philip Alston, who issued a major study on targeted killings in May 2010 that examined the practice of the United States and other

States. Alston's report specified requirements for targeting operations under human rights law (applicable in and outside armed conflict) and humanitarian law (applicable in armed conflict).

Moreover, in June 2012 U.N. High Commissioner for Human Rights Navi Pillay expressed "serious concern" over drone strikes in Pakistan, noting that it is "unclear that all persons targeted are combatants or directly participating in hostilities." She reminded States of their obligations to "take all necessary precautions to ensure that attacks comply with international law" and to "conduct investigations that are transparent, credible and independent, and provide victims with effective remedies."

Ben Emmerson, U.N. Special Rapporteur on the promotion and protection of human rights and fundamental freedoms while countering terrorism, has also expressed strong concern about the legality of the targeted killing program and will examine the legality of drone strikes this year.

V. Recommended Questions

1. Describe with specificity the legal framework the U.S. government applies to targeting operations occurring outside the context of armed conflict in Afghanistan. Clarify U.S. legal standards for who may be targeted, including whether the U.S. presumes that all military-age males in a strike zone are lawfully subject to direct attack.

2. Provide an accounting of all casualties resulting from targeting operations occurring outside of Afghanistan, including a breakdown of the number of people targeted and injured or killed as well as collateral civilian deaths and injuries.

3. Describe with specificity the measures or strategies the U.S. government applies to mitigate civilian harm in targeting operations.

4. Describe the measures in place to provide prompt, thorough, effective and independent public investigation of alleged violations of international humanitarian law and human rights resulting from targeting operations outside of Afghanistan.

5. Clarify whether a system of compensation, reparation or making amends exists in Pakistan, Yemen, Somalia or other States where targeting operations have taken place, similar to those the U.S. put in place in Iraq and Afghanistan. If no such system exists, describe what measures are being taken to expeditiously establish and implement such a system.

VI. Suggested Recommendations

1. Identify the rules of international law the government considers to provide a basis for targeting operations outside of the armed conflict in

Afghanistan. Specify the procedural safeguards in place to ensure in advance of targeted killings that they comply with international law, and the measures taken after any such killing to ensure that the government's legal justification and factual analysis was accurate.

2. Officially acknowledge drone strikes and other targeting operations in Pakistan, Yemen, Somalia and other States, including the role of the CIA and Joint Special Operations Command. Do not invoke state secrets as barriers to judicial review of targeted killings in U.S. courts.

3. Disclose all casualties resulting from targeting operations outside of Afghanistan, including a breakdown of the number of people targeted and injured or killed as well as collateral civilian deaths and injuries. Disaggregate data to identify the number of casualties resulting from the use of armed drones as well as other aircraft.

4. Disclose with specificity measures or strategies the U.S. government applies to mitigate civilian harm in targeting operations.

5. Establish a system to ensure prompt, thorough, effective and independent public investigation of alleged violations of international humanitarian law and human rights law resulting from drone strikes outside of Afghanistan.

6. Clarify whether a system of compensation, reparation or making amends exists in Pakistan, Yemen, Somalia or other States where targeting operations have taken place, similar to those the U.S. put in place in Iraq and Afghanistan. If no such system exists, expeditiously establish and implement such a system.

After receiving input from civil society, including the NGO report excerpted above, the U.N. Human Rights Committee transmitted a "List of Issues" for the United States to respond to in advance of its in-person review in Geneva. What follows are the Committee's questions related to targeted drone strikes.

U.N. HUMAN RIGHTS COMMITTEE, LIST OF ISSUES IN RELATION TO THE FOURTH PERIODIC REPORT OF THE UNITED STATES OF AMERICA
U.N. Doc. CCPR/C/USA/4 and Corr.1 (April 29, 2013).

10. Regarding the protection of life in armed conflict:

(a) Please clarify how targeted killings conducted through drone attacks on the territory of other States, as well as collateral civilian casualties are in compliance with Covenant obligations. Please clarify how the State party ensures that such use of force fully complies with its obligation to protect life.

(b) Please clarify whether the State party has effectively investigated and punished lower-ranking soldiers for unlawful killings, including possible war crimes, in its international operations, and whether it has held senior officers responsible under the doctrine of command responsibility. Please also clarify whether similar investigations have been instigated against private contractors and civilian intelligence agencies.

. . .

———————

The United States submitted a set of written responses addressing the Human Rights Committee's List of Issues. In the excerpt below, the government replies to the Committee's questions regarding the practice of targeted drone strikes.

U.N. HUMAN RIGHTS COMMITTEE, LIST OF ISSUES IN RELATION TO THE FOURTH PERIODIC REPORT OF THE UNITED STATES OF AMERICA, ADDENDUM: REPLIES OF THE UNITED STATES OF AMERICA TO THE LIST OF ISSUES

U.N. Doc. CCPR/C/USA/4 and Corr.1 (July 5, 2013).

Reply to the issues raised in paragraph 10 of the list of issues

34. *Issue 10(a).* The United States is in an armed conflict with al-Qaida, the Taliban, and associated forces, and may also use force consistent with our inherent right of national self-defense. The United States has acknowledged that it has conducted targeted strikes with remotely piloted aircraft against specific targets outside areas of active hostilities. These strikes are conducted in a manner that is consistent with all applicable domestic and international law. Please see 2011 Report, ¶¶ 506–509.

35. Presidential Policy Guidance sets out standards for the use of lethal force outside areas of active hostilities. These standards are either already in place or will be transitioned into place over time. Under these policy standards, lethal force is used only to prevent or stop attacks against U.S. persons, and even then, only when capture is not feasible and no other reasonable alternatives exist to address the threat effectively. In addition, under these standards lethal force is to be used outside areas of active hostilities only against a target that poses a continuing, imminent threat to U.S. persons. If a terrorist does not pose such a threat, the United States will not use lethal force. Importantly, these policy standards include several criteria that must be met before

lethal action may be taken, including near certainty that non-combatants will not be injured or killed. This is confirmed by the content of the policy standards and procedures, key elements of which are laid out in a document recently released by the Administration, http://www.white house.gov/the-press-office/2013/05/23/fact-sheet-us-policy-standards-and-procedures-use-force-counterterrorism.

36. U.S. military forces go to extraordinary lengths to avoid civilian casualties. Although the United States has used targeted air strikes with as much discrimination and care as possible, there have been instances where civilian casualties have occurred. The U.S. government takes seriously all credible reports of civilian deaths and investigates such claims to make a determination about civilian casualties.

37. As explained most recently in President Obama's May 23, 2013 address at the National Defense University, the U.S. military takes scrupulous care to ensure that uses of force—and, in this context, targeted strikes—conform to the principles of the law of war, including, importantly, the principles of proportionality and distinction, http://www. whitehouse.gov/the-press-office/2013/05/23/remarks-president-national-defense-university.

38. U.S. service members receive training in the principles and rules of the law of war, including the principles of proportionality and distinction, commensurate with each individual's duties and responsibilities, throughout their service in the military. Additionally, the U.S. military makes qualified legal advisers available at all levels of command to provide advice about law of war compliance during planning and execution of exercises and operations.

39. *Issue 10(b).* The United States has several judicial means by which to hold its nationals accountable for violations of the law of war, including (1) courts-martial for offenses defined by the Uniform Code of Military Justice (UCMJ), and (2) federal courts for offenses under other federal law, including the War Crimes Act of 1996. Under the UCMJ, general courts-martial have jurisdiction to try persons subject to the UCMJ for a wide variety of offenses. General courts-martial also have jurisdiction to try any person who by the law of war is subject to trial by a military tribunal and may adjudge any punishment permitted by the law of war. Federal courts have jurisdiction to try certain persons for offenses in federal law, including those who, whether inside or outside the United States, commit a war crime, if the person committing such war crime or the victim of such war crime is a U.S. service member or a national of the United States.

40. The United States has investigated U.S. military personnel and civilian personnel, including contractors, for suspected unlawful killings committed in operations conducted outside the United States. Most of the

investigations and prosecutions, including administrative and criminal inquiries and proceedings, have been carried out by [the Department of Defense], [the Department of Justice], and other U.S. government components that have jurisdiction over such actions. Some of these investigations resulted in prosecutions (some resulting in conviction and others not), and some investigations were closed without initiation of prosecutions.

. . .

42. The concept of command responsibility is implemented within the U.S. military through training and military doctrine. Additionally, the UCMJ, 10 U.S.C. Chapter 47, and other disciplinary mechanisms with the U.S. military, as well as the Military Commissions Act of 2009, P. L. 111–84, implement the concept of command responsibility. Although the concept is well-known and established under international law and is widely used by international tribunals, not all of U.S. federal criminal law specifically incorporates the concept of command responsibility. For example, the doctrine of command responsibility has not been employed by DOJ in its prosecutions. However, under U.S. federal criminal law, the conspiracy and aiding and abetting statutes may be utilized in appropriate cases to reach senior-level offenders.

43. Robust review procedures are in place to ensure appropriate training of U.S. forces in the law of armed conflict and appropriate rules of engagement and tactics, techniques, and procedures. If [the Department of Defense] has reason to believe that a crime has occurred that resulted in unlawful killings, a full investigation is initiated. If the investigation reveals allegations of criminal activity, action is taken as appropriate to hold accountable those determined to be responsible, including those deemed culpable as a function of command responsibility.

. . .

_____

After the United States submitted its written response to the U.N. Human Rights Committee's List of Issues, U.S. civil society had another opportunity to provide input for the Committee's consideration of the issue. What follows is an excerpt from the American Civil Liberties Union's shadow report to the Committee, further detailing and updating its concerns with the U.S. practice of targeted drone strikes and offering an assessment of the government's written response to the Committee's question in the List of Issues.

AMERICAN CIVIL LIBERTIES UNION, UNITED STATES
COMPLIANCE WITH THE INTERNATIONAL COVENANT ON CIVIL
AND POLITICAL RIGHTS, SHADOW REPORT TO THE FOURTH
PERIODIC REPORT OF THE UNITED STATES
(Sept. 13, 2013).

I.   Issue Summary

Targeted Killing

Since our submission to the Committee in December 2012, there have been a few positive developments with respect to long-overdue transparency concerning the United States' targeted killing program. As discussed below, however, many of these developments raise more questions than answers about the lawfulness of U.S. lethal force strikes abroad. Moreover, the United States is still keeping entirely secret from the American public and the international community basic information about lethal strikes—including the identity of targets and victims, numbers of casualties (including civilian bystanders), and the basis for strikes—and it is refusing to provide meaningful transparency and accountability in domestic courts.

On February 8, 2013, the United States officially released a white paper summarizing its claimed legal basis for the use of lethal force against a U.S. citizen abroad. It did so after a leak of the same document days earlier. On May 23, 2013, the government released a "Presidential Policy Guidance" outlining the policy standards to which it would internally adhere when using lethal force outside active hostilities. Under the new policy, the United States has said it will only use lethal force against "continuing, imminent" threats to the American people; previously, according to credible media reports, the United States had on occasion used lethal force against individuals who presented a threat not to the United States, but to the governments of states in which the killings were carried out. Importantly, the government clarified that it will apply its new, apparently more protective, rules regardless of the target's citizenship, eliminating a troubling distinction between citizens and non-citizens. In addition, President Obama announced in a speech at National Defense University that the U.S. government will only use lethal force when there is "near-certainty" that civilian bystanders will not be injured or killed.

While these new policy pronouncements were an encouraging, though belated, move toward openness about U.S. government targeted killing policies, there are disturbing indications that little has changed in practice.

As an initial matter, the new rules remain highly opaque. Most basically, it is unclear how the U.S. government defines the "places of active hostilities" in which the new rules do *not* apply. And the rules do nothing to address the fundamental problem with U.S. targeted killing policy: the standards it is using violate international human rights law, which prohibits use of lethal force outside of armed conflict unless it is a last resort, used against a specific, concrete, and imminent threat. That concern is heightened by the U.S. government's novel interpretations of human rights law. For example, according to the white paper, the U.S. government claims the authority to use lethal force against an individual who constitutes a "continuing, imminent threat"—as the government defines "imminence," it need not even have clear evidence that the threat involves a concrete and known plot. If true, the government's elastic definition of "imminence" is a clear departure from international standards, and from plain English. Additionally, though the Presidential Policy Guidance states that the government will conduct targeted killings only where capture is not feasible and no reasonable alternatives to the use of lethal force exist, the document contains no explanation of what those purported constraints mean in practice. In short, while we appreciate these efforts to explain U.S. government policy standards to the public, those explanations provoke more concerns and questions than provide answers, and do nothing to inspire confidence that the U.S. government is adhering to its international legal obligations.

Concern about the government's actual implementation of new policies was heightened when, just days after the Presidential Policy Guidance was released, officials confirmed that the government would continue to carry out so-called "signature strikes"—the targeting of unidentified individuals based on apparent behavioral patterns. On its face, the Presidential Policy Guidance appeared to have constrained the practice of signature strikes. That the U.S. government carved out an exception to an apparent restriction so soon after it was announced calls into question the extent to which the government is relying on other loopholes in its own policy constraints.

II.   Relevant Questions in the Human Rights Committee's List of Issues

The use of so-called targeted killings by the U.S. outside recognized armed conflict remains a significant threat to the right to life and continues to result in violations of the ICCPR. The Committee has asked the U.S. Government to address the following question:

10). Regarding the protection of life in armed conflict:

a.   Please clarify how targeted killings conducted through drone attacks on the territory of other States, as well as collateral civilian casualties are in compliance with Covenant obligations. Please clarify how the State party ensures that such use of force fully complies with its obligation to protect life.

III. U.S. Government Response

The U.S. government's response to the Committee emphasized that its targeted killing program is "consistent with all applicable . . . international law." But the government's policy choices on their face deviate from stringent international legal requirements, and the government has thus far refused to make public the legal memoranda containing its analysis and interpretation of the legal constraints on the use of lethal force. Perhaps most problematically, the Presidential Policy Guidance—which is invoked in the U.S. replies to the Committee's list of issues—is explicitly a government *policy*; it is not an expression of the government's view of the *law*. In the context of the government's targeted killings practices, that is a key discrepancy.

Furthermore, the government has not disclosed its selection process or evidentiary criteria for targeted killing decisions. Although the government has finally acknowledged responsibility for killing four U.S. citizens, it refuses to disclose the identity or number of non-citizens, including civilian bystanders, who have been killed. In the absence of that information, neither the Committee nor the international community at large can have confidence that the U.S. government's targeted killing actions actually adhere to the legal requirements.

Crucially, while the U.S. government continues to publicly insist that its targeted killing program complies with its international obligations to protect the right to life, it has maintained an unwavering opposition to judicial review and accountability.

. . .

IV. Recommended Questions

In addition to the questions and recommendations previously submitted:

1.   Provide the identities and numbers of non-U.S. citizens killed or injured in the government's targeted killing program, including the number of civilian bystanders who have been killed or injured. If the government refuses to disclose this information, provide an explanation of why it distinguishes between citizens and non-citizens when it comes to releasing this basic information.

2.   Describe with specificity whether and how the U.S. government may depart from the Presidential Policy Guidance and how any such departure complies with international human rights law.

3.   Describe with specificity how the U.S. government's claimed "signature strike" authority complies with international human rights law, and the circumstances under which such strikes will be conducted.

4.   Describe the measures in place to provide prompt, thorough, effective, and independent public investigations of alleged violations of international humanitarian and human rights law resulting from lethal force operations outside of Afghanistan.

5.   Explain how the U.S. government's opposition to judicial review of the lawfulness of targeted killings of its own citizens complies with its obligation under the ICCPR to provide an effective remedy for violations of the right to life.

V.   Suggested Recommendations

1.   The U.S. Government should disclose the legal and policy standards, including the OLC opinions and the rules implementing the Presidential Policy Guidance, relevant to the targeted killing program.

2.   The President should direct an end to any use of force outside of Afghanistan that does not comport with international human rights law.

3.   The Executive Branch should refrain from invoking jurisdictional, secrecy, and immunity doctrines to prevent judicial review of the merits of wrongful targeted killing claims in domestic courts.

The above exchange culminated in an in-person, interactive dialogue in Geneva between the members of the U.N. Human Rights Committee and a high-level delegation of U.S. government officials, including officials from the U.S. Department of State, the Department of Homeland Security, the Department of Defense and the Department of Justice. A few weeks after the review, the Committee issued its Concluding Observations, outlining areas of concern and offering recommendations for how the United States can improve its treaty compliance. Below are the Committee's Concluding Observations and recommendations related to the issue of targeted drone strikes.

HUMAN RIGHTS COMMITTEE, CONCLUDING OBSERVATIONS ON
THE FOURTH PERIODIC REPORT BY THE UNITED STATES
U.N. Doc. CCPR/C/USA/CO/4 (April 23, 2014).

Targeted killings using unmanned aerial vehicles (drones)

9.   The Committee is concerned about the State party's practice of targeted killings in extraterritorial counter-terrorism operations using unmanned aerial vehicles (UAV), also known as "drones", the lack of transparency regarding the criteria for drone strikes, including the legal justification for specific attacks, and the lack of accountability for the loss of life resulting from such attacks. The Committee notes the State party's position that drone strikes are conducted in the course of its armed

conflict with Al-Qaida, the Taliban and associated forces in accordance with its inherent right of national self-defence, and that they are governed by international humanitarian law as well as by the Presidential Policy Guidance that sets out standards for the use of lethal force outside areas of active hostilities. Nevertheless, the Committee remains concerned about the State party's very broad approach to the definition and geographical scope of "armed conflict", including the end of hostilities, the unclear interpretation of what constitutes an "imminent threat", who is a combatant or a civilian taking direct part in hostilities, the unclear position on the nexus that should exist between any particular use of lethal force and any specific theatre of hostilities, as well as the precautionary measures taken to avoid civilian casualties in practice (arts. 2, 6 and 14).

The State party should revisit its position regarding legal justifications for the use of deadly force through drone attacks. It should:

(a) Ensure that any use of armed drones complies fully with its obligations under article 6 of the Covenant, including, in particular, with respect to the principles of precaution, distinction and proportionality in the context of an armed conflict;

(b) Subject to operational security, disclose the criteria for drone strikes, including the legal basis for specific attacks, the process of target identification and the circumstances in which drones are used;

(c) Provide for independent supervision and oversight of the specific implementation of regulations governing the use of drone strikes;

(d) In armed conflict situations, take all feasible measures to ensure the protection of civilians in specific drone attacks and to track and assess civilian casualties, as well as all necessary precautionary measures in order to avoid such casualties;

(e) Conduct independent, impartial, prompt and effective investigations of allegations of violations of the right to life and bring to justice those responsible;

(f) Provide victims or their families with an effective remedy where there has been a violation, including adequate compensation, and establish accountability mechanisms for victims of allegedly unlawful drone attacks who are not compensated by their home governments.

. . .

NOTES & QUESTIONS

1. Do the Committee's questions in the "List of Issues" regarding targeted drone strikes reflect the concerns raised by the first NGO submission? Do they address all of the concerns raised in the submission? What considerations might have gone into the Committee's decision of which questions to ask, and how to phrase the concerns?

2. Did the government's response to the questions posed in the List of Issues fully answer the Committee's questions? The subsequent shadow report characterizes the U.S. answer as insufficiently specific. Might there be reasons that the government would leave some of its answers vague or ambiguous?

3. How do the Committee's concluding observations and recommendations compare to the questions and recommendations suggested in the ACLU's second submission? Does the Committee address the concerns raised in the ACLU submission? Do you think that the Committee's discussion of the issue in its concluding observations was influenced by the NGO submissions? In what ways?

4. What factors might influence the Committee's decision to raise an issue with the government in the list of issues for the review and in the course of the review itself? What are some factors that might go into how the government responds to the questions? For a critical assessment of the impact of the exchange between the U.N. treaty bodies and the U.S. government, see Monica Hakimi, *Secondary Human Rights Law*, 34 Yale J. Int'l L. 596 (2009).

As these materials reflect, the treaty review process offers advocates opportunities to engage with both the U.N. treaty bodies and U.S. government officials to influence the results of the review. As you read the following two passages, think about the appropriateness of NGO involvement and potential influence in the U.N. treaty body review process. Does substantial NGO involvement in this process potentially undermine the U.N. committees' legitimacy and effectiveness? What value might NGOs bring to the process?

KERSTIN MARTENS, "NGOS IN THE UN SYSTEM: EXAMINING FORMAL AND INFORMAL MECHANISMS OF INTERACTION"
2 Int'l J. of Civil Soc'y L. 11, 13–15 (2004).

A lot of NGO activity is intended to influence the political debate at the UN. By providing information, NGOs aim at initiating political activities at UN level on the issues of their concern. In order to reach their goals, NGOs often use formal ways to feed in their information. For example, the UN has established mechanisms, such as annual sessions, committees, meetings or special officials which take in NGO contributions. In addition, through informal lobbying, NGOs are also able to influence UN officials and governmental representatives. Both ways, the information provided by NGOs can be used in official reports by UN staff and by governmental representatives in their statements.

. . .

NGO reports and summaries of the human rights situation in a particular country often serve UN officials as background material. In particular, since the end of the Cold War, NGOs have been increasingly acknowledged as the primary sources of information. In fact, today "[c]ommittee members eagerly look for NGO materials before each country review, because it helps make their questioning more precise, factual, and less abstract. Nongovernmental organisations essentially serve as unofficial researchers to committee members, rendering invaluable and in place of the understaffed, poorly financed secretariat."

Such information from NGOs is necessary to make the system of human rights protection reliable, because it often is the only non-governmental source of information. "If [UN officials] were unable to obtain the relevant information from independent sources (and UN backup facilities are often unable to produce an in-depth analysis), committee members would have to take government reports at their face value and would be hard pressed to challenge them."

. . .

In addition to the formal and semi-formal channels, NGOs informally lobby governmental representatives and UN officials for their goals and objectives. Through lobbying, NGOs get in touch with UN bodies, UN officials and government representatives outside the official channels. Due to their recognition by the UN, NGOs are able to enter UN buildings and come together with official governmental representatives and intergovernmental personnel. In particular for advocacy NGOs, lobbying is an important activity at UN level. For example, human rights NGOs seek to talk to governmental representatives in order to convince them about the necessity of addressing an issue of concern to them. Again, they also provide them with thoroughly researched data, such as human rights violations in a particular country so that they can use this information in official forums.

. . .

STEVEN GROVES, "THE INEQUITIES OF THE U.N. COMMITTEE
ON THE ELIMINATION OF RACIAL DISCRIMINATION"

Heritage Foundation Backgrounder No. 2168 (Aug. 7, 2008).

The [CERD] committee's reviews of the U.S. record have bordered on the farcical. Rather than pursuing the noble goal of ending racial discrimination, the committee's members have used their position as a platform to dictate social policy to the U.S.—while ignoring evidence of U.S. compliance with the treaty.

In May 2007, the United States went to great pains to report to the CERD Committee regarding its compliance with the terms of the treaty. The U.S. report was more than a hundred pages long and detailed—article by article—U.S. compliance with each of the substantive provisions of the treaty. The U.S. report described executive decisions, judicial opinions, and legislative and administrative enactments that furthered the cause of racial equality. Actions to combat discrimination taken by the Equal Employment Opportunity Commission, the Civil Rights Division of the Department of Justice, the Department of Labor's Office of Federal Contract Compliance Programs, the Department of Housing and Urban Development, and various state agencies were set forth in great detail.

After the initial U.S. report was submitted, a committee country expert (who serves as an interlocutor and is responsible for presenting draft comments and recommendations to the CERD Committee) submitted 32 additional written questions to the U.S. inquiring on a wide range of matters, many of which are wholly unrelated to racial discrimination. Included were questions related to sexual and reproductive health, the enemy combatants held at Guantánamo Bay, the protection of "undocumented migrants crossing the borders between Mexico and the United States," and violence against women. Despite the dubious nature of these questions, the U.S. dutifully replied to each one, again at great length (the response was more than 110 pages long). Then, in February 2008, the U.S. sent a delegation of 25 officials to appear before the committee, which questioned members of the delegation at length regarding the U.S. report.

Yet when the CERD Committee issued its report on U.S. compliance, only a fraction of the report (one-half of a page of a 13-page report) took note of the lengthy and detailed U.S. submissions. The original U.S. report, the U.S.'s answers to the committee's 32 additional written questions, and the U.S. delegation's responses to the committee's oral inquiries were entirely ignored.

Instead, most of the text of the committee report is taken directly from a "shadow report" submitted to the CERD Committee by the U.S. Human Rights Network (HRN), a nongovernmental organization (NGO) that coordinated the reports of multiple NGOs in connection with the 2008 CERD review of the U.S. record. Of the 36 substantive "concerns and recommendations" made in the CERD Committee report, at least 19 echo statements or recommendations made in the HRN report. Indeed, it appears that many of the allegations made in the committee's report were lifted directly from the HRN report.

Such heavy reliance by the CERD Committee on an NGO "shadow report" deserves scrutiny, especially since the HRN report is laced with allegations, claims, and characterizations that do not reflect reality and are well outside the mainstream of U.S. public opinion regarding the current state of race relations in the United States.

. . .

It is disturbing, to say the least, that the CERD Committee relied on—and in many cases adopted wholesale—an NGO report that makes such outrageous accusations, not one of which is backed by any evidence whatsoever. The committee accepted the claims made in the HRN shadow report seemingly without deliberation or scrutiny, while the report submitted by the U.S.—all of which was verifiable and supported by documentation—was mostly dismissed.

The CERD Committee's reliance on information provided by an NGO is not necessarily improper. Many parties to CERD submit incomplete or evasive submissions to the committee or fail to provide any report at all. In such cases, it is necessary for the committee to rely on NGO submissions as its primary or even sole source of information. In the case of the 2008 review of the U.S. record, however, the CERD Committee ignored the detailed submissions made by the U.S. and based a substantial portion of its report on allegations made in the HRN report.

By becoming a party to CERD, the United States agreed to report periodically to the CERD Committee on U.S. compliance with the terms of the treaty. It stands to reason that the CERD Committee is concomitantly obligated to review the U.S. submissions fully and to base its comments and recommendations regarding U.S. compliance with the treaty primarily on those submissions. By failing to act as contemplated by the terms of the treaty, the committee has breached its obligations to the U.S. as a state party.

. . .

NOTES & QUESTIONS

1.   Should there be concern about the level of influence that NGOs appear to have over the treaty review process? To whom are NGOs and other advocates accountable? Is there a check on their influence? What ensures that their submissions and data are accurate? Should there be concern that

by relying on advocates for information, treaty experts will compromise their independence and lose legitimacy? And what ensures that a diversity of NGOs are able to participate in the process? Since a similar process is used for all of U.N. treaty monitoring, this issue strikes at the efficacy of a significant part of the U.N's monitoring and enforcement role. Are there structural changes that might improve the system while maintaining its broad contours? Is this issue similar to that faced by any policy-making body, such as the U.S. Congress, which also has to rely on the integrity of witnesses and NGOs to submit accurate information?

2.   In addition to the opportunities it offers to engage directly with the treaty bodies, the treaty review process gives U.S. activists the opportunity to network with human rights organizations around the world and connect with the broader international human rights community. What might U.S. advocates gain from such international networking?

3.   Advocating with U.N. treaty bodies does pose some significant challenges for U.S. advocates, as well. Among these are the financial challenges of U.S. advocates engaging with a system that is based primarily in Geneva, as travel to and accommodations in Geneva are quite expensive. In addition, advocates can be constrained in their advocacy by the U.S. government's pace of treaty reporting, which influences the pace of the treaty body review. Another challenge is that the U.N. treaty bodies often issue their concluding observations and recommendations to governments in the jargon of the U.N., which may be inaccessible to many and fail to excite people about important human rights concerns. Lack of familiarity with the system and skepticism of many civil society stakeholders pose challenges as well. What other challenges might U.S. advocates face in their efforts to engage with the U.N. system? What are some strategies for overcoming those obstacles?

The treaty review process provides openings for advocates to engage with the government and with the U.N. treaty bodies. But how likely is the treaty review process to result in any actual change in policy or practice? If policy change directly tied to the review is unlikely, are there other reasons why NGOs might engage in the review process? Consider the account of federal government decision-making in the context of human rights treaty reporting by Rebecca Ingber, a former lawyer in the U.S. State Department's Office of the Legal Adviser.

REBECCA INGBER, "INTERPRETATION CATALYSTS AND EXECUTIVE BRANCH LEGAL DECISIONMAKING"
38 Yale J. of Int'l L. 359, 395–97 (2013).

[T]he treaty-reporting context creates pressure and opportunity for the Administration to reach a position in a forum that prioritizes international law and human rights to the extent possible. The process reminds the U.S. government of its legal obligations and promotes compliance with respect to policies and enforcement, and can pressure U.S. officials toward interpretations of legal commitments that are more in line with the understanding of the committee and the international community.

U.S. officials tend to view the reports themselves and subsequent meetings with the committees as opportunities to highlight positive U.S. policies and practice. There is thus often a desire on the part of such officials to have certain "deliverables"—positive updates on policy, implementation, or even an evolving legal interpretation—that they can bring to the committee hearings. Moreover, advocates for change within the executive can use the process instrumentally to promote these developments.

Regular reporting on states' interpretation of treaties in addition to their implementation can be critical because new events may raise questions that states did not necessarily grapple with at the time of negotiation or ratification. Modern circumstances may call for updating the state's understanding of its obligations under a given treaty and assessing how it applies to novel situations or contexts. The evolving U.S. understanding of domestic and international law as applicable to its detention operations at Guantánamo Bay is one such example. In the early years after 9/11, the executive's positions on its legal constraints at Guantánamo included the views that neither the writ of habeas corpus nor the provisions of various human rights treaties extended to its detainee operations there. Yet over the course of a decade, these views shifted in both dramatic and nuanced ways, due to a mix of both external factors and to the executive branch's own changed positions. Such shifts can critically affect a state's interpretation of and compliance with treaty obligations, which can raise questions in multiple contexts, including but by no means limited to the reporting process. Thus, whether or not the U.S. position that ultimately arises out of a treaty reporting process conforms to the exact views of the committee, the process encourages U.S. officials to come together to coordinate and crystallize a position in an environment and through a process geared toward promotion of the U.S. record on human rights. As one recent U.S. report states, the U.S. government views the treaty reporting process as "an important tool" in the development of its human rights practices and performance, and an "opportunity to engage in a process of stock-taking and self-examination."

To be sure, the effect of treaty body reporting on legal change should not be overstated. As with other areas of executive branch legal interpretation, new interpretations of law occur quite rarely. Government lawyers, wherever they are housed throughout the executive, are inherently conservative in conceding legal constraints. Moreover, as in

other contexts, precedent plays an enormous role in the treaty body
reporting process, and great emphasis is placed on continuity in U.S.
positions. The focus on consensus means there is a high bar for changing
the government's position. If there is no consensus on taking a new
position, the status quo—or vagueness—is always a potential fallback.

Nevertheless, the executive does sometimes change course. And
unlike litigation, the treaty-body reporting catalyst brings together the
distinctive decision-making elements that are best suited to promoting
progressive change in both law and policy. Where potential "policy
windows" exist—in areas where evolving circumstances call for
innovative reasoning, or in areas of debate within the executive where
potential for change may hinge on contextual pressures, involvement of
particular players, or simply getting the issue onto the agenda—the
treaty-body reporting process provides a forum for decision-making that
permits long-term contemplation and coordination, heavy input from
"expert" agencies, room for interaction between political and career
players, and space for legal policy development in a context that
prioritizes international law compliance, the promotion of human rights,
and engagement with the international community.

. . .

NOTES & QUESTIONS

1.   Based on this account, what factors might advocates take into
consideration when deciding which issues to prioritize in the course of a
treaty review?

2.   Reconsider the exchanges between civil society, the U.N. Human
Rights Committee, and the U.S. government over targeted drone strikes in
light of Ingber's account. What impact, if any, might the reporting process
have had on the government's policy or articulated position on this issue?

———————

Short of actual policy changes, a treaty review can result in specific
recommendations from international experts. Advocates then face the
challenge of integrating the recommendations into their advocacy in U.S.
courts or with domestic policy makers. In the following excerpt, Eric Tars
provides an account of the efforts by one advocacy campaign to implement
recommendations from the reviews of the United States by the U.N.
Committee Against Torture and the U.N. Human Rights Committee.

ERIC TARS, "WHO KNOWS WHAT LURKS IN THE HEARTS OF
HUMAN RIGHTS VIOLATORS? THE SHADOW (REPORTER)
KNOWS—HUMAN RIGHTS SHADOW REPORTING:
A STRATEGIC TOOL FOR DOMESTIC JUSTICE"

42 Clearinghouse Rev. 475, 478–80 (2009).

On October 21, 2008, former Chicago Police Commander Jon Burge
was arrested for the twenty years of torture that he and his deputies
inflicted on hundreds of African American men. The arrest was in no way
guaranteed—indeed, Burge had faced minimal discipline and evaded
justice for over thirty years. He was fired, but he still continued to draw
his $3,000 per month police pension. By building on a solid base of local
organizing and legal work, however, attorneys and activists used
strategies, such as shadow reporting, that finally brought Burge to face
his day in court.

From 1972 to 1993, in Chicago's Police Area 2 under Burge's
command, 135 African American males were allegedly tortured in order
to obtain confessions. Burge's torture techniques included beatings with
telephone books; suffocation with typewriter covers; attaching alligator
clips to ears, nose, mouth, and exposed genitals; electric shock;
handcuffing arrestees to radiators, causing severe burns; and mock
executions. In numerous cases the state's attorney's office was aware of
the allegations but used the coerced statements to convict the victims at
trial.

Burge left the police force in 1993, but until October 2008 no criminal
charges were ever filed against him or his deputies. Lawyers from the
People's Law Office and activists from a number of Chicago organizations
worked tirelessly to bring Burge to justice. Although numerous internal
investigations found evidence of torture, both the state's attorney and
federal prosecutors claimed that procedural bars prevented prosecution of
Burge.

Having run into one brick wall after another in the domestic legal
system, activists turned to the international sphere. In April 2006 the
Midwest Coalition for Human Rights included complaints about the
Burge situation in a shadow report that a large number of domestic
antipolice brutality groups submitted to the Committee Against Torture.
Representing the Coalition and the People's Law Office, attorney Joey
Mogul joined a dozen other advocates in Geneva to bring the case to the
committee the following month. At briefings and through informal
conversations, Mogul moved committee members with her testimony.
During the formal hearings with the U.S. government, the committee
chair, Andreas Mavrommatis, specifically questioned the government
delegation regarding the failure to prosecute the cases. Unsatisfied with
the U.S. response, the committee noted in its official Concluding

Observations "the limited investigation and lack of prosecution in respect of the allegations of torture perpetrated in areas 2 and 3 of the Chicago Police Department (article 12)" and recommended "promptly, thoroughly and impartially" investigating to "bring perpetrators to justice." The committee also asked the United States to supply follow-up information on the outcome of such investigations.

The specific focus on the Chicago case brought vast press coverage both in Chicago and nationally. The committee's response to the shadow report critically changed the tone: from then on, whenever the Burge case was mentioned in the media, Burge's acts were referred to as "torture" rather than merely "police brutality," almost always in connection with the condemnation by the U.N. body. The tide was beginning to turn for the advocates.

Following closely on the heels of the Committee against Torture hearings were the [Human Rights Committee] hearings in July 2006. With more than sixty other U.S. advocates, Mogul returned to Geneva to repeat her call for justice in the Burge case. Once again committee members specifically questioned the U.S. delegation on the case. The hearings coincided with the release of a major report on the case by state special prosecutors, who once again claimed that they were procedurally barred from filing charges. News coverage again shined the international spotlight on Chicago. The HRC's Concluding Observations reiterated its concern about and called for increased efforts to eliminate police brutality, although the HRC did not refer specifically to the Burge case. Concluding Observations are not binding judicial decrees, however, and despite the international spotlight, in a report in July 2006, state special prosecutors continued to claim that they were procedurally barred from prosecuting Burge.

. . .

Advocates took [the] strategy of pushing good-faith local compliance to both the federal and local government. Relying on the Concluding Observations, they convinced the Cook County Board of Commissioners to hold a public hearing on July 10, 2007, at which advocates spoke of the ongoing violations and lack of justice. As a result of those hearings and citing the Committee against Torture findings, the commissioners unanimously called for (1) the U.S. Attorney's Office in the Northern District of Illinois to investigate and prosecute any federal crimes committed by former Commander Burge and his men; (2) Illinois Attorney General Lisa Madigan to initiate new hearings for the twenty-six African American torture victims who remain convicted and incarcerated, and (3) the Illinois legislature and the U.S. Congress to criminalize acts of torture with no statute of limitations. One week after the county hearings, the Chicago City Council introduced Mayor Richard

M. Daley's ordinance establishing a new city agency, the Office of Professional Standards, to investigate police abuse.

A week after that, the council held hearings on the status of the investigation and case. And on January 10, 2008, ending what one alderman called "a horrible chapter in the city's history," the Chicago City Council approved settlements totaling as much as $19.8 million with four men who said they were tortured into murder confessions by Burge and those under his command.

In September 2007 the U.S. Attorney's office finally opened an investigation and, in October 2008, indicted Burge on two counts of obstruction of justice and one count of perjury. These charges were based on allegations that Burge lied and impeded court proceedings in November 2003 when he supplied false written answers to questions in a civil lawsuit alleging that he and others engaged in torture and abuse of suspects. Although the underlying torture has not yet been charged, U.S. Attorney Patrick J. Fitzgerald said that "it is not the end of the investigation of torture and abuse."

Shadow reporting added a tangible benefit to the Burge campaign by reframing a local case of police abuse as an international issue of torture. Advocates were able to apply the abstract standards of international human rights specifically to local issues, thereby circumventing a local political system that had perpetrated and covered up these abuses. Building on years of local organizing, they held city, county, and federal government officials accountable to a higher standard and achieved justice for the victims of these crimes. As Mogul concluded in her statement to the press on Burge's arrest, "[w]e are heartened that the federal government has heeded the call of the U.N. to step in and prosecute where local and state officials have failed to do so. We are gratified that Jon Burge will finally be brought to justice for his heinous violations of human rights."

· · ·

NOTES & QUESTIONS

1. In 2010, a federal jury convicted Burge on charges of obstruction of justice and perjury, and, in 2011, a federal judge sentenced him to 4 ½ years in a federal prison. What factors might have led to advocates' success in translating their "wins" in Geneva into advocacy back home in Chicago? What challenges might the advocates have faced in their efforts to do so?

2. The advocates in Chicago engaged the U.N. human rights treaty review process after pursuing more traditional domestic strategies for twenty years. Are there ways in which they might have designed a domestic advocacy strategy from the beginning to complement and maximize the impact of U.N.-based advocacy?

B. U.N. CHARTER BODIES

In addition to the treaty-specific monitoring bodies described above, the United Nations human rights system also includes bodies authorized by the U.N. Charter. Included in these is the Human Rights Council, an inter-governmental body comprised of 47 countries elected to membership and charged with promoting and protecting human rights around the world. It was created in 2006 as a replacement to the former U.N. Commission on Human Rights, which had come under fire for being highly politicized and for failing to address serious human rights violations by its members.

The Human Rights Council's monitoring and review mechanisms include the Universal Periodic Review process and the ability to appoint "Special Procedures." Unlike treaty monitoring bodies, U.N. Charter-based mechanisms monitor countries' compliance with all of the rights contained in the Universal Declaration of Human Rights, regardless of a country's treaty ratification practices. Thus, U.S. advocates have found U.N. Charter-based mechanisms to be useful in measuring the United States' compliance with the full array of human rights standards, notwithstanding the United States' failure to ratify specific treaties, particularly those focusing on economic and social rights. In this section, we explore advocacy opportunities offered by the Universal Periodic Review and the U.N. Special Procedures. In addition to using these mechanisms, human rights advocates with the necessary U.N. credentials can engage directly with the Human Rights Council by making statements from the floor of the Council while it is in session. NGOs can also work with government officials (U.S. officials and delegations from other countries) to influence the content of resolutions considered by the Council.

i. Universal Periodic Review

The Universal Periodic Review (UPR), established by the United Nations' Human Rights Council in 2006, requires that the human rights record of each of the 193 countries belonging to the U.N. be reviewed once every four years. The UPR is based on the U.N. Charter, the UDHR, human rights instruments to which the country is a party, and any voluntary pledges and commitments made by countries, including those made when presenting candidacy for the Human Rights Council, and is intended to "promote the universality, interdependence, indivisibility and interrelatedness of all human rights."[2]

Unlike the treaty body reviews, which are conducted by committees of experts, the UPR is intended to be a "peer review," through which

---

[2] Human Rights Council Res. 5/1, Rep. of the Human Rights Council, 5th Sess., June 11–18, 2007, U.N. GAOR, 62d Sess., Supp. No. 53, A/62/53, at 49 (June 18, 2007).

representatives from every member of the U.N. have an opportunity to ask questions and make recommendations of the country under review. It is therefore considered a more political process than the treaty review process.

Under the UPR, first, the country under review offers an assessment of its own human rights record by submitting a national report. An important feature of the UPR is its requirement that governments engage "all relevant stakeholders, including non-governmental organizations" in the preparation of its report.[3] Once the country submits the national report, the other U.N. member countries have an opportunity to review the assessment, along with a compilation of findings and reports from U.N. human rights treaty bodies, special procedures and other relevant U.N. mechanisms, and a summary of reports submitted by civil society, including community groups and advocacy organizations. It should be noted that the UPR procedures place significant page limits on each of these reports. The government under review then participates in a three hour and thirty minute interactive dialogue in Geneva, during which all U.N. member countries have an opportunity to ask direct questions and the government under review may respond. The exchange is memorialized, along with the recommendations made and the response of the country under review, in a final report.

The United States' first UPR occurred in November 2010, with considerable civil society engagement. In the lead up to the review, the U.S. State Department held a series of consultations in nine cities throughout the country, in many cases organized by advocacy organizations. Advocates filed 103 stakeholder reports, which are similar to shadow reports submitted in conjunction with treaty body reviews. At the review, more than 50 countries engaged the U.S. delegation on issues ranging from U.S. detention policy and the death penalty to the United States' failure to ratify key human rights treaties and establish an independent human rights monitoring body. The review resulted in 228 Recommendations for ways in which the United States can improve human rights conditions domestically.

The following materials are from the first U.S. UPR. As you read these materials, consider the role that advocates played in shaping the U.S. report, the recommendations that resulted from the UPR, and the U.S. response to those recommendations. How might the UPR supplement treaty body reviews and related advocacy efforts of domestic human rights lawyers? In what ways does the UPR differ from the treaty body review process?

---

[3] *Id.*

U.S. DEPARTMENT OF STATE, "REPORT OF THE UNITED
STATES OF AMERICA, SUBMITTED TO THE U.N. HIGH
COMMISSIONER FOR HUMAN RIGHTS, IN CONJUNCTION
WITH THE UNIVERSAL PERIODIC REVIEW"

(Aug. 23, 2010).

I. Introduction

I.1   *A more perfect union, a more perfect world*

1.   The story of the United States of America is one guided by universal values shared the world over—that all are created equal and endowed with inalienable rights. In the United States, these values have grounded our institutions and motivated the determination of our citizens to come ever closer to realizing these ideals. Our Founders, who proclaimed their ambition "to form a more perfect Union," bequeathed to us not a static condition but a perpetual aspiration and mission.

2.   We present our first Universal Periodic Review (UPR) report in the context of our commitment to help to build a world in which universal rights give strength and direction to the nations, partnerships, and institutions that can usher us toward a more perfect world, a world characterized by, as President Obama has said, "a just peace based on the inherent rights and dignity of every individual."

3.   The U.S. has long been a cornerstone of the global economy and the global order. However, the most enduring contribution of the United States has been as a political experiment. The principles that all are created equal and endowed with inalienable rights were translated into promises and, with time, encoded into law. These simple but powerful principles have been the foundation upon which we have built the institutions of a modern state that is accountable to its citizens and whose laws are both legitimated by and limited by an enduring commitment to respect the rights of individuals. It is our political system that enables our economy and undergirds our global influence. As President Obama wrote in the preface to the recently published National Security Strategy, "democracy does not merely represent our better angels, it stands in opposition to aggression and injustice, and our support for universal rights is both fundamental to American leadership and a source of our strength in the world." Part of that strength derives from our democracy's capacity to adopt improvements based upon the firm foundation of our principled commitments. Our democracy is what allows us to acknowledge the realities of the world we live in, to recognize the opportunities to progress toward the fulfillment of an ideal, and to look to the future with pride and hope.

4.   The ideas that informed and inform the American experiment can be found all over the world, and the people who have built it over centuries have come from every continent. The American experiment is a

human experiment; the values on which it is based, including a commitment to human rights, are clearly engrained in our own national conscience, but they are also universal.

5.   Echoing Eleanor Roosevelt, whose leadership was crucial to the adoption of the Universal Declaration of Human Rights (UDHR), Secretary of State Hillary Clinton has reaffirmed that "[h]uman rights are universal, but their experience is local. This is why we are committed to holding everyone to the same standard, including ourselves." From the UDHR to the ensuing Covenants and beyond, the United States has played a central role in the internationalization of human rights law and institutions. We associate ourselves with the many countries on all continents that are sincerely committed to advancing human rights, and we hope this UPR process will help us to strengthen our own system of human rights protections and encourage others to strengthen their commitments to human rights.

I.2   The United States and the Universal Periodic Review: approach and methodology

6.   The ultimate objective of the UPR process, and of the UN Human Rights Council, is to enhance the protections for and enjoyment of human rights. Our participation signifies our commitment to that end, and we hope to contribute to it by sharing how we have made and will continue to make progress toward it. Some may say that by participating we acknowledge commonality with states that systematically abuse human rights. We do not. There is no comparison between American democracy and repressive regimes. Others will say that our participation, and our assessment of certain areas where we seek continued progress, reflects doubt in the ability of the American political system to deliver progress for its citizens. It does not. As Secretary Clinton said in a speech on human rights last year, "democracies demonstrate their greatness not by insisting they are perfect, but by using their institutions and their principles to make themselves . . . more perfect." Progress is our goal, and our expectation thereof is justified by the proven ability of our system of government to deliver the progress our people demand and deserve.

7.   This document gives a partial snapshot of the current human rights situation in the United States, including some of the areas where problems persist in our society. In addressing those areas, we use this report to explore opportunities to make further progress and also to share some of our recent progress. For us, the primary value of this report is not as a diagnosis, but rather as a roadmap for our ongoing work within our democratic system to achieve lasting change. We submit this report with confidence that the legacy of our past efforts to embrace and actualize universal rights foreshadows our continued success.

8. This report is the product of collaboration between the U.S. Government and representatives of civil society from across the United States. Over the last year, senior representatives from more than a dozen federal departments and agencies traveled the country to attend a series of UPR consultations hosted by a wide range of civil society organizations. At these gatherings, individuals presented their concerns and recommendations and often shared stories or reports as they interacted with government representatives. Those conversations shaped the substance and structure of this report. Nearly a thousand people, representing a diversity of communities and viewpoints, and voicing a wide range of concerns, attended these gatherings in New Orleans, Louisiana; New York, New York; El Paso, Texas; Albuquerque, New Mexico; Window Rock, Arizona; the San Francisco Bay Area; Detroit, Michigan; Chicago, Illinois; Birmingham, Alabama; and Washington, D.C. Information about the process was also posted on the website of the U.S. Department of State. Members of the public were encouraged to contribute questions, comments, and recommendations via that site, and many did so. The consultation process followed a familiar tradition of collaboration and discussion between government and civil society that is vital to the strength of our democracy. The U.S. Government is grateful to all those who hosted meetings and shared their views both in those consultations and online. We also welcome constructive comments and recommendations from other governments and non-governmental organizations through the UPR process.

. . .

IV. A commitment to foster a society where citizens are empowered to exercise their rights

67. The paradigm elucidated in Franklin Roosevelt's 1941 "Four Freedoms" speech became a reference point for many in the international human rights movement. On subjects such as "freedom from want," the United States has focused on democratic solutions and civil society initiatives while the U.S. courts have defined our federal constitutional obligations narrowly and primarily by focusing on procedural rights to due process and equal protection of the law. But, as a matter of public policy, our citizens have taken action through their elected representatives to help create a society in which prosperity is shared, including social benefits provided by law, so that all citizens can live what Roosevelt called "a healthy peacetime life." Often this has included safeguards for the most vulnerable in our society—including the young, the old, the poor, and the infirm. In the wake of the Civil War, legislation was passed to support the well-being of widows and veterans, and to provide land to former slaves. By the early 20th century, all of our states had recognized that children needed schooling in order to become free and engaged citizens and had instituted free education for all. During the

Great Depression, new programs were introduced to ensure the security of those who could no longer work. In the 1960s, several administrations announced a "war on poverty," and programs were established to provide health care for seniors and the very poor. And this year saw the passage of major legislation that will greatly expand the number of Americans who have health insurance. In every case, the creation of these programs has reflected a popular sense that the society in which we want to live is one in which each person has the opportunity to live a full and fulfilling life. That begins, but does not end, with the exercise of their human rights.

. . .

IV.2 Health

69. The United States has been the source of many significant innovations in modern medicine that have alleviated suffering and cured disease for millions in our own country and around the world. This year, we also made significant progress by enacting major legislation that expands access to health care for our citizens.

70. On March 23, 2010, President Obama signed the Affordable Care Act into law. The Act makes great strides toward the goal that all Americans have access to quality, affordable health care. The law is projected to expand health insurance coverage to 32 million Americans who would otherwise lack health insurance, significantly reduces disparities in accessing high-quality care, and includes substantial new investments in prevention and wellness activities to improve public health. The law also includes important consumer protections, such as prohibiting insurance companies from denying coverage to people based on pre-existing conditions or medical history, which disproportionately impacts older and sicker populations.

71. The law increases access to care for underserved populations by expanding community health centers that deliver preventive and primary care services. The law will also help our nation reduce disparities and discrimination in access to care that have contributed to poor health. For example, African Americans are 29 percent more likely to die from heart disease than non-Hispanic whites. Asian American men suffer from stomach cancer 114 percent more often than non-Hispanic white men. Hispanic women are 2.2 times more likely to be diagnosed with cervical cancer than non-Hispanic white women. American Indians and Alaska Natives are 2.2 times as likely to have diabetes as non-Hispanic whites. Additionally, these racial and ethnic groups accounted for almost 70 percent of the newly diagnosed cases of HIV and AIDS in 2003.

72. The Act will reduce disparities like these through access to preventive services; investment in chronic disease control and prevention;

enhanced data collection to support population-specific epidemiological research; and recruitment of health professionals from diverse backgrounds.

73. Implementation of the Affordable Care Act will help more Americans get the care they need to live healthy lives and ensure more Americans are free to learn, work, and contribute to their communities.

. . .

VI. Conclusion

100.   The United States views participation in this UPR process as an opportunity to discuss with our citizenry and with fellow members of the Human Rights Council our accomplishments, challenges, and vision for the future on human rights. We welcome observations and recommendations that can help us on that road to a more perfect union. Delivering on human rights has never been easy, but it is work we will continue to undertake with determination, for human rights will always undergird our national identity and define our national aspirations.

NOTES & QUESTIONS

1.   Who is the audience for the U.S. UPR report? What is the United States attempting to communicate through its report? Do you think this is an appropriate use of the mechanism? Do you think it is effective in achieving the government's goals?

2.   In engaging in its first UPR, the United States, under President Obama, sought to set the "gold standard" for government engagement with the mechanism and made extensive outreach to civil society a hallmark of its approach to the process. Why do you think this was such an important component of the U.S. approach? Why does the U.S. report go into such detail regarding the process it underwent in preparing for the UPR? Is this information relevant in evaluating the United States' human rights record? Is this an effective way of communicating the United States' commitment to the UPR process and encouraging other countries to undertake a rigorous review?

3.   How does the U.S. report characterize the United States' stance on economic, social, and cultural rights? Why does the U.S. report go into such detail about the health care law, the Affordable Care Act?

As with the treaty review process, human rights advocates, academic institutions, national human rights institutions, and other non-governmental organizations (NGOs) have an opportunity to participate in the UPR by submitting their own assessment of the human rights conditions in the country under review. The review itself is based in part on a document prepared by the Office of the High Commissioner for Human Rights summarizing these "other stakeholder" reports. NGOs can also observe the review and the subsequent Working Group sessions, and they have a limited opportunity to make statements during the session of the Human Rights Council when the UPR outcome document is adopted. Unlike the shadow reports that NGOs can submit to the human rights treaty bodies, the stakeholder submissions for the UPR must adhere to a specific format, including page limitations. The following stakeholder report was submitted by an NGO coalition addressing the United States' human rights treaty ratification practice, an issue that was the focus of a significant number of the recommendations that came out of the Review.

STAKEHOLDER REPORT ON U.S. HUMAN RIGHTS TREATY RATIFICATION, JOINT SUBMISSION TO THE UNITED NATIONS UNIVERSAL PERIODIC REVIEW, NINTH SESSION OF THE WORKING GROUP ON THE UPR, HUMAN RIGHTS COUNCIL
(Dec. 2010).

A. *The U.S. Should Take Immediate Steps to Ratify Major Human Rights Treaties.*

4.   The United States played a critical role in developing and drafting the UDHR, demonstrating an early commitment to promoting and protecting human rights. Yet since that time, the United States has had an inconsistent history of incorporating and applying international human rights standards domestically. Indeed, the U.S. has continuously refused to join with other states in taking on international human rights legal obligations through its failure to sign and/or ratify core international human rights treaties. Despite playing an influential role in the drafting and negotiation of many of these treaties, the United States has yet to take the steps necessary to demonstrate a commitment to the universality and interdependence of human rights.

. . .

6.   When presenting its candidacy to the Human Rights Council, the current Administration noted its commitment "to live up to our ideals at home and to meet our international human rights obligations" and "to work[ ] with its legislative branch to consider the possible ratification of human rights treaties, including but not limited to the Convention on the Elimination of Discrimination Against Women." The U.S. should translate this rhetoric into action by taking immediate concrete steps to sign and/or ratify international human rights treaties.

1.   *The U.S. Should Offer for Advice and Consent the Treaties it has Signed.*

7.   The U.S. has failed to move several treaties beyond the presidential signing phase of the ratification process, leaving one treaty in limbo for over 30 years. The U.S. has symbolically approved, (agreeing, at a minimum, not to violate the spirit and purpose of), but failed to ratify:

   a.   Convention on the Elimination of Discrimination Against Women (CEDAW).

8.   Among the treaties the U.S. has failed to ratify, CEDAW has made it the farthest along the track toward ratification. The United States stands with six other countries that have failed to ratify CEDAW: Iran, Somalia, Sudan, Nauru, Palau and Tonga. CEDAW contains important provisions for women's equal access to, equal opportunities and equal participation in all spheres of life on the basis of substantive equality.

9.   Signed 30 years ago and submitted for ratification in 1994, CEDAW has never gone to a full Senate vote. In the absence of ratification, independent action at the subnational level demonstrates support for the rights enshrined in this Convention. By the end of 2009 numerous subnational bodies, including cities and counties, had passed resolutions supporting CEDAW.

   b.   The Convention on the Rights of the Child (CRC).

10.   The CRC is the most widely ratified human rights treaty, leaving the United States virtually alone in its refusal to ratify. Currently, the United States and Somalia are the only states that have not ratified the CRC. In November 2009, Somalia announced its intention to ratify the Convention. The United States' failure to ratify this convention is in stark contrast to its position during the drafting and negotiation process, where the U.S. submitted more new articles than any other government and proposed language or amendments for 38 of CRC's 40 substantive provisions. Although President Clinton signed the CRC in 1995, no President has submitted it for a full Senate vote.

   c.   The Convention on the Rights of Persons with Disabilities (CRPD).

11.   President Obama, in his first year as President, has already demonstrated his support for the United States' ratification of the CRPD by signing the convention in July 2009. Further, the United States was instrumental in the development of the CRPD and has praised it as an "extraordinary treaty," recognizing the importance of equality and "the inherent dignity and worth and independence of all persons with disabilities." Despite this praise, the U.S. has not ratified the Convention.

d.   The International Covenant on Economic, Social, and Cultural Rights (ICESCR).

12. Of the three foundational human rights documents that constitute the International Bill of Human Rights, the ICESCR is the only one that the United States has not either ratified or adopted. Despite its leading role in developing the UDHR, the U.S. demanded that binding obligations with respect to the rights enumerated in the Declaration must be divided into two separate core treaties, effectively splitting economic, social and cultural rights from civil and political rights. The ICESCR has been ratified by over 160 countries from every region of the world. The U.S. signed the ICESCR over 30 years ago but has taken no further steps towards its ratification. Ratification would demonstrate a commitment to protecting fundamental rights, including the rights to education, housing, work, social security and the highest attainable standard of health as recognized under international law.

2.   *The U.S. Should Take Action on the Regional and International Agreements it Has Not Signed or Ratified.*

13. The United States' failure to engage fully with the international community is further demonstrated by the number of important regional and international agreements that it has not yet committed to uphold in the international arena. The U.S. should take immediate steps to sign and/or ratify the following international and regional agreements:

- American Convention on Human Rights
- Convention on Cluster Munitions
- Convention on the Prohibition of the Use, Stockpiling, Production and Transfer of Anti-Personnel Mines and on their Destruction
- International Convention for the Protection of all Persons from Enforced Disappearance
- International Convention on the Protection of the Rights of All Migrant Workers and Members of Their Families
- International Labor Organization Fundamental Conventions
- Protocol I and II to the Geneva Conventions
- Rome Statute of the International Criminal Court

Additionally, the U.S. should endorse the United Nations Declaration on the Rights of Indigenous Peoples.

. . .

C.   *The U.S. Should Fully Implement the Human Rights Treaties it has Ratified.*

21. For each human rights treaty the U.S. has ratified, it has entered a package of RUDs. Some of these clarify interpretations, as allowed under international law. However, several of the RUDs entered by the United States prevent legal enforcement of the treaties' provisions.

22. The most sweeping of these RUDs is the United States' understanding that human rights conventions are not "self-executing." As a result, victims of treaty violations cannot directly invoke the treaties' provisions in U.S. courts to seek legal remedies. "Non-self-executing" treaties can have direct legal effect only through independent implementing legislation understood to cover the terms of each treaty. Congress has expressly adopted legislation in some cases, such as allowing limited prosecution for torture, war crimes, and genocide to implement treaty provisions. By contrast, in over fifteen years since ratifying the CERD, the U.S. has not adopted any implementing legislation for that treaty.

. . .

The first U.S. UPR resulted in 228 recommendations from U.N. member countries—a record for any country reviewed up to that point. Many of the recommendations were similar to one another, and, indeed, several themes emerged during the course of the review, including the need for the United States to ratify core human rights treaties, abolish the death penalty, vigorously protect economic and social rights, address criminal justice concerns, and close the U.S. detention facility at Guantánamo Bay. On March 18, 2011, a delegation of U.S. officials, including the legal adviser to the State Department, appeared before the Human Rights Council in Geneva for the official adoption of the Report. The following are excerpts of the legal adviser's remarks in response to the UPR recommendations.

HAROLD HONGJU KOH, LEGAL ADVISER, U.S. DEPARTMENT OF STATE, STATEMENT UPON ADOPTION OF UNIVERSAL PERIODIC REVIEW REPORT, UNITED NATIONS HUMAN RIGHTS COUNCIL, GENEVA

(Mar 18, 2011).

We have found the Universal Periodic Review a useful tool to assess how our country can continue to improve in achieving its own human rights goals. Civil society has been involved in each and every step of our UPR: from an unprecedented series of a dozen listening sessions that involved representatives of local and national civil society organizations as well as hundreds of citizens from communities across our country, to the Town Hall gathering for civil society held here last November in Geneva, and since then our Federal agencies have held numerous meetings with civil society to discuss our response to the many recommendations.

. . .

Civil society groups hold government to our values by asking hard questions and making tough recommendations. We welcome your recommendations and thank you for them; for that is how we can learn and improve. We value our conversation with those NGOs who were able to make it to Geneva this week. We are glad to see some of you here, with the formal speaking role the UPR affords you in this session.

. . .

When we presented our initial report last November, we received 228 recommendations. We have considered the substance of each and every one of the recommendations, even those whose tone suggests they were not offered in a constructive spirit. While our written submission provides a specific response to each recommendation, in my time today, let me discuss the ten thematic areas these recommendations cover, and review significant changes that have occurred since our report last November.

. . .

Many members of civil society—and such states as Uruguay, Australia, and Israel—asked us to do more to address discrimination against lesbian, gay, bisexual, and transgender individuals. Our government has taken important recent steps in this regard, notably enactment on December 22, 2010, of the Don't Ask, Don't Tell Repeal Act, which will allow gay men and women to serve openly in our military, strengthening our national security while upholding the basic equality upon which our nation was founded.

The United States continues to strive vigorously to ensure justice and equality for all Americans. In response to the mortgage crisis, the Civil Rights Division established a new Fair Lending Unit, to address a wide range of allegations of discriminatory conduct. The Department of Justice also has stepped up its vigorous enforcement of laws prohibiting discrimination in areas including voting, employment, public accommodations, and education.

The United States continues to prosecute violations of our Federal hate crimes law, including a recent indictment involving a racially motivated assault of a Native American victim with a developmental disability.

In a second area, criminal justice, the United States continues to work—as recommended by Sweden, France, Haiti, Thailand, Belgium, Algeria, and others—to ensure protection under our Constitution and laws of the rights of those accused of committing crimes and held in prisons or jails. We set and enforce high standards of conduct for law enforcement personnel. In New Orleans, the Civil Rights Division recently secured convictions against police officers who engaged in misconduct in the wake of Hurricane Katrina. Yesterday, the Justice Department announced its findings that the New Orleans Police Department has engaged in patterns of misconduct that violate the Constitution and Federal law. Its problems include excessive force and policing inconsistencies based on race, ethnicity, sexual orientation, limited English proficiency, and gender.

About 25 countries, including close friends and allies, made recommendations concerning administration of capital punishment by those governments within our system that still apply it. Domestic civil society also raised capital punishment as an issue of concern. While we respect those who make these recommendations, as I noted last November, they reflect continuing differences of policy, not differences about what the rules of international human rights law currently require. To those who desire as a matter of policy to end capital punishment in the United States—and I count myself among those—I note the decision made by the government of Illinois on March 9 to abolish that state's death penalty.

In a third area, the rights of indigenous peoples, the United States recognizes past wrongs and has committed itself to working with tribal governments to address the many issues facing their communities, including two particular recommendations. First, the importance of tribal consultation was repeatedly stressed during our UPR listening sessions with tribal leaders and civil society. Second, reflected in recommendations from civil society and tribes and echoed by a number of countries including Finland and New Zealand, was that we support the UN Declaration on the Rights of Indigenous Peoples.

At his second White House Tribal Nations Conference last December, President Obama addressed both concerns when he announced the United States' support for the UN Declaration on the Rights of Indigenous Peoples, and issued a statement detailing U.S. support for the Declaration and ongoing work on Native American issues. His announcement capped a year in which the President had directed that consultations with tribal officials be reinvigorated throughout the U.S. Government.

Civil society and countries including Malaysia, Mexico, and Norway made recommendations to us concerning a fourth area: national security.

As I explained in November, the United States takes its obligations under international law seriously, and abides by all applicable law in its continuing armed conflicts against Al Qaeda, the Taliban, and associated forces, including those laws respecting humane treatment, detention, and use of force. It is legal under the laws of war to use detention to prevent adversaries from re-engaging in the conflict, but we do not—and we will not—tolerate torture or inhumane treatment of detainees in our custody, wherever they are held.

Ireland, Switzerland and others made recommendations about the Guantánamo detention facility. As the White House indicated last Monday, President Obama remains committed to closing that facility, although that will clearly take more time, due to restrictive legislation and complex politics. As this effort continues, we are committed to ensuring that all practices on Guantánamo fully accord with international law.

. . .

In the context of counter-terrorism, a number of U.S. civil society groups and countries—such as Egypt and Algeria—have raised concerns regarding discrimination against Muslims. The United States agrees that the problem of terrorism is not unique to members of any religious or ethnic group. Our government does not support attempts to treat entire communities as a threat to our national security, based solely on their race, religion, or ethnicity.

In a fifth area, immigration, we accepted many recommendations from civil society and from countries including Guatemala, Mexico, Brazil, Ecuador, Vietnam, Switzerland, and the United Kingdom. The contributions of immigrants have been an important element of every chapter of American history. While challenges remain, we also know that people from around the world continue to arrive on our shores in search of refuge and opportunity. What attracts immigrants to the United States—like my own parents, and those of many others in our delegation—is the promise of universal values embodied in our Constitution, with our continuing efforts to ensure that we deliver on that promise.

. . .

In a sixth area—economic, social, cultural, and environmental rights—as civil society and countries including Thailand, Norway, Morocco, and Brazil recommended, local, State, and Federal governments in the United States continue to protect the environment in which we live and to take significant action to address what President Roosevelt called "freedom from want." Recent Federal department and agency actions include: (1) the Department of Education's February 2011 announcement of an Equity and Excellence Commission to examine disparities in educational opportunities and to address the needs of children in distressed, high-poverty communities; (2) grants from the Department of Health and Human Services to support health centers around the country and improve . . . health care access for the uninsured; and (3) two recent settlements from the Environmental Protection Agency that would require new source performance standards for greenhouse gas emissions.

In a seventh area—workplace protections and the fight against human trafficking—the United States has long been a leader. We support several recommendations that concern trafficking, including one from Moldova.

. . .

We are committed to an eighth goal as well—robust domestic implementation of our international human rights obligations. In this area, we support recommendations from Egypt, Norway, Austria, and Costa Rica. We particularly appreciated Austria's recommendation that we continue consultation with civil society, which we have done and intend to continue including immediately after this presentation. Civil society has also helpfully advised us on how to take additional steps to inform local and state governments about our UPR.

As a party to several human rights treaties, the United States is bound to comply with its obligations at Federal, State, and local levels. Under our Constitution and federal system of government, the different levels and branches of our government ensure a comprehensive web of protections and enforcement mechanisms that reinforce our country's ability to guarantee respect of human rights.

The ninth and largest group of recommendations that we received concerned ratification of treaties and other international instruments. Under our Constitution, treaty ratification requires approval not only by the Executive Branch, but also a two-thirds supermajority of our Senate. Despite this high threshold, the Administration has pushed for positive Senate action on a number of human rights and other treaties that afford humanitarian protection, and will continue to do so.

. . .

Tenth and finally, we address together a number of the recommendations made at the UPR that did not fit into other categories. As our written report says, we do not support recommendations that urged particular action in pending judicial cases. Nor do we support certain other inappropriate or politically motivated recommendations. Despite some countries' desire to use the UPR for their own political ends, we have worked, with respect for the process, to consider the merits of each and every one of the 228 recommendations made to us, and to respond honestly to each.

In closing, we complete our first Universal Periodic Review proud of our heritage as a nation conceived in liberty, still dedicated to the proposition that all persons are created equal. At a time when so many nations are in turmoil, when so many are still struggling to achieve government of the people, by the people, and for the people, our constant and urgent challenge remains the same: to achieve a more perfect union and to promote a more perfect world. As a diverse democracy now well into our third century, the United States of America has been honored to present our response to the world's recommendations. We now look forward to hearing the reactions of other countries and civil society.

Thank you very much.

NOTES & QUESTIONS

1. During the U.S. review, over forty countries offered recommendations that the United States ratify core human rights agreements. While some of the recommendations were general, many focused on specific treaties, including the Convention on the Elimination of Discrimination Against Women, the Convention on the Rights of the Child, the Convention on the Rights of Persons with Disabilities, the International Covenant on Economic, Social, and Cultural Rights, the Optional Protocol to the Convention Against Torture, the International Labor Organization Fundamental Conventions, the International Convention on the Protection of the Rights of all Migrant Workers and Members of their Families, and the American Convention on Human Rights. Additionally, almost a dozen countries called on the United States to review and remove existing Reservations, Understandings, and Declarations (RUDs) attached to its treaty ratifications. Why might so many countries have focused their recommendations on U.S. ratification of human rights treaties? Do you think this is an effective way to pressure the United States to ratify human rights treaties? Are there any potential negative impacts? In its official response to the UPR recommendations, the U.S. government stated:

> We support the recommendations asking us to ratify the Convention on the Elimination of All Forms of Discrimination against Women, the Convention on the Rights of Persons with Disabilities, and ILO Convention 111. We also support the recommendations that we ratify the Convention on the Rights of the Child, as we support its goals and intend to review how we could move toward its ratification. We also support recommendations urging deliberative treaty actions, such as that we "consider ratifying" them.

U.S. Department of State, Report of the United States of America Submitted to the U.N. High Commissioner of Human Rights In Conjunction with the Universal Periodic Review, Response to the U.N. Human Rights Council Working Group Report (Mar. 10, 2011).

Does this, along with Adviser Koh's comments, reveal anything about the U.S. politics underlying human rights treaty ratification? Does the statement commit the executive branch to any action with respect to treaty ratification?

2.   Notice that in his remarks at the adoption of the final Outcome Document, Adviser Koh identifies some of the countries associated with specific recommendations. Why do you think he does this? What is the relevance of this information? Should it matter to the United States which countries made particular recommendations? Should advocates concentrate on particular countries in their lobbying efforts to urge U.N. delegates to make recommendations during the course of the review? What strategic considerations should advocates have in mind when planning a UPR lobbying effort?

3.   As Adviser Koh noted, several of the recommendations called on the United States to end a particular practice with respect to one particular country. Do you think this is an appropriate forum for countries to make such recommendations? Is the U.S. right to characterize these recommendations as "political?"

4.   Given what the U.S. characterizes as the highly politicized nature of several of the recommendations that were made during the U.S. UPR, what is the value of the review? Do you agree with the United States' position that it was important to engage with the process as a way of setting an example to other countries for how to engage in a meaningful review? Is there a potential downside to the United States' engagement?

5.   How do the recommendations resulting from the UPR differ from those that result from treaty body reviews? Is there a value in having a review process that is conducted by the countries themselves, rather than by independent human rights experts? Is there a potential downside?

6.   Based on Adviser Koh's comments at the conclusion of the U.S. UPR and the U.S. report to the working group, do you think that the UPR resulted in a "hard look" by the U.S. administration at its policies and practices? What changes do you think did or might come about as a result of the UPR? What impact might the UPR have on future treaty body reviews? On future efforts by U.S. advocates to engage the administration on issues pertaining to human rights?

7.   One concrete outcome of the UPR was the creation of a federal "Equality Working Group" which, according to the United States' periodic report to the CERD Committee in 2013, was

> [l]aunched in March 2012 by the Civil Rights Division of the Department of Justice in partnership with the Department of State's Bureau of Democracy, Human Rights, and Labor to enhance the government's domestic implementation of our international human rights obligations and commitments relating to non-discrimination and equal opportunity, with an initial focus on those

commitments that relate to combating racial discrimination, including under the CERD.

U.S. Department of State, Periodic Report of the United States of America to the United Nations Committee on the Elimination of Racial Discrimination Concerning the International Convention on the Elimination of All Forms of Racial Discrimination, ¶ 4 (June 12, 2013).

In the lead-up to the UPR and in subsequent treaty reviews, advocates urged the Administration to establish an Interagency Working Group on Human Rights to coordinate all federal agencies and departments in their engagement with and implementation of its human rights commitments, and to coordinate human rights implementation at the state and local level. (A somewhat similar body was created by Executive Order 13107 in 1998 under President Clinton but was not utilized under President Bush. *See* The Opportunity Agenda, Memorandum: Assessing Human Rights in the United States: Domestic Human Rights Indicators 4 (2011)). Does the Equality Working Group, as described in the U.S.'s report to the CERD, meet the advocates' call for a federal coordinating body for comprehensive human rights implementation? What else would you need to know in order to answer this question?

8. How tied is U.S. engagement with the UPR to the presidential administration in office at the time of the review? What might help to institutionalize U.S. involvement with the UPR and with the treaty bodies?

9. What might have motivated the United States' "deep engagement" with the UPR? How might U.S. advocates leverage this motivation?

10. The United States accepted several ESC-related recommendations resulting from the UPR, including the recommendations that it: promote "equal socio-economic as well as educational opportunities for all in both law and fact;" ensure "further measures be taken [ ] in the areas of economic and social rights for women and minorities;" and address issues in the domain of "access to housing, vital for the realization of several other rights, in order to meet the needs for adequate housing at an affordable price for all segments of the American society." U.N. Human Rights Council, Report of the Working Group on the Universal Periodic Review: United States of America, ¶¶ 92.109, 92.113, U.N. Doc. A/HRC/16/11 (Jan. 4, 2011). In accepting the recommendation that the United States ensure the realization of the rights to food and health, the United States noted that it is not a party to the ICESCR, yet recognized that the rights to food and health are contained in other human rights instruments that it has accepted. *See* U.S. Department of State, Report of the United States of America Submitted to the U.N. High Commissioner of Human Rights In Conjunction with the Universal Periodic Review, Response to the U.N. Human Rights Council Working Group Report, para. 19 (Mar. 10, 2011). It noted, too, that the rights are to be realized progressively. *Id.* How does the United States' response to the UPR recommendations differ from its discussion of ESC rights in its initial Report? What might account for this difference?

11. The questions countries asked during the course of the UPR, and the resulting recommendations, were remarkably similar to concerns raised by U.S. civil society groups in the pre-review consultations, in the over 100 reports that U.S. advocates filed in conjunction with the process, and in the town hall meeting that the U.S. delegation hosted for representatives of more than 70 U.S. non-governmental organizations just after the review. This suggests that U.S. advocates played a role in influencing the recommendations that emerged from the United States' UPR. Is this an appropriate role for U.S. advocates to play in a "peer review" process? Why did the United States highlight civil society involvement so prominently throughout the review? Should human rights advocates have any concerns about the way in which their involvement was characterized?

12. Some commentators criticized the United States for subjecting itself to scrutiny by countries with poor human rights records of their own, and they decried the "harshly critical" role that "American human rights interest groups" played in the review. *See* George Russell, *U.N. Human Rights Council Takes Aim at New Target: United States*, Fox News (Nov. 5, 2010), *available at* http://www.foxnews.com/world/2010/11/04/united-nations-human-rights-council/. Is there a value to the United States receiving and responding to input on its human rights record from countries whose own human rights records are perhaps far from exemplary? Can robust participation by the United States in the UPR answer some of the concerns of American exceptionalism that we explored in **Chapter II**, and perhaps underscore some of the more positive aspects of American exceptionalism that Harold Koh and others urge?

13. Remarkable civil society mobilization and coordination occurred in the lead up to the United States UPR. In addition to the shadow reporting effort described above, advocacy communities hosted and participated directly in conversations with federal government officials through the government's on-site consultations with civil society and in the "town hall" hosted by the U.S. government in Geneva immediately following the Review. For a detailed accounting of one U.S. advocacy organization's efforts to engage the UPR process as a way of furthering its work to establish a right to housing in the United States, see Eric S. Tars and Deodonne Bhattarai, *Opening the Door the Human Right to Housing: The Universal Periodic Review for a Rights-Based Approach to Housing*, 45 Clearinghouse Rev. 197 (2011).

14. For a more general accounting of U.S. civil society coordination and collaboration around the first U.S. UPR, see Sarah H. Paoletti, *Using the Universal Periodic Review to Advance Human Rights*, 45 Clearinghouse Rev. 268 (2011). For the U.S. Department's summary of the civil society consultations it held in advance of the Review, see *Summaries of UPR Civil Society Consultations*, U.S. Dep't of State, http://www.state.gov/j/drl/upr/archive/137900.htm. *See also* Yuri Saito and Gareth Sweeney, *An NGO Assessment of the New Mechanisms of the UN Human Rights Council*, 9 Hum. Rts. L. Rev. 203 (2009).

15. For articles examining the utility and functioning of the UPR more generally, particularly as it relates to the other U.N. human rights monitoring mechanisms, see Felice D. Gaer, *A Voice Not An Echo: Universal Periodic Review and the UN Treaty Body System*, 7 Hum. Rts. L. Rev. 109 (2007); Elvira Dominguez Redondo, *The Universal Periodic Review of the UN Human Rights Council: An Assessment of the First Session*, 7 Chinese J. Int'l L. 721 (2010).

ii. Special Procedures

Special Procedures are U.N. Charter-based mechanisms intended to serve as the U.N.'s "eyes and ears" in evaluating and addressing human rights concerns in specific countries or pertaining to particular thematic issues. Special Procedures are either an individual (usually called a Special Rapporteur or Independent Expert) or a working group with deep subject matter expertise. They serve independently of governments, as volunteers in their personal capacity. Each Special Procedure has its own mandate, defined by the resolution that created it. As of October 2013, mandates exist for thirty-seven thematic and fourteen country-specific Special Procedures. Thematic mandates cover a broad range of issues, including adequate housing, education, extreme poverty, trafficking in persons, countering terrorism, indigenous peoples, arbitrary detention, and health. There is no Special Procedure with a mandate specific to the United States.

Special Procedures base their evaluations on standards drawn from the UDHR and other human rights norms and thus are not limited by whether a country has ratified a certain treaty, a fact that is particularly relevant with respect to the United States. Their core functions include receiving information on specific human rights abuses and sending urgent appeals to governments seeking clarification on the allegations, as well as conducting country visits to investigate human rights situations on the ground. In addition, the Special Procedures develop thematic reports and guiding principles to clarify how existing human rights law applies in specific situations. The following excerpt seeks to evaluate the effectiveness of the U.N. Special Rapporteurs as a mechanism for influencing the human rights practice within a country.

TED PICCONE, "CATALYSTS FOR RIGHTS: THE UNIQUE
CONTRIBUTION OF THE U.N.'S INDEPENDENT
EXPERTS ON HUMAN RIGHTS"
Brookings Institution (Oct. 2010).

The term "Special Procedures" refers to the special rapporteurs, special representatives, independent experts and working groups mandated by the U.N.'s political bodies to monitor and report on human rights violations and to recommend ways to promote and protect human rights.

U.N. member states created these mechanisms over thirty years ago to serve as independent eyes and ears evaluating the application of international human rights norms to concrete situations.

The Special Procedures carry out this function by undertaking fact-finding missions to countries of concern; issuing communications, including urgent appeals, to governments and requesting corrective action; calling public attention to specific violations; elaborating on human rights norms; and providing periodic reports to the Human Rights Council (HRC) and General Assembly.

They operate as critical nodes in a larger system composed of treaty bodies, political resolutions, the High Commissioner for Human Rights, technical assistance, and field offices, connecting to each part in different and unique ways. They serve as the main entry point into this system for victims and human rights defenders in every corner of the world, offering a practical forum for the promotion and protection of human rights. By most accounts, they have played a critical role in shaping the content of international human rights norms, shedding light on how states comply with such norms, and advancing measures to improve respect for them. They are considered by many to be, in the words of then U.N. Secretary General Kofi Annan, "the crown jewel of the system."

. . .

A Short Summary of Special Procedures: Who They Are and What They Do

The U.N.'s system of Special Procedures is a unique and effective mechanism that allows independent, periodic, on-the-ground scrutiny of a country's record of respect for human rights. Since the appointment by the Commission on Human Rights of an Ad Hoc Working Group to inquire into the situation of human rights in Chile in 1975, followed by appointment of the first special rapporteur in 1979 on the same subject, this mechanism has grown to become one of the U.N. system's most important instruments for promotion of universal human rights norms at the national and international level.

. . .

The experts appointed by the Human Rights Council to serve as Special Procedures are independent of governments, serve in their personal capacities, and carry out their mandates on a volunteer basis. They may serve no more than six years total (thematic mandate holders typically serve two terms of three years and country-specific mandate holders typically serve for one year renewable terms). Their authority is derived from their professional qualifications to address specific human rights situations objectively as well as the political mandate they receive from the Council. Governments rely on them to gather facts, identify problems and make recommendations, but carry out little systematic follow-up. One of their greatest assets is a sense of passion and commitment to the cause of human rights which, combined with subject matter expertise, political skills and good judgment, represents a dynamic force for catalyzing attention and action to protect human rights.

. . .

The main reference points for Special Procedures' examination of a state's human rights record range broadly from the general provisions of the Universal Declaration of Human Rights and other internationally recognized human rights standards to the specific terms of their mandates from the HRC. They may rely on particular instruments of "hard" treaty law as well as "soft" law of relevant declarations, resolutions and guiding principles. In this regard, they have several important advantages over treaty bodies: they are not restricted to the text of any one convention; they may examine any U.N. member state, not just those states that have ratified a treaty; they may make *in situ* visits to any country in the world (assuming the government concerned grants permission); and they may receive and act upon individual complaints without prior exhaustion of domestic remedies. This combination of features gives them a uniquely flexible and independent role to play in a system otherwise dominated by governments. They operate, in the words of one researcher, in the space between universal norms and local realities, allowing them to elaborate and interpret international standards grounded in concrete situations, "to define rights in real time."

. . .

In carrying out their mandates, the Council's independent experts employ a variety of working methods to bridge the distance between international norms and national-level implementation. These include country visits; direct communications with victims and their representatives regarding specific violations; letters of allegation and urgent appeals to governments; thematic and country reports submitted at least annually to the Human Rights Council and where mandated, to the General Assembly; press statements, both individually and jointly; and press conferences.

. . .

Summary of Findings

1. Our research found that the U.N.'s independent experts have played a valuable and, in some cases, decisive role in drawing attention to chronic and emerging human rights issues and in catalyzing improvements in respect for human rights on the ground, including direct support to victims.

2.   At the same time, state cooperation with the Special Procedures is highly uneven and generally disappointing, with some notable exceptions. Cooperation by states ranges from regularly accepting country visits by multiple independent experts along with high response rates to their communications, to virtually zero recognition or dialogue with the rapporteurs. As further illustrated by the evidence that follows, this failure by member states to fulfill their obligations to cooperate with the Special Procedures and address the recommendations they make is the main obstacle hampering their ability to fulfill the mandates states have given them.

3.   The Special Procedures are also hobbled by a host of other challenges, including inadequate training and resources, insufficient understanding of the local context for their work, and the lack of a systematic process for following up their recommendations. Despite these obstacles, the Special Procedures mechanism represents one of the most effective tools of the international human rights system and deserves further strengthening and support.

Country Visits

   Scope of Activity

4.   The Special Procedures are prolific workers, annually conducting dozens of country visits, producing hundreds of country-specific and thematic reports, and issuing thousands of communications to individual governments.

. . .

8.   By most accounts, country visits were the most important tool in the SP toolbox. The monitoring function of a Special Procedures' country visit in and of itself has a salutary impact on the human rights situation in a given country. This is largely due to the serious attention SP visits receive from most governments, civil society and the media. The blue U.N. flag SPs carry when they land in a country allows them privileged access to key actors on the ground, granting them an elevated voice in the quest to achieve greater respect for human rights. Their physical presence in country gives victims of human rights violations and their defenders a higher platform for advocacy at the national level and a direct entry point into an otherwise complicated and bureaucratic U.N. system.

9.   Country visits by SPs, which typically last 5–15 days, allow for close examination of specific human rights situations and motivate key actors in and outside governments to concentrate their energies toward establishing facts, identifying violations and recommending remedies. The visits are especially important for civil society actors who devote considerable time and attention to informing the experts about the human rights problems in the country, preparing substantive reports,

helping them make contact with victims and suggesting ways to improve state compliance with international standards. In many cases, such visits prompt or strengthen mechanisms of collaboration among disparate nongovernmental organizations, help professionalize their work and foster ongoing cooperation that leads to more effective advocacy. The visits also allow mandate holders the opportunity to raise issues directly with government officials at the highest levels and advise them on specific reforms.

10. Because of their high profile, visiting a country as an independent U.N. expert can be a political minefield. Therefore, an effective country visit depends on thorough and substantive preparation by the independent expert and his or her staff before, during and after a visit. Close consultation with a range of relevant actors, including [the Office of the High Commissioner for Human Rights (OHCHR)], treaty bodies and U.N. country team staff, government officials, human rights defenders and experts, political party leaders and parliamentarians to understand the political context and identify the main challenges is critical to a successful mission.

11. The media play an essential role in amplifying the main points of the visit and creating some pressure for governments to respond. Typically, SPs brief the media upon arrival in a country to explain the terms of their mandate and purpose of the visit then refrain from any further public statements until a departure press conference in which the expert provides initial observations regarding the subject under review along with some recommendations. Preceding this public report, which is generally well-covered by the media, the Special Procedure briefs government officials, giving them an opportunity to provide initial reactions to the expert directly and to the press, subsequently. This process of private consultation and public reporting is well regarded by most actors involved and should be considered a good practice. Public statements by SPs before arriving in country, on the other hand, can complicate a country visit unless they are scrupulously neutral.

12. It takes several months for Special Procedures to prepare and issue their final reports, which are closely read by government officials and human rights activists alike. From the point of view of human rights advocates on the ground, however, it is the substantive public statements made by the Special Procedures while in country, particularly during the concluding press conference, that matters most. Waiting a year or more for a final report in a foreign language can often deflate the momentum generated by the visit. When it does happen, presentation of the report to the Council through brief "interactive dialogues" with member states is anticlimactic, often overshadowed by other concerns on the agenda and loses it punch, particularly for the country in question. Broad

dissemination of the final report in country is uneven and rarely available in local languages or only after much delay.

. . .

Follow Up to Country Visits

23. What happens after a country visit remains one of the most challenging questions for the U.N. human rights system. A number of good practices have been established largely on the initiative of a few rapporteurs with additional resources. These include ongoing requests for information from the government concerned, questionnaires to key stakeholders, annual reporting to the HRC on the status of a state's progress or lack thereof, and follow-up visits by the rapporteur or his or her successor.

24. There is, however, no institutionalized mechanism for follow-up to an SP's country visit. SPs themselves generally do not have the resources— time or staff—to engage in repeated visits or communications. Only in a few cases, usually when additional resources are available, has an SP methodically reported on a state's implementation of recommendations. Similarly, a current or successor SP has carried out visits to the same country two or more years later with the express purpose of tracking progress on previous recommendations.

. . .

Communications

28. According to the HRC's Code of Conduct, communications from Special Procedures should be based on information "submitted by a person or group of persons claiming to be a victim of violations or by a person or group of persons, including non-governmental organizations, acting in good faith in accordance with human rights . . . and claiming to have direct or reliable knowledge of those violations substantiated by clear information. The communication should not be exclusively based on reports disseminated by mass media." Unfortunately, there is no formalized, consistent procedure for cataloguing correspondence received from parties requesting intervention by the Special Procedures; each rapporteur ultimately has the discretion to decide which allegations to act upon.

. . .

29. Communications by SPs generally take the form of letters of allegation or urgent appeals that are transmitted to the state involved via its diplomatic mission in Geneva. Urgent appeals alert state authorities to time-sensitive and life-threatening violations of an ongoing or imminent nature while letters of allegation convey information of a past

incident of lesser urgency. They serve an important role in establishing a written record of victims' complaints and putting them into appropriate government channels. Human rights defenders complain, however, that they do not receive confirmation from OHCHR that their correspondence has been registered or what, if any, action was taken by the SP in response.

. . .

Resources

38. Although the level of support provided to the Special Procedures has improved significantly over the last ten years, severely limited resources for the SPs' work continues to be a chronic weakness that clearly undermines the effectiveness of this mechanism.

. . .

39. The HRC's independent experts work on a volunteer basis, with reimbursement only for travel-related expenses. . . . OHCHR resources available to support thematic SPs cover on average only one staff person for each mandate, further limiting their ability to carry out their functions; country-specific rapporteurs get even less staff support. Actual allocated resources vary according to a needs assessment of such elements as a rapporteur's workplan, volume of communications and extraordinary circumstances (like the earthquake disaster in Haiti). Given the heavy demands of taking on a position with virtually no compensation, some qualified experts may be dissuaded from presenting their candidacies, withdraw early from service, or curtail their activities to meet the demands of their principal professional positions.

40. Some states and a small group of non-governmental donors earmark their contributions to OHCHR for certain purposes or mandates, thereby limiting OHCHR's flexibility in allocating funds according to need. . . . Earmarking funds directly to a mandate holder has obvious benefits for the recipient but raises difficult problems regarding equity across the range of different mandates. The lack of transparency about funding sources and allocations also raises questions about who is supporting which mandates and what, if any, influence they have on their work.

. . .

NOTES & QUESTIONS

1. For a complete listing of the U.N. Special Procedures thematic mandates and the mandate holders, see *Special Procedures Assumed by the Human Rights Council,* United Nations Human Rights, http://www.ohchr.org/EN/HRBodies/SP/Pages/Welcomepage.aspx.

2. For a series of articles examining the function, utility and limitations of U.N. Special Procedures, see *Special Issue: The Role of the Special Rapporteurs of the United Nations Human Rights Council in the Development and Promotion of International Human Rights Norms*, 15 Int'l J. of Hum. Rts. 155 (2011). *See also* Ted Piccone, Catalysts for Change: How the UN's Independent Experts Promote Human Rights (2012).

3. Given the limitations that U.N. Special Procedures face in doing their work, in what ways can they supplement the monitoring functions of the U.N. treaty bodies and the UPR? Why might U.S. advocates find it useful to engage with the Special Procedures alongside other U.N. mechanisms?

In recent years, U.N. experts, including Special Rapporteurs, Independent Experts and Working Groups with mandates focused on education, extreme poverty, migrants, water and sanitation, adequate housing, violence against women, indigenous peoples, racism, and business and human rights have all made official visits to the United States. In the course of these visits, U.S. advocates have actively engaged with the experts to address core human rights concerns. Advocates provide them with information and recommendations, arrange interviews and consultations with victims of human rights violations, and encourage meetings with government officials.

At the conclusion of their visits, the U.N. experts issue reports detailing achievements, observations and concerns related to human rights in the United States. Fact-finding missions by U.N. Special Procedures present unique opportunities for domestic advocates to increase the visibility of domestic causes, garner media coverage, raise awareness of human rights violations, access government officials, and build networks.

The materials that follow pertain to an official visit to the United States by the U.N. Special Rapporteur on the human right to safe drinking water and sanitation, Catarina de Albuquerque. The Special Rapporteur visited the United States in 2011 and met with community members, government officials, and advocates in Washington, D.C., Massachusetts, California, and Maryland. As you read these materials, consider what role advocates can and should play in engaging with U.N. experts as they conduct official U.S. missions, and how U.N. Special Procedures supplement the other U.N. mechanisms discussed in this chapter.

REPORT OF THE SPECIAL RAPPORTEUR ON THE HUMAN RIGHT
TO SAFE DRINKING WATER AND SANITATION, ADDENDUM:
MISSION TO THE UNITED STATES OF AMERICA
(22 FEB.–4 MAR. 2011)

U.N. Doc. A/HRC/18/33/Add.4 (Aug. 2, 2011) (by Catarina de Albuquerque).

II.   International and domestic legal framework

6.   At the international level, the human right to safe drinking water and sanitation derives from the right to an adequate standard of living which is protected under, *inter alia*, article 25 of the Universal Declaration of Human Rights, and article 11 of the International Covenant on Economic, Social and Cultural Rights. This right was also recently recognized by the General Assembly and reaffirmed by the Human Rights Council, with the support of the United States of America, which the independent expert welcomes. States obligation with regard to the right to safe drinking water and sanitation requires that water and sanitation be available, accessible, affordable, acceptable and of good quality for everyone without discrimination. This obligation must be progressively realized to the maximum of available resources, meaning that a State must take concrete and targeted steps towards ensuring universal access to water and sanitation. Any retrogressive measure— such as in a period of economic crisis—is presumed to be a violation of the human right unless fully justified by the State. There must be opportunities for meaningful participation in decision-making; there must be transparency and access to information; and accountability mechanisms must be established to address cases where these rights are violated. Ensuring the rights to water and sanitation is closely related to the enjoyment of other human rights, including the rights to education, work, health, housing and food, among others.

7.   The legal framework governing access to water and sanitation in the United States of America is a complex amalgam of federal and state statutes and common law principles. This multi-tiered system, coupled with an array of variances available to states and private actors, make generalizations about the capacity of the United States legal framework to reflect access to safe drinking water and sanitation as human rights particularly difficult. The United States has not ratified many of the relevant treaties from which these rights are derived, including the International Covenant on Economic, Social and Cultural Rights, the Convention on the Elimination of All Forms of Discrimination against Women, the Convention on the Rights of the Child and the Convention on the Rights of Persons with Disabilities. The independent expert, nevertheless, notes that the United States has signed these instruments (in 1977, 1980, 1995 and 2009, respectively) and reminds the Government that upon signing, it assumed the obligation to refrain from acts that would defeat the object and purpose of these treaties, pending decision on

ratification. She encourages the United States to take steps towards ratifying these instruments without reservations.

8.   Existing federal laws generally focus on maintaining water quality rather than ensuring access for all citizens. Constitutional and statutory provisions that pertain to non-discrimination and equal protection of the law create a framework that allows citizens to enforce the rights to safe drinking water and sanitation indirectly, but without the ability to ground such claims as an explicit right, the success of such claims remain uncertain.

9.   While there is no federally recognized right to safe drinking water and sanitation, individual states have taken the initiative to consecrate this right. For instance, the states of Massachusetts and Pennsylvania have already recognized the right to water (though not to sanitation) in their constitutions. In California, a bill package has been introduced that recognizes the human right to water.

10.   The two primary federal statutes governing water in the United States are the Clean Water Act and the Safe Drinking Water Act. Additionally, a number of federal agencies play a role in regulating water, including the Environmental Protection Agency (EPA), the Department of Agriculture and the Department of the Interior.

. . .

III. The right to water and sanitation in the United States of America

14.   People living in the United States enjoy near universal access to safe water. Nationwide, there are an estimated 161,000 public water systems, which may be publicly or privately owned. Community water systems are public water systems that serve people year-round in their homes. The majority of people in the United States (268 million) receive their water from a community water system (54,000 systems). Approximately 15 per cent (46 million) of Americans rely on their own private drinking water supplies, and these supplies are not subject to EPA standards, although some state and local governments set rules to protect users of these wells. With no regular monitoring, the burden is on households with private systems to take precautions to ensure the protection and maintenance of their drinking water supplies. Additionally, over 53,000 rural water utilities exist, 90 per cent of which serve communities of 10,000 people or less. These figures highlight the fragmentation of the sector, which presents enormous challenges when trying to regulate, monitor and find solutions for universal access.

15.   Twenty-five percent of all households in the U.S. have on-site wastewater treatment systems, and most others are connected to sewerage networks and wastewater treatment facilities. But according to

EPA, in general, states and communities have not established adequate management programmes to assure proper functioning of onsite systems for wastewater treatment.

16. The United States has aging water and wastewater systems, with decreasing investment in research and development, coupled with an increase in the population. By the year 2020, the population will likely be over 325 million and systems will need to increase capacity. Furthermore, the population is shifting geographically, requiring rapid increases in system capacity in some parts of the country, and maintenance of aging systems in other parts of the country with diminishing populations (and a diminishing rate base).

. . .

18. The independent expert welcomes the fact that there is near universal access to water and sanitation in the United States and commends the Government for its achievements in this regard. By its nature, a human rights analysis focuses on the situation of the most marginalized and excluded. Thus, this report especially concentrates on the situation of these groups with regard to their access to water and sanitation. While these groups comprise a small proportion of the population, the independent expert emphasizes that they require priority attention.

. . .

D.   Excluded groups

27. The independent expert met with numerous communities and groups who face challenges in accessing safe water and sanitation. The situations of homeless people and indigenous persons have particular features that warrant a specific human rights analysis.

Homeless people

28. As a part of her mission, the independent expert examined the situation of the homeless with regard to access to water and sanitation. Up to 3.5 million people experience homelessness in the United States every year, and on any given night over 800,000 people are homeless. In some cities, homelessness is being increasingly criminalized. Criminalization includes fines, arrests and severance of social protection benefits or even access to employment. Local statutes prohibiting public urination and defecation—which can constitute a sexual offence in some cases—, while facially constitutional to protect public health, are often discriminatory in their effects. Such discrimination often occurs because such statutes are enforced against homeless individuals who often have no access to public restrooms and are given no alternatives. Furthermore, there is an increasing trend in local governments to limit opening hours

or close entirely public restrooms. Such decisions are contrary to the need to create an enabling environment so homeless individuals can realize their rights to water and sanitation.

29. The independent expert notes that in 2010 the Inter-Agency Council on Homelessness published the first federal plan to end homelessness. The plan includes constructive alternatives to the criminalization of homelessness.

30. Because evacuation of the bowels and bladder is a necessary biological function and because denial of opportunities to do so in a lawful and dignified manner can both compromise human dignity and cause suffering, such denial could, in some cases (e.g., where it results from deliberate actions or clear neglect) amount to cruel, inhumane or degrading treatment. Individuals are sometimes compelled to go to extraordinary lengths to prevent such suffering. The independent expert visited a community of homeless people in Sacramento, California, where she met a man who called himself the "sanitation technician" for the community.[4] He engineered a sanitation system that consists of a seat with a two-layered plastic bag underneath. Every week Tim collects the bags full of human waste, which vary in weight between 130 to 230 pounds, and hauls them on his bicycle a few miles to a local public restroom. Once a toilet becomes available, he empties the content of the bags; packs the plastic bags with leftover residue inside a third plastic bag; ties it securely and disposes of them in the garbage; then sanitizes his hands with water and lemon. He said that even though this job is difficult, he does it for the community, especially the women.

31. The fact that private citizens are compelled to provide such services is an indication of failure by the State to meet its responsibilities to ensure the provision of the most fundamental of services. The remarkable contribution of this single human rights defender to assume such a burden in defence of human dignity and the human right to sanitation in no way reduces the responsibility of public authorities to correct this and similar situations elsewhere in the country.

32. The United States, one of the wealthiest countries in the world, must ensure that everyone, without discrimination, has physical and economic access, in all spheres of life, to sanitation which is safe, hygienic, secure, socially and culturally acceptable, and which provides privacy and ensures dignity. An immediate, interim solution is to ensure access to restrooms facilities in public places, including during the night. The long-term solution to homelessness must be to ensure adequate housing.

. . .

---

[4]   [Editors' Note: This Sacramento homeless community is called "Safe Ground."]

IV. Non-discrimination and equality

42. Although the vast majority of the population in the United States enjoys regular access to safe drinking water and sanitation, the above analysis reveals categories of people who are excluded. Individuals who do not have regular access, who face obstacles in access or are otherwise deprived of the same level of access as the general population, also generally face discrimination in society more broadly. The people with whom the independent expert met and who are facing obstacles in their enjoyment of the rights to water and sanitation were disproportionately Black, Latino, American Indian, homeless or otherwise disadvantaged.

43. Human rights require a focus on the most vulnerable, those who are most often excluded from progress. Often, these people are the most difficult to reach, but this cannot be justification for neglecting them—on the contrary. Human rights require that there be universal access. Hence, merely addressing formal or direct discrimination will not ensure substantive equality. To eliminate discrimination in practice, special attention must be paid, and priority must be given, to groups of individuals who suffer historical or persistent prejudice, instead of merely comparing the formal treatment of individuals in similar situations.

44. The International Covenant on Civil and Political Rights, to which the United States is a party, states that all persons are equal before the law, and that the law shall prohibit any discrimination and guarantee to all persons equal and effective protection against discrimination on any prohibited ground (art. 26). In this regard, the Human Rights Committee has noted that article 26 does not merely duplicate the guarantee already provided for in article 2 (general guarantee against non-discrimination in the exercise of Covenant rights) but provides, in itself, an autonomous right. It prohibits discrimination in law or in fact in any field regulated and protected by public authorities. Article 26 therefore is concerned with the obligations imposed on States parties with regard to their legislation and the application thereof. Moreover, the application of the principle of non-discrimination contained in article 26 is not limited to those rights that are provided for in the Covenant, but extends to economic, social and cultural rights.

45. In the view of the independent expert, the United States has achieved significant gains in eliminating formal or direct discrimination in law. Nevertheless, she remains concerned that several laws, policies and practices, while appearing neutral, disproportionately affect the enjoyment of human rights by certain groups, or are enforced without attention to specific circumstances. Moreover, the independent expert notes that there is a lack of data regarding who does and who does not have access to water and sanitation. Availability of accurate and

disaggregated data is fundamental in the design of appropriate and efficient policies and programmes to address the many outstanding challenges related to water and sanitation.

. . .

V.   Conclusions and recommendations

. . .

92. Placing the human rights to water and sanitation at the centre of policy formulation for both domestic and international aid policies is crucial to ensure that all people in the United States, as well as those benefiting from its development assistance, have access to affordable, accessible, acceptable and safe water and sanitation in sufficient amounts to protect human health and human dignity. In this regard, the independent expert offers the following recommendations:

(a) Ratify the International Covenant on Economic, Social and Cultural Rights and the Optional Protocol thereto, as well as the other core international human rights treaties it has not ratified thus far. To this end, the Government should reconvene the Interagency Working Group on Human Rights (Executive Order 13107);

(b) Adopt a comprehensive federal law on water and sanitation guaranteeing the rights to safe water and sanitation without discrimination and clearly delineating the responsibilities of public officials at the federal, state and local levels. Such a law must prioritize water for personal and domestic use and set affordability standards, among others;

(c) Formulate a national water and sanitation policy and plan of action, guided by the normative content of the rights to water and sanitation, that devote priority attention to improving aging infrastructure, as well as innovative designs and approaches that promote human rights, are affordable and create more value in terms of public health improvements, community development and sustainability;

(d) Ensure proper regulation and monitoring of the water quality of private drinking water systems;

(e) Exemptions under the Safe Drinking Water Act, including for the oil and gas industry, must be re-assessed and repealed if resulting in a negative impact on the enjoyment of the right to water;

(f) Strengthen the regulatory system on water and sanitation to prevent upstream pollution (agricultural, industrial, chemical, including pharmaceutical, stormwater run-offs, etc.) as well as ensure adequate regulation of the bottled water industry;

(g) Engage in public education and information campaigns about water quality in the languages spoken by the community to assure people of the safety of drinking tap water;

(h) Evaluate the extent to which people living in poverty face challenges in paying for water and sanitation services, and adopt, at the federal level, a national minimum standard on affordability of water and sanitation, as well as due process guarantees in relation to disconnections;

(i) Ensure that all municipalities provide access to safe drinking water and sanitation to homeless people, including through ensuring the opening and regular maintenance and upkeep of public restrooms, as well as availability of public water fountains, including during the night;

(j) Engage in dialogue with homeless communities to assist these individuals to find more secure housing solutions, including stable access to adequate water and sanitation;

(k) Enact the necessary legal action to change the status of unrecognized and terminated tribes to enable them to realize their rights to water and sanitation, as well as express religious and cultural rights;

(l) Ensure adequate consultation and prior and informed consent of indigenous communities regarding activities affecting their access to water;

(m) Guide the ODA by human rights principles, including the rights to water and sanitation, and devote [a] larger proportion of aid to ensuring the human rights to water and sanitation to those who do not yet have access. Ensure that affected communities have access to information and opportunities to participate in the formulation, implementation and evaluation of projects.

Encouraged by de Albuquerque's findings related to the Safe Ground community of people who are homeless in Sacramento, the lawyers at Legal Services of Northern California, working together with the National Law Center on Homelessness and Poverty, filed a formal communication (complaint) with the Special Rapporteur on behalf of Safe Ground regarding the city's failure to provide access to proper water and sanitation facilities for homeless persons. Subsequently, the Special Rapporteur sent a letter directly to the mayor of Sacramento, California, reiterating the concerns expressed in her official report over city policies that potentially violate the human rights to water and sanitation of people who are homeless.

LETTER FROM CATARINA DE ALBUQUERQUE, U.N. SPECIAL RAPPORTEUR ON THE HUMAN RIGHT TO SAFE DRINKING WATER AND SANITATION, TO KEVIN JOHNSON, MAYOR OF THE CITY OF SACRAMENTO

(Jan. 23, 2012).

Dear Mayor Johnson,

I am writing to you in my capacity as United Nations Special Rapporteur on the Human Right to Safe Drinking Water and Sanitation, appointed by the United Nations Human Rights Council. It has been brought to my attention that the City of Sacramento is going to hold a public hearing in the near future to decide whether to permit the provision of water and sanitation services to homeless tent camps. I greatly appreciate this initiative and hope that your local government will take into consideration international human rights standards when making a decision on this important human rights issue. Being aware of your dream to ensure that Sacramento becomes "a city that works for everyone", I am writing to you to remind you that for your vision to become a reality, the promotion of the human rights of homeless people should become an integral part of the city's policies.

As you may know, I was on an official visit to the United States of America under my UN mandate from 22 February to 4 March 2011 where I had the opportunity to meet with the authorities and talk to local communities in Sacramento. In my final statement at the end of my mission to the USA last year I specifically referred to the situation in Sacramento, California where I visited a community of homeless people. . . .

[Here, the Special Rapporteur describes the work of Tim, who called himself the "sanitation technician" for his community, as included in paragraph 30 of her report.] Because evacuation of the bowels and bladder is a necessary biological function and because denial of opportunities to do so in a lawful and dignified manner can both compromise human dignity and cause suffering, such denial could, in some cases, amount to cruel, inhuman or degrading treatment. An immediate and interim solution for those without housing is to ensure access to restroom facilities in public places, including during the night.

Moreover, during my visit, I observed the lack of access to adequate water and sanitation and adequate housing as well as health concerns of homeless people living along the American River. As you know, there were three sources of potable water ranging from one-half mile to one-and-a-half miles away from the camp, but one of them had been allegedly removed and capped by the City of Sacramento. Many people used the river water, which often caused sickness. Many parks operated by the City and County of Sacramento had reportedly closed restrooms to public access during the evening, night-time and morning hours. As a result, the homeless people's access to the public restrooms at night-time was prevented. Private restrooms available for the homeless were also very limited. I am concerned that the closure of public restrooms and the removal of water resources in the area of the Sacramento's American River Parkway have a serious negative impact on homeless individuals' access to water and sanitation and their health.

In addition, I have been informed that the City of Sacramento enforces the Sacramento City Code (which criminalizes public urination and/or defecation, camping and storage of personal property in public spaces and parks and on private properties) customarily against homeless persons, especially those residing in tent camps along the American River Parkway and other local parks. . . . I am concerned about the disproportionate impact of the enforcement of the Code on persons living in poverty in general and on homeless persons in particular. The criminalization of life-sustaining behaviors of homeless persons in public spaces, such as sleeping, camping or public urination and defecation, in a context of lack of adequate shelter alternatives, has the potential to impede the enjoyment of human rights by poor and vulnerable groups, including the right to an adequate standard of living. The criminalization of public urination and defecation combined with a lack of public toilets leaves the homeless people in a desperate situation and without alternatives.

I would like to draw the attention of your local government to the applicable international human rights norms and standards, in particular, the following:

The human right to safe drinking water and sanitation derives from the right to an adequate standard of living which is protected under, *inter alia*, article 25 of the Universal Declaration of Human Rights, and article 11 of the International Covenant on Economic, Social and Cultural Rights (ICESCR), which the US Government signed on 5 October 1977. While it has not ratified the Covenant, upon signing the ICESCR, the US Government agreed to bind itself in good faith to ensure that nothing is done that would defeat the object and purpose of the international instrument, pending a decision on ratification. Moreover, on 28 July 2010 the United Nations General Assembly recognized water and sanitation as a human right. This decision was subsequently endorsed by the United Nations Human Rights Council in September 2010. The USA publicly declared that it was "proud to take the significant step of joining consensus" on the latter's resolution, expressing thus clear support to the recognition of this fundamental human right.

The United Nations Committee on Economic, Social and Cultural Rights (CESCR), which monitors the implementation of the ICESCR, has asserted that everyone is entitled to sufficient, safe, acceptable, physically accessible and affordable water for personal and domestic uses, which includes sanitation. In its General Comments 15 (2002), the CESCR affirmed that the right to water clearly falls within the category of guarantees essential for securing an adequate standard of living, particularly since it is one of the most fundamental conditions for survival, further explaining that this right is also inextricable related to the right to the highest attainable standard of health and the rights to adequate housing and adequate food.

. . .

I would also like to draw the attention of your local government to the principles of equality and non-discrimination, which are core elements of the international human rights normative framework and enshrined, inter alia, in article 2 of the Universal Declaration of Human Rights and articles 2 of the ICESCR and of the International Covenant on Civil and Political Rights and other human rights treaties that the USA has ratified. In its General Comment 20 (paras. 34 and 35), the CESCR noted that "place of residence" and "economic and social status" are prohibited grounds for discrimination, implied in the phrase "other status" in article 2 of the ICESCR. Thus, measures which discriminate against individuals because they live in a situation of poverty may amount to a contravention of the prohibition of discrimination. Owing to their lack of or limited access to housing, persons living in poverty rely more heavily on public spaces for their daily activities. Quoting again the statement I made at the end of my country mission to the USA last year, local statutes prohibiting public urination and defecation, while they appear constitutional are often discriminatory in their effects. Discrimination often occurs because such statutes are enforced against homeless individuals, who often have no access to public restrooms and are given no alternatives. To conclude, I call on your government to take the right decision to ensure the realization of the human rights to water and sanitation of the homeless people living in the City of Sacramento, thereby ensuring their life in dignity.

Sincerely Yours,

Catarina de Albuquerque Special Rapporteur on the human right to safe drinking water and sanitation

NOTES & QUESTIONS

1. Does the Special Rapporteur's report and subsequent letter to Mayor Johnson effectively articulate the right to water as a human rights concern in the United States? Does the letter, addressed to a city mayor on local matters, raise any federalism concerns? Would the letter be more appropriately addressed to the United States government? What role should

the U.S. government play in this exchange between a U.N. expert and a local official?

2. U.S. human rights advocates played in important role in coordinating Catarina de Albuquerque's visit to the United States. Legal services lawyers in Northern California, in particular, understood their engagement with the Special Rapporteur's U.S. mission as one piece in a broader strategy to bring the human rights concerns confronting homeless people in their region to the attention of the United Nations. *See* Mona Tawatao and Colin Bailey, *Toward a Human Rights Framework in Homelessness Advocacy: Bringing Clients Face-to-Face with the United Nations*, 45 Clearinghouse Rev. 169 (2011). Does the Special Rapporteur's reliance on civil society in this way compromise his or her independence or credibility?

3. As part of its national advocacy strategy, the National Law Center on Homelessness and Poverty worked to ensure that both de Albuquerque's report and letter to Mayor Johnson asserted that the lack of access to bathrooms "could, in some cases, amount to cruel, inhuman or degrading treatment," language which parallels the U.S. Constitution's Eighth Amendment prohibition on cruel and unusual punishment. The National Law Center has promoted adoption of this language with numerous Special Rapporteurs and U.N. treaty bodies as part of its overarching legal and policy strategy, illustrating how advocates can work across multiple human rights mechanisms to develop an advocacy strategy and advance a single issue. *See* Eric S. Tars & Kristen Blume, *Changing the Paradigm: Addressing the Criminalization of Homelessness in the United States through the U.N. Human Rights Committee Review*, 6 Housing Rights Watch 3 (Oct. 2013). Are there other U.S. legal standards that might be ripe for similar interpretative advocacy?

4. In what ways does de Albuquerque leverage the resources of her position to the benefit of U.S. advocates and the communities they serve? What are some limitations she faces in having a maximum impact in the United States? What are some of the challenges and benefits advocates might encounter in engaging with her? What are some strategic considerations advocates should attend to before undertaking an advocacy campaign that involves a U.N. Special Rapporteur?

5. Following de Albuquerque's visit to California, local advocates lobbied the state legislature to recognize the right to clean water under state law. In September 2012, California Governor Jerry Brown signed Assembly Bill 685 into law. The new law recognizes that "every human being has the right to safe, clean, affordable and accessible water adequate for human consumption, cooking and sanitary purposes," and requires state agencies to consider the human right to water when "revising, adopting, or establishing policies, regulations and grant criteria" that impact water use for domestic purposes. 2012 Cal. Stat. 91 (codified at Cal. Water Code § 106.3 (West 2012)). Catarina de Albuquerque issued a press statement supporting the law

once it was adopted, and the U.N. reported that her findings and recommendations were quoted during the introduction, discussion, and adoption of the law. *See California: New law on the human right to water sets "inspiring example for others," News and Events,* United Nations Office of High Commissioner for Human Rights (Sept. 28, 2012), http://www.ohchr.org/en/NewsEvents/Pages/DisplayNews.aspx?NewsID=12605&LangID=E.

6. In the fall of 2009, the U.N. Special Rapporteur on the right to adequate housing conducted the mandate's first official visit to the United States. *See* Special Rapporteur on the Adequate Housing as a Component of the Right to an Adequate Standard of Living, and on the Right to non-Discrimination in this Context, Addendum: Mission to the United States of America, U.N. Doc. No. A/HRC/13/20/Add.4 (Feb. 12, 2010). As with the visit by the Special Rapporteur on the right to safe drinking water and sanitation, community-based organizations played a key role in coordinating site visits and facilitating dialogue with members of impacted communities. For a report documenting this visit and the role of community-based groups in the effort, see National Economic & Social Rights Initiative (NESRI) & Campaign to Restore National Human Rights, Our Voices Must be Heard, A Grassroots Report on the U.S. Mission of the UN Special Rapporteur on the Right to Adequate Housing (Oct. 25, 2010).

7. Advocates and experts engaged in a different way with the U.N. Special Rapporteur on violence against women, Rashida Manjoo, in advance of her visit to the United States in 2011. To assist Manjoo in preparing for her U.S. mission, a number of advocates and academics drafted and submitted a series of briefing papers on five topics related to violence against women in the United States. The papers can be found at http://www.law.virginia.edu/pdf/hr/vaw.pdf.

_____

As the materials above reflect, lawyers in the United States are becoming increasingly interested in engaging with U.N. Special Procedures through their official communications function, whereby individuals and groups can submit allegations of human rights violations directly to the U.N. experts. Once a Special Procedure receives such a complaint, the expert typically sends a communication to the government in the form of a "letter of allegation" or "urgent appeal," which is transmitted to the appropriate government officials through diplomatic channels. In 2012, motivated by a thematic report on access to justice presented by the U.N. Special Rapporteur on extreme poverty and human rights to the U.N. General Assembly, a coalition of legal advocacy and social services organizations submitted a communication to the Special Rapporteur, Magdalena Sepulveda, arguing that the United States' failure to protect legal and social services providers' access to migrant farmworkers' labor camps violates the right to access to justice under human rights law. As you read the executive summary of the communication, give thought to what strategic and ethical considerations might have gone into the advocates' decision to lodge the complaint.

COMPLAINT TO U.N. SPECIAL RAPPORTEUR ON EXTREME POVERTY AND HUMAN RIGHTS REGARDING U.S. FAILURE TO PROTECT LEGAL SERVICE PROVIDERS' ACCESS TO MIGRANT FARMWORKERS

(Dec. 13, 2012).

Distinguished Special Rapporteur:

This human rights complaint is respectfully submitted to the United Nations Special Rapporteur regarding the United States' failure to protect the human rights of migrant farmworkers. By failing to protect outreach providers' unfettered access to migrant farmworkers [and] their family-members who live in agricultural labor camps supplied by their employers, the United States is complicit in violating the human rights of this vulnerable population.

. . .

EXECUTIVE SUMMARY

Between 1 and 3 million year-round and seasonal migrant farmworkers, including at least 100,000 children, are estimated to labor every year in American fields. Migrant farmworkers are one of the most vulnerable populations in American society. Yet, distressingly, they are also the least protected. Most are poor and many live and work in dangerous and dehumanizing circumstances.

Frequent migration and social, linguistic and physical isolation exacerbate this vulnerability. . . . Lack of access to migrant labor camps amounts to lack of access to justice for those migrant workers and families that live at the labor camps. It also decreases these workers' and their families' access to other services that are essential to their health, welfare and dignity.

. . .

Routinely, however, outreach workers who attempt to provide farmworkers living at labor camps with legal assistance, healthcare, education, and social and other basic services are denied access altogether or not provided meaningful access.

. . .

Farmworkers' employers commonly tell outreach workers to leave the property; accuse outreach workers of trespassing on their property; demand prior notice before visiting the property; or pressure the outreach workers to break confidentiality and infringe on the privacy of farmworkers by naming prospective clients who are seeking assistance. Outreach workers, moreover, regularly experience harassment, are threatened with arrest and even threatened with violence by owners and operators of migrant labor camps. Farmworkers also face threats of deportation; sexual violence and violence against security of person; and inhumane treatment and abuse at the hands of their employers. Further, employers may use the enforcement power of local law enforcement officials to control the access that the migrant farmworkers living on their property have to other people and services. The almost total control that some agricultural employers exert over farmworkers that live in their labor camps has been likened to an "almost slave-master relationship."

The effects of these abuses are manifold: service providers are discouraged from providing services; farmworkers' vital privacy interest and the confidential relationship between service providers and workers is undermined; and advocates are limited in their ability to identify and serve victims of labor abuses, sexual violence, child labor and human trafficking. The totality of these factors gives employers a free pass to engage in a "race to the bottom" and to exploit to an unconscionable degree the human rights of this extremely vulnerable population.

The United States does not have a consistent legal framework that mandates camp access; instead, laws and law enforcement relating to camp access is generally left up to individual states. This failure, coupled with federal and state labor laws that exacerbate the socio-economic deprivation of migrant farmworkers and discriminate against them because of their migrant status or poverty violates migrant farmworkers' human rights and the United States' obligations under the International Covenant on Civil and Political Rights (ICCPR) and the International Convention on the Elimination of All Forms of Racial Discrimination (CERD)—both treaties that the United States has signed and ratified.

As such, the signatories to this complaint recommend that the Special Rapporteur request the United States to do the following: permit a country visit by the Special Rapporteur to conduct an in-depth investigation into migrant camp-access issues; take all reasonable measures to bring United States law and regulations in compliance with treaty obligations under the ICCPR and CERD; urge strengthened enforcement of rights of migrant farmworkers by all appropriate federal and state agencies; educate and train local law enforcement about rights of migrant farmworkers to receive outreach worker visitors in their migrant camp homes.

. . .

NOTES & QUESTIONS

1.   The advocates' complaint was motivated in part by the Special Rapporteur's thematic report to the U.N. General Assembly on Access to Justice. *See* U.N Special Rapporteur on Extreme Poverty and Human Rights, *Report on Access to Justice for People Living in Poverty*, U.N. Doc. A/67/278 (Aug. 9, 2012) (by Maria Magdalena Sepúlveda Carmona). While the Special Rapporteur did not discuss the issue of migrant farmworkers' access to legal services and other community service providers in particular, advocates sought to leverage the international attention that her report brought to the issue of access to justice for vulnerable communities. What can the advocates reasonably expect to gain through their advocacy with the Special Rapporteur?

2.   Why might engagement with a U.N. expert be a useful strategy for advocates working on issues pertaining to the rights of migrant farmworkers in the United States, in particular? How is the issue of federalism, and particularly the role of the federal government, addressed in this communication? How does this compare with the approach taken by the Special Rapporteur on clean water and sanitation in her letter to the mayor of Sacramento?

C. CASE STUDY: LEVERAGING U.N. "WINS" BACK IN U.S. COURTS

Through concerted and coordinated efforts to engage the U.N. mechanisms discussed in this chapter, U.S. advocates are beginning to build an international record on a range of human rights concerns. The challenge for lawyers in the United States who seek to leverage these gains in their domestic advocacy efforts is in translating statements, observations, and recommendations made by U.N. experts and by the international community into material that is persuasive to federal, state and local policy makers and in U.S. courts. Here, we examine one effort to do so.

The following *amicus* brief was filed by a group of civil rights and human rights advocacy organizations in *National Federation of Independent Business v. Sebelius*,[5] arguing in support of the constitutionality of the Medicaid expansion provision of the Patient Protection and Affordable Care Act (ACA). The brief seeks to present the U.S. Supreme Court with U.N. experts' concerns about racial disparities in U.S. health care, and describe the ways in which the United States government has presented the ACA internationally as a response to those concerns. As you read the brief, pay particular attention to the footnotes that the *amici* include to explain the various U.N. procedures and mechanisms and provide the relevant context for the Court.

---

[5]   132 S. Ct. 2566 (2012).

BRIEF OF AMICI CURIAE THE LEADERSHIP CONFERENCE ON
CIVIL AND HUMAN RIGHTS ET AL. IN SUPPORT OF
RESPONDENTS REGARDING MEDICAID EXPANSION
NATIONAL FEDERATION OF INDEPENDENT
BUSINESS V. SEBELIUS

Supreme Court of the United States, 2012.
132 S. Ct. 2566.

ARGUMENT

I.   The International Context of the ACA is Relevant to This
Court's Consideration of the Constitutionality of the Medicaid
Expansion Provision

Beginning in 2014, eligibility for Medicaid shall extend to certain
individuals with incomes up to 133 percent of the federal poverty level.

While the Medicaid Expansion Provision is most certainly a domestic
U.S. law, its enactment and subsequent judicial consideration take place
in an international context, including relevant international law to which
the U.S. is a party, and considerable interest from the international
community. Consideration of this international context of the Medicaid
Expansion Provision would continue a "longstanding practice" of this
Court to look beyond our Nation's borders for support for its conclusions.
Graham v. Florida, 130 S. Ct. 2011, 2033 (2010); *see also* Sarah H.
Cleveland, *Our International Constitution*, 31 Yale J. Int'l L. 1, 88 (2006).
This Court has referred to international authority as "instructive for its
interpretation" of federal law. *Roper v. Simmons*, 543 U.S. 551, 575
(2005); *see Abbott v. Abbott*, 130 S. Ct. 1983, 1993–94 (2010); *see also*
Grutter v. Bollinger, 539 U.S. 306, 344 (2003) (Ginsburg, J., concurring).
Further, consistency between the Court's interpretation and international
agreements "demonstrates that the Court's rationale has respected
reasoning to support it." *Graham*, 130 S. Ct. at 2034.

II.   The   Medicaid   Expansion   Provision   Furthers   U.S.
Compliance with its International Human Rights Treaty
Obligations to Ensure Equality in Access to Adequate Health
Care Regardless of Race

A.   International Bodies and Experts Have Noted Concern Over
Racial Disparities in Access to Health Care in the U.S.

In 1994, the U.S. ratified the International Convention on the
Elimination of All Forms of Racial Discrimination (CERD), agreeing to
"undertake to guarantee the right of everyone, without distinction as to
race, colour, or national or ethnic origin, to equality before the law,
notably in the enjoyment of . . . [t]he right to public health [and] medical
care." Convention on the Elimination of All Forms of Racial Equality art.

5(e)(iv).[2] *See also* CERD General Recommendation No. 34 on Racial Discrimination Against People of African Descent, ¶¶ 50, 55 (recommending that State parties remove obstacles to enjoyment of right to health as well as ensure equal access to health care for people of African descent).

With ratification of the treaty, the U.S. agreed to submit periodic reports to the CERD Committee, the United Nations body charged with monitoring state compliance with the Convention.[3] On each occasion that the CERD Committee has conducted such a review, it has held the U.S. to its international obligations and has communicated to the U.S. its concern about the high levels of racial inequality in access to health care in the U.S.

In 2001, commenting on the U.S.'s first set of submissions concerning its compliance with CERD, the CERD Committee specifically noted its concern "about persistent disparities in the enjoyment of, in particular, . . . access to public and private health care." U.N. Comm. on the Elimination of Racial Discrimination, Concluding Observations of the Committee on the Elimination of Racial Discrimination: United States of America, ¶ 19 (Aug. 13, 2001). Reviewing the U.S.'s next submission, in 2008, the CERD Committee again noted its concern, this time in greater detail. Observing "that a large number of persons belonging to racial, ethnic and national minorities still remain without health insurance and face numerous obstacles to access to adequate health care and services," the Committee specifically recommended that the U.S. take steps to eliminate "the obstacles that currently prevent or limit [racial, ethnic and national minorities'] access to adequate health care, such as lack of health insurance, unequal distribution of health care resources, persistent racial discrimination in the provision of health care and poor quality of health care services." U.N. Comm. on the Elimination of Racial Discrimination, Concluding Observations of the Committee on the Elimination of Racial Discrimination: United States of America, ¶ 32 (May 8, 2008).

United Nations independent experts have expressed concerns similar to those raised by the CERD Committee. The Independent Expert on

---

[2] In ratifying CERD the United States attached an understanding setting forth a division of labor between federal, state and local government for domestic implementation. The record notes that the United States would implement the Covenant "to the extent that it exercises jurisdiction over the matters covered therein, otherwise by the state and local governments. To the extent that state and local governments exercise jurisdiction over such matters, the Federal Government, shall, as necessary, take appropriate measures to ensure the fulfillment of this Convention." . . . The federal government remains responsible under international law for any violations of international obligations.

[3] An obligation that a country accepts when it ratifies a human rights treaty is periodic review by the international committee of independent experts charged with monitoring treaty compliance ("the treaty body"). As part of the review, the country must submit a comprehensive report on progress that it has made towards implementing its treaty commitments. At the conclusion of the treaty review, the treaty body issues a set of concluding recommendations highlighting specific areas of concern.

Human Rights and Extreme Poverty made an official visit to the U.S. in 2005, invited by the U.S. government.[4] In his report, submitted to the U.N. Economic and Social Council, the Independent Expert noted the "significant disparity in uninsured rates between non-Hispanic Whites (11.3 per cent); African Americans (19.7 per cent) and Hispanics (32.7 per cent)," and the "deep inequalities linked to income, health insurance coverage, race, ethnicity, geography and critically-[needed] access to care." U.N. Independent Expert on Human Rights and Extreme Poverty, Report on Mission to the United States, ¶¶ 32–33 (March 27, 2006). The Independent Expert concluded that in the U.S., "[i]nequality in the health outcomes are staggering" and urged expansion of the social safety net as one approach to reducing these impacts. *Id.* at ¶¶ 33, 81.

These concerns were repeated in 2010, during a visit to the United States by the U.N. Working Group of Experts on People of African Descent, a group established in 2002 by the predecessor to the U.N. Human Rights Council. The Working Group found that access to health care is an issue of great importance to people of African descent in the United States, and based on a detailed review of relevant data, that "health disparities between people of African descent and the white population continue to be of concern." U.N. Human Rights Council, Working Group of Experts on People of African Descent, Report on Visit to the United States of America from 25 to 29 January 2010, ¶ 38 (Aug. 6, 2010). The Working Group identified several health issues that are problematic from a racial standpoint, including the fact that "minorities in the U.S. are less likely than whites to receive needed care." *Id.* at ¶ 79.

B.   Responding to International Concern, the United States Has Repeatedly Cited the ACA to Demonstrate U.S. Progress Toward Meeting Its International Obligations and Ensuring Equal Access to Health Care Regardless of Race

Since the ACA's enactment on March 23, 2010, the U.S. has repeatedly cited the legislation as a response to these international concerns and as evidence of U.S. progress toward meeting its international human rights treaty obligations to achieve racial equality in the enjoyment of public health and medical care. These Executive branch statements concerning the nature of U.S. treaty obligations and the ways in which they are served by the ACA are entitled to "great weight." *Abbott*, 130 S. Ct. at 1993 (citation omitted) (noting that the Court's conclusion was "supported and informed by the State Department's view on the issue"); *see Sumitomo Shoji America, Inc. v. Avagliano*, 457 U.S. 176, 184 n.10 (1982) (deferring to the Executive branch's interpretation of a treaty as memorialized in a brief before the Court).

---

[4]   Independent Experts under the purview of the U.N. make country visits only upon an invitation from the government.

For example, the United States' report to the U.N. Human Rights Council in conjunction with the Universal Periodic Review, submitted on August 23, 2010 ("the UPR Report"), cites the ACA as evidence of the nation's commitment to reduce discrimination in access to health care and health insurance in accordance with its international obligations.[5] Acknowledging the alarming disparities in health between minorities and the white population, the U.S. government's UPR Report specifically notes that the ACA will "help our nation reduce disparities and discrimination in access to care that have contributed to poor health."[6]

The U.S. State Department's Legal Adviser, Harold Koh, underscored this assertion in remarks formally responding to the recommendations of the U.N. Human Rights Council that resulted from the UPR. In particular, the Legal Adviser cited the "recent landmark healthcare reform" as the latest example of a U.S. federal program established to "empower our citizens to live what FDR called a 'healthy peacetime life.' "

In December 2011, the U.S. government again cited the ACA in its periodic report to the U.N. Human Rights Committee concerning U.S. compliance with its commitments under provisions of the International Covenant on Civil and Political Rights ("ICCPR"). Like CERD, the ICCPR has been ratified by the U.S.; Article 2 of the ICCPR obligates each State party to adhere to principles of nondiscrimination on the basis of race as well as other grounds. The U.S. government's ICCPR Report notes that the ACA addresses "concerns regarding racial and ethnic disparities in healthcare access" and intimates that the Medicaid Expansion Provision specifically furthers U.S. efforts to provide all children adequate health care.

Finally, speaking in a domestic forum and training his remarks toward an international audience, in March 2011, Assistant Secretary of State for Democracy, Human Rights, and Labor Michael Posner articulated the U.S. government's perspective that the ACA plays an important role in establishing the nation's international leadership on access to healthcare, asserting that,

---

[5]   The Universal Periodic Review (UPR) is a mechanism, created by the U.N. General Assembly in 2006 along with the U.N. Human Rights Council, by which the Human Rights Council facilitates an intergovernmental review of the human rights record of each U.N. member state. The United States' first UPR occurred in 2010.

[6]   For example, the report notes that African Americans are 29 percent more likely to die from heart disease than non-Hispanic whites. Asian American men suffer from stomach cancer 114 percent more often than non-Hispanic white men. Hispanic women are 2.2 times more likely to be diagnosed with cervical cancer than non-Hispanic white women. American Indians and Alaska Natives are 2.2 times as likely to have diabetes as non-Hispanic whites. Additionally, these racial and ethnic groups accounted for almost 70 percent of the newly diagnosed cases of HIV and AIDS in 2003. UPR Report at ¶ 71, *citing* U.S. Department of Health and Human Services, Office of Minority Health "Protecting the Health of Minority Communities" (2006), *available at*: www.hhs.gov/news/factsheet/minorityhealth.html.

> Our government's commitment to provide for the basic social and economic needs of our people is clear, and it reflects the will of the American people. The people ask us to care for the sick . . . and we do. In 2009, our nation spent nearly $900 billion on Medicare and Medicaid. And as you know, last year the administration passed and signed the Affordable Care Act to expand access to health care in America.

Michael Posner, Assistant Secretary of State for Human Rights, Democracy and Labor, "The Four Freedoms Turn 70: Ensuring Economic, Political, and National Security in the 21st Century," Annual Meeting of the American Society of International Law, Washington, D.C., March 24, 2011.

. . .

NOTES & QUESTIONS

1.   Do you think that the brief effectively contextualizes the concerns and findings of the international community regarding disparities in access to health care within the United States? Is it a strong assertion that the United States must follow international law? Why or why not? What is the relevance of this information to the Court?

2.   How does the articulation and use of international law in this brief compare to other examples you've explored of lawyers drawing on international and foreign law for persuasive authority in U.S. courts? What strategic considerations should go into the decision of whether and how to present such material to U.S. courts?

3.   In its decision in the case, Court did not cite to any of the international human rights material referenced in the brief. Nevertheless, the Court upheld the constitutionality of the ACA and, in principle, the Medicaid Expansion Provision (though the Court limited the ability of the federal government to penalize states that do not comply with the provision, thus making it optional rather than mandatory). Can the advocates who filed the human rights *amicus* brief take some credit for the outcome?

SKILLS EXERCISE: ENGAGING WITH U.N. MECHANISMS

You work for an advocacy organization concerned about access to justice in civil cases. Your organization is particularly concerned about the recent budget cuts to the federal Legal Services Corporation and federal restrictions on legal services providers. In this exercise, you will draft advocacy materials regarding these concerns in conjunction with the U.N. Human Rights Committee's review of the United States for its compliance with the ICCPR.

After reviewing the following research materials:

1.   Draft a short submission to the U.N. Human Rights Committee urging it to take up the issue of legal aid with the United States during its

upcoming review. Include in your submission questions you'd like the Committee to ask of the United States, and recommendations you would like it to make regarding access to legal services.

2.   Draft a short opinion piece to raise public awareness about the upcoming U.S. review under the ICCPR, and the United States' obligation to ensure procedural fairness in light of recent budget cuts and federal restrictions on LSC funded organizations.

3.   Draft a letter to the Assistant Secretary of State for the Bureau of Democracy, Labor, and Human Rights and the Senior Counselor at the Department of Justice's Access to Justice Initiative, urging the government to take certain actions in light of its obligations under the ICCPR, and in preparation for its review by the U.N. Human Rights Committee.

Research Materials

The Legal Services Corporation (LSC) is a federal independent non-profit corporation that provides grants for civil legal service assistance to low-income Americans. Over the past few years, LSC has been hit with significant cuts to its congressional appropriations. Congressional appropriations for LSC have decreased from $420 million in 2010 to $365 million in 2014. These decreases are of particular concern as they come at a time of economic crisis, when more and more Americans are falling below federal poverty guidelines and are in more need of civil legal services than ever before. Legal services providers report being flooded with a huge increase in clients seeking legal assistance for more severe legal problems. Due to funding reductions since 2010, LSC has been forced to eliminate more than 1,000 staff positions and more than thirty offices. As a result, LSC and its grantees have been unable to meet current demands for their civil legal services.

Federal restrictions prohibit the use of any LSC funds to represent most undocumented and other categories of immigrants, with a few narrow exceptions. And they prohibit LSC grantees from representing incarcerated individuals in any civil litigation or administrative challenges to the conditions of incarceration. An LSC-funded organization may not be involved in litigation involving abortion or represent someone in public housing eviction cases when the eviction is based on the public health or safety of residents or staff and the evicted person was convicted or charged of a drug crime. LSC grantees may not engage in advocacy or representation before legislative bodies on pending or proposed legislation, nor may they represent clients or client interests in front of administrative agencies that direct rulemaking. Federal restrictions forbid conducting or participating in grass roots lobbying and prohibit LSC-funded groups from initiating, participating, or engaging in class actions. These federal restrictions extend to all of an LSC grantee's activities, even those fully financed with non-LSC funding.

You are aware that the United States is currently being reviewed by the U.N. Human Rights Committee for its compliance with the ICCPR. In its official report to the Human Rights Committee, you note that the U.S. discusses the Legal Services Corporation in its recitation of ways in which it meets its obligations under Article 14 of the Covenant.

Article 14 of the ICCPR provides, in relevant part:

> All persons shall be equal before the courts and tribunals. In the determination of . . . his rights and obligations in a suit at law, everyone shall be entitled to a fair and public hearing by a competent, independent and impartial tribunal established by law.

The Human Rights Committee's General Comment 32 has interpreted the provision as follows:

> Access to administration of justice must effectively be guaranteed in all such cases to ensure that no individual is deprived, in procedural terms, of his/her right to claim justice. . . . The availability or absence of legal assistance often determines whether or not a person can access the relevant proceedings or participate in them in a meaningful way. . . . States are encouraged to provide free legal aid in [non-criminal cases], for individuals who do not have sufficient means to pay for it. In some cases, they may even be obliged to do so."

In its report to the Human Rights Committee, the U.S. states:

> The Legal Services Corporation (LSC), a non-profit corporation created by Congress, also provides civil legal aid for the poor. LSC distributes about 95 percent of its total funding to 136 independent nonprofit legal aid programs with more than 900 offices that provide legal assistance to low-income individuals and families throughout the nation.

You are aware that the U.N. CERD Committee made a recommendation regarding right to counsel in civil cases during its last review of the United States, and that several U.N. Special Procedures have commented more generally on the importance of the right to legal aid. These comments and recommendations are as follows:

Comm. On the Elimination of Racial Discrimination, *Consideration of Reports Submitted by States Parties Under Article 9 of the Convention, Concluding Observations-United States of America,* U.N. Doc. CERD/C/USA/CO/6 (May 8, 2008):

> 22. While welcoming the recent initiatives undertaken by the State party to improve the quality of criminal defence programmes for indigent persons, the Committee is concerned about the disproportionate impact that persistent systemic inadequacies in these programmes have on indigent defendants belonging to racial, ethnic and national minorities. The Committee also notes with concern the disproportionate impact that the lack of a generally recognized right to counsel in civil proceedings has on indigent

persons belonging to racial, ethnic and national minorities (art. 5 (a)).

The Committee recommends that the State party adopt all necessary measures to eliminate the disproportionate impact that persistent systemic inadequacies in criminal defence programmes for indigent persons have on defendants belonging to racial, ethnic and national minorities, inter alia, by increasing its efforts to improve the quality of legal representation provided to indigent defendants and ensuring that public legal aid systems are adequately funded and supervised. The Committee further recommends that the State party allocate sufficient resources to ensure legal representation of indigent persons belonging to racial, ethnic and national minorities in civil proceedings, with particular regard to those proceedings where basic human needs, such as housing, health care, or child custody, are at stake.

. . .

U.N. Special Rapporteur on Extreme Poverty and Human Rights, *Report on Access to Justice for People Living in Poverty*, ¶ 62, U.N Doc. A/67/278 (Aug. 9, 2012) (by Maria Magdalena Sepúlveda Carmona):

62. Lack of legal aid for civil matters can seriously prejudice the rights and interests of persons living in poverty, for example when they are unable to contest tenancy disputes, eviction decisions, immigration or asylum proceedings, eligibility for social security benefits, abusive working conditions, discrimination in the workplace or child custody decisions. Indeed, exclusion of certain categories of claims from the scope of free legal aid, such as housing or immigration proceedings, or exclusion from representation before quasi-judicial tribunals, such as welfare or employment appeal boards, discriminates against the poor. Moreover, the legal processes which relate to such civil matters are often extremely complex and their requirements onerous, creating insurmountable obstacles for those without the assistance of a lawyer, particularly if the State or other party enjoys such assistance. This is particularly troubling with respect to civil matters involving the most vulnerable groups, such as indigenous peoples, persons with disabilities and ethnic minorities, who often face serious deprivations and violations of their rights, and lack the means or ability to contest them.

. . .

Report of the Special Rapporteur on the Independence of Judges and Lawyers, U.N. Doc. A/HRC/23/43, ¶¶ 20, 28 (Mar. 15, 2013) (by Gabriela Knaul):

20. Legal aid is an essential component of a fair and efficient justice system founded on the rule of law. It is also a right in itself and an essential precondition for the exercise and enjoyment of a number of human rights, including the right to a fair trial and the right to an effective remedy. Access to legal advice and assistance is also an important safeguard that helps to ensure fairness and public trust in the administration of justice.

. . .

28. The Special Rapporteur is of the view that the right to legal aid can be construed as both a right and an essential procedural guarantee for the effective exercise of other human rights, including the right to an effective remedy, the right to liberty and security of person, the right to equality before the courts and tribunals, the right to counsel and the right to a fair trial. Owing to its importance and considering its potential scope, the right to legal aid should be recognized, guaranteed and promoted in both criminal and non-criminal cases.

. . .

Report of the Special Rapporteur on Adequate Housing as a Component of the Right to an Adequate Standard of Living, and on the Right to Non-Discrimination in this Context, U.N. Doc. A/HRC/22/46, ¶ 69 (Dec. 24, 2012) (by Raquel Rolnik):

69. Finally, while the full elaboration of the scope of—security of tenure as recognized in the framework of international human rights law presents a range of challenges that have yet to be adequately met, the Special Rapporteur nonetheless underscores that security of tenure should be understood as encompassing, at a minimum: (a) legal protection from forced eviction, harassment or other threats; (b) recognition—legally, by authorities, but also by private actors—of the right to live in a secure place in peace and dignity; this recognition includes receiving support from authorities and equal access to and availability of all public services; (c) justiciability—in other words, security of tenure must be enforceable; to make this criterion truly effective may require the provision of legal aid to facilitate access to effective remedies; and (d) any other aspect required as a step towards the enjoyment of other components of the right to adequate housing, on an equal basis with others.

. . .

U.N. Special Rapporteur on Violence against Women, its Causes and Consequences, *Annual Report to Comm. On Human Rights: International, Regional and National Developments in the Area of Violence against Women (1994–2003)*, U.N. Doc. E/CN.4/2003/75, ¶ 90 (Jan. 6, 2003) (by Radhika Coomaraswamy):

90. States should establish, strengthen or facilitate support services to respond to the needs of actual and potential victims, including appropriate protection, safe shelter, counseling, legal aid, health-care services, rehabilitation and reintegration into society.

. . .

III. THE INTER-AMERICAN HUMAN RIGHTS SYSTEM

A. INTRODUCTION

In addition to the universal (United Nations) human rights system, regional systems provide accountability mechanisms for human rights around the world. Members of the Council of Europe are bound by the European Convention on Human Rights and judgments of the European Court of Human Rights. The newer African regional system includes the African Court on Human and Peoples' Rights and the African Commission on Human and Peoples' Rights. Established by the Organization of American States (OAS), the Inter-American human rights system is the regional human rights system for North, Central, and South America as well as the Caribbean islands, and thus the United States.

The core human rights documents within the Inter-American system are the American Convention on Human Rights ("the American Convention") and the American Declaration on the Rights and Duties of Man ("The American Declaration"). The American Declaration applies to all members of the Organization of American States, including the United States, and includes the full range of rights in the Universal Declaration of Human Rights. The American Convention is binding only on countries that have ratified it. The United States has signed but not ratified the American Convention. Other important instruments within the system include the Additional Protocol to the American Convention in the Area of Economic, Social and Cultural Rights (Protocol of San Salvador) and the Inter-American Convention on the Prevention, Punishment and Eradication of Violence Against Women (Convention of Belem do Para), neither of which the United States has ratified.

The two primary organs of the Inter-American human rights system are the Inter-American Court of Human Rights, based in San Jose, Costa Rica, and the Inter-American Commission on Human Rights (IACHR), based on Washington, D.C. Because the United States is party to both the OAS Charter and the American Declaration and has signed, but not yet ratified, the American Convention, the U.S. is subject to the jurisdiction of the Inter-American Commission on Human Rights, but not the Inter-American Court. The American Declaration must serve as the primary basis for any claims brought to the IACHR against the United States, though the American Convention's provisions can be raised as additional persuasive authority in U.S. human rights advocacy.

Created in 1959 in order to "further respect" for human rights among OAS member states, the Inter-American Commission promotes human rights in the region through human rights education and technical assistance, investigates human rights violations and country conditions, and hears cases brought by individuals and groups. The Commission has the authority to examine violations of the rights listed in the American Declaration, the American Convention, and other treaties, to request information from states, make recommendations, and publish its findings. The Commission can hear petitions from individuals, groups, and NGOs alleging human rights violations, even without the consent of the named victims. The Commission may also refer cases to the Inter-American Court if the state in question has accepted the Court's contentious jurisdiction, an option not open to U.S. advocates.

Though the Inter-American Court's jurisdiction to hear contentious cases does not extend to the United States, the Court can issue advisory opinions regarding the compatibility of U.S. law with the American Convention or other human rights treaties at the request of the Commission or another OAS member state, or as a means of fleshing out obligations under a given treaty more generally.

U.S. advocates have engaged with the Inter-American system for over three decades, filing cases, requesting hearings, and seeking precautionary measures against the U.S. government on issues including the death penalty, migrants' rights, military detention and national security, juvenile life without parole, environmental justice, voting, domestic violence, and indigenous land rights. Indeed, as Professor Cynthia Soohoo notes in her history of U.S. human rights advocacy:

> The filing of cases involving the U.S. with the Inter-American Commission on Human Rights . . . is not new. However, recent years have marked significant increases in both the number and the types of U.S. cases brought before the Commission. In an article looking at U.S. cases before the Commission, law professor Rick Wilson found only seven decisions in contentious cases concerning the United States in the 1970s and 1980s. Most of the cases had an international aspect to them, such as the treatment of aliens in the United States. In 2006, seventy-five new U.S. cases were filed with the Commission involving a wide array of domestic issues.
>
> The increase in U.S. cases before the Commission started with death penalty cases in the 1980s. According to Wilson, these cases resulted from a conscious strategy choice on the part

of death penalty lawyers at the NAACP Legal Defense Fund, who were looking for "new directions." By the 1990s, death penalty cases constituted the majority of the Commission's U.S. cases, but other types of domestic cases slowly began to appear on the Commission's docket. Many of these cases reflected the limitations of domestic law and the hope that a favorable decision from the Commission would increase political pressure for change. For instance, in the 1990s, the Indian Law Resource Center brought a case challenging the seizure of tribal lands after U.S. courts had rejected their claims. Other cases filed in the 1990s argued that 1996 welfare reforms violated economic and social rights and that the lack of Congressional representation for D.C. residents violated rights to equality and political participation.

Favorable rulings and publicity around several of these cases as well as a 2002 case challenging U.S. detention policies on Guantánamo Bay have increased the Commission's profile among U.S. lawyers, expanding both the number and diversity of cases filed.

Cynthia Soohoo, *Human Rights and the Transformation of the "Civil Rights" and "Civil Liberties" Lawyer*, in 2 Bringing Human Rights Home 71, 84 (Cynthia Soohoo et al. eds., 2008). As of 2013, the Inter-American Commission had issued decisions on the merits in twenty-six contentious cases.[6]

Although the United States formally participates in cases before the IACHR, submitting legal briefs, offering hearing testimony, and attending working meetings to explore friendly settlement and implementation, because the United States has not ratified the American Convention and because there is no mechanism for enforcing Commission decisions, the U.S. government regularly asserts that the Commission's recommendations are non-binding. This leads to significant challenges for advocates seeking governmental implementation of recommendations issued by the Commission. Nevertheless, the Commission offers benefits for advocates seeking to address human rights violations in the United States. As Margaret Huang describes:

The Inter-American Commission offers individual petitioners who have been denied access to U.S. courts the opportunity to have their case heard by an official body. For many victims of human rights violations, the Inter-American Commission process offers the only formal acknowledgement of their experience. The thematic hearings before the Commission

---

[6] *See* Inter-American Commission for Human Rights, http://www.oas.org/en/iachr/decisions/merits.asp.

also offer the opportunity to raise interest in a particular human rights violation, which can be used in education and media outreach efforts. But it is important to note that the U.S. government usually does not accept the jurisdiction of the Commission and refuses to comply with any decisions taken against it. Because of the government's refusal to accept the legal authority of the Commission, advocates must have clear and limited expectations about what a Commission decision can actually accomplish.

Margaret Huang, *"Going Global": Appeals to International and Regional Human Rights Bodies, in* 2 Bringing Human Rights Home 105, 114 (Cynthia Soohoo et al. eds., 2008).

In addition to the benefits Huang describes, advocacy with the Inter-American system offers opportunities for sustained dialogue with the U.S. government over discrete human rights concerns, and findings from the Commission can contribute to the "international record" on particular human rights issues.

The following article describes the procedures of the Inter-American system. As you read, notice the differences between the Inter-American system and the U.N. system. What are the potential benefits that each offers to U.S. advocates?

CAROLINE BETTINGER-LOPEZ, "THE INTER-AMERICAN HUMAN RIGHTS SYSTEM: A PRIMER"

42 Clearinghouse Rev. 581, 583–91 (2009).

The Inter-American Commission on Human Rights was created in 1959 "to promote the observance and defense of human rights" in OAS member states. It is composed of seven commissioners, who are independent human rights experts nominated by their home countries and elected by the OAS general assembly. They serve in their personal capacity on a part-time basis for four-year terms.

. . .

The Commission has both contentious and promotional functions. It acts as an arbiter and adjudicator of cases in which discrete human rights violations are alleged against individuals or groups. It is also a forum for generalized grievances or issues that are not appropriate or ripe for adjudication but which the Commission may consider and investigate. In its latter function the Commission uses its influence to promote human rights issues in member states.

In its role as arbiter and adjudicator the Commission accepts human rights complaints, or "petitions," against OAS member states and considers them in light of relevant human rights instruments and jurisprudence. The Commission explains its decisions in published reports and recommendations that state the Commission's findings, its determination as to whether a violation occurred, and its suggested remedies. Remedies may include the payment of damages, a public apology, an investigation into the source of a violation, and suggested changes in law, action, or policy. This contentious function is unique to the Commission: it is the only international forum in which individuals, or nongovernmental organizations acting on behalf of individuals, may bring human rights complaints against the United States and have those complaints adjudicated by a decision-making body. The Commission also considers claims for "precautionary measures"—akin to temporary restraining orders or injunctions—and helps negotiate "friendly settlements" between the parties in contentious cases.

In its promotional role the Commission presides over thematic hearings (also known as "general hearings"), publishes thematic or country-specific human rights reports, and conducts on-site visits to regions with problematic human rights situations. Each commissioner also serves as a country or thematic rapporteur or both. [Rapporteurships include] freedom of expression, women's rights, migrant workers and families, children, indigenous peoples, persons deprived of liberty, human rights defenders, and racial discrimination and the rights of Afrodescendants. The Commission's promotional authority is broader and more flexible than its adjudicatory role and allows it to address large structural or historic inequities, which would not necessarily be cognizable through the individual petition process because of jurisdictional or substantive limitations.

. . .

Petitioners with claims that are against the United States or its subnational entities and are cognizable under the American Declaration may turn to the Inter-American Commission on Human Rights for relief if they have exhausted all appeals or if domestic procedural restrictions . . . or legal precedent preclude the pursuit of remedies in U.S. courts. While many U.S. advocates find that the Commission's enforcement limitations make it a less desirable forum than a domestic decision-making body, hearings before the Commission can be particularly powerful places for victims to have their "day in court". . . . And winning a case before the Commission can have far-reaching domestic and international implications and cause other regional human rights bodies and the United Nations to take notice.

Advocates may advance human rights concerns before the Commission in a number of ways. Through the Commission, they may pursue individual case adjudication, seek precautionary measures, or request thematic or general hearings on a particular issue or series of issues. They may request the Commission to conduct on-site investigations and issue reports. They may also seek Inter-American Court advisory opinions to effectuate change. . . . [A]lthough the offending actor might be a state or municipality, the U.S. government is ultimately answerable to the Commission.

. . .

A word of caution is appropriate here, however. The Inter-American human rights system is not intended to be a site of first relief for individuals complaining of human rights abuse but rather, when national safeguard mechanisms fail, provides an additional pressure point on the United States and an alternate forum for individuals and communities experiencing the effects of human rights abuses.

A.   Litigating a Contentious Case

Any individual or group, or "petitioners," may petition the Commission for adjudicatory relief, claiming that a federal government, or "respondent state," is responsible for human rights violations.

. . .

The Commission considers only petitions alleging violations of human rights by the federal government or its agents (including subnational entities, such as states and municipalities), not allegations focused on purely private conduct. In some cases causal responsibility can be imputed to the federal government through its omission or failure to respond appropriately to private conduct that violates human rights.

Individuals and groups may submit petitions on their own behalf or on behalf of third parties. Petitions may be submitted without the victim's knowledge or authorization. The Commission accepts collective petitions, indicating numerous victims of a specific incident or practice, but not "actio popularis," or class action suits that set forth generalized harms not limited to a specific group or event. Claims of widespread, generalized harm are excluded from the Commission's case-based jurisdiction and instead are considered in general hearings and country reports.

Before a petition may be filed, petitioners must "exhaust domestic legal remedies" or show that the pursuit of certain legal avenues would have been futile. Petitions must be filed within six months of notification of final judgment or, under certain circumstances, within a "reasonable period" of time thereafter. The Commission is not a "court of fourth instance" and will not substitute its judgment for that of the domestic trier-of-fact. The Commission will, however, consider cases that allege that the domestic adjudication violated the petitioner's due process or denied petitioner a fair hearing resulting in an ineffective remedy. The

Commission will not consider petitions that are duplicative of cases pending before or resolved by other international tribunals, or cases that the Commission itself has already resolved.

A contentious case before the Inter-American Commission proceeds in two phases. In the first phase, known as the "admissibility" phase, a panel of commissioners decides whether the petitioner has met the procedural requirements and whether the Commission has competence (akin to jurisdiction) to examine the human rights claims contained in the petition.

. . .

If the Commission deems a case admissible, the case enters the second, or "merits" phase, to determine whether a human rights violation took place. At the merits phase, the Commission considers evidence presented before it and may hold hearings or even conduct investigatory field or on-site visits in which it does its own fact-finding. Petitioners may also request that key local, state, or federal government officials participate as part of the government's delegation. At case-based hearings and at the working meetings described below, petitioners may have the opportunity to develop the factual record, clarify legal arguments, offer victim statements and expert testimony, and request face-to-face time with the Commissioners.

Throughout the merits phase, the Commission will encourage "friendly settlement" between the parties. The Commission may do so by granting a "working meeting" during one of its sessions in which it will meet privately with the parties to discuss progress in settlement discussions. When settlement is not possible and when the Commission determines that there is a violation, it will send the offending state a preliminary report with the proposals and recommendations it deems pertinent.

. . .

In most cases, . . . the Commission publishes a merits report on state culpability. The Commission considers the facts of the case in light of the precedential jurisprudence of the Inter-American Court and Commission and sometimes looks to other relevant human rights treaties for persuasive authority or interpretive guidance in drafting its report. If the Commission deems the state responsible for a human rights violation, the Commission then issues a recommendation outlining the general contours of a remedy that will make the victim whole and create legal and policy reforms to prevent repetition of the harm.

After the issuance of the Commission's report, petitioners may request a "working meeting" with the Commission and the state in question to discuss state progress in implementing the Commission's recommendations. The Commission continues to supervise state compliance with its recommendations and publishes statistics on compliance in its Annual Report. While no enforcement mechanism ensures state compliance with Commission decisions, the Commission's merits reports contribute to international standard setting and carry significant moral and political weight that can be useful in advocacy campaigns.

. . .

C.   Seeking Precautionary Measures

In "serious and urgent cases, and whenever necessary," the Commission can request, on its own initiative or at the request of a party, that an OAS member state take immediate precautionary measures "to prevent irreparable harm to persons." The Commission issues a report and recommendations for immediate action. Precautionary measures do not require prior exhaustion of domestic remedies and allow the system to respond rapidly to urgent human rights concerns without prejudging the merits of a case. A request for precautionary measures forces the Commission to engage immediately in a supervisory and monitoring role in a new substantive dispute and thus "can also act as a catalyst for involving the Commission . . . in new substantive areas of human rights law."

. . .

D.   Requesting a Thematic Hearing

Thematic, or general, hearings allow advocates to raise awareness about serious human rights issues that may not be justiciable due to jurisdictional bars or other reasons but nevertheless merit the Commission's attention in its promotional function. General hearings may focus on a particular human rights issue that is cross-regional or on a particular region that experiences multifaceted human rights problems. Thematic hearings allow for greater flexibility in theme, form, and structure than case-based hearings. Advocates may find more opportunities for coalition building and a broader framing of the issues at thematic hearings than before domestic tribunals.

. . .

The Commission does not issue a written report at the conclusion of a general hearing. However, the Commission does issue a press release at the end of each hearing session. The press release may refer to some or all of the general hearings that took place during the session and may even express concern regarding the matters raised at the hearings.

. . .

E.   Engaging with a Country or Thematic Rapporteur and Soliciting an On-Site Visit and Report

Individuals or groups may request that the Commission or specific commissioners, in their capacities as country or thematic rapporteurs, make on-site visits to investigate allegations of widespread human rights violations within a country or region or among a particular cross-section of a population. During the visits, Commission representatives interact with the victims, nongovernmental organizations, and government officials. The Commission often issues a press release at the conclusion of a visit and sometimes issues a country or thematic report highlighting its key findings.

The Commission's country or thematic reports offer comprehensive analyses and recommendations regarding the general human rights situation in a particular country or a specific human rights issue in one or several countries.

. . .

F.   Soliciting an Advisory Opinion from the Inter-American Court of Human Rights

Advocates may also work with foreign governments and the Commission to request advisory opinions from the Inter-American Court on matters relevant to the United States.

. . .

NOTES & QUESTIONS

1.   For more detailed discussion on the administrative functioning, jurisdiction, and procedures of the Inter-American Commission and Court, see Dinah L. Shelton, *The Inter-American Human Rights System*, *in* Guide to International Human Rights Practice 127 (Hurst Hannum ed., 4th ed. 2004). *See also* Dinah L. Shelton and Paolo Wright-Carozza, Regional Protection of Human Rights (2d ed. 2012); Tara J. Melish, *The Inter-American Commission on Human Rights: Defending Social Rights Through Case-Based Petitions*, *in* Social Rights Jurisprudence: Emerging Trends in Comparative and International Law 339–48 (Malcom Langford ed., 2008); Jo Pasqualucci, The Practice and Procedure of the Inter-American Court of Human Rights (2003).

2.   Between 2011 and 2013, the Inter-American Commission underwent a significant reform process, leading to changes to its rules of procedures. For example, the Commission is now required to provide written decisions on requests for precautionary measures. *See* Inter-American Commission on Human Rights, Modification to the Rules of the Procedure (Aug. 1, 2013), *available at* http://www.oas.org/en/iachr/mandate/Basics/ModificationsRulesIACHR2013.pdf.

3.   Although the Inter-American Court of Human Rights does not have jurisdiction to hear contentious cases brought against the United States, the Court does have the ability to issue advisory opinions on human rights concerns in the United States. For example, U.S. advocates were actively involved in a request for an Advisory Opinion brought by the government of Mexico in the wake of the U.S. Supreme Court's 2002 decision in *Hoffman Plastic Compounds v. National Labor Relations Board*, 535 U.S. 137 (2002), holding that unauthorized immigrant workers are not entitled to back pay as a remedy for unlawful firing under the National Labor Relations Act. Concerned about the impact of *Hoffman Plastics* on unauthorized immigrant workers from Mexico in the United States, the Mexican Government filed a request for an Advisory Opinion from the Inter-American Court on the question of whether governments can condition employment and labor rights on immigration status. The Court issued Advisory Opinion OC–18, holding that unauthorized immigrant workers have the same workplace rights as other employees. *See* Legal Status and Rights of Undocumented Migrants, Advisory Opinion OC–18/03, Inter-Am. Ct. H.R. (ser. A.) No. 3, ¶¶ 6, 8, 157 (Sept. 17, 2003).

4.   Over the past twenty years, U.S. advocates have found the Inter-American human rights system to be a receptive forum for engaging in advocacy concerning the rights of migrants. For a discussion of such advocacy efforts, see Beth Lyon, *Changing Tactics: Globalization and the U.S. Immigrant Worker Rights Movement*, 13 U.C.L.A. J. Int'l L. & Foreign Aff. 161 (2008) (discussing engagement of the U.S. immigrant worker rights movement within the Inter-American Human Rights System). *See also* Sarah Paoletti, *Pursuit of a Rights-Based Approach to Migration: Recent Developments at the UN and the Inter-American System*, 14 Hum. Rts. Brief 14 (2007); Sarah Paoletti, *Human Rights for All Workers: The Emergence of Protections for Unauthorized Workers in the Inter-American Human Rights System*, 12 Hum. Rts. Brief 5 (2004).

5.   In addition, U.S. advocates have engaged with the Inter-American system to challenge a range of criminal justice practices in the United States, including the death penalty, the practice of sentencing juveniles to life without parole, and the failure of the United States to inform foreign nationals of their right to consular notification. For a discussion of some of these efforts, see Sandra Babcock, *Human Rights Advocacy in United States Capital Cases, in* 3 Bringing Human Rights Home 103–09 (Soohoo et al. eds., 2008) (discussing more broadly advocates' engagement with the Inter-American system to challenge the death penalty in the United States); Sandra Babcock, *The Limits of International Law: Efforts to Enforce Rulings of the International Court of Justice in U.S. Death Penalty Cases*, 62 Syracuse L. Rev. 183 (2012) (describing international human rights advocacy, including advocacy at the Inter-American Commission on Human Rights and the International Court of Criminal Justice, to seek relief for and halt to executions of foreign nationals who were not informed of their rights to consular notification and access under Article 36 of the Vienna Convention on

Consular Relations); Richard J. Wilson, *The United States' Position on the Death Penalty in the Inter-American Human Rights System*, 42 Santa Clara L. Rev. 1159 (2002).

6.   U.S. advocates have also brought cases against the United States challenging national security-related policies and practices, including detentions at Guantánamo Bay. For discussion of some of these efforts, see Brian Tittimore, *Guantánamo Bay and Precautionary Measures of the Inter-American Commission on Human Rights: A Case for International Oversight in the Struggle Against Terrorism*, 6 Hum. Rts. L. Rev. 378 (2006); Richard J. Wilson, *Detainees at Guantánamo Bay: The Inter-American Human Rights Commission Responds to a "Legal Black Hole,"* 10 Hum. Rts. Brief 2 (2003).

7.   For strategic reasons, advocates may choose to engage with the Commission on a number of different cases in the same thematic area. By so doing, they can help to lay the foundation for the Commission to take a broader approach to an issue, for example by issuing a thematic report examining States' practice and setting forth the applicable legal standards. Such efforts have led to thematic reports by the IACHR on issues including the death penalty, immigration detention, and juvenile justice. *See* Thematic Reports, Inter-American Commission on Human Rights, http://www.oas.org/en/iachr/reports/thematic.asp.

8.   Given that there are no mechanisms available to enforce decisions of the Commission against the U.S. Government, what is the value to advocates and their clients of bringing a claim to the Commission? If the United States doesn't consider the IACHR's recommendations to be binding on it, why do you think it regularly participates and engages in the proceedings? How can advocates make the most of the United States' participation?

9.   Another challenge that advocates face in engaging with the Inter-American system is general lack of public awareness about the system, and the Commission in particular. How might this lack of awareness impact advocacy efforts? How might advocates work to overcome this challenge?

10.   Are there any advantages to engaging with a regional system over the U.N. system? Or engaging with a human rights commission over a treaty monitoring body? What are some strategic considerations U.S. advocates might weigh before committing to one forum or another? Must advocates choose?

11.   In fact, advocates often bring the same human rights issue to multiple human rights bodies, for example engaging in U.N. treaty reporting around the rights of migrant workers while simultaneously organizing a U.S. visit for the U.N. Special Rapporteur on the rights of migrants and filing a contentious case with the Inter-American Commission on Human Rights. And, many of the decisions and recommendations issued by the Inter-American system are similar to and reinforce decisions and recommendations issued by the U.N. treaty bodies and independent experts. What are the

advantages of using multiple fora (U.S. courts, the Inter-American system, and the United Nations human rights system) to advocate around the same issue? Are there any drawbacks to such an approach? How can advocates use favorable decisions from one to obtain a favorable decision in another, and then to urge changes in domestic law or policy?

12. Increasingly, there has been cooperation and collaboration between the Inter-American human rights system and the U.N. human rights system. For example, in 2013, at the urging of the Center for Constitutional Rights and the Center for Justice and International Law (CEJIL), the Inter-American Commission on Human Rights, the United Nations Working Group on Arbitrary Detention, the U.N. Special Rapporteur on human rights and counterterrorism, the U.N. Special Rapporteur on health, and the U.N. Rapporteur on torture issued a joint statement to call attention to the hunger strike of detainees at Guantánamo Bay and call on the United States Government to end indefinite detention and close the Guantánamo detention center. *See IACHR, UN Working Group on Arbitrary Detention, UN Rapporteur on Torture, UN Rapporteur on Human Rights and Counter-Terrorism, and UN Rapporteur on Health reiterate need to end the indefinite detention of individuals at Guantánamo Naval Base in light of current human rights crisis, News and Events,* United Nations Office of the High Commissioner for Human Rights (May 1, 2013), http://www.ohchr.org/EN/NewsEvents/Pages/DisplayNews.aspx?NewsID=13278&LangID=E. Also in 2013, the U.N. Special Rapporteur on solitary confinement, Juan Mendez, testified at the Inter-American Commission on Human Rights during a thematic hearing on solitary confinement in the Americas. *See UN Special Rapporteur on Torture Warns About Abuse of Solitary Confinement in the Americas, News and Events,* United Nations Office of the High Commissioner for Human Rights (Mar. 13, 2013), http://www.ohchr.org/en/NewsEvents/Pages/DisplayNews.aspx?NewsID=13134&LangID=E. How might advocates facilitate and maximize such cooperation?

B. CASE STUDY: ENGAGING THE INTER-AMERICAN SYSTEM TO ADDRESS VIOLENCE AGAINST WOMEN

Advocates have used the Inter-American system to address the issue of violence against women in a case in which U.S. courts were not available. The case of *Lenahan (Gonzales) v. The United States* was brought on behalf of Jessica Lenahan (then Gonzales), a domestic violence victim whose three daughters (Leslie, Katheryn and Rebecca) were killed after police in Colorado failed to enforce a restraining order against her estranged husband. In June 2005, in the case of *Castle Rock v. Gonzales,* 545 U.S. 748, 768 (2005), the U.S. Supreme Court upheld the lower court's grant of a motion to dismiss and rejected Lenahan's constitutional claims against the police, holding that she had no constitutionally protected due process interest in having the police enforce a domestic violence restraining order. The *Castle Rock* decision revisited a central question in *DeShaney v. Winnebago County Dep't of Soc. Servs.*, 489 U.S. 189, 195 (1989), in which the Court had held that the Due Process Clause does not impose an affirmative obligation on the government to "guarantee . . . certain minimal levels of safety and security" for individuals at risk of private, third-party violence.

Having lost the ability to bring her claims before any U.S. court, in December 2005, Lenahan and her lawyers filed a petition with the Inter-American Commission alleging human rights violations under the American Declaration. In March 2007, Lenahan had her first opportunity to tell her story to a decision-making body when she testified before the Commission in an admissibility hearing. The Commission declared her case admissible and, in 2011, issued a decision in which it found the U.S. government in violation of the rights to life and special protections for children, the right to access judicial remedies, and the right to equality and non-discrimination for its failure to prevent and eradicate violence against women. In its conclusion, the Commission issued a set of recommendations for changes to U.S. law and policy pertaining to domestic violence.

In the aftermath of the Commission's decision, U.S. advocates, including Lenahan's attorneys (the ACLU, University of Miami Human Rights Clinic, and the Columbia Law School Human Rights Clinic) are working to implement the Commission's recommendations within the United States.

Below is an excerpt from the decision by the Inter-American Commission, followed by materials reflecting some of the challenges and opportunities of implementing a decision by a regional human rights body that the United States considers "non-binding."

JESSICA LENAHAN (GONZALES) V. UNITED STATES

Inter-American Commission on Human Rights, 2011.
Case 12.626, Inter-Am. Comm'n H.R., Report No. 80/11.

110.   Gender-based violence is one of the most extreme and pervasive forms of discrimination, severely impairing and nullifying the enforcement of women's rights. The [I]nter-American system as well has consistently highlighted the strong connection between the problems of discrimination and violence against women.

111.   In the same vein, the international and regional systems have pronounced on the strong link between discrimination, violence and due diligence, emphasizing that a State's failure to act with due diligence to protect women from violence constitutes a form of discrimination, and denies women their right to equality before the law. These principles have also been applied to hold States responsible for failures to protect women from domestic violence acts perpetrated by private actors. Domestic

violence, for its part, has been recognized at the international level as a human rights violation and one of the most pervasive forms of discrimination, affecting women of all ages, ethnicities, races and social classes.

. . .

114. In light of the parties' arguments and submissions, there are three questions before the Commission under Articles I, II and VII of the American Declaration that it will review in the following section. The first is whether the obligation not to discriminate contained in Article II of the American Declaration requires member States to act to protect women from domestic violence; understanding domestic violence as an extreme form of discrimination. The second question pertains to the content and scope of this legal obligation under the American Declaration in light of the internationally recognized due diligence principle, and when analyzed in conjunction with the obligations to protect the right to life and to provide special protection contained in Articles I and VII of the American Declaration. The third is whether this obligation was met by the authorities in this case.

. . .

122. The Commission notes that the principle of due diligence has a long history in the international legal system and its standards on state responsibility. It has been applied in a range of circumstances to mandate States to prevent, punish, and provide remedies for acts of violence, when these are committed by either State or non-State actors.

. . .

125. The international community has consistently referenced the due diligence standard as a way of understanding what State's human rights obligations mean in practice when it comes to violence perpetrated against women of varying ages and in different contexts, including domestic violence. This principle has also been crucial in defining the circumstances under which a State may be obligated to prevent and respond to the acts or omissions of private actors. This duty encompasses the organization of the entire state structure—including the State's legislative framework, public policies, law enforcement machinery and judicial system—to adequately and effectively prevent and respond to these problems. Both the Inter-American Commission and the Court have invoked the due diligence principle as a benchmark to rule on cases and situations of violence against women perpetrated by private actors, including those pertaining to girl-children.

. . .

128.   The protection of the right to life is a critical component of a State's due diligence obligation to protect women from acts of violence. This legal obligation pertains to the entire state institution, including the actions of those entrusted with safeguarding the security of the State, such as the police forces. It also extends to the obligations a State may have to prevent and respond to the actions of non-state actors and private persons.

129.   The duty of protection related to the right to life is considered especially rigorous in the case of girl-children. This stems, on the one hand, from the broadly-recognized international obligation to provide special protection to children, due to their physical and emotional development. On the other, it is linked to the international recognition that the due diligence duty of States to protect and prevent violence has special connotations in the case of women, due to the historical discrimination they have faced as a group.

130.   In light of these considerations, the Commission observes that the evolving standards related to the due diligence principle are relevant to interpret the scope and reach of States' legal obligations under Articles I, II, and VII of the American Declaration in cases of violence against women and girl-children taking place in the domestic context. Cases of violence against women perpetrated by private actors require an integrated analysis of the State's legal obligations under the American Declaration to act with due diligence to prevent, investigate, sanction and offer remedies.

. . .

iii.   Conclusions

160.   Based on these considerations, the Commission concludes that even though the State recognized the necessity to protect Jessica Lenahan and Leslie, Katheryn and Rebecca Gonzales from domestic violence, it failed to meet this duty with due diligence. The state apparatus was not duly organized, coordinated, and ready to protect these victims from domestic violence by adequately and effectively implementing the restraining order at issue; failures to protect which constituted a form of discrimination in violation of Article II of the American Declaration.

161.   These systemic failures are particularly serious since they took place in a context where there has been a historical problem with the enforcement of protection orders; a problem that has disproportionately affected women—especially those pertaining to ethnic and racial minorities and to low-income groups—since they constitute the majority of the restraining order holders. Within this context, there is also a high correlation between the problem of wife battering and child abuse,

exacerbated when the parties in a marriage separate. Even though the Commission recognizes the legislation and programmatic efforts of the United States to address the problem of domestic violence, these measures had not been sufficiently put into practice in the present case.

. . .

163. The States' duties to protect and guarantee the rights of domestic violence victims must also be implemented in practice. As the Commission has established in the past, in the discharge of their duties, States must take into account that domestic violence is a problem that disproportionately affects women, since they constitute the majority of the victims. Children are also often common witnesses, victims, and casualties of this phenomenon. Restraining orders are critical in the guarantee of the due diligence obligation in cases of domestic violence. They are often the only remedy available to women victims and their children to protect them from imminent harm. They are only effective, however, if they are diligently enforced.

164. In the case of Leslie, Katheryn and Rebecca Gonzales, the Commission also establishes that the failure of the United States to adequately organize its state structure to protect them from domestic violence not only was discriminatory, but also constituted a violation of their right to life under Article I and their right to special protection as girl-children under Article VII of the American Declaration. . . .

165. The State's duty to apply due diligence to act expeditiously to protect girl-children from right to life violations requires that the authorities in charge of receiving reports of missing persons have the capacity to understand the seriousness of the phenomenon of violence perpetrated against them, and to act immediately. In this case, the police appear to have assumed that Jessica Lenahan's daughters and their friend would be safe with Simon Gonzales because he was Leslie, Katheryn and Rebecca's father. There is broad international recognition of the connection between domestic violence and fatal violence against children perpetrated by parents, and the CRPD officers should have been trained regarding this link. The police officers should also have been aware that the children were at an increased risk of violence due to the separation of their parents, Simon Gonzales' efforts to maintain contact with Jessica Lenahan, and his criminal background. Moreover, the Commission knows of no protocols and/or directives that were in place to guide the police officers at hand on how to respond to reports of missing children in the context of domestic violence and protection orders. The police officers' response throughout the evening was uncoordinated, and not conducive to ascertaining whether the terms of the order had been violated by Simon Gonzales.

. . .

169. The Commission also observes that the State's obligations to protect Jessica Lenahan and her daughters from domestic violence did not conclude that evening. They extended to offering Jessica Lenahan a remedy for these failures and to investigating the circumstances of Leslie, Katheryn and Rebecca Gonzales' death.

. . .

170. Based on these considerations, the Commission holds that the systemic failure of the United States to offer a coordinated and effective response to protect Jessica Lenahan and her daughters from domestic violence, constituted an act of discrimination, a breach of their obligation not to discriminate, and a violation of their right to equality before the law under Article II of the American Declaration. The Commission also finds that the State fail[ed] to undertake reasonable measures to protect the life of Leslie, Katheryn and Rebecca Gonzales, and that this failure constituted a violation of their right to life established in Article I of the American Declaration, in relation to their right to special protection contained in Article VII of the American Declaration.

. . .

i.   Claims related to remedies for the non-enforcement of a protection order

177. The Commission has identified the duty of State parties to adopt legal measures to prevent imminent acts of violence, as one side of their obligation to ensure that victims can adequately and effectively access judicial protection mechanisms. The Commission has identified restraining orders, and their adequate and effective enforcement, among these legal measures. According to this principle, the failures of the State in this case to adequately and effectively organize its apparatus to ensure the implementation of the restraining order also violated the right to judicial protection of Jessica Lenahan and Leslie, Katheryn and Rebecca Gonzales.

178. The Commission also considers that when there are State failures, negligence and/or omissions to protect women from imminent acts of violence, the State also has the obligation to investigate systemic failures to prevent their repetition in the future. This involves an impartial, serious and exhaustive investigation of the State structures that were involved in the enforcement of a protection order, including a thorough inquiry into the individual actions of the public officials involved. States must hold public officials accountable—administratively, disciplinarily or criminally—when they do not act in accordance with the rule of law.

. . .

ii.   The investigation of Leslie, Katheryn and Rebecca's deaths, access to information, and the right to truth

181.   The Commission has emphasized the principle that the ability of victims of violence against women to access judicial protection and remedies includes ensuring clarification of the truth of what has happened. Investigations must be serious, prompt, thorough, and impartial, and must be conducted in accordance with international standards in this area. In addition, the IACHR has established that the State must show that the investigation "was not the product of a mechanical implementation of certain procedural formalities without the State genuinely seeking the truth."

. . .

184.   [T]he United States had the duty to undertake, on its own initiative, a prompt, thorough and separate investigation aimed at clarifying the cause, time and place of the deaths of Leslie, Katheryn and Rebecca Gonzales.

. . .

194.   Eleven years have passed since the murders of Leslie, Katheryn and Rebecca Gonzales, and the State has not fully clarified the cause, time and place of their deaths. The State has not duly communicated this information to their family. The petitioners have presented information highlighting the challenges that Jessica Lenahan and her family members have faced to obtain basic information surrounding the circumstances of Leslie, Katheryn and Rebecca Gonzales' deaths. They also indicate that Leslie, Katheryn and Rebecca Gonzales' gravestones still do not contain information about the time and place of their death. . . .

195.   The Commission underscores that under the American Declaration, the State is obligated to investigate the circumstances surrounding Leslie, Katheryn and Rebecca Gonzales' deaths and to communicate the results of such an investigation to their family. Compliance with this State obligation is critical to sending a social message in the United States that violence against girl-children will not be tolerated, and will not remain in impunity, even when perpetrated by private actors.

. . .

V.   CONCLUSIONS

199.   Based on the foregoing considerations of fact and law, and having examined the evidence and arguments presented by the parties during the proceedings, the Commission concludes that the State failed to

act with due diligence to protect Jessica Lenahan and Leslie, Katheryn and Rebecca Gonzales from domestic violence, which violated the State's obligation not to discriminate and to provide for equal protection before the law under Article II of the American Declaration. The State also failed to undertake reasonable measures to prevent the death of Leslie, Katheryn and Rebecca Gonzales in violation of their right to life under Article I of the American Declaration, in conjunction with their right to special protection as girl-children under Article VII of the American Declaration. Finally, the Commission concludes that the State violated the right to judicial protection of Jessica Lenahan and her next-of kin, under Article XVIII of the American Declaration.

. . .

VI. RECOMMENDATIONS

201.   Based on the analysis and conclusions pertaining to the instant case, the Inter-American Commission on Human Rights recommends to the United States:

1.   To undertake a serious, impartial and exhaustive investigation with the objective of ascertaining the cause, time and place of the deaths of Leslie, Katheryn and Rebecca Gonzales, and to duly inform their next-of-kin of the course of the investigation.

2.   To conduct a serious, impartial and exhaustive investigation into systemic failures that took place related to the enforcement of Jessica Lenahan's protection order as a guarantee of their non-repetition, including performing an inquiry to determine the responsibilities of public officials for violating state and/or federal laws, and holding those responsible accountable.

3.   To offer full reparations to Jessica Lenahan and her next-of-kin considering their perspective and specific needs.

4.   To adopt multifaceted legislation at the federal and state levels, or to reform existing legislation, making mandatory the enforcement of protection orders and other precautionary measures to protect women from imminent acts of violence, and to create effective implementation mechanisms. These measures should be accompanied by adequate resources destined to foster their implementation; regulations to ensure their enforcement; training programs for the law enforcement and justice system officials who will participate in their execution; and the design of model protocols and directives that can be followed by police departments throughout the country.

5.   To adopt multifaceted legislation at the federal and state levels, or reform existing legislation, including protection measures for children in the context of domestic violence. Such measures should be accompanied by adequate resources destined to foster their

implementation; regulations to ensure their enforcement; training programs for the law enforcement and justice system officials who will participate in their execution; and the design of model protocols and directives that can be followed by police departments throughout the country.

6.   To continue adopting public policies and institutional programs aimed at restructuring the stereotypes of domestic violence victims, and to promote the eradication of discriminatory socio-cultural patterns that impede women and children's full protection from domestic violence acts, including programs to train public officials in all branches of the administration of justice and police, and comprehensive prevention programs.

7.   To design protocols at the federal and state levels specifying the proper components of the investigation by law enforcement officials of a report of missing children in the context of a report of a restraining order violation.

NOTES & QUESTIONS

1.   Prior to the hearing that resulted in the decision on the merits of the case, over 70 organizations and individuals joined a total of eight *amicus* briefs to the Commission, addressing issues including the pervasive and severe nature of domestic violence in the United States, the effects of domestic violence on children, and the challenges faced by women of color and immigrant women in obtaining government services to protect themselves from domestic violence. Among these, the Indian Law Resource Center and the Sacred Circle National Resource Center to End Violence Against Native Women led a coalition of Native American women's groups to file an *amicus* brief on behalf of Jessica Lenahan, informing the U.S. government concerning the epidemic of violence against Native Women and expressing concern about the impact of the U.S. Supreme Court's *Gonzales* decision on tribal protection orders. *See* http://web.law.columbia.edu/sites/default/files/ microsites/human-rights-institute/files/Gonzalesdocs/amicus%20indigenous %20women.pdf. As a result of this and other advocacy, some of these issues were addressed in the 2013 reauthorization of the Violence Against Women Act. Winter King & Sara Clark, *Navigating VAWA's New Tribal Court Jurisdictional Provision*, Indian Country Today (March 31, 2013), *available at* http://indiancountrytodaymedianetwork.com/opinion/navigating-vawas-new-tribal-court-jurisdictional-provision-148458.

2.   The *Lenahan* decision resulted in a fairly extensive set of recommendations for how the United States should address domestic violence at the local, state, and federal levels. Given that the United States considers these recommendations to be non-binding and indeed there is no mechanism for enforcement, what is the utility of such a detailed list of recommendations? How might advocates incorporate them into their

advocacy efforts to address domestic violence and violence against women more generally? What are some strategies for seeking implementation of the decision?

3.   One way in which advocates have suggested that the federal government implement the *Lenahan* decision is through issuing federal guidance to state and local law enforcement regarding gender bias in policing and developing protocols to respond to violence against women. Perhaps related to these efforts, in its comprehensive investigations of the New Orleans and Puerto Rico Police Departments, conducted in 2011, the U.S. Department of Justice's Civil Rights Division found that both the New Orleans and Puerto Rico police departments failed to respond adequately to allegations of domestic violence and sexual assaults. In 2012, the DOJ entered into consent decrees with both police departments requiring them to, *inter alia,* make broad changes in policies and practices to the ways in which they respond to calls for service related to domestic violence and sexual assault. Lawyers for Jessica Lenahan and other domestic violence advocates have urged the Department of Justice to formalize the protocols established in the New Orleans and Puerto Rico cases and create guidance for nation-wide dissemination as part of the U.S. government's efforts to implement the decision in *Lenahan.* In June 2013, the Department of Justice's Office of Victims of Crime, Office on Violence Against Women, and Office of Community Oriented Policing issued a joint statement on gender-biased policing, recognizing that under-enforcement of domestic or sexual violence laws amounts to prohibited discriminatory policing. *See* Joint Statement of The Office of Community Oriented Policing Services, The Office for Victims of Crime, and The Office on Violence Against Women on Addressing Gender-Discrimination in Policing, The OVW Blog, U.S. Department of Justice (June 20, 2013), http://blogs.justice.gov/ovw/archives/2406. For a discussion of this and other implementation strategies, see Caroline Bettinger-López, Jessica Lenahan (Gonzales) v. United States: *Implementation, Litigation and Mobilization Strategies*, 21 Am. U.J. Gender Soc. Pol'y & L. 207 (2012).

4.   In another example of cooperation and collaboration between the U.N. and Inter-American human rights systems, the U.N. Special Rapporteur on violence against women, in an official visit to the United States, recognized the issue at the core of the Inter-American Commission's decision and criticized the effect of the U.S. Supreme Court's decision in *Town of Castle Rock v. Gonzales* for refusing to recognize a federal constitutional right to enforcement of a restraining order. *See Report of the Special Rapporteur on Violence Against Women, Its Causes and Consequences, Addendum: Mission to the United States of America*, UN Doc. A/HRC/17/26/Add.5 (June 1, 2011) (by Rashida Manjoo). After the Inter-American Commission on Human Rights released its decision in *Lenahan*, Manjoo issued a statement underscoring the importance of the decision and the Commission's findings that "state inaction towards cases of violence against women fosters an environment of impunity and promotes the repetition of violence." *Violence Against Women: UN expert urges full policy review after regional body finds*

the US responsible of rights violations, News and Events, United Nations Office of the High Commissioner for Human Rights (Aug. 23, 2011), http://www.ohchr.org/en/NewsEvents/Pages/DisplayNews.aspx?NewsID=11325&LangID=E.

5. Moreover, advocates have raised the issues underlying the *Lenahan* case in U.S. human rights treaty reviews, resulting in recommendations from U.N. treaty monitoring bodies related to the issue of state responsibility in protecting and preventing against violence against women. *See* U.N. CERD Committee, *Consideration of Reports Submitted by States Parties under Article 9 of the Convention, Concluding Observations: United States of America*, U.N. Doc. CERD/C/USA/CO/6 (Mar. 5, 2008), para. 26; U.N. Human Rights Committee, *Concluding Observations on the fourth periodic report of the United States of America*, U.N. Doc. CCPR/C/USA/CO/4 (Apr. 23, 2014), Para. 16.

6. For additional discussion of the case and related advocacy strategies, see Caroline Bettinger-López, *Human Rights at Home: Domestic Violence as a Human Rights Violation*, 40 Colum. Hum. Rts. L. Rev. 19 (2008); Elizabeth M. Schneider et al., *Implementing the Inter-American Commission on Human Rights' Domestic-Violence Ruling*, 46 Clearinghouse Rev. 113, 115–16 (2012).

———

One challenge advocates face in leveraging success at the Inter-American Commission is lack of public awareness and understanding about the Commission. As you read the following materials, consider how advocates can effectively communicate the decisions and other actions undertaken by the Commission and Inter-American system more generally, and how they can minimize backlash that may result from misunderstanding or misinformation.

VINCENT CARROLL, EDITORIAL, "ON POINT: USURPING JUSTICE"
Rocky Mountain News (Mar. 2, 2007).

The murders of Jessica Gonzales' three children in 1999 rank as one of the most poignant tragedies in recent Colorado history. Now it is being used, incredibly, in an attempt to undermine U.S. legal sovereignty.

In the nation's capital this morning, the Inter-American Commission on Human Rights is scheduled to hear Jessica Gonzales v. United States of America, a case alleging that the behavior of Castle Rock police in responding to Gonzales' calls for help violated international law.

The commission is one of two organs of the Organization of American States—the other is the Inter-American Court of Human Rights in Costa Rica—that attempts to monitor and rectify human rights abuses throughout the Western Hemisphere. According to the petition asking the commission to hear the case, "the United States has failed to adequately investigate and prosecute domestic violence cases, and Ms. Gonzales is but one of many victims of this widespread and systematic failure on the part of the State."

What's happening here is a textbook case of activist lawyers hoping to expand the reach and influence of international agencies in the pursuit of their political agendas.

. . .

It doesn't particularly matter what you think of the police's performance on that tragic day. In retrospect they obviously should have responded aggressively to Gonzales' calls pleading with them to look for her estranged husband, who'd taken the children despite a court order limiting his contact with the family.

Instead of immediately beginning a search, police told Gonzales to wait. Her husband killed the 10-, 8- and 7-year-old girls eight hours later.

Do police have an affirmative duty to prevent crime—even given what little they knew about the actual danger that day? Would they have been able to find the man even if they'd looked?

Such questions have already been litigated in U.S. courts. Gonzales (her surname now is Lenahan) sued, the case made it to the U.S. Supreme Court, and two years ago it ruled 7–2 in favor of Castle Rock.

The petitioners argue that "Gender discrimination is the common thread running through the violations by the United States of Jessica Gonzales' rights," and that "Colorado police had affirmative obligations to take effective measures to prevent Mr. Gonzales from subjecting her to acts of violence." Maybe police should have such obligations (although it would open them up to nightmarish second-guessing), but if so, that's a decision that Americans and U.S. courts should decide for themselves.

The decisions shouldn't be made under pressure from international agencies that have adopted expansive theories of what count as violations of basic human rights.

EDITORIAL, "A PHONY HUMAN RIGHTS CASE"
Rocky Mountain News (Oct. 14, 2007).

The Inter-American Commission on Human Rights is an organ of the Organization of American States. Typically, human rights violations, which the commission defends, involve gross or systematic abuse of citizens by governments, or instances where private parties run roughshod over others, usually without a government stepping in to stop or punish them. The term has little in common with an incident in which a lone murderer kills his own kids and then in turn is shot by police.

The commission, which says it has more than 800 cases of alleged human rights violations pending, accepted 55 cases from 17 OAS countries in 2006. The majority concerned abuses by ruling governments, such as arrest and detention without formal charges, repression of free speech, state-approved murder, deportation and suppression of political freedom. Four of the 55 cases involved the United States (a death row inmate in Tennessee, two deportation matters and a dispute regarding World War II Japanese internment reparations), and two originated in Canada.

All are a far cry from inspecting how a local police department responded to a domestic situation in which a restraining order had been issued.

. . .

JESSICA LENAHAN, GUEST COMMENTARY, "FAILING VICTIMS OF VIOLENCE"
Denver Post (Aug. 28, 2011).

Twelve years ago, I found myself in an unthinkable situation. My husband, Simon Gonzales, whom I had known since childhood, became a possessive, controlling man I didn't recognize. When he became abusive, I feared for my safety and that of our children. I obtained a restraining order against him, and trusted the law to protect us.

But that trust was destroyed on June 22, 1999. That night, my estranged husband kidnapped our daughters—Rebecca, Katheryn and Leslie—from our front yard. Panicked, I repeatedly called the Castle Rock police for help. Over the next 10 hours, the police refused to go after Simon or try to find my daughters. Hours later, my husband drove up to the police station and opened fire. He was killed in the shootout, and the bodies of my girls were found shot to death in the back of his truck.

There wasn't even a proper investigation to determine whether my girls were killed by their father or in the hail of bullets at the station. I still don't know for certain the exact cause, time and place of my children's death.

In the hours leading up to the shootout, it became clear that my order of protection was worthless, and that the police didn't regard domestic violence as potentially lethal. I was told "the girls were with their father," that I "shouldn't worry," and that I should "give it a few hours." Meanwhile, the police responded to a fire-lane violation, looked for a lost dog, and took a two-hour dinner break.

I sued the town of Castle Rock for failing to enforce the restraining order and took my case to the U.S. Supreme Court. But the court ruled my constitutional rights had not been violated by the failure to enforce the restraining order.

I felt utterly abandoned, but I wasn't done fighting. Along with attorneys from the ACLU, I filed a petition before the Inter-American Commission on Human Rights, arguing that the police failure to enforce my restraining order, and the U.S. courts' failure to provide a remedy, constituted violations of international human rights law. After a 12-year process, the commission made public on Aug. 17 a landmark decision in which it found the U.S. had violated my human rights and those of my three children.

The commission's report said the Castle Rock Police failed in its legal obligation to protect women and children from domestic violence, and emphasized the government has a duty to protect domestic violence victims by taking steps to ensure their safety, including the enforcement of restraining orders.

In the United States, an estimated 1.3 million women are victims of physical assault by an intimate partner each year. Many of these women will, like I did, place their faith in the justice system. To tell these women they have no right to rely on their government to protect them is outrageous and cruel. Restraining orders filed by victims of domestic violence must always be enforced, and a 911 call to enforce those orders must mean something. Policies regarding domestic violence must change so no one else's rights are violated.

It is shameful that it took an international human rights commission to point out that policies meant to protect domestic violence survivors are dangerously inadequate. Despite everything I've lost, I still have hope that our government will use this ruling as an opportunity to make things right, to provide the protection and accountability that will prevent a tragedy like I suffered from occurring again.

NOTES & QUESTIONS

1.   Is the op-ed by Jessica Lenahan effective in articulating the human rights concerns at issue in the case? Does it effectively communicate the importance of the victory? Does it provide sufficiently clear and detailed information about the Commission more generally?

2.   How might advocates counter the argument that the *Lenahan* case is an attempt to undermine U.S. sovereignty? How might they counter the suggestion that the issue in *Lenahan* doesn't amount to a human rights violation worthy of international scrutiny?

SKILLS EXERCISE

You are a lawyer for the ACLU, one of the organizations that represented Jessica Lenahan in her case before the Inter-American Commission on Human Rights. Write a press release announcing and discussing the decision issued by the Commission. Be sure to explain the historic significance of the decision, as well as its relevance and effect in the United States. In drafting your press release, try to anticipate and diffuse negative publicity and messaging about the case.

In addition to urging the federal government to implement the IACHR's recommendations, advocates have sought to incorporate the Commission's findings and recommendations into state and local efforts addressing violence against women, including state court litigation and local policy making, a strategy discussed more generally in **Chapter VI**. Below is one example of an effort to incorporate the IACHR decision at the local level. What is the value added of reference to the *Lenahan* decision in the resolution below? What additional strategies might lawyers use to build on the decision in other advocacy efforts?

MIAMI-DADE BOARD OF COUNTY COMMISSIONERS, RESOLUTION EXPRESSING THE BOARD'S INTENT TO DECLARE THAT THE FREEDOM FROM DOMESTIC VIOLENCE IS A FUNDAMENTAL HUMAN RIGHT

Resolution No. R–644–12 (July 17, 2012).

WHEREAS, the Board of County Commissioners ("Board") of Miami-Dade County, Florida ("County") seeks to enhance the public welfare by declaring that the protection against domestic violence is a fundamental human right; and

WHEREAS, survivors of domestic violence must deal with the effects of physical injuries, long-term psychological damage, financial instability, and trouble finding safe housing; and

WHEREAS, more than 1 in 3 women and more than 1 in 4 men in the United States will experience rape, physical violence, and/or stalking by an intimate partner at some point in their lives; and this problem disproportionately impacts women of color, women with disabilities, women with low income, and immigrant women within Miami-Dade County, as well as their children; and

WHEREAS, according to 2011 Uniform Crime Reports, of the 111,681 reported domestic violence offenses Statewide, 9,313 occurred in Miami-Dade County, representing the highest number of domestic violence cases of any county in Florida; and

WHEREAS, of those 9,313 Miami-Dade County domestic violence offenses, about half (4,736) resulted in arrests; and of the 5,970 temporary injunctions issued in Miami-Dade County on domestic violence, dating violence, and sexual violence, twenty-three percent (1,401) resulted in the issuance of permanent injunctions; and

WHEREAS, in 2011, in Miami-Dade County, domestic violence victims made 5,567 crisis hotline and direct service calls for assistance; and shelters provided overnight protection to victims fleeing domestic violence 23,276 times; and there were 1,846 new admissions to residential and nonresidential domestic violence service facilities; and

WHEREAS, the United Nations Declaration on the Elimination of Violence Against Women recognizes the urgent need for the universal application to women of the rights and principles with regard to equality, security, liberty, integrity, and dignity of all human beings, and the United Nations Special Rapporteur on Violence Against Women has stated that "violence against women is the most pervasive human rights violation" and has urged the United States government to reassess laws and policies for protecting domestic violence survivors and for punishing abusers; and

WHEREAS, in 2011, the Inter-American Commission on Human Rights found in *Jessica Lenahan (Gonzales) v. United States* that the United States' failure to protect women from gender-based violence constitutes discrimination and a human rights violation, and urged the United States to enact law and policy reforms to protect victims of domestic violence and their children; and

WHEREAS, world leaders and leaders within the United States recognize that domestic violence is a human rights concern; and police and sheriffs departments, courts, counties, cities, social service agencies, and other local government entities constitute the first line of defense against domestic violence; and

WHEREAS, by recognizing that domestic violence is a human rights violation, Miami-Dade County will raise awareness and enhance domestic violence education in communities, the public and private sectors, and within government agencies,

NOW, THEREFORE, BE IT RESOLVED BY THE BOARD OF COUNTY COMMISSIONERS OF MIAMI-DADE COUNTY, FLORIDA, that:

Section 1. This Board expresses its intent to join world leaders and leaders [within] the United States in recognition of domestic violence as a human rights concern and declares that the freedom from domestic violence is a fundamental human right.

Section 2. This Resolution shall serve as a declaration to assure the citizens of the County that state and local governments bear a moral responsibility to secure this human right on behalf of their residents.

Section 3. This Resolution shall serve as a charge to all local government agencies to incorporate these principles into their policies and practices.

Section 4. A copy of this Resolution is to be sent to the Mayor, the Honorable Chair and Members of the Board of County Commissioners, the Director of the Miami-Dade Police Department, the Mayors and Commission and Council members of each municipality within Miami-Dade County.

NOTES & QUESTIONS

1.   Is the Miami Resolution effective in re-framing the "local" problem of domestic violence as an international human rights concern? Is the reference to the decision in *Lenahan* effective in this framing? What is the impact of framing the issue in this way?

2.   Why does the Miami Resolution place a particular emphasis on local government agencies? Is there something unique about the role of local officials in protecting against domestic violence? What can local actors do to reduce the incidence of domestic violence and provide protections and services to domestic violence victims? Are local governments obligated to address domestic violence as a human rights concern? Does Section 3 of the Miami Resolution impose a duty on local governments?

3.   How can the Miami Resolution be invoked to hold local officials accountable for human rights violations, such as the failure to protect people from domestic violence? How can lawyers representing domestic violence victims in cases seeking child custody or protective orders, or in housing cases or those seeking public benefits, integrate the Resolution into their advocacy on behalf of clients for whom domestic violence is a factor in their lives? How can the Resolution be used to raise awareness about domestic violence as a human rights concern more generally in the community?

4.   A number of other municipalities have adopted resolutions recognizing a human right to be protected from domestic violence. For a summary and the text of these resolutions, see Columbia Law School Human Rights Clinic & University of Miami School of Law Human Rights Clinic, Recognizing Freedom from Domestic Violence as a Fundamental Human Right: Local Resolutions Across the United States (as of May 14, 2014), http://web.law.columbia.edu/sites/default/files/microsites/human-rights-institute/files/2014.6.15_localdvresolutions_memo.pdf.

The *Lenahan* decision is part of an emerging jurisprudence in the Inter-American system and other jurisdictions regarding the due diligence standard in the context of violence against women. In the following brief, advocates sought to bring this jurisprudence before the New York Court of Appeals, New York's highest court. The plaintiff in the case, Carmen Valdez, sued the City of New York for breaching its duty to protect her after she notified a domestic violence detective that her former boyfriend, against whom she had an order of protection, had threatened to kill her. Despite assurances from the officer that the police would arrest the former boyfriend for violating the order of protection, the police took no action and, the next day, he shot Valdez, causing her permanent injuries. A jury found in favor of Valdez, awarding her damages, but an appellate court overturned the verdict on grounds that Valdez was not justified in relying on the police. As you read the following excerpt from an *amicus* brief filed in the appeal to the New York Court of Appeals, consider what impact the argument regarding the due diligence standard, including the citation to *Lenahan*, might have on the Court's consideration of the case.

BRIEF OF AMICI CURIAE NEW YORK CITY BAR ASSOCIATION ET AL. SUPPORTING PLAINTIFFS-APPELLANTS CARMEN VALDEZ ET AL. VALDEZ V. CITY OF NEW YORK

Court of Appeals of New York, 2011.
960 N.E.2d 356.

International law recognizes that there is a fundamental human right to be protected from gender-based violence, including domestic violence, and to effective remedies when such protection fails. This norm, as reflected in ratified treaties and other international instruments, now forms a part of customary international law, and should help guide this Court's consideration of whether withholding a remedy to a domestic violence survivor, as a matter of law, comports with governments' obligations to survivors. Amici curiae here do not cite international law as binding precedent but rather because it "cast[s] an empirical light on the consequences of different solutions to a common legal problem. . . ." Printz v. United States 521 U.S. 898, 976–77 [1997] (Breyer, J., dissenting).

Given the rich body of international law on the right to be free from gender-based violence, including victims' access to remedies, this Court can and should look to international law on this issue.

International law has long formed part of the common law of the United States. U.S. courts, including the U.S. Supreme Court and New York state courts, have routinely looked to this body of law as a guide to the proper interpretation of domestic constitutions and other laws.

Acknowledging the relevance of international law to domestic adjudication, the U.S. Supreme Court has repeatedly cited to and relied on international and foreign materials in the course of interpreting U.S. law. Most recently in *Graham v. Florida*, the Court reaffirmed its "longstanding practice" of "look[ing] beyond our Nation's borders for support for its independent conclusion that a particular sentence is cruel and unusual" for purposes of the Eighth Amendment.

New York state courts have a long history of employing foreign and international sources of law and indeed have shown "persuasive power" in the interpretation of customary international law doctrines.

. . .

The right to be protected from gender-based violence and to be afforded effective remedies when such protection fails is recognized in widely-ratified international and regional human rights treaties, including those ratified by the United States, numerous resolutions by the United Nations and other inter-governmental organizations, decisions of international tribunals, and the laws and practices of other nations. Inherent in this right is the obligation on states to undertake reasonable measures to protect women from acts of violence where there is a real and immediate risk of harm to a particular individual or family. This "due diligence" obligation requires that states adopt measures aimed at preventing such violence from occurring in the first place, investigating it when it does, and punishing perpetrators-an obligation that applies equally whether the perpetrator is a state or private actor. It also requires that states provide compensation and redress for victims and survivors of such violence. The right to be free from gender-based violence and concomitant "due diligence" obligation on states to protect victims from such violence is now [so] well established under international law that it has attained the status of customary international law.

In Ms. Valdez's case, from the issuance of the protective order and her call to the police regarding its violation, the relevant authorities knew of the risk of harm she faced and asserted that an arrest would occur immediately, yet they failed to act. Instead, the police arguably increased the risk of harm to Ms. Valdez by instructing her to return to her home, contrary to her original safety plan. In these circumstances, international law would require that the relevant authorities enforce the terms of the order of protection or otherwise take effective preventive measures, given their knowledge of the threat she faced. *See* United Nations, Report of the Special Rapporteur on Violence Against Women, Its Causes and Consequences, Rashida Manjoo, Mission to the United States of America, A/HRC/17/26/Add. 5, 13, 15, 115 (June 1, 2011)   *See e.g.* Beijing Declaration and Platform for Action, Fourth World Conference on Women, at Annex I, ch IV, 125–30, UN Doc A/CONF.177/20 and A/CONF

.177/20/Add.1 (1995) (recognizing the right of women to be free from violence by affording "women who are subjected to violence with access to mechanism of justice and . . . to just and effective remedies for the harm they have suffered."); Beijing Declaration, para 125(h); *see also* Opuz v. Turkey, App No. 33401102 [Eur Ct HR June 9, 2009].

. . .

International tribunals and bodies have repeatedly held governments accountable for their failure to act with due diligence and given victims of domestic and gender-based violence access to remedies, including compensation, against governments that failed to protect them. For example, the European Court of Human Rights issued a judgment against the government of Turkey and awarded damages to Nahide Opuz, a domestic violence survivor, because the government had failed to take adequate steps to protect her and her family from repeated violence. *Opuz v. Turkey*, App No. 33401/02 [Eur Ct HR June 9, 2009]. In *Maria da Penha Maia Fernandes v. Brazil*, the Inter-American Commission on Human Rights concluded that Brazil had violated Ms. Fernandes's rights by delaying the prosecution of her abusive husband for attempted murder for 15 years. The Commission found that Ms. Fernandes was entitled to prompt and effective compensation from the government, and that Brazil must adopt measures that would ensure actual compensation, because the government had made it impossible "to institute timely proceedings for redress and compensation in the civil sphere." Case No. 12.051, Inter-Am CHR 704, OEA/Ser. L/V/II.111Doc20 Rev. 3, 61 [Apr. 16, 2001]. Similarly, in *MC. v. Bulgaria*, the European Court ruled that the government of Bulgaria owed compensation to a rape victim based partly on its failure to fully and effectively investigate rape cases. App No. 39272/98 185–87, 191–94 [Eur Ct HR Mar. 4, 2004].

These cases establish that a remedy to victims must be available when the government does not meet its legal obligations to protect. Because remedies were unavailable in the national courts, the victims had to tum to international bodies. *See e.g. Jessica Gonzales v. United States*, Case 12.626, Inter-Am CHR, OEA/Ser./L/V/II.128 Doc 19, (July 24, 2007). Here, Ms. Valdez sought such a remedy through a state court. To set aside the jury verdict as a matter of law would severely damage the availability of recourse for New York victims as guaranteed under international law.

. . .

Accordingly, the decision of the Appellate Division undermines New York's domestic violence laws and victim safety and conflicts with international law because it releases police from their legal obligation to enforce orders of protection, even when the police make an explicit assurance to the victim and as a result, she alters her safety plan.

. . .

NOTES & QUESTIONS

1.   The Court of Appeals declined to apply the due diligence standard, and upheld the lower court's dismissal of the plaintiff's complaint. Do you think the *amicus* brief is effective in discussing the relevance of due diligence jurisprudence to the New York State court? How might the argument have been strengthened?

2.   How else might the jurisprudence surrounding the Inter-American's Commission's due diligence standard, including the *Lenahan* decision, be used in federal and state court advocacy? For a discussion of ways in which advocates might incorporate *Lenahan* into a domestic litigation strategy, see Elizabeth M. Schneider et al., *Implementing the Inter-American Commission on Human Rights' Domestic-Violence Ruling*, 46 Clearinghouse Rev. 113, 115–16 (2012).

C. CASE STUDY: USING HUMAN RIGHTS MECHANISMS TO MOBILIZE FOR DOMESTIC CHANGE: THE WESTERN SHOSHONE

In this chapter, we explored the use of international and regional human rights mechanisms to advance advocacy within the U.S. In this section, we offer a final example of how these two systems can be leveraged to achieve an advocacy objective. This example centers on the Western Shoshone people and highlights, too, the unique status of the tribes under domestic and international law and the ways in which Native Americans have long engaged these mechanisms.

In many respects, Native men and women have been leaders in utilizing human rights mechanisms to push for changes within the United States. The unique status of tribes within the U.S. as independent sovereigns invites engagement with international human rights law as a common legal ground between the U.S. and the tribes.[7]

---

[7]   For more discussion of tribes' status under U.S. law and the intersections with human rights law, *see* Aliza Gail Organick, *Listening to Indigenous Voices: What the UN Declaration on the Rights of Indigenous Peoples Means for U.S. Tribes*, 16 U.C. Davis J. Int'l L. & Pol'y 171, 175–76 (2009). *See also* Kristen A. Carpenter & Angela R. Riley, *Essay: Indigenous Peoples and the Jurisgenerative Moment in Human Rights*, 102 Calif. L. Rev. 173 (2014); Lillian Aponte Miranda, *Indigenous Peoples as International Lawmakers*, 32 U. Pa. J. Int'l L. 203 (2010). United States Courts have not always accepted the concept of tribal sovereignty. *See generally* Philip P. Frickey, *(Native) American Exceptionalism in Federal Public Law*, 119 Harv. L. Rev. 431 (2005); Zachary S. Price, *Dividing Sovereignty in Tribal and Territorial Criminal Jurisprudence*, 113 Colum. L. Rev. 657 (2013). *See also* S. James Anaya, Indigenous Peoples in International Law (2d ed. 2004).

The advocacy of the Western Shoshone people concerning their ancestral lands provides an example of the ways in which indigenous peoples have used international human rights mechanisms to raise public awareness and apply pressure on the United States government as part of a comprehensive advocacy strategy. While this case study focuses on the Western Shoshone campaign, many other tribes have made appeals to United Nations or regional human rights bodies, including the Navajo and Onondaga Nations. Often these appeals involve efforts to gain the return of historic tribal lands or to protect sacred places from environmental desecration. The human rights issues raised by Native Americans in international fora also extend to issues of violence against women and poverty, which disparately affect the tribes.[8]

Background

Legal Context

The United Nations system has often provided Native Americans a more welcoming forum than United States' domestic venues. Indeed, when the United Nations recognized the unique status of indigenous peoples in a 2007 declaration, the U.N. Declaration on the Rights of Indigenous People (UNDRIP), the U.S. was one of only four countries that voted against the measure.[9] The United States eventually endorsed the Declaration in 2010.[10]

While not a binding treaty, UNDRIP sets out a range of baseline expectations for the status and treatment of indigenous peoples, including recognition of their rights to protect their cultural heritage and ancestral lands. For example, Article 28 of the Resolution provides that

> 1. Indigenous peoples have the right to redress, by means that can include restitution or, when this is not possible, just, fair and equitable compensation, for the lands, territories and resources which they have traditionally owned or otherwise occupied or used, and which have been confiscated, taken, occupied, used or damaged without their free, prior and informed consent.

---

[8]   The issue of violence against women was discussed by Native American women's groups in a hearing before the Inter-American Commission on October 25, 2011. *See* Press Release: *IACHR Hearing on Violence Against Native Women*, Indian Law Resource Center, *available at* http://www.indianlaw.org/safewomen/iachr-hearing-violence-against-native-women-us,

[9]   United Nations Declaration on the Rights of Indigenous Peoples, G.A. Res. 61/295, U.N. Doc. A/RES/47/1 (Sept. 7, 2007). The four countries that voted against UNDRIP in 2007 were the United States, Canada, New Zealand and Australia. *See generally* Robert T. Coulter, *The U.N. Declaration on the Rights of Indigenous Peoples: A Historic Change in International Law*, 45 Idaho L. Rev. 539 (2009).

[10]   Announcement of U.S. Support for the United Nations Declaration on the Rights of Indigenous Peoples: Initiatives to Promote the Government-to-Government Relationship and to Improve the Lives of Indigenous Peoples (Nov. 2010), *available at* http://www.state.gov/r/pa/prs/ps/2010/12/153027.htm.

> 2. Unless otherwise freely agreed upon by the peoples concerned, compensation shall take the form of lands, territories and resources equal in quality, size and legal status or of monetary compensation or other appropriate redress.

United Nations Declaration on the Rights of Indigenous Peoples, G.A. Res. 61/295, U.N. Doc. A/RES/47/1 (Sept. 7, 2007), Art. 28.

Importantly, the CERD Committee has opined that UNDRIP should be viewed as a guide to State Parties' obligations relating to indigenous peoples under CERD, effectively using CERD to give UNDRIP the weight of a treaty.[11] The U.S. has declined to adopt this approach.[12]

The Western Shoshone

The Western Shoshone people comprise several distinct Shoshone tribes that share a geographic and cultural heritage. Their ancestral lands encompass significant parts of Idaho, Nevada, California and Utah.

In 1863, the U.S. Government and the Western Shoshone entered into the Ruby Valley Treaty, which granted white settlers access to Western Shoshone land but did not transfer title. However, in the 1950s, the federal Indian Claims Commission determined that the Shoshone's rights had been extinguished through gradual encroachment of outside interests. The Commission awarded $26 million in compensation for the property, depositing the funds into a U.S. Treasury trust for the tribes. The Western Shoshone challenged this process, but in 1985 the U.S. Supreme Court agreed with the Commission, ruling that the Western Shoshone's rights ended when the compensation fund was created and the money placed in trust.[13] Because the tribes refused to accept the payment, however, the funds remained in the trust fund, undisbursed.

Some members of the Western Shoshone continued to pursue legal and other remedies after the Supreme Court's ruling. Taking the lead were Carrie and Mary Dann, members of the Dann Traditional Family, also known as the Dann Band. For 30 years these two women, ranching in a remote area of Nevada, refused to submit to the federal permit system imposed by the U.S. government, arguing that it contravened their traditional land rights. Rather, they allowed their horses and cattle to roam freely without regard to federal boundaries. On several occasions,

---

[11] Comm. on the Elimination of Racial Discrimination, *Concluding Observations—United States of America*, ¶ 29, U.N. Doc. CERD/C/USA/CO/6 (May 8, 2008).

[12] Periodic Report of the United States of America to the United Nations Committee on the Elimination of Racial Discrimination, Concerning the International Convention on the Elimination of All Forms of Racial Discrimination, June 12, 2013, ¶ 176 (stating that "the United States does not consider that the Declaration—a non-legally binding, aspirational instrument that was not negotiated for the purpose of interpreting or applying the CERD—should be used to reinterpret parties' obligations under the treaty").

[13] United States v. Dann, 470 U.S. 39, 41–45 (1985) (holding that Western Shoshone had been compensated for their land even though they refused to cooperate in distribution of the funds).

including in February 2003, federal agents rounded up and confiscated their livestock grazing on the disputed lands. In all, the Dann Band accumulated federal fines for trespass and other violations totaling more than $3 million, which they vowed they would never pay.[14]

Proceedings Before the Inter-American Commission on Human Rights

The Danns and their supporters turned to international and regional human rights systems as early as 1993, when the Indian Law Resource Center submitted a petition on their behalf to the Inter-American Commission on Human Rights. The petition alleged that the restrictions on the Danns' use of the ancestral Western Shoshone lands violated their rights guaranteed by the American Declaration on the Rights and Duties of Man, including rights to equality, a fair trial, and property. The federal government responded to the petition claiming that the petitioners had not exhausted domestic remedies, that the petition was not timely, and that it did not state any violations of the American Declaration.

While the parties wrangled over these threshold issues, events continued to unfold on the ground, as the Danns' accumulated fines mounted up. On two occasions, in response to Dann Band requests, the Inter-American Commission issued precautionary measures against the United States, requesting that the government suspend any further legal action against the Danns pending the Commission's full investigation of the matter.[15] The United States government did not respond.

Finally, in 1999, the Inter-American Commission ruled that the Danns' petition was admissible, i.e., that they had stated a claim and that they had properly exhausted their domestic remedies.[16] In supplemental briefing, the Danns, represented by Professor James Anaya and the Indian Law Resource Center, reiterated their claims on the merits.[17] The Inter-American Commission issued its final decision in 2003, stating that the United States was violating the Western Shoshone tribes' human rights. According to the Commission, the United States had used

---

[14] Charlie LeDuff, *U.S. Agents Seize Horses of Two Defiant Indian Sisters*, N.Y. Times, Feb. 7, 2003.

[15] The mechanism for precautionary measures is established in Article 25 of the IACHR Rules of Procedure. Under these rules, in serious and urgent situations, the Commission may request that a State adopt measures to prevent irreparable harm to persons or to the subject matter of the proceedings in connection with a pending petition, as well as to persons under the jurisdiction of the State concerned, independently of any pending petition. The Rules specify that these measures will have no preclusive effect on parties' arguments concerning the ultimate outcome of the dispute.

[16] Inter-American Commission on Human Rights, Report No. 99/99, Case 11–140, Mary and Carrie Dann v. United States (Sept. 27, 1999), *available at* http://www.cidh.oas.org/annualrep/99eng/Admissible/U.S.11140.htm.

[17] A law professor at the University of Arizona, James Anaya, served as the U.N. Special Rapporteur on the Situation of Human Rights and Fundamental Freedoms of Indigenous People from 2008 to 2014.

illegitimate means to assert ownership of the disputed lands.[18] The Commission directed the United States to provide a fair legal process to determine the Western Shoshones' land rights and to review the United States' laws, procedures and practices regarding property rights of indigenous peoples to ensure compliance with the American Declaration on the Rights and Duties of Man.

The United States did not respond to the Inter-American Commission decision and indeed, vigorously rejected the Commission's report "in its entirety" when it was presented with the Commission's preliminary findings.[19] However, in 2004, led by U.S. Senator Harry Reid of Nevada, Congress enacted the Western Shoshone Claims Distribution Act (WSCDA). Under the Act, the trust funds set aside decades earlier were to be used to make payments of more than $22,000 each to the approximately 5000 individuals who were at least one-quarter Western Shoshone. Notably, under this scheme, payments would be made to individuals rather than to the tribes, and formal tribal membership was not required in order to qualify for a payment. Accumulated interest on the trust funds was designated for educational and other support programs directed to the Western Shoshone.

The Act was controversial within the Western Shoshone community, but by 2004, decades of litigating land rights had taken their toll. In a vote, tribal members overwhelmingly supported the payment scheme offered by the Act, effectively rejecting the Dann's position that the Western Shoshone should continue to fight for land rights. Still, payment was by no means immediate, leaving opportunity for additional advocacy by those urging the U.S. government to recognize the land rights of the Western Shoshone.

One such effort was initiated by the Inter-American Commission itself. In a continuing effort to gain implementation of its decision—a regular Commission practice—in March 2007, the Inter-American Commission convened a meeting to discuss the status of United States' compliance with the Inter-American Commission's recommendations. Carrie Dann and her lawyer, Professor Anaya, participated in the meeting, along with representatives of the U.S. Government.[20] However, the United States maintained its position rejecting the Commission's report and recommendations.

---

[18] Dann v. United States, Case 11.140, Inter-Am. Comm'n H.R., Report No. 75/02, doc. 5 rev. 1 ¶ 112 (2002) (merits decision of Dec. 27, 2002).

[19] Observations of the Government of the United States to the Inter-American Commission on Human Rights Report No. 113/01 of October 15, 2001 concerning Case No. 11.140 (Mary and Carrie Dann), *available at* http://www.state.gov/s/l/38647.htm.

[20] Mary Dann died in 2005 at age 82.

Appeals to CERD and the Human Rights Committee

The Dann Band and the Indian Law Resource Center did not limit their human rights appeals to the Inter-American Commission. In fact, they strategically appealed to other international bodies as a way to increase pressure on the U.S. government to implement the Inter-American Commission's decision.

From 1999 to 2005, the Dann Band presented several requests to the CERD under the Committee's early warning and urgent action procedure. CERD's early warning and urgent procedures mechanisms were first articulated in a working paper in 1993 and adopted as part of CERD's regular practice in 1994. According to the Committee, early warning and urgent action procedures should be invoked to "prevent[ ] existing problems from escalating into conflicts."[21] Such procedures may include requests for early reports from state parties, engagement of other human rights bodies, and direct involvement of Committee representatives in resolving a conflict.

The CERD invited the United States government to submit responses to the Danns' requests for urgent action, but the government did not do so. In 2006, the CERD issued a decision recommending, among other things, that the United States "take immediate action to initiate a dialogue with the representatives of the Western Shoshone peoples," "[f]reeze any plan to privatize the Western Shoshone ancestral lands", and "[s]top imposing grazing fees . . . on the Western Shoshone people."[22]

The U.S. did not respond immediately to the Committee's recommendations, but over the next few years, the topic of Western Shoshone land rights was repeatedly addressed by both the United States and the CERD. When United States' compliance with the CERD treaty was reviewed in 2008, the U.S. attached a separate annex to its submission discussing the case. Members of the Dann Band and their lawyers attended the United States review hearings in Geneva to further press their case before the Committee. At the end of the proceeding, the Committee's Concluding Observations again expressed concern over the United States' position and asked for additional information on United States compliance with the CERD Convention within one year.[23]

---

[21] *CERD, Guidelines for the Early Warning and Urgent Action Procedures, Annual report A/62/18, Annexes, Chapter III.*

[22] Comm. for the Elimination of Racial Discrimination, Early Warning and Urgent Action Procedure Decision 1, 68th Sess., Feb. 20–Mar. 10, 2006, CERD/C/USA/DEC/1 (Apr. 11, 2006) (finding that United States' continued efforts to privatize Western Shoshone lands and allow for destructive activities on them, such as nuclear testing, violated the Western Shoshone's right to equal treatment under the law).

[23] Comm. on the Elimination of Racial Discrimination, *Concluding Observations—United States of America,* ¶¶ 19 45, U.N. Doc. CERD/C/USA/CO/6 (May 8, 2008).

In 2009, the U.S. government included the following paragraphs in its follow-up report to the Committee, stressing the growing internal divisions within the Western Shoshone tribe:

As explained in a special annex to its most recent periodic report, the United States recognizes, as a historical matter, that indigenous people throughout the world have been unfairly deprived of lands they once habitually occupied or roamed. Such ancestral lands once constituted most of the Western Hemisphere. In 1946, recognizing that many Indian tribes in the United States had been unfairly deprived of such lands, the United States Congress established a special body, the Indian Claims Commission ("ICC"), to hear such claims by Indian tribes, bands, or other identifiable groups for compensation of lands that had been taken by private individuals or the government. In 1951, the Western Shoshone, represented by the Te-Moak Bands, successfully brought such a claim. The parties to the litigation stipulated that the lands were taken in 1872. A valuation trial was held and the ICC declared the value of the lands and sub-surface rights as of the valuation date.

The petitions submitted by certain Western Shoshone descendants to the CERD concern an internal dispute among Western Shoshone descendants about the litigation strategy pursued in that claim. However, they failed to raise their objections in a timely manner. Specifically, the ICC and appellate court found that their attempt to intervene in the proceedings was untimely because: (1) they had waited 23 years from the start of the case before seeking to participate, despite admitting in their filings to the court that they had been aware of the ICC proceedings; (2) they had not presented an excuse to the court for the delay; and (3) they had not demonstrated fraud or collusion by the representatives of the Western Shoshone in the litigation. Because they have been unsuccessful in pursuing their objections, certain Western Shoshone descendants who disagreed with the litigation strategy now seek to bring the issue of an 1872 land taking claim to the CERD Committee, despite ample recourse before U.S. courts, including the United States Supreme Court, and despite the fact that their position does not represent the views of all Western Shoshone descendants, most of whom wish to receive the compensation awarded by the ICC.

Periodic Report of the United States of America to the United Nations Committee on the Elimination of Racial Discrimination, Concerning the International Convention on the Elimination of All Forms of Racial Discrimination, June 12, 2013, ¶ 176.

The Dann's international advocacy also extended beyond the CERD. In 2006, the Dann Band submitted reports to the U.N. Human Rights Committee concerning U.S. compliance with the ICCPR, arguing that the policies affecting indigenous people violated United States' obligations under that treaty. And in 2006, the Danns submitted an urgent appeal to the U.N. Special Rapporteur on indigenous peoples to speak out on their behalf.

Subsequent Developments

Significantly delayed by the difficulty of making eligibility determinations and other bureaucratic challenges, the final distribution of the Treasury trust fund payments was not completed until 2012. Western Shoshone resistance to federal land rights continues in some quarters—Carrie Dann, in particular, continues to resist—but the fact that so many individuals within the tribe accepted federal payments for the land has muted the continued pursuit of international human rights remedies for violations of Western Shoshone land rights arising from the Ruby Valley Treaty.

Groups of Western Shoshone nevertheless continue to vigorously pursue international remedies for other claims, such as environmental degradation of sacred lands.[24] Further, other indigenous groups continue to actively pursue international human rights remedies, including, as discussed below, advocacy by the Navajo Nation objecting to commercial uses of the San Francisco Peaks within their ancestral territory.

NOTES & QUESTIONS

1.   Did the human rights advocacy of the Western Shoshone appear to make a difference in their situation? Did international involvement contribute to a resolution of the land rights dispute? Can an international human rights body effectively intervene in a domestic dispute between a government and indigenous populations? Note that the Inter-American Commission was careful to focus its attention on processes rather than on the merits of the Ruby Valley Treaty and subsequent interpretations.

2.   What recourse does a litigant have when the U.S. government simply refuses to comply with an order issued by an international human rights body such as the Inter-American Commission? What is the impact of such refusal on the international institution issuing the order and on the perceived efficacy of international human rights law in general? When individuals and groups see a value in appealing to international human rights bodies, is there a way for them to mitigate such negative impacts? Note that the issue of non-compliance is not unique to the U.S. or to indigenous issues. For example, the European Court of Human Rights has

---

[24] *See, e.g.,* South Fork Band Council of Western Shoshone of Nevada v. U.S. Dept. of Interior, 2012 WL 13780 (D.Nev., 2012) (suit to enjoin mining operations on disputed lands).

ruled repeatedly that blanket disenfranchisement of prisoners violates the European Convention on Human Rights, to which the United Kingdom is a party, yet the U.K. has failed to alter its laws and policies allowing such disenfranchisement. See Ruvi Ziegler, *UK vs ECtHR: The Prisoner Voting Saga Continues*, (OxHRH Blog, Aug. 14, 2014) <http://ohrh.law.ox.ac.uk/?p= 13089> [Aug. 16, 2014].

3. The Western Shoshone engaged human rights mechanisms alongside non-governmental organizations and other members of civil society. But are the tribes, with specific property claims against the government and quasi-sovereign status, really like other advocacy and activist groups? Should there be different human rights processes crafted for indigenous groups? If so, what should they look like?

4. For more background and history regarding the Western Shoshone's engagement with the regional and international human rights systems to defend their land rights, see Julie Cavanaugh-Hill, *Defining Human Rights When Economic Interests are High: the Case of the Western Shoshone*, *in* The Local Relevance of Human Rights 208–239 (De Feyter, et al., eds. 2011).

5. In May 2013, representatives of the Navajo Nation met with the U.N. Working Group on Business and Human Rights during the group's official visit to the United States. *See* Statement at the end of visit to the United States, U.N. Working Group on Business and Human Rights, Washington D.C. (May 1, 2013). The U.N. Working Group's mandate is focused on implementation of the U.N. Guiding Principles on Business and Human Rights. The Guiding Principles are discussed in detail in **Chapter XI**, *infra*, where their significance for legal ethics is examined. In this instance, however, the Navajo Nation raised substantive concerns about business practices under the Guiding Principles. Among the issues raised by the Navajo representatives was the commercial use of reclaimed wastewater in snowmaking by the ski resorts on the San Francisco Peaks, an area that is sacred to the Navajo and Hopi tribes. The U.S. Forest Service has concluded that use of wastewater in this way may be a responsible business practice given the dearth of available water in desert areas. However, some scientists have reported that the reclaimed wastewater is a breeding ground for antibiotic resistant bacteria. To consider the relevance of the Guiding Principles to this situation, you may now want to review the excerpts of the Principles set out in **Chapter XI, Part II**. The Guiding Principles are human rights guidelines for businesses, not a binding treaty. How might the Guiding Principles on Business and Human Rights be effectively utilized by native advocates in this context?

CHAPTER IX

HUMAN RIGHTS FACT-FINDING AND REPORTING

■ ■ ■

I. INTRODUCTION

Fact-finding and reporting are cornerstones of human rights advocacy, enabling activists to identify and expose human rights concerns and leverage greater awareness into a broader strategy. These projects have several phases. Human rights fact-finding involves identifying, collecting, and verifying information on human rights concerns. Reporting involves analyzing and presenting the collected information with an eye towards the relevant human rights standards, and developing recommendations based on field observations.

Human rights fact-finding and reporting may take different forms and be aimed at various and multiple audiences including governments, NGOs, U.N. and regional human rights bodies, and the media. For example, an advocacy organization seeking to protect voting rights may *collect* information on voting rights violations by conducting on-the-ground interviews and analyzing social science data, *frame* the findings in terms of internationally recognized human rights standards, and *present* the information in a report to the U.N. Human Rights Committee during its review of U.S. compliance with the International Covenant on Civil and Political Rights (ICCPR), urging specific recommendations for federal action and reform. The organization may use the same report as a basis for lobbying the U.S. Department of Justice to launch an investigation into violations identified in the report. And through press releases and other media outreach, it may use the report as a basis for media advocacy and a public awareness campaign, seeking to generate public support and pressure for the government to address the concerns identified in the report.

Human rights fact-finding and reporting often involve intense advance preparation and require advocates to be adept at interviewing, research, and analysis. They also require a strong grounding in the relevant human rights standards. The approach places a premium on credibility and accuracy, and implicates unique ethical and strategic concerns. While fact-finding and reporting projects need not involve lawyers, people with legal training bring relevant skills to these processes, including a nuanced understanding of human rights standards, training in fact-gathering and analysis, and professional attention to ethics. In this chapter, we explore some of these considerations and examine two human rights reports and the questions and critiques that they invite.

II. ESTABLISHING CREDIBILITY

The legitimacy and impact of human rights fact-finding and reporting depends on the fact-finders' credibility, accuracy, and impartiality. In the following article, Professor Diane Orentlicher discusses some of the important ways in which NGOs can establish and maintain legitimacy through fact-finding and analysis. Most of the examples that Professor Orentlicher relies upon involve fact-finding of significant and dramatic human rights violations, often in the context of armed conflict between or within countries other than the United States. As you read the following, consider whether the same issues and concerns are relevant for advocates engaged in human rights fact-finding and reporting related to activities occurring within or conducted by the United States.

DIANE F. ORENTLICHER, "BEARING WITNESS: THE ART AND SCIENCE OF HUMAN RIGHTS FACT-FINDING"
3 Harv. Hum. Rts. J. 83, 92–101 (1990).

The credibility of [NGOs'] fact-finding is their stock-in-trade. Broadly stated, the chief objective of human rights NGOs is to promote compliance with international human rights standards. As self-appointed watchdogs, NGOs have no "authority" to compel governments to bring their practices into compliance with those standards; NGOs can aspire only to *persuade* governments to respect the rights of individuals subject to the governments' jurisdictions. To this end, NGOs appeal to governments believed to be responsible for abuses to cease the violations. NGOs also frequently marshal external sources of pressure, such as the intervention of other governments or intergovernmental bodies. Fact-finding lies at the heart of these efforts, and the fact-finding "works" when it convinces the target audience that the published allegations are well founded.

Although critiques of NGO reporting do not reflect a coherent set of commonly acknowledged standards, it is possible to identify factors that figure prominently in public assessments of NGO fact-finding. The most frequently cited criteria fall into two categories. One relates to the integrity of an NGO's fact-finding methodology; the other takes account of various factors that are thought to indicate whether the NGO has an institutional bias—other than a bias in favor of human rights—that may taint the credibility of its conclusions.

. . .

A. Fact-Finding Methodology

Several aspects of the methodology underlying country reports tend to make even the most meticulous NGOs vulnerable to credibility challenges. . . .

1. The Effects of Government Secrecy and Intimidation

First, the fact-finding activities of the most prominent human rights NGOs tend to focus on violations of physical integrity, such as torture, extrajudicial executions, "disappearances," and arbitrary detention. The facts surrounding reported violations of this sort are rarely beyond dispute, in large part because the violations themselves are often deliberately shrouded in secrecy. . . . The obstacles to fact-finding posed by the state's nearly exclusive control of essential information are often compounded by other, related circumstances. In a context of widespread state lawlessness, for example, witnesses and victims often are afraid to provide testimony to human rights investigators, fearing retaliation by government forces. Moreover, a substantial number of countries in which gross violations are practiced on a systematic basis are closed to foreign investigators. In many countries, political repression is so severe that independent human rights monitors either cannot operate internally or do so under enormous constraints and at great personal risk. And in countries with serious systematic abuses, a bridled press often does not— because it cannot—provide independent accounts of human rights violations.

Thus, the circumstances in which human rights investigation is undertaken typically place substantial limitations on fact-finding. Though such constraints may be unavoidable, their effect on NGO methodology can invite challenge from a critical audience.

2. The Role of Interpretation

Second, the role of interpretation in the preparation of country reports contributes to their vulnerability to challenge. While it may be a truism that there are no "pure facts" and that any attempt to describe factual conditions entails substantial interpretation, the role of interpretation is particularly large in the context of human rights country reports. Because country reports aspire to describe broad patterns, the finder of fact must attempt not only to verify individual incidents of abuse, but also to reach more sweeping judgments about the extent of the violations, the nature of government (and, where relevant, insurgent) responsibility for the abuses, and the significance of apparent trends.

. . .

The point is that, however objective an NGO's methodology in ascertaining the "facts" about alleged human rights violations, its final conclusions draw upon qualitative interpretation of the data. While unavoidable, the substantial role of interpretation in human rights fact-finding leaves room for observers to reach different conclusions about the significance of even agreed upon facts.

Divergent conclusions about the "same" facts may also reflect differing judgments about a government's degree of moral culpability, or about the relative efficacy of alternative characterizations in promoting the institutional objectives of the fact-finding organization.

. . .

3. Applying Abstract Human Rights Standards

A third aspect of human rights fact-finding further increases the potential for different conclusions to emerge from the same facts: the investigator must measure facts against an abstract standard. Most NGOs evaluate states' compliance with internationally recognized human rights standards. Some NGOs also assess state practices in light of protections embodied in domestic law. Thus, in seeking to verify a reported violation, NGOs must attempt to determine both what actually happened, and whether the facts, under all the attendant circumstances, constitute a violation of relevant standards. These determinations often require difficult judgment calls, and it is scarcely surprising that different analysts sometimes reach different judgments about the legality of particular conduct.

B. Institutional Credibility

Recent critiques of NGO fact-finding have focused as much on indicia of institutional credibility as on methodology. Challenges to the institutional credibility of NGOs have focused on two charges in particular.

1. Political "Balance"

The first charge is that a survey of an NGO's work betrays a high degree of selectivity in the countries that are monitored, and that the selection is driven by a decided political slant. When applying this measure, critics often make reference to both the range of countries which an NGO has scrutinized and the evenhandedness of the organization's application of international standards to different countries' human rights records. Thus, even NGOs that attempt to monitor countries of every political orientation have been criticized for "going easier" on countries of one political shading than another. Sometimes the apparent disparity has been largely a matter of tone—a difference in the moral fervor of an NGO's respective condemnations of similar violations by different governments. But in human rights reporting, in which shadings of language convey varying levels of opprobrium, tone is substance.

2. Anti-Government Bias

The second charge is that an NGO's work on a particular country betrays a political bias against the government and in favor of its opponents. The criticism often arises with respect to reports that examine countries in which the most serious abuses occur in a context of civil war. In these circumstances, government officials have frequently charged that an NGO report is biased if it criticizes only abuses by government forces, and not those of their armed adversaries.

. . .

There are, however, principled reasons for NGOs to monitor violations attributable only to government forces, and most domestic NGOs, as well as many international NGOs, follow this practice. These organizations base their work on international human rights law, which establishes international responsibility for violations only on the part of governments, in contrast to the laws of war (also known as humanitarian law), which generate international responsibility for violations by all sides to an armed conflict. Thus an NGO that bases its mandate exclusively on international human rights law is faithful to the law by focusing on government conduct.

. . .

3. Acknowledgment of Contextual Factors

Beyond such considerations as whether NGOs monitor both sides to an armed conflict or whether they monitor governments of the right and left with equal vigor, more subtle factors affect public perceptions of NGOs' credibility. Governments that are the subject of scrutiny as well as other audiences often evaluate NGO reporting according to its "fairness" in a particular sense: whether it acknowledges contextual factors that place violations "in perspective."

. . .

While signaling that the NGOs' motive in publicizing government abuses is not political, these types of "contextual" observations serve a separate function as well: they anticipate and address the target government's (or other target audiences') possible inclination to dismiss the NGO's reports as politically motivated, naive, inappropriate, or irrelevant. By addressing the government's dilemma head on, NGOs recognize its predicament without accepting the abuses of its armed opponents as justification for state-sponsored violations of fundamental rights.

Inclusion of textual information to this end reflects a peculiar aspect of NGO reports: they form part of an ongoing dialogue with the target government and, often, with other audiences. By acknowledging that the government has committed human rights violations as a response to circumstances that help explain its behavior, the NGO has anticipated the next stage in the dialogue—the government's response—and answered it.

A key point to be made here is that human rights reports are not merely abstract factual accounts. The reports are advocacy tools, designed to promote change in government practices. As such, their presentation of facts is designed to respond to factors likely to affect the report's impact.

Emerging standards used to judge institutional credibility place somewhat conflicting demands on NGOs concerned with maximizing the persuasive impact of their reports. In principle, the public judges NGO reporting as "fair" and "balanced" if the organization measures every government's record against the same, universal standards; in practice, however, the perceived fairness or balance of particular reports often depends upon the extent to which the report takes account of contextual factors that are peculiar to the country concerned. Thus public perceptions of "fair" and "balanced" reporting is often a relative matter, and even NGOs that are genuinely committed to the principle that human rights fact-finding must be politically neutral face substantial challenges in their efforts to appear so.

To the extent that an NGO's reports explicitly address a current policy debate, there are even more substantial risks that the report will be discredited as politically motivated.

. . .

NOTES & QUESTIONS

1.   Professor Orentlicher notes that most of the prominent human rights NGOs focus their fact-finding activities on violations of physical integrity. In the years since her article was published, many human rights organizations have widened the focus of their fact-finding efforts. Many now engage in fact-finding on issues related to labor rights and other economic, social, and cultural rights. Similarly, Orentlicher's excerpt discusses NGO fact-finding efforts which focus exclusively on governments. Today, many human rights NGOs document abuses by business entities (many with related government violations through the failure to protect). For an example of a fact-finding report that does both, see Human Rights Watch, Blood, Sweat and Fear: Workers' Rights in the U.S. Meat and Poultry Plants (Jan. 25, 2005), *available at* http://www.hrw.org/en/reports/2005/01/24/blood-sweat-and-fear. Are the concerns with methodology and institutional credibility that Orentlicher raises relevant to fact-finding on matters related to economic,

social, and cultural rights and abuses by business entities? Are there additional, or different, concerns that might be relevant?

2. Another critique of human rights fact-finding focuses on the relationship between the researchers and their subjects. Professor David Kennedy argues that reporting on the "victims" of human rights abuses is an "[i]nherently voyeuristic or pornographic practice" which inevitably "transforms the position of the victim in his or her society and produces a language of victimization for him or her to speak on the international stage." David Kennedy, The Dark Sides of Virtue: Reassessing International Humanitarianism 29 (2004). Barbora Bukovska, a human rights advocate who works in Central and Eastern Europe, agrees with Kennedy's critique. She argues that by "discussing victims as objects of research rather than giving them the opportunity to be subjects of a whole process, the human rights reporters maintain control over them, their reports perpetuating the image of victims as incapable individuals or groups that must be saved from their misery by human rights advocates." Barbora Bukovska, *Perpetrating Good: Unintended Consequences of International Human Rights Advocacy*, 9 Sur Int'l J. on Hum. Rts. 7, 12 (2008). Moreover, in her personal experience, "the contacts that international organizations producing reports have with victims stop with the end of their fact-finding missions. The victims are almost never subsequently visited and are not given help either with the documented problems or with the potential backlash that they might face because of the report." *Id.* Thus, Bukovska suggests that the reporting process can itself result in a new form of victimization for its subjects. *Id.* Kennedy and Bukovska are focused on international human rights fact-finding. Do you think these critiques are equally applicable in the context of domestic human rights lawyering? See, for example, some of the critiques of advocacy following Hurricane Katrina, explored in **Chapter X**.

3. When domestic lawyers are engaged in human rights fact-finding and monitoring, there may be additional ethical considerations. Are any of the Rules of Professional Conduct that govern lawyers pertinent here? Suppose a domestic lawyer is employed by the ACLU to oversee a human rights monitoring and documentation project targeting the treatment of employees in catfish factories in Mississippi. She would like to use a testing process to gather information, placing ACLU representatives in jobs in the factories so that they can report first-hand on the conditions. Is the ACLU her client? What is the testers' relationship to the catfish factories? Should she be concerned about her state's version of Model Rule 4.1, which provides that "[i]n the course of representing a client a lawyer shall not knowingly make a false statement of material fact or law to a third person." Would she be precluded from engaging in her monitoring project if other lawyers from the ACLU filed a class action suit against the same catfish factories in Mississippi that she is targeting? What impact might the lawyer's fact-finding activities have in the litigation context? For example, is the information subject to discovery? Are there any other ethical concerns? *See Apple Corps Ltd. v. International Collectors Soc.*, 15 F. Supp. 2d 456, 475–476

(D.N.J. 1998) (Rule "8.4(c) does not apply to misrepresentations solely as to identity of purpose and solely for evidence gathering purposes."); Ala. State Bar's Office of the General Counsel, Ethics Opinion No. RO–89–31 (1989) (it is permissible for a lawyer to direct an investigator to pose as a customer in order to determine whether the plaintiff lied about injuries). *See also* David B. Isbell and Lucantonio N. Salvi, *Ethical Responsibility of Lawyers for Deception by Undercover Investigators and Discrimination Testers: An Analysis of the Provisions Prohibiting Misrepresentations Under the Model Rules of Professional Conduct*, 8 Geo. J. Legal Ethics 791, 816 (1995). *But see In re Conduct of Gatti*, 330 Or. 517, 8 P.3d 966 (2000) (Oregon Supreme Court reprimanded lawyer for lying when he posed as a doctor during telephone calls to an insurance company he was preparing to sue). In response to the decision in *In re Gatti*, the Oregon legislature passed into law House Bill 3857 (signed into law June 28, 2001) which authorizes prosecutors and other government lawyers to "participate in covert activities that are conducted by public bodies . . . for the purpose of enforcing laws, or in covert activities that are conducted by the federal government for the purpose of enforcing laws, even though the participation may require the use of deceit or misrepresentation." H.B. 3857, 2001 Leg., Reg. Sess. (Or. 2001). H.B. 3857 leaves the holding of *In re Gatti* intact for private lawyers in cases not connected to governmental activities.

III. GUIDELINES FOR CONDUCTING HUMAN RIGHTS FACT-FINDING

Though there are no general binding rules for advocates seeking to engage in human rights fact-finding, the U.N. Office of the High Commissioner for Human Rights has developed a set of guidelines for human rights monitoring conducted by U.N. human rights officers ("HROs"). Despite the stated focus on HROs working under the mandate of the U.N., the introduction to the manual indicates that the guidelines are relevant to non-governmental organizations, as well. As you read the following, think about the implications of each principle for U.S. advocates seeking to engage in domestic human rights fact-finding.

U.N. OFFICE OF THE HIGH COMMISSIONER FOR HUMAN RIGHTS, CHAPTER 5: BASIC PRINCIPLES OF MONITORING

Training Manual on Human Rights Monitoring, No. 7 (2001).

A. Introduction

1. This chapter identifies eighteen basic principles of monitoring which HROs should keep in mind as they pursue their monitoring functions as described in the following chapters, including information gathering, interviewing, visits to persons in detention, visits to internally displaced persons and/or refugees in camps, monitoring the return of refugees and/or internally displaced persons, trial observation, election

observation, monitoring demonstrations, monitoring economic, social and cultural rights, monitoring during periods of armed conflict, verification and assessment of the information collected, and use of the information to address human rights problems.

B.   Monitoring as a method of improving the protection of human rights

2.   Monitoring is a method of improving the protection of human rights. The principal objective of human rights monitoring is to reinforce State responsibility to protect human rights. HROs can also perform a preventative role through their presence. When a Government official or other responsible actor is monitored, s/he becomes more careful about her/his conduct.

3.   HROs must relate their work to the overall objective of human rights protection. They can record observations and collect information for immediate action and later use. They can communicate the information to the appropriate authorities or other bodies. HROs should not only observe developments, collect information, and perceive patterns of conduct, but should, as far as their mandate allows and their competence permits, identify problems, diagnose their causes, consider potential solutions, and assist in problem solving. While exercising good judgement at all times, HROs should take initiative in solving problems and, provided they are acting within their authority and competence, should not wait for a specific instruction or express permission before acting.

C.   Do no harm

4.   HROs and the operation they are assigned to should make every effort to address effectively each situation arising under their mandate. Yet, in reality, HROs will not be in a position to guarantee the human rights and safety of all persons. Despite their best intentions and efforts, HROs may not have the means to ensure the safety of victims and witnesses of violations. It is critical to remember that the foremost duty of the officer is to the victims and potential victims of human rights violations. For example, a possible conflict of interest is created by the HRO's need for information and the potential risk to an informant (victim or witness of the violation). The HRO should keep in mind the safety of the people who provide information. At a minimum, the action or inaction of HROs should not jeopardize the safety of victims, witnesses or other individuals with whom they come into contact, or the sound functioning of the human rights operation.

D.   Respect the mandate

5.   A detailed mandate facilitates dealing with UN headquarters, other UN bodies (especially those less sensitive to human rights imperatives), and all other involved parties. Every HRO should make an

effort to understand the mandate, bear it in mind at all times, and learn how to apply and interpret it in the particular situations s/he will encounter. In evaluating the situation, HROs should consider such questions as: What are the relevant terms of the mandate? What are the relevant international standards underlying and explicating the mandate? How will the mandate be served by making a particular inquiry, by pursuing discussions with the authorities, or by taking any other course of action? What action am I authorized to undertake under the mandate? What are the ethical implications, if any, of that course of action? How will the action being considered by the HRO be received by the host Government? What potential harm could be caused by the action under consideration?

E.   Know the standards

6.   HROs should be fully familiar with the international human rights standards which are relevant to their mandate and applicable to the country of operation. International human rights standards not only define the HROs' mandate, but also provide sound legal basis and legitimacy to the work of the HRO and the UN operation in a specific country, in that they reflect the will (or the agreement) of the international community and define the legal obligations of the Government.

F.   Exercise good judgement

7.   Whatever their number, their relevance and their precision, rules cannot substitute for the good personal judgement and common sense of the human rights officer. HROs should exercise their good judgement at all times and in all circumstances.

G.   Seek consultation

8.   Wisdom springs from discussion and consultation. When an HRO is dealing with a difficult case, a case on the borderline of the mandate or a case which could be doubtful, it is always wise to consult other officers and, whenever possible, superiors. Similarly, HROs will ordinarily work in the field with several UN and other humanitarian organizations; they should consult or make sure that there has been appropriate consultation with those organizations to avoid duplication or potentially contradictory activity.

H.   Respect the authorities

9.   HROs should keep in mind that one of their objectives and the principal role of the UN operation is to encourage the authorities to improve their behaviour. In general, the role envisaged for HROs does not call for officers to take over governmental responsibilities or services. Instead, HROs should respect the proper functioning of the authorities, should welcome improvements, should seek ways to encourage

governmental policies and practices which will continue to implement human rights after the operation has completed its work.

I. Credibility

10. The HRO's credibility is crucial to successful monitoring. HROs should be sure not to make any promises they are unlikely or unable to keep and to follow through on any promise that they make. Individuals must trust the HROs or they will not be as willing to cooperate and to produce reliable information. When interviewing victims and witnesses of violations, the HRO should introduce him/herself, briefly explain the mandate, describe what can and cannot be done by the HRO, emphasize the confidentiality of the information received, and stress the importance of obtaining as many details as possible to establish the facts (for example, whether there has been a human rights violation).

J. Confidentiality

11. Respect for the confidentiality of information is essential because any breach of this principle could have very serious consequences: (a) for the person interviewed and for the victim; (b) for the HROs' credibility and safety; (c) for the level of confidence enjoyed by the operation in the minds of the local population; and thus (d) for the effectiveness of the operation. The HRO should assure the witness that the information s/he is communicating will be treated as strictly confidential. The HRO should ask persons they interview whether they would consent to the use of information they provide for human rights reporting or other purposes. If the individual would not want the information attributed to him or her, s/he might agree that the information may be used in some other, more generalized fashion which does not reveal the source. The HRO should take care not to communicate his/her judgements or conclusions on the specific case to those s/he interviews.

12. Special measures should also be taken to safeguard the confidentiality of recorded information, including identities of victims, witnesses, etc. The use of coded language and passwords, as well as keeping documents which identify persons in separate records from facts about those persons, may be useful means to protect the confidentiality of information collected.

K. Security

13. This basic principle refers both to the security of the HRO and of the persons who come in contact with him/her .... HROs should protect themselves by taking common-sense security measures, such as avoiding travelling alone, reducing risks of getting lost, and getting caught in cross-fire during an armed conflict.

14. HROs should always bear in mind the security of the people who provide information. They should obtain the consent of witnesses to

interview and assure them about confidentiality. Security measures should also be put in place to protect the identity of informants, interviewees, witnesses, etc. The human rights officer should not offer unrealistic guarantees concerning the safety of a witness or other individual, should avoid raising false hopes, and should be sure that any undertakings (such as keeping in touch) to protect the victim or witness can be kept.

L. Understand the country

15. HROs should endeavour to understand the country in which they work, including its people, history, governmental structure, culture, customs, language, etc. HROs will be more effective, and more likely to receive the cooperation of the local population, the deeper their understanding of the country.

M. Need for consistency, persistence and patience

16. The collection of sound and precise information to document human rights situations can be a long and difficult process. Generally, a variety of sources will have to be approached and the information received from them will have to be examined carefully, compared and verified. Immediate results cannot always be expected. The HRO should continue his/her efforts until a comprehensive and thorough inquiry has been completed, all possible sources of information have been explored, and a clear understanding of the situation has been obtained. Persistence may be particularly necessary in raising concerns with the Government. Of course, cases will arise in which urgent action is required (e.g., if there is evidence of an imminent threat to a particular individual or group). The HRO should promptly respond to such urgent cases.

N. Accuracy and precision

17. A central goal of the HRO is to provide sound and precise information. The information produced by the HRO will serve as the basis for the officer's immediate or future action with the local authorities, or the action of his/her superiors, or action by the Headquarters of the operation, or by other UN bodies. The provision of sound and precise information requires thorough and well-documented reports. The HRO should always be sure to ask precise questions (e.g., not just whether a person was beaten, but how many times, with what weapon, to what parts of the body, with what consequences, by whom, etc.).

18. Written communication is always essential to avoid lack of precision, rumours and misunderstandings. Reports prepared by HROs should reflect thorough inquiries, should be promptly submitted, and should contain specific facts, careful analysis and useful recommendations. Reports should avoid vague allusions and general

descriptions. All conclusions should be based on detailed information included in the report.

O. Impartiality

19. The HRO should keep in mind that the UN operation is an impartial body. Each task or interview should be approached with an attitude of impartiality with regard to the application of the mandate and the underlying international standards. Violations and/or abuses by all parties should be investigated with equal thoroughness. The HRO should not be seen as siding with one party over another.

P. Objectivity

20. The HRO should maintain an objective attitude and appearance at all times. When collecting and weighing information, the HRO should objectively consider all the facts. The HRO should apply the standard adopted by the UN operation to the information received in an unbiased and impartial way.

Q. Sensitivity

21. When interviewing victims and witnesses, the HRO should be sensitive to the suffering which an individual may have experienced, as well as to the need to take the necessary steps to protect the security of the individual—at least by keeping in contact. The HRO must be particularly sensitive to the problems of retraumatization and vicarious victimization. . . . HROs should also be very careful about any conduct or words/phrases which might indicate that their concern for human rights is not impartial or that they are prejudiced.

R. Integrity

22. The HRO should treat all informants, interviewees and co-workers with decency and respect. In addition, the officer should carry out the tasks assigned to him/her in an honest and honourable manner.

S. Professionalism

24. The HRO should approach each task with a professional manner. The officer should be knowledgeable, diligent, competent and fastidious about details.

T. Visibility

25. HROs should be sure that both the authorities and the local population are aware of the work pursued by the UN operation. The presence of visible HROs can deter human rights violations. As a general rule, a visibly active monitoring presence on the ground can provide some degree of protection to the local population since potential violators do not want to be observed. Also, a highly visible monitoring presence can reassure individuals or groups who are potential victims. Moreover, a

visible monitoring presence can help to inspire confidence in crucial post-conflict processes, such as elections, reconstruction and development. Hence, effective monitoring means both seeing and being seen.

In 2009, the International Bar Association's Human Rights Institute and the Raoul Wallenberg Institute released a set of guidelines for NGOs and individuals engaged in human rights fact-finding and reporting. Unlike the U.N. guidelines, these standards, known as the Lund-London Guidelines, are aimed directly at NGOs and individuals, rather than U.N. human rights officers. The stated objective of the guidelines is to establish a standard for ensuring accuracy and credibility in fact-finding activities. How do the Lund-London Guidelines differ from the U.N. guidelines? What might account for the differences?

GUIDELINES FOR INTERNATIONAL HUMAN RIGHTS FACT-FINDING VISITS AND REPORTS (THE LUND-LONDON GUIDELINES)

Raoul Wallenberg Institute of Human Rights and Humanitarian Law
and the International Bar Association, 2009.

Definition of Fact Finding

1.   For the purpose of these guidelines, fact-finding means a mission or visit mandated by an NGO to ascertain the relevant facts relating to and elucidating a situation of human rights concern, whether allegedly committed by state or non-state actors. In many instances this activity will result in a report. These guidelines do not prejudice the use of other methods of collecting information, other ventures or the use of fact finding in other contexts.

Instigation of a Fact-Finding Mission

2.   Where a situation of concern is identified, a fact-finding mission should be considered in the light of the mandate, priorities, resources and procedures of the NGO. The NGO should consider the possible negative consequences of undertaking a mission.

3.   The NGO should take into account the work that other relevant organisations have done or are doing on the same situation and of the effect any previous missions or public statements relating to the situation have had. In order to strengthen efforts and maximise the effective use of resources, cooperation with those other organisations should be considered.

Terms of Reference for the Mission

4. The terms of reference must be determined prior to the mission. These should relate to the specific situations under investigation bearing in mind the NGO's mandate.

5. The terms of reference must not reflect any predetermined conclusions about the situation under investigation.

6. The terms of reference should be clear, concise and relevant. However, they should be sufficiently flexible to permit the investigation of and reporting on any other related relevant circumstances.

7. If unforeseen situations arise which are outside of the mission's terms of reference the delegation should report those to the relevant NGO contact person as soon as possible. If the new situation falls within the mandate and expertise of the NGO, it may decide to extend the terms of reference or create a second mission. If the former, the NGO should be confident that the delegation has the competence and expertise to deal with the new situation. If the new situation falls outside the mandate and expertise of the NGO, it should refer the matter to another organisation which can take action.

Composition of the Delegation

8. The mission's delegation should comprise individuals who are and are seen to be unbiased. The NGO should be confident that the delegation members have the competence, experience and expertise relevant to the matters pertaining to the terms of reference.

9. The NGO should ensure that delegation members have sufficient time for pre-mission briefings and/or training for implementation of the mission and any proposed follow-up work, including contributing to the report.

10. The NGO should ensure that all members of the delegation are aware that they must, at all times, act in an independent, unbiased, objective, lawful and ethical manner.

11. The NGO should ensure appropriate gender balance in the composition of the delegation. Where relevant, the NGO may wish to consider such issues as geographic, racial, ethnic or other types of balance and diversity when selecting the delegation members. The NGO may also wish to consider the importance of linguistic expertise and/or in-country knowledge.

12. The NGO should identify a leader of the delegation and/or a rapporteur.

13. As and where appropriate, delegations should be comprised of people with relevant expertise and skills in interviewing members of specific victim groups, especially when these are children, women, victims of

torture or other vulnerable groups and internally displaced persons. See also paragraph 45.

14. When appointing a member of a delegation, the NGO should take into account any potential risk in appointing people of specific nationalities or members of particular religious groups, and any other reasons which might make it too dangerous for an individual to participate in the mission, or create danger for that person's family or others. This possibility should always be kept under review by the delegation and the NGO both before and during the visit.

Interpreters and Other Persons Associated with the Mission and/or Report

15. The NGO should ensure that all persons associated with a mission and/or a report are aware that they must, at all times, act in an independent, unbiased, objective, lawful and ethical manner.

. . .

18. Where necessary, interpreters should be used during the course of the mission. Every care must be taken in selection to ensure that interpreters are expert in the required languages and relevant technical concepts, as well as independent and professional.

. . .

Pre-Visit

20. The NGO should provide a pre-visit briefing for members of the delegation, which includes balanced material relating to the reason for the visit and any relevant cultural, economic, political, historical and legal information. Where necessary, any relevant material should be translated.

21. The NGO should also provide a briefing on local logistical issues, operating procedures, medical issues (including preparation for travel), appropriate conduct in-country and other relevant matters. All members of the delegation should be provided with a copy of these guidelines.

22. The NGO should ensure that the members of the delegation are confident that they have been adequately briefed and understand the terms of reference, the initial reason for the visit and the mandate of the NGO. If any member of the delegation is not sufficiently confident that their briefing has been adequate, the NGO should be informed and it should then provide additional briefing.

23. The NGO should ensure that the members of the delegation understand the need to be unbiased and not pre-judge any issues during the mission. The NGO must also ensure that the delegation understands the need to act in an ethical manner and in accordance with the laws of the country and internationally accepted human rights standards.

Awareness training, including gender sensitivity, should be provided where necessary.

24. The NGO should ensure that members of the delegation and persons associated with the mission receive clear and consistent messages about the mission, specifically its objectives and limitations, to ensure that the mission can be clearly explained to the people with whom they meet, so as to manage expectations and avoid miscommunication.

25. Where necessary, the NGO should ensure that all members of the delegation are fully briefed on recognising and managing stress and psychosocial trauma to prepare them properly for the realities of the situation and to promote the well-being of persons they interview, persons otherwise associated with the mission, and themselves.

26. The NGO is responsible for organising the visit, including the security, health and safety of the delegation. The NGO should ensure that appropriate emergency procedures are in place and that the delegation is fully briefed. It is the responsibility of the members of the delegation to act in accordance with any risk assessment made by the NGO and any formal requirements such as visa conditions as required by the laws of the country.

27. The NGO should as appropriate inform the government of the state in which the mission is to take place or any other relevant authorities that the mission will take place.

28. The NGO should consider what, if any, media strategy is appropriate for the delegation and for the mission overall. The NGO should ensure that all members of the mission are familiar with any strategy adopted.

Working Methods

General

29. The NGO has overall responsibility for the delegation and the mission.

30. The members of the delegation must conduct themselves with integrity, professionalism and in accordance with international human rights law standards at all times during the mission.

31. If a member of the delegation, or any other person associated with the mission, conducts him-or herself in a way which jeopardises the mission, the safety of others or the confidentiality of sources, or in any other way acts without sufficient professionalism or integrity, that person should be required to leave the mission. In such situations it will be for the NGO, in consultation with the leader of the delegation, to determine whether to abandon the mission or replace that person. If the team leader is implicated, or is otherwise unavailable, any other member of the delegation may draw the matter to the attention of the NGO.

32. If it transpires during the course of the mission that there is a conflict of interest or other circumstances involving any member of the delegation which might jeopardise their independence and impartiality, or which might give the appearance that their independence and integrity is compromised, the leader of the delegation should inform the NGO and that member should desist from participating in a particular meeting, or where necessary from the remainder of the mission. If the team leader is implicated, or is otherwise unavailable, any other members of the delegation may draw the matter to the attention of the NGO.

33. Any threats to, or intimidation of, the delegation must be reported immediately to the NGO. Where appropriate, the NGO will need to seek assurances from the government as to the safety of the delegation and should initiate emergency procedures should they be required.

Agenda

34. The NGO, in collaboration with the delegation, should determine criteria for selecting the people and locations it wishes to visit, make the necessary arrangements and draw up a schedule for the visit, as far as possible. In so doing, the NGO should take into account the safety and security of potential interviewees and persons associated with them. It may be necessary to amend the schedule as the mission progresses.

35. Wherever possible the delegation should interview all parties relevant to the situation under consideration in order to achieve a balanced, comprehensive picture. This might include members of the government, judiciary, parliamentarians, opposition party members, journalists, NGO personnel, academics, staff of intergovernmental organisations, or any other person who could reliably shed light on the situation under review.

36. The delegation is under no obligation to advise the government of the people it intends to meet. If the government or any other party finds out this information and there are concerns as to the safety of an interviewee, then the NGO may wish to cancel the interview or to abandon the mission and should seek a guarantee from the government that the interviewee or prospective interviewee will not be persecuted, victimised or otherwise put in a worse position for having been willing to cooperate with the delegation. The same principle applies if the interviewee is threatened as a result of identification by other people.

37. The delegation may wish to operate as a whole group, or may wish to separate into smaller groups for specific assignments.

Interviews

38. The delegation must take into account the safety and security of the interviewees.

39. The delegation should be mindful that the venues for interviews will ensure the protection and confidentiality of all involved and are culturally appropriate.

40. Interviews should be scheduled with sufficient time for the ascertainment of all the relevant facts and to give the interviewee an opportunity to express their opinion.

41. The delegation should inform interviewees of the terms of reference, as well as giving reasons for the visit, prior to or at the meeting, in a language they understand.

42. The delegation should take a careful note of whether an interviewee provides informed consent to be interviewed and identified or quoted and of future possible uses of their statements. If they do not consent, their wishes must be respected.

43. Where appropriate, interviews should be conducted by at least two members of the delegation. It should be clarified in all cases whether interviewees wish to have a supporting person present, or wish for some person to absent themselves during the interview.

44. Interviews should be consistent and thorough and be conducted in a professional manner.

45. Members of the mission should be especially aware of the vulnerabilities of particular categories of potential interviewees and such interviewees should be approached with the utmost care. Interviews of vulnerable groups must only be undertaken by those with the relevant expertise and skill (see paragraph 13). Particular methodological techniques should be considered in certain cases: for example, female victims of sexual abuse should be offered the choice of being interviewed by a female member of the delegation and a clear explanation given of the possible future need for testimony in criminal or other proceedings.

46. Members of the delegation should be alert to the possibility of stress or trauma experienced by interviewees and be ready to terminate the interview if necessary. Wherever possible, the delegation members should ensure that interviewees are referred to appropriate victim support services.

47. Members of the delegation should be alert to the humanitarian needs of interviewees and, wherever possible, should ensure that interviewees are referred to appropriate humanitarian or other organisations which might be able to meet those needs.

Information Gathering

48. It is essential that the delegation make use of all data collection techniques available. In addition to interviews, these may include site visits, collation of documents, or assessment of local laws and practices.

Where the delegation relies upon information gathered by a third party, the delegation should take all reasonable measures to verify the objectivity of that information gathering process in order to rely on the evidence collected. . . .

49. The delegation should take full and fair notes or, where necessary, ensure that these are being taken on the delegation's behalf.

50. The delegation should endeavour to obtain and review all relevant written materials and documents.

51. The delegation must ensure that all materials and information are collated for the drafter of the report.

52. All notes, transcripts and documents, including electronic date, together with other materials from the visit, should be kept secure at all times. If confidentiality cannot be secured, the interviewee should be informed in accordance with paragraph 42.

53. The delegation should document any relevant obstacles it has met during its visit and in relation to the collection of information.

54. In making their findings the delegation should try to verify alleged facts with an independent third party or otherwise. Where this is not possible, it should be noted.

55. In making their findings the delegation should work independently having regard to the terms of reference, the situation giving rise to the visit, and the mandate of any reasonable directions from the NGO.

56. The delegation should assess all the information gathered and reach conclusions to its reasonable satisfaction based on this assessment.

. . .

NOTES & QUESTIONS

1. Is there a need for international or universal norms for human rights fact-finding? What challenges might there be in developing and implementing such guidelines? Do the OHCHR guidelines address the methodological concerns raised in Professor Orentlicher's article? What about the Lund-London guidelines? If not, what additions to the principles would you propose?

2. Do the OHCHR and Lund-London guidelines seem sensible to you? Do they pose any potential challenges for advocacy organizations seeking to engage in human rights fact-finding? Do some provisions seem more important than others? Are all of the provisions relevant to advocates engaged in fact-finding in the U.S.?

3. Compare the OHCHR guidelines with the Lund-London guidelines. In what ways are they similar? How do they differ? What might account for the differences?

4.   Human rights fact-finding provides the basis for many of the NGO reports submitted to the U.N. treaty bodies as part of their review of U.S. compliance. Should the treaty bodies evaluate the NGO reports based on the U.N. principles? How might that influence NGO participation in the reporting process?

5.   In 2013, a group of U.N. and government officials, jurists, attorneys, and scholars gathered in Siracusa, Italy, to discuss best practices for international and national commissions of inquiry on issues related to investigations, data collection, and reporting. The experts' meeting resulted in a set of guiding principles for investigative commissions and fact-finding bodies, called the Siracusa Guidelines for International, Regional and National Fact-Finding Bodies. *See* International Institute for Higher Studies in Criminal Sciences (ISISC), Siracusa Guidelines for International, Regional and National Fact-finding Bodies (M. Cherif Bassiouni & Christina Abraham eds., 2013). To what extent should the guidelines developed by and for inter-governmental organizations such as the United Nations and national and regional fact-finding bodies apply to NGOs? Do NGOs have the same objectives, interests, and constraints as inter-governmental organizations and national bodies, particularly with respect to their fact-finding activities? For a discussion of some of the potential differences, and additional proposed standards for fact-finding by NGOs, see David Weissbrodt & James McCarthy, *Fact-Finding by Nongovernmental Organizations*, *in* International Law and Fact-Finding in the Field Of Human Rights 186, 186–230 (B.G. Ramcharan ed., 1982).

IV. THE IMPORTANCE OF METHODOLOGY

The methodology used for any human rights fact-finding project will depend on the focus, scope, and objective of the project, as well as the resources available to support it. Possible methodologies include observation, surveys, interviews, and document review, as well as quantitative social science research methods and use of social media and other newer technologies. Whatever the methodology chosen, prior to developing a research protocol, advocates should clearly identify the focus and goal of the project, develop a clear understanding of the relevant international human rights standards, domestic law, and other legal contexts, and assess the available resources, including time, expertise, and finances. The methodology underlying a human rights fact-finding project is critical to the credibility and accuracy of the resulting report.

Below, we present the methodology section of a report by a human rights advocacy organization documenting civilian casualties caused by U.S. drones strikes in Pakistan. In recent years, several human rights advocacy organizations have challenged the U.S. government's use of weaponized drone technology in Yemen, Afghanistan, and Pakistan. Under the Obama administration, the United States dramatically increased its use of drone technology to conduct targeting operations, with the stated goal of killing militant leaders. The legality of these strikes is a matter of debate, due to the complex nature of the law and limited information about who is killed. In addition, there has been significant debate on the efficacy of the strikes to disrupt and dismantle militant groups and the extent of unintended civilian deaths.

The methodology section is followed by a critique of the report written by a law professor who was a former navy pilot. The critique focuses primarily on the report's methodology. In reading these materials, assess what impact the critique has on the validity of the report's findings and the credibility of the advocacy organization. Consider what challenges the researchers faced in conducting the interviews underlying their findings, and also what factors might be motivating the critique.

AMNESTY INTERNATIONAL, "WILL I BE NEXT?": U.S. DRONE STRIKES IN PAKISTAN?

(Amnesty International Publications 2013).

1.1 Methodology

Amnesty International conducted research for this report from late 2012 to September 2013. The organization carried out over 60 interviews with survivors of drone strikes, relatives of victims, eyewitnesses, residents of affected areas, members of armed groups and Pakistani government officials. These took place in North Waziristan, neighboring areas of Khyber Pakhtunkhwa province, Islamabad and Rawalpindi. Interviews were conducted in Pashto, Urdu, and English.

Amnesty International obtained rare access to some parts of North Waziristan, where more drone strikes have occurred over the past two years than anywhere else in Pakistan. Amnesty International corroborated written and oral testimony against photographic and video evidence and satellite imagery for every strike discussed in this report. Through this research, Amnesty International was able to determine the exact locations of the two main drone strikes documented in this report.

Obtaining reliable information about drone strikes in North Waziristan is extremely difficult due to ongoing insecurity and barriers on independent monitoring imposed by armed groups like the Taliban and the Pakistani military. Independent observers risk accusations of espionage, abduction and death at the hands of these actors for seeking to shed light on human rights in North Waziristan. In addition, the Pakistani military restricts access to the region on the grounds of security risks, which are a legitimate concern, but also to tightly manage reporting on the area. Given the highly politicized debate around the US drones program in Pakistan, Amnesty International was also concerned that local actors would seek to influence its research by coercing those interviewed for this report, or providing false or inaccurate information.

To address this, Amnesty International assembled a number of local investigative teams, which worked independently from one other, and then cross-corroborated the information they gathered, including against other sources.

The Pakistan armed forces did not allow Amnesty International to travel to North Waziristan with them, citing security concerns. However, it agreed in principle to escort the organization to South Waziristan, which has also faced significant drone strikes. In any event, victims and residents said that they were reluctant to meet in North Waziristan during any visit facilitated by and under escort from the armed forces out of fear of retribution from them or from armed groups; for example, if they criticized the conduct of Pakistani forces, or armed groups, or for being seen as aligned with the Pakistani military. Given these obstacles, Amnesty International was not able to conduct on-site investigations in all areas targeted by drone strikes documented in this report, especially those carried out in 2013.

Many of the people interviewed for this report did so at great personal risk, knowing that they might face reprisals from US or Pakistani authorities, the Taliban, or other groups. They spoke out because they were anxious to make known the human cost of the drone program, and the impact on themselves and their communities of living in a state of fear. One witness said:

> It is difficult to trust anyone. I can't even trust my own brother. . . . After I spoke to you some men in plain clothes visited me [in North Waziristan]. I don't know who they were, whether they were Taliban or someone else; they were not from our village. I was clearly warned not to give any more information about the victims of drone strikes. They told me it is fine if I continue to do my work but I should not share any information with the people who come here.

Amnesty International discussed the possible risks carefully with the people who provided information for this report, and wishes to thank all those who shared their stories with us despite the dangers, as well as those who assisted in the research in other ways. However, because of ongoing security concerns, many of the names in this report have been changed to protect the identity of those who spoke with us, and we continue to monitor the situation of our contacts. Most of the Pakistani officials we spoke to also requested anonymity due to the sensitivity of the issues.

Amnesty International wrote to the relevant authorities in the USA and Pakistan regarding the specific cases documented in this report and the overall US drone program in Pakistan. The organization wishes to thank the Governor of Khyber Pakhtunkhwa province, the Secretariat of the Federally Administered Tribal Areas, and the Pakistan Foreign Ministry for speaking candidly and on the record regarding the US drone program in Pakistan and the broader law and order situation in the tribal areas. However, despite written requests and a number of follow ups by Amnesty International, none of the Pakistani authorities answered questions regarding specific drone strikes or the possible role of some Pakistani officials or private citizens in the US drone program.

The US government's utter lack of transparency about its drone program posed a significant research challenge. The USA refuses to make public even basic information about the program, and does not release legal or factual information about specific strikes. None of the US authorities contacted by Amnesty International were willing to provide information regarding the specific cases documented in this report or the legal and policy basis for the drone program in Pakistan. The Central Intelligence Agency (CIA), which is believed to be responsible for the US drone program in Pakistan, said that questions regarding the drone program should be put to the White House. As at time of publication, the White House had not responded to Amnesty International's repeated requests for comment.

. . .

MICHAEL W. LEWIS, "THE MISLEADING HUMAN RIGHTS WATCH AND AMNESTY INTERNATIONAL REPORTS ON U.S. DRONES"
(Nov. 8, 2013, 12:28 PM), *available at* http://opiniojuris.org.

The Amnesty International study displays methodological flaws similar to those of [a previous study by Stanford and NYU] of drone strikes in the FATA region that was published last year. Like the Stanford/NYU study, Amnesty received no input from anyone in the US government. It is not clear whether the authors of the Amnesty report received input from current or former members of the military, although some of the errors contained in the report would make it appear unlikely.

The problem with Amnesty's willingness to uncritically credit information provided by their group of interviewees is best illustrated when the reader understands a little bit about how drones actually work.

. . .

Amnesty accepts the assumption that its witnesses make that any airstrike conducted in the FATA regions of Pakistan is carried out by American drones. Yet . . . the Pakistani Air Force (PAF) also frequently operates in the FATA region and according to its own reporting has struck thousands of targets in that region compared with less than 400 attributable to drones. The manned aircraft flown by the PAF like the F-

16 and the Mirage III are much more easily seen and heard than solitary drones. Drones fly at high altitudes, always above 10,000 feet and in most cases above 20,000 feet, making them very difficult to see with the naked eye and usually inaudible to the human ear. Manned aircraft almost always fly in formation, and seldom operate alone. Drones are not capable of flying in formation and often operate alone. Lastly, manned aircraft like the Pakistani Air Force's (PAF) F-16's typically employ 500 lb. laser guided bombs or Maverick air-to-ground missiles that carry warheads of between 125 and 300 lbs. In contrast the primary weapon used by drones is the Hellfire missile which weighs approximately 100 lbs. and carries a 20 lb. warhead.

Yet many of the observations in the Amnesty report discuss numerous drones acting together including this description from one of the two strikes that feature prominently in the report (the killing of Mamana Bibi): "The drone planes were flying over our village all day and night, flying in pairs, sometimes three together." This description appears to be of a formation of aircraft, which means that they must have been manned aircraft of the PAF, not US drones. Further, according to Amnesty this strike "left a big crater" in the field near where Mamana was working. A "big crater" and a formation of aircraft easily visible and audible from the ground is far more consistent with the detonation of a 200 lb. warhead from a bomb dropped by PAF manned aircraft than it is with the explosion of a 20 lb. warhead from a drone-launched Hellfire missile. But Amnesty does not even mention the possibility of PAF involvement as it directs its demands for disclosure exclusively to US authorities.

The Amnesty report also contains a section on the fear of drones. Parroting the Stanford/NYU report's claim that the US drone program interferes with educational opportunities for girls and women because they fear to go outside, Amnesty's report describes "frequent attacks by drones". It also describes fear and sleeplessness caused by the "constant whine of drones overhead". Again, Amnesty ignores the much larger presence of the Pakistani military in the region. Pakistani Army artillery frequently shells targets in FATA and the PAF has conducted thousands of strikes there while there have been less than 25 US drone strikes throughout the entire region this year. PAF aircraft, which since 2009 have included the Italian-built Falco drones that fly at lower altitudes than US drones, constantly patrol the region. Contrary to Amnesty's assertions, the fear and disruption of daily life that it attributes to the US drone program in fact has far more to do with the continuing conflict between the Taliban and the Pakistani government.

Both [the Amnesty and Human Rights Watch] reports have significant flaws that undermine their objectivity and overall credibility. This is particularly unfortunate because both organizations have historically done some excellent work in uncovering and reporting on human rights violations throughout the world. That standard of excellence is far from met here.

NOTES & QUESTIONS

1.   The Amnesty report, as well as a related report by Human Rights Watch, generated significant media attention. *See* Declan Walsh & Ihsanullah Tipu Mehsud, *Civilian Deaths in Drone Strikes Cited in Report*, New York Times, Oct. 22, 2013, *available at* http://www.nytimes.com/2013/10/22/world/asia/civilian-deaths-in-drone-strikes-cited-in-report.html?_r=0; Craig Whitlock, *Drone Strikes Killing More Civilians than US Admits, Human Rights Groups Say*, The Washington Post, Oct, 21, 2013, *available at* http://www.washingtonpost.com/world/national-security/drone-strikes-killing-more-civilians-than-us-admits-human-rights-groups-say/2013/10/21/a99cbe78-3a81-11e3-b7ba-503fb5822c3e_story.html.

2.   Do you find Professor Lewis' critique of the Amnesty report to be effective? Could the researchers have rectified the issues raised in the critique? As you read the methodology section of the report by Amnesty International, did you identify any other potential concerns?

3.   What factors or considerations might motivate critiques of human rights reports? Is it only a respect for and insistence on methodological accuracy and purity? Might some critiques be motivated by political considerations? *See, e.g.*, Stanley Cohen, *Government Responses to Human Rights Reports: Claims, Denials, and Counterclaims*, 18 Hum. Rts. Qtrly. 517–43 (1996). How might an NGO respond to politically motivated critiques of methodology or findings?

4.   An important consideration that researchers often face in planning and conducting fact-finding missions is choosing and cultivating local partners. Why might it be important for national and international NGOs to engage local partners when conducting fact-finding missions? What criteria should national and international NGOs use to evaluate the appropriate local partner organizations? What might be some of the challenges for national and international NGOs in identifying and working with local partners? What are potential challenges for local organizations working with national and international NGOs as they conduct local fact-finding missions?

5.   In addition to raising concerns about bias and credibility, fact-finding methodology can also have a significant impact on witnesses and victims. How witness testimony is obtained, how it is used, and the resulting relationship between the witness and the fact-finders are all challenging considerations requiring human rights researchers to strike a careful balance between objective investigation and the interests of the victims of human rights abuses. For example, one issue that arises is whether a researcher's effort to gather information will trigger re-traumatization of victims and witnesses. This is of particular concern for research that might involve gender-based violence. For resources that discuss the need for gender

sensitivity and the potential for re-traumatization, see Amnesty International, Methodology for Gender-Sensitive Research (1999); Rights & Democracy and Women Living under Muslim Laws (WLUML), Documenting Women's Rights Violations by Non-State Actors (2006), *available at* http://www.wluml.org/sites/wluml.org/files/import/english/pubs/pdf/misc/non-state-actors.pdf; World Health Organization, Ethical and Safety Recommendations for Interviewing Trafficked Women (2003), *available at* http://www.who.int/gender/documents/en/final%20recommendations%2023%20oct.pdf; World Health Organization and PATH, Researching Violence against Women: A Practical Guide for Researchers and Activists (2005), *available at* http://whql ibdoc.who.int/publications/2005/9241546476_eng.pdf?ua=1.

6. Other significant issues that arise in crafting fact-finding methodology are the role of social science quantitative research methods and the use of social media and other new technologies. *See, e.g.*, Ryan Goodman, Derek Jinks & Andrew K. Woods, *Introduction: Social Science and Human Rights, in* Understanding Social Action, Promoting Human Rights 3–22 (Ryan Goodman, Derek Jinks & Andrew K. Woods eds., 2012); Malcom Langford & Sakiko Fukuda-Parr, *The Turn to Metrics*, 30 Nordic J. Hum. Rts 222 (2012); Molly Land et al., #ICT4HR: Information and Communications Technologies for Human Rights (World Bank Institute et al. 2012).

7. There are a number of resources for practitioners seeking guidance on how to develop a fact-finding and documentation project. *See, e.g.,* Office of the High Commissioner for Human Rights, Training Manual on Human Rights Monitoring, Sales No. E.01.XIV.2 (2001); Handbook on Fact-Finding and Documentation of Human Rights Violations (D. Ravindran, Manuel Guzman & Babes Ignacio eds., Asian Forum for Human Rights and Development 1994); Karyn Kaplan, Human Rights Documentation and Advocacy: A Guide for Organizations of People who Use Drugs, Harm Reduction Field Guide (Open Society Institute Feb. 2009); Amnesty International & CODESRIA, Monitoring and Documenting Human Rights Violations in Africa, A Handbook (2000), http://www.hrea.org/erc/Library/Ukweli/ukweli-en.pdf; The Advocates for Human Rights and the United States Human Rights Network, A Practitioner's Guide to Human Rights Monitoring, Documentation, and Advocacy (Jan. 2011), http://www.theadvocatesforhumanrights.org/uploads/final_report_3.pdf. *See also* International Law and Fact-Finding in the Field of Human Rights (B.G. Ramcharan ed., 1982).

V. CASE STUDY: HUMAN RIGHTS WATCH REPORT ON ALABAMA'S IMMIGRATION LAW

In June 2011, Alabama joined several states, including Arizona and Georgia, in enacting highly restrictive immigration provisions. The law, known as House Bill 56 (HB 56), included a host of provisions that touched on all aspects of the lives of immigrants living in the state. In legislative debate surrounding the bill, its sponsor stated "[t]his bill is designed to make it difficult for 'undocumented immigrants' to live here so they will deport themselves."[1]

Among its provisions, the Alabama statute required law enforcement officers stopping a person for a traffic violation or other infraction to detain and verify the person's immigration status if they suspected him or her of being in the country illegally. In addition, the law required public elementary and secondary schools to determine the immigration status of students; prohibited courts from enforcing contracts by unauthorized immigrants; criminalized transporting undocumented immigrants or providing them with accommodations or renting housing to them; and prohibited undocumented immigrants from working, looking for work, or doing any business transaction with a government agency, including applying for a driver's license, identification card, license plate, or a business license.[2]

As soon as it was enacted, civil rights advocates challenged the law. Advocacy organizations, including the ACLU, ACLU of Alabama, Southern Poverty Law Center, Asian Law Caucus, Mexican American Legal Defense and Education Fund, National Immigration Law Center, and LatinoJustice/PLDEF, filed lawsuits against the state, as did the U.S. Justice Department, challenging the statute on constitutional grounds. Local organizations engaged in grassroots advocacy and a media campaign through the Alabama Coalition for Justice.

In December 2011, Human Rights Watch issued a report documenting the ways in which the immigration law impacted immigrants living in the state. As you read the report's summary and description of methodology, below, as well as an editorial from a local newspaper discussing the report, consider how the fact-finding and reporting effort may have contributed to other advocacy efforts challenging the law.

HUMAN RIGHTS WATCH, NO WAY TO LIVE: ALABAMA'S IMMIGRANT LAW
(December 14, 2011).

Summary

On September 28, 2011, the state of Alabama began implementing a law intended by its sponsors to make everyday life unlivable for unauthorized immigrants to the United States. Every provision of this law, the "Beason-Hammon Alabama Taxpayer and Citizen Protection Act," Act No. 2011–535 (the "Beason-Hammon Act" or "Alabama

---

[1] Kim Chandler, *Alabama House Passes Arizona-style immigration law*, Birmingham News, April 5, 2011, http://blog.al.com/spotnews/2011/04/alabama_house_passes_arizona-s.html.
[2] See II.D. 56, 2011 Leg., Reg. Sess. (Ala. 2011).

immigrant law," also commonly known as "HB 56"), calls for unauthorized immigrants to be treated differently than other residents of Alabama, whether they are applying for a state-regulated service or seeking justice in court. The law denies unauthorized immigrants equal protection of the law guaranteed under the US constitution and applicable international human rights law. And it has encouraged local and state officials to deny unauthorized immigrants basic rights such as access to water and housing. Although the law is new and its full impact unclear, it has already severely affected the state's unauthorized immigrants, their children, many of whom are US citizens, and the broader community linked to this population.

Every country has the authority to regulate the entry of immigrants into its territory, to deport those who have made an unauthorized entry, and to enforce its immigration laws against those no longer authorized to remain. At the same time, international law requires that all persons, by virtue of their humanity, enjoy fundamental human rights. In the United States, these rights are reflected in US constitutional law as well as US international legal obligations which, in setting forth protections for fundamental rights, make clear that such rights apply to "persons," "people," and "everyone," with only a few distinctions allowed between citizens and non-citizens, such as in the areas of voting rights and deportation procedures. These legal obligations bind states and local governments as well. Thus, while every state in the United States has a population of people who entered the country illegally who may lawfully be subject to deportation, no federal or state law may create a situation in which fundamental rights due all persons are infringed upon.

Alabama's immigrant law, however, does just that. As made explicit in the quote above from Representative Mickey Hammon, one of the law's sponsors in the Alabama House of Representatives, the law aims to attack "every aspect of an illegal alien's life." That goal was underscored by the comments of State Senator Scott Beason, a co-author of the law, who stated that the best way to address the problem of illegal immigration is to "empty the clip, and do what has to be done."

The breadth of the law is staggering. Like Arizona's highly problematic immigrant law (popularly known as "SB 1070"), the Beason-Hammon Act requires the police to determine the citizenship and immigration status of anyone they stop or arrest if they have "reasonable suspicion" the person is unauthorized. But the Alabama law reaches far beyond immigrant interactions with law enforcement officials. Unauthorized immigrants are prohibited from entering into broadly defined "business transactions" with the state. Schools are required to check the immigration status of children. Seeking work as an unauthorized immigrant constitutes a misdemeanor crime. Unauthorized immigrants who have had a contract violated, whether an employment contract or a lease, are not to receive protection from the courts. An unauthorized immigrant arrested for any offense, even one as minor as not having a driver's license, will automatically be denied bail. The law further makes it a crime for US citizens and legal residents to knowingly help unauthorized immigrants, such as by giving them a ride or helping them sign up for water service.

And these are merely the intended consequences of the law. The actual consequences, which continue to unfold, remain unclear. Much may ultimately depend on which provisions of the law survive review by the courts. As noted below, courts have preliminarily enjoined enforcement of some provisions; at the time of writing, it is unclear whether they will be permanently struck down. In the meantime, other provisions remain in effect or are due to go into effect in 2012, and many people's lives have already been drastically changed.

Supporters of the law make no allowance for the fact that many unauthorized immigrants in Alabama—as in other states—have long been integrated into their communities. Most of the 50 unauthorized immigrants Human Rights Watch interviewed for this report have lived in the United States for more than 10 years, and in some cases, for more than 20. The majority have US citizen or permanent resident family members—not only children but also siblings and parents. One unauthorized immigrant said he had US citizen children, a US citizen father, a permanent resident mother, and four permanent resident siblings.

Because the US immigration system functions so slowly, he has been "waiting in line" for residency status for nearly 19 years, since his father first petitioned for him. These numbers are echoed by recent research that indicate that nearly two-thirds of unauthorized immigrants in the US have lived in the country for at least 10 years, and that nearly half are parents of minor children.

These immigrants work for, and sometimes own, Alabama businesses. They are important participants in local religious, educational, and civic life. Many described a fierce attachment to Alabama, and not just to the US. One 19-year-old, brought to the US when he was nine, struggled to articulate what Alabama meant for him: "It's just home. I love here." A 27-year-old father of two, who came to the US when he was 15, felt the same way: "Others go to Michigan, Florida. This is my home."

For years, Alabama has implicitly acknowledged their presence, as well as accepted their labor, taxes, and various state fees. But now, Alabama has decided that many state protections will not apply to these residents.

Shortly before this report went to press, Alabama Attorney General Luther Strange issued memorandums interpreting some provisions of the Beason-Hammon Act more narrowly than had been interpreted by local and state officials, and he recommended some provisions to be modified or repealed. As this report shows, however, the law both denies fundamental rights and encourages interpretations of the law that make violations of these rights more likely. The human rights of all residents in Alabama cannot be protected simply with modifications to a law that is grounded in discrimination.

Human Rights Concerns

The new law contains provisions that have been interpreted in a manner to prevent unauthorized immigrants from engaging in necessary everyday transactions, which denies them fundamental rights.

For instance, the law as implemented in the first two months barred unauthorized immigrants in some parts of the state from signing up for water or other utility service, as such service was considered a prohibited "business transaction" with the state. The law was similarly interpreted to deprive them of their ability to live in the homes they own: unauthorized immigrants were told they could not renew the registration tags on mobile homes they own, nor pay property taxes for their homes as they had for years. The attorney general in December issued a guidance letter stating that the phrase "business transaction" does not encompass access to water and other utility services. A federal court also temporarily enjoined enforcement of the "business transaction" provision as applied to mobile homes. At the time of writing, it remains unclear how these directives will be implemented at the local level.

The Beason-Hammon Act more explicitly denies equal protection of the law in several ways. Some unauthorized immigrants who are victims of wage theft and other crimes, having heard that Alabama courts will not uphold their contracts and that the police will engage in federal immigration enforcement, have decided not to report the crimes to the authorities. Judges and attorneys have raised concerns that the law might prevent them from fulfilling their legal duties towards unauthorized immigrants.

The people most affected by the law are overwhelmingly Hispanic, an ethnic minority in Alabama. While discrimination against Hispanics and other minorities has a long history in Alabama, passage of the Beason-Hammon Act appears to have given police and private individuals a license to harass and abuse unauthorized immigrants as well as minority US citizens and permanent residents. Several Hispanics told Human Rights Watch that since the law went into effect, the police stopped or arrested them for no reason or on pretext. They also reported harassment by private individuals. Some reported discrimination in private business transactions, such as one woman, a permanent resident, who was unable to get her prescription filled at a major discount store chain because she could not prove US citizenship.

Particularly hard hit have been the children of unauthorized immigrants, an especially vulnerable population, including the many such children who are US citizens. As their parents curtail driving, some no longer receive timely medical care. Although the provision requiring schools to check the immigration status of their students was enjoined by the courts, many families withdrew their children while that provision was in effect, and the remaining students struggle to understand what has happened to their classmates and what may happen to their own families. Such difficulties are exacerbated by bullying from classmates who question other children, even US citizen children, asking: "What are you doing here? Why don't you go back?"

That unauthorized immigrants could avoid many of these abuses by returning to their countries does not justify Alabama's denial of their basic rights. The fact that the Alabama law also effectively infringes on the rights of many US citizens and permanent residents is additional cause for concern.

A Climate of Fear

In the first two months since the law went into effect, unauthorized immigrants, their families, and their communities have seen their lives changed in profound ways. Schools, businesses, and landlords have all reported a significant exodus of people from the state. Patricia T., a US citizen married to an undocumented Mexican, watched her neighbors move away the very night the law went into effect with only their cars and the clothes on their backs, leaving behind their homes, furniture, and other belongings. Families left behind not only all of their possessions, but also communities and school children traumatized by the sudden disappearance of their friends. One minister's congregation decreased from 100 members to 25.

Those who remain avoid as much contact with government officials as possible by adopting "underground" lives. One woman, describing the atmosphere in her community, stated, "We live in terror." Nearly every unauthorized immigrant interviewed by Human Rights Watch reported curtailing everyday activities. To minimize the risk of being stopped by the police while driving, families reported staying home as much as possible, driving only to go to work or buy necessities. One couple shops at Walmart, a discount store chain, only under cover of darkness, when it is harder for the police to identify them as Latino.

Fear has also infringed upon the spiritual lives of Alabama's unauthorized immigrants. Church is often an important source of solace and strength for many immigrant families. As one man put it, "There is a

God and He won't ask for papers." But in one rural community, several families decided the church was too far away to risk driving. Although the priest is now conducting Mass in one family's trailer once a month, that family decided their child could not attend Communion classes.

The impact on family life has been severe. Several families reported their children no longer participate in activities like soccer, cheerleading, and Boy Scouts, because they do not want to risk more driving. Not surprisingly, children have become anxious and fearful.

One mother reported that when she is out of the house, her children call constantly, asking, "Mommy, are you coming? Where are you? When are you coming home?"

There has been important opposition to the law in the state. Many Alabamians, including educators and police officers, have spoken out publicly against the law. Several unauthorized immigrants reported that many more unnamed individuals have softened the blow of the law by giving them a ride to work, taking children to school or soccer practice, signing powers of attorney to help take care of children in the event of a parent's arrest, or signing up for water service in their own names. Sadly, many of these actions, done out of a sense of kindness and decency, are actions the Beason-Hammon Act seeks to criminalize.

As severe as the impact has been in the first two months, the effects of the law are likely to get worse as time goes on. Unless the courts intervene and the preliminary injunctions become permanent ones, more people will be denied access to utilities, more people will find themselves unable to renew their business permits and mobile home tags, and more people will become victims of crime, abuse, and harassment without any meaningful legal recourse.

Some of the state legislators who voted for the bill are now having second thoughts. State Senator Gerald Dial recently created a package of amendments to address "unintended consequences." He has stated, "We're loving, caring, compassionate people in Alabama, not hateful and mean as we've been painted by this bill. I want to remove some of that stigma." And as this report went to press, Attorney General Strange recommended repeal or modification of certain provisions, including some analyzed in this report. He also issued guidance letters that would limit the impact of the law on some rights. At the same time, however, supporters of the law insist they are open only to minor changes that would make the law more enforceable. Sen. Beason stated, "I have no intention of weakening the anti-illegal immigration law."

The government of Alabama's recognition that there are serious problems with the Beason-Hammon Act may eliminate some "worst case" scenarios. But the proposed modifications do not change the fundamental intent and impact of the law: to deprive unauthorized immigrants of basic rights and equal protection of the law so as to make it difficult or nearly impossible for them to live in the state. Given the all-encompassing nature of the law, the only appropriate solution is an equally comprehensive one: repealing the Beason-Hammon Act altogether.

Recommendations

To the State of Alabama

    To the Alabama State Legislature

- Promptly repeal the Beason-Hammon Alabama Taxpayer and Citizen Protection Act, Act No. 2011–535.

To Alabama Governor Robert Bentley and Law Enforcement Officials

    Even before repeal,

- Direct all state and local officials to ensure all residents, regardless of immigration status, are able to access necessities like water and housing.

- Train local law enforcement on how to avoid illegal racial profiling and collect data on police stops and arrests to ensure racial profiling is not occurring.

To Alabama Attorney General Luther Strange

- Ensure that local and state officials implement policies in accordance with the attorney general's guidance letters that more narrowly interpret some provisions of the Beason-Hammon Act.

To All US State and Local Governments

- Repeal or oppose efforts to enact legislation that would infringe upon the fundamental rights of unauthorized immigrants guaranteed under the US constitution or international human rights law.

To the US Congress

- Enact comprehensive immigration reform in keeping with US obligations under international human rights law.

To the US President

- Direct the Department of Homeland Security and other US agencies not to participate in the enforcement of the Alabama immigrant law, and, specifically, ensure that unauthorized immigrants arrested under the law are not placed in removal proceedings.

- Direct the Department of Justice to continue to vigorously investigate all allegations of civil rights violations due to the Alabama law.

Methodology

This report is based on research conducted by Human Rights Watch in Alabama from October 26 to November 4, 2011. Human Rights Watch researchers visited several cities and towns in Alabama, including Birmingham and several of its suburbs, as well as Albertville, Decatur, Tuscaloosa, Troy, Dothan, and Foley. The report is also based on telephone interviews with Alabama residents in October and November 2011, as well as reports by local and national media and by other advocacy organizations.

Human Rights Watch conducted 57 interviews with people who reported they had personally experienced discrimination or abuses because of the new immigrant law, including 50 unauthorized immigrants and seven US citizens and lawful permanent residents living in Alabama. We also received over a dozen reports of discrimination and abuses from individuals who had personal knowledge of incidents experienced by others.

We further interviewed people familiar with the application of Alabama's law, including lawyers, ministers, teachers, community leaders, and local immigrant advocates. Many of these people helped us identify the unauthorized immigrants whom we interviewed. We also interviewed judges, police officers, and school administrators. We did not investigate specific incidents of police harassment where the person reporting the incident had requested anonymity, but we did interview ranking officers at police departments about their general policies regarding the Beason-Hammon Act and their response to allegations of racial profiling or abuse. We also visited local permit offices and utility boards in two towns and inquired into what documents were required for service and renewal. In total, we interviewed over 90 people.

Interviews were conducted in English, Spanish, or a combination of the two, depending on the interviewee's preferences. Most interviews were done individually, except in a few instances where interviewees preferred to speak with their spouses or in small groups. No interviewee received compensation for providing information. Where appropriate, Human Rights Watch provided contact information for organizations offering legal or other services, including information on hotlines to report abuses to the US Department of Justice and to the Southern Poverty Law Center.

We have used pseudonyms for every unauthorized immigrant interviewed so as to protect their privacy. A few legal residents and US citizens also requested anonymity for privacy reasons. All interviews were conducted in Alabama, except where we specifically note that we conducted the interview by telephone. The exact location of some interviews has been withheld, as have some identifying details, to protect the identity of interviewees.

. . .

JOEY KENNEDY, EDITORIAL, "BEAR WITNESS TO A WRONG, THEN TELL ALL"
Birmingham News, December 18, 2011.

A week ago today, I received a heads-up from Grace Meng with Human Rights Watch letting me know her organization, well-known and respected across the globe, would be issuing a report on Alabama's dreadful immigration law. Meng sent links to the embargoed report, and, sadly, what I read didn't surprise me one bit.

It was more bad news—and bad publicity—on the way for Alabama.

Meng is a researcher in the U.S. Program at Human Rights Watch. She and her crew spent 10 days in the state in late October and early November, talking with Alabama people—U.S. citizens, permanent residents and undocumented folks—who said they personally experienced discrimination or abuses because of the immigration law.

Too many Alabamians are in denial about this atrocious law. They claim because the law itself prohibits racial profiling or discrimination, it isn't happening. That's bunk, of course. It's not what a law says, but what a law does. Many supporters say people here without documents should be chased out by practically any means; humane treatment isn't necessary. They claim an outrageous cost of undocumented residents and workers, when many of these hardworking people actually contribute positively to the state's economy and to the communities in which they live.

Still, our leaders in the Legislature and Gov. Robert Bentley wanted the toughest immigration law in the land, and they got it.

Congratulations, and welcome to an Alabama we've seen before.

The awful immigration law does awful things, and Meng found a bunch of those.

People who are victims of crimes are afraid to report those crimes to the authorities. Others were victims of wage theft, but they didn't believe they could recover that pay because the law denies undocumented workers the right to enforce contracts in Alabama courts.

"The new law has given police and private citizens effective license to discriminate against unauthorized immigrants, as well as minority US citizens and permanent residents," said a release from Human Rights

Watch as the 52-page report—"No Way to Live: Alabama's Immigrant Law"—was released last Wednesday.

This was Meng's first trip to Alabama, and she was impressed by many of the people and stories she heard.

"One man I spoke to, he was just very, very grateful to Alabama and the local community," Meng says. "He said others can go (self-deport) to Michigan or Florida, but he could not leave his home. He also said he just did not believe that the same people who had been so good to him and were helping him could support this law."

While in Birmingham, Meng enjoyed the vegetables at Niki's West. Her visit, though, wasn't about fine food or good people.

It was about bad law.

"We commented on Arizona's law," Meng says, "but really, Alabama is the only state where we saw so many provisions go into effect. We're going to use Alabama as Exhibit A as to why other states shouldn't pass a similar law."

The goal of Human Rights Watch, however, is to make sure people understand this isn't just an Alabama thing.

"There may be people who think this is just something Alabama is doing, and Alabama has this history," Meng says. "What's happening in Alabama could happen elsewhere. We don't see this as just an Alabama issue, but a national issue."

Meng, who has a law degree from Yale Law School and previously practiced immigration law, has been investigating and writing about abuses in the U.S. immigration system for a while. She hopes the spotlight put on the state by Human Rights Watch will encourage state leaders to scrap the law.

"I understand the way people can feel about an outsider criticizing them," Meng says, "but if that weren't the case, there would be so many human rights abuses that would go unnoticed. The whole human rights movement grew out of the ideal that everybody who can should bear witness."

Of course, Meng is right. If we stay silent after we witness a wrong, we're no better than the wrongdoer.

We can be better.

NOTES & QUESTIONS

1. As the Human Rights Watch report and the editorial indicate, prior to the issuance of the report, state officials had already begun to question the law and consider changes to it. Given this, what (if anything) is the "value

added" of a human rights fact-finding report on the issue? Were there any potential downsides to the report, given the political climate in the state and the pending litigation? Note that Human Rights Watch was not one of the advocacy organizations directly involved in the litigation.

2.   Consider the report in light of Diane Orentlicher's article. Do you think the report's authors gave sufficient context for the report? Is the report susceptible to any of the critiques that Orentlicher suggests?

3.   The editorial suggests and implicitly dismisses a possible critique of the report: unwarranted scrutiny of local practice by an outside human rights "professional." Is this a valid critique of human rights fact-finding endeavors? Is it a critique of methodology, politics, or something else? How can human rights researchers and advocates diffuse or head off such a critique?

4.   In August 2012, the 11th Circuit Court of Appeals blocked portions of Alabama's HB 56, and, in October 2013, civil rights organizations and the Department of Justice reached a settlement agreement with the State of Alabama to permanently block most aspects of the law. Certain aspects of the law that had been temporarily enjoined by federal courts were permanently enjoined under the agreement. These include the provisions authorizing police to detain people to check immigration status, requiring schools to verify the immigration status of newly enrolled students, criminalizing the solicitation of work by unauthorized immigrants, criminalizing the provision of a ride to undocumented immigrants or renting to them, and criminalizing failure to register immigration status. Several sections of the law remain unaffected by the settlement, including provisions barring unauthorized immigrants from attending a state university or college, and the provision requiring proof of citizenship for certain transactions with the state, including obtaining a drivers' license or business license. *See* Joint Report Regarding Case Status and Disposition, Hispanic Interest Coalition v. Bentley (N.D. Ala. Oct. 29, 2013) (Case Num. 5:11–cv–02484–SLB).

CHAPTER X

MOBILIZING COMMUNITIES

■ ■ ■

Beyond human rights' status as formal law, human rights concepts have been important tools for organizing and supporting social movements. Global examples abound. Effective use of human rights concepts and framing enabled Korean residents of Japan in the 1970s to transform their activism for minority rights into a human rights movement resonating with the broader Japanese public.[1] Similarly, human rights frames have supported local and national feminist organizing in Ireland.[2] Another example is the Human Rights Cities model, used worldwide, which encourages local coalitions to engage a human rights framework to guide city policymaking.[3]

There are also many instances where human rights concepts have been used in organizing and mobilizing social movements in the United States. Examples include Los Angeles parents concerned about school discipline who used a human rights model to critique expulsion and suspension policies; displaced tenants in New Orleans who raised their human right to housing as a rallying cry in their efforts to return to their homes after Hurricane Katrina; and low wage workers in the Baltimore, Maryland inner harbor area who established a "human rights zone" around their workplace to pressure their employers for improvements and educate visitors about their working conditions.[4]

These examples may seem out of place in a law school casebook, given that they don't include standard "legal" strategies. In fact, many of the groups that use human rights for organizing and mobilization purposes do so very successfully without any lawyer involvement at all. Nonetheless, as this chapter will demonstrate, lawyers often do interact directly and indirectly with grassroots groups and social movement

---

[1]   Kiyoteru Tsutsui and Hwa-Ji Shin, Global Norms, *Local Activism and Social Movement Outcomes: Global Human Rights and Resident Koreans in Japan*, 55 Social Problems 391 (2008).

[2]   Niamh Reilly, *Linking Local and Global Feminist Advocacy: Framing Women's Rights and Human Rights in the Republic of Ireland*, Women's Studies International Forum 30 (2007). *See generally* Beth A. Simmons, Mobilizing for Human Rights: International Law in Domestic Politics (2009) (including case studies of Colombia and Japan).

[3]   Stephen P. Marks and Kathleen A. Modrowski, Human Rights Cities: Civic Engagement for Societal Development, UN Societal Development, UNHABITAT and PDHRE (2008).

[4]   More in-depth treatment of these and other examples are available on the website of the National Economic and Social Rights Initiative, www.nesri.org.

activists, and lawyers may often be in the position of adapting human rights approaches to respond to community needs.

Part I of this chapter offers some successful examples of human rights organizing in the U.S., spanning a range of contexts from immigration to universal health care. Part II provides some examples of human rights mobilization that were less successful. While human rights is often an effective tool, some U.S. activists report that human rights concepts do not resonate with their constituencies; among other things, "human rights" may seem a poor stand-in for well-established civil rights concepts that have more cultural meaning in the United States. Part III examines these challenges from a communications perspective. Finally, Part IV sets out a case study of human rights mobilization following Hurricane Katrina. As you read this material, consider what factors contribute to successful use of human rights for mobilization in the U.S. and what factors may spell failure. Also reflect on what a lawyer might learn from these accounts about how to best use all of the tools available, including human rights law, to further the agenda of a client group. Consider, too, how lawyers might contribute to these organizing campaigns.

I. ACCOUNTS OF HUMAN RIGHTS AND MOBILIZATION IN THE UNITED STATES

Activists have effectively used human rights approaches to support grassroots organizing in a variety of settings around the country. The readings that follow provide a snapshot of the ways in which human rights have been used to mobilize communities around issues of common concern, both with and without lawyer involvement. The first excerpt describes the role of human rights in supporting immigrants' organizing at the U.S.-Mexico border. The article's author, Fernando Garcia, is the founder of the Border Network for Human Rights (BNHR), a human rights and immigration advocacy organization based in El Paso, Texas. BNHR is a membership organization that includes more than 4000 individuals and families in West Texas and Southern New Mexico.

FERNANDO GARCIA, "HUMAN RIGHTS AND IMMIGRATION IN
THE U.S.: AN EXPERIENCE OF BORDER
IMMIGRANT COMMUNITIES"
22 Geo. Immigr. L. J. 405, 405–06 (2008).

It is, indeed, at the U.S.-Mexico border where the irrational contradictions of our American society and policies are expressed in a very dramatic way, and where border residents and immigrants pay the price with their rights and lives. As founding director of BNHR, my learning process has evolved in well-defined stages. It began almost 10 years ago, with the idea to build a human rights organization based on the participation and leadership of immigrants and border residents, with the main purpose to deter, through community education and organizing, human rights violations and the pathology of abuse fostered by U.S. immigration and border enforcement policies.

BNHR has been extremely successful in accomplishing that goal by consolidating a grassroots community structure in the form of Human Rights Community Committees. This structure has not only provided human rights education to many immigrant families, but has also developed generations of community leaders, known as Human Rights Promoters. Moreover, these Human Rights Committees have learned to question, for instance, the motives of the lack of accountability and oversight of U.S. border policy; the "American Exceptionalism" with regard to the enforcement of human rights; and the limitations of the international human rights framework in reference to the protection of immigrants.

. . .

For years, immigrant families and border residents have confronted the very real limitations of the U.S. national legal framework that meant to protect them from random searches and detentions inside their homes, places of worship, employment and schools. All along the border region, the expanded and overgrown U.S. Border Patrol and Immigration and Customs Enforcement Agency (ICE), previously known as INS, have become synonymous with impunity and lack of accountability. A climate of fear and persecution can be felt throughout border cities. Incidents of human and civil rights abuses ranging from racial profiling, wrongful searches and detentions, beatings and insults, raids, and killings have marked the recent historical record of those border enforcement and immigration agencies.

It is in this context and climate that in 1998 the Border Network for Human Rights started its human rights organizing, focusing primarily on immigrant communities of West Texas and Southern New Mexico. Since the beginning of the organizing work, the challenge was to confront a culture of pandemic abuse imposed at the border with a culture of human rights and, more importantly, to directly engage those impacted communities in the process of reaffirming, defending, and reclaiming their human rights. This did not look to be an easy task.

The early stage of the community organizing process was to connect people and issues, and to engage them in intensive dialogues and discussion. At this point, BNHR families and members framed their immigrant struggle within three primary sources of rights, as a way to react and respond to the culture of abuse. These conceptualization processes started with rather simple questions related to the origin of rights, the historical alienation of those rights, the reaffirmation of the individual and his/her community, and the analysis of the national and international framework of rights and liberties.

These members of the BNHR, mostly immigrants, reached an important breakthrough by internalizing the first source of rights. The most important thing for those harassed and persecuted immigrants emerged from the violation of their human needs and from their quest to actively reclaim dignity and rights. In other words, in our case, human rights are born out of the resistance and experiences of the organized impacted immigrant and border communities, as well from the struggle of other peoples and communities. As a result of this understanding, BNHR membership prioritized demands around the struggle to change U.S. immigration law, more concretely, for the U.S. government to recognize the work and contributions of undocumented immigrants by legalizing them and giving them a right place in society. At the same time, Border Network members reacted to the abusive border reality in which they live by calling for change in current border policy and practices, focusing on alternatives that would create a climate of accountability, oversight, community security, and human rights within their corresponding border communities.

These demands were always placed in the larger context of human rights, and, after long discussions and consultations, BNHR members developed a comprehensive list of thirteen community priorities or demands central to the work of the Border Network.

These 13 fundamental priorities were developed parallel to the organizing process and through the direct involvement and participation of communities, reflecting the core issues that affect the well-being of immigrants on the U.S.-Mexico Border. For BNHR families, these priorities defined their *basic human rights* and their aspiration of a better society: Permanent Residency-Legalization, Civil and Constitutional Rights, Labor Rights, Dignified Housing, Access to Education, Healthy Communities, Nutrition, Public Services, Culture and Language, Civic Community Participation, Human Mobility, Dignity and Respect, and Peace with Justice.

As a second source of rights, individuals and families of the BNHR use the principles and articles contained within the Universal Declaration of Human Rights. Even though I made a critical evaluation of the current international human rights framework, BNHR members still use the Declaration to place the issues and problems they face in the U.S. Article 13 of the Universal Declaration states: "Everyone has the right to freedom of movement and residence within the borders of each State and that everyone has the right to leave any country, including his own, and to return to his country." BNHR is using this Article to further frame one of the most important demands of the immigrant movement in the U.S.—immigrant workers and their families should be able to enter the U.S. legally, in a regulated way, free of violence, and with rights. As part of this analysis, keep in mind that today the entry of immigrant workers to the U.S. is taking place in an unregulated manner, with grave consequences to human rights and with denial of basic protections.

Article 13 also mentions the Right to Permanent Residency, although quite superficially due to the previously mentioned limitations. Article 15 of the Universal Declaration explains the "right to change nationality," but in a very limited context. And, most importantly, the Universal Declaration mirrors the social, political and economical demands that BNHR members have naturally identified in their struggle for a better life (the 13 Priorities).

Finally, the third source of rights for the BNHR comes from the U.S. Constitution, in particular from some of the amendments that integrate the Bill of Rights. It was evident for our immigrant families that the Constitution does not go far enough in granting rights, but it has become a legal tool to help them protect themselves from wrongful searches, questionings, and detentions which are a daily occurrence in immigrant communities.

The Border Network for Human Rights: An Experience of Immigrant Communities Internalizing Human Rights.

In the last six years, through a series of human rights trainings, the Border Network for Human Rights went from 0 to almost 100 active *Human Rights Promoters* working in the border region of West Texas-Southern New Mexico. These *Promoters* became effective community organizers and leaders in their communities. The BNHR human rights trainings provided *Promoters* with the educational values to internalize rights, to educate their communities through collective dynamics, and to understand and apply the Bill of Rights and the Universal Declaration in their local and practical realities. Moreover, it offered organizational values and principles to build a highly participatory process to defend these rights with internal democracy, accountability, consultation, and responsibility.

It is because of their work and commitment as human rights presenters and organizers that the *Human Right Promoters* brought together self-sustained *Human Rights Community Based Committees* in neighborhoods, barrios and colonias. Over time, these committees created the Border Network for Human Rights. Several of those *Promoters* have become significant members of the Board of Directors and Executive Committee of the BNHR. . . . Today, the structure of the Border Network integrates more than 20 Human Rights Community Based Committees in which more than 500 immigrant families participate throughout West Texas and Southern New Mexico.

. . .

A powerful and relevant change has occurred with individuals and families that decided to participate, either as members of the Human Rights Committees or as Human Rights Promoters, in the Border Network for Human Rights. Most of them come from a background of despair, abuse and loss of hope; the vast majority had never been involved in any kind of social or political struggle before joining the Network. What they bring to BNHR are hopes of a better future for their family and that last fragment of dignity that still remains intact from the constant journey that began when they left their home country.

The knowledge of rights and the constant collective discussion and trainings on the U.S. Constitution and the Universal Declaration for Human Rights has significantly reduced BNHR members' fears of abuse and increased their hopes and participation in the struggle for a better society. An important gain of BNHR's educational process is represented in the internalization of this sentiment: "I am a human being and member of this society. I do have legal and human rights granted by the U.S. Constitution and the International Human Rights Law."

Such internalization has led members of our impacted communities to defend, exercise and promote rights actively, by reporting incidents of abuse occurring in their neighborhoods. The incidents reported have included illegal entries in houses, wrongful searches, and physical and psychological aggression. Members have reaffirmed their rights during such incidents by asking for validity, legality and humanity in any action taken by law enforcement authorities. Furthermore, they are engaging in specific campaigns to change the policies and practices that foster human rights violations, such as the immigration law enforcement abuse documentation campaigns and access to permanent residency and legal status campaigns.

. . .

Final Thoughts

The human rights framework, although limited, has provided BNHR with key values for immigrant communities to assert and reclaim their human rights in their new home. It has given them a comprehensive perspective of their humanity and dignity, and it has provided the conceptual tool to engage in the larger question of common well being. Immigrants in the United States are beginning to sustain a push for a very complex social and political struggle, in which, for instance, they are asking U.S. society to recognize them as human beings with rights, while at the same time questioning the overall fairness of such a society by demanding to incorporate human rights values in the construction of a better one.

And finally, what is most fascinating is the realization that through a very intense and permanent educational and organizing process, immigrants are reclaiming the concepts, values, and principles of human rights independently of the effectiveness of the international framework and institutions. Even more importantly, they are becoming an energized and essential sector within the human rights movement in the United States.

———————

The next excerpt describes human rights organizing by the Coalition of Immokalee Workers (CIW), a worker-led organization of low wage agricultural laborers in Florida who have successfully mobilized for increased wages and improved working conditions. Greg Asbed, the author of this article, was a lawyer with Florida Rural Legal Services until he co-founded the CIW in 1996. Asbed's colleague and co-founder of CIW, Lucas Benitez, was a migrant farmworker who came to the United States from Mexico at age 17. Benitez's activism in the face of worker abuse and exploitation was the spark that ignited early organizing efforts.[5]

GREG ASBED, "COALITION OF IMMOKALEE WORKERS: *'¡GOLPEAR A UNO ES GOLPEAR A TODOS!'* TO BEAT ONE OF US IT TO BEAT US ALL!"

3 Bringing Human Rights Home 1, 5–6 (Cynthia Soohoo, et al., eds 2008).

Today, the Southeastern United States is home to some of the most rapidly growing Latino and indigenous communities in the country. Almost without exception, employment has been the magnet drawing these new immigrants to communities throughout the region. From the carpet factories of Dalton, Georgia, to the poultry plants of Sand Mountain, Alabama, from the watermelon fields of Kennet, Missouri, to the tobacco farms of Clinton, North Carolina, recent immigrants from Mexico and Central America hold a growing majority of the local economy's back-breaking, low-paying jobs. But the list does not stop there. In construction, health care, landscaping, janitorial, and restaurant work and throughout the service sector—Caribbean, Guatemalan, Salvadoran, and Mexican immigrants are by far the fastest growing sector of the work force in today's low-wage South. Urban or rural, it's the same story.

———————

[5] More information about CIW's history and current organizing efforts can be found at its website, www.ciw-online.org.

Immokalee, the heart of Florida's tomato and citrus industries, and the place where the CIW [Coalition of Immokalee Workers] was born, is no exception. And to understand the CIW—what it is and what it isn't—it is important to understand the community from which it emerged.

Immokalee is more a labor reserve than a town. It is an unincorporated place where the population nearly doubles (to somewhere between 20,000 and 30,000 people) during the nine months of the year from September to June that the agricultural industry needs workers. (From June through August, most farmworkers migrate north to states along the length of the East Coast for the shorter northern harvest season.)

The workforce is 85 to 90 percent male. The median age is twenty-four and falling (in fact, according to one local health official, the average age of Immokalee's farmworkers is closer to twenty-one). The vast majority of the young, single males living and working in Immokalee come from rural, farming communities in Mexico, Guatemala, and Haiti, in that order. Most are very recent immigrants, with many only a few days or weeks from having arrived in the country. And while Immokalee may be the first destination for many recent immigrants, many will not remain here for long. The turnover in our community is unparalleled, as workers are lured away daily by the call of higher wages and more favorable working conditions in just about any industry other than the fields.

In a cultural sense, Immokalee is one of the most cosmopolitan communities in the U.S. South, despite the fact that the town has only four traffic lights (all on Highway 29, the main road through town), and the biggest store in town is the Winn Dixie supermarket. Indeed, if you stand on just about any street corner in Immokalee you can easily hear four or five different languages—Spanish, Haitian Creole, Mixtec, Kanjobal, Quiche, Tztotzil, and more.

In short, Immokalee is a crossroads between the rural poverty of the global South and the promise of a modern job paying a minor fortune in American dollars. It is an employer's dream, and an organizer's nightmare. Ethnically and linguistically divided, documented and undocumented (with many still in debt to their "coyotes," the people who lead undocumented immigrants across the border and across the country to Florida), highly mobile, dirt-poor, largely non-literate and culturally isolated from the mainstream community of Southwest Florida, the Immokalee farmworker community could not be more challenging to traditional organizers armed with traditional organizing approach.

What's more, farm labor is excluded from the National Labor Relations Act, denying farmworkers the legal rights and protections that have made it possible for almost all other American workers to organize and join unions since 1935. Complicating matters yet further, the agricultural labor force in Immokalee is structured as one big labor pool, where thousands of people wake up at 4:00 A.M. every morning to beg for a day's labor at the central parking lot in town, and where workers pick up paychecks from as many as three or four different companies every Friday evening. This means that virtually none of the major agricultural corporations that operate in Southwest Florida has a fixed work force. There is no such thing as "Pacific Land Co.'s workers" or "Gargiulo's crews," there are only Immokalee workers and changing faces picking, planting, and pulling plastic in company fields on any given day. Put all this together, and you have a town where workplace organizing in any normal sense of the term is effectively impossible.

And that is why the country's worst-paid, least-protected workers remained unorganized for so long. Until, that is, about ten years ago, when a small group of workers with experience in organizing back home in Guatemala, Haiti, and Mexico, started to bring that experience to their lives as farmworkers here in the United States.

Reverse Technology Transfer—New Wave Of Latin American Immigrants Brings Organizing Experience, Tools To Bear On U.S. Agricultural Exploitation

In the early 1990s, Haiti was undergoing another wave of intense political unrest and violence. . . . As a result, a new wave of Haitian "boat people" set out for the shores of Florida, among them many seasoned veterans of some of the most intense grassroots political organizing in this hemisphere's recent history. Many of those new Haitian refugees made their way to Immokalee, as there was already a significant Haitian community established here during an earlier wave of immigration in the 1980s. Once in Immokalee, they joined Guatemalan and Salvadoran refugees fleeing war and human rights attacks against peasant organizations in their own countries, as well as an increasing influx of indigenous immigrants from southern Mexico, many of whom came from the soon-to-be-famous state of Chiapas and had participated in the rapidly evolving Zapatista movement.

A history of struggle united many of these new immigrants, but it was a history that, for the most part, people did their best to forget and leave behind as they scratched out a living in the harsh fields of Florida's tomato and citrus industries. And what immigrants found in those fields in the early 1990s was anything but refuge—instead they found conditions even crueler and more brutal than today. On top of the sub-poverty wages, decrepit housing, and humiliating labor relations that still characterize farm work today, workers also faced frequent violence at the hands of their employers and widespread wage theft. In the early days of the CIW, Immokalee was a vicious, dog-eat-dog world where each worker faced the full brunt of the forces arrayed against him on his own. No individual worker stood a chance against those forces, consequently survival meant finding a way out of the fields and out of town as quickly as one's ingenuity and familial connections would allow.

But not everyone had left their tools of struggle at home. A small group of workers, including Haitian peasant "animators" (trained organizers from the Mouvman Peyizan Papay, Haiti's largest peasant movement) and members of rural organizations from Guatemala, Mexico, and Haiti began meeting to discuss their new situation as immigrants. These workers were determined to find solutions to some of the most pressing problems facing the Immokalee farmworker community, and to do so they decided it would be necessary to finally "unpack" their organizing experience from their home countries and put it to use here in Florida. From a room borrowed from Immokalee's Catholic church, the workers launched an organizing process that drew directly from Latin American and Caribbean organizing traditions for both its methods and its overall, long-term strategy.

Specifically, these experienced organizers employed three key tools common to their organizing experiences at home to forge a movement for grassroots, democratic, worker-led change in the United States: (1) popular education, used to provoke participatory analysis of the problems facing farmworkers in Immokalee; (2) leadership development, to guarantee a constantly growing, broad base of leadership in the high-turnover worker community; and (3) powerful protest actions, both to serve as an additional tool for building awareness and leadership within the movement, and to create a growing pressure on the agricultural industry to negotiate fundamental changes for farm labor in the absence of the traditional organizing tools most other American workers have had at their disposal since 1935 to legally compel their employers to the table (signature cards, elections, the NLRB, etc.).

. . .

Two Lands, One Movement: Human Rights In Latin America And Immokalee

It is possible to define . . . the abysmal working conditions in Florida's fields as a series of violations of particular articles of the United Nations Universal Declaration on Human Rights, and the CIW does speak in those terms in certain organizing contexts.

But the use and meaning of human rights language in the CIW's overall organizing approach is in fact far broader than those narrowly defined legal terms. This broader use is central to our organizing success, both internally, organizing in the Immokalee community, and externally, organizing in the various communities of allies that have been so crucial to the success of the Taco Bell campaign and its aftermath.

Internally, the notion of human rights within the CIW organizing approach is very similar to its definition and role in the Latin American popular movements that inspired the CIW. In those movements, the idea of human rights is not viewed through a legalistic lens, dividing rights into economic, social, and political categories. Rather, it is a much more holistic idea that is rooted in a fundamental belief in the equality and dignity of all human beings. This idea informs both the movements' organizing objectives as well as their internal structures.

The late 1960s saw the emergence of strong social movements across Latin America that gave voice to the grievances of the region's desperately poor peasant and urban underclasses. Through adult literacy approaches that combined reading and writing with political and social analysis, peasant organizing that focused as much on economic justice as on economic development, and urban development efforts that questioned the authority of the region's many military and family dictatorships, a broad array of movements came to be known as one popular movement loosely united around the goal of winning human rights—the right to a dignified existence—for all.

The religious/political philosophy known as liberation theology provided those movements with a theological foundation and institutional credibility in the highly religious communities of the poor, the same communities that would send their sons and daughters to Immokalee to search for a better life. Together, church-based organizing driven by the tenets of liberation theology and popular organizing outside the four walls of the church helped spread the notion of human rights throughout Latin America and made the idea that we are all born with the equal right to lead a dignified life, a life free of degradation—in all the political, social, and economic expressions of that idea—the defining concept of those emerging movements. By the late 1980s, popular movements had grown into powerful social forces in countries throughout Central America and the Caribbean.

This broad notion of human rights was reflected not just in the objectives of popular organization in Latin America but in its practice as well. The structure and function of many of these organizations tended to emphasize broad-based participation and grassroots, nonhierarchical leadership—two very concrete expressions of the principle of equality in practice—in a way totally unfamiliar to traditional U.S. forms of organizing. In contrast, U.S. organizing approaches during this same period tended to focus on hierarchical structures, boards of directors, and incremental, measurable organizing goals, à la Saul Alinsky and his widely read "Rules for Radicals."

Meanwhile, in Immokalee itself, where even Alinsky-style organization had never dared to tread, efforts to reform migrant farmworker exploitation had been dominated by the legal "advocate" model, driven primarily by a generation of attorneys inspired by the famous 1960 documentary "Harvest of Shame." In this model, the problem of farmworker exploitation is approached as a series of legal violations to be remedied, usually by legal action and occasionally, when the advocates were feeling frisky, by political or media pressure.

In the early 1990s, however, the workers who gathered to confront exploitation in Florida's tomato fields had never read "Rules for Radicals," nor had they much faith in the U.S. legal system. Rather, they came to Immokalee equipped with Latin American tools of struggle—many with direct experience in the powerful Latin American popular movements of the 1980s—and set about to work with a community that spoke the same organizing language.

To the workers that formed the Coalition of Immokalee Workers, ramshackle, overcrowded housing, for example, wasn't a distinct problem to be addressed by code inspectors, political pressure, and exposés in the press. Rather, it was a symptom of a much more profound violation of workers' human rights, one concrete expression of a system that locked farmworkers in poverty and fundamentally failed to recognize their dignity. The same could be said for the myriad conditions—from pesticide poisoning and dangerous transportation to wage theft and violence in the fields—of farmworker exploitation that for so many years had been addressed as particular legal violations to be attacked on an individual, case by case, basis. All the specific excesses of farmworker exploitation were understood by these new organizers as branches of the same condition, all rooted in the poverty and powerlessness that was their fate in their adopted country, in the denial of their fundamental equality and dignity as human beings—their human rights. The most effective way to address the many particular aspects of farmworker exploitation, from the perspective of these new immigrant organizers, was to attack them at their common root, that is, to redress the immense imbalance of power between farmworkers and their employers and so begin to win back the dignity and human rights that had been for so long denied farmworkers in this country.

This new perspective resulted in a shift in Immokalee from an extremely atomized, U.S.-style emphasis on specific farmworker legal rights to a more community-wide, Latin American-style, holistic understanding of human rights, and that shift gave birth to the CIW. It's the shift from suing in court to assure that workers receive the minimum wage guaranteed by law, to fighting in the street as a community for a living wage; the shift from accepting as a given that farmworkers are excluded from the laws that protect the right to collective bargaining, to organizing general strikes demanding the right to bargain as a collective.

. . .

And the workers discovered a great new efficacy in their organizing, as many of the most vexing human rights violations that had been ineffectually addressed through legal avenues for decades were virtually eliminated overnight through an approach that took aim at the underlying power relations, the roots of the violations.

The success of the initial organizing against exploitation at the hands of the local crewleaders encouraged CIW members and gave form to the continuation of our efforts, aimed after 1996 at the next level of power, at the growers. Here again, over the next several years, the Latin American roots of the CIW's organizing approach manifested themselves in every aspect of our work, from our demands to the very actions we employed to advance our campaign.

Our demands were captured in the name of the campaign that gave shape to the four years from 1997 to 2000: "Campaign for Dignity, Dialogue, and a Living Wage." Dignity was the overarching theme of our demands, tied to the idea of human rights as the universal standards by which a dignified existence is defined. This use of dignity in the U.S. organizing context is generally seen as too vague, far from the concrete, measurable demands typical of Alinsky-style organizing. But for workers in Immokalee, the denial of dignity, felt in virtually every aspect of relations with employers at work and with the powers that ruled community life, was the most humiliating condition of existence as a farmworker in the United States. Like the sanitation workers in Memphis who captured their struggle in the famous Civil Rights movement slogan "I Am a Man," workers in Immokalee chose "dignity" as the primary demand of their movement for human rights in the fields.

"Dialogue," like dignity, is also far too vague a term for most U.S.-style organizing. Collective bargaining has long been the gold standard of labor negotiation, and given the U.S. legal framework for labor organizing, the entire legal structure of union representation and recognition is set up with collective bargaining as its end. Dialogue, on the other hand, has no legal definition, and no structural mechanisms or institutional support to foster its practice.

But farmworkers are excluded from the National Labor Relations Act that gives unions the legal mechanisms necessary to compel employers to recognize the union as the collective bargaining agent for their labor. Consequently, not only can farmworkers be fired with no legal recourse if they attempt to organize or even ask for a raise, but farmworkers cannot access the National Labor Relations Board or any of its processes to compel their employers to bargain. What's more, Immokalee's function as a massive labor pool for dozens of agricultural employers makes workplace-specific organizing effectively impossible as virtually no workers have any lasting relationship to any particular employer.

Dialogue, therefore, is perhaps the closest that a community that is a labor pool for multiple employers, without the organizing rights and protections granted by the NLRA, can get to collective bargaining. Dialogue as a means to address the systematic, community-wide violation of human rights also has strong roots in the Latin American organizing experience, as community movements in Latin American often frame talks with authorities in terms of dialogue or "platicas." Dialogue also carries with it the implication of dignity as its suggestion of talks among equals was an important reason for its choice as a frame for our demands.

But not only were our demands framed in terms familiar to veterans of the Latin American human rights experience, the actions that CIW members chose to promote our campaign were likewise clearly not the product of the U.S. organizing tradition. In the four years from 1997 to 2000, the CIW organized a number of high-profile actions, including two more community-wide general strikes, a thirty-day hunger strike by six CIW members, and a fourteen-day march across the state of Florida to the offices of the growers' lobbying association, the Florida Fruit and Vegetable Association.

. . .

[In the years that followed, CIW also staged a series of successful boycotts, starting with the organized boycott of Taco Bell.] And running throughout the boycott as the thread that tied it all together was the theme of human rights. The CIW's framing of the campaign as a struggle of human rights versus corporate profits—not simply a struggle for farmworker rights—provided the broader analytical context that made the notion of alliance, as opposed to the more traditional and vertical solidarity, possible. The CIW's history of struggle for human rights both in Immokalee and beyond the level of farmworker grievances gave that frame legitimacy.

. . .

The third excerpt reviews the successful use of a human rights framework to support state-wide adoption of universal health care coverage in Vermont. In this case the author, Mariah McGill, is a lawyer and academic researcher rather than a movement activist. The Vermont Workers Center, whose work she chronicles, was founded in 1998. Just ten years later, led by Executive Director James Haslam, the Center

launched its campaign to adopt universal health care in the State of
Vermont. As described below, human rights were at the center of that
ongoing effort, though the movement was not led by lawyers.[6]

MARIAH MCGILL, "HUMAN RIGHTS FROM THE GRASSROOTS UP: VERMONT'S CAMPAIGN FOR UNIVERSAL HEALTH CARE"

14 Health and Hum. Rts.: An Int'l J.106, 106–07 (2012).

[I]n 2008, the Vermont Workers' Center launched the "Healthcare Is
a Human Right" Campaign (HCHR), which resulted in the 2010 passage
of health care legislation that incorporates human rights principles into
Vermont law and provides a framework for universal health care. By
framing health care as a human right, the center mobilized thousands of
state residents—many of whom had no prior involvement with political
campaigning—making it possible for the center to change the political
environment and pressure the state legislature to enact laws that may
lead to universal health care.

Vermont is a small rural state along the northeast border of the
United States. The 625,000 residents are primarily white and fairly well-
educated. The state has a strong tradition of direct democracy and local
control; the state's voters tend to be center-left on the political spectrum
and have twice elected a socialist, Senator Bernie Sanders, to serve in the
United States Senate. Vermont has frequently led the nation in issues
such as the abolition of slavery and marriage equality for same-sex
couples, and has repeatedly attempted to improve its health care system
over the past few decades.

In the 2000s, health care access and affordability was an issue of
primary importance to Vermonters, and a number of grassroots advocacy
groups began to push for health care reform. The member-run Vermont
Workers' Center, founded by a group of low-income Vermonters in 1996 to
address socioeconomic issues including livable wages, affordable housing,
and health care, fosters leadership in as many people as possible. The
center emphasizes transparency and participation in order to build a
sustainable grassroots movement. In the mid-2000s, staff noticed that
they were receiving frequent requests for assistance on health care
matters. When it became clear that health care was a major issue for
working Vermonters, the center focused its efforts on achieving universal
health care. In launching the new campaign, the center decided to use a
human rights framework inspired by the right to health as it is defined in
international law.

In developing their human rights framework, the center looked to
international treaties and documents that recognized the right to health,

---

[6] For updates on implementation efforts in Vermont, see www.workerscenter.org/
healthcare.

including the Universal Declaration of Human Rights and the International Covenant on Economic, Social, and Cultural Rights (ICESCR). Article 12 of the Covenant recognizes the right of everyone to the enjoyment of the highest attainable standard of physical and mental health.

The Covenant requires governments to progressively realize the right to health, as well as other economic and social rights. It recognizes that immediate implementation of all aspects may be impossible, but calls for governments to take steps that will over time lead to the full enjoyment of the right to health.

. . .

While the United States Senate has not ratified the ICESCR and therefore is not bound by the terms of the Convention, the Vermont Workers' Center chose to develop a human rights framework for its health care organizing. Rather than advocating for a particular form of universal health care, the center focused on ensuring that human rights principles would be incorporated into any universal health care system that the government adopted. The human rights principles at the center of the Vermont Workers' Center's framework are universality, equity, transparency, accountability, and participation.

Specifically, the campaign asserts that health care should be available to all Vermonters regardless of their ability to pay; that the cost of the health care system should be shared fairly; that Vermonters should participate in the design and implementation of the health care system; that the system should be transparent, efficient, and accountable to the people it serves; and that government should be responsible for ensuring that the health care system complies with these principles.

. . .

While other groups in the state are advocating for health care reform, the Vermont Workers' Center is the only group organizing around a human right to health care. The center chose to use a human rights framework because it wants to ensure that people are at the center of the debate. Previous health care reform debates in Vermont have focused on costs and financing mechanisms, such as single-payer health care, rather than on how the current health care system impacts people and what any proposed reforms would do to improve their health. While ordinary Vermonters might not relate to terms like "single-payer" or the "public option," they understand that the current system is causing needless suffering in their communities. The center asserts that the human rights framework has enabled the campaign to effectively organize and mobilize working people by making health care policy more accessible.

. . .

During the first year of the campaign, organizers focused on mobilizing state residents, believing that reform would be impossible without strong, sustained grassroots pressure. The center's emphasis on engaging the grassroots stemmed from previous failed efforts to introduce universal health care. In 2005, advocacy groups including the Vermont Workers' Center successfully pressured the Vermont state legislature to pass a single-payer health care bill, only to have the legislation vetoed by Governor James Douglas, a Republican. The center believed that the veto and the legislature's failure to override it were due to the influence of hospital, health insurance, and pharmaceutical lobbyists, whose industries benefited financially from the current system. While universal health care advocates had succeeded in getting single-payer health care legislation passed, it was defeated because there was not a strong grassroots base of support demanding health care reform.

. . .

To mobilize Vermonters, the campaign used a variety of strategies, including recruiting volunteers to staff tables at grocery stores and farmers' markets, march in local parades, and write letters to the editor. The center built relationships with other health care reform groups, unions, religious communities, and Vermont businesses. The campaign received endorsements from more than 100 organizations, businesses, faith communities, and labor unions, including Vermont Health Care for All and the Vermont Nurses' Union.

The center also developed a "People's Toolkit," which provided information on human rights and the campaign goals. One of the most effective organizing tools was "human rights hearings," which were held across the state. At these hearings, residents testified to community leaders about their experiences with the health care system; the hearings gave the center an opportunity to educate everyone in attendance on the human right to health care. The hearings demonstrated how the current health care system was harming thousands of Vermonters, and built solidarity among residents from all socioeconomic backgrounds.

Throughout 2008, campaign volunteers also asked Vermonters to complete a short survey and share personal stories about how the current health care system jeopardized their health and their finances. The campaign compiled over 1,500 surveys by the end of 2008. The survey results highlighted the links between the health care crisis and other social problems including homelessness, employment discrimination, bankruptcy, and domestic violence. For example, some residents without dental care reported social stigma and employment discrimination because they had missing or unsightly teeth. Some also reported becoming homeless after severe illnesses because they could not afford to pay for both housing and medical treatment. Finally, many reported staying in abusive relationships because they or their children needed medical care that they could not afford without the abusive partner's employer-sponsored health care plan.

> My father was an abusive alcoholic. My father would constantly threaten my mother that without him and his health insurance, she would never be able to make it on her own . . . The fear of not having health care prevents us from [from having] the freedom to make choices.

—Survey respondent

These personal stories humanized the health care crisis and helped the center explain the connection between human rights principles and the suffering of individual residents. The survey results were compiled in a report entitled "Voices of the Vermont Health Care Crisis," which was released to wide distribution in December 2008 in celebration of the 60th anniversary of the Universal Declaration of Human Rights.

In the fall of 2009, the campaign reached out to legislators to demand legislative reform in the 2010 session. When center organizers first approached legislators about enacting universal health care, they were discouraged by the response. Legislators argued, first, that universal health care was too controversial to tackle in an election year, and, second, that the legislature should focus on addressing the state budget crisis caused by the global economic crisis.

Although legislators were initially resistant, the strength of the grassroots social movement for "Healthcare as a Human Right" made it impossible for legislators to ignore the demand for universal health care. In the fall of 2009, the campaign also organized a series of "people's forums" throughout the state and invited local legislators to hear testimony from their constituents regarding their experiences with the health care system.

While many legislators had previously argued that health care reform was unnecessary, their argument became more difficult when confronted with voter testimony on the system's shortcomings. Many legislators began to express support for the notion of health care as a human right and publicly pledged to work on health care reform in the 2010 legislative session.

When the session began that January, the legislature did take up a variety of health care bills. The campaign used a variety of organizing tactics to place pressure on legislators to pass a bill that provided for universal health care, organizing a "People's Team" of volunteers who maintained a constant presence at the State House and attended every committee meeting related to health care during the 2010 session. The team tried to ensure that different campaign volunteers attended each meeting, illustrating that the campaign was not a fringe group, but that it represented the views of thousands of state residents.

The People's Team also made it easier for residents to engage in the political process. They revised the Toolkit to analyze the proposed health care bills from a human rights perspective, using language that was easy to read for those unfamiliar with health care policy.

. . .

H.100/S.88, which received the highest scores, was passed by both the House and the Senate. It became law on May 27, 2010, without the signature of Governor Douglas.

The new law, Act 128, does not explicitly state that health care is a human right, but it states that health care is a public good for all Vermonters, and incorporates the human rights principles advanced by the campaign. It clearly notes that it is state policy to ensure universal access to health care, and that systemic barriers must not prevent people from accessing health care. It also states that any health care plan must be transparent in design, efficient in operation, and accountable to the people it serves. Additionally, the government is held responsible for ensuring residents' ability to participate in the design, implementation, and accountability mechanisms of the health care system; the government must ensure that the health care system satisfies all these principles.

Act 128 established a health care commission charged with hiring an independent consultant to design three universal health care models, each of which was to incorporate the human rights principles laid out in the legislation. Dr. William Hsiao, the independent consultant hired to design the models, presented three models to the legislature and the general public in January 2011. He recommended that Vermont adopt a "public/private" single-payer health care system with a standard benefits package and a uniform payment system.

In November 2010, Peter Shumlin was elected governor after campaigning in support of a single-payer health care system. On February 11, 2011, the new governor unveiled H.202, a bill that established a single-payer health care system modeled after Hsiao's recommendations. Although the proposed legislation had the potential to move Vermont towards a universal health care system, the campaign offered a number of critiques. For example, the campaign expressed concern that the legislation did not attempt to provide universal health care coverage for all Vermonters until 2017. In addition, Green Mountain Care, the proposed universal health care system, required cost-sharing, which the Vermont Workers' Center asserted would make it more difficult for low-income residents to access care.

Despite these concerns, the campaign supported the bill and continued to mobilize residents to improve it and to ensure its passage. Throughout the 2011 legislative session, the campaign employed the strategies that had proven so successful the year before. Organizers drafted editorials, recruited volunteers to attend public hearings, and held a number of rallies. State and national groups working on health care reform also contributed to the effort to pass H.202. Dr. Deb Richter, founder of Vermont Health Care for All and long-time advocate for single-payer health care, delivered more than 500 talks to medical providers around the state, convincing many to support the legislation. Physicians for a National Health Program and the American Medical Student Association sponsored a rally drawing medical providers and students from across New England to the State House in support of a single-payer system. In March, the legislature teamed up with Vermont Interactive Television to host a statewide public hearing that used televisions to link legislators and residents at 15 locations around the state. The Rutland Herald reported that more than half the Vermonters who spoke were affiliated with the campaign and that the hearing was "as much a testimony to the organizing power of the 'Healthcare is a Human Right Campaign' as it was an indictment of the current health care system."

H.202 passed in the Vermont House on March 24, 2011, and the Vermont Senate on April 26, 2011. A last-minute amendment was added to the Senate version that excluded undocumented immigrants from coverage under the universal health care system. In the early days of the campaign, center organizers had identified health care for immigrants as a potential wedge issue, and to prepare, had educated organizers and members on the universality of human rights. The campaign responded to the amendment by reminding residents that all people are entitled to health care regardless of immigration status. The message resonated, and thousands signed petitions against the amendment and more than 40 volunteers lobbied at the State House to ensure that the amendment was stripped. The campaign mobilization against this amendment was so successful that Senator Richard Sears, one of the amendment's two co-sponsors, withdrew his support and instead introduced a resolution calling for federal immigration reform. On May 1, the campaign held a rally that attracted more than 2,000 attendees. After the House and Senate versions were reconciled in conference committee and again passed, Governor Shumlin signed H.202 into law on May 26. In a period of less than three years, the Vermont Workers' Center had successfully mobilized thousands of Vermonters to change what was politically possible and ensure that human rights principles were incorporated into state law.

The center's campaign is not the first campaign for universal health care in Vermont, but it has been the most effective because it has not wavered from the simple message that health care is a universal human right. The simplicity of this message has transformed the way Vermont residents and policy makers view health care, and has shifted the debate from cost-control and financing mechanisms to providing access to health care as a basic human right.

. . .

NOTES & QUESTIONS

1.   What role do/should lawyers play in grassroots campaigns of the kinds described above? Is this different than lawyers' roles in other social justice efforts? How do social mobilization efforts complement other human rights advocacy efforts in which lawyers might be involved?

2.   Lawyers are typically far from the center of grassroots campaigns such as those mounted by BNHR, CIW and the Vermont Workers Center. Yet these campaigns have explicitly adopted recognizable legal standards such as "dignity" and "universality" as their goals. Is it just happenstance that these goals have specific legal meanings and weight? How could the legal meanings of these terms be used in ways that contribute to the organizing campaigns of the grassroots groups involved?

3.   Fernando Garcia describes the way in which legal concepts like "rights" can empower individuals, even as their rights continue to go unrecognized by those in power. As a practical matter, is that "empowerment effect" dependent upon the involvement of lawyers in the movement? Can activists get as much mileage using "law without lawyers"? What role do lawyers play in advocates' use of legal concepts to mobilize and empower constituencies?

4.   What barriers did organizers face in mobilizing these constituencies? Was a human rights frame particularly suited to respond to the challenges that these groups faced? Or were these groups so marginalized that a human rights framework was really a last resort?

5.   In recent years, the CIW has had a number of high-profile successes. For example, CIW's Fair Food Campaign has led to agreements with many multi-billion dollar food retailers to establish more humane standards and fairer wages for farmworkers in their supply chains. Walmart, McDonalds, Subway and Whole Foods are among the parties to these agreements; Yum Brands was the first company to participate in 2005. These agreements include specific monitoring mechanisms to ensure that companies abide by their obligations. A complete list of participating companies is available at www.ciw-online.org/campaign-for-fair-food/. Interestingly, the Fair Food Campaign eschewed government-oriented regulatory approaches to the problems facing farmworkers and instead sought private agreements. Is the human rights framework particularly adapted to campaigns focused away from government and toward private actors, including corporations?

II. HUMAN RIGHTS IN U.S. ORGANIZING:
UNEVEN ACCEPTANCE

This section explores the challenges of using human rights in the U.S as a tool for organizing grassroots communities. After reviewing data from Boston about organizers' perceptions of human rights, this section introduces a case study from New York City of a human rights organizing campaign that had mixed results in reaching its goal. Finally, this section examines U.S. public awareness and understanding of human rights norms, using survey data compiled by the Opportunity Agenda.

In the United States, civil rights norms have long been a tool for mobilization and organizing, as well as legal action. Given this, why might grassroots groups choose to shift to a human rights frame?

A Boston-based study conducted in 2008 surveyed individuals associated with 42 organizations, and found that 43 percent of the interviewees "typified a human rights frame as a weak, irrelevant, or abstract set of discursive and analytical tools."[7] Among other things, interviewees identified the "lack of US cultural resonance" with human rights as a factor in their assessment, as well as the persistent notion that human rights abuses take place outside of the United States. The fact that the United States has ratified relatively few international human rights conventions also contributed to these reactions.

Despite these perceptions, 36 percent of the organizations studied were shifting their focus toward a human rights frame, and 62 percent of individuals interviewed indicated that the human rights frame informed their thinking about their own work. Interviewees identified the universality of, and interconnections between, human rights as important to their work. Activists also appreciated the potential for international connections that the human rights frame provided. Further, the activists identified a number of specific areas where they believed the human rights frame has significant potential utility, leading the study's authors to conclude that the engagement with human rights norms may grow over time.

A.C. Finnegan, et al., "Negotiating Politics and
Culture: The Utility of Human Rights for
Activist Organizing in the United States"

2 J. of Hum. Rts. Practice 307, 325–26 (2010).

One immigration activist explained how she saw her work connected to the UDHR: "that's exactly why it's not a matter of whether you're here legally or illegally; but [rather] what are we to do as far as [showing] that

---

[7]   A.C. Finnegan, et al., *Negotiating Politics and Culture: The Utility of Human Rights for Activist Organizing in the United States*, 2 J. of Hum. Rts. Practice 307 (2010).

your rights as a human being are respected?" An LGBT activist similarly shared how a human rights frame is valuable for constituencies like transgender people who like "illegal immigrants" are often portrayed as subhuman in US society. He said: "For some transgender folks, the myth has been perpetuated that we deserve to be treated badly so I think that being able to say that you have the right as a human being to live this kind of way is a good starting point to help people build self-esteem."

Other audiences that interviewees mentioned as resonating with human rights are young people, the medical community and advocates of social justice. One LGBT activist explained her thinking about youth: "Youth love the human rights framework because it is practical and it speaks to their mindset and that is [the perspective] from where youth are coming to us." Regarding the medical community, one health activist replied: "I can use that more successfully with medical people, because medical people by and large still have that ethical sense that people have the right to have a shot at good health." Pertaining to those who embody a social justice ethos, a few interviewees mentioned how the World Social Forum, an entity born in the anti-globalization movement and held in high esteem by many progressive social justice activists, has a framework that is "really rooted in expanding the human rights agenda."

In general, this study suggests that the potential of a human rights framework within the United States lies with grassroots efforts. If US-based organizers are willing to take on the human rights frame in their work, it has promise for bringing groups together across multiple issues. Furthermore, the human rights frame already appears to have resonance with those working on immigration issues, with young people, with the medical community, and with social justice advocates. It is these potential spaces and the fact that many activists are already using the framework to inform their own thinking which suggests that the human rights framework—despite its ambivalent history and perceived limitations—can still play a critical role in progressive efforts within the United States.

. . .

NOTES & QUESTIONS

1. The study cited above was based on research completed in 2008. Do you think opinions have changed in the intervening years? Would researchers find more or less interest in human rights frames if they repeated their study today?

2. The researchers for this study suggested that the human rights framework is most suited to grassroots mobilization. But consider the fact that one of the most publicized domestic social movements in recent years, Occupy Wall Street, did not explicitly invoke human rights language to

support its calls for redistribution of wealth. Was that an oversight or a missed opportunity, or a calculated move to broaden their appeal by not cabining their cause as a human rights claim? For a discussion of the international law relevant to the Occupy Movement, see Martha F. Davis, *Occupy Wall Street and International Human Rights*, 39 Fordham Urb. L.J. 931 (2012) (concluding that the Occupy's challenges to the wealth gap fall into a gray area of international law).

3.   Some of the organizers interviewed for the Boston study shied away from human rights frames because they believe that human rights are perceived as "liberal" or "progressive," and they hope to position themselves and their organization as neutral or a-political. Is this "liberal" quality inherent in human rights, or has it been imposed from the outside by cultural norms and domestic politics? Is there are way to redeem human rights as a neutral framework? Would that be a worthwhile goal?

4.   Professor Johanna Kalb has observed that subnational efforts to implement human rights norms have been most vigorous in subject matter areas where the U.S. has failed to act. As Kalb explains, states and localities are more likely to take steps to implement the provisions of CEDAW or to endorse the substance of the CRC—which the U.S. has not ratified—than they are to take concrete steps to implement U.S. obligations under CERD, which the U.S. has ratified. *See* Johanna Kalb, *The Persistence of Dualism*, 30 Yale L. & Pol'y J. 71 (2011). Kalb argues that this phenomenon arises, at least in part, from the residual effects of dualism, the idea that the federal government bears primary, or even sole, responsibility for human rights compliance. Interestingly, at least some of the activists interviewed in the article excerpted above also speak to this issue. They bemoan the fact that the U.S. has not ratified the full range of human rights treaties and say that they would be more likely to use these treaties in advocacy if the U.S. had ratified them. Is this because these activists also subscribe to the dualism paradigm?

5.   The study excerpted above was conducted in Boston, Massachusetts, one of the more politically progressive large cities in the country. Would you expect organizers in a so-called Red State to differ in their views of human rights from the organizers interviewed in Boston? In what ways?

The next excerpt focuses on another city: New York. In 2008, Professor Sally Merry, a legal anthropologist, and several colleagues published a detailed study of the NYC Human Rights Initiative (NYC HRI), an effort to enact a human rights law in New York modeled loosely on San Francisco's city-level CEDAW. Among other things, the study observed the ways in which legal organizations and grassroots groups engaged (or didn't) with various dimensions of human rights law. The excerpt below provides some details of Merry's study and her conclusions. In particular, Merry and her colleagues identified three dimensions of human rights law that come into play when advocates use human rights to mount a campaign for social change: (1) law; (2) values; and (3) good governance. Each of these played a role in the NYC HRI campaign, not always with expected results. As you read this piece, consider what "added-value" lawyers bring to a multi-dimensional campaign of this kind, where the greatest successes are in the area of education and values, rather than traditional areas of lawyer expertise such as law and governance.

SALLY ENGLE MERRY, PEGGY LEVITT, MIHAELA SERBAN ROSEN AND DIANA H. YOON, "WOMEN'S HUMAN RIGHTS AND SOCIAL MOVEMENTS IN NEW YORK CITY"

44 Law & Soc'y Rev.101, 102, 109 (2010).

For social movements, human rights are simultaneously a system of law, a set of values, and a vision of good governance. Each of these dimensions of human rights offers resources for grassroots social movements, but in quite different ways. Distinguishing them allows a clearer understanding of the way human rights work as law from below.

. . .

Our study . . . suggests that the values side of human rights is more open to mobilization by grassroots social movements than the law side, but that using either dimension depends on collaboration among social movement leaders, grassroots activists, and legal experts. This collaboration enables relatively powerless actors to mobilize human rights law and discourse from below. However, emphasizing human rights as good governance can derail attention from human rights values.

. . .

In its early stages, the NYC HRI was an ambitious attempt to change the anti-discrimination paradigm in New York City, to merge due process and equal protection, to bring in social and economic rights, and to shift from a focus on gender discrimination to one that stressed the intersectionality of race and gender. In the process of translating CEDAW and CERD into a city ordinance, there were necessary compromises with U.S. law, New York City politics, and the differences between civil and human rights, with ongoing questions about how international language or mechanisms can work in a domestic context. Some wanted to pass a law and others to use the law to develop a human rights consciousness. Although the drafting committee and the political strategy outreach committee worked together, the former focused on producing a legal text while the latter worked on public education and training human rights awareness to foster social transformation. For the latter committee, the law was an opportunity to mobilize support for an intersectional, human rights approach to inequality. This group valued the opportunities for public debate provided by the bill's monitoring system and sought to develop human rights consciousness.

. . .

There were also divisions based on race, social class, education, and professional status as well as the relative status, funding, and national visibility of the partnering NGOs. By and large, those who focused on legal perspectives were more elite, legally skilled, and more national and international in orientation. They were at the center of the NYC HRI during the drafting process. Those concerned with building a social movement came from less elite backgrounds and had experience with building social movements. In a sense, there was a division between those more focused on values and participation versus those more concerned with law and regulation of city agencies.

The movement changed as it intersected the state. The attempt to gain the City Council's support reshaped the project. The more radical idea of a CEDAW/CERD ordinance was domesticated by the City Council Legal Department that rewrote it in more conservative terms that conformed to New York City law. Tailoring the ordinance to fit into the city's political process changed and ultimately weakened it. The bill went from being a statement of human rights focusing on the intersection between race and gender to a document specifying processes for good governance and auditing. Grassroots participation in oversight was eliminated because the mayor was granted the power to appoint task force members.

. . .

Law, Values, and Governance

The NYC HRI and its coalition were both a legal campaign and a social movement. Together they tried to implement human rights law and mobilize support for the ideals of human rights. In addition to drafting the ordinance, the NYC HRI held public education and training sessions for city employees and NGOs in its coalition. Local NGOs working on a variety of justice projects concerning education, housing, poverty, welfare, and domestic violence received human rights training. Many added this framework to their previous repertoire of discourses and strategies. Human rights shifted rather than replaced these groups' frames, however, adding new tactics to existing ones. This combination of a legal approach and human rights awareness work served as an effective organizing strategy. Had the group focused only on law, it would have been more vulnerable to defeat in the face of resistance such as that of the New York City Council and the mayor's office. Clearly, developing rights consciousness is an integral part of social movement change through law.

Nevertheless, there were tensions between those working with human rights as law and those who saw it as values. The former wanted to draft a viable piece of legislation, while the latter were more concerned about mobilizing a social movement. The drafters worked with the social movement to "produce a document that would serve clients." The movement people considered this approach too instrumental and technical, preferring to concentrate on public awareness of injustice. Although, as one funder noted, human rights "has the potential to bring all progressive groups and issues together," this initiative demonstrated significant differences in the way human rights are conceived. These differences pervaded the entire initiative.

This was clearly not entirely a movement from below, nor was it exclusively an elite-driven initiative. Instead, it was a collaboration between elite legal experts and grassroots leaders rooted in local political struggles.

. . .

The collaboration was not free of hierarchies of expertise, connections, and status, but these diverse individuals and organizations were able to forge common ground in human rights ideals and governance principles, despite their differences in status and power. Indeed, the ideological commitment to equality and participation facilitated efforts to incorporate a variety of perspectives and issues. Here the values of human rights and its principles of governance facilitated collaboration among a highly diverse set of participants, including faculty in elite law schools, community organizers, experienced litigators in powerful national NGOs, and working-class members of community organizations in New York City.

. . .

Conclusions: Law From Below?

This case study suggests that the tripartite shape of human rights facilitates its capacity to respond to the concerns of less powerful people. Its values are accessible to those without legal expertise. Its ideology and governance principles foster collaborative work, which creates new alliances and coalitions. In New York City, it drew together groups working on a wide range of civil liberties and social and economic justice issues. Despite tensions between those with legal expertise and community organizing expertise as well as between members of large, relatively wealthy organizations and those of local ones with fewer resources, it generated ongoing cooperation over several years. The ideology of human rights itself, with its emphasis on equality and inclusion and its international grounding, contributed to this cooperation.

Thus, human rights ideology facilitates coalition work that brings different values and political strategies to the work of social movements.

However, human rights law, when confronting the law of the city or the nation, had more limited success. Although social movements are unlikely to abandon law as a path to power, mobilizing law demands pragmatic compromises and accommodations to the state and state law. Using human rights law as a social movement strategy domesticated human rights ideology. As the human rights framework became more firmly integrated into the state political and legal process, it lost some of its idealism and radical vision. The [human rights] law became a reformist document seeking to reshape existing institutions and increase participation rather than one that fundamentally challenged racial and gender discrimination in the city and state government as a whole. Thus, the capacious nature of human rights as law, values, and governance facilitates their mobilization. Individuals use their varied dimensions to promote social change.

Yet there is also skepticism and suspicion. Not all lawyers are sure that social movements matter or that these movements have understood human rights correctly. As legal reforms are passed, they are domesticated by the state and lose some of their critical capacity. Idealists in social movements find the pragmatic compromises required to implement human rights law discouraging. On the other hand, social movement activists think that passing laws without new forms of rights consciousness and mobilization is likely to be ineffective. They know that individuals will not pursue human rights cases unless they understand themselves to be rights-bearing subjects. The law, value, and governance sides of human rights are uneasy bedfellows, not always companionable but unable to act alone.

Indeed, the nonlaw dimensions of human rights are more accessible to the poor than the law dimensions. These values are central to mobilizing grassroots participation. Through coalitions and collaboration, relatively powerless groups can appropriate the moral strength and legitimacy of international human rights law. Their efforts to harness human rights in all its complexity constitute mobilization of law "from below."

NOTES & QUESTIONS

1.   After its introduction, the NYC HRI initiative that Merry, *et al.*, studied lay dormant for many years, at least in part because of mayoral opposition to the measure. Why would this proposal be so controversial? And why hasn't grassroots support been sufficient to overcome mayoral opposition? Is "good governance," which is clearly part of a worldwide human rights agenda, inherently a non-starter when it comes to mobilization of social movements?

2.   Professor Merry is an anthropologist and Professor Finnegan, primary author of the earlier excerpt, is a sociologist. What can lawyers learn from the observations of experts from other disciplines, like anthropology, about how to work with social movements? Are there other disciplines lawyer should seek out for advice about working with social movements? For lawyers, what are the practical implications of Professor Merry's work?

III. HUMAN RIGHTS IN THE U.S.: RE-FRAMING THE CONVERSATION

In the excerpt at the beginning of the preceding section, Professor Finnegan observed that activists are deliberately choosing "frames" to further their work, and that some in the U.S. have not found the human rights frame to be particularly useful. Polling data developed by the Opportunity Agenda confirms that in some areas, Americans are reluctant to fully support human rights. In a 2009 report entitled *How to Discuss Specific Social Justice Issues within a Human Rights Framework: Public Opinion Research Findings*, the Opportunity Agenda summarized their findings:

> We found that these audiences generally see human rights as the rights you have by virtue of being born. However, as the discussions move from initial reactions to the phrase "human rights" to more in-depth discussions of applying human rights to a range of social justice issues in the United States, participants' views of human rights become more complex. In particular, when members of the key audiences begin to distinguish between rights which are *protected*—freedom from torture, freedom of speech, etc.—from rights which are *provided*—health care, education, etc.—we begin to see some hesitation about calling the latter human rights.

> Many of the participants also held a conditional view of who should have certain human rights. For example, undocumented immigrants, in the minds of most of the key audience members, have forfeited some of their human rights because they have broken the law to be in the United States. Therefore, many question, and even object to, undocumented immigrants receiving health care. There are some human rights, however, that most of the members of the key audiences believe should be guaranteed to *all*, including due process rights, freedom from discrimination, and freedom from mistreatment.[8]

Following their initial findings, the Opportunity Agenda examined the issue of "framing," exploring the question of whether different

---

[8]   For a more detailed description of the Opportunity Agenda's research and findings, visit their website at http://opportunityagenda.org/public_opinion_research_2009.

approaches to framing human rights might influence public opinion and mobilize communities. In the excerpt below, the Opportunity Agenda explores the question of how to most effectively talk about human rights with a U.S. audience. By virtue of their training, lawyers tend to focus on laws. These findings suggest, however, that successful community organizing, mobilization and more general public engagement may require a different framework.

OPPORTUNITY AGENDA, "TALKING HUMAN RIGHTS IN THE UNITED STATES: A COMMUNICATION TOOLKIT FROM THE OPPORTUNITY AGENDA"
(2009).

We often talk about "framing" or "reframing" the debate on social issues. But what exactly does that mean? And how can it promote support for human rights?

Framing is the idea that communications—whether in a news story, a speech, an op-ed, or a water cooler conversation—carry implicit values, stories, and world views that shape the terms of debate and determine whether problems and solutions are part of the conversation. Framing taps into stories that we carry in our heads, with heroes, villains, morals, causes, and solutions.

Framing or reframing a debate takes time, repetition, and "message discipline." It does not mean that we should all mindlessly mouth the exact same words or avoid answering tough questions honestly.

But it does mean that all of our communications should carry common values and themes.

Human rights are just such a theme. By consistently calling up the values represented by a human rights approach, we can start to reframe a number of debates in favor of upholding human rights for all. Identifying those values and developing messages and stories that showcase them are key strategies to shaping the national dialogue.

As we work to start a conversation about human rights, it's important to understand the barriers and opportunities identified through public opinion research and on-the-ground experience. It's unlikely that we can immediately or dramatically change the frame of a particular argument in favor of a human rights frame if our audiences currently do not connect the issue to human rights. That's why it's encouraging that audiences *are* receptive to talking about due process, health care, racial profiling, and some other issues in specific human rights terms. It's also why we need to open conversations about other issues, such as immigration and sentencing youth to life without parole, with care and build more slowly toward an understanding of how they intersect with human rights.

Promoting values, concerns, and solutions in the public discourse is a long-term effort. Successful narratives about civil rights and environmentalism, for example, took decades to establish. We now know enough about how key audiences receive human rights messages to start strategically a HUMAN RIGHTS NARRATIVE.

. . .

HUMAN RIGHTS MESSAGING CORE MESSAGE:

It is better for everyone to live in a society that pays attention to human rights, rather than one that ignores human rights.

Our research shows that the American public is ready to hear more about upholding and promoting human rights at home. Americans hold a clear and positive concept of human rights and place social justice issues in a human rights framework—including economic and social rights. However, this understanding of and support for human rights is not rooted in treaties and does not translate to urgency in moving forward with an explicit human rights agenda. To build a case for doing so, we recommend that advocates both connect human rights to familiar and core values and make the case for a human rights approach with concrete examples of how using such a framework can have a positive and concrete effect on people's lives.

Themes to Guide Message Development

Lead with values. Fairness, dignity and opportunity, and pride in America's heritage and founding principles, were ranked highly by all audiences as a reason why human rights are important. Connect human rights issues to these values, drawing particularly on American experiences and history and our continuing struggle to make our founding ideals a reality.

Begin with supportive audiences and work outward.

. . .

Emphasize consensus issues to introduce the idea of human rights generally. Equal opportunity, freedom from torture, education, and health care are each widely accepted as human rights.

Start conversations with the goal—upholding human rights—rather than the process. Audiences have almost no knowledge of treaties and mechanisms and care less about their existence than they do about the conditions such vehicles are meant to address.

Then move to specific examples. This will illustrate the effectiveness of thinking about social justice issues though a human rights lens. Audiences do not immediately see the implication of viewing an issue as a human right and are likely to view human rights merely as inspiring ideals without concrete examples of their impact.

. . .

NOTES & QUESTIONS

1.   In 2011, the Council on Foreign Relations (CFR) conducted worldwide polling on attitudes regarding the United Nations and human rights. While world opinion was generally more supportive than U.S. public opinion, the U.S. respondents nevertheless gave strong support to the idea that the U.N. should seek to promote the principles in the UDHR. According to the CFR report,

> Americans express support for the United Nations playing an active role in promoting human rights and reject the argument that this would be improper interference in the internal affairs of a country. A large majority favors the UN playing a larger role than it presently does to promote human rights and favor giving it greater power to go into countries to investigate human rights abuses. A substantial majority of Americans believe that the UN should try to further women's rights even when presented with the argument that this would conflict with the principle of national sovereignty. When asked which entity should make decisions on matters related to human rights, more Americans prefer giving this role to the UN or regional organizations than to national governments.

Council on Foreign Relations, Digest of International Opinion on Human Rights, http://www.worldpublicopinion.org/pipa/articles/btjusticehuman_right sra/701.php?lb=bthr&pnt=701&nid=&id=.

What accounts for the differences between this poll and that conducted by the Opportunity Agenda? Are there framing differences in the questions presented that might drive responses in different directions, to be either more or less supportive of a broad range of human rights? What do these differences suggest about how to gain acceptance for human rights campaigns within the U.S.?

2.   The Opportunity Agenda suggests focusing on the goal rather than the process of human rights. Similarly, Professor Merry's study found that the values of human rights were its most effective dimension in the NYC HRI campaign. Values were also featured in the examples of grassroots mobilization mounted by the Border Network for Human Rights, the Coalition of Immokalee Workers and the Vermont Workers' Center. Is it up to lawyers to also engage in mobilizing grassroots communities by emphasizing values over process, or should lawyers stick to law? Does this emphasis on values suggest that it is simply too soon in the integration of human rights

into U.S. culture to take up legal campaigns directed at implementing human rights in this country? What is the counter-argument to the assertion that law and legal talk should take a back seat in human rights advocacy efforts, at least for the time being?

IV. CASE STUDY: MOBILIZATION, HUMAN RIGHTS AND LEGAL ADVOCACY AFTER HURRICANES KATRINA AND RITA

The following case study gives you a chance to apply these materials to a real-life human rights challenge: the aftermath of Hurricanes Katrina and Rita. As you read, consider the various dimensions of human rights involved in responding to this catastrophe, and how lawyers can be supportive of community mobilization around human rights.

Hurricane Katrina, which struck the Louisiana coast in August 2005, was the deadliest and most destructive hurricane in the history of the United States. At least 1833 people died in the hurricane and subsequent floods. Total property damage was estimated at $81 billion. Tens of thousands of individuals were displaced from their homes, often for prolonged periods. In many instances, they had no habitable homes to which to return.

Just weeks later, Hurricane Rita struck. Less powerful than Katrina, it was nevertheless the fourth largest Atlantic hurricane ever recorded. The storm surge from Rita inundated coastal Louisiana communities that were still reeling from Katrina's effects. As Rita bore down on the Texas coast, evacuees who had only recently relocated from communities in Louisiana were uprooted again, along with more than three million residents of coastal Texas, Galveston and Houston who fled north along crowded highways. A total of 120 deaths have been attributed to Hurricane Rita, seven of which were directly related to flooding, wind and other weather conditions. The remaining deaths were primarily traced to the evacuations. The National Hurricane Center estimated Rita's damage to coastal communities at $12 billion.

Years after the hurricanes, New Orleans and other communities that suffered major losses are still recovering. More than a million people were displaced. While some returned to their homes quickly, more than 600,000 households were displaced for a month or more. The U.S. Census Bureau reported in 2009 that 7 percent of those who evacuated with Katrina did not, even four years later, consider themselves to be permanently re-settled. Within the first year after Katrina/Rita, New Orleans lost over half of its population. By July 2012, the population had recovered somewhat but was still just 76 percent of pre-disaster numbers.

The federal response to these twin disasters was widely criticized as both slow and ineffective. After criticism in the media and by Congress and state governments, FEMA's own Inspector General joined the chorus, stating that "much of the criticism is warranted."

In the wake of these disasters, both local and out-of-state lawyers rallied to help the local communities. Ethical rules that would have otherwise prevented out-of-state lawyers from practicing in Louisiana were relaxed so that large law firms and law schools from outside of the region were able to send contingents to help. And the local lawyers, legal workers, and organizers went to great lengths to set up projects, help to coordinate volunteers and otherwise support the work of visiting lawyers.

In the local community, the human rights framework resonated as individuals and organizations sought to come to grips with their new daily challenges. Yet the excerpts below suggest that the human rights frame was sometimes perceived as coming from advocacy professionals—and even from out-of-state advocates—rather than from the local grassroots, despite the fact that the initial integration of human rights concepts into local advocacy agendas was accomplished before Katrina and Rita hit.

DAVIDA FINGER AND RACHEL E. LUFT, "NO SHELTER: DISASTER POLITICS IN LOUISIANA AND THE STRUGGLE FOR HUMAN RIGHTS"

Human Rights in the United States: Beyond Exceptionalism 291, 300–01
(Shareen Hertel, et al., eds., 2011).

Within days of Hurricane Katrina's landfall, AEHR [Advocates for Environmental Human Rights], USHRN [U.S. Human Rights Network], and other U.S. social justice advocates and organizers were framing the disaster in human rights terms. They emphasized different rights frameworks in accord with their respective organizational orientations. For example, the National Economic and Social Rights Initiative concentrated on the absence of economic rights that even prior to the hurricane had produced poverty and greatly enhanced disaster vulnerability. A notable number of black liberation organizations condemned the events in the language of human rights and national oppression. Saladin Muhammad of Black Workers for Justice, for instance, issued a searing critique of national policy called "The Black Nation's 9/11". He placed Katrina in a long history of racism and imperialism, concluding with the link between human rights and black self-determination that has been central to black liberation human rights articulations. The political diversity of this early Katrina framing reflects the vibrancy and heterogeneity of the U.S. human rights movement.

. . .

[Here], we describe the development of these frameworks within the grassroots movement struggling for a just reconstruction in New Orleans. In the five years since Hurricane Katrina, some local movement groups have begun to adopt the discourse of human rights in their resistance efforts. We find a hybrid approach: local groups use some human rights *language* but have not for the most part adopted human rights *strategy* or *tactics,* staying focused instead on conventional civil rights-based goals and methods.

. . .

When Katrina struck land in August 2005, New Orleans was already home to legal advocates working on a domestic human rights agenda. Few though they were, these advocates had strong ties to local grassroots organizers. Although New Orleans movement culture itself was overwhelmingly oriented to local issues of racial and economic justice and cultural survival, the human rights advocates were part of broader national networks. These ties would be important conduits of human rights activity after the storm.

Days after Hurricane Katrina, dozens of local and regional far left groups came together to form a movement coalition called the People's Hurricane Relief Fund (PHRF). It was founded by leaders of the black liberation movement, some of whom had political roots in the black liberation human rights tradition. Within weeks PHRF organizers had carefully chosen the language of "Right to Return" as their motto. Coined to assert the contested, political, and interconnected web of obstacles to returning home, the phrase placed displacement at the center of the recovery and rights at the center of displacement. The saying became the slogan of local and national Katrina resistance activity. By December 2005, at the height of PHRF's role as the New Orleans post-Katrina justice movement coalition, the human rights orientation was central to its articulation of grievances and its reconstruction agenda. One significant action was to convene human rights tribunals—part of a two-pronged effort to sustain international attention on Katrina-related U.S. rights violations and to advance a local, popular, human rights political education campaign.

Between Hurricane Katrina in 2005 and Hurricane Gustav in September 2008, human rights activism in New Orleans proliferated. It included the use of traditional human rights tactics such as testimony before UN committees and the submission of shadow reports, visits by several UN Special Rapporteurs, a proposed resolution to the People's Assembly of the United States Social Forum, the PHRF Tribunals, and grassroots public forums designed to educate New Orleanians about international human rights standards and to demand U.S. accountability to them. In addition to these more formal human rights mechanisms, this period also witnessed a growing use of human rights language in meetings, rallies, and marches supporting the movement for a just reconstruction. This discursive development suggests a cultural shift that human rights advocates and scholars have argued is a central component of human rights movement-building. Post-Katrina New Orleans, we found, is the site of an emergent human rights culture.

By human rights culture we mean an engagement—philosophical, moral, and political, if not legal or systematic—with the notion that human beings are entitled to a broader category of rights than those promised by the U.S. Constitution. This orientation reveals itself in the growing use of human rights framing devices by grassroots movement activists. We believe this development has the potential to become part of what Cass Sunstein terms "constitutive commitments" toward what USHRN calls the necessary "transform[ation of] U.S. political culture."

The human rights agenda was still foreign to most New Orleanians and the community's grassroots leadership before Katrina, steeped like most U.S. citizens in a civil rights framework. But at the time of this writing, at the fifth anniversary of Katrina, the effects of the popular education campaign are discernible. In the rest of this [essay], we examine this development and describe two characteristics. The first is that human rights frames are entering communities through professional human rights advocates via local movement leadership; it is not a bottom-up phenomenon. Human rights do not constitute the political habitus of most Americans for specific historical reasons documented by Carol Anderson and others. However, the advocates who have played the greatest role in New Orleans are those with strong movement ties; their priority is domestic human rights movement-building in and among poor black communities.

The second characteristic is the coexistence of proto-human rights consciousness with more conventional strategies and tactics. Discursive inclusion of human rights in the political vocabulary of movement participants does not necessarily signal a human rights strategic orientation or use of formal human rights instruments. Instead, we find a hybrid approach. We take each of these characteristics in turn.

Human rights consciousness is spreading in top-down fashion as movement leaders become educated to human rights frameworks through the explicit efforts of local and nonlocal advocates. Monique Harden of AEHR and Kali Akuno of PHRF and USHRN have each played an instrumental role in introducing human rights concepts and reframing local issues in human rights terms. Each has pursued formal human rights mechanisms—shadow reports, Special Rapporteur visits, tribunals—as political education and base-building opportunities for local activists and residents. Local movement leadership, in turn, has taken to the framework more quickly than the base.

An example of the vertical nature of the flow of human rights acculturation is apparent in Voice of the Ex-Offender (V.O.T.E.), a local criminal justice reform organization. Founder Norris Henderson does not draw directly on human rights frameworks in his own work, which is focused on civil and political rights, but he understands their value:

> The first word is human. Everyone is on the same level. That gives us more protection. We've been fascinated by civil rights. And it did that, it got us civically engaged. But we're still shut out. So we need something else. I see the benefits of being called an [Internally Displaced Person]. If I'm an IDP, then all these things should happen. We have a lack of human rights education. We need more training. People just get accustomed to what they've been doing.

Although Henderson appreciates the political possibilities offered by human rights frames, they are still foreign to his membership. Two days after Henderson voiced the distinction between civil and human rights, when one member of his organization was asked the same question about whether human rights had a role in V.O.T.E.'s work, the member replied, "Absolutely. We fight for human rights more than anything. We're not supposed to see a color. We see this happening with Mexicans now. They're not getting what they deserve." His answer suggested a conflation of human rights with a civil rights politic and a post-civil rights colorblindness; he responded from the domestic framework with which he was familiar. There is still a gap in familiarity with human rights between the leadership and its constituency. We describe this feature of local human rights culture because of the political delicacy of movement-building with non-indigenous frames. Because of the history of political culture in the United States, spontaneous human rights discourse is unlikely. We have sought to document patterns in its reception once the framework is introduced.

The second characteristic of the emergent human rights culture is a burgeoning human rights consciousness that exists together with traditional U.S.-based movement strategies and tactics rooted in local or domestic agendas. Adoption of human rights terms does not necessarily signal adoption of the legal, formal, or transnational agenda and methods that have usually accompanied them. Instead, at this stage, they communicate a more general sense that people betrayed by the U.S. government have rights that transcend its jurisdiction and to which it must be accountable. Henderson, for example, the grassroots organizer who founded V.O.T.E., has a national vision for enfranchising formerly incarcerated persons. The work is consummate political rights activity based on voter education and registration, although he understands it to be a part of the broader struggle for human rights. Although most New Orleans movement groups maintain their strategic and programmatic focus locally and domestically, we see signs that the language of human rights is becoming a more generalized movement vocabulary for politicizing hurricane-related events and other forms of injustice.

The second characteristic is consistent with the literature on grassroots domestic human rights movements in the United States. Use of formal human rights instruments such as international rights documents and presentations to international human rights bodies still represents quintessential human rights activity. However, as the U.S. human rights movement grows, formal mechanisms are becoming de-centered, taking their place in a larger repertoire of social movement tactics. Human rights scholarship suggests that it is ultimately human rights framing more than strategy, and strategy more than tactics, that marks a shift in political culture, at least at the emergent stage. In New Orleans, human rights strategy and tactics are still the purview of professional human rights advocates.

———————

Despite the perception in some quarters that outside activists were trying to take leadership of post-Katrina responses,[9] including utilizing human rights strategies that were not fully understood or supported by the affected communities, some community activists clearly embraced human rights approaches. For example, three years after Katrina, Hurricane Gustav hit the same region of Louisiana, wreaking dramatic damage. Stand with Dignity, a local Louisiana coalition, employed widely-accepted human rights techniques when it conducted an independent evaluation of evacuation shelters, assessing their compliance with human rights standards. As you read this report, think about what specific human rights norms it invokes, even as it stops short of using treaty language or other explicit legal frameworks.

---

[9] *See, e.g.*, Sean Benjamin et al., *Points for Visiting Activists to Consider* (Oct. 15, 2005), *available at* http://katrinareader.org/points-visiting-activists-consider (urging visiting volunteers to be "respectful" of those living in the community).

STAND WITH DIGNITY, "THROUGH MY EYES: LOUISIANA'S FIRST INDEPENDENT EVACUATION SHELTER MONITORING REPORT"

(2010).

"Access to a humane and comprehensive evacuation plan is a basic human right of all evacuees."

Purpose

Evacuation can never be effective, humane or legal without prioritizing community input and decision making in evacuation planning, preparation, and implementation. This grassroots monitoring report is one step towards building adequate transparency and accountability into Louisiana's emergency preparedness and response.

The purpose of this report is to provide families of Southeast Louisiana with a comprehensive and honest assessment of Louisiana's evacuation plan and sheltering readiness prior to a mandatory evacuation. The information comes from community assessors—90% were former evacuees in state run shelters during the 2008 mandatory Gustav evacuation.

STAND's specific priorities were (1) to determine the readiness of the state of Louisiana's 2009 Evacuation and Sheltering Plan; (2) to assess the humanitarian standards in place at 'State-run' Critical Transportation Needs Shelters (CTNS) and Medical Special Needs Shelters; and (3) to evaluate the state's shelter management and organization.

Background

On August 4, 2009, STAND led an independent community assessment and inspection of three state-run shelter facilities. Community assessors accompanied the Louisiana's Department of Social Services, the Governor's Office of Homeland Security and Emergency Preparedness, and other supportive state partners. The community assessment delegation, comprised of 90% former evacuees, along with their allies, conducted the shelter inspections in Monroe, Shreveport, and Alexandria.

Although disasters may be 'natural,' preparation and government policies shape their impact on communities. In the midst of the mandatory evacuation during Hurricane Gustav, STAND's independent shelter monitoring exposed how the poorest and most vulnerable evacuees suffered the most devastating effects of the disaster because of the state policy that directed them to the least prepared state shelters that failed to meet basic humanitarian standards.

Based on this experience, STAND committed to two main goals. First, STAND challenged the state's practice of unequally disadvantaging the most-vulnerable communities with its evacuation policies. Second, STAND pressured the state to establish basic minimum standards for all evacuation shelters housing Louisiana evacuees.

The determination of STAND's community leaders and organizers over the past year has been critical in exposing Louisiana's lack of preparation and response, advancing the rights of evacuees to access humane and equal conditions and treatment, and ensuring the state adopts best-practice emergency shelter standards and conditions.

As discussed herein, the 2009 sheltering improvements, while significant, leave room for improvement, particularly in the areas of safety and security, shelter infrastructure, and environmental health. The improvements thus far evidence the critical importance of community inclusion and accountability that are necessary to ensure a humane and comprehensive evacuation and recovery plan for Louisiana's coastal residents.

. . .

We STAND Upon Six Rights to a Dignified Evacuation

1.   *The right to complete and transparent planning and preparation prior to Hurricane Season.*

Evacuees have a right to know the short and long term plan for sheltering and humanitarian relief including the location of shelters (both in-state and out of state) and the basic standards that set conditions and treatment of evacuees. Evacuees also have a right to know local options for protection in the city and the responsibility of city, parish, and state officials.

2.   *The right to full inclusion and community participation in decision making regarding evacuation planning and preparation.* Evacuees know best how to articulate and assist their families' needs. Many mistakes were made during Gustav that could have been prevented if evacuees were included in the planning and decision making. While the sheltering plans have improved, important work remains on state plans for safety and security, shelter infrastructure, and environmental health.

3.   *The right to humane conditions and treatment during and after a hurricane.*

Disaster relief must be provided for all victims despite a [person's] economic, race, criminal background and immigration status and relief must meet accepted, basic humanitarian standards.

4.   *The right to humane security and safety services from all law enforcement officers and disaster relief staff.* Evacuees should be treated

with dignity and respect—as human beings. Evacuating and trying to survive does not make evacuees criminals, and they should not be treated that way. All law enforcement, shelter staff, and relief agencies must take [responsibility] for protecting evacuees both during and after hurricanes.

5. *The right to community health and environmental standards within all disaster facilities and servicing stations.* This includes waiting, transportation, servicing centers, and shelters. Transportation must include ventilation that meets health code, adequate personal space, basic sanitary resources, and bathrooms. Holding and waiting sites should have hydration, bathrooms, and onsite medical personnel.

6. *The right to transparency, dialogue, and direct accountability with all officials governing the system.* Evacuees must be guaranteed the right to transparency, dialogue, and accountability from the agencies involved planning, preparing and implementing the state and local government's responsibilities. No evacuee should have to use the media and public protest to open dialogue with the Governor and other [responsible] authorities.

. . .

Evacuation can never be effective, humane or legal without prioritizing community input and decision making in evacuation planning, preparation, and implementation. Never again will we allow our families and Louisiana's poorest and most-vulnerable evacuees to arrive at warehouses converted into emergencies shelters lacking the most basic service and infrastructure.

STAND believes it is the community's responsibility to hold the government accountable for providing humane, fair, and equitable conditions. This independent monitoring report is the first step in a process to build transparency and accountability into Louisiana's emergency preparedness and response. While some substantial sheltering improvements were evident during STAND's tour of model shelter facilities, more community inclusion and accountability are necessary to ensure a humane and comprehensive evacuation and recovery plan for Louisiana's coastal residents.

. . .

NOTES & QUESTIONS

1. Veteran activist, lawyer and law professor William Quigley, a New Orleans resident, offers the following general suggestions to public interest lawyers:

Learning to join rather than lead, learning to listen rather than to speak, learning to assist people in empowering themselves rather than manipulating the levers of power for them, these are the elements of lawyering for empowerment. By mastering their elements, a lawyer can help people join together and control those forces influencing their daily lives. By helping people in a community organized process to recognize common challenges, they can work together to formulate common strategies to combat these challenges.

William Quigley, *Reflections of Community Organizers: Lawyering for Empowerment of Community Organizations,* 21 Ohio N. Univ. L. Rev. 455, 479 (1995).

How could you translate these general admonitions into specific approaches for lawyers in New Orleans post-Katrina?

2.   Drawing on the work of constitutional law scholar Professor Robert Cover, Professor Katharine Young recently proposed a working dichotomy of "redemptive" and "rejectionist" frames in the context of ESC rights. According to Young,

> Redemptive frames can be understood as those that seek to reinterpret or change laws to emphasize incipient constitutional, statutory, common law, and international protections of economic, social, and cultural rights. Rejectionist frames, on the other hand, expose the lack of legal protections under current constitutional, statutory, common law, or internationally binding arrangements. The first frame proposes a way forward within current legal institutions, but may be vulnerable to co-optation by the very institutions in which change is sought. The second frame opposes the current structures of law and the state yet may be no less immune from co-optation. Like the notions of accommodation versus resistance, or of amelioration versus opposition, these concepts serve as heuristics to facilitate our understanding of the assumptions that undergird particular strategies of mobilization or advocacy, each sharing features of its apparent counterpart.

Katharine G. Young, *Redemptive and Rejectionist Frames: Framing Economic, Social, and Cultural Rights for Advocacy and Mobilization in the United States,* 4 Northeastern L.J. 323 (2013).

In her article, Young examines the Occupy movement using these frameworks. Is this dichotomy also useful for understanding post-Katrina activism in New Orleans—or is a different analysis required when communities are responding to a natural disaster rather than a failure of government? Are there examples of both redemptive and rejectionist frames in the struggles that followed the hurricane? Which approach do you believe is more effective for mobilization? For achieving social change? What differing roles might lawyers have within these alternative frames?

3.   An important and devastating aspect of the post-Katrina/Rita struggle was the displacement of hundreds of thousands of former New Orleans residents. Popular media often referred to these individuals as

refugees. A more accurate term drawing on international law would have
been Internally Displaced Persons (IDPs). IDPs are defined as "persons or
groups of persons who have been forced or obliged to flee or to leave their
homes or places of habitual residence, in particular as the result of or in order
to avoid the effects of armed conflict, situations of generalised violence,
violations of human rights or natural or human-made disasters, and who
have not crossed an internationally recognised State border." U.N.
Commission on Human Rights, Report of the Representative of the Secretary-
General, Mr. Francis M. Deng, submitted pursuant to Commission resolution
1997/39. Addendum: Guiding Principles on Internal Displacement, 11
February 1998, E/CN.4/1998/53/Add.2, *available at* http://www.refworld.
org/docid/3d4f95e11.html. While no international treaty specifically covers
the rights of IDPs displaced by natural disasters, IDPs are protected under
any international treaties to which their country is party. *See* Frederic L.
Kirgis, *Hurricane Katrina and Internally Displaced Persons*, 9 ASIL Insights
(Sept. 21, 2005). The Office of the United Nations High Commissioner for
Refugees has released Guiding Principles to specify rights for IDPs. The
Guiding Principles have not been placed in a treaty but the United Nations
General Assembly adopted a resolution in 2003 affirming these Guiding
Principles. U.N. General Assembly, UN Doc. A/RES/58/177, preambular
paragraphs.

4.   After the Katrina disaster, the National Social and Economic Rights
Initiative circulated a policy statement that drew on the human rights
principles developed internationally to address IDPs. Challenges and
Potential for a Human Rights Response to Hurricane Katrina, https://www.
nesri.org/sites/default/files/Challenges%20and%20Potential%20for%20a
%20HR%20Response%20to%20Hurricane%20Katrina.pdf.

The U.S. Human Rights Network, an umbrella organization of domestic
human rights organizations, also took this approach, issuing a statement
entitled "Hold the US Accountable: IDP Human Rights Campaign." What
impact might the IDP frame have in the context of an organizing strategy
post-Katrina? What impact might the framework have on a legal strategy?
What advocacy opportunities does it offer? Accepting the IDP categorization
for the time being, what messages/frames might the Opportunity Agenda
report suggest for post-Katrina advocacy and mobilization in New Orleans to
address IDP issues?

5.   Imagine that a foundation has invited you to design a legal
organization located in New Orleans focused on providing continuing redress
for individual Hurricane Katrina victims while also targeting the overarching
economic factors that contributed to the disparate racial impact of the
hurricane's aftermath. Money is no object as you put together your plans, but
you will need community buy-in in order to identify potential clients and
accomplish your goals. How will human rights approaches figure, if at all, in
the strategic plans for your legal organization? Would it be more effective to
allocate the funds to an existing organization or to create a new initiative?
What factors will you consider as you make these decisions?

CHAPTER XI

ETHICS AND DOMESTIC HUMAN RIGHTS LAWYERING

■ ■ ■

Ethical issues pervade the practice of law, including domestic human rights lawyering. Some of the issues faced by domestic human rights lawyers are familiar, and perhaps indistinguishable, from other areas of practice, *e.g.*, client communication, candor to the tribunal, confidentiality. However, some of the ethical issues faced by domestic human rights lawyers will have a spin that differs from domestic practice. For example, domestic human rights lawyers may want to ensure that their interactions with clients respect human rights norms while also conforming to binding legal ethics codes. Further, the boundaries between legal advice and moral advice may be particularly blurry in the human rights arena. Some even argue that human rights work done by lawyers is not truly lawyering at all, and therefore not governed by the legal profession's ethics guidelines.[1]

Part I examines human rights law itself as a source of legal ethics norms, specifically considering the intersections between human rights norms and domestic ethics codes. In particular, you are invited to think about how human rights might fit within existing ethics codes, or whether there are tensions between existing legal ethics norms and human rights. Part II then looks at how human rights norms designed to guide corporations—the U.N. Guiding Principles on Business and Human Rights—may influence the practice of law, both by regulating law firms as corporate entities and by structuring the advice that lawyers may ethically offer. Finally, Part III examines human rights lawyering as a type of public interest lawyering, and considers the ways in which issues like client-centered lawyering, group representation and cultural competence may play out in the domestic human rights context.

This chapter is included not because human rights supersedes binding domestic ethical obligations, but because it is clear that as human rights gain purchase in the U.S. and internationally, these norms will have to be reconciled, particularly in the area of business and human

---

[1] *See* Beth Lyons, *Human Rights Aspirations, Professional Obligations: Practitioner Survey on the Ethics of Domestic Human Rights*, 1 Notre Dame J. of Int'l, Comp. & Hum. Rts. L. 114, 128 (2011) (one survey participant observed that proceeding in a supranational forum is "more akin to calling a press conference than winning a case").

rights. Furthermore, looking at legal ethics through a human rights lens illuminates some of the choices made by the legal profession, and opens up further dialogue on two fronts: the content of lawyers' ethical behavior, and the status of human rights as real law.

I. PROFESSIONAL ETHICS CODES AND HUMAN RIGHTS

Lawyers worldwide are required to conform to professional ethical standards in their practice of law. Attorney discipline for non-compliance with these standards is a key part of the self-regulation that marks lawyers' status as members of an independent profession. In many jurisdictions around the globe, the efforts to maintain ethical standards of practice date back hundreds of years, to the very origin of the legal profession.[2]

Enforceable disciplinary standards are generally established by the jurisdiction that issues the attorney's license to practice. In the United States, ethics standards are promulgated at the state level and enforced against lawyers licensed in the state by state bar disciplinary bodies and ultimately, state supreme courts. Sanctions for disciplinary violations may include public censure, suspension or even disbarment.

A. A SURVEY OF LEGAL ETHICS CODES

The American Bar Association, the largest professional organization in the world, maintains detailed Model Rules of Professional Conduct upon which states often draw as they revise their own particularized disciplinary codes. The current Model Rules, completed in 1983, are the ABA's most recent effort to support codification of universal ethics standards—a project that began in 1908 with the original Canons of Professional Ethics and continued with the Model Code of Professional Responsibility before the current Model Rules superseded those earlier efforts.

i.   The ABA Model Rules

The ABA's Model Rules address topics from confidentiality to unauthorized practice of law, but do not explicitly reference human rights as a norm for ethical legal practice. Earlier ABA efforts—the Canons and the Model Code—were similarly devoid of references to human rights, though the Preamble to the Model Code did mention the "dignity of the individual" as a touchstone of legal practice. There is no record of why that language was deleted in more recent versions of the ethics provisions.

---

[2]   For more background information on this, see Carol Rice Andrews, *Standards of Conduct for Lawyers: An 800-Year Evolution*, 57 SMU L. Rev. 1385 (2004).

However, the ABA standards clearly draw on moral philosophy and political theory, as well as the law of agency, criminal law and other existing legal standards, to establish guidelines for attorney behavior. For example, the Preamble to the current Model Rules admonishes that

> [A] lawyer should further the public's understanding of and confidence in the rule of law and the justice system because legal institutions in a constitutional democracy depend on popular participation and support to maintain their authority. A lawyer should be mindful of deficiencies in the administration of justice and of the fact that the poor, and sometimes persons who are not poor, cannot afford adequate legal assistance.

Likewise, the ABA Model Rules and accompanying commentary detail the role of lawyers as "counselors" and "advisors" in ways that suggest a role for human rights norms. For example, Rule 2.1 of the Model Rules provides that "[i]n representing a client, a lawyer shall exercise independent professional judgment and render candid advice. In rendering advice, a lawyer may refer not only to law but to other considerations such as moral, economic, social and political factors that may be relevant to the client's situation." The Commentary to Rule 2.1 expands on this provision, making clear that lawyers "may" offer a broader range of assistance to clients beyond technical legal advice:

> [2] Advice couched in narrow legal terms may be of little value to a client, especially where practical considerations, such as cost or effects on other people, are predominant. Purely technical legal advice, therefore, can sometimes be inadequate. It is proper for a lawyer to refer to relevant moral and ethical considerations in giving advice. Although a lawyer is not a moral advisor as such, moral and ethical considerations impinge upon most legal questions and may decisively influence how the law will be applied.

> [3] A client may expressly or impliedly ask the lawyer for purely technical advice. When such a request is made by a client experienced in legal matters, the lawyer may accept it at face value. When such a request is made by a client inexperienced in legal matters, however, the lawyer's responsibility as advisor may include indicating that more may be involved than strictly legal considerations.

> [4] Matters that go beyond strictly legal questions may also be in the domain of another profession. Family matters can involve problems within the professional competence of psychiatry, clinical psychology or social work; business matters can involve problems within the competence of the accounting profession or of financial specialists. Where consultation with a professional in

another field is itself something a competent lawyer would recommend, the lawyer should make such a recommendation. At the same time, a lawyer's advice at its best often consists of recommending a course of action in the face of conflicting recommendations of experts.

ABA Model Rules of Prof'l Conduct, R.2.1, cmt. 2 (2013).

Finally, Rule 6.1 of the ABA Model Rules, addressing lawyers' obligation to contribute pro bono assistance, suggests another role for human rights, though explicit human rights language is missing from the Rule. According to Rule 6.1:

> Every lawyer has a professional responsibility to provide legal services to those unable to pay. A lawyer should aspire to render at least (50) hours of pro bono publico legal services per year. In fulfilling this responsibility, the lawyer should:
>
> (a) provide a substantial majority of the (50) hours of legal services without fee or expectation of fee to:
>
>> (1) persons of limited means or
>>
>> (2) charitable, religious, civic, community, governmental and educational organizations in matters that are designed primarily to address the needs of persons of limited means; and
>
> (b) provide any additional services through:
>
>> (1) delivery of legal services at no fee or substantially reduced fee to individuals, groups or organizations seeking to secure or protect civil rights, civil liberties or public rights, or charitable, religious, civic, community, governmental and educational organizations in matters in furtherance of their organizational purposes, where the payment of standard legal fees would significantly deplete the organization's economic resources or would be otherwise inappropriate. . . .

The Commentary to Rule 6.1 explains that "the types of issues that may be addressed under [paragraph b] include First Amendment claims, Title VII claims and environmental protection claims. Additionally, a wide range of organizations may be represented, including social service, medical research, cultural and religious groups."

NOTES & COMMENTS

1.   Do Model Rule 2.1's references to moral and ethical considerations encompass human rights? Does the suggestion that "human rights" has a place under ABA Model Rule 2.1 rest on the assumption that human rights

law is not real law, and that it is not relevant to other aspects of the Model Rules? Note that under Rule 2.1, lawyers "may" offer advice concerning morality but that they "shall" provide competent legal advice.

2.   The Commentary to Rule 2.1 suggests that in some situations, lawyers should draw on the expertise of other professionals such as social workers or accountants. Are there particular professionals to whom lawyers might look for further insights into human rights norms? Some commentators suggest looking to the medical profession, journalism, humanitarian practices and academics for pertinent standards. *See* Caroline Bettinger-López et al., *Redefining Human Rights Lawyering Through the Lens of Critical Theory: Lessons for Pedagogy and Practice*, 18 Geo. J. on Poverty L. & Pol'y 337, 384 (2011).

3.   Rule 6.1 addressing pro bono work does not list human rights work as an area for lawyers' pro bono assistance. Is this omission significant? Is there any organization that might be excluded from pro bono assistance because of the absence of human rights language from Rule 6.1?

ii.   The Japanese Regulations

The ABA Model Rules are simply models that are not attached to any particular jurisdiction and not binding on any lawyers. However, some of the binding legal ethics codes established at the national level do incorporate human rights. The European Code references human rights in a rhetorical way, providing that each lawyer has legal and moral obligations towards "the public for whom the existence of a free and independent legal profession . . . is an essential means of safeguarding human rights in face of the power of the state and other interests in society."[3] The Japanese attorney regulations go further, specifically setting out a role for human rights in attorney practice. The excerpt below highlights the obligation of government and corporate attorneys to incorporate a human rights mission into their practice.

BASIC REGULATIONS FOR ATTORNEYS' DUTIES
(BENGOSHI SHOKUMU KIHON KITEI)

Adopted on November 10, 2004, at the Extraordinary General Meeting of the Japan Federation of Bar Associations.

The mission of an attorney is to protect fundamental human rights and realize social justice. To attain this mission, an attorney is granted freedom and independence in his or her duties, and is guaranteed a high degree of autonomy. An attorney is socially responsible for being aware of such mission and disciplining his or her behavior. Therefore, we hereby provide the basic provisions for attorneys' duties in order to clarify the ethics and the standard of conduct with respect to attorneys' duties.

---

[3]   Council of Bars and Law Societies of Europe (CCBE) Code of Conduct, Section 1.1.

. . .

Article 50.   Freedom and independence

An attorney who is a staff member or an employee, or a director or any other member of the board of directors (hereinafter "an attorney in an organization") in a public agency or a public or private group (except an attorney's corporation, hereinafter "organization") shall not lose sight of the mission of attorneys and the freedom and independence that are essential for attorneys and shall strive to perform his or her duties following the dictates of his or her conscience.

NOTES & COMMENTS

1.   Japan's post-World War II history may have set the stage for such explicit references to human rights in the regulation of lawyers. The Japanese Constitution, approved in 1947, revolves around the concepts of human rights that were particularly influential at the time. *See* Fritz Snyder, *The Fundamental Human Rights Compared in Two Progressive Constitutions: Japan and Montana*, 14 Int'l Legal Persp. 30 (2004).

2.   Still, it is worth asking whether even under Japan's binding legal ethics regime, the ethical provisions referencing human rights are simply aspirational. The Japanese regulations explicitly purport to incorporate human rights, but are the Japanese rules substantively different from professional legal ethics rules such as the ABA Model Rules that do not explicitly reference human rights?

iii. The International Bar Association Principles

In 2011, the International Bar Association—established in 1947 as a global network of bar associations and individual lawyers—promulgated a set of universal principles of legal ethics, set out below. While the phrase "human rights" does not appear in the principles themselves, the official Commentary to the principles indicates that the Universal Declaration of Human Rights was one of the guiding documents consulted during drafting. As you review the IBA Principles, try to identify the ways in which these principles both reflect and complement the UDHR.

INTERNATIONAL BAR ASSOCIATION: INTERNATIONAL
PRINCIPLES ON CONDUCT FOR THE LEGAL PROFESSION
(2011).

Lawyers throughout the world are specialised professionals who place the interests of their clients above their own, and strive to obtain respect for the Rule of Law. They have to combine a continuous update on legal developments with service to their clients, respect for the courts, and the legitimate aspiration to maintain a reasonable standard of living.

Between these elements there is often tension. These principles aim at establishing a generally accepted framework to serve as a basis on which codes of conduct may be established by the appropriate authorities for lawyers in any part of the world. In addition, the purpose of adopting these International Principles is to promote and foster the ideals of the legal profession. These International Principles are not intended to replace or limit a lawyer's obligation under applicable laws or rules of professional conduct. Nor are they to be used as criteria for imposing liability, sanctions, or disciplinary measures of any kind.

1. Independence

A lawyer shall maintain independence and be afforded the protection such independence offers in giving clients unbiased advice and representation. A lawyer shall exercise independent, unbiased professional judgment in advising a client, including as to the likelihood of success of the client's case.

2. Honesty, integrity and fairness

A lawyer shall at all times maintain the highest standards of honesty, integrity and fairness towards the lawyer's clients, the court, colleagues and all those with whom the lawyer comes into professional contact.

3. Conflicts of interest

A lawyer shall not assume a position in which a client's interests conflict with those of the lawyer, another lawyer in the same firm, or another client, unless otherwise permitted by law, applicable rules of professional conduct, or, if permitted, by client's authorisation.

4. Confidentiality/professional secrecy

A lawyer shall at all times maintain and be afforded protection of confidentiality regarding the affairs of present or former clients, unless otherwise allowed or required by law and/or applicable rules of professional conduct.

5. Clients' interest

A lawyer shall treat client interests as paramount, subject always to there being no conflict with the lawyer's duties to the court and the interests of justice, to observe the law, and to maintain ethical standards.

6. Lawyers' undertaking

A lawyer shall honour any undertaking given in the course of the lawyer's practice in a timely manner, until the undertaking is performed, released or excused.

7.   Clients' freedom

A lawyer shall respect the freedom of clients to be represented by the lawyer of their choice. Unless prevented by professional conduct rules or by law, a lawyer shall be free to take on or reject a case.

8.   Property of clients and third parties

A lawyer shall account promptly and faithfully for and prudently hold any property of clients or third parties that comes into the lawyer's trust, and shall keep it separate from the lawyer's own property.

9.   Competence

A lawyer's work shall be carried out in a competent and timely manner. A lawyer shall not take on work that the lawyer does not reasonably believe can be carried out in that manner.

10.   Fees

Lawyers are entitled to a reasonable fee for their work, and shall not charge an unreasonable fee. A lawyer shall not generate unnecessary work.

NOTES & QUESTIONS

1.   The IBA was established by lawyers who were "inspired by the vision of the United Nations (UN)," with "the aim of supporting the establishment of law and administration of justice worldwide." *See* International Bar Association, http://www.ibanet.org/About_the_IBA/About_ the_IBA.aspx. More than 200 bar associations and 50,000 individuals are now members of the IBA. Do you agree with the instinct of the IBA's founders that lawyers worldwide should ascribe to the same basic principles in their work? Andrew Boon and John Flood assert that the impetus for such international ethics codes comes from lawyers engaged in international commerce and finance working on cross-border issues. They ask, then, "Do these initiatives pave the way for collaboration between lawyers and professional bodies concerned about wider spheres of activity, for example in relation to human rights?" Andrew Boon & John Flood, *The Globalization of Professional Ethics? The Significance of Lawyers' International Codes of Conduct*, 2 Legal Ethics 29, 30 (1999), Is there a case to be made that human rights law practice worldwide would benefit from these sorts of international ethics principles? If so, is the absence of human rights from the ABA Model Rules another instance of American exceptionalism?

2.   More than four decades after the IBA's creation, in 1990, the Eighth United Nations Congress on the Prevention of Crime and the Treatment of Offenders adopted a statement of Basic Principles on the Role of Lawyers. Most sections of the Basic Principles address government responsibilities vis à-vis lawyers, in recognition of the fact that "adequate protection of the human rights and fundamental freedoms to which all persons are entitled, be

they economic, social and cultural, or civil and political, requires that all persons have effective access to legal services provided by an independent legal profession." The Basic Principles call on governments to provide adequate funding of legal aid, to ensure that lawyers have adequate education and training, and to maintain the legal profession's self-governance and independence. In addition, the Basic Principles set out some baseline principles of lawyer conduct:

> 12. Lawyers shall at all times maintain the honour and dignity of their profession as essential agents of the administration of justice.

> 13. The duties of lawyers towards their clients shall include:

> (a) Advising clients as to their legal rights and obligations, and as to the working of the legal system in so far as it is relevant to the legal rights and obligations of the clients;

> (b) Assisting clients in every appropriate way, and taking legal action to protect their interests;

> (c) Assisting clients before courts, tribunals or administrative authorities, where appropriate.

> 14. Lawyers, in protecting the rights of their clients and in promoting the cause of justice, shall seek to uphold human rights and fundamental freedoms recognized by national and international law and shall at all times act freely and diligently in accordance with the law and recognized standards and ethics of the legal profession.

> 15. Lawyers shall always loyally respect the interests of their clients.

Basic Principles on the Role of Lawyers, U.N. Hum. Rts. (1990), *available at*: http://www.ohchr.org/EN/ProfessionalInterest/Pages/RoleofLawyers.aspx.

These Basic Principles have been promulgated by the U.N. Office of the High Commissioner for Human Rights. The principles are indeed quite basic, and it's hard to imagine anyone objecting to the vague ideas that, for example, lawyers should "uphold the honour and dignity of their profession" and "assist clients in every appropriate way." But what about the provision calling on lawyers to "loyally respect the interests of their clients"? Many state ethics codes in the United States call on lawyers to "zealously represent" their clients' interests. *See*, *e.g.*, Ind. Rules of Professional Conduct, R.1.3; D.C. Rules of Professional Conduct R. 1.6. Is "loyal respect" a lower or a higher standard than "zealous representation"? Is it important to reconcile these standards? Should the international standard be given any weight domestically?

3. Lawyers are not the only legal professionals who have taken steps to create an international ethics code. In 2001 and 2002, the world's Chief Justices were brought together by the United Nations Centre for International Crime Prevention and drafted the Bangalore Principles of

Judicial Conduct, http://www.unodc.org/pdf/crime/corruption/judicial_group/ Bangalore_principles.pdf. In drafting the principles, the jurists consulted both international documents and domestic judicial standards; for example, the Iowa Code of Judicial Conduct is among the references listed. The Preamble to the Bangalore Principles ties them directly to human rights, citing the UDHR and the ICCPR, and noting that "the implementation of all the other rights ultimately depends upon the proper administration of justice." The substantive provisions of the Bangalore Principles address familiar issues such as judicial independence, impartiality, integrity, propriety, equality, competence and diligence. Some of the prescriptions in the Bangalore Principles are quite specific; for example, the Principles state that "A judge shall not practise law whilst the holder of judicial office." *Id.* at 4.12. Interestingly in light of the domestic U.S. debate concerning citation of international law in judicial opinions, Principle 6.4 provides that "A judge shall keep himself or herself informed about relevant developments of international law, including international conventions and other instruments establishing human rights norms."

B. WOULD LAWYERS BEHAVE DIFFERENTLY IF ETHICS RULES REFERENCED HUMAN RIGHTS?

Now that you have considered the Japanese legal ethics provisions and the IBA's model principles, consider whether the ABA Model Rules would look any different, or have any different effect, if the Rules explicitly drew on human rights norms.

i.   Specific Ethics Standards

Professor Martha Davis has speculated about the revisions that might be necessary to the ABA Model Rules if they were scrutinized through a human rights lens. As you read this excerpt, ask yourself whether there are reasons that justify keeping human rights norms completely out of domestic legal ethics standards.

MARTHA F. DAVIS, "HUMAN RIGHTS AND THE MODEL RULES
OF PROFESSIONAL CONDUCT: INTERSECTION
AND INTEGRATION"
42 Colum. Hum. Rts. L. Rev. 157, 178–81 (2010).

Incorporation of human rights norms into the ABA's professional code could begin with a review of the ways in which such norms might inform and infuse attorney-client relationships. Rather than focusing on human rights ends, this approach to incorporation of human rights norms would emphasize the means, or processes, of human rights and their relevance to the processes of legal representation. Human rights principles with substantial relevance to process include respect for human dignity, participation (and leadership) of those most affected in crafting solutions to their problems, and recognition of the interrelationships between the full range of human rights.

. . .

There are a number of ways in which human rights norms could be operationalized in the text of the ABA's professional code. First, the pre-1983 language that identified the protection of individual dignity as an element of legal representation should be restored to the Preamble to the Model Rules. This simple change, entirely consistent with the thrust of the Model Rules and with broader developments in modern law practice concerning client-centered lawyering, would provide a basis for evaluating legal representation in human rights terms. The reference to dignity would not only add shape to legal representation through its direct meaning, but would also draw in the extensive law, both domestic and international, on human dignity, ranging from *Lawrence v. Texas* to the Universal Declaration of Human Rights. This approach to incorporation within the Model Rules is not novel. Familiar common law concepts such as "reasonableness" or "fraud" are similarly incorporated into the ABA Rules, bringing with them extensive interpretations that are external to the four corners of the professional code but that directly and indirectly inform its interpretation.

A prefatory reference to dignity in the ABA Model Rules would also inform the meaning of subsequent, more specific provisions of the Model Rules, such as Rule 1.4 addressing Communication. Thus, the lawyer's obligation to "keep a client reasonably informed" and to "explain a matter to the extent reasonably necessary" would arise from the recognition of the client's individual dignity consistent with human rights norms, not merely from common law principles of agency. This reformulation of attorney-client obligations would also be tied to human rights norms valuing participation in problem-solving of those most affected by the problems at issue. In the current Model Rules, the moderating qualification of "reasonableness" sits in tension with a human rights value—derived from the concept of human dignity—of ensuring participation and, where feasible, leadership by those most affected by rights violations. Changing the terrain underlying the requirement of "reasonableness" in Rule 1.4 to reflect these human rights norms would likely shift the content of the reasonableness standard toward greater expectations for communication and client participation.

The third human rights principle identified above, the recognition of the interrelationships within the range of human rights, comes into play in evaluating Model Rule 1.8. The comment to current Model Rule 1.8 admonishes:

> Lawyers may not subsidize lawsuits or administrative proceedings brought, on behalf of their clients, including making

or guaranteeing loans to their clients for living expenses, because to do so would encourage clients to pursue lawsuits that might not otherwise be brought and because such assistance gives lawyers too great a financial stake in the litigation.

ABA Model Rule 1.8.

Instead of focusing on potential conflicts of interest and the integrity of the judicial system, a human rights approach to the question of subsidy would acknowledge the inequality of power and resources between the lawyer and client, and would take into account that a *meritorious* lawsuit might be thwarted if the client cannot subsist during its pendency. Further, viewed through a human rights lens, it is clear that a client's lack of access to subsistence support (that is, access to economic rights) has a critical impact on his or her ability to vindicate other procedural or substantive legal rights. A human rights approach would reformulate this rule, explicitly balancing the importance of a lawyer's independence with competing considerations regarding the practical availability of legal processes to litigants who are seeking to defend important rights. Such a rule could explicitly encourage lawyers to extend subsistence support to clients when such support would contribute to vindicating important human rights.

. . .

NOTES & QUESTIONS

1.   Besides revising the existing provisions of the ABA Model Rules, can you think of new rules that would be suggested by a human rights approach to legal ethics? Is the exercise of reconciling human rights with domestic legal ethics made more difficult by the tension between human rights norms and the U.S.'s adversarial justice system, ultimately based on lawyers' zealous representation of their clients? Why might U.S. lawyers resist the inclusion of human rights norms as an aspect of their binding ethical obligations? What are the arguments for and against a human rights approach to legal ethics on the state level, where bar disciplinary committees may review individual compliance and issue sanctions for violations?

2.   Working in law school-based human rights law clinics, some students and professors have questioned the fit between legal ethics rules and human rights practice. One law student proposed an alternative framework, drawing "eleven principles from various professions to guide the ethical behavior of international human rights lawyers: exercise competence; undertake effective communication; maintain independence; engage in zealous advocacy; do no harm; protect life, health and dignity; assess risks/benefits to the population; guarantee fully informed consent; ensure accuracy and objectivity; practice cultural sensitivity; avoid conflicts of interest; and take steps to ensure accountability." Caroline Bettinger-López, et al., *Redefining Human Rights Lawyering Through the Lens of Critical*

Theory: Lessons for Pedagogy and Practice, 18 Geo. J. on Poverty L. & Pol'y 337, 384 (2011). How are these principles different from those articulated by the ABA or the IBA?

3.   Notably, Professor David Luban, a leading figure in the field of legal ethics, has in recent years shifted his proposed ethical framework for lawyers from one that seeks "justice" to one that emphasizes and honors "human dignity." Professor Luban observes that invoking dignity has the rhetorical advantage of suggesting an affinity between legal ethics and the field of international human rights. What is the advantage that Professor Luban perceives? Why might he want to emphasize such a connection? Note that Professor Luban contends in his book, Legal Ethics and Human Dignity (2007), that society's success in "securing human rights and human dignity" is dependent upon "the ethical character of the legal profession."

ii.   The Torture Memos

One explanation for the turn toward human rights in the domestic legal ethics literature may be the notorious "Torture Memos" affair, in which U.S. government lawyers were central to a controversy over aggressive interrogation techniques used on suspected terrorists.

In the days immediately following the September 11, 2001 attacks on the U.S., the Bush Administration attempted to obtain intelligence concerning the terrorists who mounted the attacks and to learn about any further attacks that might be planned. Within a few days of the attacks, President Bush announced that the U.S. was declaring a general "War on Terror," opening the door to a broader campaign against terrorist activity.

As the executive branch initiated these activities, one question was what law constrained the methods that the U.S. government could permissibly use to interrogate prisoners and detainees suspected of having knowledge of terrorist activities. On the one hand were U.S. human rights treaty obligations. The U.S. ratified the Convention Against Torture in 1994, which bars both torture and cruel and degrading treatment of detainees. "Torture" is defined in the treaty as

> [a]ny act by which severe pain or suffering, whether physical or mental, is intentionally inflicted on a person for such purposes as obtaining from him or a third person information or a confession, punishing him for an act he or a third person has committed or is suspected of having committed, or intimidating or coercing him or a third person, or for any reason based on discrimination of any kind, when such pain or suffering is inflicted by or at the instigation of or with the consent or acquiescence of a public official or other person acting in an official capacity. It does not include pain or suffering arising only from, inherent in or incidental to lawful sanctions.

Convention Against Torture, Art. 1, A/RES/39/46 (Dec. 10, 1984).

Further, the treaty makes clear that the bar on torture is absolute, not conditional. According to Article 2 of the Convention, "[n]o exceptional circumstances whatsoever, whether a state of war or a threat of war, internal political instability or any other public emergency, may be invoked as a justification of torture." In addition to the Convention Against Torture, the U.S. has ratified the 1949 Fourth Geneva Convention, which governs the treatment of individuals in the context of war. Domestic statutes adopted pursuant to these international obligations, such as 18 U.S.C. §§ 2340–2340A (2013), also criminalize the use of torture.

These international and domestic legal obligations were well-known to the Administration. In fact, one month after the September 11 attacks, the U.N. High Commissioner for Human Rights wrote U.N. member states, including the U.S., to remind them of the "non-derogable nature of the obligations undertaken by them in ratifying the Convention against Torture." Despite the clear international and domestic legal framework, within the executive branch, government lawyers drafted a series of analyses attempting to reconcile the CAT, the Geneva obligations, and the domestic statutory provisions with the government's aggressive pursuit of information about terrorists and terrorism. Two memos prepared in August 2002 by Jay Bybee, head of the Office of Legal Counsel, were entitled "Standards of Conduct for Interrogation under 18 U.S.C. sections 2340–2340A" and "Interrogation of al Qaeda." John Yoo, also of the Office of Legal Counsel, drafted additional analysis for then-White House Counsel Alberto Gonzales. (Over time, further internal memos have been released that address these subjects in similar ways.) These memos advised the Central Intelligence Agency, the U.S. Department of Defense, and the President on the use of "enhanced interrogation techniques," mental and physical torment and coercion such as waterboarding and sleep deprivation. The memos concluded that these acts might be legally permissible under an expansive interpretation of presidential authority justified by the War on Terror. Drawing on these analyses, White House Counsel Gonzales determined that any U.S. obligations to refrain from torture under the Fourth Geneva Convention or the Convention Against Torture were superseded in the context of a War on Terror. He wrote in a January 25, 2002 memo to President Bush that "[t]his new paradigm renders obsolete Geneva's strict limitations on questioning of enemy prisoners and renders quaint some of its provisions requiring that captured enemy be afforded such things as commissary privileges."

In 2003, Bybee was appointed to the U.S. Court of Appeals for the Ninth Circuit. Even before these internal memos became public in 2004,

Bybee's successor at the Office of Legal Counsel, Jack Goldsmith, withdrew the memos as flawed.

Once the memos became public, they were widely condemned both as poorly reasoned and bad policy. Nonetheless, the positions taken in these legal memos were initially endorsed by President Bush and formed the operative framework for government interrogations for more than a year. Some argue that the shadow cast by the memos contributed to the excesses at Abu Ghraib prison in 2003–2004, where military personnel abused Iraqi prisoners, and to the inhumane treatment of detainees at the Guantánamo detention facility.[4] Their influence may also be seen in assertions of Presidential power to gather intelligence through warrantless domestic wiretaps or to oversee remote-controlled targeted killing of terror suspects by unmanned aerial drones.[5]

Beyond the merits of the administration's torture policy, many commentators addressed whether lawyers Yoo and Bybee had acted improperly by failing to give their client, the White House, objective legal advice. Professor David Luban testified before the Senate Committee on the Judiciary on May 13, 2009, that "the memos are an ethical trainwreck." According to Luban,

> the interrogation memos fall far short of professional standards of candid advice and independent judgment. They involve a selective and in places deeply eccentric reading of the law. The memos cherry-pick sources of law that back their conclusions, and leave out sources of law that do not. They read as if they were reverse engineered to reach a pre-determined outcome: approval of waterboarding and the other CIA techniques.

What Went Wrong: Torture and the Office of Legal Counsel in the Bush Administration: Hearing Before the Subcomm. on Administrative Oversight and the Courts of the S. Comm. on the Judiciary, 111th Cong., May 13, 2009 (Statement of David Luban, Prof. of Law, Geo. U. L. Center).

Professor Stephen Gillers concurred with this ethical assessment, suggesting that that the memos represent a "perversion of law and legal duty, a betrayal of the client and professional norms."[6]

In contrast, Professors Eric Posner and Adrian Vermuele called the idea that the Office of Legal Counsel should provide "disinterested" advice "sentimental" and "self-serving." They labeled the memos' analysis "routine," and argued that "there is nothing particularly problematic

---

[4] *See* Andrew Cohen, *The Torture Memos, Ten Years Later*, The Atlantic (Feb. 12, 2012).

[5] *See* Jane Mayer, *Torture and Obama's Drone Program*, The New Yorker (Feb. 15, 2013).

[6] Stephen Gillers, *The Torture Memo*, The Nation (April 28, 2008).

about the . . . conclusion that the President cannot be bound by federal laws prohibiting torture overseas."[7]

NOTES & QUESTIONS

1.   Consider whether the Torture Memos reflect negatively on the legal profession more broadly and if so, in what ways. What steps might the legal profession have taken to encourage a different approach by the government lawyers who authored the Torture Memos? For proposed standards for the Office of Legal Counsel, see Dawn Johnsen, *Guidelines for the President's Legal Advisors (Including Principles to Guide the Office of Legal Counsel)*, 81 Ind. L.J. 1835 (2006).

2.   The lawyers who wrote the Torture Memos were licensed members of their state Bars, subject to discipline in their home jurisdictions. There were calls for disbarment when the memos came to light and an advocacy group filed complaints against the lawyers, but neither Jay Bybee nor John Yoo were subjected to any bar discipline for their work on the Torture Memos. The Department of Justice's Office of Professional Responsibility (OPR) concluded in a 261-page report dated July 29, 2009, that Yoo committed "intentional professional misconduct" when he "knowingly failed to provide a thorough, objective, and candid interpretation of the law," and it recommended a referral to the Pennsylvania Bar for disciplinary action. But David Margolis, the career Justice Department attorney charged with resolving challenges to OPR's finding, countermanded the recommended referral. Do you agree that Judge Bybee and Professor Yoo did not violate any disciplinary rules? What about the state analogs to Model Rule 2.1, which indicates that lawyers "shall" exercise independent judgment and give candid advice, which "may" address moral considerations?

3.   Even if these attorneys did not violate any disciplinary rules, would an emphasis on human rights in their state bar ethics code have made a difference in their approach to these issues? The ABA requires that lawyers pass an ethics exam as part of their bar exam; as a precursor to that, law students are required to complete a law school course on legal ethics. If human rights norms were part of the required legal ethics course and the ethics exam, would these lawyers have approached their advice-giving function more reflectively? Regardless of its impact on individual lawyers' behavior, would inclusion of human rights in the ABA Model Rules now, after the Torture Memos, send a message to the public that lawyers should consider the human rights implications of their advice? Or would it simply serve to dilute lawyers' obligation to zealously serve their clients?

4.   As mentioned above, Jay Bybee, who authored some of the Torture Memos, is now a federal appellate judge. He has said that he regrets the contents of the memos, as well as their misuse. *See* Karl Vick, *Amid Outcry on Memo, Signer's Private Regret*, Washington Post (April 25, 2000). John Yoo

---

[7]   Eric Posner and Adrian Vermuele, *A "Torture" Memo and its Tortuous Critics*, Wall Street Journal, July 6, 2004, at A22.

is a Professor of Law at Boalt College of Law, Berkeley. He continues to be a vocal defender of the positions on presidential power and human rights expressed in the Torture Memos.

II. CORPORATE SOCIAL RESPONSIBILITY AND LEGAL PRACTICE

While ethics codes in the U.S. steer clear of direct reference to human rights, human rights norms are directly pertinent to legal practice through the Guiding Principles on Business and Human Rights (the Guiding Principles), endorsed by the U.N. in 2011, and the Organization for Economic Cooperation and Development (OECD) Guidelines for Multinational Enterprises which incorporate the Guiding Principles. The non-binding Guiding Principles apply to all businesses, including law firms. For lawyers, these principles provide guidance on the sorts of substantive advice to give business clients; they may also indicate specific internal practices for law firms as well as ethical standards for individual lawyers and firms. Indeed, when the ABA endorsed these Guiding Principles it explicitly connected the dots between these principles and lawyers' ethical obligations as advisors under ABA Model Rule 2.1.

The Guiding Principles were developed in several stages under the direction of Professor John Ruggie, who served as the Special Representative of the U.N. Secretary-General for Business and Human Rights from 2005 to 2011. In 2008, Professor Ruggie proposed that principles of business and human rights be organized around three pillars already fundamental to the U.N.:

> — The state duty to **protect** against human rights abuses by third parties, including business, through appropriate policies, regulation, and adjudication;

> — The corporate responsibility to **respect** human rights, that is, to act with due diligence to avoid infringing on the rights of others and address adverse impacts with which they are involved; and

> — The need for greater access by victims to effective **remedy**, both judicial and non-judicial.

In 2011, Professor Ruggie proposed the Guiding Principles as a means to implement the "Protect, Respect, and Remedy" pillars in the business realm. The following excerpt from the Guiding Principles highlights one key aspect of the framework, the corporate responsibility to respect human rights. As you review these Principles, keep in mind that law firms are, as businesses, subject to these standards and consider whether firms would face any unique challenges in seeking to comply.

JOHN RUGGIE, REPORT OF THE SPECIAL REPRESENTATIVE OF
THE SECRETARY-GENERAL ON THE ISSUE OF HUMAN RIGHTS
AND TRANSNATIONAL CORPORATIONS AND OTHER
BUSINESS ENTERPRISES

March 21, 2011.

A.   Foundational principles

. . .

11. Business enterprises should respect human rights. This means that they should avoid infringing on the human rights of others and should address adverse human rights impacts with which they are involved.

Commentary

The responsibility to respect human rights is a global standard of expected conduct for all business enterprises wherever they operate. It exists independently of States' abilities and/or willingness to fulfill their own human rights obligations, and does not diminish those obligations. And it exists over and above compliance with national laws and regulations protecting human rights.

Addressing adverse human rights impacts requires taking adequate measures for their prevention, mitigation and, where appropriate, remediation. Business enterprises may undertake other commitments or activities to support and promote human rights, which may contribute to the enjoyment of rights. But this does not offset a failure to respect human rights throughout their operations. Business enterprises should not undermine States' abilities to meet their own human rights obligations, including by actions that might weaken the integrity of judicial processes.

. . .

13. The responsibility to respect human rights requires that business enterprises:

(a) Avoid causing or contributing to adverse human rights impacts through their own activities, and address such impacts when they occur;

(b) Seek to prevent or mitigate adverse human rights impacts that are directly linked to their operations, products or services by their business relationships, even if they have not contributed to those impacts.

Commentary

Business enterprises may be involved with adverse human rights impacts either through their own activities or as a result of their business relationships with other parties. Guiding Principle 19 elaborates further on the implications for how business enterprises should address these situations. For the purpose of these Guiding Principles a business enterprise's "activities" are understood to include both actions and omissions; and its "business relationships" are understood to include relationships with business partners, entities in its value chain, and any other non-State or State entity directly linked to its business operations, products or services.

14. The responsibility of business enterprises to respect human rights applies to all enterprises regardless of their size, sector, operational context, ownership and structure. Nevertheless, the scale and complexity of the means through which enterprises meet that responsibility may vary according to these factors and with the severity of the enterprise's adverse human rights impacts.

Commentary

The means through which a business enterprise meets its responsibility to respect human rights will be proportional to, among other factors, its size. Small and medium-sized enterprises may have less capacity as well as more informal processes and management structures than larger companies, so their respective policies and processes will take on different forms. But some small and medium-sized enterprises can have severe human rights impacts, which will require corresponding measures regardless of their size. Severity of impacts will be judged by their scale, scope and irremediable character.

The means through which a business enterprise meets its responsibility to respect human rights may also vary depending on whether, and the extent to which, it conducts business through a corporate group or individually. However, the responsibility to respect human rights applies fully and equally to all business enterprises.

15. In order to meet their responsibility to respect human rights, business enterprises should have in place policies and processes appropriate to their size and circumstances, including:

(a) A policy commitment to meet their responsibility to respect human rights;

(b) A human rights due diligence process to identify, prevent, mitigate and account for how they address their impacts on human rights;

(c) Processes to enable the remediation of any adverse human rights impacts they cause or to which they contribute.

Commentary

Business enterprises need to know and show that they respect human rights. They cannot do so unless they have certain policies and processes in place. Principles 16 to 24 elaborate further on these.

B.   Operational principles

. . .

Human rights due diligence

17. In order to identify, prevent, mitigate and account for how they address their adverse human rights impacts, business enterprises should carry out human rights due diligence. The process should include assessing actual and potential human rights impacts, integrating and acting upon the findings, tracking responses, and communicating how impacts are addressed.

Human rights due diligence:

> (a) Should cover adverse human rights impacts that the business enterprise may cause or contribute to through its own activities, or which may be directly linked to its operations, products or services by its business relationships;

> (b) Will vary in complexity with the size of the business enterprise, the risk of severe human rights impacts, and the nature and context of its operations;

> (c) Should be ongoing, recognizing that the human rights risks may change over time as the business enterprise's operations and operating context evolve.

Commentary

This Principle defines the parameters for human rights due diligence, while Principles 18 through 21 elaborate its essential components. Human rights risks are understood to be the business enterprise's potential adverse human rights impacts. Potential impacts should be addressed through prevention or mitigation, while actual impacts—those that have already occurred—should be a subject for remediation (Principle 22). Human rights due diligence can be included within broader enterprise risk management systems, provided that it goes beyond simply identifying and managing material risks to the company itself, to include risks to rights-holders. Human rights due diligence should be initiated as early as possible in the development of a new activity or relationship, given that human rights risks can be increased or mitigated already at the stage of structuring contracts or other agreements, and may be inherited through mergers or acquisitions.

Where business enterprises have large numbers of entities in their value chains it may be unreasonably difficult to conduct due diligence for adverse human rights impacts across them all. If so, business enterprises should identify general areas where the risk of adverse human rights impacts is most significant, whether due to certain suppliers' or clients' operating context, the particular operations, products or services involved, or other relevant considerations, and prioritize these for human rights due diligence.

Questions of complicity may arise when a business enterprise contributes to, or is seen as contributing to, adverse human rights impacts caused by other parties. Complicity has both non-legal and legal meanings. As a nonlegal matter, business enterprises may be perceived as being "complicit" in the acts of another party where, for example, they are seen to benefit from an abuse committed by that party.

As a legal matter, most national jurisdictions prohibit complicity in the commission of a crime, and a number allow for criminal liability of business enterprises in such cases. Typically, civil actions can also be based on an enterprise's alleged contribution to a harm, although these may not be framed in human rights terms. The weight of international criminal law jurisprudence indicates that the relevant standard for aiding and abetting is knowingly providing practical assistance or encouragement that has a substantial effect on the commission of a crime.

Conducting appropriate human rights due diligence should help business enterprises address the risk of legal claims against them by showing that they took every reasonable step to avoid involvement with an alleged human rights abuse. However, business enterprises conducting such due diligence should not assume that, by itself, this will automatically and fully absolve them from liability for causing or contributing to human rights abuses.

18. In order to gauge human rights risks, business enterprises should identify and assess any actual or potential adverse human rights impacts with which they may be involved either through their own activities or as a result of their business relationships. This process should:

(a) Draw on internal and/or independent external human rights expertise;

(b) Involve meaningful consultation with potentially affected groups and other relevant stakeholders, as appropriate to the size of the business enterprise and the nature and context of the operation.

Commentary

The initial step in conducting human rights due diligence is to identify and assess the nature of the actual and potential adverse human rights impacts with which a business enterprise may be involved. The purpose is to understand the specific impacts on specific people, given a specific context of operations. Typically this includes assessing the human rights context prior to a proposed business activity, where possible; identifying who may be affected; cataloguing the relevant human rights standards and issues; and projecting how the proposed activity and associated business relationships could have adverse human rights impacts on those identified.

In this process, business enterprises should pay special attention to any particular human rights impacts on individuals from groups or populations that may be at heightened risk of vulnerability or marginalization, and bear in mind the different risks that may be faced by women and men.

While processes for assessing human rights impacts can be incorporated within other processes such as risk assessments or environmental and social impact assessments, they should include all internationally recognized human rights as a reference point, since enterprises may potentially impact virtually any of these rights.

Because human rights situations are dynamic, assessments of human rights impacts should be undertaken at regular intervals: prior to a new activity or relationship; prior to major decisions or changes in the operation (e.g. market entry, product launch, policy change, or wider changes to the business); in response to or anticipation of changes in the operating environment (e.g. rising social tensions); and periodically throughout the life of an activity or relationship. To enable business enterprises to assess their human rights impacts accurately, they should seek to understand the concerns of potentially affected stakeholders by consulting them directly in a manner that takes into account language and other potential barriers to effective engagement.

In situations where such consultation is not possible, business enterprises should consider reasonable alternatives such as consulting credible, independent expert resources, including human rights defenders and others from civil society. The assessment of human rights impacts informs subsequent steps in the human rights due diligence process.

19. In order to prevent and mitigate adverse human rights impacts, business enterprises should integrate the findings from their impact assessments across relevant internal functions and processes, and take appropriate action.

    (a) Effective integration requires that:

        (i) Responsibility for addressing such impacts is assigned to the appropriate level and function within the business enterprise;

(ii) Internal decision-making, budget allocations and oversight processes enable effective responses to such impacts.

(b) Appropriate action will vary according to:

(i) Whether the business enterprise causes or contributes to an adverse impact, or whether it is involved solely because the impact is directly linked to its operations, products or services by a business relationship;

(ii) The extent of its leverage in addressing the adverse impact.

Commentary

The horizontal integration across the business enterprise of specific findings from assessing human rights impacts can only be effective if its human rights policy commitment has been embedded into all relevant business functions. This is required to ensure that the assessment findings are properly understood, given due weight, and acted upon. In assessing human rights impacts, business enterprises will have looked for both actual and potential adverse impacts. Potential impacts should be prevented or mitigated through the horizontal integration of findings across the business enterprise, while actual impacts—those that have already occurred—should be a subject for remediation (Principle 22).

Where a business enterprise causes or may cause an adverse human rights impact, it should take the necessary steps to cease or prevent the impact. Where a business enterprise contributes or may contribute to an adverse human rights impact, it should take the necessary steps to cease or prevent its contribution and use its leverage to mitigate any remaining impact to the greatest extent possible. Leverage is considered to exist where the enterprise has the ability to effect change in the wrongful practices of an entity that causes a harm. Where a business enterprise has not contributed to an adverse human rights impact, but that impact is nevertheless directly linked to its operations, products or services by its business relationship with another entity, the situation is more complex. Among the factors that will enter into the determination of the appropriate action in such situations are the enterprise's leverage over the entity concerned, how crucial the relationship is to the enterprise, the severity of the abuse, and whether terminating the relationship with the entity itself would have adverse human rights consequences.

The more complex the situation and its implications for human rights, the stronger is the case for the enterprise to draw on independent expert advice in deciding how to respond.

If the business enterprise has leverage to prevent or mitigate the adverse impact, it should exercise it. And if it lacks leverage there may be ways for the enterprise to increase it. Leverage may be increased by, for example, offering capacity-building or other incentives to the related entity, or collaborating with other actors. There are situations in which the enterprise lacks the leverage to prevent or mitigate adverse impacts and is unable to increase its leverage. Here, the enterprise should consider ending the relationship, taking into account credible assessments of potential adverse human rights impacts of doing so. Where the relationship is "crucial" to the enterprise, ending it raises further challenges. A relationship could be deemed as crucial if it provides a product or service that is essential to the enterprise's business, and for which no reasonable alternative source exists. Here the severity of the adverse human rights impact must also be considered: the more severe the abuse, the more quickly the enterprise will need to see change before it takes a decision on whether it should end the relationship. In any case, for as long as the abuse continues and the enterprise remains in the relationship, it should be able to demonstrate its own ongoing efforts to mitigate the impact and be prepared to accept any consequences—reputational, financial or legal—of the continuing connection.

. . .

The ABA endorsed the Guiding Principles in 2012. Among other things, the ABA's Report noted that the legal field of Corporate Social Responsibility (CSR) is burgeoning. As more and more corporations are devoting resources to CSR, in part responding to the momentum generated by the Guiding Principles, the large law firms that serve these corporations have responded by establishing new CSR practice groups to provide advice in navigating this field. However, as noted above, the Guiding Principles are not limited to mega-corporations and large law firms. All law firms are subject to the Principles. Further, Footnote 1 of the ABA's Report, briefly excerpted below, tentatively identifies a connection between the Guiding Principles and legal ethics codes that is pertinent to all corporate legal representation and advising. Recall that Rule 2.1 was also cited in consideration of whether the Torture Memos conformed to legal ethics standards.

AMERICAN BAR ASSOCIATION REPORT ACCOMPANYING THE RESOLUTION ENDORSING THE GUIDING PRINCIPLES
2012.

The UN *Framework* is likely to influence legal regulations and processes; corporations may find more clarity in standards and compliance requirements, states may step-up investigation and enforcement, and individuals harmed by corporate activities may benefit from enhanced causes of action and access to justice. Indeed, for most businesses, CSR is a voluntary, market-driven, and discretionary standard of conduct that varies greatly from company to company. The *Framework* and *Guiding Principles,* in contrast, constitute a baseline standard of conduct that applies to all businesses, whatever their sector, whatever their size, and wherever they operate (Guiding Principle 14).[FN 1]

> FN 1: It bears noting here that ABA Model Rule of Professional Conduct 2.1 may well apply in this context. It requires lawyers to exercise "independent professional judgment and render candid advice" and permits them to "refer not only to law but to other considerations such as moral, economic, social and political factors that may be relevant to the client's situation." See ABA Model R. Prof'l Con. R. 2.1. This imperative logically would include applicable international standards in the conduct of a client's affairs, including the Framework and Guiding Principles where corporate clients are concerned.

. . .

NOTES & QUESTIONS

1.   Does the ABA view the Guiding Principles as "law" or as "other considerations" under Rule 2.1? What do you make of the use of the word "imperative" in the Footnote 1?

2.   Is it realistic to think that all lawyers will advise all business clients concerning the Guiding Principles? What sort of training would be appropriate to prepare lawyers for this role? A practitioners' advisory group has been set up to inform the future work of the Law Society of England and Wales on business and human rights issues, including advice and guidance aimed at the legal profession. In setting up the group, the Law Society has become the first bar association in the world to systematically review the approach of the legal services sector to the U.N. Guiding Principles on Business and Human Rights.

The U.S. legal profession is still in the early stages of grappling with the implications of the Guiding Principles for legal practice, but lawyers in the U. K. and Europe have already initiated important conversations about these implications. For example, the organization Advocates for International Development: Lawyers Eradicating Poverty (A4ID), has developed an initial guide to lawyers' implementation of the Guiding Principles; the International Bar Association has announced that it is developing a model human rights code for law firms; and several prominent U. K. firms have announced that they are breaking new ground by developing their own freestanding law-firm-specific codes, believed to be the first such codes in the world.[8]

A4ID's analysis provides a starting place for these bar initiatives.[9] According to A4ID, once a law firm determines, based on an initial human rights assessment, that it is involved in actual adverse human rights impacts of the client or that there is a human rights risk—that is, a potential impact in which the firm may be involved—it should take concrete action. In the case of on-going services to a client, the firm is required to take action, regardless of whether the law firm contributes or is linked to the client's adverse human rights impacts through its services. However, where a prospective client has adverse human rights impacts, the law firm does not have any responsibility to take action unless it enters into a relationship with the client.

A4ID makes a distinction between those circumstances where the firm contributes to the adverse impact and those where it is involved solely because the impact is directly linked to its services to the client by its business relationship [*see* Guiding Principle 19(b)]. Where the firm's involvement in the adverse human rights impact would arise because of its contribution to the impact then the law firm should take steps to cease or prevent its contribution and then use its leverage or influence with the client to mitigate the client's impact [*see* Commentary to Guiding Principle 19]. In a case where the firm is directly linked to the adverse human rights impact as a result of its services to the client, the firm is not responsible for the impact or for taking remedial measures, but instead must use its leverage with the client to mitigate the client's adverse human rights impacts [*see* Commentary to Guiding Principle 19].

According to A4ID, leverage should not be interpreted as simply a threat to withdraw service. Convincing the client of the need for change, influencing the clients' policy or practice, promoting an alternative course of action or triggering further advice, either from the law firm or another service, will be the more usual form of leverage used by firms. The A4D report gives the following examples of leverage for firms:

- Raising an issue of adverse human rights impacts with a client;

- Suggesting the firm can provide advice to client on said issue;

---

[8]   For more information, see the website of Shift, a center for business and human rights practice, http://www.shiftproject.org/article/professional-responsibility-lawyers-under-guiding-principles.

[9]   Advocates for International Development, The U.N. Guiding Principles on Business and Human Rights. A Guide for the Legal Profession, *available at* http://a4id.org/sites/default/files/user/A4ID%20Business%20and%20Human%20Rights%20Guide%202013%20(web).pdf.

- Advising the client of the consequent impacts on the individuals;

- Advising the client of the potential reputational impacts on the client;

- Advising the client on measures to avoid/mitigate/remedy adverse impacts; persuading the client to take such measures.[10]

Though A4ID has initiated a conversation in the European legal community about the scope of lawyer responsibility to mitigate their clients' human rights violations, the Guiding Principles have not been without controversy and some members of the legal profession are concerned about tensions between the U.N. principles and binding legal ethics rules that govern attorney practice. In particular, commentators ask, how can a law firm "know and show" its own human rights compliance consistent with its obligations of client confidentiality and the overriding principle of access to representation, itself a matter of human rights. The article below, by a leading British solicitor, articulates these concerns.

JONATHAN GOLDSMITH, "WHEN HUMAN RIGHTS AND CLIENTS' RIGHTS CONFLICT"
The Law Society Gazette (2012).

Corporate social responsibility (CSR) is a fashionable concept. Big firms flaunt their CSR credentials, and no one knows whether it is a marketing strategy to make us buy their goods and services, or a serious attempt to promote a better society. It was only a matter of time before law firms came into the cross-hairs of the CSR industry.

However, there is a big, unresolved problem about lawyers and CSR. No one can complain about efforts to make law firms comply with CSR standards in relation, say, to employees. In other words, the rights of staff must be protected, and there should be policies in place, for instance in relation to diversity, discrimination and harassment.

But can CSR apply also to dealings with clients? It is no secret that there are seriously suspect clients out there, the most obvious being governments who flout even the most basic human rights principles. Are they to be denied access to legal advice and representation because of their actions?

. . .

---

[10] *Id.* at 22–23.

There are a number of problems around the issue of CSR and the client. First, no one disputes that even the most heinous criminal is entitled to a defence lawyer. But does the same principle apply to a heinous company which is not breaching the criminal law but is undertaking a transaction which most people think is wrong. The A4ID report gives the example of so-called 'vulture funds' that target poor countries which are receiving international debt relief, buy their debt, often just before those debts are to be written off, and then sue the country for the full amount. Shame! Horrible! But do 'vulture funds' deserve to receive legal advice and assistance if their actions are lawful?

Apparently some law firms have said that they will not act for them, and there has been naming and shaming in the press of those which have acted for them in the past. But would it be right if *all* lawyers said that they would not act for such funds (always on the basis that the funds' actions are lawful)? What would that say about our legal system?

Then there is the problem of finding midway through the representation that a client has been abusing human rights. Again assuming that this does not involve a breach of the law, do you withdraw from representation? Under the Solicitors Regulation Authority rules, you cannot do this "without good reason and without providing reasonable notice." The guiding principles include a human rights due diligence— rather like that undertaken for different reasons under anti-money laundering legislation—to be effected in advance of agreeing to represent a client. The range of due diligence is growing!

A core component of the guiding principles is that companies should both know and show that they are respecting human rights. The "know" is covered by due diligence. But can law firms *show* that they have respected human rights matters in relation to clients without breaching client confidentiality?

These are serious matters. CSR is an important exercise to address corporate misbehaviour. Professional rules like client confidentiality are essential to the rule of law. What happens when the two conflict? At present, CSR is restricted to guidance, but we know that human nature often leads people to turn guidance into binding rules. It is for this reason that lawyers should watch these developments closely, and participate in them.

NOTES & QUESTIONS

1. Does lawyers' compliance with the Guiding Principles require a fundamental shift in the traditional view of lawyers as their clients' agents? Or does it simply require that lawyers take a broader view of their sphere of advice to business clients, while leaving the agency relationship intact? How

might the role of inside counsel differ from the role of outside counsel in providing this advice?

2. The ABA endorsement of the Guiding Principles cites Model Rule 2.1 as supporting lawyers' advice on human rights compliance. In a state jurisdiction that has adopted a version of Model Rule 2.1 as a binding provision, would lawyers be ethically required to provide such advice to their clients?

3. How do you respond to the challenges posed by Jonathan Goldsmith? Should lawyers be exempt from the Guiding Principles insofar as lawyers are protecting client confidences? Is the fact that the Principles simply offer guidance, not a mandatory regime, a sufficient answer to Goldsmith's concerns?

SKILLS EXERCISE

You work at a U.S.-based non-profit legal organization that provides advice to corporations on how to bring their business practices into conformity with the Guiding Principles. How would you advise the following companies?

1. MallTemps is a new start-up that places temporary workers into sales positions in shopping malls across the U.S. MallTemps contracts with mall-based stores to provide this service; MallTemps sales workers are then paid by MallTemps. Participating stores are required to sign a general non-discrimination pledge agreeing to treat workers fairly. Further, MallTemps has a company policy of paying workers a living wage. MallTemps would like advice about what more they should do, as a relatively small company providing a service to much larger companies, to comply with the Guiding Principles?

2. A regional firm of 150 lawyers, Smith & Jacobs (S&J), represents UWeb, a company that contracts with governments around the world to design and maintain the governments' websites. UWeb has asked S&J to draw up a contract between UWeb and the government of China for an English-language government website. The Chinese government will provide the technical specifications and content for the website, and UWeb will prepare a website frame and launch consistent with the specifications provided. Among other things, the Chinese government has specified that it must be able to edit the contents of any external news feed before it is linked to the site.[11] UWeb is prepared to comply with those requirements and the specifications will be an appendix to the contract that S&J has been asked to

---

[11] While this example is fictional, there has been significant coverage of internet censorship in China consistent with this hypothetical. *See generally* Isabella Bennett, Backgrounder: Media Censorship in China (Council on Foreign Relations 2013), http://www.cfr.org/china/media-censorship-china/p11515 (describing imprisonment of Chinese journalists who overstep the government's restrictions and harassment of foreign journalists).

draft. What should S&J do to honor the Guiding Principles in this situation?

III. HUMAN RIGHTS AND PUBLIC INTEREST LAWYERING

In addition to its impact on corporate representation, the human rights framework also has the potential to inject new considerations into traditional domestic public interest lawyering. Some public interest organizations have embraced this. For example, as we saw in **Chapter VII**, the Maryland Legal Aid Bureau (MLAB), founded in 1911, recently adopted a human rights framework for its work on behalf of low income clients. According to attorney Seri Wilpone of MLAB, "Clients tell us they have needs for basic human rights and for us to make lasting changes for them we need to keep human right norms in mind as we look at legal remedies—poor housing, poor remuneration, unaffordable medical treatment."[12]

In part, then, MLAB uses the human rights framework to help it keep a focus on the big picture as it works on behalf of low income individuals on many fronts.

But is attention to the big picture, to the overall housing market or the overall health care situation or structural factors that promote poverty, in tension with lawyers' obligations to individual clients?

For more than thirty years, the concept of "client-centered lawyering" has been a touchstone of legal services practice and clinical legal education.[13] Client-centeredness has two key aspects. First, it underscores and expands the role of the client as the decisionmaker in his or her matter. In theory, human rights norms seem entirely consistent with this aspect of client-centered representation, since they include the right of those most affected to participate in decisionmaking.[14] The challenge is to ensure that the client can fully participate when dealing with unfamiliar institutions and procedures in the human rights realm.

The second aspect of client-centeredness maintains that the focus of the legal representation must be on the client and the achievement of the client's goals. At first blush, this seems to be a given. A lawyer should not take on representation that is shaped by her own goals of raising her profile or enhancing her reputation or making herself rich or even achieving her personal social and policy goals. But the issue may not be

---

[12] Joe Surkiewicz, *Commentary: Of Service: Addressing Needs and Rights*, The Daily Record (Baltimore, Maryland), June 8, 2009.

[13] *See* David Binder and Susan Price, Legal Interviewing and Counseling: A Client Centered Approach (1977).

[14] *See, e.g.*, Office of the High Commissioner of Human Rights, Good Governance Practices for the Protection of Human Rights (2007).

so simple. Should, for example, a lawyer handling individual representation take into account larger community goals (perhaps framed as human rights considerations), or does even this depart from the accepted model of client-centered lawyering?

The excerpts below explore both of these aspects of client-centered lawyering and its "fit" with human rights approaches.

DINA F. HAYNES, "CLIENT-CENTERED HUMAN RIGHTS ADVOCACY"
13 Clinical L. Rev. 379, 412–13 (2006).

As much as I hold that client-centered lawyering principles bring necessary practice skills to human rights advocacy, I want to acknowledge and highlight some aspects of human rights law and practice that make client-centered lawyering very challenging. Client-centered lawyering imagines that the client be at least an equal partner in the development of the case theory, legal approach and remedies that will be sought, and that identification of the remedies will flow organically from the process of interviewing and counseling. In true client-centered lawyering, then, the client's goals would emerge through open-ended interviewing. Discussion of remedies would come much later, after a thorough understanding of the client's life, situation and goals.

The first difficulty with employing client-centered lawyering in human rights practice comes with identifying the client. . . . [I]t is often a struggle to identify who the client is, which I do not think is a struggle limited to human rights practice. Specific to human rights practice, however, is the fact that the average client will have little to no understanding of the various human rights institutions and mechanisms available and applicable to their case. As a consequence, it may be necessary for the human rights lawyer to begin earlier discussions about the existence and practicability of the various human rights institutions and relevant legal systems that might remedy the harm, a conversation that might not ever take place in a truly client-centered interview. Because of this, the client-centered human rights lawyer must take extra precaution against playing a larger role than desirable in guiding the client to select or acquiesce to a potential course of action, and to do this, must take more time explaining the possibilities to the client, so that the client can retain agency in securing his solution to the human rights problem.

. . .

Professor Scott Cummings also examines the tension between cause lawyering and individual representation in public interest law, but draws on the larger context of the internationalization of public interest law to make his point. The internationalization phenomenon may be a driver of greater engagement with human rights norms, but at the same time may create more pressures on public interest lawyers to, for example, represent more clients with more diverse needs or to engage in more efficient triage or to prioritize causes and impacts over individuals. As you read the excerpt below, consider whether human rights norms of the sort adopted by MLAB provide any guidance to public interest lawyers dealing with the pressures of internationalization and globalization of the issues their clients face.

SCOTT CUMMINGS, "THE INTERNATIONALIZATION OF PUBLIC INTEREST LAW"
57 Duke L. J. 891, 1027–34 (2008).

A central tension of public interest law is how lawyers balance professional obligations to clients with personal commitments to causes. Lawyering in the international sphere reproduces these tensions on a wider stage, raising distinct challenges to the norm of client accountability and influencing professional motivations for pursuing global causes.

1.   *Representation.*   The conventional view of the lawyer's professional role emphasizes the obligation to place the client's interests above the lawyer's political or personal aspirations. Public interest practice tests this view by substituting moral *neutrality* with moral *commitment* as the defining feature of legal advocacy. Commitment to cause, however, does not mean that public interest lawyers reject professional norms; rather, public interest practice operates along a spectrum of client-centeredness, with legal services lawyers who privilege access to individual client services at one end and law reformers who care chiefly about the political ends of representation at the other. From the perspective of client accountability, the central concern across the spectrum is lawyer power. At the client service end, the main issue is *private* accountability: How do lawyers exercise their power to choose poor clients and make decisions on their behalf? At the law reform end, the question is one of *public* accountability: Who defines the cause and resolves conflicts over how to pursue it? Public interest lawyers operating in global arenas face challenges across both dimensions of accountability.

At frontline legal services offices, where priority is given to client service over systemwide reform, globalization has meant responding to the legal needs of the expanding base of immigrant clients. This has generated a dilemma of access. Lawyers faced with expanding immigrant demand for services confront difficult questions of triage. which immigrants get served and in what types of cases? The answer to this question depends in part on lawyer location. Within federally funded legal services programs, LSC [Legal Services Corporation] policy mandates the triage decision, with lawyers limited to the representation of legal immigrants or those whose undocumented status is connected to morally sympathetic circumstances (for instance, victims of trafficking and family abuse). Lawyers committed to less constrained advocacy for undocumented immigrants look for more supportive organizational locales, but outside of LSC programs, triage decisions are often driven as much by the availability of funding as by an assessment of client needs. Advocates complain that resources for assistance with workplace abuse, the defining injustice of the undocumented immigrant experience, are limited, while funders are attracted to support "victimization" projects—asylum, trafficking, domestic violence, and juvenile neglect. In the face of resource constraints, lawyers committed to workers' rights formulate other triage strategies, such as taking on cases based on their potential to achieve systemwide impacts or conditioning representation on client agreements to help run workers' rights organizations.

Language access also defines the boundaries of legal services provision. Organizations that lack bilingual lawyers or staff members in languages relevant to immigrant client communities impose significant barriers to access for monolingual clients. Legal services groups have attempted to respond to this problem by actively recruiting bilingual staff and conducting targeted outreach to immigrant communities. The multiplicity of Asian languages is a particular concern. In response, legal aid groups like Greater Boston Legal Services and the Legal Aid Foundation of Los Angeles have established Asian outreach projects in which lawyers who speak Cantonese, Mandarin, and Vietnamese provide community education and direct services to clients. There are also fledgling efforts to use technology to extend bilingual services: the LSC-funded Legal Services for New York City, in conjunction with the New York State Bar and probono.net, launched a free on-line referral and information service in Spanish. Yet as limited English proficient immigrants grow in number and diversity, while fanning out to nontraditional settlement states, legal services programs continue to struggle to meet the goal of equal access. Once immigrant clients are accepted for representation, language difference compromises communication about case strategies and goals, which renders poor clients more vulnerable to lawyer influence over the basic terms of representation. Though legal services programs have made efforts to address language access by setting guidelines for translation, commentators note that in practice translation services are frequently unavailable and—when they are available—often involve nonprofessionals who inject third party viewpoints into the lawyer-client relationship, thus challenging the aims of client-centered service.

At the other end of the public interest spectrum are those lawyers who view representation as a means to the end of legal and political reform. Domestic reform lawyers have been the subject of two basic criticisms. The first questions the systemic legitimacy of small groups of lawyers pursuing their own version of social change without significant political checks. On the one hand, this concern is heightened in the global context to the degree that U.S. lawyers are seen intervening as legal crusaders in countries around the world. Why should U.S. lawyers be involved in setting human rights standards in Burma and Nigeria, policing labor and environmental practices in Mexico, protesting World Bank projects in India, or asserting reproductive rights on behalf of women in Africa? In this spirit, critics assail the use of the ATS to advance human rights claims, emphasizing the undemocratic nature of U.S. lawyers asking judges to adjudicate international norms. On the other hand, however, public interest lawyering in the international arena can be seen as promoting democracy to the extent that it challenges the exclusion of less powerful groups from bodies of international decisionmaking and counteracts the negative impact of U.S. policy abroad in cases where domestic channels of redress are blocked. Reform lawyering can also be seen as advancing the democratically formulated goals of the international community to the extent that lawyers attempt to enforce universal human rights in countries where egregious abuse cannot be remedied by the political process.

The second major criticism of reform lawyering centers not on democratic legitimacy, but rather on client group accountability. Here, reform lawyers are faulted for pursuing causes in a top-down fashion, generating advocacy agendas without input from affected communities. Reform lawyering in the international arena reproduces, and in some situations heightens, this concern. The nature of human rights lawyering, in particular, raises challenges for client accountability. In terms of agenda setting, the project of human rights tends to be top-down, with lawyers seeking to build international law either out of a normative commitment to universality or as a pragmatic alternative to domestic constitutionalism. The execution of human rights advocacy also raises issues of client accountability: human rights lawyers chart test cases to push the boundaries of international law and exert control over questions of goals, strategy, and venues. In addition, the transnational nature of human rights litigation tends to increase complexity, which operates in favor of greater lawyer control. Particularly with respect to ATS cases, questions of jurisdiction, immunity, and enforcement are highly arcane, requiring deference to lawyer expertise. There are also logistical barriers that make client input more difficult. At one extreme are the Guantanamo cases, in which lawyers are limited in the ability to communicate with clients by government fiat; but even in less unique situations, the transnational scope of litigation makes coordination with clients more complex, particularly when access to technology is not readily available.

There are countervailing international dynamics that operate to ground lawyering more firmly in grassroots activity. As seen in the labor context, the development of sophisticated and cohesive transnational activist networks around maquiladora and sweatshop issues offers a counterweight to lawyer power in the design and execution of reform campaigns. As transnational human rights, environmental, and other networks continue to grow and develop mechanisms for coordination, they can more effectively demand lawyer responsiveness to network-defined decisions. Yet the rise of transnational networks also magnifies the accountability problems inherent in group representation, with lawyers placed in the position of navigating conflicts among network members and having to discern the collective will from fluid and informal decisionmaking processes.

2. *Motivation.* Motivation is a central component of professional identity, distinguishing the work of public interest lawyers, who are moved by a calling to pursue some version of social justice. In the pursuit of justice, however, there are multiple routes to take, not all of which involve global engagement. What factors shape the decisions of public interest lawyers to pursue international advocacy?

At the ideological level, the increasing salience of global interconnections may influence how lawyers perceive their advocacy role, injecting new explanations of injustice and presenting new prescriptions for reform. In this sense, "globalization" becomes a way of both understanding abuse and motivating efforts to fight it: workers' rights advocates thus describe the need to fight globally linked garment sweatshops with global activism, while environmentalists emphasize the global struggle to combat transborder pollution. From an advocacy perspective, exposure to international human rights further reframes the way lawyers view possibilities for reform, legitimizing the notion that the United States must adhere to its international obligations, and reviving efforts to stimulate more proactive economic and social rights agendas.

Motivation is also shaped by organizational context. For frontline legal services attorneys, global engagement is largely reactive, driven by the logic of individual case representation. For instance, lawyers at legal services groups on the border, like Texas RioGrande Legal Aid, report entering Mexico to pursue cases involving transnational kidnapping, while lawyers representing migrant farmworkers follow their clients to their home countries in the conduct of wage-and-hour cases. Yet organizational norms can influence how far legal services lawyers are willing to travel in the pursuit of client service. In the economic development context, some legal services groups are eager to help promote investment projects by HTAs [Hometown Associations] to benefit communities in Mexico, while others view their missions in strictly domestic terms and therefore limit their services to HTAs that focus their work primarily on helping immigrants in the United States.

For law reform groups, global engagement is largely a matter of deliberate strategic choice, with international advocacy guided by an impulse to press new claims and test new venues. Here, too, organizational norms are an important factor in lawyer receptivity to international opportunities. Lawyers in reform organizations like CCR [Center for Constitutional Rights] and the ACLU, with organizational histories of international work and funding commitments to promote human rights, have moved most aggressively. Lawyers in civil rights groups like the NAACP LDF, in contrast, have entered the international domain more slowly out of concern for reneging on the fight for domestic legal justice.

Although public interest lawyers are influenced by ideological and organizational factors, their decisions to engage globally are also shaped by personal and professional motives. International advocacy harbors the promise of adventure and the exotic. Particularly for public interest lawyers whose lower salaries make foreign travel more difficult, opportunities to travel abroad in connection with work are coveted. The chance to connect with foreign counterparts, share domestic experiences, and see new locales is a powerful draw. To the extent that advocacy in the global arena is seen as the vanguard of new social movements, lawyers are attracted out of a desire to be a part of something that gives larger meaning to individual efforts. Moreover, there is professional prestige associated with the international sphere and opportunities to parlay international experiences into better jobs at home. Lawyers who forge new international paths by using human rights laws, bringing cases in international venues, or creating connections with transnational groups receive professional attention in the form of conference invitations, media opportunities, fellowships, and academic jobs. From these platforms, lawyers tout accomplishments and legitimize global strategies—adding further momentum to public interest law's internationalization.

· · ·

NOTES & QUESTIONS

1.   Professor Haynes suggests that clients' likely unfamiliarity of international mechanisms may inhibit client-centered lawyering. But isn't this just one of many areas in which lawyers bring special expertise to a lawyer-client relationship? For example, few clients will be readily familiar with the particulars of the Federal Rules of Civil Procedure, so lawyers must draw on their own knowledge of these rules to provide adequate

representation. Is a client's unfamiliarity with human rights mechanisms any different?

2. An additional issue may be that clients misapprehend the strength of human rights claims. As lawyers found when litigating to stop public housing demolition following Hurricane Katrina, "[t]he guarantees of the Guiding Principles [on Internal Displacement], even when coupled with strong movement organizing, could not provide displaced persons with necessary short or long term housing relief following the hurricanes. Lack of enforceability of the relevant human rights norms was at odds with displaced persons' urgency for immediate safe and affordable shelter. This amplified a basic tension with pursuing human rights in the United States. Without government acceptance and commitment to enforcement and oversight, the visionary Guiding Principles could not offer hurricane survivors the realization of decent post-disaster housing." Caroline Bettinger-López, *et al.*, *Redefining Human Rights Lawyering Through the Lens of Critical Theory: Lessons for Pedagogy and Practice*, 18 Geo. J. on Poverty L. & Pol'y 337, 372 (2011). When clients are facing urgent needs as they were post-Katrina, does reliance on human rights claims create false hopes, perhaps even skirting ethical obligations regarding competence and communication?

3. Professor Cummings goes farther and speculates that some domestic public interest lawyers may be attracted to human rights approaches for their own reasons, because such approaches are "exotic" and hold the promise of international travel, as well as because such approaches may promote the lawyers' political and social worldview. Would such an interest by the lawyer create a personal conflict of interest, as a matter of legal ethics? Is one remedy simply to identify clients who share the lawyers' agenda?

4. Note that even if a U.S. human rights lawyer's work is domestically oriented, he or she may be involved in legal work outside of the U.S.—for example, appearing before the Inter-American Commission or traveling to Geneva for a U.N. meeting. Rule 8.5 of the Model Rules of Professional Conduct is a "choice of law" provision that governs the applicable ethics rules. According to the commentary, Rule 8.5 "applies to lawyers engaged in transnational practice, unless international law, treaties or other agreements between competent regulatory authorities in the affected jurisdictions provide otherwise." In general, a lawyer is subject to the disciplinary authority of the jurisdiction where he or she is admitted, and may also be subject to discipline in the jurisdiction where the conduct occurs. *See* David Weissbrodt, *Ethical Problems of an International Human Rights Law Practice*, 7 Mich. YBI Legal Stud. 217, 244–51 (1985). Professor Beth Lyon argues that the "provide otherwise" language attached to Rule 8.5 may create difficulties for practitioners, since "American lawyers may be required to conform to irrelevant and unfamiliar rules when practicing in an international forum, if the international forum has not explicitly ruled out their use." Beth Lyon, *Human Rights Aspirations, Professional Obligations:*

Practitioner Survey on the Ethics of Domestic Human Rights, 1 Notre Dame J. of Int'l Comp. & Hum. Rts. L. 114, 135–36 (2011).

SKILLS EXERCISE

You are admitted to practice law in a state that has fully adopted the provisions of the ABA's Model Rules of Professional Conduct. On a pro bono basis, you represent a group of adult, non-citizen immigrant detainees facing removal from the U.S. who have been denied appointment of counsel in their pending proceedings. The detainees are being held in New York City.

After exhausting your remedies in federal court, where your clients were unsuccessfully pursuing right to counsel claims under the 5th Amendment due process clause, you file a petition before the Inter-American Commission on Human Rights (IACHR). (The IACHR is located in Washington, D.C. but, like the United Nations headquarters in New York City, the IACHR location is considered to be extraterritorial.) The petition names the United States as a respondent and alleges that the U.S. policy of denying appointed counsel to adult immigrants in removal proceedings violates U.S. obligations under the American Convention on the Rights and Duties of Man. After the petition is filed, you are contacted by administrative staff of the Commission, who would like to set up an *ex parte* meeting between you and several of the Commission's staff attorneys to discuss your claims. Such meetings are viewed as routine by the Commission.

Does this situation raise any legal ethics concerns? Note that the ABA Model Rules provide in Rule 3.5 that "[a] lawyer shall not . . . communicate *ex parte*" with a judge or other officials during a proceeding "unless authorized to do so by law or court order." The Comments to the Rule make clear that this prohibition on *ex parte* communication extends to all "persons serving in an official capacity in the proceeding."

APPENDIX A

SELECT HUMAN RIGHTS INSTRUMENTS OF THE UNITED NATIONS

■ ■ ■

Table of Contents

INTERNATIONAL COVENANT ON CIVIL AND POLITICAL RIGHTS

Adopted and opened for signature, ratification and accession by
General Assembly resolution 2200A (XXI) of 16 December 1966
entry into force 23 March 1976, in accordance with Article 49

PREAMBLE

The States Parties to the present Covenant,

Considering that, in accordance with the principles proclaimed in the
Charter of the United Nations, recognition of the inherent dignity and of

the equal and inalienable rights of all members of the human family is the foundation of freedom, justice and peace in the world,

Recognizing that these rights derive from the inherent dignity of the human person,

Recognizing that, in accordance with the Universal Declaration of Human Rights, the ideal of free human beings enjoying civil and political freedom and freedom from fear and want can only be achieved if conditions are created whereby everyone may enjoy his civil and political rights, as well as his economic, social and cultural rights,

Considering the obligation of States under the Charter of the United Nations to promote universal respect for, and observance of, human rights and freedoms,

Realizing that the individual, having duties to other individuals and to the community to which he belongs, is under a responsibility to strive for the promotion and observance of the rights recognized in the present Covenant,

Agree upon the following articles:

PART I

Article 1

1. All peoples have the right of self-determination. By virtue of that right they freely determine their political status and freely pursue their economic, social and cultural development.

2. All peoples may, for their own ends, freely dispose of their natural wealth and resources without prejudice to any obligations arising out of international economic co-operation, based upon the principle of mutual benefit, and international law. In no case may a people be deprived of its own means of subsistence.

3. The States Parties to the present Covenant, including those having responsibility for the administration of Non-Self-Governing and Trust Territories, shall promote the realization of the right of self-determination, and shall respect that right, in conformity with the provisions of the Charter of the United Nations.

PART II

Article 2

1. Each State Party to the present Covenant undertakes to respect and to ensure to all individuals within its territory and subject to its jurisdiction the rights recognized in the present Covenant, without distinction of any kind, such as race, colour, sex, language, religion, political or other opinion, national or social origin, property, birth or other status.

2. Where not already provided for by existing legislative or other measures, each State Party to the present Covenant undertakes to take the necessary steps, in accordance with its constitutional processes and with the provisions of the present Covenant, to adopt such laws or other measures as may be necessary to give effect to the rights recognized in the present Covenant.

3. Each State Party to the present Covenant undertakes:

(a) To ensure that any person whose rights or freedoms as herein recognized are violated shall have an effective remedy, notwithstanding that the violation has been committed by persons acting in an official capacity;

(b) To ensure that any person claiming such a remedy shall have his right thereto determined by competent judicial, administrative or legislative authorities, or by any other competent authority provided for by the legal system of the State, and to develop the possibilities of judicial remedy;

(c) To ensure that the competent authorities shall enforce such remedies when granted.

Article 3

The States Parties to the present Covenant undertake to ensure the equal right of men and women to the enjoyment of all civil and political rights set forth in the present Covenant.

Article 4

1. In time of public emergency which threatens the life of the nation and the existence of which is officially proclaimed, the States Parties to the present Covenant may take measures derogating from their obligations under the present Covenant to the extent strictly required by the exigencies of the situation, provided that such measures are not inconsistent with their other obligations under international law and do not involve discrimination solely on the ground of race, colour, sex, language, religion or social origin.

2. No derogation from articles 6, 7, 8 (paragraphs 1 and 2), 11, 15, 16 and 18 may be made under this provision.

3. Any State Party to the present Covenant availing itself of the right of derogation shall immediately inform the other States Parties to the present Covenant, through the intermediary of the Secretary-General of the United Nations, of the provisions from which it has derogated and of the reasons by which it was actuated. A further communication shall be made, through the same intermediary, on the date on which it terminates such derogation.

Article 5

1. Nothing in the present Covenant may be interpreted as implying for any State, group or person any right to engage in any activity or perform any act aimed at the destruction of any of the rights and freedoms recognized herein or at their limitation to a greater extent than is provided for in the present Covenant.

2. There shall be no restriction upon or derogation from any of the fundamental human rights recognized or existing in any State Party to the present Covenant pursuant to law, conventions, regulations or custom on the pretext that the present Covenant does not recognize such rights or that it recognizes them to a lesser extent.

PART III

Article 6

1. Every human being has the inherent right to life. This right shall be protected by law. No one shall be arbitrarily deprived of his life.

2. In countries which have not abolished the death penalty, sentence of death may be imposed only for the most serious crimes in accordance with the law in force at the time of the commission of the crime and not contrary to the provisions of the present Covenant and to the Convention on the Prevention and Punishment of the Crime of Genocide. This penalty can only be carried out pursuant to a final judgement rendered by a competent court.

3. When deprivation of life constitutes the crime of genocide, it is understood that nothing in this article shall authorize any State Party to the present Covenant to derogate in any way from any obligation assumed under the provisions of the Convention on the Prevention and Punishment of the Crime of Genocide.

4. Anyone sentenced to death shall have the right to seek pardon or commutation of the sentence. Amnesty, pardon or commutation of the sentence of death may be granted in all cases.

5. Sentence of death shall not be imposed for crimes committed by persons below eighteen years of age and shall not be carried out on pregnant women.

6. Nothing in this article shall be invoked to delay or to prevent the abolition of capital punishment by any State Party to the present Covenant.

Article 7

No one shall be subjected to torture or to cruel, inhuman or degrading treatment or punishment. In particular, no one shall be subjected without his free consent to medical or scientific experimentation.

Article 8

1. No one shall be held in slavery; slavery and the slave-trade in all their forms shall be prohibited.

2. No one shall be held in servitude.

3. (a) No one shall be required to perform forced or compulsory labour;

(b) Paragraph 3 (a) shall not be held to preclude, in countries where imprisonment with hard labour may be imposed as a punishment for a crime, the performance of hard labour in pursuance of a sentence to such punishment by a competent court;

(c) For the purpose of this paragraph the term "forced or compulsory labour" shall not include:

(i) Any work or service, not referred to in subparagraph (b), normally required of a person who is under detention in consequence of a lawful order of a court, or of a person during conditional release from such detention;

(ii) Any service of a military character and, in countries where conscientious objection is recognized, any national service required by law of conscientious objectors;

(iii) Any service exacted in cases of emergency or calamity threatening the life or well-being of the community;

(iv) Any work or service which forms part of normal civil obligations.

Article 9

1. Everyone has the right to liberty and security of person. No one shall be subjected to arbitrary arrest or detention. No one shall be deprived of his liberty except on such grounds and in accordance with such procedure as are established by law.

2. Anyone who is arrested shall be informed, at the time of arrest, of the reasons for his arrest and shall be promptly informed of any charges against him.

3. Anyone arrested or detained on a criminal charge shall be brought promptly before a judge or other officer authorized by law to exercise judicial power and shall be entitled to trial within a reasonable time or to release. It shall not be the general rule that persons awaiting

trial shall be detained in custody, but release may be subject to guarantees to appear for trial, at any other stage of the judicial proceedings, and, should occasion arise, for execution of the judgement.

4. Anyone who is deprived of his liberty by arrest or detention shall be entitled to take proceedings before a court, in order that that court may decide without delay on the lawfulness of his detention and order his release if the detention is not lawful.

5. Anyone who has been the victim of unlawful arrest or detention shall have an enforceable right to compensation.

Article 10

1. All persons deprived of their liberty shall be treated with humanity and with respect for the inherent dignity of the human person.

2. (a) Accused persons shall, save in exceptional circumstances, be segregated from convicted persons and shall be subject to separate treatment appropriate to their status as unconvicted persons;

(b) Accused juvenile persons shall be separated from adults and brought as speedily as possible for adjudication.

3. The penitentiary system shall comprise treatment of prisoners the essential aim of which shall be their reformation and social rehabilitation. Juvenile offenders shall be segregated from adults and be accorded treatment appropriate to their age and legal status.

Article 11

No one shall be imprisoned merely on the ground of inability to fulfill a contractual obligation.

Article 12

1. Everyone lawfully within the territory of a State shall, within that territory, have the right to liberty of movement and freedom to choose his residence.

2. Everyone shall be free to leave any country, including his own.

3. The above-mentioned rights shall not be subject to any restrictions except those which are provided by law, are necessary to protect national security, public order (ordre public), public health or morals or the rights and freedoms of others, and are consistent with the other rights recognized in the present Covenant.

4. No one shall be arbitrarily deprived of the right to enter his own country.

Article 13

An alien lawfully in the territory of a State Party to the present Covenant may be expelled therefrom only in pursuance of a decision reached in accordance with law and shall, except where compelling reasons of national security otherwise require, be allowed to submit the reasons against his expulsion and to have his case reviewed by, and be represented for the purpose before, the competent authority or a person or persons especially designated by the competent authority.

Article 14

1. All persons shall be equal before the courts and tribunals. In the determination of any criminal charge against him, or of his rights and obligations in a suit at law, everyone shall be entitled to a fair and public hearing by a competent, independent and impartial tribunal established by law. The press and the public may be excluded from all or part of a trial for reasons of morals, public order (ordre public) or national security in a democratic society, or when the interest of the private lives of the parties so requires, or to the extent strictly necessary in the opinion of the court in special circumstances where publicity would prejudice the interests of justice; but any judgement rendered in a criminal case or in a suit at law shall be made public except where the interest of juvenile persons otherwise requires or the proceedings concern matrimonial disputes or the guardianship of children.

2. Everyone charged with a criminal offence shall have the right to be presumed innocent until proved guilty according to law.

3. In the determination of any criminal charge against him, everyone shall be entitled to the following minimum guarantees, in full equality:

(a) To be informed promptly and in detail in a language which he understands of the nature and cause of the charge against him;

(b) To have adequate time and facilities for the preparation of his defence and to communicate with counsel of his own choosing;

(c) To be tried without undue delay;

(d) To be tried in his presence, and to defend himself in person or through legal assistance of his own choosing; to be informed, if he does not have legal assistance, of this right; and to have legal assistance assigned to him, in any case where the interests of justice so require, and without payment by him in any such case if he does not have sufficient means to pay for it;

(e) To examine, or have examined, the witnesses against him and to obtain the attendance and examination of witnesses on his behalf under the same conditions as witnesses against him;

(f) To have the free assistance of an interpreter if he cannot understand or speak the language used in court;

(g) Not to be compelled to testify against himself or to confess guilt.

4. In the case of juvenile persons, the procedure shall be such as will take account of their age and the desirability of promoting their rehabilitation.

5. Everyone convicted of a crime shall have the right to his conviction and sentence being reviewed by a higher tribunal according to law.

6. When a person has by a final decision been convicted of a criminal offence and when subsequently his conviction has been reversed or he has been pardoned on the ground that a new or newly discovered fact shows conclusively that there has been a miscarriage of justice, the person who has suffered punishment as a result of such conviction shall be compensated according to law, unless it is proved that the non-disclosure of the unknown fact in time is wholly or partly attributable to him.

7. No one shall be liable to be tried or punished again for an offence for which he has already been finally convicted or acquitted in accordance with the law and penal procedure of each country.

Article 15

1. No one shall be held guilty of any criminal offence on account of any act or omission which did not constitute a criminal offence, under national or international law, at the time when it was committed. Nor shall a heavier penalty be imposed than the one that was applicable at the time when the criminal offence was committed. If, subsequent to the commission of the offence, provision is made by law for the imposition of the lighter penalty, the offender shall benefit thereby.

2. Nothing in this article shall prejudice the trial and punishment of any person for any act or omission which, at the time when it was committed, was criminal according to the general principles of law recognized by the community of nations.

Article 16

Everyone shall have the right to recognition everywhere as a person before the law.

Article 17

1. No one shall be subjected to arbitrary or unlawful interference with his privacy, family, home or correspondence, nor to unlawful attacks on his honour and reputation.

2.   Everyone has the right to the protection of the law against such interference or attacks.

Article 18

1.   Everyone shall have the right to freedom of thought, conscience and religion. This right shall include freedom to have or to adopt a religion or belief of his choice, and freedom, either individually or in community with others and in public or private, to manifest his religion or belief in worship, observance, practice and teaching.

2.   No one shall be subject to coercion which would impair his freedom to have or to adopt a religion or belief of his choice.

3.   Freedom to manifest one's religion or beliefs may be subject only to such limitations as are prescribed by law and are necessary to protect public safety, order, health, or morals or the fundamental rights and freedoms of others.

4.   The States Parties to the present Covenant undertake to have respect for the liberty of parents and, when applicable, legal guardians to ensure the religious and moral education of their children in conformity with their own convictions.

Article 19

1.   Everyone shall have the right to hold opinions without interference.

2.   Everyone shall have the right to freedom of expression; this right shall include freedom to seek, receive and impart information and ideas of all kinds, regardless of frontiers, either orally, in writing or in print, in the form of art, or through any other media of his choice.

3.   The exercise of the rights provided for in paragraph 2 of this article carries with it special duties and responsibilities. It may therefore be subject to certain restrictions, but these shall only be such as are provided by law and are necessary:

(a) For respect of the rights or reputations of others;

(b) For the protection of national security or of public order (ordre public), or of public health or morals.

Article 20

1.   Any propaganda for war shall be prohibited by law.

2.   Any advocacy of national, racial or religious hatred that constitutes incitement to discrimination, hostility or violence shall be prohibited by law.

Article 21

The right of peaceful assembly shall be recognized. No restrictions may be placed on the exercise of this right other than those imposed in conformity with the law and which are necessary in a democratic society in the interests of national security or public safety, public order (ordre public), the protection of public health or morals or the protection of the rights and freedoms of others.

Article 22

1.   Everyone shall have the right to freedom of association with others, including the right to form and join trade unions for the protection of his interests.

2.   No restrictions may be placed on the exercise of this right other than those which are prescribed by law and which are necessary in a democratic society in the interests of national security or public safety, public order (ordre public), the protection of public health or morals or the protection of the rights and freedoms of others. This article shall not prevent the imposition of lawful restrictions on members of the armed forces and of the police in their exercise of this right.

3.   Nothing in this article shall authorize States Parties to the International Labour Organisation Convention of 1948 concerning Freedom of Association and Protection of the Right to Organize to take legislative measures which would prejudice, or to apply the law in such a manner as to prejudice, the guarantees provided for in that Convention.

Article 23

1.   The family is the natural and fundamental group unit of society and is entitled to protection by society and the State.

2.   The right of men and women of marriageable age to marry and to found a family shall be recognized.

3.   No marriage shall be entered into without the free and full consent of the intending spouses.

4.   States Parties to the present Covenant shall take appropriate steps to ensure equality of rights and responsibilities of spouses as to marriage, during marriage and at its dissolution. In the case of dissolution, provision shall be made for the necessary protection of any children.

Article 24

1.   Every child shall have, without any discrimination as to race, colour, sex, language, religion, national or social origin, property or birth, the right to such measures of protection as are required by his status as a minor, on the part of his family, society and the State.

2.   Every child shall be registered immediately after birth and shall have a name.

3.   Every child has the right to acquire a nationality.

Article 25

Every citizen shall have the right and the opportunity, without any of the distinctions mentioned in article 2 and without unreasonable restrictions:

(a) To take part in the conduct of public affairs, directly or through freely chosen representatives;

(b) To vote and to be elected at genuine periodic elections which shall be by universal and equal suffrage and shall be held by secret ballot, guaranteeing the free expression of the will of the electors;

(c) To have access, on general terms of equality, to public service in his country.

Article 26

All persons are equal before the law and are entitled without any discrimination to the equal protection of the law. In this respect, the law shall prohibit any discrimination and guarantee to all persons equal and effective protection against discrimination on any ground such as race, colour, sex, language, religion, political or other opinion, national or social origin, property, birth or other status.

Article 27

In those States in which ethnic, religious or linguistic minorities exist, persons belonging to such minorities shall not be denied the right, in community with the other members of their group, to enjoy their own culture, to profess and practise their own religion, or to use their own language.

PART IV

Article 28

1.   There shall be established a Human Rights Committee (hereafter referred to in the present Covenant as the Committee). It shall consist of eighteen members and shall carry out the functions hereinafter provided.

2.   The Committee shall be composed of nationals of the States Parties to the present Covenant who shall be persons of high moral character and recognized competence in the field of human rights, consideration being given to the usefulness of the participation of some persons having legal experience.

3. The members of the Committee shall be elected and shall serve in their personal capacity.

Article 29

1. The members of the Committee shall be elected by secret ballot from a list of persons possessing the qualifications prescribed in article 28 and nominated for the purpose by the States Parties to the present Covenant.

2. Each State Party to the present Covenant may nominate not more than two persons. These persons shall be nationals of the nominating State.

3. A person shall be eligible for renomination.

Article 30

1. The initial election shall be held no later than six months after the date of the entry into force of the present Covenant.

2. At least four months before the date of each election to the Committee, other than an election to fill a vacancy declared in accordance with article 34, the Secretary-General of the United Nations shall address a written invitation to the States Parties to the present Covenant to submit their nominations for membership of the Committee within three months.

3. The Secretary-General of the United Nations shall prepare a list in alphabetical order of all the persons thus nominated, with an indication of the States Parties which have nominated them, and shall submit it to the States Parties to the present Covenant no later than one month before the date of each election.

4. Elections of the members of the Committee shall be held at a meeting of the States Parties to the present Covenant convened by the Secretary General of the United Nations at the Headquarters of the United Nations. At that meeting, for which two thirds of the States Parties to the present Covenant shall constitute a quorum, the persons elected to the Committee shall be those nominees who obtain the largest number of votes and an absolute majority of the votes of the representatives of States Parties present and voting.

Article 31

1. The Committee may not include more than one national of the same State.

2. In the election of the Committee, consideration shall be given to equitable geographical distribution of membership and to the representation of the different forms of civilization and of the principal legal systems.

Article 32

1.   The members of the Committee shall be elected for a term of four years. They shall be eligible for re-election if renominated. However, the terms of nine of the members elected at the first election shall expire at the end of two years; immediately after the first election, the names of these nine members shall be chosen by lot by the Chairman of the meeting referred to in article 30, paragraph 4.

2.   Elections at the expiry of office shall be held in accordance with the preceding articles of this part of the present Covenant.

Article 33

1.   If, in the unanimous opinion of the other members, a member of the Committee has ceased to carry out his functions for any cause other than absence of a temporary character, the Chairman of the Committee shall notify the Secretary-General of the United Nations, who shall then declare the seat of that member to be vacant.

2.   In the event of the death or the resignation of a member of the Committee, the Chairman shall immediately notify the Secretary-General of the United Nations, who shall declare the seat vacant from the date of death or the date on which the resignation takes effect.

Article 34

1.   When a vacancy is declared in accordance with article 33 and if the term of office of the member to be replaced does not expire within six months of the declaration of the vacancy, the Secretary-General of the United Nations shall notify each of the States Parties to the present Covenant, which may within two months submit nominations in accordance with article 29 for the purpose of filling the vacancy.

2.   The Secretary-General of the United Nations shall prepare a list in alphabetical order of the persons thus nominated and shall submit it to the States Parties to the present Covenant. The election to fill the vacancy shall then take place in accordance with the relevant provisions of this part of the present Covenant.

3.   A member of the Committee elected to fill a vacancy declared in accordance with article 33 shall hold office for the remainder of the term of the member who vacated the seat on the Committee under the provisions of that article.

Article 35

The members of the Committee shall, with the approval of the General Assembly of the United Nations, receive emoluments from United Nations resources on such terms and conditions as the General Assembly may decide, having regard to the importance of the Committee's responsibilities.

Article 36

The Secretary-General of the United Nations shall provide the necessary staff and facilities for the effective performance of the functions of the Committee under the present Covenant.

Article 37

1. The Secretary-General of the United Nations shall convene the initial meeting of the Committee at the Headquarters of the United Nations.

2. After its initial meeting, the Committee shall meet at such times as shall be provided in its rules of procedure.

3. The Committee shall normally meet at the Headquarters of the United Nations or at the United Nations Office at Geneva.

Article 38

Every member of the Committee shall, before taking up his duties, make a solemn declaration in open committee that he will perform his functions impartially and conscientiously.

Article 39

1. The Committee shall elect its officers for a term of two years. They may be re-elected.

2. The Committee shall establish its own rules of procedure, but these rules shall provide, inter alia, that:

    (a) Twelve members shall constitute a quorum;

    (b) Decisions of the Committee shall be made by a majority vote of the members present.

Article 40

1. The States Parties to the present Covenant undertake to submit reports on the measures they have adopted which give effect to the rights recognized herein and on the progress made in the enjoyment of those rights:

    (a) Within one year of the entry into force of the present Covenant for the States Parties concerned;

    (b) Thereafter whenever the Committee so requests.

2. All reports shall be submitted to the Secretary-General of the United Nations, who shall transmit them to the Committee for consideration. Reports shall indicate the factors and difficulties, if any, affecting the implementation of the present Covenant.

3. The Secretary General of the United Nations may, after consultation with the Committee, transmit to the specialized agencies

concerned copies of such parts of the reports as may fall within their field of competence.

4.   The Committee shall study the reports submitted by the States Parties to the present Covenant. It shall transmit its reports, and such general comments as it may consider appropriate, to the States Parties. The Committee may also transmit to the Economic and Social Council these comments along with the copies of the reports it has received from States Parties to the present Covenant.

5.   The States Parties to the present Covenant may submit to the Committee observations on any comments that may be made in accordance with paragraph 4 of this article.

Article 41

1.   A State Party to the present Covenant may at any time declare under this article that it recognizes the competence of the Committee to receive and consider communications to the effect that a State Party claims that another State Party is not fulfilling its obligations under the present Covenant. Communications under this article may be received and considered only if submitted by a State Party which has made a declaration recognizing in regard to itself the competence of the Committee. No communication shall be received by the Committee if it concerns a State Party which has not made such a declaration. Communications received under this article shall be dealt with in accordance with the following procedure:

(a) If a State Party to the present Covenant considers that another State Party is not giving effect to the provisions of the present Covenant, it may, by written communication, bring the matter to the attention of that State Party. Within three months after the receipt of the communication the receiving State shall afford the State which sent the communication an explanation, or any other statement in writing clarifying the matter which should include, to the extent possible and pertinent, reference to domestic procedures and remedies taken, pending, or available in the matter;

(b) If the matter is not adjusted to the satisfaction of both States Parties concerned within six months after the receipt by the receiving State of the initial communication, either State shall have the right to refer the matter to the Committee, by notice given to the Committee and to the other State;

(c) The Committee shall deal with a matter referred to it only after it has ascertained that all available domestic remedies have been invoked and exhausted in the matter, in conformity with the generally recognized principles of international law.

This shall not be the rule where the application of the remedies is unreasonably prolonged;

(d) The Committee shall hold closed meetings when examining communications under this article;

(e) Subject to the provisions of subparagraph (c), the Committee shall make available its good offices to the States Parties concerned with a view to a friendly solution of the matter on the basis of respect for human rights and fundamental freedoms as recognized in the present Covenant;

(f) In any matter referred to it, the Committee may call upon the States Parties concerned, referred to in subparagraph (b), to supply any relevant information;

(g) The States Parties concerned, referred to in subparagraph (b), shall have the right to be represented when the matter is being considered in the Committee and to make submissions orally and/or in writing;

(h) The Committee shall, within twelve months after the date of receipt of notice under subparagraph (b), submit a report:

(i) If a solution within the terms of subparagraph (e) is reached, the Committee shall confine its report to a brief statement of the facts and of the solution reached;

(ii) If a solution within the terms of subparagraph (e) is not reached, the Committee shall confine its report to a brief statement of the facts; the written submissions and record of the oral submissions made by the States Parties concerned shall be attached to the report. In every matter, the report shall be communicated to the States Parties concerned.

2. The provisions of this article shall come into force when ten States Parties to the present Covenant have made declarations under paragraph I of this article. Such declarations shall be deposited by the States Parties with the Secretary-General of the United Nations, who shall transmit copies thereof to the other States Parties. A declaration may be withdrawn at any time by notification to the Secretary-General. Such a withdrawal shall not prejudice the consideration of any matter which is the subject of a communication already transmitted under this article; no further communication by any State Party shall be received after the notification of withdrawal of the declaration has been received by the Secretary-General, unless the State Party concerned has made a new declaration.

Article 42

1. (a) If a matter referred to the Committee in accordance with article 41 is not resolved to the satisfaction of the States Parties concerned, the Committee may, with the prior consent of the States Parties concerned, appoint an ad hoc Conciliation Commission (hereinafter referred to as the Commission). The good offices of the Commission shall be made available to the States Parties concerned with a view to an amicable solution of the matter on the basis of respect for the present Covenant;

(b) The Commission shall consist of five persons acceptable to the States Parties concerned. If the States Parties concerned fail to reach agreement within three months on all or part of the composition of the Commission, the members of the Commission concerning whom no agreement has been reached shall be elected by secret ballot by a two-thirds majority vote of the Committee from among its members.

2. The members of the Commission shall serve in their personal capacity. They shall not be nationals of the States Parties concerned, or of a State not Party to the present Covenant, or of a State Party which has not made a declaration under article 41.

3. The Commission shall elect its own Chairman and adopt its own rules of procedure.

4. The meetings of the Commission shall normally be held at the Headquarters of the United Nations or at the United Nations Office at Geneva. However, they may be held at such other convenient places as the Commission may determine in consultation with the Secretary-General of the United Nations and the States Parties concerned.

5. The secretariat provided in accordance with article 36 shall also service the commissions appointed under this article.

6. The information received and collated by the Committee shall be made available to the Commission and the Commission may call upon the States Parties concerned to supply any other relevant information.

7. When the Commission has fully considered the matter, but in any event not later than twelve months after having been seized of the matter, it shall submit to the Chairman of the Committee a report for communication to the States Parties concerned:

(a) If the Commission is unable to complete its consideration of the matter within twelve months, it shall confine its report to a brief statement of the status of its consideration of the matter;

(b) If an amicable solution to the matter on the basis of respect for human rights as recognized in the present Covenant is reached, the Commission shall confine its report to a brief statement of the facts and of the solution reached;

(c) If a solution within the terms of subparagraph (b) is not reached, the Commission's report shall embody its findings on all questions of fact relevant to the issues between the States Parties concerned, and its views on the possibilities of an amicable solution of the matter. This report shall also contain the written submissions and a record of the oral submissions made by the States Parties concerned;

(d) If the Commission's report is submitted under subparagraph (c), the States Parties concerned shall, within three months of the receipt of the report, notify the Chairman of the Committee whether or not they accept the contents of the report of the Commission.

8.   The provisions of this article are without prejudice to the responsibilities of the Committee under article 41.

9.   The States Parties concerned shall share equally all the expenses of the members of the Commission in accordance with estimates to be provided by the Secretary-General of the United Nations.

10. The Secretary-General of the United Nations shall be empowered to pay the expenses of the members of the Commission, if necessary, before reimbursement by the States Parties concerned, in accordance with paragraph 9 of this article.

Article 43

The members of the Committee, and of the ad hoc conciliation commissions which may be appointed under article 42, shall be entitled to the facilities, privileges and immunities of experts on mission for the United Nations as laid down in the relevant sections of the Convention on the Privileges and Immunities of the United Nations.

Article 44

The provisions for the implementation of the present Covenant shall apply without prejudice to the procedures prescribed in the field of human rights by or under the constituent instruments and the conventions of the United Nations and of the specialized agencies and shall not prevent the States Parties to the present Covenant from having recourse to other procedures for settling a dispute in accordance with general or special international agreements in force between them.

Article 45

The Committee shall submit to the General Assembly of the United Nations, through the Economic and Social Council, an annual report on its activities.

PART V

Article 46

Nothing in the present Covenant shall be interpreted as impairing the provisions of the Charter of the United Nations and of the constitutions of the specialized agencies which define the respective responsibilities of the various organs of the United Nations and of the specialized agencies in regard to the matters dealt with in the present Covenant.

Article 47

Nothing in the present Covenant shall be interpreted as impairing the inherent right of all peoples to enjoy and utilize fully and freely their natural wealth and resources.

PART VI

Article 48

1. The present Covenant is open for signature by any State Member of the United Nations or member of any of its specialized agencies, by any State Party to the Statute of the International Court of Justice, and by any other State which has been invited by the General Assembly of the United Nations to become a Party to the present Covenant.

2. The present Covenant is subject to ratification. Instruments of ratification shall be deposited with the Secretary-General of the United Nations.

3. The present Covenant shall be open to accession by any State referred to in paragraph 1 of this article.

4. Accession shall be effected by the deposit of an instrument of accession with the Secretary-General of the United Nations.

5. The Secretary-General of the United Nations shall inform all States which have signed this Covenant or acceded to it of the deposit of each instrument of ratification or accession.

Article 49

1. The present Covenant shall enter into force three months after the date of the deposit with the Secretary-General of the United Nations of the thirty-fifth instrument of ratification or instrument of accession.

2. For each State ratifying the present Covenant or acceding to it after the deposit of the thirty-fifth instrument of ratification or instrument of accession, the present Covenant shall enter into force three months after the date of the deposit of its own instrument of ratification or instrument of accession.

Article 50

The provisions of the present Covenant shall extend to all parts of federal States without any limitations or exceptions.

Article 51

1. Any State Party to the present Covenant may propose an amendment and file it with the Secretary-General of the United Nations. The Secretary-General of the United Nations shall thereupon communicate any proposed amendments to the States Parties to the present Covenant with a request that they notify him whether they favour a conference of States Parties for the purpose of considering and voting upon the proposals. In the event that at least one third of the States Parties favours such a conference, the Secretary-General shall convene the conference under the auspices of the United Nations. Any amendment adopted by a majority of the States Parties present and voting at the conference shall be submitted to the General Assembly of the United Nations for approval.

2. Amendments shall come into force when they have been approved by the General Assembly of the United Nations and accepted by a two-thirds majority of the States Parties to the present Covenant in accordance with their respective constitutional processes.

3. When amendments come into force, they shall be binding on those States Parties which have accepted them, other States Parties still being bound by the provisions of the present Covenant and any earlier amendment which they have accepted.

Article 52

1. Irrespective of the notifications made under article 48, paragraph 5, the Secretary-General of the United Nations shall inform all States referred to in paragraph I of the same article of the following particulars:

(a) Signatures, ratifications and accessions under article 48;

(b) The date of the entry into force of the present Covenant under article 49 and the date of the entry into force of any amendments under article 51.

Article 53

1. The present Covenant, of which the Chinese, English, French, Russian and Spanish texts are equally authentic, shall be deposited in the archives of the United Nations.

2. The Secretary-General of the United Nations shall transmit certified copies of the present Covenant to all States referred to in article 48.

INTERNATIONAL COVENANT ON ECONOMIC, SOCIAL AND CULTURAL RIGHTS

Adopted and opened for signature, ratification and accession by
General Assembly resolution 2200A (XXI) of 16 December 1966
entry into force 3 January 1976, in accordance with article 27

PREAMBLE

The States Parties to the present Covenant,

Considering that, in accordance with the principles proclaimed in the Charter of the United Nations, recognition of the inherent dignity and of the equal and inalienable rights of all members of the human family is the foundation of freedom, justice and peace in the world,

Recognizing that these rights derive from the inherent dignity of the human person,

Recognizing that, in accordance with the Universal Declaration of Human Rights, the ideal of free human beings enjoying freedom from fear and want can only be achieved if conditions are created whereby everyone may enjoy his economic, social and cultural rights, as well as his civil and political rights,

Considering the obligation of States under the Charter of the United Nations to promote universal respect for, and observance of, human rights and freedoms,

Realizing that the individual, having duties to other individuals and to the community to which he belongs, is under a responsibility to strive for the promotion and observance of the rights recognized in the present Covenant,

Agree upon the following articles:

PART I

Article 1

1.   All peoples have the right of self-determination. By virtue of that right they freely determine their political status and freely pursue their economic, social and cultural development.

2.   All peoples may, for their own ends, freely dispose of their natural wealth and resources without prejudice to any obligations arising out of international economic co-operation, based upon the principle of mutual benefit, and international law. In no case may a people be deprived of its own means of subsistence.

3.   The States Parties to the present Covenant, including those having responsibility for the administration of Non-Self-Governing and

Trust Territories, shall promote the realization of the right of self-determination, and shall respect that right, in conformity with the provisions of the Charter of the United Nations.

PART II

Article 2

1.   Each State Party to the present Covenant undertakes to take steps, individually and through international assistance and co-operation, especially economic and technical, to the maximum of its available resources, with a view to achieving progressively the full realization of the rights recognized in the present Covenant by all appropriate means, including particularly the adoption of legislative measures.

2.   The States Parties to the present Covenant undertake to guarantee that the rights enunciated in the present Covenant will be exercised without discrimination of any kind as to race, colour, sex, language, religion, political or other opinion, national or social origin, property, birth or other status.

3.   Developing countries, with due regard to human rights and their national economy, may determine to what extent they would guarantee the economic rights recognized in the present Covenant to non-nationals.

Article 3

The States Parties to the present Covenant undertake to ensure the equal right of men and women to the enjoyment of all economic, social and cultural rights set forth in the present Covenant.

Article 4

The States Parties to the present Covenant recognize that, in the enjoyment of those rights provided by the State in conformity with the present Covenant, the State may subject such rights only to such limitations as are determined by law only in so far as this may be compatible with the nature of these rights and solely for the purpose of promoting the general welfare in a democratic society.

Article 5

1.   Nothing in the present Covenant may be interpreted as implying for any State, group or person any right to engage in any activity or to perform any act aimed at the destruction of any of the rights or freedoms recognized herein, or at their limitation to a greater extent than is provided for in the present Covenant.

2.   No restriction upon or derogation from any of the fundamental human rights recognized or existing in any country in virtue of law, conventions, regulations or custom shall be admitted on the pretext that

the present Covenant does not recognize such rights or that it recognizes them to a lesser extent.

PART III

Article 6

1.   The States Parties to the present Covenant recognize the right to work, which includes the right of everyone to the opportunity to gain his living by work which he freely chooses or accepts, and will take appropriate steps to safeguard this right.

2.   The steps to be taken by a State Party to the present Covenant to achieve the full realization of this right shall include technical and vocational guidance and training programmes, policies and techniques to achieve steady economic, social and cultural development and full and productive employment under conditions safeguarding fundamental political and economic freedoms to the individual.

Article 7

The States Parties to the present Covenant recognize the right of everyone to the enjoyment of just and favourable conditions of work which ensure, in particular:

(a) Remuneration   which   provides   all   workers,   as   a minimum, with:

(i) Fair wages and equal remuneration for work of equal value without distinction of any kind, in particular women being guaranteed conditions of work not inferior to those enjoyed by men, with equal pay for equal work;

(ii) A decent living for themselves and their families in accordance with the provisions of the present Covenant;

(b) Safe and healthy working conditions;

(c) Equal opportunity for everyone to be promoted in his employment to an appropriate higher level, subject to no considerations other than those of seniority and competence;

(d) Rest, leisure and reasonable limitation of working hours and periodic holidays with pay, as well as remuneration for public holidays

Article 8

1.   The States Parties to the present Covenant undertake to ensure:

(a) The right of everyone to form trade unions and join the trade union of his choice, subject only to the rules of the organization concerned, for the promotion and protection of his economic and social interests. No restrictions may be placed on the exercise of this right other than those prescribed by law and which are necessary in a democratic society in the interests of national security or public order or for the protection of the rights and freedoms of others;

(b) The right of trade unions to establish national federations or confederations and the right of the latter to form or join international trade-union organizations;

(c) The right of trade unions to function freely subject to no limitations other than those prescribed by law and which are necessary in a democratic society in the interests of national security or public order or for the protection of the rights and freedoms of others;

(d) The right to strike, provided that it is exercised in conformity with the laws of the particular country.

2. This article shall not prevent the imposition of lawful restrictions on the exercise of these rights by members of the armed forces or of the police or of the administration of the State.

3. Nothing in this article shall authorize States Parties to the International Labour Organisation Convention of 1948 concerning Freedom of Association and Protection of the Right to Organize to take legislative measures which would prejudice, or apply the law in such a manner as would prejudice, the guarantees provided for in that Convention.

Article 9

The States Parties to the present Covenant recognize the right of everyone to social security, including social insurance.

Article 10

The States Parties to the present Covenant recognize that:

1. The widest possible protection and assistance should be accorded to the family, which is the natural and fundamental group unit of society, particularly for its establishment and while it is responsible for the care and education of dependent children. Marriage must be entered into with the free consent of the intending spouses.

2. Special protection should be accorded to mothers during a reasonable period before and after childbirth. During such period working mothers should be accorded paid leave or leave with adequate social security benefits.

3. Special measures of protection and assistance should be taken on behalf of all children and young persons without any discrimination for reasons of parentage or other conditions. Children and young persons

should be protected from economic and social exploitation. Their employment in work harmful to their morals or health or dangerous to life or likely to hamper their normal development should be punishable by law. States should also set age limits below which the paid employment of child labour should be prohibited and punishable by law.

Article 11

1.   The States Parties to the present Covenant recognize the right of everyone to an adequate standard of living for himself and his family, including adequate food, clothing and housing, and to the continuous improvement of living conditions. The States Parties will take appropriate steps to ensure the realization of this right, recognizing to this effect the essential importance of international co-operation based on free consent.

2.   The States Parties to the present Covenant, recognizing the fundamental right of everyone to be free from hunger, shall take, individually and through international co-operation, the measures, including specific programmes, which are needed:

(a) To improve methods of production, conservation and distribution of food by making full use of technical and scientific knowledge, by disseminating knowledge of the principles of nutrition and by developing or reforming agrarian systems in such a way as to achieve the most efficient development and utilization of natural resources;

(b) Taking into account the problems of both food-importing and food-exporting countries, to ensure an equitable distribution of world food supplies in relation to need.

Article 12

1.   The States Parties to the present Covenant recognize the right of everyone to the enjoyment of the highest attainable standard of physical and mental health.

2.   The steps to be taken by the States Parties to the present Covenant to achieve the full realization of this right shall include those necessary for:

(a) The provision for the reduction of the stillbirth-rate and of infant mortality and for the healthy development of the child;

(b) The improvement of all aspects of environmental and industrial hygiene;

(c) The prevention, treatment and control of epidemic, endemic, occupational and other diseases;

(d) The creation of conditions which would assure to all medical service and medical attention in the event of sickness.

Article 13

1.   The States Parties to the present Covenant recognize the right of everyone to education. They agree that education shall be directed to the full development of the human personality and the sense of its dignity, and shall strengthen the respect for human rights and fundamental freedoms. They further agree that education shall enable all persons to participate effectively in a free society, promote understanding, tolerance and friendship among all nations and all racial, ethnic or religious groups, and further the activities of the United Nations for the maintenance of peace.

2.   The States Parties to the present Covenant recognize that, with a view to achieving the full realization of this right:

(a) Primary education shall be compulsory and available free to all;

(b) Secondary education in its different forms, including technical and vocational secondary education, shall be made generally available and accessible to all by every appropriate means, and in particular by the progressive introduction of free education;

(c) Higher education shall be made equally accessible to all, on the basis of capacity, by every appropriate means, and in particular by the progressive introduction of free education;

(d) Fundamental education shall be encouraged or intensified as far as possible for those persons who have not received or completed the whole period of their primary education;

(e) The development of a system of schools at all levels shall be actively pursued, an adequate fellowship system shall be established, and the material conditions of teaching staff shall be continuously improved.

3.   The States Parties to the present Covenant undertake to have respect for the liberty of parents and, when applicable, legal guardians to choose for their children schools, other than those established by the public authorities, which conform to such minimum educational standards as may be laid down or approved by the State and to ensure the religious and moral education of their children in conformity with their own convictions.

4.   No part of this article shall be construed so as to interfere with the liberty of individuals and bodies to establish and direct educational

institutions, subject always to the observance of the principles set forth in paragraph I of this article and to the requirement that the education given in such institutions shall conform to such minimum standards as may be laid down by the State.

Article 14

Each State Party to the present Covenant which, at the time of becoming a Party, has not been able to secure in its metropolitan territory or other territories under its jurisdiction compulsory primary education, free of charge, undertakes, within two years, to work out and adopt a detailed plan of action for the progressive implementation, within a reasonable number of years, to be fixed in the plan, of the principle of compulsory education free of charge for all.

Article 15

1.   The States Parties to the present Covenant recognize the right of everyone:

(a) To take part in cultural life;

(b) To enjoy the benefits of scientific progress and its applications;

(c) To benefit from the protection of the moral and material interests resulting from any scientific, literary or artistic production of which he is the author.

2.   The steps to be taken by the States Parties to the present Covenant to achieve the full realization of this right shall include those necessary for the conservation, the development and the diffusion of science and culture.

3.   The States Parties to the present Covenant undertake to respect the freedom indispensable for scientific research and creative activity.

4.   The States Parties to the present Covenant recognize the benefits to be derived from the encouragement and development of international contacts and co-operation in the scientific and cultural fields.

PART IV

Article 16

1.   The States Parties to the present Covenant undertake to submit in conformity with this part of the Covenant reports on the measures which they have adopted and the progress made in achieving the observance of the rights recognized herein.

2.   (a) All reports shall be submitted to the Secretary-General of the United Nations, who shall transmit copies to the Economic and Social

Council for consideration in accordance with the provisions of the present Covenant;

(b) The Secretary-General of the United Nations shall also transmit to the specialized agencies copies of the reports, or any relevant parts therefrom, from States Parties to the present Covenant which are also members of these specialized agencies in so far as these reports, or parts therefrom, relate to any matters which fall within the responsibilities of the said agencies in accordance with their constitutional instruments.

Article 17

1.   The States Parties to the present Covenant shall furnish their reports in stages, in accordance with a programme to be established by the Economic and Social Council within one year of the entry into force of the present Covenant after consultation with the States Parties and the specialized agencies concerned.

2.   Reports may indicate factors and difficulties affecting the degree of fulfilment of obligations under the present Covenant.

3.   Where relevant information has previously been furnished to the United Nations or to any specialized agency by any State Party to the present Covenant, it will not be necessary to reproduce that information, but a precise reference to the information so furnished will suffice.

Article 18

Pursuant to its responsibilities under the Charter of the United Nations in the field of human rights and fundamental freedoms, the Economic and Social Council may make arrangements with the specialized agencies in respect of their reporting to it on the progress made in achieving the observance of the provisions of the present Covenant falling within the scope of their activities. These reports may include particulars of decisions and recommendations on such implementation adopted by their competent organs.

Article 19

The Economic and Social Council may transmit to the Commission on Human Rights for study and general recommendation or, as appropriate, for information the reports concerning human rights submitted by States in accordance with articles 16 and 17, and those concerning human rights submitted by the specialized agencies in accordance with article 18.

Article 20

The States Parties to the present Covenant and the specialized agencies concerned may submit comments to the Economic and Social Council on any general recommendation under article 19 or reference to such general recommendation in any report of the Commission on Human Rights or any documentation referred to therein.

Article 21

The Economic and Social Council may submit from time to time to the General Assembly reports with recommendations of a general nature and a summary of the information received from the States Parties to the present Covenant and the specialized agencies on the measures taken and the progress made in achieving general observance of the rights recognized in the present Covenant.

Article 22

The Economic and Social Council may bring to the attention of other organs of the United Nations, their subsidiary organs and specialized agencies concerned with furnishing technical assistance any matters arising out of the reports referred to in this part of the present Covenant which may assist such bodies in deciding, each within its field of competence, on the advisability of international measures likely to contribute to the effective progressive implementation of the present Covenant.

Article 23

The States Parties to the present Covenant agree that international action for the achievement of the rights recognized in the present Covenant includes such methods as the conclusion of conventions, the adoption of recommendations, the furnishing of technical assistance and the holding of regional meetings and technical meetings for the purpose of consultation and study organized in conjunction with the Governments concerned.

Article 24

Nothing in the present Covenant shall be interpreted as impairing the provisions of the Charter of the United Nations and of the constitutions of the specialized agencies which define the respective responsibilities of the various organs of the United Nations and of the specialized agencies in regard to the matters dealt with in the present Covenant.

Article 25

Nothing in the present Covenant shall be interpreted as impairing the inherent right of all peoples to enjoy and utilize fully and freely their natural wealth and resources.

PART V

Article 26

1. The present Covenant is open for signature by any State Member of the United Nations or member of any of its specialized agencies, by any State Party to the Statute of the International Court of Justice, and by any other State which has been invited by the General Assembly of the United Nations to become a party to the present Covenant.

2. The present Covenant is subject to ratification. Instruments of ratification shall be deposited with the Secretary-General of the United Nations.

3. The present Covenant shall be open to accession by any State referred to in paragraph 1 of this article.

4. Accession shall be effected by the deposit of an instrument of accession with the Secretary-General of the United Nations.

5. The Secretary-General of the United Nations shall inform all States which have signed the present Covenant or acceded to it of the deposit of each instrument of ratification or accession.

Article 27

1. The present Covenant shall enter into force three months after the date of the deposit with the Secretary-General of the United Nations of the thirty-fifth instrument of ratification or instrument of accession.

2. For each State ratifying the present Covenant or acceding to it after the deposit of the thirty-fifth instrument of ratification or instrument of accession, the present Covenant shall enter into force three months after the date of the deposit of its own instrument of ratification or instrument of accession.

Article 28

The provisions of the present Covenant shall extend to all parts of federal States without any limitations or exceptions.

Article 29

1. Any State Party to the present Covenant may propose an amendment and file it with the Secretary-General of the United Nations. The Secretary-General shall thereupon communicate any proposed amendments to the States Parties to the present Covenant with a request that they notify him whether they favour a conference of States Parties for the purpose of considering and voting upon the proposals. In the event that at least one third of the States Parties favours such a conference, the Secretary-General shall convene the conference under the auspices of the United Nations. Any amendment adopted by a majority of the States

Parties present and voting at the conference shall be submitted to the General Assembly of the United Nations for approval.

2.   Amendments shall come into force when they have been approved by the General Assembly of the United Nations and accepted by a two-thirds majority of the States Parties to the present Covenant in accordance with their respective constitutional processes.

3.   When amendments come into force they shall be binding on those States Parties which have accepted them, other States Parties still being bound by the provisions of the present Covenant and any earlier amendment which they have accepted.

Article 30

Irrespective of the notifications made under article 26, paragraph 5, the Secretary-General of the United Nations shall inform all States referred to in paragraph I of the same article of the following particulars:

(a) Signatures, ratifications and accessions under article 26;

(b) The date of the entry into force of the present Covenant under article 27 and the date of the entry into force of any amendments under article 29.

Article 31

1.   The present Covenant, of which the Chinese, English, French, Russian and Spanish texts are equally authentic, shall be deposited in the archives of the United Nations.

2.   The Secretary-General of the United Nations shall transmit certified copies of the present Covenant to all States referred to in article 26.

INTERNATIONAL CONVENTION ON THE ELIMINATION OF ALL FORMS OF RACIAL DISCRIMINATION

Adopted and opened for signature and ratification by General
Assembly resolution 2106 (XX) of 21 December 1965
entry into force 4 January 1969, in accordance with Article 19

The States Parties to this Convention,

Considering that the Charter of the United Nations is based on the principles of the dignity and equality inherent in all human beings, and that all Member States have pledged themselves to take joint and separate action, in co-operation with the Organization, for the achievement of one of the purposes of the United Nations which is to promote and encourage universal respect for and observance of human rights and fundamental freedoms for all, without distinction as to race, sex, language or religion,

Considering that the Universal Declaration of Human Rights proclaims that all human beings are born free and equal in dignity and rights and that everyone is entitled to all the rights and freedoms set out therein, without distinction of any kind, in particular as to race, colour or national origin,

Considering that all human beings are equal before the law and are entitled to equal protection of the law against any discrimination and against any incitement to discrimination,

Considering that the United Nations has condemned colonialism and all practices of segregation and discrimination associated therewith, in whatever form and wherever they exist, and that the Declaration on the Granting of Independence to Colonial Countries and Peoples of 14 December 1960 (General Assembly resolution 1514 (XV)) has affirmed and solemnly proclaimed the necessity of bringing them to a speedy and unconditional end,

Considering that the United Nations Declaration on the Elimination of All Forms of Racial Discrimination of 20 November 1963 (General Assembly resolution 1904 (XVIII)) solemnly affirms the necessity of speedily eliminating racial discrimination throughout the world in all its forms and manifestations and of securing understanding of and respect for the dignity of the human person,

Convinced that any doctrine of superiority based on racial differentiation is scientifically false, morally condemnable, socially unjust and dangerous, and that there is no justification for racial discrimination, in theory or in practice, anywhere,

Reaffirming that discrimination between human beings on the grounds of race, colour or ethnic origin is an obstacle to friendly and peaceful relations among nations and is capable of disturbing peace and security among peoples and the harmony of persons living side by side even within one and the same State,

Convinced that the existence of racial barriers is repugnant to the ideals of any human society,

Alarmed by manifestations of racial discrimination still in evidence in some areas of the world and by governmental policies based on racial superiority or hatred, such as policies of apartheid, segregation or separation,

Resolved to adopt all necessary measures for speedily eliminating racial discrimination in all its forms and manifestations, and to prevent and combat racist doctrines and practices in order to promote understanding between races and to build an international community free from all forms of racial segregation and racial discrimination,

Bearing in mind the Convention concerning Discrimination in respect of Employment and Occupation adopted by the International Labour Organisation in 1958, and the Convention against Discrimination in Education adopted by the United Nations Educational, Scientific and Cultural Organization in 1960,

Desiring to implement the principles embodied in the United Nations Declaration on the Elimination of All Forms of Racial Discrimination and to secure the earliest adoption of practical measures to that end,

Have agreed as follows:

PART I

Article 1

1.   In this Convention, the term "racial discrimination" shall mean any distinction, exclusion, restriction or preference based on race, colour, descent, or national or ethnic origin which has the purpose or effect of nullifying or impairing the recognition, enjoyment or exercise, on an equal footing, of human rights and fundamental freedoms in the political, economic, social, cultural or any other field of public life.

2.   This Convention shall not apply to distinctions, exclusions, restrictions or preferences made by a State Party to this Convention between citizens and non-citizens.

3.   Nothing in this Convention may be interpreted as affecting in any way the legal provisions of States Parties concerning nationality, citizenship or naturalization, provided that such provisions do not discriminate against any particular nationality.

4.   Special measures taken for the sole purpose of securing adequate advancement of certain racial or ethnic groups or individuals requiring such protection as may be necessary in order to ensure such groups or individuals equal enjoyment or exercise of human rights and fundamental freedoms shall not be deemed racial discrimination, provided, however, that such measures do not, as a consequence, lead to the maintenance of separate rights for different racial groups and that they shall not be continued after the objectives for which they were taken have been achieved.

Article 2

1.   States Parties condemn racial discrimination and undertake to pursue by all appropriate means and without delay a policy of eliminating racial discrimination in all its forms and promoting understanding among all races, and, to this end:

(a) Each State Party undertakes to engage in no act or practice of racial discrimination against persons, groups of persons or institutions and to en sure that all public authorities and public institutions, national and local, shall act in conformity with this obligation;

(b) Each State Party undertakes not to sponsor, defend or support racial discrimination by any persons or organizations;

(c) Each State Party shall take effective measures to review governmental, national and local policies, and to amend, rescind or nullify any laws and regulations which have the effect of creating or perpetuating racial discrimination wherever it exists;

(d) Each State Party shall prohibit and bring to an end, by all appropriate means, including legislation as required by circumstances, racial discrimination by any persons, group or organization;

(e) Each State Party undertakes to encourage, where appropriate, integrationist multiracial organizations and movements and other means of eliminating barriers between races, and to discourage anything which tends to strengthen racial division.

2.   States Parties shall, when the circumstances so warrant, take, in the social, economic, cultural and other fields, special and concrete measures to ensure the adequate development and protection of certain racial groups or individuals belonging to them, for the purpose of guaranteeing them the full and equal enjoyment of human rights and fundamental freedoms. These measures shall in no case entail as a consequence the maintenance of unequal or separate rights for different racial groups after the objectives for which they were taken have been achieved.

Article 3

States Parties particularly condemn racial segregation and apartheid and undertake to prevent, prohibit and eradicate all practices of this nature in territories under their jurisdiction.

Article 4

States Parties condemn all propaganda and all organizations which are based on ideas or theories of superiority of one race or group of persons of one colour or ethnic origin, or which attempt to justify or promote racial hatred and discrimination in any form, and undertake to adopt immediate and positive measures designed to eradicate all incitement to, or acts of, such discrimination and, to this end, with due regard to the principles embodied in the Universal Declaration of Human

Rights and the rights expressly set forth in article 5 of this Convention, inter alia:

(a) Shall declare an offence punishable by law all dissemination of ideas based on racial superiority or hatred, incitement to racial discrimination, as well as all acts of violence or incitement to such acts against any race or group of persons of another colour or ethnic origin, and also the provision of any assistance to racist activities, including the financing thereof;

(b) Shall declare illegal and prohibit organizations, and also organized and all other propaganda activities, which promote and incite racial discrimination, and shall recognize participation in such organizations or activities as an offence punishable by law;

(c) Shall not permit public authorities or public institutions, national or local, to promote or incite racial discrimination.

Article 5

In compliance with the fundamental obligations laid down in article 2 of this Convention, States Parties undertake to prohibit and to eliminate racial discrimination in all its forms and to guarantee the right of everyone, without distinction as to race, colour, or national or ethnic origin, to equality before the law, notably in the enjoyment of the following rights:

(a) The right to equal treatment before the tribunals and all other organs administering justice;

(b) The right to security of person and protection by the State against violence or bodily harm, whether inflicted by government officials or by any individual group or institution;

(c) Political rights, in particular the right to participate in elections-to vote and to stand for election-on the basis of universal and equal suffrage, to take part in the Government as well as in the conduct of public affairs at any level and to have equal access to public service;

(d) Other civil rights, in particular:

(i) The right to freedom of movement and residence within the border of the State;

(ii) The right to leave any country, including one's own, and to return to one's country;

(iii) The right to nationality;

(iv) The right to marriage and choice of spouse;

(v) The right to own property alone as well as in association with others;

(vi) The right to inherit;

(vii) The right to freedom of thought, conscience and religion;

(viii) The right to freedom of opinion and expression;

(ix) The right to freedom of peaceful assembly and association;

(e) Economic, social and cultural rights, in particular:

(i) The rights to work, to free choice of employment, to just and favourable conditions of work, to protection against unemployment, to equal pay for equal work, to just and favourable remuneration;

(ii) The right to form and join trade unions;

(iii) The right to housing;

(iv) The right to public health, medical care, social security and social services;

(v) The right to education and training;

(vi) The right to equal participation in cultural activities;

(f) The right of access to any place or service intended for use by the general public, such as transport hotels, restaurants, cafes, theatres and parks.

Article 6

States Parties shall assure to everyone within their jurisdiction effective protection and remedies, through the competent national tribunals and other State institutions, against any acts of racial discrimination which violate his human rights and fundamental freedoms contrary to this Convention, as well as the right to seek from such tribunals just and adequate reparation or satisfaction for any damage suffered as a result of such discrimination.

Article 7

States Parties undertake to adopt immediate and effective measures, particularly in the fields of teaching, education, culture and information, with a view to combating prejudices which lead to racial discrimination and to promoting understanding, tolerance and friendship among nations and racial or ethnical groups, as well as to propagating the purposes and principles of the Charter of the United Nations, the Universal Declaration of Human Rights, the United Nations Declaration on the Elimination of All Forms of Racial Discrimination, and this Convention.

PART II

Article 8

1.   There shall be established a Committee on the Elimination of Racial Discrimination (hereinafter referred to as the Committee) consisting of eighteen experts of high moral standing and acknowledged impartiality elected by States Parties from among their nationals, who shall serve in their personal capacity, consideration being given to equitable geographical distribution and to the representation of the different forms of civilization as well as of the principal legal systems.

2.   The members of the Committee shall be elected by secret ballot from a list of persons nominated by the States Parties. Each State Party may nominate one person from among its own nationals.

3.   The initial election shall be held six months after the date of the entry into force of this Convention. At least three months before the date of each election the Secretary-General of the United Nations shall address a letter to the States Parties inviting them to submit their nominations within two months. The Secretary-General shall prepare a list in alphabetical order of all persons thus nominated, indicating the States Parties which have nominated them, and shall submit it to the States Parties.

4.   Elections of the members of the Committee shall be held at a meeting of States Parties convened by the Secretary-General at United Nations Headquarters. At that meeting, for which two thirds of the States Parties shall constitute a quorum, the persons elected to the Committee shall be nominees who obtain the largest number of votes and an absolute majority of the votes of the representatives of States Parties present and voting.

5.   (a) The members of the Committee shall be elected for a term of four years. However, the terms of nine of the members elected at the first election shall expire at the end of two years; immediately after the first election the names of these nine members shall be chosen by lot by the Chairman of the Committee;

(b) For the filling of casual vacancies, the State Party whose expert has ceased to function as a member of the Committee shall appoint another expert from among its nationals, subject to the approval of the Committee.

6.   States Parties shall be responsible for the expenses of the members of the Committee while they are in performance of Committee duties.

Article 9

1.   States Parties undertake to submit to the Secretary-General of the United Nations, for consideration by the Committee, a report on the legislative, judicial, administrative or other measures which they have adopted and which give effect to the provisions of this Convention:

(a) within one year after the entry into force of the Convention for the State concerned; and

(b) thereafter every two years and whenever the Committee so requests. The Committee may request further information from the States Parties.

2.   The Committee shall report annually, through the Secretary General, to the General Assembly of the United Nations on its activities and may make suggestions and general recommendations based on the examination of the reports and information received from the States Parties. Such suggestions and general recommendations shall be reported to the General Assembly together with comments, if any, from States Parties.

Article 10

1.   The Committee shall adopt its own rules of procedure.

2.   The Committee shall elect its officers for a term of two years.

3.   The secretariat of the Committee shall be provided by the Secretary General of the United Nations.

4.   The meetings of the Committee shall normally be held at United Nations Headquarters.

Article 11

1.   If a State Party considers that another State Party is not giving effect to the provisions of this Convention, it may bring the matter to the attention of the Committee. The Committee shall then transmit the communication to the State Party concerned. Within three months, the receiving State shall submit to the Committee written explanations or statements clarifying the matter and the remedy, if any, that may have been taken by that State.

2.   If the matter is not adjusted to the satisfaction of both parties, either by bilateral negotiations or by any other procedure open to them, within six months after the receipt by the receiving State of the initial communication, either State shall have the right to refer the matter again to the Committee by notifying the Committee and also the other State.

3.   The Committee shall deal with a matter referred to it in accordance with paragraph 2 of this article after it has ascertained that all available domestic remedies have been invoked and exhausted in the

case, in conformity with the generally recognized principles of international law. This shall not be the rule where the application of the remedies is unreasonably prolonged.

4. In any matter referred to it, the Committee may call upon the States Parties concerned to supply any other relevant information.

5. When any matter arising out of this article is being considered by the Committee, the States Parties concerned shall be entitled to send a representative to take part in the proceedings of the Committee, without voting rights, while the matter is under consideration.

Article 12

1. (a) After the Committee has obtained and collated all the information it deems necessary, the Chairman shall appoint an ad hoc Conciliation Commission (hereinafter referred to as the Commission) comprising five persons who may or may not be members of the Committee. The members of the Commission shall be appointed with the unanimous consent of the parties to the dispute, and its good offices shall be made available to the States concerned with a view to an amicable solution of the matter on the basis of respect for this Convention;

(b) If the States parties to the dispute fail to reach agreement within three months on all or part of the composition of the Commission, the members of the Commission not agreed upon by the States parties to the dispute shall be elected by secret ballot by a two-thirds majority vote of the Committee from among its own members.

2. The members of the Commission shall serve in their personal capacity. They shall not be nationals of the States parties to the dispute or of a State not Party to this Convention.

3. The Commission shall elect its own Chairman and adopt its own rules of procedure.

4. The meetings of the Commission shall normally be held at United Nations Headquarters or at any other convenient place as determined by the Commission.

5. The secretariat provided in accordance with article 10, paragraph 3, of this Convention shall also service the Commission whenever a dispute among States Parties brings the Commission into being.

6. The States parties to the dispute shall share equally all the expenses of the members of the Commission in accordance with estimates to be provided by the Secretary-General of the United Nations.

7. The Secretary-General shall be empowered to pay the expenses of the members of the Commission, if necessary, before reimbursement by

the States parties to the dispute in accordance with paragraph 6 of this article.

8.   The information obtained and collated by the Committee shall be made available to the Commission, and the Commission may call upon the States concerned to supply any other relevant information.

Article 13

1.   When the Commission has fully considered the matter, it shall prepare and submit to the Chairman of the Committee a report embodying its findings on all questions of fact relevant to the issue between the parties and containing such recommendations as it may think proper for the amicable solution of the dispute.

2.   The Chairman of the Committee shall communicate the report of the Commission to each of the States parties to the dispute. These States shall, within three months, inform the Chairman of the Committee whether or not they accept the recommendations contained in the report of the Commission.

3.   After the period provided for in paragraph 2 of this article, the Chairman of the Committee shall communicate the report of the Commission and the declarations of the States Parties concerned to the other States Parties to this Convention.

Article 14

1.   A State Party may at any time declare that it recognizes the competence of the Committee to receive and consider communications from individuals or groups of individuals within its jurisdiction claiming to be victims of a violation by that State Party of any of the rights set forth in this Convention. No communication shall be received by the Committee if it concerns a State Party which has not made such a declaration.

2.   Any State Party which makes a declaration as provided for in paragraph I of this article may establish or indicate a body within its national legal order which shall be competent to receive and consider petitions from individuals and groups of individuals within its jurisdiction who claim to be victims of a violation of any of the rights set forth in this Convention and who have exhausted other available local remedies.

3.   A declaration made in accordance with paragraph 1 of this article and the name of any body established or indicated in accordance with paragraph 2 of this article shall be deposited by the State Party concerned with the Secretary-General of the United Nations, who shall transmit copies thereof to the other States Parties. A declaration may be withdrawn at any time by notification to the Secretary General, but such

a withdrawal shall not affect communications pending before the Committee.

4. A register of petitions shall be kept by the body established or indicated in accordance with paragraph 2 of this article, and certified copies of the register shall be filed annually through appropriate channels with the Secretary-General on the understanding that the contents shall not be publicly disclosed.

5. In the event of failure to obtain satisfaction from the body established or indicated in accordance with paragraph 2 of this article, the petitioner shall have the right to communicate the matter to the Committee within six months.

6. (a) The Committee shall confidentially bring any communication referred to it to the attention of the State Party alleged to be violating any provision of this Convention, but the identity of the individual or groups of individuals concerned shall not be revealed without his or their express consent. The Committee shall not receive anonymous communications;

(b) Within three months, the receiving State shall submit to the Committee written explanations or statements clarifying the matter and the remedy, if any, that may have been taken by that State.

7. (a) The Committee shall consider communications in the light of all information made available to it by the State Party concerned and by the petitioner. The Committee shall not consider any communication from a petitioner unless it has ascertained that the petitioner has exhausted all available domestic remedies. However, this shall not be the rule where the application of the remedies is unreasonably prolonged;

(b) The Committee shall forward its suggestions and recommendations, if any, to the State Party concerned and to the petitioner.

8. The Committee shall include in its annual report a summary of such communications and, where appropriate, a summary of the explanations and statements of the States Parties concerned and of its own suggestions and recommendations.

9. The Committee shall be competent to exercise the functions provided for in this article only when at least ten States Parties to this Convention are bound by declarations in accordance with paragraph I of this article.

Article 15

1. Pending the achievement of the objectives of the Declaration on the Granting of Independence to Colonial Countries and Peoples, contained in General Assembly resolution 1514 (XV) of 14 December

1960, the provisions of this Convention shall in no way limit the right of petition granted to these peoples by other international instruments or by the United Nations and its specialized agencies.

2. (a) The Committee established under article 8, paragraph 1, of this Convention shall receive copies of the petitions from, and submit expressions of opinion and recommendations on these petitions to, the bodies of the United Nations which deal with matters directly related to the principles and objectives of this Convention in their consideration of petitions from the inhabitants of Trust and Non-Self-Governing Territories and all other territories to which General Assembly resolution 1514 (XV) applies, relating to matters covered by this Convention which are before these bodies;

(b) The Committee shall receive from the competent bodies of the United Nations copies of the reports concerning the legislative, judicial, administrative or other measures directly related to the principles and objectives of this Convention applied by the administering Powers within the Territories mentioned in subparagraph (a) of this paragraph, and shall express opinions and make recommendations to these bodies.

3. The Committee shall include in its report to the General Assembly a summary of the petitions and reports it has received from United Nations bodies, and the expressions of opinion and recommendations of the Committee relating to the said petitions and reports.

4. The Committee shall request from the Secretary-General of the United Nations all information relevant to the objectives of this Convention and available to him regarding the Territories mentioned in paragraph 2 (a) of this article.

Article 16

The provisions of this Convention concerning the settlement of disputes or complaints shall be applied without prejudice to other procedures for settling disputes or complaints in the field of discrimination laid down in the constituent instruments of, or conventions adopted by, the United Nations and its specialized agencies, and shall not prevent the States Parties from having recourse to other procedures for settling a dispute in accordance with general or special international agreements in force between them.

PART III

Article 17

1. This Convention is open for signature by any State Member of the United Nations or member of any of its specialized agencies, by any

State Party to the Statute of the International Court of Justice, and by any other State which has been invited by the General Assembly of the United Nations to become a Party to this Convention.

2.   This Convention is subject to ratification. Instruments of ratification shall be deposited with the Secretary-General of the United Nations.

Article 18

1.   This Convention shall be open to accession by any State referred to in article 17, paragraph 1, of the Convention. 2. Accession shall be effected by the deposit of an instrument of accession with the Secretary-General of the United Nations.

Article 19

1.   This Convention shall enter into force on the thirtieth day after the date of the deposit with the Secretary-General of the United Nations of the twenty-seventh instrument of ratification or instrument of accession.

2.   For each State ratifying this Convention or acceding to it after the deposit of the twenty-seventh instrument of ratification or instrument of accession, the Convention shall enter into force on the thirtieth day after the date of the deposit of its own instrument of ratification or instrument of accession.

Article 20

1.   The Secretary-General of the United Nations shall receive and circulate to all States which are or may become Parties to this Convention reservations made by States at the time of ratification or accession. Any State which objects to the reservation shall, within a period of ninety days from the date of the said communication, notify the Secretary-General that it does not accept it.

2.   A reservation incompatible with the object and purpose of this Convention shall not be permitted, nor shall a reservation the effect of which would inhibit the operation of any of the bodies established by this Convention be allowed. A reservation shall be considered incompatible or inhibitive if at least two thirds of the States Parties to this Convention object to it.

3.   Reservations may be withdrawn at any time by notification to this effect addressed to the Secretary-General. Such notification shall take effect on the date on which it is received.

Article 21

A State Party may denounce this Convention by written notification to the Secretary-General of the United Nations. Denunciation shall take effect one year after the date of receipt of the notification by the Secretary General.

Article 22

Any dispute between two or more States Parties with respect to the interpretation or application of this Convention, which is not settled by negotiation or by the procedures expressly provided for in this Convention, shall, at the request of any of the parties to the dispute, be referred to the International Court of Justice for decision, unless the disputants agree to another mode of settlement.

Article 23

1. A request for the revision of this Convention may be made at any time by any State Party by means of a notification in writing addressed to the Secretary-General of the United Nations.

2. The General Assembly of the United Nations shall decide upon the steps, if any, to be taken in respect of such a request.

Article 24

The Secretary-General of the United Nations shall inform all States referred to in article 17, paragraph 1, of this Convention of the following particulars:

(a) Signatures, ratifications and accessions under articles 17 and 18;

(b) The date of entry into force of this Convention under article 19;

(c) Communications and declarations received under articles 14, 20 and 23;

(d) Denunciations under article 21.

Article 25

1. This Convention, of which the Chinese, English, French, Russian and Spanish texts are equally authentic, shall be deposited in the archives of the United Nations.

2. The Secretary-General of the United Nations shall transmit certified copies of this Convention to all States belonging to any of the categories mentioned in article 17, paragraph 1, of the Convention.

CONVENTION ON THE ELIMINATION OF ALL FORMS OF DISCRIMINATION AGAINST WOMEN

Adopted and opened for signature, ratification and accession by
United Nations General Assembly Resolution 34/180 of 18
December 1979
entry into force on 3 September 1982,
in accordance with Article 27(1)

The States Parties to the present Convention,

Noting that the Charter of the United Nations reaffirms faith in fundamental human rights, in the dignity and worth of the human person and in the equal rights of men and women,

Noting that the Universal Declaration of Human Rights affirms the principle of the inadmissibility of discrimination and proclaims that all human beings are born free and equal in dignity and rights and that everyone is entitled to all the rights and freedoms set forth therein, without distinction of any kind, including distinction based on sex,

Noting that the States Parties to the International Covenants on Human Rights have the obligation to ensure the equal rights of men and women to enjoy all economic, social, cultural, civil and political rights,

Considering the international conventions concluded under the auspices of the United Nations and the specialized agencies promoting equality of rights of men and women,

Noting also the resolutions, declarations and recommendations adopted by the United Nations and the specialized agencies promoting equality of rights of men and women,

Concerned, however, that despite these various instruments extensive discrimination against women continues to exist,

Recalling that discrimination against women violates the principles of equality of rights and respect for human dignity, is an obstacle to the participation of women, on equal terms with men, in the political, social, economic and cultural life of their countries, hampers the growth of the prosperity of society and the family and makes more difficult the full development of the potentialities of women in the service of their countries and of humanity,

Concerned that in situations of poverty women have the least access to food, health, education, training and opportunities for employment and other needs,

Convinced that the establishment of the new international economic order based on equity and justice will contribute significantly towards the promotion of equality between men and women,

Emphasizing that the eradication of apartheid, all forms of racism, racial discrimination, colonialism, neo-colonialism, aggression, foreign occupation and domination and interference in the internal affairs of States is essential to the full enjoyment of the rights of men and women,

Affirming that the strengthening of international peace and security, the relaxation of international tension, mutual co-operation among all States irrespective of their social and economic systems, general and complete disarmament, in particular nuclear disarmament under strict and effective international control, the affirmation of the principles of justice, equality and mutual benefit in relations among countries and the realization of the right of peoples under alien and colonial domination and foreign occupation to self-determination and independence, as well as respect for national sovereignty and territorial integrity, will promote social progress and development and as a consequence will contribute to the attainment of full equality between men and women,

Convinced that the full and complete development of a country, the welfare of the world and the cause of peace require the maximum participation of women on equal terms with men in all fields,

Bearing in mind the great contribution of women to the welfare of the family and to the development of society, so far not fully recognized, the social significance of maternity and the role of both parents in the family and in the upbringing of children, and aware that the role of women in procreation should not be a basis for discrimination but that the upbringing of children requires a sharing of responsibility between men and women and society as a whole,

Aware that a change in the traditional role of men as well as the role of women in society and in the family is needed to achieve full equality between men and women,

Determined to implement the principles set forth in the Declaration on the Elimination of Discrimination against Women and, for that purpose, to adopt the measures required for the elimination of such discrimination in all its forms and manifestations,

Have agreed on the following:

PART I

Article I

For the purposes of the present Convention, the term "discrimination against women" shall mean any distinction, exclusion or restriction made on the basis of sex which has the effect or purpose of impairing or nullifying the recognition, enjoyment or exercise by women, irrespective of their marital status, on a basis of equality of men and women, of human rights and fundamental freedoms in the political, economic, social, cultural, civil or any other field.

Article 2

States Parties condemn discrimination against women in all its forms, agree to pursue by all appropriate means and without delay a policy of eliminating discrimination against women and, to this end, undertake:

(a) To embody the principle of the equality of men and women in their national constitutions or other appropriate legislation if not yet incorporated therein and to ensure, through law and other appropriate means, the practical realization of this principle;

(b) To adopt appropriate legislative and other measures, including sanctions where appropriate, prohibiting all discrimination against women;

(c) To establish legal protection of the rights of women on an equal basis with men and to ensure through competent national tribunals and other public institutions the effective protection of women against any act of discrimination;

(d) To refrain from engaging in any act or practice of discrimination against women and to ensure that public authorities and institutions shall act in conformity with this obligation;

(e) To take all appropriate measures to eliminate discrimination against women by any person, organization or enterprise;

(f) To take all appropriate measures, including legislation, to modify or abolish existing laws, regulations, customs and practices which constitute discrimination against women;

(g) To repeal all national penal provisions which constitute discrimination against women.

Article 3

States Parties shall take in all fields, in particular in the political, social, economic and cultural fields, all appropriate measures, including legislation, to en sure the full development and advancement of women, for the purpose of guaranteeing them the exercise and enjoyment of human rights and fundamental freedoms on a basis of equality with men.

Article 4

1.   Adoption by States Parties of temporary special measures aimed at accelerating de facto equality between men and women shall not be

considered discrimination as defined in the present Convention, but shall in no way entail as a consequence the maintenance of unequal or separate standards; these measures shall be discontinued when the objectives of equality of opportunity and treatment have been achieved.

2. Adoption by States Parties of special measures, including those measures contained in the present Convention, aimed at protecting maternity shall not be considered discriminatory.

Article 5

States Parties shall take all appropriate measures:

(a) To modify the social and cultural patterns of conduct of men and women, with a view to achieving the elimination of prejudices and customary and all other practices which are based on the idea of the inferiority or the superiority of either of the sexes or on stereotyped roles for men and women;

(b) To ensure that family education includes a proper understanding of maternity as a social function and the recognition of the common responsibility of men and women in the upbringing and development of their children, it being understood that the interest of the children is the primordial consideration in all cases.

Article 6

States Parties shall take all appropriate measures, including legislation, to suppress all forms of traffic in women and exploitation of prostitution of women.

PART II

Article 7

States Parties shall take all appropriate measures to eliminate discrimination against women in the political and public life of the country and, in particular, shall ensure to women, on equal terms with men, the right:

(a) To vote in all elections and public referenda and to be eligible for election to all publicly elected bodies;

(b) To participate in the formulation of government policy and the implementation thereof and to hold public office and perform all public functions at all levels of government;

(c) To participate in non-governmental organizations and associations concerned with the public and political life of the country.

Article 8

States Parties shall take all appropriate measures to ensure to women, on equal terms with men and without any discrimination, the opportunity to represent their Governments at the international level and to participate in the work of international organizations.

Article 9

1.   States Parties shall grant women equal rights with men to acquire, change or retain their nationality. They shall ensure in particular that neither marriage to an alien nor change of nationality by the husband during marriage shall automatically change the nationality of the wife, render her stateless or force upon her the nationality of the husband.

2.   States Parties shall grant women equal rights with men with respect to the nationality of their children.

PART III

Article 10

States Parties shall take all appropriate measures to eliminate discrimination against women in order to ensure to them equal rights with men in the field of education and in particular to ensure, on a basis of equality of men and women:

(a) The same conditions for career and vocational guidance, for access to studies and for the achievement of diplomas in educational establishments of all categories in rural as well as in urban areas; this equality shall be ensured in pre-school, general, technical, professional and higher technical education, as well as in all types of vocational training;

(b) Access to the same curricula, the same examinations, teaching staff with qualifications of the same standard and school premises and equipment of the same quality;

(c) The elimination of any stereotyped concept of the roles of men and women at all levels and in all forms of education by encouraging coeducation and other types of education which will help to achieve this aim and, in particular, by the revision of textbooks and school programmes and the adaptation of teaching methods;

(d) The same opportunities to benefit from scholarships and other study grants;

(e) The same opportunities for access to programmes of continuing education, including adult and functional literacy programmes, particularly those aimed at reducing, at the earliest possible time, any gap in education existing between men and women;

(f) The reduction of female student drop-out rates and the organization of programmes for girls and women who have left school prematurely;

(g) The same opportunities to participate actively in sports and physical education;

(h) Access to specific educational information to help to ensure the health and well-being of families, including information and advice on family planning.

Article 11

1. States Parties shall take all appropriate measures to eliminate discrimination against women in the field of employment in order to ensure, on a basis of equality of men and women, the same rights, in particular:

(a) The right to work as an inalienable right of all human beings;

(b) The right to the same employment opportunities, including the application of the same criteria for selection in matters of employment;

(c) The right to free choice of profession and employment, the right to promotion, job security and all benefits and conditions of service and the right to receive vocational training and retraining, including apprenticeships, advanced vocational training and recurrent training;

(d) The right to equal remuneration, including benefits, and to equal treatment in respect of work of equal value, as well as equality of treatment in the evaluation of the quality of work;

(e) The right to social security, particularly in cases of retirement, unemployment, sickness, invalidity and old age and other incapacity to work, as well as the right to paid leave;

(f) The right to protection of health and to safety in working conditions, including the safeguarding of the function of reproduction.

2. In order to prevent discrimination against women on the grounds of marriage or maternity and to ensure their effective right to work, States Parties shall take appropriate measures:

(a) To prohibit, subject to the imposition of sanctions, dismissal on the grounds of pregnancy or of maternity leave and discrimination in dismissals on the basis of marital status;

(b) To introduce maternity leave with pay or with comparable social benefits without loss of former employment, seniority or social allowances;

(c) To encourage the provision of the necessary supporting social services to enable parents to combine family obligations with work responsibilities and participation in public life, in particular through promoting the establishment and development of a network of child-care facilities;

(d) To provide special protection to women during pregnancy in types of work proved to be harmful to them.

3. Protective legislation relating to matters covered in this article shall be reviewed periodically in the light of scientific and technological knowledge and shall be revised, repealed or extended as necessary.

Article 12

1. States Parties shall take all appropriate measures to eliminate discrimination against women in the field of health care in order to ensure, on a basis of equality of men and women, access to health care services, including those related to family planning.

2. Notwithstanding the provisions of paragraph I of this article, States Parties shall ensure to women appropriate services in connection with pregnancy, confinement and the post-natal period, granting free services where necessary, as well as adequate nutrition during pregnancy and lactation.

Article 13 States Parties shall take all appropriate measures to eliminate discrimination against women in other areas of economic and social life in order to ensure, on a basis of equality of men and women, the same rights, in particular:

(a) The right to family benefits;

(b) The right to bank loans, mortgages and other forms of financial credit;

(c) The right to participate in recreational activities, sports and all aspects of cultural life.

Article 14

1. States Parties shall take into account the particular problems faced by rural women and the significant roles which rural women play in the economic survival of their families, including their work in the non-monetized sectors of the economy, and shall take all appropriate measures to ensure the application of the provisions of the present Convention to women in rural areas.

2. States Parties shall take all appropriate measures to eliminate discrimination against women in rural areas in order to ensure, on a basis of equality of men and women, that they participate in and benefit from rural development and, in particular, shall ensure to such women the right:

(a) To participate in the elaboration and implementation of development planning at all levels;

(b) To have access to adequate health care facilities, including information, counselling and services in family planning;

(c) To benefit directly from social security programmes;

(d) To obtain all types of training and education, formal and non-formal, including that relating to functional literacy, as well as, inter alia, the benefit of all community and extension services, in order to increase their technical proficiency;

(e) To organize self-help groups and co-operatives in order to obtain equal access to economic opportunities through employment or self employment;

(f) To participate in all community activities;

(g) To have access to agricultural credit and loans, marketing facilities, appropriate technology and equal treatment in land and agrarian reform as well as in land resettlement schemes;

(h) To enjoy adequate living conditions, particularly in relation to housing, sanitation, electricity and water supply, transport and communications.

PART IV

Article 15

1. States Parties shall accord to women equality with men before the law.

2. States Parties shall accord to women, in civil matters, a legal capacity identical to that of men and the same opportunities to exercise that capacity. In particular, they shall give women equal rights to conclude contracts and to administer property and shall treat them equally in all stages of procedure in courts and tribunals.

3. States Parties agree that all contracts and all other private instruments of any kind with a legal effect which is directed at restricting the legal capacity of women shall be deemed null and void.

4. States Parties shall accord to men and women the same rights with regard to the law relating to the movement of persons and the freedom to choose their residence and domicile.

Article 16

1. States Parties shall take all appropriate measures to eliminate discrimination against women in all matters relating to marriage and family relations and in particular shall ensure, on a basis of equality of men and women:

(a) The same right to enter into marriage;

(b) The same right freely to choose a spouse and to enter into marriage only with their free and full consent;

(c) The same rights and responsibilities during marriage and at its dissolution;

(d) The same rights and responsibilities as parents, irrespective of their marital status, in matters relating to their children; in all cases the interests of the children shall be paramount;

(e) The same rights to decide freely and responsibly on the number and spacing of their children and to have access to the information, education and means to enable them to exercise these rights;

(f) The same rights and responsibilities with regard to guardianship, wardship, trusteeship and adoption of children, or similar institutions where these concepts exist in national legislation; in all cases the interests of the children shall be paramount;

(g) The same personal rights as husband and wife, including the right to choose a family name, a profession and an occupation;

(h) The same rights for both spouses in respect of the ownership, acquisition, management, administration, enjoyment and disposition of property, whether free of charge or for a valuable consideration.

2. The betrothal and the marriage of a child shall have no legal effect, and all necessary action, including legislation, shall be taken to specify a minimum age for marriage and to make the registration of marriages in an official registry compulsory.

PART V

Article 17

1. For the purpose of considering the progress made in the implementation of the present Convention, there shall be established a Committee on the Elimination of Discrimination against Women (hereinafter referred to as the Committee) consisting, at the time of entry into force of the Convention, of eighteen and, after ratification of or accession to the Convention by the thirty-fifth State Party, of twenty-three experts of high moral standing and competence in the field covered by the Convention. The experts shall be elected by States Parties from among their nationals and shall serve in their personal capacity, consideration being given to equitable geographical distribution and to the representation of the different forms of civilization as well as the principal legal systems.

2. The members of the Committee shall be elected by secret ballot from a list of persons nominated by States Parties. Each State Party may nominate one person from among its own nationals.

3. The initial election shall be held six months after the date of the entry into force of the present Convention. At least three months before the date of each election the Secretary-General of the United Nations shall address a letter to the States Parties inviting them to submit their nominations within two months. The Secretary-General shall prepare a list in alphabetical order of all persons thus nominated, indicating the States Parties which have nominated them, and shall submit it to the States Parties.

4. Elections of the members of the Committee shall be held at a meeting of States Parties convened by the Secretary-General at United Nations Headquarters. At that meeting, for which two thirds of the States Parties shall constitute a quorum, the persons elected to the Committee shall be those nominees who obtain the largest number of votes and an absolute majority of the votes of the representatives of States Parties present and voting.

5. The members of the Committee shall be elected for a term of four years. However, the terms of nine of the members elected at the first election shall expire at the end of two years; immediately after the first election the names of these nine members shall be chosen by lot by the Chairman of the Committee.

6. The election of the five additional members of the Committee shall be held in accordance with the provisions of paragraphs 2, 3 and 4 of this article, following the thirty-fifth ratification or accession. The terms of two of the additional members elected on this occasion shall expire at

the end of two years, the names of these two members having been chosen by lot by the Chairman of the Committee.

7.   For the filling of casual vacancies, the State Party whose expert has ceased to function as a member of the Committee shall appoint another expert from among its nationals, subject to the approval of the Committee.

8.   The members of the Committee shall, with the approval of the General Assembly, receive emoluments from United Nations resources on such terms and conditions as the Assembly may decide, having regard to the importance of the Committee's responsibilities.

9.   The Secretary-General of the United Nations shall provide the necessary staff and facilities for the effective performance of the functions of the Committee under the present Convention.

Article 18

1.   States Parties undertake to submit to the Secretary-General of the United Nations, for consideration by the Committee, a report on the legislative, judicial, administrative or other measures which they have adopted to give effect to the provisions of the present Convention and on the progress made in this respect:

(a) Within one year after the entry into force for the State concerned;

(b) Thereafter at least every four years and further whenever the Committee so requests.

2.   Reports may indicate factors and difficulties affecting the degree of fulfilment of obligations under the present Convention.

Article 19

1.   The Committee shall adopt its own rules of procedure.

2.   The Committee shall elect its officers for a term of two years.

Article 20

1.   The Committee shall normally meet for a period of not more than two weeks annually in order to consider the reports submitted in accordance with article 18 of the present Convention.

2.   The meetings of the Committee shall normally be held at United Nations Headquarters or at any other convenient place as determined by the Committee.

Article 21

1.   The Committee shall, through the Economic and Social Council, report annually to the General Assembly of the United Nations on its activities and may make suggestions and general recommendations based

on the examination of reports and information received from the States Parties. Such suggestions and general recommendations shall be included in the report of the Committee together with comments, if any, from States Parties.

2.   The Secretary-General of the United Nations shall transmit the reports of the Committee to the Commission on the Status of Women for its information.

Article 22

The specialized agencies shall be entitled to be represented at the consideration of the implementation of such provisions of the present Convention as fall within the scope of their activities. The Committee may invite the specialized agencies to submit reports on the implementation of the Convention in areas falling within the scope of their activities.

PART VI

Article 23

Nothing in the present Convention shall affect any provisions that are more conducive to the achievement of equality between men and women which may be contained:

(a) In the legislation of a State Party; or

(b) In any other international convention, treaty or agreement in force for that State.

Article 24

States Parties undertake to adopt all necessary measures at the national level aimed at achieving the full realization of the rights recognized in the present Convention.

Article 25

1.   The present Convention shall be open for signature by all States.

2.   The Secretary-General of the United Nations is designated as the depositary of the present Convention.

3.   The present Convention is subject to ratification. Instruments of ratification shall be deposited with the Secretary-General of the United Nations.

4.   The present Convention shall be open to accession by all States. Accession shall be effected by the deposit of an instrument of accession with the Secretary-General of the United Nations.

Article 26

1. A request for the revision of the present Convention may be made at any time by any State Party by means of a notification in writing addressed to the Secretary-General of the United Nations.

2. The General Assembly of the United Nations shall decide upon the steps, if any, to be taken in respect of such a request.

Article 27

1. The present Convention shall enter into force on the thirtieth day after the date of deposit with the Secretary-General of the United Nations of the twentieth instrument of ratification or accession.

2. For each State ratifying the present Convention or acceding to it after the deposit of the twentieth instrument of ratification or accession, the Convention shall enter into force on the thirtieth day after the date of the deposit of its own instrument of ratification or accession.

Article 28

1. The Secretary-General of the United Nations shall receive and circulate to all States the text of reservations made by States at the time of ratification or accession.

2. A reservation incompatible with the object and purpose of the present Convention shall not be permitted.

3. Reservations may be withdrawn at any time by notification to this effect addressed to the Secretary-General of the United Nations, who shall then inform all States thereof. Such notification shall take effect on the date on which it is received.

Article 29

1. Any dispute between two or more States Parties concerning the interpretation or application of the present Convention which is not settled by negotiation shall, at the request of one of them, be submitted to arbitration. If within six months from the date of the request for arbitration the parties are unable to agree on the organization of the arbitration, any one of those parties may refer the dispute to the International Court of Justice by request in conformity with the Statute of the Court.

2. Each State Party may at the time of signature or ratification of the present Convention or accession thereto declare that it does not consider itself bound by paragraph I of this article. The other States Parties shall not be bound by that paragraph with respect to any State Party which has made such a reservation.

3. Any State Party which has made a reservation in accordance with paragraph 2 of this article may at any time withdraw that

reservation by notification to the Secretary-General of the United Nations.

Article 30

The present Convention, the Arabic, Chinese, English, French, Russian and Spanish texts of which are equally authentic, shall be deposited with the Secretary-General of the United Nations.

CONVENTION AGAINST TORTURE AND OTHER CRUEL, INHUMAN OR DEGRADING TREATMENT OR PUNISHMENT

Adopted and opened for signature, ratification and accession by
General Assembly resolution 39/46 of 10 December 1984
entry into force 26 June 1987, in accordance with article 27 (1)

The States Parties to this Convention,

Considering that, in accordance with the principles proclaimed in the Charter of the United Nations, recognition of the equal and inalienable rights of all members of the human family is the foundation of freedom, justice and peace in the world,

Recognizing that those rights derive from the inherent dignity of the human person,

Considering the obligation of States under the Charter, in particular Article 55, to promote universal respect for, and observance of, human rights and fundamental freedoms,

Having regard to article 5 of the Universal Declaration of Human Rights and article 7 of the International Covenant on Civil and Political Rights, both of which provide that no one shall be subjected to torture or to cruel, inhuman or degrading treatment or punishment,

Having regard also to the Declaration on the Protection of All Persons from Being Subjected to Torture and Other Cruel, Inhuman or Degrading Treatment or Punishment, adopted by the General Assembly on 9 December 1975,

Desiring to make more effective the struggle against torture and other cruel, inhuman or degrading treatment or punishment throughout the world,

Have agreed as follows:

PART I

Article 1

1. For the purposes of this Convention, the term "torture" means any act by which severe pain or suffering, whether physical or mental, is

intentionally inflicted on a person for such purposes as obtaining from him or a third person information or a confession, punishing him for an act he or a third person has committed or is suspected of having committed, or intimidating or coercing him or a third person, or for any reason based on discrimination of any kind, when such pain or suffering is inflicted by or at the instigation of or with the consent or acquiescence of a public official or other person acting in an official capacity. It does not include pain or suffering arising only from, inherent in or incidental to lawful sanctions.

2.   This article is without prejudice to any international instrument or national legislation which does or may contain provisions of wider application.

Article 2

1.   Each State Party shall take effective legislative, administrative, judicial or other measures to prevent acts of torture in any territory under its jurisdiction.

2.   No exceptional circumstances whatsoever, whether a state of war or a threat of war, internal political instability or any other public emergency, may be invoked as a justification of torture.

3.   An order from a superior officer or a public authority may not be invoked as a justification of torture.

Article 3

1.   No State Party shall expel, return ("refouler") or extradite a person to another State where there are substantial grounds for believing that he would be in danger of being subjected to torture.

2.   For the purpose of determining whether there are such grounds, the competent authorities shall take into account all relevant considerations including, where applicable, the existence in the State concerned of a consistent pattern of gross, flagrant or mass violations of human rights.

Article 4

1.   Each State Party shall ensure that all acts of torture are offences under its criminal law. The same shall apply to an attempt to commit torture and to an act by any person which constitutes complicity or participation in torture.

2.   Each State Party shall make these offences punishable by appropriate penalties which take into account their grave nature.

Article 5

1. Each State Party shall take such measures as may be necessary to establish its jurisdiction over the offences referred to in article 4 in the following cases:

(a) When the offences are committed in any territory under its jurisdiction or on board a ship or aircraft registered in that State;

(b) When the alleged offender is a national of that State;

(c) When the victim is a national of that State if that State considers it appropriate.

2. Each State Party shall likewise take such measures as may be necessary to establish its jurisdiction over such offences in cases where the alleged offender is present in any territory under its jurisdiction and it does not extradite him pursuant to article 8 to any of the States mentioned in paragraph I of this article.

3. This Convention does not exclude any criminal jurisdiction exercised in accordance with internal law.

Article 6

1. Upon being satisfied, after an examination of information available to it, that the circumstances so warrant, any State Party in whose territory a person alleged to have committed any offence referred to in article 4 is present shall take him into custody or take other legal measures to ensure his presence. The custody and other legal measures shall be as provided in the law of that State but may be continued only for such time as is necessary to enable any criminal or extradition proceedings to be instituted.

2. Such State shall immediately make a preliminary inquiry into the facts.

3. Any person in custody pursuant to paragraph I of this article shall be assisted in communicating immediately with the nearest appropriate representative of the State of which he is a national, or, if he is a stateless person, with the representative of the State where he usually resides.

4. When a State, pursuant to this article, has taken a person into custody, it shall immediately notify the States referred to in article 5, paragraph 1, of the fact that such person is in custody and of the circumstances which warrant his detention. The State which makes the preliminary inquiry contemplated in paragraph 2 of this article shall promptly report its findings to the said States and shall indicate whether it intends to exercise jurisdiction.

Article 7

1.   The State Party in the territory under whose jurisdiction a person alleged to have committed any offence referred to in article 4 is found shall in the cases contemplated in article 5, if it does not extradite him, submit the case to its competent authorities for the purpose of prosecution.

2.   These authorities shall take their decision in the same manner as in the case of any ordinary offence of a serious nature under the law of that State. In the cases referred to in article 5, paragraph 2, the standards of evidence required for prosecution and conviction shall in no way be less stringent than those which apply in the cases referred to in article 5, paragraph 1.

3.   Any person regarding whom proceedings are brought in connection with any of the offences referred to in article 4 shall be guaranteed fair treatment at all stages of the proceedings.

Article 8

1.   The offences referred to in article 4 shall be deemed to be included as extraditable offences in any extradition treaty existing between States Parties. States Parties undertake to include such offences as extraditable offences in every extradition treaty to be concluded between them.

2.   If a State Party which makes extradition conditional on the existence of a treaty receives a request for extradition from another State Party with which it has no extradition treaty, it may consider this Convention as the legal basis for extradition in respect of such offences. Extradition shall be subject to the other conditions provided by the law of the requested State.

3.   States Parties which do not make extradition conditional on the existence of a treaty shall recognize such offences as extraditable offences between themselves subject to the conditions provided by the law of the requested State.

4.   Such offences shall be treated, for the purpose of extradition between States Parties, as if they had been committed not only in the place in which they occurred but also in the territories of the States required to establish their jurisdiction in accordance with article 5, paragraph 1.

Article 9

1.   States Parties shall afford one another the greatest measure of assistance in connection with criminal proceedings brought in respect of any of the offences referred to in article 4, including the supply of all evidence at their disposal necessary for the proceedings.

2. States Parties shall carry out their obligations under paragraph I of this article in conformity with any treaties on mutual judicial assistance that may exist between them.

Article 10

1. Each State Party shall ensure that education and information regarding the prohibition against torture are fully included in the training of law enforcement personnel, civil or military, medical personnel, public officials and other persons who may be involved in the custody, interrogation or treatment of any individual subjected to any form of arrest, detention or imprisonment.

2. Each State Party shall include this prohibition in the rules or instructions issued in regard to the duties and functions of any such person.

Article 11

Each State Party shall keep under systematic review interrogation rules, instructions, methods and practices as well as arrangements for the custody and treatment of persons subjected to any form of arrest, detention or imprisonment in any territory under its jurisdiction, with a view to preventing any cases of torture.

Article 12

Each State Party shall ensure that its competent authorities proceed to a prompt and impartial investigation, wherever there is reasonable ground to believe that an act of torture has been committed in any territory under its jurisdiction.

Article 13

Each State Party shall ensure that any individual who alleges he has been subjected to torture in any territory under its jurisdiction has the right to complain to, and to have his case promptly and impartially examined by, its competent authorities. Steps shall be taken to ensure that the complainant and witnesses are protected against all ill-treatment or intimidation as a consequence of his complaint or any evidence given.

Article 14

1. Each State Party shall ensure in its legal system that the victim of an act of torture obtains redress and has an enforceable right to fair and adequate compensation, including the means for as full rehabilitation as possible. In the event of the death of the victim as a result of an act of torture, his dependents shall be entitled to compensation.

2. Nothing in this article shall affect any right of the victim or other persons to compensation which may exist under national law.

Article 15

Each State Party shall ensure that any statement which is established to have been made as a result of torture shall not be invoked as evidence in any proceedings, except against a person accused of torture as evidence that the statement was made.

Article 16

1.   Each State Party shall undertake to prevent in any territory under its jurisdiction other acts of cruel, inhuman or degrading treatment or punishment which do not amount to torture as defined in article I, when such acts are committed by or at the instigation of or with the consent or acquiescence of a public official or other person acting in an official capacity. In particular, the obligations contained in articles 10, 11, 12 and 13 shall apply with the substitution for references to torture of references to other forms of cruel, inhuman or degrading treatment or punishment.

2.   The provisions of this Convention are without prejudice to the provisions of any other international instrument or national law which prohibits cruel, inhuman or degrading treatment or punishment or which relates to extradition or expulsion.

PART II

Article 17

1.   There shall be established a Committee against Torture (hereinafter referred to as the Committee) which shall carry out the functions hereinafter provided. The Committee shall consist of ten experts of high moral standing and recognized competence in the field of human rights, who shall serve in their personal capacity. The experts shall be elected by the States Parties, consideration being given to equitable geographical distribution and to the usefulness of the participation of some persons having legal experience.

2.   The members of the Committee shall be elected by secret ballot from a list of persons nominated by States Parties. Each State Party may nominate one person from among its own nationals. States Parties shall bear in mind the usefulness of nominating persons who are also members of the Human Rights Committee established under the International Covenant on Civil and Political Rights and who are willing to serve on the Committee against Torture.

3.   Elections of the members of the Committee shall be held at biennial meetings of States Parties convened by the Secretary-General of the United Nations. At those meetings, for which two thirds of the States Parties shall constitute a quorum, the persons elected to the Committee shall be those who obtain the largest number of votes and an absolute

majority of the votes of the representatives of States Parties present and voting.

4. The initial election shall be held no later than six months after the date of the entry into force of this Convention. At least four months before the date of each election, the Secretary-General of the United Nations shall address a letter to the States Parties inviting them to submit their nominations within three months. The Secretary-General shall prepare a list in alphabetical order of all persons thus nominated, indicating the States Parties which have nominated them, and shall submit it to the States Parties.

5. The members of the Committee shall be elected for a term of four years. They shall be eligible for re-election if renominated. However, the term of five of the members elected at the first election shall expire at the end of two years; immediately after the first election the names of these five members shall be chosen by lot by the chairman of the meeting referred to in paragraph 3 of this article.

6. If a member of the Committee dies or resigns or for any other cause can no longer perform his Committee duties, the State Party which nominated him shall appoint another expert from among its nationals to serve for the remainder of his term, subject to the approval of the majority of the States Parties. The approval shall be considered given unless half or more of the States Parties respond negatively within six weeks after having been informed by the Secretary-General of the United Nations of the proposed appointment.

7. States Parties shall be responsible for the expenses of the members of the Committee while they are in performance of Committee duties.

Article 18

1. The Committee shall elect its officers for a term of two years. They may be re-elected.

2. The Committee shall establish its own rules of procedure, but these rules shall provide, inter alia, that:

(a) Six members shall constitute a quorum;

(b) Decisions of the Committee shall be made by a majority vote of the members present.

3. The Secretary-General of the United Nations shall provide the necessary staff and facilities for the effective performance of the functions of the Committee under this Convention.

4. The Secretary-General of the United Nations shall convene the initial meeting of the Committee. After its initial meeting, the Committee shall meet at such times as shall be provided in its rules of procedure.

5. The States Parties shall be responsible for expenses incurred in connection with the holding of meetings of the States Parties and of the Committee, including reimbursement to the United Nations for any expenses, such as the cost of staff and facilities, incurred by the United Nations pursuant to paragraph 3 of this article.

Article 19

1. The States Parties shall submit to the Committee, through the Secretary-General of the United Nations, reports on the measures they have taken to give effect to their undertakings under this Convention, within one year after the entry into force of the Convention for the State Party concerned. Thereafter the States Parties shall submit supplementary reports every four years on any new measures taken and such other reports as the Committee may request.

2. The Secretary-General of the United Nations shall transmit the reports to all States Parties.

3. Each report shall be considered by the Committee which may make such general comments on the report as it may consider appropriate and shall forward these to the State Party concerned. That State Party may respond with any observations it chooses to the Committee.

4. The Committee may, at its discretion, decide to include any comments made by it in accordance with paragraph 3 of this article, together with the observations thereon received from the State Party concerned, in its annual report made in accordance with article 24. If so requested by the State Party concerned, the Committee may also include a copy of the report submitted under paragraph I of this article.

Article 20

1. If the Committee receives reliable information which appears to it to contain well-founded indications that torture is being systematically practised in the territory of a State Party, the Committee shall invite that State Party to co-operate in the examination of the information and to this end to submit observations with regard to the information concerned.

2. Taking into account any observations which may have been submitted by the State Party concerned, as well as any other relevant information available to it, the Committee may, if it decides that this is warranted, designate one or more of its members to make a confidential inquiry and to report to the Committee urgently.

3. If an inquiry is made in accordance with paragraph 2 of this article, the Committee shall seek the co-operation of the State Party concerned. In agreement with that State Party, such an inquiry may include a visit to its territory.

4.   After examining the findings of its member or members submitted in accordance with paragraph 2 of this article, the Commission shall transmit these findings to the State Party concerned together with any comments or suggestions which seem appropriate in view of the situation.

5.   All the proceedings of the Committee referred to in paragraphs I to 4 of this article shall be confidential, and at all stages of the proceedings the co-operation of the State Party shall be sought. After such proceedings have been completed with regard to an inquiry made in accordance with paragraph 2, the Committee may, after consultations with the State Party concerned, decide to include a summary account of the results of the proceedings in its annual report made in accordance with article 24.

Article 21

1.   A State Party to this Convention may at any time declare under this article that it recognizes the competence of the Committee to receive and consider communications to the effect that a State Party claims that another State Party is not fulfilling its obligations under this Convention. Such communications may be received and considered according to the procedures laid down in this article only if submitted by a State Party which has made a declaration recognizing in regard to itself the competence of the Committee. No communication shall be dealt with by the Committee under this article if it concerns a State Party which has not made such a declaration. Communications received under this article shall be dealt with in accordance with the following procedure;

(a) If a State Party considers that another State Party is not giving effect to the provisions of this Convention, it may, by written communication, bring the matter to the attention of that State Party. Within three months after the receipt of the communication the receiving State shall afford the State which sent the communication an explanation or any other statement in writing clarifying the matter, which should include, to the extent possible and pertinent, reference to domestic procedures and remedies taken, pending or available in the matter;

(b) If the matter is not adjusted to the satisfaction of both States Parties concerned within six months after the receipt by the receiving State of the initial communication, either State shall have the right to refer the matter to the Committee, by notice given to the Committee and to the other State;

(c) The Committee shall deal with a matter referred to it under this article only after it has ascertained that all domestic remedies have been invoked and exhausted in the matter, in conformity with the generally recognized principles of international law. This shall not be the rule where the application of the remedies is unreasonably prolonged or is unlikely to bring effective relief to the person who is the victim of the violation of this Convention;

(d) The Committee shall hold closed meetings when examining communications under this article;

(e) Subject to the provisions of subparagraph (c), the Committee shall make available its good offices to the States Parties concerned with a view to a friendly solution of the matter on the basis of respect for the obligations provided for in this Convention. For this purpose, the Committee may, when appropriate, set up an ad hoc conciliation commission;

(f) In any matter referred to it under this article, the Committee may call upon the States Parties concerned, referred to in subparagraph (b), to supply any relevant information;

(g) The States Parties concerned, referred to in subparagraph (b), shall have the right to be represented when the matter is being considered by the Committee and to make submissions orally and/or in writing;

(h) The Committee shall, within twelve months after the date of receipt of notice under subparagraph (b), submit a report:

(i) If a solution within the terms of subparagraph (e) is reached, the Committee shall confine its report to a brief statement of the facts and of the solution reached;

(ii) If a solution within the terms of subparagraph (e) is not reached, the Committee shall confine its report to a brief statement of the facts; the written submissions and record of the oral submissions made by the States Parties concerned shall be attached to the report.

In every matter, the report shall be communicated to the States Parties concerned.

2.   The provisions of this article shall come into force when five States Parties to this Convention have made declarations under paragraph 1 of this article. Such declarations shall be deposited by the States Parties with the Secretary-General of the United Nations, who shall transmit copies thereof to the other States Parties. A declaration may be withdrawn at any time by notification to the Secretary-General. Such a withdrawal shall not prejudice the consideration of any matter which is the subject of a communication already transmitted under this article; no further communication by any State Party shall be received under this article after the notification of withdrawal of the declaration

has been received by the Secretary-General, unless the State Party concerned has made a new declaration.

Article 22

1.   A State Party to this Convention may at any time declare under this article that it recognizes the competence of the Committee to receive and consider communications from or on behalf of individuals subject to its jurisdiction who claim to be victims of a violation by a State Party of the provisions of the Convention. No communication shall be received by the Committee if it concerns a State Party which has not made such a declaration.

2.   The Committee shall consider inadmissible any communication under this article which is anonymous or which it considers to be an abuse of the right of submission of such communications or to be incompatible with the provisions of this Convention.

3.   Subject to the provisions of paragraph 2, the Committee shall bring any communications submitted to it under this article to the attention of the State Party to this Convention which has made a declaration under paragraph 1 and is alleged to be violating any provisions of the Convention. Within six months, the receiving State shall submit to the Committee written explanations or statements clarifying the matter and the remedy, if any, that may have been taken by that State.

4.   The Committee shall consider communications received under this article in the light of all information made available to it by or on behalf of the individual and by the State Party concerned.

5.   The Committee shall not consider any communications from an individual under this article unless it has ascertained that:

(a) The same matter has not been, and is not being, examined under another procedure of international investigation or settlement;

(b) The individual has exhausted all available domestic remedies; this shall not be the rule where the application of the remedies is unreasonably prolonged or is unlikely to bring effective relief to the person who is the victim of the violation of this Convention.

6.   The Committee shall hold closed meetings when examining communications under this article.

7.   The Committee shall forward its views to the State Party concerned and to the individual.

8.   The provisions of this article shall come into force when five States Parties to this Convention have made declarations under

paragraph 1 of this article. Such declarations shall be deposited by the States Parties with the Secretary-General of the United Nations, who shall transmit copies thereof to the other States Parties. A declaration may be withdrawn at any time by notification to the Secretary-General. Such a withdrawal shall not prejudice the consideration of any matter which is the subject of a communication already transmitted under this article; no further communication by or on behalf of an individual shall be received under this article after the notification of withdrawal of the declaration has been received by the Secretary-General, unless the State Party has made a new declaration.

Article 23

The members of the Committee and of the ad hoc conciliation commissions which may be appointed under article 21, paragraph 1 (e), shall be entitled to the facilities, privileges and immunities of experts on mission for the United Nations as laid down in the relevant sections of the Convention on the Privileges and Immunities of the United Nations.

Article 24

The Committee shall submit an annual report on its activities under this Convention to the States Parties and to the General Assembly of the United Nations.

PART III

Article 25

1.   This Convention is open for signature by all States.

2.   This Convention is subject to ratification. Instruments of ratification shall be deposited with the Secretary-General of the United Nations.

Article 26

This Convention is open to accession by all States. Accession shall be effected by the deposit of an instrument of accession with the Secretary-General of the United Nations.

Article 27

1.   This Convention shall enter into force on the thirtieth day after the date of the deposit with the Secretary-General of the United Nations of the twentieth instrument of ratification or accession.

2.   For each State ratifying this Convention or acceding to it after the deposit of the twentieth instrument of ratification or accession, the Convention shall enter into force on the thirtieth day after the date of the deposit of its own instrument of ratification or accession.

Article 28

1. Each State may, at the time of signature or ratification of this Convention or accession thereto, declare that it does not recognize the competence of the Committee provided for in article 20.

2. Any State Party having made a reservation in accordance with paragraph I of this article may, at any time, withdraw this reservation by notification to the Secretary-General of the United Nations.

Article 29

1. Any State Party to this Convention may propose an amendment and file it with the Secretary-General of the United Nations. The Secretary-General shall thereupon communicate the proposed amendment to the States Parties with a request that they notify him whether they favour a conference of States Parties for the purpose of considering and voting upon the proposal. In the event that within four months from the date of such communication at least one third of the States Parties favours such a conference, the Secretary-General shall convene the conference under the auspices of the United Nations. Any amendment adopted by a majority of the States Parties present and voting at the conference shall be submitted by the Secretary-General to all the States Parties for acceptance.

2. An amendment adopted in accordance with paragraph 1 of this article shall enter into force when two thirds of the States Parties to this Convention have notified the Secretary-General of the United Nations that they have accepted it in accordance with their respective constitutional processes.

3. When amendments enter into force, they shall be binding on those States Parties which have accepted them, other States Parties still being bound by the provisions of this Convention and any earlier amendments which they have accepted.

Article 30

1. Any dispute between two or more States Parties concerning the interpretation or application of this Convention which cannot be settled through negotiation shall, at the request of one of them, be submitted to arbitration. If within six months from the date of the request for arbitration the Parties are unable to agree on the organization of the arbitration, any one of those Parties may refer the dispute to the International Court of Justice by request in conformity with the Statute of the Court.

2. Each State may, at the time of signature or ratification of this Convention or accession thereto, declare that it does not consider itself bound by paragraph 1 of this article. The other States Parties shall not be

bound by paragraph 1 of this article with respect to any State Party having made such a reservation.

3. Any State Party having made a reservation in accordance with paragraph 2 of this article may at any time withdraw this reservation by notification to the Secretary-General of the United Nations.

Article 31

1. A State Party may denounce this Convention by written notification to the Secretary-General of the United Nations. Denunciation becomes effective one year after the date of receipt of the notification by the Secretary-General.

2. Such a denunciation shall not have the effect of releasing the State Party from its obligations under this Convention in regard to any act or omission which occurs prior to the date at which the denunciation becomes effective, nor shall denunciation prejudice in any way the continued consideration of any matter which is already under consideration by the Committee prior to the date at which the denunciation becomes effective.

3. Following the date at which the denunciation of a State Party becomes effective, the Committee shall not commence consideration of any new matter regarding that State.

Article 32

The Secretary-General of the United Nations shall inform all States Members of the United Nations and all States which have signed this Convention or acceded to it of the following:

(a) Signatures, ratifications and accessions under articles 25 and 26;

(b) The date of entry into force of this Convention under article 27 and the date of the entry into force of any amendments under article 29;

(c) Denunciations under article 31.

Article 33

1. This Convention, of which the Arabic, Chinese, English, French, Russian and Spanish texts are equally authentic, shall be deposited with the Secretary-General of the United Nations.

2. The Secretary-General of the United Nations shall transmit certified copies of this Convention to all States.

CONVENTION ON THE RIGHTS OF THE CHILD

Adopted and opened for signature, ratification and accession by
General Assembly resolution 44/25 of 20 November 1989
entry into force 2 September 1990, in accordance with article 49

PREAMBLE

The States Parties to the present Convention,

Considering that, in accordance with the principles proclaimed in the
Charter of the United Nations, recognition of the inherent dignity and of
the equal and inalienable rights of all members of the human family is
the foundation of freedom, justice and peace in the world,

Bearing in mind that the peoples of the United Nations have, in the
Charter, reaffirmed their faith in fundamental human rights and in the
dignity and worth of the human person, and have determined to promote
social progress and better standards of life in larger freedom,

Recognizing that the United Nations has, in the Universal
Declaration of Human Rights and in the International Covenants on
Human Rights, proclaimed and agreed that everyone is entitled to all the
rights and freedoms set forth therein, without distinction of any kind,
such as race, colour, sex, language, religion, political or other opinion,
national or social origin, property, birth or other status,

Recalling that, in the Universal Declaration of Human Rights, the
United Nations has proclaimed that childhood is entitled to special care
and assistance,

Convinced that the family, as the fundamental group of society and
the natural environment for the growth and well-being of all its members
and particularly children, should be afforded the necessary protection and
assistance so that it can fully assume its responsibilities within the
community,

Recognizing that the child, for the full and harmonious development
of his or her personality, should grow up in a family environment, in an
atmosphere of happiness, love and understanding,

Considering that the child should be fully prepared to live an
individual life in society, and brought up in the spirit of the ideals
proclaimed in the Charter of the United Nations, and in particular in the
spirit of peace, dignity, tolerance, freedom, equality and solidarity,

Bearing in mind that the need to extend particular care to the child
has been stated in the Geneva Declaration of the Rights of the Child of
1924 and in the Declaration of the Rights of the Child adopted by the
General Assembly on 20 November 1959 and recognized in the Universal
Declaration of Human Rights, in the International Covenant on Civil and
Political Rights (in particular in articles 23 and 24), in the International

Covenant on Economic, Social and Cultural Rights (in particular in article 10) and in the statutes and relevant instruments of specialized agencies and international organizations concerned with the welfare of children,

Bearing in mind that, as indicated in the Declaration of the Rights of the Child, "the child, by reason of his physical and mental immaturity, needs special safeguards and care, including appropriate legal protection, before as well as after birth",

Recalling the provisions of the Declaration on Social and Legal Principles relating to the Protection and Welfare of Children, with Special Reference to Foster Placement and Adoption Nationally and Internationally; the United Nations Standard Minimum Rules for the Administration of Juvenile Justice (The Beijing Rules); and the Declaration on the Protection of Women and Children in Emergency and Armed Conflict, Recognizing that, in all countries in the world, there are children living in exceptionally difficult conditions, and that such children need special consideration,

Taking due account of the importance of the traditions and cultural values of each people for the protection and harmonious development of the child, Recognizing the importance of international co-operation for improving the living conditions of children in every country, in particular in the developing countries,

Have agreed as follows:

PART I

Article 1

For the purposes of the present Convention, a child means every human being below the age of eighteen years unless under the law applicable to the child, majority is attained earlier.

Article 2

1.   States Parties shall respect and ensure the rights set forth in the present Convention to each child within their jurisdiction without discrimination of any kind, irrespective of the child's or his or her parent's or legal guardian's race, colour, sex, language, religion, political or other opinion, national, ethnic or social origin, property, disability, birth or other status.

2.   States Parties shall take all appropriate measures to ensure that the child is protected against all forms of discrimination or punishment on the basis of the status, activities, expressed opinions, or beliefs of the child's parents, legal guardians, or family members.

Article 3

1.   In all actions concerning children, whether undertaken by public or private social welfare institutions, courts of law, administrative authorities or legislative bodies, the best interests of the child shall be a primary consideration.

2.   States Parties undertake to ensure the child such protection and care as is necessary for his or her well-being, taking into account the rights and duties of his or her parents, legal guardians, or other individuals legally responsible for him or her, and, to this end, shall take all appropriate legislative and administrative measures.

3.   States Parties shall ensure that the institutions, services and facilities responsible for the care or protection of children shall conform with the standards established by competent authorities, particularly in the areas of safety, health, in the number and suitability of their staff, as well as competent supervision.

Article 4

States Parties shall undertake all appropriate legislative, administrative, and other measures for the implementation of the rights recognized in the present Convention. With regard to economic, social and cultural rights, States Parties shall undertake such measures to the maximum extent of their available resources and, where needed, within the framework of international co-operation.

Article 5

States Parties shall respect the responsibilities, rights and duties of parents or, where applicable, the members of the extended family or community as provided for by local custom, legal guardians or other persons legally responsible for the child, to provide, in a manner consistent with the evolving capacities of the child, appropriate direction and guidance in the exercise by the child of the rights recognized in the present Convention.

Article 6

1.   States Parties recognize that every child has the inherent right to life.

2.   States Parties shall ensure to the maximum extent possible the survival and development of the child.

Article 7

1.   The child shall be registered immediately after birth and shall have the right from birth to a name, the right to acquire a nationality and. as far as possible, the right to know and be cared for by his or her parents.

2.   States Parties shall ensure the implementation of these rights in accordance with their national law and their obligations under the relevant international instruments in this field, in particular where the child would otherwise be stateless.

Article 8

1.   States Parties undertake to respect the right of the child to preserve his or her identity, including nationality, name and family relations as recognized by law without unlawful interference.

2.   Where a child is illegally deprived of some or all of the elements of his or her identity, States Parties shall provide appropriate assistance and protection, with a view to re-establishing speedily his or her identity.

Article 9

1.   States Parties shall ensure that a child shall not be separated from his or her parents against their will, except when competent authorities subject to judicial review determine, in accordance with applicable law and procedures, that such separation is necessary for the best interests of the child. Such determination may be necessary in a particular case such as one involving abuse or neglect of the child by the parents, or one where the parents are living separately and a decision must be made as to the child's place of residence.

2.   In any proceedings pursuant to paragraph 1 of the present article, all interested parties shall be given an opportunity to participate in the proceedings and make their views known.

3.   States Parties shall respect the right of the child who is separated from one or both parents to maintain personal relations and direct contact with both parents on a regular basis, except if it is contrary to the child's best interests.

4.   Where such separation results from any action initiated by a State Party, such as the detention, imprisonment, exile, deportation or death (including death arising from any cause while the person is in the custody of the State) of one or both parents or of the child, that State Party shall, upon request, provide the parents, the child or, if appropriate, another member of the family with the essential information concerning the whereabouts of the absent member(s) of the family unless the provision of the information would be detrimental to the well-being of the child. States Parties shall further ensure that the submission of such a request shall of itself entail no adverse consequences for the person(s) concerned.

Article 10

1.   In accordance with the obligation of States Parties under article 9, paragraph 1, applications by a child or his or her parents to enter or

leave a State Party for the purpose of family reunification shall be dealt with by States Parties in a positive, humane and expeditious manner. States Parties shall further ensure that the submission of such a request shall entail no adverse consequences for the applicants and for the members of their family.

2.   A child whose parents reside in different States shall have the right to maintain on a regular basis, save in exceptional circumstances personal relations and direct contacts with both parents. Towards that end and in accordance with the obligation of States Parties under article 9, paragraph 1, States Parties shall respect the right of the child and his or her parents to leave any country, including their own, and to enter their own country. The right to leave any country shall be subject only to such restrictions as are prescribed by law and which are necessary to protect the national security, public order (ordre public), public health or morals or the rights and freedoms of others and are consistent with the other rights recognized in the present Convention.

Article 11

1.   States Parties shall take measures to combat the illicit transfer and non-return of children abroad.

2.   To this end, States Parties shall promote the conclusion of bilateral or multilateral agreements or accession to existing agreements.

Article 12

1.   States Parties shall assure to the child who is capable of forming his or her own views the right to express those views freely in all matters affecting the child, the views of the child being given due weight in accordance with the age and maturity of the child.

2.   For this purpose, the child shall in particular be provided the opportunity to be heard in any judicial and administrative proceedings affecting the child, either directly, or through a representative or an appropriate body, in a manner consistent with the procedural rules of national law.

Article 13

1.   The child shall have the right to freedom of expression; this right shall include freedom to seek, receive and impart information and ideas of all kinds, regardless of frontiers, either orally, in writing or in print, in the form of art, or through any other media of the child's choice.

2.   The exercise of this right may be subject to certain restrictions, but these shall only be such as are provided by law and are necessary:

(a) For respect of the rights or reputations of others; or

(b) For the protection of national security or of public order (ordre public), or of public health or morals.

Article 14

1.   States Parties shall respect the right of the child to freedom of thought, conscience and religion.

2.   States Parties shall respect the rights and duties of the parents and, when applicable, legal guardians, to provide direction to the child in the exercise of his or her right in a manner consistent with the evolving capacities of the child.

3.   Freedom to manifest one's religion or beliefs may be subject only to such limitations as are prescribed by law and are necessary to protect public safety, order, health or morals, or the fundamental rights and freedoms of others.

Article 15

1.   States Parties recognize the rights of the child to freedom of association and to freedom of peaceful assembly.

2.   No restrictions may be placed on the exercise of these rights other than those imposed in conformity with the law and which are necessary in a democratic society in the interests of national security or public safety, public order (ordre public), the protection of public health or morals or the protection of the rights and freedoms of others.

Article 16

1.   No child shall be subjected to arbitrary or unlawful interference with his or her privacy, family, or correspondence, nor to unlawful attacks on his or her honour and reputation.

2.   The child has the right to the protection of the law against such interference or attacks.

Article 17

States Parties recognize the important function performed by the mass media and shall ensure that the child has access to information and material from a diversity of national and international sources, especially those aimed at the promotion of his or her social, spiritual and moral well-being and physical and mental health.

To this end, States Parties shall:

(a) Encourage the mass media to disseminate information and material of social and cultural benefit to the child and in accordance with the spirit of article 29;

(b) Encourage international co-operation in the production, exchange and dissemination of such information and material from a diversity of cultural, national and international sources;

(c) Encourage the production and dissemination of children's books;

(d) Encourage the mass media to have particular regard to the linguistic needs of the child who belongs to a minority group or who is indigenous;

(e) Encourage the development of appropriate guidelines for the protection of the child from information and material injurious to his or her well-being, bearing in mind the provisions of articles 13 and 18.

Article 18

1. States Parties shall use their best efforts to ensure recognition of the principle that both parents have common responsibilities for the upbringing and development of the child. Parents or, as the case may be, legal guardians, have the primary responsibility for the upbringing and development of the child. The best interests of the child will be their basic concern.

2. For the purpose of guaranteeing and promoting the rights set forth in the present Convention, States Parties shall render appropriate assistance to parents and legal guardians in the performance of their child-rearing responsibilities and shall ensure the development of institutions, facilities and services for the care of children.

3. States Parties shall take all appropriate measures to ensure that children of working parents have the right to benefit from child-care services and facilities for which they are eligible.

Article 19

1. States Parties shall take all appropriate legislative, administrative, social and educational measures to protect the child from all forms of physical or mental violence, injury or abuse, neglect or negligent treatment, maltreatment or exploitation, including sexual abuse, while in the care of parent(s), legal guardian(s) or any other person who has the care of the child.

2. Such protective measures should, as appropriate, include effective procedures for the establishment of social programmes to provide necessary support for the child and for those who have the care of the child, as well as for other forms of prevention and for identification, reporting, referral, investigation, treatment and follow-up of instances of child maltreatment described heretofore, and, as appropriate, for judicial involvement.

Article 20

1. A child temporarily or permanently deprived of his or her family environment, or in whose own best interests cannot be allowed to remain in that environment, shall be entitled to special protection and assistance provided by the State.

2. States Parties shall in accordance with their national laws ensure alternative care for such a child.

3. Such care could include, inter alia, foster placement, kafalah of Islamic law, adoption or if necessary placement in suitable institutions for the care of children. When considering solutions, due regard shall be paid to the desirability of continuity in a child's upbringing and to the child's ethnic, religious, cultural and linguistic background.

Article 21

States Parties that recognize and/or permit the system of adoption shall ensure that the best interests of the child shall be the paramount consideration and they shall:

(a) Ensure that the adoption of a child is authorized only by competent authorities who determine, in accordance with applicable law and procedures and on the basis of all pertinent and reliable information, that the adoption is permissible in view of the child's status concerning parents, relatives and legal guardians and that, if required, the persons concerned have given their informed consent to the adoption on the basis of such counselling as may be necessary;

(b) Recognize that inter-country adoption may be considered as an alternative means of child's care, if the child cannot be placed in a foster or an adoptive family or cannot in any suitable manner be cared for in the child's country of origin;

(c) Ensure that the child concerned by inter-country adoption enjoys safeguards and standards equivalent to those existing in the case of national adoption;

(d) Take all appropriate measures to ensure that, in inter-country adoption, the placement does not result in improper financial gain for those involved in it;

(e) Promote, where appropriate, the objectives of the present article by concluding bilateral or multilateral arrangements or agreements, and endeavour, within this framework, to ensure that the placement of the child in another country is carried out by competent authorities or organs.

Article 22

1. States Parties shall take appropriate measures to ensure that a child who is seeking refugee status or who is considered a refugee in accordance with applicable international or domestic law and procedures shall, whether unaccompanied or accompanied by his or her parents or by any other person, receive appropriate protection and humanitarian assistance in the enjoyment of applicable rights set forth in the present Convention and in other international human rights or humanitarian instruments to which the said States are Parties.

2. For this purpose, States Parties shall provide, as they consider appropriate, co-operation in any efforts by the United Nations and other competent intergovernmental organizations or non-governmental organizations co-operating with the United Nations to protect and assist such a child and to trace the parents or other members of the family of any refugee child in order to obtain information necessary for reunification with his or her family. In cases where no parents or other members of the family can be found, the child shall be accorded the same protection as any other child permanently or temporarily deprived of his or her family environment for any reason, as set forth in the present Convention.

Article 23

1. States Parties recognize that a mentally or physically disabled child should enjoy a full and decent life, in conditions which ensure dignity, promote self-reliance and facilitate the child's active participation in the community.

2. States Parties recognize the right of the disabled child to special care and shall encourage and ensure the extension, subject to available resources, to the eligible child and those responsible for his or her care, of assistance for which application is made and which is appropriate to the child's condition and to the circumstances of the parents or others caring for the child.

3. Recognizing the special needs of a disabled child, assistance extended in accordance with paragraph 2 of the present article shall be provided free of charge, whenever possible, taking into account the financial resources of the parents or others caring for the child, and shall be designed to ensure that the disabled child has effective access to and receives education, training, health care services, rehabilitation services, preparation for employment and recreation opportunities in a manner conducive to the child's achieving the fullest possible social integration and individual development, including his or her cultural and spiritual development.

4.   States Parties shall promote, in the spirit of international cooperation, the exchange of appropriate information in the field of preventive health care and of medical, psychological and functional treatment of disabled children, including dissemination of and access to information concerning methods of rehabilitation, education and vocational services, with the aim of enabling States Parties to improve their capabilities and skills and to widen their experience in these areas. In this regard, particular account shall be taken of the needs of developing countries.

Article 24

1.   States Parties recognize the right of the child to the enjoyment of the highest attainable standard of health and to facilities for the treatment of illness and rehabilitation of health. States Parties shall strive to ensure that no child is deprived of his or her right of access to such health care services.

2.   States Parties shall pursue full implementation of this right and, in particular, shall take appropriate measures:

(a) To diminish infant and child mortality;

(b) To ensure the provision of necessary medical assistance and health care to all children with emphasis on the development of primary health care;

(c) To combat disease and malnutrition, including within the framework of primary health care, through, inter alia, the application of readily available technology and through the provision of adequate nutritious foods and clean drinking-water, taking into consideration the dangers and risks of environmental pollution;

(d) To ensure appropriate pre-natal and post-natal health care for mothers;

(e) To ensure that all segments of society, in particular parents and children, are informed, have access to education and are supported in the use of basic knowledge of child health and nutrition, the advantages of breastfeeding, hygiene and environmental sanitation and the prevention of accidents;

(f) To develop preventive health care, guidance for parents and family planning education and services.

3.   States Parties shall take all effective and appropriate measures with a view to abolishing traditional practices prejudicial to the health of children.

4.   States Parties undertake to promote and encourage international co-operation with a view to achieving progressively the full

realization of the right recognized in the present article. In this regard, particular account shall be taken of the needs of developing countries.

Article 25

States Parties recognize the right of a child who has been placed by the competent authorities for the purposes of care, protection or treatment of his or her physical or mental health, to a periodic review of the treatment provided to the child and all other circumstances relevant to his or her placement.

Article 26

1.   States Parties shall recognize for every child the right to benefit from social security, including social insurance, and shall take the necessary measures to achieve the full realization of this right in accordance with their national law.

2.   The benefits should, where appropriate, be granted, taking into account the resources and the circumstances of the child and persons having responsibility for the maintenance of the child, as well as any other consideration relevant to an application for benefits made by or on behalf of the child.

Article 27

1.   States Parties recognize the right of every child to a standard of living adequate for the child's physical, mental, spiritual, moral and social development.

2.   The parent(s) or others responsible for the child have the primary responsibility to secure, within their abilities and financial capacities, the conditions of living necessary for the child's development.

3.   States Parties, in accordance with national conditions and within their means, shall take appropriate measures to assist parents and others responsible for the child to implement this right and shall in case of need provide material assistance and support programmes, particularly with regard to nutrition, clothing and housing.

4.   States Parties shall take all appropriate measures to secure the recovery of maintenance for the child from the parents or other persons having financial responsibility for the child, both within the State Party and from abroad. In particular, where the person having financial responsibility for the child lives in a State different from that of the child, States Parties shall promote the accession to international agreements or the conclusion of such agreements, as well as the making of other appropriate arrangements.

Article 28

1.   States Parties recognize the right of the child to education, and with a view to achieving this right progressively and on the basis of equal opportunity, they shall, in particular:

(a) Make primary education compulsory and available free to all;

(b) Encourage the development of different forms of secondary education, including general and vocational education, make them available and accessible to every child, and take appropriate measures such as the introduction of free education and offering financial assistance in case of need;

(c) Make higher education accessible to all on the basis of capacity by every appropriate means;

(d) Make educational and vocational information and guidance available and accessible to all children;

(e) Take measures to encourage regular attendance at schools and the reduction of drop-out rates.

2.   States Parties shall take all appropriate measures to ensure that school discipline is administered in a manner consistent with the child's human dignity and in conformity with the present Convention.

3.   States Parties shall promote and encourage international cooperation in matters relating to education, in particular with a view to contributing to the elimination of ignorance and illiteracy throughout the world and facilitating access to scientific and technical knowledge and modern teaching methods. In this regard, particular account shall be taken of the needs of developing countries.

Article 29

1.   States Parties agree that the education of the child shall be directed to:

(a) The development of the child's personality, talents and mental and physical abilities to their fullest potential;

(b) The development of respect for human rights and fundamental freedoms, and for the principles enshrined in the Charter of the United Nations;

(c) The development of respect for the child's parents, his or her own cultural identity, language and values, for the national values of the country in which the child is living, the country from which he or she may originate, and for civilizations different from his or her own;

(d) The preparation of the child for responsible life in a free society, in the spirit of understanding, peace, tolerance, equality of sexes, and friendship among all peoples, ethnic, national and religious groups and persons of indigenous origin;

(e) The development of respect for the natural environment.

2.   No part of the present article or article 28 shall be construed so as to interfere with the liberty of individuals and bodies to establish and direct educational institutions, subject always to the observance of the principle set forth in paragraph 1 of the present article and to the requirements that the education given in such institutions shall conform to such minimum standards as may be laid down by the State.

Article 30

In those States in which ethnic, religious or linguistic minorities or persons of indigenous origin exist, a child belonging to such a minority or who is indigenous shall not be denied the right, in community with other members of his or her group, to enjoy his or her own culture, to profess and practise his or her own religion, or to use his or her own language.

Article 31

1.   States Parties recognize the right of the child to rest and leisure, to engage in play and recreational activities appropriate to the age of the child and to participate freely in cultural life and the arts.

2.   States Parties shall respect and promote the right of the child to participate fully in cultural and artistic life and shall encourage the provision of appropriate and equal opportunities for cultural, artistic, recreational and leisure activity.

Article 32

1.   States Parties recognize the right of the child to be protected from economic exploitation and from performing any work that is likely to be hazardous or to interfere with the child's education, or to be harmful to the child's health or physical, mental, spiritual, moral or social development.

2.   States Parties shall take legislative, administrative, social and educational measures to ensure the implementation of the present article. To this end, and having regard to the relevant provisions of other international instruments, States Parties shall in particular:

(a) Provide for a minimum age or minimum ages for admission to employment;

(b) Provide for appropriate regulation of the hours and conditions of employment;

(c) Provide for appropriate penalties or other sanctions to ensure the effective enforcement of the present article.

Article 33

States Parties shall take all appropriate measures, including legislative, administrative, social and educational measures, to protect children from the illicit use of narcotic drugs and psychotropic substances as defined in the relevant international treaties, and to prevent the use of children in the illicit production and trafficking of such substances.

Article 34

States Parties undertake to protect the child from all forms of sexual exploitation and sexual abuse. For these purposes, States Parties shall in particular take all appropriate national, bilateral and multilateral measures to prevent:

(a) The inducement or coercion of a child to engage in any unlawful sexual activity;

(b) The exploitative use of children in prostitution or other unlawful sexual practices;

(c) The exploitative use of children in pornographic performances and materials.

Article 35

States Parties shall take all appropriate national, bilateral and multilateral measures to prevent the abduction of, the sale of or traffic in children for any purpose or in any form.

Article 36

States Parties shall protect the child against all other forms of exploitation prejudicial to any aspects of the child's welfare.

Article 37

States Parties shall ensure that:

(a) No child shall be subjected to torture or other cruel, inhuman or degrading treatment or punishment. Neither capital punishment nor life imprisonment without possibility of release shall be imposed for offences committed by persons below eighteen years of age;

(b) No child shall be deprived of his or her liberty unlawfully or arbitrarily. The arrest, detention or imprisonment of a child shall be in conformity with the law and shall be used only as a measure of last resort and for the shortest appropriate period of time;

(c) Every child deprived of liberty shall be treated with humanity and respect for the inherent dignity of the human person, and in a manner which takes into account the needs of persons of his or her age. In particular, every child deprived of liberty shall be separated from adults unless it is considered in the child's best interest not to do so and shall have the right to maintain contact with his or her family through correspondence and visits, save in exceptional circumstances;

(d) Every child deprived of his or her liberty shall have the right to prompt access to legal and other appropriate assistance, as well as the right to challenge the legality of the deprivation of his or her liberty before a court or other competent, independent and impartial authority, and to a prompt decision on any such action.

Article 38

1. States Parties undertake to respect and to ensure respect for rules of international humanitarian law applicable to them in armed conflicts which are relevant to the child.

2. States Parties shall take all feasible measures to ensure that persons who have not attained the age of fifteen years do not take a direct part in hostilities.

3. States Parties shall refrain from recruiting any person who has not attained the age of fifteen years into their armed forces. In recruiting among those persons who have attained the age of fifteen years but who have not attained the age of eighteen years, States Parties shall endeavour to give priority to those who are oldest.

4. In accordance with their obligations under international humanitarian law to protect the civilian population in armed conflicts, States Parties shall take all feasible measures to ensure protection and care of children who are affected by an armed conflict.

Article 39

States Parties shall take all appropriate measures to promote physical and psychological recovery and social reintegration of a child victim of: any form of neglect, exploitation, or abuse; torture or any other form of cruel, inhuman or degrading treatment or punishment; or armed conflicts. Such recovery and reintegration shall take place in an environment which fosters the health, self-respect and dignity of the child.

Article 40

1. States Parties recognize the right of every child alleged as, accused of, or recognized as having infringed the penal law to be treated

in a manner consistent with the promotion of the child's sense of dignity and worth, which reinforces the child's respect for the human rights and fundamental freedoms of others and which takes into account the child's age and the desirability of promoting the child's reintegration and the child's assuming a constructive role in society.

2.   To this end, and having regard to the relevant provisions of international instruments, States Parties shall, in particular, ensure that:

(a) No child shall be alleged as, be accused of, or recognized as having infringed the penal law by reason of acts or omissions that were not prohibited by national or international law at the time they were committed;

(b) Every child alleged as or accused of having infringed the penal law has at least the following guarantees:

(i) To be presumed innocent until proven guilty according to law;

(ii) To be informed promptly and directly of the charges against him or her, and, if appropriate, through his or her parents or legal guardians, and to have legal or other appropriate assistance in the preparation and presentation of his or her defence;

(iii) To have the matter determined without delay by a competent, independent and impartial authority or judicial body in a fair hearing according to law, in the presence of legal or other appropriate assistance and, unless it is considered not to be in the best interest of the child, in particular, taking into account his or her age or situation, his or her parents or legal guardians;

(iv) Not to be compelled to give testimony or to confess guilt; to examine or have examined adverse witnesses and to obtain the participation and examination of witnesses on his or her behalf under conditions of equality;

(v) If considered to have infringed the penal law, to have this decision and any measures imposed in consequence thereof reviewed by a higher competent, independent and impartial authority or judicial body according to law;

(vi) To have the free assistance of an interpreter if the child cannot understand or speak the language used;

(vii) To have his or her privacy fully respected at all stages of the proceedings.

3.   States Parties shall seek to promote the establishment of laws, procedures, authorities and institutions specifically applicable to children alleged as, accused of, or recognized as having infringed the penal law, and, in particular:

(a) The establishment of a minimum age below which children shall be presumed not to have the capacity to infringe the penal law;

(b) Whenever appropriate and desirable, measures for dealing with such children without resorting to judicial proceedings, providing that human rights and legal safeguards are fully respected.

4.   A variety of dispositions, such as care, guidance and supervision orders; counselling; probation; foster care; education and vocational training programmes and other alternatives to institutional care shall be available to ensure that children are dealt with in a manner appropriate to their well-being and proportionate both to their circumstances and the offence.

Article 41

Nothing in the present Convention shall affect any provisions which are more conducive to the realization of the rights of the child and which may be contained in:

(a) The law of a State party; or

(b) International law in force for that State.

PART II

Article 42

States Parties undertake to make the principles and provisions of the Convention widely known, by appropriate and active means, to adults and children alike.

Article 43

1.   For the purpose of examining the progress made by States Parties in achieving the realization of the obligations undertaken in the present Convention, there shall be established a Committee on the Rights of the Child, which shall carry out the functions hereinafter provided.

2.   The Committee shall consist of eighteen experts of high moral standing and recognized competence in the field covered by this Convention.1/ The members of the Committee shall be elected by States Parties from among their nationals and shall serve in their personal capacity, consideration being given to equitable geographical distribution, as well as to the principal legal systems.

3.   The members of the Committee shall be elected by secret ballot from a list of persons nominated by States Parties. Each State Party may nominate one person from among its own nationals.

4.   The initial election to the Committee shall be held no later than six months after the date of the entry into force of the present Convention and thereafter every second year. At least four months before the date of each election, the Secretary-General of the United Nations shall address a letter to States Parties inviting them to submit their nominations within two months. The Secretary-General shall subsequently prepare a list in alphabetical order of all persons thus nominated, indicating States Parties which have nominated them, and shall submit it to the States Parties to the present Convention.

5.   The elections shall be held at meetings of States Parties convened by the Secretary-General at United Nations Headquarters. At those meetings, for which two thirds of States Parties shall constitute a quorum, the persons elected to the Committee shall be those who obtain the largest number of votes and an absolute majority of the votes of the representatives of States Parties present and voting.

6.   The members of the Committee shall be elected for a term of four years. They shall be eligible for re-election if renominated. The term of five of the members elected at the first election shall expire at the end of two years; immediately after the first election, the names of these five members shall be chosen by lot by the Chairman of the meeting.

7.   If a member of the Committee dies or resigns or declares that for any other cause he or she can no longer perform the duties of the Committee, the State Party which nominated the member shall appoint another expert from among its nationals to serve for the remainder of the term, subject to the approval of the Committee.

8.   The Committee shall establish its own rules of procedure.

9.   The Committee shall elect its officers for a period of two years.

10. The meetings of the Committee shall normally be held at United Nations Headquarters or at any other convenient place as determined by the Committee. The Committee shall normally meet annually. The duration of the meetings of the Committee shall be determined, and reviewed, if necessary, by a meeting of the States Parties to the present Convention, subject to the approval of the General Assembly.

11. The Secretary-General of the United Nations shall provide the necessary staff and facilities for the effective performance of the functions of the Committee under the present Convention.

12. With the approval of the General Assembly, the members of the Committee established under the present Convention shall receive

emoluments from United Nations resources on such terms and conditions as the Assembly may decide.

Article 44

1.   States Parties undertake to submit to the Committee, through the Secretary-General of the United Nations, reports on the measures they have adopted which give effect to the rights recognized herein and on the progress made on the enjoyment of those rights

(a) Within two years of the entry into force of the Convention for the State Party concerned;

(b) Thereafter every five years.

2.   Reports made under the present article shall indicate factors and difficulties, if any, affecting the degree of fulfilment of the obligations under the present Convention. Reports shall also contain sufficient information to provide the Committee with a comprehensive understanding of the implementation of the Convention in the country concerned.

3.   A State Party which has submitted a comprehensive initial report to the Committee need not, in its subsequent reports submitted in accordance with paragraph 1 (b) of the present article, repeat basic information previously provided.

4.   The Committee may request from States Parties further information relevant to the implementation of the Convention.

5.   The Committee shall submit to the General Assembly, through the Economic and Social Council, every two years, reports on its activities.

6.   States Parties shall make their reports widely available to the public in their own countries.

Article 45

In order to foster the effective implementation of the Convention and to encourage international co-operation in the field covered by the Convention:

(a) The specialized agencies, the United Nations Children's Fund, and other United Nations organs shall be entitled to be represented at the consideration of the implementation of such provisions of the present Convention as fall within the scope of their mandate. The Committee may invite the specialized agencies, the United Nations Children's Fund and other competent bodies as it may consider appropriate to provide expert advice on the implementation of the Convention in areas falling within the scope of their respective mandates. The

Committee may invite the specialized agencies, the United Nations Children's Fund, and other United Nations organs to submit reports on the implementation of the Convention in areas falling within the scope of their activities;

(b) The Committee shall transmit, as it may consider appropriate, to the specialized agencies, the United Nations Children's Fund and other competent bodies, any reports from States Parties that contain a request, or indicate a need, for technical advice or assistance, along with the Committee's observations and suggestions, if any, on these requests or indications;

(c) The Committee may recommend to the General Assembly to request the Secretary-General to undertake on its behalf studies on specific issues relating to the rights of the child;

(d) The Committee may make suggestions and general recommendations based on information received pursuant to articles 44 and 45 of the present Convention. Such suggestions and general recommendations shall be transmitted to any State Party concerned and reported to the General Assembly, together with comments, if any, from States Parties.

PART III

Article 46

The present Convention shall be open for signature by all States.

Article 47

The present Convention is subject to ratification. Instruments of ratification shall be deposited with the Secretary-General of the United Nations.

Article 48

The present Convention shall remain open for accession by any State. The instruments of accession shall be deposited with the Secretary-General of the United Nations.

Article 49

1. The present Convention shall enter into force on the thirtieth day following the date of deposit with the Secretary-General of the United Nations of the twentieth instrument of ratification or accession.

2. For each State ratifying or acceding to the Convention after the deposit of the twentieth instrument of ratification or accession, the Convention shall enter into force on the thirtieth day after the deposit by such State of its instrument of ratification or accession.

Article 50

1.   Any State Party may propose an amendment and file it with the Secretary-General of the United Nations. The Secretary-General shall thereupon communicate the proposed amendment to States Parties, with a request that they indicate whether they favour a conference of States Parties for the purpose of considering and voting upon the proposals. In the event that, within four months from the date of such communication, at least one third of the States Parties favour such a conference, the Secretary-General shall convene the conference under the auspices of the United Nations. Any amendment adopted by a majority of States Parties present and voting at the conference shall be submitted to the General Assembly for approval.

2.   An amendment adopted in accordance with paragraph 1 of the present article shall enter into force when it has been approved by the General Assembly of the United Nations and accepted by a two-thirds majority of States Parties.

3.   When an amendment enters into force, it shall be binding on those States Parties which have accepted it, other States Parties still being bound by the provisions of the present Convention and any earlier amendments which they have accepted.

Article 51

1.   The Secretary-General of the United Nations shall receive and circulate to all States the text of reservations made by States at the time of ratification or accession.

2.   A reservation incompatible with the object and purpose of the present Convention shall not be permitted.

3.   Reservations may be withdrawn at any time by notification to that effect addressed to the Secretary-General of the United Nations, who shall then inform all States. Such notification shall take effect on the date on which it is received by the Secretary-General

Article 52

A State Party may denounce the present Convention by written notification to the Secretary-General of the United Nations. Denunciation becomes effective one year after the date of receipt of the notification by the Secretary-General.

Article 53

The Secretary-General of the United Nations is designated as the depositary of the present Convention.

Article 54

The original of the present Convention, of which the Arabic, Chinese, English, French, Russian and Spanish texts are equally authentic, shall be deposited with the Secretary-General of the United Nations. In witness thereof the undersigned plenipotentiaries, being duly authorized thereto by their respective Governments, have signed the present Convention.

***

OPTIONAL PROTOCOL TO THE CONVENTION ON THE RIGHTS OF THE CHILD ON THE INVOLVEMENT OF CHILDREN IN ARMED CONFLICT

Adopted and opened for signature, ratification and accession by
General Assembly resolution A/RES/54/263 of 25 May 2000
entry into force 12 February 2002 in accordance with Article 10

The States Parties to the present Protocol,

Encouraged by the overwhelming support for the Convention on the Rights of the Child, demonstrating the widespread commitment that exists to strive for the promotion and protection of the rights of the child,

Reaffirming that the rights of children require special protection, and calling for continuous improvement of the situation of children without distinction, as well as for their development and education in conditions of peace and security,

Disturbed by the harmful and widespread impact of armed conflict on children and the long-term consequences this has for durable peace, security and development,

Condemning the targeting of children in situations of armed conflict and direct attacks on objects protected under international law, including places generally having a significant presence of children, such as schools and hospitals,

Noting the adoption of the Statute of the International Criminal Court, and, in particular, its inclusion as a war crime of conscripting or enlisting children under the age of 15 years or using them to participate actively in hostilities in both international and non-international armed conflicts,

Considering, therefore, that to strengthen further the implementation of rights recognized in the Convention on the Rights of the Child there is a need to increase the protection of children from involvement in armed conflict,

Noting that article 1 of the Convention on the Rights of the Child specifies that, for the purposes of that Convention, a child means every human being below the age of 18 years unless, under the law applicable to the child, majority is attained earlier,

Convinced that an optional protocol to the Convention raising the age of possible recruitment of persons into armed forces and their participation in hostilities will contribute effectively to the implementation of the principle that the best interests of the child are to be a primary consideration in all actions concerning children,

Noting that the twenty-sixth international Conference of the Red Cross and Red Crescent in December 1995 recommended, inter alia, that parties to conflict take every feasible step to ensure that children under the age of 18 years do not take part in hostilities,

Welcoming the unanimous adoption, in June 1999, of International Labour Organization Convention No. 182 on the Prohibition and Immediate Action for the Elimination of the Worst Forms of Child Labour, which prohibits, inter alia, forced or compulsory recruitment of children for use in armed conflict,

Condemning with the gravest concern the recruitment, training and use within and across national borders of children in hostilities by armed groups distinct from the armed forces of a State, and recognizing the responsibility of those who recruit, train and use children in this regard,

Recalling the obligation of each party to an armed conflict to abide by the provisions of international humanitarian law,

Stressing that this Protocol is without prejudice to the purposes and principles contained in the Charter of the United Nations, including Article 51, and relevant norms of humanitarian law,

Bearing in mind that conditions of peace and security based on full respect of the purposes and principles contained in the Charter and observance of applicable human rights instruments are indispensable for the full protection of children, in particular during armed conflicts and foreign occupation,

Recognizing the special needs of those children who are particularly vulnerable to recruitment or use in hostilities contrary to this Protocol owing to their economic or social status or gender,

Mindful of the necessity of taking into consideration the economic, social and political root causes of the involvement of children in armed conflicts,

Convinced of the need to strengthen international cooperation in the implementation of this Protocol, as well as the physical and psychosocial rehabilitation and social reintegration of children who are victims of armed conflict,

Encouraging the participation of the community and, in particular, children and child victims in the dissemination of informational and educational programmes concerning the implementation of the Protocol,

Have agreed as follows:

Article 1

States Parties shall take all feasible measures to ensure that members of their armed forces who have not attained the age of 18 years do not take a direct part in hostilities.

Article 2

States Parties shall ensure that persons who have not attained the age of 18 years are not compulsorily recruited into their armed forces.

Article 3

1.   States Parties shall raise the minimum age for the voluntary recruitment of persons into their national armed forces from that set out in article 38, paragraph 3, of the Convention on the Rights of the Child, taking account of the principles contained in that article and recognizing that under the Convention persons under 18 are entitled to special protection.

2.   Each State Party shall deposit a binding declaration upon ratification of or accession to this Protocol that sets forth the minimum age at which it will permit voluntary recruitment into its national armed forces and a description of the safeguards that it has adopted to ensure that such recruitment is not forced or coerced.

3.   States Parties that permit voluntary recruitment into their national armed forces under the age of 18 shall maintain safeguards to ensure, as a minimum, that:

   a.   Such recruitment is genuinely voluntary;

   b.   Such recruitment is done with the informed consent of the person's parents or legal guardians;

   c.   Such persons are fully informed of the duties involved in such military service;

   d.   Such persons provide reliable proof of age prior to acceptance into national military service.

4.   Each State Party may strengthen its declaration at any time by notification to that effect addressed to the Secretary-General of the United Nations, who shall inform all States Parties. Such notification shall take effect on the date on which it is received by the Secretary-General.

5. The requirement to raise the age in paragraph 1 of the present article does not apply to schools operated by or under the control of the armed forces of the States Parties, in keeping with articles 28 and 29 of the Convention on the Rights of the Child.

Article 4

1. Armed groups that are distinct from the armed forces of a State should not, under any circumstances, recruit or use in hostilities persons under the age of 18 years.

2. States Parties shall take all feasible measures to prevent such recruitment and use, including the adoption of legal measures necessary to prohibit and criminalize such practices.

3. The application of the present article under this Protocol shall not affect the legal status of any party to an armed conflict.

Article 5

Nothing in the present Protocol shall be construed as precluding provisions in the law of a State Party or in international instruments and international humanitarian law that are more conducive to the realization of the rights of the child.

Article 6

1. Each State Party shall take all necessary legal, administrative and other measures to ensure the effective implementation and enforcement of the provisions of this Protocol within its jurisdiction.

2. States Parties undertake to make the principles and provisions of the present Protocol widely known and promoted by appropriate means, to adults and children alike.

3. States Parties shall take all feasible measures to ensure that persons within their jurisdiction recruited or used in hostilities contrary to this Protocol are demobilized or otherwise released from service. States Parties shall, when necessary, accord to these persons all appropriate assistance for their physical and psychological recovery and their social reintegration.

Article 7

1. States Parties shall cooperate in the implementation of the present Protocol, including in the prevention of any activity contrary to the Protocol and in the rehabilitation and social reintegration of persons who are victims of acts contrary to this Protocol, including through technical cooperation and financial assistance. Such assistance and cooperation will be undertaken in consultation with concerned States Parties and relevant international organizations.

2.   States Parties in a position to do so shall provide such assistance through existing multilateral, bilateral or other programmes, or, inter alia, through a voluntary fund established in accordance with the rules of the General Assembly.

Article 8

1.   Each State Party shall submit, within two years following the entry into force of the Protocol for that State Party, a report to the Committee on the Rights of the Child providing comprehensive information on the measures it has taken to implement the provisions of the Protocol, including the measures taken to implement the provisions on participation and recruitment.

2.   Following the submission of the comprehensive report, each State Party shall include in the reports they submit to the Committee on the Rights of the Child, in accordance with article 44 of the Convention, any further information with respect to the implementation of the Protocol. Other States Parties to the Protocol shall submit a report every five years.

3.   The Committee on the Rights of the Child may request from States Parties further information relevant to the implementation of this Protocol.

Article 9

1.   The present Protocol is open for signature by any State that is a party to the Convention or has signed it.

2.   The present Protocol is subject to ratification and is open to accession by any State. Instruments of ratification or accession shall be deposited with the Secretary-General of the United Nations.

3.   The Secretary-General, in his capacity as depositary of the Convention and the Protocol, shall inform all States Parties to the Convention and all States that have signed the Convention of each instrument of declaration pursuant to article 13.

Article 10

1.   The present Protocol shall enter into force three months after the deposit of the tenth instrument of ratification or accession.

2.   For each State ratifying the present Protocol or acceding to it after its entry into force, the present Protocol shall enter into force one month after the date of the deposit of its own instrument of ratification or accession.

Article 11

1.   Any State Party may denounce the present Protocol at any time by written notification to the Secretary-General of the United Nations,

who shall thereafter inform the other States Parties to the Convention and all States that have signed the Convention. The denunciation shall take effect one year after the date of receipt of the notification by the Secretary-General. If, however, on the expiry of that year the denouncing State Party is engaged in armed conflict, the denunciation shall not take effect before the end of the armed conflict.

2. Such a denunciation shall not have the effect of releasing the State Party from its obligations under the present Protocol in regard to any act that occurs prior to the date on which the denunciation becomes effective. Nor shall such a denunciation prejudice in any way the continued consideration of any matter that is already under consideration by the Committee prior to the date on which the denunciation becomes effective.

Article 12

1. Any State Party may propose an amendment and file it with the Secretary-General of the United Nations. The Secretary-General shall thereupon communicate the proposed amendment to States Parties, with a request that they indicate whether they favour a conference of States Parties for the purpose of considering and voting upon the proposals. In the event that, within four months from the date of such communication, at least one third of the States Parties favour such a conference, the Secretary-General shall convene the conference under the auspices of the United Nations. Any amendment adopted by a majority of States Parties present and voting at the conference shall be submitted to the General Assembly for approval.

2. An amendment adopted in accordance with paragraph 1 of the present article shall enter into force when it has been approved by the General Assembly of the United Nations and accepted by a two-thirds majority of States Parties.

3. When an amendment enters into force, it shall be binding on those States Parties that have accepted it, other States Parties still being bound by the provisions of the present Protocol and any earlier amendments that they have accepted.

Article 13

1. The present Protocol, of which the Arabic, Chinese, English, French, Russian and Spanish texts are equally authentic, shall be deposited in the archives of the United Nations.

2. The Secretary-General of the United Nations shall transmit certified copies of the present Protocol to all States Parties to the Convention and all States that have signed the Convention

OPTIONAL PROTOCOL TO THE CONVENTION ON THE RIGHTS OF THE CHILD ON THE SALE OF CHILDREN, CHILD PROSTITUTION AND CHILD PORNOGRAPHY

Adopted and opened for signature, ratification and accession by
General Assembly resolution A/RES/54/263 of 25 May 2000
entry into force on 18 January 2002 in accordance with Article 14

The States Parties to the present Protocol,

Considering that, in order further to achieve the purposes of the Convention on the Rights of the Child and the implementation of its provisions, especially articles 1, 11, 21, 32, 33, 34, 35 and 36, it would be appropriate to extend the measures that States Parties should undertake in order to guarantee the protection of the child from the sale of children, child prostitution and child pornography,

Considering also that the Convention on the Rights of the Child recognizes the right of the child to be protected from economic exploitation and from performing any work that is likely to be hazardous or to interfere with the child's education, or to be harmful to the child's health or physical, mental, spiritual, moral or social development,

Gravely concerned at the significant and increasing international traffic of children for the purpose of the sale of children, child prostitution and child pornography,

Deeply concerned at the widespread and continuing practice of sex tourism, to which children are especially vulnerable, as it directly promotes the sale of children, child prostitution and child pornography,

Recognizing that a number of particularly vulnerable groups, including girl children, are at greater risk of sexual exploitation, and that girl children are disproportionately represented among the sexually exploited,

Concerned about the growing availability of child pornography on the Internet and other evolving technologies, and recalling the International Conference on Combating Child Pornography on the Internet (Vienna, 1999) and, in particular, its conclusion calling for the worldwide criminalization of the production, distribution, exportation, transmission, importation, intentional possession and advertising of child pornography, and stressing the importance of closer cooperation and partnership between Governments and the Internet industry,

Believing that the elimination of the sale of children, child prostitution and child pornography will be facilitated by adopting a holistic approach, addressing the contributing factors, including underdevelopment, poverty, economic disparities, inequitable socio-economic structure, dysfunctioning families, lack of education, urban-rural migration, gender discrimination, irresponsible adult sexual behaviour, harmful traditional practices, armed conflicts and trafficking of children,

Believing that efforts to raise public awareness are needed to reduce consumer demand for the sale of children, child prostitution and child pornography, and also believing in the importance of strengthening global partnership among all actors and of improving law enforcement at the national level,

Noting the provisions of international legal instruments relevant to the protection of children, including the Hague Convention on the Protection of Children and Cooperation with Respect to Inter-Country Adoption, the Hague Convention on the Civil Aspects of International Child Abduction, the Hague Convention on Jurisdiction, Applicable Law, Recognition, Enforcement and Cooperation in Respect of Parental Responsibility and Measures for the Protection of Children, and International Labour Organization Convention No. 182 on the Prohibition and Immediate Action for the Elimination of the Worst Forms of Child Labour,

Encouraged by the overwhelming support for the Convention on the Rights of the Child, demonstrating the widespread commitment that exists for the promotion and protection of the rights of the child,

Recognizing the importance of the implementation of the provisions of the Programme of Action for the Prevention of the Sale of Children, Child Prostitution and Child Pornography/3 and the Declaration and Agenda for Action adopted at the World Congress against Commercial Sexual Exploitation of Children, held at Stockholm from 27 to 31 August 1996,/4 and the other relevant decisions and recommendations of pertinent international bodies,

Taking due account of the importance of the traditions and cultural values of each people for the protection and harmonious development of the child,

Have agreed as follows:

Article 1

States Parties shall prohibit the sale of children, child prostitution and child pornography as provided for by the present Protocol.

Article 2

For the purpose of the present Protocol:

a.   Sale of children means any act or transaction whereby a child is transferred by any person or group of persons to another for remuneration or any other consideration;

b. Child prostitution means the use of a child in sexual activities for remuneration or any other form of consideration;

c. Child pornography means any representation, by whatever means, of a child engaged in real or simulated explicit sexual activities or any representation of the sexual parts of a child for primarily sexual purposes.

Article 3

1. Each State Party shall ensure that, as a minimum, the following acts and activities are fully covered under its criminal or penal law, whether these offences are committed domestically or transnationally or on an individual or organized basis:

a. In the context of sale of children as defined in article 2:

i. The offering, delivering or accepting, by whatever means, a child for the purpose of:

a. Sexual exploitation of the child;

b. Transfer of organs of the child for profit;

c. Engagement of the child in forced labour;

ii. Improperly inducing consent, as an intermediary, for the adoption of a child in violation of applicable international legal instruments on adoption;

b. Offering, obtaining, procuring or providing a child for child prostitution, as defined in article 2;

c. Producing, distributing, disseminating, importing, exporting, offering, selling or possessing for the above purposes child pornography as defined in article 2.

2. Subject to the provisions of a State Party's national law, the same shall apply to an attempt to commit any of these acts and to complicity or participation in any of these acts.

3. Each State Party shall make these offences punishable by appropriate penalties that take into account their grave nature.

4. Subject to the provisions of its national law, each State Party shall take measures, where appropriate, to establish the liability of legal persons for offences established in paragraph 1 of the present article. Subject to the legal principles of the State Party, this liability of legal persons may be criminal, civil or administrative.

5. States Parties shall take all appropriate legal and administrative measures to ensure that all persons involved in the adoption of a child act in conformity with applicable international legal instruments.

Article 4

1.   Each State Party shall take such measures as may be necessary to establish its jurisdiction over the offences referred to in article 3, paragraph 1, when the offences are committed in its territory or on board a ship or aircraft registered in that State.

2.   Each State Party may take such measures as may be necessary to establish its jurisdiction over the offences referred to in article 3, paragraph 1, in the following cases:

   a.   When the alleged offender is a national of that State or a person who has his habitual residence in its territory;

   b.   When the victim is a national of that State.

3.   Each State Party shall also take such measures as may be necessary to establish its jurisdiction over the above-mentioned offences when the alleged offender is present in its territory and it does not extradite him or her to another State Party on the ground that the offence has been committed by one of its nationals.

4.   This Protocol does not exclude any criminal jurisdiction exercised in accordance with internal law.

Article 5

1.   The offences referred to in article 3, paragraph 1, shall be deemed to be included as extraditable offences in any extradition treaty existing between States Parties and shall be included as extraditable offences in every extradition treaty subsequently concluded between them, in accordance with the conditions set forth in those treaties.

2.   If a State Party that makes extradition conditional on the existence of a treaty receives a request for extradition from another State Party with which it has no extradition treaty, it may consider this Protocol as a legal basis for extradition in respect of such offences. Extradition shall be subject to the conditions provided by the law of the requested State.

3.   States Parties that do not make extradition conditional on the existence of a treaty shall recognize such offences as extraditable offences between themselves subject to the conditions provided by the law of the requested State.

4.   Such offences shall be treated, for the purpose of extradition between States Parties, as if they had been committed not only in the place in which they occurred but also in the territories of the States required to establish their jurisdiction in accordance with article 4.

5.   If an extradition request is made with respect to an offence described in article 3, paragraph 1, and if the requested State Party does

not or will not extradite on the basis of the nationality of the offender, that State shall take suitable measures to submit the case to its competent authorities for the purpose of prosecution.

Article 6

1.   States Parties shall afford one another the greatest measure of assistance in connection with investigations or criminal or extradition proceedings brought in respect of the offences set forth in article 3, paragraph 1, including assistance in obtaining evidence at their disposal necessary for the proceedings.

2.   States Parties shall carry out their obligations under paragraph 1 of the present article in conformity with any treaties or other arrangements on mutual legal assistance that may exist between them. In the absence of such treaties or arrangements, States Parties shall afford one another assistance in accordance with their domestic law.

Article 7

States Parties shall, subject to the provisions of their national law:

a.   Take measures to provide for the seizure and confiscation, as appropriate, of:

i.   Goods such as materials, assets and other instrumentalities used to commit or facilitate offences under the present protocol;

ii.   Proceeds derived from such offences;

b.   Execute requests from another State Party for seizure or confiscation of goods or proceeds referred to in subparagraph (a) (i);

c.   Take measures aimed at closing, on a temporary or definitive basis, premises used to commit such offences.

Article 8

1.   States Parties shall adopt appropriate measures to protect the rights and interests of child victims of the practices prohibited under the present Protocol at all stages of the criminal justice process, in particular by:

a.   Recognizing the vulnerability of child victims and adapting procedures to recognize their special needs, including their special needs as witnesses;

b.   Informing child victims of their rights, their role and the scope, timing and progress of the proceedings and of the disposition of their cases;

c. Allowing the views, needs and concerns of child victims to be presented and considered in proceedings where their personal interests are affected, in a manner consistent with the procedural rules of national law;

d. Providing appropriate support services to child victims throughout the legal process;

e. Protecting, as appropriate, the privacy and identity of child victims and taking measures in accordance with national law to avoid the inappropriate dissemination of information that could lead to the identification of child victims;

f. Providing, in appropriate cases, for the safety of child victims, as well as that of their families and witnesses on their behalf, from intimidation and retaliation;

g. Avoiding unnecessary delay in the disposition of cases and the execution of orders or decrees granting compensation to child victims.

2. States Parties shall ensure that uncertainty as to the actual age of the victim shall not prevent the initiation of criminal investigations, including investigations aimed at establishing the age of the victim.

3. States Parties shall ensure that, in the treatment by the criminal justice system of children who are victims of the offences described in the present Protocol, the best interest of the child shall be a primary consideration.

4. States Parties shall take measures to ensure appropriate training, in particular legal and psychological training, for the persons who work with victims of the offences prohibited under the present Protocol.

5. States Parties shall, in appropriate cases, adopt measures in order to protect the safety and integrity of those persons and/or organizations involved in the prevention and/or protection and rehabilitation of victims of such offences.

6. Nothing in the present article shall be construed as prejudicial to or inconsistent with the rights of the accused to a fair and impartial trial.

Article 9

1. States Parties shall adopt or strengthen, implement and disseminate laws, administrative measures, social policies and programmes to prevent the offences referred to in the present Protocol. Particular attention shall be given to protect children who are especially vulnerable to these practices.

2. States Parties shall promote awareness in the public at large, including children, through information by all appropriate means, education and training, about the preventive measures and harmful effects of the offences referred to in the present Protocol. In fulfilling their obligations under this article, States Parties shall encourage the participation of the community and, in particular, children and child victims, in such information and education and training programmes, including at the international level.

3. States Parties shall take all feasible measures with the aim of ensuring all appropriate assistance to victims of such offences, including their full social reintegration and their full physical and psychological recovery.

4. States Parties shall ensure that all child victims of the offences described in the present Protocol have access to adequate procedures to seek, without discrimination, compensation for damages from those legally responsible.

5. States Parties shall take appropriate measures aimed at effectively prohibiting the production and dissemination of material advertising the offences described in the present Protocol.

Article 10

1. States Parties shall take all necessary steps to strengthen international cooperation by multilateral, regional and bilateral arrangements for the prevention, detection, investigation, prosecution and punishment of those responsible for acts involving the sale of children, child prostitution, child pornography and child sex tourism. States Parties shall also promote international cooperation and coordination between their authorities, national and international non-governmental organizations and international organizations.

2. States Parties shall promote international cooperation to assist child victims in their physical and psychological recovery, social reintegration and repatriation.

3. States Parties shall promote the strengthening of international cooperation in order to address the root causes, such as poverty and underdevelopment, contributing to the vulnerability of children to the sale of children, child prostitution, child pornography and child sex tourism.

4. States Parties in a position to do so shall provide financial, technical or other assistance through existing multilateral, regional, bilateral or other programmes.

Article 11

Nothing in the present Protocol shall affect any provisions that are more conducive to the realization of the rights of the child and that may be contained in:

a.   The law of a State Party;

b.   International law in force for that State.

Article 12

1.   Each State Party shall submit, within two years following the entry into force of the Protocol for that State Party, a report to the Committee on the Rights of the Child providing comprehensive information on the measures it has taken to implement the provisions of the Protocol.

2.   Following the submission of the comprehensive report, each State Party shall include in the reports they submit to the Committee on the Rights of the Child, in accordance with article 44 of the Convention, any further information with respect to the implementation of the Protocol. Other States Parties to the Protocol shall submit a report every five years.

3.   The Committee on the Rights of the Child may request from States Parties further information relevant to the implementation of this Protocol.

Article 13

1.   The present Protocol is open for signature by any State that is a party to the Convention or has signed it.

2.   The present Protocol is subject to ratification and is open to accession by any State that is a party to the Convention or has signed it. Instruments of ratification or accession shall be deposited with the Secretary-General of the United Nations.

Article 14

1.   The present Protocol shall enter into force three months after the deposit of the tenth instrument of ratification or accession.

2.   For each State ratifying the present Protocol or acceding to it after its entry into force, the present Protocol shall enter into force one month after the date of the deposit of its own instrument of ratification or accession.

Article 15

1.   Any State Party may denounce the present Protocol at any time by written notification to the Secretary-General of the United Nations, who shall thereafter inform the other States Parties to the Convention

and all States that have signed the Convention. The denunciation shall take effect one year after the date of receipt of the notification by the Secretary-General of the United Nations.

2.   Such a denunciation shall not have the effect of releasing the State Party from its obligations under this Protocol in regard to any offence that occurs prior to the date on which the denunciation becomes effective. Nor shall such a denunciation prejudice in any way the continued consideration of any matter that is already under consideration by the Committee prior to the date on which the denunciation becomes effective.

Article 16

1.   Any State Party may propose an amendment and file it with the Secretary-General of the United Nations. The Secretary-General shall thereupon communicate the proposed amendment to States Parties, with a request that they indicate whether they favour a conference of States Parties for the purpose of considering and voting upon the proposals. In the event that, within four months from the date of such communication, at least one third of the States Parties favour such a conference, the Secretary-General shall convene the conference under the auspices of the United Nations. Any amendment adopted by a majority of States Parties present and voting at the conference shall be submitted to the General Assembly for approval.

2.   An amendment adopted in accordance with paragraph 1 of the present article shall enter into force when it has been approved by the General Assembly of the United Nations and accepted by a two-thirds majority of States Parties.

3.   When an amendment enters into force, it shall be binding on those States Parties that have accepted it, other States Parties still being bound by the provisions of the present Protocol and any earlier amendments that they have accepted.

Article 17

1.   The present Protocol, of which the Arabic, Chinese, English, French, Russian and Spanish texts are equally authentic, shall be deposited in the archives of the United Nations.

2.   The Secretary-General of the United Nations shall transmit certified copies of the present Protocol to all States Parties to the Convention and all States that have signed the Convention.

CONVENTION ON THE RIGHTS OF PERSONS WITH DISABILITIES

Adopted by United Nations General Assembly Resolution 61/106
of 13 December 2006, opened for signature on 30 March 2007
entry into force on 3 May 2008 in accordance with Article 45

Preamble

The States Parties to the present Convention,

a.   *Recalling* the principles proclaimed in the Charter of the United Nations which recognize the inherent dignity and worth and the equal and inalienable rights of all members of the human family as the foundation of freedom, justice and peace in the world,

b.   *Recognizing* that the United Nations, in the Universal Declaration of Human Rights and in the International Covenants on Human Rights, has proclaimed and agreed that everyone is entitled to all the rights and freedoms set forth therein, without distinction of any kind,

c.   *Reaffirming* the universality, indivisibility, interdependence and interrelatedness of all human rights and fundamental freedoms and the need for persons with disabilities to be guaranteed their full enjoyment without discrimination,

d.   *Recalling* the International Covenant on Economic, Social and Cultural Rights, the International Covenant on Civil and Political Rights, the International Convention on the Elimination of All Forms of Racial Discrimination, the Convention on the Elimination of All Forms of Discrimination against Women, the Convention against Torture and Other Cruel, Inhuman or Degrading Treatment or Punishment, the Convention on the Rights of the Child, and the International Convention on the Protection of the Rights of All Migrant Workers and Members of Their Families,

e.   *Recognizing* that disability is an evolving concept and that disability results from the interaction between persons with impairments and attitudinal and environmental barriers that hinders their full and effective participation in society on an equal basis with others,

f.   *Recognizing* the importance of the principles and policy guidelines contained in the World Programme of Action concerning Disabled Persons and in the Standard Rules on the Equalization of Opportunities for Persons with Disabilities in influencing the promotion, formulation and evaluation of the policies, plans, programmes and actions at the national, regional and international levels to further equalize opportunities for persons with disabilities,

g.   *Emphasizing* the importance of mainstreaming disability issues as an integral part of relevant strategies of sustainable development,

h. *Recognizing* also that discrimination against any person on the basis of disability is a violation of the inherent dignity and worth of the human person,

i. *Recognizing* further the diversity of persons with disabilities,

j. *Recognizing* the need to promote and protect the human rights of all persons with disabilities, including those who require more intensive support,

k. *Concerned* that, despite these various instruments and undertakings, persons with disabilities continue to face barriers in their participation as equal members of society and violations of their human rights in all parts of the world,

l. *Recognizing* the importance of international cooperation for improving the living conditions of persons with disabilities in every country, particularly in developing countries,

m. *Recognizing* the valued existing and potential contributions made by persons with disabilities to the overall well-being and diversity of their communities, and that the promotion of the full enjoyment by persons with disabilities of their human rights and fundamental freedoms and of full participation by persons with disabilities will result in their enhanced sense of belonging and in significant advances in the human, social and economic development of society and the eradication of poverty,

n. *Recognizing* the importance for persons with disabilities of their individual autonomy and independence, including the freedom to make their own choices,

o. *Considering* that persons with disabilities should have the opportunity to be actively involved in decision-making processes about policies and programmes, including those directly concerning them,

p. *Concerned* about the difficult conditions faced by persons with disabilities who are subject to multiple or aggravated forms of discrimination on the basis of race, colour, sex, language, religion, political or other opinion, national, ethnic, indigenous or social origin, property, birth, age or other status,

q. *Recognizing* that women and girls with disabilities are often at greater risk, both within and outside the home of violence, injury or abuse, neglect or negligent treatment, maltreatment or exploitation,

r. *Recognizing* that children with disabilities should have full enjoyment of all human rights and fundamental freedoms on an equal basis with other children, and recalling obligations to that end undertaken by States Parties to the Convention on the Rights of the Child,

s. *Emphasizing* the need to incorporate a gender perspective in all efforts to promote the full enjoyment of human rights and fundamental freedoms by persons with disabilities,

t. *Highlighting* the fact that the majority of persons with disabilities live in conditions of poverty, and in this regard recognizing the critical need to address the negative impact of poverty on persons with disabilities,

u. *Bearing* in mind that conditions of peace and security based on full respect for the purposes and principles contained in the Charter of the United Nations and observance of applicable human rights instruments are indispensable for the full protection of persons with disabilities, in particular during armed conflicts and foreign occupation,

v. *Recognizing* the importance of accessibility to the physical, social, economic and cultural environment, to health and education and to information and communication, in enabling persons with disabilities to fully enjoy all human rights and fundamental freedoms,

w. *Realizing* that the individual, having duties to other individuals and to the community to which he or she belongs, is under a responsibility to strive for the promotion and observance of the rights recognized in the International Bill of Human Rights,

x. *Convinced* that the family is the natural and fundamental group unit of society and is entitled to protection by society and the State, and that persons with disabilities and their family members should receive the necessary protection and assistance to enable families to contribute towards the full and equal enjoyment of the rights of persons with disabilities,

y. *Convinced* that a comprehensive and integral international convention to promote and protect the rights and dignity of persons with disabilities will make a significant contribution to redressing the profound social disadvantage of persons with disabilities and promote their participation in the civil, political, economic, social and cultural spheres with equal opportunities, in both developing and developed countries,

Have agreed as follows:

Article 1—Purpose

The purpose of the present Convention is to promote, protect and ensure the full and equal enjoyment of all human rights and fundamental freedoms by all persons with disabilities, and to promote respect for their inherent dignity.

Persons with disabilities include those who have long-term physical, mental, intellectual or sensory impairments which in interaction with various barriers may hinder their full and effective participation in society on an equal basis with others.

Article 2—Definitions

For the purposes of the present Convention:

"Communication" includes languages, display of text, Braille, tactile communication, large print, accessible multimedia as well as written, audio, plain-language, human-reader and augmentative and alternative modes, means and formats of communication, including accessible information and communication technology;

"Language" includes spoken and signed languages and other forms of non spoken languages;

"Discrimination on the basis of disability" means any distinction, exclusion or restriction on the basis of disability which has the purpose or effect of impairing or nullifying the recognition, enjoyment or exercise, on an equal basis with others, of all human rights and fundamental freedoms in the political, economic, social, cultural, civil or any other field. It includes all forms of discrimination, including denial of reasonable accommodation;

"Reasonable accommodation" means necessary and appropriate modification and adjustments not imposing a disproportionate or undue burden, where needed in a particular case, to ensure to persons with disabilities the enjoyment or exercise on an equal basis with others of all human rights and fundamental freedoms;

"Universal design" means the design of products, environments, programmes and services to be usable by all people, to the greatest extent possible, without the need for adaptation or specialized design. "Universal design" shall not exclude assistive devices for particular groups of persons with disabilities where this is needed.

Article 3—General principles

The principles of the present Convention shall be:

a.   Respect for inherent dignity, individual autonomy including the freedom to make one's own choices, and independence of persons;

b.   Non-discrimination;

c.   Full and effective participation and inclusion in society;

d.   Respect for difference and acceptance of persons with disabilities as part of human diversity and humanity;

e.   Equality of opportunity;

f.   Accessibility;

g.   Equality between men and women;

h.   Respect for the evolving capacities of children with disabilities and respect for the right of children with disabilities to preserve their identities.

Article 4—General obligations

1.   States Parties undertake to ensure and promote the full realization of all human rights and fundamental freedoms for all persons with disabilities without discrimination of any kind on the basis of disability. To this end, States Parties undertake:

a.   To adopt all appropriate legislative, administrative and other measures for the implementation of the rights recognized in the present Convention;

b.   To take all appropriate measures, including legislation, to modify or abolish existing laws, regulations, customs and practices that constitute discrimination against persons with disabilities;

c.   To take into account the protection and promotion of the human rights of persons with disabilities in all policies and programmes;

d.   To refrain from engaging in any act or practice that is inconsistent with the present Convention and to ensure that public authorities and institutions act in conformity with the present Convention;

e.   To take all appropriate measures to eliminate discrimination on the basis of disability by any person, organization or private enterprise;

f.   To undertake or promote research and development of universally designed goods, services, equipment and facilities, as defined in article 2 of the present Convention, which should require the minimum possible adaptation and the least cost to meet the specific needs of a person with disabilities, to promote their availability and use, and to promote universal design in the development of standards and guidelines;

g.   To undertake or promote research and development of, and to promote the availability and use of new technologies, including information and communications technologies, mobility aids, devices and assistive technologies, suitable for persons with disabilities, giving priority to technologies at an affordable cost;

h.   To provide accessible information to persons with disabilities about mobility aids, devices and assistive technologies, including new technologies, as well as other forms of assistance, support services and facilities;

    i.   To promote the training of professionals and staff working with persons with disabilities in the rights recognized in this Convention so as to better provide the assistance and services guaranteed by those rights.

    2.   With regard to economic, social and cultural rights, each State Party undertakes to take measures to the maximum of its available resources and, where needed, within the framework of international cooperation, with a view to achieving progressively the full realization of these rights, without prejudice to those obligations contained in the present Convention that are immediately applicable according to international law.

    3.   In the development and implementation of legislation and policies to implement the present Convention, and in other decision-making processes concerning issues relating to persons with disabilities, States Parties shall closely consult with and actively involve persons with disabilities, including children with disabilities, through their representative organizations.

    4.   Nothing in the present Convention shall affect any provisions which are more conducive to the realization of the rights of persons with disabilities and which may be contained in the law of a State Party or international law in force for that State. There shall be no restriction upon or derogation from any of the human rights and fundamental freedoms recognized or existing in any State Party to the present Convention pursuant to law, conventions, regulation or custom on the pretext that the present Convention does not recognize such rights or freedoms or that it recognizes them to a lesser extent.

    5.   The provisions of the present Convention shall extend to all parts of federal states without any limitations or exceptions.

Article 5—Equality and non-discrimination

    1.   States Parties recognize that all persons are equal before and under the law and are entitled without any discrimination to the equal protection and equal benefit of the law.

    2.   States Parties shall prohibit all discrimination on the basis of disability and guarantee to persons with disabilities equal and effective legal protection against discrimination on all grounds.

    3.   In order to promote equality and eliminate discrimination, States Parties shall take all appropriate steps to ensure that reasonable accommodation is provided.

4. Specific measures which are necessary to accelerate or achieve de facto equality of persons with disabilities shall not be considered discrimination under the terms of the present Convention.

Article 6—Women with disabilities

1. States Parties recognize that women and girls with disabilities are subject to multiple discrimination, and in this regard shall take measures to ensure the full and equal enjoyment by them of all human rights and fundamental freedoms.

2. States Parties shall take all appropriate measures to ensure the full development, advancement and empowerment of women, for the purpose of guaranteeing them the exercise and enjoyment of the human rights and fundamental freedoms set out in the present Convention.

Article 7—Children with disabilities

1. States Parties shall take all necessary measures to ensure the full enjoyment by children with disabilities of all human rights and fundamental freedoms on an equal basis with other children.

2. In all actions concerning children with disabilities, the best interests of the child shall be a primary consideration.

3. States Parties shall ensure that children with disabilities have the right to express their views freely on all matters affecting them, their views being given due weight in accordance with their age and maturity, on an equal basis with other children, and to be provided with disability and age-appropriate assistance to realize that right.

Article 8—Awareness-raising

1. States Parties undertake to adopt immediate, effective and appropriate measures:

    a. To raise awareness throughout society, including at the family level, regarding persons with disabilities, and to foster respect for the rights and dignity of persons with disabilities;

    b. To combat stereotypes, prejudices and harmful practices relating to persons with disabilities, including those based on sex and age, in all areas of life;

    c. To promote awareness of the capabilities and contributions of persons with disabilities.

Measures to this end include:

    a. Initiating and maintaining effective public awareness campaigns designed:

        i. To nurture receptiveness to the rights of persons with disabilities;

    ii.   To promote positive perceptions and greater social awareness towards persons with disabilities;

    iii. To promote recognition of the skills, merits and abilities of persons with disabilities, and of their contributions to the workplace and the labour market;

    b.   Fostering at all levels of the education system, including in all children from an early age, an attitude of respect for the rights of persons with disabilities;

    c.   Encouraging all organs of the media to portray persons with disabilities in a manner consistent with the purpose of the present Convention;

    d.   Promoting awareness-training programmes regarding persons with disabilities and the rights of persons with disabilities.

Article 9—Accessibility

1.   To enable persons with disabilities to live independently and participate fully in all aspects of life, States Parties shall take appropriate measures to ensure to persons with disabilities access, on an equal basis with others, to the physical environment, to transportation, to information and communications, including information and communications technologies and systems, and to other facilities and services open or provided to the public, both in urban and in rural areas. These measures, which shall include the identification and elimination of obstacles and barriers to accessibility, shall apply to, inter alia:

    a.   Buildings, roads, transportation and other indoor and outdoor facilities, including schools, housing, medical facilities and workplaces;

    b.   Information, communications and other services, including electronic services and emergency services.

2.   States Parties shall also take appropriate measures to:

    a.   Develop, promulgate and monitor the implementation of minimum standards and guidelines for the accessibility of facilities and services open or provided to the public;

    b.   Ensure that private entities that offer facilities and services which are open or provided to the public take into account all aspects of accessibility for persons with disabilities;

    c.   Provide training for stakeholders on accessibility issues facing persons with disabilities;

d. Provide in buildings and other facilities open to the public signage in Braille and in easy to read and understand forms;

e. Provide forms of live assistance and intermediaries, including guides, readers and professional sign language interpreters, to facilitate accessibility to buildings and other facilities open to the public;

f. Promote other appropriate forms of assistance and support to persons with disabilities to ensure their access to information;

g. Promote access for persons with disabilities to new information and communications technologies and systems, including the Internet;

h. Promote the design, development, production and distribution of accessible information and communications technologies and systems at an early stage, so that these technologies and systems become accessible at minimum cost.

Article 10—Right to life

States Parties reaffirm that every human being has the inherent right to life and shall take all necessary measures to ensure its effective enjoyment by persons with disabilities on an equal basis with others.

Article 11—Situations of risk and humanitarian emergencies

States Parties shall take, in accordance with their obligations under international law, including international humanitarian law and international human rights law, all necessary measures to ensure the protection and safety of persons with disabilities in situations of risk, including situations of armed conflict, humanitarian emergencies and the occurrence of natural disasters.

Article 12—Equal recognition before the law

1. States Parties reaffirm that persons with disabilities have the right to recognition everywhere as persons before the law.

2. States Parties shall recognize that persons with disabilities enjoy legal capacity on an equal basis with others in all aspects of life.

3. States Parties shall take appropriate measures to provide access by persons with disabilities to the support they may require in exercising their legal capacity.

4. States Parties shall ensure that all measures that relate to the exercise of legal capacity provide for appropriate and effective safeguards to prevent abuse in accordance with international human rights law. Such safeguards shall ensure that measures relating to the exercise of

legal capacity respect the rights, will and preferences of the person, are free of conflict of interest and undue influence, are proportional and tailored to the person's circumstances, apply for the shortest time possible and are subject to regular review by a competent, independent and impartial authority or judicial body. The safeguards shall be proportional to the degree to which such measures affect the person's rights and interests.

5.   Subject to the provisions of this article, States Parties shall take all appropriate and effective measures to ensure the equal right of persons with disabilities to own or inherit property, to control their own financial affairs and to have equal access to bank loans, mortgages and other forms of financial credit, and shall ensure that persons with disabilities are not arbitrarily deprived of their property.

Article 13—Access to justice

1.   States Parties shall ensure effective access to justice for persons with disabilities on an equal basis with others, including through the provision of procedural and age-appropriate accommodations, in order to facilitate their effective role as direct and indirect participants, including as witnesses, in all legal proceedings, including at investigative and other preliminary stages.

2.   In order to help to ensure effective access to justice for persons with disabilities, States Parties shall promote appropriate training for those working in the field of administration of justice, including police and prison staff.

Article 14—Liberty and security of the person

1.   States Parties shall ensure that persons with disabilities, on an equal basis with others:

a.   Enjoy the right to liberty and security of person;

b.   Are not deprived of their liberty unlawfully or arbitrarily, and that any deprivation of liberty is in conformity with the law, and that the existence of a disability shall in no case justify a deprivation of liberty.

2.   States Parties shall ensure that if persons with disabilities are deprived of their liberty through any process, they are, on an equal basis with others, entitled to guarantees in accordance with international human rights law and shall be treated in compliance with the objectives and principles of this Convention, including by provision of reasonable accommodation.

*Article 15—Freedom from torture or cruel, inhuman
or degrading treatment or punishment*

1.   No one shall be subjected to torture or to cruel, inhuman or degrading treatment or punishment. In particular, no one shall be subjected without his or her free consent to medical or scientific experimentation.

2.   States Parties shall take all effective legislative, administrative, judicial or other measures to prevent persons with disabilities, on an equal basis with others, from being subjected to torture or cruel, inhuman or degrading treatment or punishment.

Article 16—Freedom from exploitation, violence and abuse

1.   States Parties shall take all appropriate legislative, administrative, social, educational and other measures to protect persons with disabilities, both within and outside the home, from all forms of exploitation, violence and abuse, including their gender-based aspects.

2.   States Parties shall also take all appropriate measures to prevent all forms of exploitation, violence and abuse by ensuring, inter alia, appropriate forms of gender- and age-sensitive assistance and support for persons with disabilities and their families and caregivers, including through the provision of information and education on how to avoid, recognize and report instances of exploitation, violence and abuse. States Parties shall ensure that protection services are age-, gender- and disability-sensitive.

3.   In order to prevent the occurrence of all forms of exploitation, violence and abuse, States Parties shall ensure that all facilities and programmes designed to serve persons with disabilities are effectively monitored by independent authorities.

4.   States Parties shall take all appropriate measures to promote the physical, cognitive and psychological recovery, rehabilitation and social reintegration of persons with disabilities who become victims of any form of exploitation, violence or abuse, including through the provision of protection services. Such recovery and reintegration shall take place in an environment that fosters the health, welfare, self-respect, dignity and autonomy of the person and takes into account gender- and age-specific needs.

5.   States Parties shall put in place effective legislation and policies, including women- and child-focused legislation and policies, to ensure that instances of exploitation, violence and abuse against persons with disabilities are identified, investigated and, where appropriate, prosecuted.

Article 17—Protecting the integrity of the person

Every person with disabilities has a right to respect for his or her physical and mental integrity on an equal basis with others.

Article 18—Liberty of movement and nationality

1. States Parties shall recognize the rights of persons with disabilities to liberty of movement, to freedom to choose their residence and to a nationality, on an equal basis with others, including by ensuring that persons with disabilities:

a. Have the right to acquire and change a nationality and are not deprived of their nationality arbitrarily or on the basis of disability;

b. Are not deprived, on the basis of disability, of their ability to obtain, possess and utilize documentation of their nationality or other documentation of identification, or to utilize relevant processes such as immigration proceedings, that may be needed to facilitate exercise of the right to liberty of movement;

c. Are free to leave any country, including their own;

d. Are not deprived, arbitrarily or on the basis of disability, of the right to enter their own country.

2. Children with disabilities shall be registered immediately after birth and shall have the right from birth to a name, the right to acquire a nationality and, as far as possible, the right to know and be cared for by their parents.

Article 19—Living independently and being included in the community

States Parties to this Convention recognize the equal right of all persons with disabilities to live in the community, with choices equal to others, and shall take effective and appropriate measures to facilitate full enjoyment by persons with disabilities of this right and their full inclusion and participation in the community, including by ensuring that:

a. Persons with disabilities have the opportunity to choose their place of residence and where and with whom they live on an equal basis with others and are not obliged to live in a particular living arrangement;

b. Persons with disabilities have access to a range of in-home, residential and other community support services, including personal assistance necessary to support living and inclusion in the community, and to prevent isolation or segregation from the community;

c. Community services and facilities for the general population are available on an equal basis to persons with disabilities and are responsive to their needs.

Article 20—Personal mobility

States Parties shall take effective measures to ensure personal mobility with the greatest possible independence for persons with disabilities, including by:

a. Facilitating the personal mobility of persons with disabilities in the manner and at the time of their choice, and at affordable cost;

b. Facilitating access by persons with disabilities to quality mobility aids, devices, assistive technologies and forms of live assistance and intermediaries, including by making them available at affordable cost;

c. Providing training in mobility skills to persons with disabilities and to specialist staff working with persons with disabilities;

d. Encouraging entities that produce mobility aids, devices and assistive technologies to take into account all aspects of mobility for persons with disabilities.

Article 21—Freedom of expression and opinion, and access to information

States Parties shall take all appropriate measures to ensure that persons with disabilities can exercise the right to freedom of expression and opinion, including the freedom to seek, receive and impart information and ideas on an equal basis with others and through all forms of communication of their choice, as defined in article 2 of the present Convention, including by:

a. Providing information intended for the general public to persons with disabilities in accessible formats and technologies appropriate to different kinds of disabilities in a timely manner and without additional cost;

b. Accepting and facilitating the use of sign languages, Braille, augmentative and alternative communication, and all other accessible means, modes and formats of communication of their choice by persons with disabilities in official interactions;

c. Urging private entities that provide services to the general public, including through the Internet, to provide information and services in accessible and usable formats for persons with disabilities;

d. Encouraging the mass media, including providers of information through the Internet, to make their services accessible to persons with disabilities;

e. Recognizing and promoting the use of sign languages.

Article 22—Respect for privacy

1. No person with disabilities, regardless of place of residence or living arrangements, shall be subjected to arbitrary or unlawful interference with his or her privacy, family, home or correspondence or other types of communication or to unlawful attacks on his or her honour and reputation. Persons with disabilities have the right to the protection of the law against such interference or attacks.

2. States Parties shall protect the privacy of personal, health and rehabilitation information of persons with disabilities on an equal basis with others.

Article 23—Respect for home and the family

1. States Parties shall take effective and appropriate measures to eliminate discrimination against persons with disabilities in all matters relating to marriage, family, parenthood and relationships, on an equal basis with others, so as to ensure that:

a. The right of all persons with disabilities who are of marriageable age to marry and to found a family on the basis of free and full consent of the intending spouses is recognized;

b. The rights of persons with disabilities to decide freely and responsibly on the number and spacing of their children and to have access to age-appropriate information, reproductive and family planning education are recognized, and the means necessary to enable them to exercise these rights are provided;

c. Persons with disabilities, including children, retain their fertility on an equal basis with others.

2. States Parties shall ensure the rights and responsibilities of persons with disabilities, with regard to guardianship, wardship, trusteeship, adoption of children or similar institutions, where these concepts exist in national legislation; in all cases the best interests of the child shall be paramount. States Parties shall render appropriate assistance to persons with disabilities in the performance of their child-rearing responsibilities.

3. States Parties shall ensure that children with disabilities have equal rights with respect to family life. With a view to realizing these rights, and to prevent concealment, abandonment, neglect and segregation of children with disabilities, States Parties shall undertake to

provide early and comprehensive information, services and support to children with disabilities and their families.

4.   States Parties shall ensure that a child shall not be separated from his or her parents against their will, except when competent authorities subject to judicial review determine, in accordance with applicable law and procedures, that such separation is necessary for the best interests of the child. In no case shall a child be separated from parents on the basis of a disability of either the child or one or both of the parents.

5.   States Parties shall, where the immediate family is unable to care for a child with disabilities, undertake every effort to provide alternative care within the wider family, and failing that, within the community in a family setting.

Article 24—Education

1.   States Parties recognize the right of persons with disabilities to education. With a view to realizing this right without discrimination and on the basis of equal opportunity, States Parties shall ensure an inclusive education system at all levels and life long learning directed to:

a.   The full development of human potential and sense of dignity and self-worth, and the strengthening of respect for human rights, fundamental freedoms and human diversity;

b.   The development by persons with disabilities of their personality, talents and creativity, as well as their mental and physical abilities, to their fullest potential;

c.   Enabling persons with disabilities to participate effectively in a free society.

2.   In realizing this right, States Parties shall ensure that:

a.   Persons with disabilities are not excluded from the general education system on the basis of disability, and that children with disabilities are not excluded from free and compulsory primary education, or from secondary education, on the basis of disability;

b.   Persons with disabilities can access an inclusive, quality and free primary education and secondary education on an equal basis with others in the communities in which they live;

c.   Reasonable accommodation of the individual's requirements is provided;

d.   Persons with disabilities receive the support required, within the general education system, to facilitate their effective education;

e. Effective individualized support measures are provided in environments that maximize academic and social development, consistent with the goal of full inclusion.

3. States Parties shall enable persons with disabilities to learn life and social development skills to facilitate their full and equal participation in education and as members of the community. To this end, States Parties shall take appropriate measures, including:

a. Facilitating the learning of Braille, alternative script, augmentative and alternative modes, means and formats of communication and orientation and mobility skills, and facilitating peer support and mentoring;

b. Facilitating the learning of sign language and the promotion of the linguistic identity of the deaf community;

c. Ensuring that the education of persons, and in particular children, who are blind, deaf or deafblind, is delivered in the most appropriate languages and modes and means of communication for the individual, and in environments which maximize academic and social development.

4. In order to help ensure the realization of this right, States Parties shall take appropriate measures to employ teachers, including teachers with disabilities, who are qualified in sign language and/or Braille, and to train professionals and staff who work at all levels of education. Such training shall incorporate disability awareness and the use of appropriate augmentative and alternative modes, means and formats of communication, educational techniques and materials to support persons with disabilities.

5. States Parties shall ensure that persons with disabilities are able to access general tertiary education, vocational training, adult education and lifelong learning without discrimination and on an equal basis with others. To this end, States Parties shall ensure that reasonable accommodation is provided to persons with disabilities.

Article 25—Health

States Parties recognize that persons with disabilities have the right to the enjoyment of the highest attainable standard of health without discrimination on the basis of disability. States Parties shall take all appropriate measures to ensure access for persons with disabilities to health services that are gender-sensitive, including health-related rehabilitation. In particular, States Parties shall:

a. Provide persons with disabilities with the same range, quality and standard of free or affordable health care and programmes as provided to other persons, including in the area of sexual and reproductive health and population-based public health programmes;

b. Provide those health services needed by persons with disabilities specifically because of their disabilities, including early identification and intervention as appropriate, and services designed to minimize and prevent further disabilities, including among children and older persons;

c. Provide these health services as close as possible to people's own communities, including in rural areas;

d. Require health professionals to provide care of the same quality to persons with disabilities as to others, including on the basis of free and informed consent by, inter alia, raising awareness of the human rights, dignity, autonomy and needs of persons with disabilities through training and the promulgation of ethical standards for public and private health care;

e. Prohibit discrimination against persons with disabilities in the provision of health insurance, and life insurance where such insurance is permitted by national law, which shall be provided in a fair and reasonable manner;

f. Prevent discriminatory denial of health care or health services or food and fluids on the basis of disability.

Article 26—Habilitation and rehabilitation

1. States Parties shall take effective and appropriate measures, including through peer support, to enable persons with disabilities to attain and maintain maximum independence, full physical, mental, social and vocational ability, and full inclusion and participation in all aspects of life. To that end, States Parties shall organize, strengthen and extend comprehensive habilitation and rehabilitation services and programmes, particularly in the areas of health, employment, education and social services, in such a way that these services and programmes:

a. Begin at the earliest possible stage, and are based on the multidisciplinary assessment of individual needs and strengths;

b. Support participation and inclusion in the community and all aspects of society, are voluntary, and are available to persons with disabilities as close as possible to their own communities, including in rural areas.

2. States Parties shall promote the development of initial and continuing training for professionals and staff working in habilitation and rehabilitation services.

3.   States Parties shall promote the availability, knowledge and use of assistive devices and technologies, designed for persons with disabilities, as they relate to habilitation and rehabilitation.

Article 27—Work and employment

1.   States Parties recognize the right of persons with disabilities to work, on an equal basis with others; this includes the right to the opportunity to gain a living by work freely chosen or accepted in a labour market and work environment that is open, inclusive and accessible to persons with disabilities. States Parties shall safeguard and promote the realization of the right to work, including for those who acquire a disability during the course of employment, by taking appropriate steps, including through legislation, to, inter alia:

a.   Prohibit discrimination on the basis of disability with regard to all matters concerning all forms of employment, including conditions of recruitment, hiring and employment, continuance of employment, career advancement and safe and healthy working conditions;

b.   Protect the rights of persons with disabilities, on an equal basis with others, to just and favourable conditions of work, including equal opportunities and equal remuneration for work of equal value, safe and healthy working conditions, including protection from harassment, and the redress of grievances;

c.   Ensure that persons with disabilities are able to exercise their labour and trade union rights on an equal basis with others;

d.   Enable persons with disabilities to have effective access to general technical and vocational guidance programmes, placement services and vocational and continuing training;

e.   Promote employment opportunities and career advancement for persons with disabilities in the labour market, as well as assistance in finding, obtaining, maintaining and returning to employment;

f.   Promote opportunities for self-employment, entrepreneurship, the development of cooperatives and starting one's own business;

g.   Employ persons with disabilities in the public sector;

h.   Promote the employment of persons with disabilities in the private sector through appropriate policies and measures, which may include affirmative action programmes, incentives and other measures;

    i.   Ensure that reasonable accommodation is provided to persons with disabilities in the workplace;

    j.   Promote the acquisition by persons with disabilities of work experience in the open labour market;

    k.   Promote vocational and professional rehabilitation, job retention and return-to-work programmes for persons with disabilities.

2.   States Parties shall ensure that persons with disabilities are not held in slavery or in servitude, and are protected, on an equal basis with others, from forced or compulsory labour.

Article 28—Adequate standard of living and social protection

1.   States Parties recognize the right of persons with disabilities to an adequate standard of living for themselves and their families, including adequate food, clothing and housing, and to the continuous improvement of living conditions, and shall take appropriate steps to safeguard and promote the realization of this right without discrimination on the basis of disability.

2.   States Parties recognize the right of persons with disabilities to social protection and to the enjoyment of that right without discrimination on the basis of disability, and shall take appropriate steps to safeguard and promote the realization of this right, including measures:

    a.   To ensure equal access by persons with disabilities to clean water services, and to ensure access to appropriate and affordable services, devices and other assistance for disability-related needs;

    b.   To ensure access by persons with disabilities, in particular women and girls with disabilities and older persons with disabilities, to social protection programmes and poverty reduction programmes;

    c.   To ensure access by persons with disabilities and their families living in situations of poverty to assistance from the State with disability-related expenses, including adequate training, counselling, financial assistance and respite care;

    d.   To ensure access by persons with disabilities to public housing programmes;

    e.   To ensure equal access by persons with disabilities to retirement benefits and programmes.

Article 29—Participation in political and public life

States Parties shall guarantee to persons with disabilities political rights and the opportunity to enjoy them on an equal basis with others, and shall undertake to:

a. Ensure that persons with disabilities can effectively and fully participate in political and public life on an equal basis with others, directly or through freely chosen representatives, including the right and opportunity for persons with disabilities to vote and be elected, inter alia, by:

i. Ensuring that voting procedures, facilities and materials are appropriate, accessible and easy to understand and use;

ii. Protecting the right of persons with disabilities to vote by secret ballot in elections and public referendums without intimidation, and to stand for elections, to effectively hold office and perform all public functions at all levels of government, facilitating the use of assistive and new technologies where appropriate;

iii. Guaranteeing the free expression of the will of persons with disabilities as electors and to this end, where necessary, at their request, allowing assistance in voting by a person of their own choice;

b. Promote actively an environment in which persons with disabilities can effectively and fully participate in the conduct of public affairs, without discrimination and on an equal basis with others, and encourage their participation in public affairs, including:

i. Participation in non-governmental organizations and associations concerned with the public and political life of the country, and in the activities and administration of political parties;

ii. Forming and joining organizations of persons with disabilities to represent persons with disabilities at international, national, regional and local levels.

Article 30—Participation in cultural life, recreation, leisure and sport

1. States Parties recognize the right of persons with disabilities to take part on an equal basis with others in cultural life, and shall take all appropriate measures to ensure that persons with disabilities:

a. Enjoy access to cultural materials in accessible formats;

    b.   Enjoy access to television programmes, films, theatre and other cultural activities, in accessible formats;

    c.   Enjoy access to places for cultural performances or services, such as theatres, museums, cinemas, libraries and tourism services, and, as far as possible, enjoy access to monuments and sites of national cultural importance.

    2.   States Parties shall take appropriate measures to enable persons with disabilities to have the opportunity to develop and utilize their creative, artistic and intellectual potential, not only for their own benefit, but also for the enrichment of society.

    3.   States Parties shall take all appropriate steps, in accordance with international law, to ensure that laws protecting intellectual property rights do not constitute an unreasonable or discriminatory barrier to access by persons with disabilities to cultural materials.

    4.   Persons with disabilities shall be entitled, on an equal basis with others, to recognition and support of their specific cultural and linguistic identity, including sign languages and deaf culture.

    5.   With a view to enabling persons with disabilities to participate on an equal basis with others in recreational, leisure and sporting activities, States Parties shall take appropriate measures:

    a.   To encourage and promote the participation, to the fullest extent possible, of persons with disabilities in mainstream sporting activities at all levels;

    b.   To ensure that persons with disabilities have an opportunity to organize, develop and participate in disability-specific sporting and recreational activities and, to this end, encourage the provision, on an equal basis with others, of appropriate instruction, training and resources;

    c.   To ensure that persons with disabilities have access to sporting, recreational and tourism venues;

    d.   To ensure that children with disabilities have equal access with other children to participation in play, recreation and leisure and sporting activities, including those activities in the school system;

    e.   To ensure that persons with disabilities have access to services from those involved in the organization of recreational, tourism, leisure and sporting activities.

Article 31—Statistics and data collection

    1.   States Parties undertake to collect appropriate information, including statistical and research data, to enable them to formulate and

implement policies to give effect to the present Convention. The process of collecting and maintaining this information shall:

a. Comply with legally established safeguards, including legislation on data protection, to ensure confidentiality and respect for the privacy of persons with disabilities;

b. Comply with internationally accepted norms to protect human rights and fundamental freedoms and ethical principles in the collection and use of statistics.

2. The information collected in accordance with this article shall be disaggregated, as appropriate, and used to help assess the implementation of States Parties' obligations under the present Convention and to identify and address the barriers faced by persons with disabilities in exercising their rights.

3. States Parties shall assume responsibility for the dissemination of these statistics and ensure their accessibility to persons with disabilities and others.

Article 32—International cooperation

1. States Parties recognize the importance of international cooperation and its promotion, in support of national efforts for the realization of the purpose and objectives of the present Convention, and will undertake appropriate and effective measures in this regard, between and among States and, as appropriate, in partnership with relevant international and regional organizations and civil society, in particular organizations of persons with disabilities. Such measures could include, inter alia:

a. Ensuring that international cooperation, including international development programmes, is inclusive of and accessible to persons with disabilities;

b. Facilitating and supporting capacity-building, including through the exchange and sharing of information, experiences, training programmes and best practices;

c. Facilitating cooperation in research and access to scientific and technical knowledge;

d. Providing, as appropriate, technical and economic assistance, including by facilitating access to and sharing of accessible and assistive technologies, and through the transfer of technologies.

2. The provisions of this article are without prejudice to the obligations of each State Party to fulfill its obligations under the present Convention.

Article 33—National implementation and monitoring

1.   States Parties, in accordance with their system of organization, shall designate one or more focal points within government for matters relating to the implementation of the present Convention, and shall give due consideration to the establishment or designation of a coordination mechanism within government to facilitate related action in different sectors and at different levels.

2.   States Parties shall, in accordance with their legal and administrative systems, maintain, strengthen, designate or establish within the State Party, a framework, including one or more independent mechanisms, as appropriate, to promote, protect and monitor implementation of the present Convention. When designating or establishing such a mechanism, States Parties shall take into account the principles relating to the status and functioning of national institutions for protection and promotion of human rights.

3.   Civil society, in particular persons with disabilities and their representative organizations, shall be involved and participate fully in the monitoring process.

Article 34—Committee on the Rights of Persons with Disabilities

1.   There shall be established a Committee on the Rights of Persons with Disabilities (hereafter referred to as "the Committee"), which shall carry out the functions hereinafter provided.

2.   The Committee shall consist, at the time of entry into force of the present Convention, of twelve experts. After an additional sixty ratifications or accessions to the Convention, the membership of the Committee shall increase by six members, attaining a maximum number of eighteen members.

3.   The members of the Committee shall serve in their personal capacity and shall be of high moral standing and recognized competence and experience in the field covered by the present Convention. When nominating their candidates, States Parties are invited to give due consideration to the provision set out in article 4.3 of the present Convention.

4.   The members of the Committee shall be elected by States Parties, consideration being given to equitable geographical distribution, representation of the different forms of civilization and of the principal legal systems, balanced gender representation and participation of experts with disabilities.

5.   The members of the Committee shall be elected by secret ballot from a list of persons nominated by the States Parties from among their nationals at meetings of the Conference of States Parties. At those

meetings, for which two thirds of States Parties shall constitute a quorum, the persons elected to the Committee shall be those who obtain the largest number of votes and an absolute majority of the votes of the representatives of States Parties present and voting.

6.   The initial election shall be held no later than six months after the date of entry into force of the present Convention. At least four months before the date of each election, the Secretary-General of the United Nations shall address a letter to the States Parties inviting them to submit the nominations within two months. The Secretary-General shall subsequently prepare a list in alphabetical order of all persons thus nominated, indicating the State Parties which have nominated them, and shall submit it to the States Parties to the present Convention.

7.   The members of the Committee shall be elected for a term of four years. They shall be eligible for re-election once. However, the term of six of the members elected at the first election shall expire at the end of two years; immediately after the first election, the names of these six members shall be chosen by lot by the chairperson of the meeting referred to in paragraph 5 of this article.

8.   The election of the six additional members of the Committee shall be held on the occasion of regular elections, in accordance with the relevant provisions of this article.

9.   If a member of the Committee dies or resigns or declares that for any other cause she or he can no longer perform her or his duties, the State Party which nominated the member shall appoint another expert possessing the qualifications and meeting the requirements set out in the relevant provisions of this article, to serve for the remainder of the term.

10. The Committee shall establish its own rules of procedure.

11. The Secretary-General of the United Nations shall provide the necessary staff and facilities for the effective performance of the functions of the Committee under the present Convention, and shall convene its initial meeting.

12. With the approval of the General Assembly, the members of the Committee established under the present Convention shall receive emoluments from United Nations resources on such terms and conditions as the Assembly may decide, having regard to the importance of the Committee's responsibilities.

13. The members of the Committee shall be entitled to the facilities, privileges and immunities of experts on mission for the United Nations as laid down in the relevant sections of the Convention on the Privileges and Immunities of the United Nations.

Article 35—Reports by States Parties

1.   Each State Party shall submit to the Committee, through the Secretary-General of the United Nations, a comprehensive report on measures taken to give effect to its obligations under the present Convention and on the progress made in that regard, within two years after the entry into force of the present Convention for the State Party concerned.

2.   Thereafter, States Parties shall submit subsequent reports at least every four years and further whenever the Committee so requests.

3.   The Committee shall decide any guidelines applicable to the content of the reports.

4.   A State Party which has submitted a comprehensive initial report to the Committee need not, in its subsequent reports, repeat information previously provided. When preparing reports to the Committee, States Parties are invited to consider doing so in an open and transparent process and to give due consideration to the provision set out in article 4.3 of the present Convention.

5.   Reports may indicate factors and difficulties affecting the degree of fulfilment of obligations under the present Convention.

Article 36—Consideration of reports

1.   Each report shall be considered by the Committee, which shall make such suggestions and general recommendations on the report as it may consider appropriate and shall forward these to the State Party concerned. The State Party may respond with any information it chooses to the Committee. The Committee may request further information from States Parties relevant to the implementation of the present Convention.

2.   If a State Party is significantly overdue in the submission of a report, the Committee may notify the State Party concerned of the need to examine the implementation of the present Convention in that State Party, on the basis of reliable information available to the Committee, if the relevant report is not submitted within three months following the notification. The Committee shall invite the State Party concerned to participate in such examination. Should the State Party respond by submitting the relevant report, the provisions of paragraph 1 of this article will apply.

3.   The Secretary-General of the United Nations shall make available the reports to all States Parties.

4.   States Parties shall make their reports widely available to the public in their own countries and facilitate access to the suggestions and general recommendations relating to these reports.

5.   The Committee shall transmit, as it may consider appropriate, to the specialized agencies, funds and programmes of the United Nations, and other competent bodies, reports from States Parties in order to address a request or indication of a need for technical advice or assistance contained therein, along with the Committee's observations and recommendations, if any, on these requests or indications.

Article 37—Cooperation between States Parties and the Committee

1.   Each State Party shall cooperate with the Committee and assist its members in the fulfilment of their mandate.

2.   In its relationship with States Parties, the Committee shall give due consideration to ways and means of enhancing national capacities for the implementation of the present Convention, including through international cooperation.

Article 38—Relationship of the Committee with other bodies

In order to foster the effective implementation of the present Convention and to encourage international cooperation in the field covered by the present Convention:

a.   The specialized agencies and other United Nations organs shall be entitled to be represented at the consideration of the implementation of such provisions of the present Convention as fall within the scope of their mandate. The Committee may invite the specialized agencies and other competent bodies as it may consider appropriate to provide expert advice on the implementation of the Convention in areas falling within the scope of their respective mandates. The Committee may invite specialized agencies and other United Nations organs to submit reports on the implementation of the Convention in areas falling within the scope of their activities;

b.   The Committee, as it discharges its mandate, shall consult, as appropriate, other relevant bodies instituted by international human rights treaties, with a view to ensuring the consistency of their respective reporting guidelines, suggestions and general recommendations, and avoiding duplication and overlap in the performance of their functions.

Article 39—Report of the Committee

The Committee shall report every two years to the General Assembly and to the Economic and Social Council on its activities, and may make suggestions and general recommendations based on the examination of reports and information received from the States Parties. Such suggestions and general recommendations shall be included in the report of the Committee together with comments, if any, from States Parties.

Article 40—Conference of States Parties

1. The States Parties shall meet regularly in a Conference of States Parties in order to consider any matter with regard to the implementation of the present Convention.

2. No later than six months after the entry into force of the present Convention, the Conference of the States Parties shall be convened by the Secretary-General of the United Nations. The subsequent meetings shall be convened by the Secretary-General of the United Nations biennially or upon the decision of the Conference of States Parties.

Article 41—Depositary

The Secretary-General of the United Nations shall be the depositary of the present Convention.

Article 42—Signature

The present Convention shall be open for signature by all States and by regional integration organizations at United Nations Headquarters in New York as of 30 March 2007.

Article 43—Consent to be bound

The present Convention shall be subject to ratification by signatory States and to formal confirmation by signatory regional integration organizations. It shall be open for accession by any State or regional integration organization which has not signed the Convention.

Article 44—Regional integration organizations

1. "Regional integration organization" shall mean an organization constituted by sovereign States of a given region, to which its member States have transferred competence in respect of matters governed by this Convention. Such organizations shall declare, in their instruments of formal confirmation or accession, the extent of their competence with respect to matters governed by this Convention. Subsequently, they shall inform the depositary of any substantial modification in the extent of their competence.

2. References to "States Parties" in the present Convention shall apply to such organizations within the limits of their competence.

3. For the purposes of article 45, paragraph 1, and article 47, paragraphs 2 and 3, any instrument deposited by a regional integration organization shall not be counted.

4. Regional integration organizations, in matters within their competence, may exercise their right to vote in the Conference of States Parties, with a number of votes equal to the number of their member States that are Parties to this Convention. Such an organization shall not

exercise its right to vote if any of its member States exercises its right, and vice versa.

Article 45—Entry into force

1. The present Convention shall enter into force on the thirtieth day after the deposit of the twentieth instrument of ratification or accession.

2. For each State or regional integration organization ratifying, formally confirming or acceding to the Convention after the deposit of the twentieth such instrument, the Convention shall enter into force on the thirtieth day after the deposit of its own such instrument.

Article 46—Reservations

1. Reservations incompatible with the object and purpose of the present Convention shall not be permitted.

2. Reservations may be withdrawn at any time.

Article 47—Amendments

1. Any State Party may propose an amendment to the present Convention and submit it to the Secretary-General of the United Nations. The Secretary-General shall communicate any proposed amendments to States Parties, with a request to be notified whether they favour a conference of States Parties for the purpose of considering and deciding upon the proposals. In the event that, within four months from the date of such communication, at least one third of the States Parties favour such a conference, the Secretary-General shall convene the conference under the auspices of the United Nations. Any amendment adopted by a majority of two thirds of the States Parties present and voting shall be submitted by the Secretary-General to the General Assembly for approval and thereafter to all States Parties for acceptance.

2. An amendment adopted and approved in accordance with paragraph 1 of this article shall enter into force on the thirtieth day after the number of instruments of acceptance deposited reaches two thirds of the number of States Parties at the date of adoption of the amendment. Thereafter, the amendment shall enter into force for any State Party on the thirtieth day following the deposit of its own instrument of acceptance. An amendment shall be binding only on those States Parties which have accepted it.

3. If so decided by the Conference of States Parties by consensus, an amendment adopted and approved in accordance with paragraph 1 of this article which relates exclusively to articles 34, 38, 39 and 40 shall enter into force for all States Parties on the thirtieth day after the number of instruments of acceptance deposited reaches two thirds of the number of States Parties at the date of adoption of the amendment.

Article 48—Denunciation

A State Party may denounce the present Convention by written notification to the Secretary-General of the United Nations. The denunciation shall become effective one year after the date of receipt of the notification by the Secretary-General.

Article 49—Accessible format

The text of the present Convention shall be made available in accessible formats.

Article 50—Authentic texts

The Arabic, Chinese, English, French, Russian and Spanish texts of the present Convention shall be equally authentic.

UNITED NATIONS DECLARATION ON THE RIGHTS OF INDIGENOUS PEOPLES

Adopted by the United Nations General Assembly Resolution
61/295 of 13 September 2007

Affirming that indigenous peoples are equal to all other peoples, while recognizing the right of all peoples to be different, to consider themselves different, and to be respected as such,

Affirming also that all peoples contribute to the diversity and richness of civilizations and cultures, which constitute the common heritage of humankind,

Affirming further that all doctrines, policies and practices based on or advocating superiority of peoples or individuals on the basis of national origin, racial, religious, ethnic or cultural differences are racist, scientifically false, legally invalid, morally condemnable and socially unjust,

Reaffirming also that indigenous peoples, in the exercise of their rights, should be free from discrimination of any kind,

Concerned that indigenous peoples have suffered from historic injustices as a result of, inter alia, their colonization and dispossession of their lands, territories and resources, thus preventing them from exercising, in particular, their right to development in accordance with their own needs and interests,

Recognizing the urgent need to respect and promote the inherent rights of indigenous peoples which derive from their political, economic and social structures and from their cultures, spiritual traditions, histories and philosophies, especially their rights to their lands, territories and resources,

Further recognizing the urgent need to respect and promote the rights of indigenous peoples affirmed in treaties, agreements and other constructive arrangements with States,

Welcoming the fact that indigenous peoples are organizing themselves for political, economic, social and cultural enhancement and in order to bring an end to all forms of discrimination and oppression wherever they occur,

Convinced that control by indigenous peoples over developments affecting them and their lands, territories and resources will enable them to maintain and strengthen their institutions, cultures and traditions, and to promote their development in accordance with their aspirations and needs,

Recognizing also that respect for indigenous knowledge, cultures and traditional practices contributes to sustainable and equitable development and proper management of the environment,

Emphasizing the contribution of the demilitarization of the lands and territories of indigenous peoples to peace, economic and social progress and development, understanding and friendly relations among nations and peoples of the world,

Recognizing in particular the right of indigenous families and communities to retain shared responsibility for the upbringing, training, education and well-being of their children, consistent with the rights of the child,

Recognizing also that indigenous peoples have the right freely to determine their relationships with States in a spirit of coexistence, mutual benefit and full respect,

Considering that the rights affirmed in treaties, agreements and constructive arrangements between States and indigenous peoples are, in some situations, matters of international concern, interest, responsibility and character,

Also considering that treaties, agreements and other constructive arrangements, and the relationship they represent, are the basis for a strengthened partnership between indigenous peoples and States,

Acknowledging that the Charter of the United Nations, the International Covenant on Economic, Social and Cultural Rights and the International Covenant on Civil and Political Rights affirm the fundamental importance of the right of self-determination of all peoples, by virtue of which they freely determine their political status and freely pursue their economic, social and cultural development,

Bearing in mind that nothing in this Declaration may be used to deny any peoples their right of self-determination, exercised in conformity with international law,

Convinced that the recognition of the rights of indigenous peoples in this Declaration will enhance harmonious and cooperative relations between the State and indigenous peoples, based on principles of justice, democracy, respect for human rights, non-discrimination and good faith,

Encouraging States to comply with and effectively implement all their obligations as they apply to indigenous peoples under international instruments, in particular those related to human rights, in consultation and cooperation with the peoples concerned,

Emphasizing that the United Nations has an important and continuing role to play in promoting and protecting the rights of indigenous peoples,

Believing that this Declaration is a further important step forward for the recognition, promotion and protection of the rights and freedoms of indigenous peoples and in the development of relevant activities of the United Nations system in this field,

Recognizing and reaffirming that indigenous individuals are entitled without discrimination to all human rights recognized in international law, and that indigenous peoples possess collective rights which are indispensable for their existence, well-being and integral development as peoples,

Solemnly proclaims the following United Nations Declaration on the Rights of Indigenous Peoples as a standard of achievement to be pursued in a spirit of partnership and mutual respect,

Article 1

Indigenous peoples have the right to the full enjoyment, as a collective or as individuals, of all human rights and fundamental freedoms as recognized in the Charter of the United Nations, the Universal Declaration of Human Rights and international human rights law.

Article 2

Indigenous peoples and individuals are free and equal to all other peoples and individuals and have the right to be free from any kind of discrimination, in the exercise of their rights, in particular that based on their indigenous origin or identity.

Article 3

Indigenous peoples have the right of self-determination. By virtue of that right they freely determine their political status and freely pursue their economic, social and cultural development.

Article 4

Indigenous peoples, in exercising their right to self-determination, have the right to autonomy or self-government in matters relating to their internal and local affairs, as well as ways and means for financing their autonomous functions.

Article 5

Indigenous peoples have the right to maintain and strengthen their distinct political, legal, economic, social and cultural institutions, while retaining their rights to participate fully, if they so choose, in the political, economic, social and cultural life of the State.

Article 6

Every indigenous individual has the right to a nationality.

Article 7

1.   Indigenous individuals have the rights to life, physical and mental integrity, liberty and security of person.

2.   Indigenous peoples have the collective right to live in freedom, peace and security as distinct peoples and shall not be subjected to any act of genocide or any other act of violence, including forcibly removing children of the group to another group.

Article 8

1.   Indigenous peoples and individuals have the right not to be subjected to forced assimilation or destruction of their culture.

2.   States shall provide effective mechanisms for prevention of, and redress for:

(a) Any action which has the aim or effect of depriving them of their integrity as distinct peoples, or of their cultural values or ethnic identities;

(b) Any action which has the aim or effect of dispossessing them of their lands, territories or resources;

(c) Any form of forced population transfer which has the aim or effect of violating or undermining any of their rights;

(d) Any form of forced assimilation or integration by other cultures or ways of life imposed on them by legislative, administrative or other measures;

(*e*) Any form of propaganda designed to promote or incite racial or ethnic discrimination directed against them.

Article 9

Indigenous peoples and individuals have the right to belong to an indigenous community or nation, in accordance with the traditions and customs of the community or nation concerned. No discrimination of any kind may arise from the exercise of such a right.

Article 10

Indigenous peoples shall not be forcibly removed from their lands or territories. No relocation shall take place without the free, prior and informed consent of the indigenous peoples concerned and after agreement on just and fair compensation and, where possible, with the option of return.

Article 11

1.   Indigenous peoples have the right to practice and revitalize their cultural traditions and customs. This includes the right to maintain, protect and develop the past, present and future manifestations of their cultures, such as archaeological and historical sites, artefacts, designs, ceremonies, technologies and visual and performing arts and literature.

2.   States shall provide redress through effective mechanisms, which may include restitution, developed in conjunction with indigenous peoples, with respect to their cultural, intellectual, religious and spiritual property taken without their free, prior and informed consent or in violation of their laws, traditions and customs.

Article 12

1.   Indigenous peoples have the right to manifest, practice, develop and teach their spiritual and religious traditions, customs and ceremonies; the right to maintain, protect, and have access in privacy to their religious and cultural sites; the right to the use and control of their ceremonial objects; and the right to the repatriation of their human remains.

2.   States shall seek to enable the access and/or repatriation of ceremonial objects and human remains in their possession through fair, transparent and effective mechanisms developed in conjunction with indigenous peoples concerned.

Article 13

1.   Indigenous peoples have the right to revitalize, use, develop and transmit to future generations their histories, languages, oral traditions, philosophies, writing systems and literatures, and to designate and retain their own names for communities, places and persons.

2. States shall take effective measures to ensure this right is protected and also to ensure that indigenous peoples can understand and be understood in political, legal and administrative proceedings, where necessary through the provision of interpretation or by other appropriate means.

Article 14

1. Indigenous peoples have the right to establish and control their educational systems and institutions providing education in their own languages, in a manner appropriate to their cultural methods of teaching and learning.

2. Indigenous individuals, particularly children, have the right to all levels and forms of education of the State without discrimination.

3. States shall, in conjunction with indigenous peoples, take effective measures, in order for indigenous individuals, particularly children, including those living outside their communities, to have access, when possible, to an education in their own culture and provided in their own language.

Article 15

1. Indigenous peoples have the right to the dignity and diversity of their cultures, traditions, histories and aspirations which shall be appropriately reflected in education and public information.

2. States shall take effective measures, in consultation and cooperation with the indigenous peoples concerned, to combat prejudice and eliminate discrimination and to promote tolerance, understanding and good relations among indigenous peoples and all other segments of society.

Article 16

1. Indigenous peoples have the right to establish their own media in their own languages and to have access to all forms of non-indigenous media without discrimination.

2. States shall take effective measures to ensure that State-owned media duly reflect indigenous cultural diversity. States, without prejudice to ensuring full freedom of expression, should encourage privately-owned media to adequately reflect indigenous cultural diversity.

Article 17

1. Indigenous individuals and peoples have the right to enjoy fully all rights established under applicable international and domestic labour law.

2. States shall in consultation and cooperation with indigenous peoples take specific measures to protect indigenous children from

economic exploitation and from performing any work that is likely to be hazardous or to interfere with the child's education, or to be harmful to the child's health or physical, mental, spiritual, moral or social development, taking into account their special vulnerability and the importance of education for their empowerment.

3.   Indigenous individuals have the right not to be subjected to any discriminatory conditions of labour and, inter alia, employment or salary.

Article 18

Indigenous peoples have the right to participate in decision-making in matters which would affect their rights, through representatives chosen by themselves in accordance with their own procedures, as well as to maintain and develop their own indigenous decision-making institutions.

Article 19

States shall consult and cooperate in good faith with the indigenous peoples concerned through their own representative institutions in order to obtain their free, prior and informed consent before adopting and implementing legislative or administrative measures that may affect them.

Article 20

1.   Indigenous peoples have the right to maintain and develop their political, economic and social systems or institutions, to be secure in the enjoyment of their own means of subsistence and development, and to engage freely in all their traditional and other economic activities.

2.   Indigenous peoples deprived of their means of subsistence and development are entitled to just and fair redress.

Article 21

1.   Indigenous peoples have the right, without discrimination, to the improvement of their economic and social conditions, including, inter alia, in the areas of education, employment, vocational training and retraining, housing, sanitation, health and social security.

2.   States shall take effective measures and, where appropriate, special measures to ensure continuing improvement of their economic and social conditions. Particular attention shall be paid to the rights and special needs of indigenous elders, women, youth, children and persons with disabilities.

Article 22

1.   Particular attention shall be paid to the rights and special needs of indigenous elders, women, youth, children and persons with disabilities in the implementation of this Declaration.

2. States shall take measures, in conjunction with indigenous peoples, to ensure that indigenous women and children enjoy the full protection and guarantees against all forms of violence and discrimination.

Article 23

Indigenous peoples have the right to determine and develop priorities and strategies for exercising their right to development. In particular, indigenous peoples have the right to be actively involved in developing and determining health, housing and other economic and social programmes affecting them and, as far as possible, to administer such programmes through their own institutions.

Article 24

1. Indigenous peoples have the right to their traditional medicines and to maintain their health practices, including the conservation of their vital medicinal plants, animals and minerals. Indigenous individuals also have the right to access, without any discrimination, to all social and health services.

2. Indigenous individuals have an equal right to the enjoyment of the highest attainable standard of physical and mental health. States shall take the necessary steps with a view to achieving progressively the full realization of this right.

Article 25

Indigenous peoples have the right to maintain and strengthen their distinctive spiritual relationship with their traditionally owned or otherwise occupied and used lands, territories, waters and coastal seas and other resources and to uphold their responsibilities to future generations in this regard.

Article 26

1. Indigenous peoples have the right to the lands, territories and resources which they have traditionally owned, occupied or otherwise used or acquired.

2. Indigenous peoples have the right to own, use, develop and control the lands, territories and resources that they possess by reason of traditional ownership or other traditional occupation or use, as well as those which they have otherwise acquired.

3. States shall give legal recognition and protection to these lands, territories and resources. Such recognition shall be conducted with due respect to the customs, traditions and land tenure systems of the indigenous peoples concerned.

Article 27

States shall establish and implement, in conjunction with indigenous peoples concerned, a fair, independent, impartial, open and transparent process, giving due recognition to indigenous peoples' laws, traditions, customs and land tenure systems, to recognize and adjudicate the rights of indigenous peoples pertaining to their lands, territories and resources, including those which were traditionally owned or otherwise occupied or used. Indigenous peoples shall have the right to participate in this process.

Article 28

1.   Indigenous peoples have the right to redress, by means that can include restitution or, when this is not possible, of a just, fair and equitable compensation, for the lands, territories and resources which they have traditionally owned or otherwise occupied or used, and which have been confiscated, taken, occupied, used or damaged without their free, prior and informed consent.

2.   Unless otherwise freely agreed upon by the peoples concerned, compensation shall take the form of lands, territories and resources equal in quality, size and legal status or of monetary compensation or other appropriate redress.

Article 29

1.   Indigenous peoples have the right to the conservation and protection of the environment and the productive capacity of their lands or territories and resources. States shall establish and implement assistance programmes for indigenous peoples for such conservation and protection, without discrimination.

2.   States shall take effective measures to ensure that no storage or disposal of hazardous materials shall take place in the lands or territories of indigenous peoples without their free, prior and informed consent.

3.   States shall also take effective measures to ensure, as needed, that programmes for monitoring, maintaining and restoring the health of indigenous peoples, as developed and implemented by the peoples affected by such materials, are duly implemented.

Article 30

1.   Military activities shall not take place in the lands or territories of indigenous peoples, unless justified by a significant threat to relevant public interest or otherwise freely agreed with or requested by the indigenous peoples concerned.

2.   States shall undertake effective consultations with the indigenous peoples concerned, through appropriate procedures and in

particular through their representative institutions, prior to using their lands or territories for military activities.

Article 31

1. Indigenous peoples have the right to maintain, control, protect and develop their cultural heritage, traditional knowledge and traditional cultural expressions, as well as the manifestations of their sciences, technologies and cultures, including human and genetic resources, seeds, medicines, knowledge of the properties of fauna and flora, oral traditions, literatures, designs, sports and traditional games and visual and performing arts. They also have the right to maintain, control, protect and develop their intellectual property over such cultural heritage, traditional knowledge, and traditional cultural expressions.

2. In conjunction with indigenous peoples, States shall take effective measures to recognize and protect the exercise of these rights.

Article 32

1. Indigenous peoples have the right to determine and develop priorities and strategies for the development or use of their lands or territories and other resources.

2. States shall consult and cooperate in good faith with the indigenous peoples concerned through their own representative institutions in order to obtain their free and informed consent prior to the approval of any project affecting their lands or territories and other resources, particularly in connection with the development, utilization or exploitation of their mineral, water or other resources.

3. States shall provide effective mechanisms for just and fair redress for any such activities, and appropriate measures shall be taken to mitigate adverse environmental, economic, social, cultural or spiritual impact.

Article 33

1. Indigenous peoples have the right to determine their own identity or membership in accordance with their customs and traditions. This does not impair the right of indigenous individuals to obtain citizenship of the States in which they live.

2. Indigenous peoples have the right to determine the structures and to select the membership of their institutions in accordance with their own procedures.

Article 34

Indigenous peoples have the right to promote, develop and maintain their institutional structures and their distinctive customs, spirituality, traditions, procedures, practices and, in the cases where they exist, juridical systems or customs, in accordance with international human rights standards.

Article 35

Indigenous peoples have the right to determine the responsibilities of individuals to their communities.

Article 36

1. Indigenous peoples, in particular those divided by international borders, have the right to maintain and develop contacts, relations and cooperation, including activities for spiritual, cultural, political, economic and social purposes, with their own members as well as other peoples across borders.

2. States, in consultation and cooperation with indigenous peoples, shall take effective measures to facilitate the exercise and ensure the implementation of this right.

Article 37

1. Indigenous peoples have the right to the recognition, observance and enforcement of Treaties, Agreements and Other Constructive Arrangements concluded with States or their successors and to have States honour and respect such Treaties, Agreements and other Constructive Arrangements.

2. Nothing in this Declaration may be interpreted as to diminish or eliminate the rights of Indigenous Peoples contained in Treaties, Agreements and Constructive Arrangements.

Article 38

States in consultation and cooperation with indigenous peoples, shall take the appropriate measures, including legislative measures, to achieve the ends of this Declaration.

Article 39

Indigenous peoples have the right to have access to financial and technical assistance from States and through international cooperation, for the enjoyment of the rights contained in this Declaration.

Article 40

Indigenous peoples have the right to have access to and prompt decision through just and fair procedures for the resolution of conflicts and disputes with States or other parties, as well as to effective remedies for all infringements of their individual and collective rights. Such a decision shall give due consideration to the customs, traditions, rules and legal systems of the indigenous peoples concerned and international human rights.

Article 41

The organs and specialized agencies of the United Nations system and other intergovernmental organizations shall contribute to the full realization of the provisions of this Declaration through the mobilization, inter alia, of financial cooperation and technical assistance. Ways and means of ensuring participation of indigenous peoples on issues affecting them shall be established.

Article 42

The United Nations, its bodies, including the Permanent Forum on Indigenous Issues, and specialized agencies, including at the country level, and States, shall promote respect for and full application of the provisions of this Declaration and follow up the effectiveness of this Declaration.

Article 43

The rights recognized herein constitute the minimum standards for the survival, dignity and well-being of the indigenous peoples of the world.

Article 44

All the rights and freedoms recognized herein are equally guaranteed to male and female indigenous individuals.

Article 45

Nothing in this Declaration may be construed as diminishing or extinguishing the rights indigenous peoples have now or may acquire in the future.

Article 46

1. Nothing in this Declaration may be interpreted as implying for any State, people, group or person any right to engage in any activity or to perform any act contrary to the Charter of the United Nations.

2. In the exercise of the rights enunciated in the present Declaration, human rights and fundamental freedoms of all shall be respected. The exercise of the rights set forth in this Declaration shall be subject only to such limitations as are determined by law, in accordance with international human rights obligations. Any such limitations shall be non-discriminatory and strictly necessary solely for the purpose of securing due recognition and respect for the rights and freedoms of others and for meeting the just and most compelling requirements of a democratic society.

3. The provisions set forth in this Declaration shall be interpreted in accordance with the principles of justice, democracy, respect for human rights, equality, non-discrimination, good governance and good faith.

APPENDIX B

SELECT INSTRUMENTS OF THE INTER-AMERICAN HUMAN RIGHTS SYSTEM

■ ■ ■

Table of Contents

AMERICAN DECLARATION OF THE RIGHTS AND DUTIES OF MAN

Adopted by the Ninth International Conference of American States, Bogotá, Colombia, 1948

PREAMBLE

All men are born free and equal, in dignity and in rights, and, being endowed by nature with reason and conscience, they should conduct themselves as brothers one to another.

The fulfillment of duty by each individual is a prerequisite to the rights of all. Rights and duties are interrelated in every social and political activity of man. While rights exalt individual liberty, duties express the dignity of that liberty.

Duties of a juridical nature presuppose others of a moral nature which support them in principle and constitute their basis.

Inasmuch as spiritual development is the supreme end of human existence and the highest expression thereof, it is the duty of man to serve that end with all his strength and resources.

Since culture is the highest social and historical expression of that spiritual development, it is the duty of man to preserve, practice and foster culture by every means within his power.

And, since moral conduct constitutes the noblest flowering of culture, it is the duty of every man always to hold it in high respect.

CHAPTER ONE

Rights

Article I. Right to life, liberty and personal security

Every human being has the right to life, liberty and the security of his person.

Article II. Right to equality before law

All persons are equal before the law and have the rights and duties established in this Declaration, without distinction as to race, sex, language, creed or any other factor.

Article III. Right to religious freedom and worship.

Every person has the right freely to profess a religious faith, and to manifest and practice it both in public and in private.

Article IV. Right to freedom of investigation, opinion,
expression and dissemination.

Every person has the right to freedom of investigation, of opinion, and of the expression and dissemination of ideas, by any medium whatsoever.

Article V. Right to protection of honor, personal reputation,
and private and family life

Every person has the right to the protection of the law against abusive attacks upon his honor, his reputation, and his private and family life.

Article VI. Right to a family and to protection thereof.

Every person has the right to establish a family, the basic element of society, and to receive protection therefore.

Article VII. Right to protection for mothers and children.

All women, during pregnancy and the nursing period, and all children have the right to special protection, care and aid.

Article VIII. Right to residence and movement.

Every person has the right to fix his residence within the territory of the state of which he is a national, to move about freely within such territory, and not to leave it except by his own will.

Article IX. Right to inviolability of the home.

Every person has the right to the inviolability of his home.

Article X. Right to the inviolability and transmission of correspondence.

Every person has the right to the inviolability and transmission of his correspondence.

Article XI. Right to the preservation of health and to well-being.

Every person has the right to the preservation of his health through sanitary and social measures relating to food, clothing, housing and medical care, to the extent permitted by public and community resources.

Article XII. Right to education.

Every person has the right to an education, which should be based on the principles of liberty, morality and human solidarity.

Likewise every person has the right to an education that will prepare him to attain a decent life, to raise his standard of living, and to be a useful member of society.

The right to an education includes the right to equality of opportunity in every case, in accordance with natural talents, merit and the desire to utilize the resources that the state or the community is in a position to provide.

Every person has the right to receive, free, at least a primary education.

Article XIII. Right to the benefits of culture.

Every person has the right to take part in the cultural life of the community, to enjoy the arts, and to participate in the benefits that result from intellectual progress, especially scientific discoveries.

He likewise has the right to the protection of his moral and material interests as regards his inventions or any literary, scientific or artistic works of which he is the author.

Article XIV. Right to work and to fair remuneration.

Every person has the right to work, under proper conditions, and to follow his vocation freely, insofar as existing conditions of employment permit.

Every person who works has the right to receive such remuneration as will, in proportion to his capacity and skill, assure him a standard of living suitable for himself and for his family.

Article XV. Right to leisure time and to the use thereof.

Every person has the right to leisure time, to wholesome recreation, and to the opportunity for advantageous use of his free time to his spiritual, cultural and physical benefit.

Article XVI. Right to social security.

Every person has the right to social security which will protect him from the consequences of unemployment, old age, and any disabilities arising from causes beyond his control that make it physically or mentally impossible for him to earn a living.

Article XVII. Right to recognition of juridical personality and civil rights.

Every person has the right to be recognized everywhere as a person having rights and obligations, and to enjoy the basic civil rights.

Article XVIII. Right to a fair trial.

Every person may resort to the courts to ensure respect for his legal rights. There should likewise be available to him a simple, brief procedure whereby the courts will protect him from acts of authority that, to his prejudice, violate any fundamental constitutional rights.

Article XIX. Right to nationality.

Every person has the right to the nationality to which he is entitled by law and to change it, if he so wishes, for the nationality of any other country that is willing to grant it to him.

Article XX. Right to vote and to participate in government.

Every person having legal capacity is entitled to participate in the government of his country, directly or through his representatives, and to take part in popular elections, which shall be by secret ballot, and shall be honest, periodic and free.

Article XXI. Right of assembly.

Every person has the right to assemble peaceably with others in a formal public meeting or an informal gathering, in connection with matters of common interest of any nature.

Article XXII. Right of association.

Every person has the right to associate with others to promote, exercise and protect his legitimate interests of a political, economic, religious, social, cultural, professional, labor union or other nature.

Article XXIII. Right to property.

Every person has a right to own such private property as meets the essential needs of decent living and helps to maintain the dignity of the individual and of the home.

Article XXIV. Right of petition.

Every person has the right to submit respectful petitions to any competent authority, for reasons of either general or private interest, and the right to obtain a prompt decision thereon.

Article XXV. Right of protection from arbitrary arrest.

No person may be deprived of his liberty except in the cases and according to the procedures established by pre-existing law.

No person may be deprived of liberty for nonfulfillment of obligations of a purely civil character.

Every individual who has been deprived of his liberty has the right to have the legality of his detention ascertained without delay by a court, and the right to be tried without undue delay or, otherwise, to be released. He also has the right to humane treatment during the time he is in custody.

Article XXVI. Right to due process of law.

Every accused person is presumed to be innocent until proved guilty.

Every person accused of an offense has the right to be given an impartial and public hearing, and to be tried by courts previously established in accordance with pre-existing laws, and not to receive cruel, infamous or unusual punishment.

Article XXVII. Right of asylum.

Every person has the right, in case of pursuit not resulting from ordinary crimes, to seek and receive asylum in foreign territory, in accordance with the laws of each country and with international agreements.

Article XXVIII. Scope of the rights of man.

The rights of man are limited by the rights of others, by the security of all, and by the just demands of the general welfare and the advancement of democracy.

CHAPTER TWO

Duties

Article XXIX. Duties to society.

It is the duty of the individual so to conduct himself in relation to others that each and every one may fully form and develop his personality.

Article XXX. Duties toward children and parents.

It is the duty of every person to aid, support, educate and protect his minor children, and it is the duty of children to honor their parents always and to aid, support and protect them when they need it.

Article XXXI. Duty to receive instruction.

It is the duty of every person to acquire at least an elementary education.

Article XXXII. Duty to vote.

It is the duty of every person to vote in the popular elections of the country of which he is a national, when he is legally capable of doing so.

Article XXXIII. Duty to obey the law.

It is the duty of every person to obey the law and other legitimate commands of the authorities of his country and those of the country in which he may be.

Article XXXIV. Duty to serve the community and the nation.

It is the duty of every able-bodied person to render whatever civil and military service his country may require for its defense and preservation, and, in case of public disaster, to render such services as may be in his power.

It is likewise his duty to hold any public office to which he may be elected by popular vote in the state of which he is a national.

Article XXXV. Duties with respect to social security and welfare

It is the duty of every person to cooperate with the state and the community with respect to social security and welfare, in accordance with his ability and with existing circumstances.

Article XXXVI. Duty to pay taxes.

It is the duty of every person to pay the taxes established by law for the support of public services.

Article XXXVII. Duty to work.

It is the duty of every person to work, as far as his capacity and possibilities permit, in order to obtain the means of livelihood or to benefit his community.

*Article XXXVIII. Duty to refrain from political activities
in a foreign country.*

It is the duty of every person to refrain from taking part in political activities that, according to law, are reserved exclusively to the citizens of the state in which he is an alien.

AMERICAN CONVENTION ON HUMAN RIGHTS

Signed at the Inter-American Specialized Conference on Human
Rights, San José, Costa Rica, 22 November 1969

PREAMBLE

The American states signatory to the present Convention,

Reaffirming their intention to consolidate in this hemisphere, within the framework of democratic institutions, a system of personal liberty and social justice based on respect for the essential rights of man;

Recognizing that the essential rights of man are not derived from one's being a national of a certain state, but are based upon attributes of the human personality, and that they therefore justify international protection in the form of a convention reinforcing or complementing the protection provided by the domestic law of the American states;

Considering that these principles have been set forth in the Charter of the Organization of American States, in the American Declaration of the Rights and Duties of Man, and in the Universal Declaration of Human Rights, and that they have been reaffirmed and refined in other international instruments, worldwide as well as regional in scope;

Reiterating that, in accordance with the Universal Declaration of Human Rights, the ideal of free men enjoying freedom from fear and want can be achieved only if conditions are created whereby everyone may enjoy his economic, social, and cultural rights, as well as his civil and political rights; and

Considering that the Third Special Inter-American Conference (Buenos Aires, 1967) approved the incorporation into the Charter of the Organization itself of broader standards with respect to economic, social, and educational rights and resolved that an inter-American convention on human rights should determine the structure, competence, and procedure of the organs responsible for these matters,

Have agreed upon the following:

PART I: STATE OBLIGATIONS AND RIGHTS PROTECTED

CHAPTER I: GENERAL OBLIGATIONS

Article 1. Obligation to Respect Rights

1. The States Parties to this Convention undertake to respect the rights and freedoms recognized herein and to ensure to all persons subject to their jurisdiction the free and full exercise of those rights and freedoms, without any discrimination for reasons of race, color, sex, language, religion, political or other opinion, national or social origin, economic status, birth, or any other social condition.

2. For the purposes of this Convention, "person" means every human being.

Article 2. Domestic Legal Effects

Where the exercise of any of the rights or freedoms referred to in Article 1 is not already ensured by legislative or other provisions, the States Parties undertake to adopt, in accordance with their constitutional processes and the provisions of this Convention, such legislative or other measures as may be necessary to give effect to those rights or freedoms.

CHAPTER II: CIVIL AND POLITICAL RIGHTS

Article 3. Right to Juridical Personality

Every person has the right to recognition as a person before the law.

Article 4. Right to Life

1.   Every person has the right to have his life respected. This right shall be protected by law and, in general, from the moment of conception. No one shall be arbitrarily deprived of his life.

2.   In countries that have not abolished the death penalty, it may be imposed only for the most serious crimes and pursuant to a final judgment rendered by a competent court and in accordance with a law establishing such punishment, enacted prior to the commission of the crime. The application of such punishment shall not be extended to crimes to which it does not presently apply.

3.   The death penalty shall not be reestablished in states that have abolished it.

4.   In no case shall capital punishment be inflicted for political offenses or related common crimes.

5.   Capital punishment shall not be imposed upon persons who, at the time the crime was committed, were under 18 years of age or over 70 years of age; nor shall it be applied to pregnant women.

6.   Every person condemned to death shall have the right to apply for amnesty, pardon, or commutation of sentence, which may be granted in all cases. Capital punishment shall not be imposed while such a petition is pending decision by the competent authority.

Article 5. Right to Humane Treatment

1.   Every person has the right to have his physical, mental, and moral integrity respected.

2.   No one shall be subjected to torture or to cruel, inhuman, or degrading punishment or treatment. All persons deprived of their liberty shall be treated with respect for the inherent dignity of the human person.

3.   Punishment shall not be extended to any person other than the criminal.

4.   Accused persons shall, save in exceptional circumstances, be segregated from convicted persons, and shall be subject to separate treatment appropriate to their status as unconvicted persons.

5.   Minors while subject to criminal proceedings shall be separated from adults and brought before specialized tribunals, as speedily as

possible, so that they may be treated in accordance with their status as minors.

6.   Punishments consisting of deprivation of liberty shall have as an essential aim the reform and social readaptation of the prisoners.

Article 6. Freedom from Slavery

1.   No one shall be subject to slavery or to involuntary servitude, which are prohibited in all their forms, as are the slave trade and traffic in women.

2.   No one shall be required to perform forced or compulsory labor. This provision shall not be interpreted to mean that, in those countries in which the penalty established for certain crimes is deprivation of liberty at forced labor, the carrying out of such a sentence imposed by a competent court is prohibited. Forced labor shall not adversely affect the dignity or the physical or intellectual capacity of the prisoner.

3.   For the purposes of this article, the following do not constitute forced or compulsory labor:

    1.   work or service normally required of a person imprisoned in execution of a sentence or formal decision passed by the competent judicial authority. Such work or service shall be carried out under the supervision and control of public authorities, and any persons performing such work or service shall not be placed at the disposal of any private party, company, or juridical person;

    2.   military service and, in countries in which conscientious objectors are recognized, national service that the law may provide for in lieu of military service;

    3.   service exacted in time of danger or calamity that threatens the existence or the well-being of the community; or

    4.   work or service that forms part of normal civic obligations.

Article 7. Right to Personal Liberty

1.   Every person has the right to personal liberty and security.

2.   No one shall be deprived of his physical liberty except for the reasons and under the conditions established beforehand by the constitution of the State Party concerned or by a law established pursuant thereto.

3.   No one shall be subject to arbitrary arrest or imprisonment.

4. Anyone who is detained shall be informed of the reasons for his detention and shall be promptly notified of the charge or charges against him.

5. Any person detained shall be brought promptly before a judge or other officer authorized by law to exercise judicial power and shall be entitled to trial within a reasonable time or to be released without prejudice to the continuation of the proceedings. His release may be subject to guarantees to assure his appearance for trial.

6. Anyone who is deprived of his liberty shall be entitled to recourse to a competent court, in order that the court may decide without delay on the lawfulness of his arrest or detention and order his release if the arrest or detention is unlawful. In States Parties whose laws provide that anyone who believes himself to be threatened with deprivation of his liberty is entitled to recourse to a competent court in order that it may decide on the lawfulness of such threat, this remedy may not be restricted or abolished. The interested party or another person in his behalf is entitled to seek these remedies.

7. No one shall be detained for debt. This principle shall not limit the orders of a competent judicial authority issued for nonfulfillment of duties of support.

Article 8. Right to a Fair Trial

1. Every person has the right to a hearing, with due guarantees and within a reasonable time, by a competent, independent, and impartial tribunal, previously established by law, in the substantiation of any accusation of a criminal nature made against him or for the determination of his rights and obligations of a civil, labor, fiscal, or any other nature.

2. Every person accused of a criminal offense has the right to be presumed innocent so long as his guilt has not been proven according to law. During the proceedings, every person is entitled, with full equality, to the following minimum guarantees:

   1. the right of the accused to be assisted without charge by a translator or interpreter, if he does not understand or does not speak the language of the tribunal or court;

   2. prior notification in detail to the accused of the charges against him;

   3. adequate time and means for the preparation of his defense;

   4. the right of the accused to defend himself personally or to be assisted by legal counsel of his own choosing, and to communicate freely and privately with his counsel;

5.   the inalienable right to be assisted by counsel provided by the state, paid or not as the domestic law provides, if the accused does not defend himself personally or engage his own counsel within the time period established by law;

6.   the right of the defense to examine witnesses present in the court and to obtain the appearance, as witnesses, of experts or other persons who may throw light on the facts;

7.   the right not to be compelled to be a witness against himself or to plead guilty; and

8.   the right to appeal the judgment to a higher court.

3.   A confession of guilt by the accused shall be valid only if it is made without coercion of any kind.

4.   An accused person acquitted by a nonappealable judgment shall not be subjected to a new trial for the same cause.

5.   Criminal proceedings shall be public, except insofar as may be necessary to protect the interests of justice.

Article 9. Freedom from Ex Post Facto Laws

No one shall be convicted of any act or omission that did not constitute a criminal offense, under the applicable law, at the time it was committed. A heavier penalty shall not be imposed than the one that was applicable at the time the criminal offense was committed. If subsequent to the commission of the offense the law provides for the imposition of a lighter punishment, the guilty person shall benefit therefrom.

Article 10. Right to Compensation

Every person has the right to be compensated in accordance with the law in the event he has been sentenced by a final judgment through a miscarriage of justice.

Article 11. Right to Privacy

1.   Everyone has the right to have his honor respected and his dignity recognized.

2.   No one may be the object of arbitrary or abusive interference with his private life, his family, his home, or his correspondence, or of unlawful attacks on his honor or reputation.

3.   Everyone has the right to the protection of the law against such interference or attacks.

Article 12. Freedom of Conscience and Religion

1.   Everyone has the right to freedom of conscience and of religion. This right includes freedom to maintain or to change one's religion or

beliefs, and freedom to profess or disseminate one's religion or beliefs, either individually or together with others, in public or in private.

2.   No one shall be subject to restrictions that might impair his freedom to maintain or to change his religion or beliefs.

3.   Freedom to manifest one's religion and beliefs may be subject only to the limitations prescribed by law that are necessary to protect public safety, order, health, or morals, or the rights or freedoms of others.

4.   Parents or guardians, as the case may be, have the right to provide for the religious and moral education of their children or wards that is in accord with their own convictions.

Article 13. Freedom of Thought and Expression

1.   Everyone has the right to freedom of thought and expression. This right includes freedom to seek, receive, and impart information and ideas of all kinds, regardless of frontiers, either orally, in writing, in print, in the form of art, or through any other medium of one's choice.

2.   The exercise of the right provided for in the foregoing paragraph shall not be subject to prior censorship but shall be subject to subsequent imposition of liability, which shall be expressly established by law to the extent necessary to ensure:

1.   respect for the rights or reputations of others; or

2.   the protection of national security, public order, or public health or morals.

3.   The right of expression may not be restricted by indirect methods or means, such as the abuse of government or private controls over newsprint, radio broadcasting frequencies, or equipment used in the dissemination of information, or by any other means tending to impede the communication and circulation of ideas and opinions.

4.   Notwithstanding the provisions of paragraph 2 above, public entertainments may be subject by law to prior censorship for the sole purpose of regulating access to them for the moral protection of childhood and adolescence.

5.   Any propaganda for war and any advocacy of national, racial, or religious hatred that constitute incitements to lawless violence or to any other similar action against any person or group of persons on any grounds including those of race, color, religion, language, or national origin shall be considered as offenses punishable by law.

Article 14. Right of Reply

1.   Anyone injured by inaccurate or offensive statements or ideas disseminated to the public in general by a legally regulated medium of communication has the right to reply or to make a correction using the

same communications outlet, under such conditions as the law may establish.

2.   The correction or reply shall not in any case remit other legal liabilities that may have been incurred.

3.   For the effective protection of honor and reputation, every publisher, and every newspaper, motion picture, radio, and television company, shall have a person responsible who is not protected by immunities or special privileges.

Article 15. Right of Assembly

The right of peaceful assembly, without arms, is recognized. No restrictions may be placed on the exercise of this right other than those imposed in conformity with the law and necessary in a democratic society in the interest of national security, public safety or public order, or to protect public health or morals or the rights or freedom of others.

Article 16. Freedom of Association

1.   Everyone has the right to associate freely for ideological, religious, political, economic, labor, social, cultural, sports, or other purposes.

2.   The exercise of this right shall be subject only to such restrictions established by law as may be necessary in a democratic society, in the interest of national security, public safety or public order, or to protect public health or morals or the rights and freedoms of others.

3.   The provisions of this article do not bar the imposition of legal restrictions, including even deprivation of the exercise of the right of association, on members of the armed forces and the police.

Article 17. Rights of the Family

1.   The family is the natural and fundamental group unit of society and is entitled to protection by society and the state.

2.   The right of men and women of marriageable age to marry and to raise a family shall be recognized, if they meet the conditions required by domestic laws, insofar as such conditions do not affect the principle of nondiscrimination established in this Convention.

3.   No marriage shall be entered into without the free and full consent of the intending spouses.

4.   The States Parties shall take appropriate steps to ensure the equality of rights and the adequate balancing of responsibilities of the spouses as to marriage, during marriage, and in the event of its dissolution. In case of dissolution, provision shall be made for the necessary protection of any children solely on the basis of their own best interests.

5.   The law shall recognize equal rights for children born out of wedlock and those born in wedlock.

Article 18. Right to a Name

Every person has the right to a given name and to the surnames of his parents or that of one of them. The law shall regulate the manner in which this right shall be ensured for all, by the use of assumed names if necessary.

Article 19. Rights of the Child

Every minor child has the right to the measures of protection required by his condition as a minor on the part of his family, society, and the state.

Article 20. Right to Nationality

1.   Every person has the right to a nationality.

2.   Every person has the right to the nationality of the state in whose territory he was born if he does not have the right to any other nationality.

3.   No one shall be arbitrarily deprived of his nationality or of the right to change it.

Article 21. Right to Property

1.   Everyone has the right to the use and enjoyment of his property. The law may subordinate such use and enjoyment to the interest of society.

2.   No one shall be deprived of his property except upon payment of just compensation, for reasons of public utility or social interest, and in the cases and according to the forms established by law.

3.   Usury and any other form of exploitation of man by man shall be prohibited by law.

Article 22. Freedom of Movement and Residence

1.   Every person lawfully in the territory of a State Party has the right to move about in it, and to reside in it subject to the provisions of the law.

2.   Every person has the right to leave any country freely, including his own.

3.   The exercise of the foregoing rights may be restricted only pursuant to a law to the extent necessary in a democratic society to prevent crime or to protect national security, public safety, public order, public morals, public health, or the rights or freedoms of others.

4.   The exercise of the rights recognized in paragraph 1 may also be restricted by law in designated zones for reasons of public interest.

5.   No one can be expelled from the territory of the state of which he is a national or be deprived of the right to enter it.

6.   An alien lawfully in the territory of a State Party to this Convention may be expelled from it only pursuant to a decision reached in accordance with law.

7.   Every person has the right to seek and be granted asylum in a foreign territory, in accordance with the legislation of the state and international conventions, in the event he is being pursued for political offenses or related common crimes.

8.   In no case may an alien be deported or returned to a country, regardless of whether or not it is his country of origin, if in that country his right to life or personal freedom is in danger of being violated because of his race, nationality, religion, social status, or political opinions.

9.   The collective expulsion of aliens is prohibited.

Article 23. Right to Participate in Government

1.   Every citizen shall enjoy the following rights and opportunities:

1.   to take part in the conduct of public affairs, directly or through freely chosen representatives;

2.   to vote and to be elected in genuine periodic elections, which shall be by universal and equal suffrage and by secret ballot that guarantees the free expression of the will of the voters; and

3.   to have access, under general conditions of equality, to the public service of his country.

2.   The law may regulate the exercise of the rights and opportunities referred to in the preceding paragraph only on the basis of age, nationality, residence, language, education, civil and mental capacity, or sentencing by a competent court in criminal proceedings.

Article 24. Right to Equal Protection

All persons are equal before the law. Consequently, they are entitled, without discrimination, to equal protection of the law.

Article 25. Right to Judicial Protection

1.   Everyone has the right to simple and prompt recourse, or any other effective recourse, to a competent court or tribunal for protection against acts that violate his fundamental rights recognized by the constitution or laws of the state concerned or by this Convention, even

though such violation may have been committed by persons acting in the course of their official duties.

2.   The States Parties undertake:

1.   to ensure that any person claiming such remedy shall have his rights determined by the competent authority provided for by the legal system of the state;

2.   to develop the possibilities of judicial remedy; and

3.   to ensure that the competent authorities shall enforce such remedies when granted.

CHAPTER III
ECONOMIC, SOCIAL, AND CULTURAL RIGHTS

Article 26. Progressive Development

The States Parties undertake to adopt measures, both internally and through international cooperation, especially those of an economic and technical nature, with a view to achieving progressively, by legislation or other appropriate means, the full realization of the rights implicit in the economic, social, educational, scientific, and cultural standards set forth in the Charter of the Organization of American States as amended by the Protocol of Buenos Aires.

CHAPTER IV
SUSPENSION OF GUARANTEES, INTERPRETATION, AND APPLICATION

Article 27. Suspension of Guarantees

1.   In time of war, public danger, or other emergency that threatens the independence or security of a State Party, it may take measures derogating from its obligations under the present Convention to the extent and for the period of time strictly required by the exigencies of the situation, provided that such measures are not inconsistent with its other obligations under international law and do not involve discrimination on the ground of race, color, sex, language, religion, or social origin.

2.   The foregoing provision does not authorize any suspension of the following articles: Article 3 (Right to Juridical Personality), Article 4 (Right to Life), Article 5 (Right to Humane Treatment), Article 6 (Freedom from Slavery), Article 9 (Freedom from Ex Post Facto Laws), Article 12 (Freedom of Conscience and Religion), Article 17 (Rights of the Family), Article 18 (Right to a Name), Article 19 (Rights of the Child), Article 20 (Right to Nationality), and Article 23 (Right to Participate in Government), or of the judicial guarantees essential for the protection of such rights.

3.   Any State Party availing itself of the right of suspension shall immediately inform the other States Parties, through the Secretary General of the Organization of American States, of the provisions the application of which it has suspended, the reasons that gave rise to the suspension, and the date set for the termination of such suspension.

Article 28. Federal Clause

1.   Where a State Party is constituted as a federal state, the national government of such State Party shall implement all the provisions of the Convention over whose subject matter it exercises legislative and judicial jurisdiction.

2.   With respect to the provisions over whose subject matter the constituent units of the federal state have jurisdiction, the national government shall immediately take suitable measures, in accordance with its constitution and its laws, to the end that the competent authorities of the constituent units may adopt appropriate provisions for the fulfillment of this Convention.

3.   Whenever two or more States Parties agree to form a federation or other type of association, they shall take care that the resulting federal or other compact contains the provisions necessary for continuing and rendering effective the standards of this Convention in the new state that is organized.

Article 29. Restrictions Regarding Interpretation

No provision of this Convention shall be interpreted as:

1.   permitting any State Party, group, or person to suppress the enjoyment or exercise of the rights and freedoms recognized in this Convention or to restrict them to a greater extent than is provided for herein;

2.   restricting the enjoyment or exercise of any right or freedom recognized by virtue of the laws of any State Party or by virtue of another convention to which one of the said states is a party;

3.   precluding other rights or guarantees that are inherent in the human personality or derived from representative democracy as a form of government; or

4.   excluding or limiting the effect that the American Declaration of the Rights and Duties of Man and other international acts of the same nature may have.

Article 30. Scope of Restrictions

The restrictions that, pursuant to this Convention, may be placed on the enjoyment or exercise of the rights or freedoms recognized herein may not be applied except in accordance with laws enacted for reasons of general interest and in accordance with the purpose for which such restrictions have been established.

Article 31. Recognition of Other Rights

Other rights and freedoms recognized in accordance with the procedures established in Articles 76 and 77 may be included in the system of protection of this Convention.

CHAPTER V
PERSONAL RESPONSIBILITIES

Article 32. Relationship between Duties and Rights

1. Every person has responsibilities to his family, his community, and mankind.

2. The rights of each person are limited by the rights of others, by the security of all, and by the just demands of the general welfare, in a democratic society.

PART II
MEANS OF PROTECTION

CHAPTER VI
COMPETENT ORGANS

Article 33

The following organs shall have competence with respect to matters relating to the fulfillment of the commitments made by the States Parties to this Convention:

1. the Inter-American Commission on Human Rights, referred to as "The Commission;" and

2. the Inter-American Court of Human Rights, referred to as "The Court."

CHAPTER VII
INTER-AMERICAN COMMISSION ON HUMAN RIGHTS

Section 1. Organization

Article 34

The Inter-American Commission on Human Rights shall be composed of seven members, who shall be persons of high moral character and recognized competence in the field of human rights.

Article 35

The Commission shall represent all the member countries of the Organization of American States.

Article 36

1.   The members of the Commission shall be elected in a personal capacity by the General Assembly of the Organization from a list of candidates proposed by the governments of the member states.

2.   Each of those governments may propose up to three candidates, who may be nationals of the states proposing them or of any other member state of the Organization of American States. When a slate of three is proposed, at least one of the candidates shall be a national of a state other than the one proposing the slate.

Article 37

1.   The members of the Commission shall be elected for a term of four years and may be reelected only once, but the terms of three of the members chosen in the first election shall expire at the end of two years. Immediately following that election the General Assembly shall determine the names of those three members by lot.

2.   No two nationals of the same state may be members of the Commission.

Article 38

Vacancies that may occur on the Commission for reasons other than the normal expiration of a term shall be filled by the Permanent Council of the Organization in accordance with the provisions of the Statute of the Commission.

Article 39

The Commission shall prepare its Statute, which it shall submit to the General Assembly for approval. It shall establish its own Regulations.

Article 40

Secretariat services for the Commission shall be furnished by the appropriate specialized unit of the General Secretariat of the Organization. This unit shall be provided with the resources required to accomplish the tasks assigned to it by the Commission.

Section 2.   Functions

Article 41

The main function of the Commission shall be to promote respect for and defense of human rights. In the exercise of its mandate, it shall have the following functions and powers:

1.   to develop an awareness of human rights among the peoples of America;

2.   to make recommendations to the governments of the member states, when it considers such action advisable, for the adoption of

progressive measures in favor of human rights within the framework of their domestic law and constitutional provisions as well as appropriate measures to further the observance of those rights;

3. to prepare such studies or reports as it considers advisable in the performance of its duties;

4. to request the governments of the member states to supply it with information on the measures adopted by them in matters of human rights;

5. to respond, through the General Secretariat of the Organization of American States, to inquiries made by the member states on matters related to human rights and, within the limits of its possibilities, to provide those states with the advisory services they request;

6. to take action on petitions and other communications pursuant to its authority under the provisions of Articles 44 through 51 of this Convention; and

7. to submit an annual report to the General Assembly of the Organization of American States.

Article 42

The States Parties shall transmit to the Commission a copy of each of the reports and studies that they submit annually to the Executive Committees of the Inter-American Economic and Social Council and the Inter-American Council for Education, Science, and Culture, in their respective fields, so that the Commission may watch over the promotion of the rights implicit in the economic, social, educational, scientific, and cultural standards set forth in the Charter of the Organization of American States as amended by the Protocol of Buenos Aires.

Article 43

The States Parties undertake to provide the Commission with such information as it may request of them as to the manner in which their domestic law ensures the effective application of any provisions of this Convention.

Section 3.   Competence

Article 44

Any person or group of persons, or any nongovernmental entity legally recognized in one or more member states of the Organization, may lodge petitions with the Commission containing denunciations or complaints of violation of this Convention by a State Party.

Article 45

1.   Any State Party may, when it deposits its instrument of ratification of or adherence to this Convention, or at any later time, declare that it recognizes the competence of the Commission to receive and examine communications in which a State Party alleges that another State Party has committed a violation of a human right set forth in this Convention.

2.   Communications presented by virtue of this article may be admitted and examined only if they are presented by a State Party that has made a declaration recognizing the aforementioned competence of the Commission. The Commission shall not admit any communication against a State Party that has not made such a declaration.

3.   A declaration concerning recognition of competence may be made to be valid for an indefinite time, for a specified period, or for a specific case.

4.   Declarations shall be deposited with the General Secretariat of the Organization of American States, which shall transmit copies thereof to the member states of that Organization.

Article 46

1.   Admission by the Commission of a petition or communication lodged in accordance with Articles 44 or 45 shall be subject to the following requirements:

   1.   that the remedies under domestic law have been pursued and exhausted in accordance with generally recognized principles of international law;

   2.   that the petition or communication is lodged within a period of six months from the date on which the party alleging violation of his rights was notified of the final judgment;

   3.   that the subject of the petition or communication is not pending in another international proceeding for settlement; and

   4.   that, in the case of Article 44, the petition contains the name, nationality, profession, domicile, and signature of the person or persons or of the legal representative of the entity lodging the petition.

2.   The provisions of paragraphs 1.a and 1.b of this article shall not be applicable when:

   1.   the domestic legislation of the state concerned does not afford due process of law for the protection of the right or rights that have allegedly been violated;

2. the party alleging violation of his rights has been denied access to the remedies under domestic law or has been prevented from exhausting them; or

3. there has been unwarranted delay in rendering a final judgment under the aforementioned remedies.

Article 47

The Commission shall consider inadmissible any petition or communication submitted under Articles 44 or 45 if:

1. any of the requirements indicated in Article 46 has not been met;

2. the petition or communication does not state facts that tend to establish a violation of the rights guaranteed by this Convention;

3. the statements of the petitioner or of the state indicate that the petition or communication is manifestly groundless or obviously out of order; or

4. the petition or communication is substantially the same as one previously studied by the Commission or by another international organization.

Section 4. Procedure

Article 48

1. When the Commission receives a petition or communication alleging violation of any of the rights protected by this Convention, it shall proceed as follows:

   1. If it considers the petition or communication admissible, it shall request information from the government of the state indicated as being responsible for the alleged violations and shall furnish that government a transcript of the pertinent portions of the petition or communication. This information shall be submitted within a reasonable period to be determined by the Commission in accordance with the circumstances of each case.

   2. After the information has been received, or after the period established has elapsed and the information has not been received, the Commission shall ascertain whether the grounds for the petition or communication still exist. If they do not, the Commission shall order the record to be closed.

   3. The Commission may also declare the petition or communication inadmissible or out of order on the basis of information or evidence subsequently received.

   4. If the record has not been closed, the Commission shall, with the knowledge of the parties, examine the matter set forth

in the petition or communication in order to verify the facts. If necessary and advisable, the Commission shall carry out an investigation, for the effective conduct of which it shall request, and the states concerned shall furnish to it, all necessary facilities.

    5.   The Commission may request the states concerned to furnish any pertinent information and, if so requested, shall hear oral statements or receive written statements from the parties concerned.

    6.   The Commission shall place itself at the disposal of the parties concerned with a view to reaching a friendly settlement of the matter on the basis of respect for the human rights recognized in this Convention.

2.   However, in serious and urgent cases, only the presentation of a petition or communication that fulfills all the formal requirements of admissibility shall be necessary in order for the Commission to conduct an investigation with the prior consent of the state in whose territory a violation has allegedly been committed.

Article 49

If a friendly settlement has been reached in accordance with paragraph 1.f of Article 48, the Commission shall draw up a report, which shall be transmitted to the petitioner and to the States Parties to this Convention, and shall then be communicated to the Secretary General of the Organization of American States for publication. This report shall contain a brief statement of the facts and of the solution reached. If any party in the case so requests, the fullest possible information shall be provided to it.

Article 50

1.   If a settlement is not reached, the Commission shall, within the time limit established by its Statute, draw up a report setting forth the facts and stating its conclusions. If the report, in whole or in part, does not represent the unanimous agreement of the members of the Commission, any member may attach to it a separate opinion. The written and oral statements made by the parties in accordance with paragraph 1.e of Article 48 shall also be attached to the report.

2.   The report shall be transmitted to the states concerned, which shall not be at liberty to publish it.

3.   In transmitting the report, the Commission may make such proposals and recommendations as it sees fit.

Article 51

1. If, within a period of three months from the date of the transmittal of the report of the Commission to the states concerned, the matter has not either been settled or submitted by the Commission or by the state concerned to the Court and its jurisdiction accepted, the Commission may, by the vote of an absolute majority of its members, set forth its opinion and conclusions concerning the question submitted for its consideration.

2. Where appropriate, the Commission shall make pertinent recommendations and shall prescribe a period within which the state is to take the measures that are incumbent upon it to remedy the situation examined.

3. When the prescribed period has expired, the Commission shall decide by the vote of an absolute majority of its members whether the state has taken adequate measures and whether to publish its report.

CHAPTER VIII
INTER-AMERICAN COURT OF HUMAN RIGHTS

Section 1.   Organization

Article 52

1. The Court shall consist of seven judges, nationals of the member states of the Organization, elected in an individual capacity from among jurists of the highest moral authority and of recognized competence in the field of human rights, who possess the qualifications required for the exercise of the highest judicial functions in conformity with the law of the state of which they are nationals or of the state that proposes them as candidates.

2. No two judges may be nationals of the same state.

Article 53

1. The judges of the Court shall be elected by secret ballot by an absolute majority vote of the States Parties to the Convention, in the General Assembly of the Organization, from a panel of candidates proposed by those states.

2. Each of the States Parties may propose up to three candidates, nationals of the state that proposes them or of any other member state of the Organization of American States. When a slate of three is proposed, at least one of the candidates shall be a national of a state other than the one proposing the slate.

Article 54

1. The judges of the Court shall be elected for a term of six years and may be reelected only once. The term of three of the judges chosen in

the first election shall expire at the end of three years. Immediately after the election, the names of the three judges shall be determined by lot in the General Assembly.

2. A judge elected to replace a judge whose term has not expired shall complete the term of the latter.

3. The judges shall continue in office until the expiration of their term. However, they shall continue to serve with regard to cases that they have begun to hear and that are still pending, for which purposes they shall not be replaced by the newly elected judges.

Article 55

1. If a judge is a national of any of the States Parties to a case submitted to the Court, he shall retain his right to hear that case.

2. If one of the judges called upon to hear a case should be a national of one of the States Parties to the case, any other State Party in the case may appoint a person of its choice to serve on the Court as an ad hoc judge.

3. If among the judges called upon to hear a case none is a national of any of the States Parties to the case, each of the latter may appoint an ad hoc judge.

4. An ad hoc judge shall possess the qualifications indicated in Article 52.

5. If several States Parties to the Convention should have the same interest in a case, they shall be considered as a single party for purposes of the above provisions. In case of doubt, the Court shall decide.

Article 56

Five judges shall constitute a quorum for the transaction of business by the Court.

Article 57

The Commission shall appear in all cases before the Court.

Article 58

1. The Court shall have its seat at the place determined by the States Parties to the Convention in the General Assembly of the Organization; however, it may convene in the territory of any member state of the Organization of American States when a majority of the Court considers it desirable, and with the prior consent of the state concerned. The seat of the Court may be changed by the States Parties to the Convention in the General Assembly by a two-thirds vote.

2. The Court shall appoint its own Secretary.

3.   The Secretary shall have his office at the place where the Court has its seat and shall attend the meetings that the Court may hold away from its seat.

Article 59

The Court shall establish its Secretariat, which shall function under the direction of the Secretary of the Court, in accordance with the administrative standards of the General Secretariat of the Organization in all respects not incompatible with the independence of the Court. The staff of the Court's Secretariat shall be appointed by the Secretary General of the Organization, in consultation with the Secretary of the Court.

Article 60

The Court shall draw up its Statute which it shall submit to the General Assembly for approval. It shall adopt its own Rules of Procedure.

Section 2.   Jurisdiction and Functions

Article 61

1.   Only the States Parties and the Commission shall have the right to submit a case to the Court.

2.   In order for the Court to hear a case, it is necessary that the procedures set forth in Articles 48 and 50 shall have been completed.

Article 62

1.   A State Party may, upon depositing its instrument of ratification or adherence to this Convention, or at any subsequent time, declare that it recognizes as binding, ipso facto, and not requiring special agreement, the jurisdiction of the Court on all matters relating to the interpretation or application of this Convention.

2.   Such declaration may be made unconditionally, on the condition of reciprocity, for a specified period, or for specific cases. It shall be presented to the Secretary General of the Organization, who shall transmit copies thereof to the other member states of the Organization and to the Secretary of the Court.

3.   The jurisdiction of the Court shall comprise all cases concerning the interpretation and application of the provisions of this Convention that are submitted to it, provided that the States Parties to the case recognize or have recognized such jurisdiction, whether by special declaration pursuant to the preceding paragraphs, or by a special agreement.

Article 63

1.   If the Court finds that there has been a violation of a right or freedom protected by this Convention, the Court shall rule that the injured party be ensured the enjoyment of his right or freedom that was violated. It shall also rule, if appropriate, that the consequences of the measure or situation that constituted the breach of such right or freedom be remedied and that fair compensation be paid to the injured party.

2.   In cases of extreme gravity and urgency, and when necessary to avoid irreparable damage to persons, the Court shall adopt such provisional measures as it deems pertinent in matters it has under consideration. With respect to a case not yet submitted to the Court, it may act at the request of the Commission.

Article 64

1.   The member states of the Organization may consult the Court regarding the interpretation of this Convention or of other treaties concerning the protection of human rights in the American states. Within their spheres of competence, the organs listed in Chapter X of the Charter of the Organization of American States, as amended by the Protocol of Buenos Aires, may in like manner consult the Court.

2.   The Court, at the request of a member state of the Organization, may provide that state with opinions regarding the compatibility of any of its domestic laws with the aforesaid international instruments.

Article 65

To each regular session of the General Assembly of the Organization of American States the Court shall submit, for the Assembly's consideration, a report on its work during the previous year. It shall specify, in particular, the cases in which a state has not complied with its judgments, making any pertinent recommendations.

Section 3.   Procedure

Article 66

1.   Reasons shall be given for the judgment of the Court.

2.   If the judgment does not represent in whole or in part the unanimous opinion of the judges, any judge shall be entitled to have his dissenting or separate opinion attached to the judgment.

Article 67

The judgment of the Court shall be final and not subject to appeal. In case of disagreement as to the meaning or scope of the judgment, the Court shall interpret it at the request of any of the parties, provided the request is made within ninety days from the date of notification of the judgment.

Article 68

1.   The States Parties to the Convention undertake to comply with the judgment of the Court in any case to which they are parties.

2.   That part of a judgment that stipulates compensatory damages may be executed in the country concerned in accordance with domestic procedure governing the execution of judgments against the state.

Article 69

The parties to the case shall be notified of the judgment of the Court and it shall be transmitted to the States Parties to the Convention.

CHAPTER IX
COMMON PROVISIONS

Article 70

1.   The judges of the Court and the members of the Commission shall enjoy, from the moment of their election and throughout their term of office, the immunities extended to diplomatic agents in accordance with international law. During the exercise of their official function they shall, in addition, enjoy the diplomatic privileges necessary for the performance of their duties.

2.   At no time shall the judges of the Court or the members of the Commission be held liable for any decisions or opinions issued in the exercise of their functions.

Article 71

The position of judge of the Court or member of the Commission is incompatible with any other activity that might affect the independence or impartiality of such judge or member, as determined in the respective statutes.

Article 72

The judges of the Court and the members of the Commission shall receive emoluments and travel allowances in the form and under the conditions set forth in their statutes, with due regard for the importance and independence of their office. Such emoluments and travel allowances shall be determined in the budget of the Organization of American States, which shall also include the expenses of the Court and its Secretariat. To this end, the Court shall draw up its own budget and submit it for approval to the General Assembly through the General Secretariat. The latter may not introduce any changes in it.

Article 73

The General Assembly may, only at the request of the Commission or the Court, as the case may be, determine sanctions to be applied against members of the Commission or judges of the Court when there are justifiable grounds for such action as set forth in the respective statutes. A vote of a two-thirds majority of the member states of the Organization shall be required for a decision in the case of members of the Commission and, in the case of judges of the Court, a two-thirds majority vote of the States Parties to the Convention shall also be required.

PART III
GENERAL AND TRANSITORY PROVISIONS
CHAPTER X
SIGNATURE, RATIFICATION, RESERVATIONS, AMENDMENTS, PROTOCOLS, AND DENUNCIATION

Article 74

1. This Convention shall be open for signature and ratification by or adherence of any member state of the Organization of American States.

2. Ratification of or adherence to this Convention shall be made by the deposit of an instrument of ratification or adherence with the General Secretariat of the Organization of American States. As soon as eleven states have deposited their instruments of ratification or adherence, the Convention shall enter into force. With respect to any state that ratifies or adheres thereafter, the Convention shall enter into force on the date of the deposit of its instrument of ratification or adherence. Ratification of or adherence to this Convention shall be made by the deposit of an instrument of ratification or adherence with the General Secretariat of the Organization of American States. As soon as eleven states have deposited their instruments of ratification or adherence, the Convention shall enter into force. With respect to any state that ratifies or adheres thereafter, the Convention shall enter into force on the date of the deposit of its instrument of ratification or adherence.

3. The Secretary General shall inform all member states of the Organization of the entry into force of the Convention.

Article 75

This Convention shall be subject to reservations only in conformity with the provisions of the Vienna Convention on the Law of Treaties signed on May 23, 1969.

Article 76

1. Proposals to amend this Convention may be submitted to the General Assembly for the action it deems appropriate by any State Party directly, and by the Commission or the Court through the Secretary General.

2.   Amendments shall enter into force for the States ratifying them on the date when two-thirds of the States Parties to this Convention have deposited their respective instruments of ratification. With respect to the other States Parties, the amendments shall enter into force on the dates on which they deposit their respective instruments of ratification.

Article 77

1.   In accordance with Article 31, any State Party and the Commission may submit proposed protocols to this Convention for consideration by the States Parties at the General Assembly with a view to gradually including other rights and freedoms within its system of protection.

2.   Each protocol shall determine the manner of its entry into force and shall be applied only among the States Parties to it.

Article 78

1.   The States Parties may denounce this Convention at the expiration of a five-year period from the date of its entry into force and by means of notice given one year in advance. Notice of the denunciation shall be addressed to the Secretary General of the Organization, who shall inform the other States Parties.

2.   Such a denunciation shall not have the effect of releasing the State Party concerned from the obligations contained in this Convention with respect to any act that may constitute a violation of those obligations and that has been taken by that state prior to the effective date of denunciation.

CHAPTER XI
TRANSITORY PROVISIONS

Section 1.   Inter-American Commission on Human Rights

Article 79

Upon the entry into force of this Convention, the Secretary General shall, in writing, request each member state of the Organization to present, within ninety days, its candidates for membership on the Inter-American Commission on Human Rights. The Secretary General shall prepare a list in alphabetical order of the candidates presented, and transmit it to the member states of the Organization at least thirty days prior to the next session of the General Assembly.

Article 80

The members of the Commission shall be elected by secret ballot of the General Assembly from the list of candidates referred to in Article 79. The candidates who obtain the largest number of votes and an absolute majority of the votes of the representatives of the member states shall be declared elected. Should it become necessary to have several ballots in order to elect all the members of the Commission, the candidates who receive the smallest number of votes shall be eliminated successively, in the manner determined by the General Assembly.

Section 2. Inter-American Court of Human Rights

Article 81

Upon the entry into force of this Convention, the Secretary General shall, in writing, request each State Party to present, within ninety days, its candidates for membership on the Inter-American Court of Human Rights. The Secretary General shall prepare a list in alphabetical order of the candidates presented and transmit it to the States Parties at least thirty days prior to the next session of the General Assembly.

Article 82

The judges of the Court shall be elected from the list of candidates referred to in Article 81, by secret ballot of the States Parties to the Convention in the General Assembly. The candidates who obtain the largest number of votes and an absolute majority of the votes of the representatives of the States Parties shall be declared elected. Should it become necessary to have several ballots in order to elect all the judges of the Court, the candidates who receive the smallest number of votes shall be eliminated successively, in the manner determined by the States Parties.

INDEX

References are to Pages

Reservations, understandings, and declarations, 146
State and local implementation, 354

CONVENTION ON THE RIGHTS OF THE CHILD (CRC)
Customary international law embodied in, 335
Customary international law treatment of, 234
Juvenile death penalty, 149
Local level strategic employments, 392
Ratification
    Generally, 107, 434
    Nonratification effects, 147
Reporting obligations of state and local authorities, 428
State and local implementation, 334
State court
    Applications, 357
    Persuasive authority, 236, 282

CONVENTIONS
See Treaties, this index

CORPORATIONS
Customary International law enforcement against, 249
Social responsibility, UN guiding principles on business and human rights, 628, 727 et seq.

CRIMINAL LAW
Capital Punishment, this index
Consular rights of alien arrestees, 157
Drug trafficking laws implementing treaties, 188
Juvenile Sentencing, this index
Mentally retarded persons sentencing, 285
Prison Conditions, this index

CRITIQUING HUMAN RIGHTS
Generally, 27 et seq.
Cultural relativism and essentialism, 38 et seq.
Feminism, 28 et seq.

CRPD
See Convention on the Rights of Persons with Disabilities, this index

CULTURAL RELATIVISM AND ESSENTIALISM
Critiquing human rights, 38 et seq.

CULTURAL RIGHTS
See Economic, Social and Cultural Rights, this index

CUSTOMARY INTERNATIONAL LAW (CIL)
Generally, 209 et seq.
Alien Tort Statute, 239 et seq.
Charming Betsy canon, 232, 238
Construction of US laws, effects on

Generally, 232, 238
    Federal courts, 285
    State courts, 349
Corporations, enforcement against, 249
CRC as expressing, 234, 335
Critiques of US application, 228
Customs and usages of nations, 237
Definitions, 209 et seq., 334
Enforcing CIL
    Generally, 232
    Alien Tort Statute, 239 et seq.
    Charming Betsy canon, 232, 238
    Construction of US laws, effects on, above
    Corporations, enforcement against, 249
    Persuasive Authority, Foreign and International Law as, this index
    Torture Victim Protection Act, 263
Erie doctrine and, 226
Federal common law and, 247, 370
Federal common law compared, 221, 224
Juveniles, capital punishment, 218
Peremptory or jus cogens norms, 211, 218
Proof issues, 337
Restatement (Third) of Foreign Relations Law, 210
Sources, 212
State and local courts applications, 230
State courts, 334
Torture, 213
Torture Victim Protection Act, 263
Treaty law distinguished, 232
US legal system
    Generally, 75, 220 et seq.
    Construction of US laws, effects on, above
    Critiques of US application, 228
    Enforcing CIL, above
    Erie doctrine and, 226
    Persuasive Authority, Foreign and International Law as, this index
    State and local courts, 230
World War II expansion of, 224, 228

DEATH PENALTY
See Capital Punishment, this index

DECLARATION OF INDEPENDENCE
United States human rights law, 72

DEVELOPMENTALLY DISABLED PERSONS
See also Convention on the Rights of Persons with Disabilities, this index
Capital punishment, international law as persuasive authority, 285

DIGNITY
Norms and standards, 9, 12